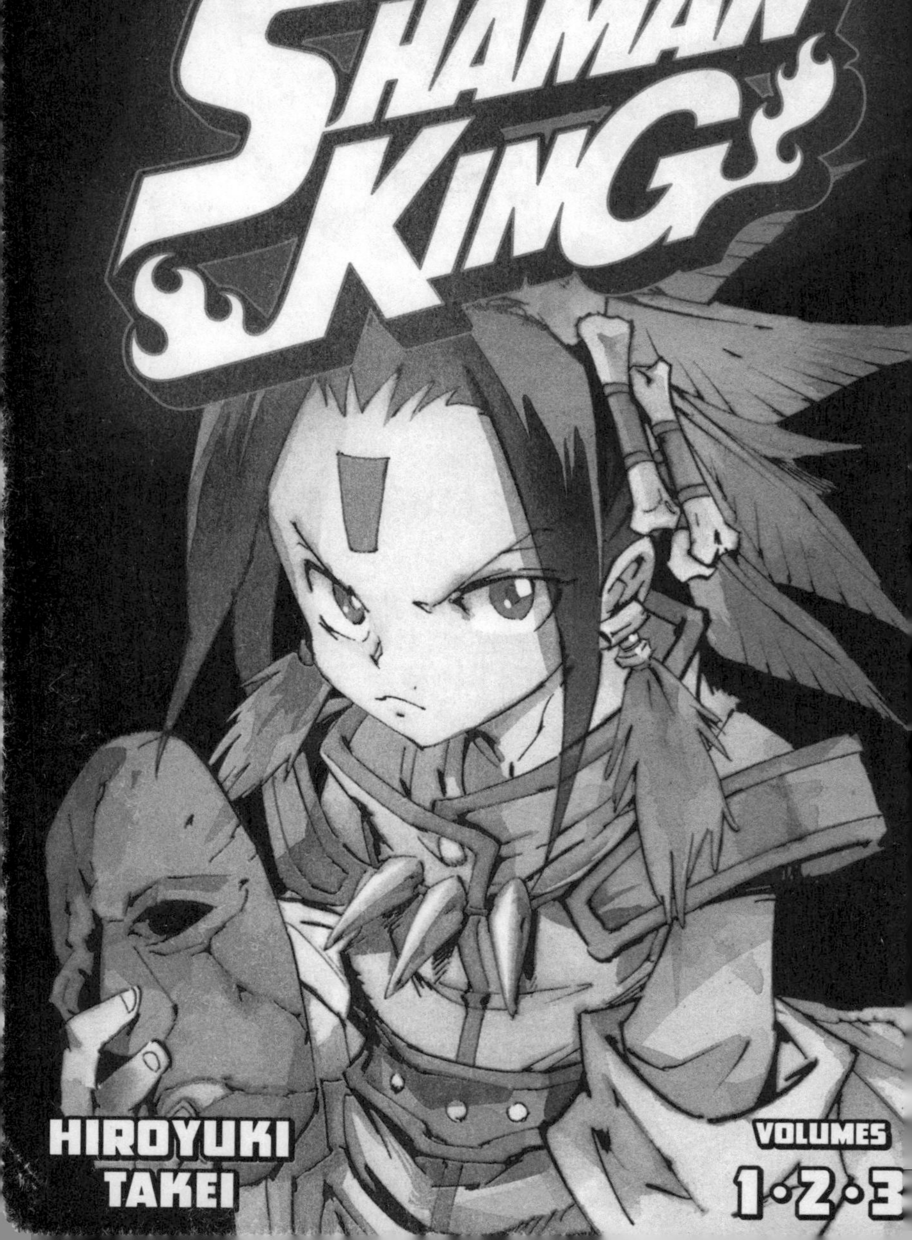
SHAMAN KING
HIROYUKI TAKEI
VOLUMES 1·2·3

SHAMAN KING

**VOLUMES
1 · 2 · 3**

TABLE OF CONTENTS

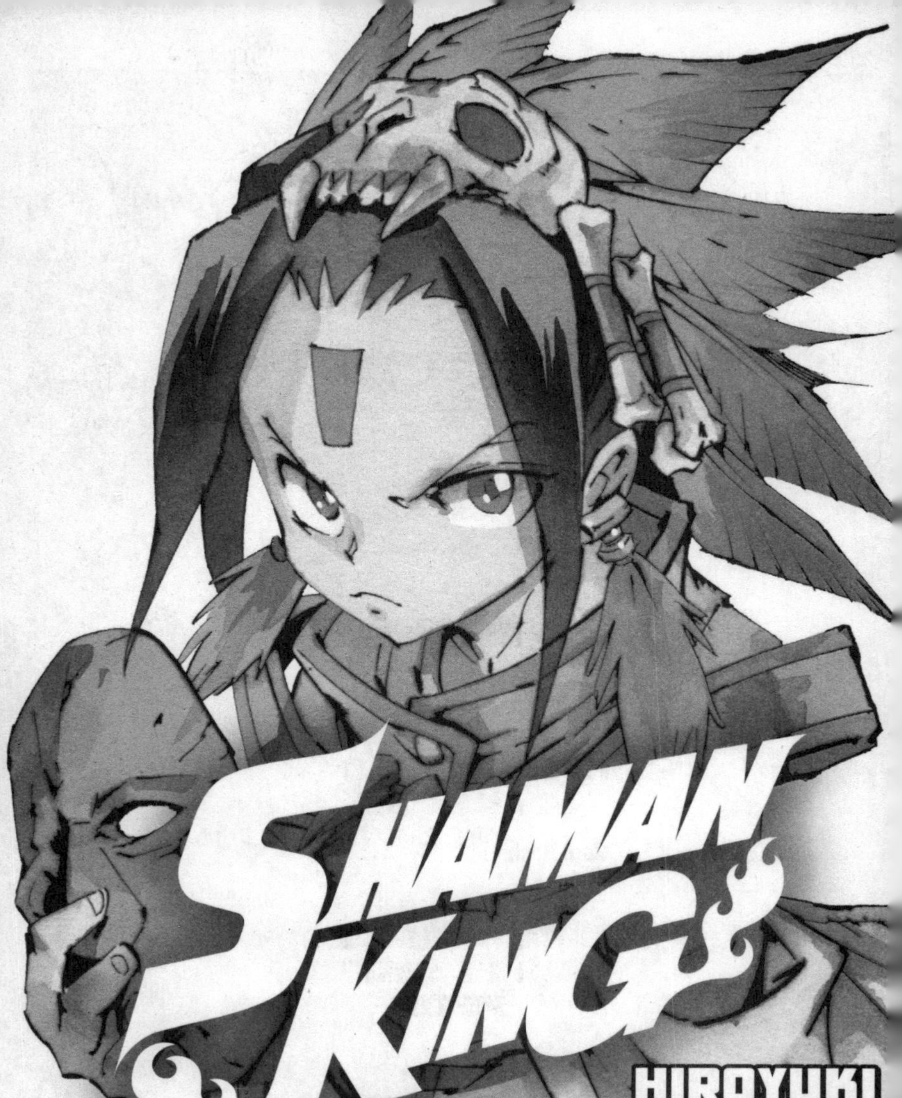
SHAMAN KING
HIROYUKI TAKEI

1 The Boy Who Dances With Ghosts

SHAMAN KING

The Boy Who Dances With Ghosts

1

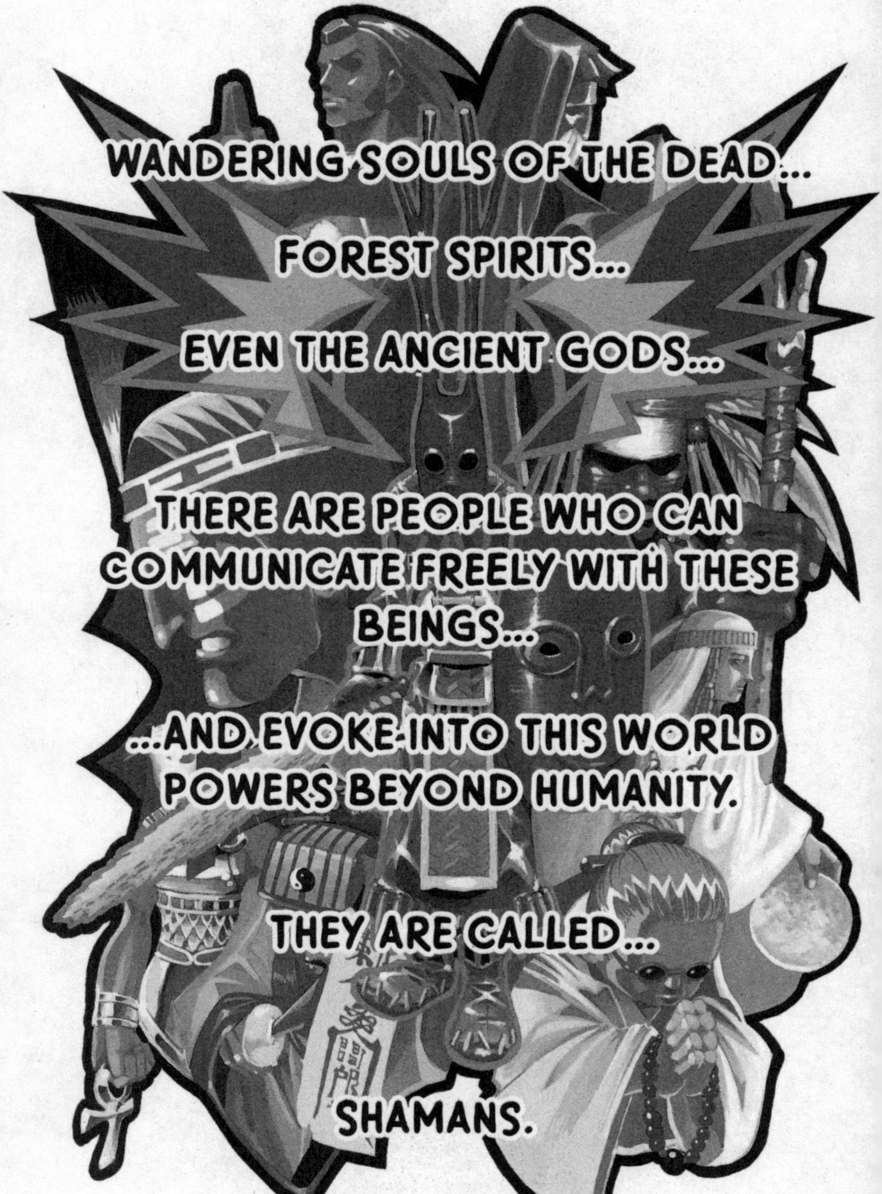
WANDERING SOULS OF THE DEAD...
FOREST SPIRITS...
EVEN THE ANCIENT GODS...
THERE ARE PEOPLE WHO CAN COMMUNICATE FREELY WITH THESE BEINGS...
...AND EVOKE INTO THIS WORLD POWERS BEYOND HUMANITY.
THEY ARE CALLED...
SHAMANS.

Chapter 1: The Boy Who Dances With Ghosts

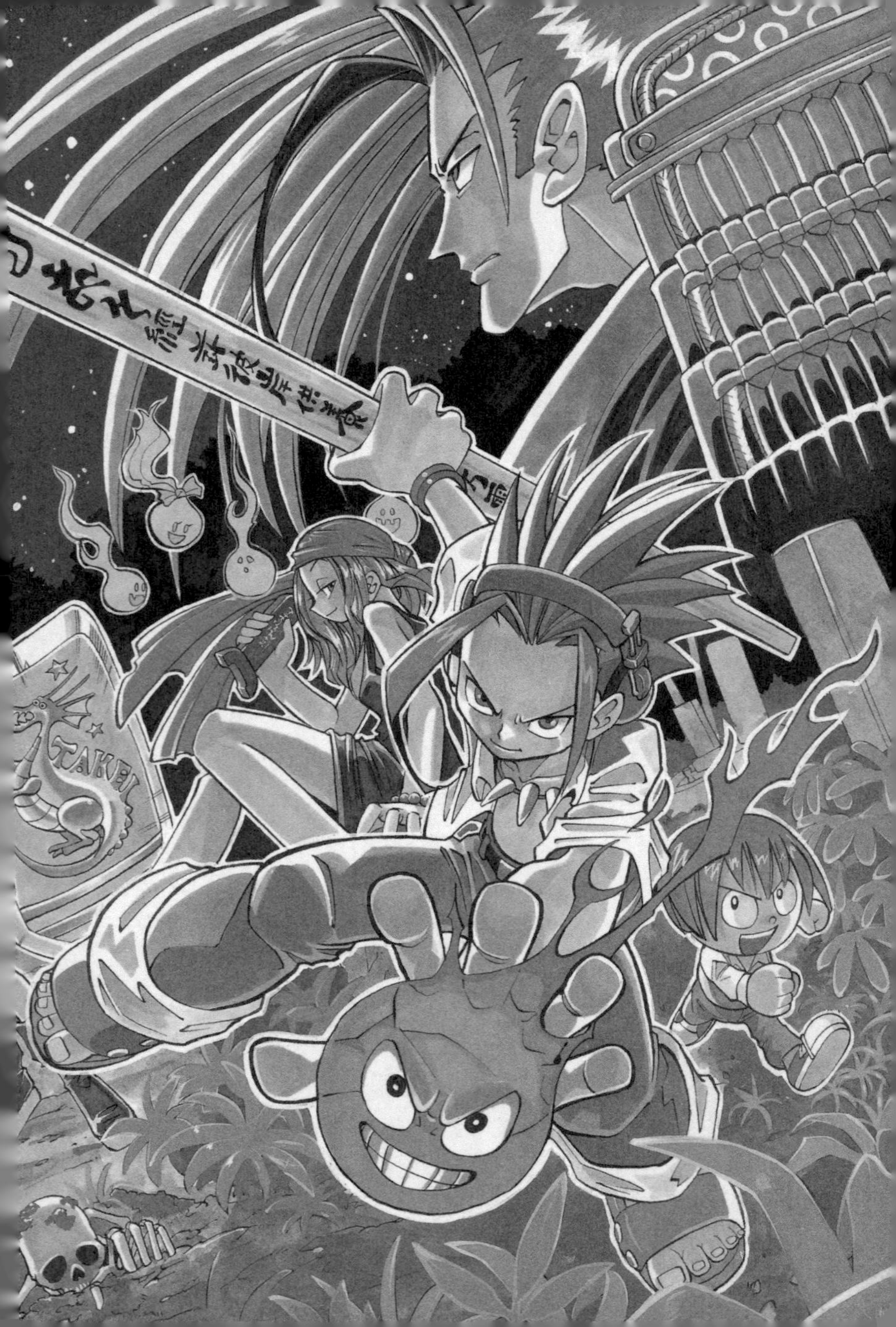
TAKEI

Chapter 1: The Boy Who Dances With Ghosts

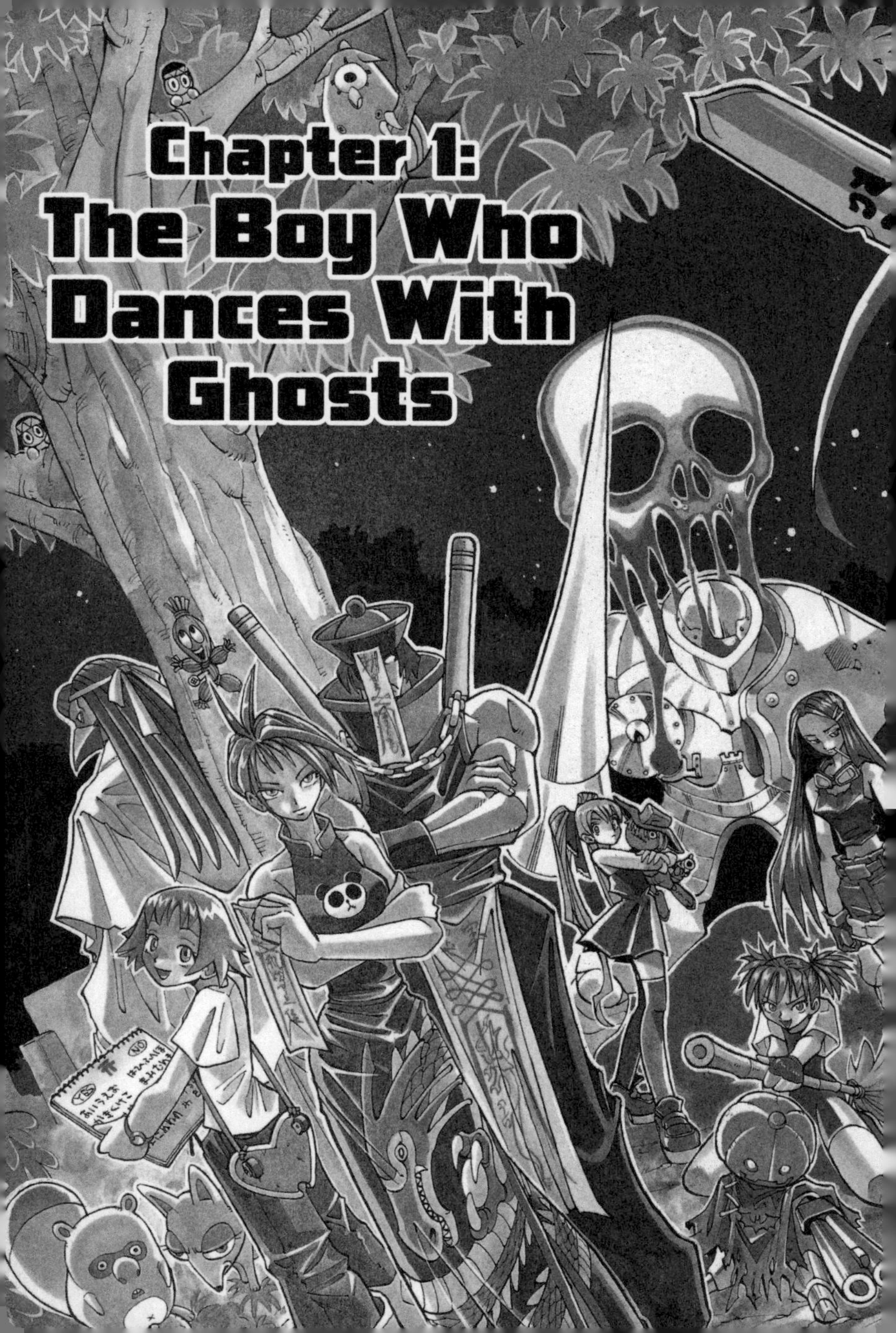

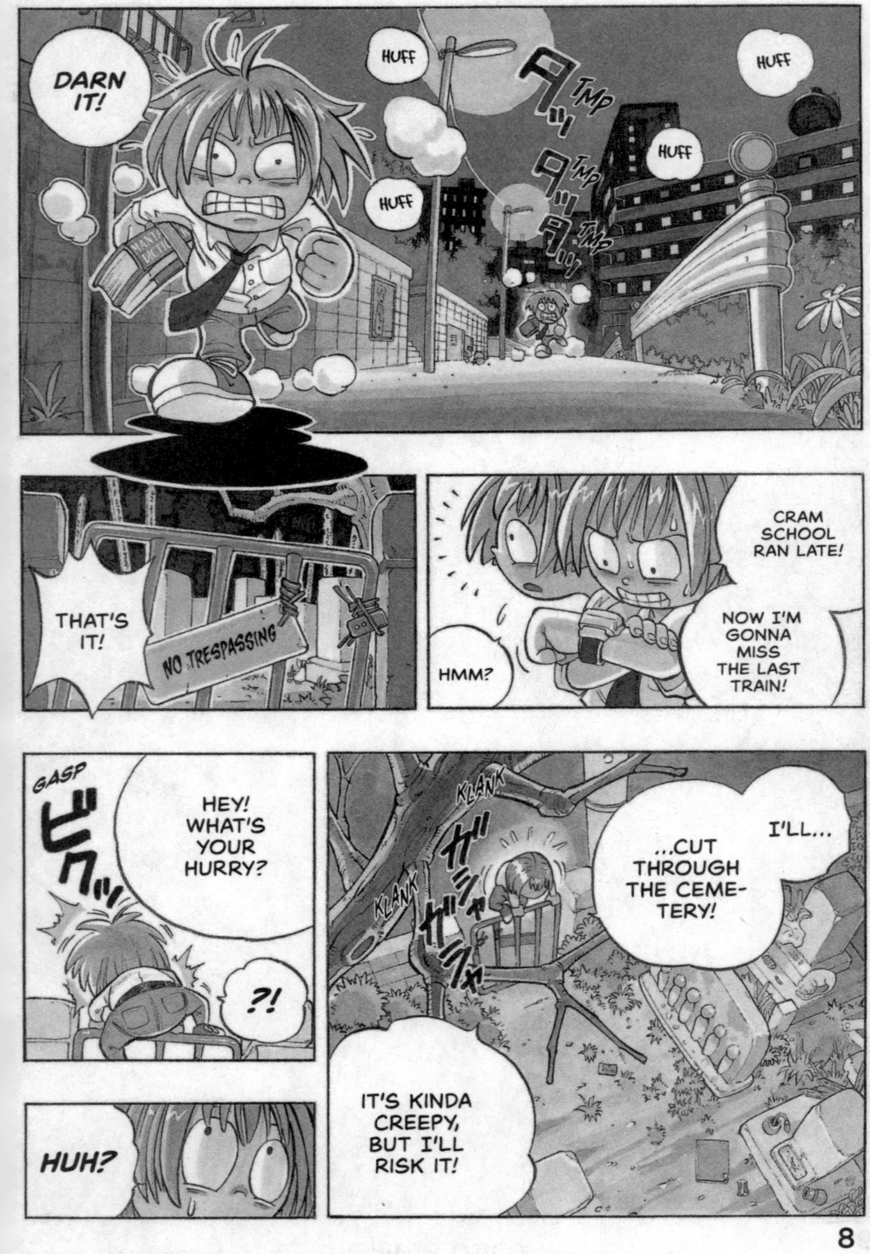
HUFF
HUFF
TMP
TMP
TMP
HUFF
HUFF
DARN IT!
CRAM SCHOOL RAN LATE!
NOW I'M GONNA MISS THE LAST TRAIN!
HMM?
THAT'S IT!
NO TRESPASSING
I'LL...
...CUT THROUGH THE CEME-TERY!
KLANK
KLANK
IT'S KINDA CREEPY, BUT I'LL RISK IT!
HEY! WHAT'S YOUR HURRY?
GASP
?!
HUH?

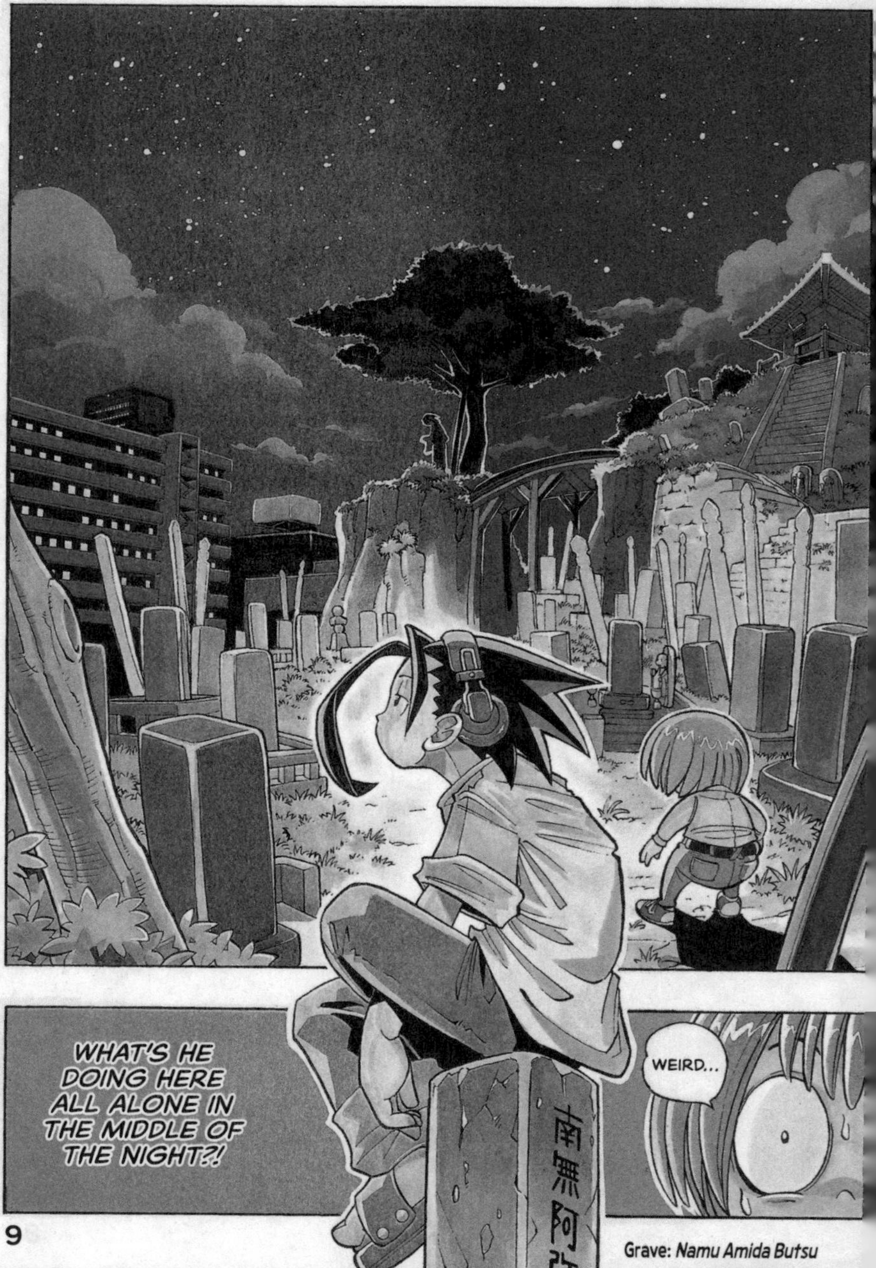
WEIRD...
WHAT'S HE DOING HERE ALL ALONE IN THE MIDDLE OF THE NIGHT?!

Grave: *Namu Amida Butsu*

SHAMAN
KING
1

Leaves

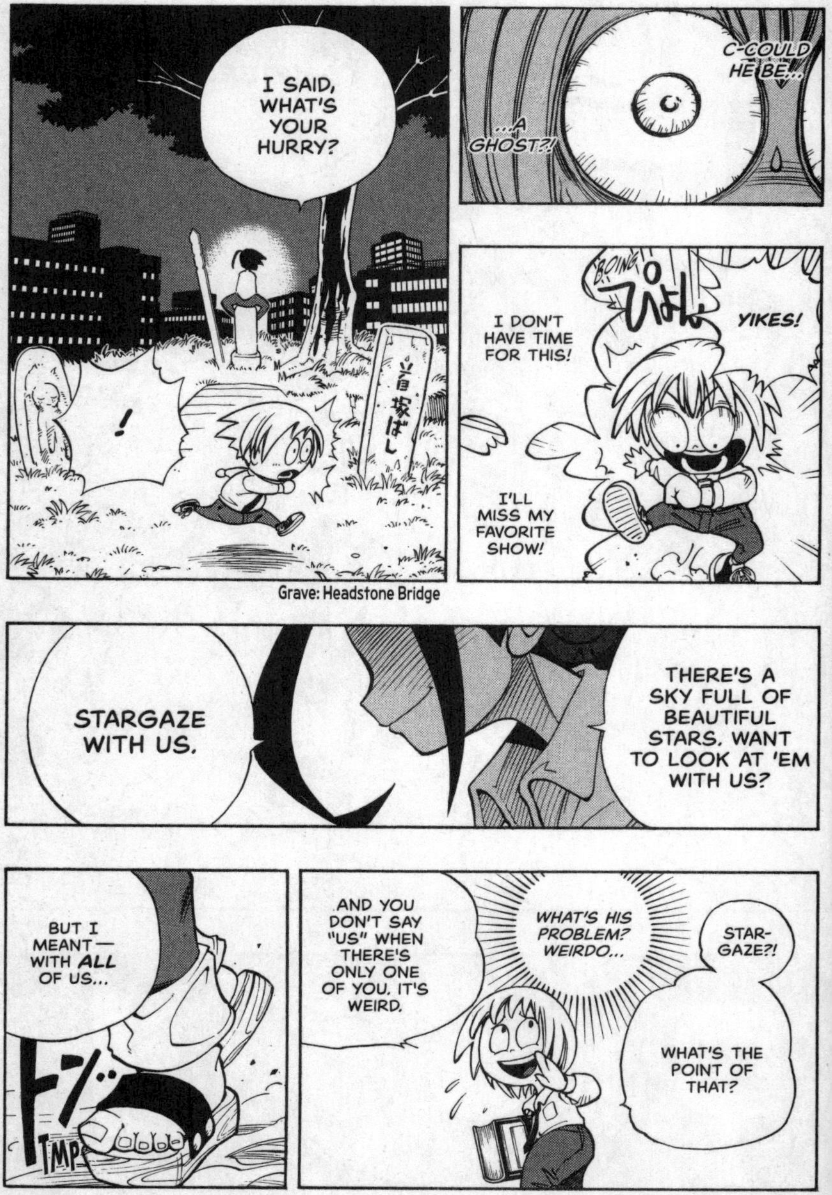
C-COULD HE BE...
...A GHOST?!
BOING
ぴょん
YIKES!
I DON'T HAVE TIME FOR THIS!
I'LL MISS MY FAVORITE SHOW!
I SAID, WHAT'S YOUR HURRY?
!
首塚ばし
THERE'S A SKY FULL OF BEAUTIFUL STARS. WANT TO LOOK AT 'EM WITH US?
STARGAZE WITH US.
STAR-GAZE?!
WHAT'S THE POINT OF THAT?
WHAT'S HIS PROBLEM? WEIRDO...
AND YOU DON'T SAY "US" WHEN THERE'S ONLY ONE OF YOU. IT'S WEIRD.
BUT I MEANT— WITH **ALL** OF US...
ドン
TMP

Grave: Headstone Bridge

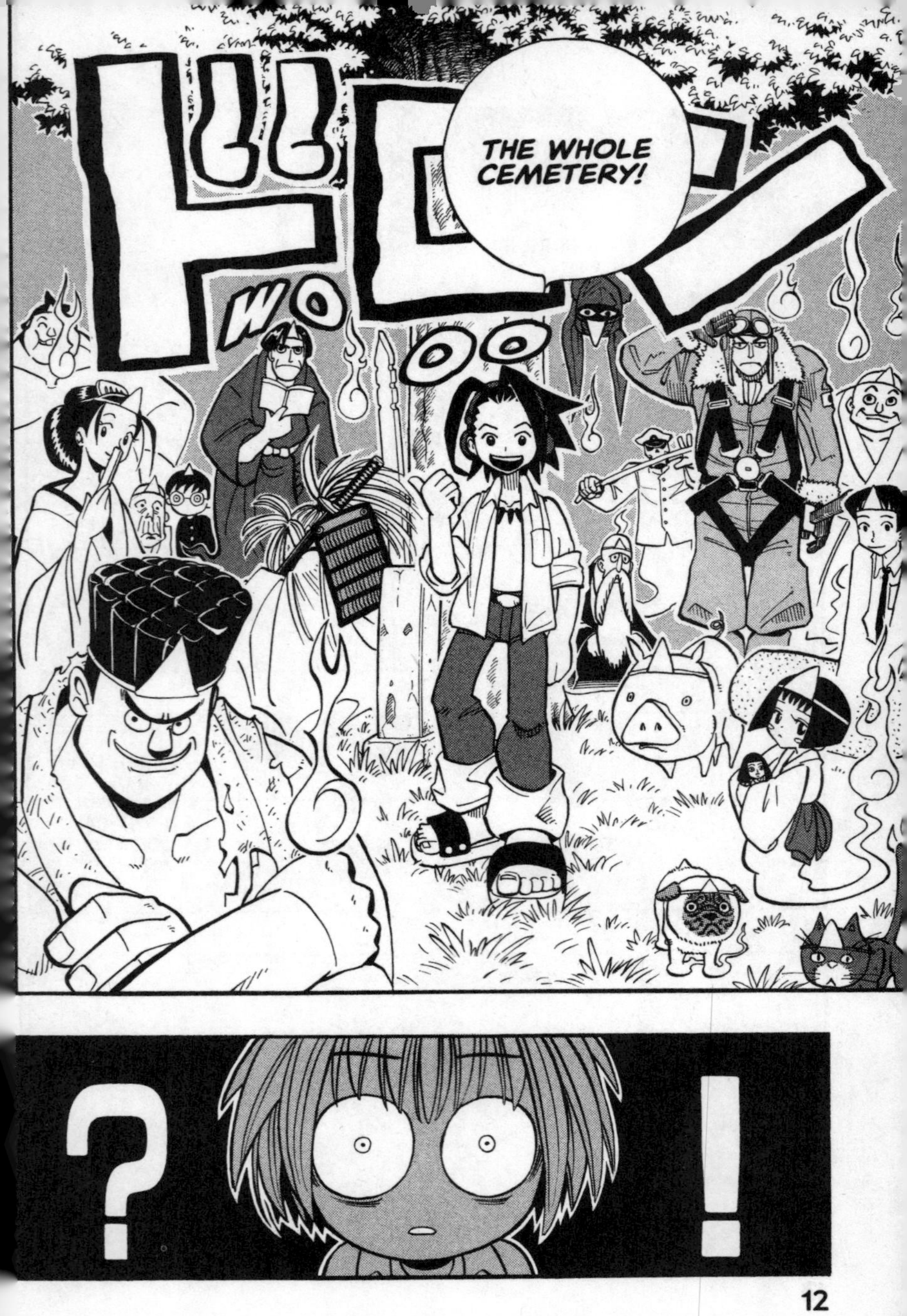
WOOOO
THE WHOLE CEMETERY!
?!

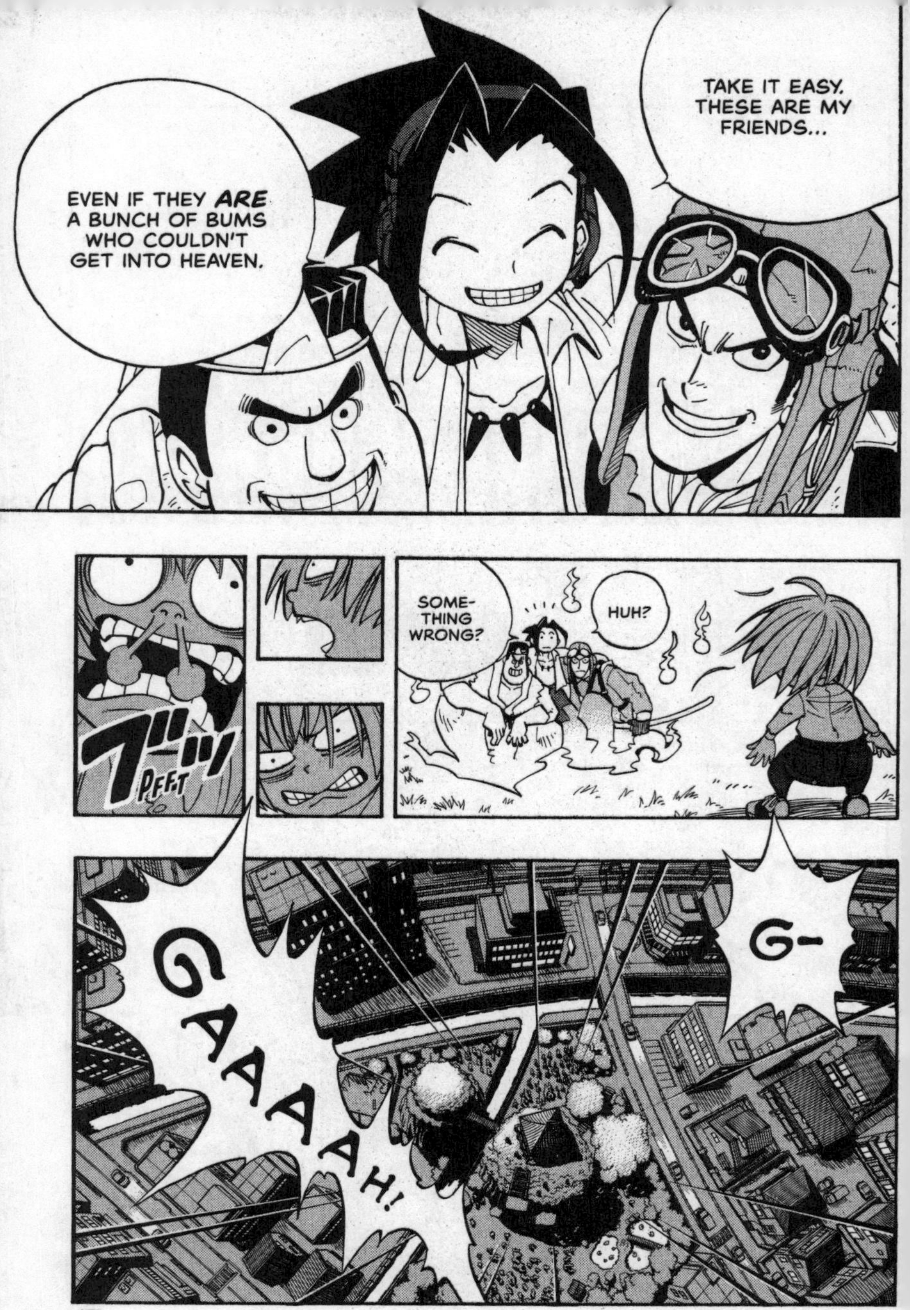
TAKE IT EASY. THESE ARE MY FRIENDS...
EVEN IF THEY **ARE** A BUNCH OF BUMS WHO COULDN'T GET INTO HEAVEN.
HUH?
SOME-THING WRONG?
PFFT
G-
GAAAAAH!

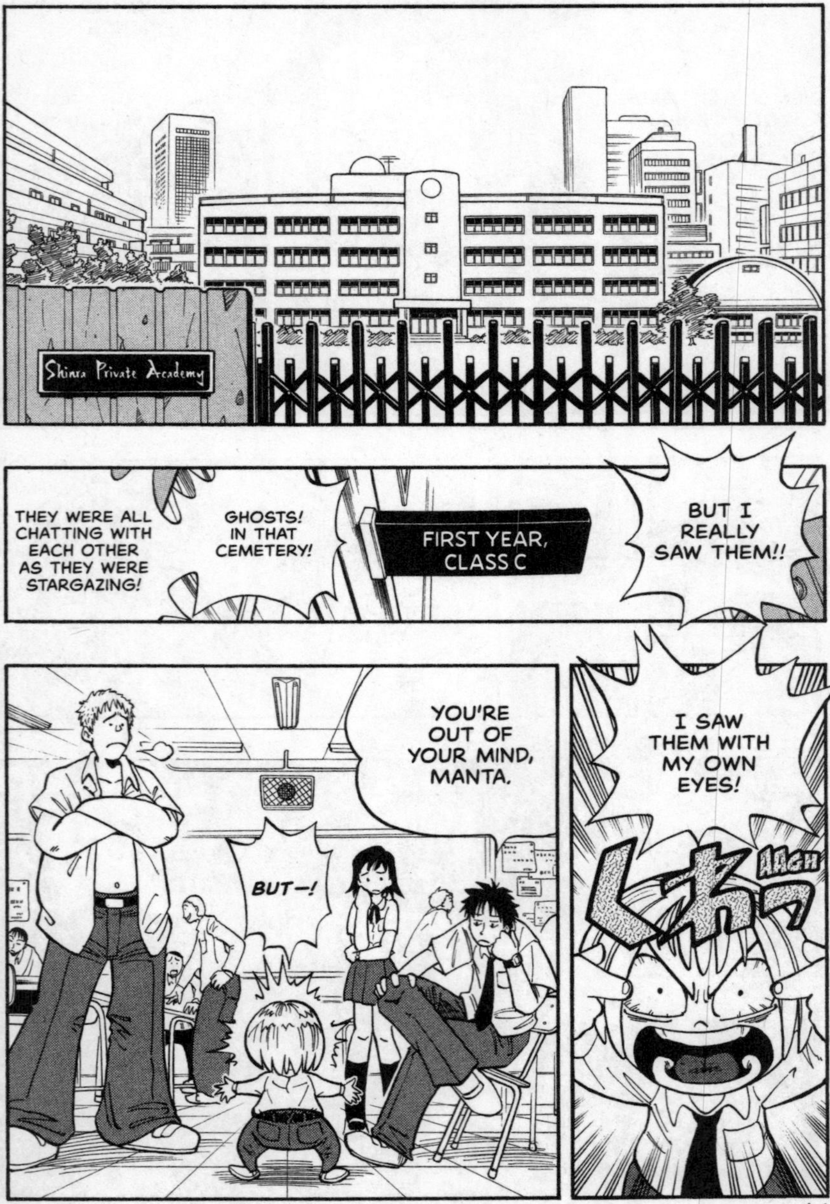
Shinra Private Academy
BUT I REALLY SAW THEM!!
FIRST YEAR, CLASS C
GHOSTS! IN THAT CEMETERY!
THEY WERE ALL CHATTING WITH EACH OTHER AS THEY WERE STARGAZING!
I SAW THEM WITH MY OWN EYES!
AAGH
YOU'RE OUT OF YOUR MIND, MANTA.
BUT—!

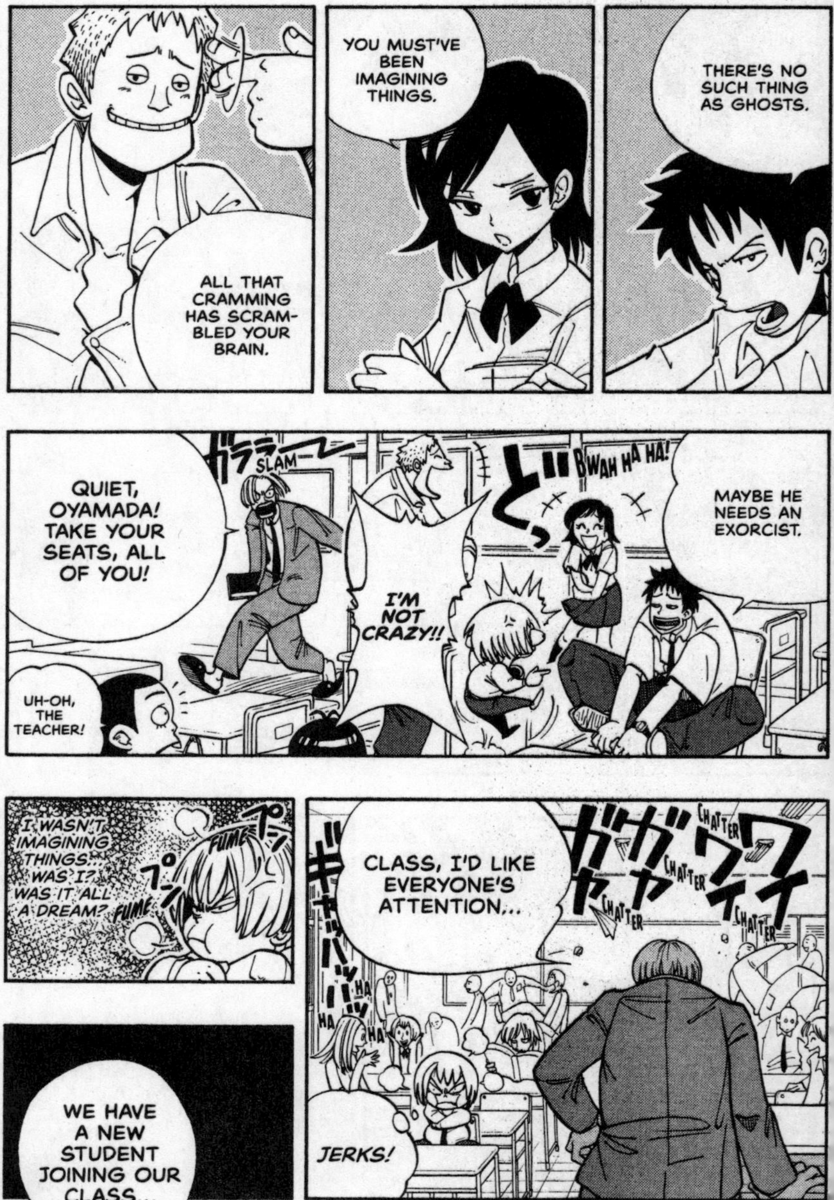
THERE'S NO SUCH THING AS GHOSTS.
YOU MUST'VE BEEN IMAGINING THINGS.
ALL THAT CRAMMING HAS SCRAMBLED YOUR BRAIN.
MAYBE HE NEEDS AN EXORCIST.
BWAH HA HA!
I'M NOT CRAZY!!
SLAM
QUIET, OYAMADA! TAKE YOUR SEATS, ALL OF YOU!
UH-OH, THE TEACHER!
CHATTER
CHATTER
CHATTER
CHATTER
CLASS, I'D LIKE EVERYONE'S ATTENTION,...
HA
HA
HA
JERKS!
FUME
FUME
I WASN'T IMAGINING THINGS... WAS I? WAS IT ALL A DREAM?
WE HAVE A NEW STUDENT JOINING OUR CLASS...

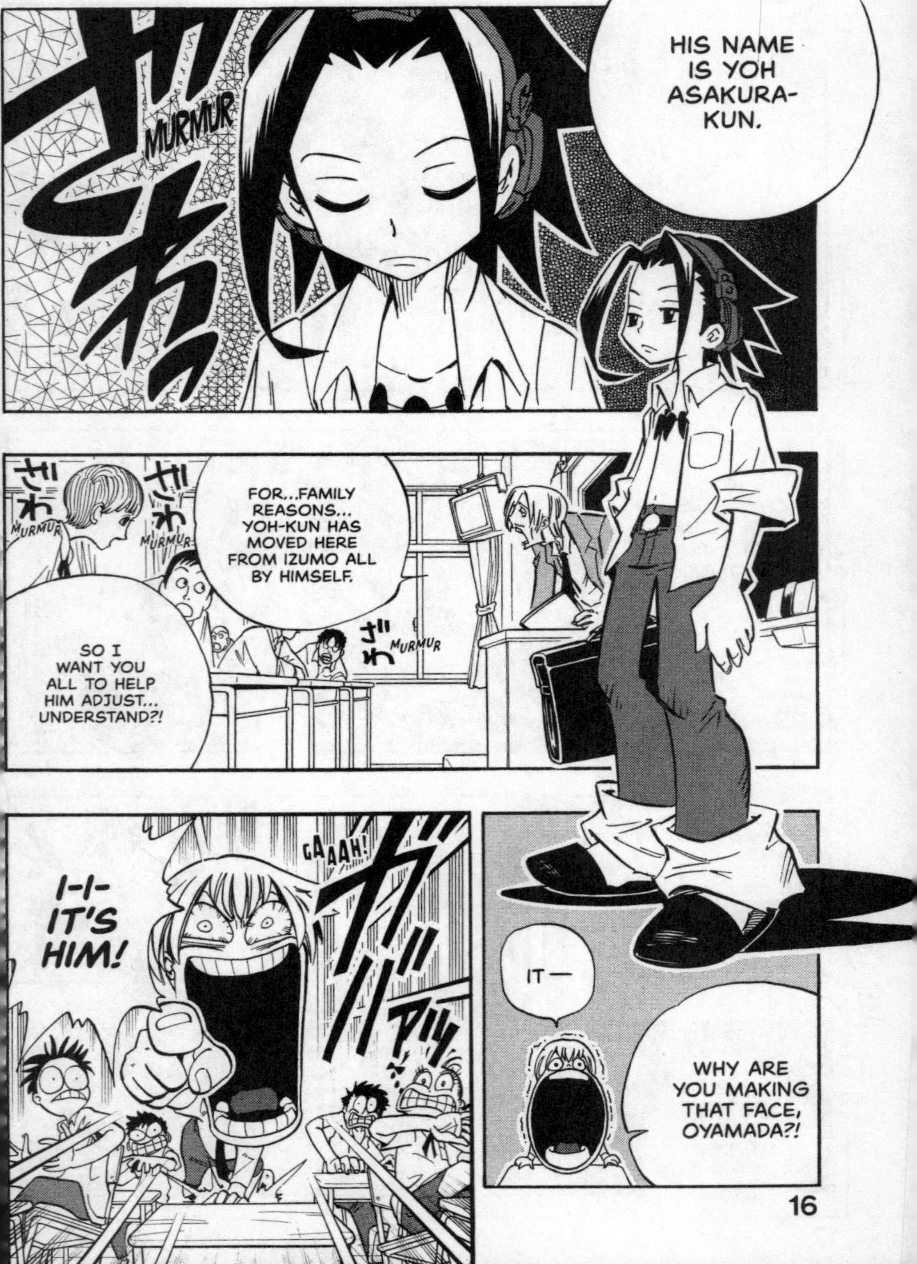
HIS NAME IS YOH ASAKURA-KUN.
MURMUR
FOR...FAMILY REASONS... YOH-KUN HAS MOVED HERE FROM IZUMO ALL BY HIMSELF.
MURMUR
MURMUR
MURMUR
SO I WANT YOU ALL TO HELP HIM ADJUST... UNDERSTAND?!
IT—
WHY ARE YOU MAKING THAT FACE, OYAMADA?!
GAAAH!
I-I-IT'S HIM!

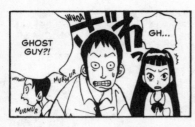

YOU GUYS!
HE'S THE GHOST GUY!
WHOA
GH...
GHOST GUY?!
MURMUR
MURMUR
MURMUR
...
THERE'S NO SUCH THING AS GHOSTS.
I'VE NEVER SEEN YOU BEFORE IN MY LIFE.
WA HA HA!
WHAT?!
BAM
LET IT GO, MANTA.
YOU HEARD WHAT HE SAID. YOU WERE OUT OF YOUR HEAD LAST NIGHT.
NO!!
IT WAS HIM! HE'S PRETENDING NOT TO KNOW ME! I WANT TO QUESTION HIM, BUT...!
BUT I CAN'T, BECAUSE...!

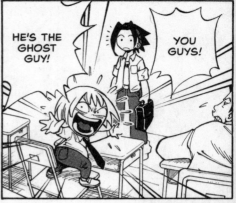

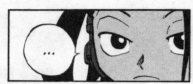

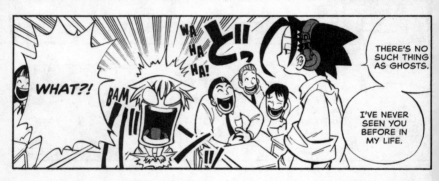

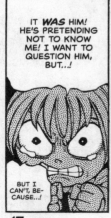

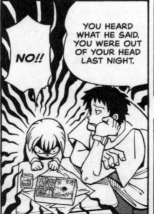

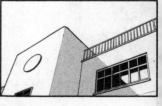

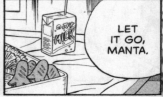

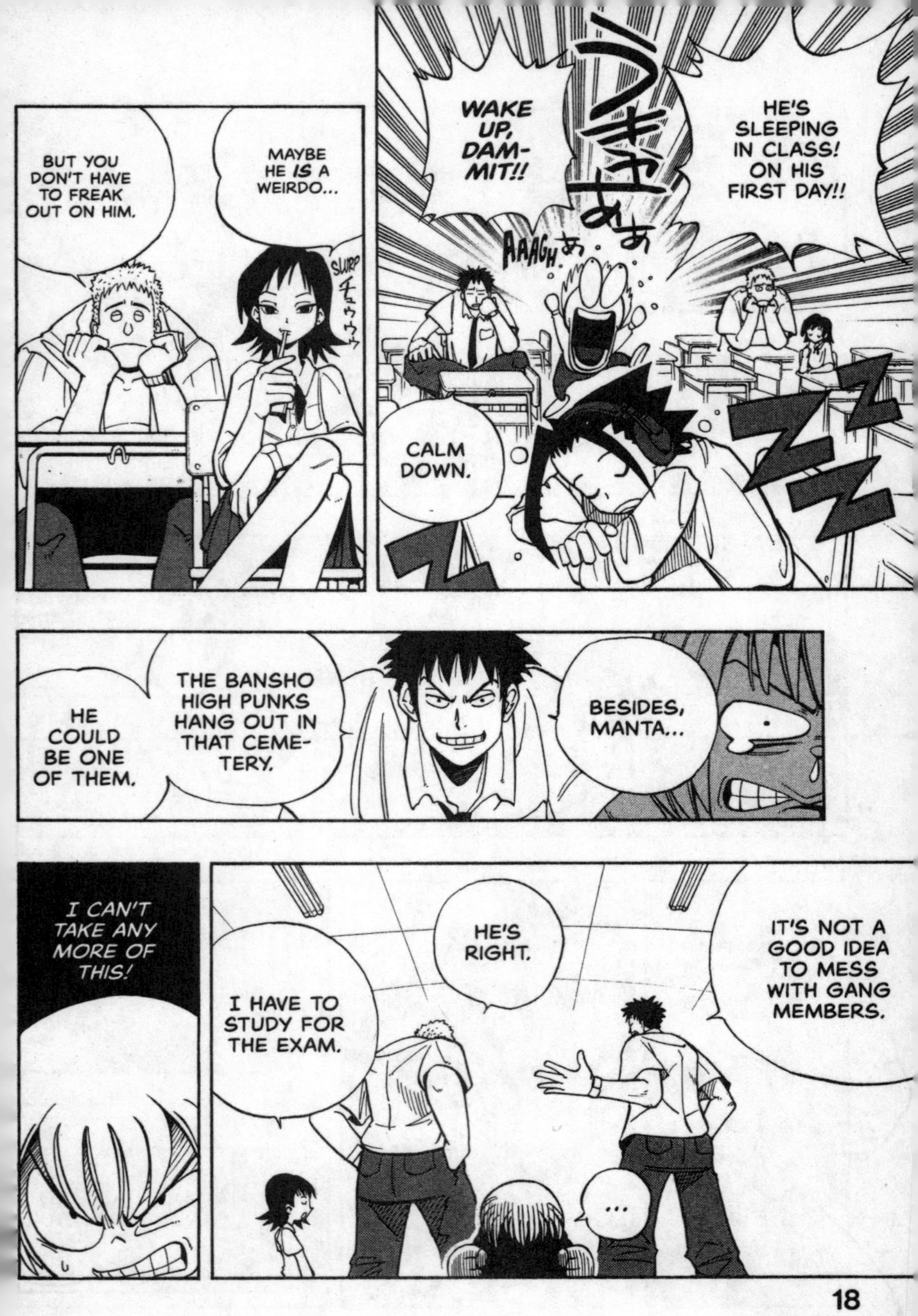
HE'S SLEEPING IN CLASS! ON HIS FIRST DAY!!
WAKE UP, DAM-MIT!!
うきゃああ
AAAGH あ
CALM DOWN.
ZZZ
MAYBE HE *IS* A WEIRDO...
BUT YOU DON'T HAVE TO FREAK OUT ON HIM.
SLURP チュウウウ
BESIDES, MANTA...
THE BANSHO HIGH PUNKS HANG OUT IN THAT CEME-TERY.
HE COULD BE ONE OF THEM.
IT'S NOT A GOOD IDEA TO MESS WITH GANG MEMBERS.
HE'S RIGHT.
I HAVE TO STUDY FOR THE EXAM.
...
I CAN'T TAKE ANY MORE OF THIS!

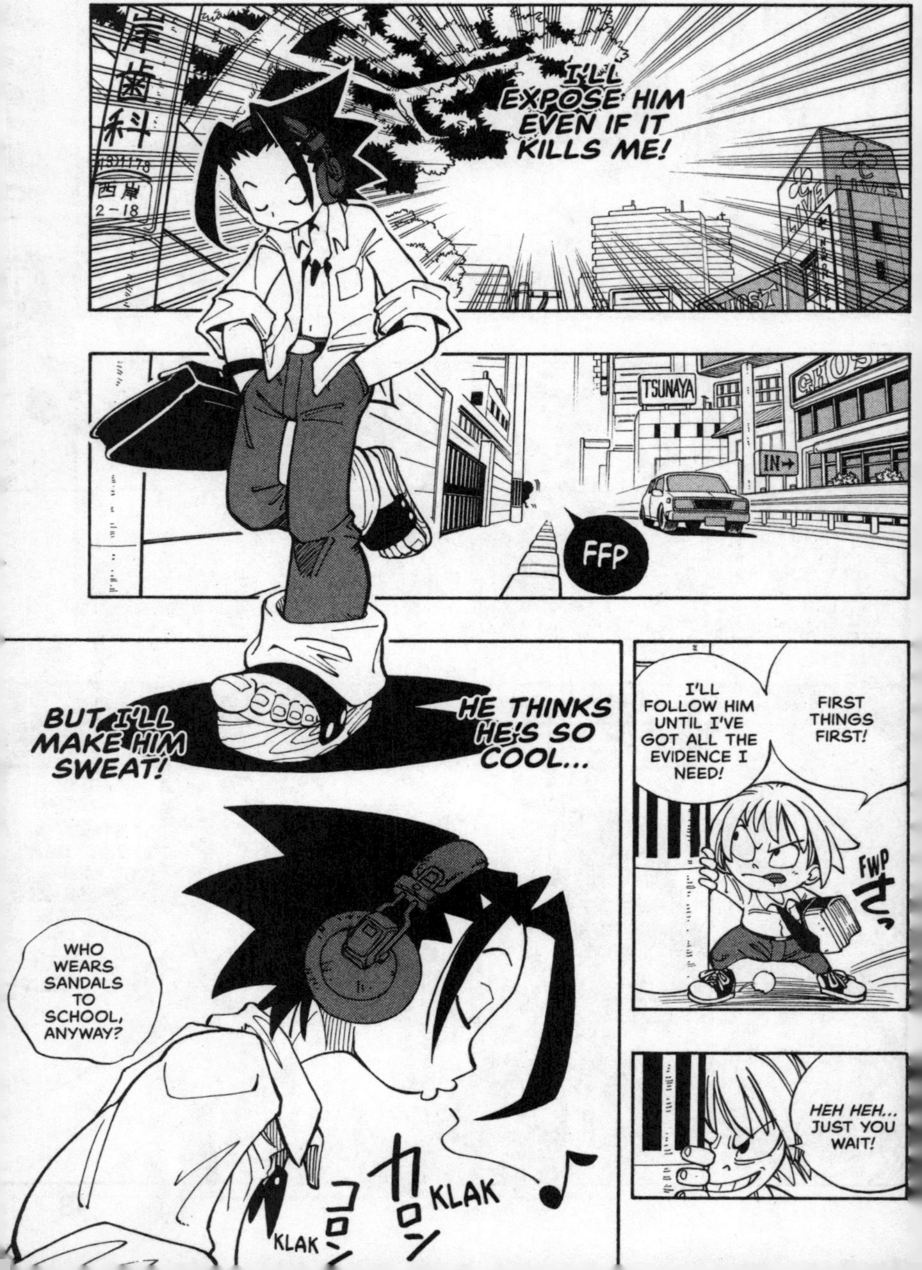

I'LL EXPOSE HIM EVEN IF IT KILLS ME!
TSUNAYA
IN→
FFP
FIRST THINGS FIRST!
I'LL FOLLOW HIM UNTIL I'VE GOT ALL THE EVIDENCE I NEED!
FWP
さっ
HEH HEH... JUST YOU WAIT!
HE THINKS HE'S SO COOL...
BUT I'LL MAKE HIM SWEAT!
WHO WEARS SANDALS TO SCHOOL, ANYWAY?
カロン
KLAK
コロン
KLAK

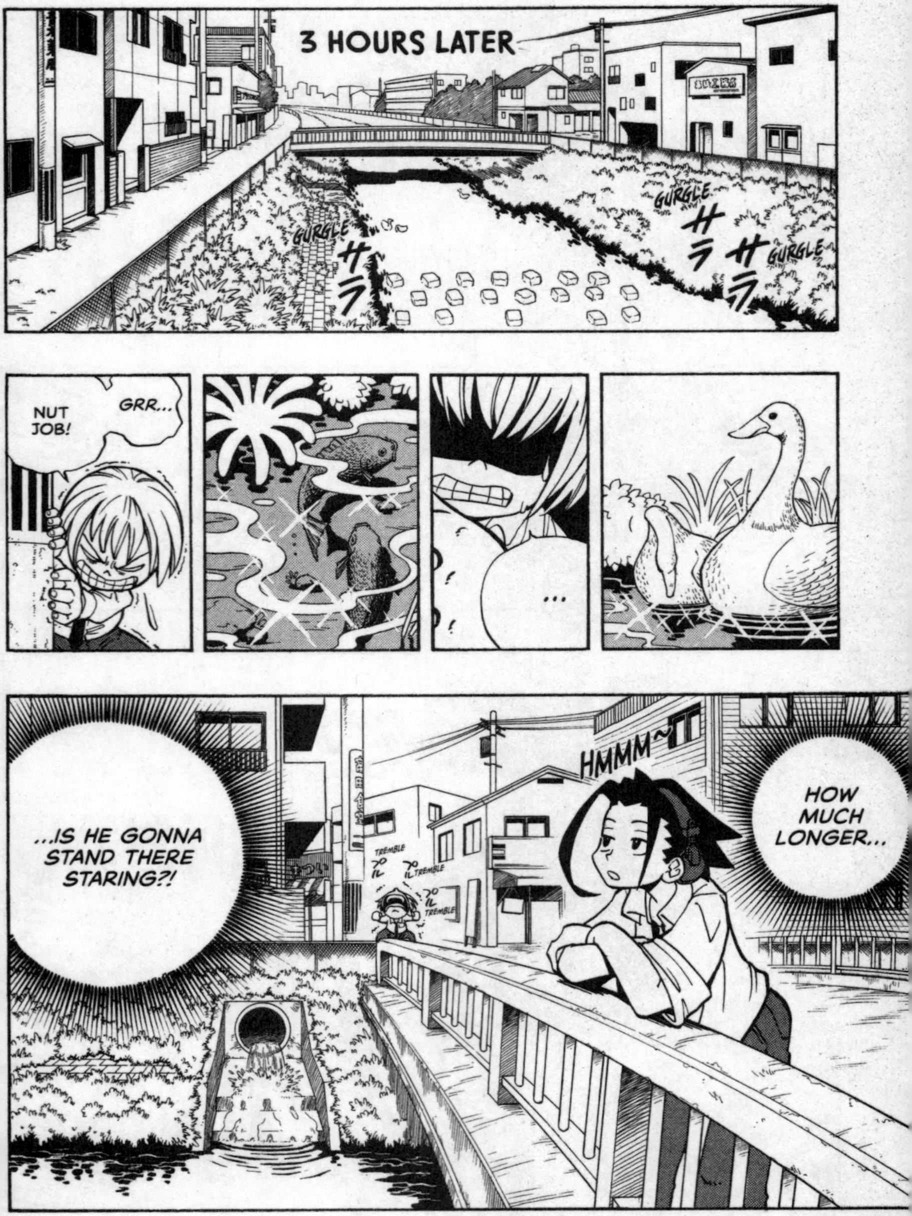

3 HOURS LATER
GURGLE
サラ
サラ
GURGLE
GURGLE
サラ
...
GRR...
NUT JOB!
HOW MUCH LONGER...
HMMM~
TREMBLE
TREMBLE
TREMBLE
...IS HE GONNA STAND THERE STARING?!

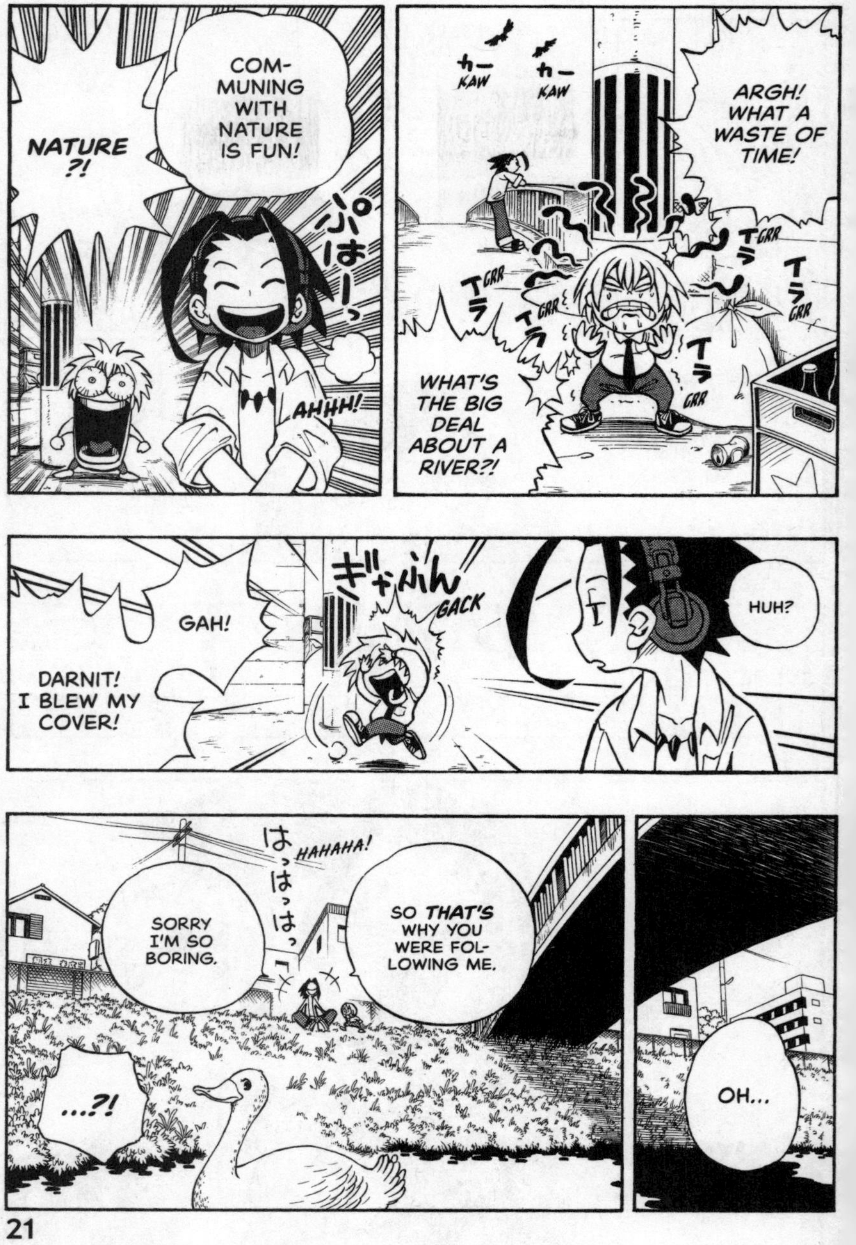

カー KAW
カー KAW
ARGH! WHAT A WASTE OF TIME!
GRR
GRR
GRR
GRR
GRR
WHAT'S THE BIG DEAL ABOUT A RIVER?!
COM-MUNING WITH NATURE IS FUN!
NATURE ?!
ぷはーっ AHHH!
HUH?
ぎゃふん GACK
GAH!
DARNIT! I BLEW MY COVER!
OH...
SO THAT'S WHY YOU WERE FOL-LOWING ME.
はっはっ HAHAHA!
SORRY I'M SO BORING.
...?!

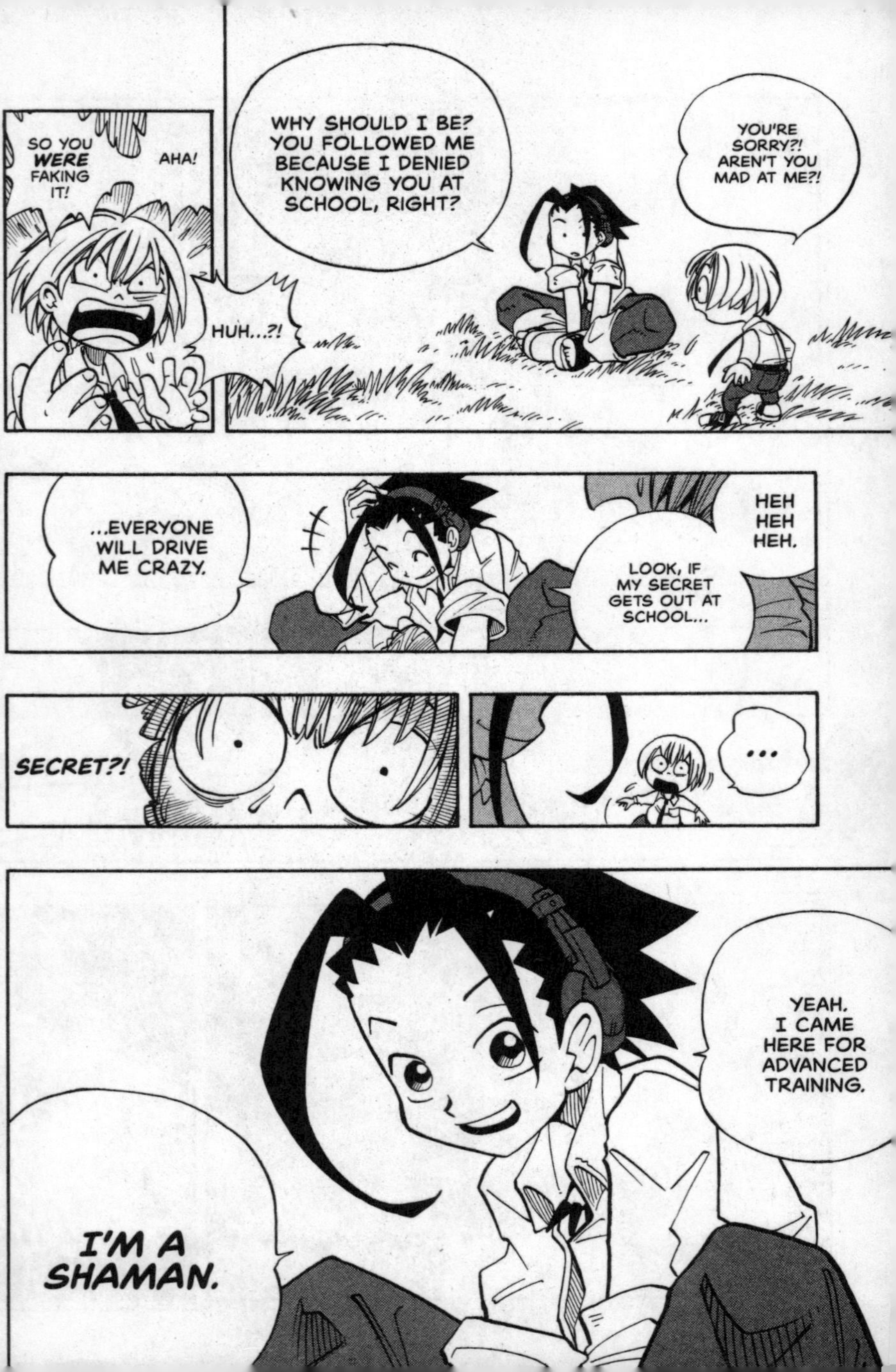
YOU'RE SORRY?! AREN'T YOU MAD AT ME?!
WHY SHOULD I BE? YOU FOLLOWED ME BECAUSE I DENIED KNOWING YOU AT SCHOOL, RIGHT?
AHA!
SO YOU *WERE* FAKING IT!
HUH...?!
HEH HEH HEH.
LOOK, IF MY SECRET GETS OUT AT SCHOOL...
...EVERYONE WILL DRIVE ME CRAZY.
...
SECRET?!
YEAH. I CAME HERE FOR ADVANCED TRAINING.
I'M A SHAMAN.

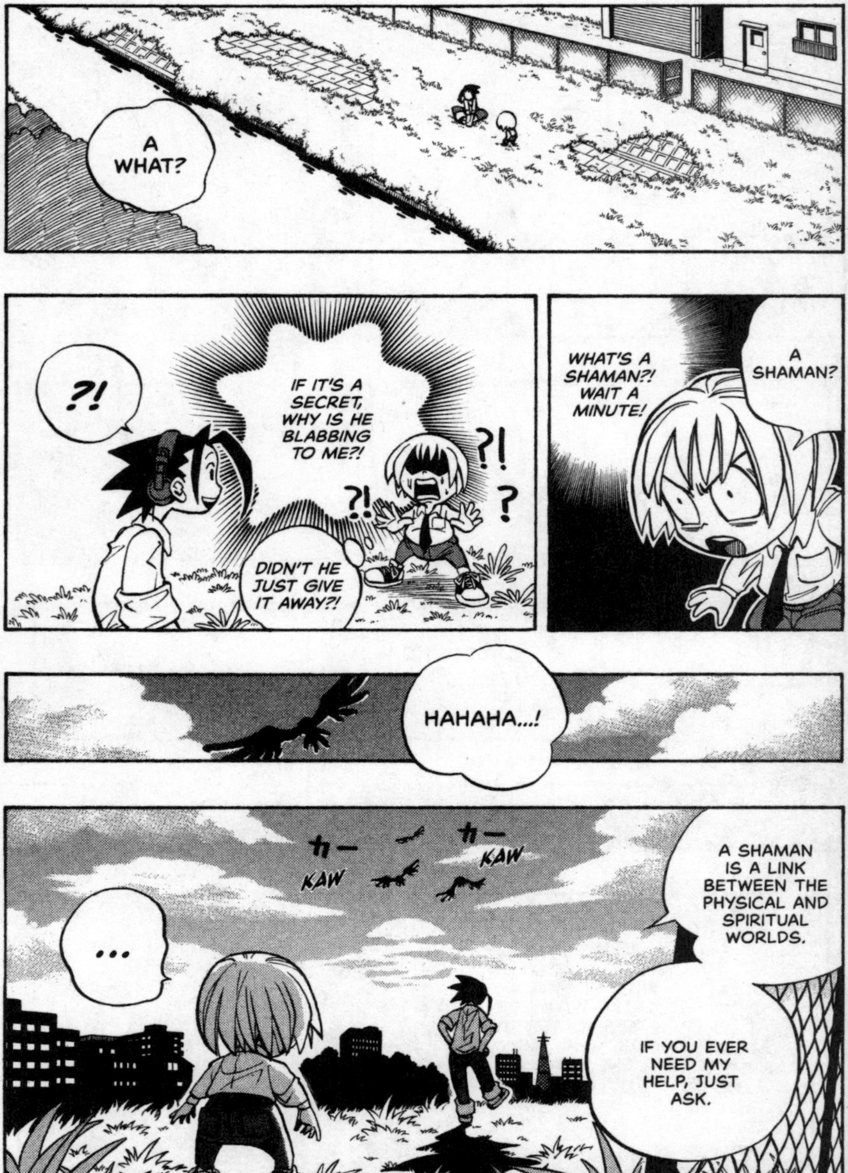
A WHAT?
A SHAMAN?
WHAT'S A SHAMAN?! WAIT A MINUTE!
?! ?
IF IT'S A SECRET, WHY IS HE BLABBING TO ME?!
?!
DIDN'T HE JUST GIVE IT AWAY?!
?!
HAHAHA...!
A SHAMAN IS A LINK BETWEEN THE PHYSICAL AND SPIRITUAL WORLDS.
IF YOU EVER NEED MY HELP, JUST ASK.
カー KAW
カー KAW
...

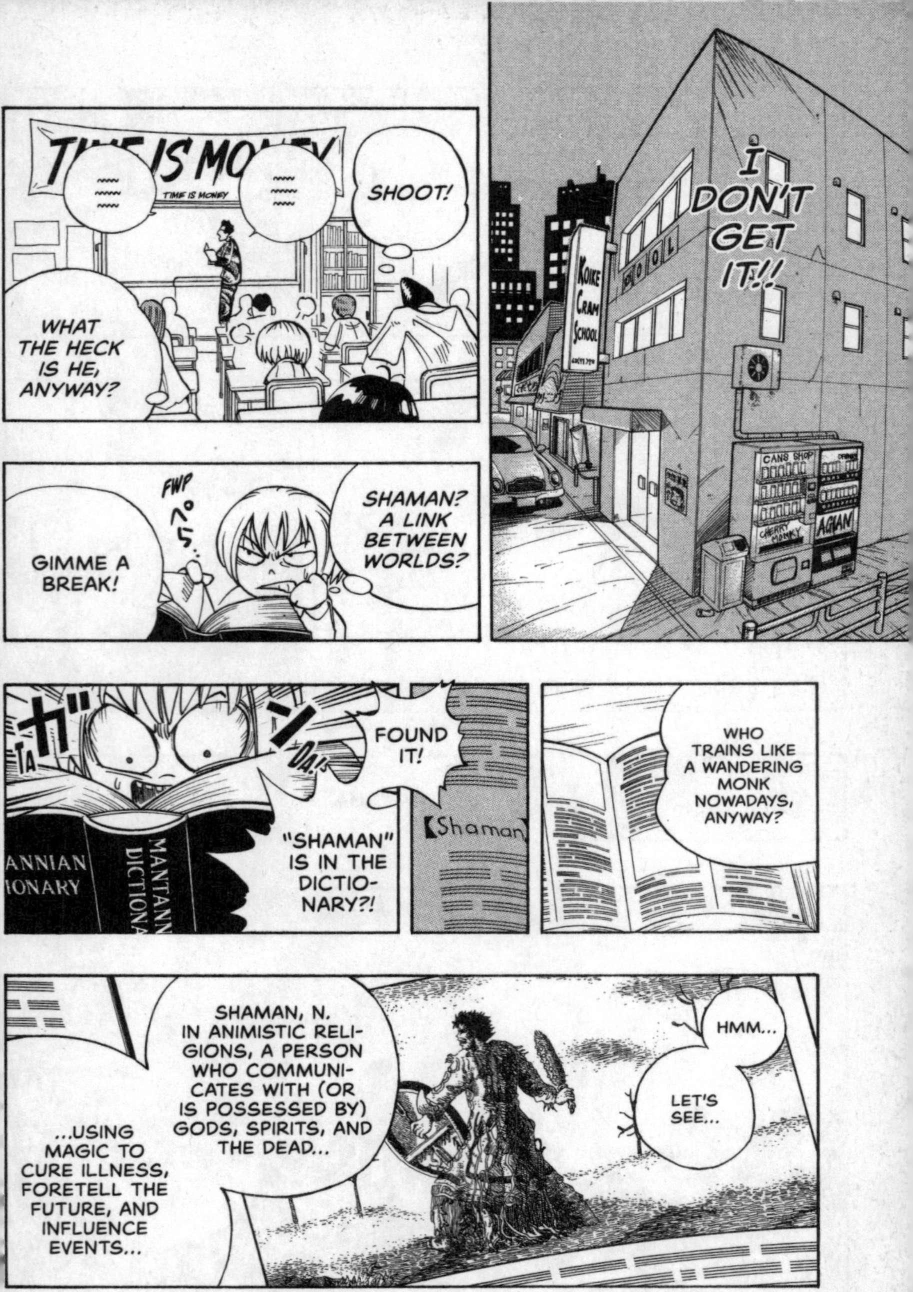
I DON'T GET IT!!
KOIKE CRAM SCHOOL
CANS SHOP
TIME IS MONEY
SHOOT!
WHAT THE HECK IS HE, ANYWAY?
SHAMAN? A LINK BETWEEN WORLDS?
FWP
GIMME A BREAK!
WHO TRAINS LIKE A WANDERING MONK NOWADAYS, ANYWAY?
【Shaman】
TA
DA!
FOUND IT!
"SHAMAN" IS IN THE DICTIONARY?!
HMM...
LET'S SEE...
SHAMAN, N. IN ANIMISTIC RELIGIONS, A PERSON WHO COMMUNICATES WITH (OR IS POSSESSED BY) GODS, SPIRITS, AND THE DEAD...
...USING MAGIC TO CURE ILLNESS, FORETELL THE FUTURE, AND INFLUENCE EVENTS...

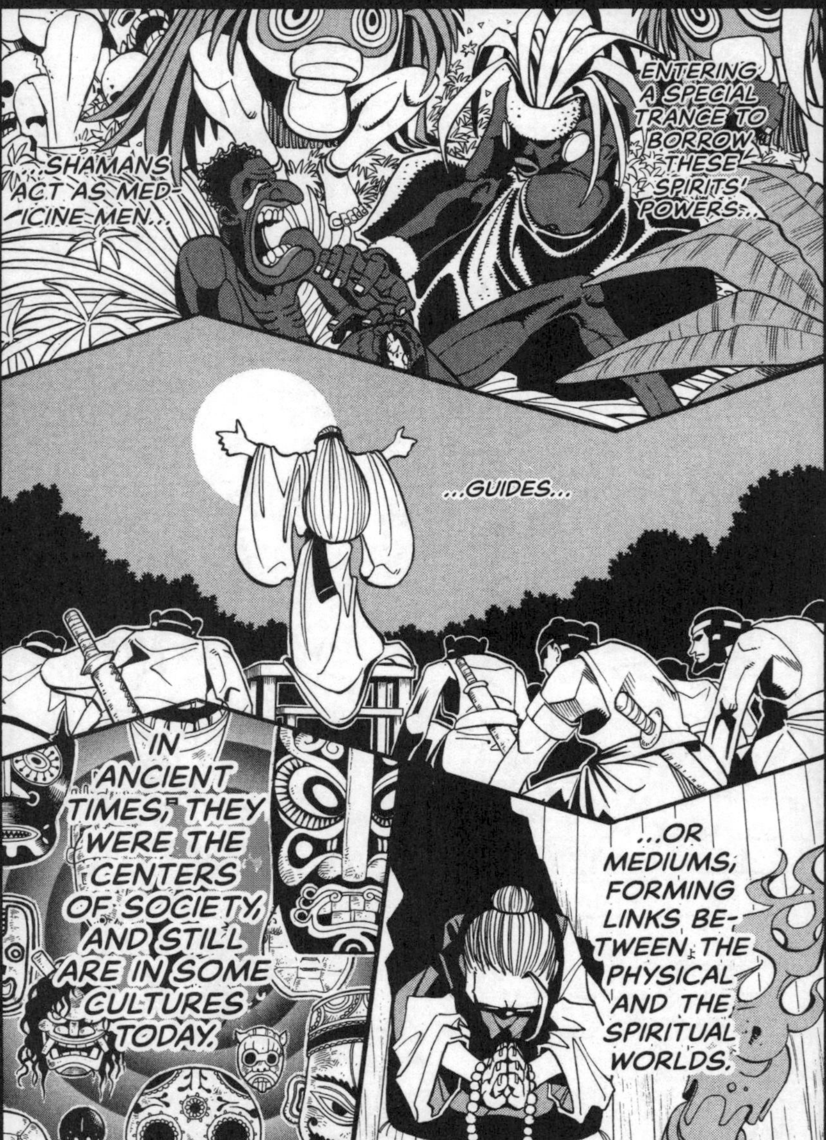
ENTERING A SPECIAL TRANCE TO BORROW THESE SPIRITS' POWERS...
...SHAMANS ACT AS MEDICINE MEN...
...GUIDES...
...OR MEDIUMS, FORMING LINKS BETWEEN THE PHYSICAL AND THE SPIRITUAL WORLDS.
IN ANCIENT TIMES, THEY WERE THE CENTERS OF SOCIETY, AND STILL ARE IN SOME CULTURES TODAY.

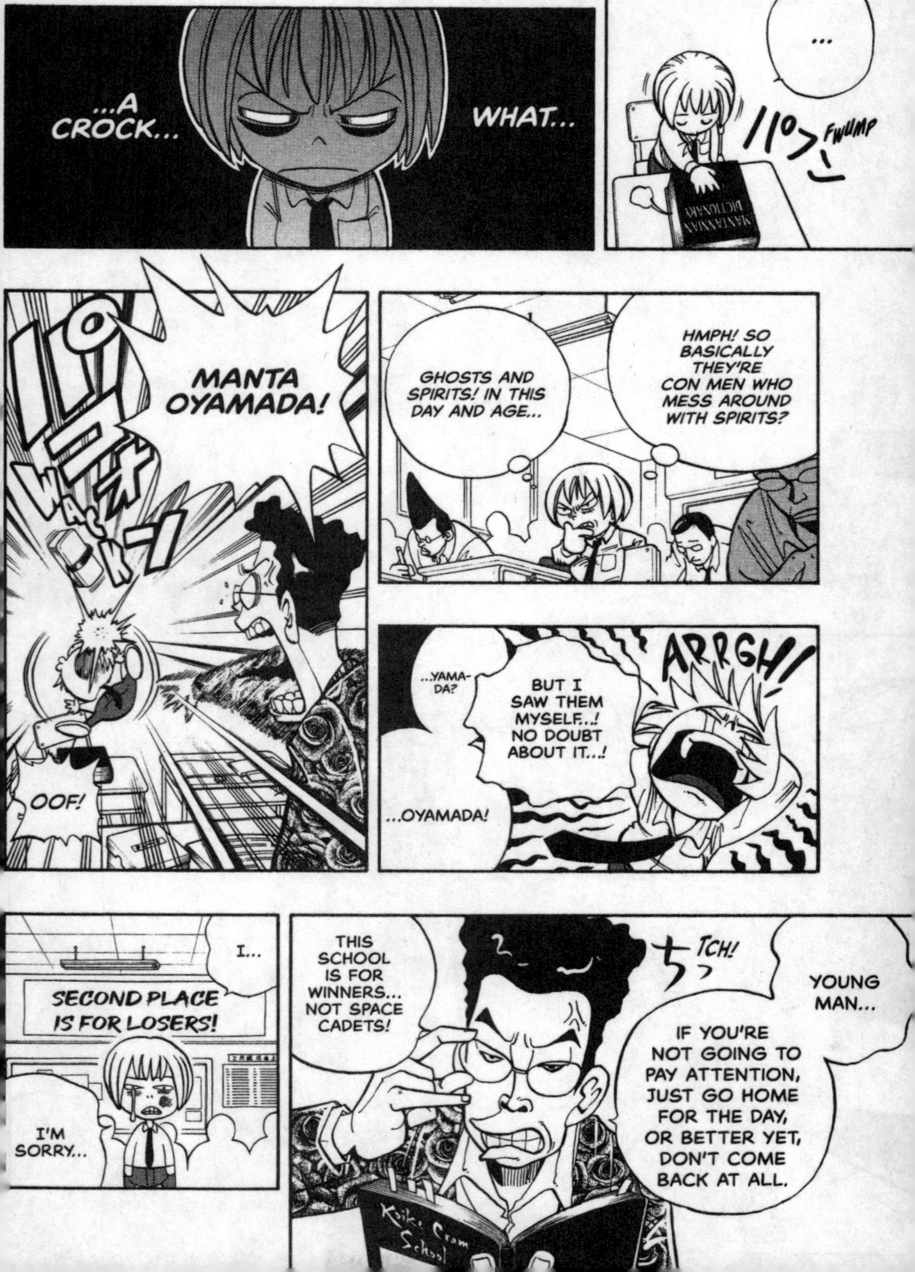
...
FWUMP
WHAT...
...A CROCK...
HMPH! SO BASICALLY THEY'RE CON MEN WHO MESS AROUND WITH SPIRITS?
GHOSTS AND SPIRITS! IN THIS DAY AND AGE...
ARRGH!
BUT I SAW THEM MYSELF...! NO DOUBT ABOUT IT...!
...YAMA-DA?
...OYAMADA!
MANTA OYAMADA!
WACK
OOF!
TCH!
YOUNG MAN...
IF YOU'RE NOT GOING TO PAY ATTENTION, JUST GO HOME FOR THE DAY, OR BETTER YET, DON'T COME BACK AT ALL.
THIS SCHOOL IS FOR WINNERS... NOT SPACE CADETS!
Koike Cram School
I...
SECOND PLACE IS FOR LOSERS!
I'M SORRY...

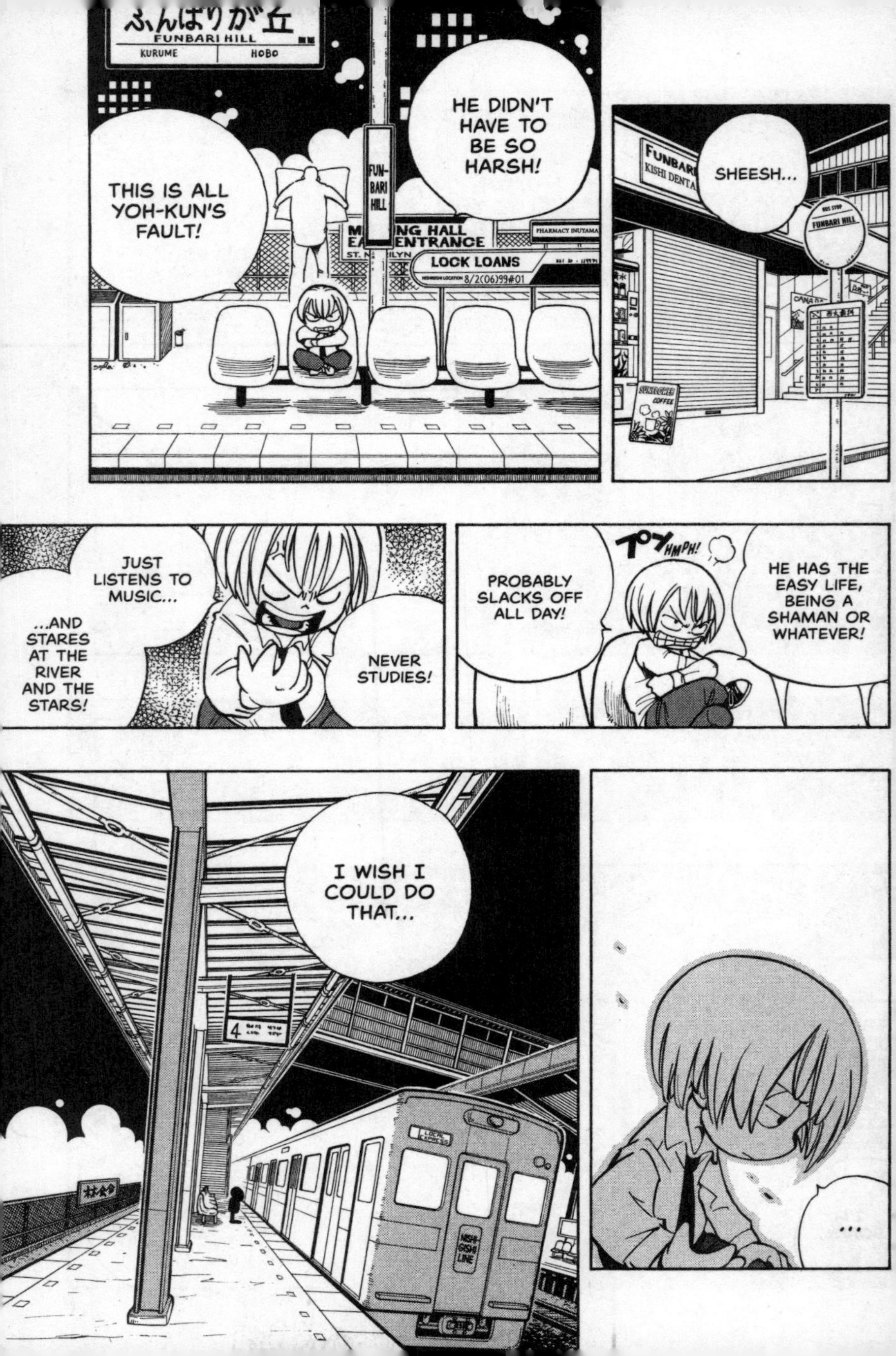
FUNBARI
KISHI DENTA
SHEESH...
BUS STOP
FUNBARI HILL
SUNFLOWER COFFEE
ふんばりが丘
FUNBARI HILL
KURUME
HOBO
HE DIDN'T HAVE TO BE SO HARSH!
FUN-BARI HILL
THIS IS ALL YOH-KUN'S FAULT!
PHARMACY INUYAMA
LOCK LOANS
HE HAS THE EASY LIFE, BEING A SHAMAN OR WHATEVER!
HMPH!
PROBABLY SLACKS OFF ALL DAY!
JUST LISTENS TO MUSIC...
...AND STARES AT THE RIVER AND THE STARS!
NEVER STUDIES!
...
I WISH I COULD DO THAT...
LOCAL EXPRESS
NISHI-GISHI LINE

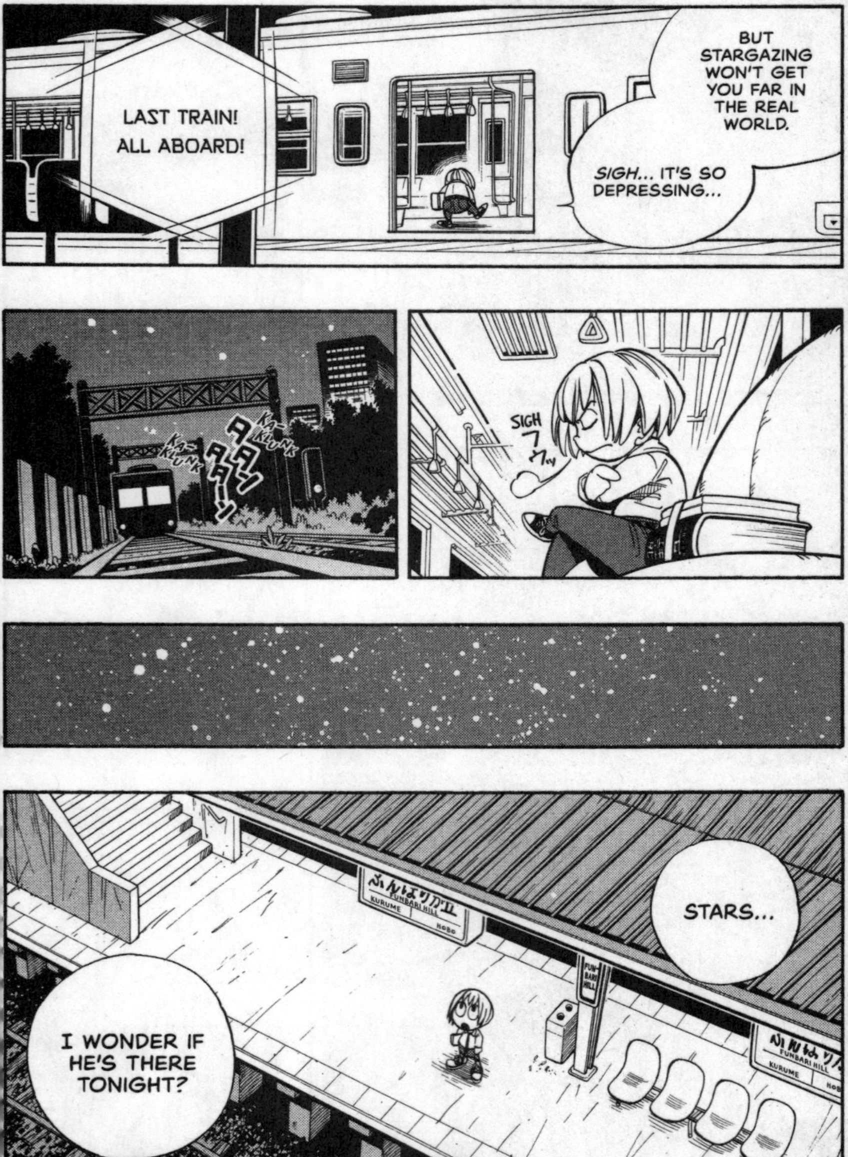
BUT STARGAZING WON'T GET YOU FAR IN THE REAL WORLD.
SIGH... IT'S SO DEPRESSING...
LAST TRAIN! ALL ABOARD!
SIGH
KA-KLUNK
KA-KLUNK
ふんばりが丘
FUNBARI HILL
KURUME
HOBO
STARS...
FUN-BARI HILL
FUNBARI HILL
KURUME
I WONDER IF HE'S THERE TONIGHT?

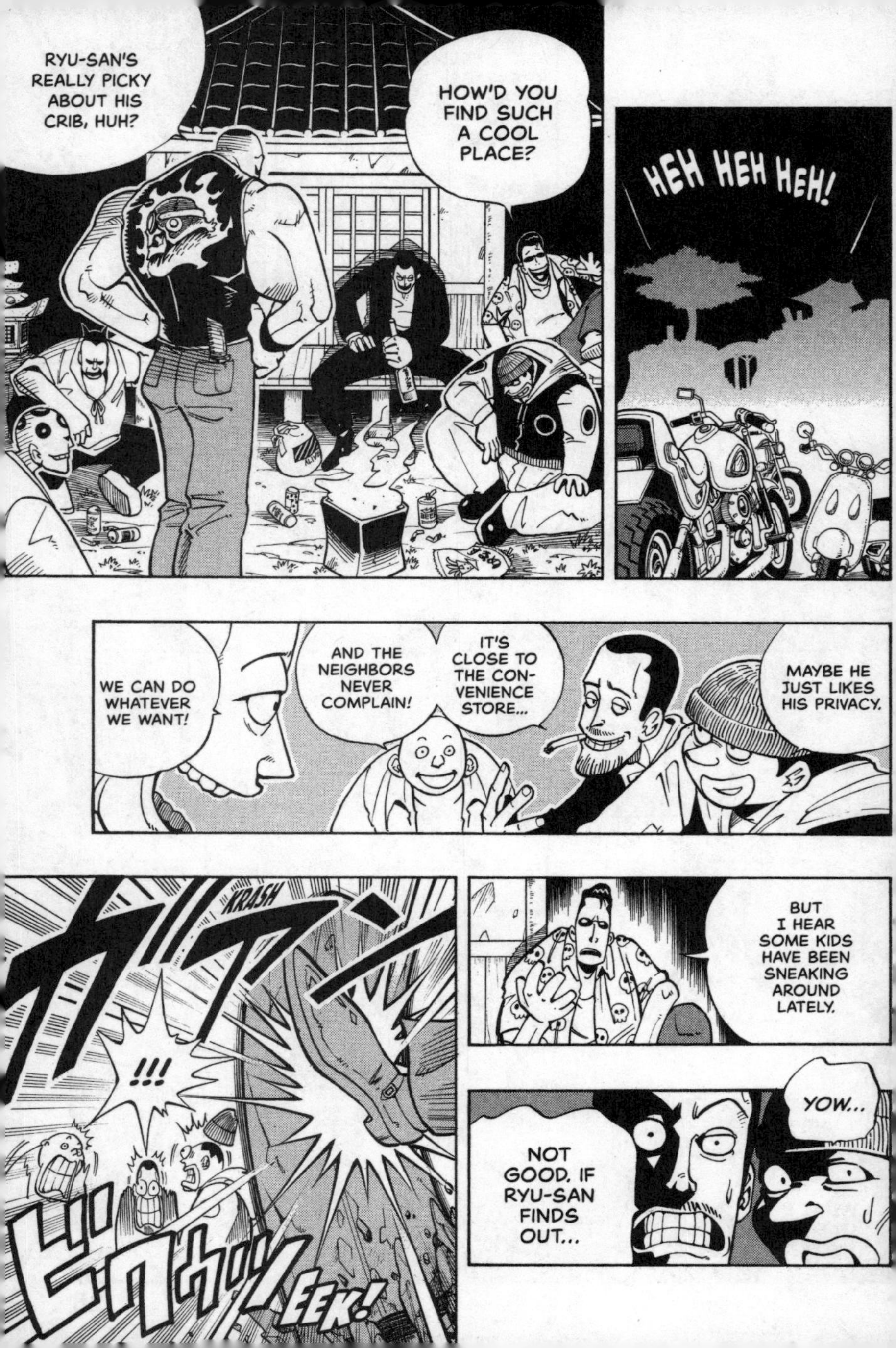
HEH HEH HEH!
HOW'D YOU FIND SUCH A COOL PLACE?
RYU-SAN'S REALLY PICKY ABOUT HIS CRIB, HUH?
MAYBE HE JUST LIKES HIS PRIVACY.
IT'S CLOSE TO THE CON-VENIENCE STORE...
AND THE NEIGHBORS NEVER COMPLAIN!
WE CAN DO WHATEVER WE WANT!
BUT I HEAR SOME KIDS HAVE BEEN SNEAKING AROUND LATELY.
YOW...
NOT GOOD. IF RYU-SAN FINDS OUT...
KRASH
!!!
EEK!

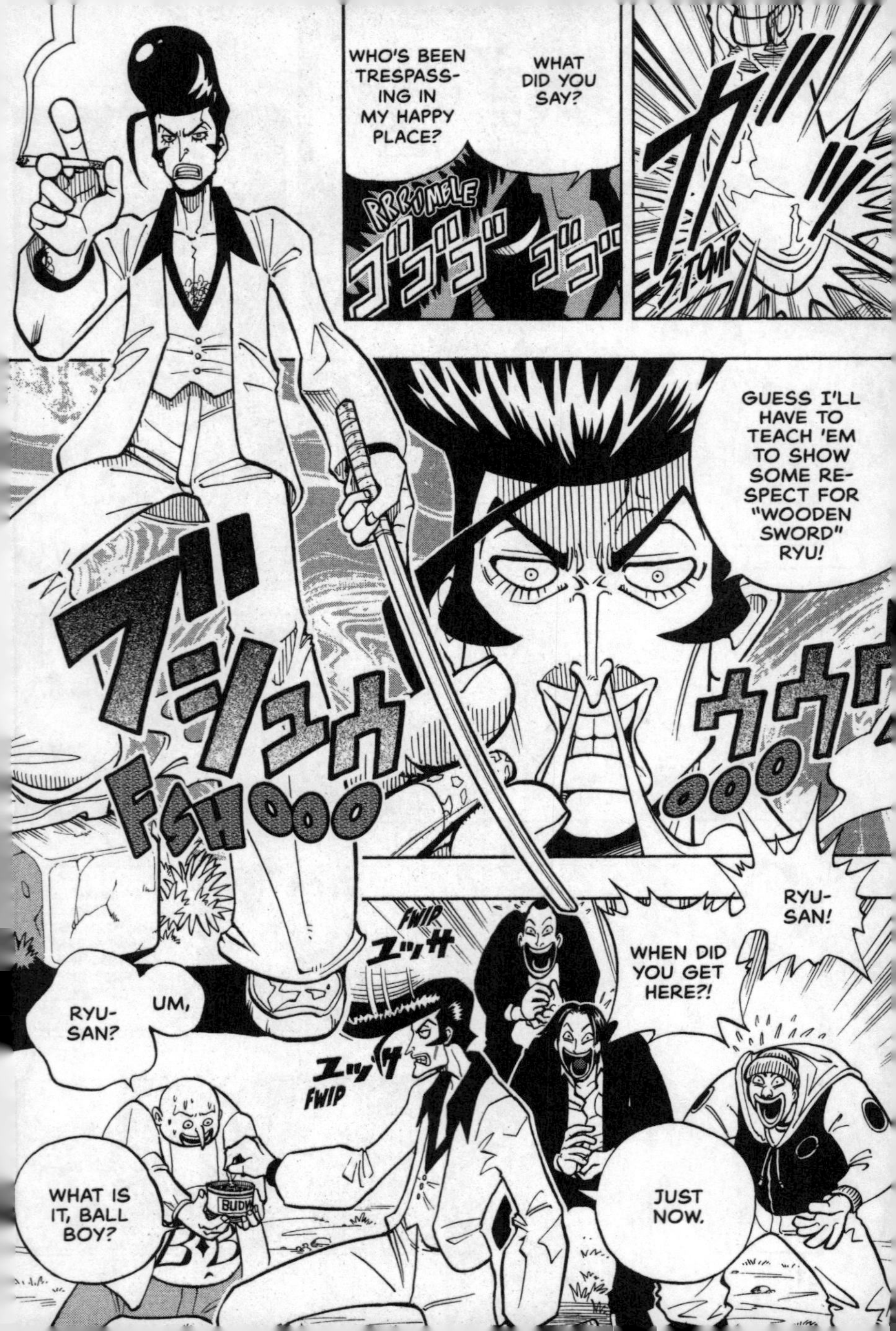
STOMP
WHAT DID YOU SAY?
WHO'S BEEN TRESPASSING IN MY HAPPY PLACE?
RRRUMBLE
ゴゴゴ ゴゴ
GUESS I'LL HAVE TO TEACH 'EM TO SHOW SOME RESPECT FOR "WOODEN SWORD" RYU!
ブシュウウウ
FSHOOOOOOO
RYU-SAN!
WHEN DID YOU GET HERE?!
JUST NOW.
ユッサ
FWIP
ユッサ
FWIP
UM,
RYU-SAN?
WHAT IS IT, BALL BOY?

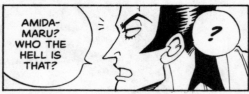

TH-THAT GRAVE!
THAT'S AMIDAMARU'S GRAVE!
AMIDAMARU? WHO THE HELL IS THAT?
?
THE FIEND, AMIDAMARU.
IT'S THE LOCAL SAMURAI LEGEND...
Grave: *Namu Amida Butsu*
SIX HUNDRED YEARS AGO, THERE WAS A REALLY TOUGH SAMURAI WHO KILLED A LOT OF PEOPLE... EVERYBODY WAS AFRAID OF HIM. THEY WERE EVEN SCARED OF HIM AFTER THEY EXECUTED HIM!
SO THEY SET UP THIS STONE IN HIS HONOR SO HIS ANGRY GHOST WOULDN'T HAUNT THEM! YOU MIGHT GET CURSED IF YOU STEP ON IT!
"THE FIEND AMIDAMARU" — PAINTING IN SAIGAN TEMPLE
CURSED, HUH?
HUH?

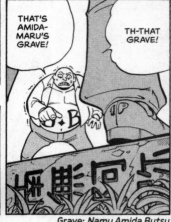

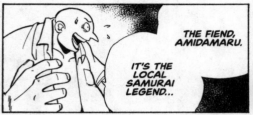

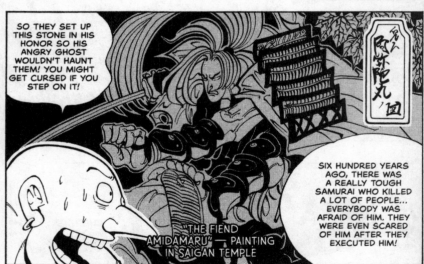

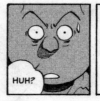

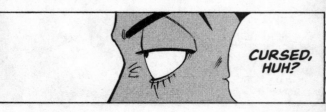

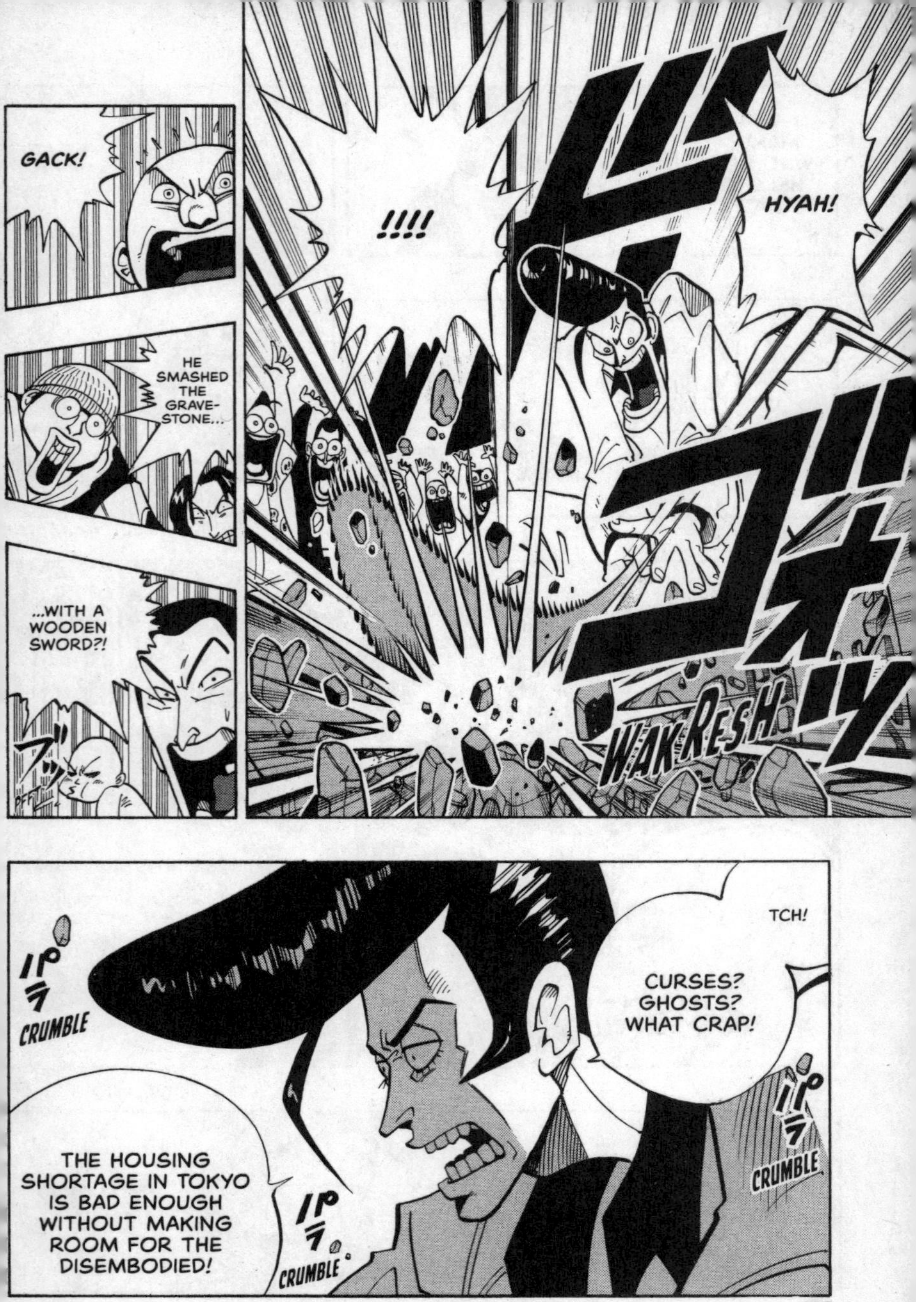
HYAH!
!!!!
WAKRESH
GACK!
HE SMASHED THE GRAVESTONE...
...WITH A WOODEN SWORD?!
TCH!
CURSES? GHOSTS? WHAT CRAP!
CRUMBLE
CRUMBLE
THE HOUSING SHORTAGE IN TOKYO IS BAD ENOUGH WITHOUT MAKING ROOM FOR THE DISEMBODIED!
CRUMBLE

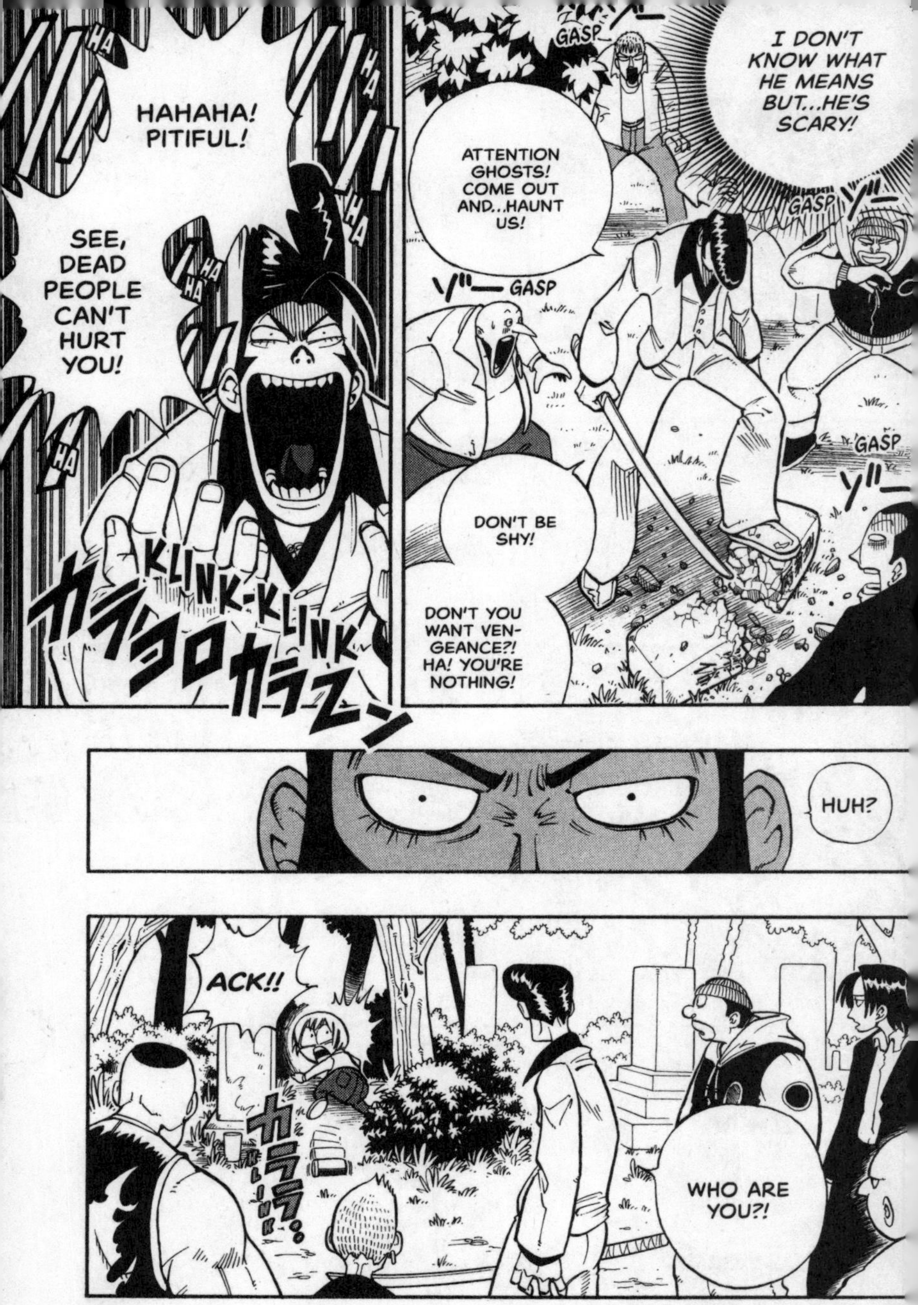

I DON'T KNOW WHAT HE MEANS BUT...HE'S SCARY!
GASP
ATTENTION GHOSTS! COME OUT AND...HAUNT US!
GASP
GASP
GASP
DON'T BE SHY!
DON'T YOU WANT VEN-GEANCE?! HA! YOU'RE NOTHING!
HA HA HA HA HA HA HA
HAHAHA! PITIFUL!
SEE, DEAD PEOPLE CAN'T HURT YOU!
KLINK-KLINK-KLINK
HUH?
WHO ARE YOU?!
ACK!!

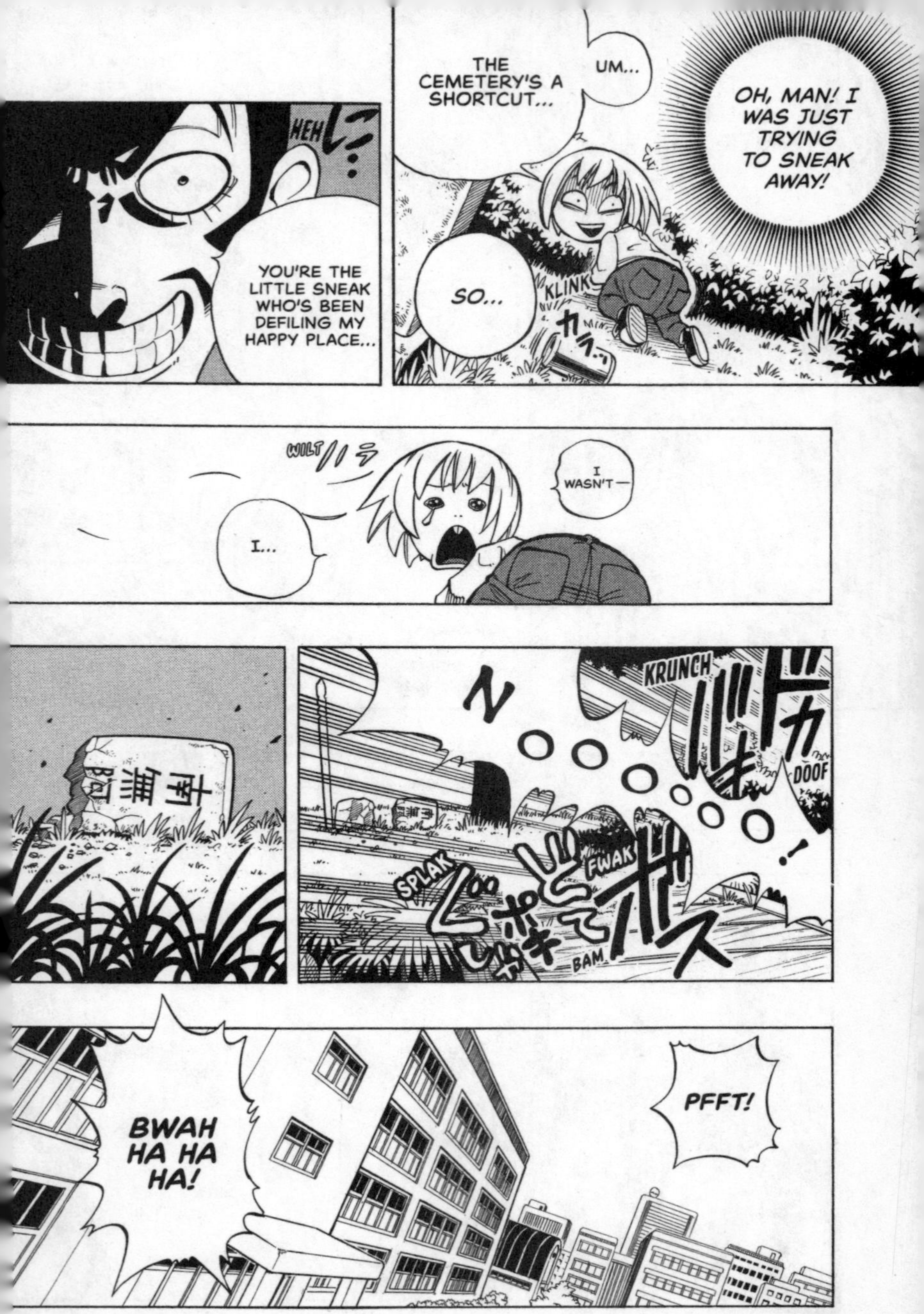
OH, MAN! I WAS JUST TRYING TO SNEAK AWAY!
UM...
THE CEMETERY'S A SHORTCUT...
SO...
KLINK
HEH
YOU'RE THE LITTLE SNEAK WHO'S BEEN DEFILING MY HAPPY PLACE...
WILT
I WASN'T—
I...
KRUNCH
DOOF
NOOOOOOOO!
FWAK
SPLAK
BAM
PFFT!
BWAH HA HA HA!

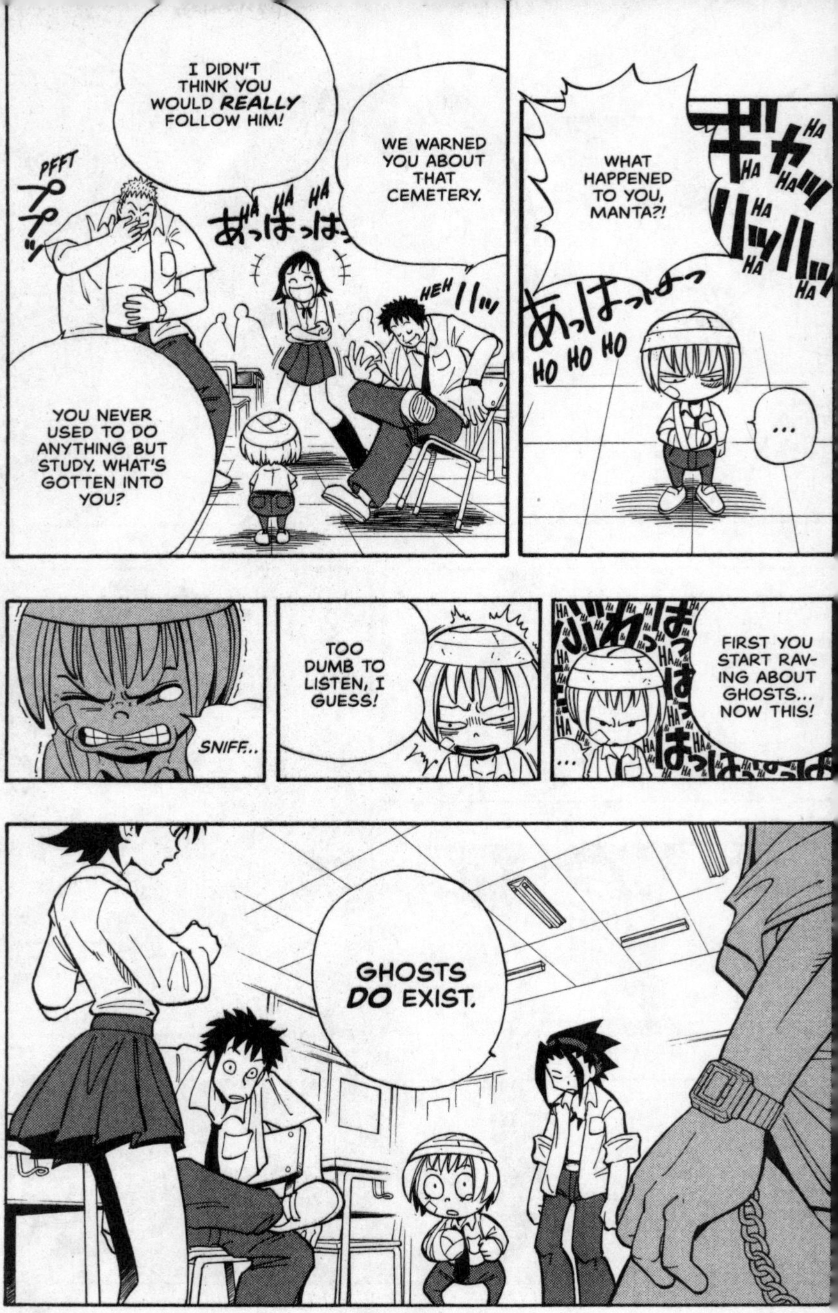
WHAT HAPPENED TO YOU, MANTA?!
HA HA HA HA HA HA
あっはっはっ
HO HO HO
...
I DIDN'T THINK YOU WOULD **REALLY** FOLLOW HIM!
WE WARNED YOU ABOUT THAT CEMETERY.
HA HA HA
あっはっはっ
PFFT
HEH
YOU NEVER USED TO DO ANYTHING BUT STUDY. WHAT'S GOTTEN INTO YOU?
FIRST YOU START RAVING ABOUT GHOSTS... NOW THIS!
...
TOO DUMB TO LISTEN, I GUESS!
SNIFF...
GHOSTS **DO** EXIST.

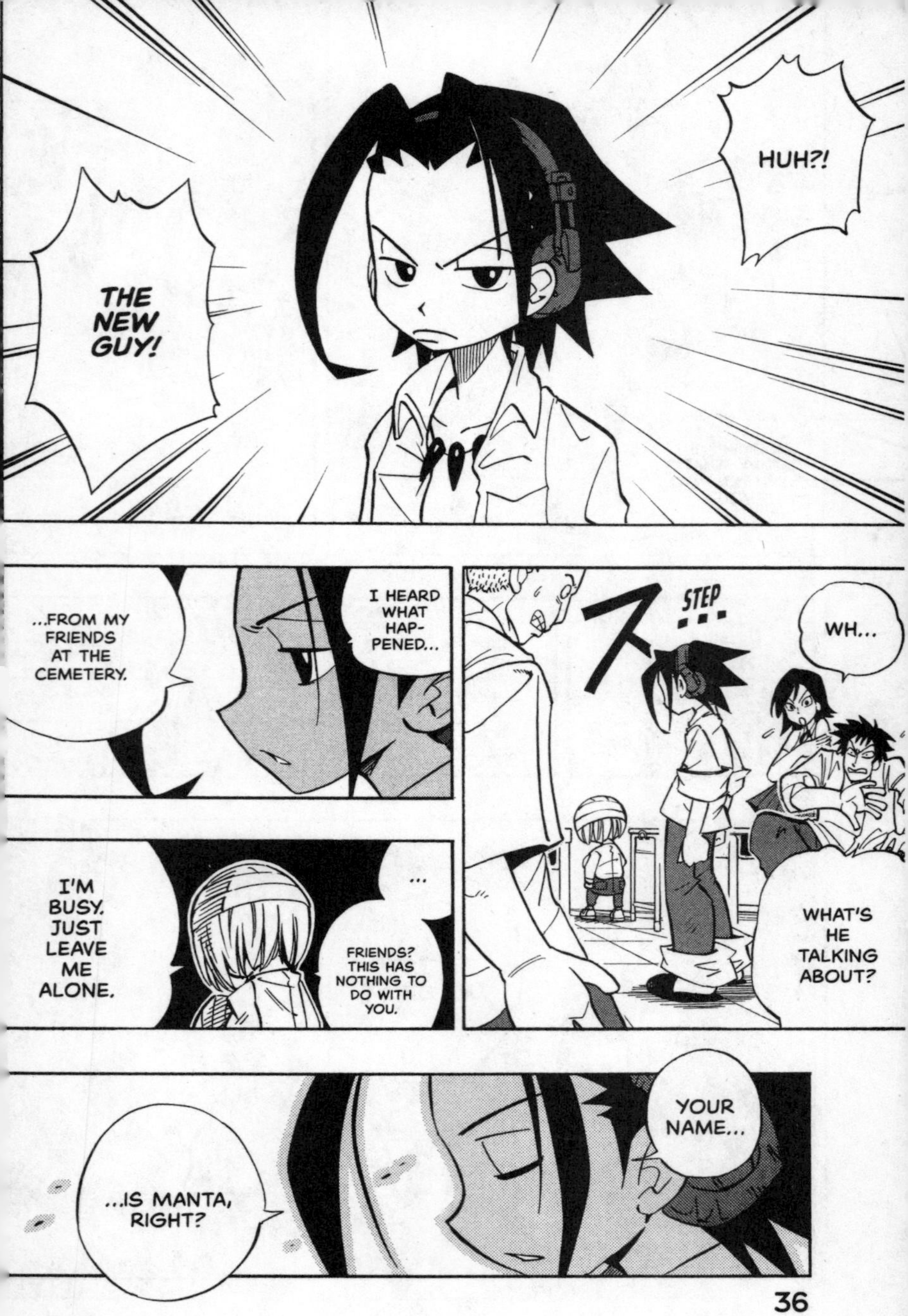
HUH?!
THE NEW GUY!
STEP
WH...
WHAT'S HE TALKING ABOUT?
I HEARD WHAT HAP-PENED...
...FROM MY FRIENDS AT THE CEMETERY.
...
FRIENDS? THIS HAS NOTHING TO DO WITH YOU.
I'M BUSY. JUST LEAVE ME ALONE.
YOUR NAME...
...IS MANTA, RIGHT?

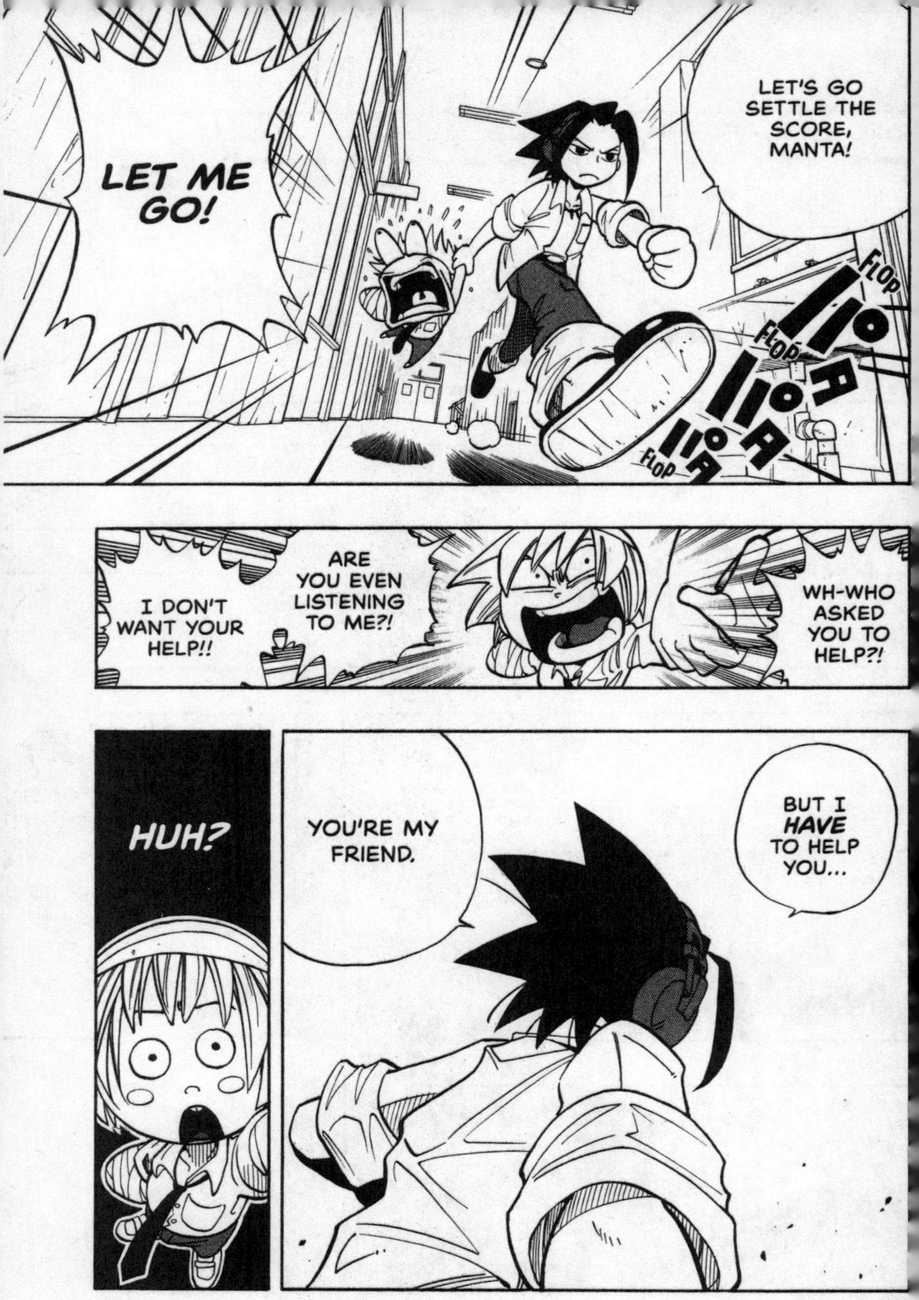
LET'S GO SETTLE THE SCORE, MANTA!
LET ME GO!
FLOP
FLOP
FLOP
WH-WHO ASKED YOU TO HELP?!
ARE YOU EVEN LISTENING TO ME?!
I DON'T WANT YOUR HELP!!
BUT I *HAVE* TO HELP YOU...
YOU'RE MY FRIEND.
HUH?

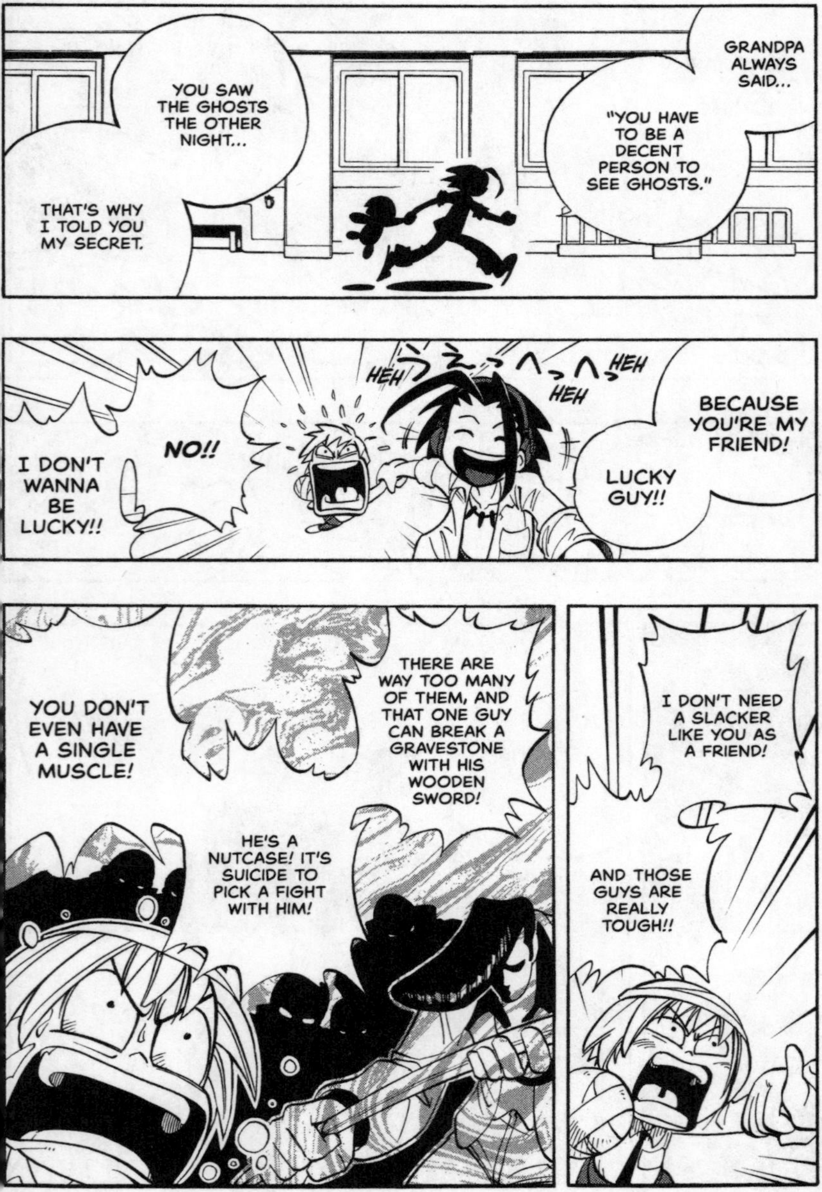
GRANDPA ALWAYS SAID...
"YOU HAVE TO BE A DECENT PERSON TO SEE GHOSTS."
YOU SAW THE GHOSTS THE OTHER NIGHT...
THAT'S WHY I TOLD YOU MY SECRET.
BECAUSE YOU'RE MY FRIEND!
LUCKY GUY!!
HEH HEH HEH
NO!!
I DON'T WANNA BE LUCKY!!
I DON'T NEED A SLACKER LIKE YOU AS A FRIEND!
AND THOSE GUYS ARE REALLY TOUGH!!
THERE ARE WAY TOO MANY OF THEM, AND THAT ONE GUY CAN BREAK A GRAVESTONE WITH HIS WOODEN SWORD!
YOU DON'T EVEN HAVE A SINGLE MUSCLE!
HE'S A NUTCASE! IT'S SUICIDE TO PICK A FIGHT WITH HIM!

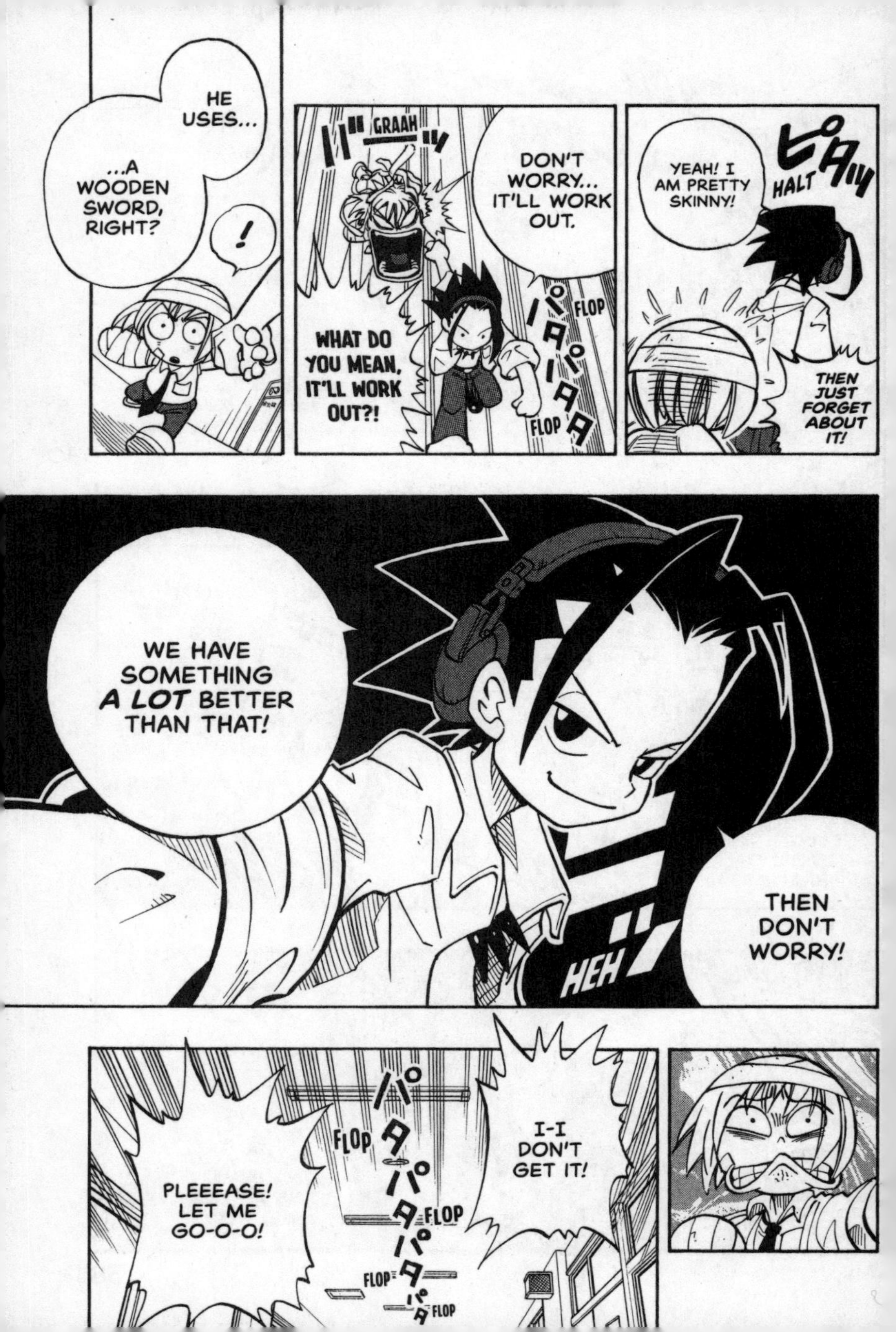
HALT
YEAH! I AM PRETTY SKINNY!
THEN JUST FORGET ABOUT IT!
DON'T WORRY... IT'LL WORK OUT.
GRAAH
WHAT DO YOU MEAN, IT'LL WORK OUT?!
FLOP
FLOP
HE USES...
...A WOODEN SWORD, RIGHT?
!
WE HAVE SOMETHING *A LOT* BETTER THAN THAT!
HEH
THEN DON'T WORRY!
I-I DON'T GET IT!
FLOP
FLOP
PLEEEASE! LET ME GO-O-O!
FLOP
FLOP

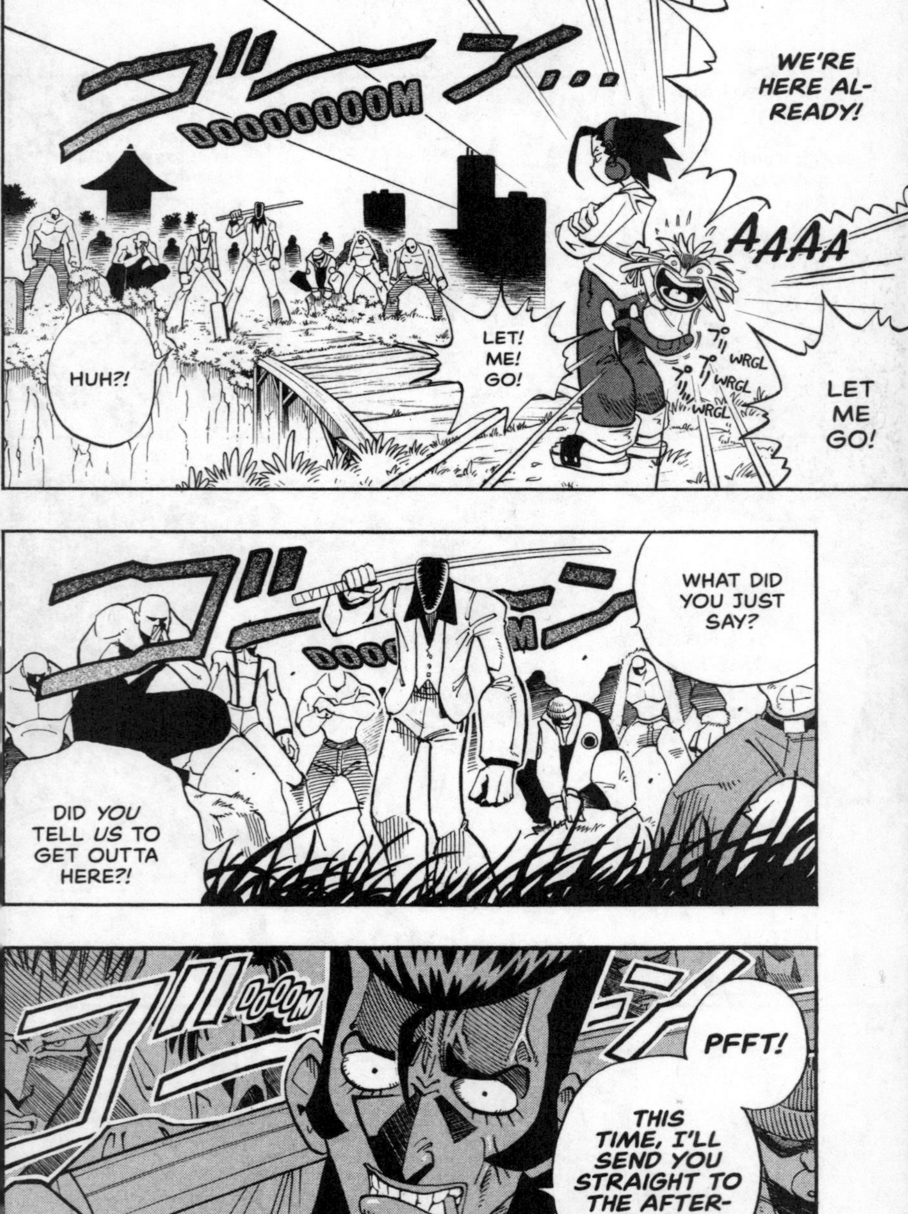
WE'RE HERE AL-READY!
DOOOOOOOOM
AAAA
LET ME GO!
WRGL
WRGL
WRGL
LET! ME! GO!
HUH?!
WHAT DID YOU JUST SAY?
DID *YOU* TELL *US* TO GET OUTTA HERE?!
PFFT!
THIS TIME, I'LL SEND YOU STRAIGHT TO THE AFTER-LIFE, PUNK.
DOOOM

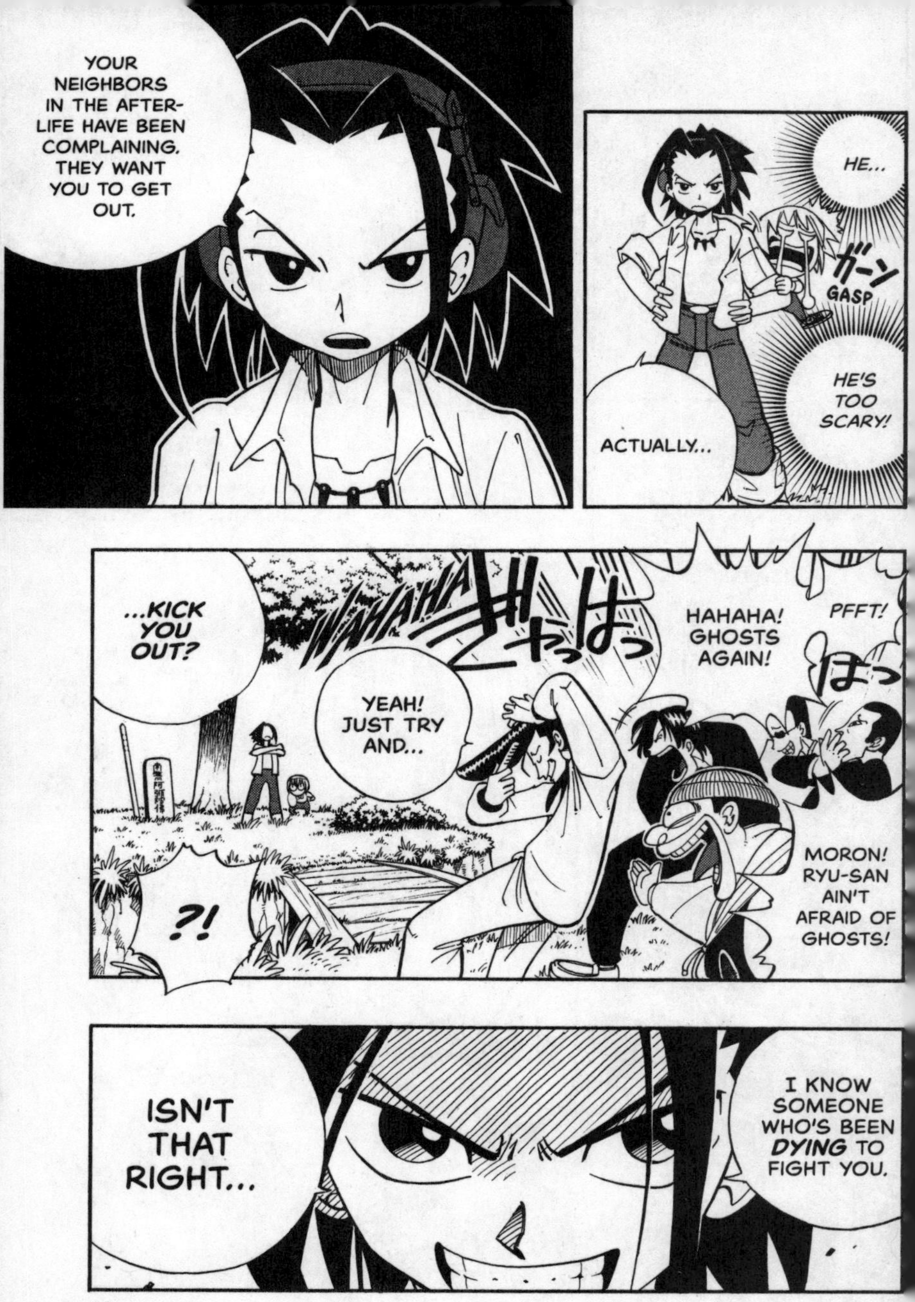
HE...
ガーン
GASP
HE'S TOO SCARY!
ACTUALLY...
YOUR NEIGHBORS IN THE AFTER-LIFE HAVE BEEN COMPLAINING. THEY WANT YOU TO GET OUT.
PFFT!
はっ
HAHAHA! GHOSTS AGAIN!
ぎゃっはっ
WAHAHA
MORON! RYU-SAN AIN'T AFRAID OF GHOSTS!
YEAH! JUST TRY AND...
...KICK YOU OUT?
?!
I KNOW SOMEONE WHO'S BEEN *DYING* TO FIGHT YOU.
ISN'T THAT RIGHT...

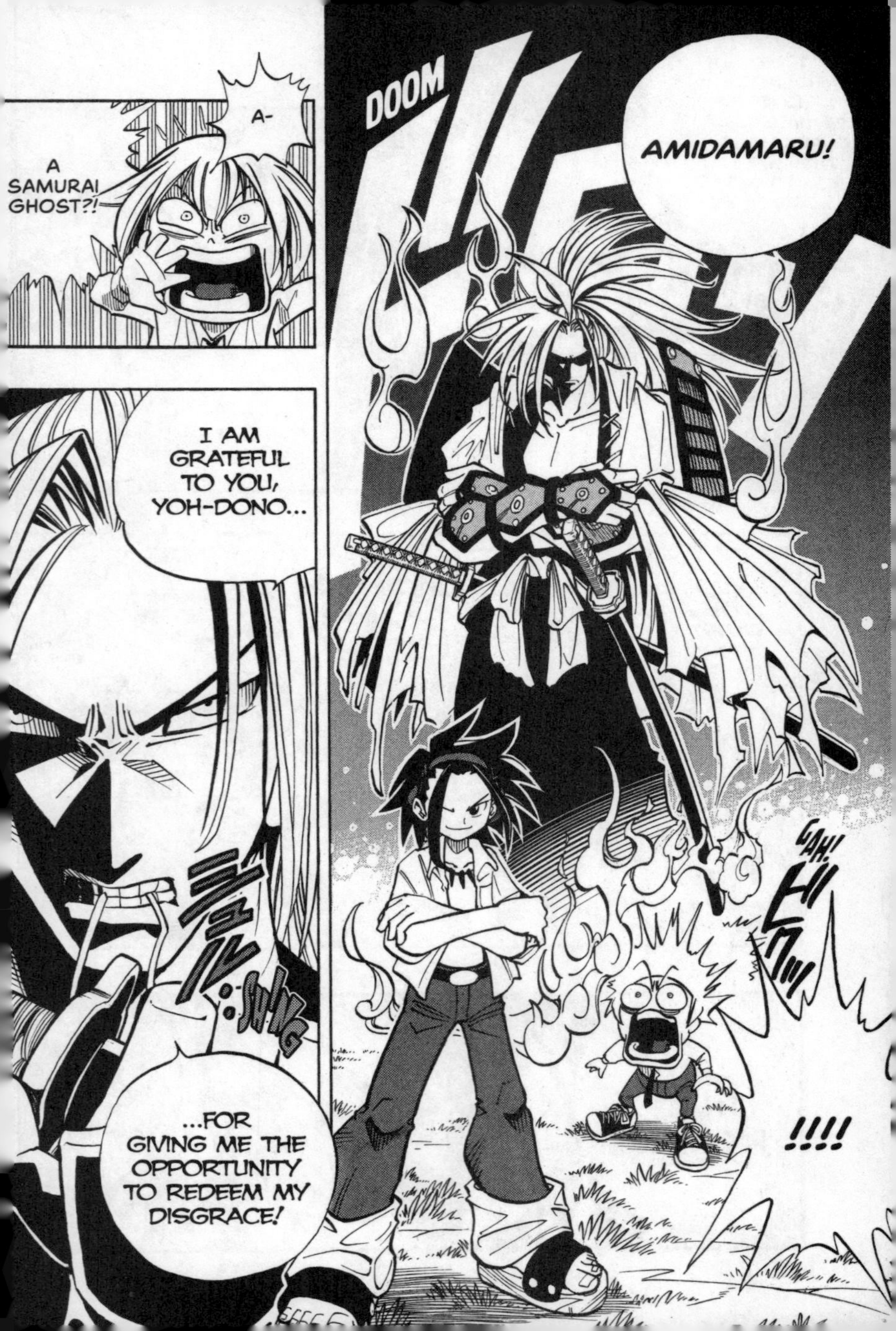
DOOM
AMIDAMARU!
GAH!
!!!!
A-
A SAMURAI GHOST?!
I AM GRATEFUL TO YOU, YOH-DONO...
SHING
...FOR GIVING ME THE OPPORTUNITY TO REDEEM MY DISGRACE!

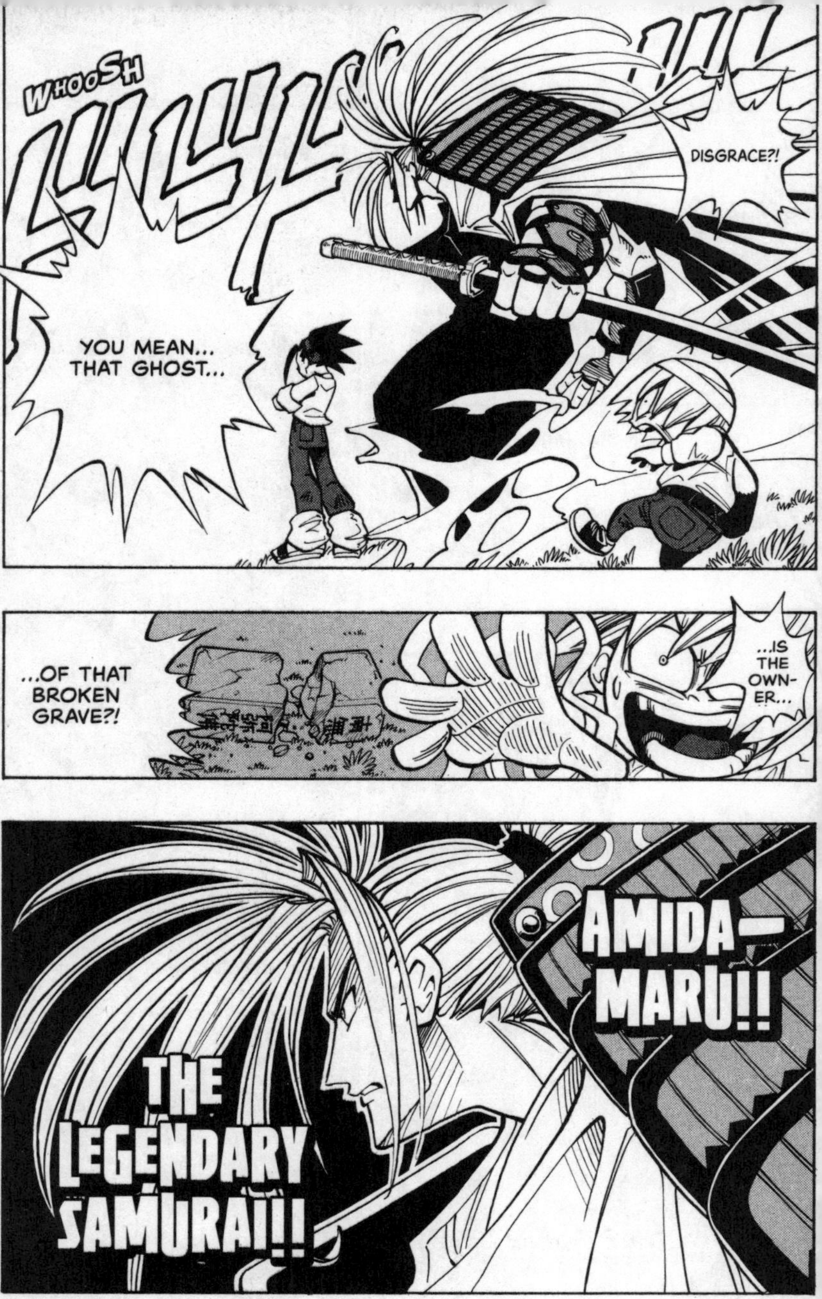
DISGRACE?!
WHOOSH
YOU MEAN... THAT GHOST...
...IS THE OWN-ER...
...OF THAT BROKEN GRAVE?!
AMIDA-MARU!!
THE LEGENDARY SAMURAI!!

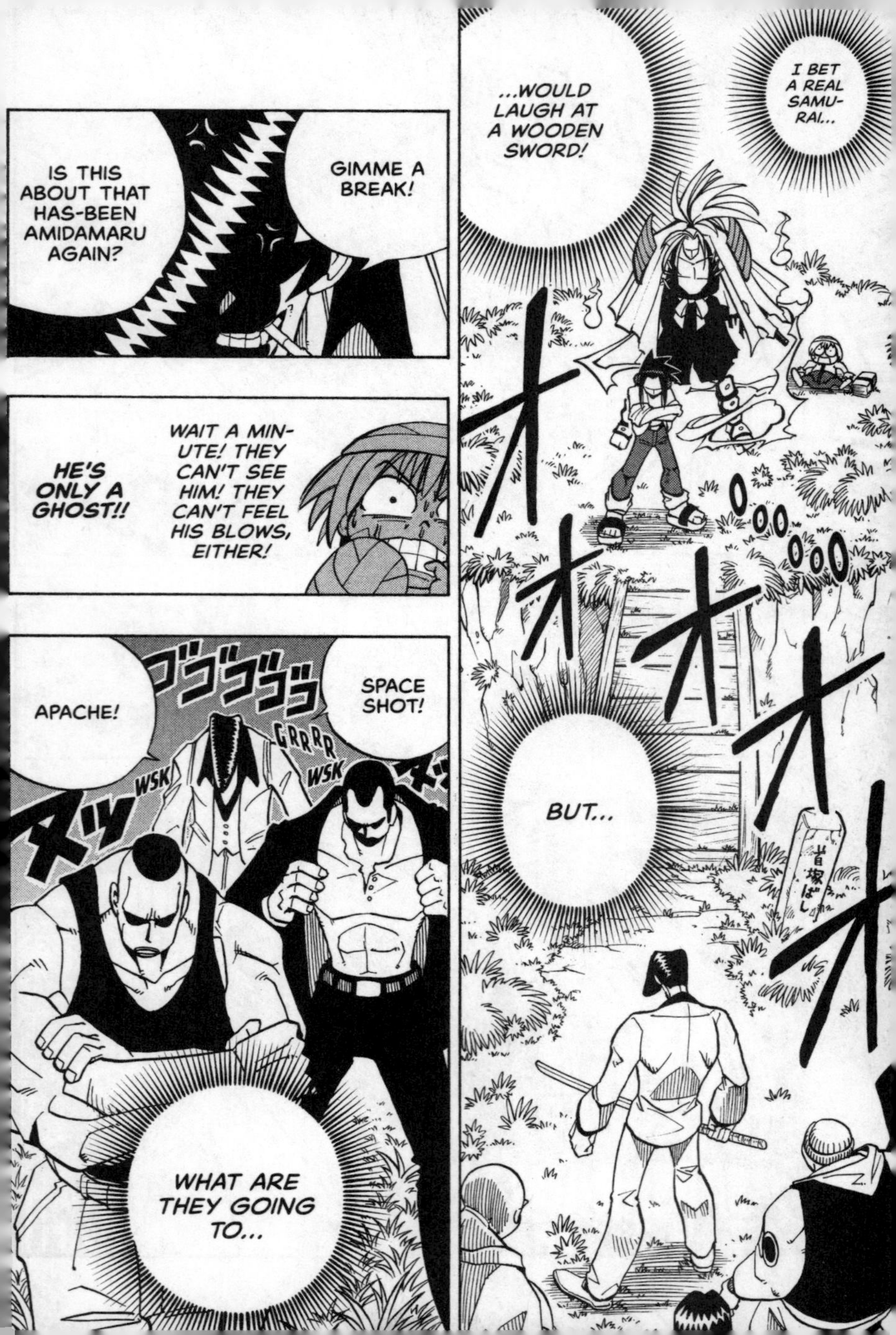
I BET A REAL SAMURAI...
...WOULD LAUGH AT A WOODEN SWORD!
オ オ オ オ オ
OOOOOO
BUT...
首塚ばし
GIMME A BREAK!
IS THIS ABOUT THAT HAS-BEEN AMIDAMARU AGAIN?
WAIT A MINUTE! THEY CAN'T SEE HIM! THEY CAN'T FEEL HIS BLOWS, EITHER!
HE'S ONLY A GHOST!!
SPACE SHOT!
ゴゴゴゴゴ
GRRRR
WSK
APACHE!
WSK
WHAT ARE THEY GOING TO...

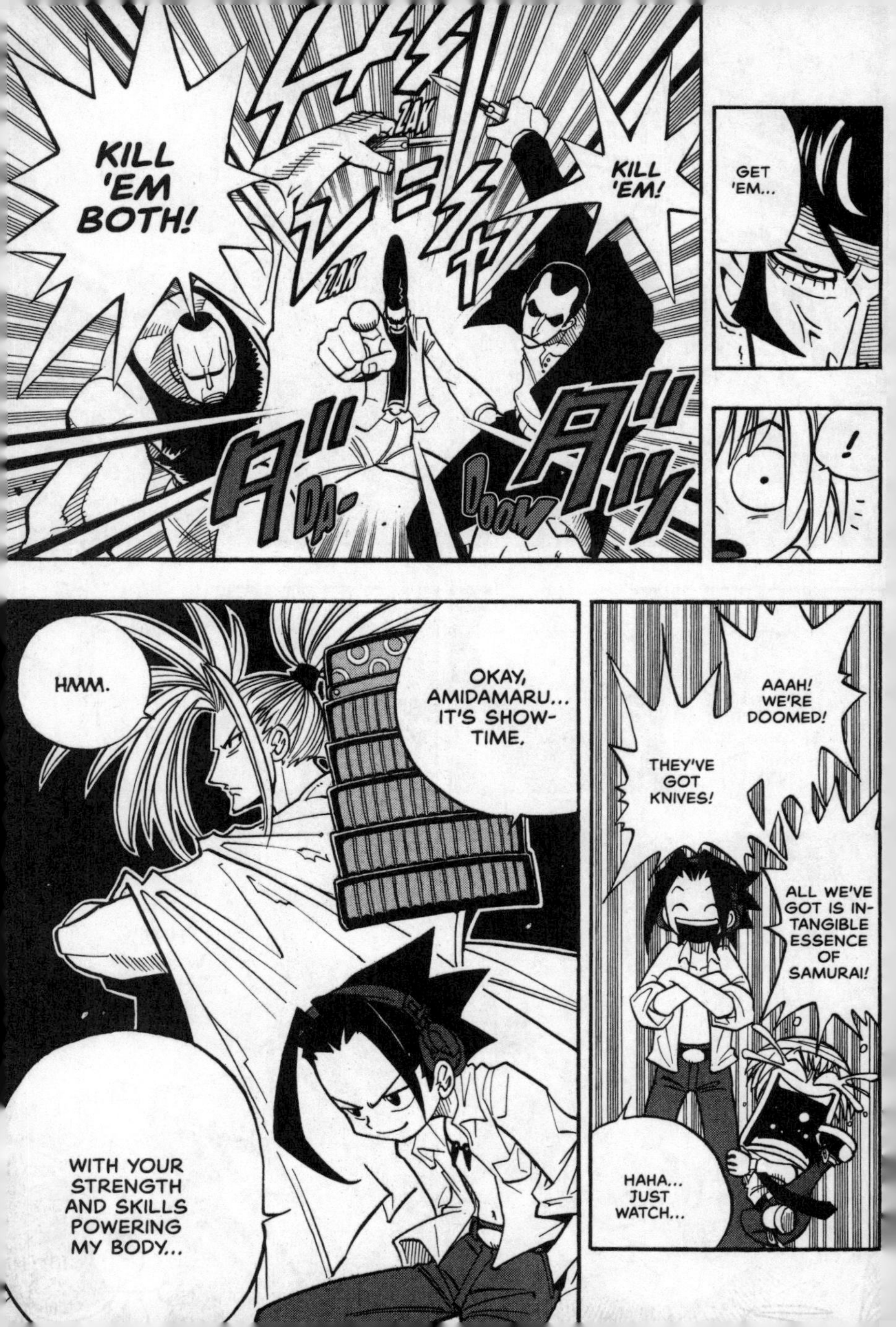
GET 'EM...
!
KILL 'EM!
ZAK
KILL 'EM BOTH!
ZAK
DA-
DOOM
AAAH! WE'RE DOOMED!
THEY'VE GOT KNIVES!
ALL WE'VE GOT IS IN-TANGIBLE ESSENCE OF SAMURAI!
HAHA... JUST WATCH...
OKAY, AMIDAMARU... IT'S SHOW-TIME.
HMM.
WITH YOUR STRENGTH AND SKILLS POWERING MY BODY...

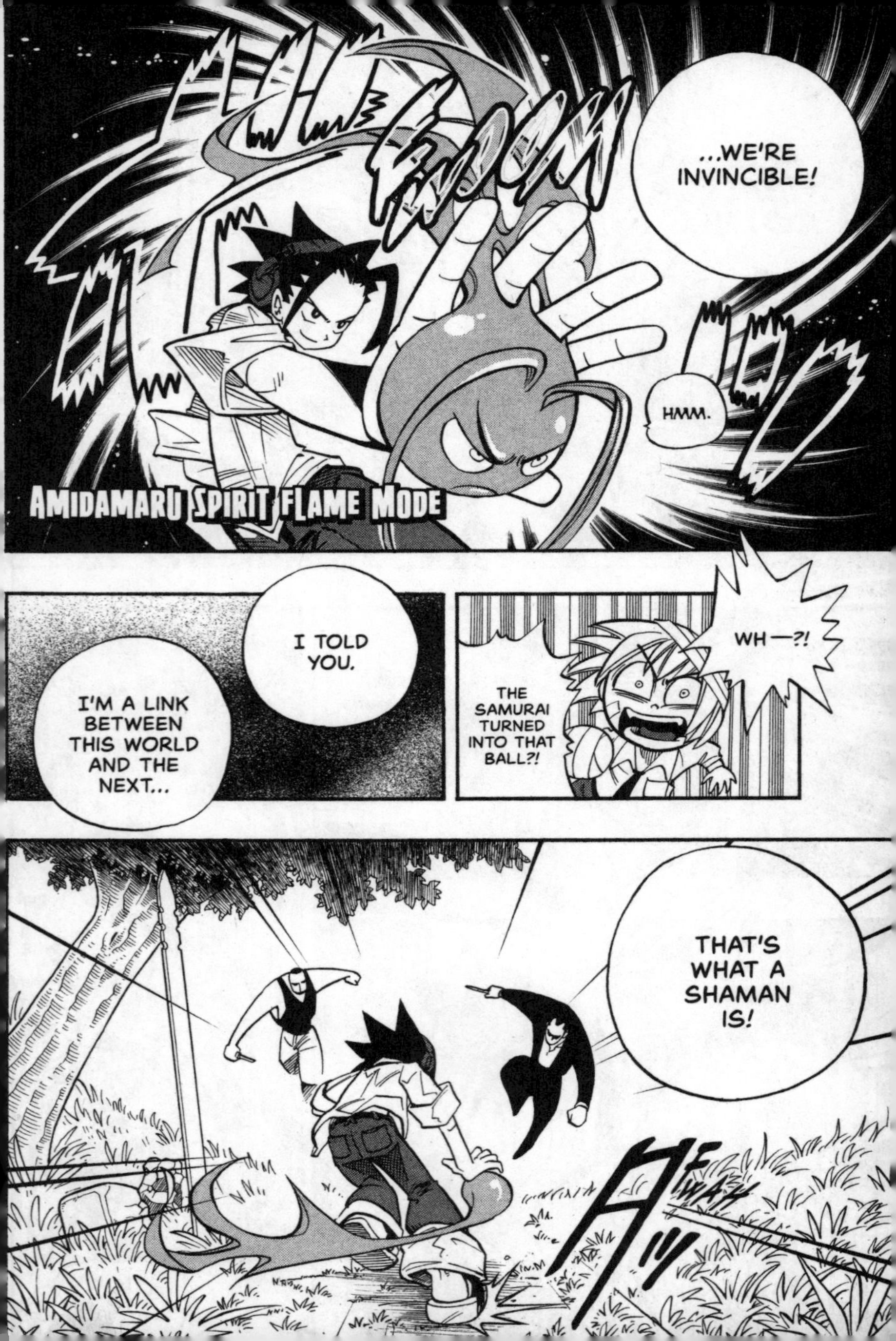
...WE'RE INVINCIBLE!
HMM.
AMIDAMARU SPIRIT FLAME MODE
WH—?!
THE SAMURAI TURNED INTO THAT BALL?!
I TOLD YOU.
I'M A LINK BETWEEN THIS WORLD AND THE NEXT...
THAT'S WHAT A SHAMAN IS!

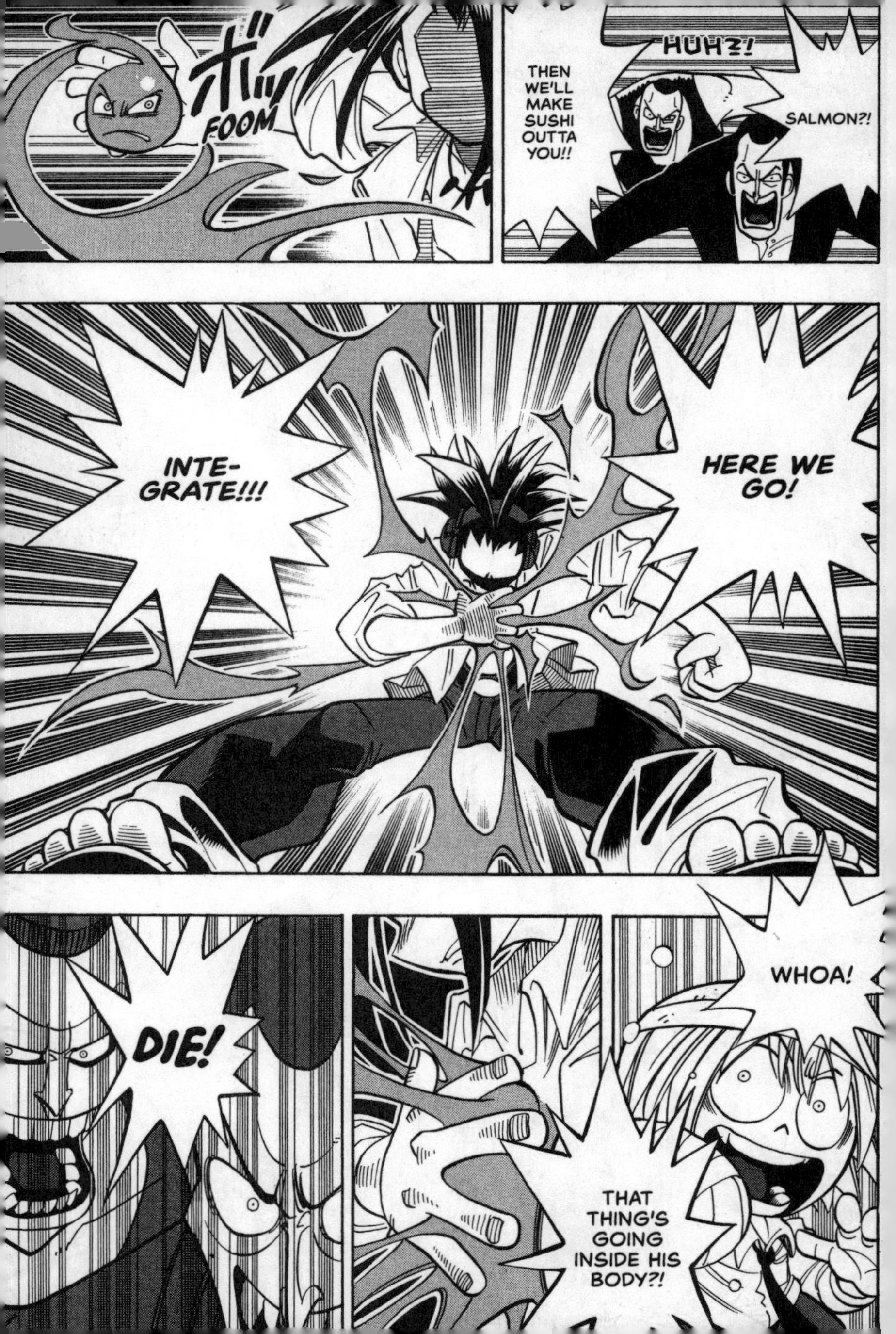
HUH?!
SALMON?!
THEN WE'LL MAKE SUSHI OUTTA YOU!!
ボッ
FOOM
HERE WE GO!
INTE-GRATE!!!
WHOA!
THAT THING'S GOING INSIDE HIS BODY?!
DIE!

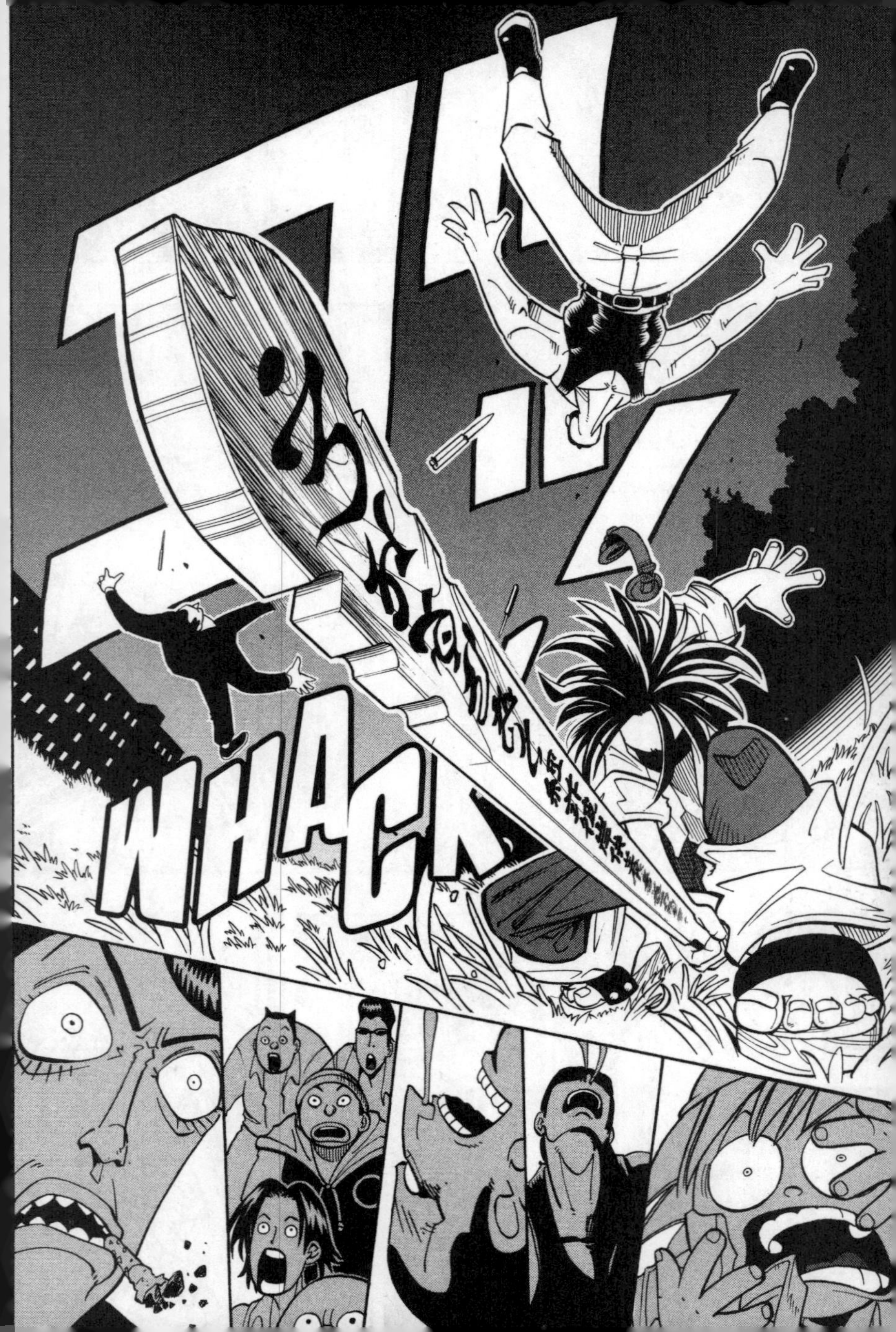
WHAC

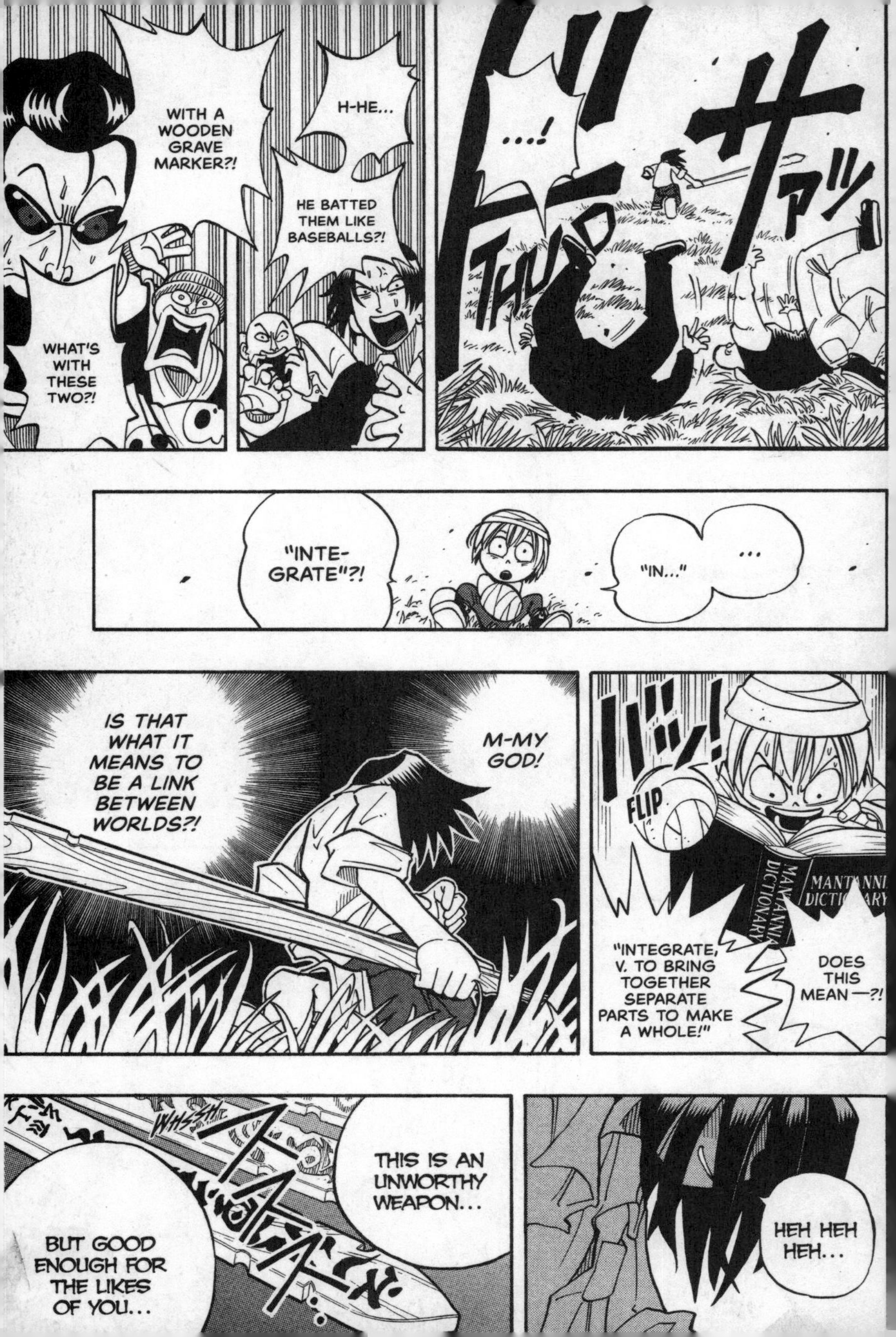
...!
THUD
H-HE...
HE BATTED THEM LIKE BASEBALLS?!
WITH A WOODEN GRAVE MARKER?!
WHAT'S WITH THESE TWO?!
...
"IN..."
"INTE-GRATE"?!
FLIP
"INTEGRATE, V. TO BRING TOGETHER SEPARATE PARTS TO MAKE A WHOLE!"
DOES THIS MEAN—?!
M-MY GOD!
IS THAT WHAT IT MEANS TO BE A LINK BETWEEN WORLDS?!
HEH HEH HEH...
THIS IS AN UNWORTHY WEAPON...
WHSSH
BUT GOOD ENOUGH FOR THE LIKES OF YOU...

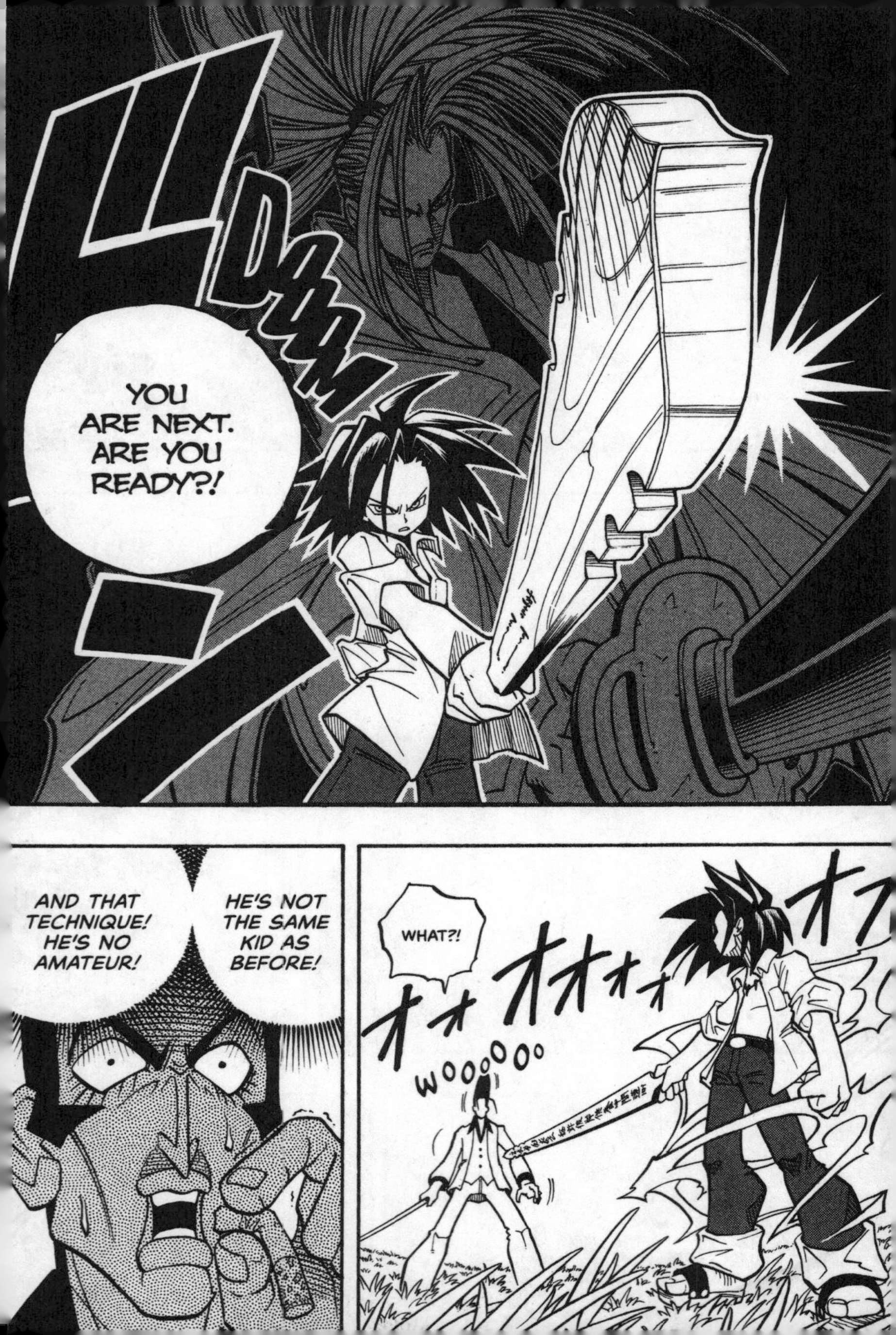
DOOM
YOU ARE NEXT. ARE YOU READY?!
WHAT?!
WOOOOOO
HE'S NOT THE SAME KID AS BEFORE!
AND THAT TECHNIQUE! HE'S NO AMATEUR!

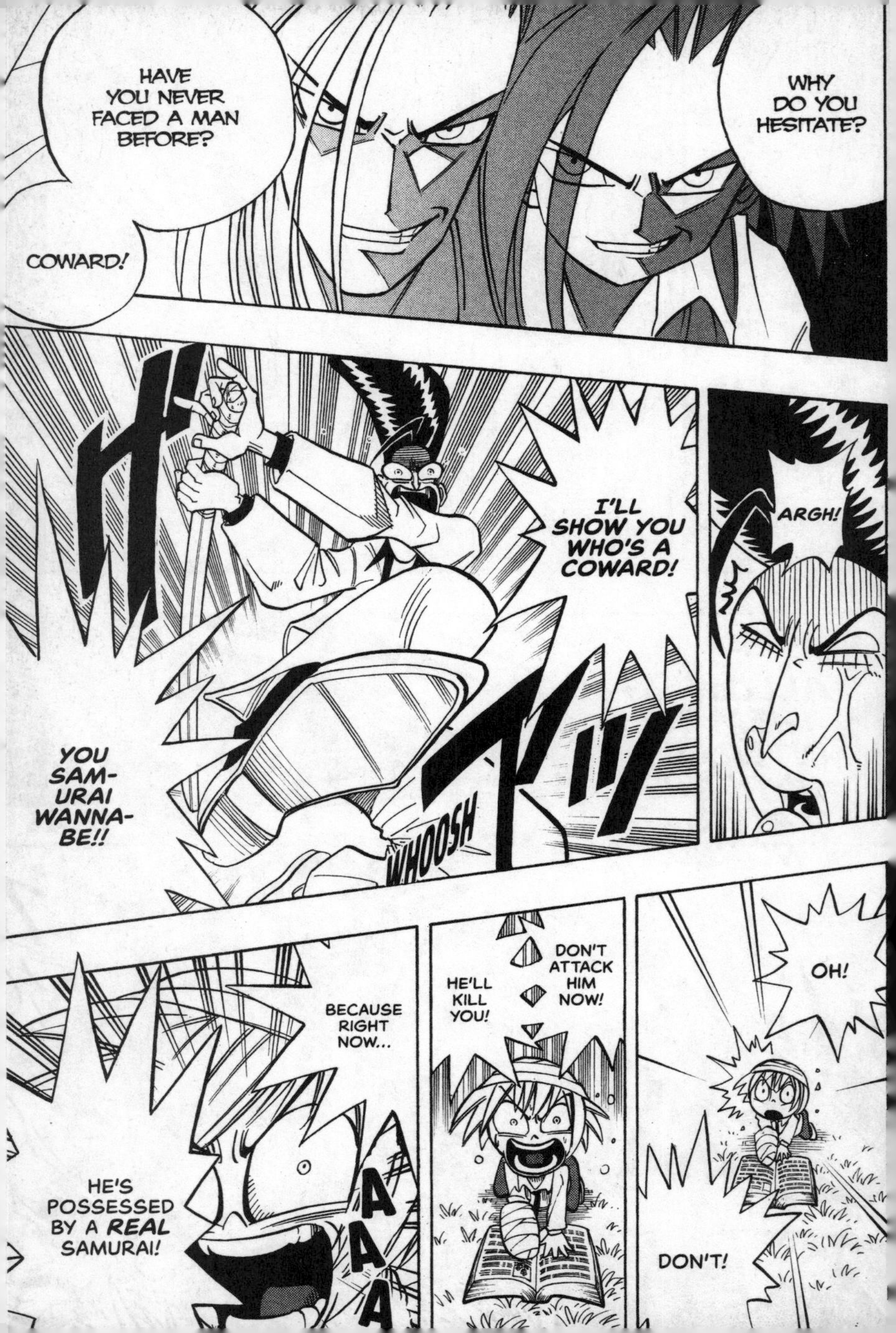
WHY DO YOU HESITATE?
HAVE YOU NEVER FACED A MAN BEFORE?
COWARD!
ARGH!
I'LL SHOW YOU WHO'S A COWARD!
YOU SAMURAI WANNABE!!
WHOOSH
OH!
DON'T!
DON'T ATTACK HIM NOW!
HE'LL KILL YOU!
BECAUSE RIGHT NOW...
HE'S POSSESSED BY A REAL SAMURAI!
AAAA

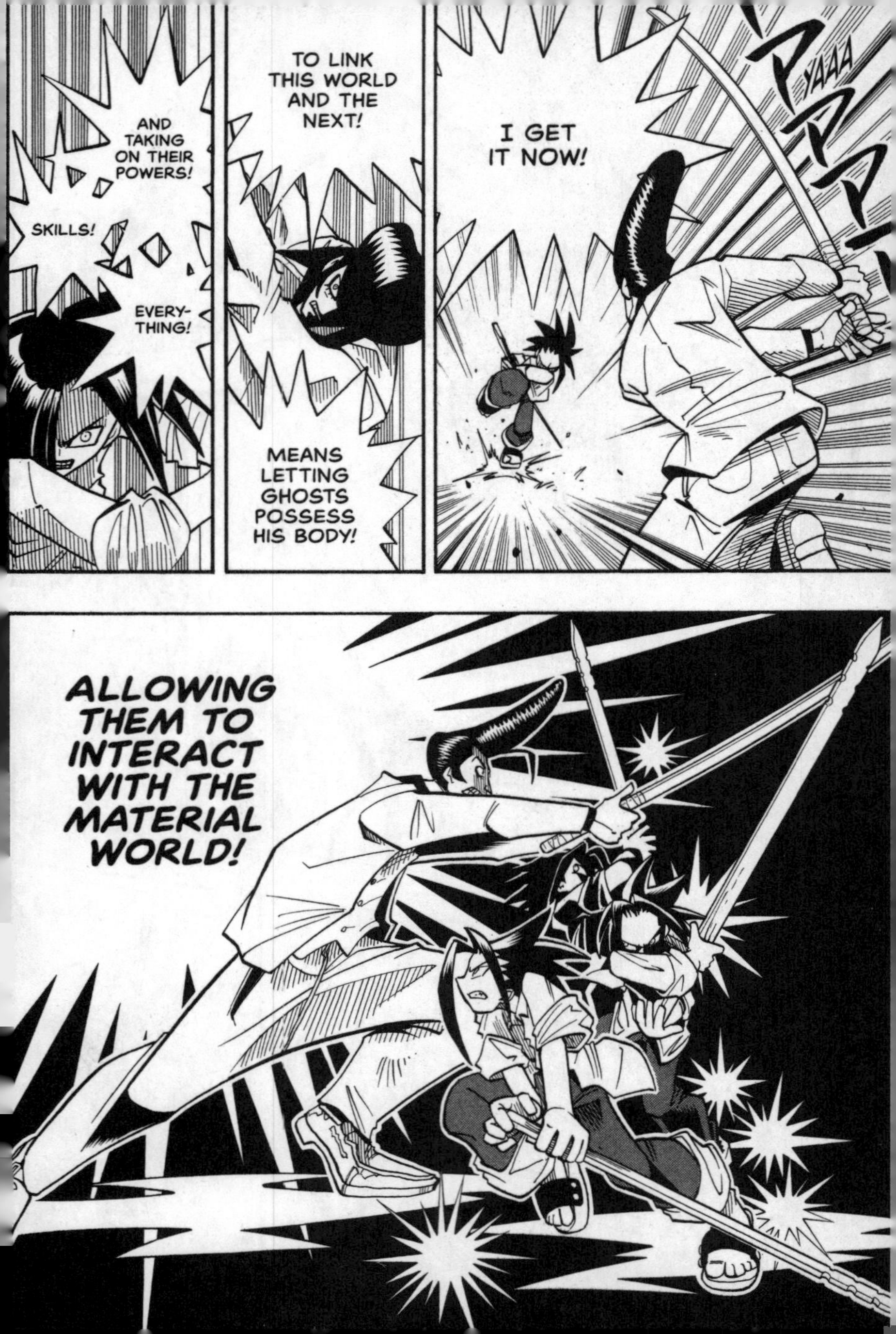
YAAA
I GET IT NOW!
TO LINK THIS WORLD AND THE NEXT!
MEANS LETTING GHOSTS POSSESS HIS BODY!
AND TAKING ON THEIR POWERS!
SKILLS!
EVERY-THING!
ALLOWING THEM TO INTERACT WITH THE MATERIAL WORLD!

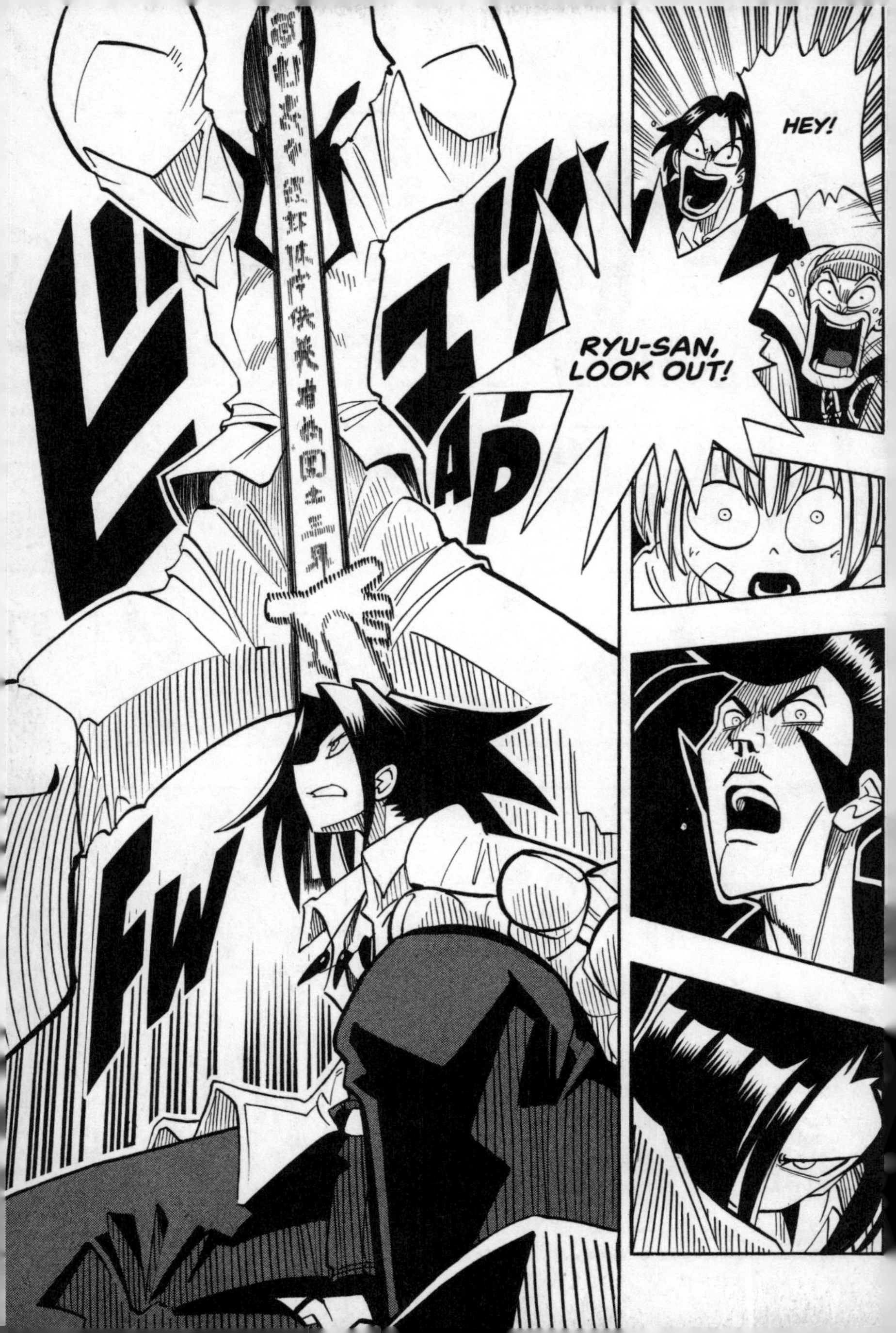
HEY!
RYU-SAN, LOOK OUT!

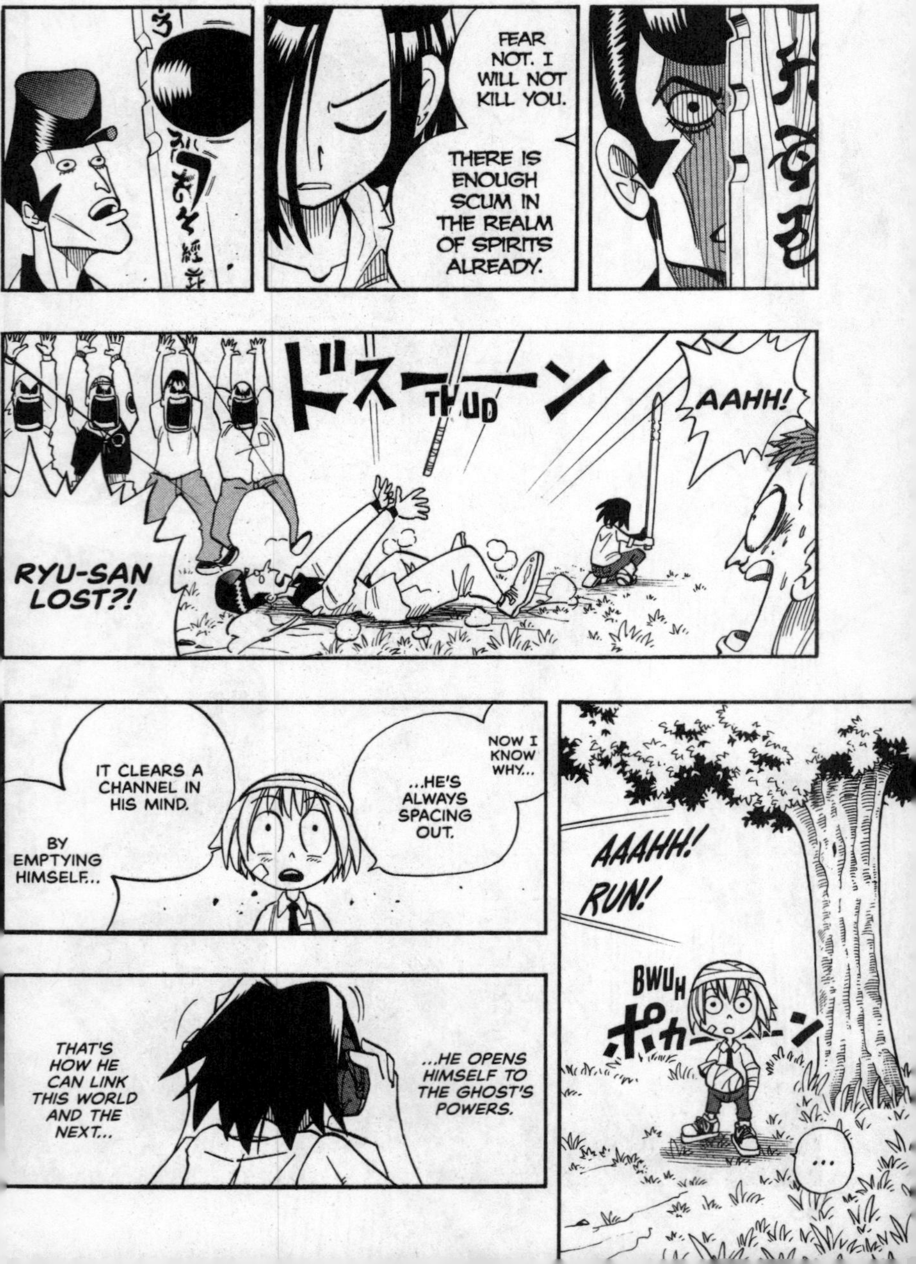
FEAR NOT. I WILL NOT KILL YOU.
THERE IS ENOUGH SCUM IN THE REALM OF SPIRITS ALREADY.
AAHH!
ドスーーン
THUD
RYU-SAN LOST?!
AAAHH! RUN!
BWUH
ポカーーン
...
NOW I KNOW WHY...
...HE'S ALWAYS SPACING OUT.
IT CLEARS A CHANNEL IN HIS MIND.
BY EMPTYING HIMSELF...
...HE OPENS HIMSELF TO THE GHOST'S POWERS.
THAT'S HOW HE CAN LINK THIS WORLD AND THE NEXT...

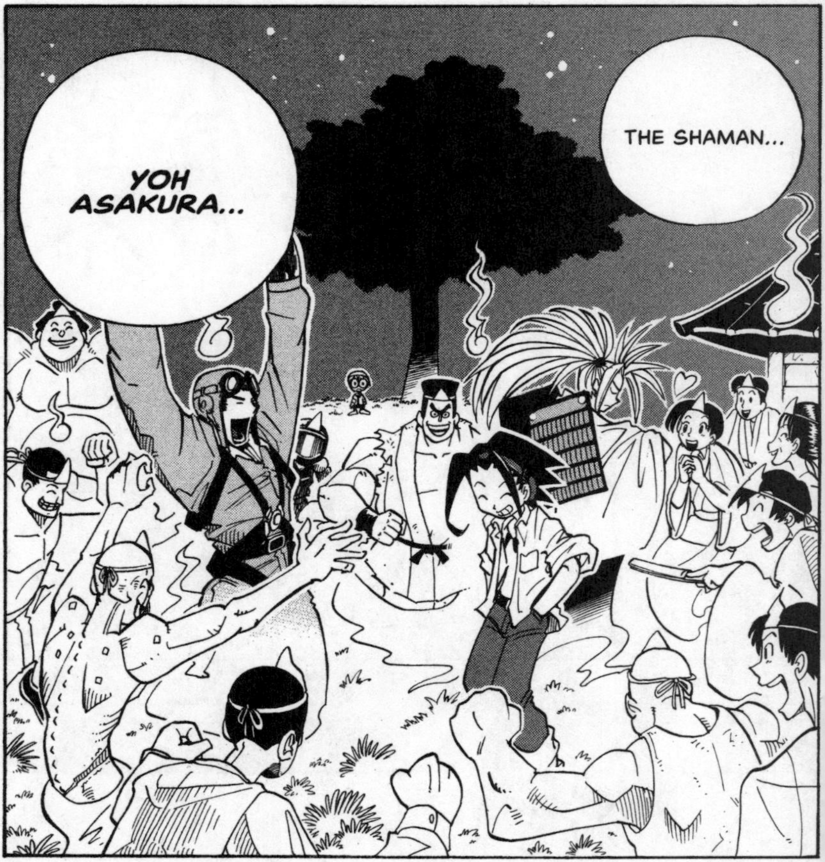
THE SHAMAN...
YOH ASAKURA...

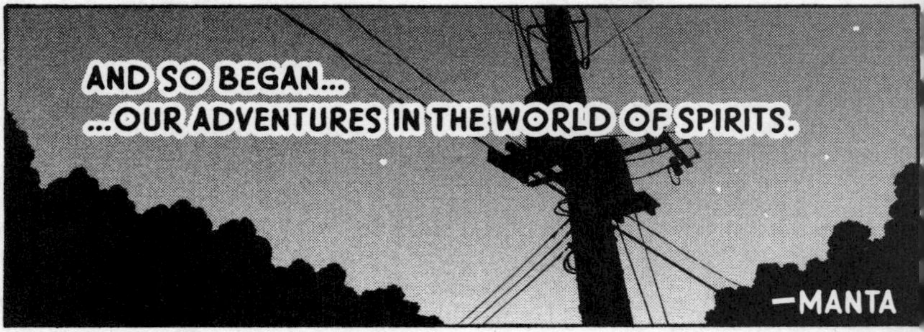
AND SO BEGAN...
...OUR ADVENTURES IN THE WORLD OF SPIRITS.
—MANTA

麻倉葉

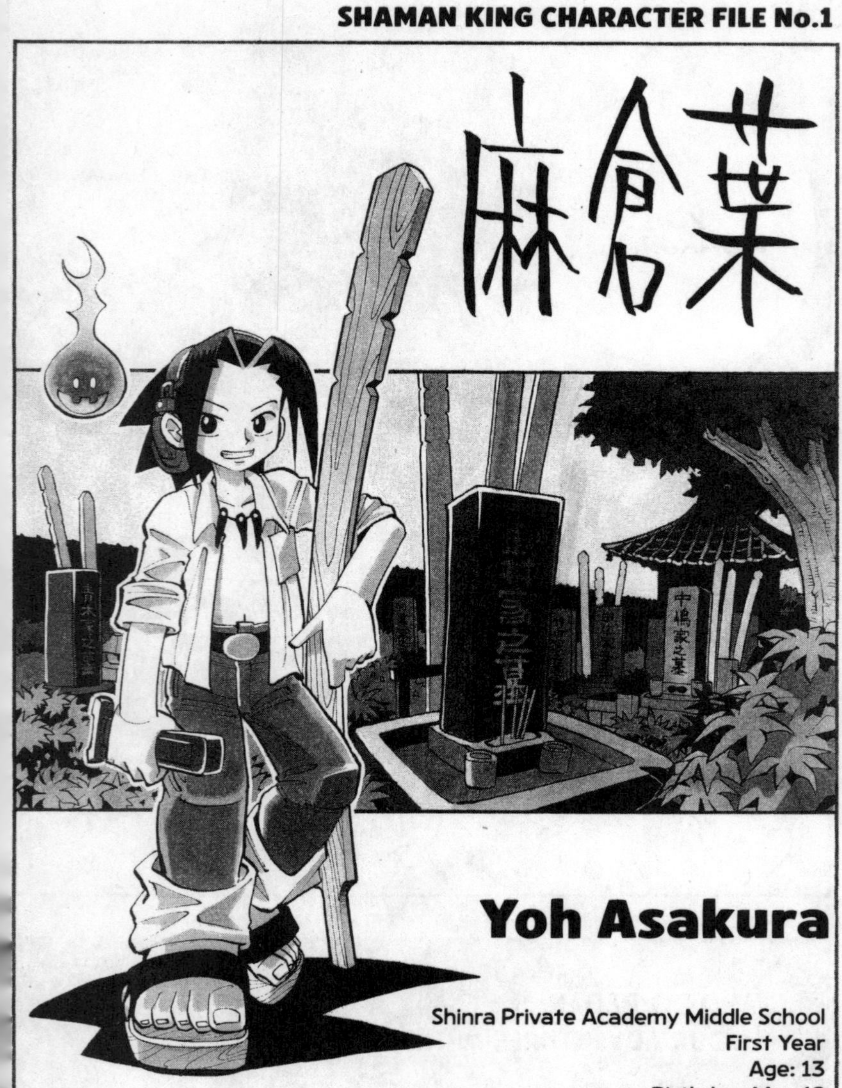

Yoh Asakura

Shinra Private Academy Middle School
First Year
Age: 13
Birthday: May 12
Blood Type: A

Chapter 2: The Waiting Samurai

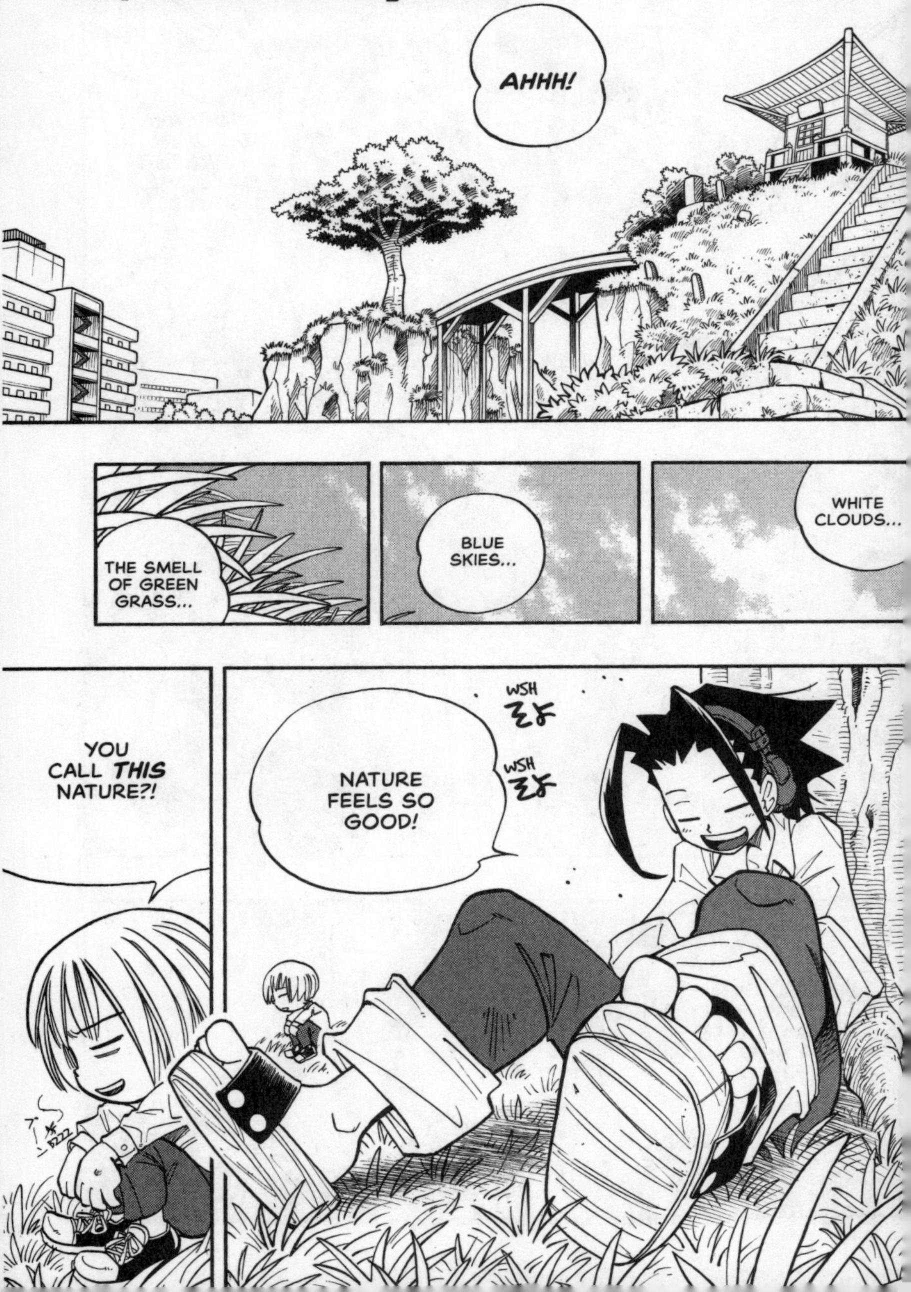
AHHH!
WHITE CLOUDS...
BLUE SKIES...
THE SMELL OF GREEN GRASS...
WSH
WSH
NATURE FEELS SO GOOD!
YOU CALL THIS NATURE?!

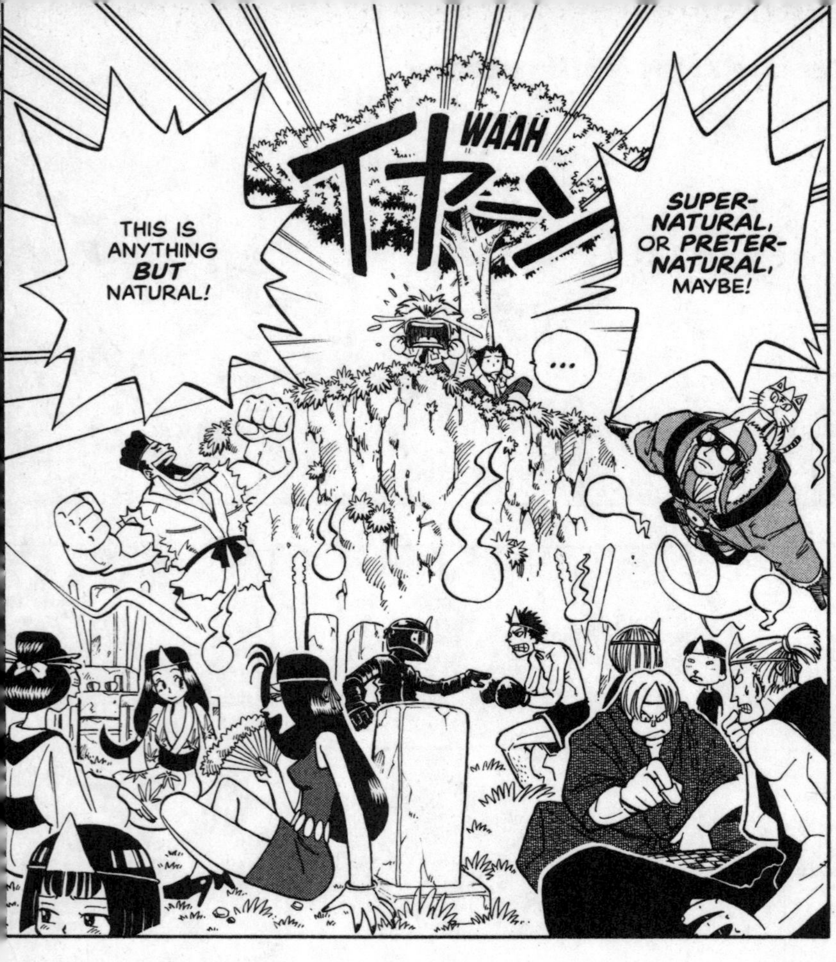
イヤーン
WAAH
SUPER-NATURAL, OR PRETER-NATURAL, MAYBE!
THIS IS ANYTHING BUT NATURAL!
...

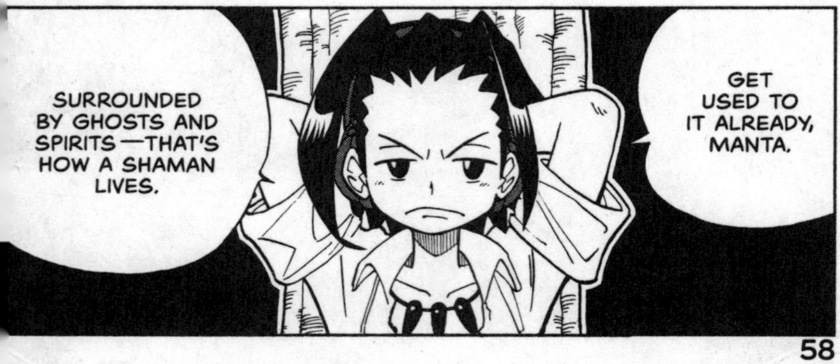
GET USED TO IT ALREADY, MANTA.
SURROUNDED BY GHOSTS AND SPIRITS—THAT'S HOW A SHAMAN LIVES.

Chapter 2:

The Waiting Samurai

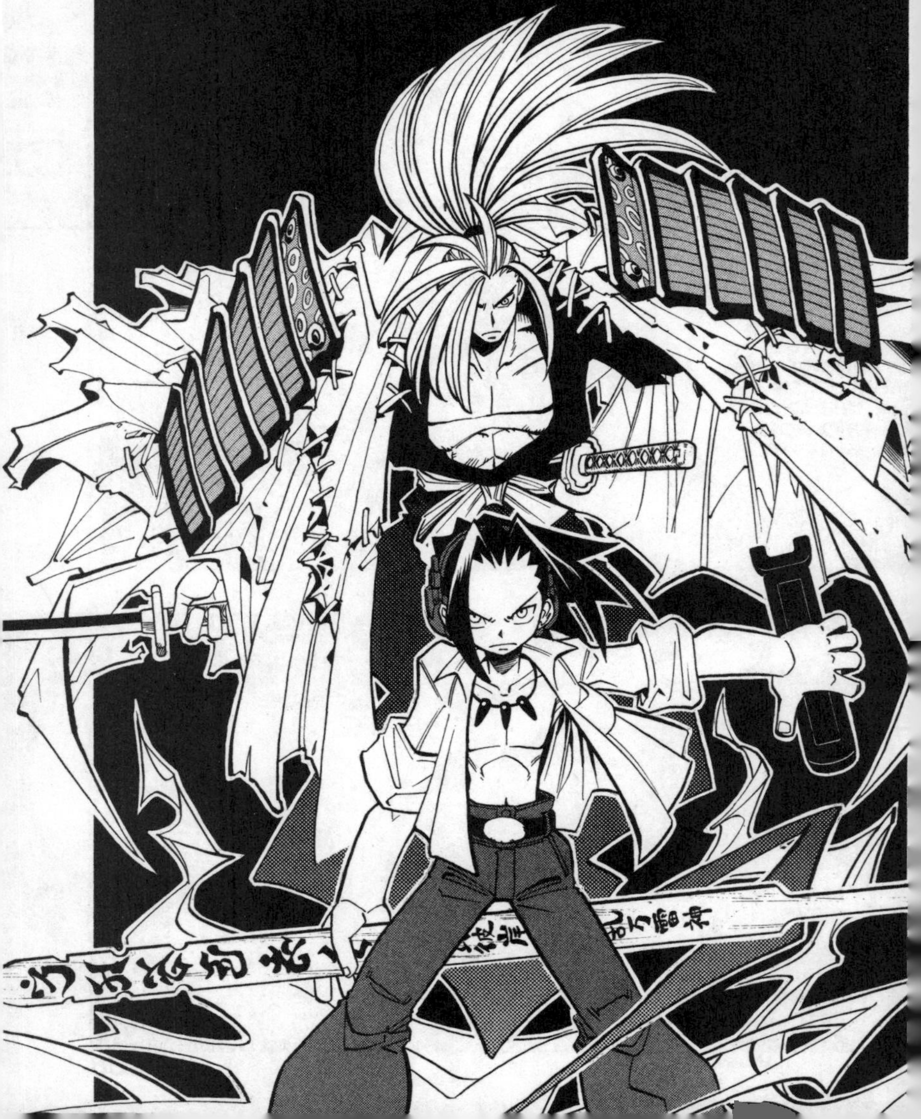

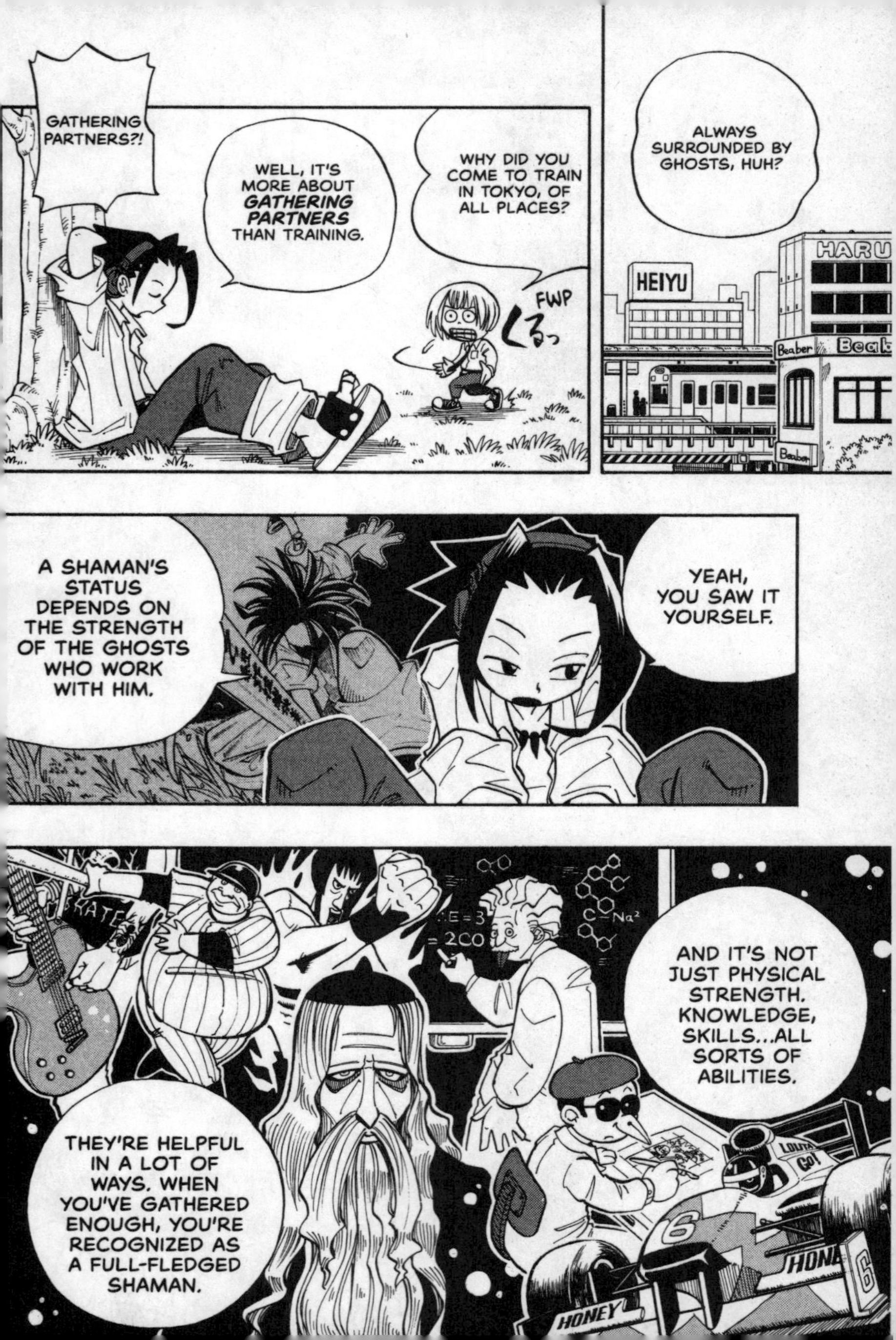
ALWAYS SURROUNDED BY GHOSTS, HUH?
HARU
HEIYU
Beaber
WHY DID YOU COME TO TRAIN IN TOKYO, OF ALL PLACES?
FWP
くるっ
WELL, IT'S MORE ABOUT GATHERING PARTNERS THAN TRAINING.
GATHERING PARTNERS?!
YEAH, YOU SAW IT YOURSELF.
A SHAMAN'S STATUS DEPENDS ON THE STRENGTH OF THE GHOSTS WHO WORK WITH HIM.
AND IT'S NOT JUST PHYSICAL STRENGTH. KNOWLEDGE, SKILLS...ALL SORTS OF ABILITIES.
THEY'RE HELPFUL IN A LOT OF WAYS. WHEN YOU'VE GATHERED ENOUGH, YOU'RE RECOGNIZED AS A FULL-FLEDGED SHAMAN.

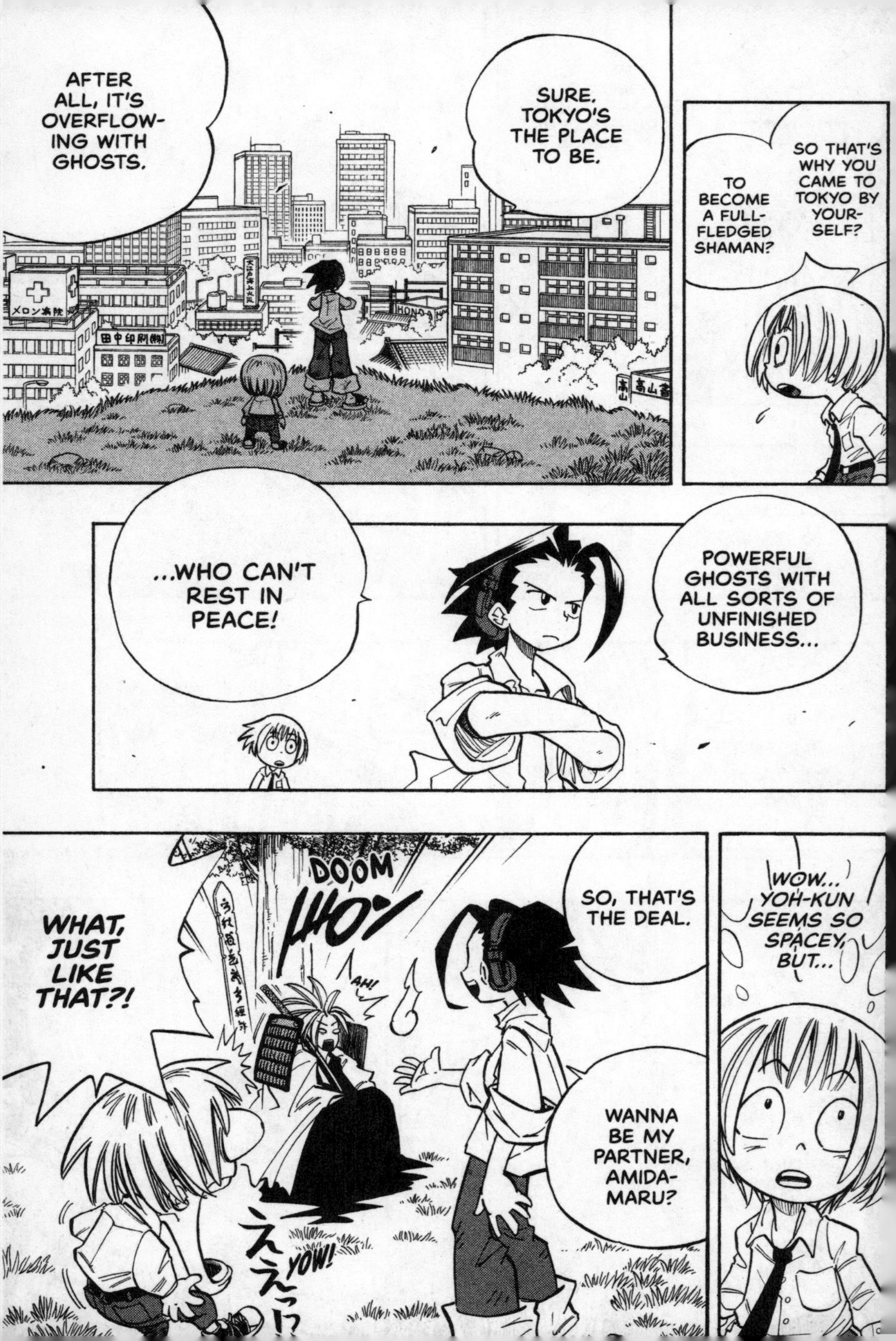
SO THAT'S WHY YOU CAME TO TOKYO BY YOUR-SELF?
TO BECOME A FULL-FLEDGED SHAMAN?
SURE. TOKYO'S THE PLACE TO BE.
AFTER ALL, IT'S OVERFLOW-ING WITH GHOSTS.
メロン病院
田中印刷㈱
POWERFUL GHOSTS WITH ALL SORTS OF UNFINISHED BUSINESS...
...WHO CAN'T REST IN PEACE!
WOW... YOH-KUN SEEMS SO SPACEY, BUT...
SO, THAT'S THE DEAL.
DOOM
WANNA BE MY PARTNER, AMIDA-MARU?
AH!
WHAT, JUST LIKE THAT?!
YOW!

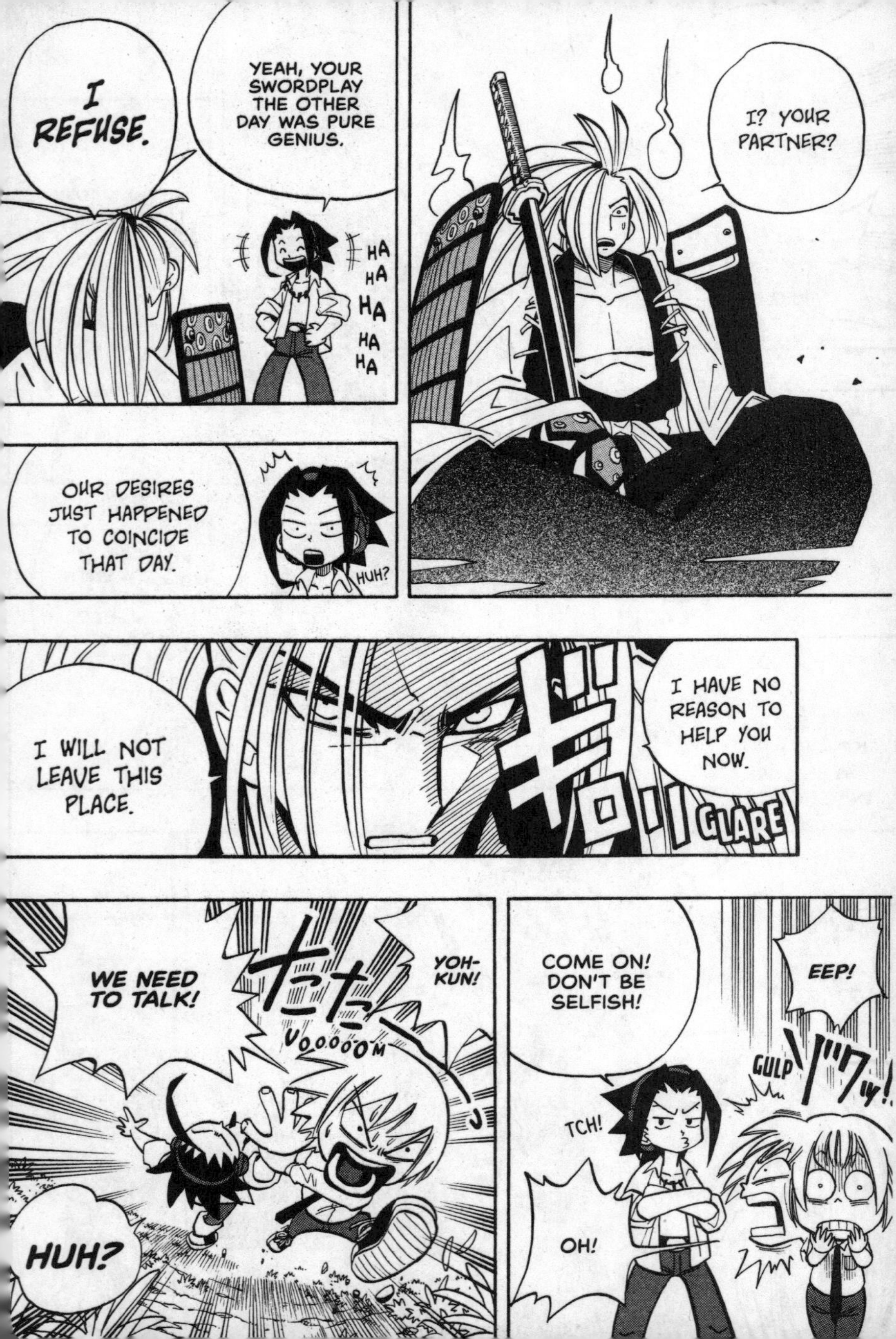

I? YOUR PARTNER?
YEAH, YOUR SWORDPLAY THE OTHER DAY WAS PURE GENIUS.
HA HA HA HA HA
I REFUSE.
HUH?
OUR DESIRES JUST HAPPENED TO COINCIDE THAT DAY.
I HAVE NO REASON TO HELP YOU NOW.
GLARE
I WILL NOT LEAVE THIS PLACE.
EEP!
GULP
COME ON! DON'T BE SELFISH!
TCH!
OH!
YOH-KUN!
VOOOOOM
WE NEED TO TALK!
HUH?

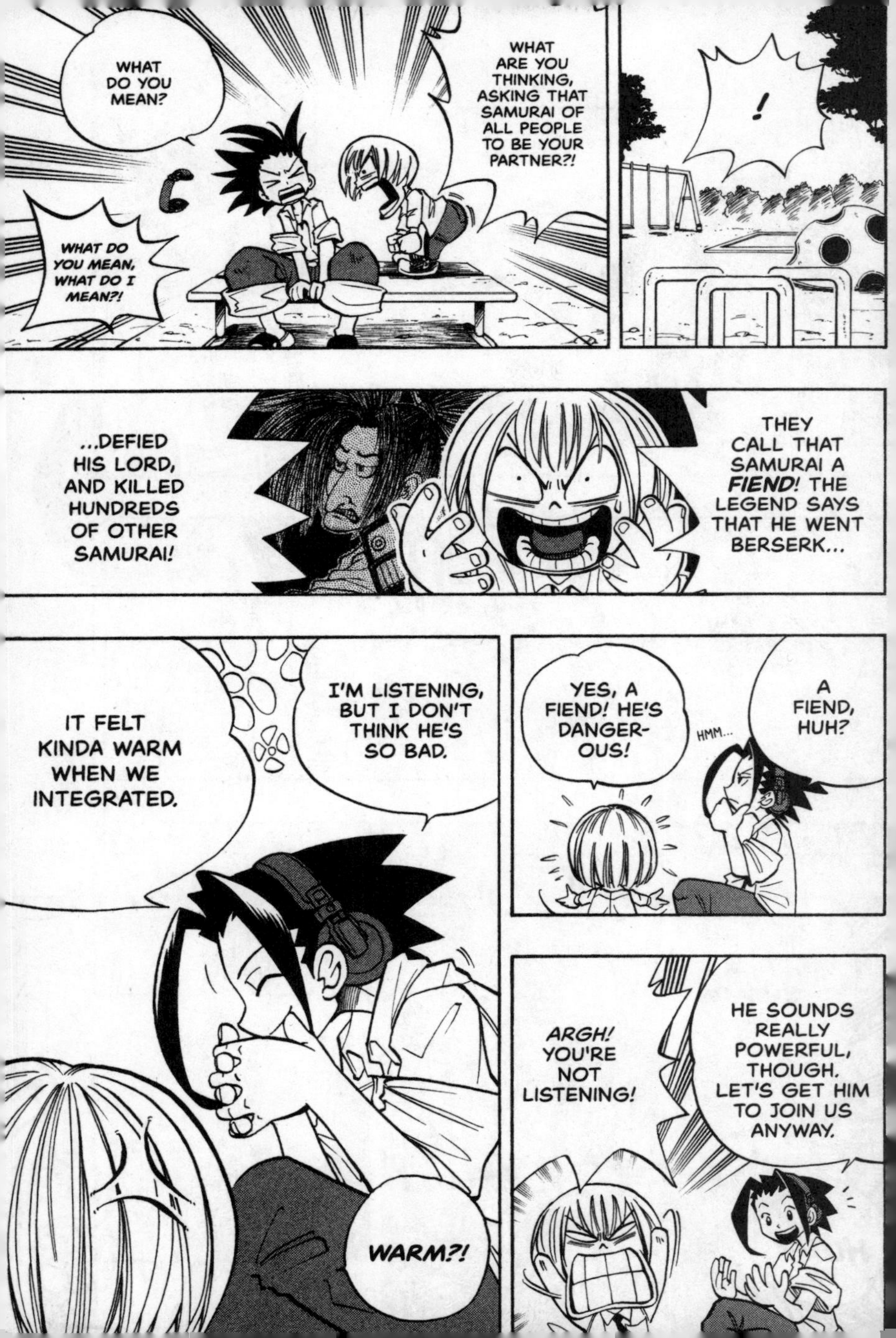
!
WHAT ARE YOU THINKING, ASKING THAT SAMURAI OF ALL PEOPLE TO BE YOUR PARTNER?!
WHAT DO YOU MEAN?
WHAT DO YOU MEAN, WHAT DO I MEAN?!
THEY CALL THAT SAMURAI A ***FIEND!*** THE LEGEND SAYS THAT HE WENT BERSERK...
...DEFIED HIS LORD, AND KILLED HUNDREDS OF OTHER SAMURAI!
A FIEND, HUH?
HMM...
YES, A FIEND! HE'S DANGER-OUS!
HE SOUNDS REALLY POWERFUL, THOUGH. LET'S GET HIM TO JOIN US ANYWAY.
ARGH! YOU'RE NOT LISTENING!
I'M LISTENING, BUT I DON'T THINK HE'S SO BAD.
IT FELT KINDA WARM WHEN WE INTEGRATED.
WARM?!

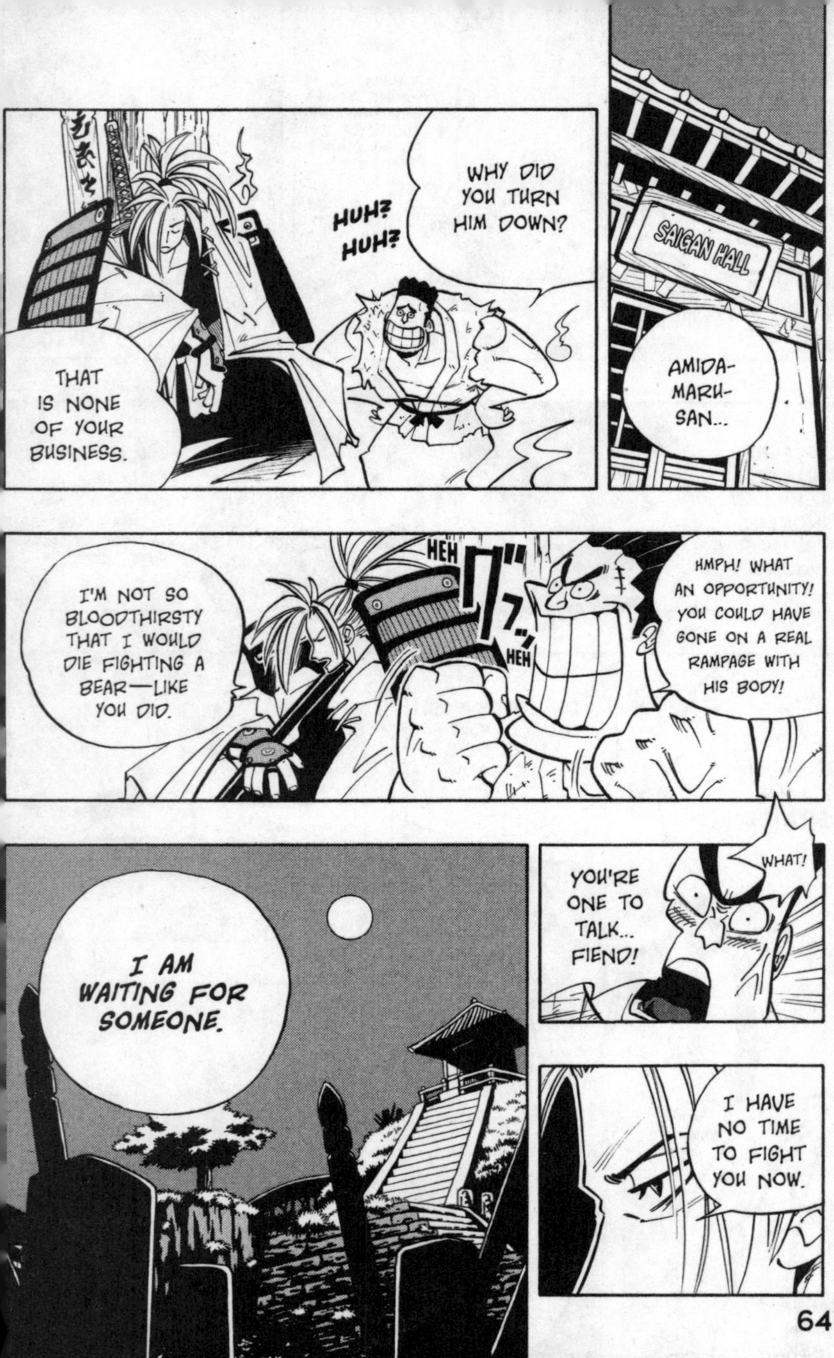
SAIGAN HALL
AMIDA-MARU-SAN...
WHY DID YOU TURN HIM DOWN?
HUH? HUH?
THAT IS NONE OF YOUR BUSINESS.
HMPH! WHAT AN OPPORTUNITY! YOU COULD HAVE GONE ON A REAL RAMPAGE WITH HIS BODY!
HEH HEH
I'M NOT SO BLOODTHIRSTY THAT I WOULD DIE FIGHTING A BEAR—LIKE YOU DID.
WHAT!
YOU'RE ONE TO TALK... FIEND!
I HAVE NO TIME TO FIGHT YOU NOW.
I AM WAITING FOR SOMEONE.

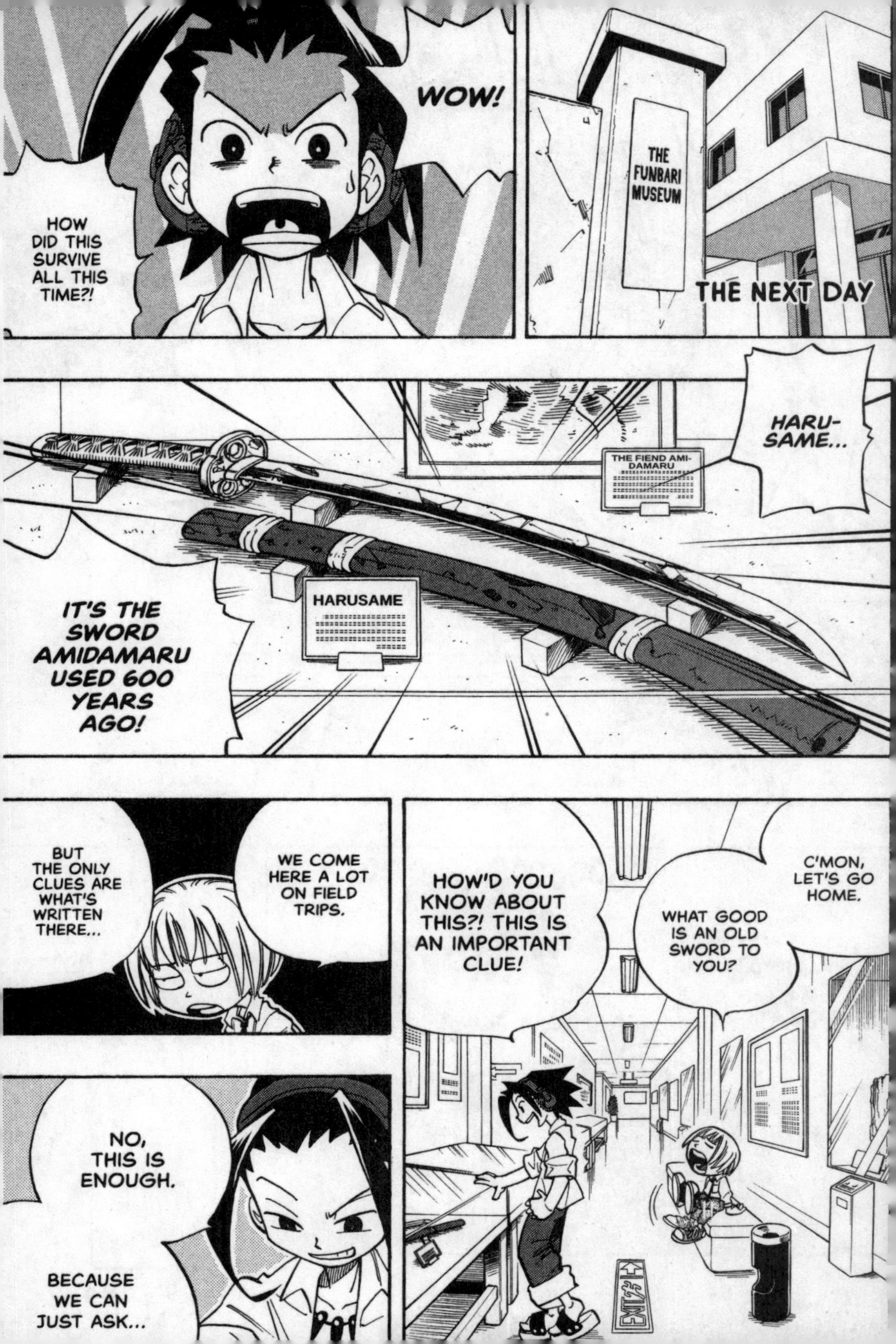
THE FUNBARI MUSEUM
THE NEXT DAY
WOW!
HOW DID THIS SURVIVE ALL THIS TIME?!
HARU-SAME...
THE FIEND AMI-DAMARU
HARUSAME
IT'S THE SWORD AMIDAMARU USED 600 YEARS AGO!
C'MON, LET'S GO HOME.
WHAT GOOD IS AN OLD SWORD TO YOU?
HOW'D YOU KNOW ABOUT THIS?! THIS IS AN IMPORTANT CLUE!
WE COME HERE A LOT ON FIELD TRIPS.
BUT THE ONLY CLUES ARE WHAT'S WRITTEN THERE...
NO, THIS IS ENOUGH.
BECAUSE WE CAN JUST ASK...

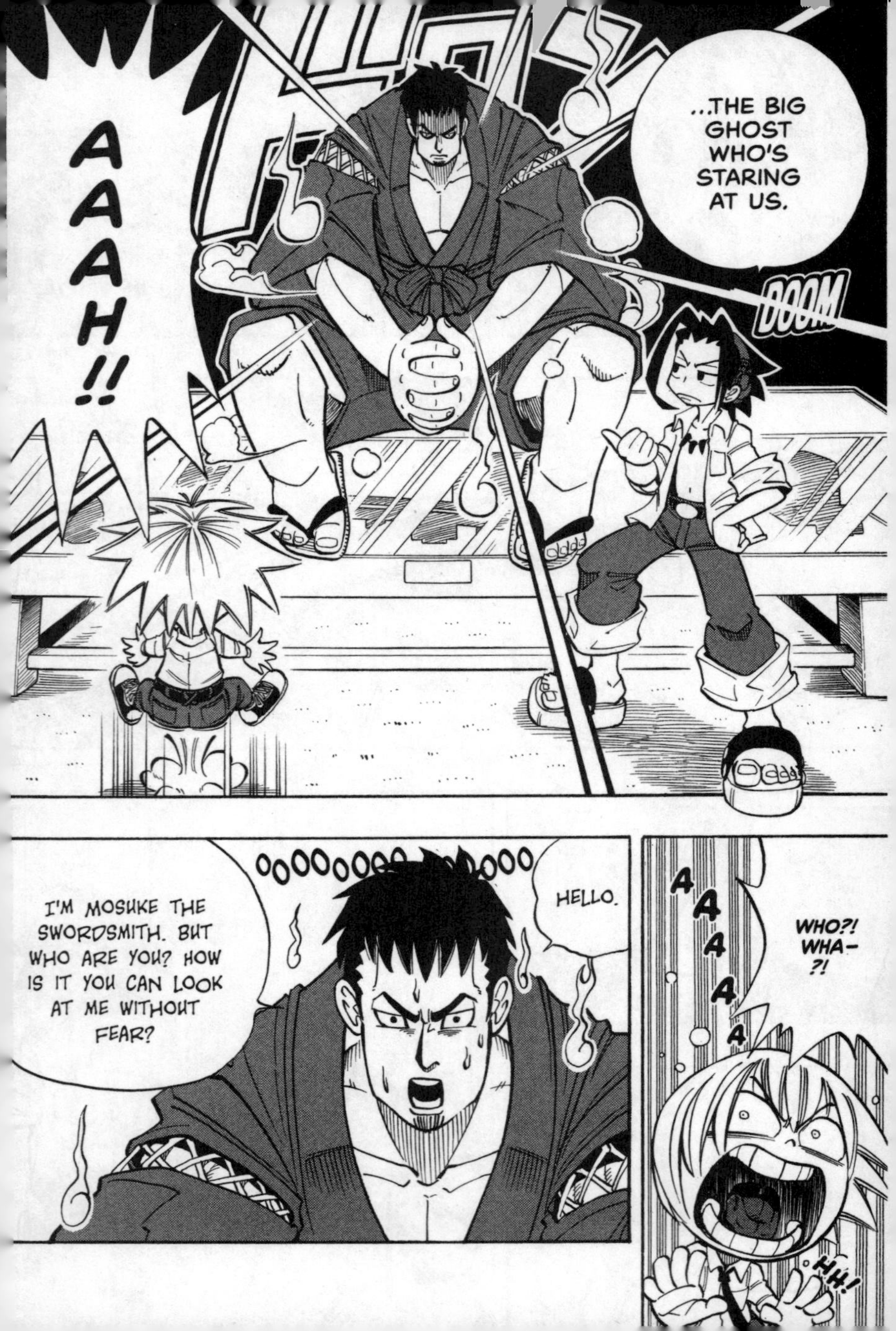

...THE BIG GHOST WHO'S STARING AT US.
DOOM
AAAAH!!
WHO?! WHA-?!
AAAAAAHH!
HELLO.
I'M MOSUKE THE SWORDSMITH. BUT WHO ARE YOU? HOW IS IT YOU CAN LOOK AT ME WITHOUT FEAR?

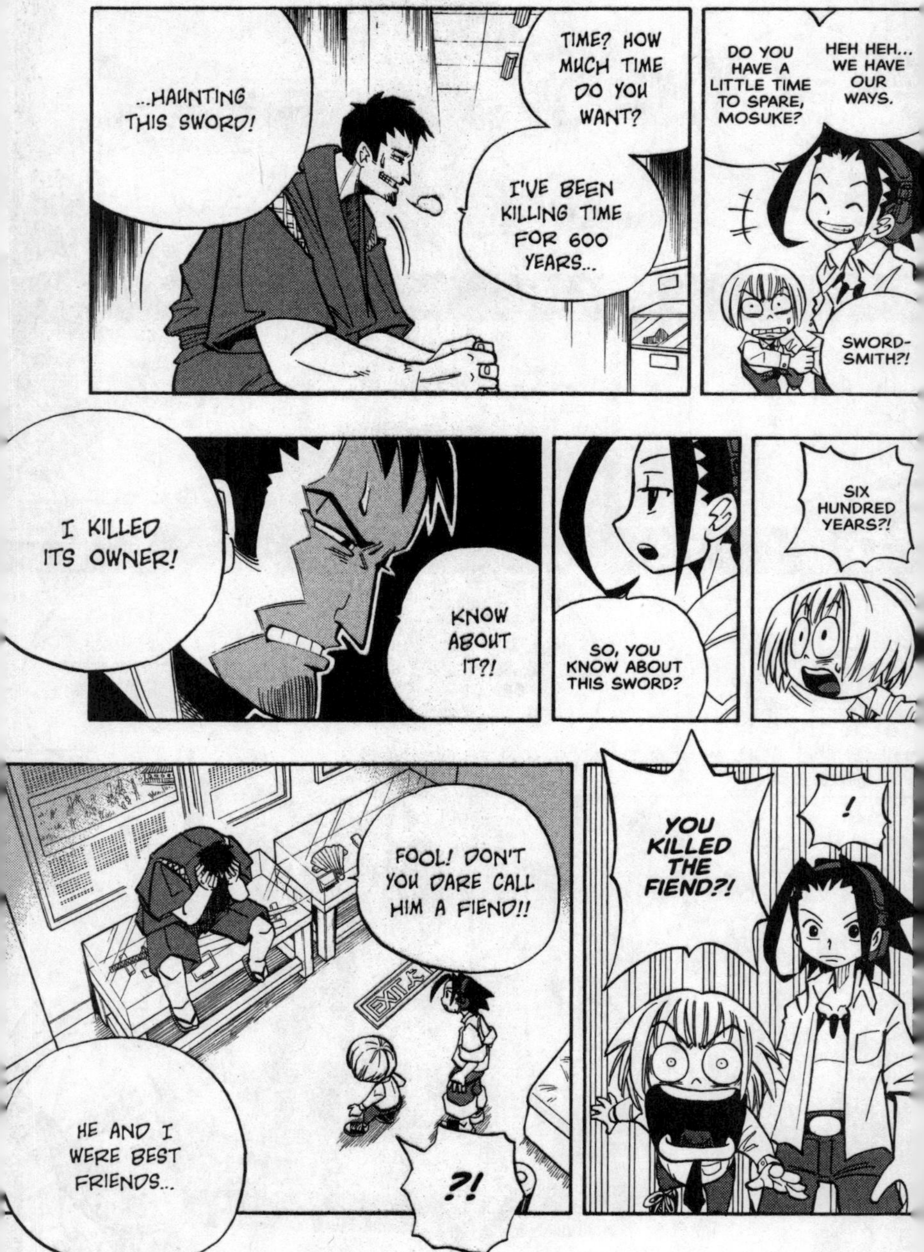
HEH HEH... WE HAVE OUR WAYS.
DO YOU HAVE A LITTLE TIME TO SPARE, MOSUKE?
SWORD-SMITH?!
TIME? HOW MUCH TIME DO YOU WANT?
I'VE BEEN KILLING TIME FOR 600 YEARS...
...HAUNTING THIS SWORD!
SIX HUNDRED YEARS?!
SO, YOU KNOW ABOUT THIS SWORD?
KNOW ABOUT IT?!
I KILLED ITS OWNER!
!
YOU KILLED THE FIEND?!
FOOL! DON'T YOU DARE CALL HIM A FIEND!!
?!
HE AND I WERE BEST FRIENDS...

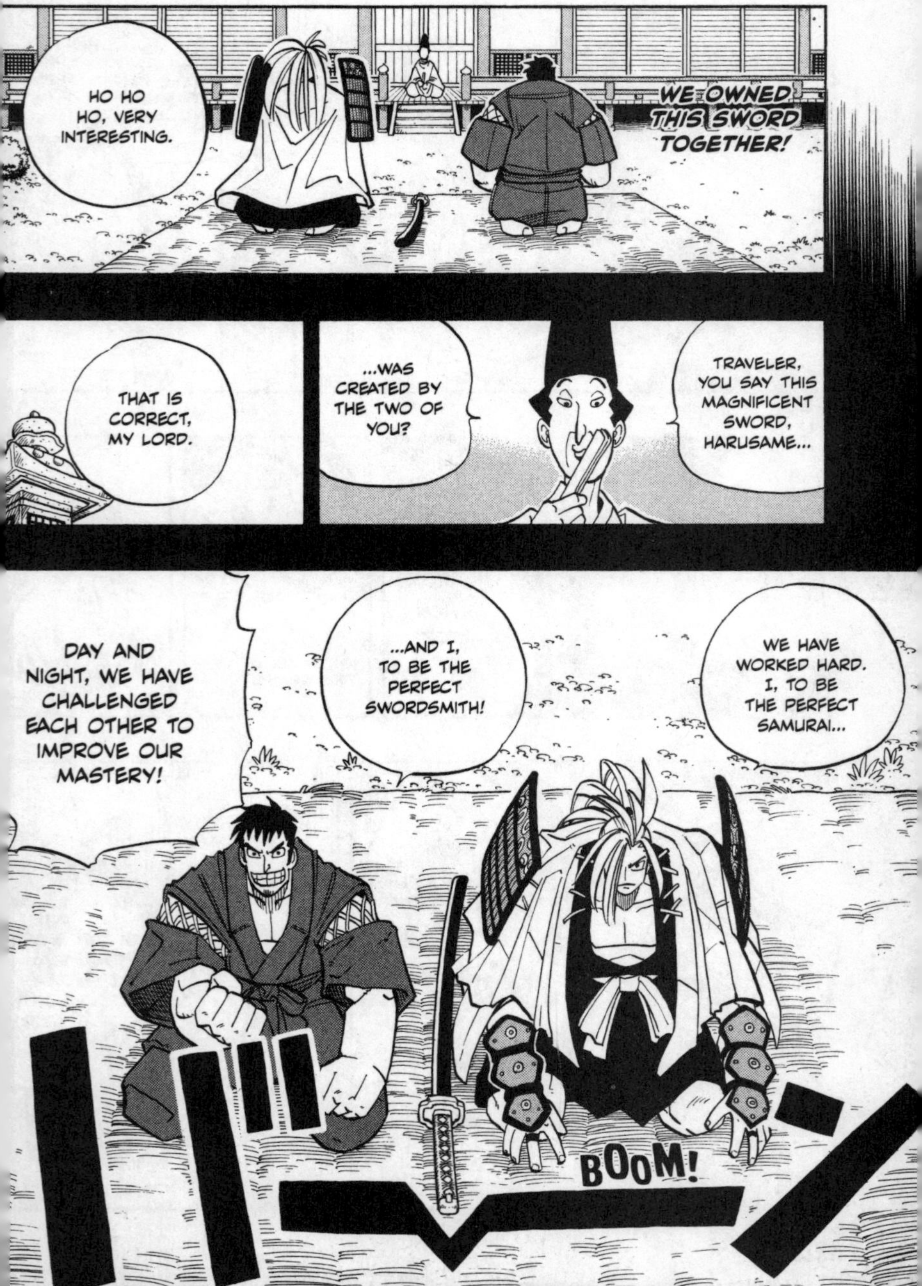
WE OWNED THIS SWORD TOGETHER!
HO HO HO, VERY INTERESTING.
TRAVELER, YOU SAY THIS MAGNIFICENT SWORD, HARUSAME...
...WAS CREATED BY THE TWO OF YOU?
THAT IS CORRECT, MY LORD.
WE HAVE WORKED HARD. I, TO BE THE PERFECT SAMURAI...
...AND I, TO BE THE PERFECT SWORDSMITH!
DAY AND NIGHT, WE HAVE CHALLENGED EACH OTHER TO IMPROVE OUR MASTERY!
BOOM!

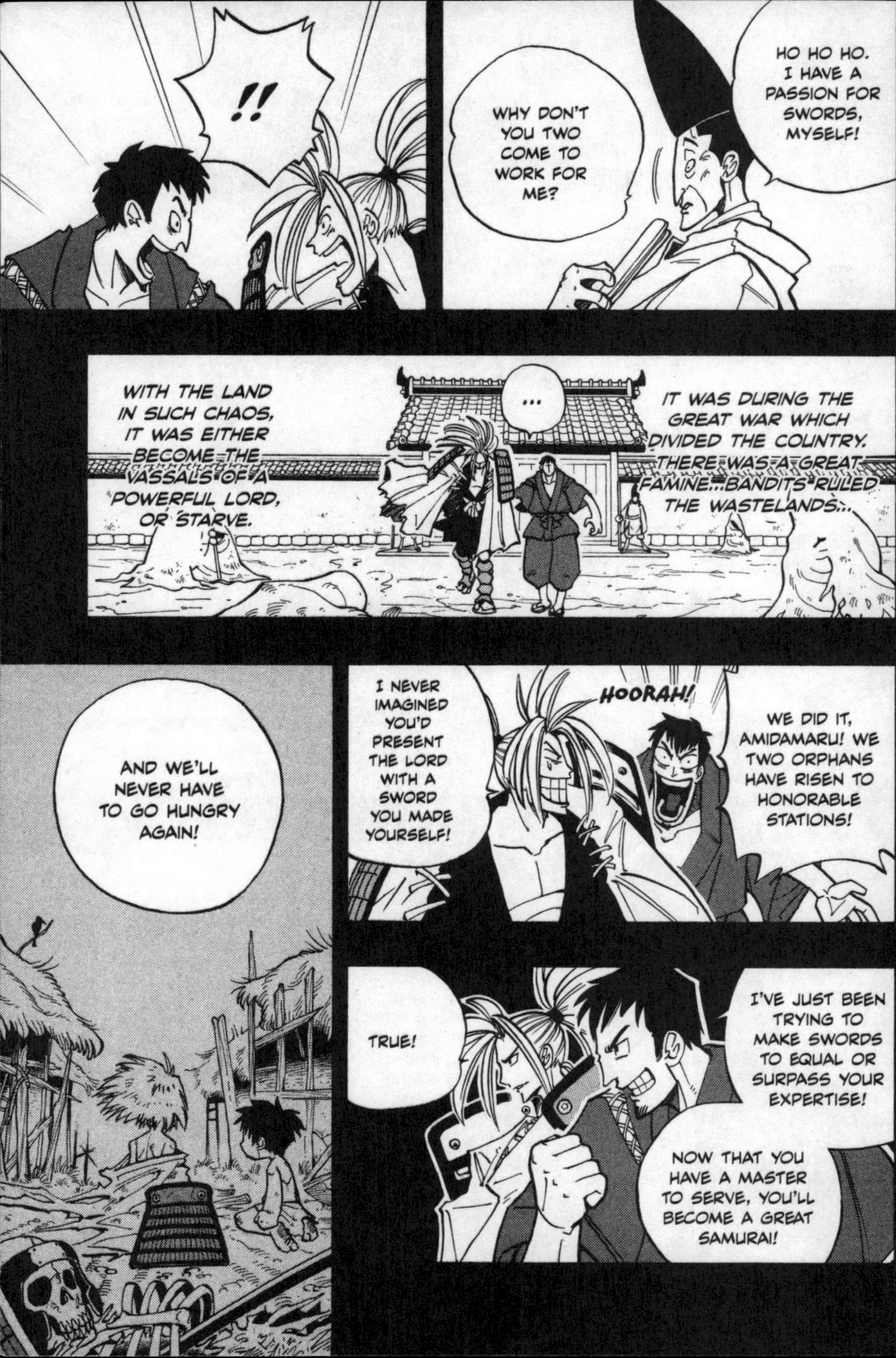

HO HO HO. I HAVE A PASSION FOR SWORDS, MYSELF!
WHY DON'T YOU TWO COME TO WORK FOR ME?
!!
IT WAS DURING THE GREAT WAR WHICH DIVIDED THE COUNTRY. THERE WAS A GREAT FAMINE...BANDITS RULED THE WASTELANDS...
...
WITH THE LAND IN SUCH CHAOS, IT WAS EITHER BECOME THE VASSALS OF A POWERFUL LORD, OR STARVE.
HOORAH!
WE DID IT, AMIDAMARU! WE TWO ORPHANS HAVE RISEN TO HONORABLE STATIONS!
I NEVER IMAGINED YOU'D PRESENT THE LORD WITH A SWORD YOU MADE YOURSELF!
I'VE JUST BEEN TRYING TO MAKE SWORDS TO EQUAL OR SURPASS YOUR EXPERTISE!
TRUE!
NOW THAT YOU HAVE A MASTER TO SERVE, YOU'LL BECOME A GREAT SAMURAI!
AND WE'LL NEVER HAVE TO GO HUNGRY AGAIN!

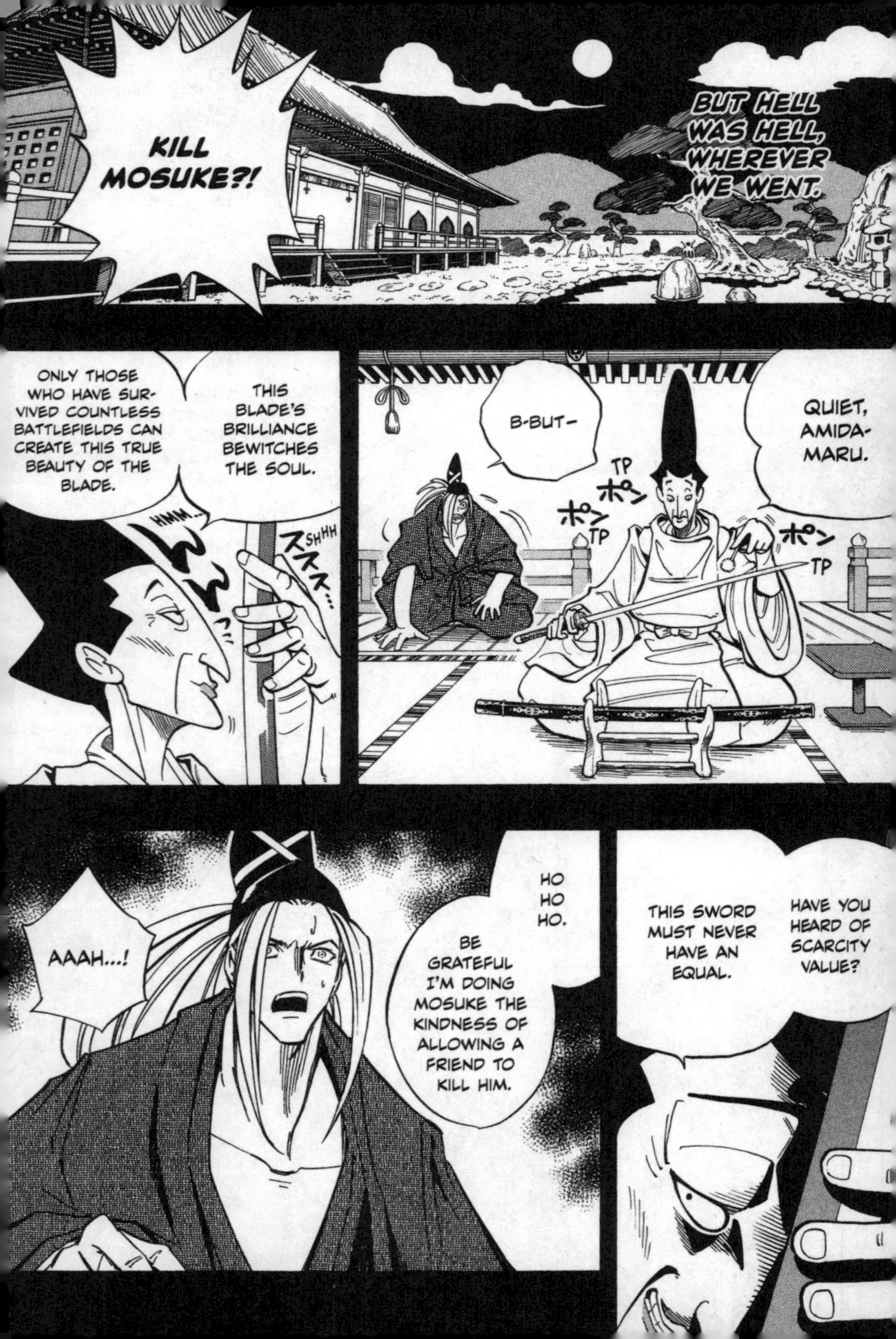
BUT HELL WAS HELL, WHEREVER WE WENT.
KILL MOSUKE?!
QUIET, AMIDA-MARU.
TP ポン
TP ポン
TP ポン
B-BUT-
THIS BLADE'S BRILLIANCE BEWITCHES THE SOUL.
ONLY THOSE WHO HAVE SURVIVED COUNTLESS BATTLEFIELDS CAN CREATE THIS TRUE BEAUTY OF THE BLADE.
HMM...
SHHH ススス...
HAVE YOU HEARD OF SCARCITY VALUE?
THIS SWORD MUST NEVER HAVE AN EQUAL.
HO HO HO.
BE GRATEFUL I'M DOING MOSUKE THE KINDNESS OF ALLOWING A FRIEND TO KILL HIM.
AAAH...!

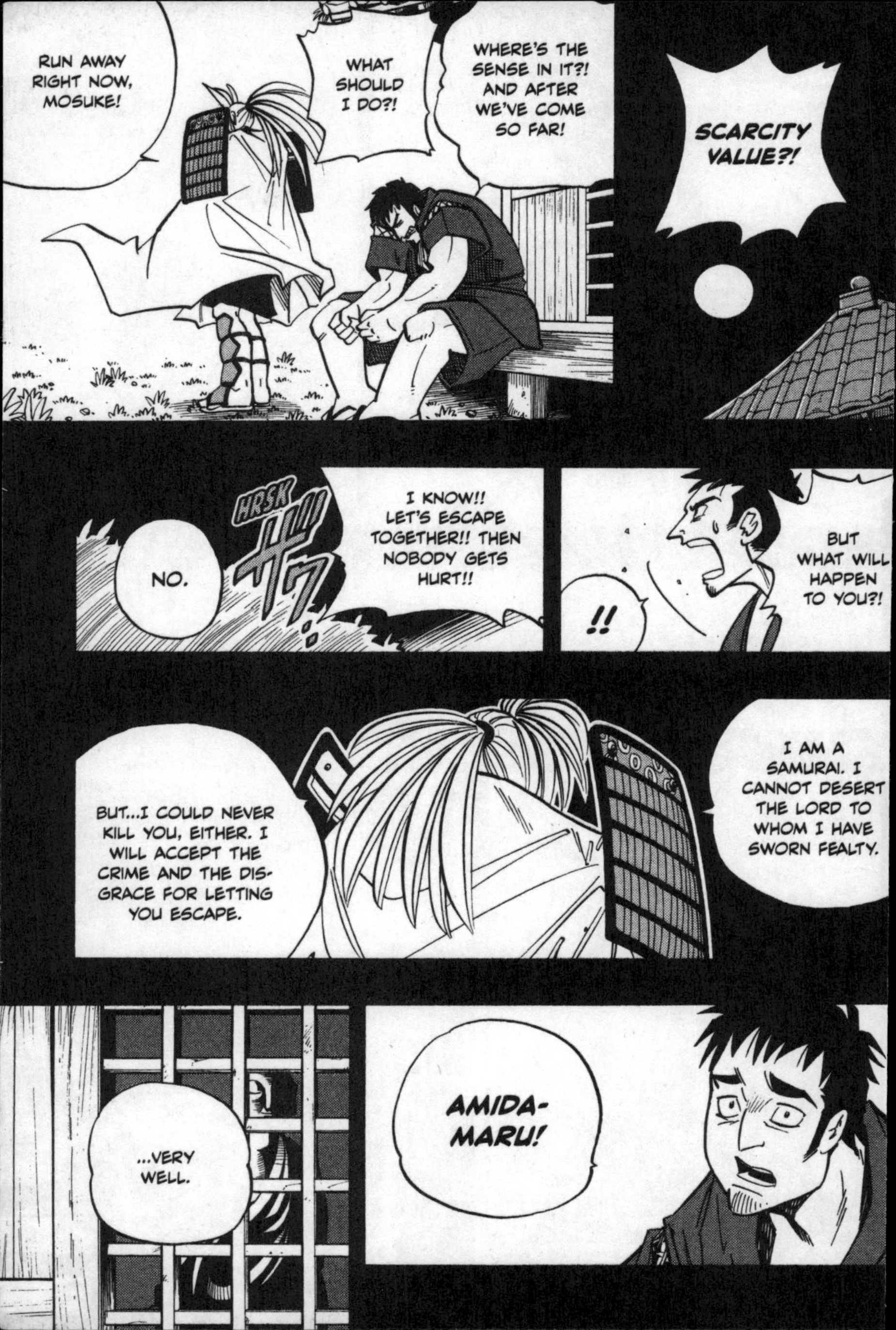
SCARCITY VALUE?!
WHERE'S THE SENSE IN IT?! AND AFTER WE'VE COME SO FAR!
WHAT SHOULD I DO?!
RUN AWAY RIGHT NOW, MOSUKE!
BUT WHAT WILL HAPPEN TO YOU?!
!!
I KNOW!! LET'S ESCAPE TOGETHER!! THEN NOBODY GETS HURT!!
HRSK
NO.
I AM A SAMURAI. I CANNOT DESERT THE LORD TO WHOM I HAVE SWORN FEALTY.
BUT...I COULD NEVER KILL YOU, EITHER. I WILL ACCEPT THE CRIME AND THE DIS-GRACE FOR LETTING YOU ESCAPE.
AMIDA-MARU!
...VERY WELL.

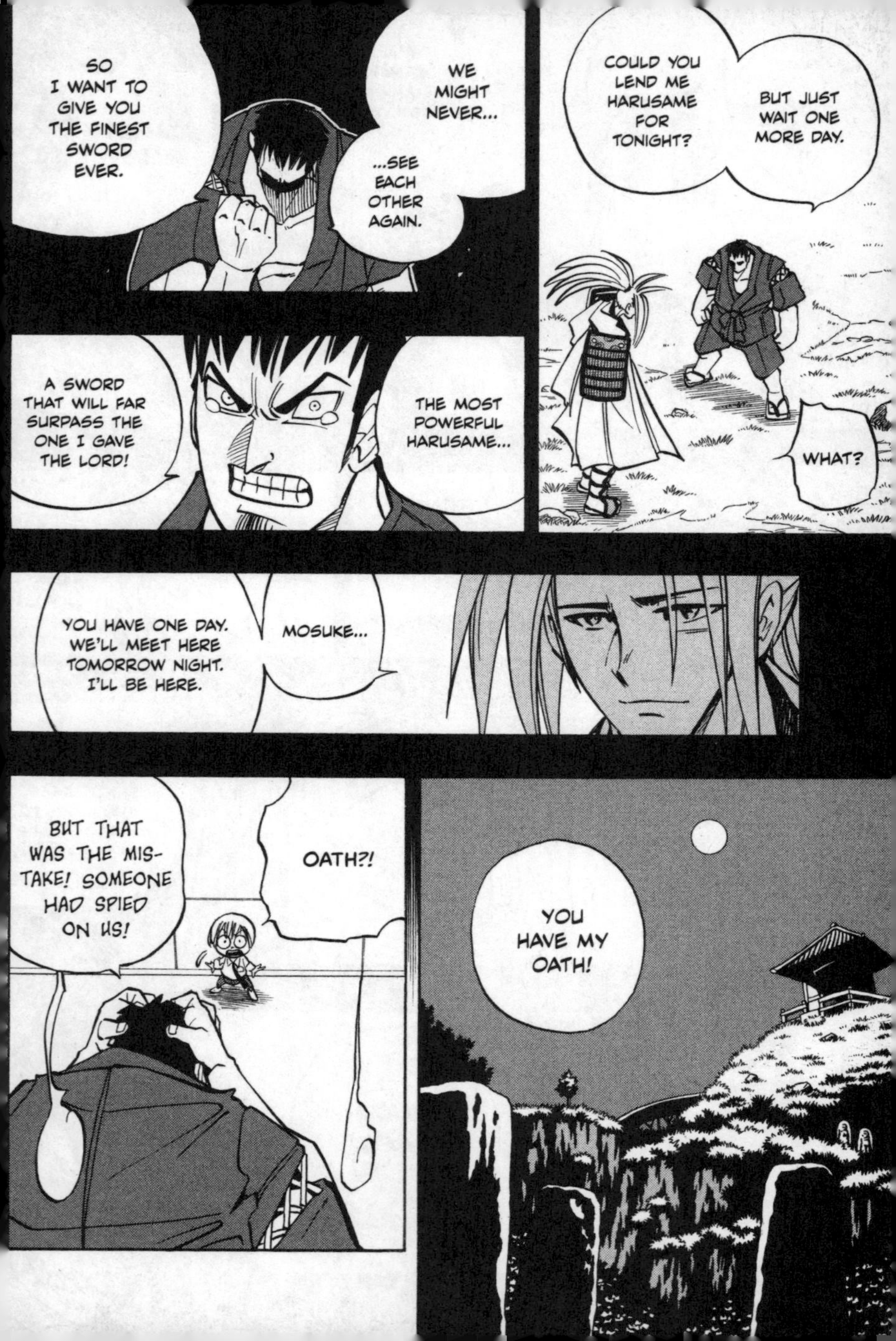
BUT JUST WAIT ONE MORE DAY.
COULD YOU LEND ME HARUSAME FOR TONIGHT?
WHAT?
WE MIGHT NEVER...
...SEE EACH OTHER AGAIN.
SO I WANT TO GIVE YOU THE FINEST SWORD EVER.
THE MOST POWERFUL HARUSAME...
A SWORD THAT WILL FAR SURPASS THE ONE I GAVE THE LORD!
MOSUKE...
YOU HAVE ONE DAY. WE'LL MEET HERE TOMORROW NIGHT. I'LL BE HERE.
YOU HAVE MY OATH!
OATH?!
BUT THAT WAS THE MIS-TAKE! SOMEONE HAD SPIED ON US!

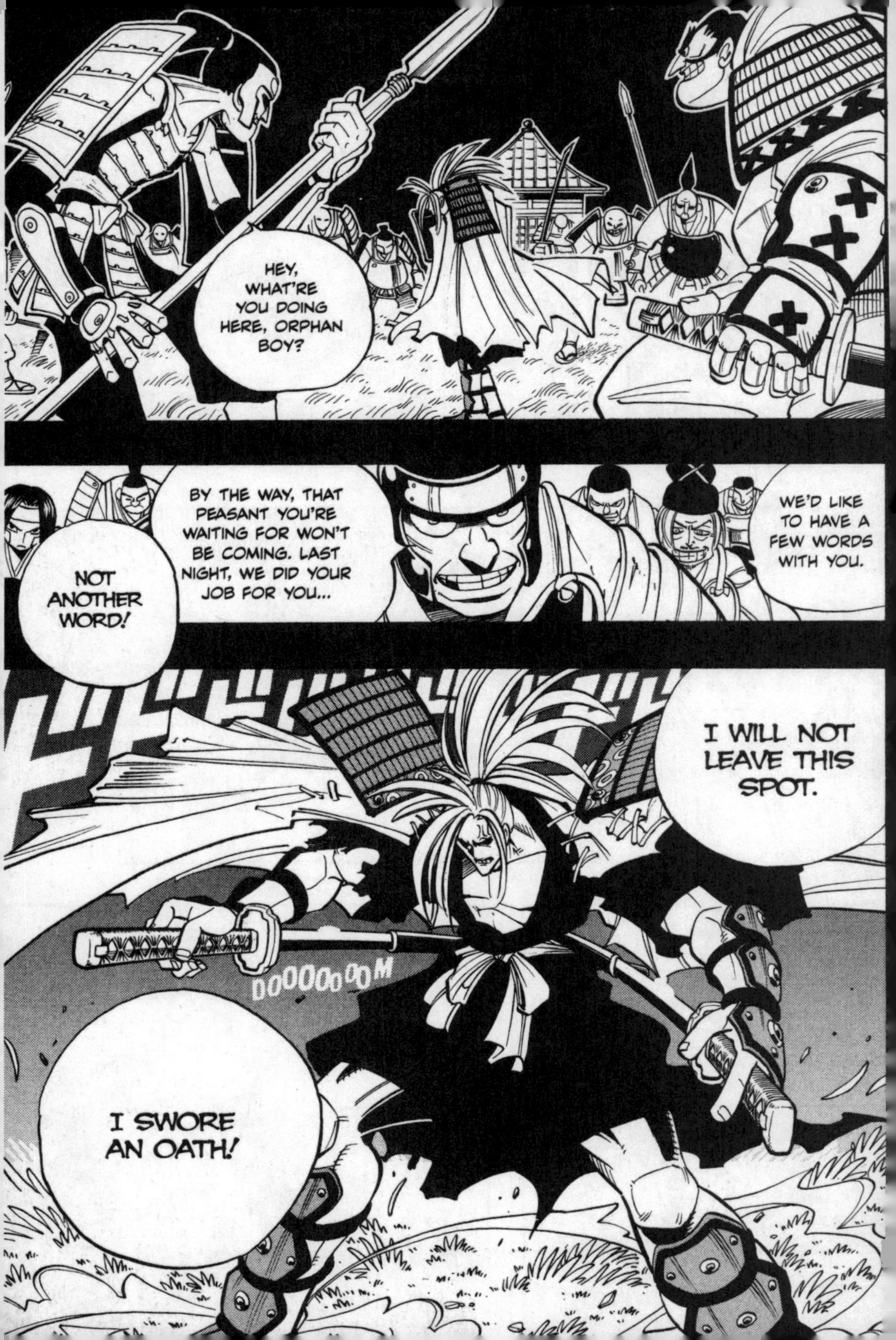
HEY, WHAT'RE YOU DOING HERE, ORPHAN BOY?
WE'D LIKE TO HAVE A FEW WORDS WITH YOU.
BY THE WAY, THAT PEASANT YOU'RE WAITING FOR WON'T BE COMING. LAST NIGHT, WE DID YOUR JOB FOR YOU...
NOT ANOTHER WORD!
I WILL NOT LEAVE THIS SPOT.
DOOOOOOOM
I SWORE AN OATH!

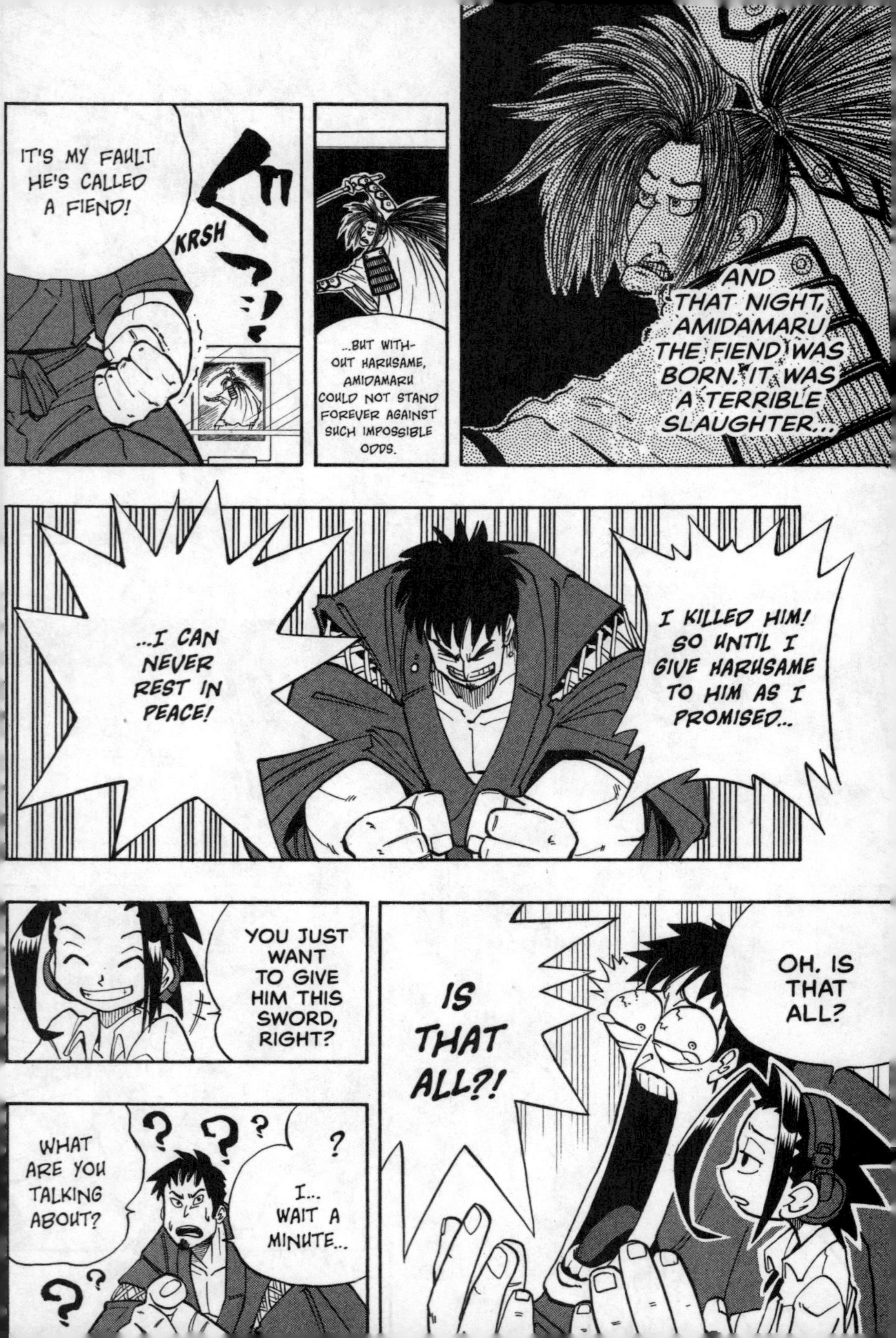
AND THAT NIGHT, AMIDAMARU THE FIEND WAS BORN. IT WAS A TERRIBLE SLAUGHTER...
...BUT WITH-OUT HARUSAME, AMIDAMARU COULD NOT STAND FOREVER AGAINST SUCH IMPOSSIBLE ODDS.
IT'S MY FAULT HE'S CALLED A FIEND!
KRSH
I KILLED HIM! SO UNTIL I GIVE HARUSAME TO HIM AS I PROMISED...
...I CAN NEVER REST IN PEACE!
OH. IS THAT ALL?
IS THAT ALL?!
YOU JUST WANT TO GIVE HIM THIS SWORD, RIGHT?
I... WAIT A MINUTE...
WHAT ARE YOU TALKING ABOUT?

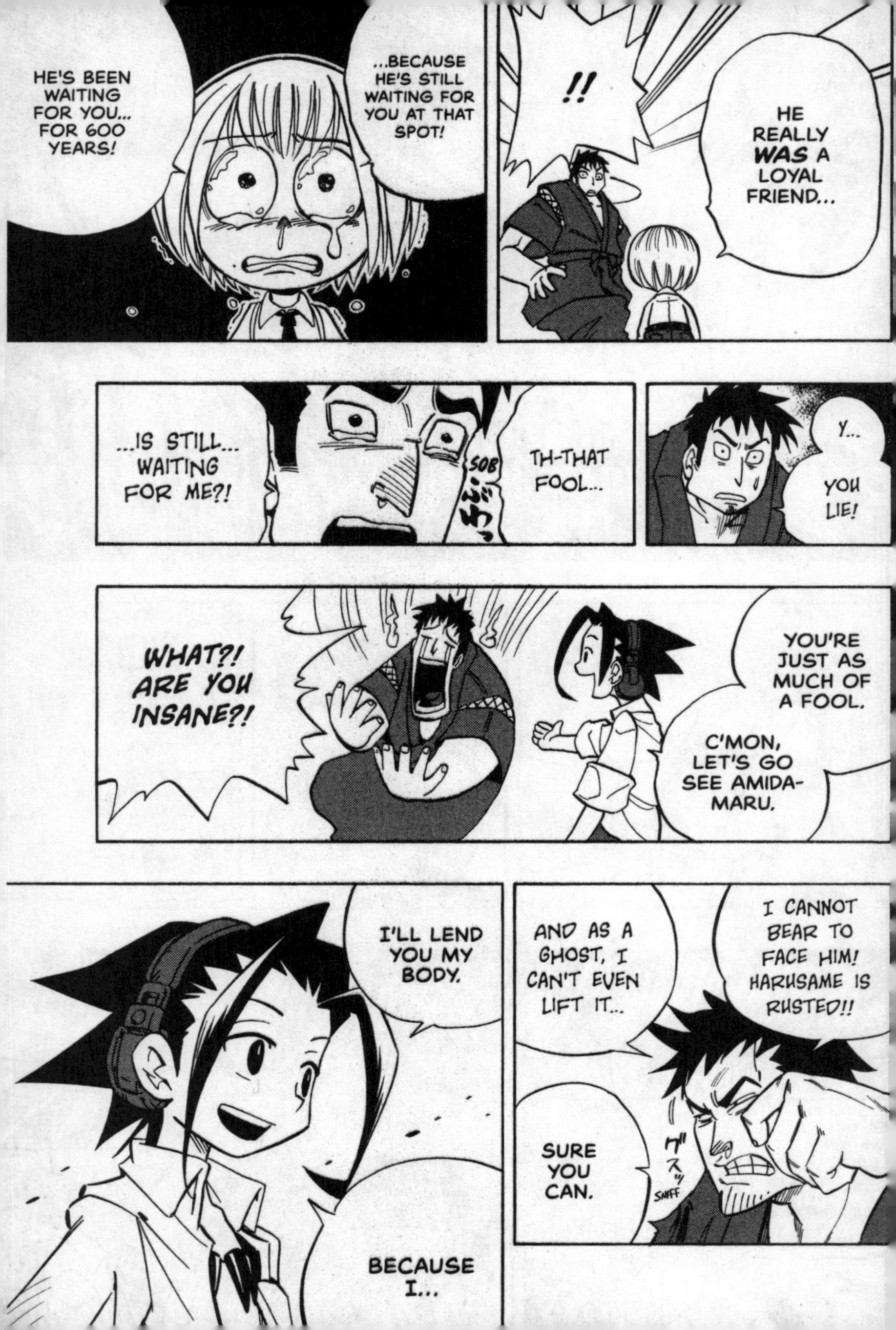
HE REALLY WAS A LOYAL FRIEND...
!!
...BECAUSE HE'S STILL WAITING FOR YOU AT THAT SPOT!
HE'S BEEN WAITING FOR YOU... FOR 600 YEARS!
Y... YOU LIE!
TH-THAT FOOL...
SOB
...IS STILL... WAITING FOR ME?!
YOU'RE JUST AS MUCH OF A FOOL.
C'MON, LET'S GO SEE AMIDA-MARU.
WHAT?! ARE YOU INSANE?!
I CANNOT BEAR TO FACE HIM! HARUSAME IS RUSTED!!
AND AS A GHOST, I CAN'T EVEN LIFT IT...
SNIFF
SURE YOU CAN.
I'LL LEND YOU MY BODY.
BECAUSE I...

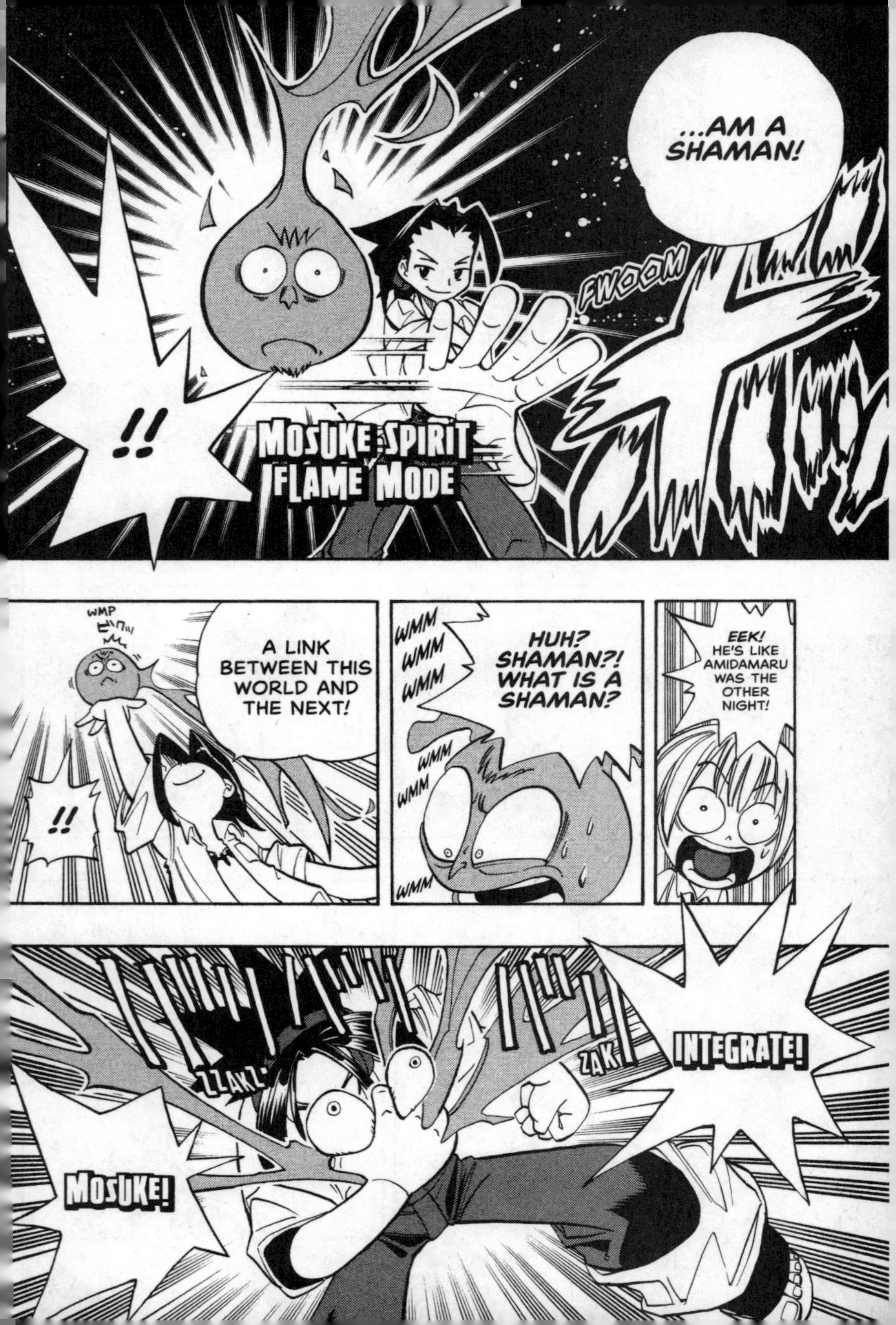
...AM A SHAMAN!
FWOOM
MOSUKE SPIRIT FLAME MODE
!!
EEK! HE'S LIKE AMIDAMARU WAS THE OTHER NIGHT!
WMM WMM WMM
HUH? SHAMAN?! WHAT IS A SHAMAN?
WMM WMM
WMM
A LINK BETWEEN THIS WORLD AND THE NEXT!
WMP
!!
INTEGRATE!
ZAK
ZZAKZ
MOSUKE!

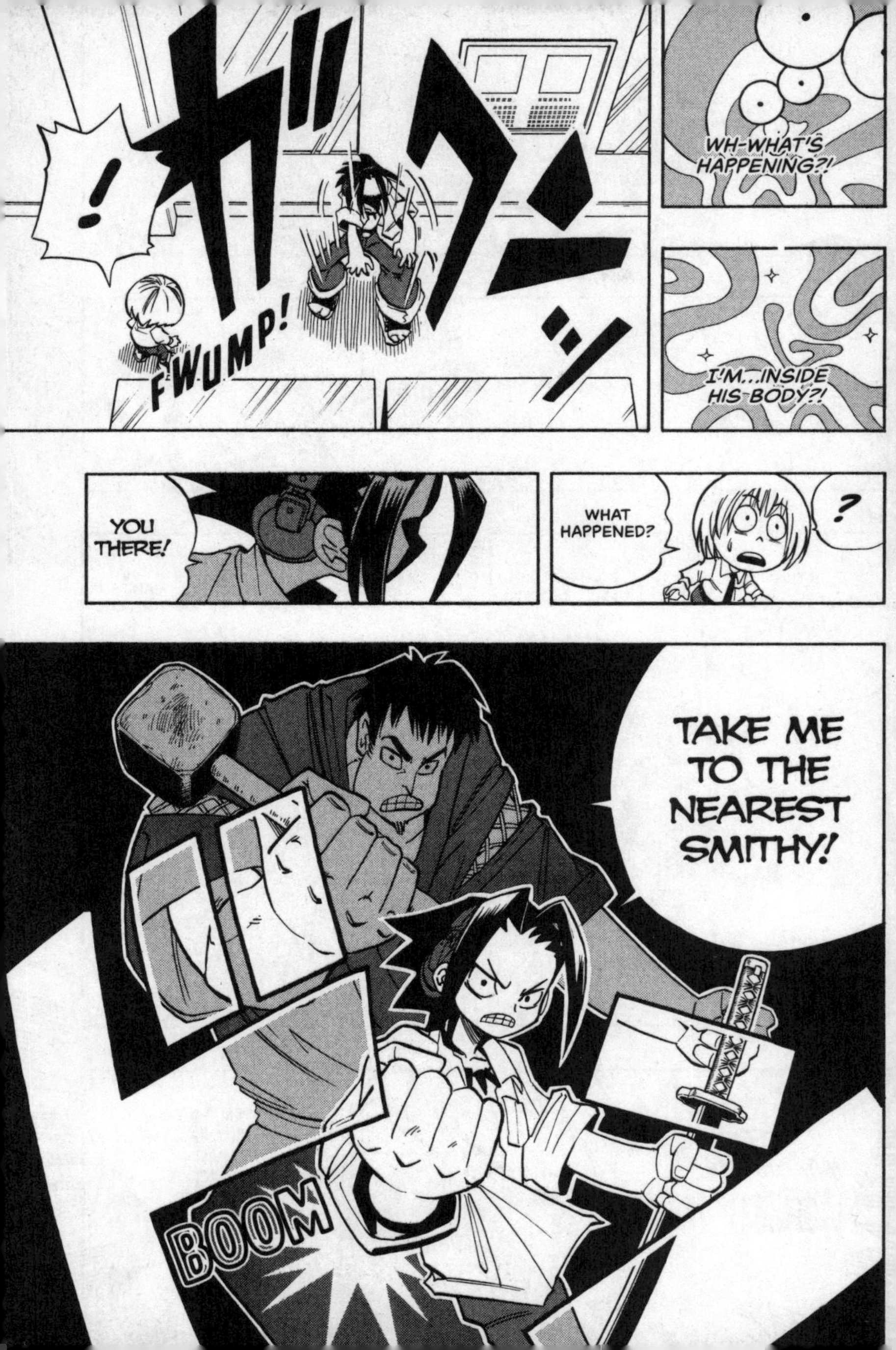
WH-WHAT'S HAPPENING?!
I'M...INSIDE HIS BODY?!
!
FWUMP!
?
WHAT HAPPENED?
YOU THERE!
TAKE ME TO THE NEAREST SMITHY!
BOOM

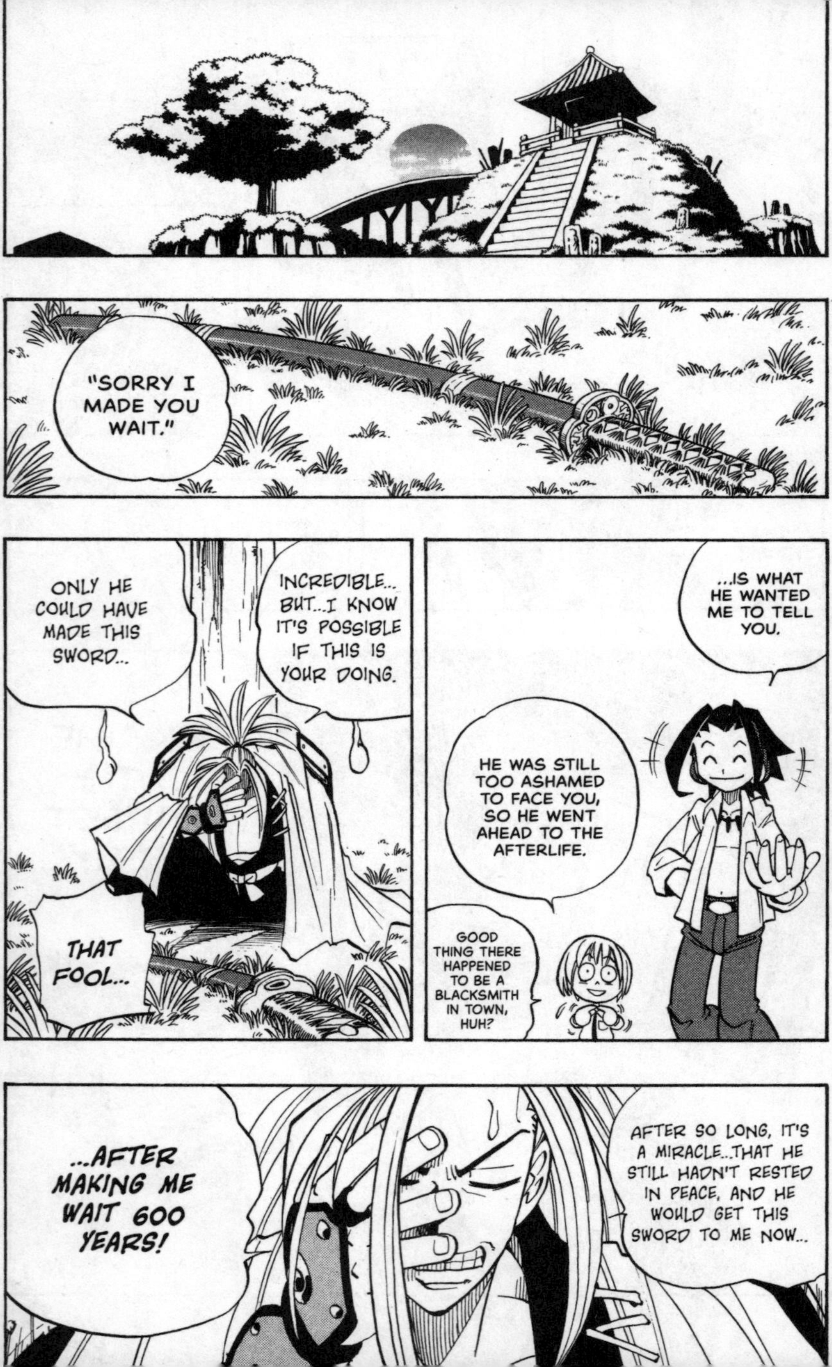
"SORRY I MADE YOU WAIT."
...IS WHAT HE WANTED ME TO TELL YOU.
HE WAS STILL TOO ASHAMED TO FACE YOU, SO HE WENT AHEAD TO THE AFTERLIFE.
GOOD THING THERE HAPPENED TO BE A BLACKSMITH IN TOWN, HUH?
INCREDIBLE... BUT...I KNOW IT'S POSSIBLE IF THIS IS YOUR DOING.
ONLY HE COULD HAVE MADE THIS SWORD...
THAT FOOL...
AFTER SO LONG, IT'S A MIRACLE...THAT HE STILL HADN'T RESTED IN PEACE, AND HE WOULD GET THIS SWORD TO ME NOW...
...AFTER MAKING ME WAIT 600 YEARS!

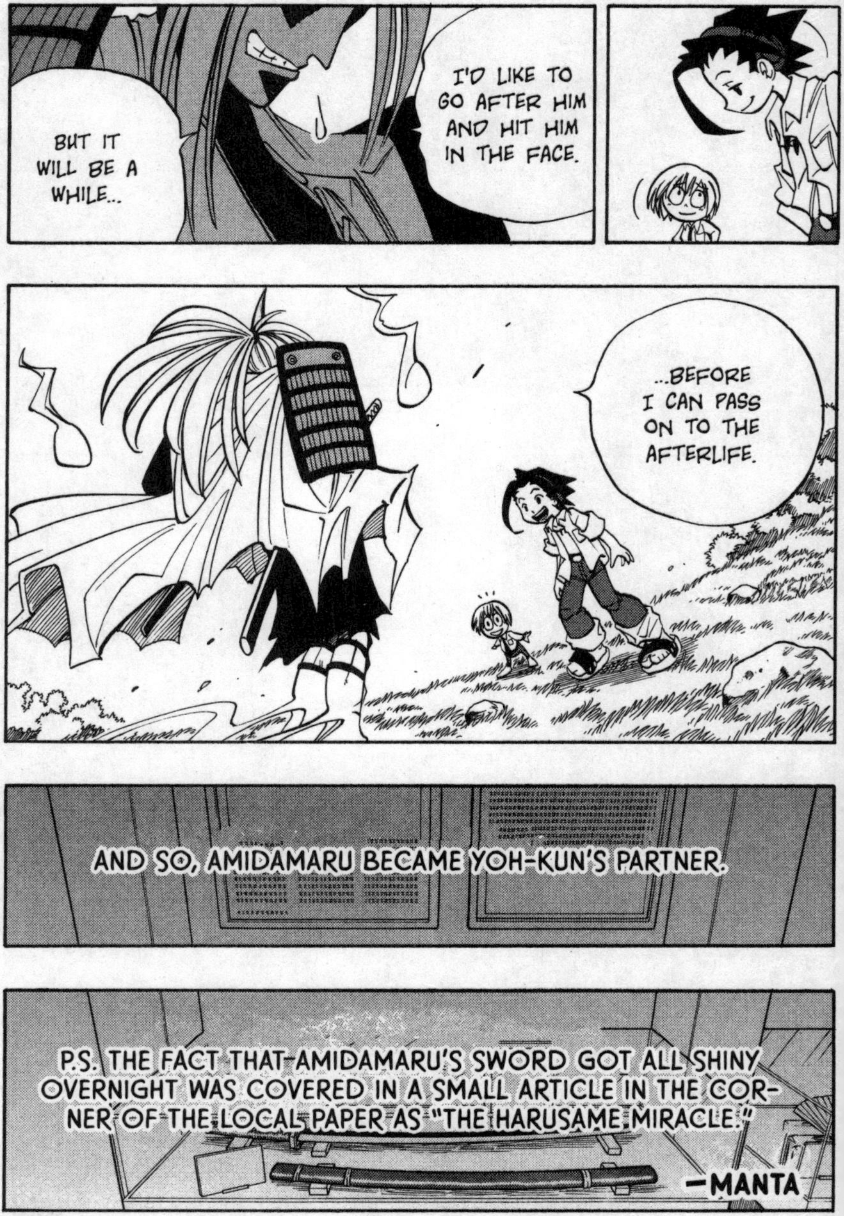
I'D LIKE TO GO AFTER HIM AND HIT HIM IN THE FACE.
BUT IT WILL BE A WHILE...
...BEFORE I CAN PASS ON TO THE AFTERLIFE.
AND SO, AMIDAMARU BECAME YOH-KUN'S PARTNER.
P.S. THE FACT THAT AMIDAMARU'S SWORD GOT ALL SHINY OVERNIGHT WAS COVERED IN A SMALL ARTICLE IN THE CORNER OF THE LOCAL PAPER AS "THE HARUSAME MIRACLE."
—MANTA

SHAMAN
KING
1

Headphones

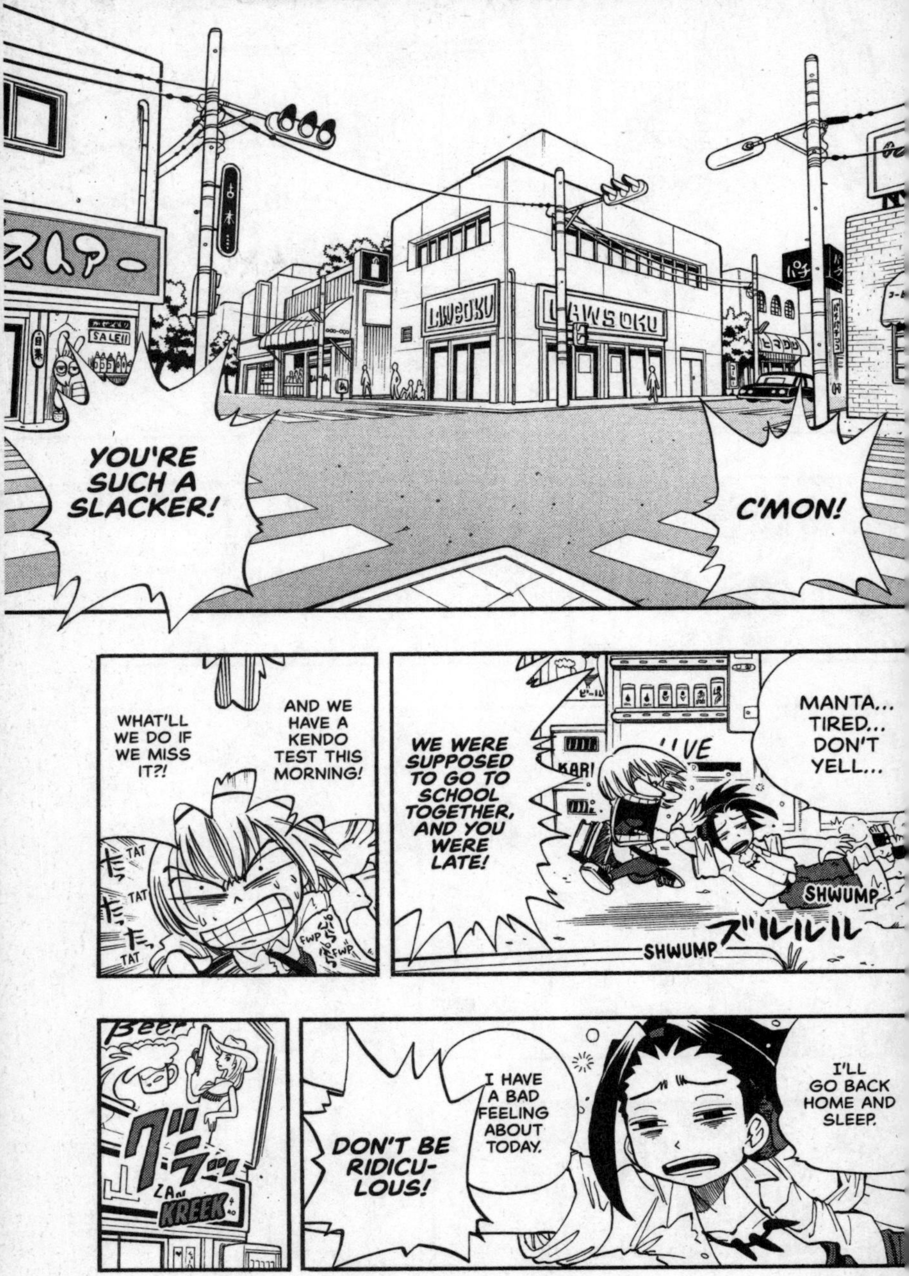
C'MON!
YOU'RE SUCH A SLACKER!
MANTA... TIRED... DON'T YELL...
WE WERE SUPPOSED TO GO TO SCHOOL TOGETHER, AND YOU WERE LATE!
SHWUMP
ズルルルル
SHWUMP
AND WE HAVE A KENDO TEST THIS MORNING!
WHAT'LL WE DO IF WE MISS IT?!
TAT
TAT
TAT
FWP
FWP
I'LL GO BACK HOME AND SLEEP.
I HAVE A BAD FEELING ABOUT TODAY.
DON'T BE RIDICU-LOUS!
Beer
ZAN
KREEK

Chapter 3: The Unfinished Billboard

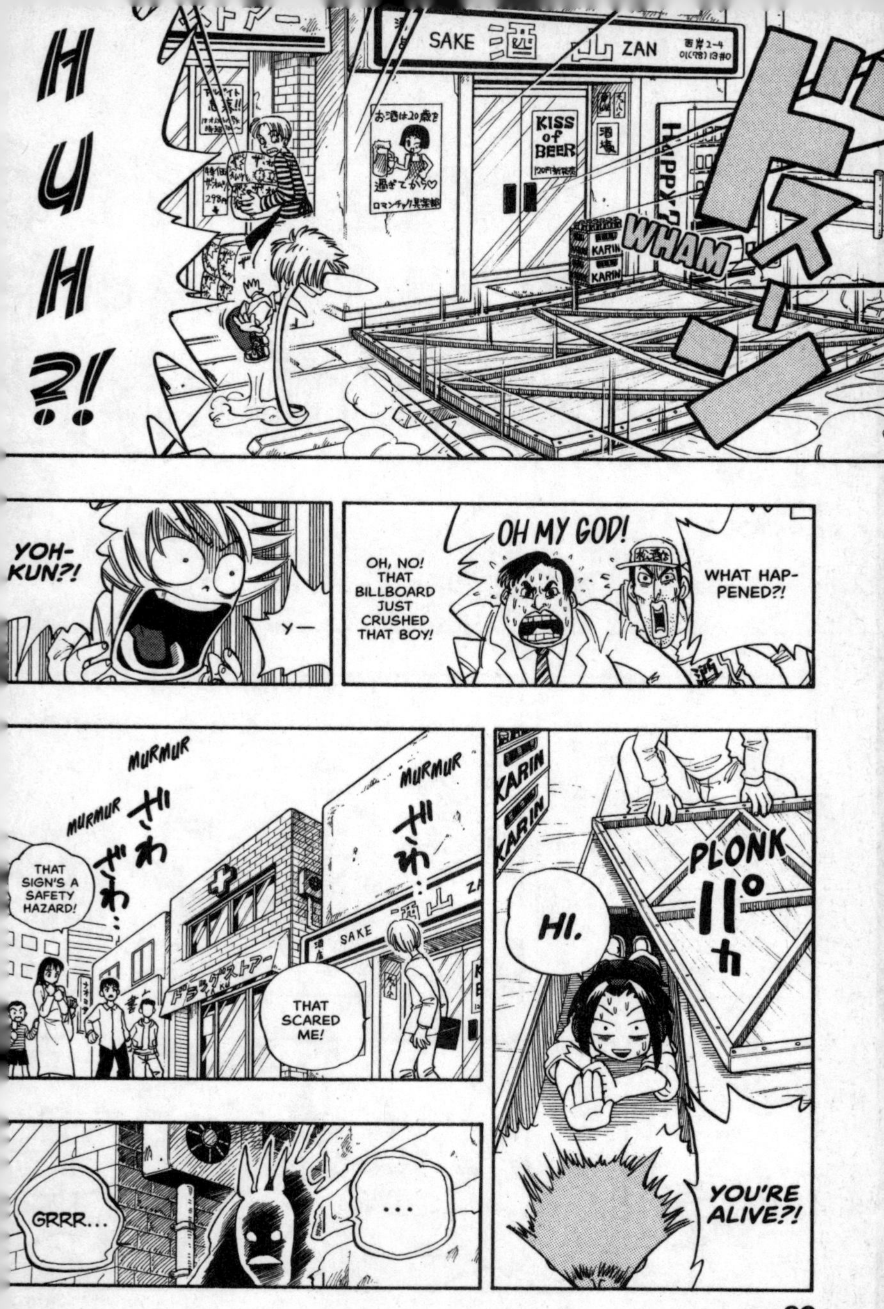
ドスーン
WHAM
SAKE 酒山 ZAN
KISS of BEER
HUH?!
WHAT HAP-PENED?!
OH MY GOD!
OH, NO! THAT BILLBOARD JUST CRUSHED THAT BOY!
Y—
YOH-KUN?!
PLONK
パカ
HI.
YOU'RE ALIVE?!
MURMUR
ざわ…
MURMUR
MURMUR
ざわ ざわ…
THAT SCARED ME!
THAT SIGN'S A SAFETY HAZARD!
...
GRRR...

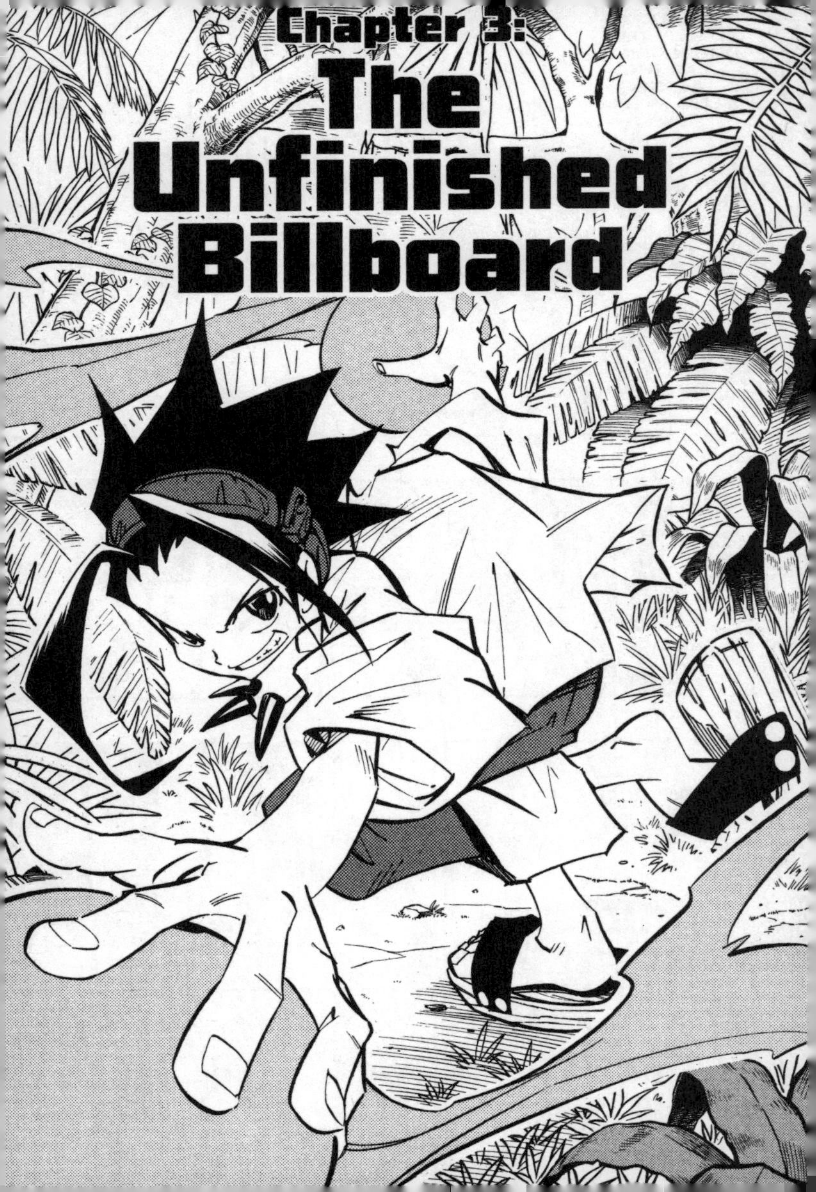
Chapter 3:
The Unfinished Billboard

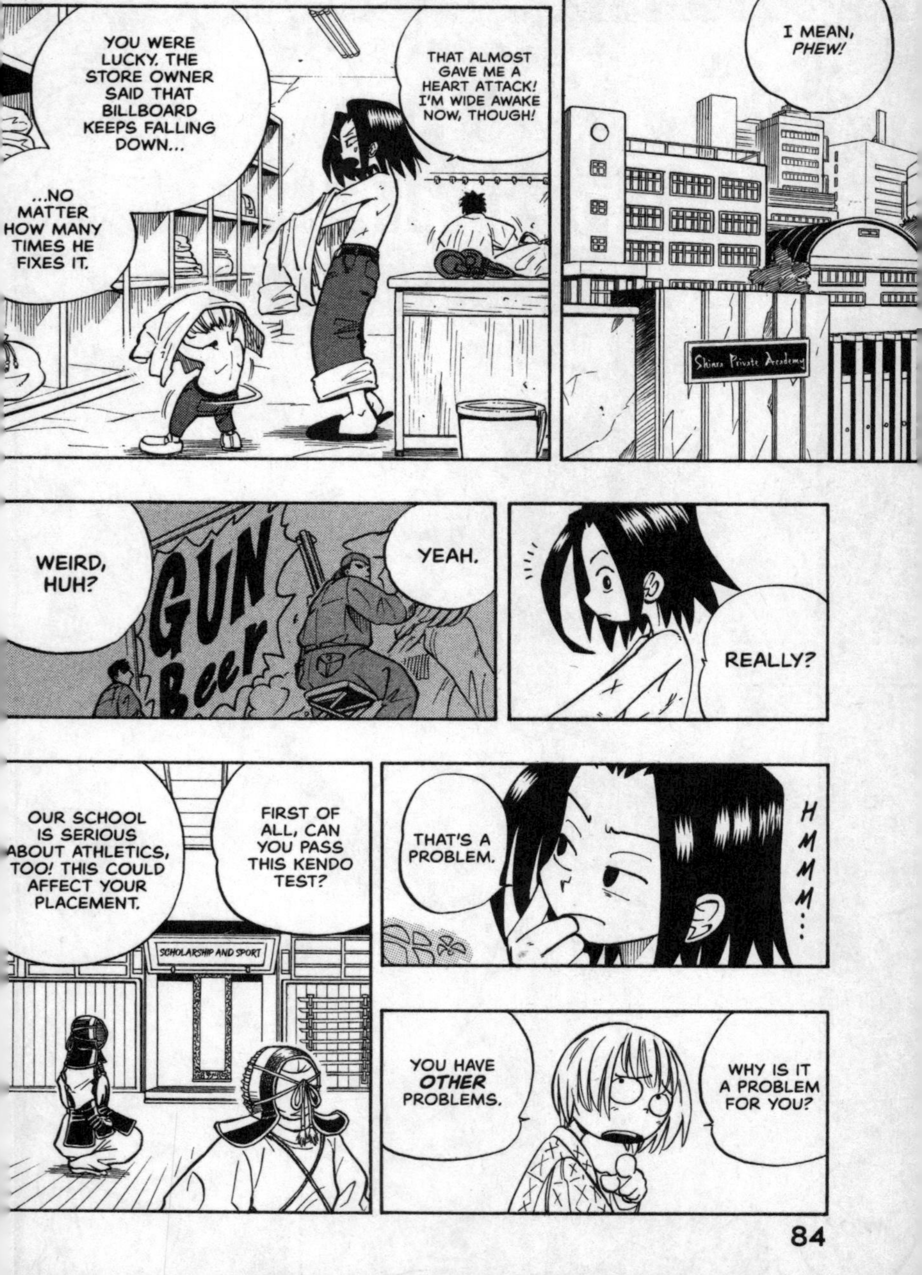
YOU WERE LUCKY. THE STORE OWNER SAID THAT BILLBOARD KEEPS FALLING DOWN...
...NO MATTER HOW MANY TIMES HE FIXES IT.
THAT ALMOST GAVE ME A HEART ATTACK! I'M WIDE AWAKE NOW, THOUGH!
I MEAN, *PHEW!*
Shinra Private Academy
WEIRD, HUH?
GUN Beer
YEAH.
REALLY?
FIRST OF ALL, CAN YOU PASS THIS KENDO TEST?
OUR SCHOOL IS SERIOUS ABOUT ATHLETICS, TOO! THIS COULD AFFECT YOUR PLACEMENT.
SCHOLARSHIP AND SPORT
THAT'S A PROBLEM.
HMMM...
WHY IS IT A PROBLEM FOR YOU?
YOU HAVE ***OTHER*** PROBLEMS.

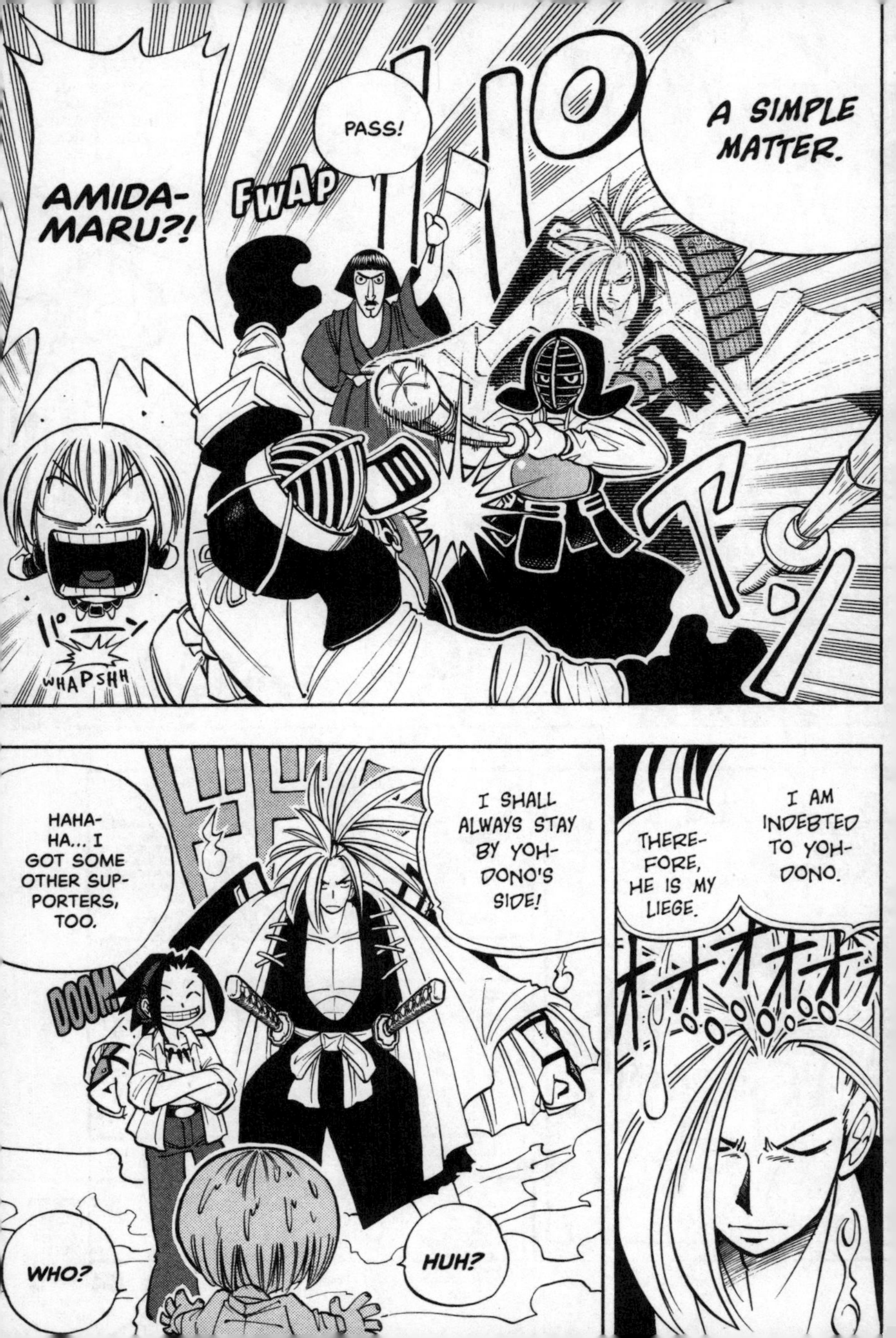
A SIMPLE MATTER.
PASS!
FWAP
AMIDA-MARU?!
WHAPSHH
I AM INDEBTED TO YOH-DONO.
THERE-FORE, HE IS MY LIEGE.
I SHALL ALWAYS STAY BY YOH-DONO'S SIDE!
HAHA-HA... I GOT SOME OTHER SUP-PORTERS, TOO.
DOOM
HUH?
WHO?

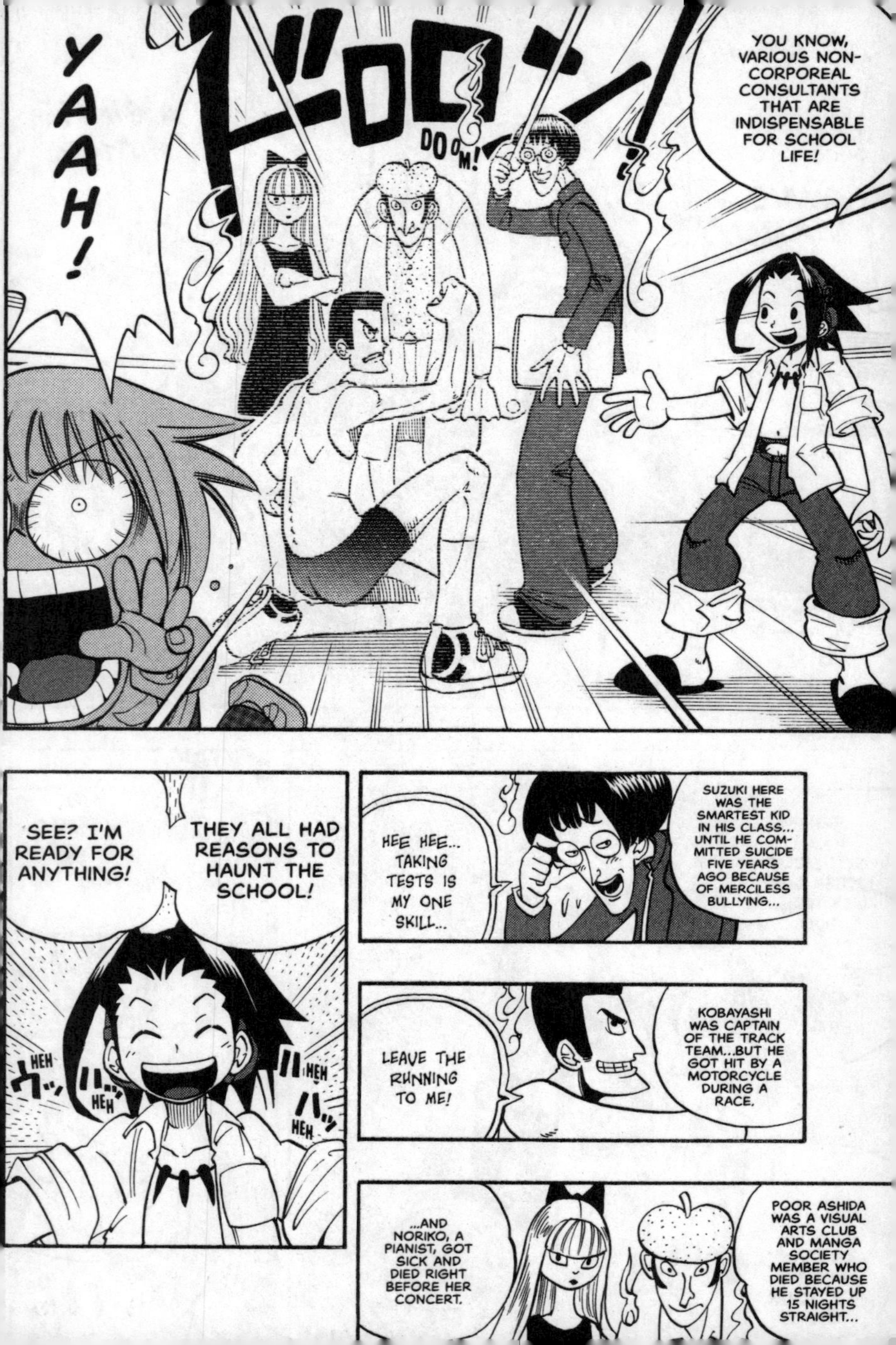
YOU KNOW, VARIOUS NON-CORPOREAL CONSULTANTS THAT ARE INDISPENSABLE FOR SCHOOL LIFE!
ドロロン!
DOOOM!
YAAAH!
SUZUKI HERE WAS THE SMARTEST KID IN HIS CLASS... UNTIL HE COMMITTED SUICIDE FIVE YEARS AGO BECAUSE OF MERCILESS BULLYING...
HEE HEE... TAKING TESTS IS MY ONE SKILL...
KOBAYASHI WAS CAPTAIN OF THE TRACK TEAM...BUT HE GOT HIT BY A MOTORCYCLE DURING A RACE.
LEAVE THE RUNNING TO ME!
POOR ASHIDA WAS A VISUAL ARTS CLUB AND MANGA SOCIETY MEMBER WHO DIED BECAUSE HE STAYED UP 15 NIGHTS STRAIGHT...
...AND NORIKO, A PIANIST, GOT SICK AND DIED RIGHT BEFORE HER CONCERT.
THEY ALL HAD REASONS TO HAUNT THE SCHOOL!
SEE? I'M READY FOR ANYTHING!
HEH HEH HEH HEH HEH

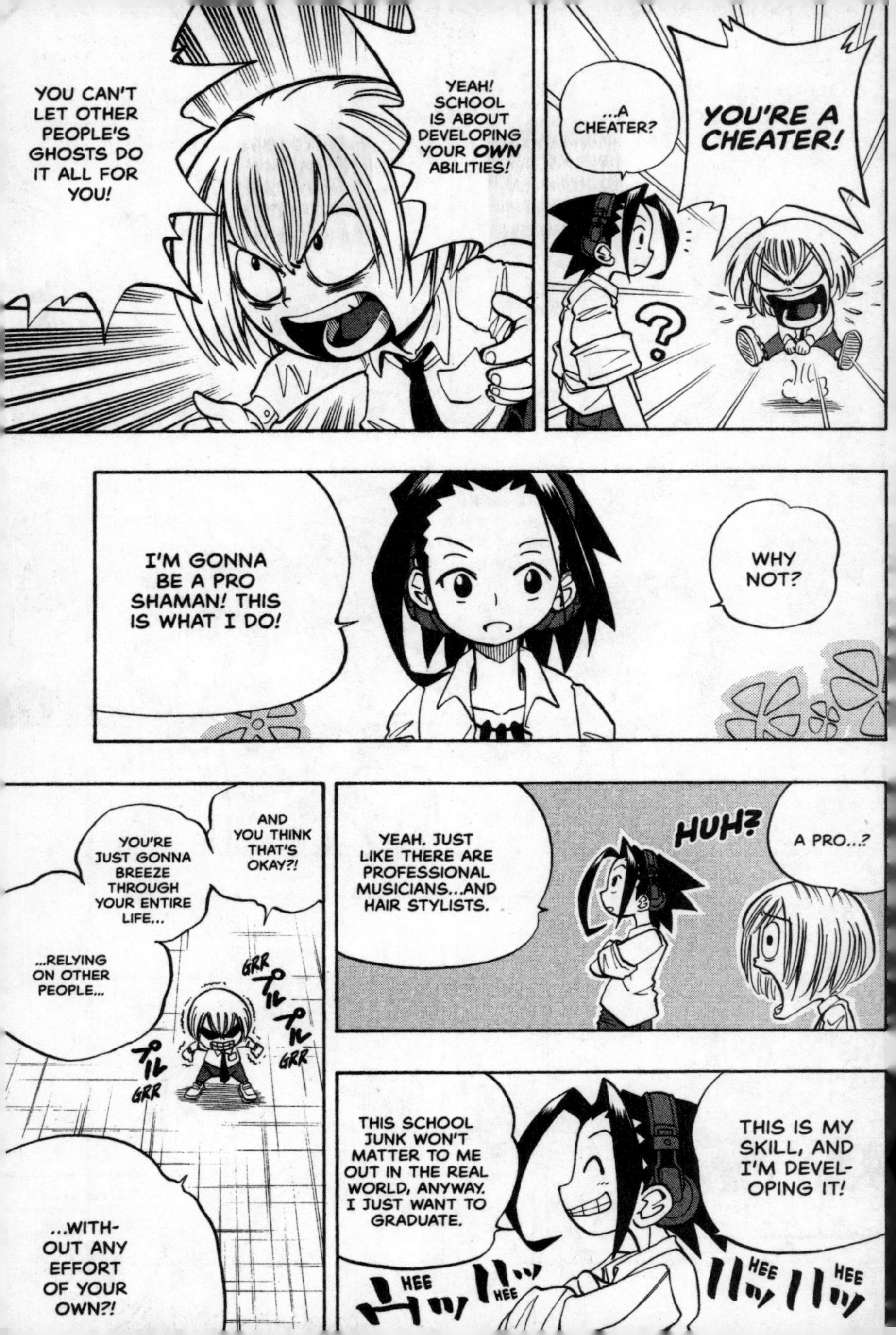
YOU'RE A CHEATER!
...A CHEATER?
YEAH! SCHOOL IS ABOUT DEVELOPING YOUR *OWN* ABILITIES!
YOU CAN'T LET OTHER PEOPLE'S GHOSTS DO IT ALL FOR YOU!
WHY NOT?
I'M GONNA BE A PRO SHAMAN! THIS IS WHAT I DO!
A PRO...?
HUH?
YEAH. JUST LIKE THERE ARE PROFESSIONAL MUSICIANS...AND HAIR STYLISTS.
THIS IS MY SKILL, AND I'M DEVEL-OPING IT!
THIS SCHOOL JUNK WON'T MATTER TO ME OUT IN THE REAL WORLD, ANYWAY. I JUST WANT TO GRADUATE.
HEE
HEE
HEE
HEE
AND YOU THINK THAT'S OKAY?!
YOU'RE JUST GONNA BREEZE THROUGH YOUR ENTIRE LIFE...
...RELYING ON OTHER PEOPLE...
GRR
GRR
GRR
...WITH-OUT ANY EFFORT OF YOUR OWN?!

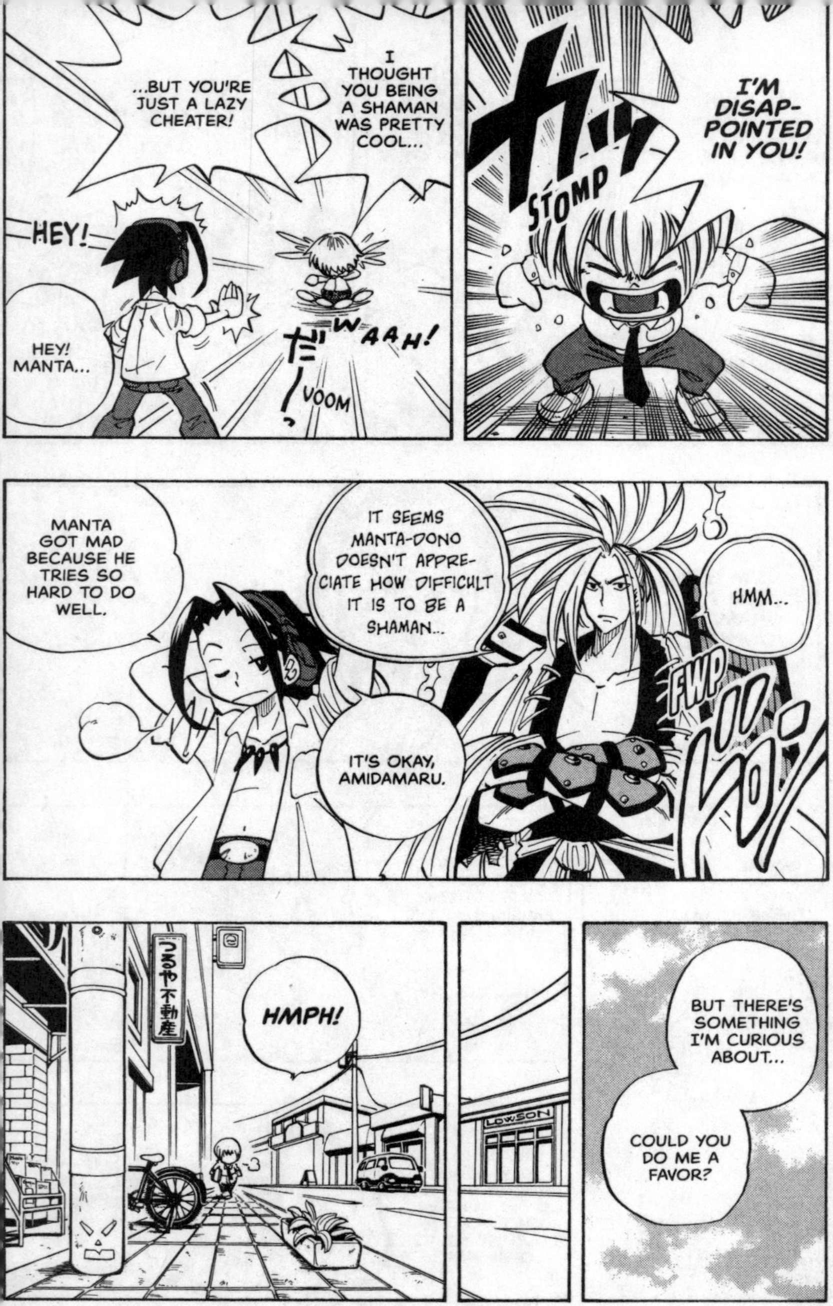
I'M DISAPPOINTED IN YOU!
STOMP
I THOUGHT YOU BEING A SHAMAN WAS PRETTY COOL...
...BUT YOU'RE JUST A LAZY CHEATER!
HEY!
WAAH!
VOOM
HEY! MANTA...
HMM...
FWP
IT SEEMS MANTA-DONO DOESN'T APPRECIATE HOW DIFFICULT IT IS TO BE A SHAMAN...
MANTA GOT MAD BECAUSE HE TRIES SO HARD TO DO WELL.
IT'S OKAY, AMIDAMARU.
BUT THERE'S SOMETHING I'M CURIOUS ABOUT...
COULD YOU DO ME A FAVOR?
LOWSON
HMPH!
つるや不動産

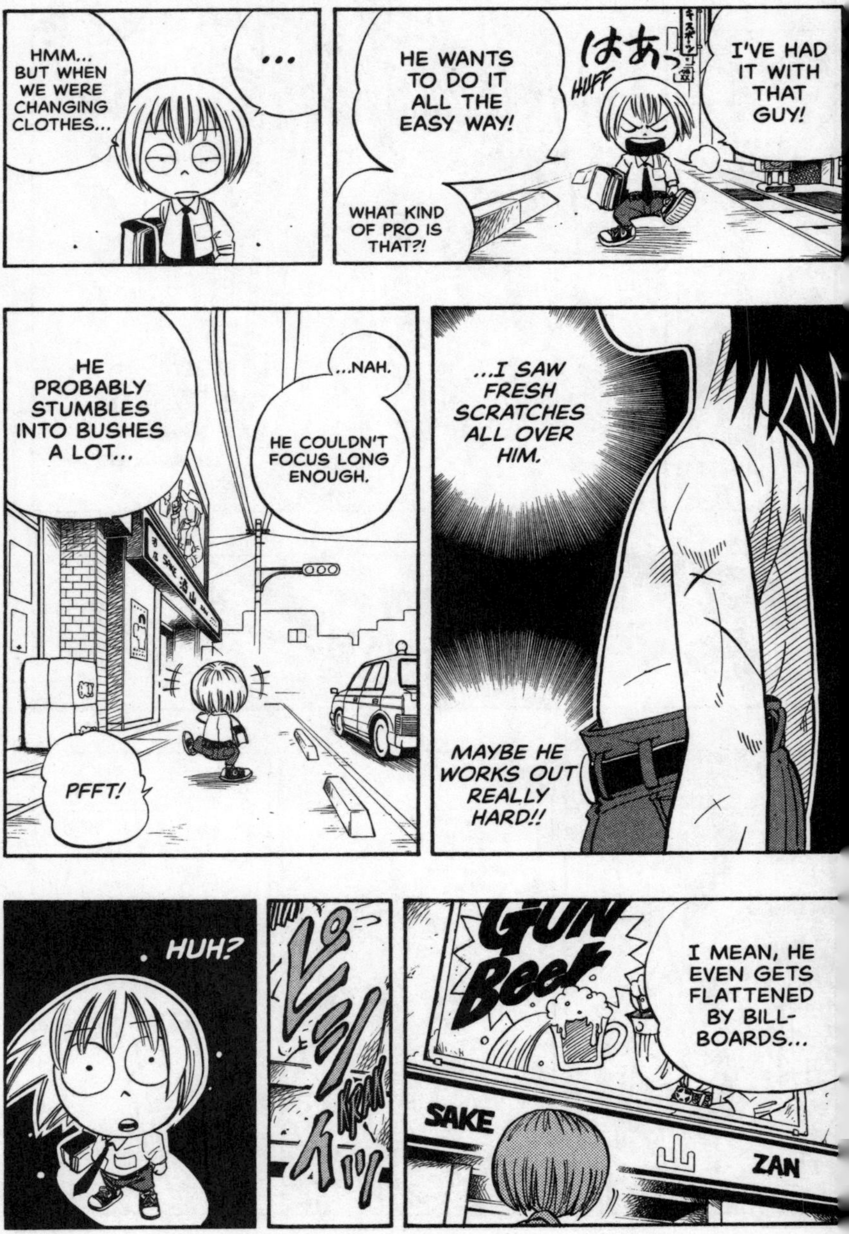
I'VE HAD IT WITH THAT GUY!
はあっ
HUFF
HE WANTS TO DO IT ALL THE EASY WAY!
WHAT KIND OF PRO IS THAT?!
...
HMM... BUT WHEN WE WERE CHANGING CLOTHES...
...I SAW FRESH SCRATCHES ALL OVER HIM.
MAYBE HE WORKS OUT REALLY HARD!!
...NAH.
HE COULDN'T FOCUS LONG ENOUGH.
HE PROBABLY STUMBLES INTO BUSHES A LOT...
PFFT!
I MEAN, HE EVEN GETS FLATTENED BY BILL-BOARDS...
GUN Beer
SAKE
ZAN
HUH?

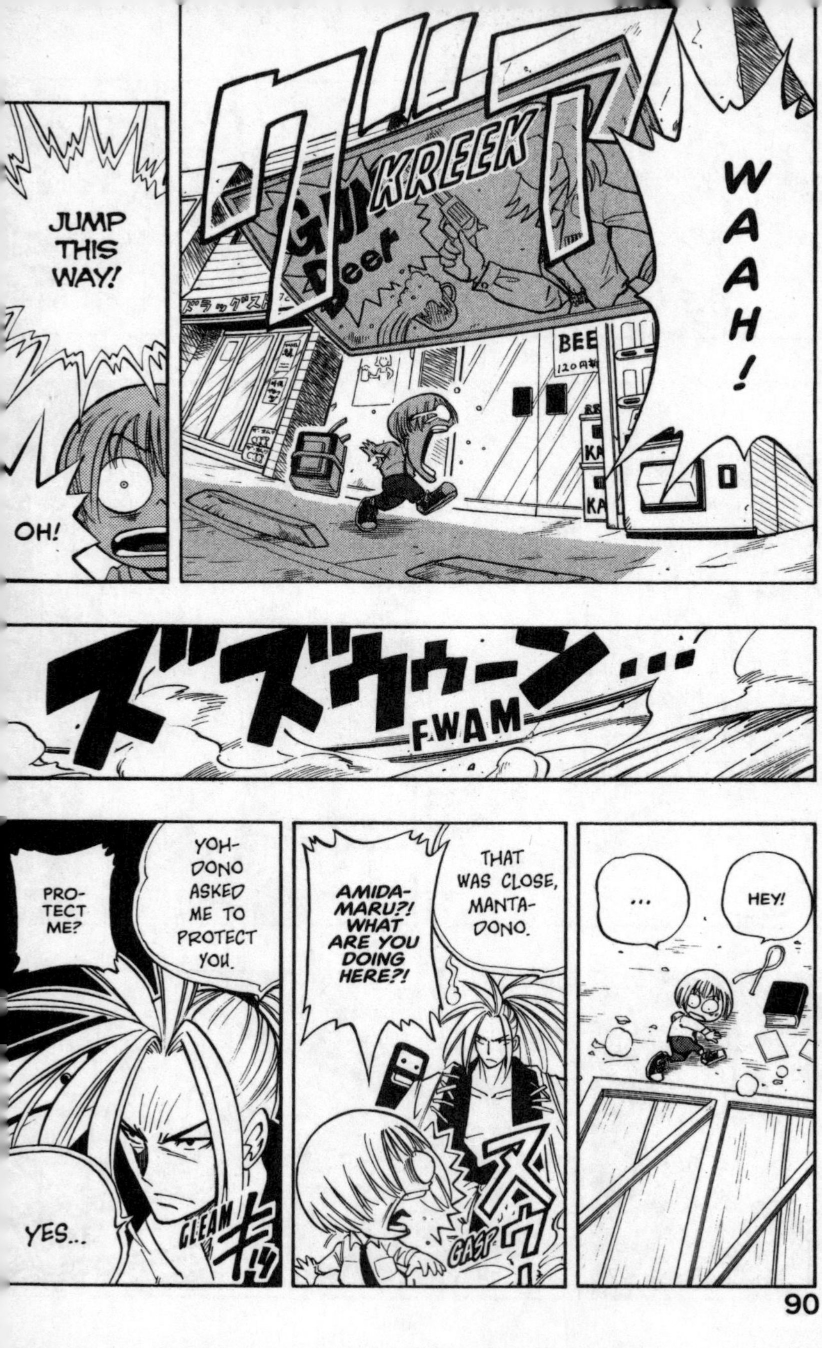

WAAH!
KREEK
JUMP THIS WAY!
OH!
FWAM
HEY!
...
THAT WAS CLOSE, MANTA-DONO.
AMIDA-MARU?! WHAT ARE YOU DOING HERE?!
GASP
YOH-DONO ASKED ME TO PROTECT YOU.
PROTECT ME?
GLEAM
YES...

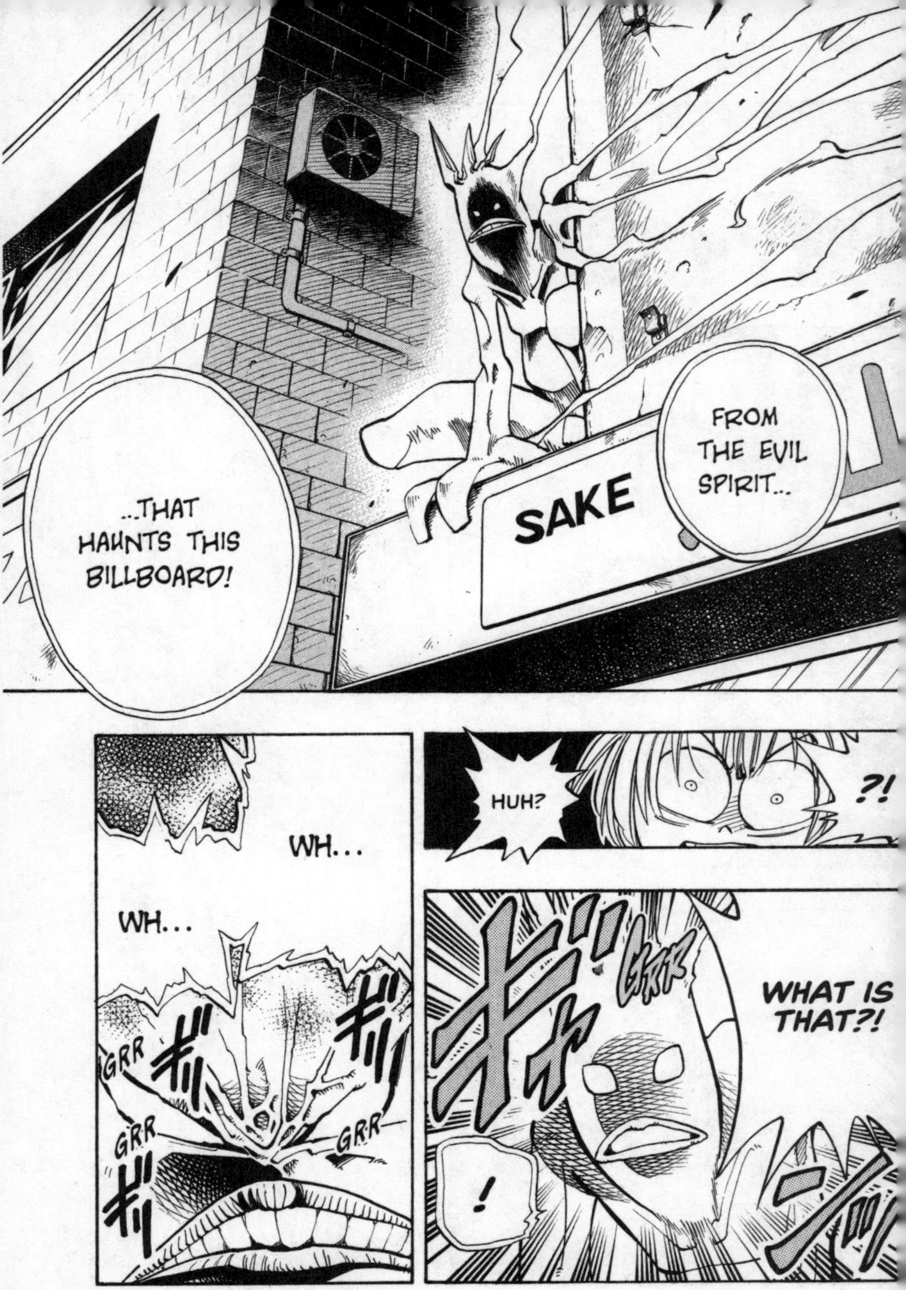
FROM THE EVIL SPIRIT...
SAKE
...THAT HAUNTS THIS BILLBOARD!
HUH?
?!
GRR
WHAT IS THAT?!
!
WH...
WH...
GRR
GR-R
GR-R

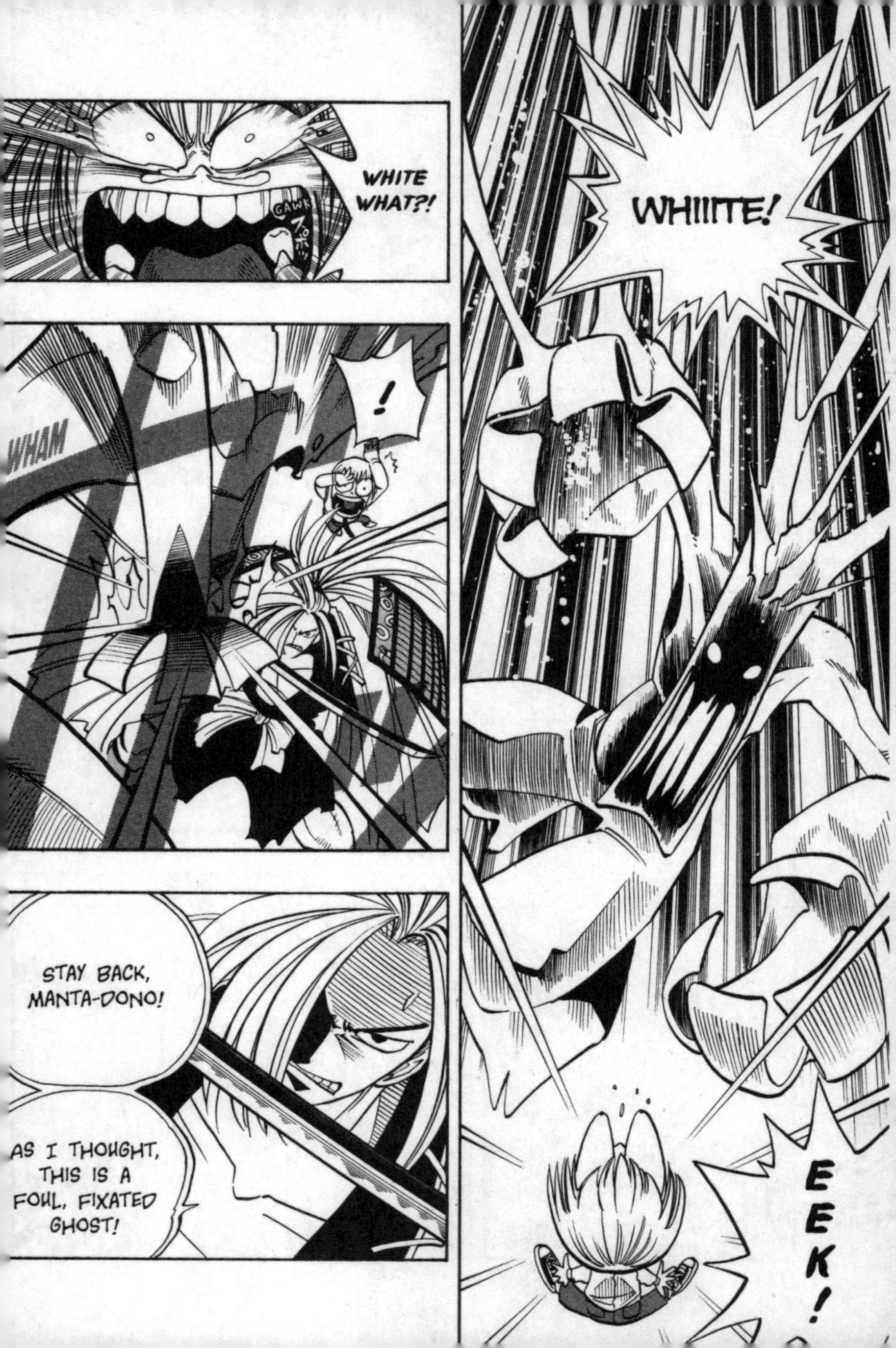
WHIIITE!
EEK!
WHITE WHAT?!
GAWK
WHAM
!
STAY BACK, MANTA-DONO!
AS I THOUGHT, THIS IS A FOUL, FIXATED GHOST!

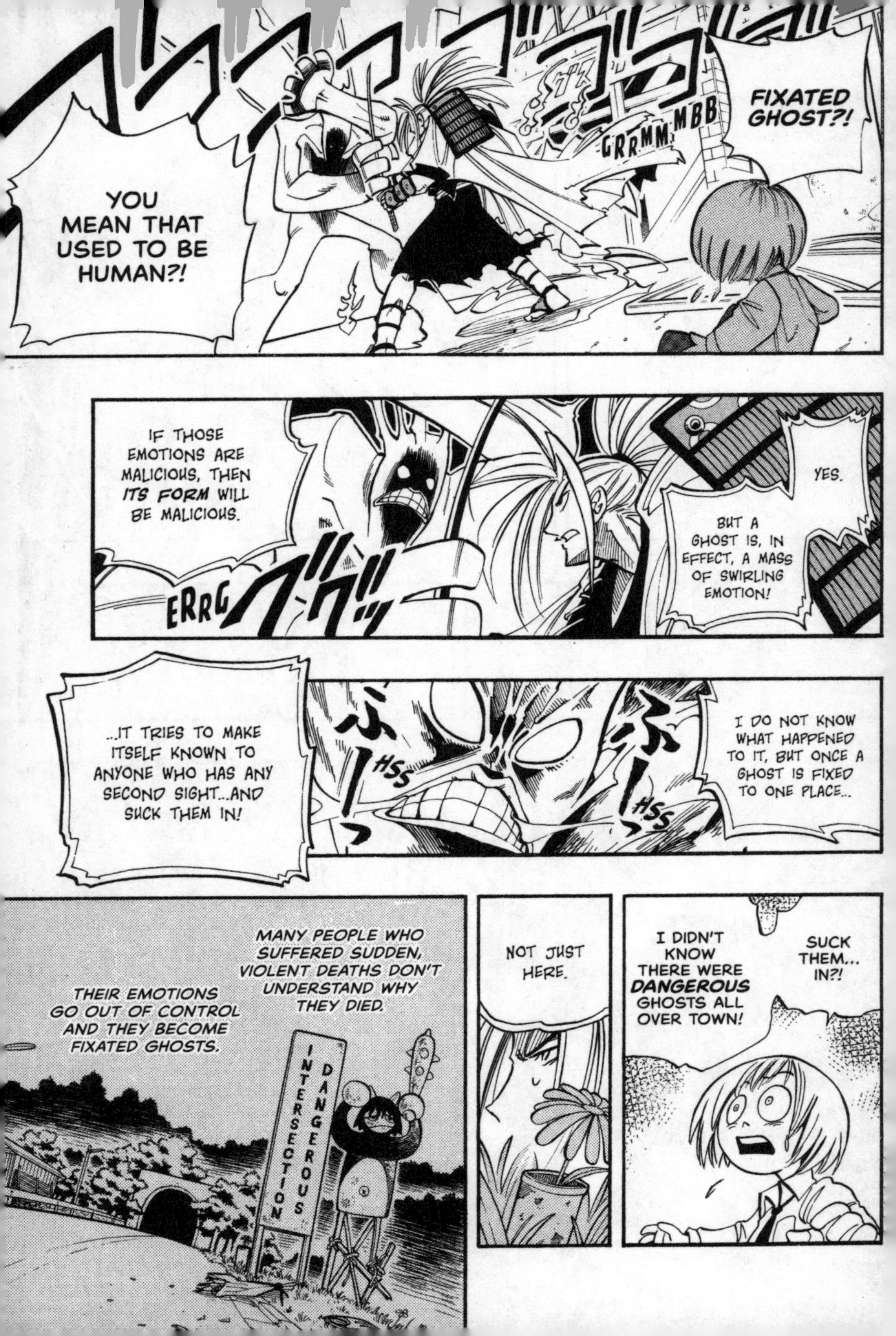

FIXATED GHOST?!
GRRMMMBB
YOU MEAN THAT USED TO BE HUMAN?!
YES.
BUT A GHOST IS, IN EFFECT, A MASS OF SWIRLING EMOTION!
IF THOSE EMOTIONS ARE MALICIOUS, THEN ITS FORM WILL BE MALICIOUS.
ERRG
I DO NOT KNOW WHAT HAPPENED TO IT, BUT ONCE A GHOST IS FIXED TO ONE PLACE...
HSS
HSS
...IT TRIES TO MAKE ITSELF KNOWN TO ANYONE WHO HAS ANY SECOND SIGHT...AND SUCK THEM IN!
SUCK THEM... IN?!
I DIDN'T KNOW THERE WERE DANGEROUS GHOSTS ALL OVER TOWN!
NOT JUST HERE.
MANY PEOPLE WHO SUFFERED SUDDEN, VIOLENT DEATHS DON'T UNDERSTAND WHY THEY DIED.
THEIR EMOTIONS GO OUT OF CONTROL AND THEY BECOME FIXATED GHOSTS.
DANGEROUS
INTERSECTION

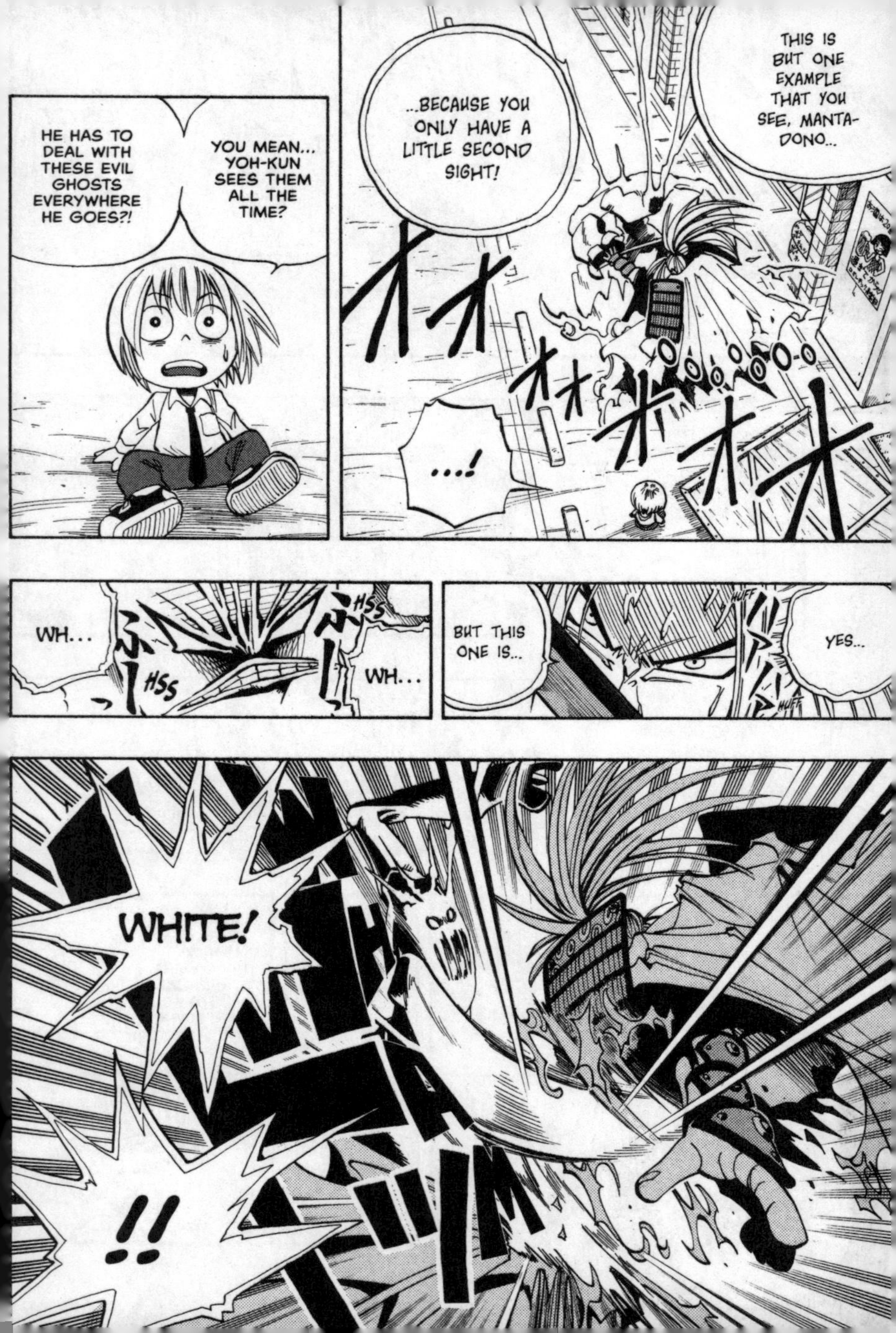
THIS IS BUT ONE EXAMPLE THAT YOU SEE, MANTA-DONO...
...BECAUSE YOU ONLY HAVE A LITTLE SECOND SIGHT!
...!
YOU MEAN... YOH-KUN SEES THEM ALL THE TIME?
HE HAS TO DEAL WITH THESE EVIL GHOSTS EVERYWHERE HE GOES?!
YES...
HUFF
HUFF
BUT THIS ONE IS...
HSS
WH...
HSS
WH...
WHITE!
!!

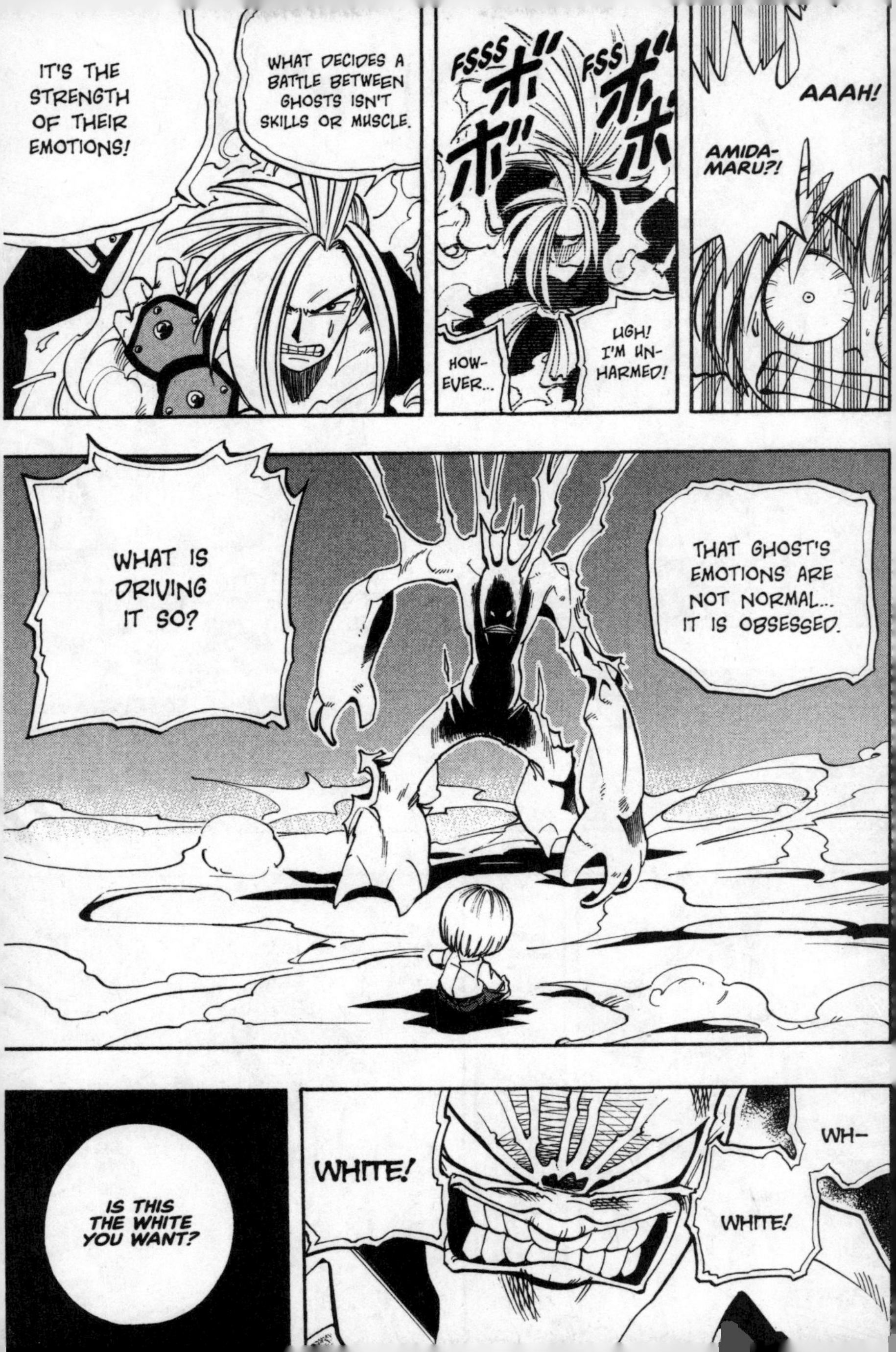
AAAH!
AMIDA-MARU?!
FSSS
ボボ
FSS
ボボ
UGH! I'M UN-HARMED!
HOW-EVER...
WHAT DECIDES A BATTLE BETWEEN GHOSTS ISN'T SKILLS OR MUSCLE.
IT'S THE STRENGTH OF THEIR EMOTIONS!
THAT GHOST'S EMOTIONS ARE NOT NORMAL... IT IS OBSESSED.
WHAT IS DRIVING IT SO?
WH-
WHITE!
WHITE!
IS THIS THE WHITE YOU WANT?

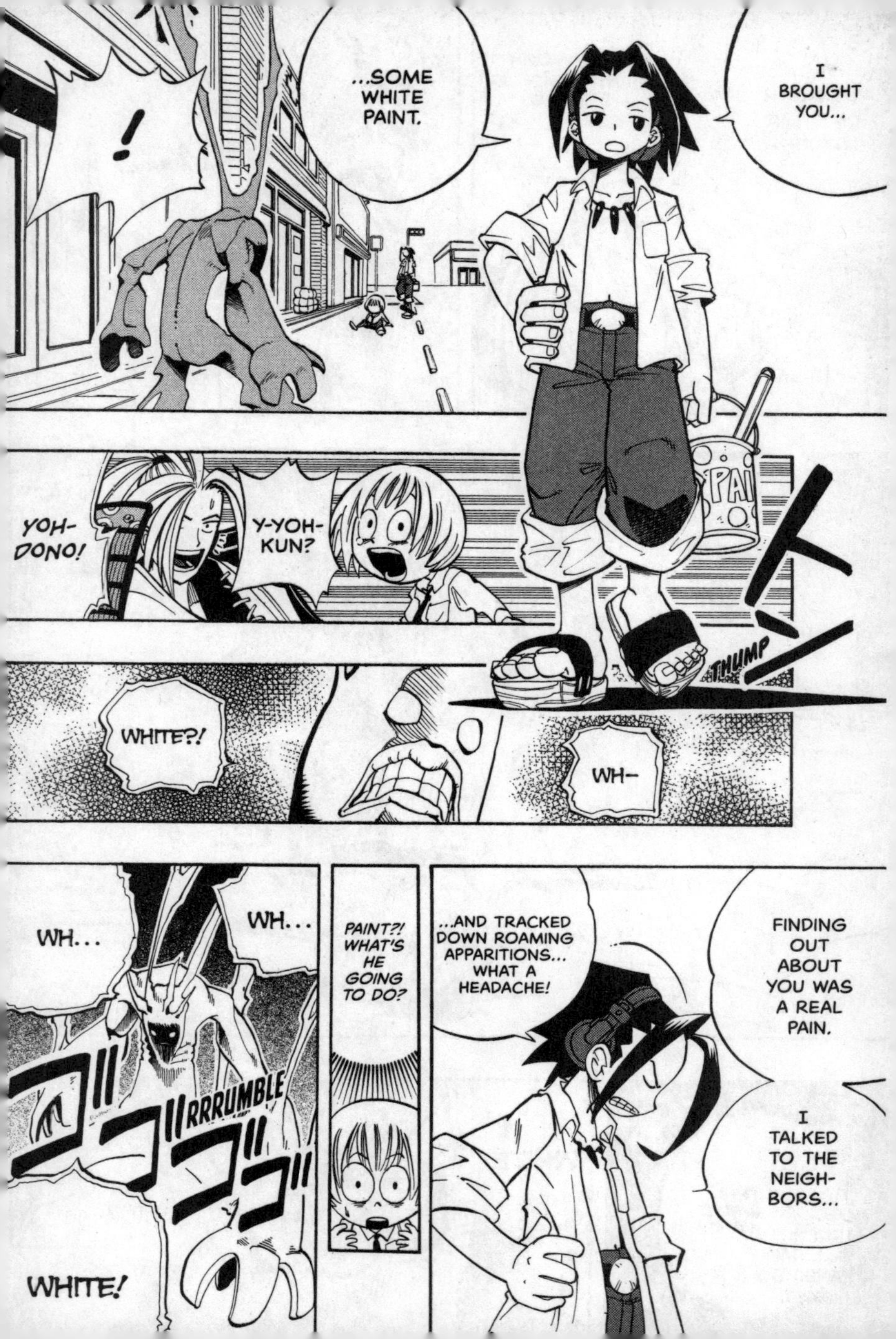
I BROUGHT YOU...
...SOME WHITE PAINT.
!
THUMP
Y-YOH-KUN?
YOH-DONO!
WH-
WHITE?!
FINDING OUT ABOUT YOU WAS A REAL PAIN.
I TALKED TO THE NEIGHBORS...
...AND TRACKED DOWN ROAMING APPARITIONS... WHAT A HEADACHE!
PAINT?! WHAT'S HE GOING TO DO?
WH...
WH...
RRRUMBLE
WHITE!

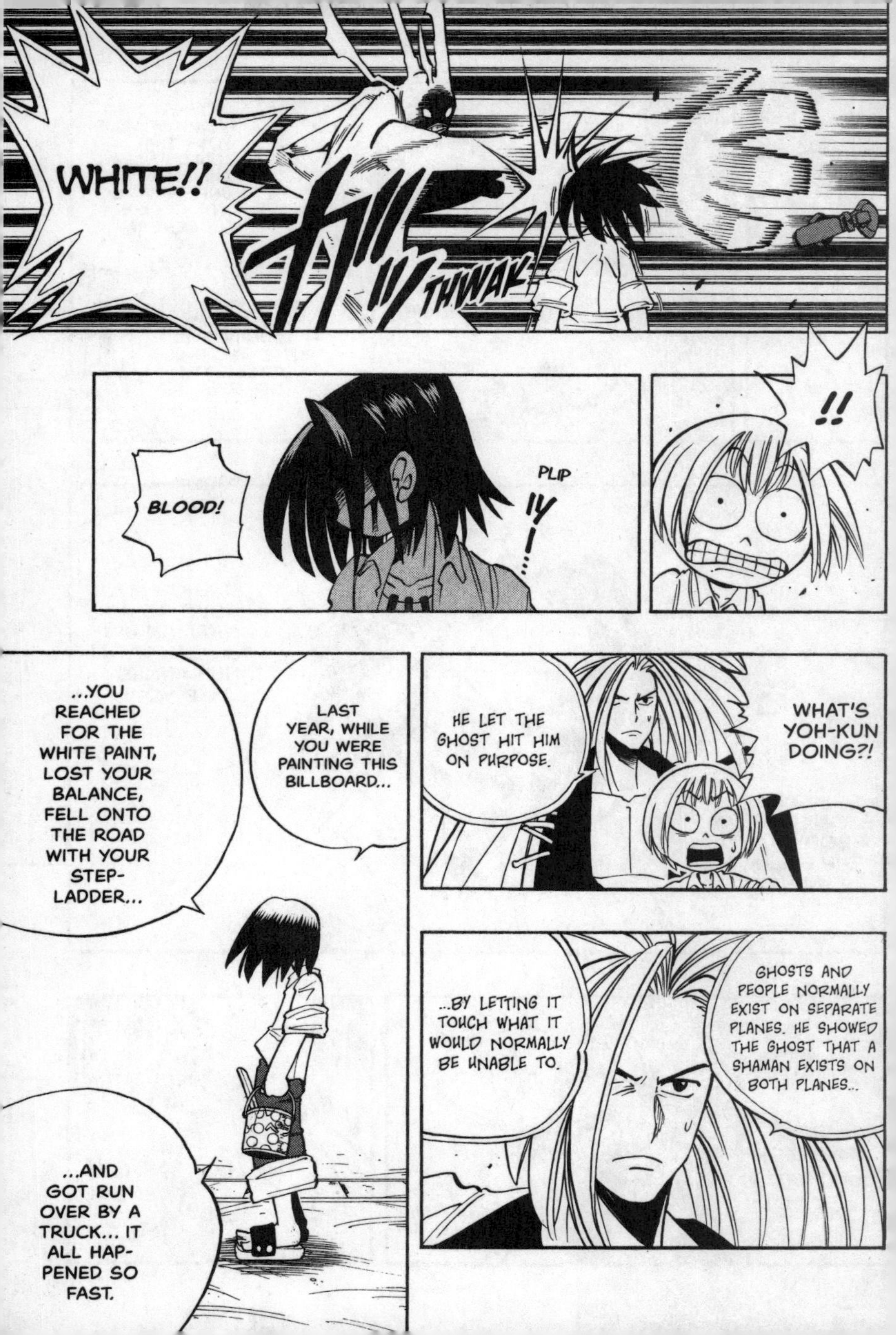
WHITE!!
THWAK
!!
PLIP
BLOOD!
WHAT'S YOH-KUN DOING?!
HE LET THE GHOST HIT HIM ON PURPOSE.
GHOSTS AND PEOPLE NORMALLY EXIST ON SEPARATE PLANES. HE SHOWED THE GHOST THAT A SHAMAN EXISTS ON BOTH PLANES...
...BY LETTING IT TOUCH WHAT IT WOULD NORMALLY BE UNABLE TO.
LAST YEAR, WHILE YOU WERE PAINTING THIS BILLBOARD...
...YOU REACHED FOR THE WHITE PAINT, LOST YOUR BALANCE, FELL ONTO THE ROAD WITH YOUR STEP-LADDER...
...AND GOT RUN OVER BY A TRUCK... IT ALL HAP-PENED SO FAST.

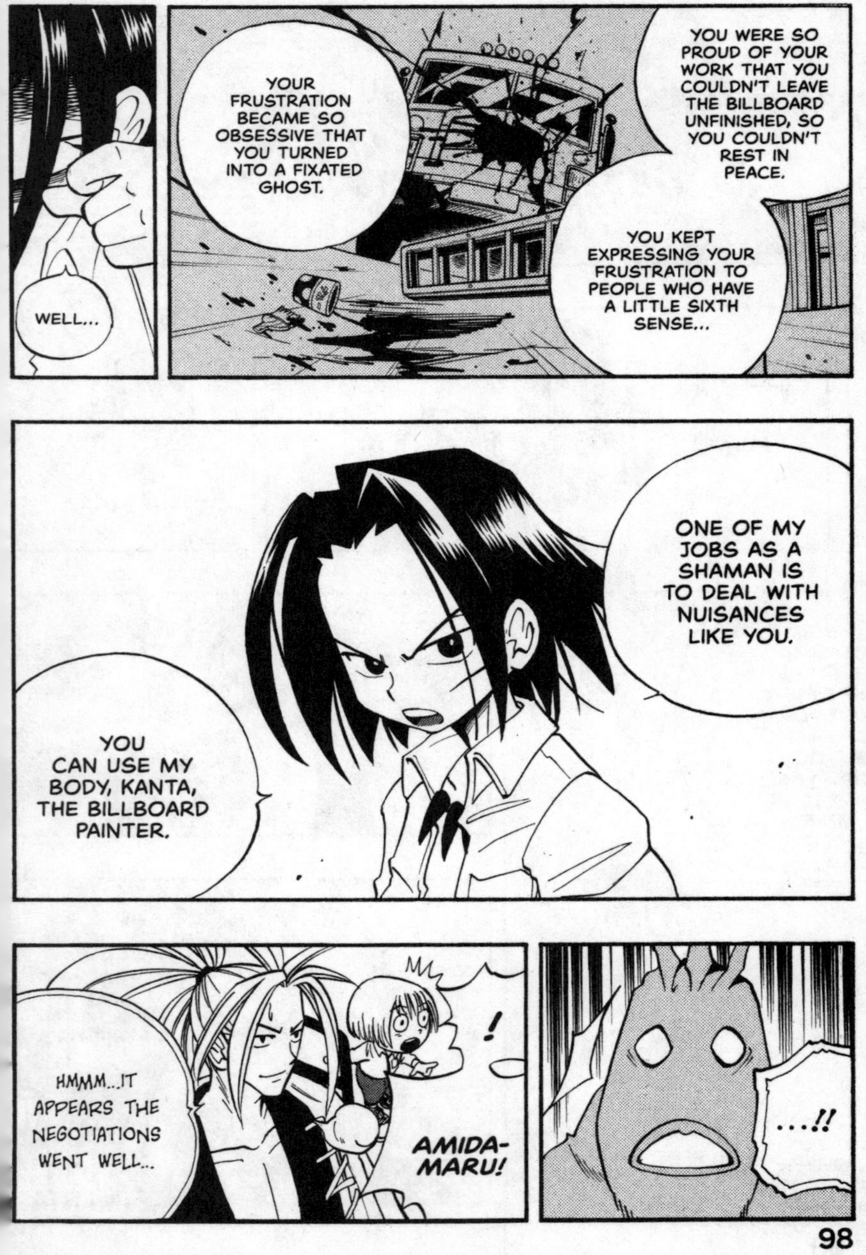
YOU WERE SO PROUD OF YOUR WORK THAT YOU COULDN'T LEAVE THE BILLBOARD UNFINISHED, SO YOU COULDN'T REST IN PEACE.
YOUR FRUSTRATION BECAME SO OBSESSIVE THAT YOU TURNED INTO A FIXATED GHOST.
YOU KEPT EXPRESSING YOUR FRUSTRATION TO PEOPLE WHO HAVE A LITTLE SIXTH SENSE...
WELL...
ONE OF MY JOBS AS A SHAMAN IS TO DEAL WITH NUISANCES LIKE YOU.
YOU CAN USE MY BODY, KANTA, THE BILLBOARD PAINTER.
...!!
!
AMIDA-MARU!
HMMM...IT APPEARS THE NEGOTIATIONS WENT WELL...

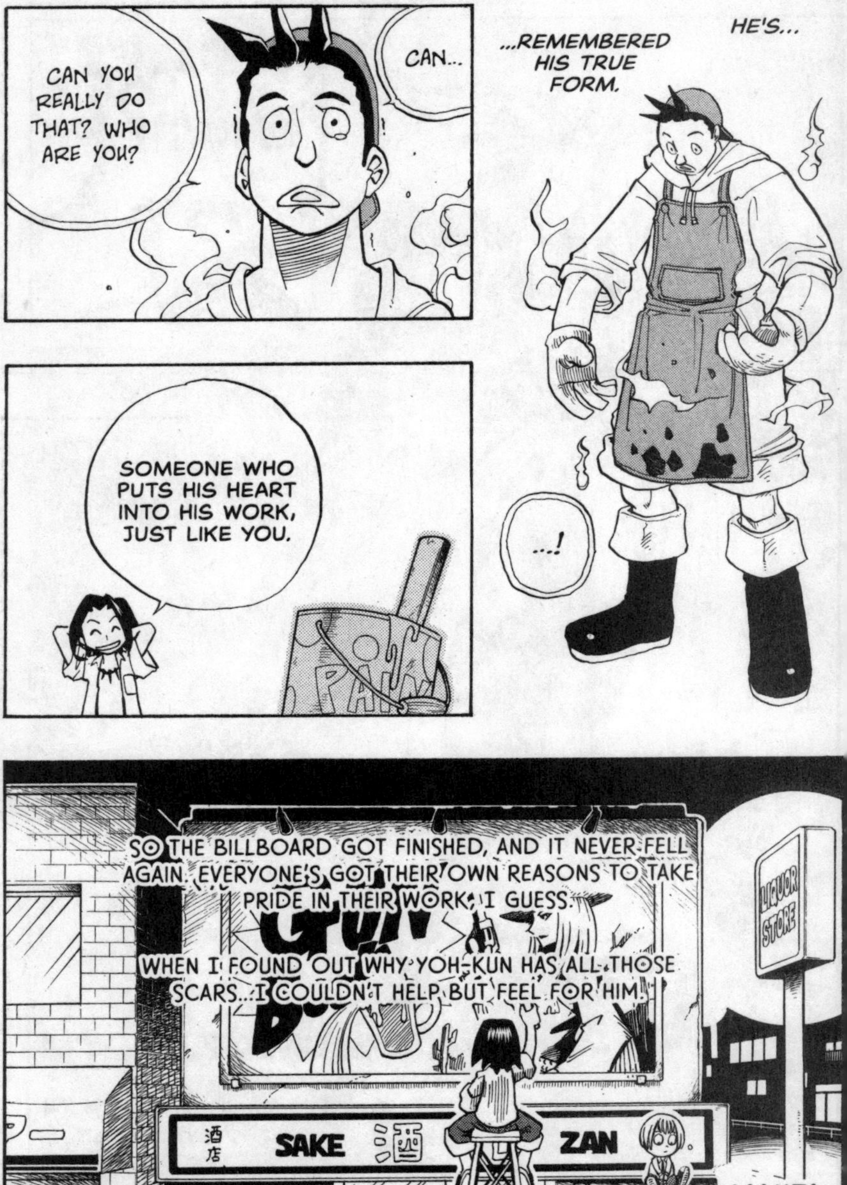
HE'S...
...REMEMBERED HIS TRUE FORM.
...!
CAN...
CAN YOU REALLY DO THAT? WHO ARE YOU?
SOMEONE WHO PUTS HIS HEART INTO HIS WORK, JUST LIKE YOU.
PAIN
SO THE BILLBOARD GOT FINISHED, AND IT NEVER FELL AGAIN. EVERYONE'S GOT THEIR OWN REASONS TO TAKE PRIDE IN THEIR WORK, I GUESS.
WHEN I FOUND OUT WHY YOH-KUN HAS ALL THOSE SCARS... I COULDN'T HELP BUT FEEL FOR HIM.
LIQUOR STORE
酒店
SAKE
酒
ZAN
MANTA

SHAMAN KING CHARACTER FILE No.2

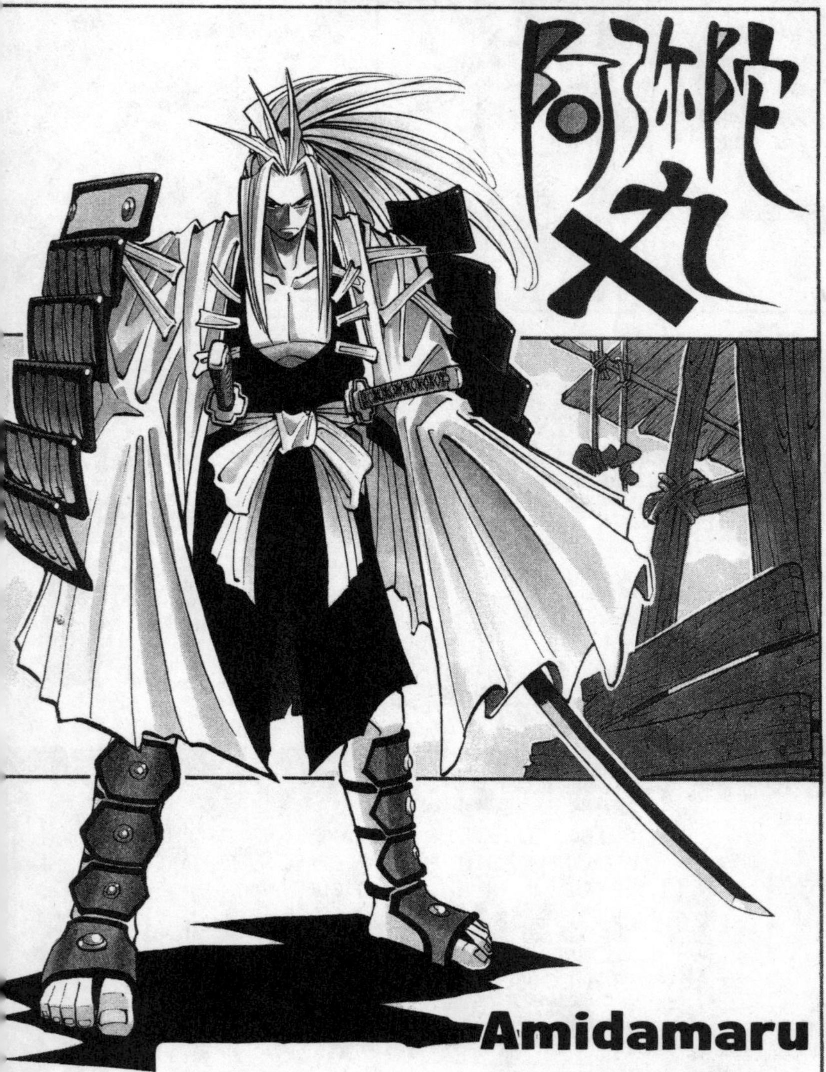
阿弥陀丸

Amidamaru

Age (at time of death): 24
Birthday: January 6
Blood Type: A

Chapter 4: Soul Boxing!

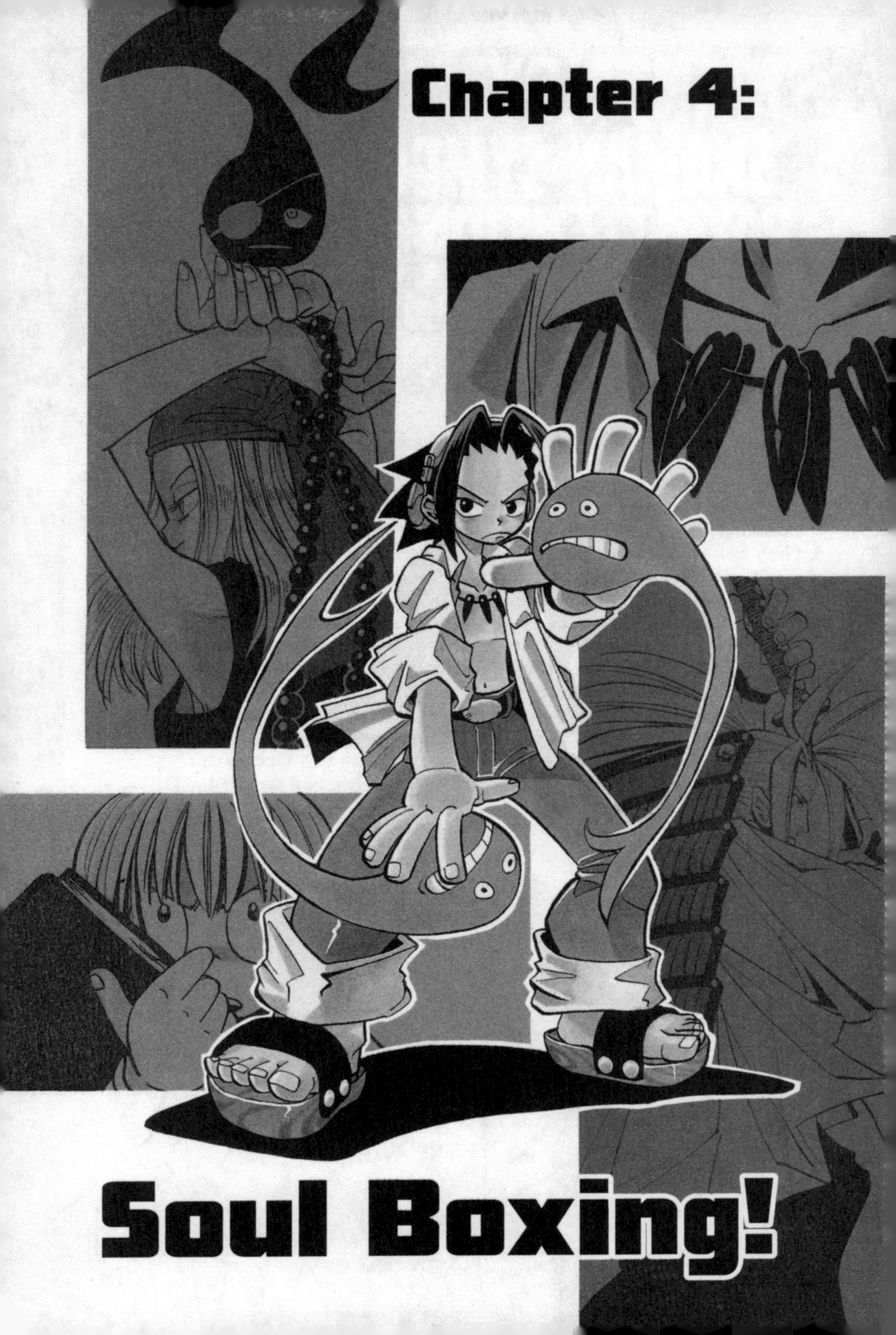

MANTA OYAMADA'S SHAMAN SYMPOSIUM PAY ATTENTION, THERE WILL BE A TEST!

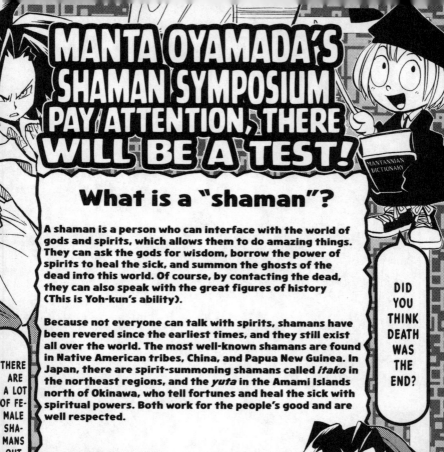

What is a "shaman"?

A shaman is a person who can interface with the world of gods and spirits, which allows them to do amazing things. They can ask the gods for wisdom, borrow the power of spirits to heal the sick, and summon the ghosts of the dead into this world. Of course, by contacting the dead, they can also speak with the great figures of history (This is Yoh-kun's ability).

Because not everyone can talk with spirits, shamans have been revered since the earliest times, and they still exist all over the world. The most well-known shamans are found in Native American tribes, China, and Papua New Guinea. In Japan, there are spirit-summoning shamans called *itako* in the northeast regions, and the *yuta* in the Amami Islands north of Okinawa, who tell fortunes and heal the sick with spiritual powers. Both work for the people's good and are well respected.

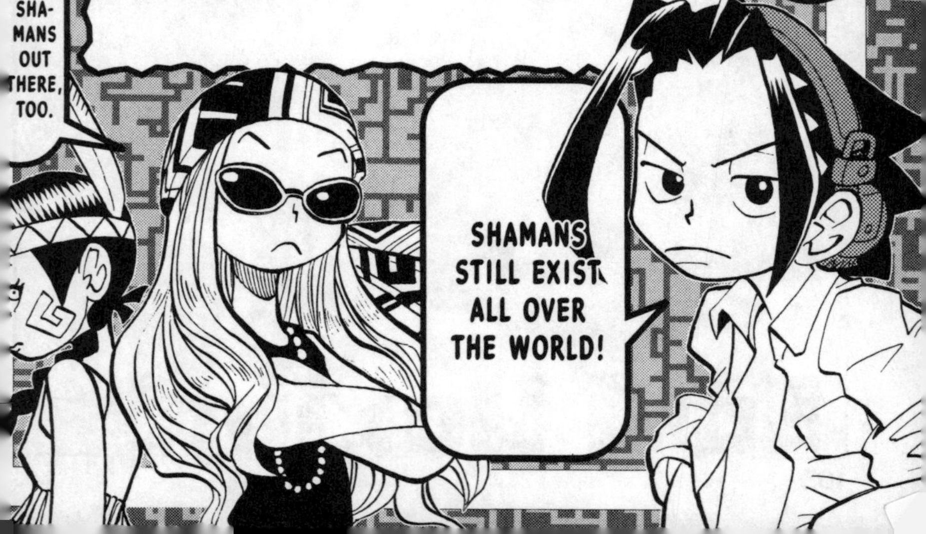

MANTANNIAN DICTIONARY
DID YOU THINK DEATH WAS THE END?
SHAMANS STILL EXIST ALL OVER THE WORLD!
THERE ARE A LOT OF FEMALE SHAMANS OUT THERE, TOO.

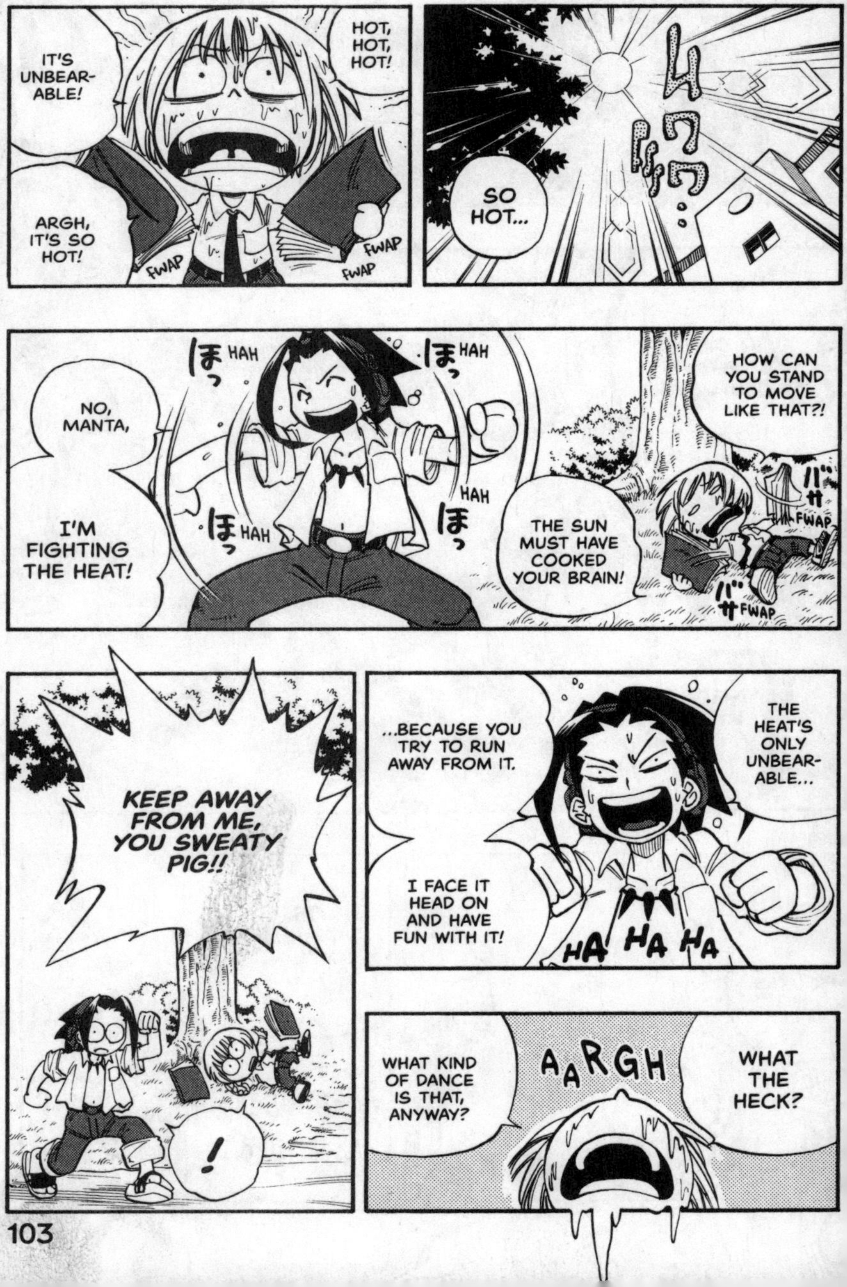
SO HOT...
HOT, HOT, HOT!
IT'S UNBEARABLE!
ARGH, IT'S SO HOT!
FWAP
FWAP
FWAP
HOW CAN YOU STAND TO MOVE LIKE THAT?!
バサ FWAP
THE SUN MUST HAVE COOKED YOUR BRAIN!
バサ FWAP
ほっ HAH
ほっ HAH
NO, MANTA,
ほっ HAH
ほっ HAH
I'M FIGHTING THE HEAT!
THE HEAT'S ONLY UNBEARABLE...
...BECAUSE YOU TRY TO RUN AWAY FROM IT.
I FACE IT HEAD ON AND HAVE FUN WITH IT!
HA HA HA
WHAT THE HECK?
AARGH
WHAT KIND OF DANCE IS THAT, ANYWAY?
KEEP AWAY FROM ME, YOU SWEATY PIG!!
!

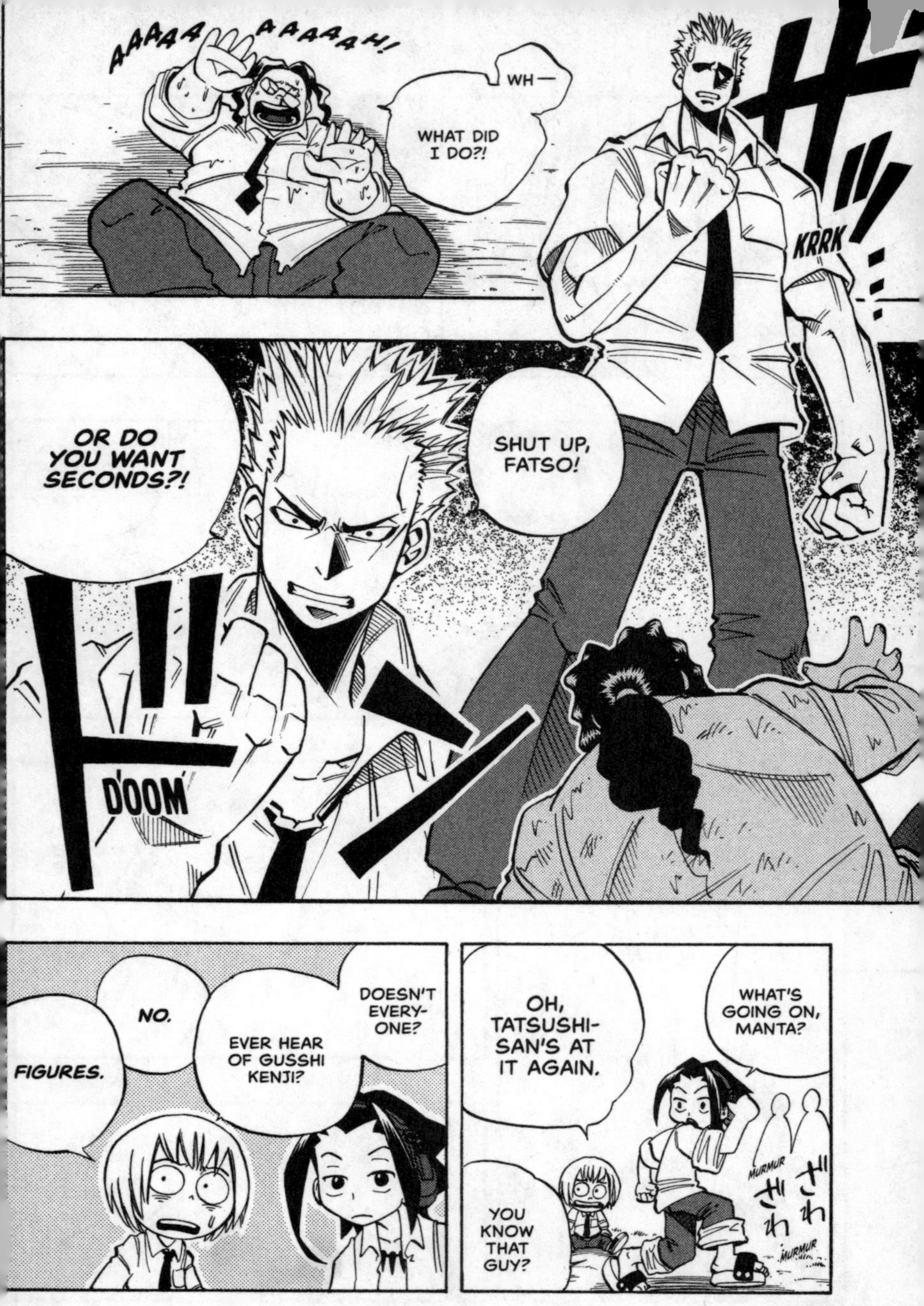
AAAAA AAAAAH!
WH—
WHAT DID I DO?!
KRRK
SHUT UP, FATSO!
OR DO YOU WANT SECONDS?!
D'OOM
WHAT'S GOING ON, MANTA?
OH, TATSUSHI-SAN'S AT IT AGAIN.
MURMUR
ざわ ざわ
MURMUR
YOU KNOW THAT GUY?
DOESN'T EVERY-ONE?
EVER HEAR OF GUSSHI KENJI?
NO.
FIGURES.

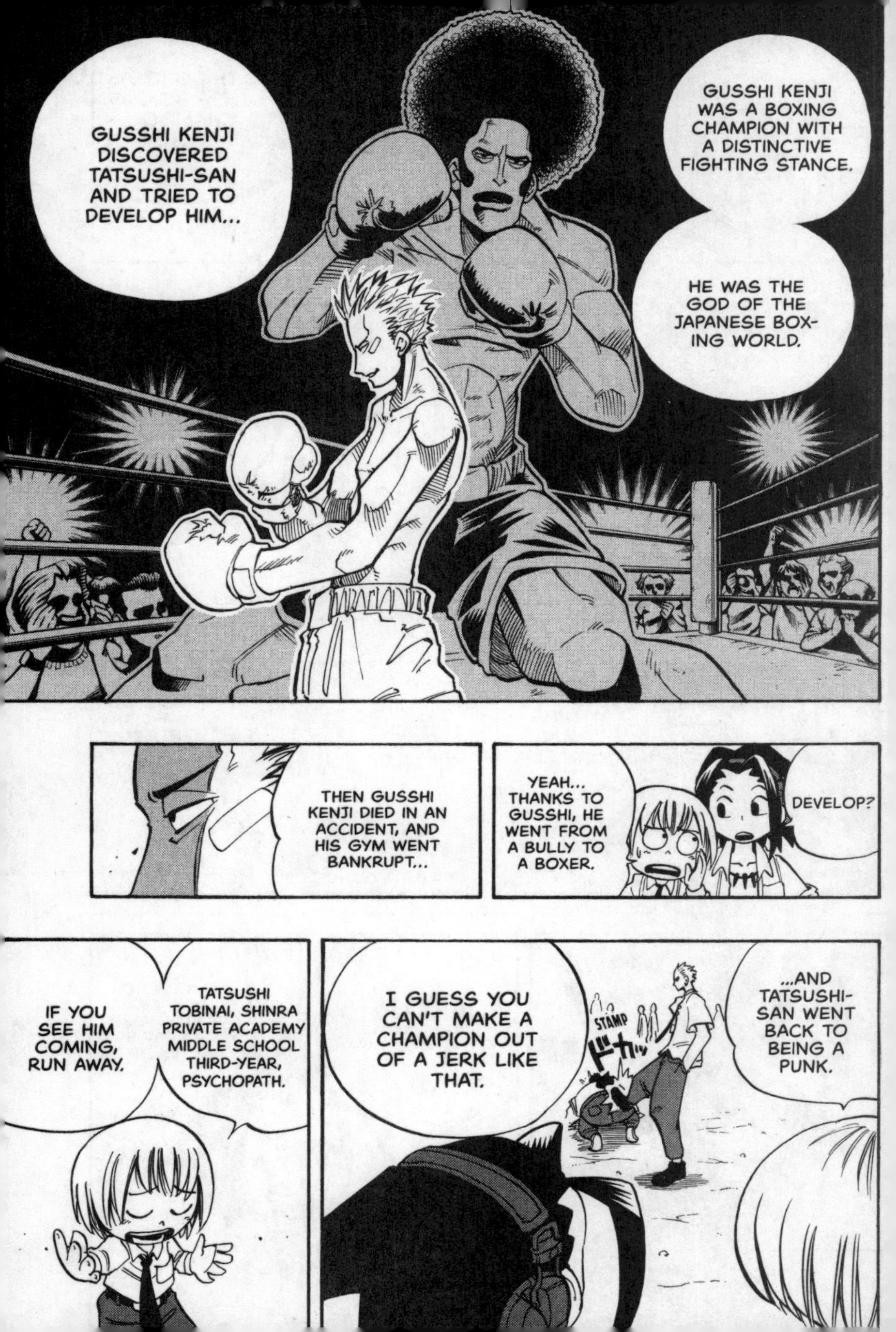
GUSSHI KENJI WAS A BOXING CHAMPION WITH A DISTINCTIVE FIGHTING STANCE.
HE WAS THE GOD OF THE JAPANESE BOX-ING WORLD.
GUSSHI KENJI DISCOVERED TATSUSHI-SAN AND TRIED TO DEVELOP HIM...
DEVELOP?
YEAH... THANKS TO GUSSHI, HE WENT FROM A BULLY TO A BOXER.
THEN GUSSHI KENJI DIED IN AN ACCIDENT, AND HIS GYM WENT BANKRUPT...
...AND TATSUSHI-SAN WENT BACK TO BEING A PUNK.
STAMP
ドカッ
I GUESS YOU CAN'T MAKE A CHAMPION OUT OF A JERK LIKE THAT.
TATSUSHI TOBINAI, SHINRA PRIVATE ACADEMY MIDDLE SCHOOL THIRD-YEAR, PSYCHOPATH.
IF YOU SEE HIM COMING, RUN AWAY.

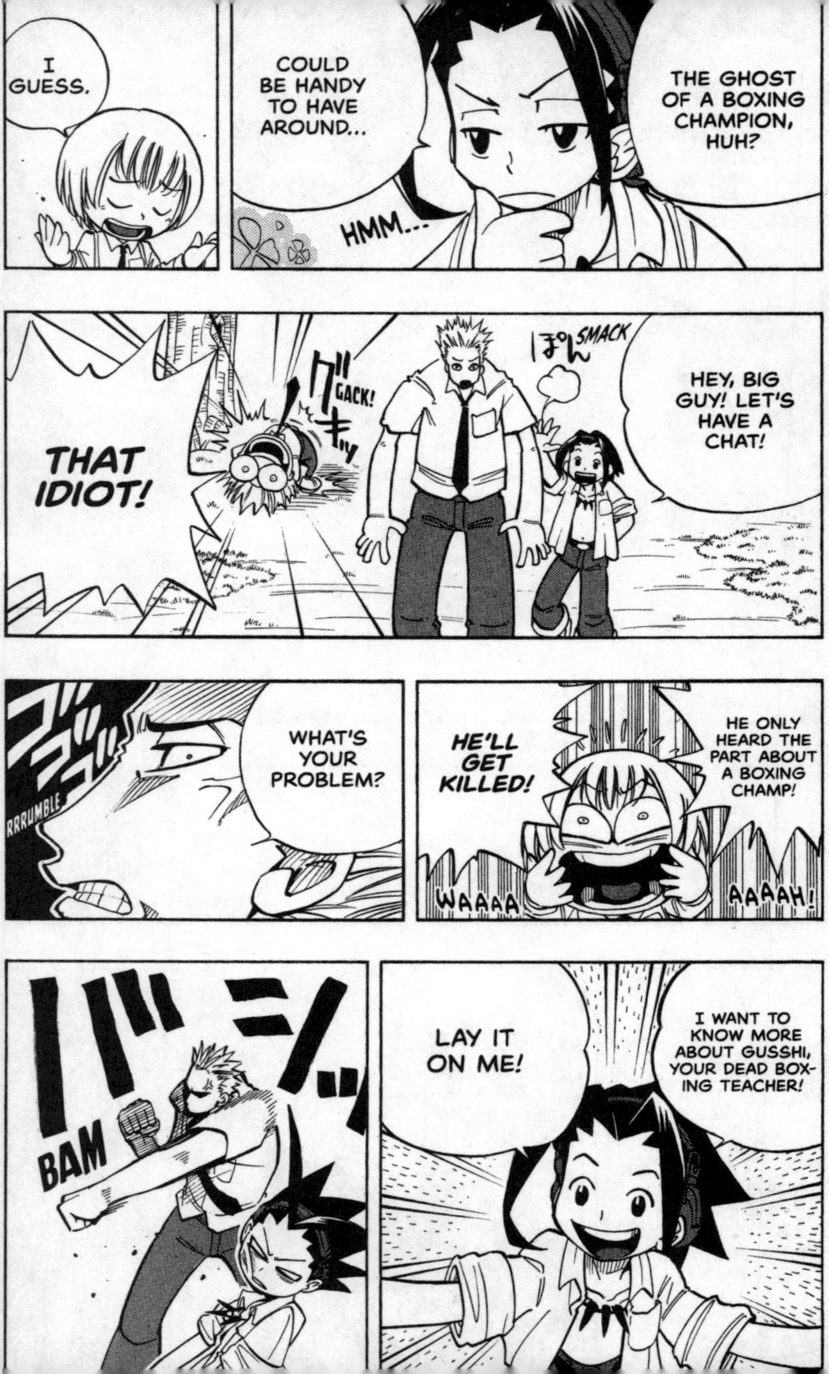
THE GHOST OF A BOXING CHAMPION, HUH?
COULD BE HANDY TO HAVE AROUND...
HMM...
I GUESS.
HEY, BIG GUY! LET'S HAVE A CHAT!
ぽん SMACK
GACK!
THAT IDIOT!
HE ONLY HEARD THE PART ABOUT A BOXING CHAMP!
HE'LL GET KILLED!
AAAAH!
WAAAA
WHAT'S YOUR PROBLEM?
RRRUMBLE
I WANT TO KNOW MORE ABOUT GUSSHI, YOUR DEAD BOX-ING TEACHER!
LAY IT ON ME!
BAM

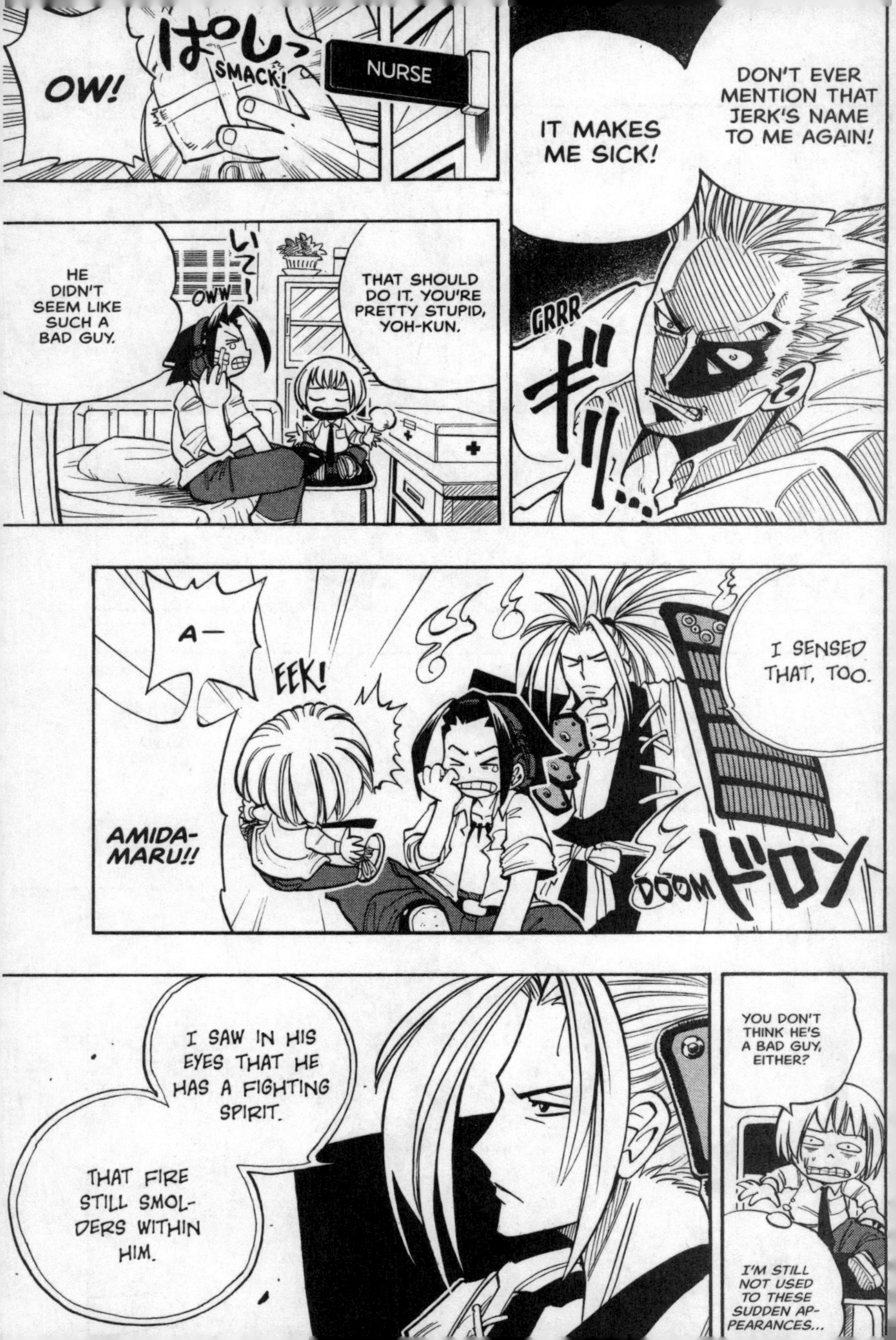
DON'T EVER MENTION THAT JERK'S NAME TO ME AGAIN!
IT MAKES ME SICK!
GRRR
ギリ...
OW!
ぱしっ
SMACK!
NURSE
THAT SHOULD DO IT. YOU'RE PRETTY STUPID, YOH-KUN.
OWW
HE DIDN'T SEEM LIKE SUCH A BAD GUY.
I SENSED THAT, TOO.
DOOM
ドロン
EEK!
A—
AMIDA-MARU!!
YOU DON'T THINK HE'S A BAD GUY, EITHER?
I'M STILL NOT USED TO THESE SUDDEN AP-PEARANCES...
I SAW IN HIS EYES THAT HE HAS A FIGHTING SPIRIT.
THAT FIRE STILL SMOL-DERS WITHIN HIM.

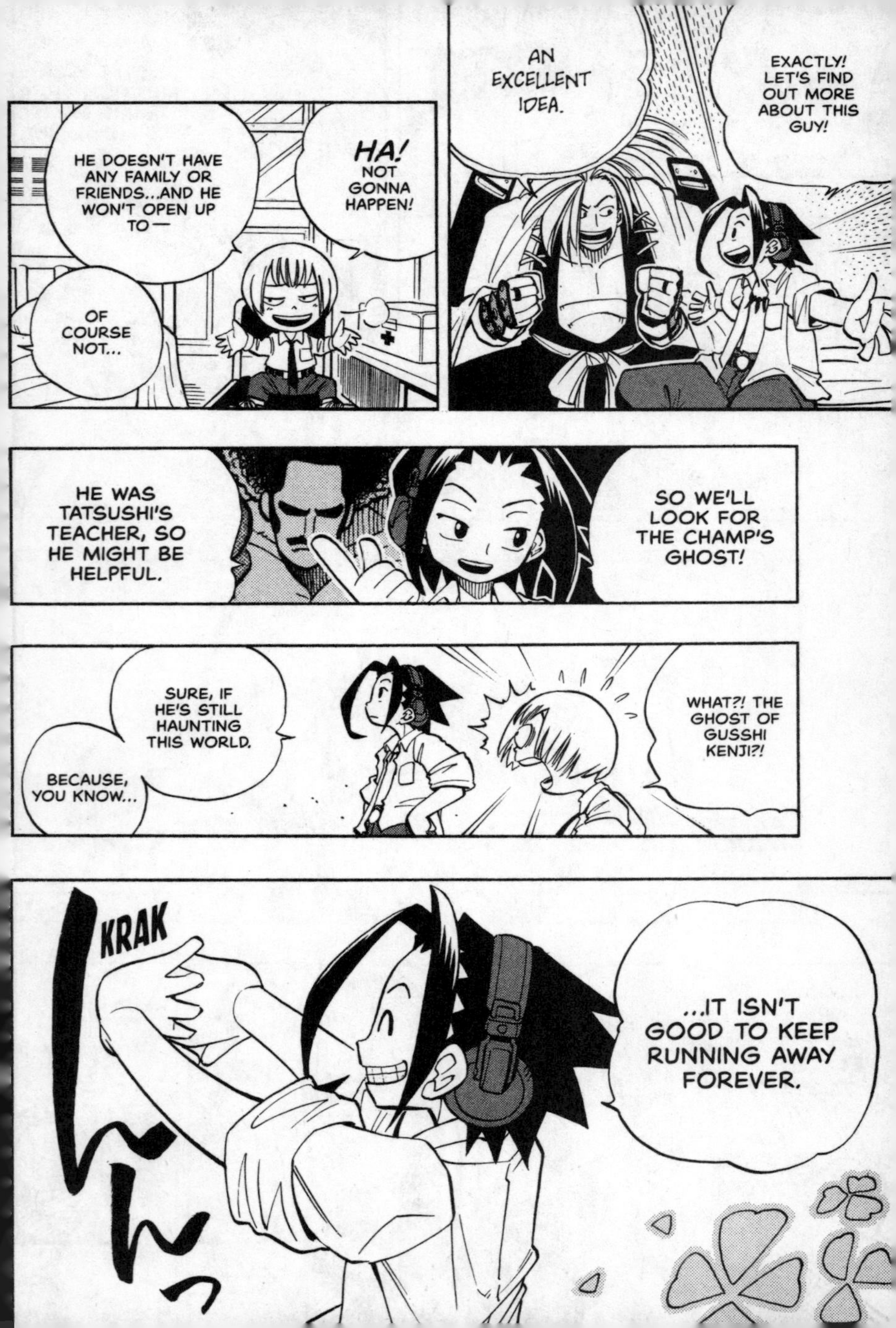
EXACTLY! LET'S FIND OUT MORE ABOUT THIS GUY!
AN EXCELLENT IDEA.
HA! NOT GONNA HAPPEN!
HE DOESN'T HAVE ANY FAMILY OR FRIENDS...AND HE WON'T OPEN UP TO—
OF COURSE NOT...
SO WE'LL LOOK FOR THE CHAMP'S GHOST!
HE WAS TATSUSHI'S TEACHER, SO HE MIGHT BE HELPFUL.
WHAT?! THE GHOST OF GUSSHI KENJI?!
SURE, IF HE'S STILL HAUNTING THIS WORLD.
BECAUSE, YOU KNOW...
...IT ISN'T GOOD TO KEEP RUNNING AWAY FOREVER.
KRAK

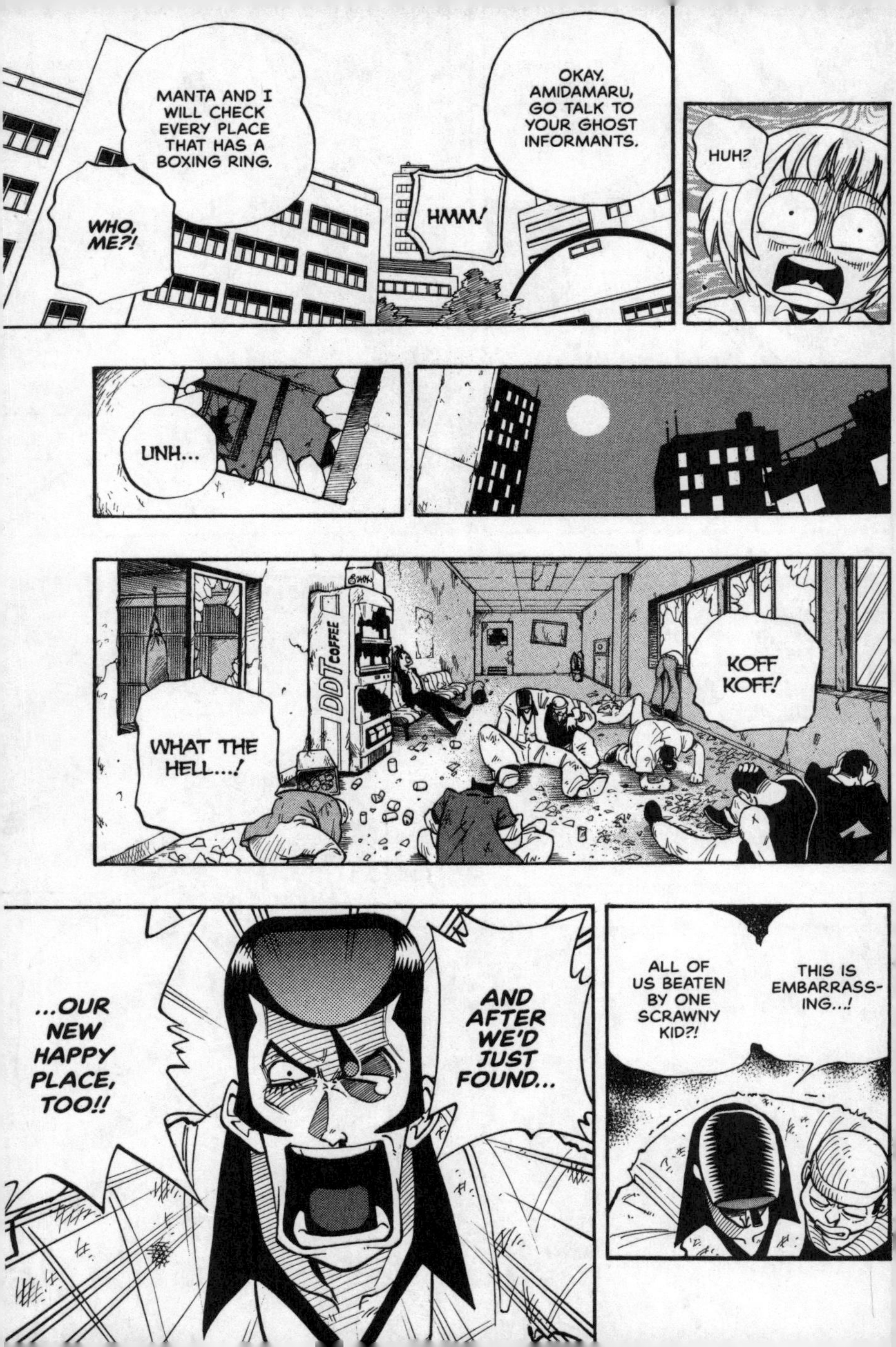
HUH?
OKAY. AMIDAMARU, GO TALK TO YOUR GHOST INFORMANTS.
HMM!
MANTA AND I WILL CHECK EVERY PLACE THAT HAS A BOXING RING.
WHO, ME?!
UNH...
KOFF KOFF!
DDT COFFEE
WHAT THE HELL...!
THIS IS EMBARRASS-ING...!
ALL OF US BEATEN BY ONE SCRAWNY KID?!
AND AFTER WE'D JUST FOUND...
...OUR NEW HAPPY PLACE, TOO!!

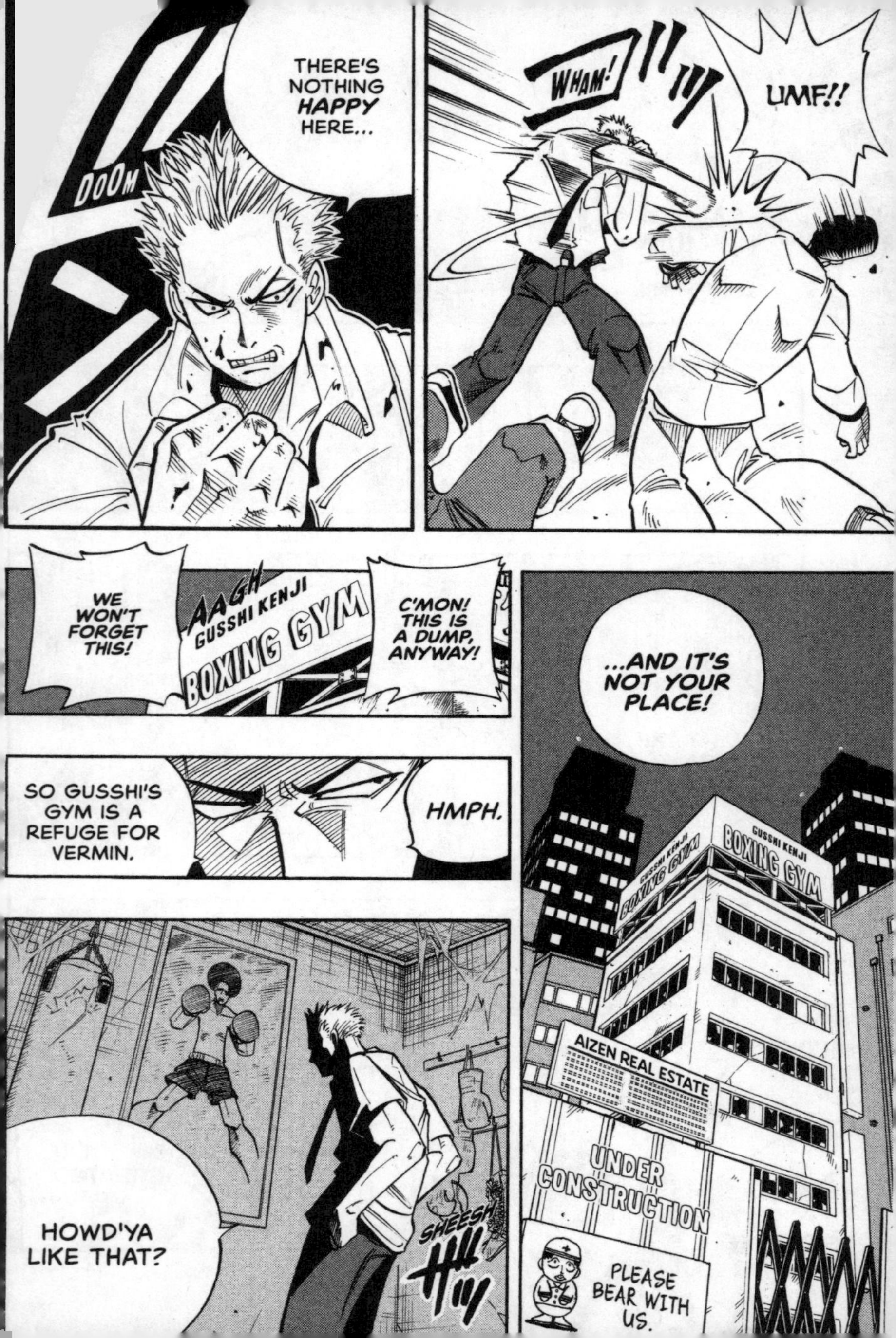
WHAM!
UMF!!
THERE'S NOTHING *HAPPY* HERE...
DOOM
...AND IT'S NOT YOUR PLACE!
GUSSHI KENJI BOXING GYM
GUSSHI BOXING GYM
AIZEN REAL ESTATE
UNDER CONSTRUCTION
PLEASE BEAR WITH US.
C'MON! THIS IS A DUMP, ANYWAY!
AAGH
GUSSHI KENJI BOXING GYM
WE WON'T FORGET THIS!
HMPH.
SO GUSSHI'S GYM IS A REFUGE FOR VERMIN.
SHEESH
HOWD'YA LIKE THAT?

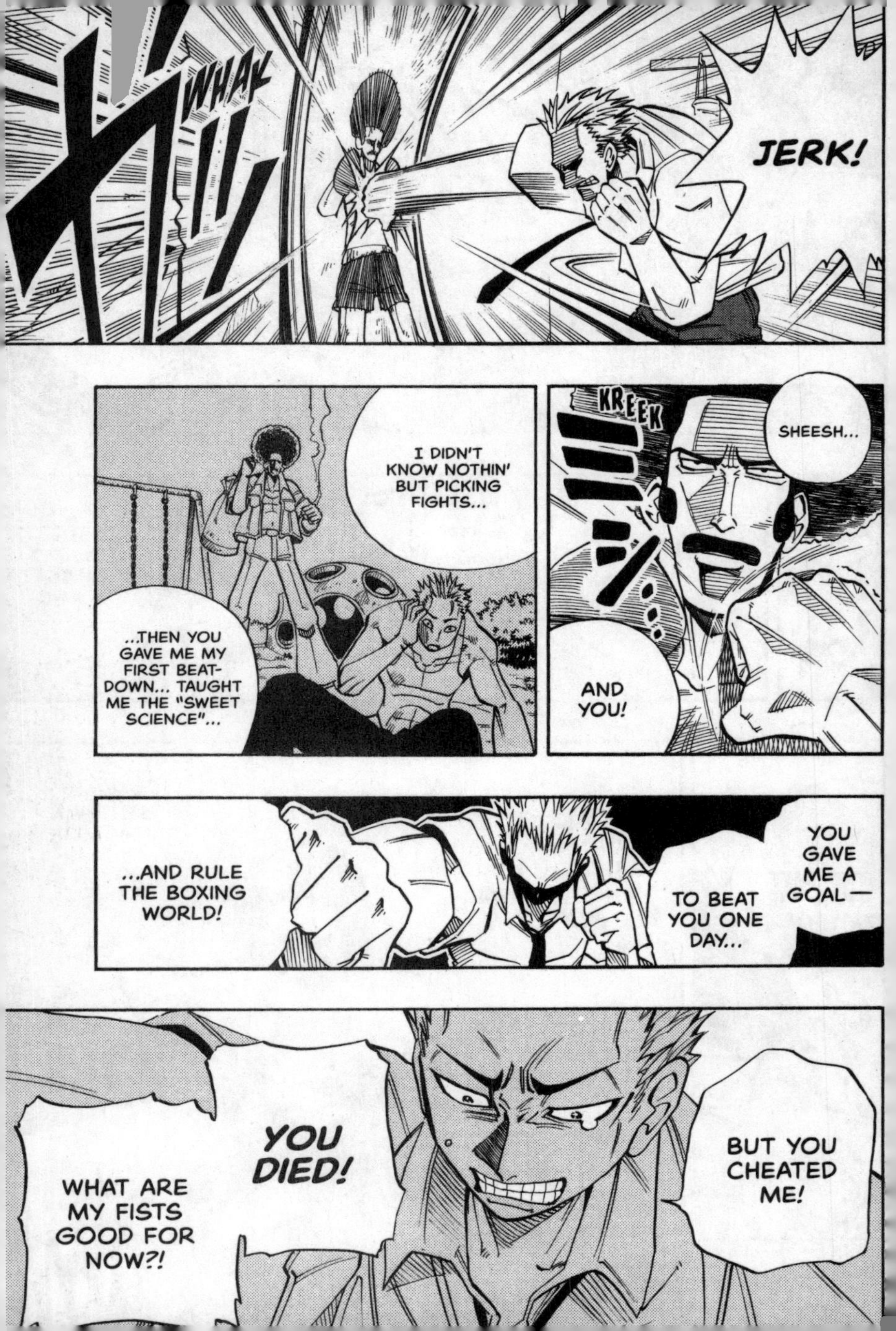
JERK!
WHAK
KREEK
SHEESH...
AND YOU!
I DIDN'T KNOW NOTHIN' BUT PICKING FIGHTS...
...THEN YOU GAVE ME MY FIRST BEAT-DOWN... TAUGHT ME THE "SWEET SCIENCE"...
YOU GAVE ME A GOAL—
TO BEAT YOU ONE DAY...
...AND RULE THE BOXING WORLD!
BUT YOU CHEATED ME!
YOU DIED!
WHAT ARE MY FISTS GOOD FOR NOW?!

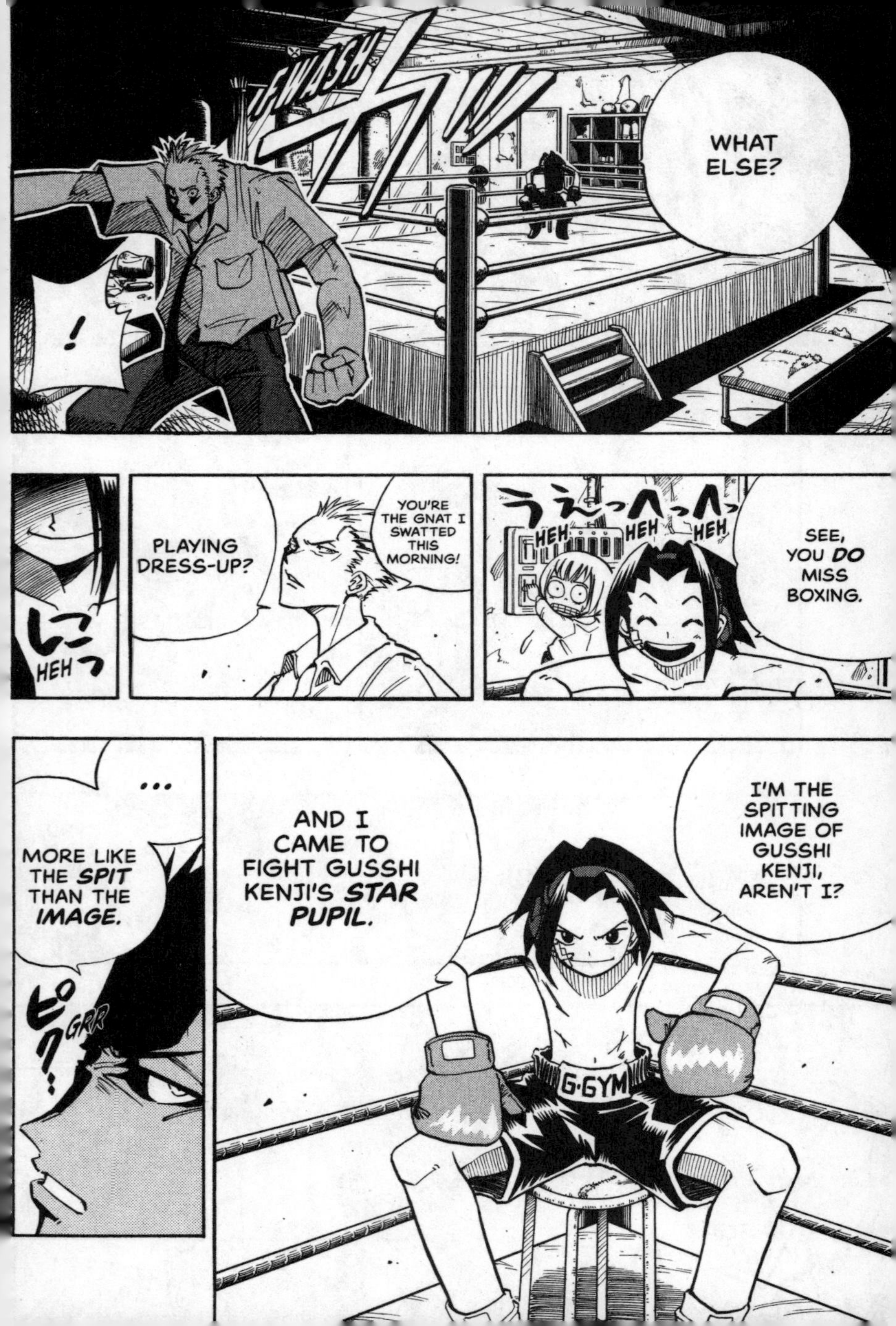
WHAT ELSE?
FWASH
!
うえっへっへっ
HEH HEH HEH
SEE, YOU DO MISS BOXING.
YOU'RE THE GNAT I SWATTED THIS MORNING!
PLAYING DRESS-UP?
しっ
HEH
I'M THE SPITTING IMAGE OF GUSSHI KENJI, AREN'T I?
AND I CAME TO FIGHT GUSSHI KENJI'S STAR PUPIL.
G·GYM
...
MORE LIKE THE SPIT THAN THE IMAGE.
ピクッ
GRR

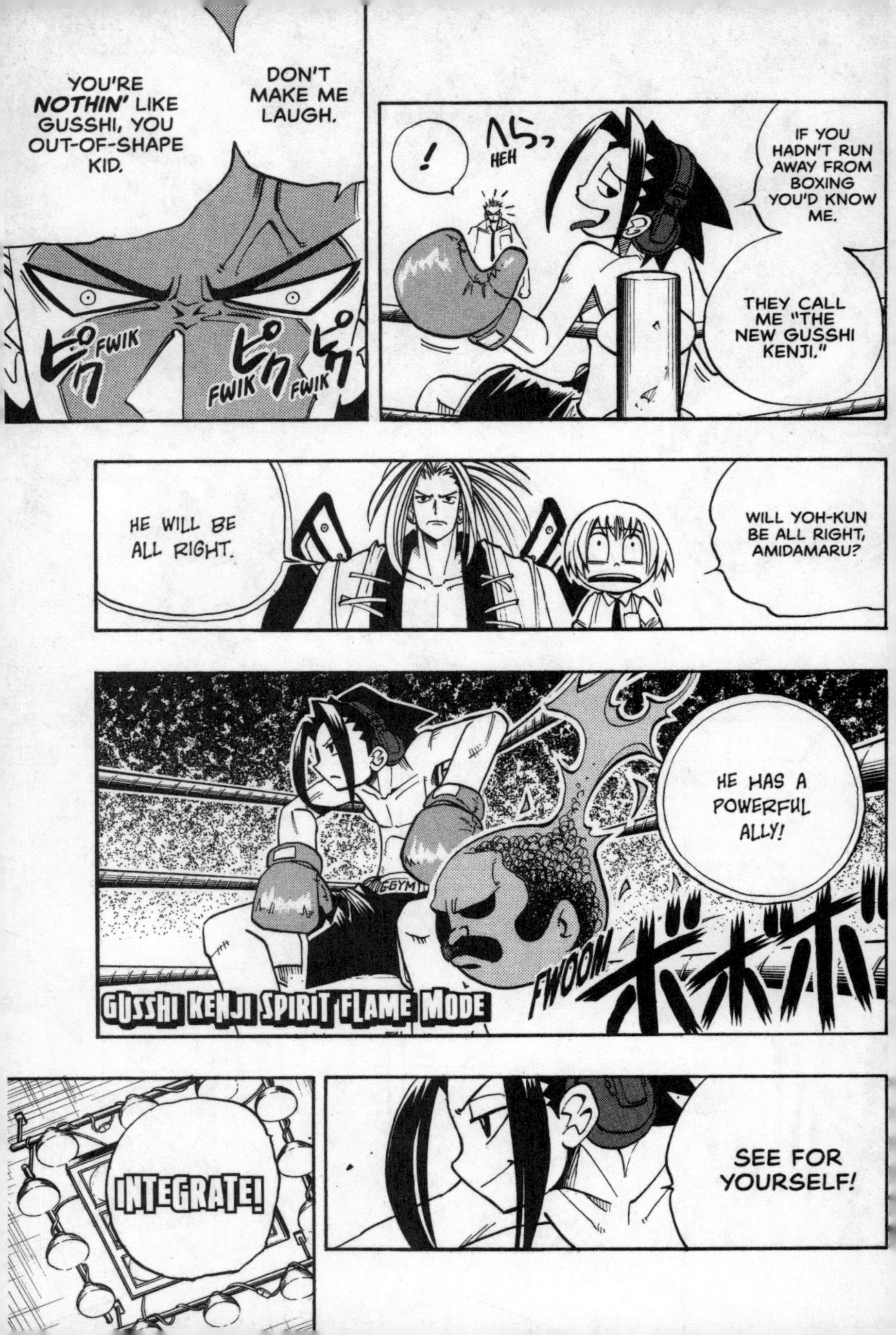
!
へらっ HEH
IF YOU HADN'T RUN AWAY FROM BOXING YOU'D KNOW ME.
THEY CALL ME "THE NEW GUSSHI KENJI."
DON'T MAKE ME LAUGH.
YOU'RE NOTHIN' LIKE GUSSHI, YOU OUT-OF-SHAPE KID.
ピク FWIK
ピク FWIK
ピク FWIK
WILL YOH-KUN BE ALL RIGHT, AMIDAMARU?
HE WILL BE ALL RIGHT.
HE HAS A POWERFUL ALLY!
FWOOM
GUSSHI KENJI SPIRIT FLAME MODE
SEE FOR YOURSELF!
INTEGRATE!

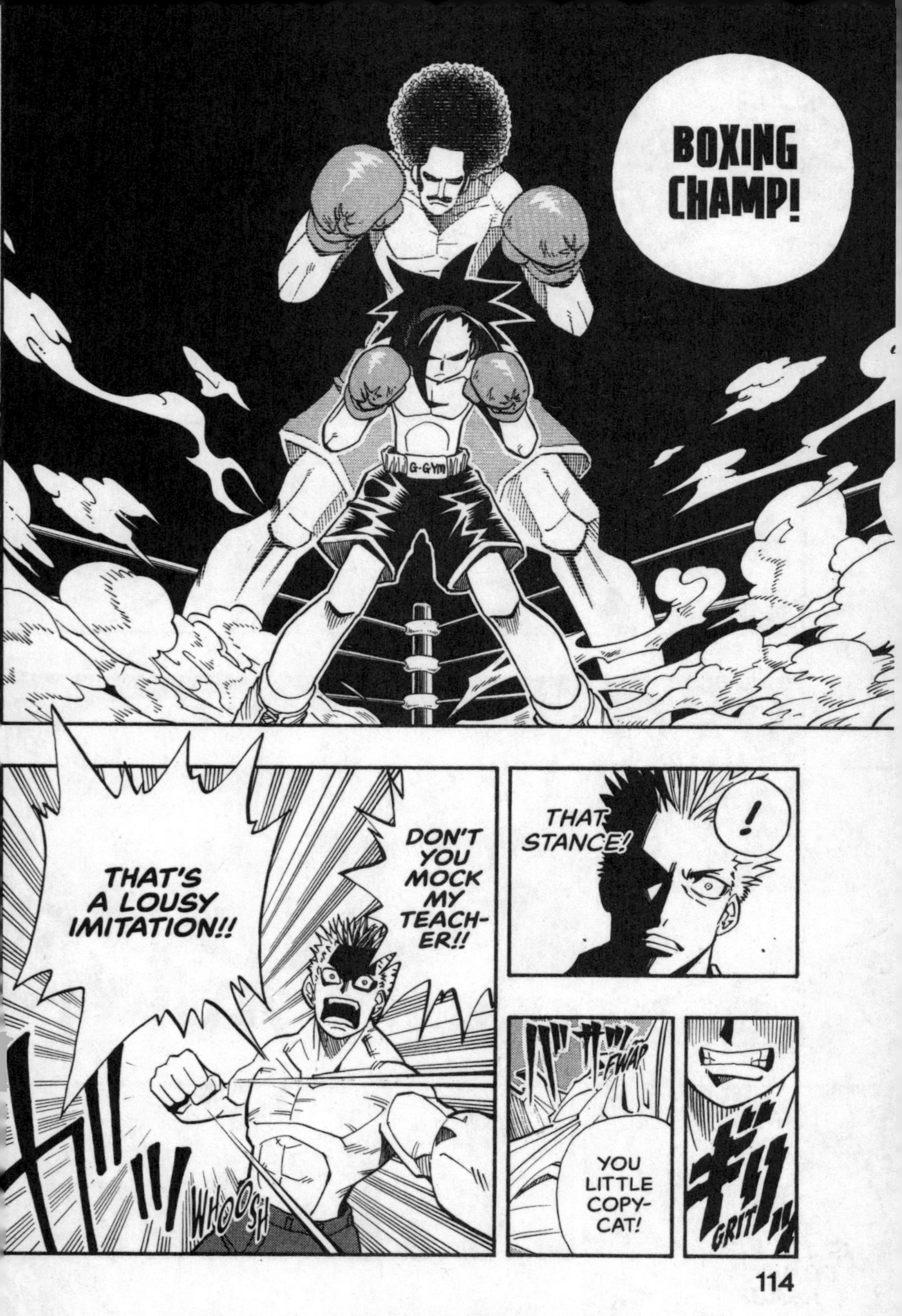
BOXING CHAMP!
!
THAT STANCE!
GRIT
FWAP
YOU LITTLE COPY-CAT!
DON'T YOU MOCK MY TEACHER!!
THAT'S A LOUSY IMITATION!!
WHOOSH

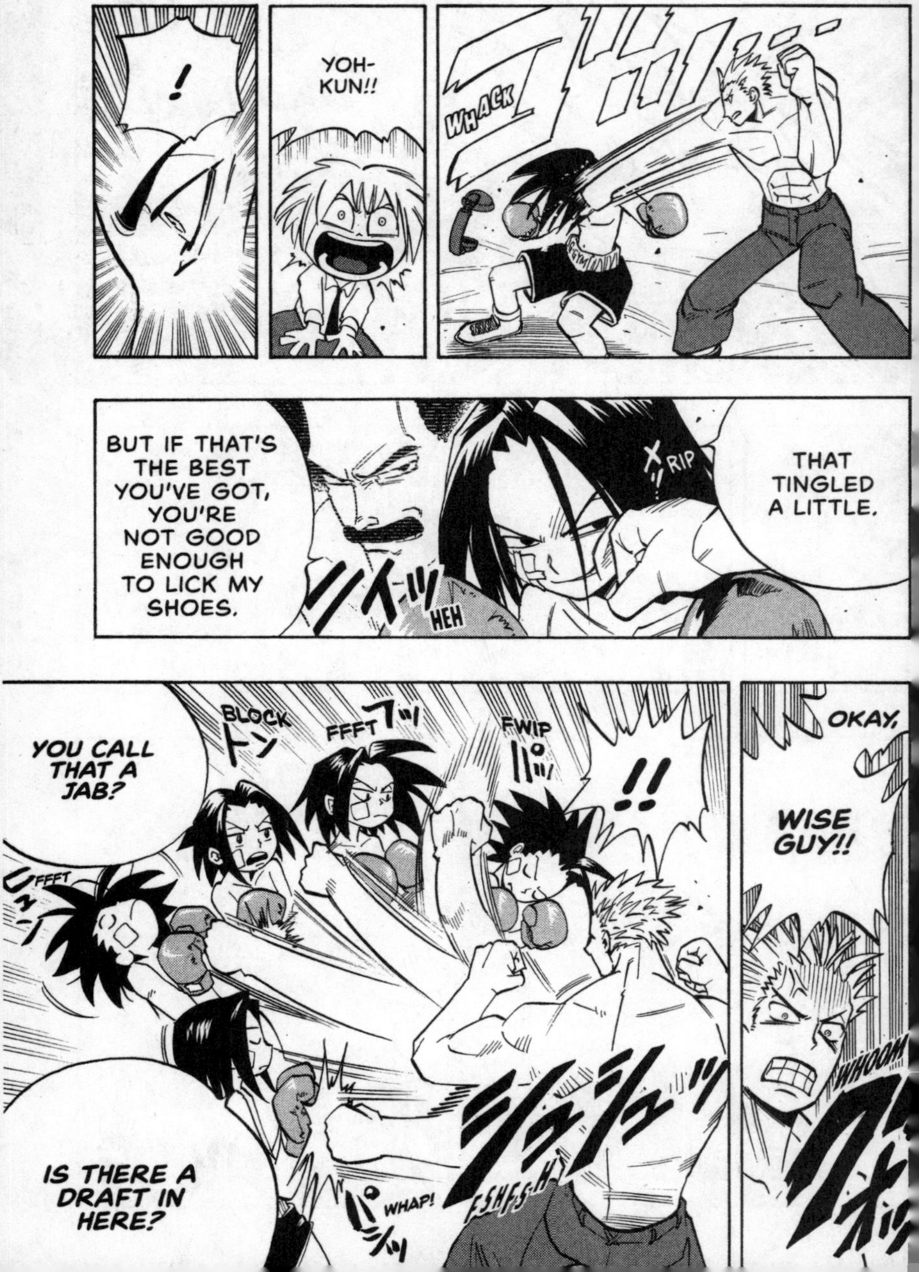
WHACK
YOH-KUN!!
!
THAT TINGLED A LITTLE.
RIP
HEH
BUT IF THAT'S THE BEST YOU'VE GOT, YOU'RE NOT GOOD ENOUGH TO LICK MY SHOES.
OKAY, WISE GUY!!
WHOOM
FWIP
!!
FFFT
BLOCK
YOU CALL THAT A JAB?
UFFFT
FSHFSH
WHAP!
IS THERE A DRAFT IN HERE?

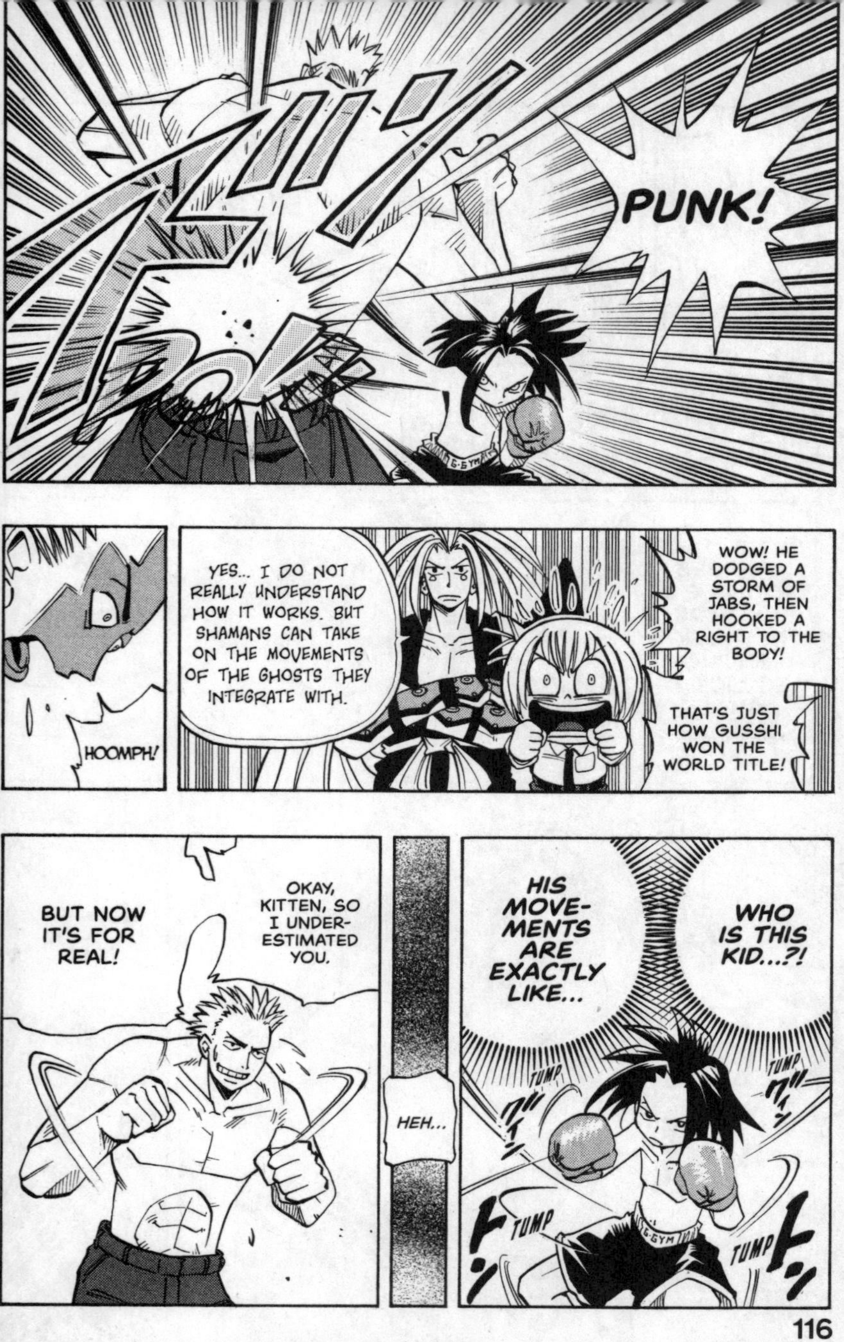
PUNK!
WOW! HE DODGED A STORM OF JABS, THEN HOOKED A RIGHT TO THE BODY!
THAT'S JUST HOW GUSSHI WON THE WORLD TITLE!
YES... I DO NOT REALLY UNDERSTAND HOW IT WORKS. BUT SHAMANS CAN TAKE ON THE MOVEMENTS OF THE GHOSTS THEY INTEGRATE WITH.
HOOMPH!
WHO IS THIS KID...?!
HIS MOVEMENTS ARE EXACTLY LIKE...
TUMP
TUMP
TUMP
TUMP
HEH...
OKAY, KITTEN, SO I UNDERESTIMATED YOU.
BUT NOW IT'S FOR REAL!

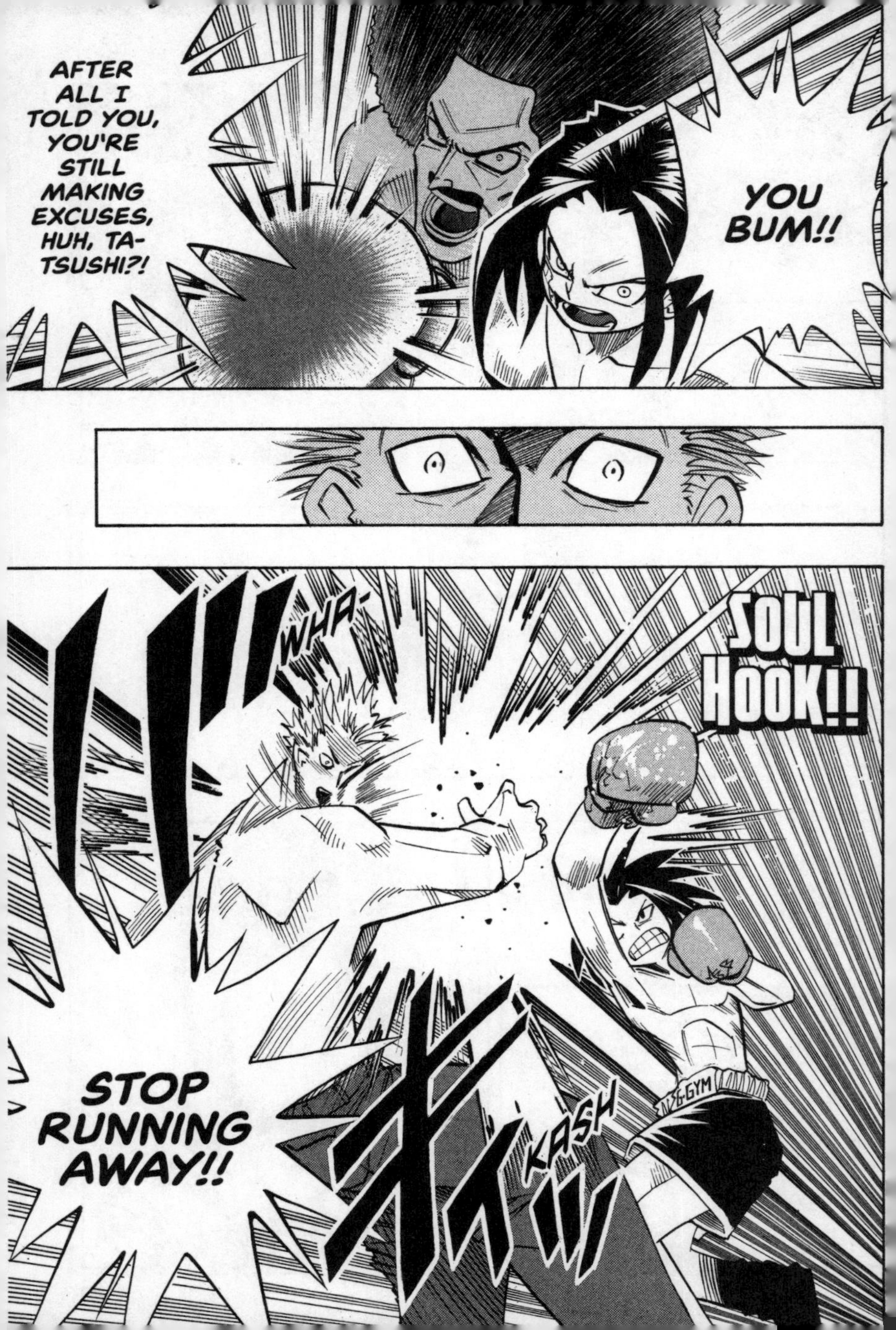
AFTER ALL I TOLD YOU, YOU'RE STILL MAKING EXCUSES, HUH, TA-TSUSHI?!
YOU BUM!!
SOUL HOOK!!
WHA-
KASH
STOP RUNNING AWAY!!

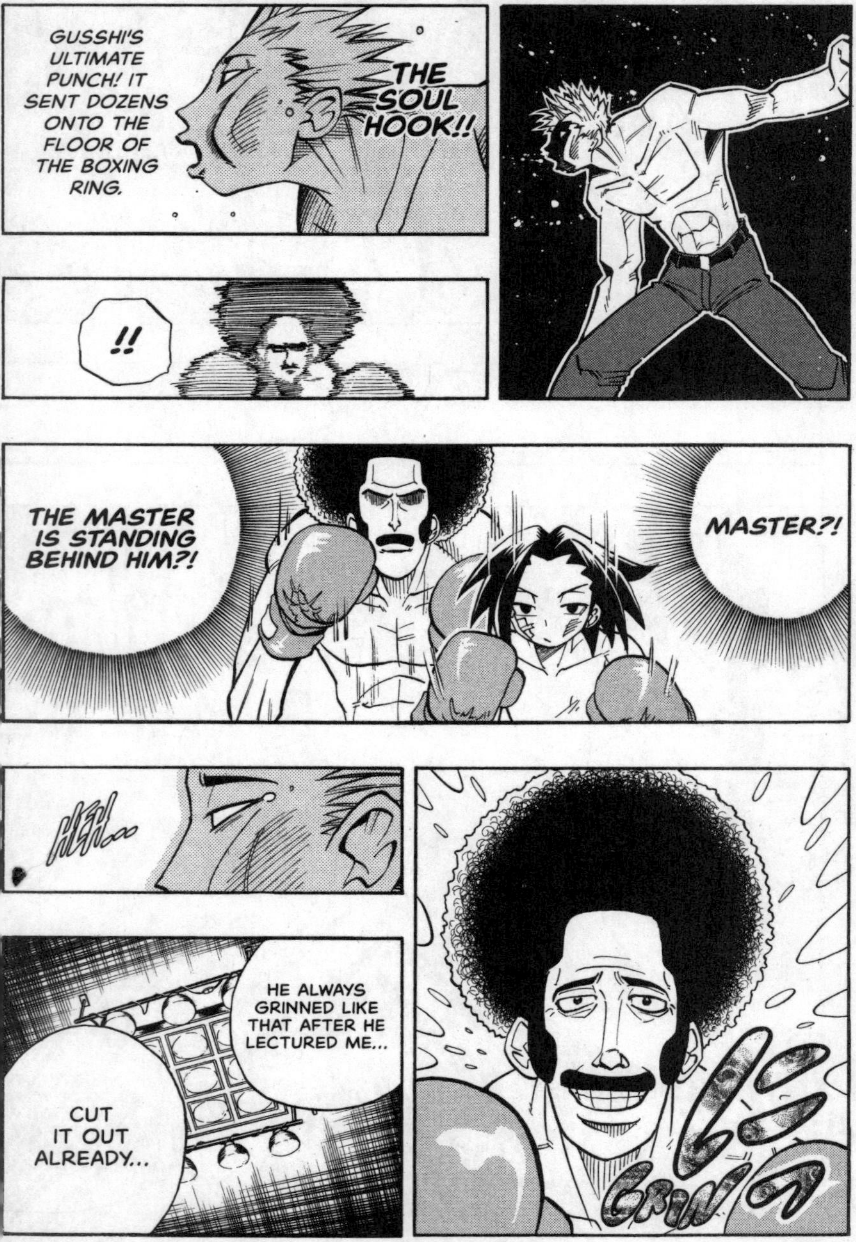
GUSSHI'S ULTIMATE PUNCH! IT SENT DOZENS ONTO THE FLOOR OF THE BOXING RING.
THE SOUL HOOK!!
!!
MASTER?!
THE MASTER IS STANDING BEHIND HIM?!
GRIN
HE ALWAYS GRINNED LIKE THAT AFTER HE LECTURED ME...
CUT IT OUT ALREADY...

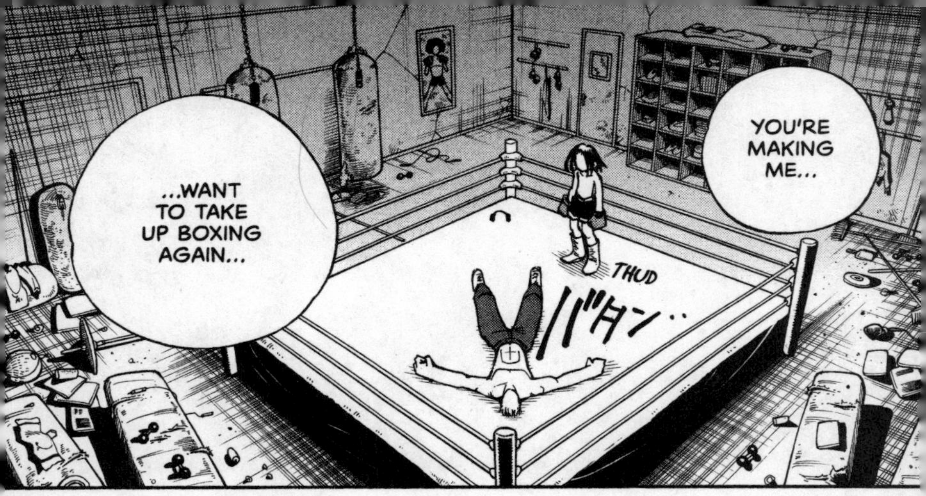
YOU'RE MAKING ME...
...WANT TO TAKE UP BOXING AGAIN...
THUD
バタン

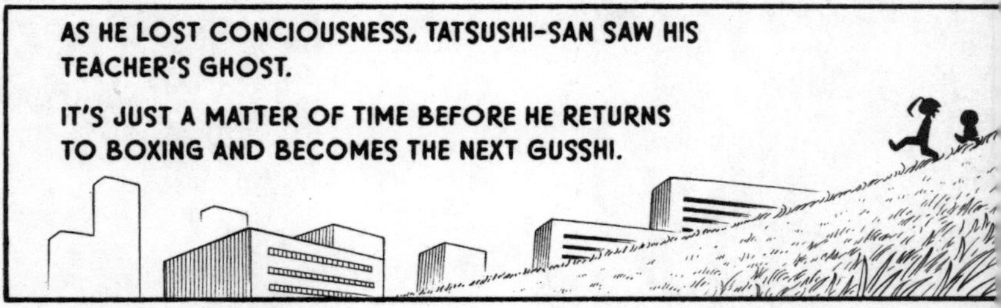
AS HE LOST CONCIOUSNESS, TATSUSHI-SAN SAW HIS TEACHER'S GHOST.
IT'S JUST A MATTER OF TIME BEFORE HE RETURNS TO BOXING AND BECOMES THE NEXT GUSSHI.

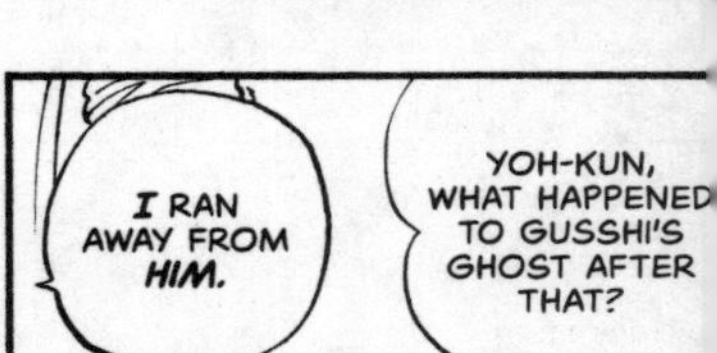
YOH-KUN, WHAT HAPPENED TO GUSSHI'S GHOST AFTER THAT?
I RAN AWAY FROM HIM.
CLENCH

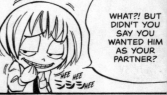

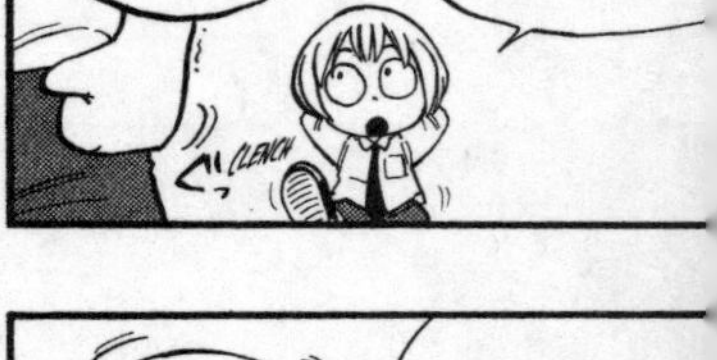
WHAT?! BUT DIDN'T YOU SAY YOU WANTED HIM AS YOUR PARTNER?
HEE HEE HEE

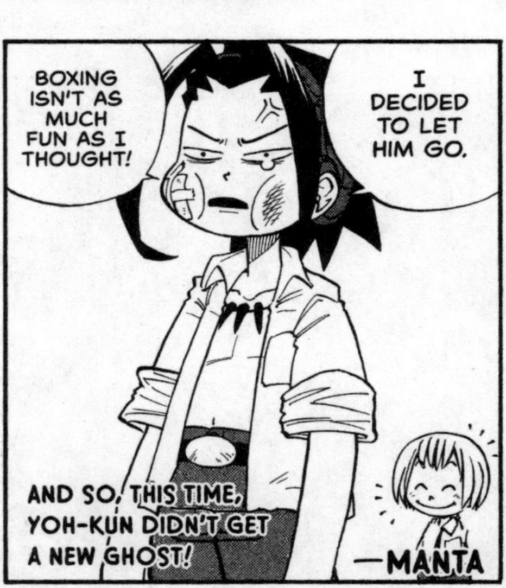
I DECIDED TO LET HIM GO.
BOXING ISN'T AS MUCH FUN AS I THOUGHT!
AND SO, THIS TIME, YOH-KUN DIDN'T GET A NEW GHOST!
—MANTA

SHAMAN
KING
1

**Bear Claw
Necklace**

Chapter 5: Samurai Bodyguard

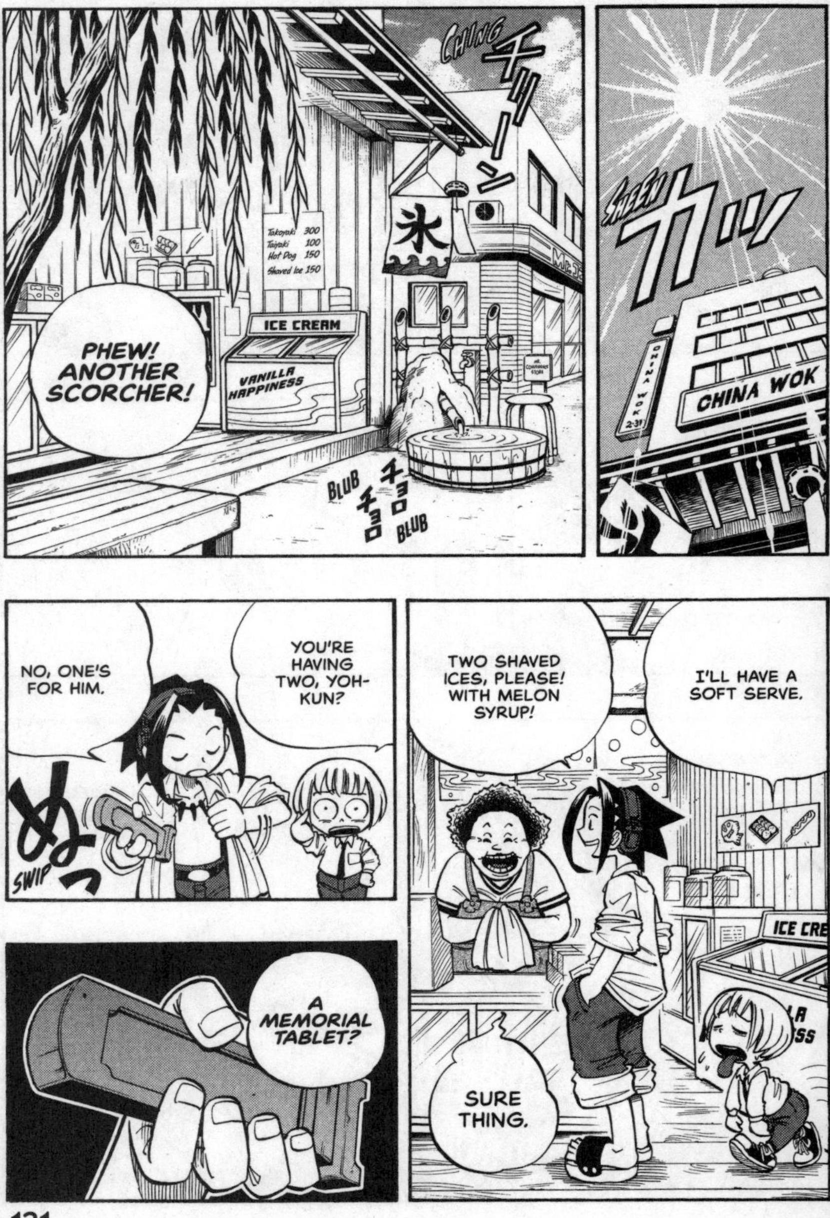
カッ
SHEEN
CHINA WOK
CHINA WOK
チリーン
CHING
氷
Takoyaki 300
Taiyaki 100
Hot Dog 150
Shaved Ice 150
ICE CREAM
VANILLA HAPPINESS
PHEW! ANOTHER SCORCHER!
チョロ チョロ
BLUB
BLUB
I'LL HAVE A SOFT SERVE.
TWO SHAVED ICES, PLEASE! WITH MELON SYRUP!
SURE THING.
ICE CRE
YOU'RE HAVING TWO, YOH-KUN?
NO, ONE'S FOR HIM.
ぬっ
SWIP
A MEMORIAL TABLET?

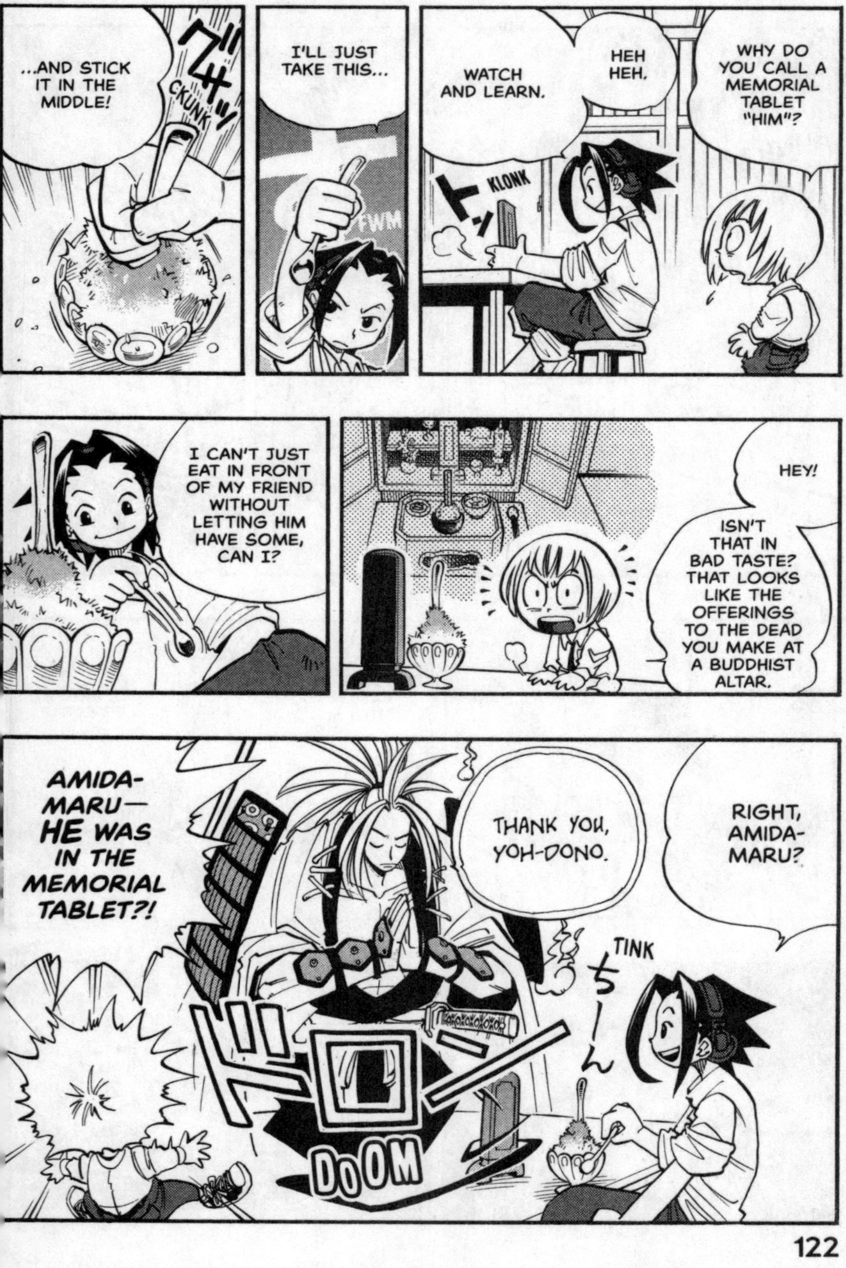
WHY DO YOU CALL A MEMORIAL TABLET "HIM"?
HEH HEH.
WATCH AND LEARN.
KLONK
I'LL JUST TAKE THIS...
FWM
...AND STICK IT IN THE MIDDLE!
CKUNK
HEY!
ISN'T THAT IN BAD TASTE? THAT LOOKS LIKE THE OFFERINGS TO THE DEAD YOU MAKE AT A BUDDHIST ALTAR.
I CAN'T JUST EAT IN FRONT OF MY FRIEND WITHOUT LETTING HIM HAVE SOME, CAN I?
RIGHT, AMIDA-MARU?
THANK YOU, YOH-DONO.
TINK
AMIDA-MARU— HE WAS IN THE MEMORIAL TABLET?!
DOOM

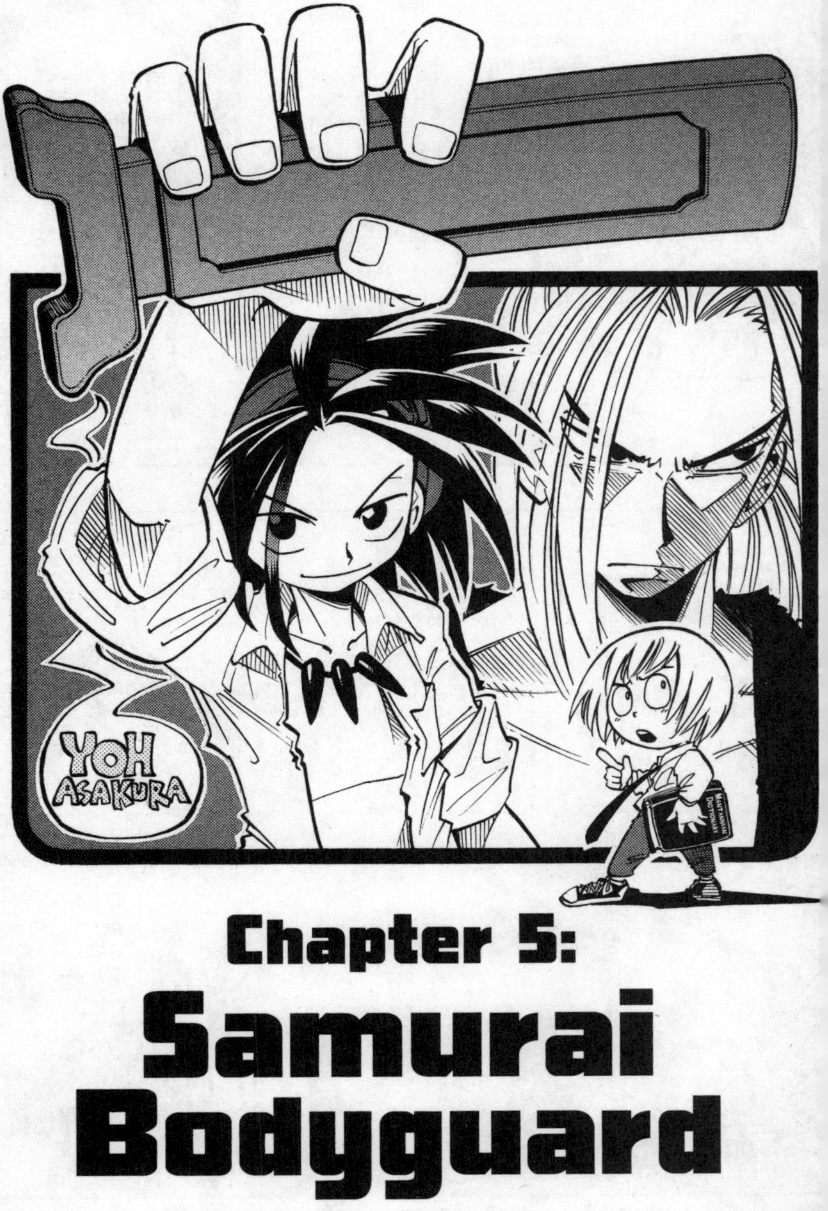
YOH ASAKURA
MANTAANNAN DICTIONARY

Chapter 5:
Samurai Bodyguard

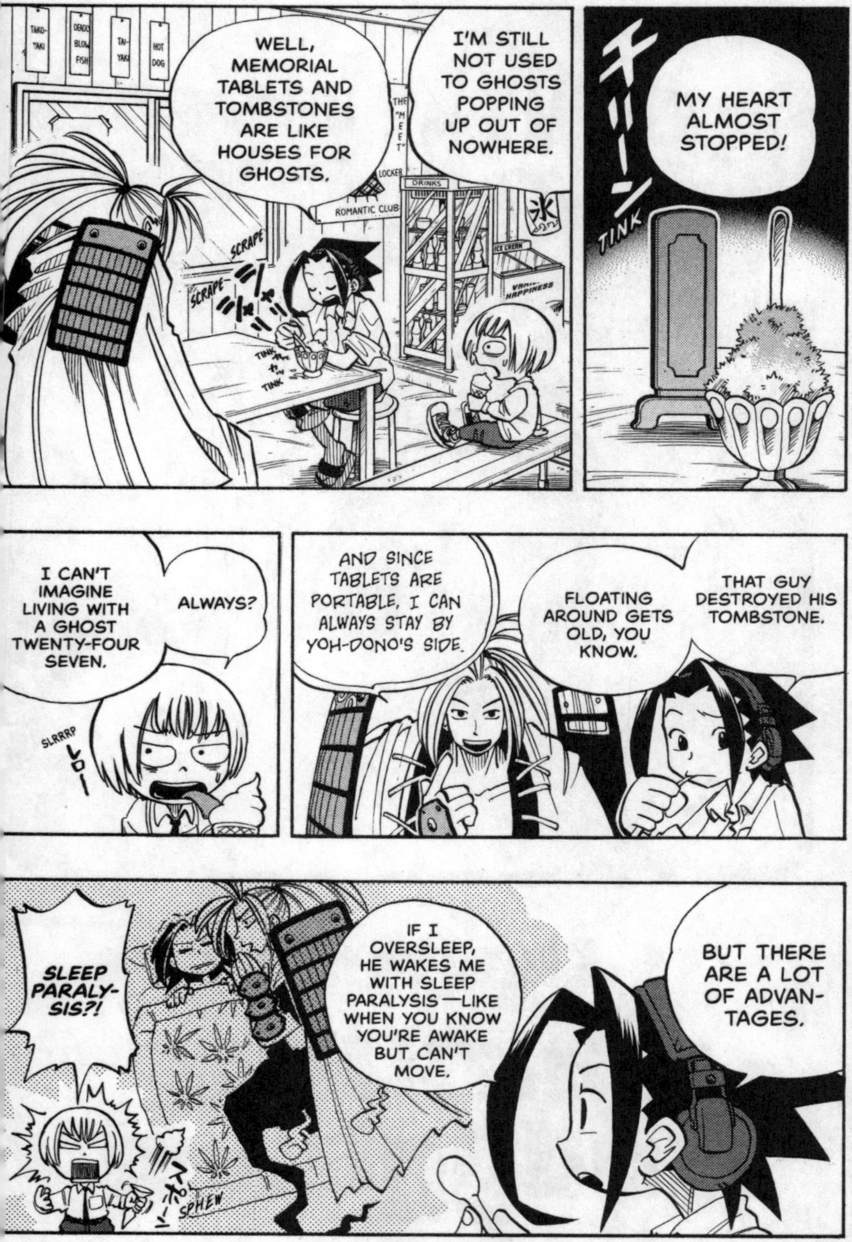
TINK
MY HEART ALMOST STOPPED!
I'M STILL NOT USED TO GHOSTS POPPING UP OUT OF NOWHERE.
WELL, MEMORIAL TABLETS AND TOMBSTONES ARE LIKE HOUSES FOR GHOSTS.
TAKO-YAKI
DEADLY BLOW FISH
TAI-YAKI
HOT DOG
THE "MEET" LOCKER
ROMANTIC CLUB
DRINKS
ICE CREAM
SCRAPE
SCRAPE
TINK
TINK
THAT GUY DESTROYED HIS TOMBSTONE.
FLOATING AROUND GETS OLD, YOU KNOW.
AND SINCE TABLETS ARE PORTABLE, I CAN ALWAYS STAY BY YOH-DONO'S SIDE.
ALWAYS?
I CAN'T IMAGINE LIVING WITH A GHOST TWENTY-FOUR SEVEN.
SLRRRP
BUT THERE ARE A LOT OF ADVAN-TAGES.
IF I OVERSLEEP, HE WAKES ME WITH SLEEP PARALYSIS—LIKE WHEN YOU KNOW YOU'RE AWAKE BUT CAN'T MOVE.
SLEEP PARALY-SIS?!
SPHEW

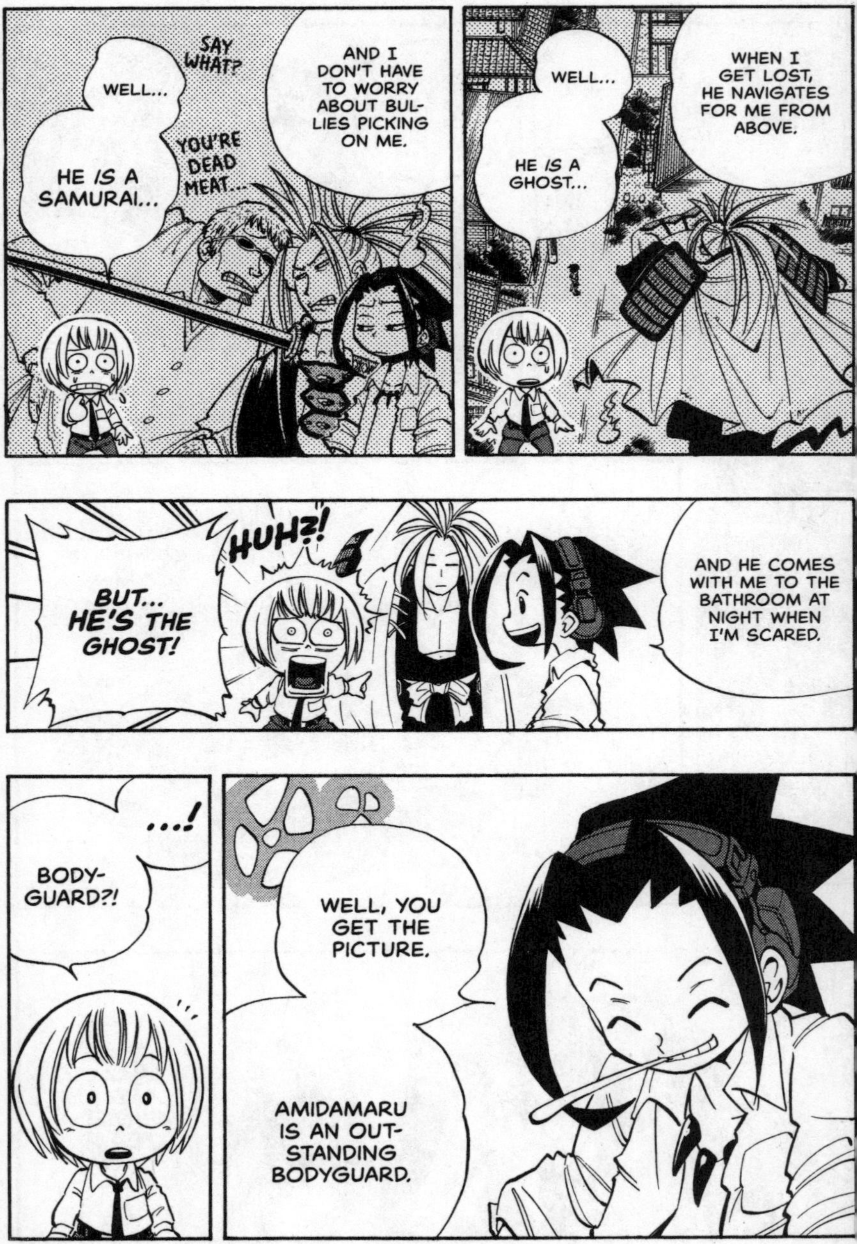
WHEN I GET LOST, HE NAVIGATES FOR ME FROM ABOVE.
WELL...
HE *IS* A GHOST...
AND I DON'T HAVE TO WORRY ABOUT BULLIES PICKING ON ME.
SAY WHAT?
YOU'RE DEAD MEAT...
WELL...
HE *IS* A SAMURAI...
AND HE COMES WITH ME TO THE BATHROOM AT NIGHT WHEN I'M SCARED.
HUH?!
BUT... *HE'S* THE GHOST!
WELL, YOU GET THE PICTURE.
AMIDAMARU IS AN OUTSTANDING BODYGUARD.
...!
BODYGUARD?!

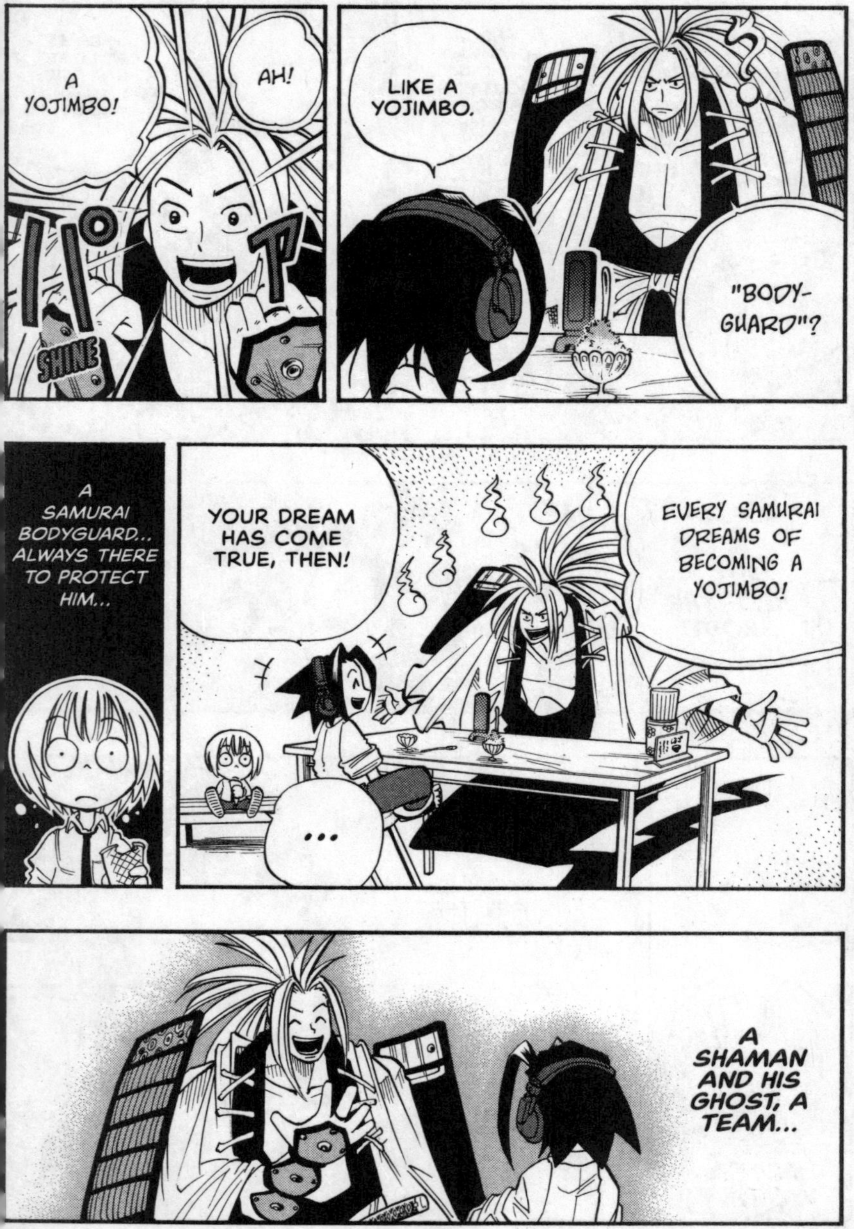
"BODY-GUARD"?
LIKE A YOJIMBO.
AH!
A YOJIMBO!
SHINE
EVERY SAMURAI DREAMS OF BECOMING A YOJIMBO!
YOUR DREAM HAS COME TRUE, THEN!
...
A SAMURAI BODYGUARD... ALWAYS THERE TO PROTECT HIM...
A SHAMAN AND HIS GHOST, A TEAM...

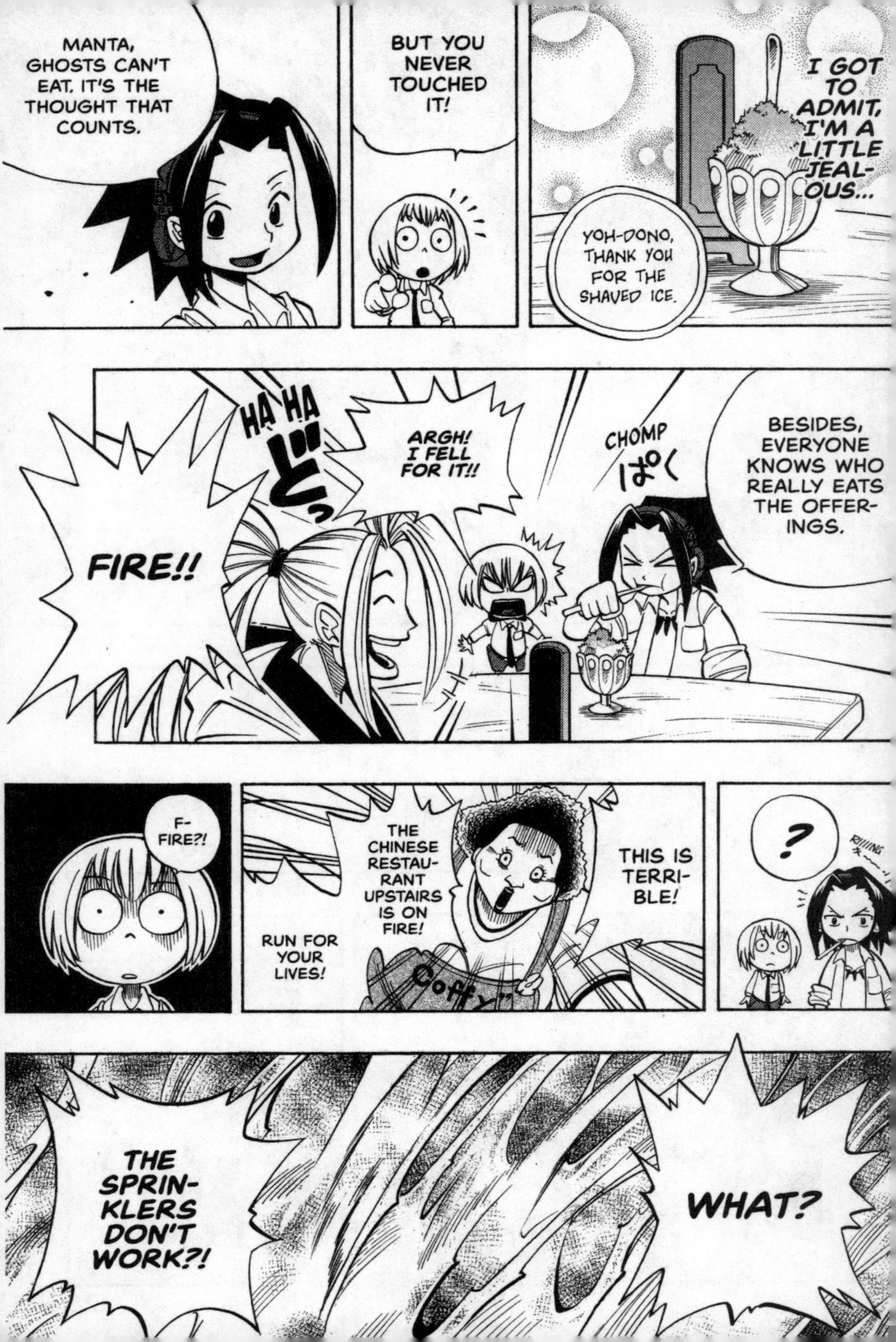
I GOT TO ADMIT, I'M A LITTLE JEALOUS...
YOH-DONO, THANK YOU FOR THE SHAVED ICE.
BUT YOU NEVER TOUCHED IT!
MANTA, GHOSTS CAN'T EAT. IT'S THE THOUGHT THAT COUNTS.
BESIDES, EVERYONE KNOWS WHO REALLY EATS THE OFFERINGS.
CHOMP
ぱく
ARGH! I FELL FOR IT!!
HA HA
どっ
FIRE!!
?
RIIING
THIS IS TERRIBLE!
THE CHINESE RESTAURANT UPSTAIRS IS ON FIRE!
RUN FOR YOUR LIVES!
Coffy
F-FIRE?!
WHAT?
THE SPRINKLERS DON'T WORK?!

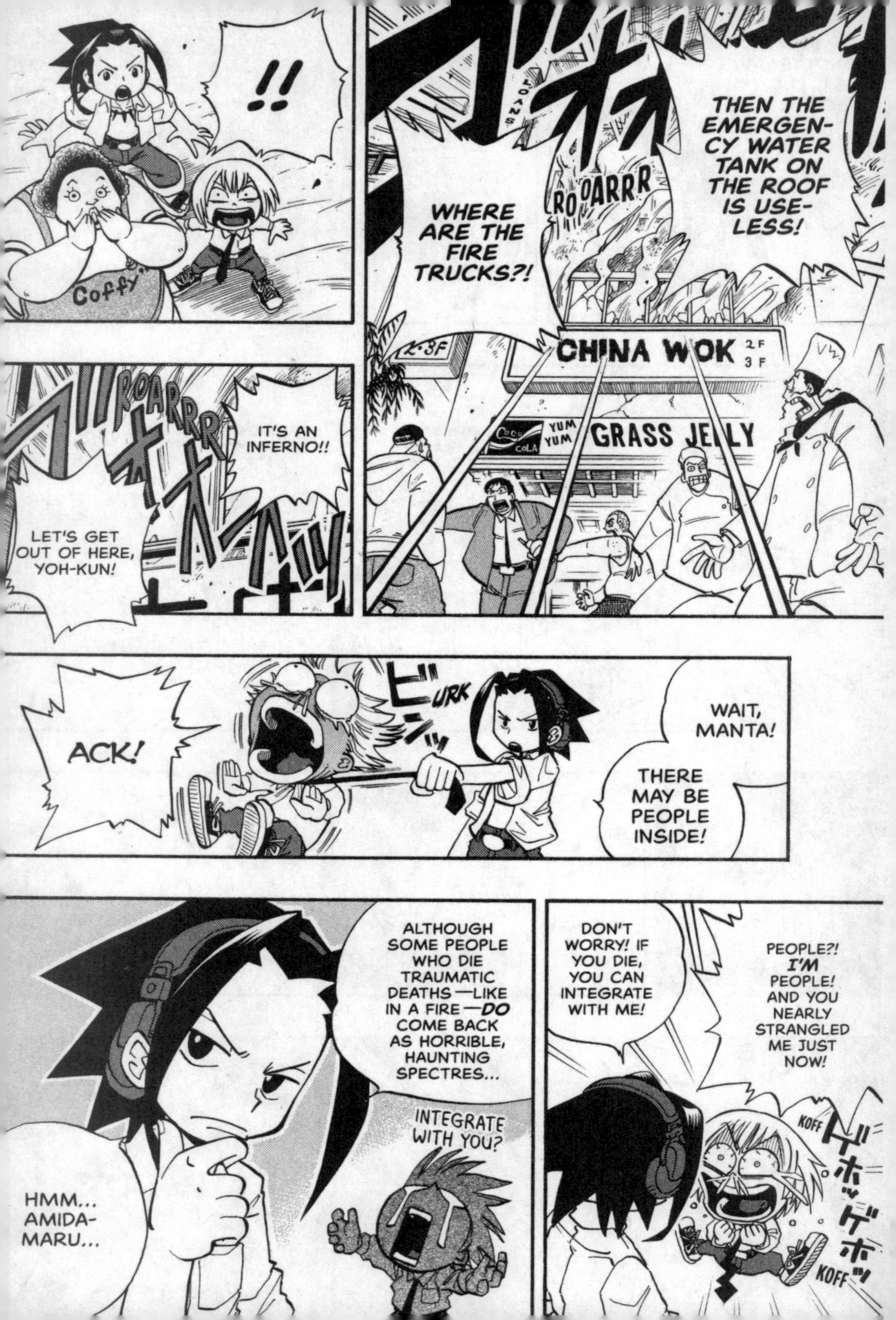
ROOARRR
THEN THE EMERGENCY WATER TANK ON THE ROOF IS USELESS!
LOANS
WHERE ARE THE FIRE TRUCKS?!
CHINA WOK 2F 3F
2·3F
YUM YUM
GRASS JELLY
!!
Coffy
ROARRR
IT'S AN INFERNO!!
LET'S GET OUT OF HERE, YOH-KUN!
WAIT, MANTA!
THERE MAY BE PEOPLE INSIDE!
URK
ACK!
PEOPLE?! *I'M* PEOPLE! AND YOU NEARLY STRANGLED ME JUST NOW!
DON'T WORRY! IF YOU DIE, YOU CAN INTEGRATE WITH ME!
KOFF
KOFF
ALTHOUGH SOME PEOPLE WHO DIE TRAUMATIC DEATHS—LIKE IN A FIRE—*DO* COME BACK AS HORRIBLE, HAUNTING SPECTRES...
INTEGRATE WITH YOU?
HMM... AMIDAMARU...

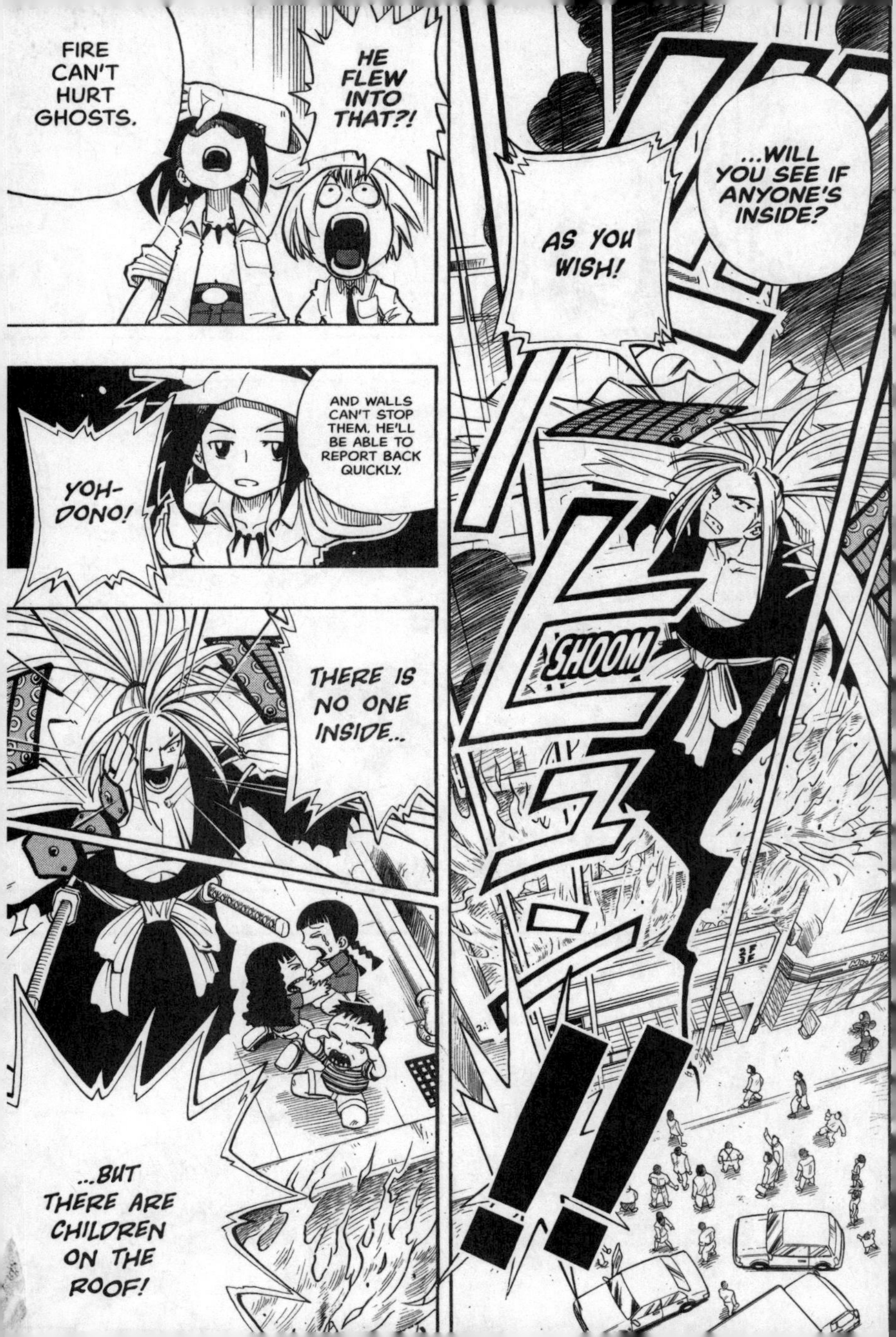
...WILL YOU SEE IF ANYONE'S INSIDE?
AS YOU WISH!
SHOOM
HE FLEW INTO THAT?!
FIRE CAN'T HURT GHOSTS.
AND WALLS CAN'T STOP THEM. HE'LL BE ABLE TO REPORT BACK QUICKLY.
YOH-DONO!
THERE IS NO ONE INSIDE...
...BUT THERE ARE CHILDREN ON THE ROOF!

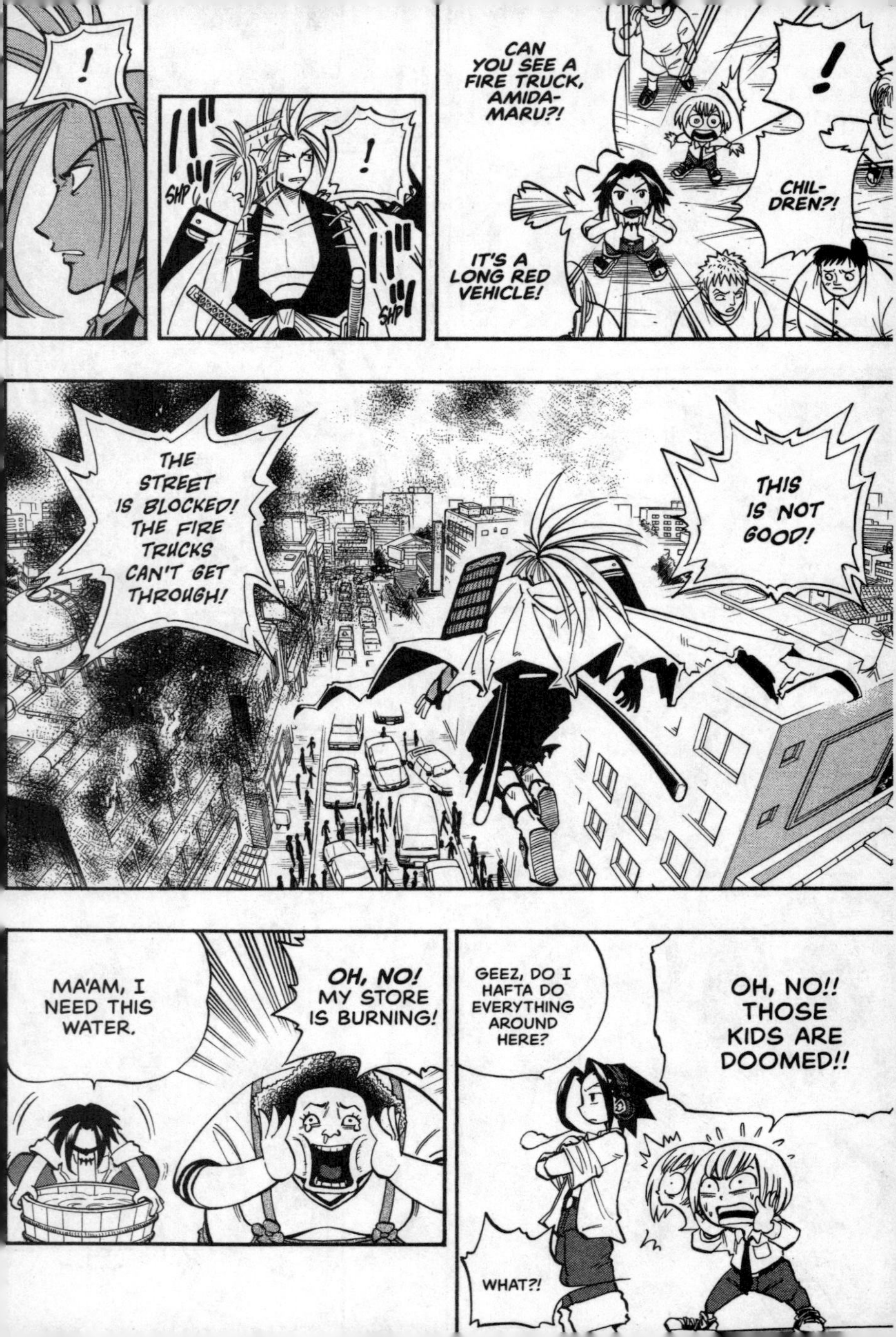
!
CHIL-DREN?!
CAN YOU SEE A FIRE TRUCK, AMIDA-MARU?!
IT'S A LONG RED VEHICLE!
!
SHP
SHP
!
THIS IS NOT GOOD!
THE STREET IS BLOCKED! THE FIRE TRUCKS CAN'T GET THROUGH!
OH, NO!! THOSE KIDS ARE DOOMED!!
GEEZ, DO I HAFTA DO EVERYTHING AROUND HERE?
WHAT?!
OH, NO! MY STORE IS BURNING!
MA'AM, I NEED THIS WATER.

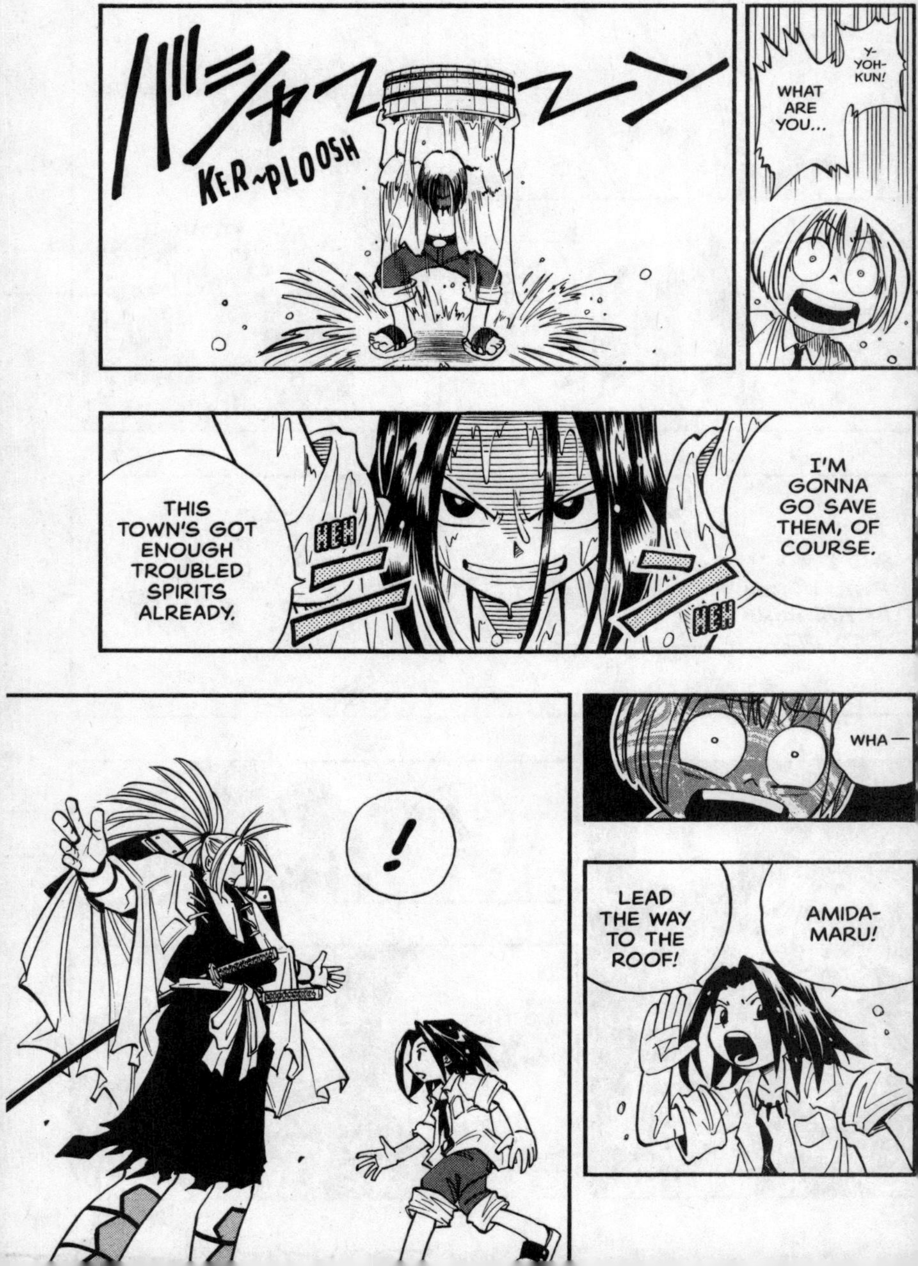
Y-YOH-KUN!
WHAT ARE YOU...
バシャーン
KER~PLOOSH
I'M GONNA GO SAVE THEM, OF COURSE.
HEH
HEH
THIS TOWN'S GOT ENOUGH TROUBLED SPIRITS ALREADY.
WHA—
AMIDA-MARU!
LEAD THE WAY TO THE ROOF!
!

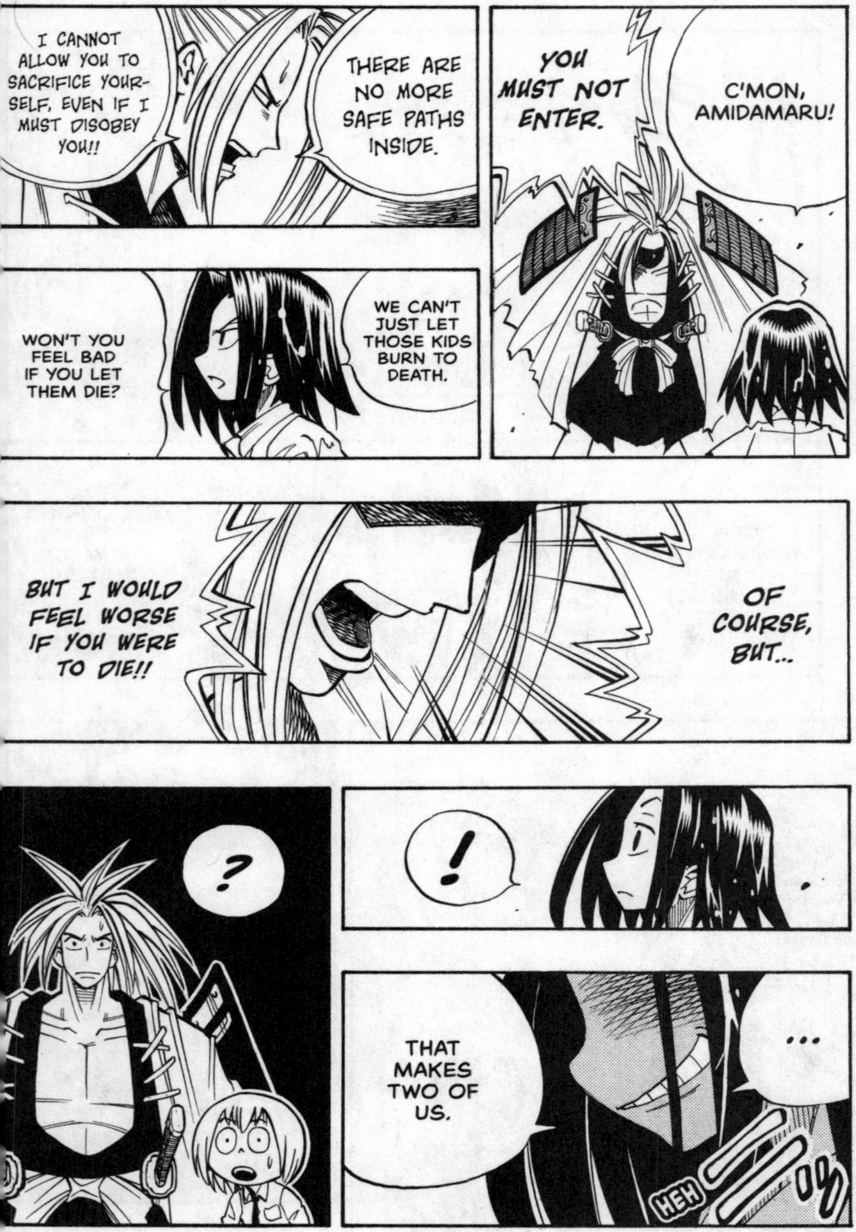
C'MON, AMIDAMARU!
YOU MUST NOT ENTER.
THERE ARE NO MORE SAFE PATHS INSIDE.
I CANNOT ALLOW YOU TO SACRIFICE YOUR-SELF, EVEN IF I MUST DISOBEY YOU!!
WE CAN'T JUST LET THOSE KIDS BURN TO DEATH.
WON'T YOU FEEL BAD IF YOU LET THEM DIE?
OF COURSE, BUT...
BUT I WOULD FEEL WORSE IF YOU WERE TO DIE!!
!
...
THAT MAKES TWO OF US.
HEH
?

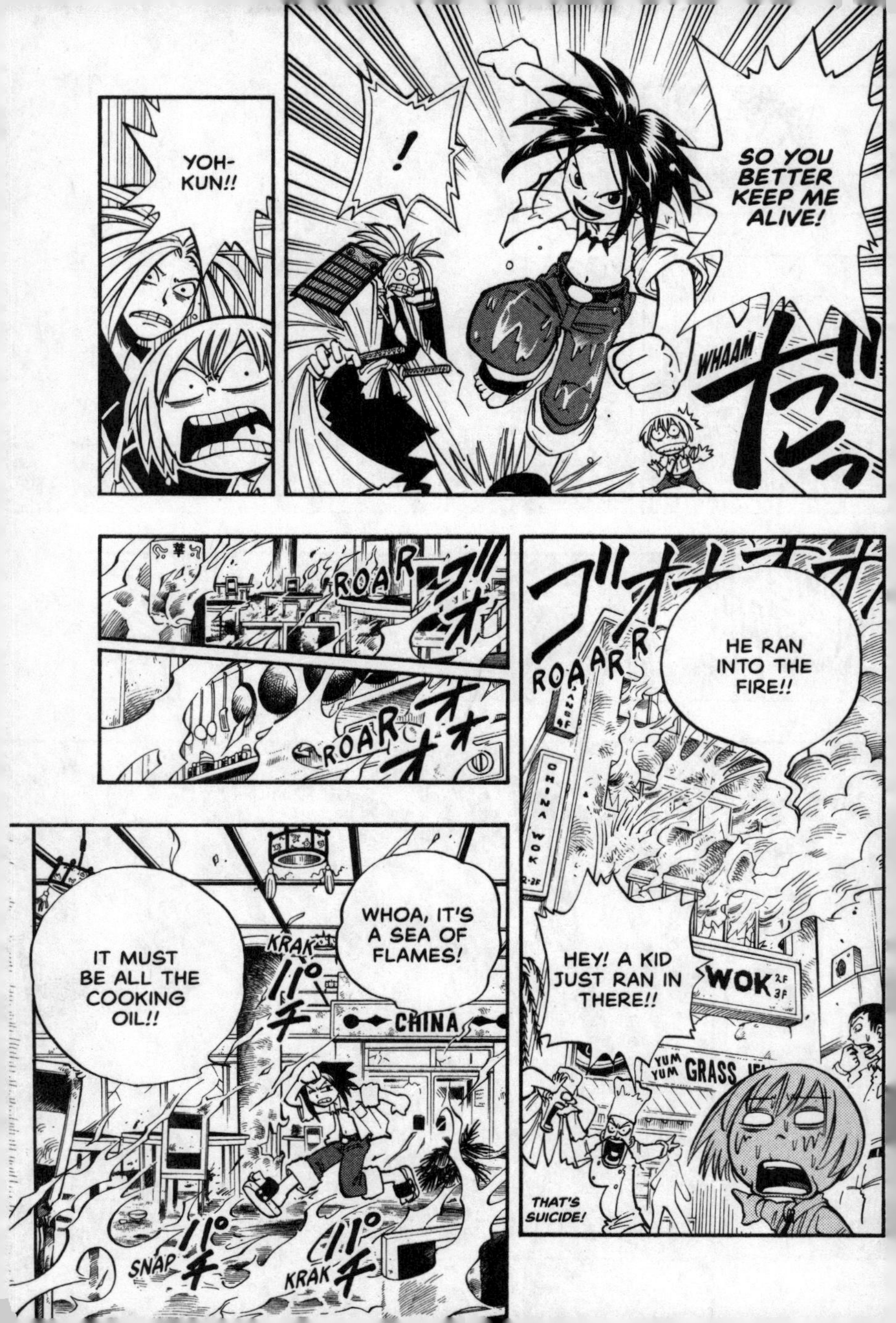
SO YOU BETTER KEEP ME ALIVE!
!
WHAAM
YOH-KUN!!
HE RAN INTO THE FIRE!!
ROAARR
CHINA WOK
HEY! A KID JUST RAN IN THERE!!
WOK 2F 3F
YUM YUM GRASS
THAT'S SUICIDE!
ROAR
ROAR
WHOA, IT'S A SEA OF FLAMES!
IT MUST BE ALL THE COOKING OIL!!
KRAK
CHINA
SNAP
KRAK

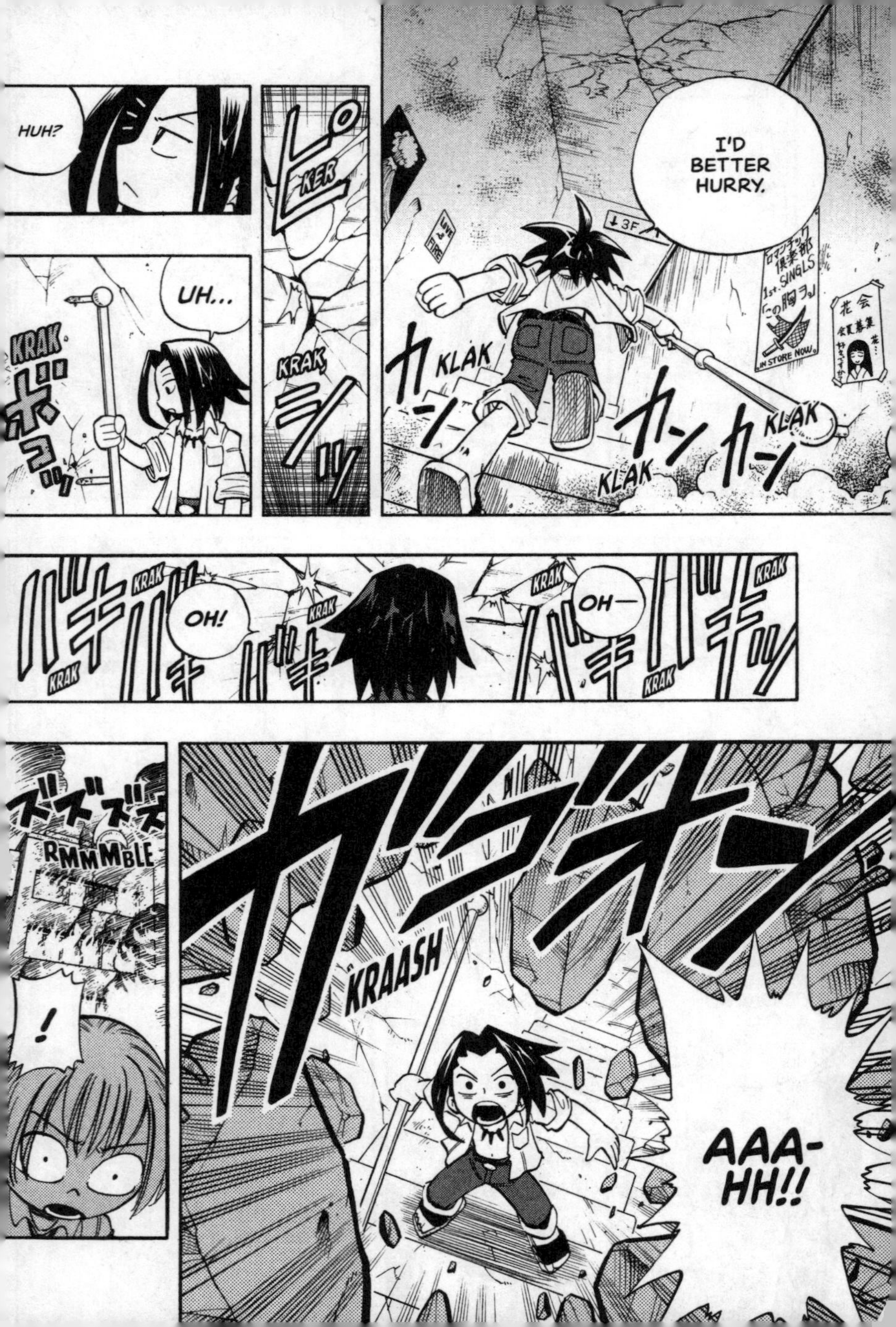

I'D BETTER HURRY.
↓3F
LOVE & FIRE
ロマンチック倶楽部
1st. SINGLS
「この胸ヲ」
IN STORE NOW
花会
会員募集
KLAK
KLAK
KLAK
KLAK
KER
KRAK
HUH?
UH...
KRAK
KRAK
OH—
KRAK
KRAK
OH!
KRAK
KRAASH
AAA-HH!!
RMMMBLE
!

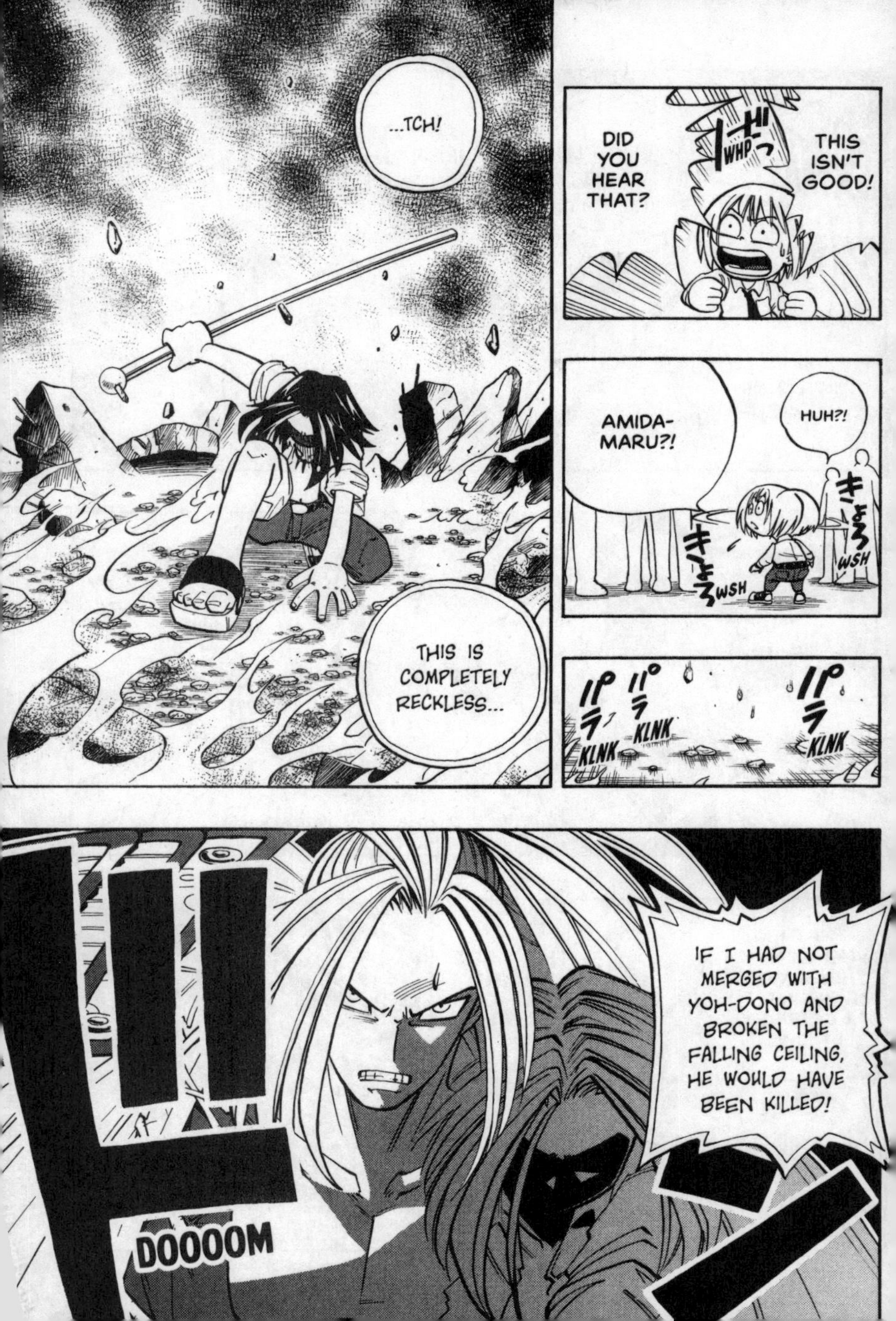
THIS ISN'T GOOD!
WHP
DID YOU HEAR THAT?
HUH?!
AMIDA-MARU?!
きょろ
WSH
きょろ
WSH
パラ
KLNK
パラ
KLNK
パラ
KLNK
...TCH!
THIS IS COMPLETELY RECKLESS...
IF I HAD NOT MERGED WITH YOH-DONO AND BROKEN THE FALLING CEILING, HE WOULD HAVE BEEN KILLED!
DOOOOM

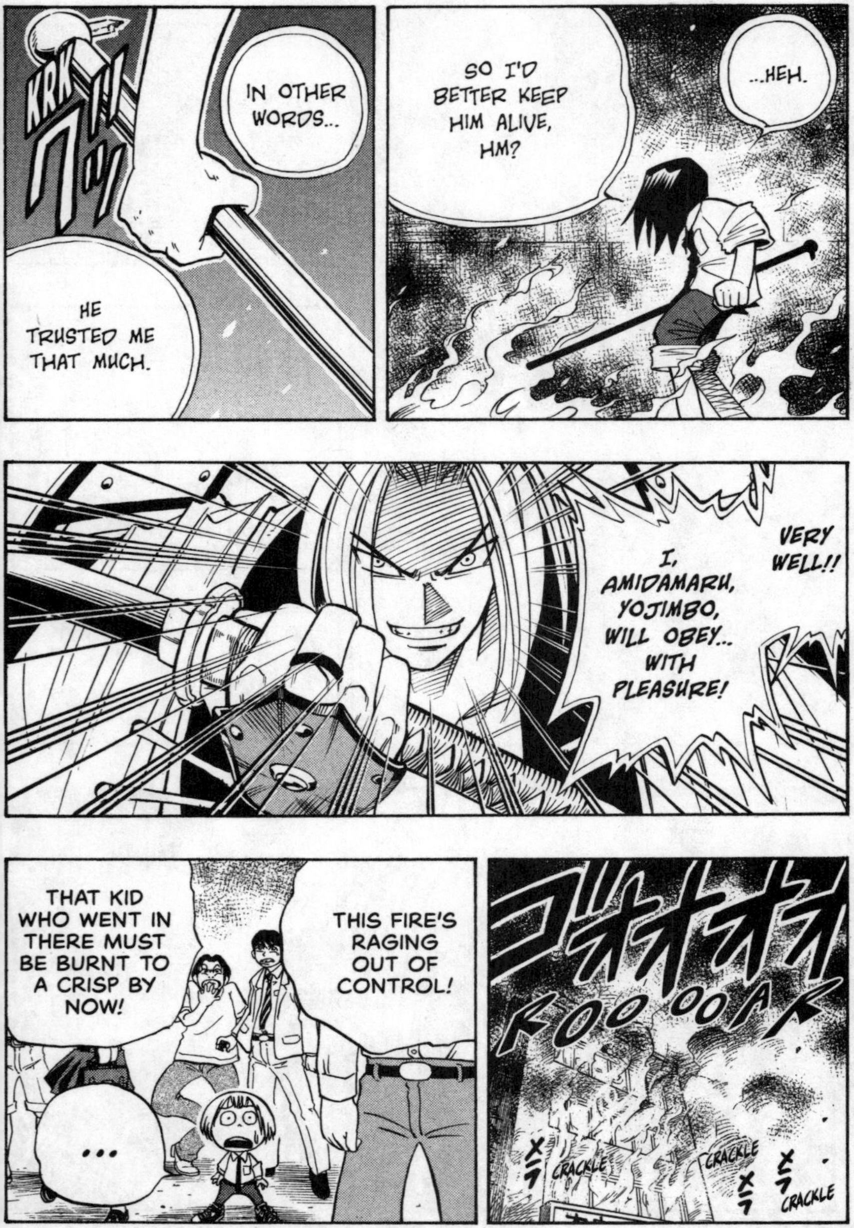
KRK
IN OTHER WORDS...
HE TRUSTED ME THAT MUCH.
SO I'D BETTER KEEP HIM ALIVE, HM?
...HEH.
VERY WELL!!
I, AMIDAMARU, YOJIMBO, WILL OBEY... WITH PLEASURE!
THAT KID WHO WENT IN THERE MUST BE BURNT TO A CRISP BY NOW!
THIS FIRE'S RAGING OUT OF CONTROL!
...
KROOOOAR
CRACKLE
CRACKLE
CRACKLE

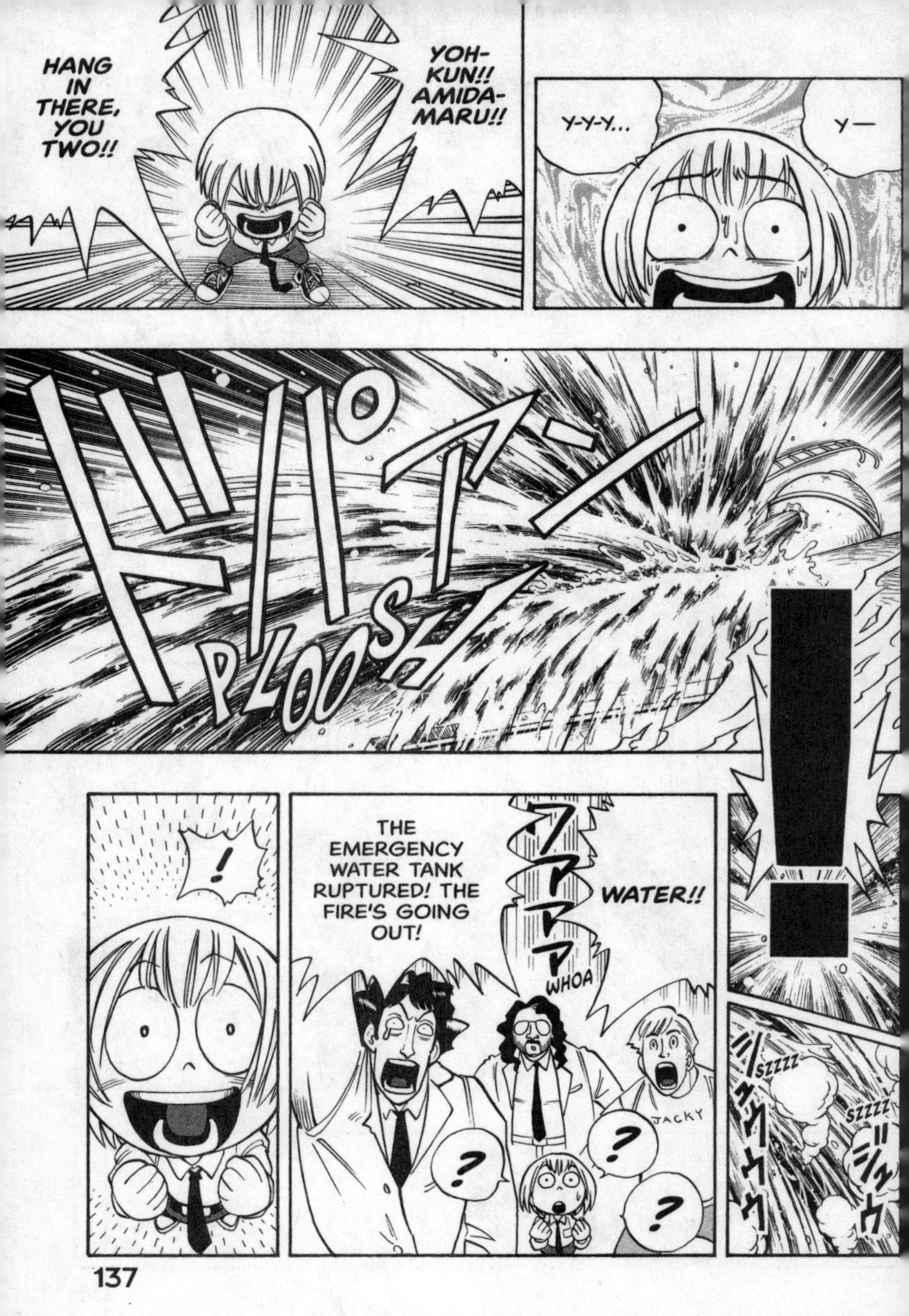
Y-Y-Y...
Y—
YOH-KUN!! AMIDA-MARU!!
HANG IN THERE, YOU TWO!!
PLOOSH
!!
SZZZZ
SZZZZ
WATER!!
WHOA
THE EMERGENCY WATER TANK RUPTURED! THE FIRE'S GOING OUT!
JACKY
?
?
?
!

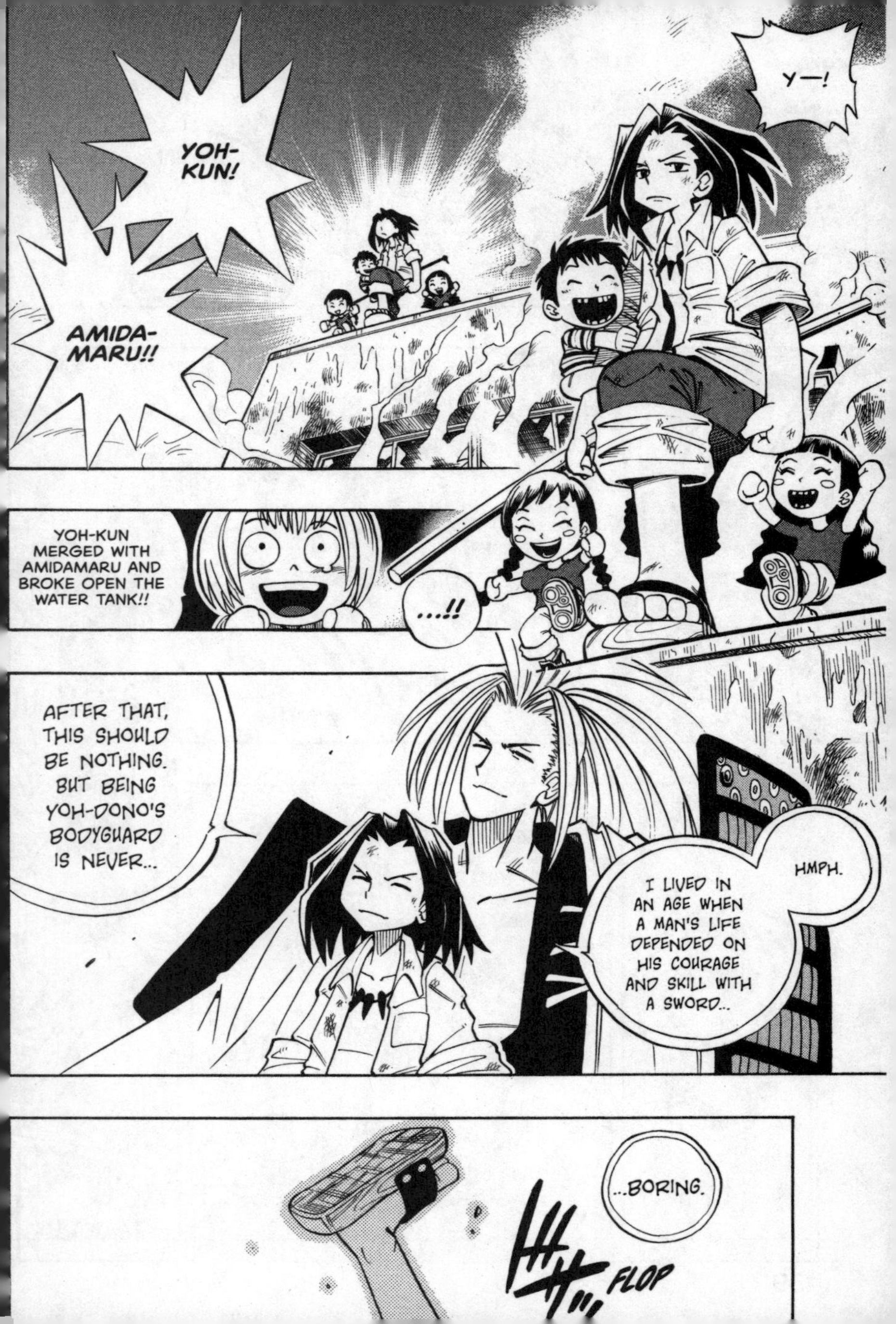
Y—!
YOH-KUN!
AMIDA-MARU!!
...!!
YOH-KUN MERGED WITH AMIDAMARU AND BROKE OPEN THE WATER TANK!!
HMPH.
I LIVED IN AN AGE WHEN A MAN'S LIFE DEPENDED ON HIS COURAGE AND SKILL WITH A SWORD...
AFTER THAT, THIS SHOULD BE NOTHING. BUT BEING YOH-DONO'S BODYGUARD IS NEVER...
...BORING.
FLOP

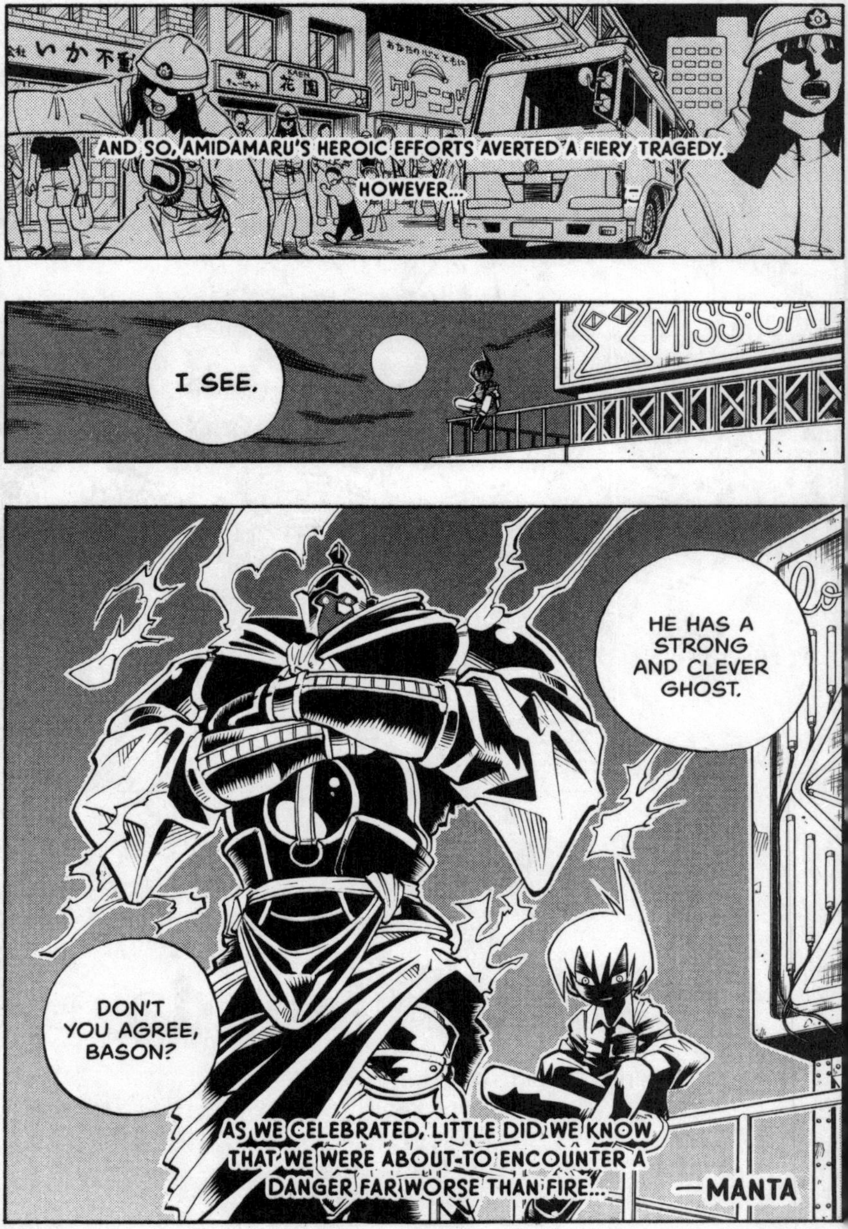

AND SO, AMIDAMARU'S HEROIC EFFORTS AVERTED A FIERY TRAGEDY.
HOWEVER...
花園
I SEE.
HE HAS A STRONG AND CLEVER GHOST.
DON'T YOU AGREE, BASON?
AS WE CELEBRATED, LITTLE DID WE KNOW THAT WE WERE ABOUT TO ENCOUNTER A DANGER FAR WORSE THAN FIRE...
—MANTA

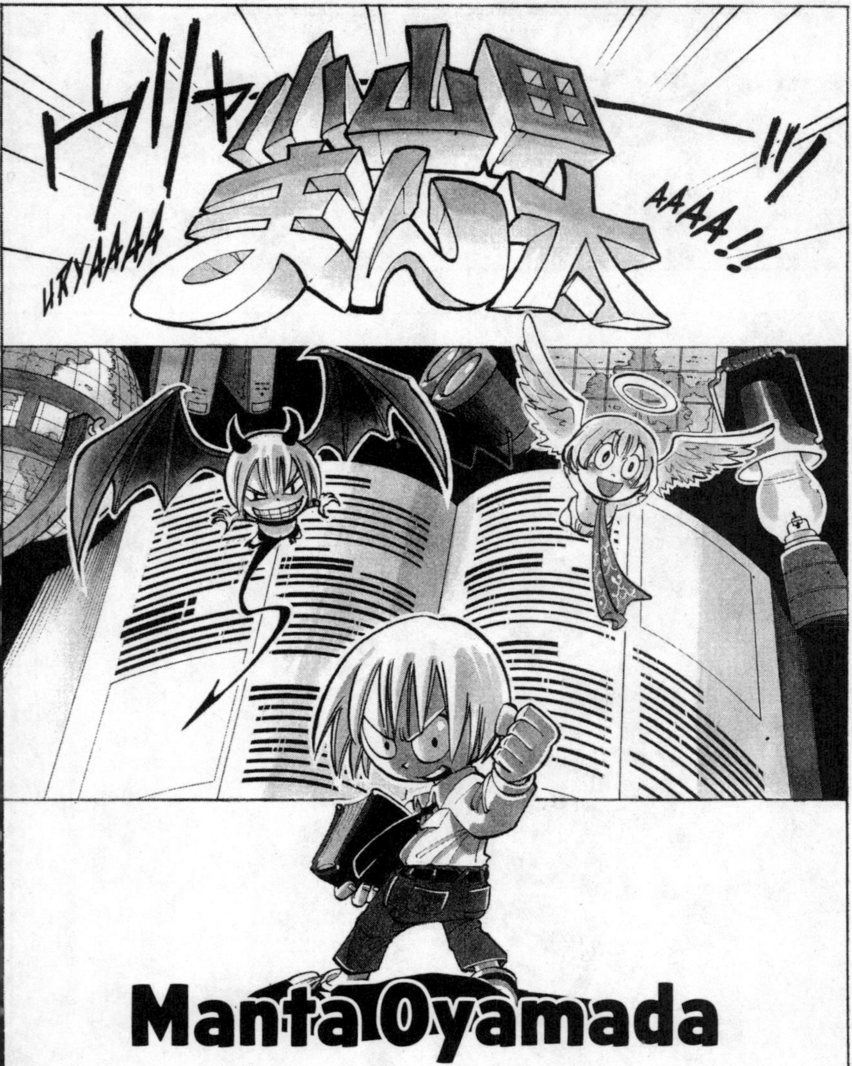
ウリャー小山田まん太ーーッ
URYAAAA
AAAA!!!

Manta Oyamada

Shinra Private Academy Middle School
First Year
Age: 13
Birthday: September 5
Blood Type: O

Chapter 6: Another Shaman

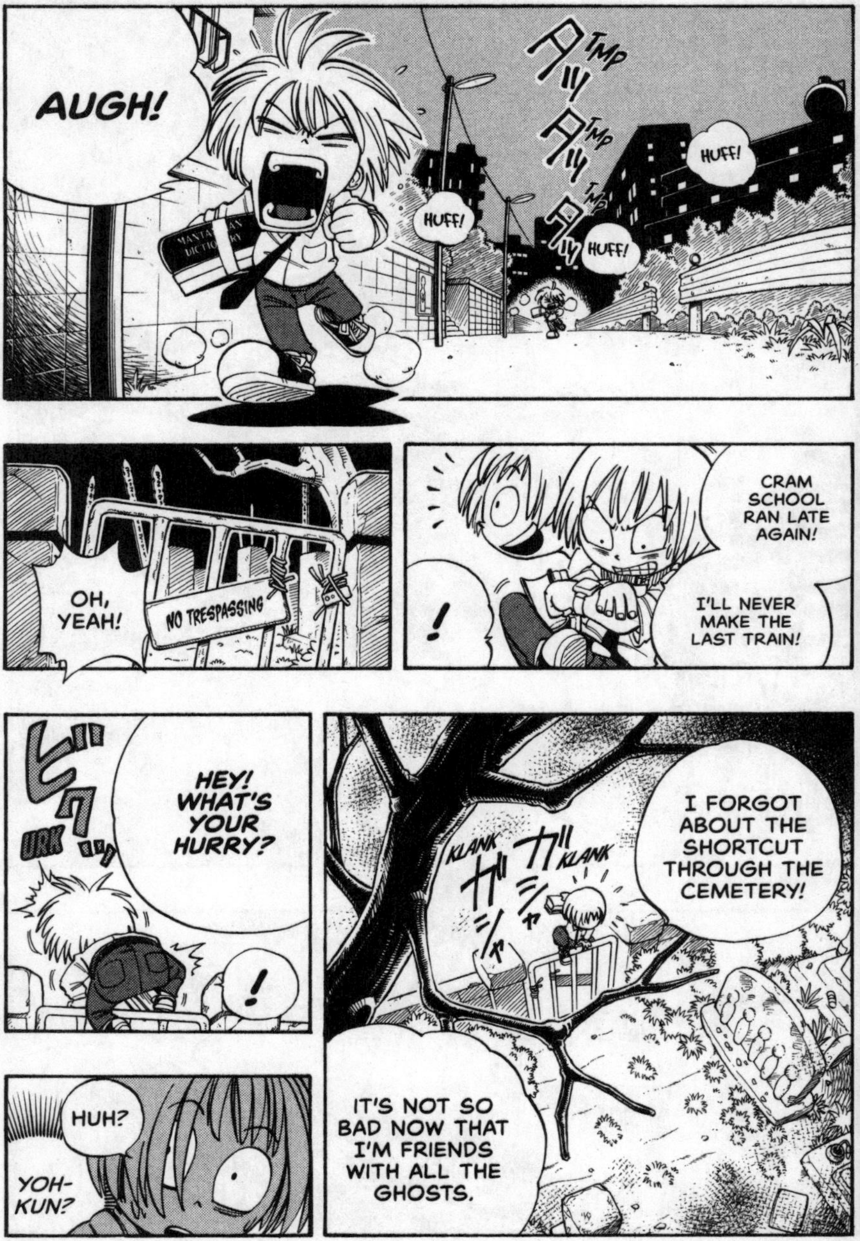
AUGH!
TMP
TMP
TMP
HUFF!
HUFF!
HUFF!
CRAM SCHOOL RAN LATE AGAIN!
I'LL NEVER MAKE THE LAST TRAIN!
!
OH, YEAH!
NO TRESPASSING
I FORGOT ABOUT THE SHORTCUT THROUGH THE CEMETERY!
KLANK
KLANK
IT'S NOT SO BAD NOW THAT I'M FRIENDS WITH ALL THE GHOSTS.
HEY! WHAT'S YOUR HURRY?
URK
!
HUH?
YOH-KUN?

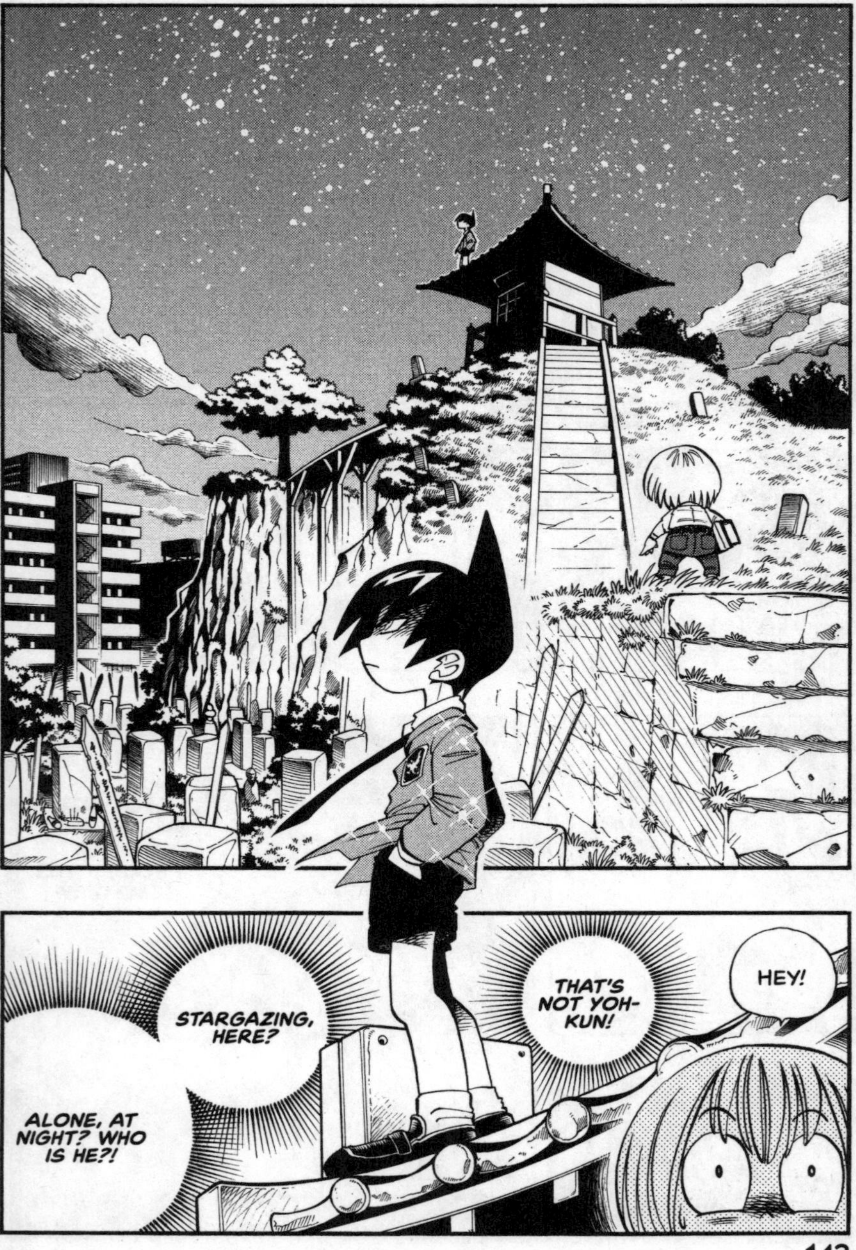
HEY!
THAT'S NOT YOH-KUN!
STARGAZING, HERE?
ALONE, AT NIGHT? WHO IS HE?!

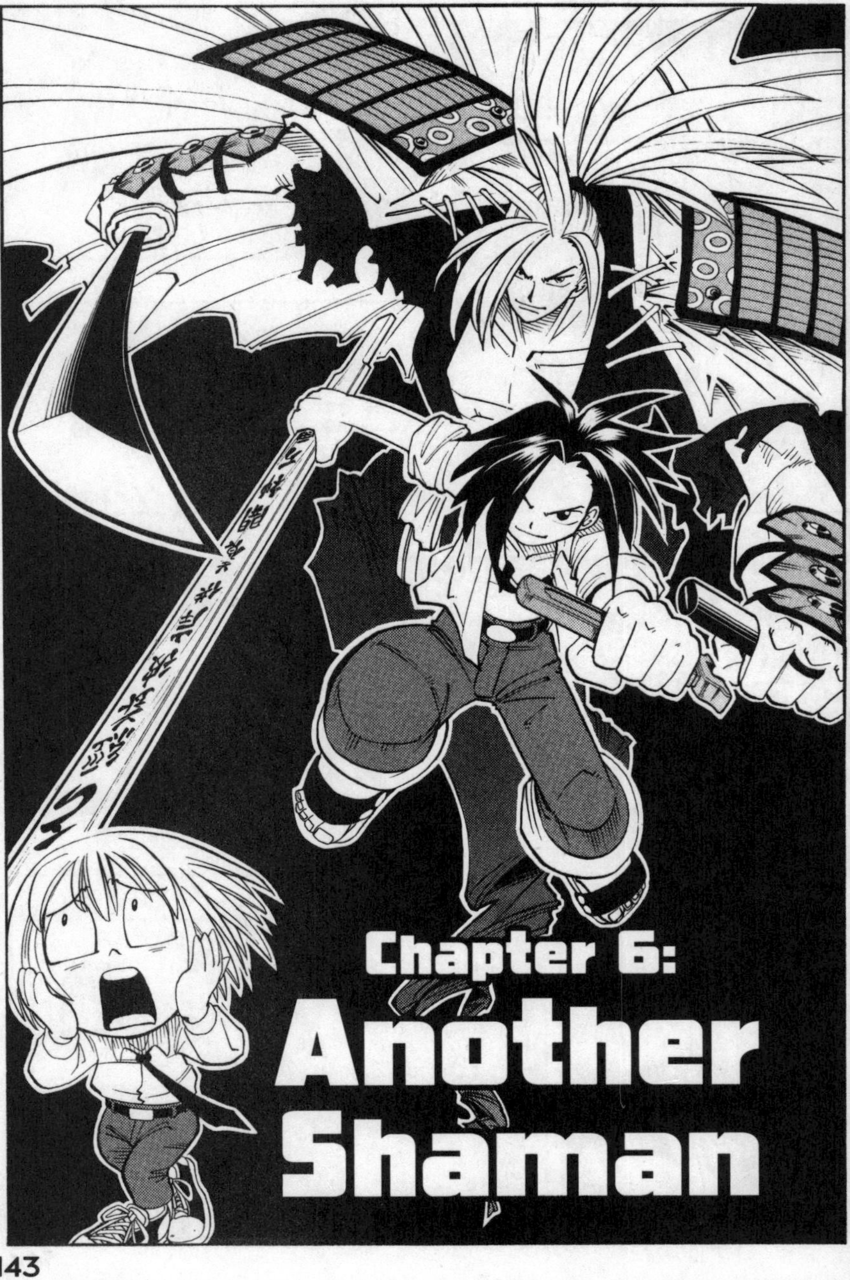
Chapter 6:
Another Shaman

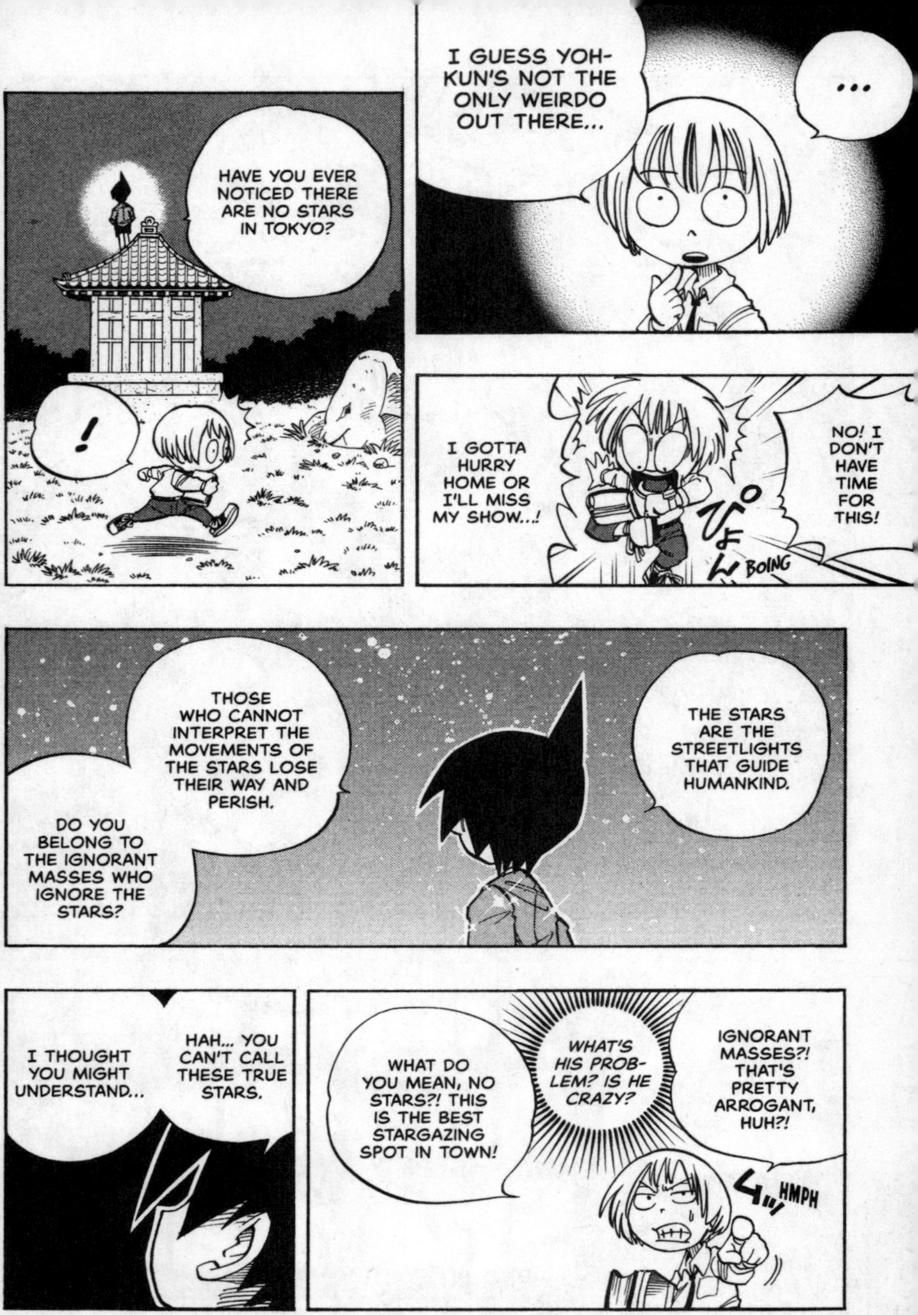
I GUESS YOH-KUN'S NOT THE ONLY WEIRDO OUT THERE...
...
NO! I DON'T HAVE TIME FOR THIS!
I GOTTA HURRY HOME OR I'LL MISS MY SHOW...!
BOING
HAVE YOU EVER NOTICED THERE ARE NO STARS IN TOKYO?
!
THE STARS ARE THE STREETLIGHTS THAT GUIDE HUMANKIND.
THOSE WHO CANNOT INTERPRET THE MOVEMENTS OF THE STARS LOSE THEIR WAY AND PERISH.
DO YOU BELONG TO THE IGNORANT MASSES WHO IGNORE THE STARS?
IGNORANT MASSES?! THAT'S PRETTY ARROGANT, HUH?!
WHAT'S HIS PROBLEM? IS HE CRAZY?
WHAT DO YOU MEAN, NO STARS?! THIS IS THE BEST STARGAZING SPOT IN TOWN!
HMPH
HAH... YOU CAN'T CALL THESE TRUE STARS.
I THOUGHT YOU MIGHT UNDERSTAND...

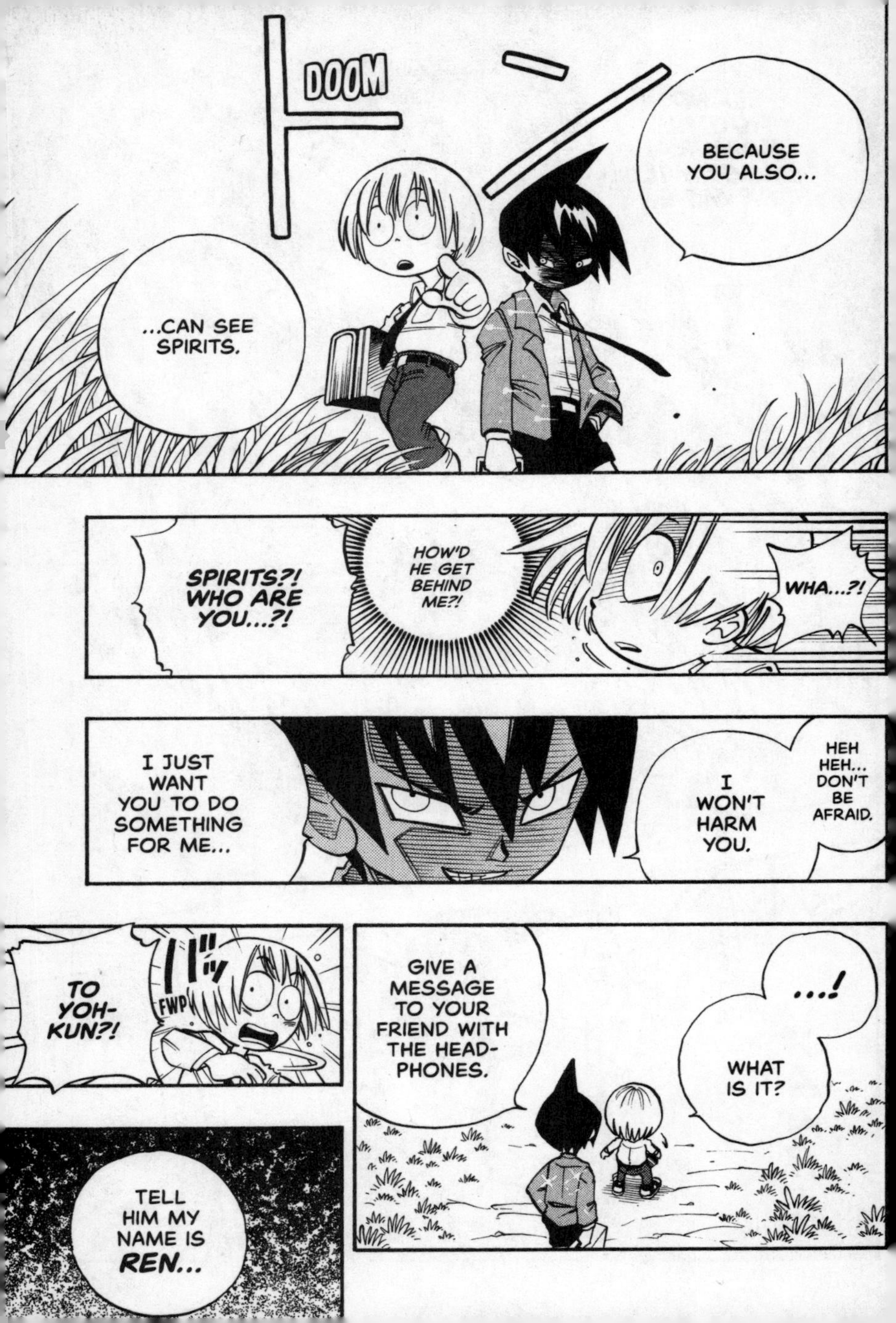
BECAUSE YOU ALSO...
DOOM
...CAN SEE SPIRITS.
WHA...?!
HOW'D HE GET BEHIND ME?!
SPIRITS?! WHO ARE YOU...?!
HEH HEH... DON'T BE AFRAID.
I WON'T HARM YOU.
I JUST WANT YOU TO DO SOMETHING FOR ME...
...!
WHAT IS IT?
GIVE A MESSAGE TO YOUR FRIEND WITH THE HEAD-PHONES.
TO YOH-KUN?!
FWP
TELL HIM MY NAME IS REN...

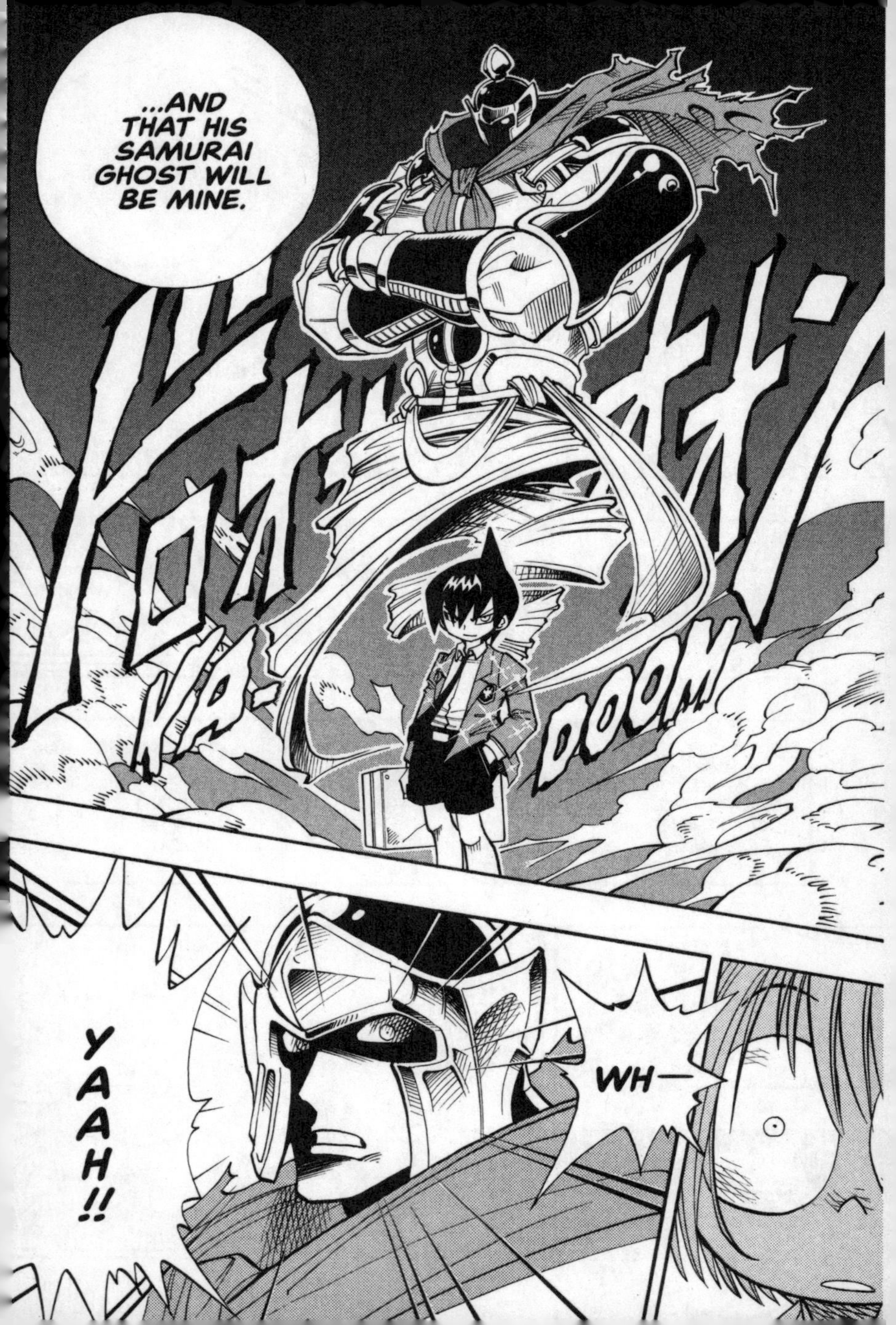
...AND THAT HIS SAMURAI GHOST WILL BE MINE.
KA-DOOM
WH—
YAAAH!!

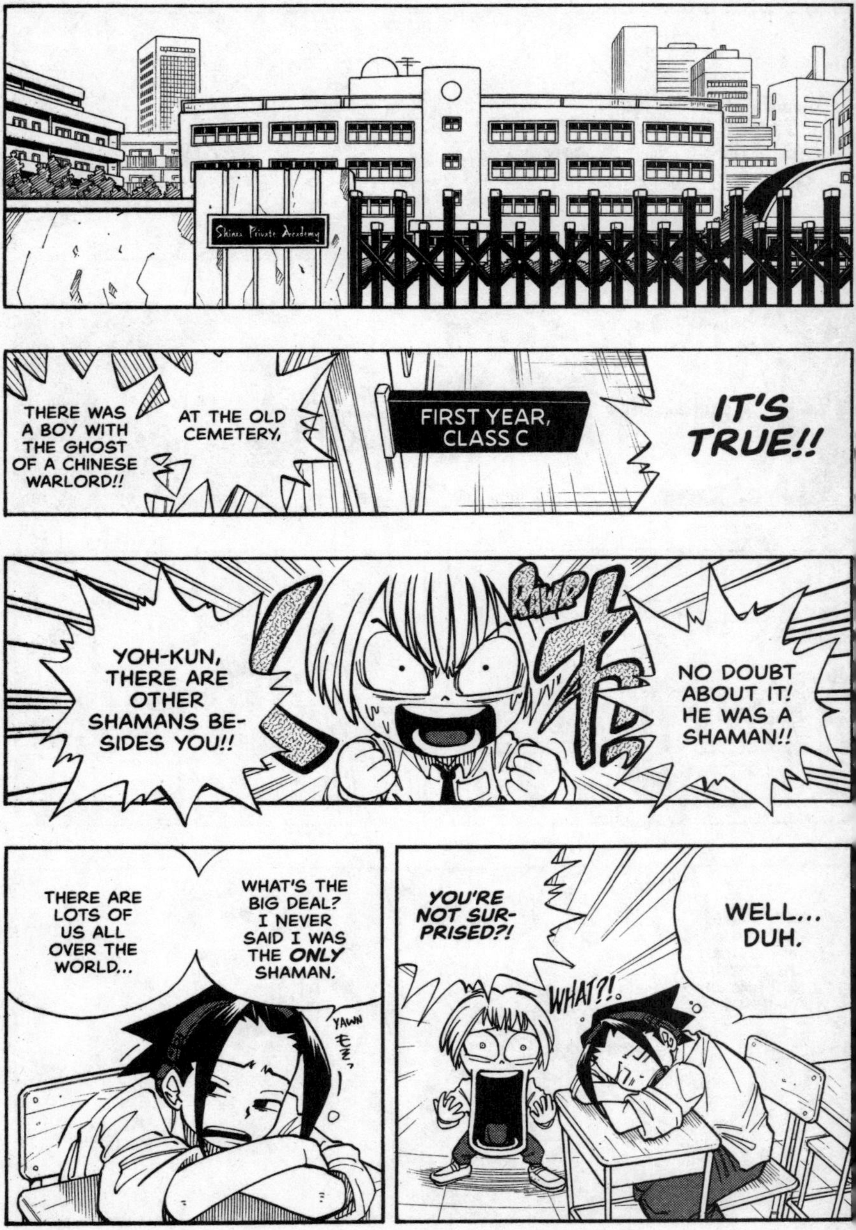
Shinra Private Academy
IT'S TRUE!!
FIRST YEAR, CLASS C
AT THE OLD CEMETERY,
THERE WAS A BOY WITH THE GHOST OF A CHINESE WARLORD!!
NO DOUBT ABOUT IT! HE WAS A SHAMAN!!
RAWR
YOH-KUN, THERE ARE OTHER SHAMANS BE-SIDES YOU!!
WELL... DUH.
WHAT?!
YOU'RE NOT SUR-PRISED?!
WHAT'S THE BIG DEAL? I NEVER SAID I WAS THE ONLY SHAMAN.
YAWN
THERE ARE LOTS OF US ALL OVER THE WORLD...

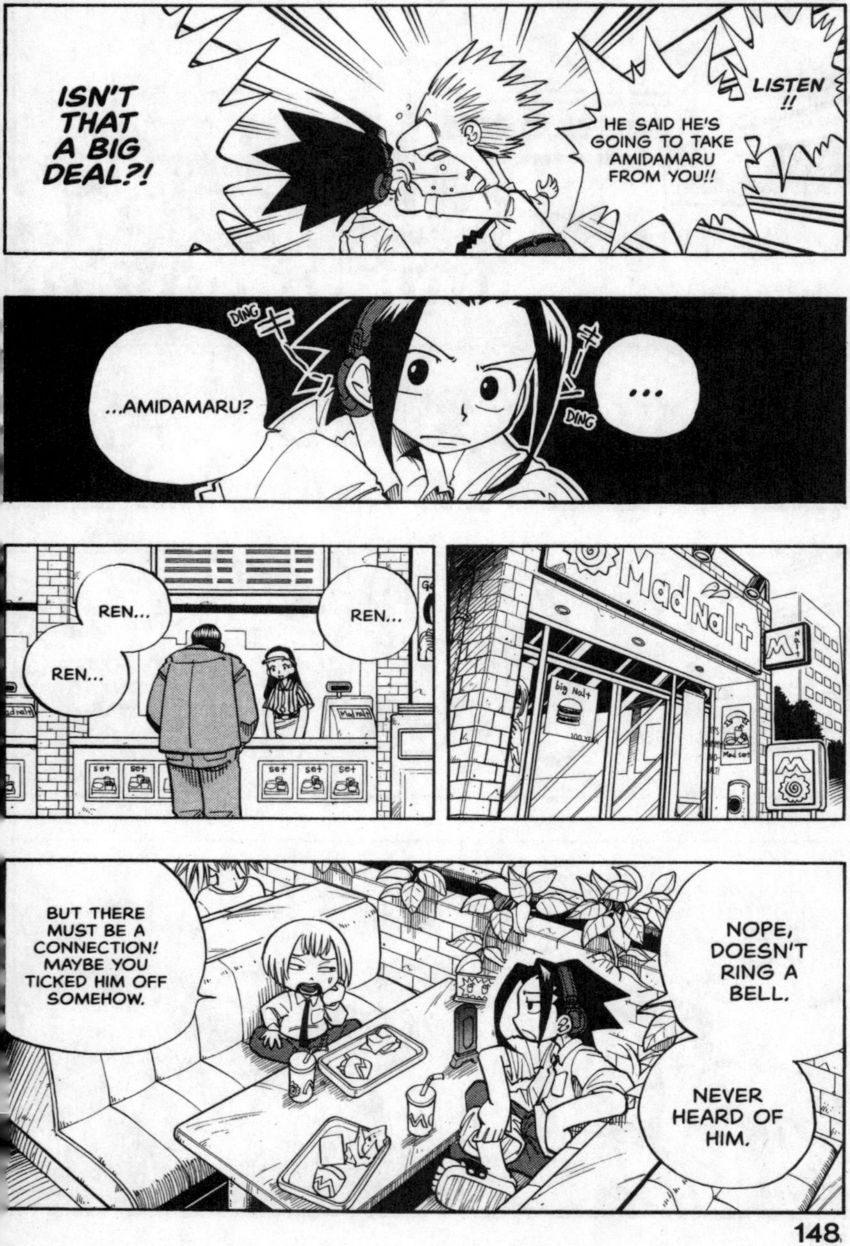
LISTEN!!
HE SAID HE'S GOING TO TAKE AMIDAMARU FROM YOU!!
ISN'T THAT A BIG DEAL?!
...
DING
DING
...AMIDAMARU?
Mad Nalt
big Nalt
REN...
REN...
REN...
NOPE, DOESN'T RING A BELL.
NEVER HEARD OF HIM.
BUT THERE MUST BE A CONNECTION! MAYBE YOU TICKED HIM OFF SOMEHOW.

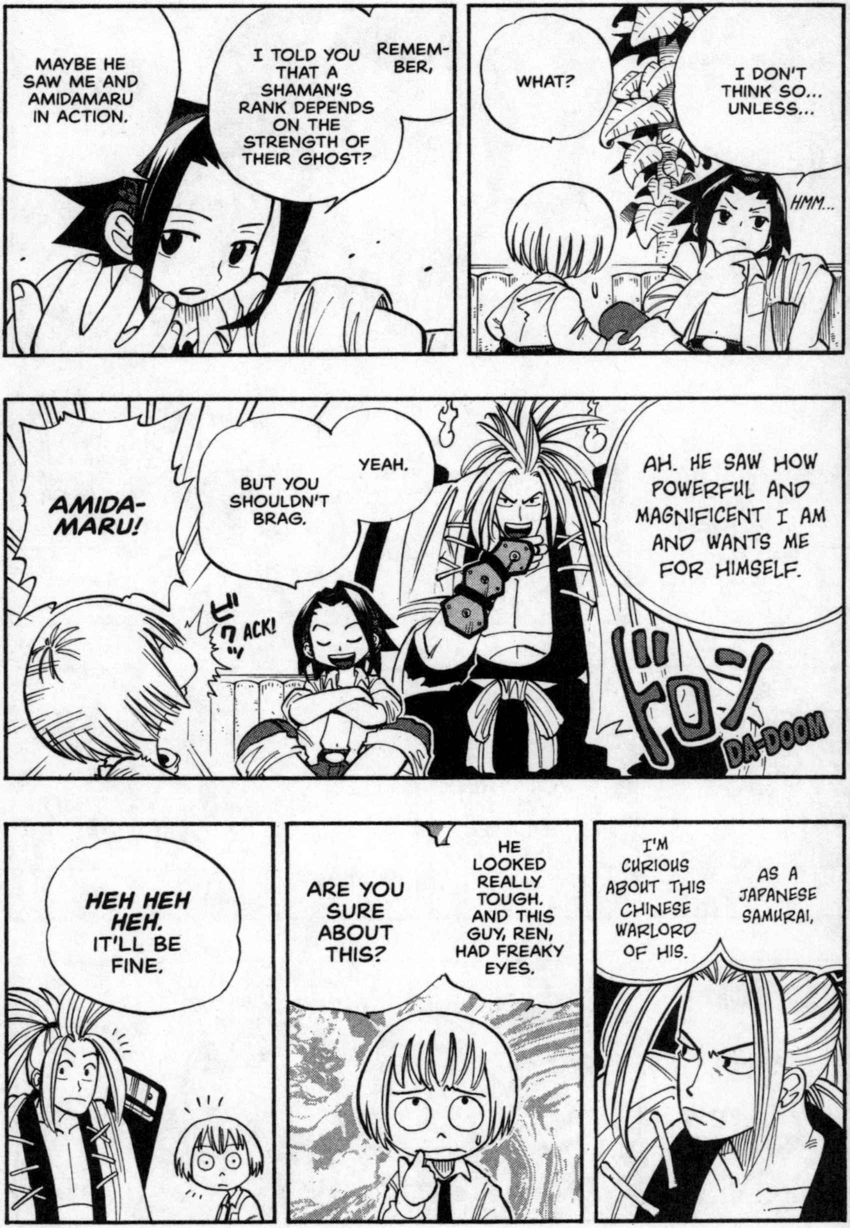
I DON'T THINK SO... UNLESS...
WHAT?
HMM...
REMEMBER,
I TOLD YOU THAT A SHAMAN'S RANK DEPENDS ON THE STRENGTH OF THEIR GHOST?
MAYBE HE SAW ME AND AMIDAMARU IN ACTION.
AH. HE SAW HOW POWERFUL AND MAGNIFICENT I AM AND WANTS ME FOR HIMSELF.
ドローン
DA-DOOM
YEAH.
BUT YOU SHOULDN'T BRAG.
ビクッ
ACK!
AMIDA-MARU!
AS A JAPANESE SAMURAI,
I'M CURIOUS ABOUT THIS CHINESE WARLORD OF HIS.
HE LOOKED REALLY TOUGH. AND THIS GUY, REN, HAD FREAKY EYES.
ARE YOU SURE ABOUT THIS?
HEH HEH HEH. IT'LL BE FINE.

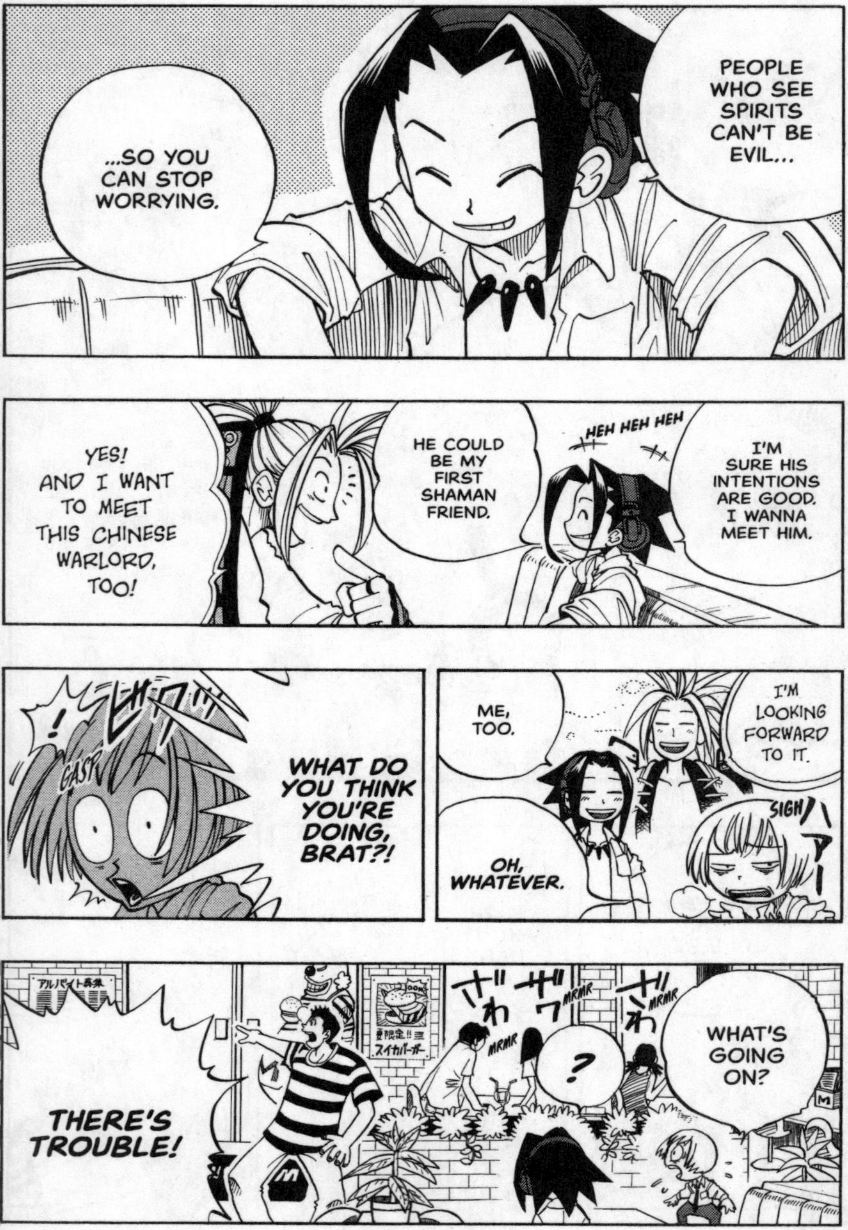
PEOPLE WHO SEE SPIRITS CAN'T BE EVIL...
...SO YOU CAN STOP WORRYING.
HEH HEH HEH
I'M SURE HIS INTENTIONS ARE GOOD. I WANNA MEET HIM.
HE COULD BE MY FIRST SHAMAN FRIEND.
YES! AND I WANT TO MEET THIS CHINESE WARLORD, TOO!
I'M LOOKING FORWARD TO IT.
ME, TOO.
SIGH
OH, WHATEVER.
!
GASP
WHAT DO YOU THINK YOU'RE DOING, BRAT?!
WHAT'S GOING ON?
MRMR
MRMR
MRMR
?
THERE'S TROUBLE!

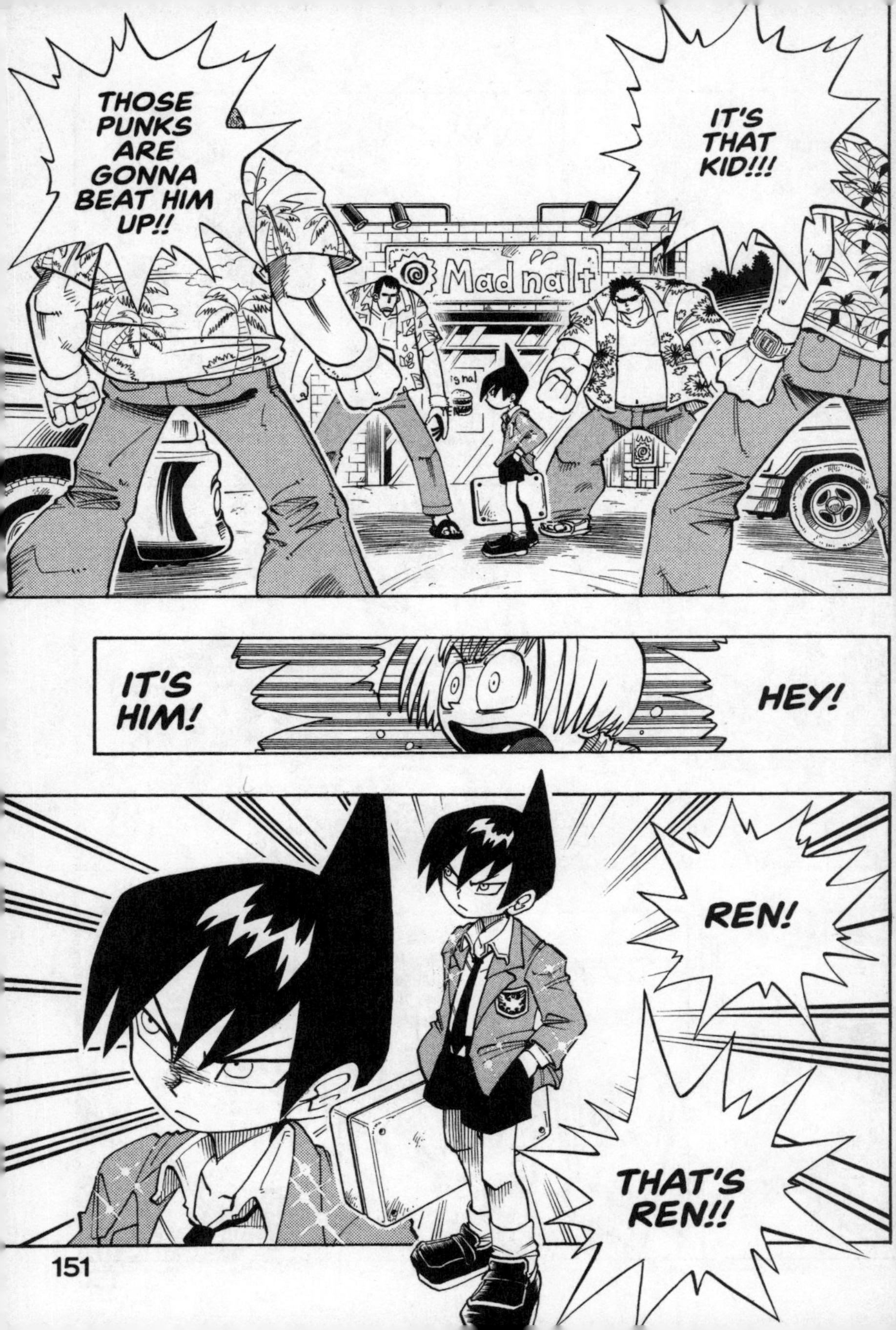
IT'S THAT KID!!!
THOSE PUNKS ARE GONNA BEAT HIM UP!!
Mad nalt
HEY!
IT'S HIM!
REN!
THAT'S REN!!

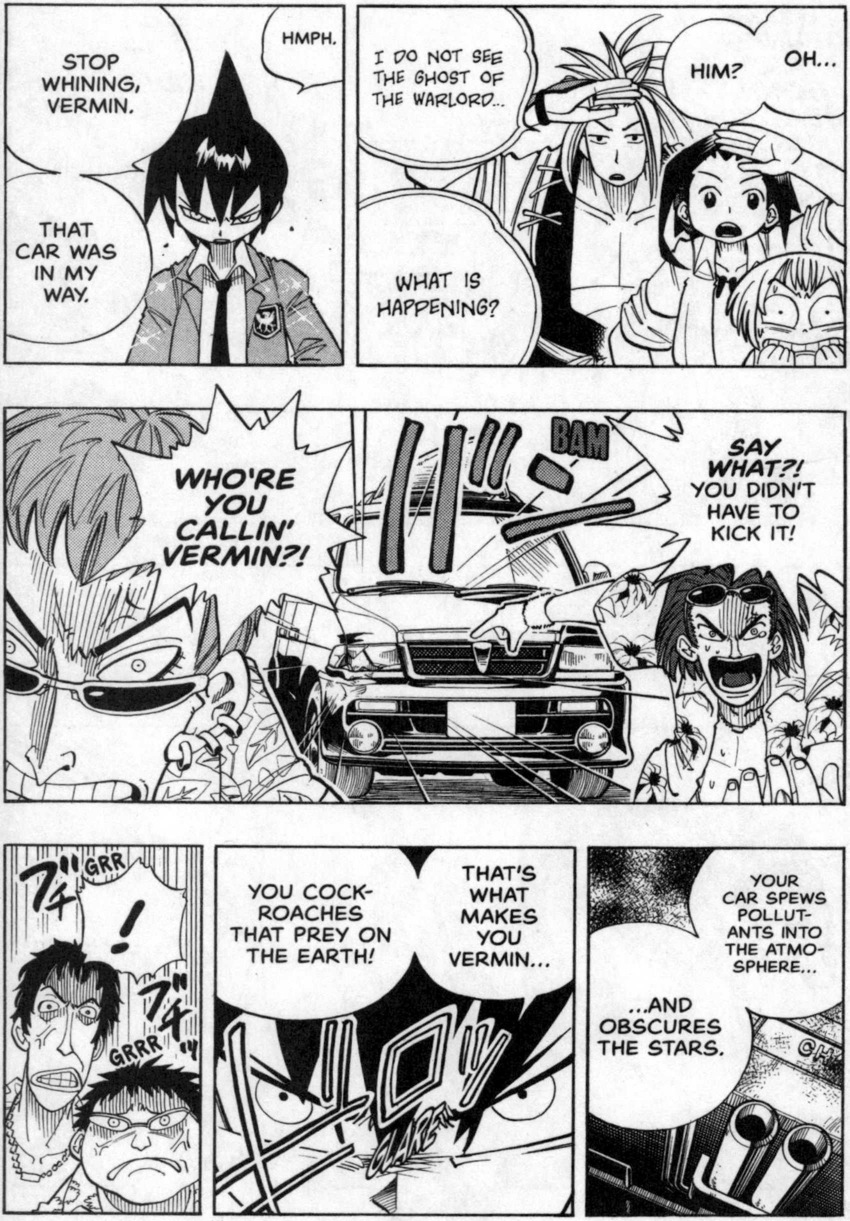
OH...
HIM?
I DO NOT SEE THE GHOST OF THE WARLORD...
WHAT IS HAPPENING?
HMPH.
STOP WHINING, VERMIN.
THAT CAR WAS IN MY WAY.
SAY WHAT?! YOU DIDN'T HAVE TO KICK IT!
BAM
WHO'RE YOU CALLIN' VERMIN?!
YOUR CAR SPEWS POLLUT-ANTS INTO THE ATMO-SPHERE...
...AND OBSCURES THE STARS.
THAT'S WHAT MAKES YOU VERMIN...
YOU COCK-ROACHES THAT PREY ON THE EARTH!
GLARE
GRR
!
GRRR

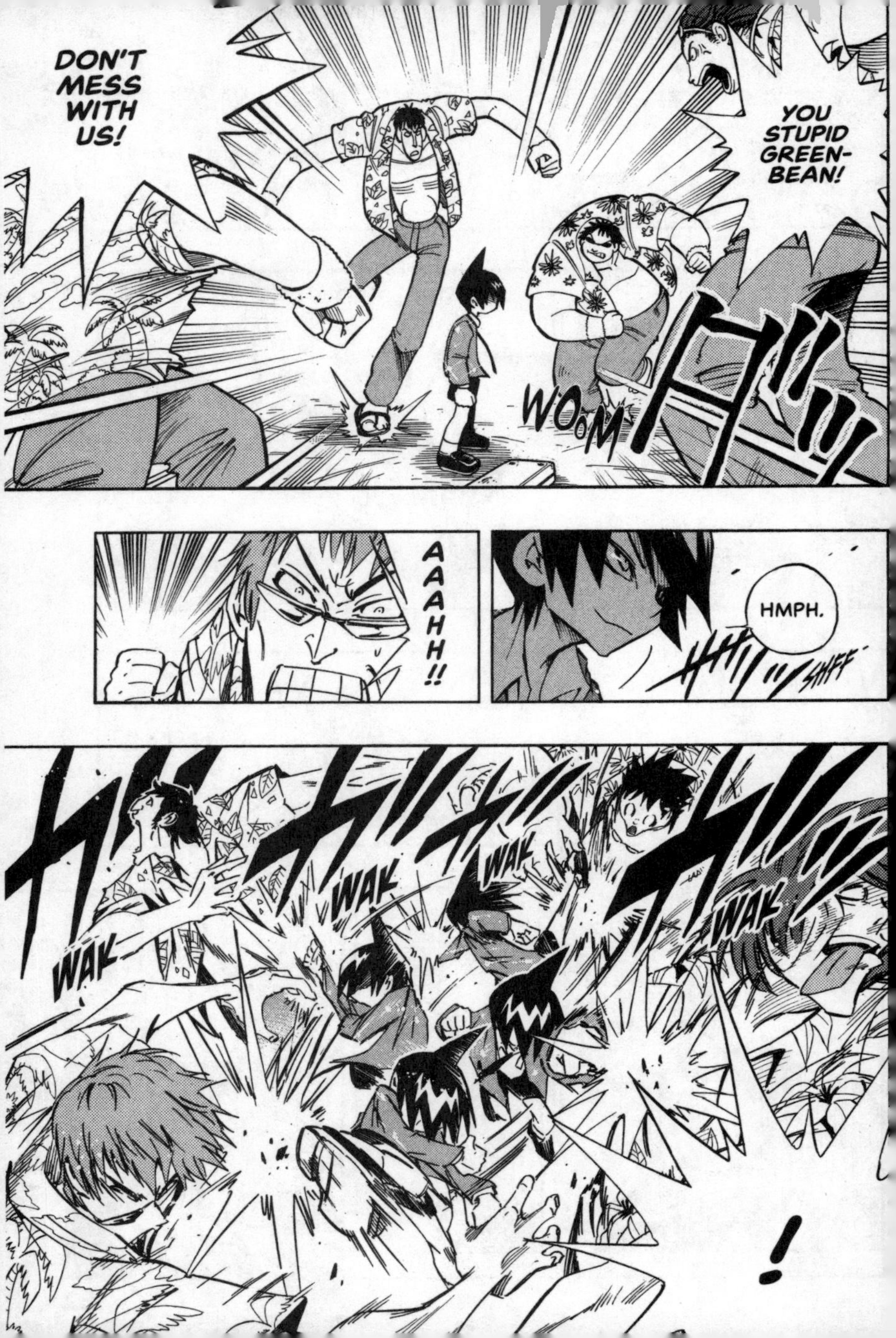
YOU STUPID GREEN-BEAN!
DON'T MESS WITH US!
WOOM
HMPH.
SHFF
AAAAHH!!
WAK
WAK
WAK
WAK
!

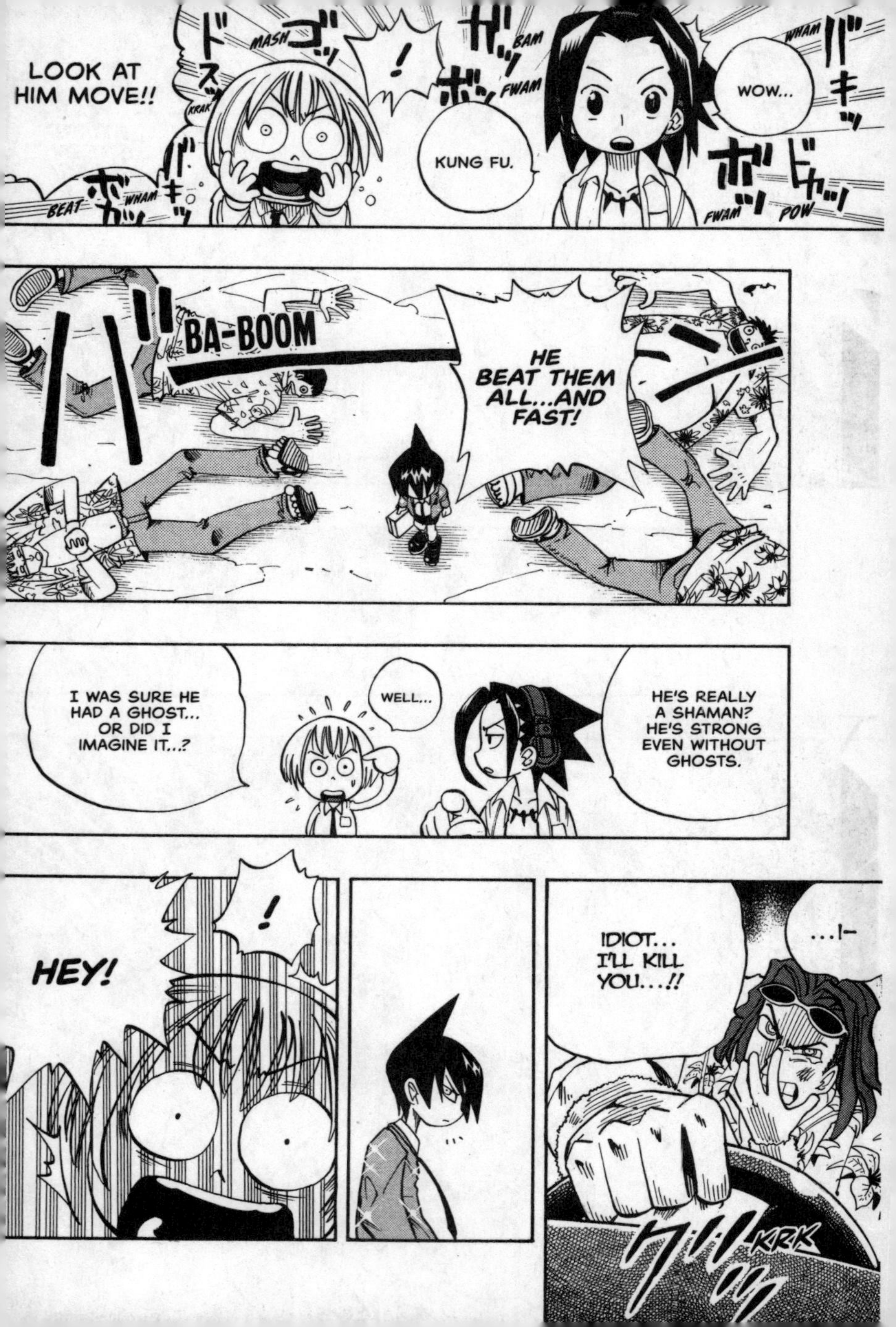
WHAM
WOW...
FWAM
POW
KUNG FU.
BAM
FWAM
!
MASH
KRAK
LOOK AT HIM MOVE!!
BEAT
WHAM
HE BEAT THEM ALL...AND FAST!
BA-BOOM
HE'S REALLY A SHAMAN? HE'S STRONG EVEN WITHOUT GHOSTS.
WELL...
I WAS SURE HE HAD A GHOST... OR DID I IMAGINE IT...?
...!–
IDIOT... I'LL KILL YOU...!!
KRK
!
HEY!

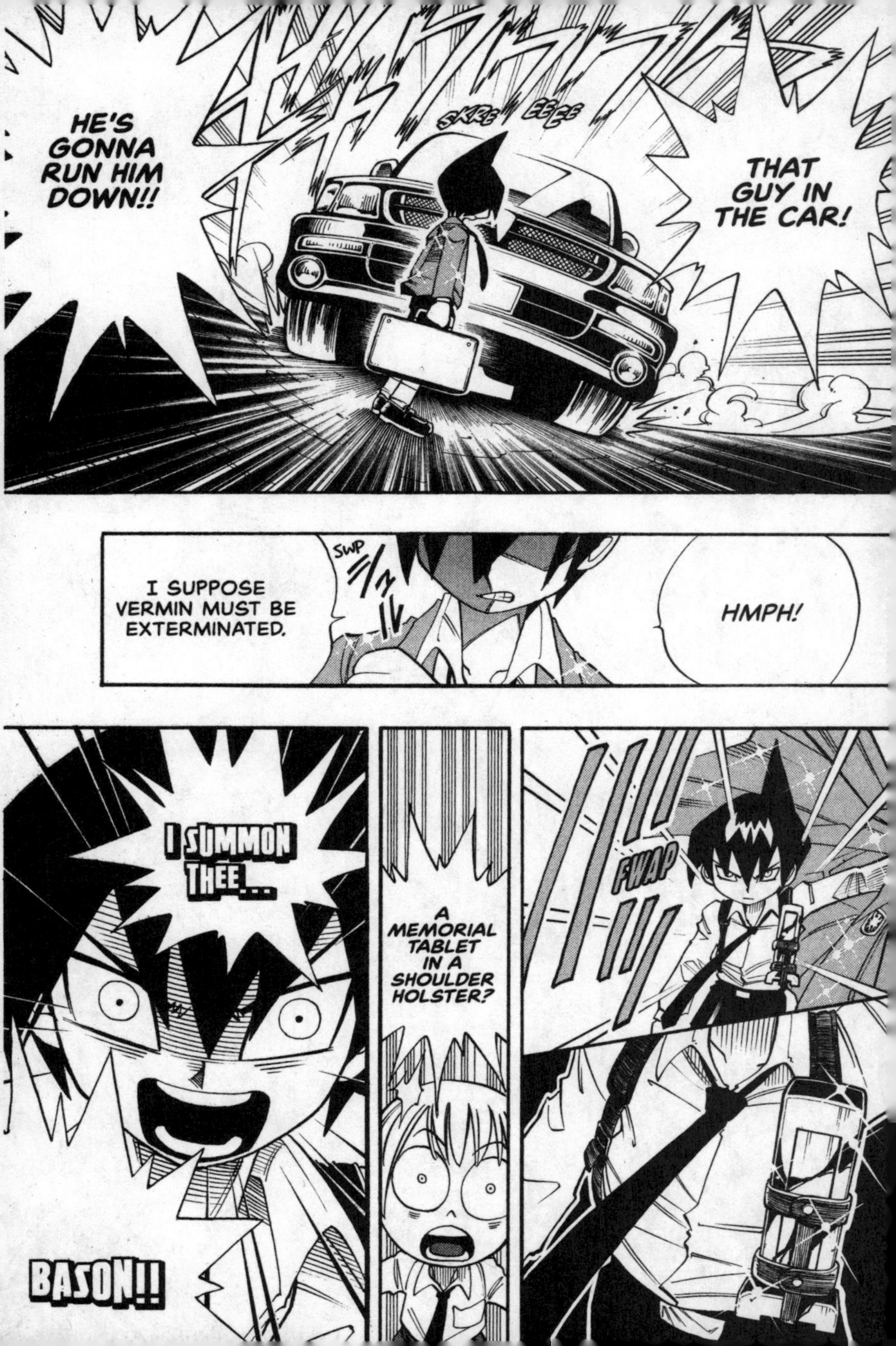
THAT GUY IN THE CAR!
SKREE EEEE
HE'S GONNA RUN HIM DOWN!!
HMPH!
SWP
I SUPPOSE VERMIN MUST BE EXTERMINATED.
FWAP
A MEMORIAL TABLET IN A SHOULDER HOLSTER?
I SUMMON THEE...
BASON!!!

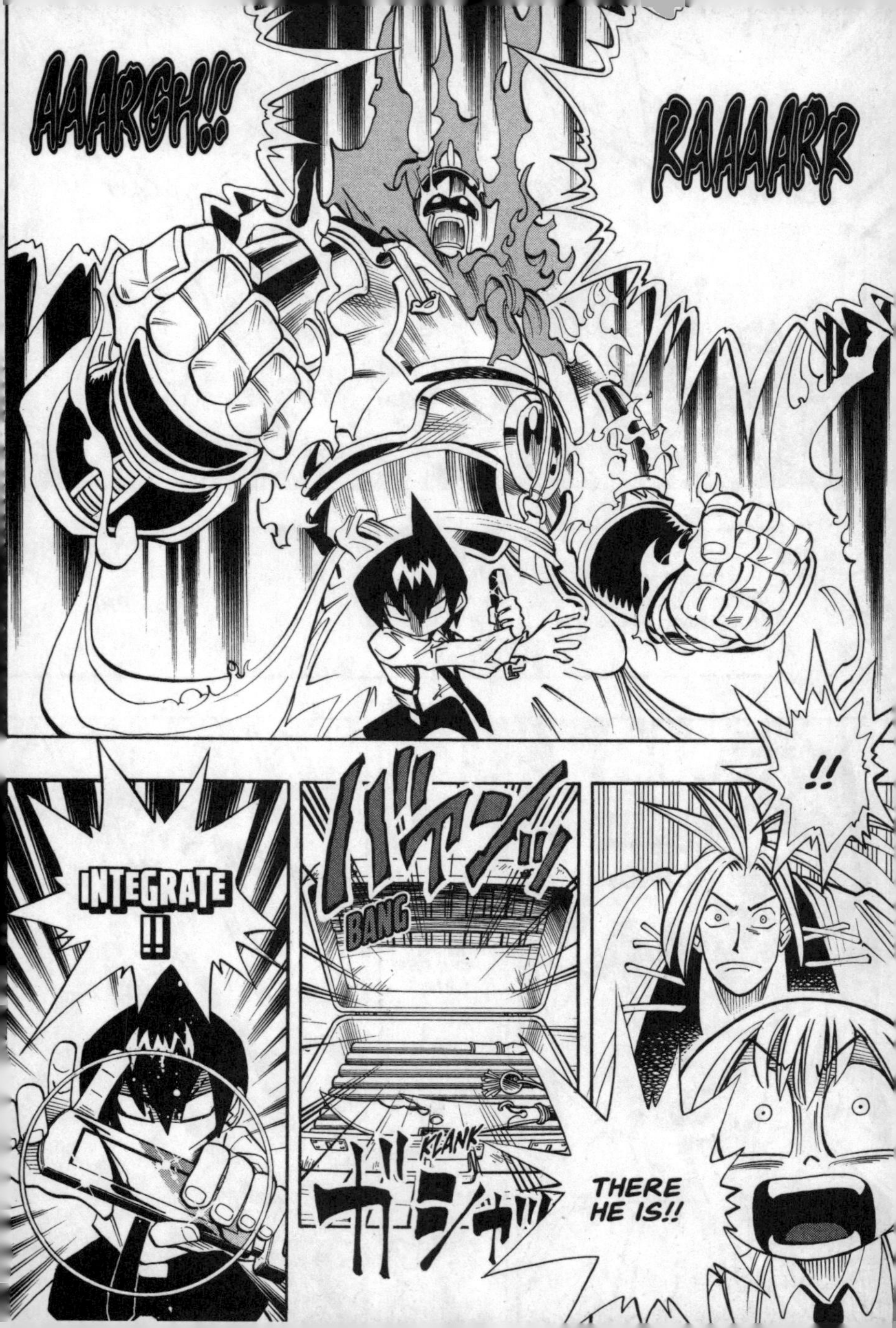
RAAAARR
AAARGH!!
!!
THERE HE IS!!
バァン!!
BANG
ガシャ!!
KLANK
INTEGRATE !!

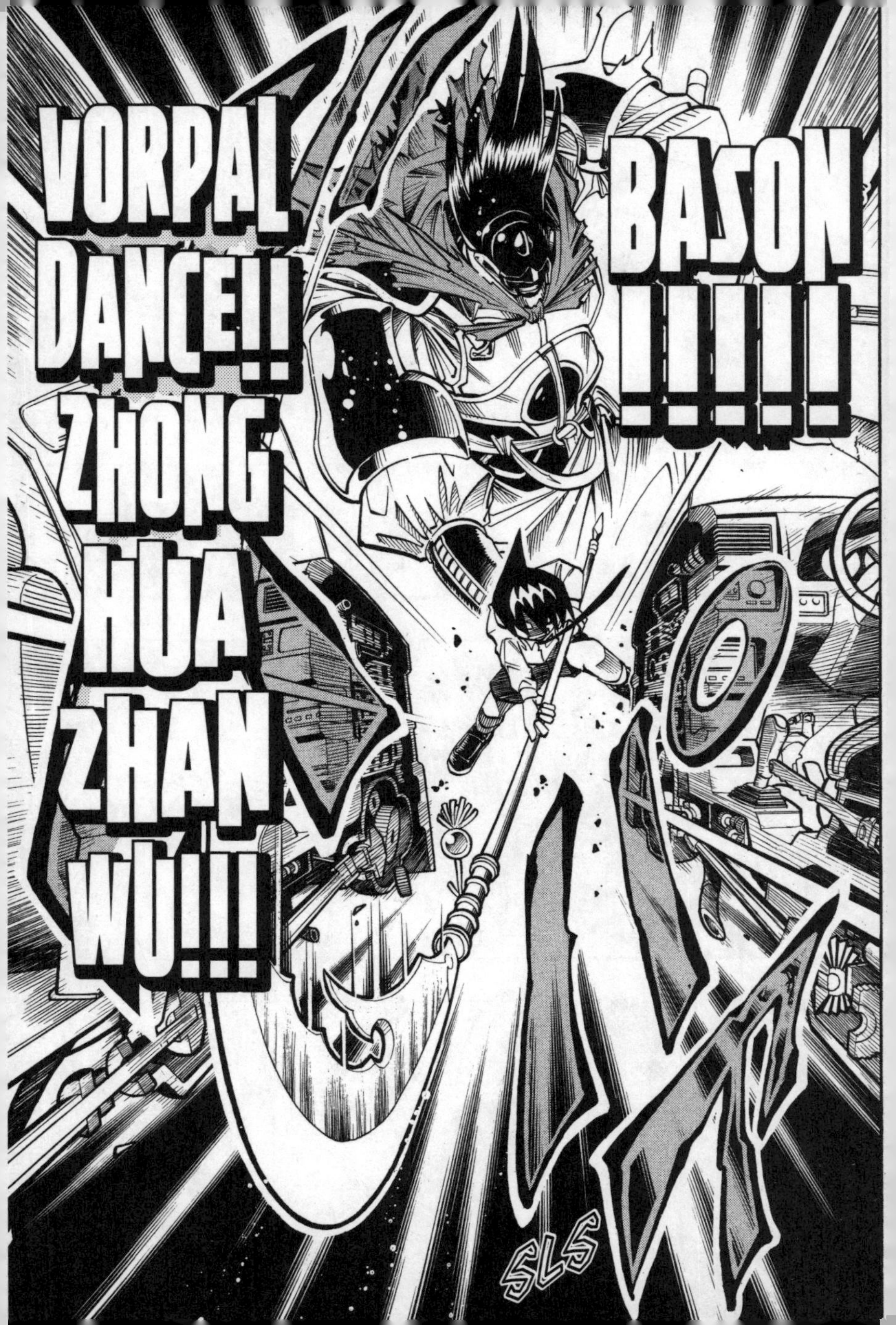
BASON!!!!!
VORPAL DANCE!! ZHONG HUA ZHAN WU!!!
SLS

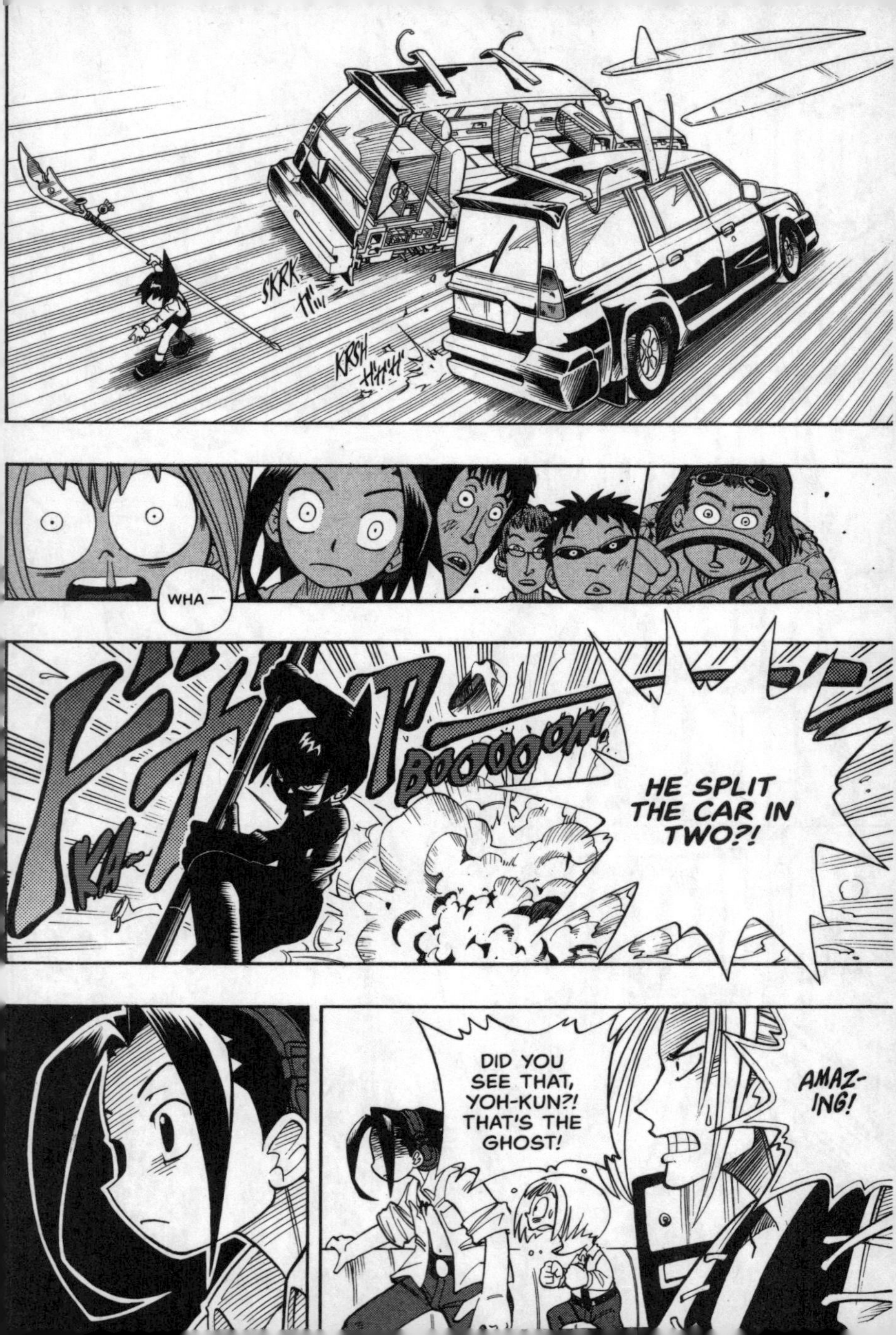
SKRK
KRSH
WHA—
HE SPLIT THE CAR IN TWO?!
BOOOOOM
KA-
AMAZ-ING!
DID YOU SEE THAT, YOH-KUN?! THAT'S THE GHOST!

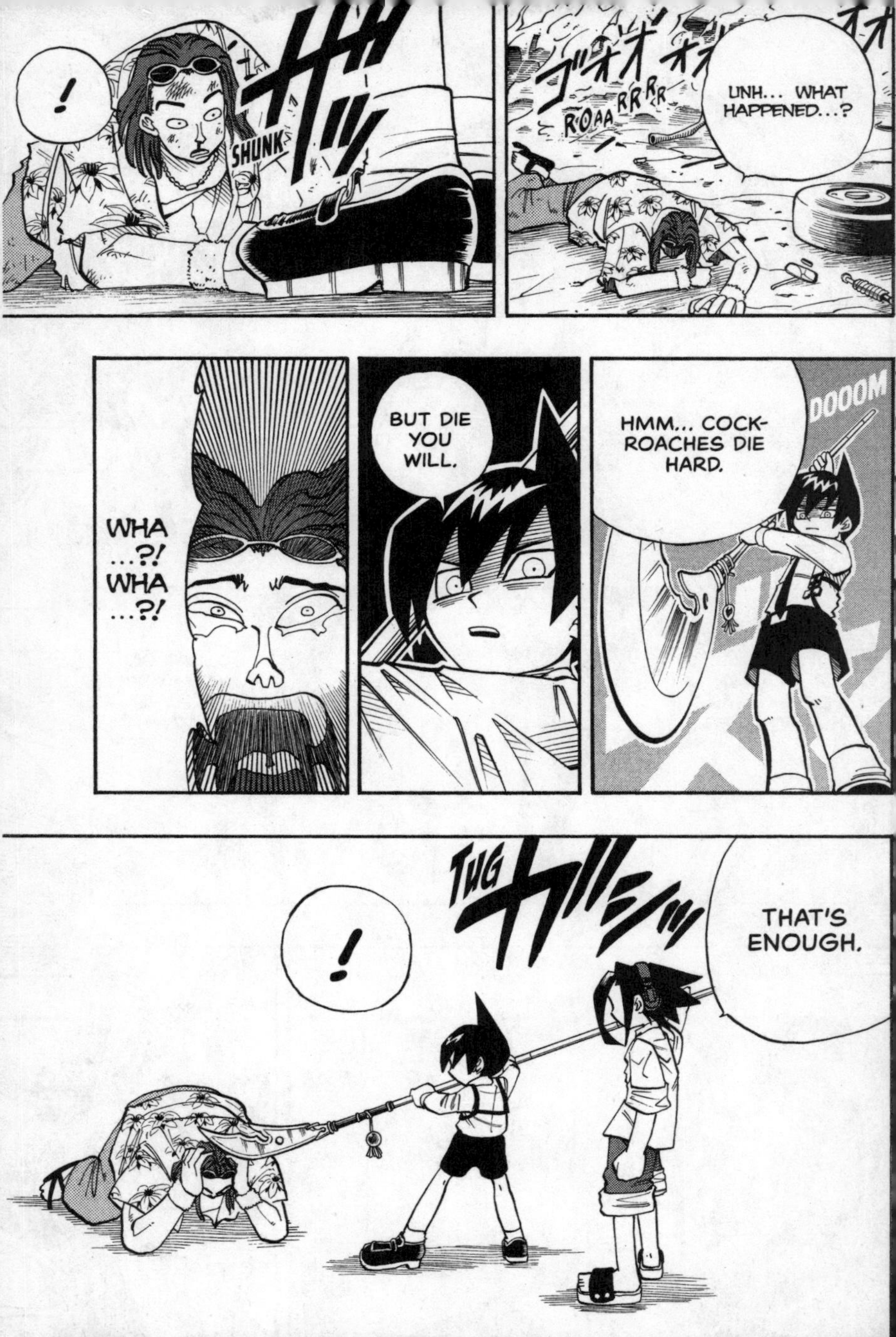
UNH... WHAT HAPPENED...?
ROAARRRR
!
SHUNK
DOOOM
HMM... COCK-ROACHES DIE HARD.
BUT DIE YOU WILL.
WHA ...?! WHA ...?!
THAT'S ENOUGH.
TUG
!

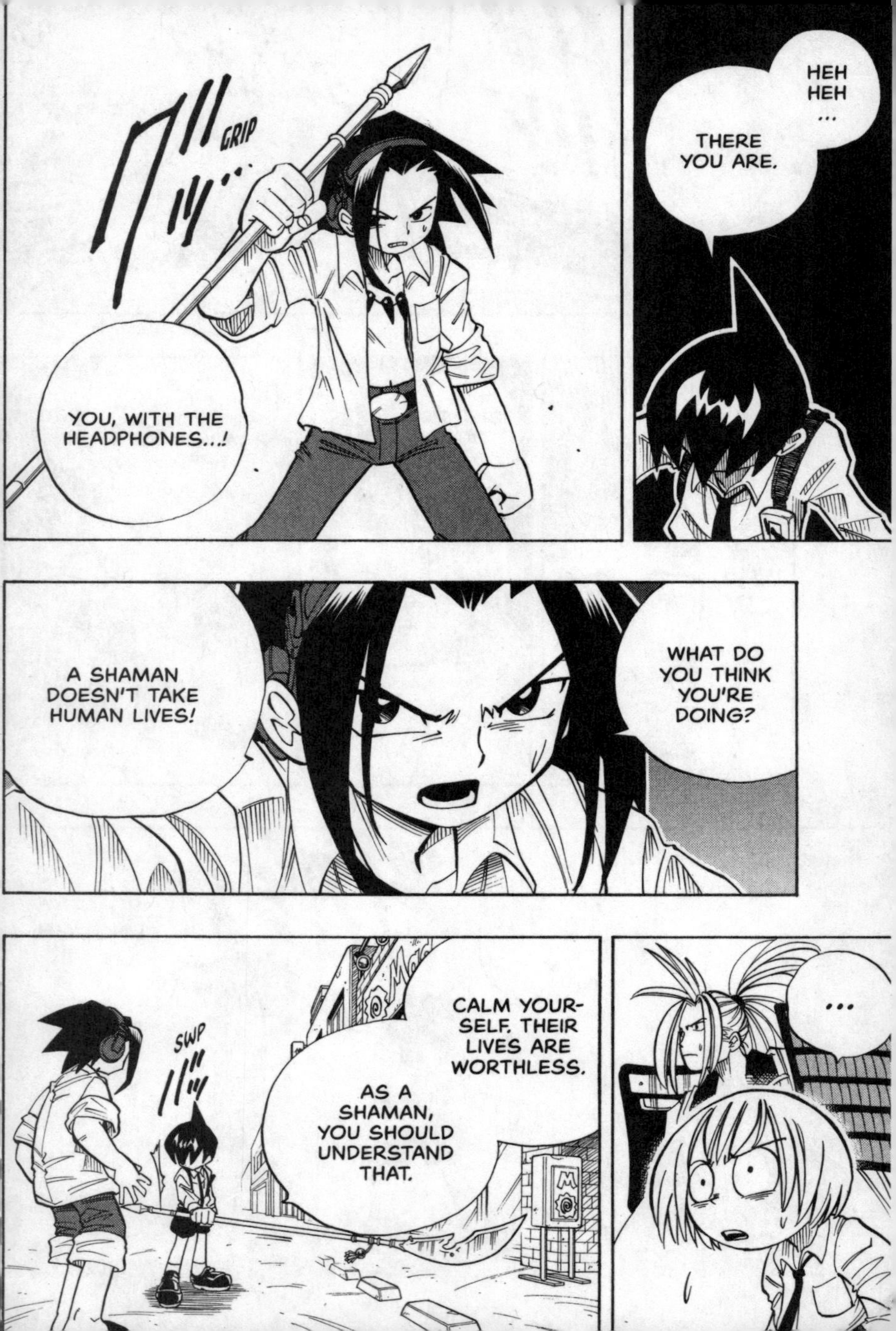
HEH HEH ...
THERE YOU ARE.
GRIP
YOU, WITH THE HEADPHONES...!
WHAT DO YOU THINK YOU'RE DOING?
A SHAMAN DOESN'T TAKE HUMAN LIVES!
...
CALM YOURSELF. THEIR LIVES ARE WORTHLESS.
AS A SHAMAN, YOU SHOULD UNDERSTAND THAT.
SWP

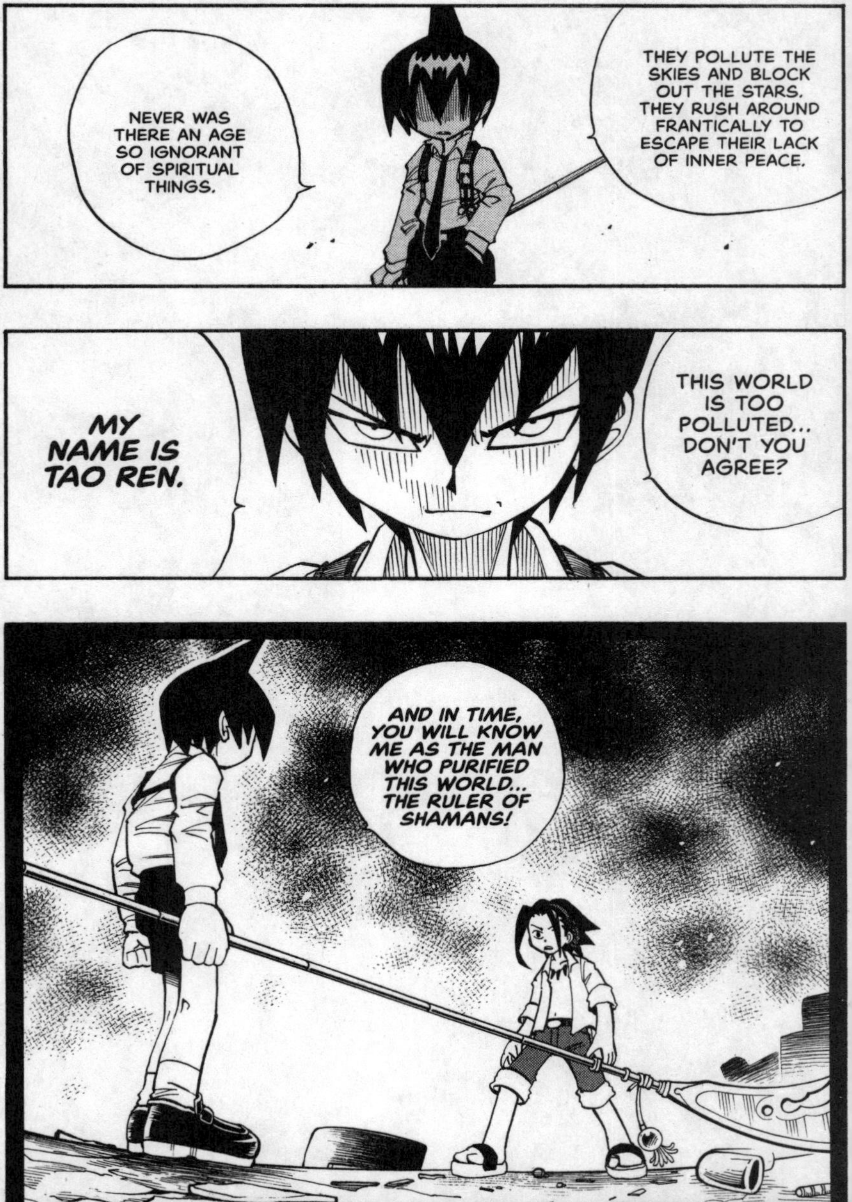
THEY POLLUTE THE SKIES AND BLOCK OUT THE STARS. THEY RUSH AROUND FRANTICALLY TO ESCAPE THEIR LACK OF INNER PEACE.
NEVER WAS THERE AN AGE SO IGNORANT OF SPIRITUAL THINGS.
THIS WORLD IS TOO POLLUTED... DON'T YOU AGREE?
MY NAME IS TAO REN.
AND IN TIME, YOU WILL KNOW ME AS THE MAN WHO PURIFIED THIS WORLD... THE RULER OF SHAMANS!

SHAMAN
KING
1

**Memorial
Tablet**

Chapter 7: Shaman Vs. Shaman

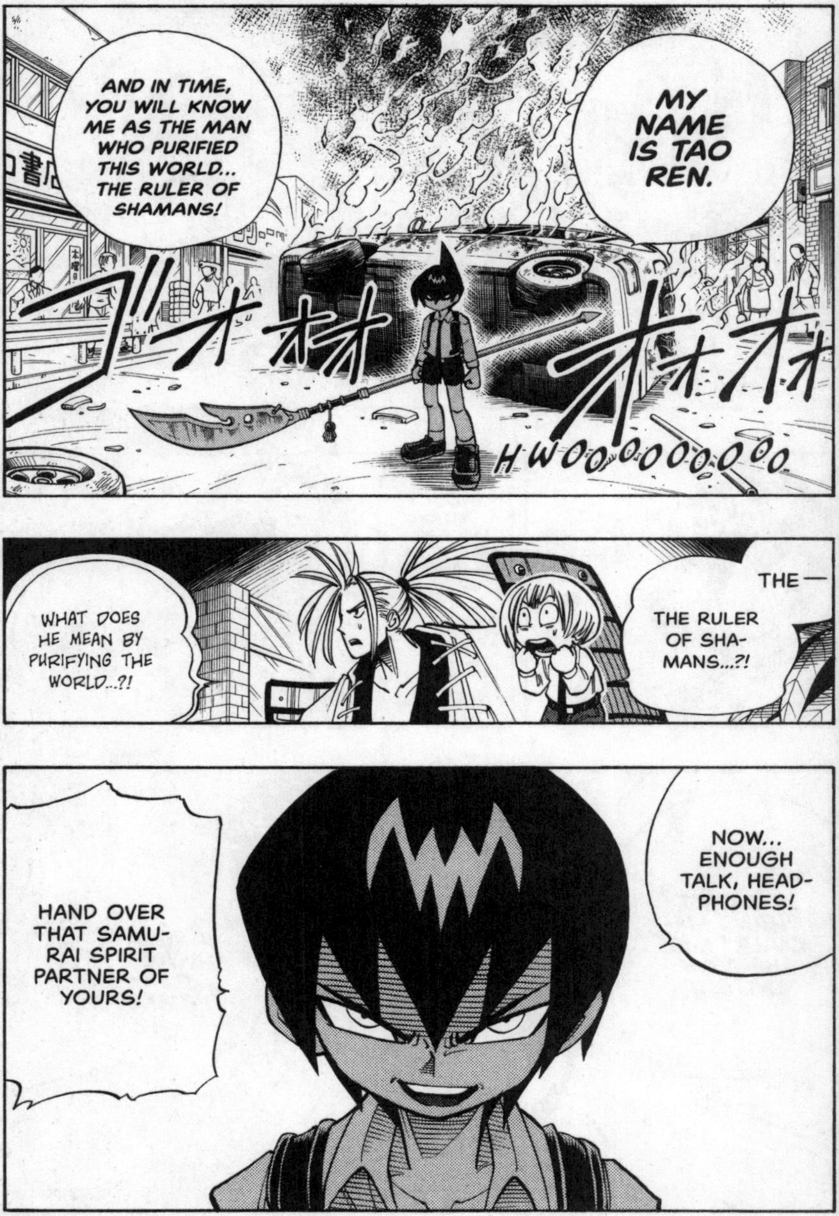

MY NAME IS TAO REN.
AND IN TIME, YOU WILL KNOW ME AS THE MAN WHO PURIFIED THIS WORLD... THE RULER OF SHAMANS!
HWOOOOOOOOOO
THE—
THE RULER OF SHA-MANS...?!
WHAT DOES HE MEAN BY PURIFYING THE WORLD...?!
NOW... ENOUGH TALK, HEAD-PHONES!
HAND OVER THAT SAMU-RAI SPIRIT PARTNER OF YOURS!

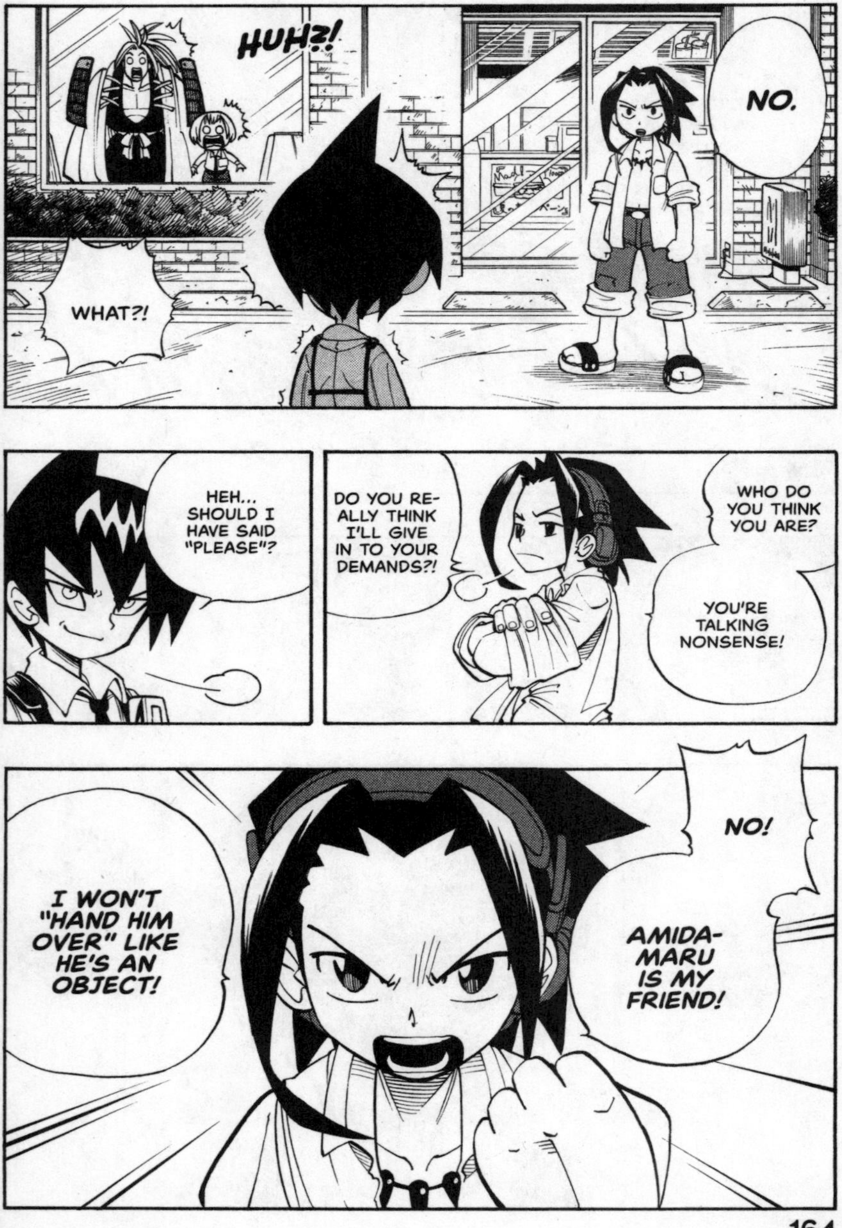
NO.
HUH?!
WHAT?!
WHO DO YOU THINK YOU ARE?
YOU'RE TALKING NONSENSE!
DO YOU REALLY THINK I'LL GIVE IN TO YOUR DEMANDS?!
HEH... SHOULD I HAVE SAID "PLEASE"?
NO!
AMIDAMARU IS MY FRIEND!
I WON'T "HAND HIM OVER" LIKE HE'S AN OBJECT!

Chapter 7:

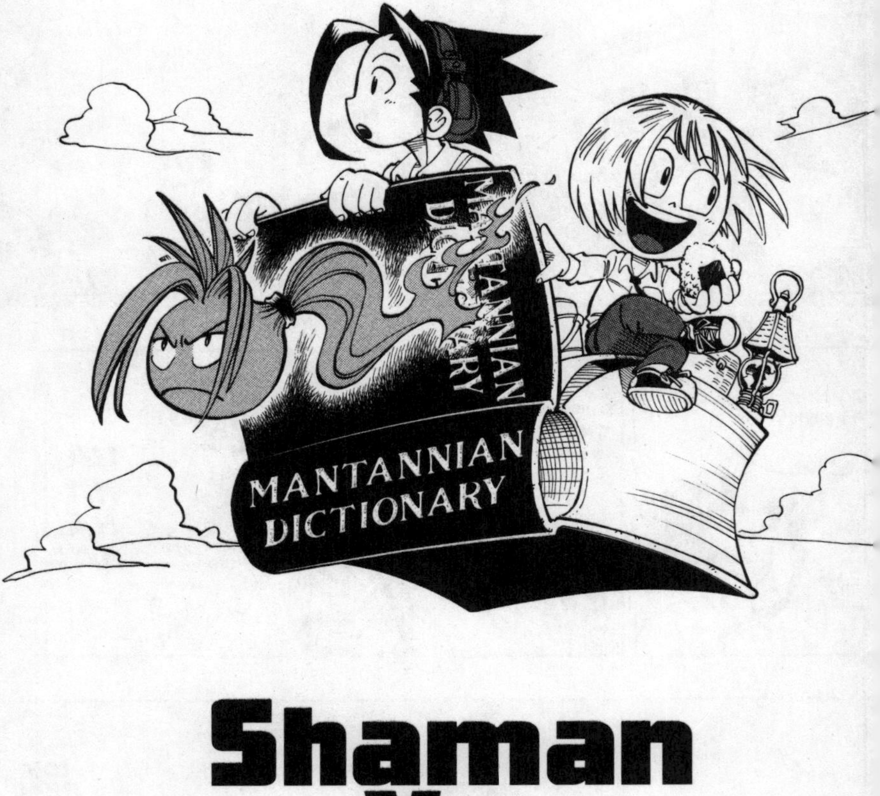
MANTANNIAN
DICTIONARY

Shaman Vs. Shaman

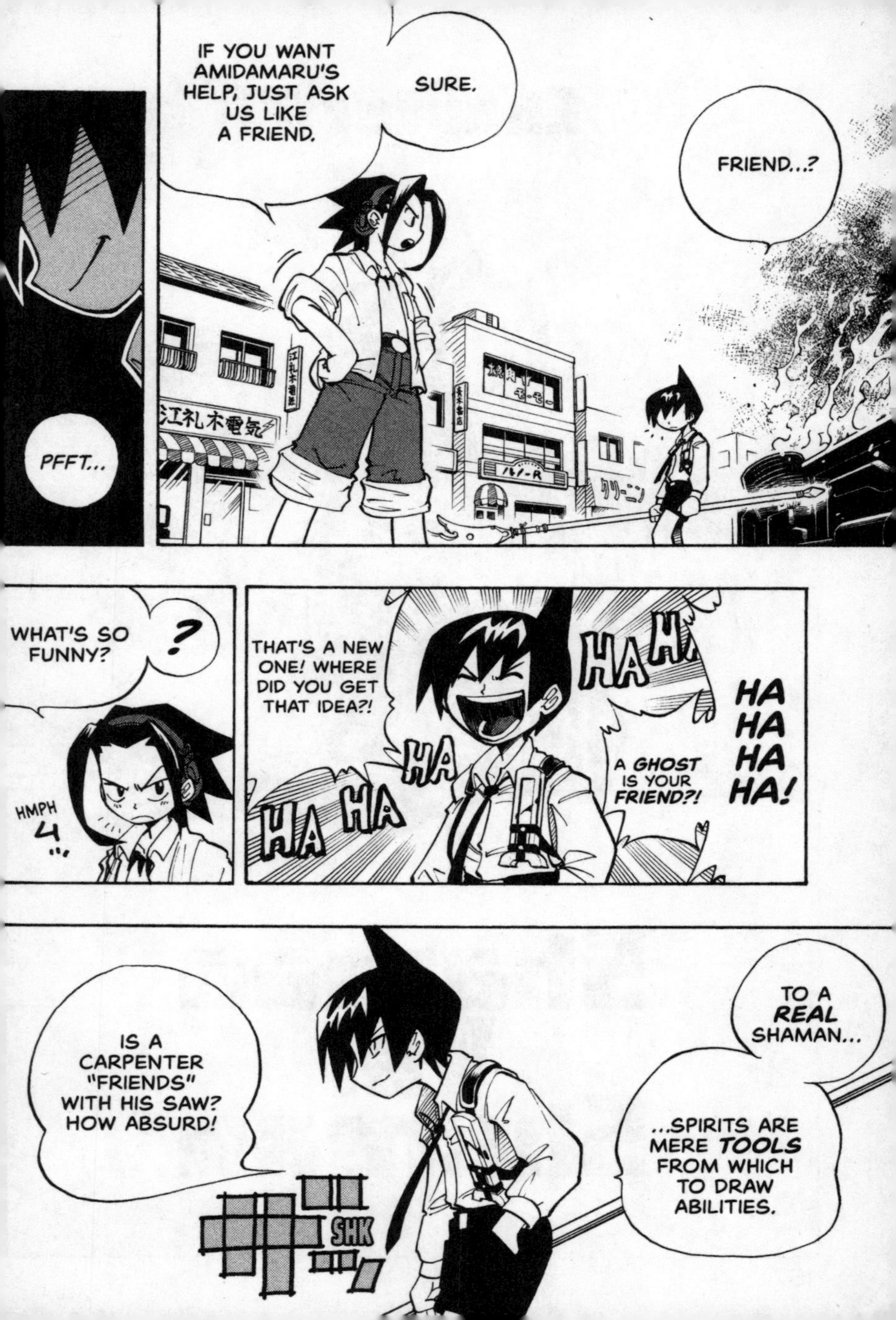
SURE.
IF YOU WANT AMIDAMARU'S HELP, JUST ASK US LIKE A FRIEND.
FRIEND...?
江礼木電気
PFFT...
HA HA
THAT'S A NEW ONE! WHERE DID YOU GET THAT IDEA?!
HA HA HA HA!
A *GHOST* IS YOUR *FRIEND?!*
HA
HA HA
WHAT'S SO FUNNY?
?
HMPH
TO A *REAL* SHAMAN...
...SPIRITS ARE MERE *TOOLS* FROM WHICH TO DRAW ABILITIES.
IS A CARPENTER "FRIENDS" WITH HIS SAW? HOW ABSURD!
SHK

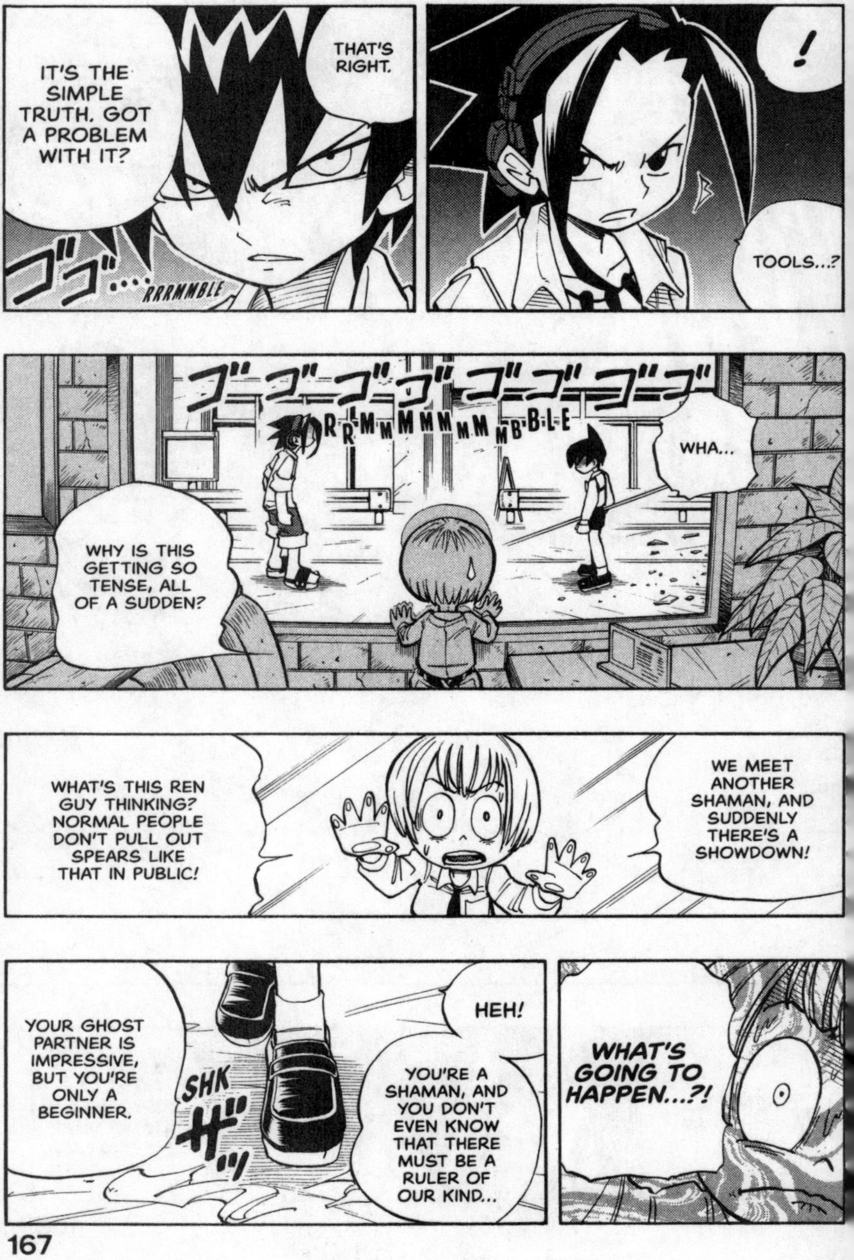
!
TOOLS...?
THAT'S RIGHT.
IT'S THE SIMPLE TRUTH. GOT A PROBLEM WITH IT?
ゴゴ....
RRRMMBLE
ゴゴゴゴゴゴゴゴ
RRMMMMMMMMMBBLE
WHA...
WHY IS THIS GETTING SO TENSE, ALL OF A SUDDEN?
WE MEET ANOTHER SHAMAN, AND SUDDENLY THERE'S A SHOWDOWN!
WHAT'S THIS REN GUY THINKING? NORMAL PEOPLE DON'T PULL OUT SPEARS LIKE THAT IN PUBLIC!
WHAT'S GOING TO HAPPEN...?!
HEH!
YOU'RE A SHAMAN, AND YOU DON'T EVEN KNOW THAT THERE MUST BE A RULER OF OUR KIND...
YOUR GHOST PARTNER IS IMPRESSIVE, BUT YOU'RE ONLY A BEGINNER.
SHK
ザッ

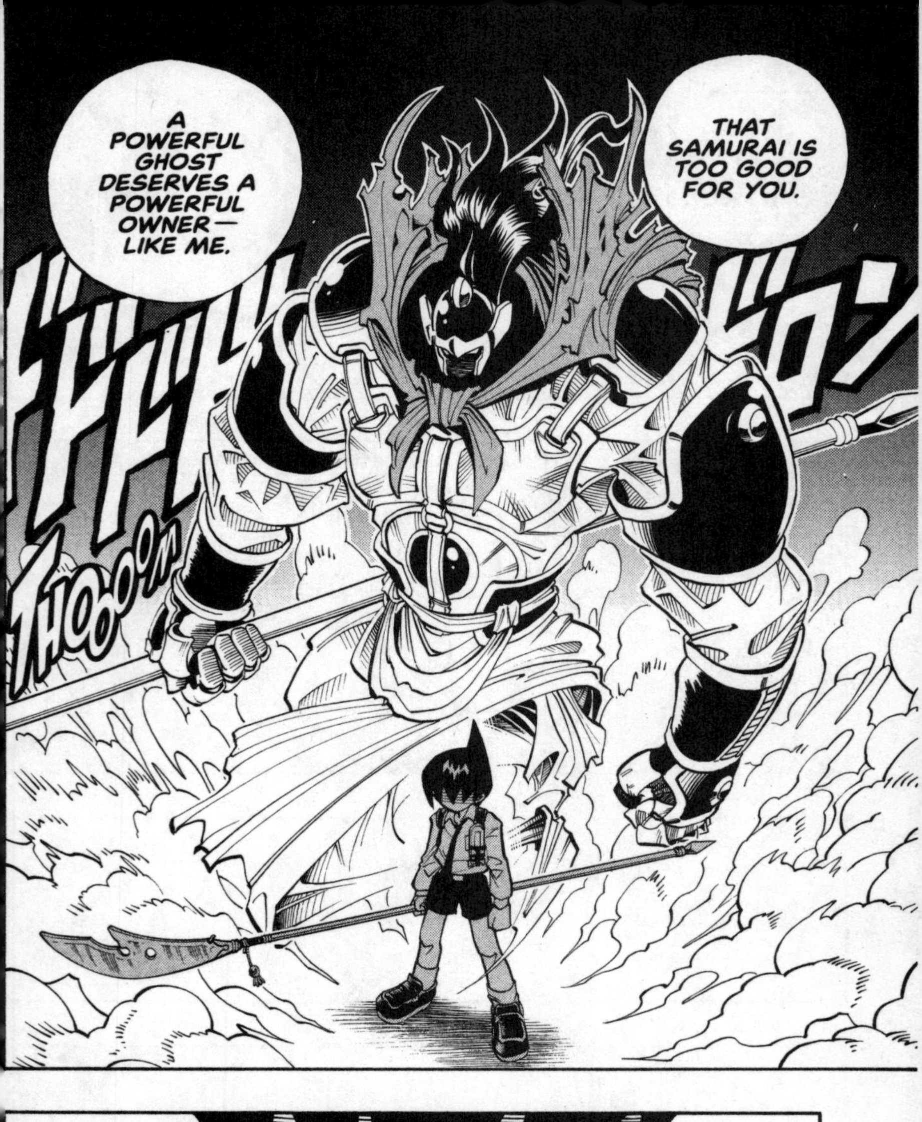
THAT SAMURAI IS TOO GOOD FOR YOU.
A POWERFUL GHOST DESERVES A POWERFUL OWNER— LIKE ME.
THOOOOM

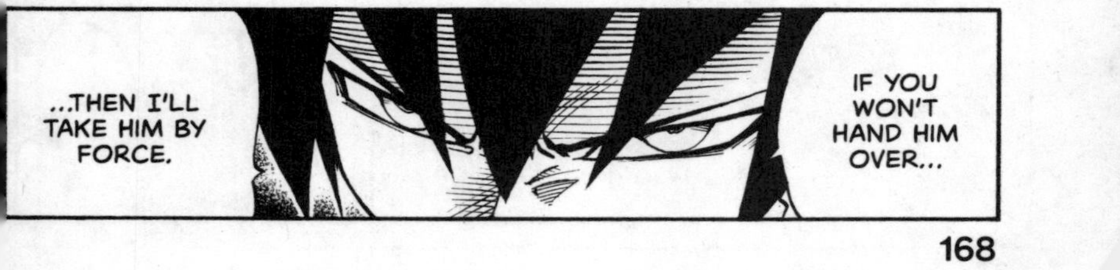
IF YOU WON'T HAND HIM OVER...
...THEN I'LL TAKE HIM BY FORCE.

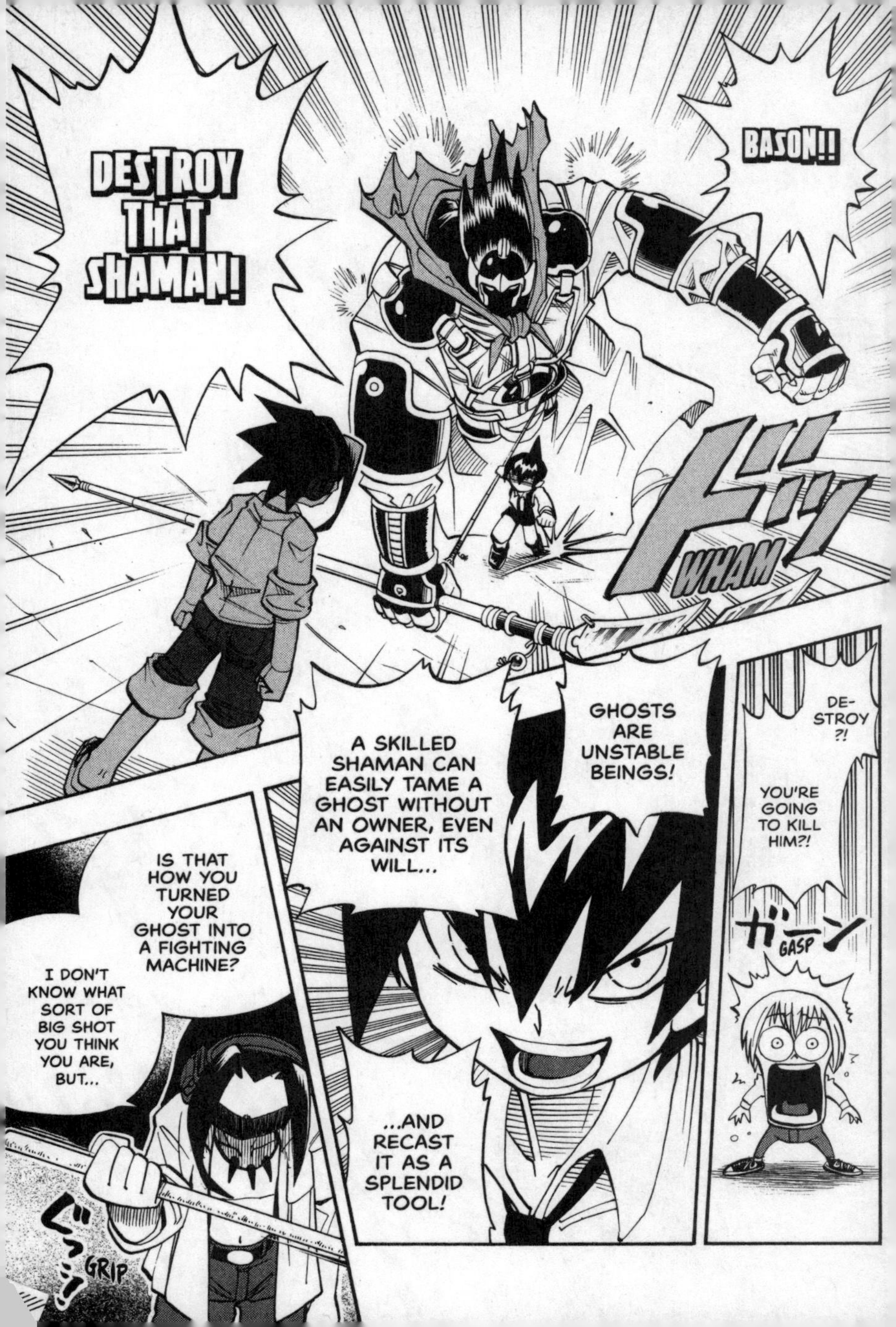
BASON!!
DESTROY THAT SHAMAN!
ドッ
WHAM!!
DE-STROY?!
YOU'RE GOING TO KILL HIM?!
ガーン
GASP
GHOSTS ARE UNSTABLE BEINGS!
A SKILLED SHAMAN CAN EASILY TAME A GHOST WITHOUT AN OWNER, EVEN AGAINST ITS WILL...
...AND RECAST IT AS A SPLENDID TOOL!
IS THAT HOW YOU TURNED YOUR GHOST INTO A FIGHTING MACHINE?
I DON'T KNOW WHAT SORT OF BIG SHOT YOU THINK YOU ARE, BUT...
ぐっ
GRIP

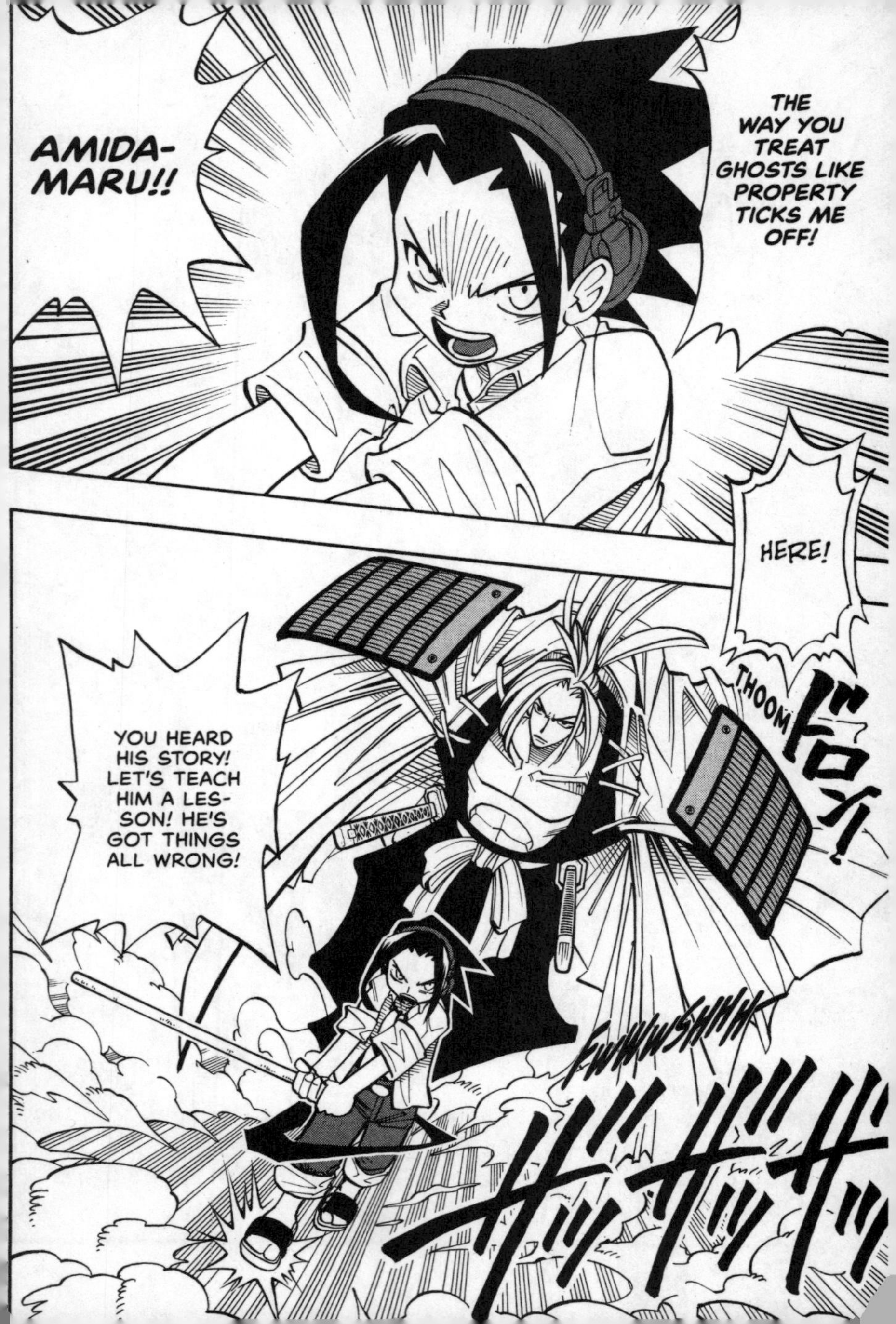
THE WAY YOU TREAT GHOSTS LIKE PROPERTY TICKS ME OFF!
AMIDA-MARU!!
HERE!
THOOM
ドロン!
YOU HEARD HIS STORY! LET'S TEACH HIM A LES-SON! HE'S GOT THINGS ALL WRONG!
ザッザッザッ

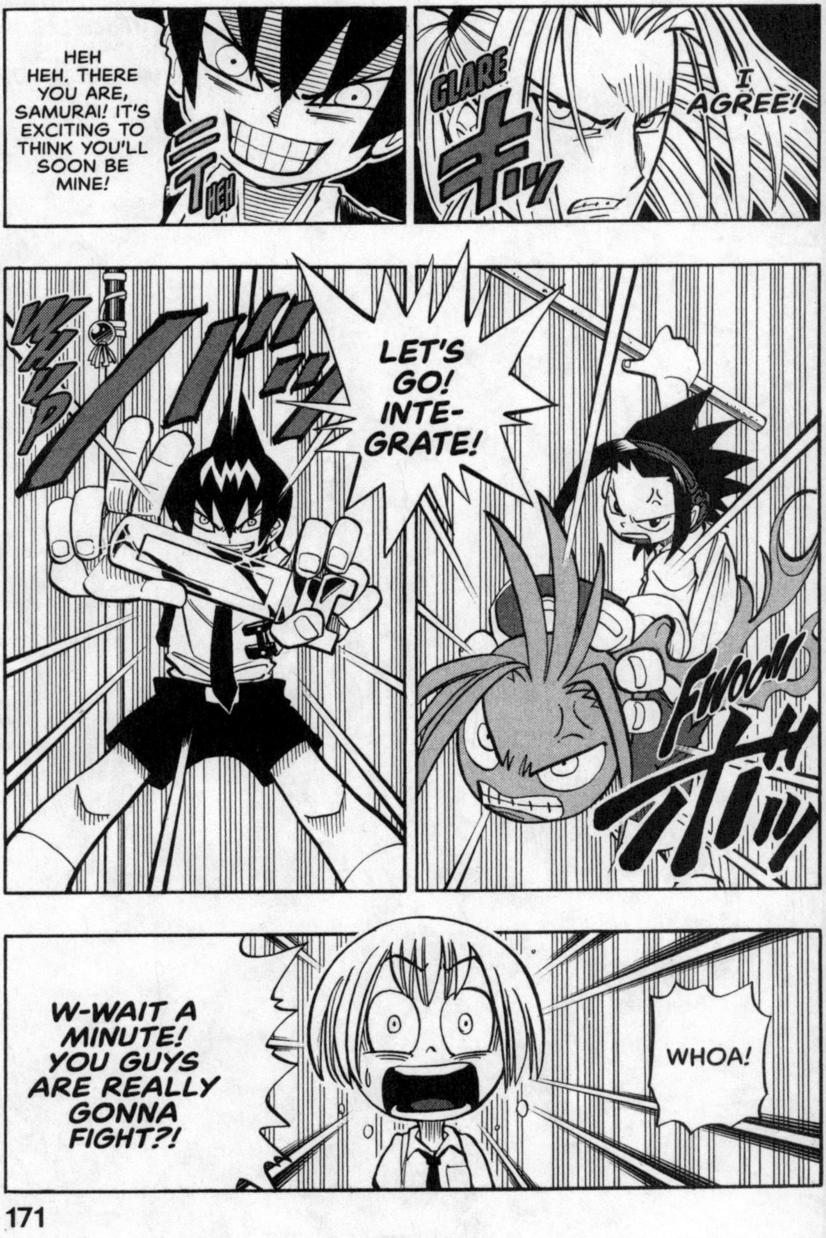
GLARE
I AGREE!
HEH HEH. THERE YOU ARE, SAMURAI! IT'S EXCITING TO THINK YOU'LL SOON BE MINE!
HEH
FWOOM
LET'S GO! INTE-GRATE!
WHUP
WHOA!
W-WAIT A MINUTE! YOU GUYS ARE REALLY GONNA FIGHT?!

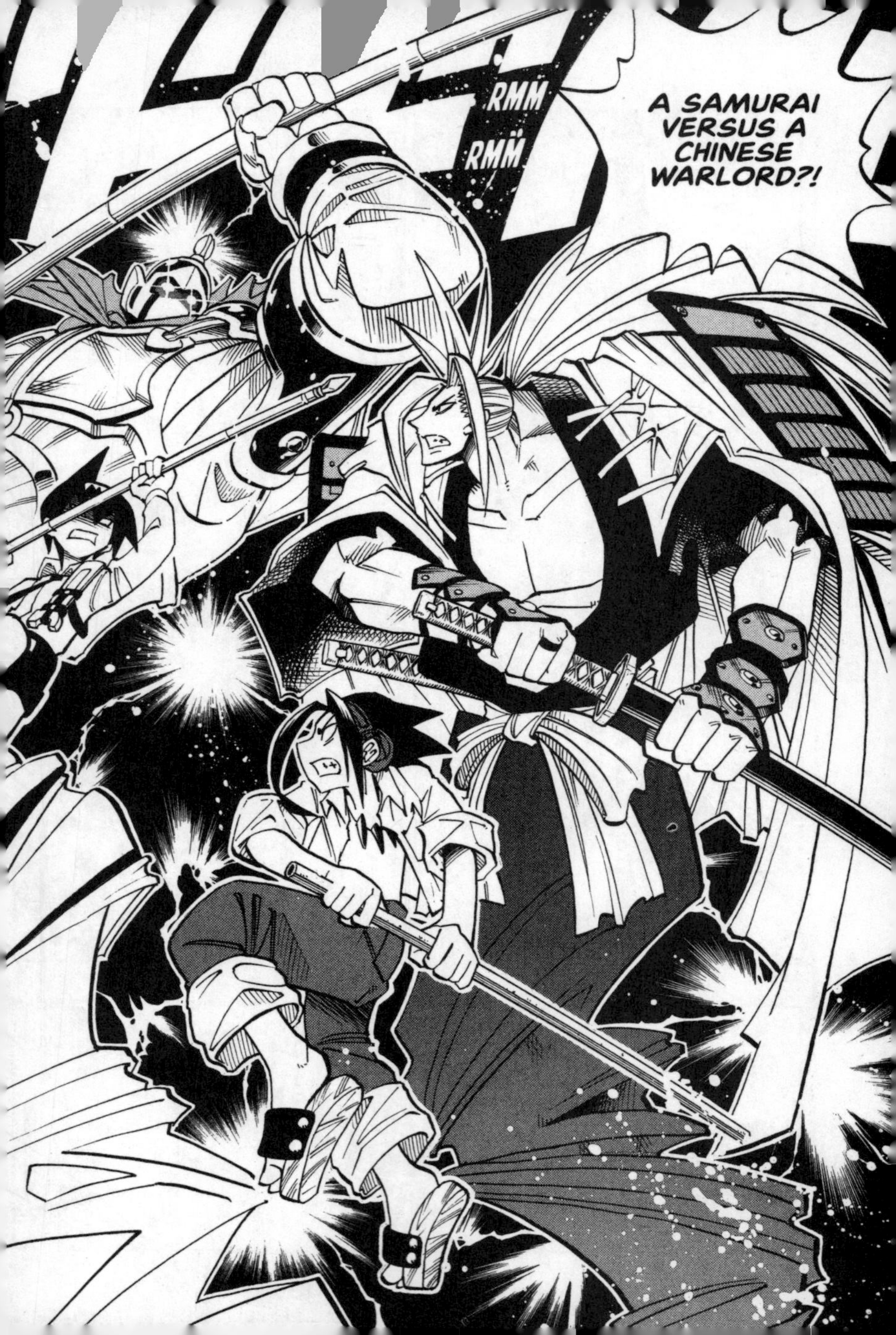
A SAMURAI VERSUS A CHINESE WARLORD?!
RMM
RMM

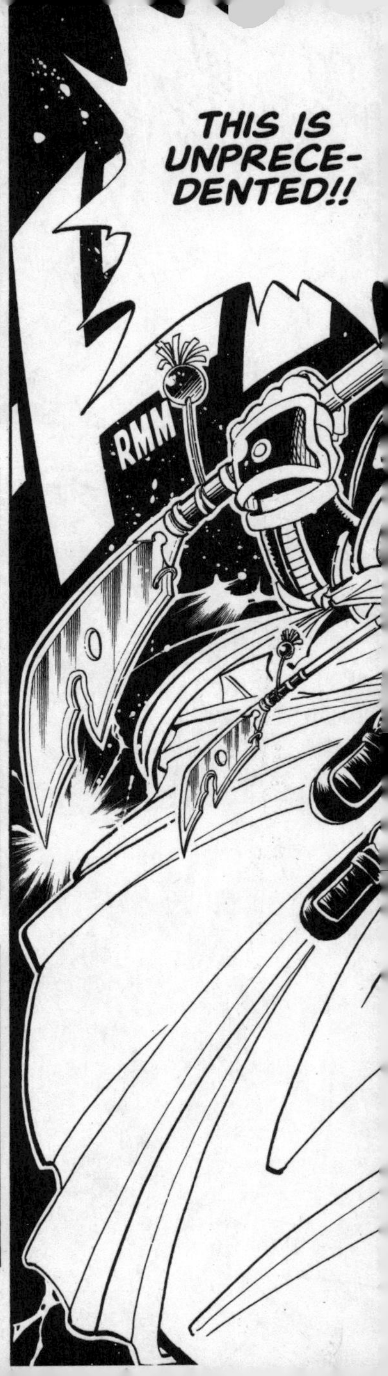
THIS IS UNPRECE-DENTED!!
RMM

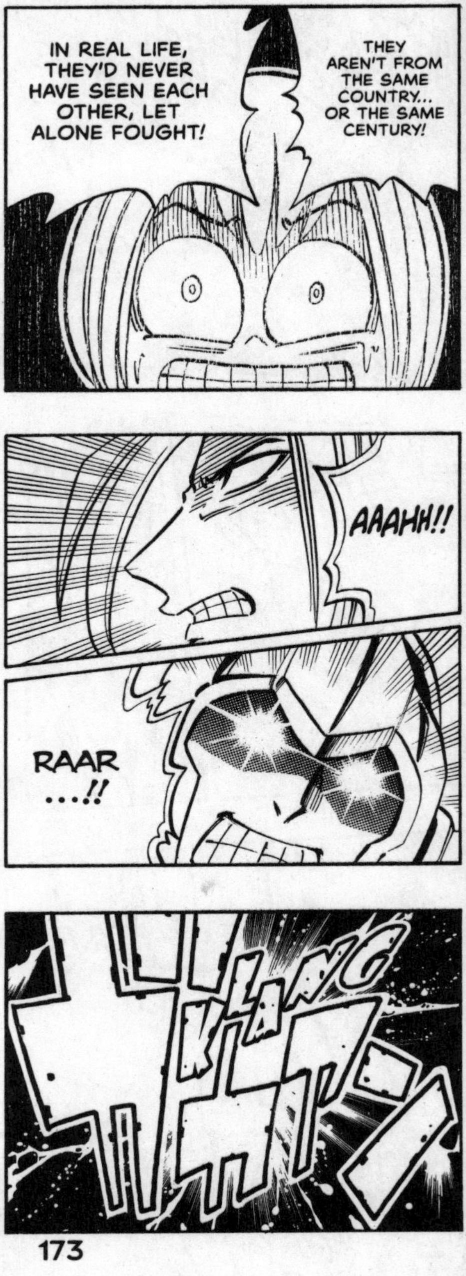
THEY AREN'T FROM THE SAME COUNTRY... OR THE SAME CENTURY!
IN REAL LIFE, THEY'D NEVER HAVE SEEN EACH OTHER, LET ALONE FOUGHT!
AAAHH!!
RAAR ...!!
KLANG

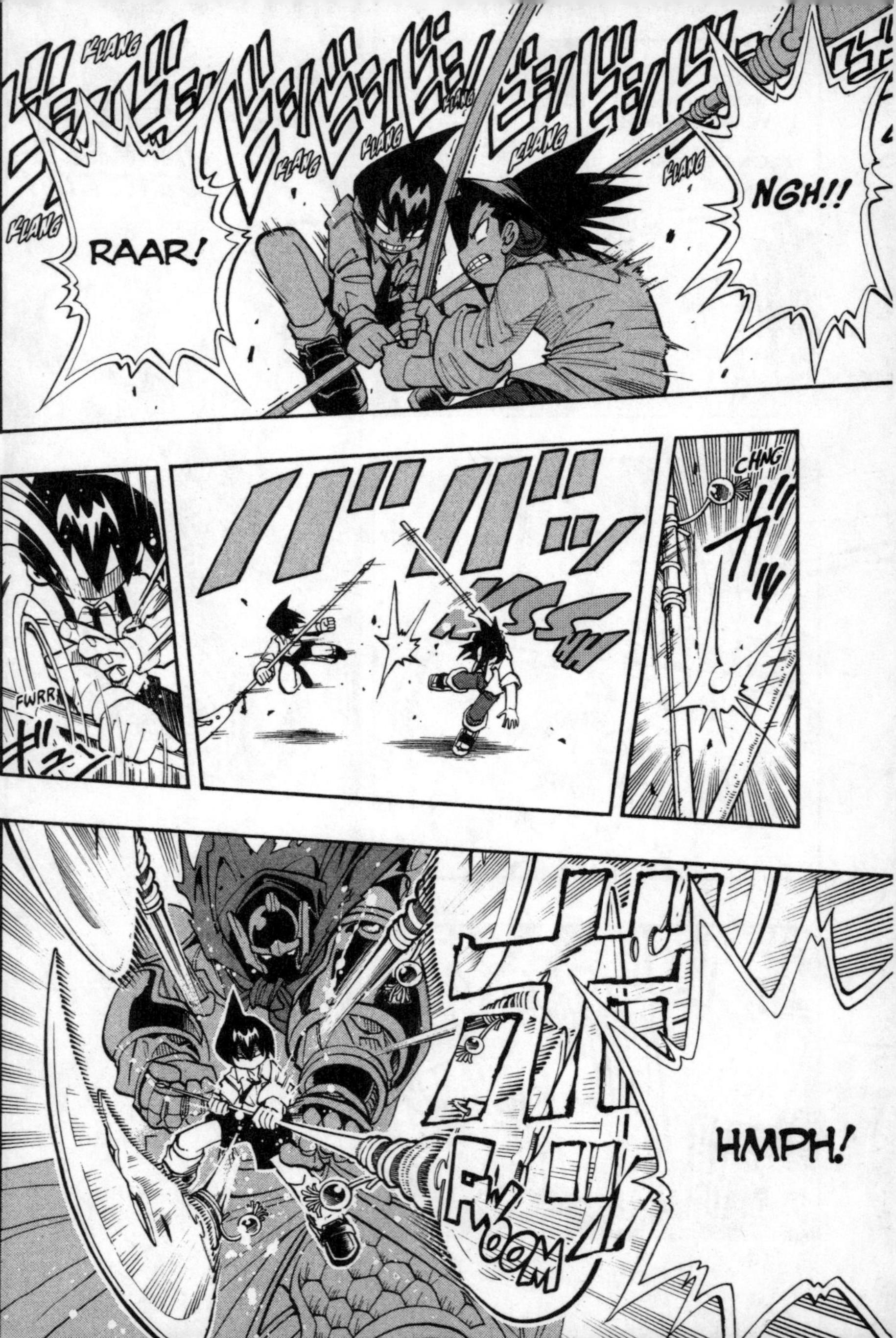
NGH!!
KLANG
KLANG
KLANG
KLANG
KLANG
KLANG
RAAR!
CHNG
FWRR
HMPH!
FWOOM

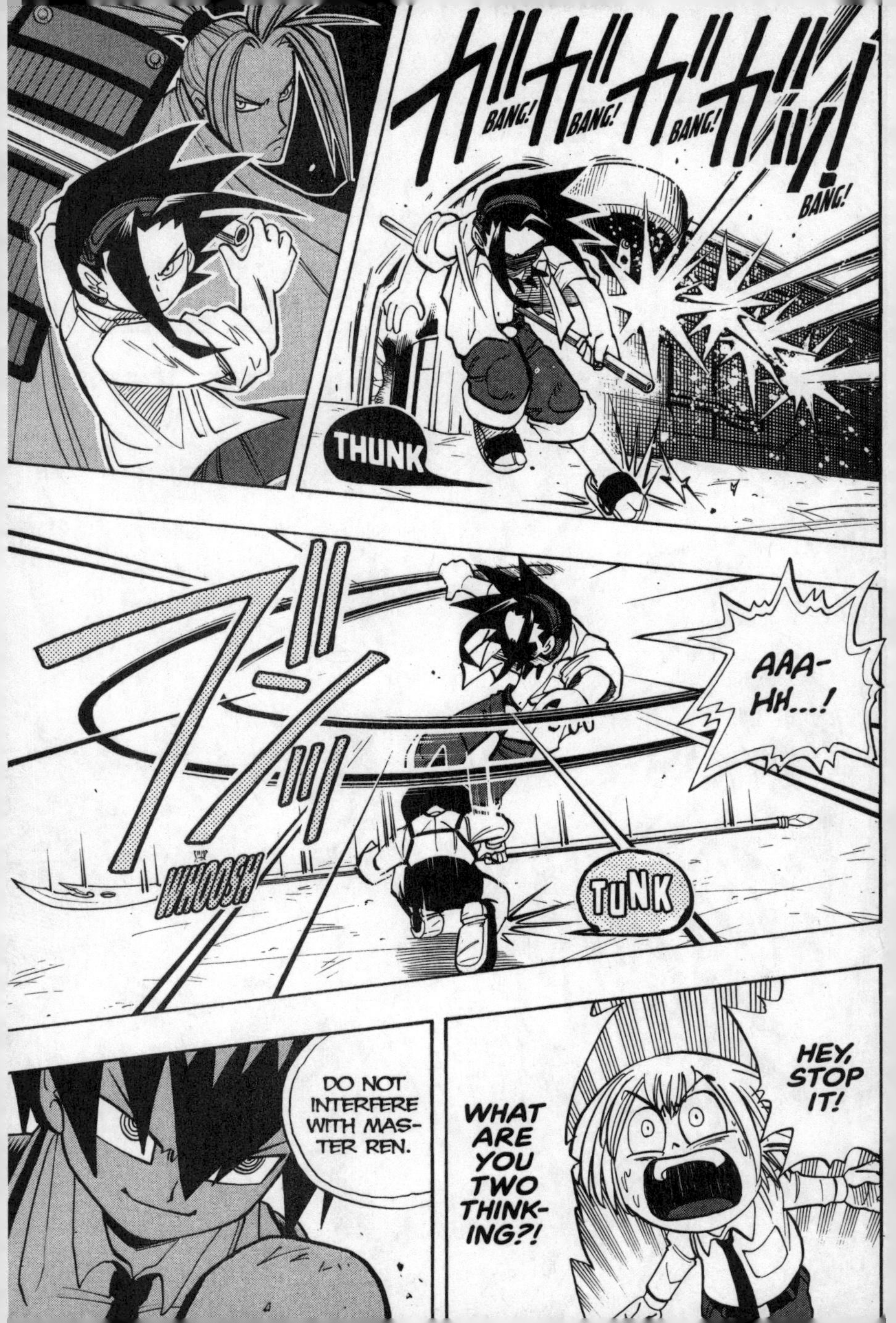
BANG!
BANG!
BANG!
BANG!
THUNK
AAA-HH...!
TUNK
WHOOSH
HEY, STOP IT!
WHAT ARE YOU TWO THINKING?!
DO NOT INTERFERE WITH MAS-TER REN.

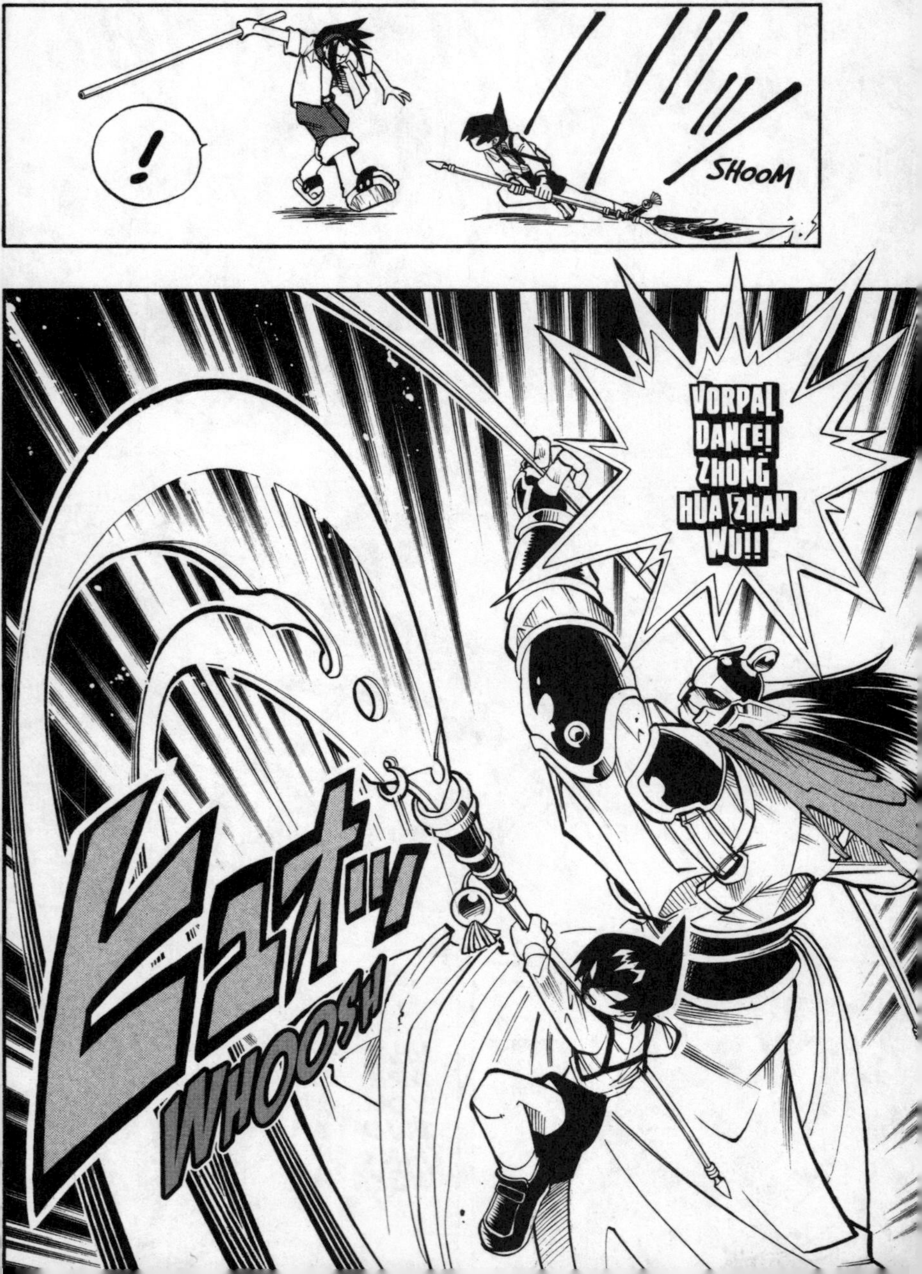
SHOOM
!
VORPAL DANCE! ZHONG HUA ZHAN WU!!
シュオッ
WHOOSH

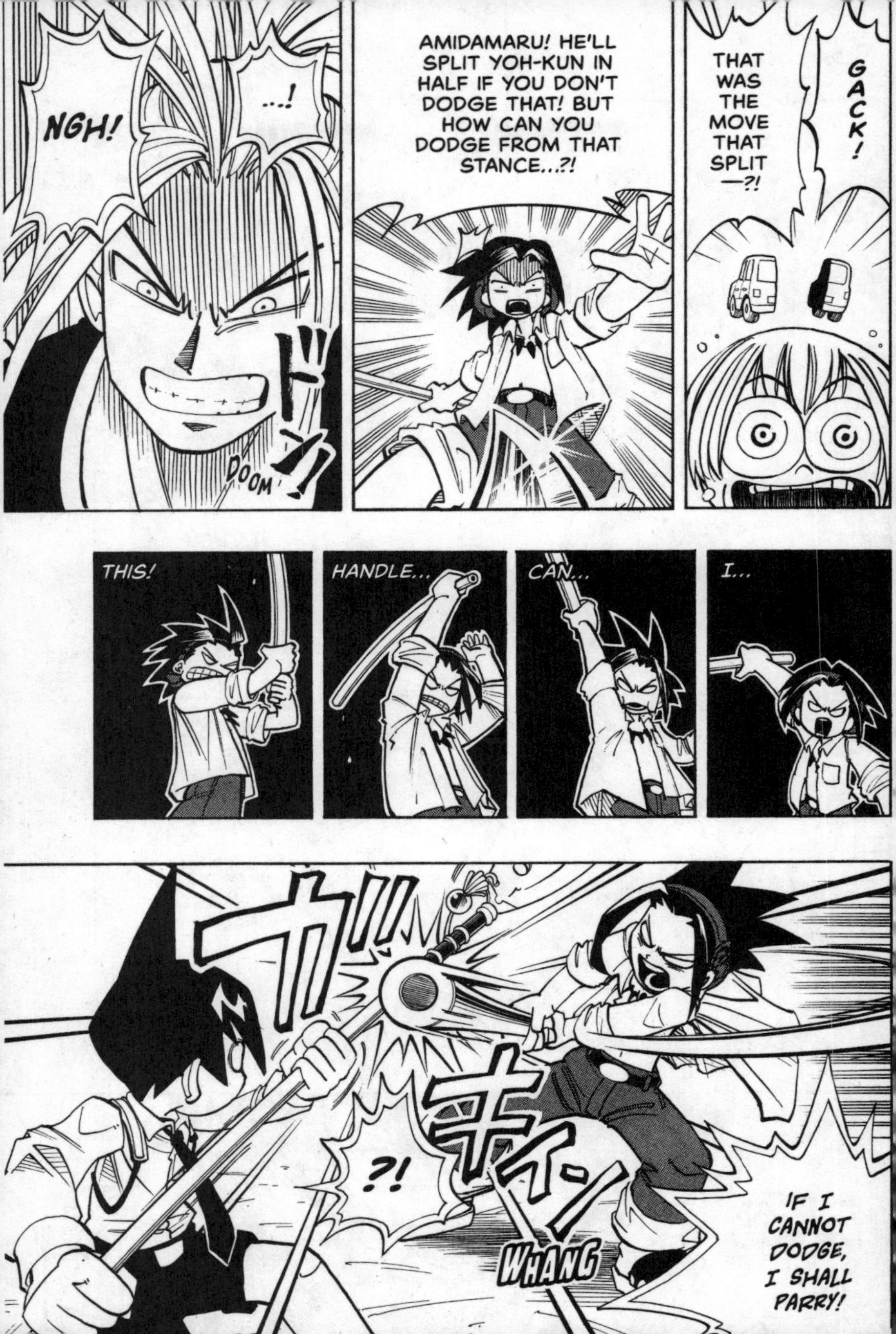
THAT WAS THE MOVE THAT SPLIT —?!
GACK!
AMIDAMARU! HE'LL SPLIT YOH-KUN IN HALF IF YOU DON'T DODGE THAT! BUT HOW CAN YOU DODGE FROM THAT STANCE...?!
...!
NGH!
DOOM
I...
CAN...
HANDLE...
THIS!
IF I CANNOT DODGE, I SHALL PARRY!
WHANG
?!

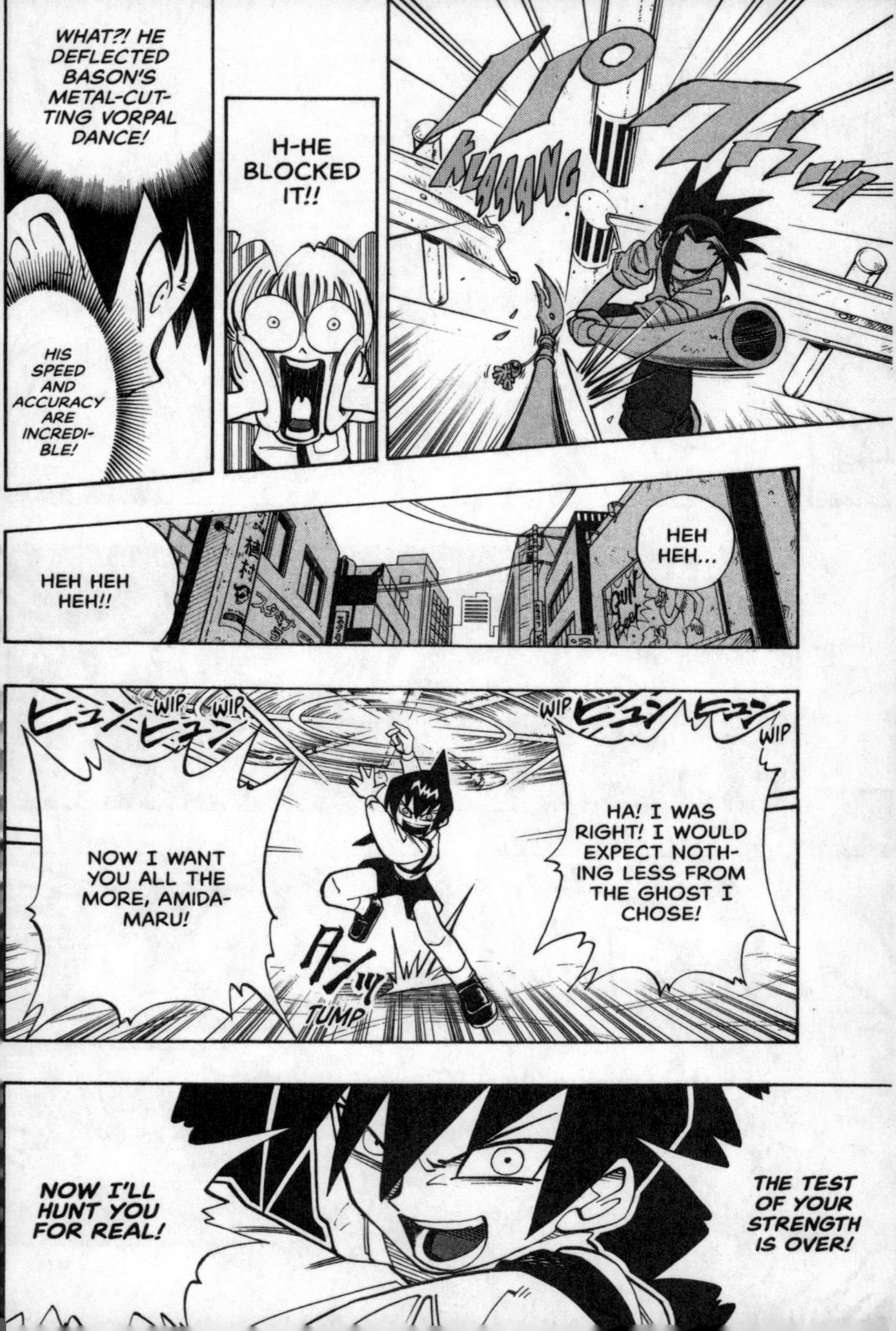

KLAAAANG
H-HE BLOCKED IT!!
WHAT?! HE DEFLECTED BASON'S METAL-CUT-TING VORPAL DANCE!
HIS SPEED AND ACCURACY ARE INCREDI-BLE!
HEH HEH...
HEH HEH HEH!!
WIP
WIP
WIP
WIP
HA! I WAS RIGHT! I WOULD EXPECT NOTH-ING LESS FROM THE GHOST I CHOSE!
NOW I WANT YOU ALL THE MORE, AMIDA-MARU!
TUMP
THE TEST OF YOUR STRENGTH IS OVER!
NOW I'LL HUNT YOU FOR REAL!

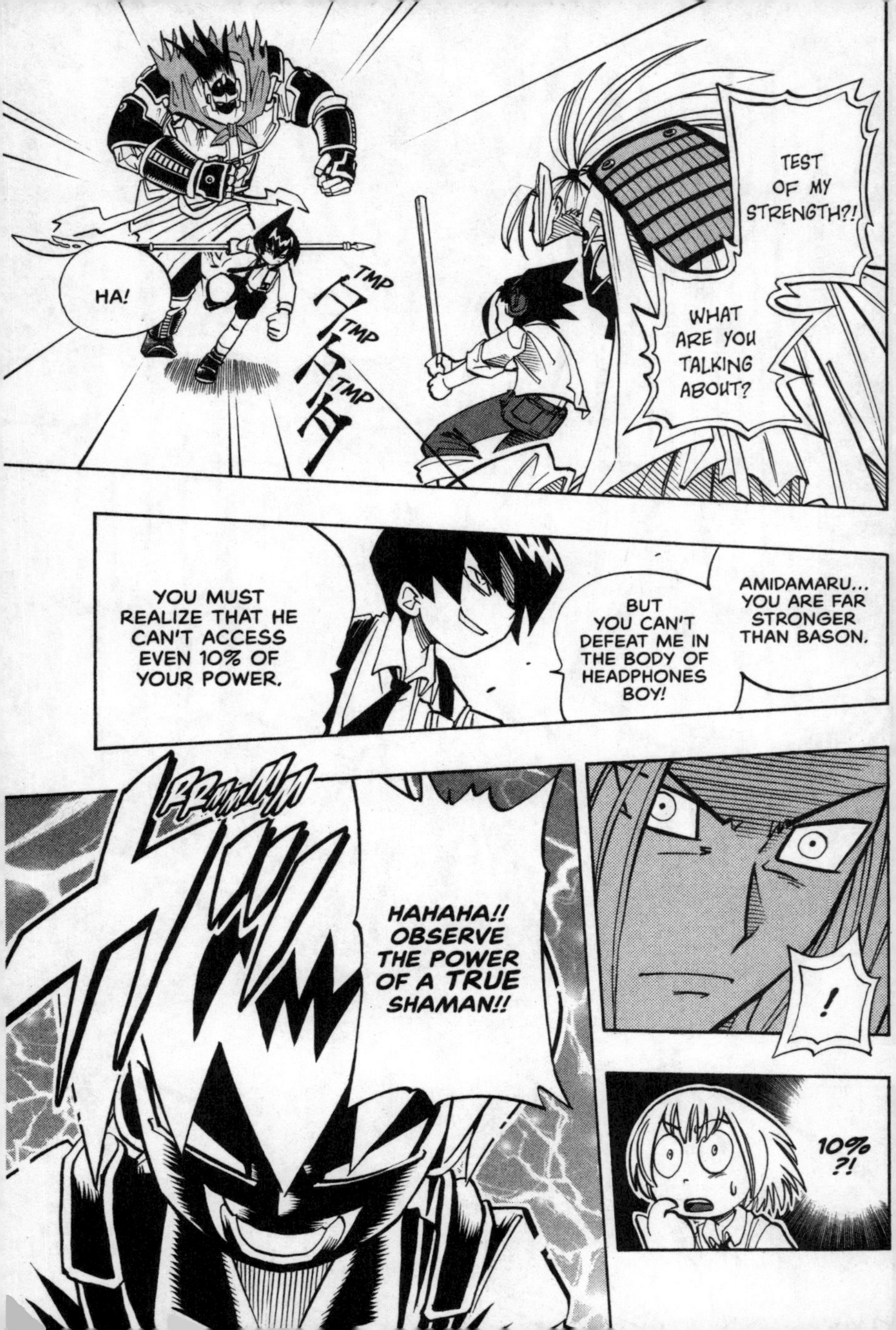
TEST OF MY STRENGTH?!
WHAT ARE YOU TALKING ABOUT?
TMP
TMP
TMP
HA!
AMIDAMARU... YOU ARE FAR STRONGER THAN BASON.
BUT YOU CAN'T DEFEAT ME IN THE BODY OF HEADPHONES BOY!
YOU MUST REALIZE THAT HE CAN'T ACCESS EVEN 10% OF YOUR POWER.
!
10% ?!
HAHAHA!! OBSERVE THE POWER OF A TRUE SHAMAN!!

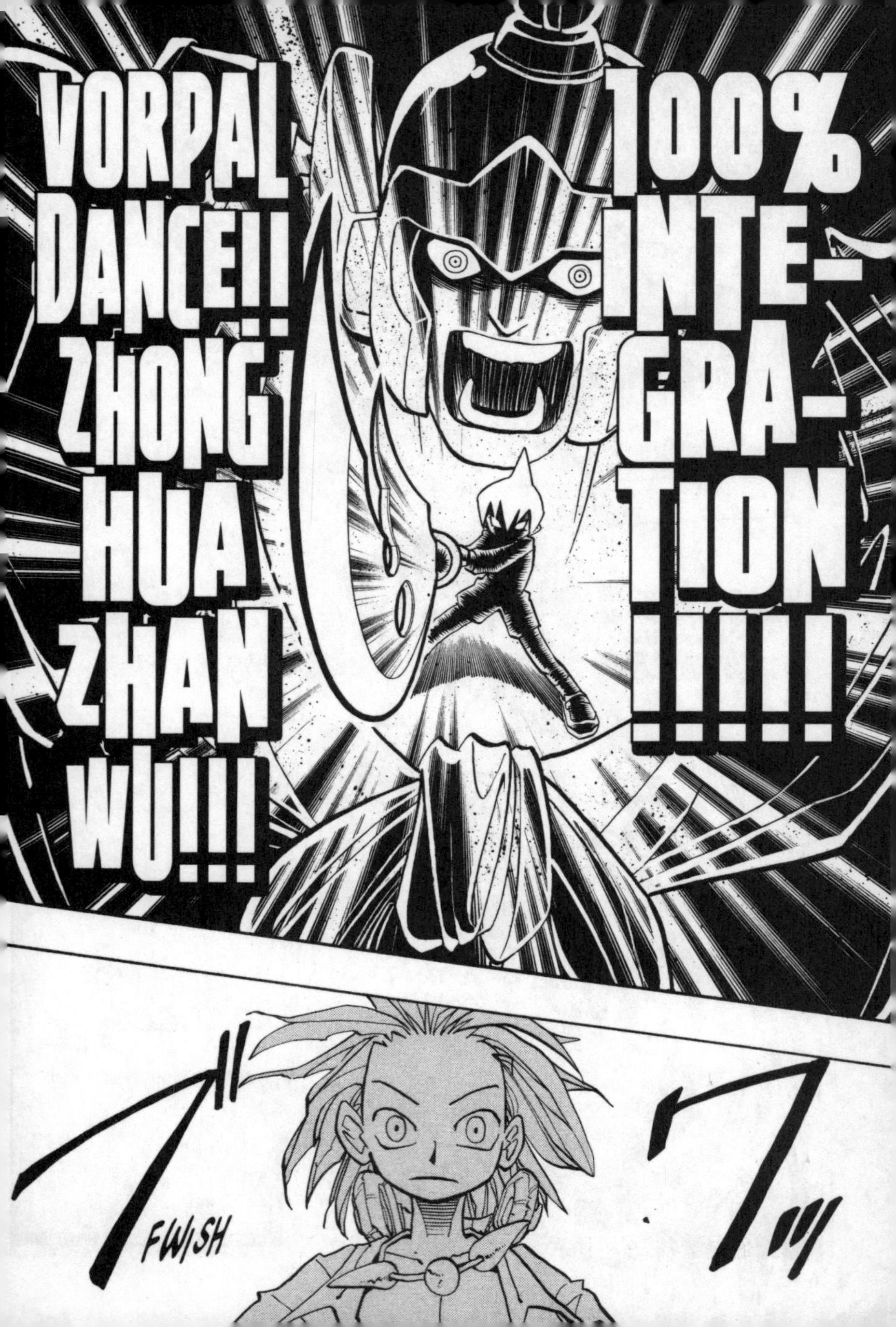
100% INTE-GRA-TION!!!!!!
VORPAL DANCE!! ZHONG HUA ZHAN WU!!!
FWISH

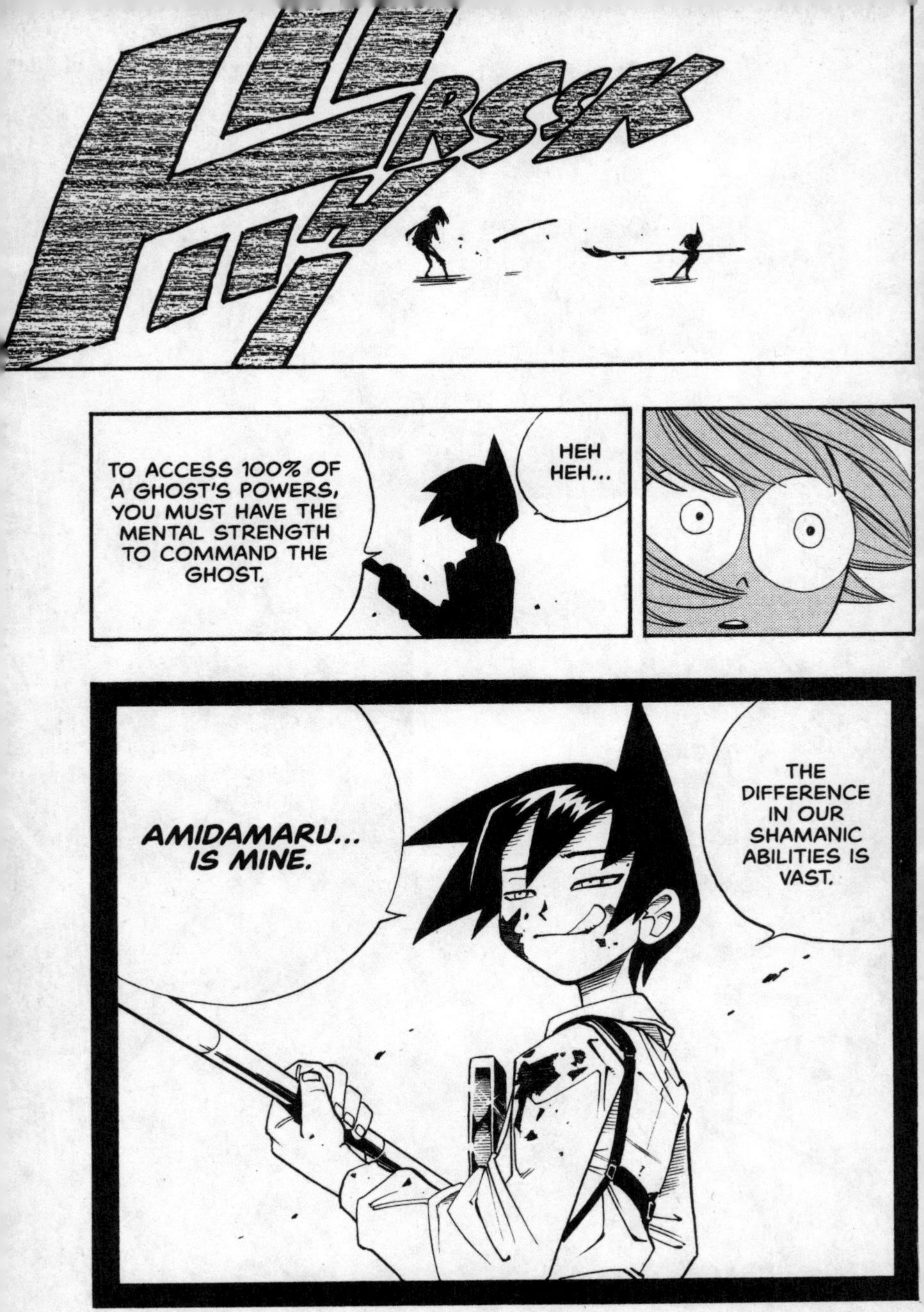
HEH HEH...
TO ACCESS 100% OF A GHOST'S POWERS, YOU MUST HAVE THE MENTAL STRENGTH TO COMMAND THE GHOST.
THE DIFFERENCE IN OUR SHAMANIC ABILITIES IS VAST.
AMIDAMARU... IS MINE.

SHAMAN
KING
1

**Bathroom
Sandals**

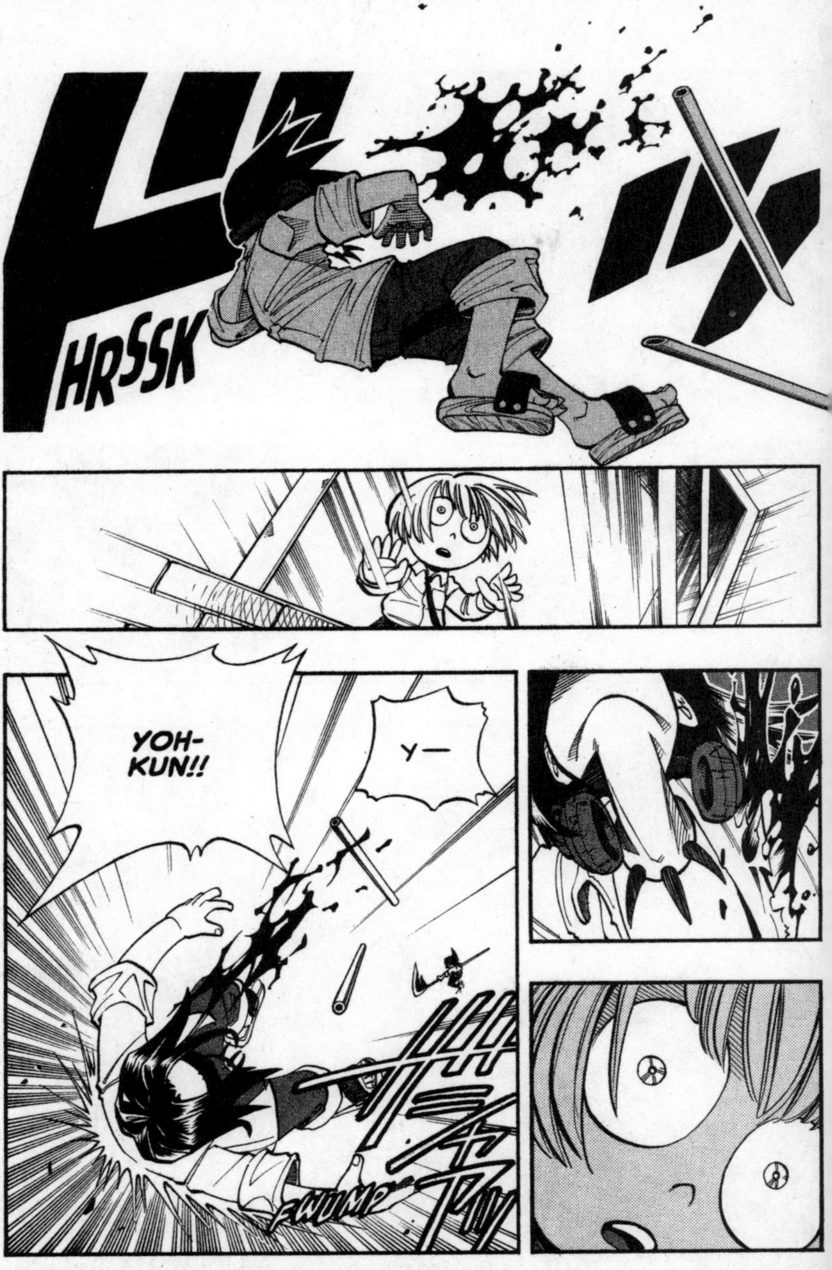
HRSSK
Y—
YOH-KUN!!
FWUMP

Chapter 8: 100% Integration

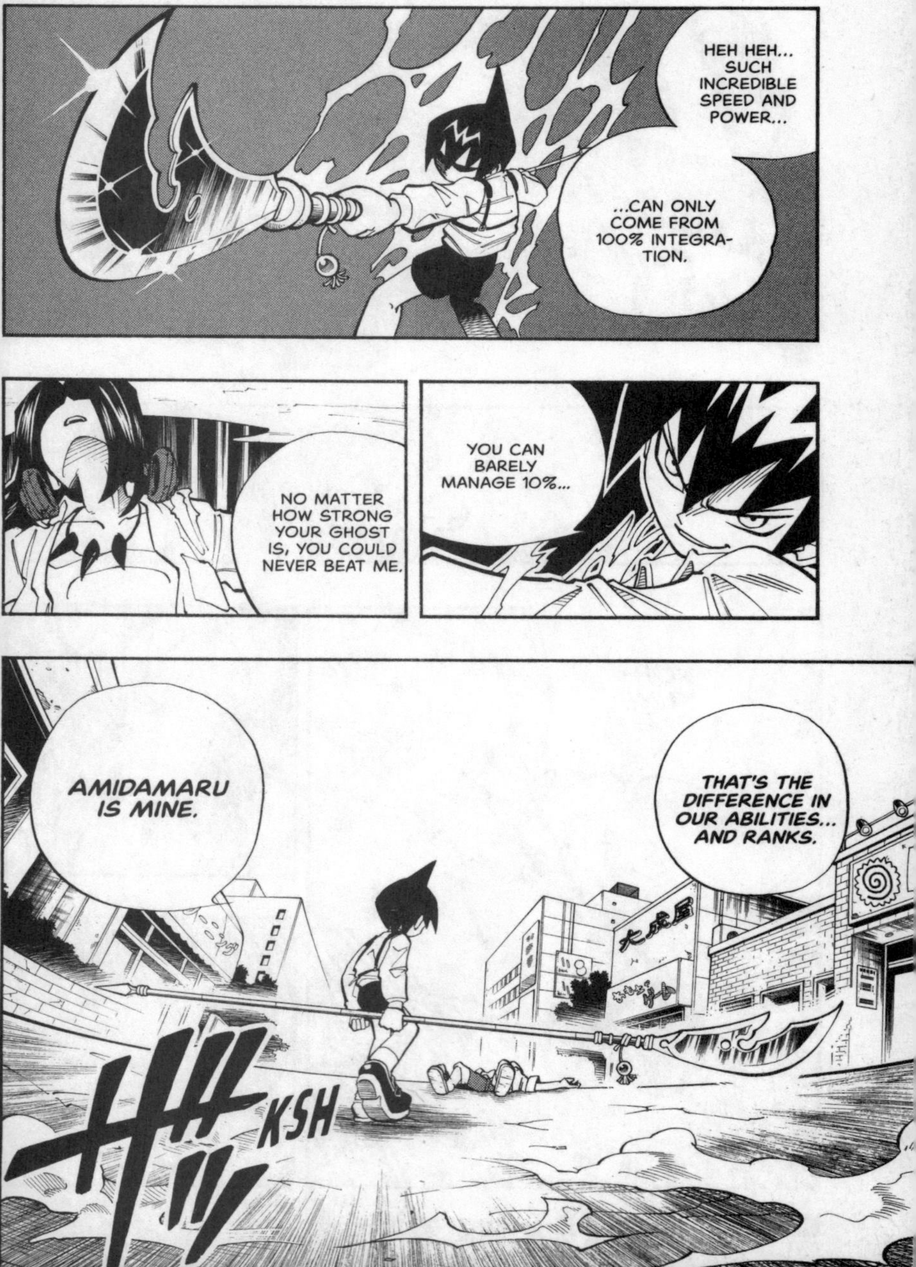
HEH HEH... SUCH INCREDIBLE SPEED AND POWER...
...CAN ONLY COME FROM 100% INTEGRA-TION.
YOU CAN BARELY MANAGE 10%...
NO MATTER HOW STRONG YOUR GHOST IS, YOU COULD NEVER BEAT ME.
THAT'S THE DIFFERENCE IN OUR ABILITIES... AND RANKS.
AMIDAMARU IS MINE.
K'SH

Chapter 8:

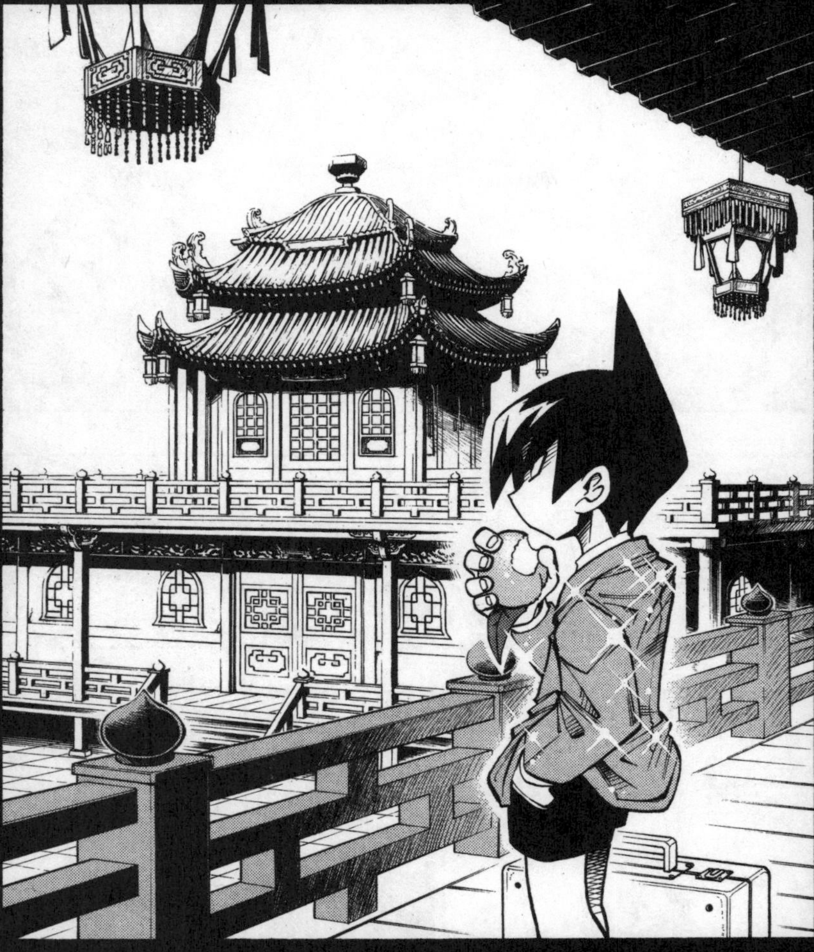

100% Integration

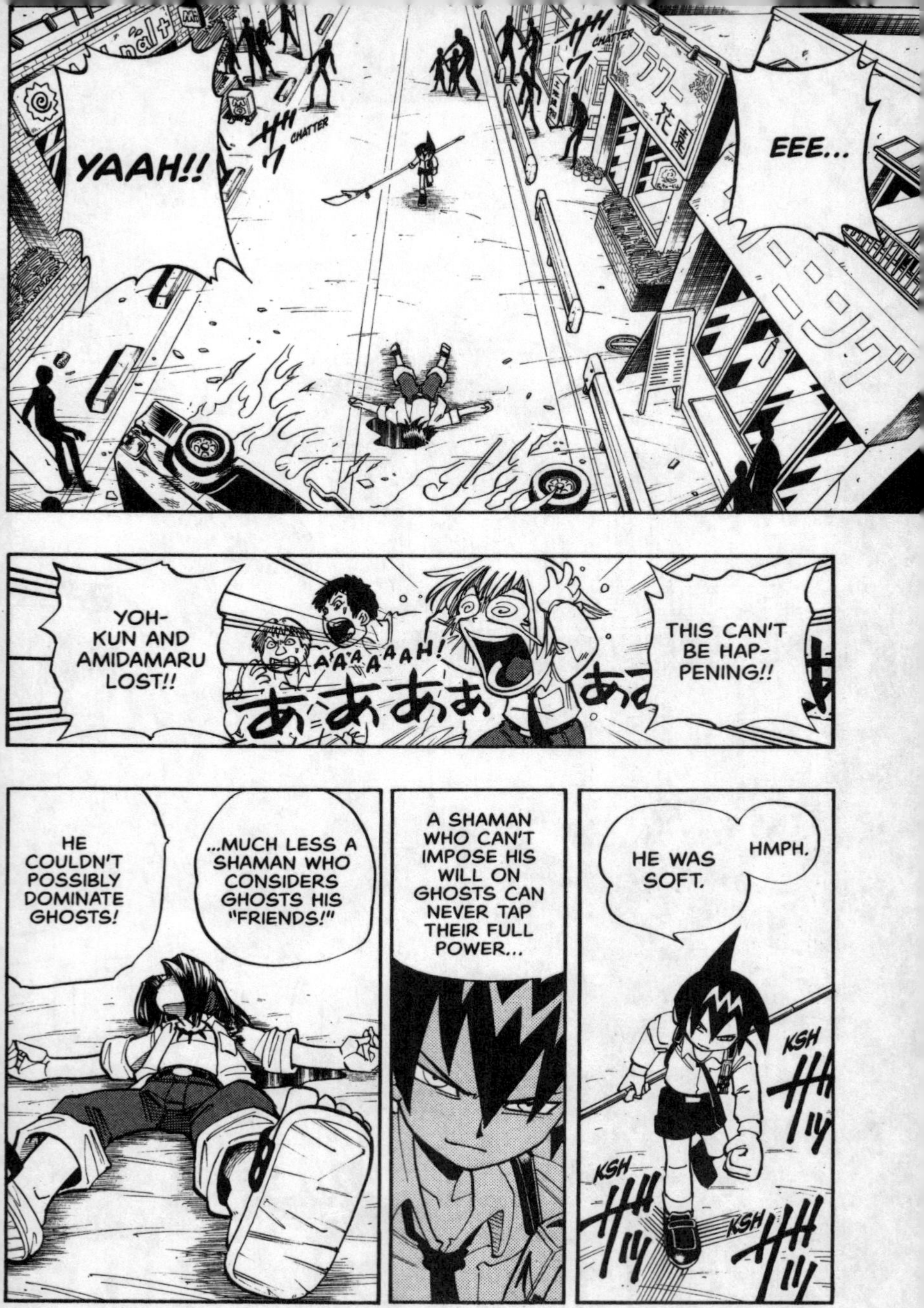
EEE...
CHATTER
YAAH!!
CHATTER
THIS CAN'T BE HAP-PENING!!
AAAAAAH!
あああああ
YOH-KUN AND AMIDAMARU LOST!!
HMPH.
HE WAS SOFT.
KSH
KSH
KSH
A SHAMAN WHO CAN'T IMPOSE HIS WILL ON GHOSTS CAN NEVER TAP THEIR FULL POWER...
...MUCH LESS A SHAMAN WHO CONSIDERS GHOSTS HIS "FRIENDS!"
HE COULDN'T POSSIBLY DOMINATE GHOSTS!

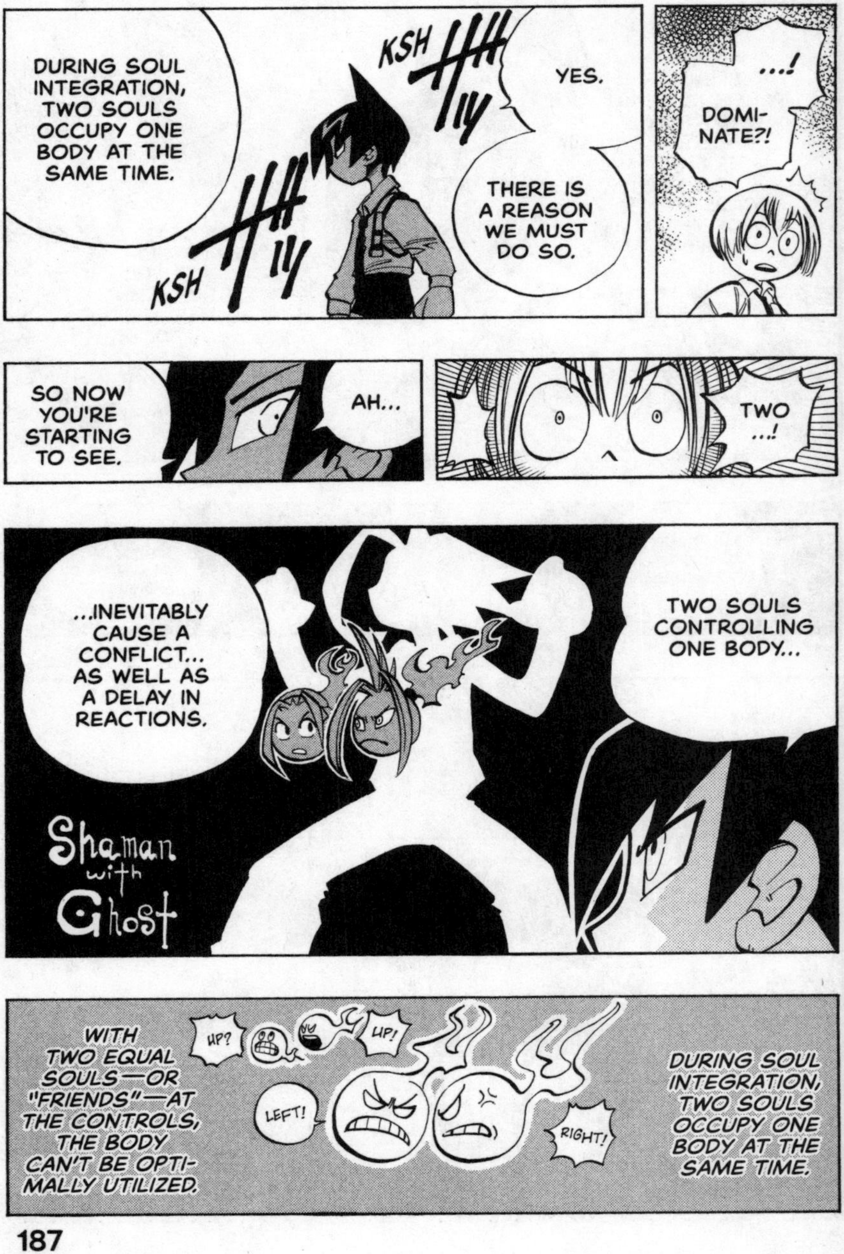
...!
DOMI-NATE?!
YES.
KSH
THERE IS A REASON WE MUST DO SO.
DURING SOUL INTEGRATION, TWO SOULS OCCUPY ONE BODY AT THE SAME TIME.
KSH
TWO ...!
AH...
SO NOW YOU'RE STARTING TO SEE.
TWO SOULS CONTROLLING ONE BODY...
...INEVITABLY CAUSE A CONFLICT... AS WELL AS A DELAY IN REACTIONS.
Shaman with Ghost
DURING SOUL INTEGRATION, TWO SOULS OCCUPY ONE BODY AT THE SAME TIME.
UP!
UP?
RIGHT!
LEFT!
WITH TWO EQUAL SOULS—OR "FRIENDS"—AT THE CONTROLS, THE BODY CAN'T BE OPTI-MALLY UTILIZED.

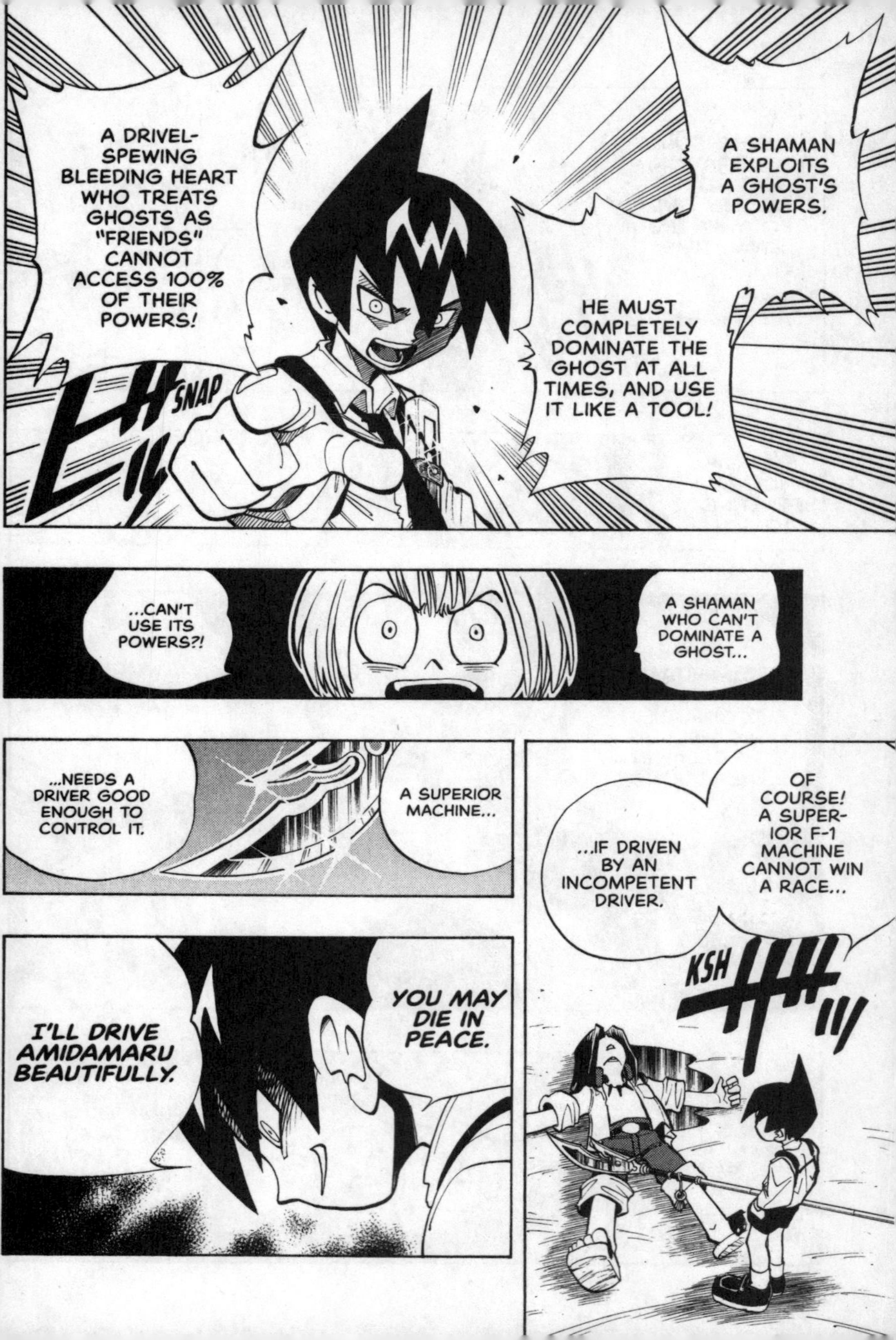
A SHAMAN EXPLOITS A GHOST'S POWERS.
HE MUST COMPLETELY DOMINATE THE GHOST AT ALL TIMES, AND USE IT LIKE A TOOL!
A DRIVEL-SPEWING BLEEDING HEART WHO TREATS GHOSTS AS "FRIENDS" CANNOT ACCESS 100% OF THEIR POWERS!
SNAP
A SHAMAN WHO CAN'T DOMINATE A GHOST...
...CAN'T USE ITS POWERS?!
OF COURSE! A SUPER-IOR F-1 MACHINE CANNOT WIN A RACE...
...IF DRIVEN BY AN INCOMPETENT DRIVER.
KSH
A SUPERIOR MACHINE...
...NEEDS A DRIVER GOOD ENOUGH TO CONTROL IT.
YOU MAY DIE IN PEACE.
I'LL DRIVE AMIDAMARU BEAUTIFULLY.

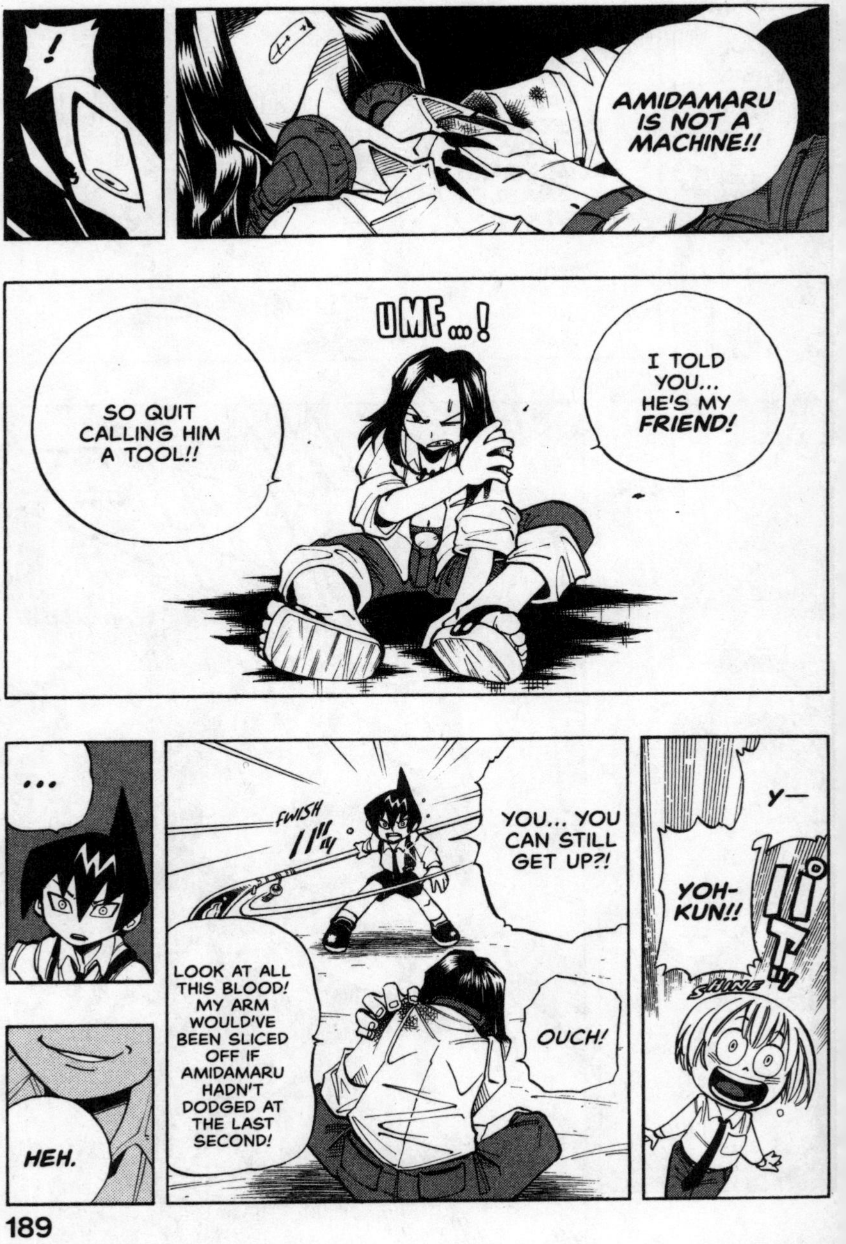
AMIDAMARU IS NOT A MACHINE!!
!
I TOLD YOU... HE'S MY FRIEND!
UMF...!
SO QUIT CALLING HIM A TOOL!!
Y—
YOH-KUN!!
SHINE
YOU... YOU CAN STILL GET UP?!
FWISH
OUCH!
LOOK AT ALL THIS BLOOD! MY ARM WOULD'VE BEEN SLICED OFF IF AMIDAMARU HADN'T DODGED AT THE LAST SECOND!
...
HEH.

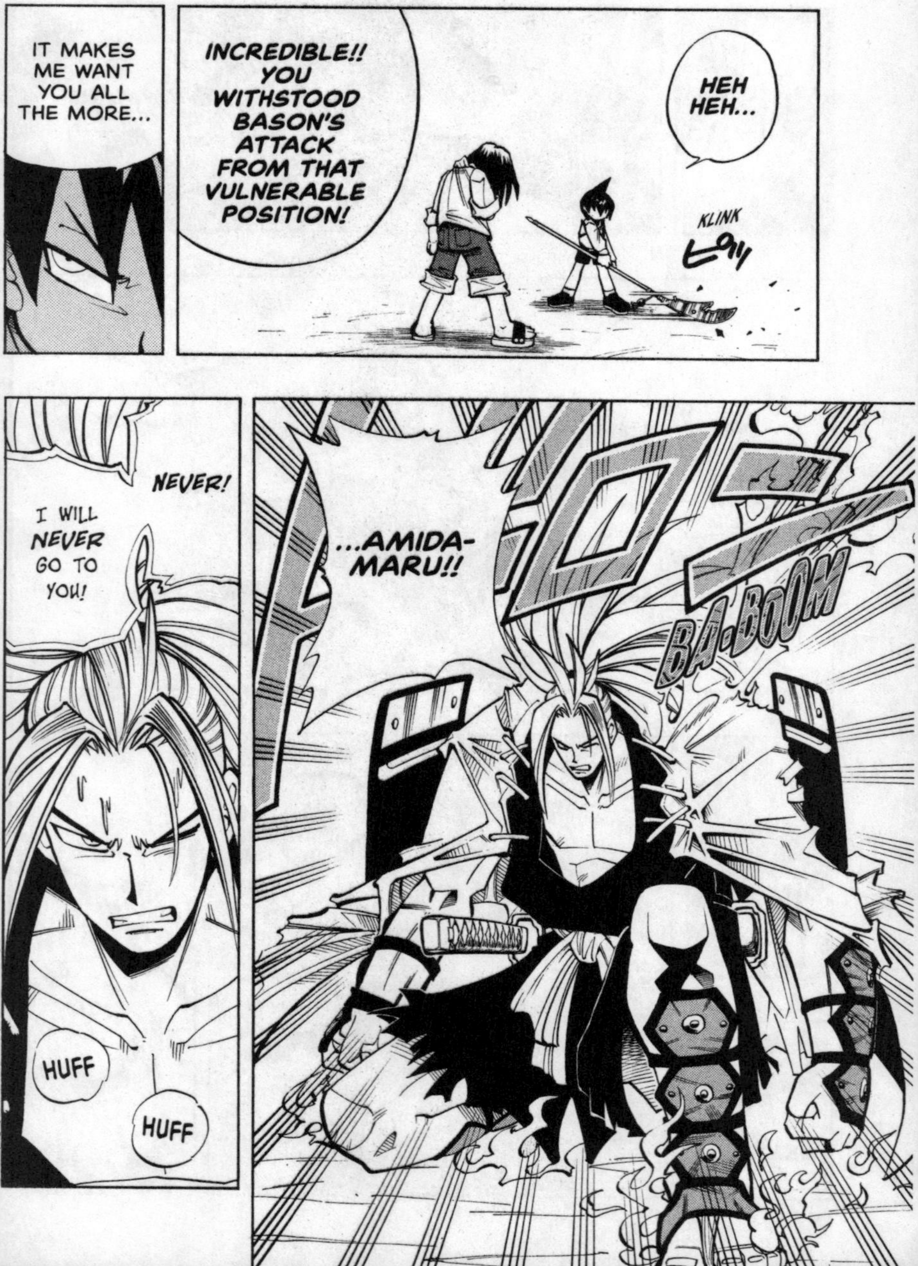
HEH HEH...
KLINK
INCREDIBLE!! YOU WITHSTOOD BASON'S ATTACK FROM THAT VULNERABLE POSITION!
IT MAKES ME WANT YOU ALL THE MORE...
...AMIDA-MARU!!
BA-BOOM
NEVER!
I WILL NEVER GO TO YOU!
HUFF
HUFF

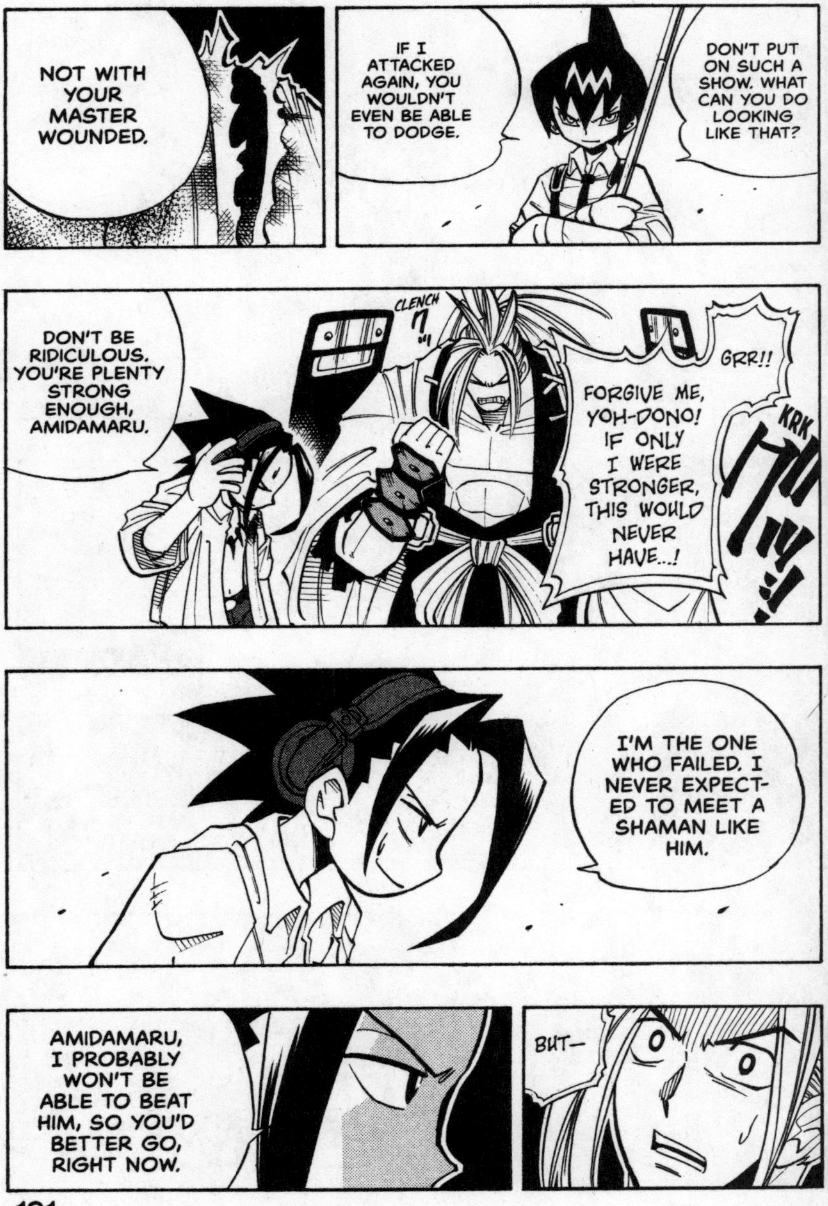
DON'T PUT ON SUCH A SHOW. WHAT CAN YOU DO LOOKING LIKE THAT?
IF I ATTACKED AGAIN, YOU WOULDN'T EVEN BE ABLE TO DODGE.
NOT WITH YOUR MASTER WOUNDED.
KRK
GRR!!
FORGIVE ME, YOH-DONO! IF ONLY I WERE STRONGER, THIS WOULD NEVER HAVE...!
CLENCH
DON'T BE RIDICULOUS. YOU'RE PLENTY STRONG ENOUGH, AMIDAMARU.
I'M THE ONE WHO FAILED. I NEVER EXPECT-ED TO MEET A SHAMAN LIKE HIM.
BUT—
AMIDAMARU, I PROBABLY WON'T BE ABLE TO BEAT HIM, SO YOU'D BETTER GO, RIGHT NOW.

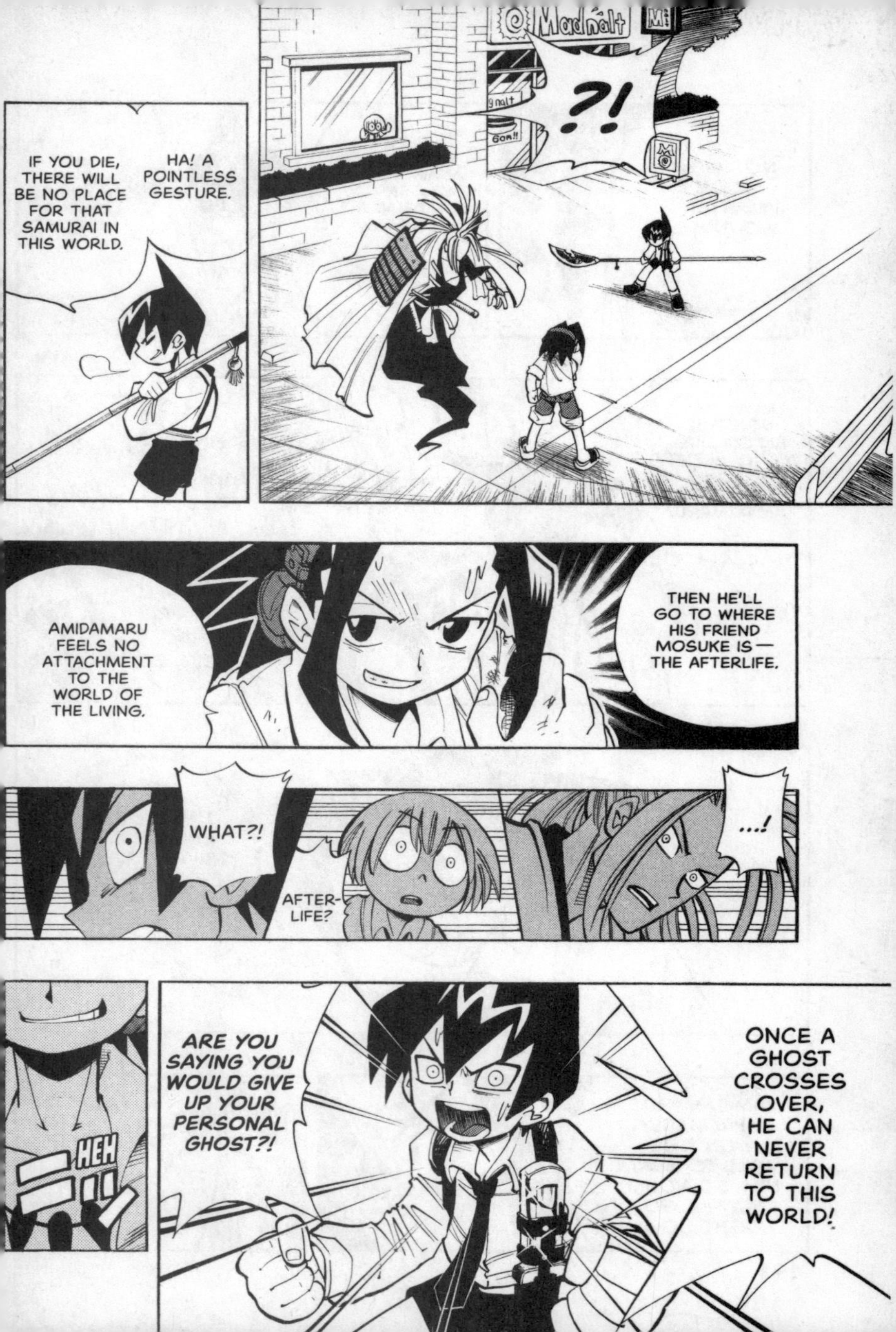
Madnalt
?!
HA! A POINTLESS GESTURE.
IF YOU DIE, THERE WILL BE NO PLACE FOR THAT SAMURAI IN THIS WORLD.
THEN HE'LL GO TO WHERE HIS FRIEND MOSUKE IS— THE AFTERLIFE.
AMIDAMARU FEELS NO ATTACHMENT TO THE WORLD OF THE LIVING.
...!
AFTER-LIFE?
WHAT?!
ONCE A GHOST CROSSES OVER, HE CAN NEVER RETURN TO THIS WORLD!
ARE YOU SAYING YOU WOULD GIVE UP YOUR PERSONAL GHOST?!
HEH

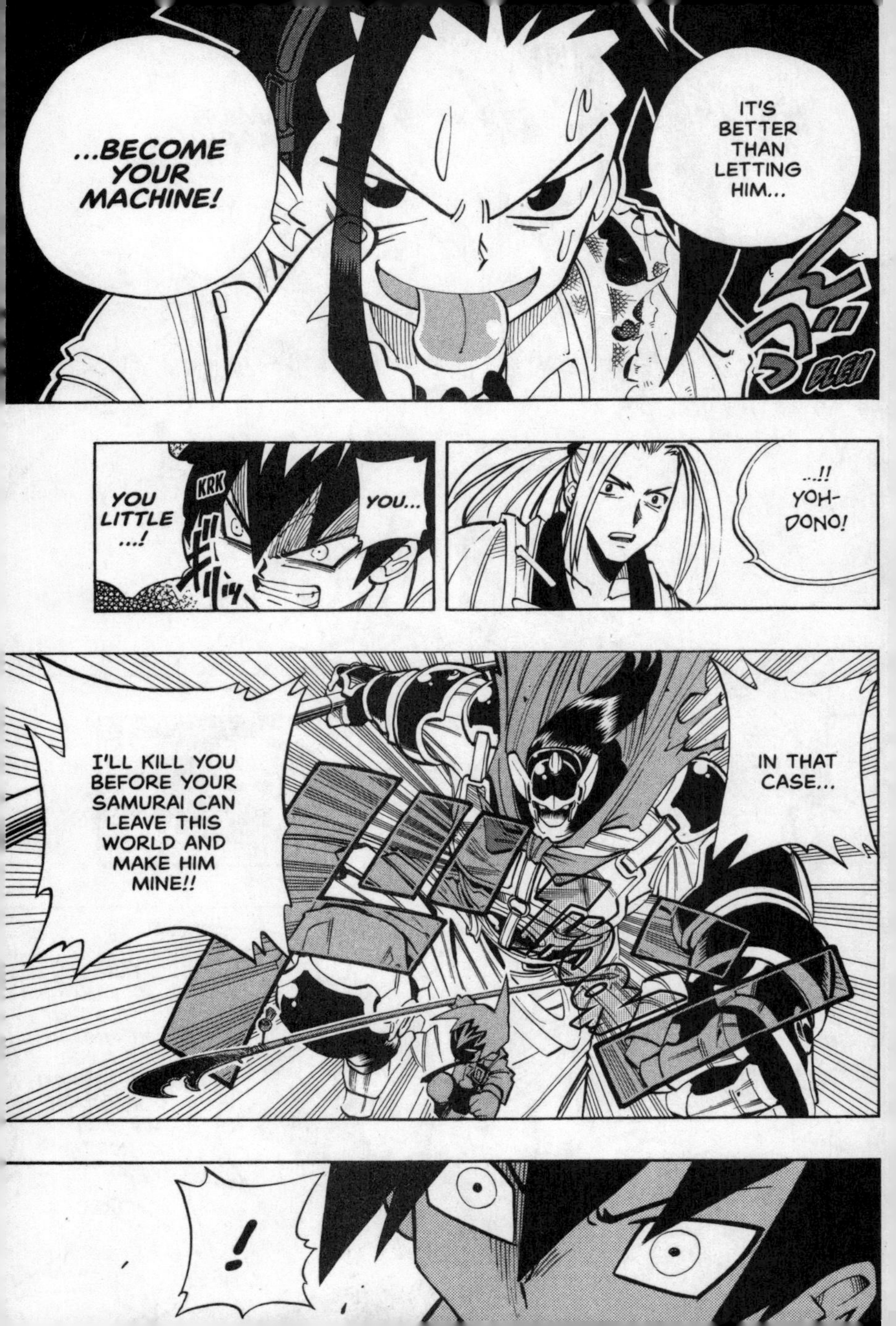
IT'S BETTER THAN LETTING HIM...
...BECOME YOUR MACHINE!
ELEH
...!! YOH-DONO!
YOU...
KRK
YOU LITTLE ...!
IN THAT CASE...
I'LL KILL YOU BEFORE YOUR SAMURAI CAN LEAVE THIS WORLD AND MAKE HIM MINE!!
!

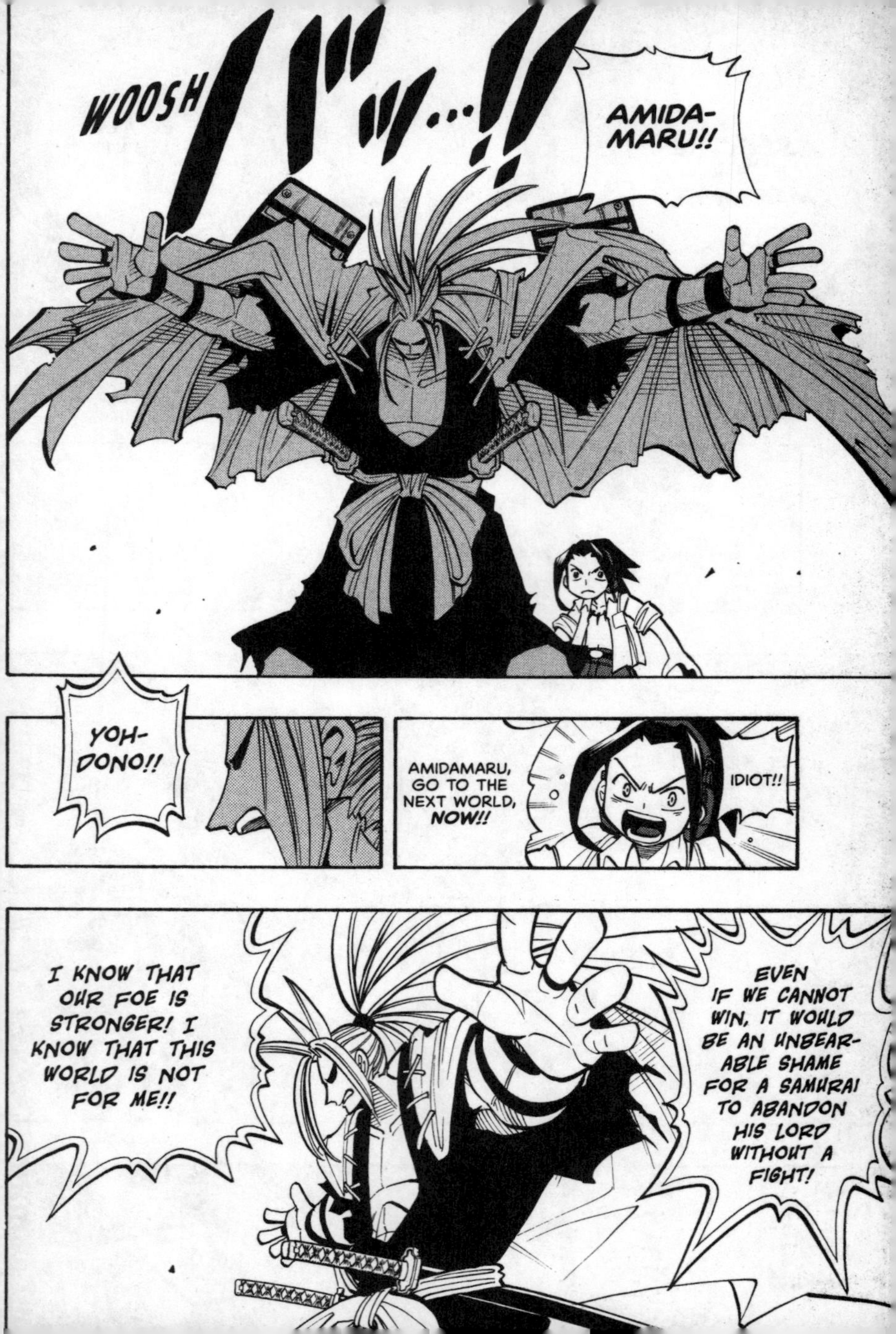
AMIDA-
MARU!!
バッ…!!
WOOSH
IDIOT!!
AMIDAMARU, GO TO THE NEXT WORLD, NOW!!
YOH-DONO!!
EVEN IF WE CANNOT WIN, IT WOULD BE AN UNBEARABLE SHAME FOR A SAMURAI TO ABANDON HIS LORD WITHOUT A FIGHT!
I KNOW THAT OUR FOE IS STRONGER! I KNOW THAT THIS WORLD IS NOT FOR ME!!

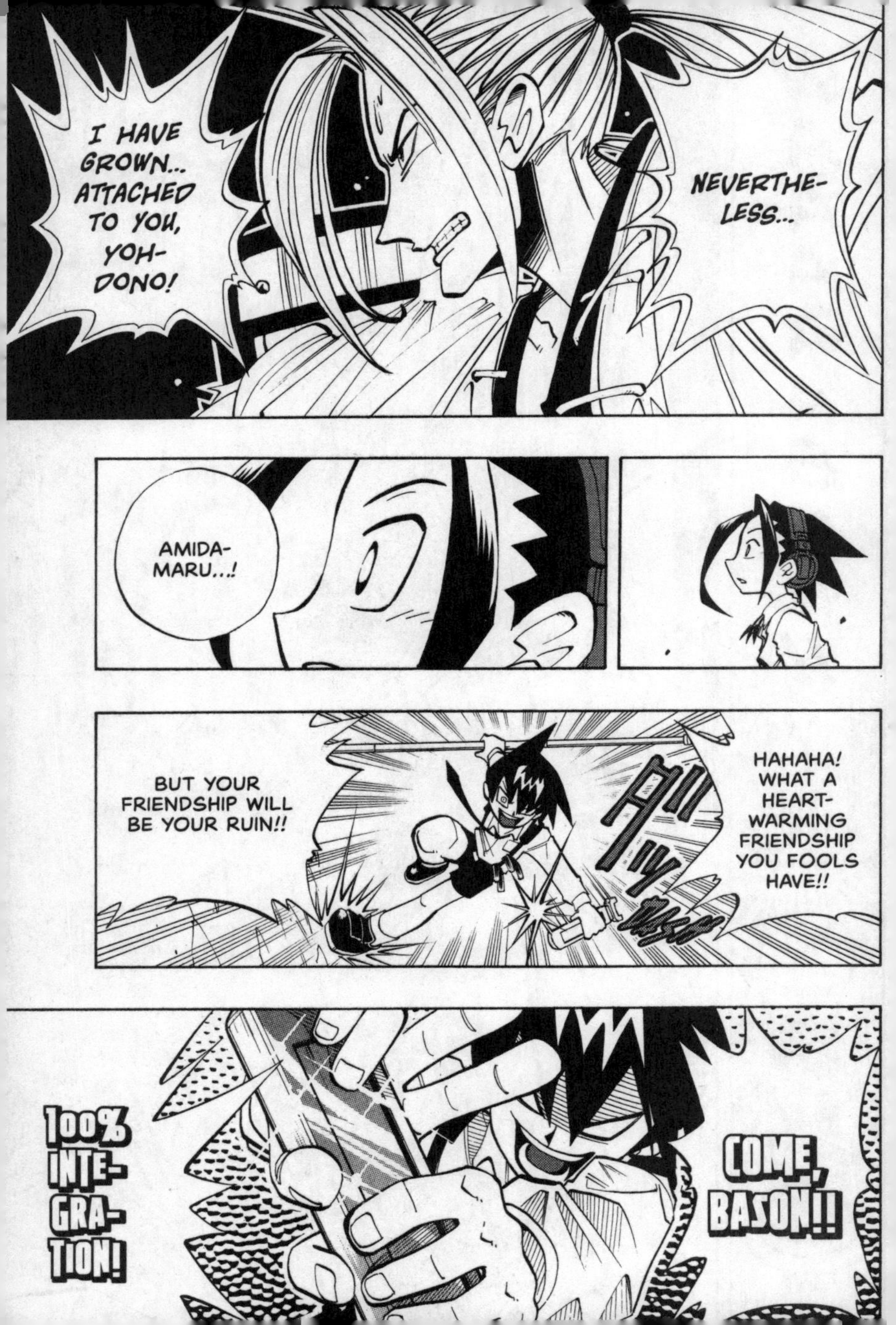
I HAVE GROWN... ATTACHED TO YOU, YOH-DONO!
NEVERTHE-LESS...
AMIDA-MARU...!
HAHAHA! WHAT A HEART-WARMING FRIENDSHIP YOU FOOLS HAVE!!
BUT YOUR FRIENDSHIP WILL BE YOUR RUIN!!
COME, BASON!!
100% INTE-GRA-TION!

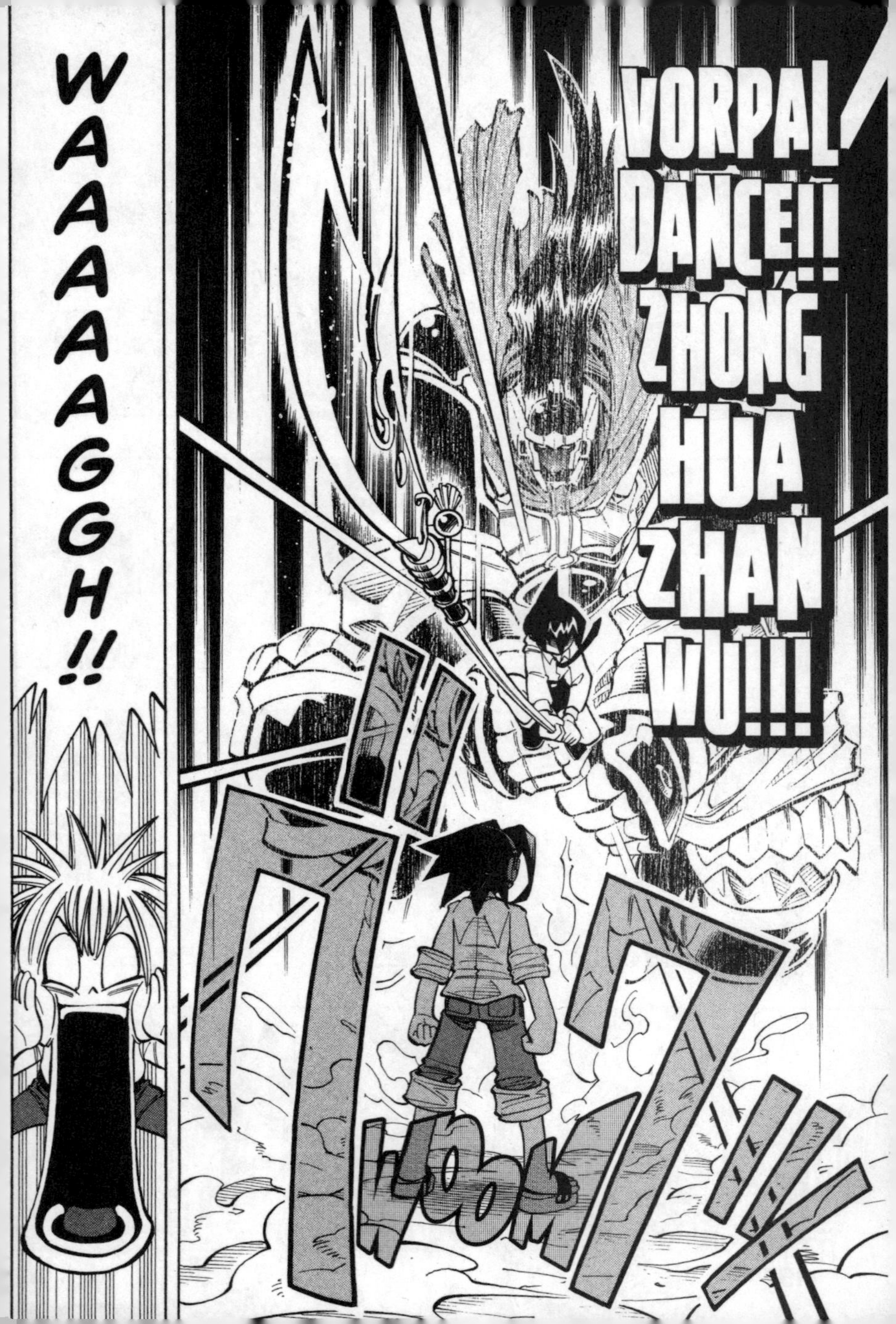
VORPAL DANCE!! ZHONG HUA ZHAN WU!!!
WOOM
WAAAAAAGGH!!

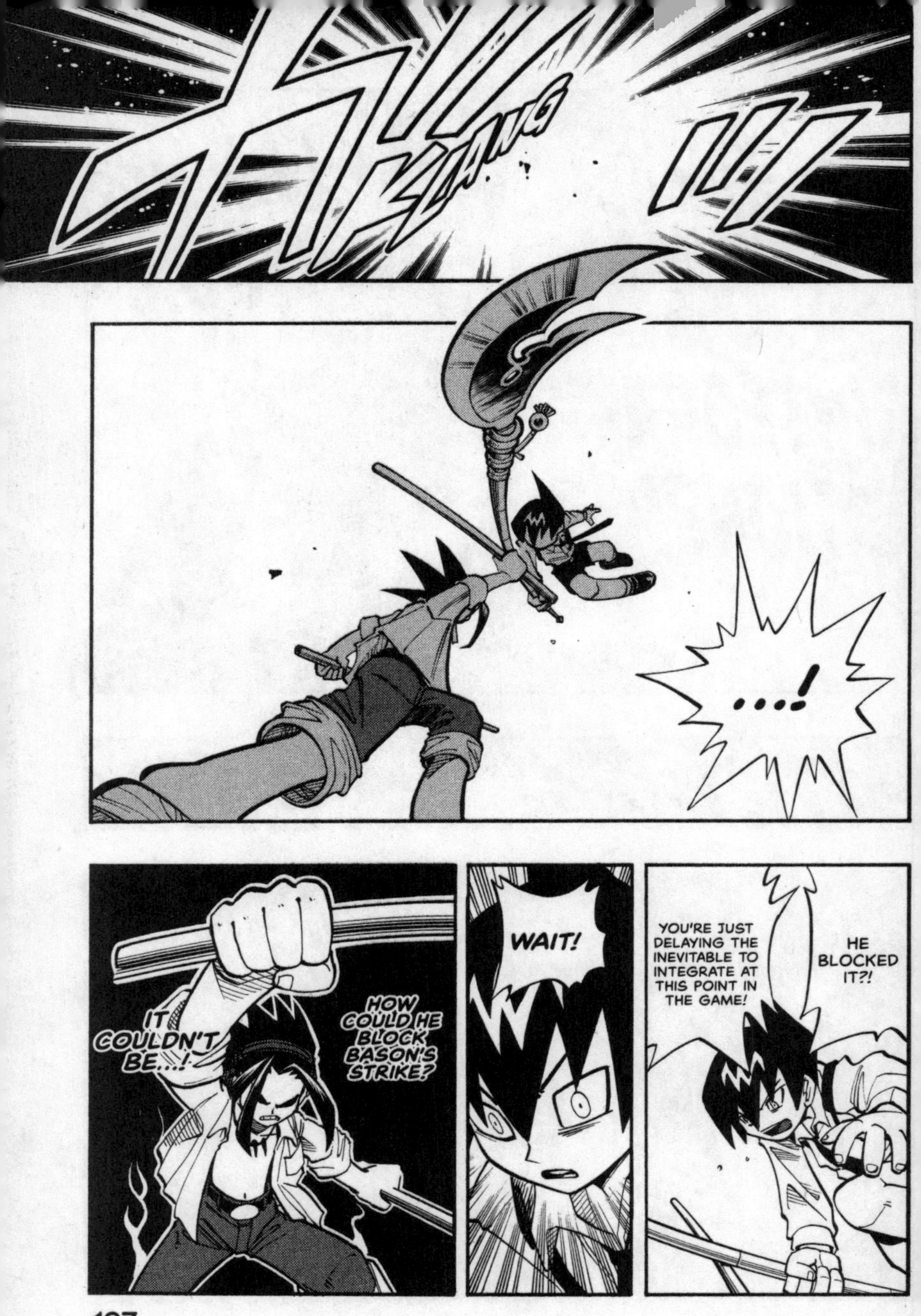
...!
HE BLOCKED IT?!
YOU'RE JUST DELAYING THE INEVITABLE TO INTEGRATE AT THIS POINT IN THE GAME!
WAIT!
HOW COULD HE BLOCK BASON'S STRIKE?
IT COULDN'T BE...!

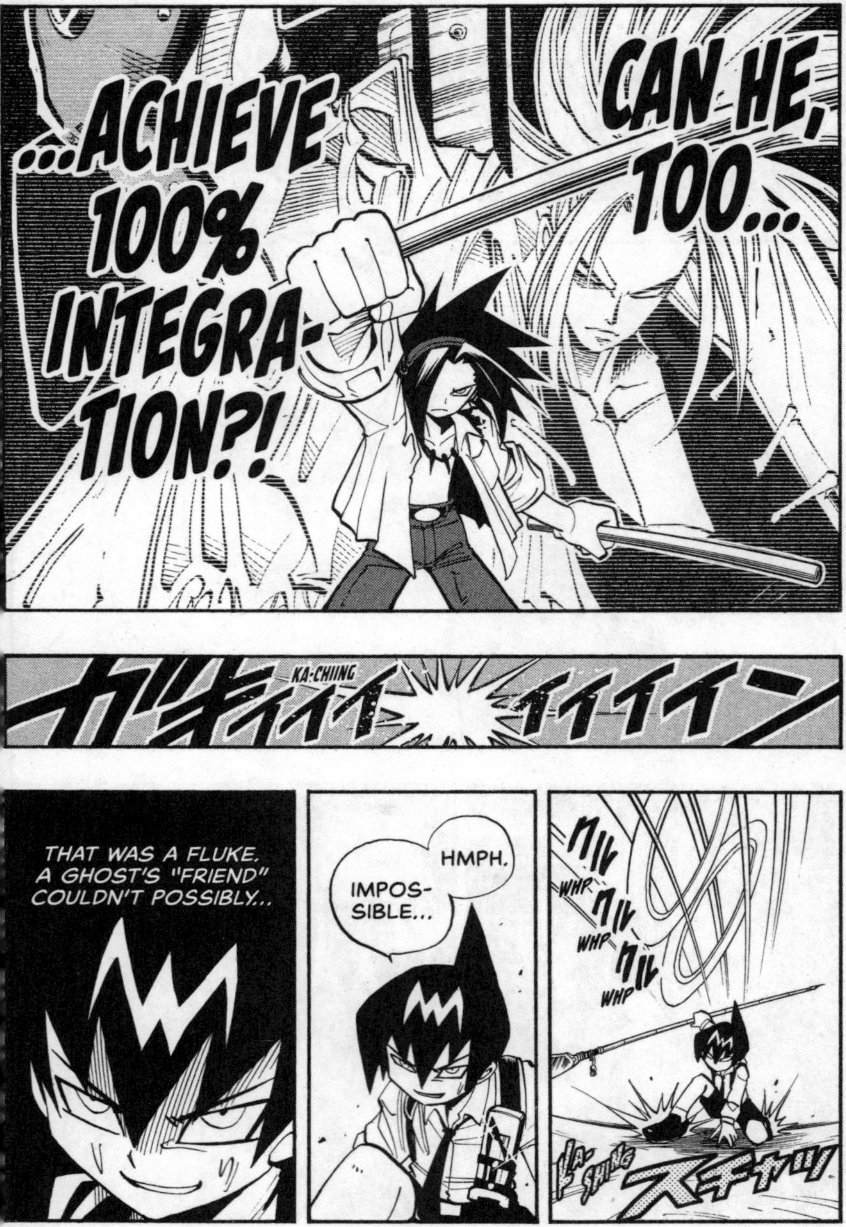
CAN HE, TOO...
...ACHIEVE 100% INTEGRATION?!
KA-CHIING
WHP WHP WHP
KA-SHING
HMPH.
IMPOSSIBLE...
THAT WAS A FLUKE. A GHOST'S "FRIEND" COULDN'T POSSIBLY...

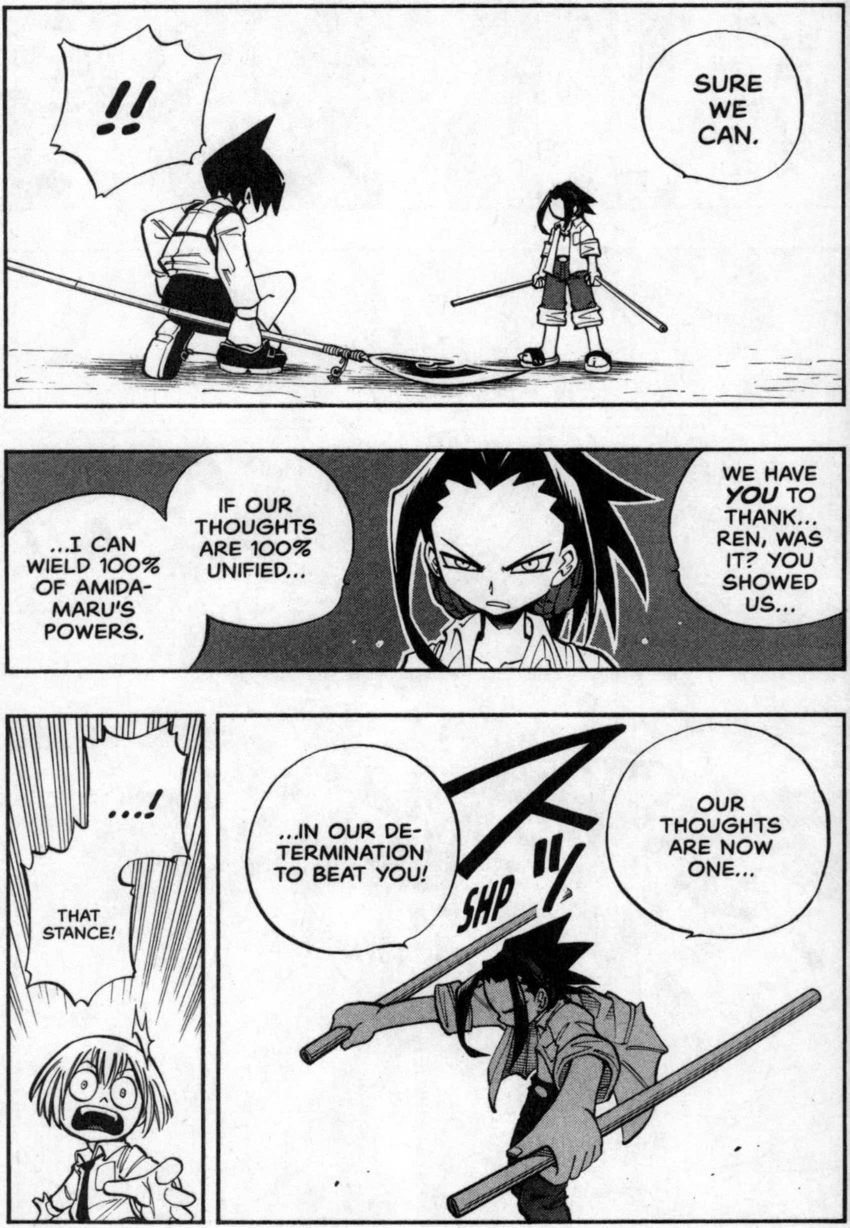
SURE WE CAN.
!!
WE HAVE YOU TO THANK... REN, WAS IT? YOU SHOWED US...
IF OUR THOUGHTS ARE 100% UNIFIED...
...I CAN WIELD 100% OF AMIDA-MARU'S POWERS.
OUR THOUGHTS ARE NOW ONE...
...IN OUR DE-TERMINATION TO BEAT YOU!
SHP
...!
THAT STANCE!

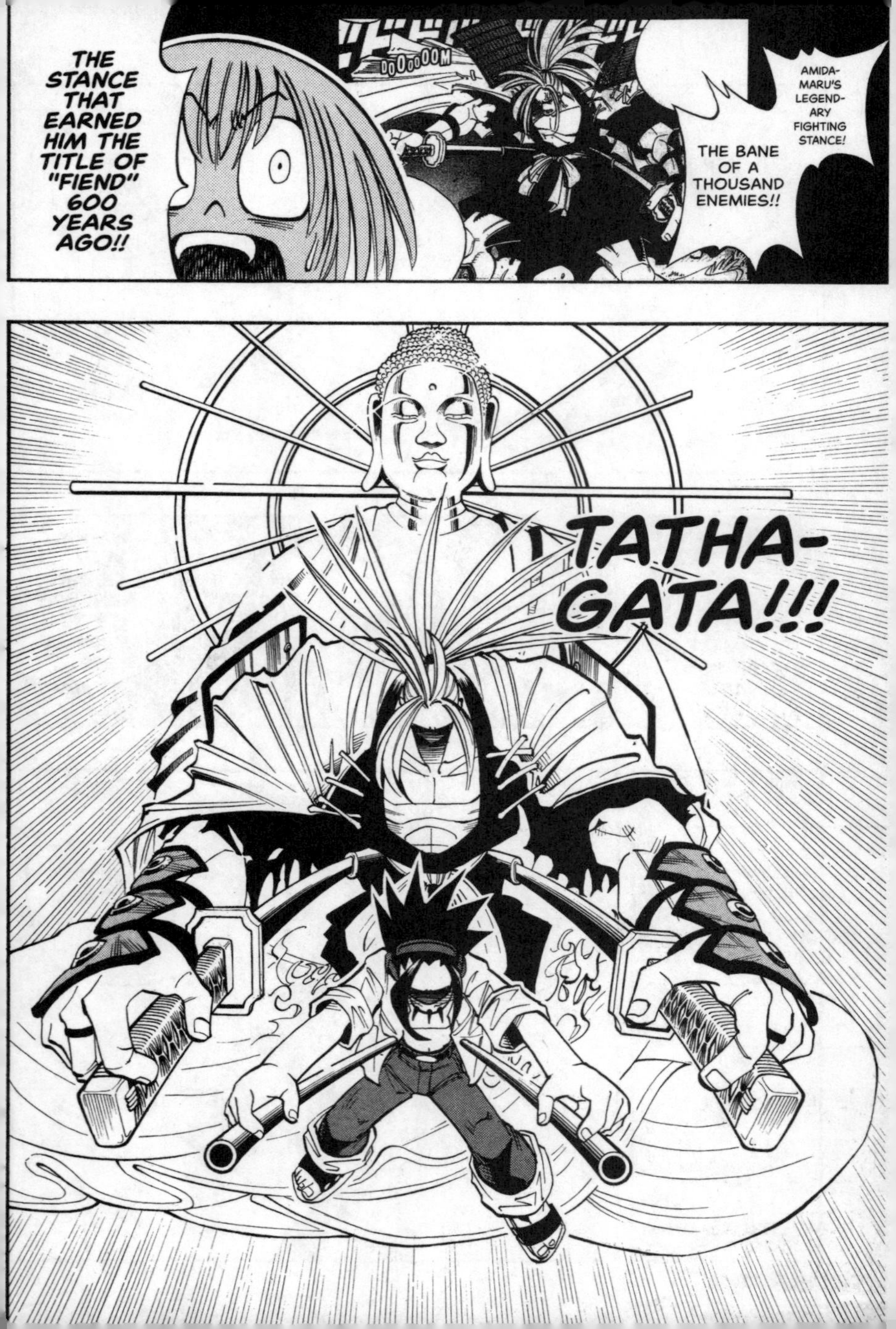
AMIDA-MARU'S LEGEND-ARY FIGHTING STANCE!
THE BANE OF A THOUSAND ENEMIES!!
DOOOOOOM
THE STANCE THAT EARNED HIM THE TITLE OF "FIEND" 600 YEARS AGO!!
TATHA-GATA!!!

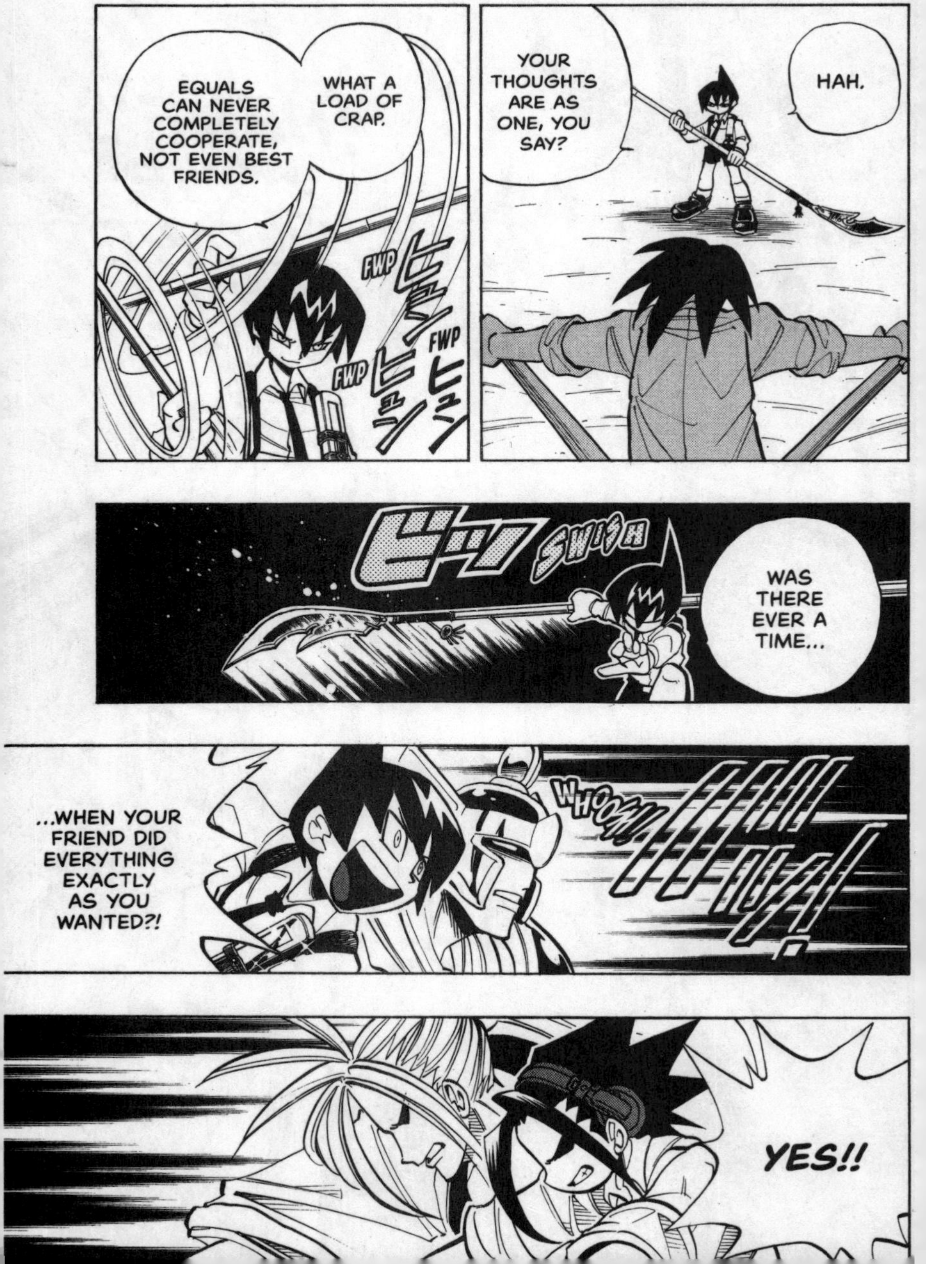
HAH.
YOUR THOUGHTS ARE AS ONE, YOU SAY?
WHAT A LOAD OF CRAP.
EQUALS CAN NEVER COMPLETELY COOPERATE, NOT EVEN BEST FRIENDS.
FWP
FWP
FWP
WAS THERE EVER A TIME...
SWISH
WHOOSH!!
...WHEN YOUR FRIEND DID EVERYTHING EXACTLY AS YOU WANTED?!
YES!!

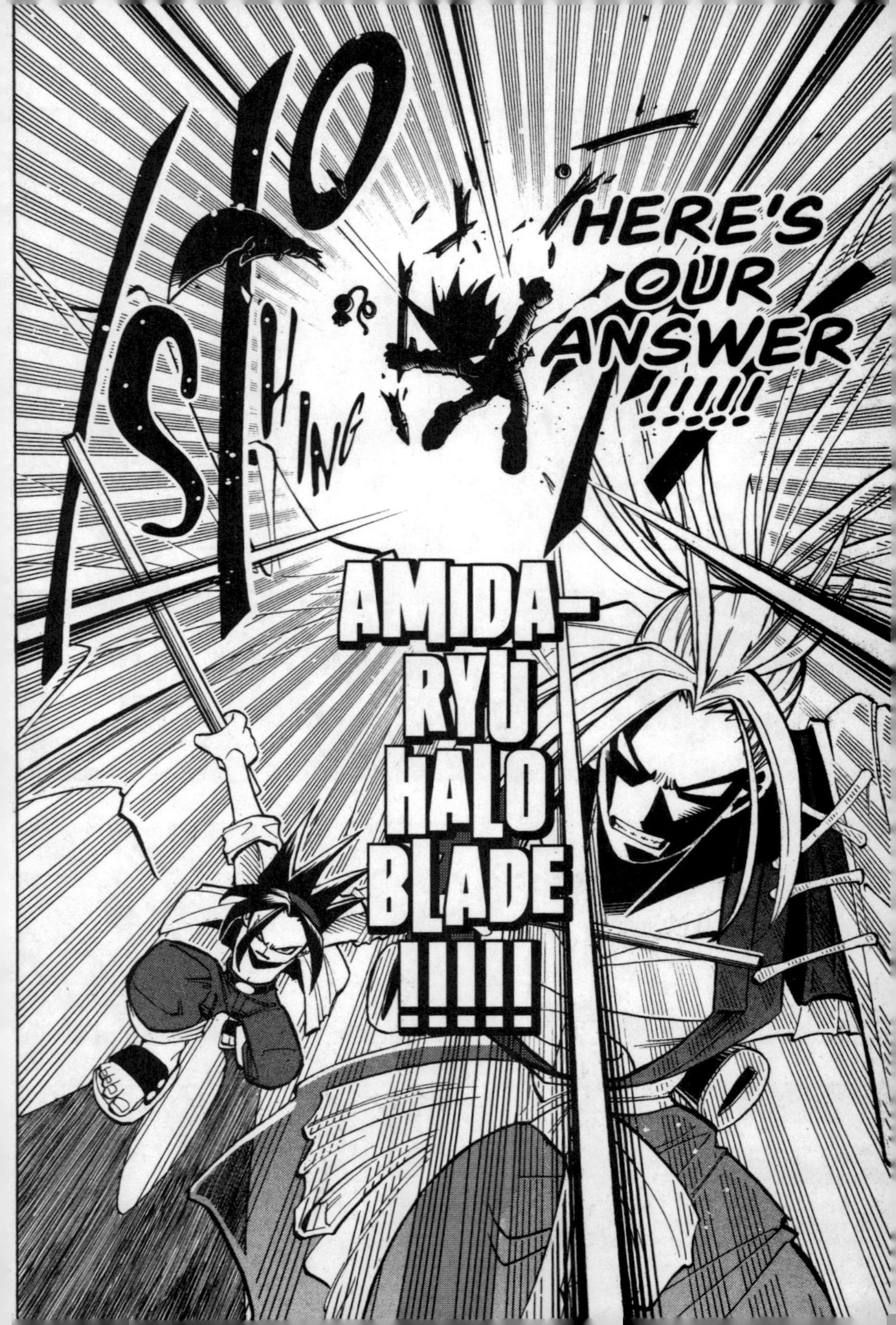
HERE'S OUR ANSWER !!!!!!
SHING
AMIDA-RYU HALO BLADE !!!!!

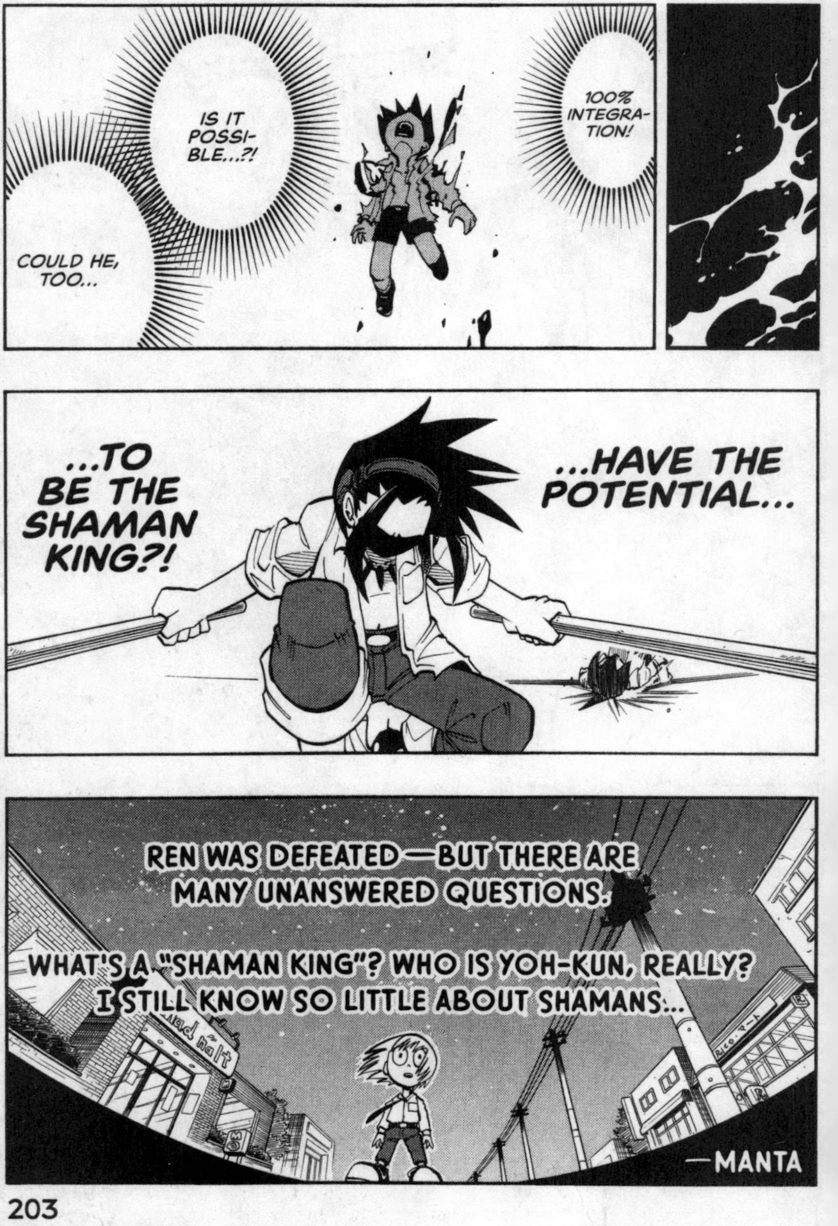
100% INTEGRATION!
IS IT POSSIBLE...?!
COULD HE, TOO...
...HAVE THE POTENTIAL...
...TO BE THE SHAMAN KING?!
REN WAS DEFEATED—BUT THERE ARE MANY UNANSWERED QUESTIONS.
WHAT'S A "SHAMAN KING"? WHO IS YOH-KUN, REALLY? I STILL KNOW SO LITTLE ABOUT SHAMANS...
—MANTA

Bonus Page!
SHAMAN KING CHARACTER FILE No.4

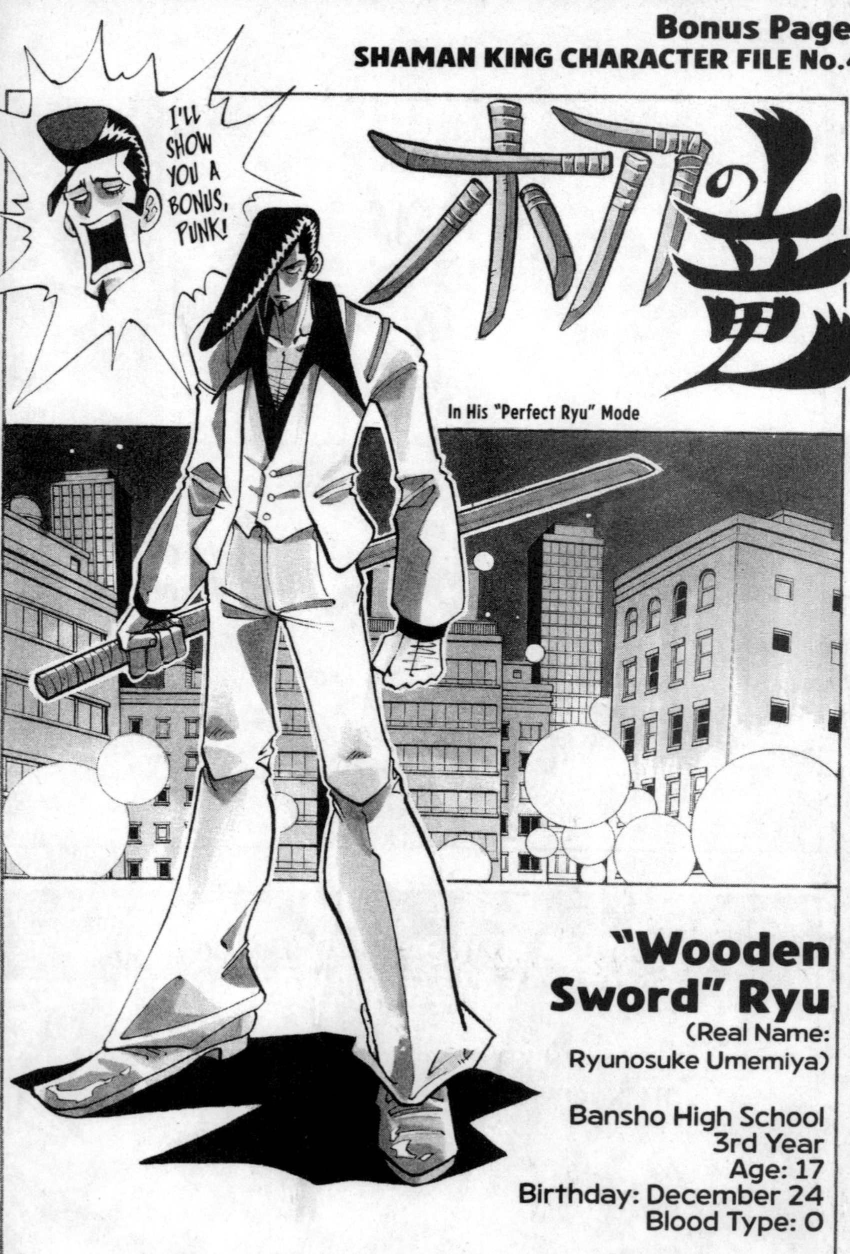
I'LL SHOW YOU A BONUS, PUNK!
木刀の竜
In His "Perfect Ryu" Mode
"Wooden Sword" Ryu
(Real Name: Ryunosuke Umemiya)
Bansho High School
3rd Year
Age: 17
Birthday: December 24
Blood Type: O

SPECIAL INFO! RYU'S COMPANIONS ON HIS SEARCH FOR THE "HAPPY PLACE"!

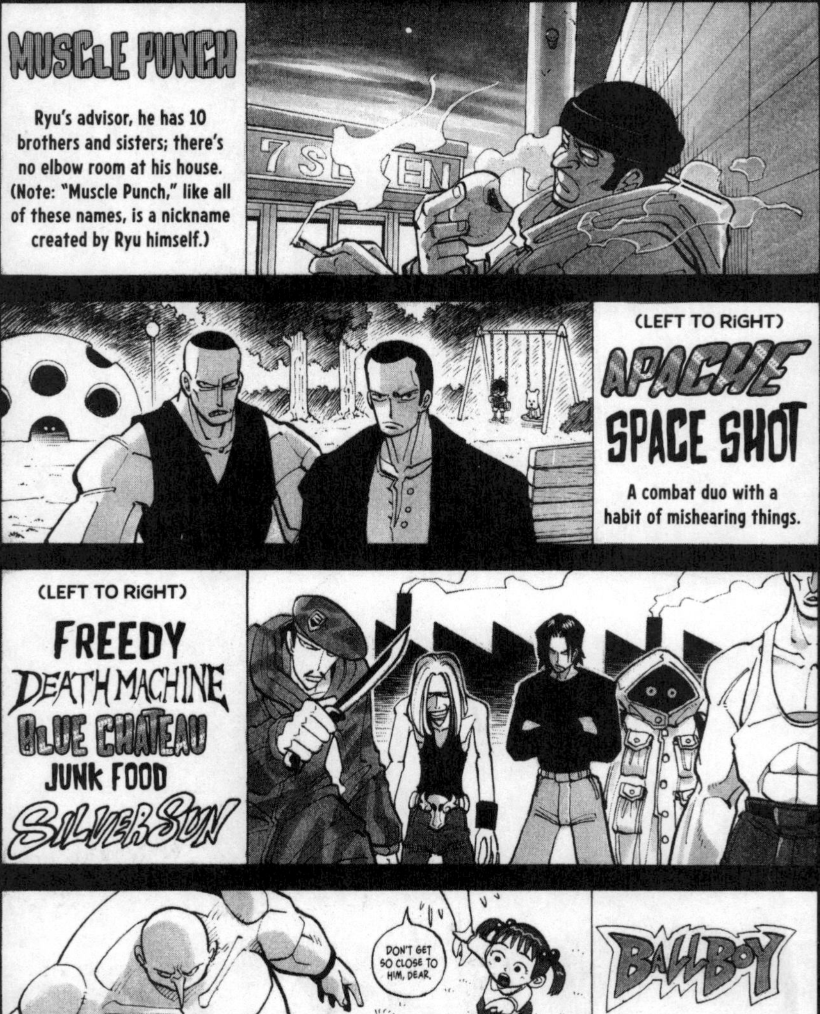
MUSCLE PUNCH
Ryu's advisor, he has 10 brothers and sisters; there's no elbow room at his house. (Note: "Muscle Punch," like all of these names, is a nickname created by Ryu himself.)
(LEFT TO RIGHT)
APACHE
SPACE SHOT
A combat duo with a habit of mishearing things.
(LEFT TO RIGHT)
FREEDY
DEATH MACHINE
BLUE CHATEAU
JUNK FOOD
SILVER SUN
BALLBOY
He's quite superstitious for his age—plus he's a grandma's boy and a coward! But he's really very kind.
DON'T GET SO CLOSE TO HIM, DEAR.
MOMMY, WHY DOESN'T HE HAVE ANY CLOTHES?
B-B

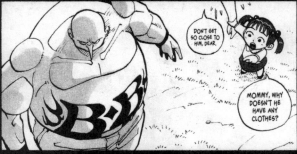

SHAMAN KING

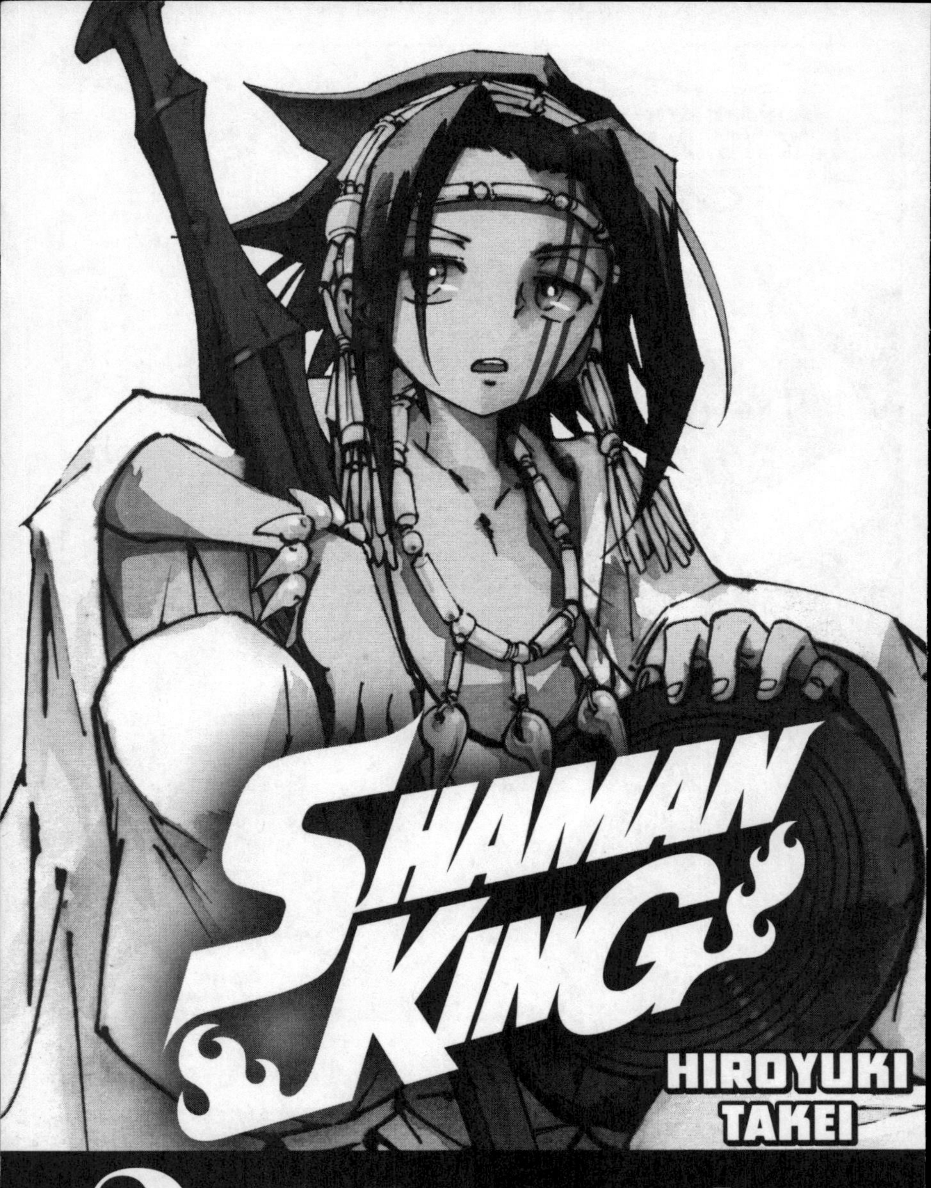
SHAMAN KING
HIROYUKI TAKEI

2 A Shaman's Ambition

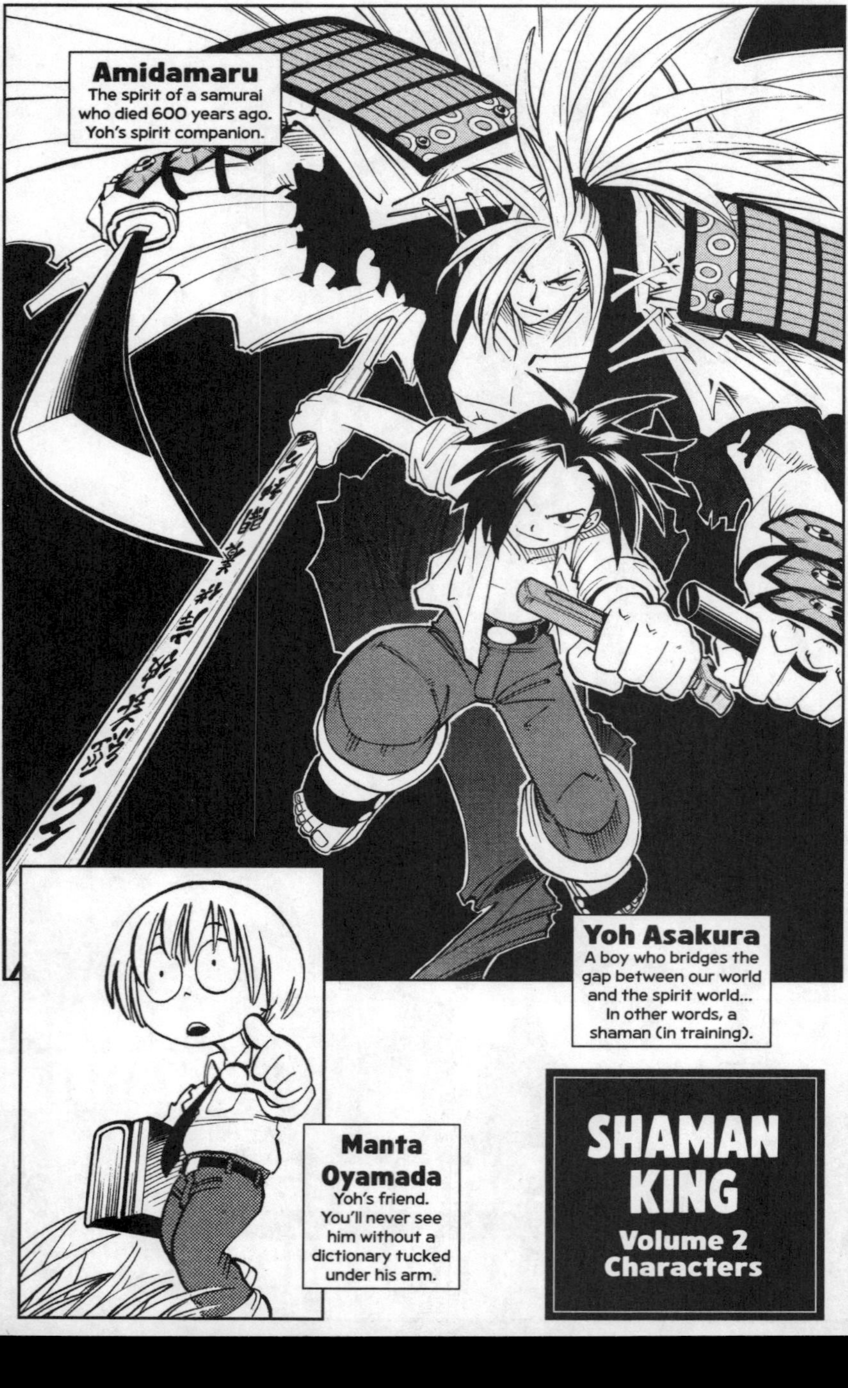
Amidamaru
The spirit of a samurai who died 600 years ago. Yoh's spirit companion.
Yoh Asakura
A boy who bridges the gap between our world and the spirit world... In other words, a shaman (in training).
SHAMAN KING
Volume 2 Characters
Manta Oyamada
Yoh's friend. You'll never see him without a dictionary tucked under his arm.

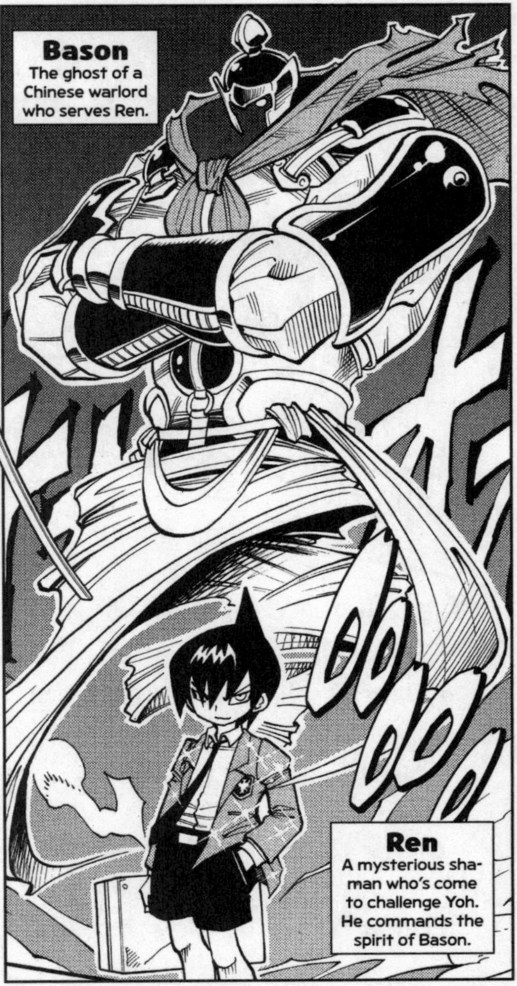

Bason
The ghost of a Chinese warlord who serves Ren.
Ren
A mysterious shaman who's come to challenge Yoh. He commands the spirit of Bason.

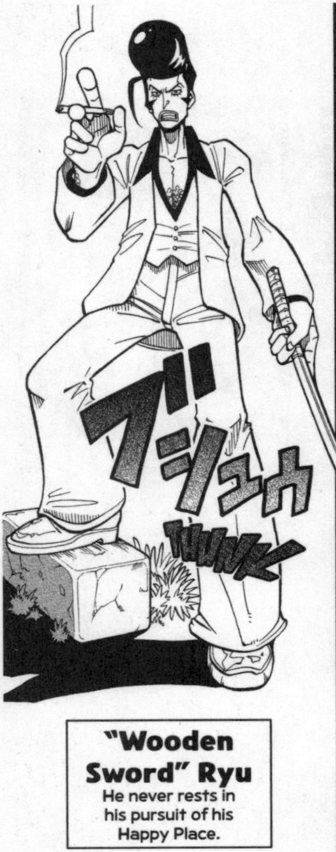

ブシュウ
THUNK
"Wooden Sword" Ryu
He never rests in his pursuit of his Happy Place.

THE STORY SO FAR

This kid named Yoh Asakura-kun transferred to my class from Izumo... and it turns out he's a shaman! It seems shamans can bridge the gap between the spirit world and our world, commune with gods and spirits, and even draw on their strength. He came here to hone his abilities and took the ghost of Amidamaru, a samurai who died 600 years ago, as his spirit companion. But just as soon as he'd done that, Ren, another shaman, showed up to steal Amidamaru! It was a long, hard-fought battle, and Yoh went down by the end of it... but not without putting Ren in his place!

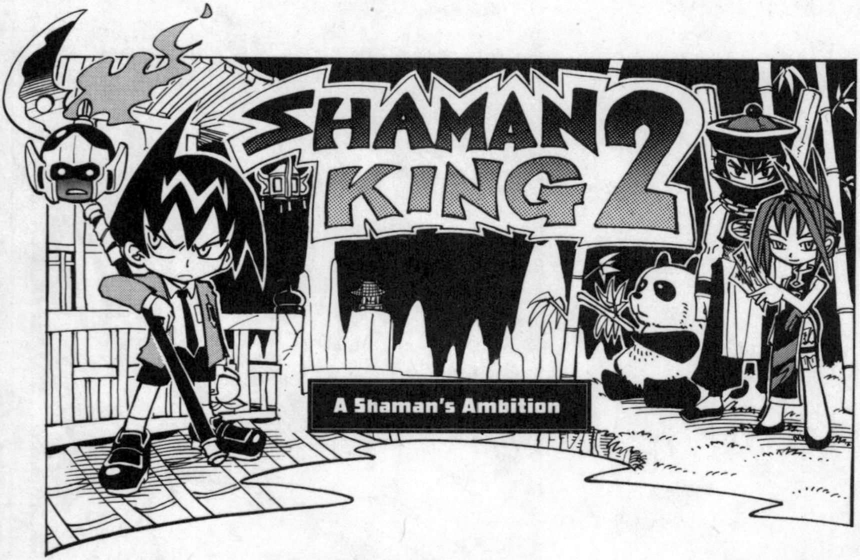
SHAMAN KING 2
A Shaman's Ambition

Chapter 9: The Shaman King

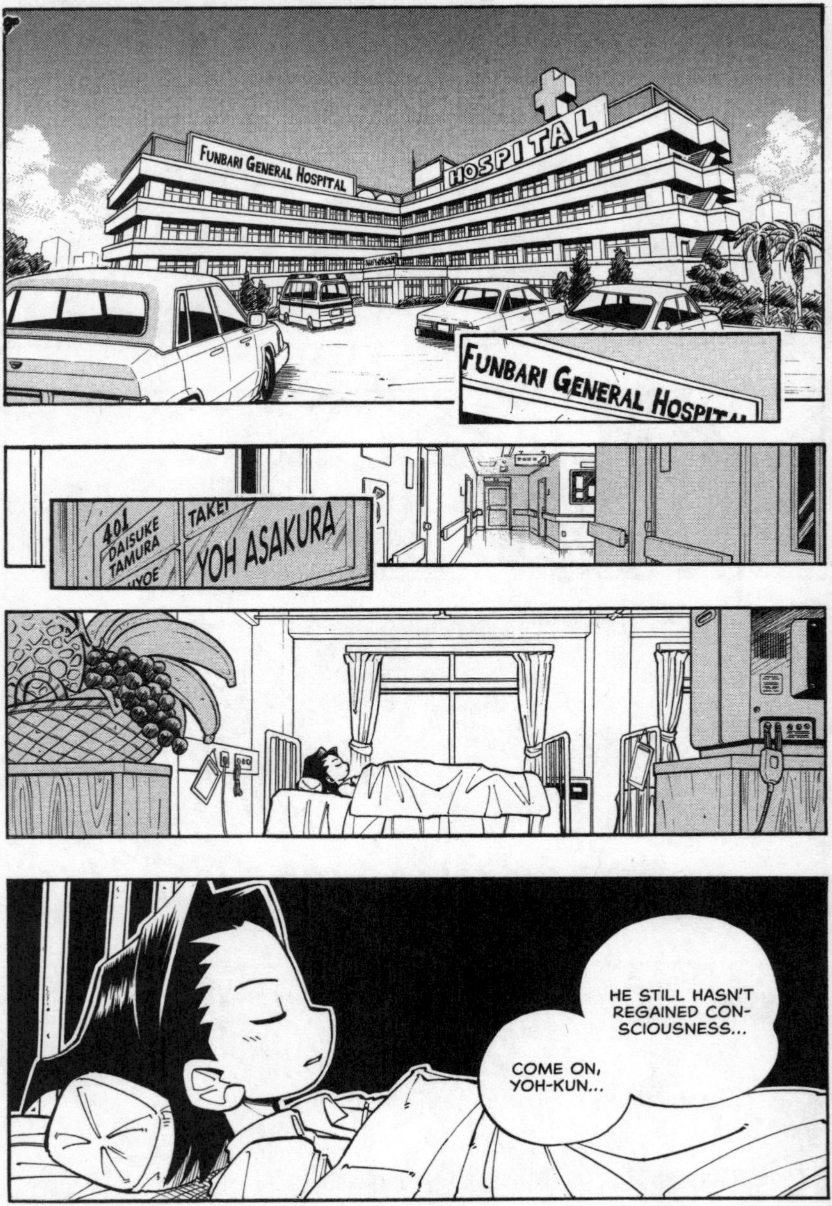

FUNBARI GENERAL HOSPITAL
HOSPITAL
FUNBARI GENERAL
401
DAISUKE TAMURA
TAKEI
YOH ASAKURA
HE STILL HASN'T REGAINED CON-SCIOUSNESS...
COME ON, YOH-KUN...

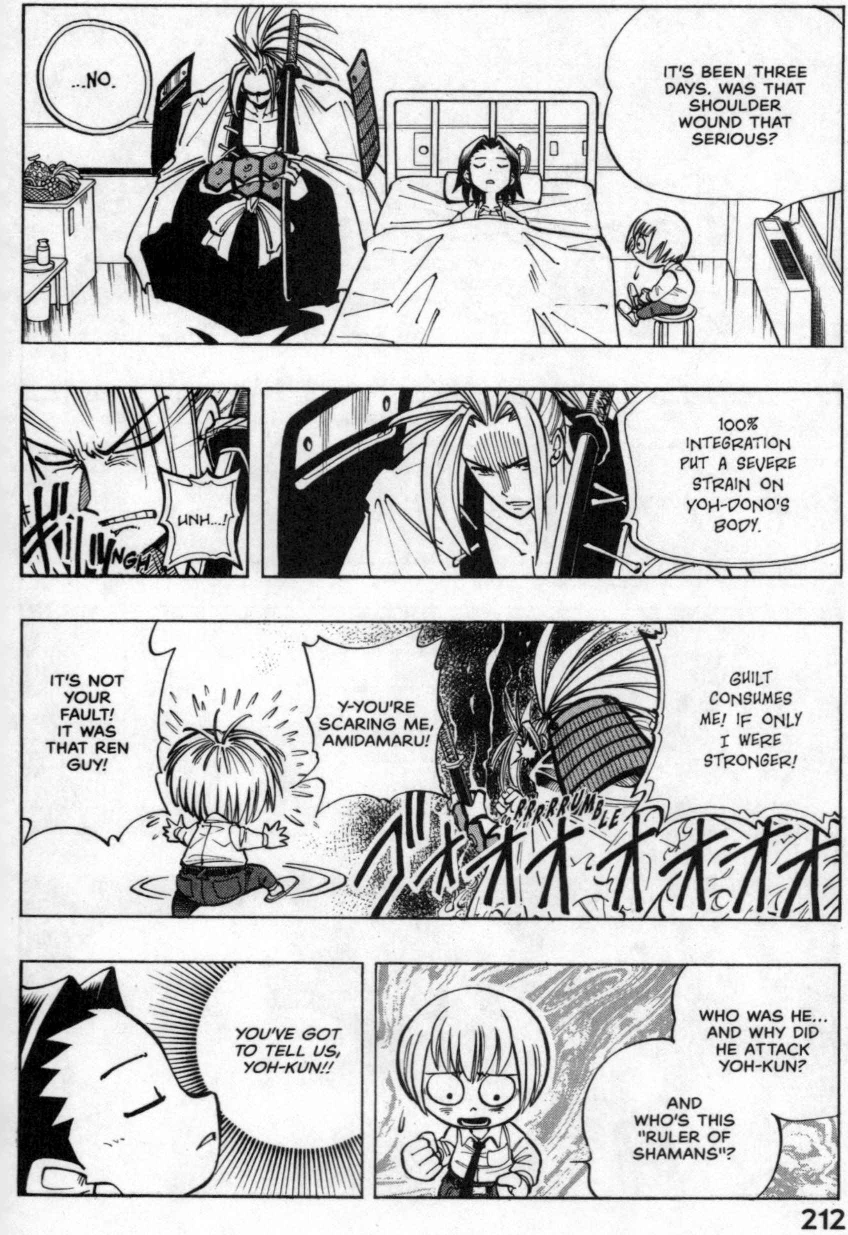
IT'S BEEN THREE DAYS. WAS THAT SHOULDER WOUND THAT SERIOUS?
...NO.
100% INTEGRATION PUT A SEVERE STRAIN ON YOH-DONO'S BODY.
UNH...!
NGH
GUILT CONSUMES ME! IF ONLY I WERE STRONGER!
RRRRRUMBLE
Y-YOU'RE SCARING ME, AMIDAMARU!
IT'S NOT YOUR FAULT! IT WAS THAT REN GUY!
WHO WAS HE... AND WHY DID HE ATTACK YOH-KUN?
AND WHO'S THIS "RULER OF SHAMANS"?
YOU'VE GOT TO TELL US, YOH-KUN!!

Chapter 9:

The Shaman King

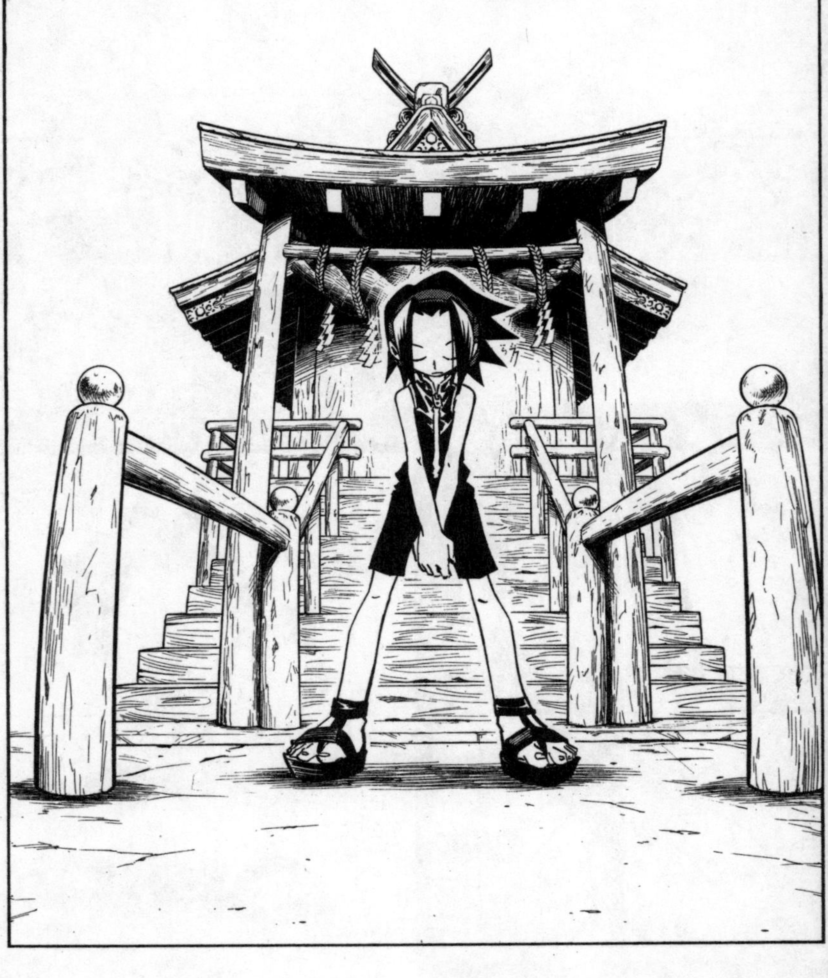

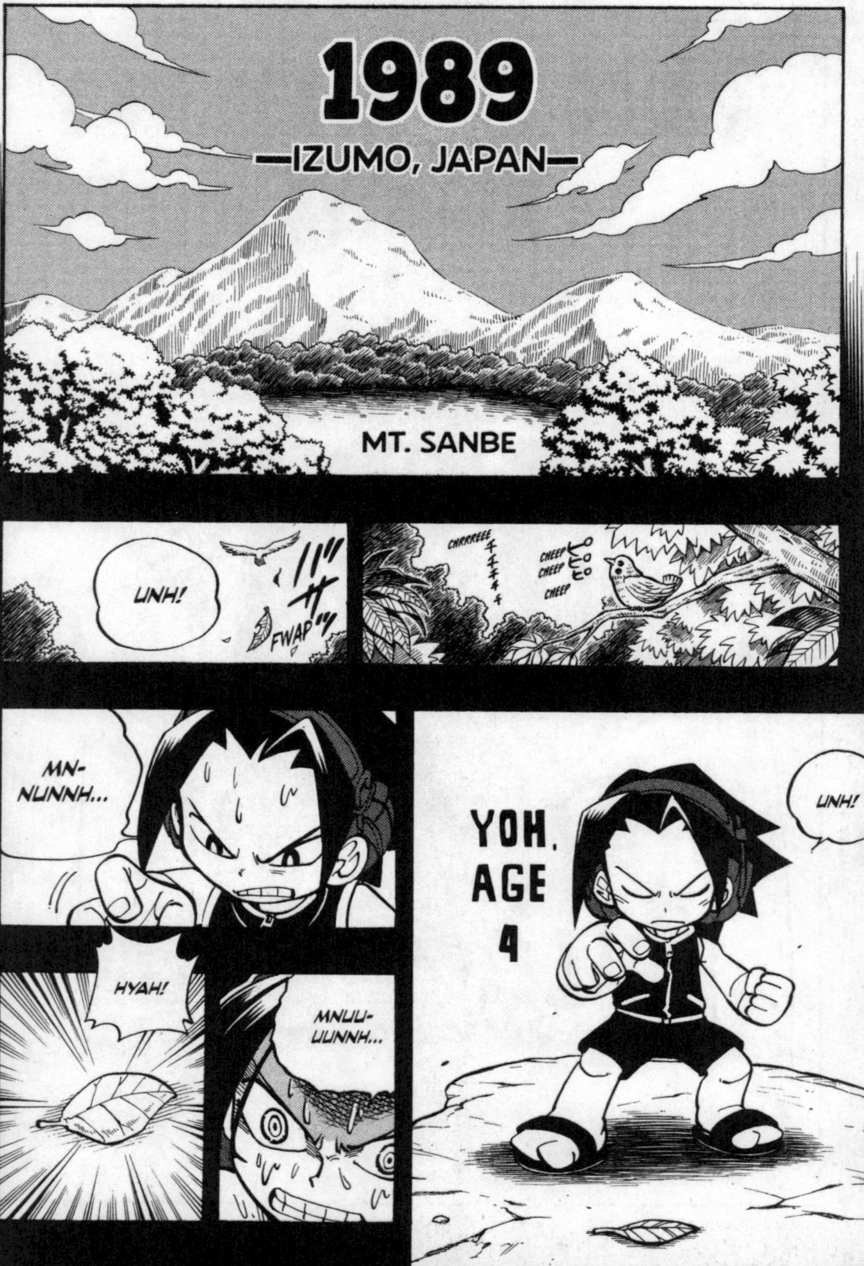
1989
—IZUMO, JAPAN—
MT. SANBE
CHRRREEE
CHEEP CHEEP CHEEP
UNH!
FWAP
YOH, AGE 4
UNH!
MN-NUNNH...
MNUU-UUNNH...
HYAH!

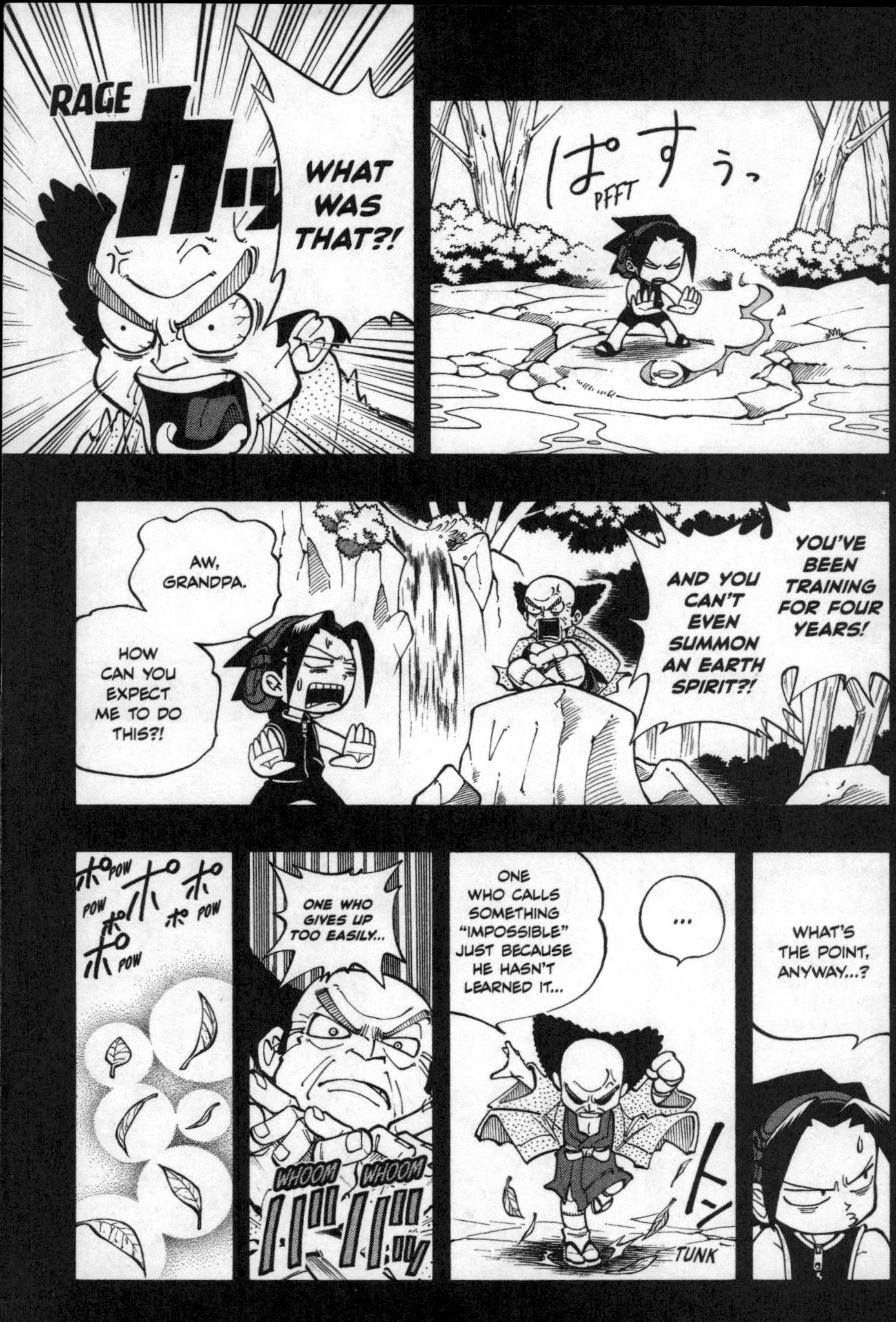
ぱすぅっ
PFFT
RAGE
カッ
WHAT WAS THAT?!
YOU'VE BEEN TRAINING FOR FOUR YEARS!
AND YOU CAN'T EVEN SUMMON AN EARTH SPIRIT?!
AW, GRANDPA.
HOW CAN YOU EXPECT ME TO DO THIS?!
WHAT'S THE POINT, ANYWAY...?
...
ONE WHO CALLS SOMETHING "IMPOSSIBLE" JUST BECAUSE HE HASN'T LEARNED IT...
トン
TUNK
ONE WHO GIVES UP TOO EASILY...
WHOOM WHOOM
ポポポポポ
POW POW POW POW POW

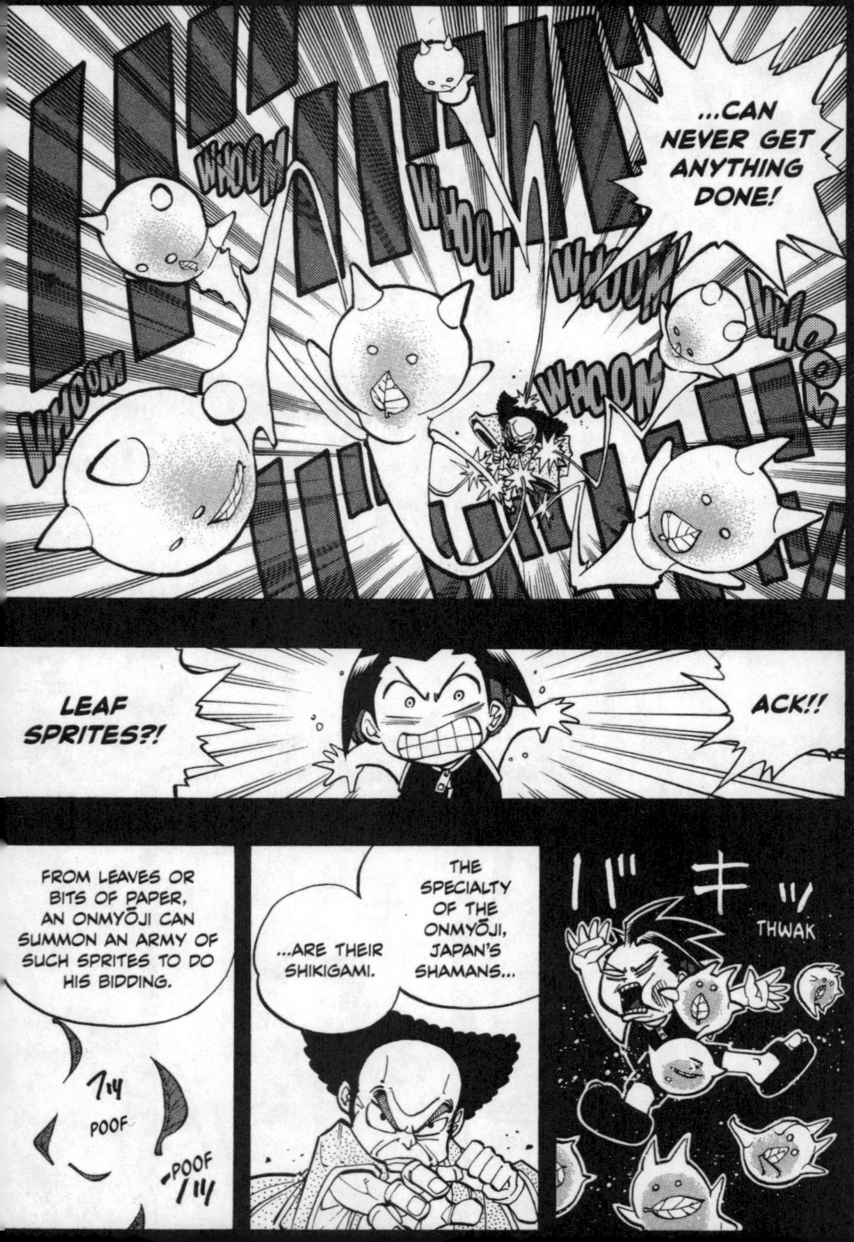
...CAN NEVER GET ANYTHING DONE!
WHOOM
WHOOM
WHOOM
WHOOM
WHOOM
WHOOM
WHOOM
ACK!!
LEAF SPRITES?!
バキッ
THWAK
THE SPECIALTY OF THE ONMYŌJI, JAPAN'S SHAMANS...
...ARE THEIR SHIKIGAMI.
FROM LEAVES OR BITS OF PAPER, AN ONMYŌJI CAN SUMMON AN ARMY OF SUCH SPRITES TO DO HIS BIDDING.
POOF
POOF

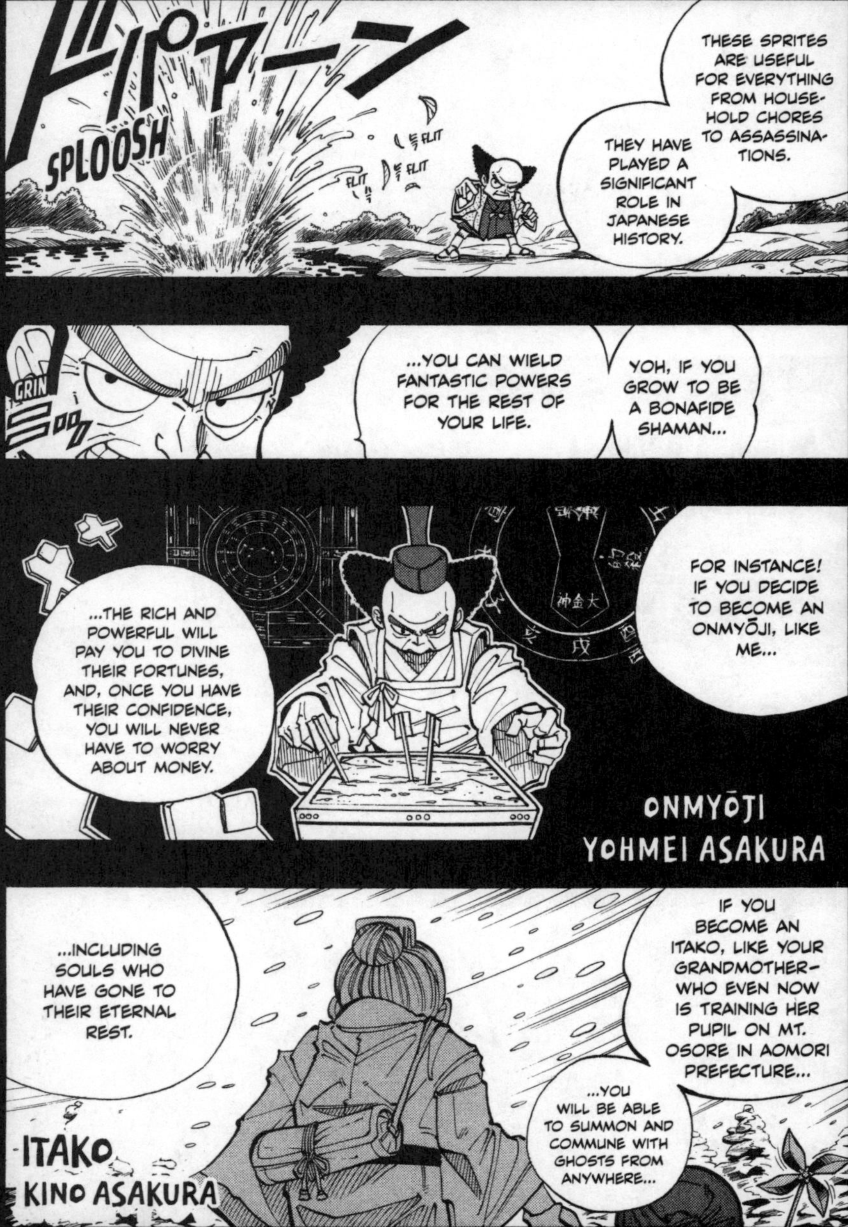

THESE SPRITES ARE USEFUL FOR EVERYTHING FROM HOUSE-HOLD CHORES TO ASSASSINA-TIONS.
THEY HAVE PLAYED A SIGNIFICANT ROLE IN JAPANESE HISTORY.
FLIT
FLIT
FLIT
SPLOOSH
YOH, IF YOU GROW TO BE A BONAFIDE SHAMAN...
...YOU CAN WIELD FANTASTIC POWERS FOR THE REST OF YOUR LIFE.
GRIN
FOR INSTANCE! IF YOU DECIDE TO BECOME AN ONMYŌJI, LIKE ME...
...THE RICH AND POWERFUL WILL PAY YOU TO DIVINE THEIR FORTUNES, AND, ONCE YOU HAVE THEIR CONFIDENCE, YOU WILL NEVER HAVE TO WORRY ABOUT MONEY.
ONMYŌJI
YOHMEI ASAKURA
IF YOU BECOME AN ITAKO, LIKE YOUR GRANDMOTHER-WHO EVEN NOW IS TRAINING HER PUPIL ON MT. OSORE IN AOMORI PREFECTURE...
...YOU WILL BE ABLE TO SUMMON AND COMMUNE WITH GHOSTS FROM ANYWHERE...
...INCLUDING SOULS WHO HAVE GONE TO THEIR ETERNAL REST.
ITAKO
KINO ASAKURA

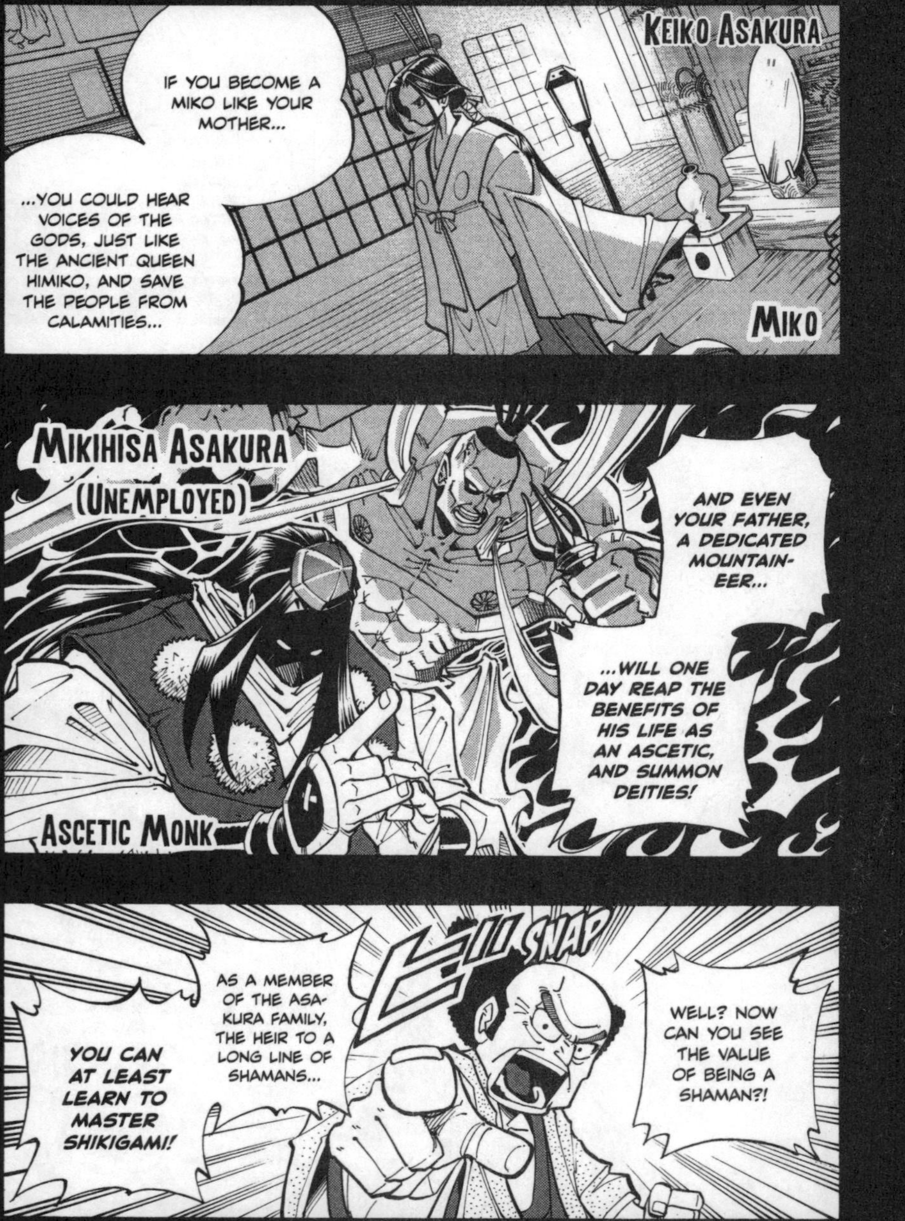
KEIKO ASAKURA
IF YOU BECOME A MIKO LIKE YOUR MOTHER...
...YOU COULD HEAR VOICES OF THE GODS, JUST LIKE THE ANCIENT QUEEN HIMIKO, AND SAVE THE PEOPLE FROM CALAMITIES...
MIKO
AND EVEN YOUR FATHER, A DEDICATED MOUNTAIN-EER...
...WILL ONE DAY REAP THE BENEFITS OF HIS LIFE AS AN ASCETIC, AND SUMMON DEITIES!
MIKIHISA ASAKURA
(UNEMPLOYED)
ASCETIC MONK
SNAP
WELL? NOW CAN YOU SEE THE VALUE OF BEING A SHAMAN?!
AS A MEMBER OF THE ASA-KURA FAMILY, THE HEIR TO A LONG LINE OF SHAMANS...
YOU CAN AT LEAST LEARN TO MASTER SHIKIGAMI!

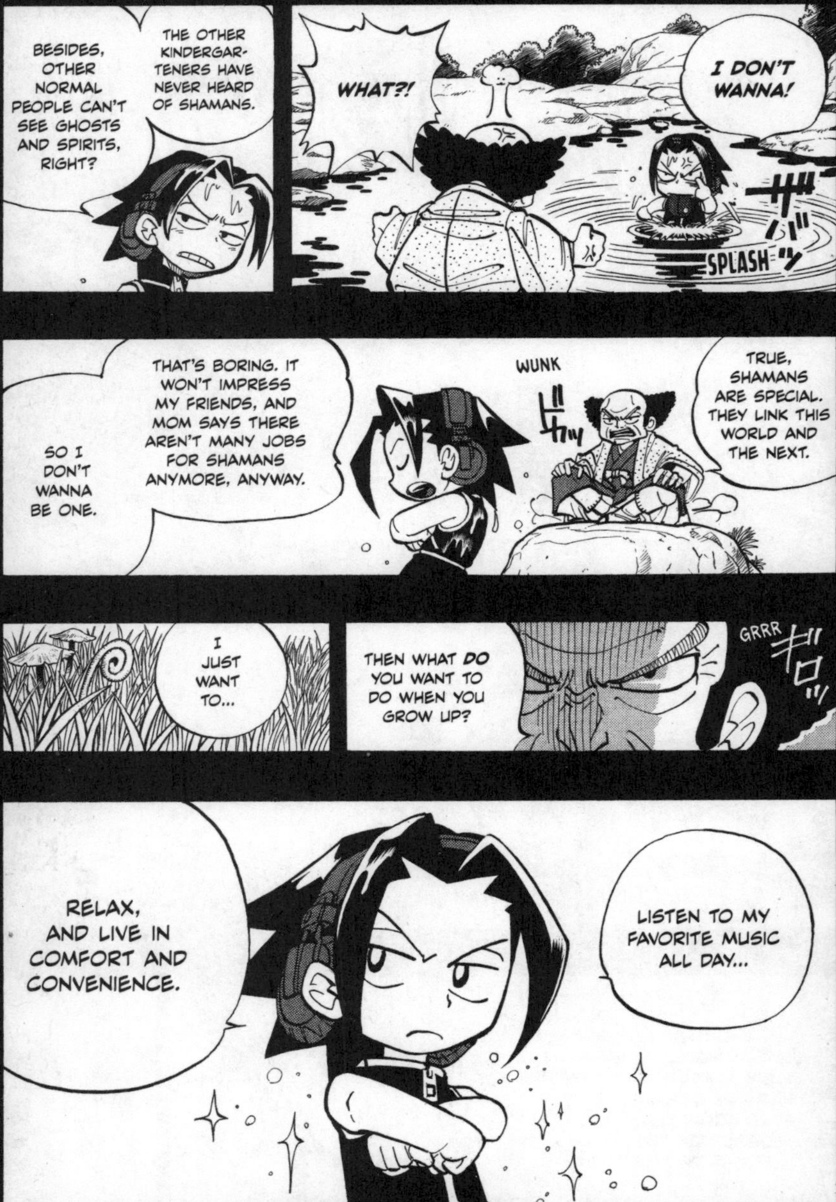
I DON'T WANNA!
WHAT?!
SPLASH
THE OTHER KINDERGAR-TENERS HAVE NEVER HEARD OF SHAMANS.
BESIDES, OTHER NORMAL PEOPLE CAN'T SEE GHOSTS AND SPIRITS, RIGHT?
TRUE, SHAMANS ARE SPECIAL. THEY LINK THIS WORLD AND THE NEXT.
WUNK
THAT'S BORING. IT WON'T IMPRESS MY FRIENDS, AND MOM SAYS THERE AREN'T MANY JOBS FOR SHAMANS ANYMORE, ANYWAY.
SO I DON'T WANNA BE ONE.
GRRR
THEN WHAT DO YOU WANT TO DO WHEN YOU GROW UP?
I JUST WANT TO...
LISTEN TO MY FAVORITE MUSIC ALL DAY...
RELAX, AND LIVE IN COMFORT AND CONVENIENCE.

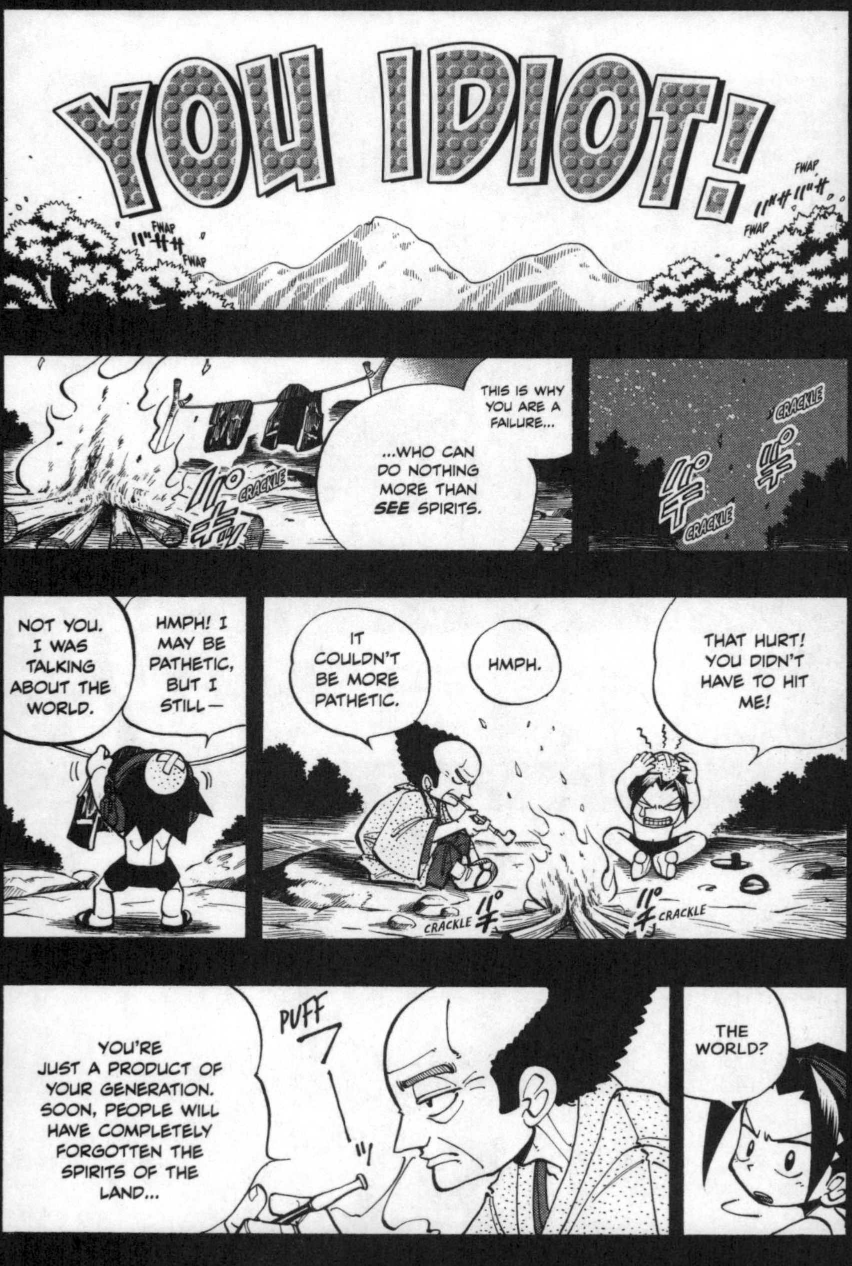
YOU IDIOT!
FWAP
FWAP
FWAP
FWAP
CRACKLE
CRACKLE
THIS IS WHY YOU ARE A FAILURE...
...WHO CAN DO NOTHING MORE THAN SEE SPIRITS.
CRACKLE
THAT HURT! YOU DIDN'T HAVE TO HIT ME!
HMPH.
IT COULDN'T BE MORE PATHETIC.
CRACKLE
CRACKLE
HMPH! I MAY BE PATHETIC, BUT I STILL—
NOT YOU. I WAS TALKING ABOUT THE WORLD.
THE WORLD?
PUFF
YOU'RE JUST A PRODUCT OF YOUR GENERATION. SOON, PEOPLE WILL HAVE COMPLETELY FORGOTTEN THE SPIRITS OF THE LAND...

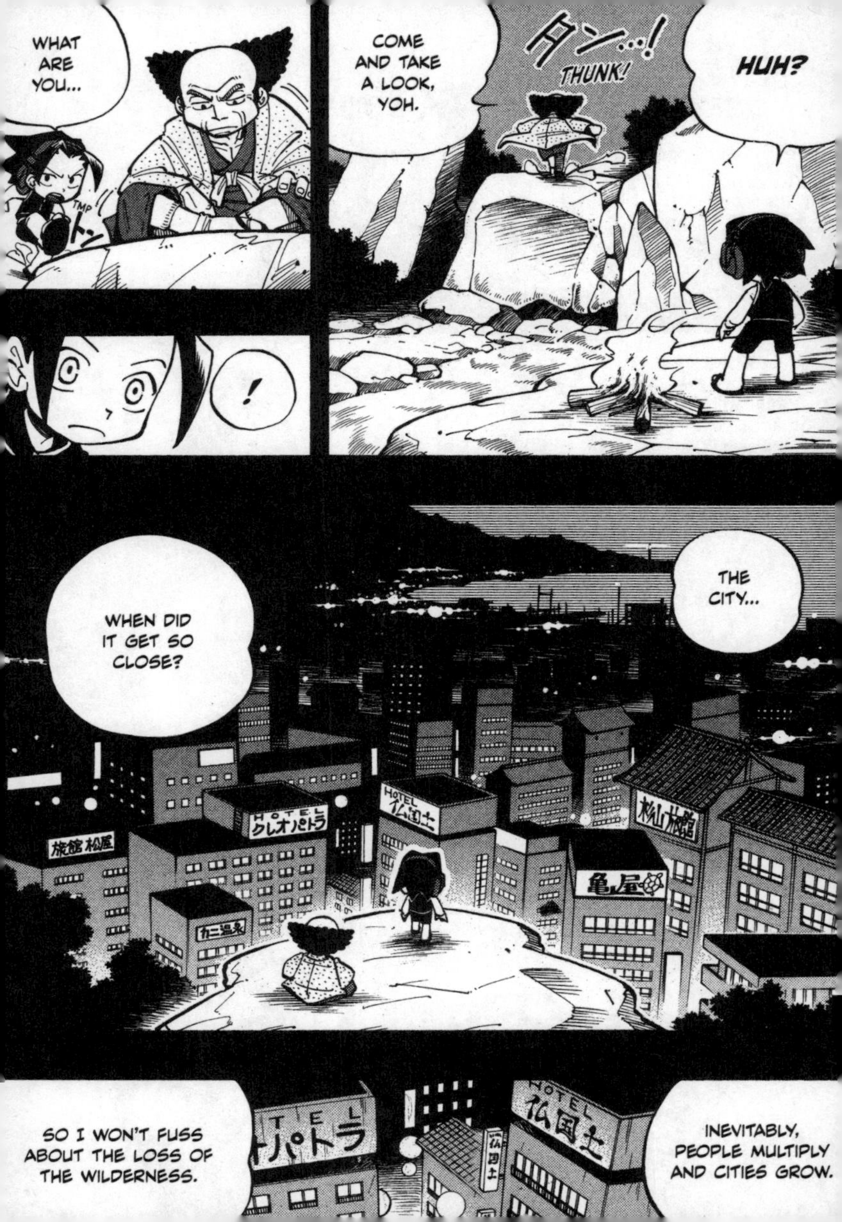
HUH?
タン…!
THUNK!
COME AND TAKE A LOOK, YOH.
WHAT ARE YOU...
TMP
トン
!
THE CITY...
WHEN DID IT GET SO CLOSE?
松山旅館
HOTEL 仏国土
HOTEL クレオパトラ
旅館 松屋
亀屋
カニ温泉
INEVITABLY, PEOPLE MULTIPLY AND CITIES GROW.
SO I WON'T FUSS ABOUT THE LOSS OF THE WILDERNESS.

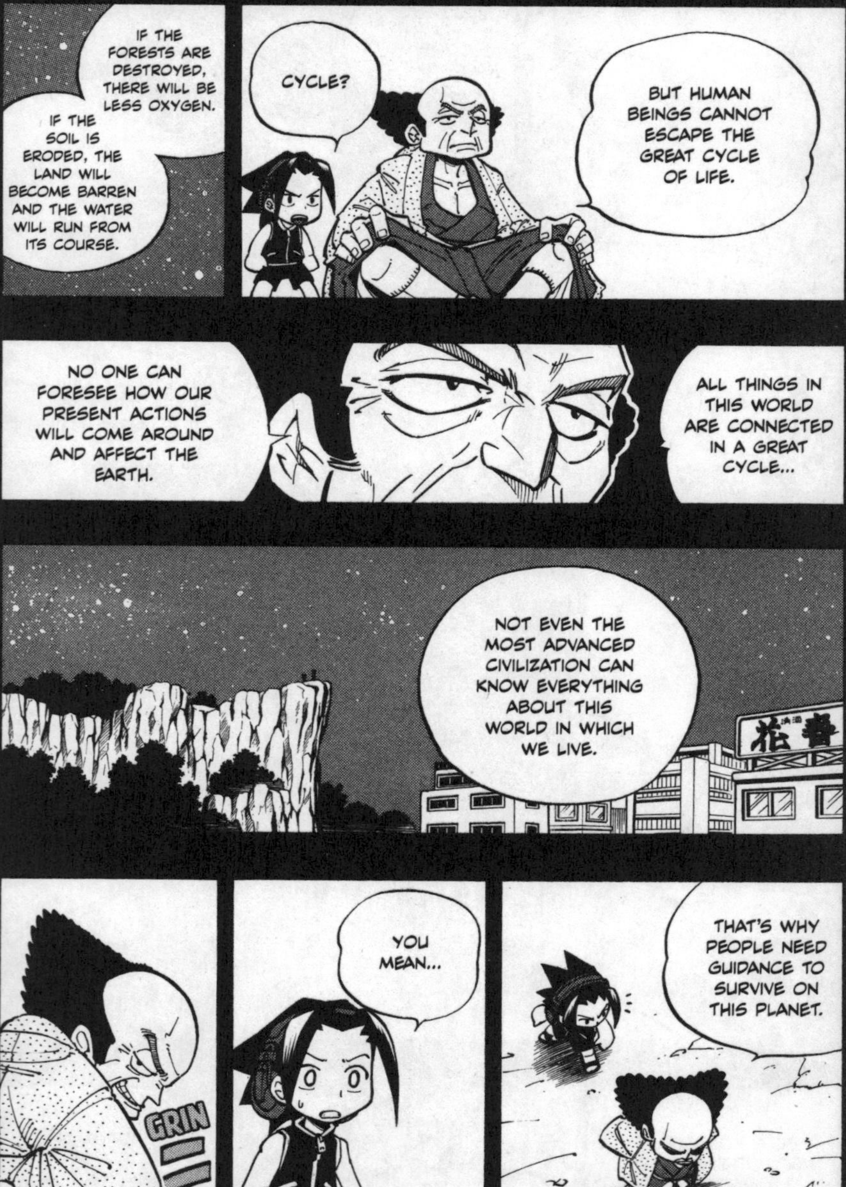

BUT HUMAN BEINGS CANNOT ESCAPE THE GREAT CYCLE OF LIFE.
CYCLE?
IF THE FORESTS ARE DESTROYED, THERE WILL BE LESS OXYGEN.
IF THE SOIL IS ERODED, THE LAND WILL BECOME BARREN AND THE WATER WILL RUN FROM ITS COURSE.
ALL THINGS IN THIS WORLD ARE CONNECTED IN A GREAT CYCLE...
NO ONE CAN FORESEE HOW OUR PRESENT ACTIONS WILL COME AROUND AND AFFECT THE EARTH.
NOT EVEN THE MOST ADVANCED CIVILIZATION CAN KNOW EVERYTHING ABOUT THIS WORLD IN WHICH WE LIVE.
THAT'S WHY PEOPLE NEED GUIDANCE TO SURVIVE ON THIS PLANET.
YOU MEAN...
GRIN

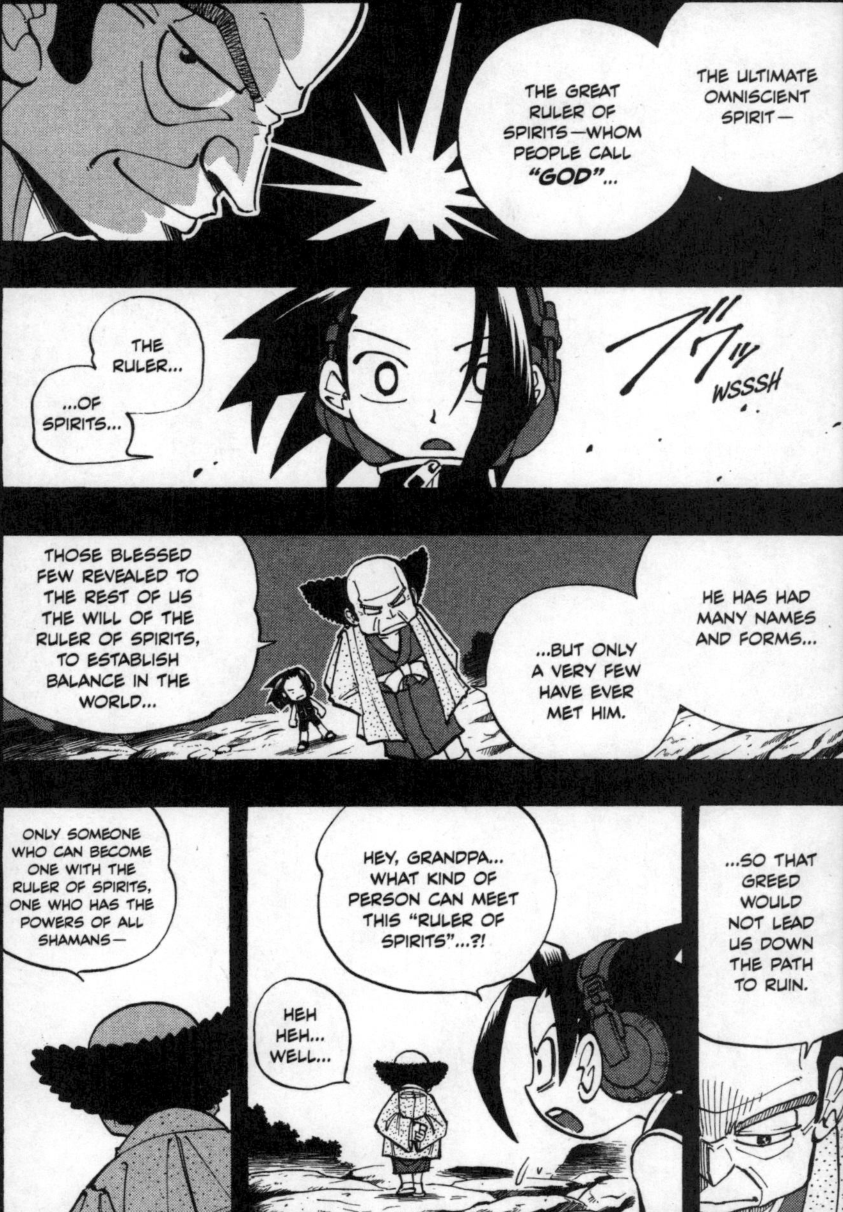
THE ULTIMATE OMNISCIENT SPIRIT—
THE GREAT RULER OF SPIRITS—WHOM PEOPLE CALL "GOD"...
WSSSH
THE RULER...
...OF SPIRITS...
HE HAS HAD MANY NAMES AND FORMS...
...BUT ONLY A VERY FEW HAVE EVER MET HIM.
THOSE BLESSED FEW REVEALED TO THE REST OF US THE WILL OF THE RULER OF SPIRITS, TO ESTABLISH BALANCE IN THE WORLD...
...SO THAT GREED WOULD NOT LEAD US DOWN THE PATH TO RUIN.
HEY, GRANDPA... WHAT KIND OF PERSON CAN MEET THIS "RULER OF SPIRITS"...?!
HEH HEH... WELL...
ONLY SOMEONE WHO CAN BECOME ONE WITH THE RULER OF SPIRITS, ONE WHO HAS THE POWERS OF ALL SHAMANS—

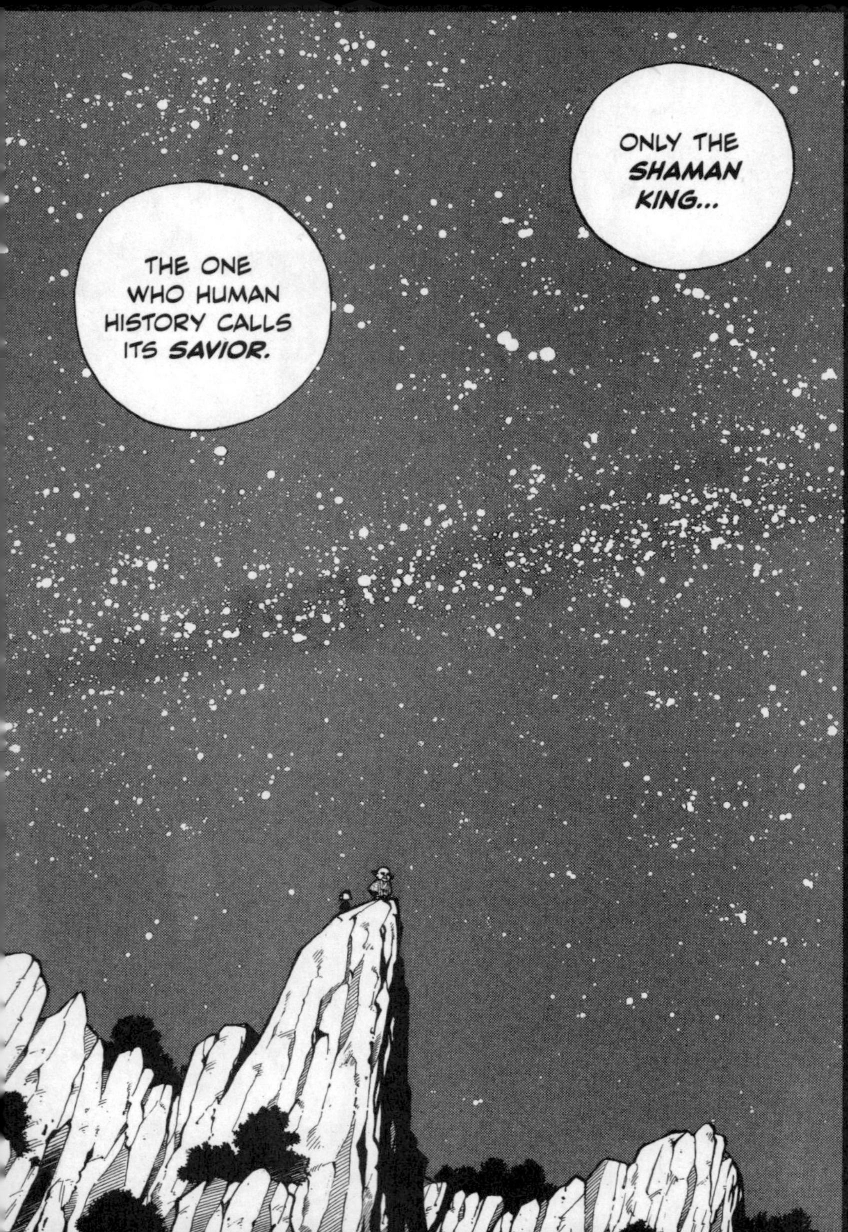
ONLY THE SHAMAN KING...
THE ONE WHO HUMAN HISTORY CALLS ITS SAVIOR.

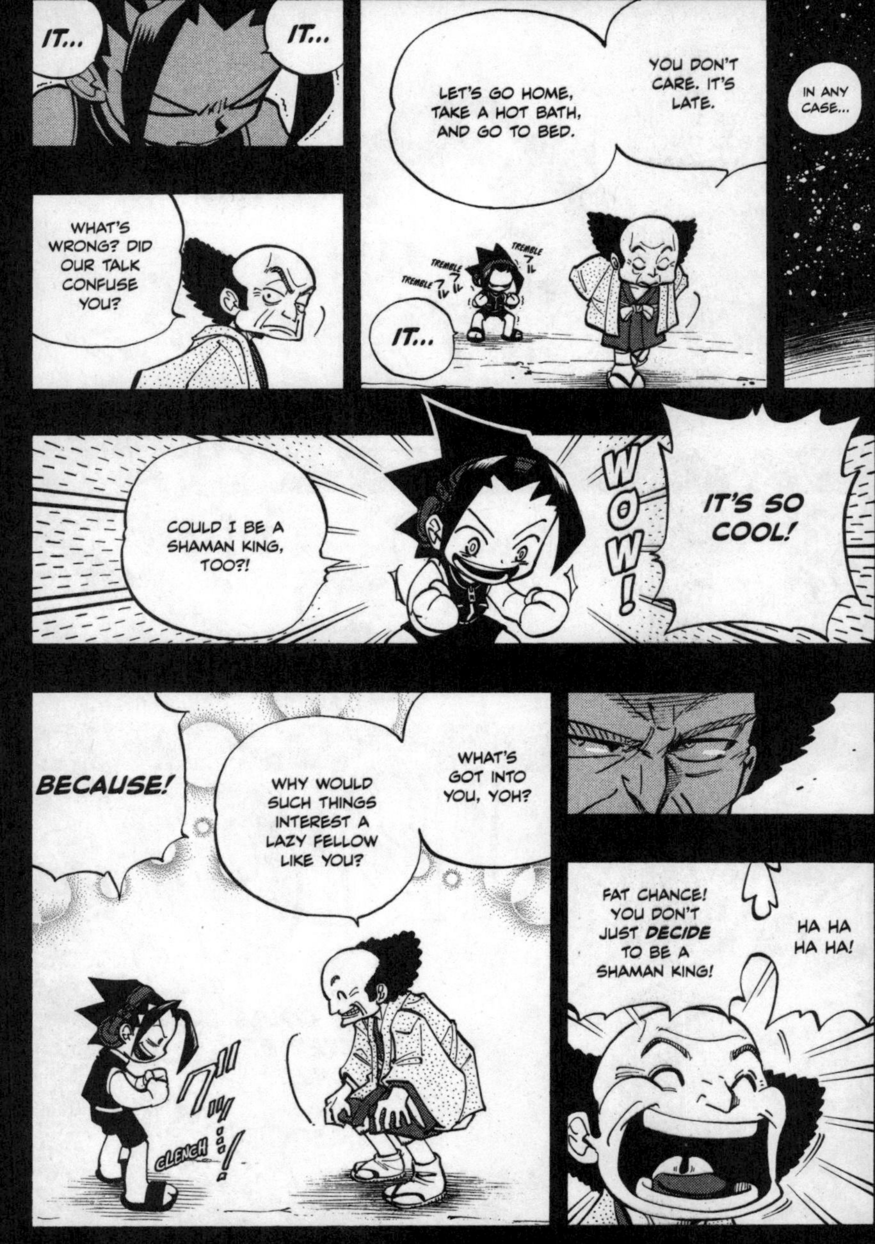

IN ANY CASE...
YOU DON'T CARE. IT'S LATE.
LET'S GO HOME, TAKE A HOT BATH, AND GO TO BED.
TREMBLE
TREMBLE
TREMBLE
IT...
IT...
IT...
WHAT'S WRONG? DID OUR TALK CONFUSE YOU?
IT'S SO COOL!
WOW!
COULD I BE A SHAMAN KING, TOO?!
HA HA HA HA!
FAT CHANCE! YOU DON'T JUST DECIDE TO BE A SHAMAN KING!
WHAT'S GOT INTO YOU, YOH?
WHY WOULD SUCH THINGS INTEREST A LAZY FELLOW LIKE YOU?
BECAUSE!
CLENCH

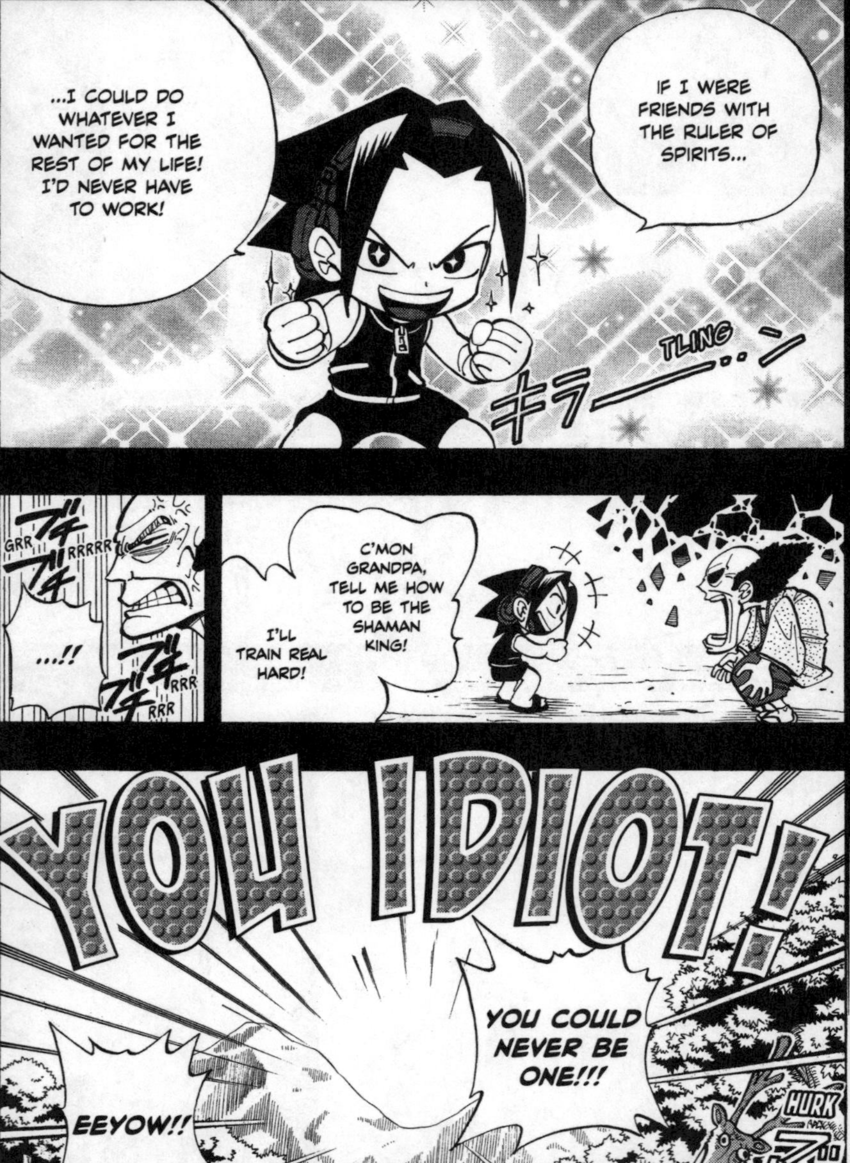
IF I WERE FRIENDS WITH THE RULER OF SPIRITS...
...I COULD DO WHATEVER I WANTED FOR THE REST OF MY LIFE! I'D NEVER HAVE TO WORK!
TLING
キラー
C'MON GRANDPA, TELL ME HOW TO BE THE SHAMAN KING!
I'LL TRAIN REAL HARD!
GRR
RRRRR
...!!
RRR
RRR
YOU IDIOT!
YOU COULD NEVER BE ONE!!!
HURK
EEYOW!!

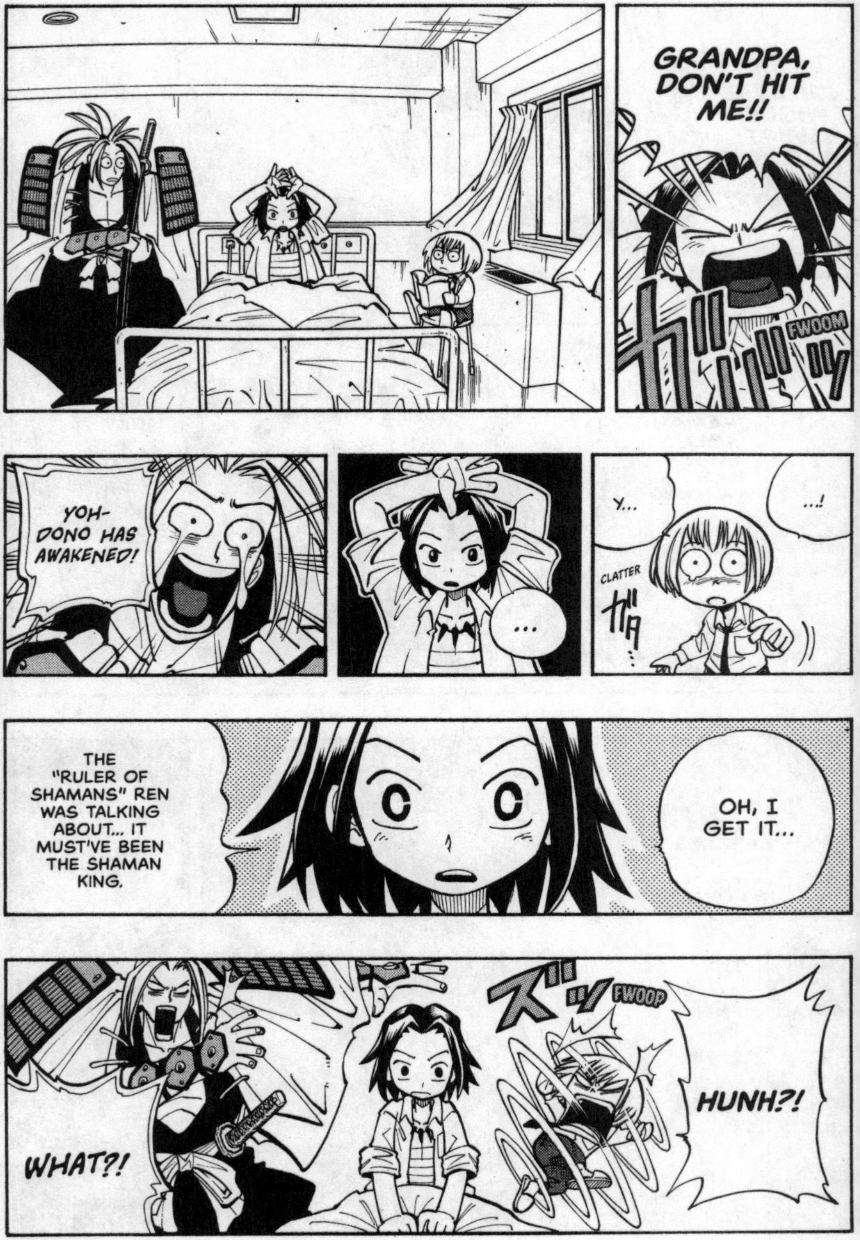
GRANDPA, DON'T HIT ME!!
FWOOM
...!
Y...
CLATTER
...
YOH-DONO HAS AWAKENED!
OH, I GET IT...
THE "RULER OF SHAMANS" REN WAS TALKING ABOUT... IT MUST'VE BEEN THE SHAMAN KING.
FWOOP
HUNH?!
WHAT?!

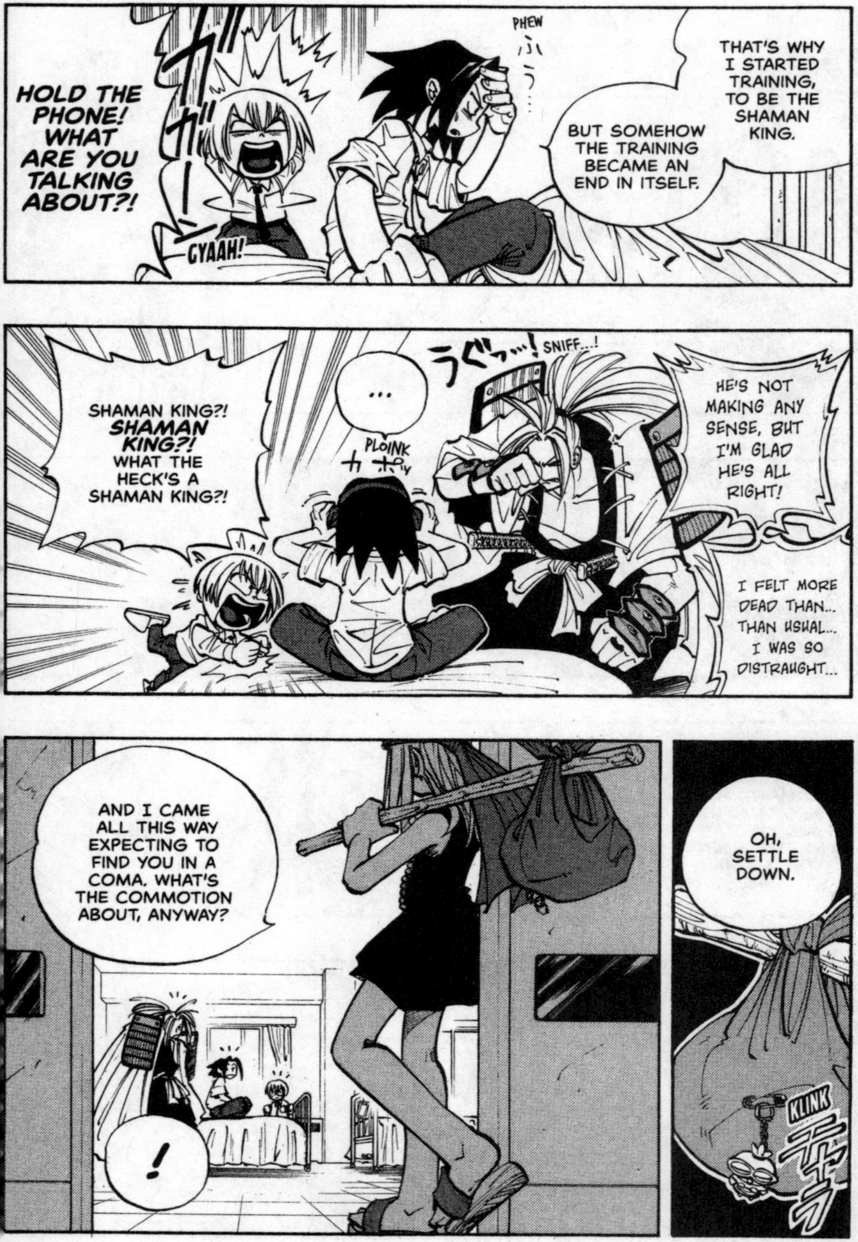
THAT'S WHY I STARTED TRAINING, TO BE THE SHAMAN KING.
BUT SOMEHOW THE TRAINING BECAME AN END IN ITSELF.
PHEW
ふう…
HOLD THE PHONE! WHAT ARE YOU TALKING ABOUT?!
GYAAH!
HE'S NOT MAKING ANY SENSE, BUT I'M GLAD HE'S ALL RIGHT!
SNIFF...!
I FELT MORE DEAD THAN... THAN USUAL... I WAS SO DISTRAUGHT...
...
PLOINK
SHAMAN KING?! SHAMAN KING?! WHAT THE HECK'S A SHAMAN KING?!
OH, SETTLE DOWN.
KLINK
AND I CAME ALL THIS WAY EXPECTING TO FIND YOU IN A COMA. WHAT'S THE COMMOTION ABOUT, ANYWAY?
!

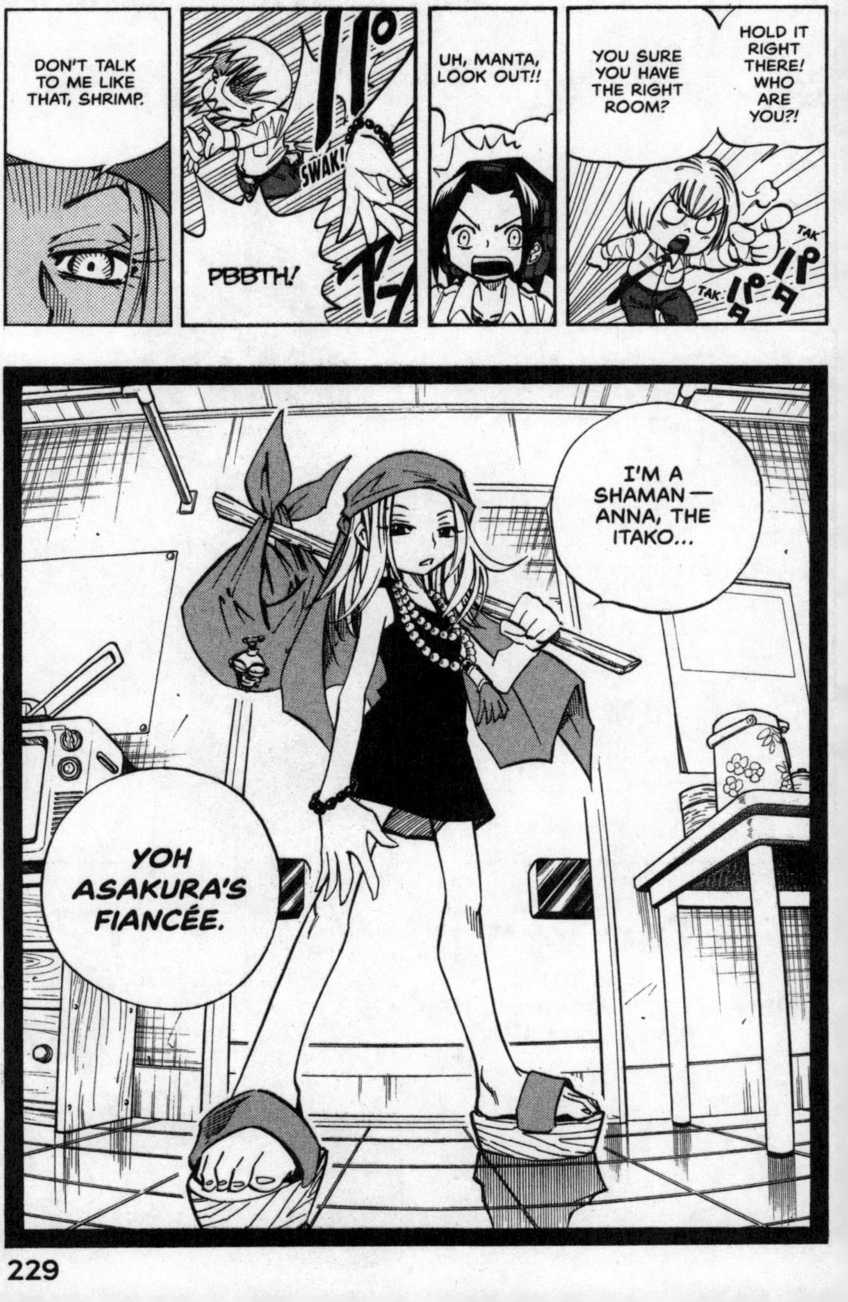
HOLD IT RIGHT THERE! WHO ARE YOU?!
YOU SURE YOU HAVE THE RIGHT ROOM?
TAK
TAK
UH, MANTA, LOOK OUT!!
SWAK!
PBBTH!
DON'T TALK TO ME LIKE THAT, SHRIMP.
I'M A SHAMAN— ANNA, THE ITAKO...
YOH ASAKURA'S FIANCÉE.

SHAMAN KING CHARACTER FILE No.5

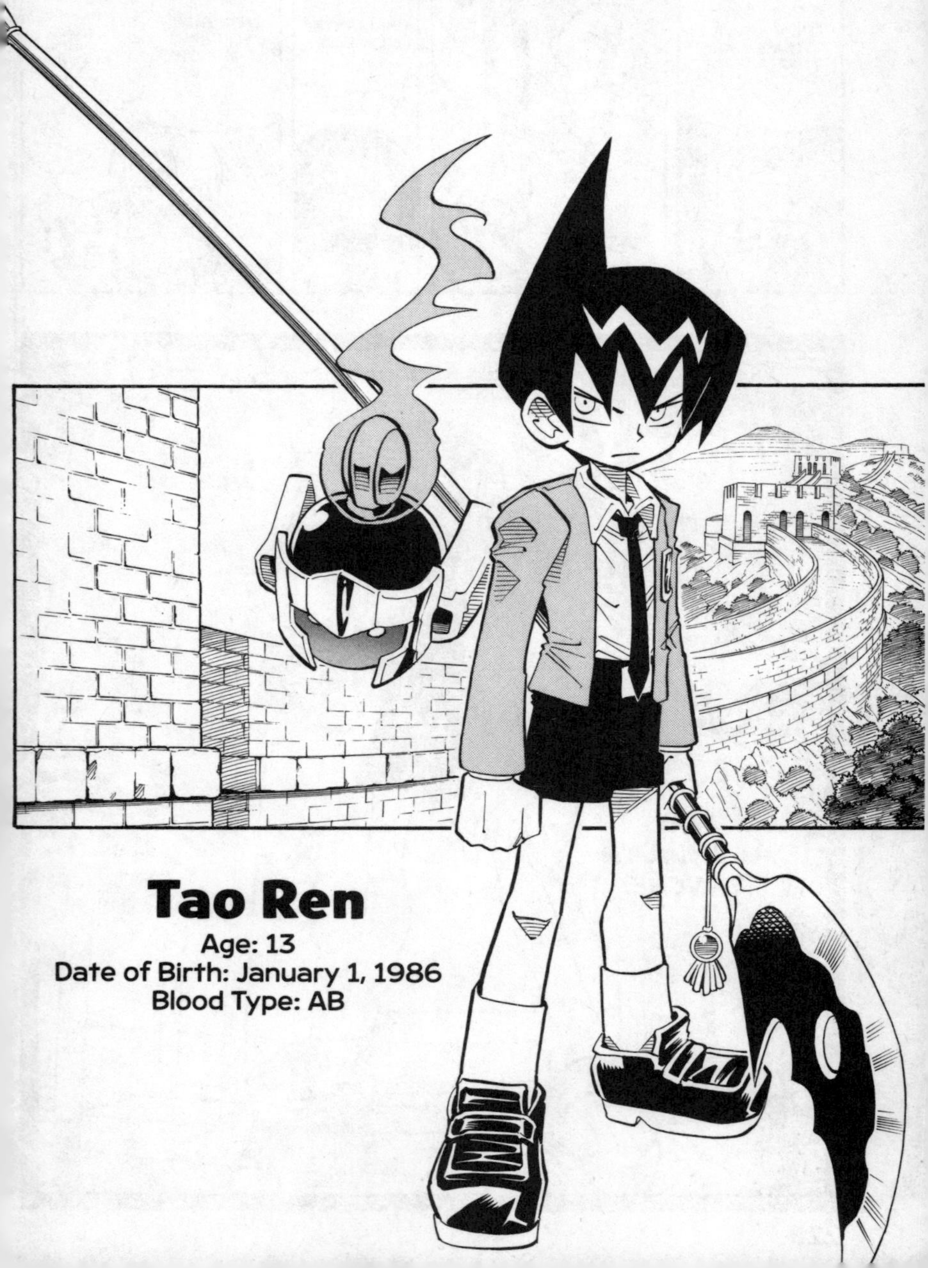

Tao Ren

Age: 13
Date of Birth: January 1, 1986
Blood Type: AB

Chapter 10: A Shaman's Ambition

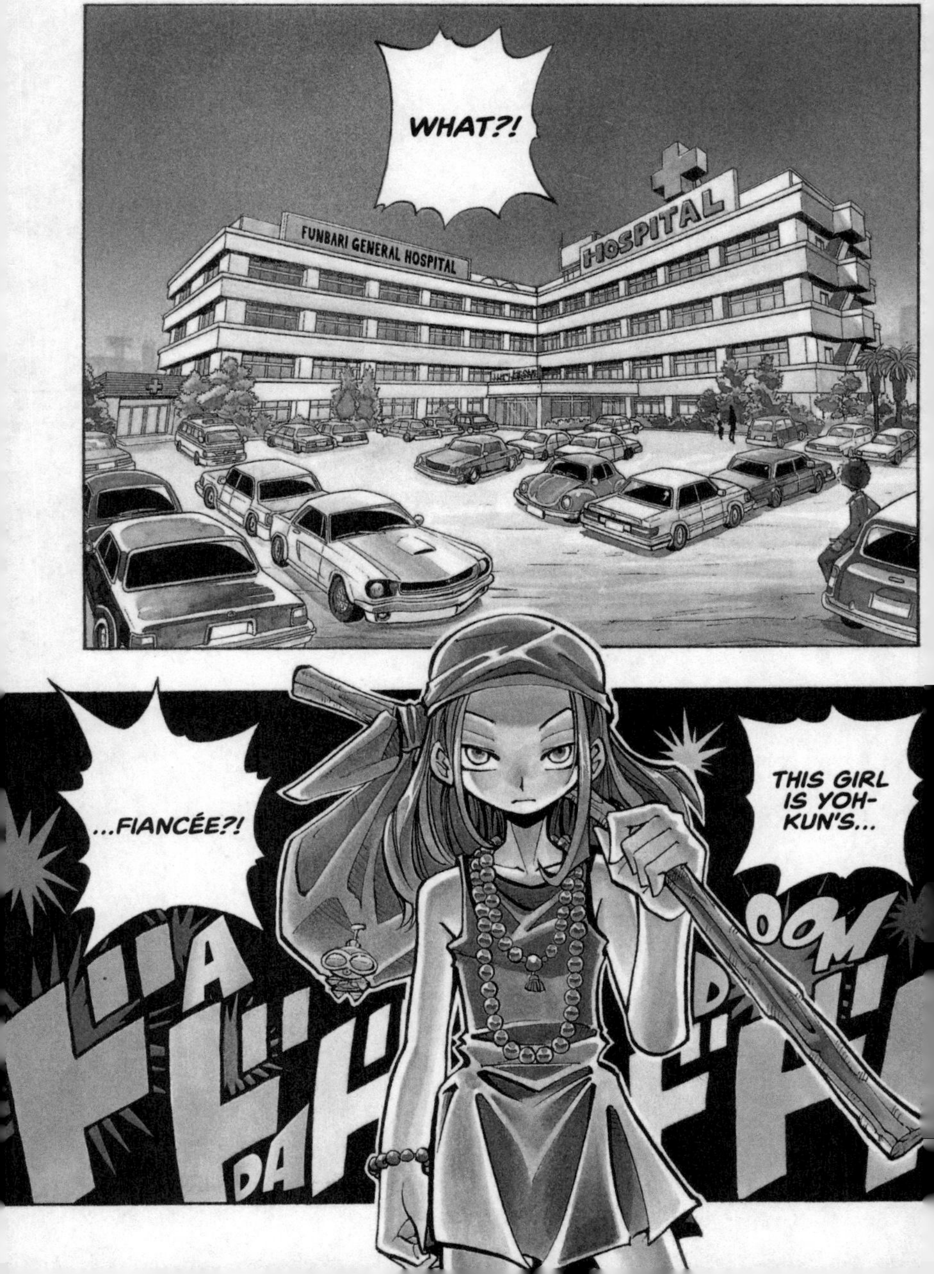
WHAT?!
HOSPITAL
FUNBARI GENERAL HOSPITAL
THIS GIRL IS YOH-KUN'S...
...FIANCÉE?!

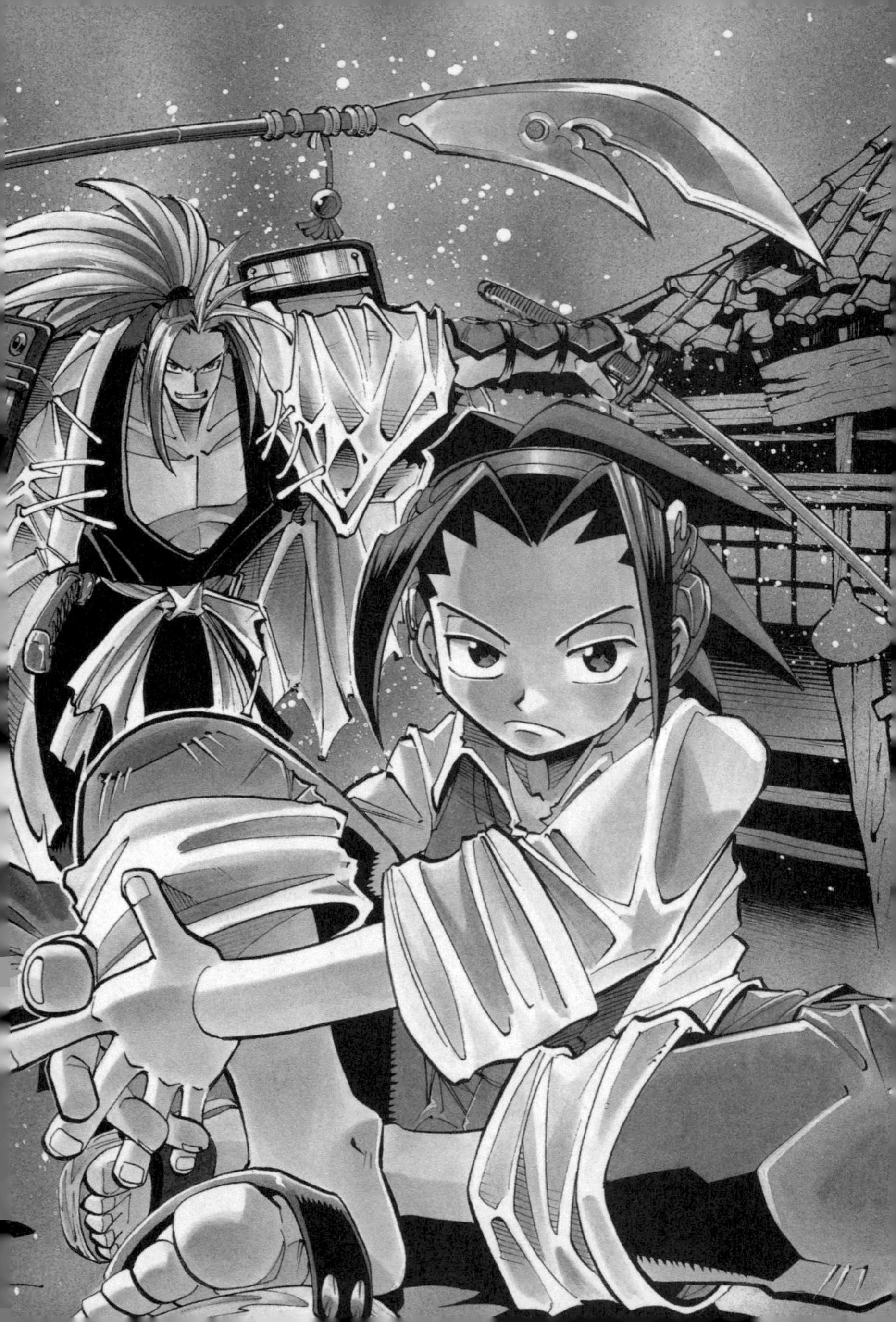

Chapter 10:
A Shaman's Ambition

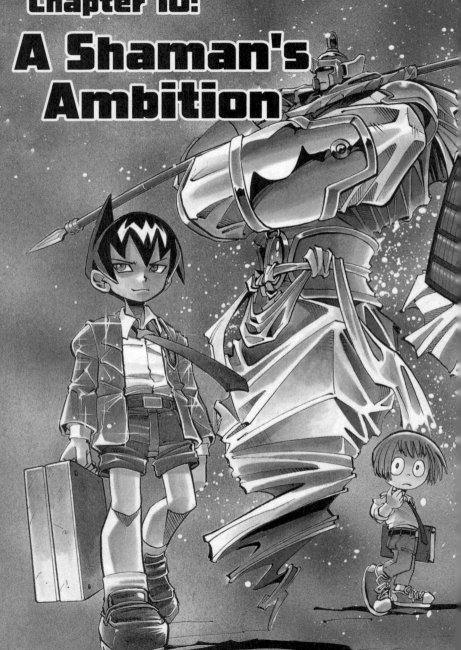

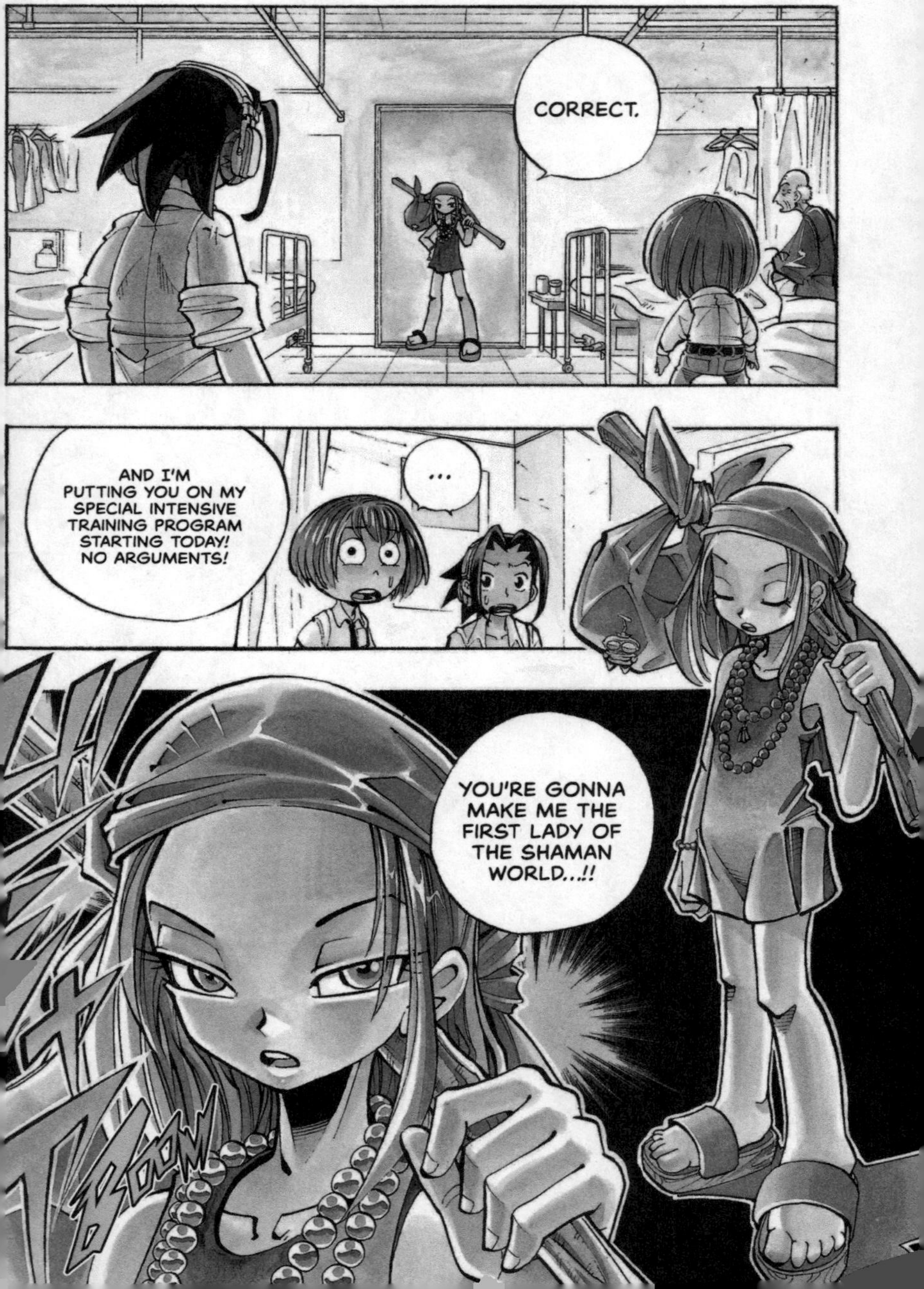
CORRECT.
...
AND I'M PUTTING YOU ON MY SPECIAL INTENSIVE TRAINING PROGRAM STARTING TODAY! NO ARGUMENTS!
YOU'RE GONNA MAKE ME THE FIRST LADY OF THE SHAMAN WORLD...!!
BOOM

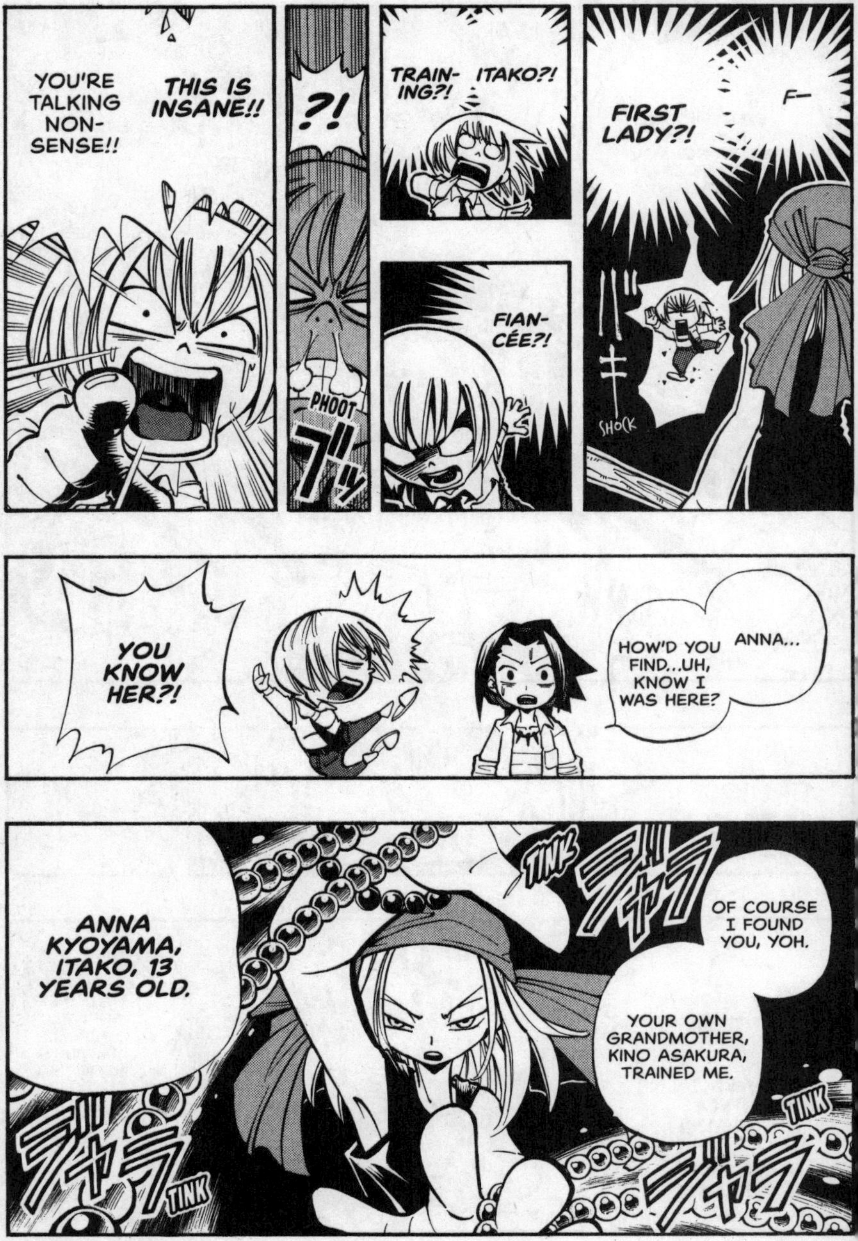
F—
FIRST LADY?!
SHOCK
ITAKO?!
TRAINING?!
FIANCÉE?!
?!
PHOOT
THIS IS INSANE!!
YOU'RE TALKING NONSENSE!!
ANNA...
HOW'D YOU FIND...UH, KNOW I WAS HERE?
YOU KNOW HER?!
TINK
OF COURSE I FOUND YOU, YOH.
YOUR OWN GRANDMOTHER, KINO ASAKURA, TRAINED ME.
TINK
ANNA KYOYAMA, ITAKO, 13 YEARS OLD.
TINK

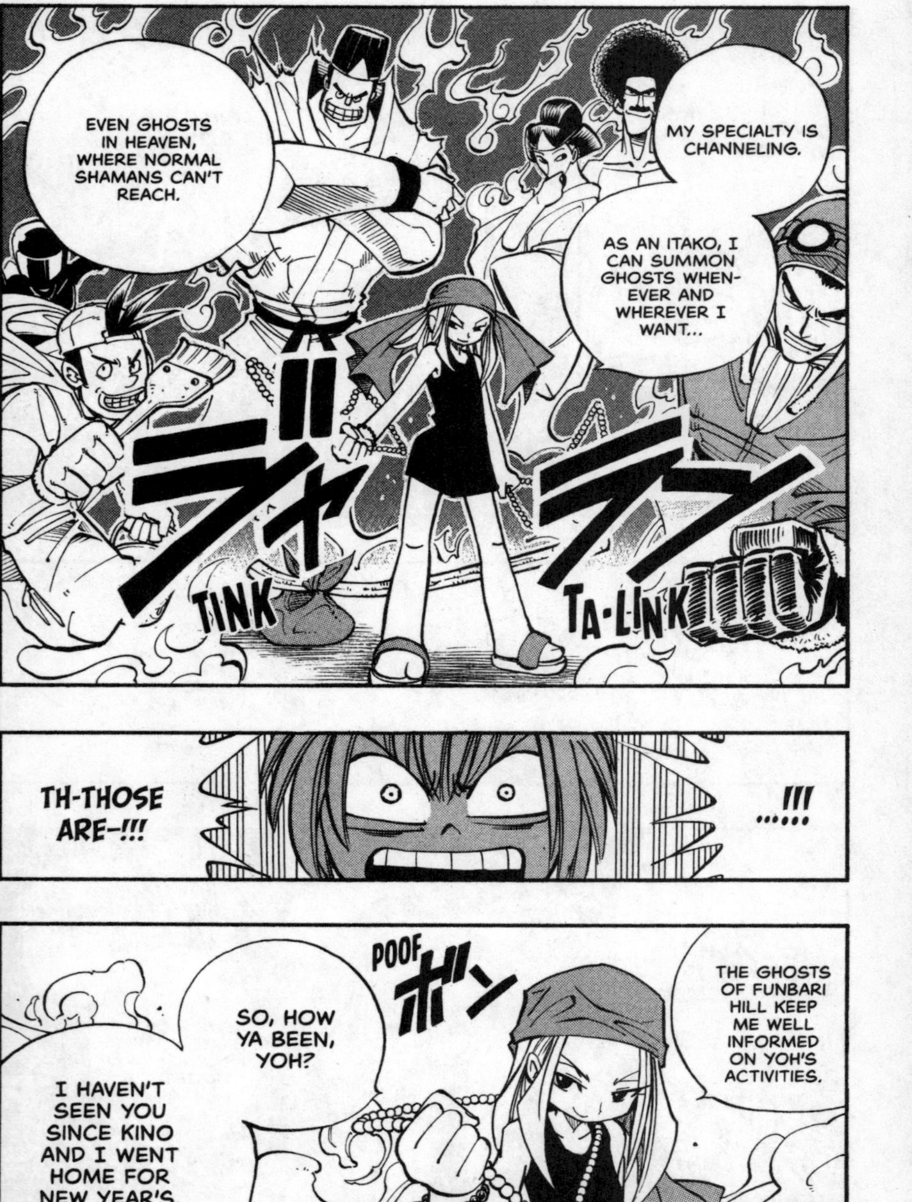
MY SPECIALTY IS CHANNELING.
AS AN ITAKO, I CAN SUMMON GHOSTS WHEN-EVER AND WHEREVER I WANT...
EVEN GHOSTS IN HEAVEN, WHERE NORMAL SHAMANS CAN'T REACH.
ジャラ
TA-LINK
TINK
...!!!
TH-THOSE ARE-!!!
THE GHOSTS OF FUNBARI HILL KEEP ME WELL INFORMED ON YOH'S ACTIVITIES.
POOF
ボン
SO, HOW YA BEEN, YOH?
I HAVEN'T SEEN YOU SINCE KINO AND I WENT HOME FOR NEW YEAR'S.

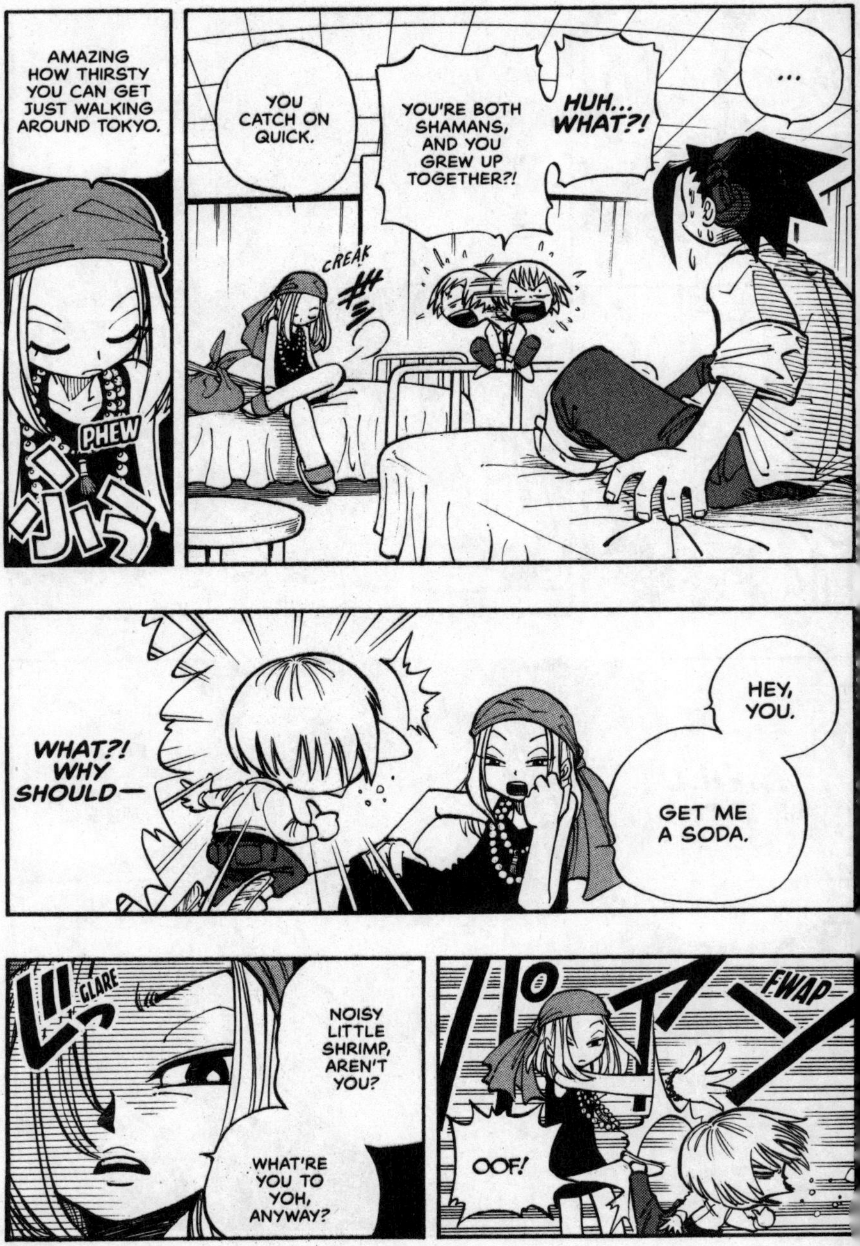
...
HUH... WHAT?!
YOU'RE BOTH SHAMANS, AND YOU GREW UP TOGETHER?!
YOU CATCH ON QUICK.
CREAK
AMAZING HOW THIRSTY YOU CAN GET JUST WALKING AROUND TOKYO.
PHEW
HEY, YOU.
GET ME A SODA.
WHAT?! WHY SHOULD—
FWAP
OOF!
GLARE
NOISY LITTLE SHRIMP, AREN'T YOU?
WHAT'RE YOU TO YOH, ANYWAY?

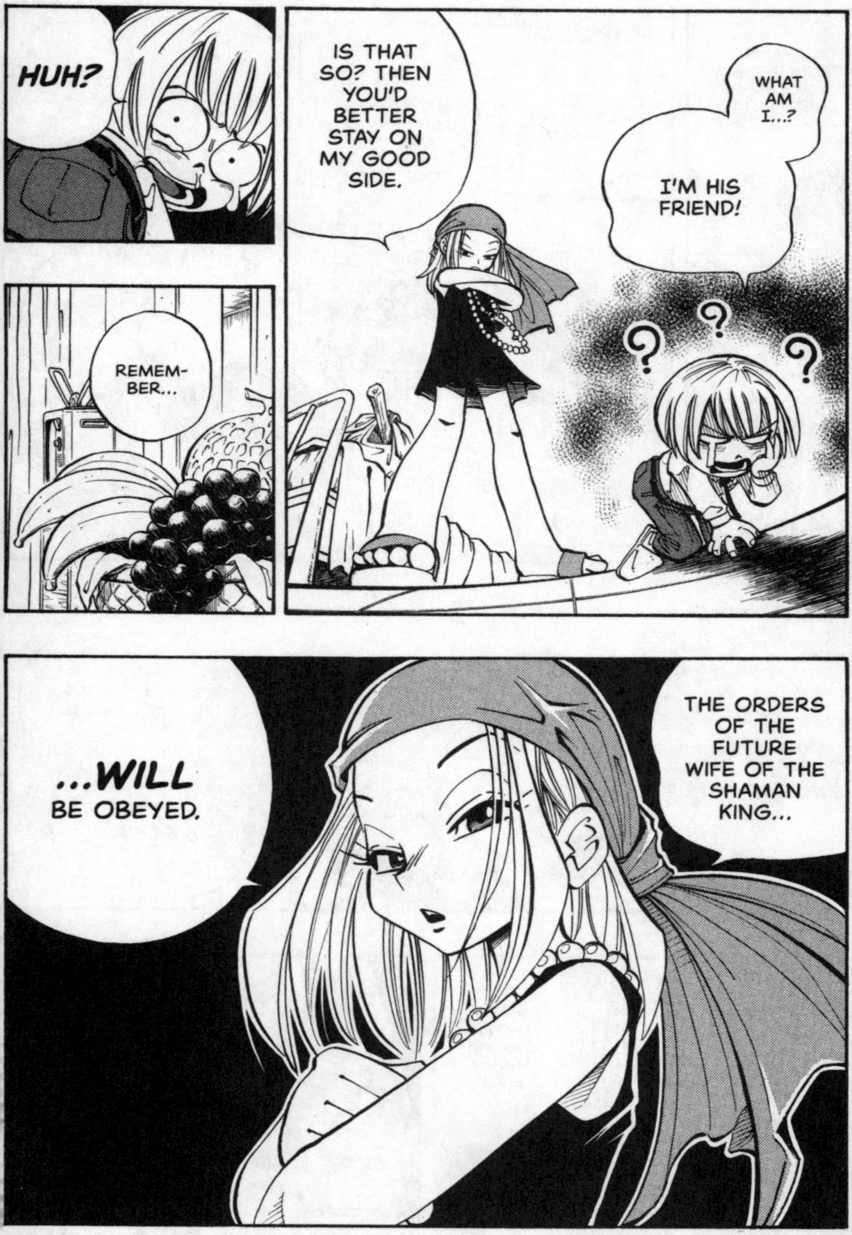
WHAT AM I...?
I'M HIS FRIEND!
IS THAT SO? THEN YOU'D BETTER STAY ON MY GOOD SIDE.
HUH?
REMEMBER...
THE ORDERS OF THE FUTURE WIFE OF THE SHAMAN KING...
...WILL BE OBEYED.

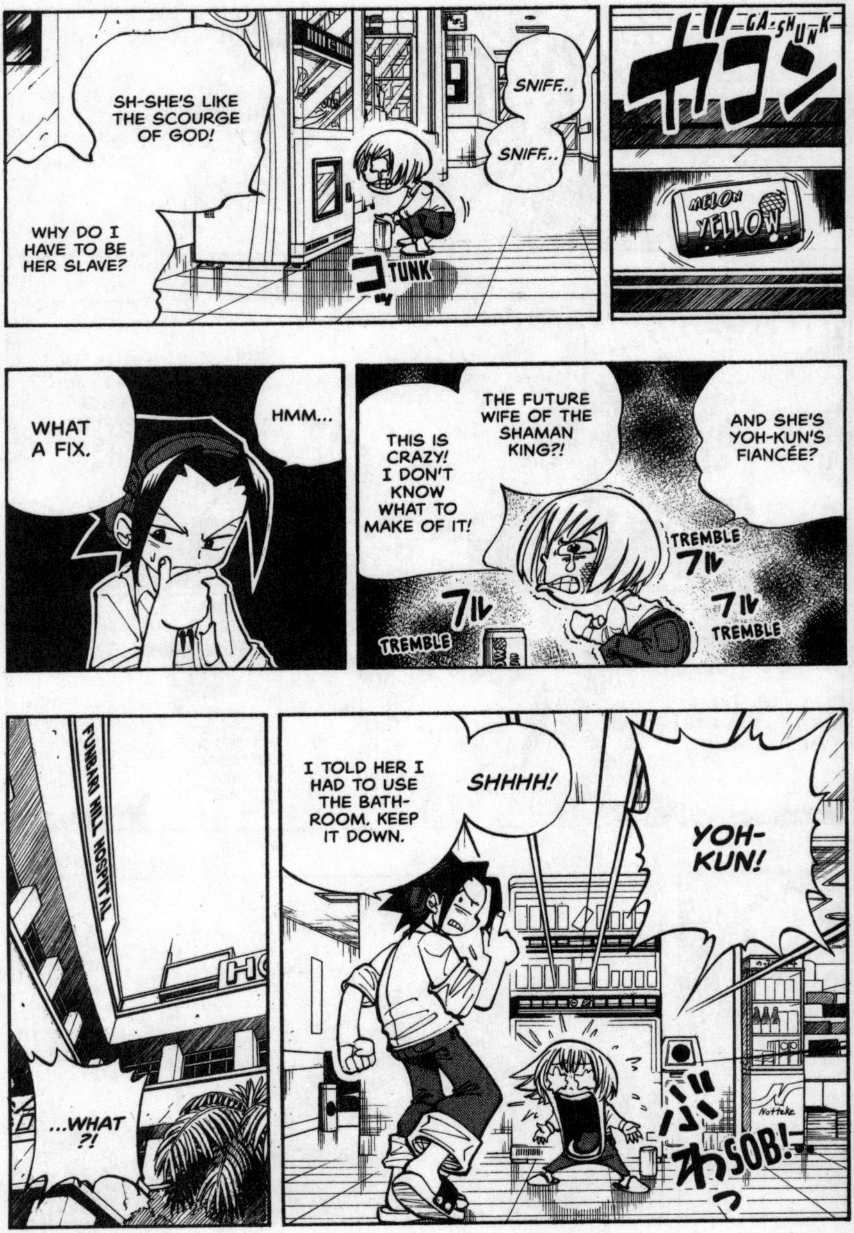
GA-SHUNK
ガコン
MELON YELLOW
SNIFF..
SNIFF..
SH-SHE'S LIKE THE SCOURGE OF GOD!
WHY DO I HAVE TO BE HER SLAVE?
コ TUNK
AND SHE'S YOH-KUN'S FIANCÉE?
THE FUTURE WIFE OF THE SHAMAN KING?!
THIS IS CRAZY! I DON'T KNOW WHAT TO MAKE OF IT!
TREMBLE フル
フル TREMBLE
フル TREMBLE
HMM...
WHAT A FIX.
YOH-KUN!
SHHHH!
I TOLD HER I HAD TO USE THE BATH-ROOM. KEEP IT DOWN.
ぶわっ SOB!
FUNBARI HILL HOSPITAL
...WHAT?!

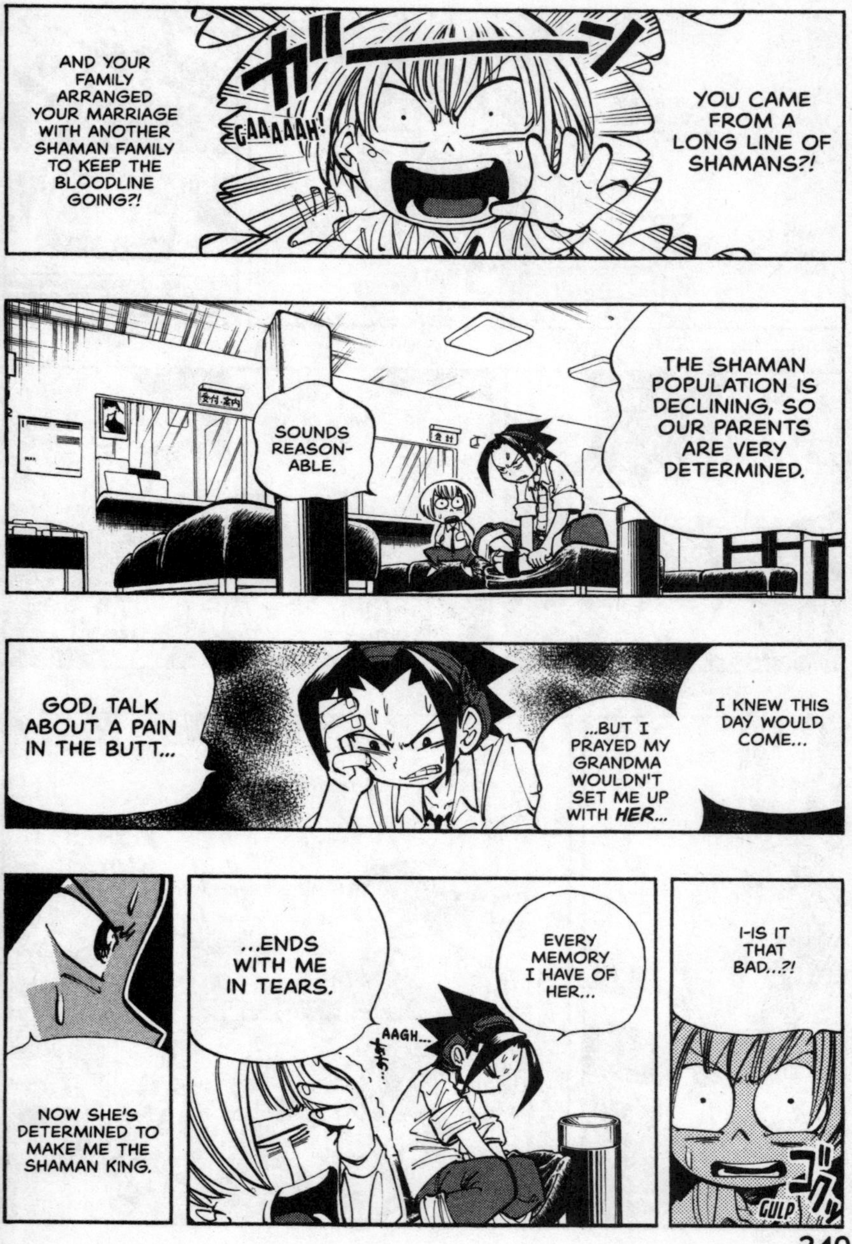
YOU CAME FROM A LONG LINE OF SHAMANS?!
GAAAAAH!
AND YOUR FAMILY ARRANGED YOUR MARRIAGE WITH ANOTHER SHAMAN FAMILY TO KEEP THE BLOODLINE GOING?!
THE SHAMAN POPULATION IS DECLINING, SO OUR PARENTS ARE VERY DETERMINED.
SOUNDS REASON-ABLE.
I KNEW THIS DAY WOULD COME...
...BUT I PRAYED MY GRANDMA WOULDN'T SET ME UP WITH *HER*...
GOD, TALK ABOUT A PAIN IN THE BUTT...
I-IS IT THAT BAD...?!
GULP
EVERY MEMORY I HAVE OF HER...
...ENDS WITH ME IN TEARS.
AAGH...
NOW SHE'S DETERMINED TO MAKE ME THE SHAMAN KING.

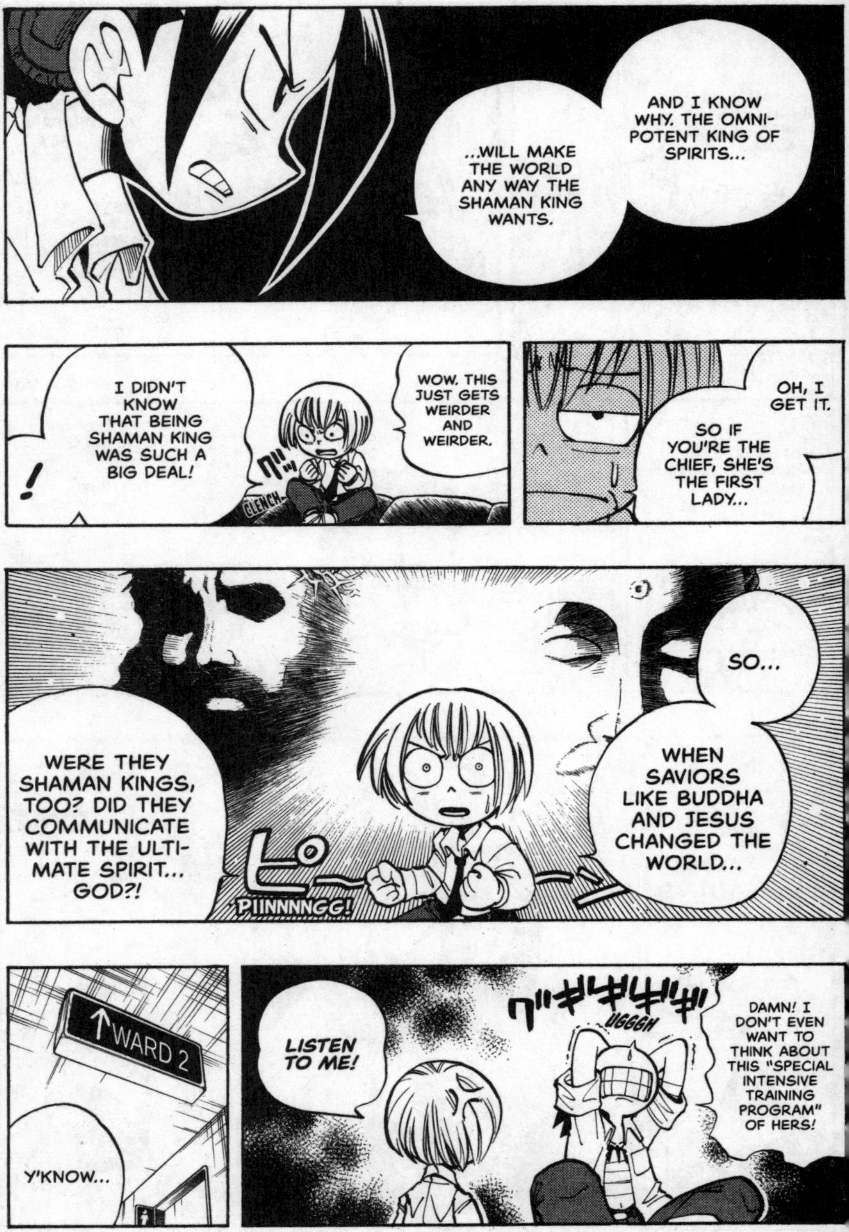
AND I KNOW WHY. THE OMNI-POTENT KING OF SPIRITS...
...WILL MAKE THE WORLD ANY WAY THE SHAMAN KING WANTS.
OH, I GET IT.
SO IF YOU'RE THE CHIEF, SHE'S THE FIRST LADY...
WOW. THIS JUST GETS WEIRDER AND WEIRDER.
CLENCH
I DIDN'T KNOW THAT BEING SHAMAN KING WAS SUCH A BIG DEAL!
!
SO...
WHEN SAVIORS LIKE BUDDHA AND JESUS CHANGED THE WORLD...
PIINNNNGG!
WERE THEY SHAMAN KINGS, TOO? DID THEY COMMUNICATE WITH THE ULTI-MATE SPIRIT... GOD?!
DAMN! I DON'T EVEN WANT TO THINK ABOUT THIS "SPECIAL INTENSIVE TRAINING PROGRAM" OF HERS!
UGGGH
LISTEN TO ME!
WARD 2
Y'KNOW...

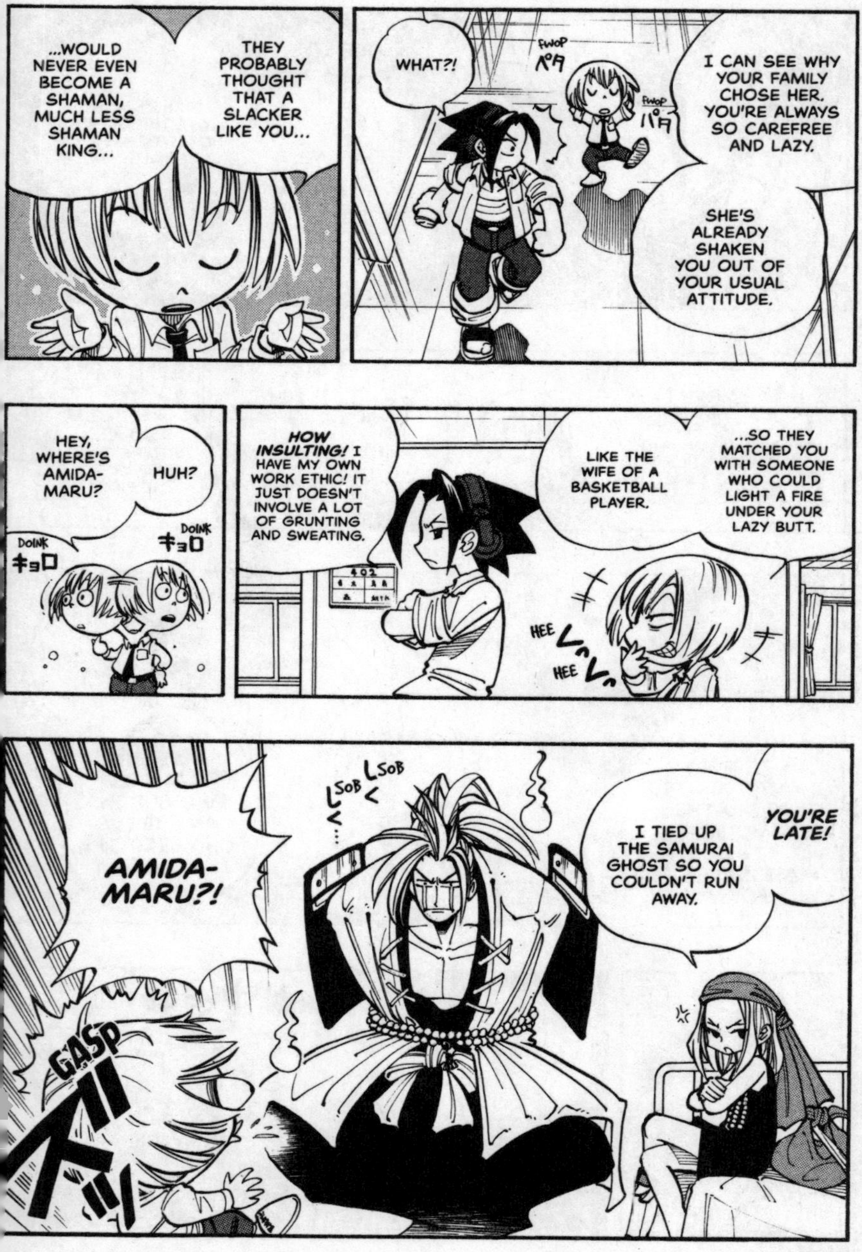
I CAN SEE WHY YOUR FAMILY CHOSE HER. YOU'RE ALWAYS SO CAREFREE AND LAZY.
FWOP
パタ
FWOP
パタ
SHE'S ALREADY SHAKEN YOU OUT OF YOUR USUAL ATTITUDE.
WHAT?!
THEY PROBABLY THOUGHT THAT A SLACKER LIKE YOU...
...WOULD NEVER EVEN BECOME A SHAMAN, MUCH LESS SHAMAN KING...
...SO THEY MATCHED YOU WITH SOMEONE WHO COULD LIGHT A FIRE UNDER YOUR LAZY BUTT.
LIKE THE WIFE OF A BASKETBALL PLAYER.
HOW INSULTING! I HAVE MY OWN WORK ETHIC! IT JUST DOESN'T INVOLVE A LOT OF GRUNTING AND SWEATING.
HEE
HEE
HUH?
HEY, WHERE'S AMIDA-MARU?
DOINK
キョロ
DOINK
キョロ
YOU'RE LATE!
I TIED UP THE SAMURAI GHOST SO YOU COULDN'T RUN AWAY.
SOB
SOB
AMIDA-MARU?!
GASP

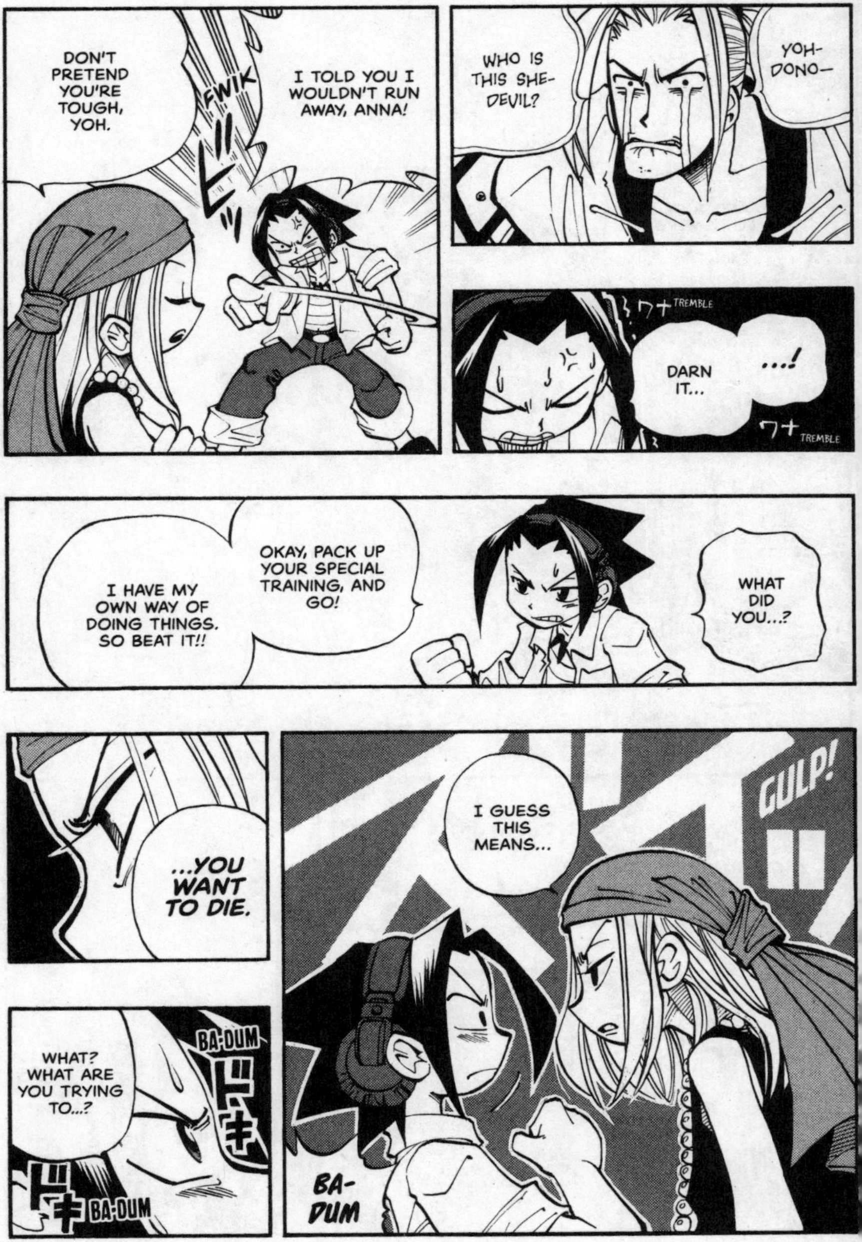

YOH-DONO—
WHO IS THIS SHE-DEVIL?
ワナ TREMBLE
...!
DARN IT...
ワナ TREMBLE
I TOLD YOU I WOULDN'T RUN AWAY, ANNA!
FWIK
DON'T PRETEND YOU'RE TOUGH, YOH.
WHAT DID YOU...?
OKAY, PACK UP YOUR SPECIAL TRAINING, AND GO!
I HAVE MY OWN WAY OF DOING THINGS. SO BEAT IT!!
GULP!
I GUESS THIS MEANS...
BA-DUM
...YOU WANT TO DIE.
BA-DUM
WHAT? WHAT ARE YOU TRYING TO...?
BA-DUM

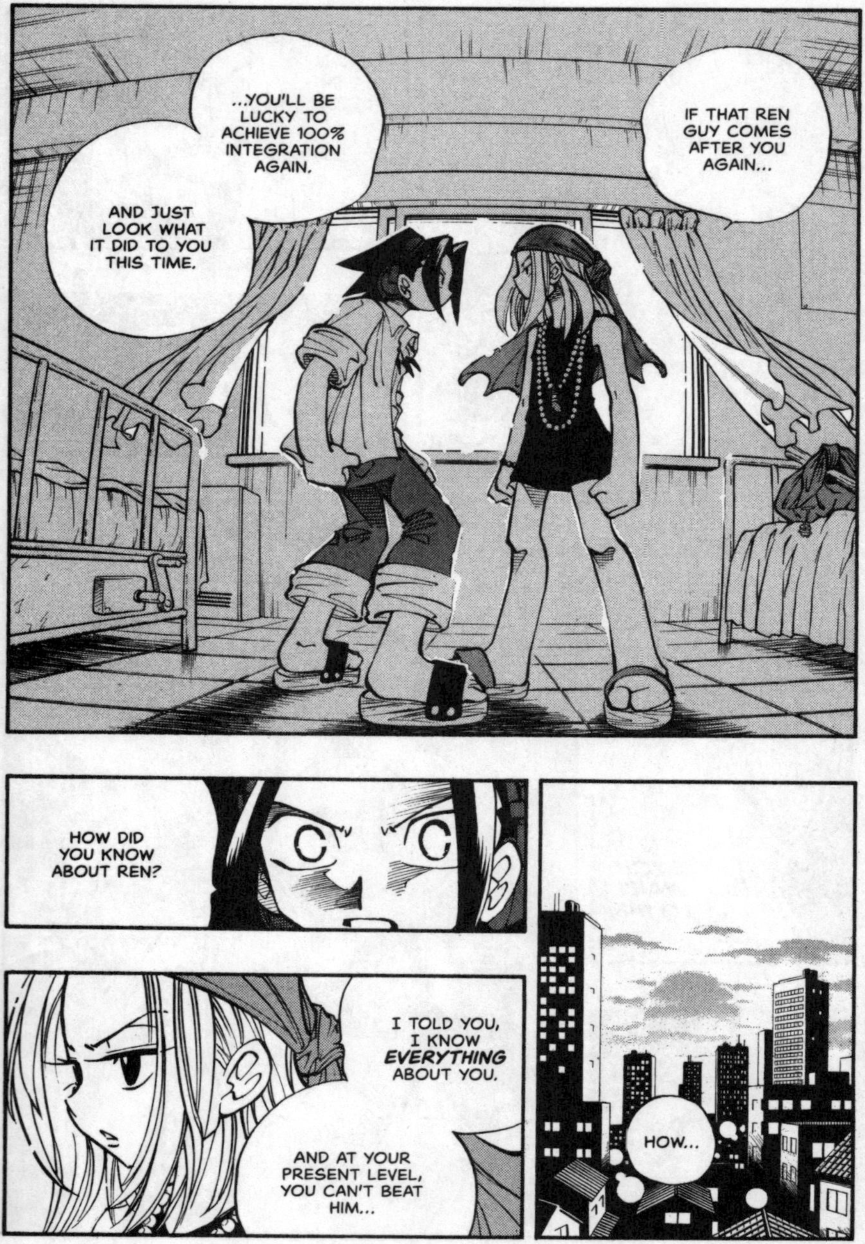
IF THAT REN GUY COMES AFTER YOU AGAIN...
...YOU'LL BE LUCKY TO ACHIEVE 100% INTEGRATION AGAIN.
AND JUST LOOK WHAT IT DID TO YOU THIS TIME.
HOW...
HOW DID YOU KNOW ABOUT REN?
I TOLD YOU, I KNOW *EVERYTHING* ABOUT YOU.
AND AT YOUR PRESENT LEVEL, YOU CAN'T BEAT HIM...

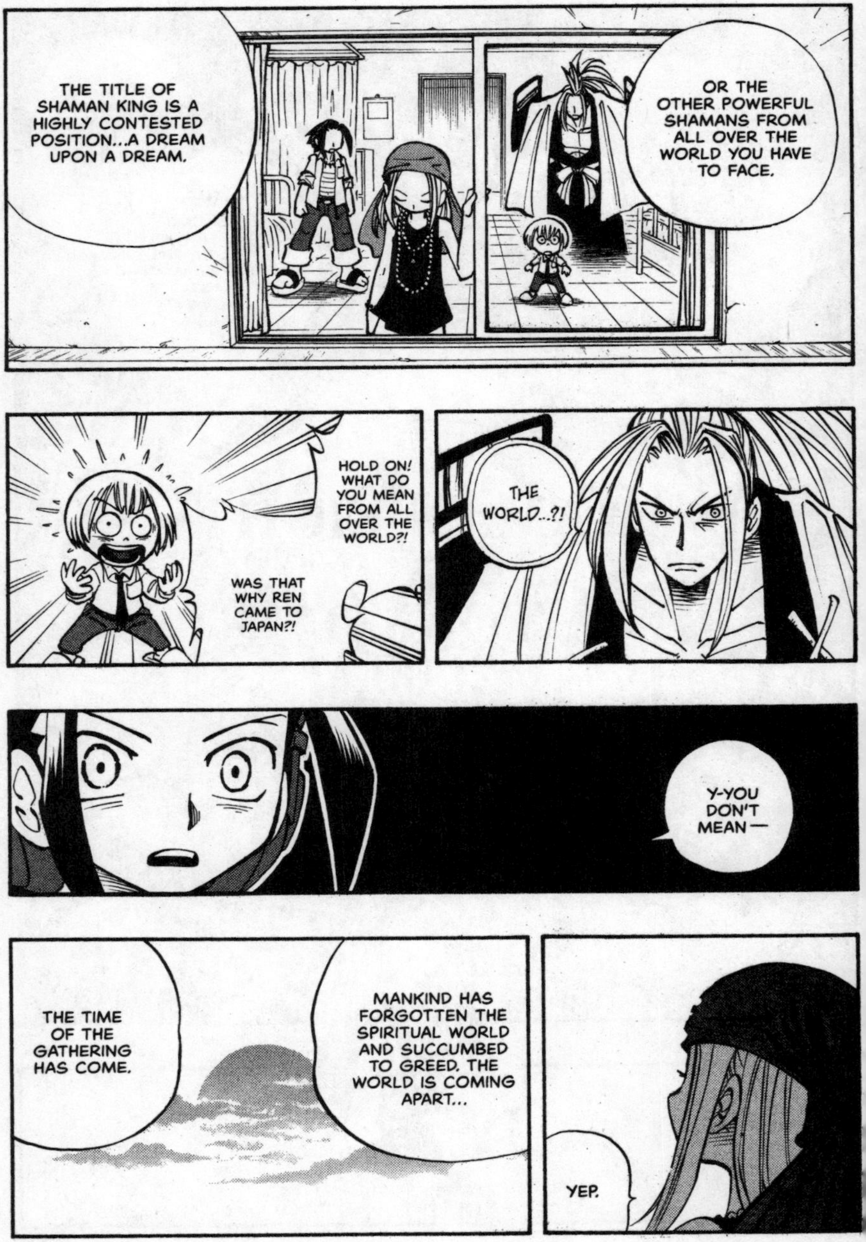
OR THE OTHER POWERFUL SHAMANS FROM ALL OVER THE WORLD YOU HAVE TO FACE.
THE TITLE OF SHAMAN KING IS A HIGHLY CONTESTED POSITION...A DREAM UPON A DREAM.
THE WORLD...?!
HOLD ON! WHAT DO YOU MEAN FROM ALL OVER THE WORLD?!
WAS THAT WHY REN CAME TO JAPAN?!
Y-YOU DON'T MEAN—
YEP.
MANKIND HAS FORGOTTEN THE SPIRITUAL WORLD AND SUCCUMBED TO GREED. THE WORLD IS COMING APART...
THE TIME OF THE GATHERING HAS COME.

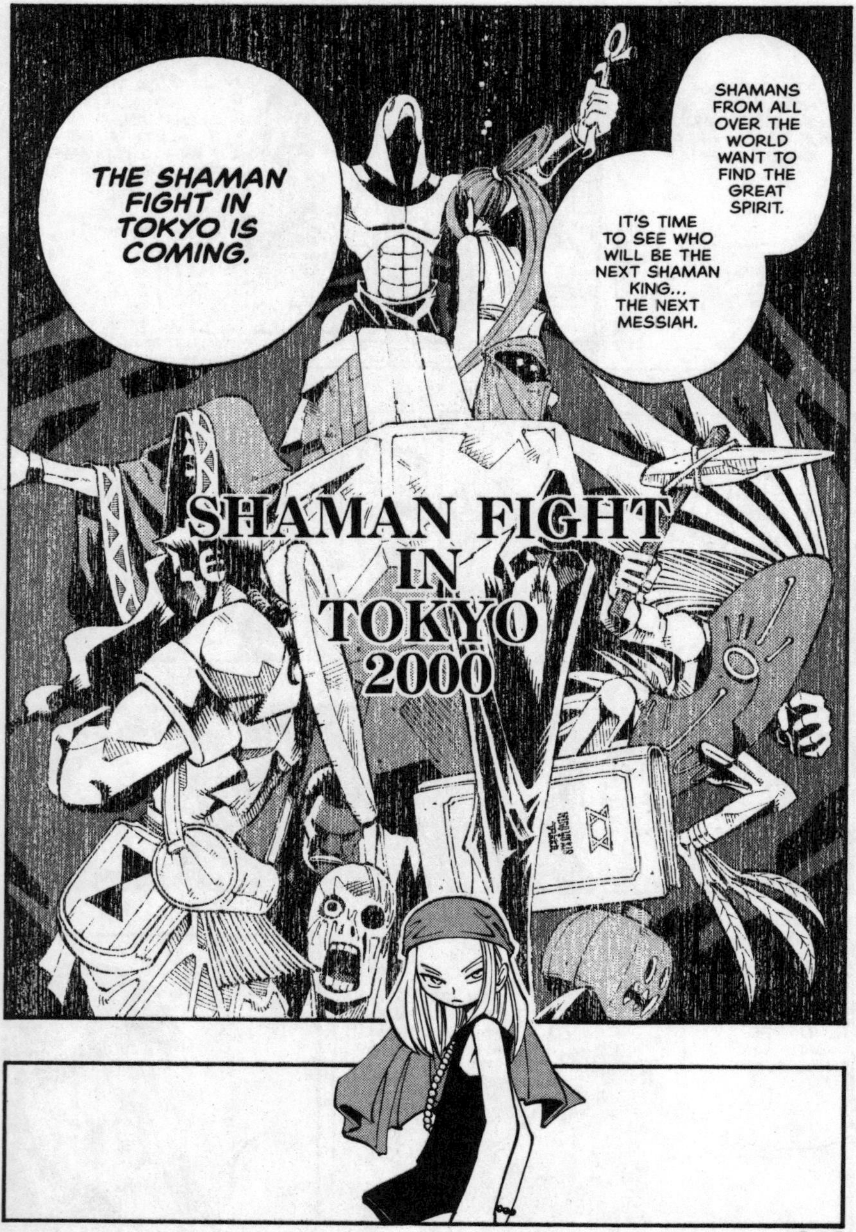
SHAMANS FROM ALL OVER THE WORLD WANT TO FIND THE GREAT SPIRIT.
IT'S TIME TO SEE WHO WILL BE THE NEXT SHAMAN KING... THE NEXT MESSIAH.
THE SHAMAN FIGHT IN TOKYO IS COMING.
SHAMAN FIGHT IN TOKYO 2000

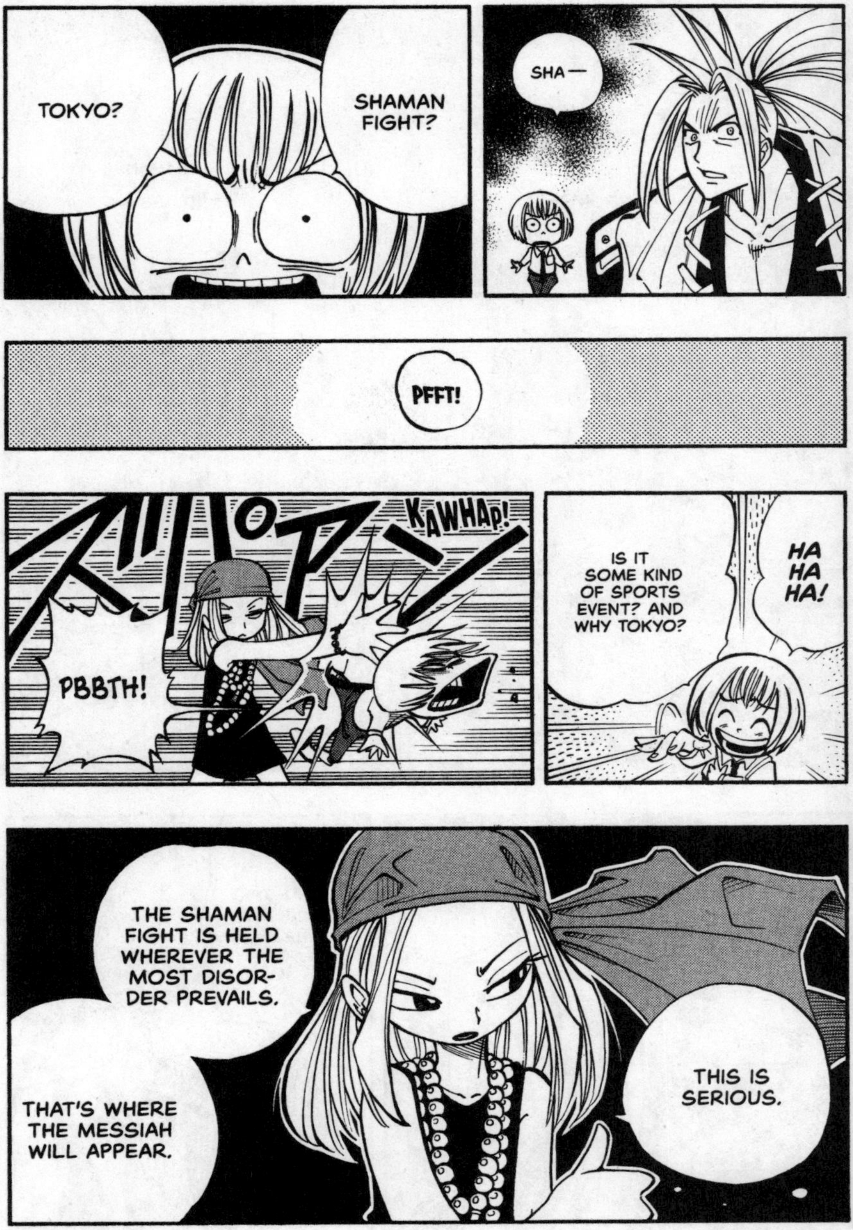
SHA—
SHAMAN FIGHT?
TOKYO?
PFFT!
HA HA HA!
IS IT SOME KIND OF SPORTS EVENT? AND WHY TOKYO?
KAWHAP!
PBBTH!
THIS IS SERIOUS.
THE SHAMAN FIGHT IS HELD WHEREVER THE MOST DISORDER PREVAILS.
THAT'S WHERE THE MESSIAH WILL APPEAR.

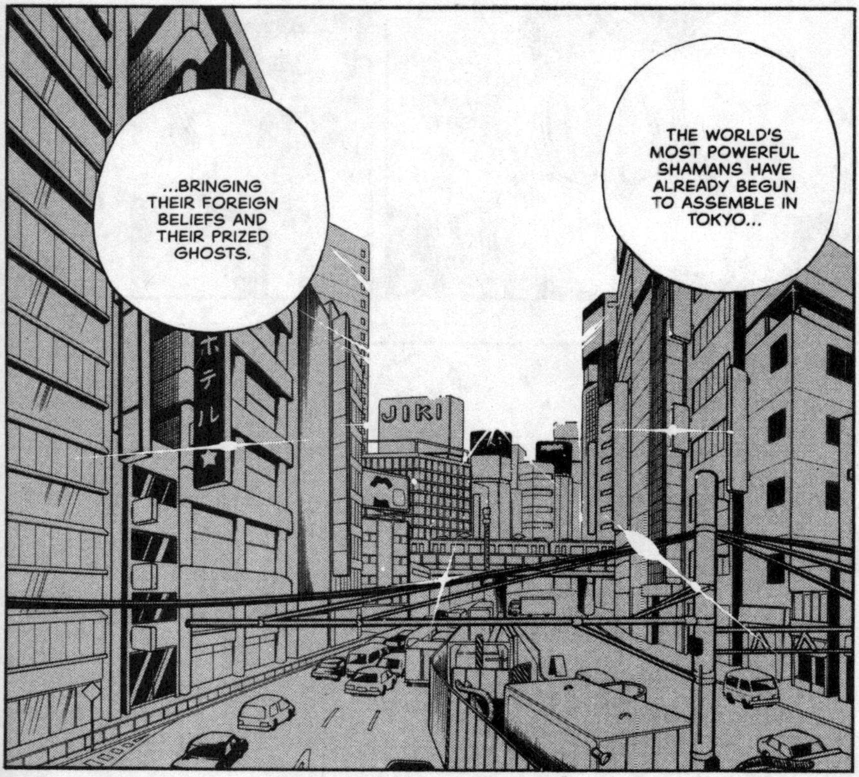
THE WORLD'S MOST POWERFUL SHAMANS HAVE ALREADY BEGUN TO ASSEMBLE IN TOKYO...
...BRINGING THEIR FOREIGN BELIEFS AND THEIR PRIZED GHOSTS.
ホテル
JIKI

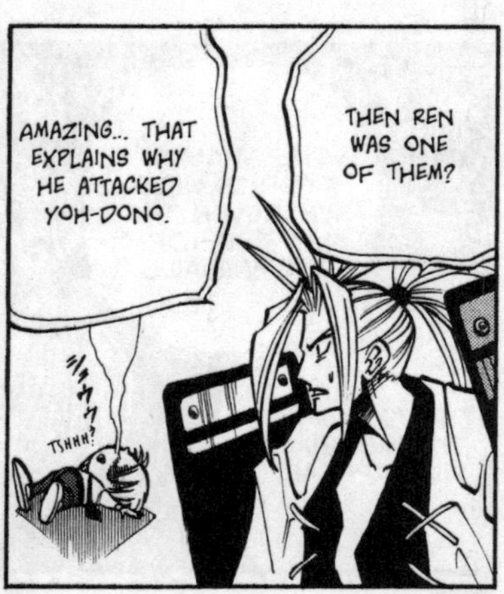
THEN REN WAS ONE OF THEM?
AMAZING... THAT EXPLAINS WHY HE ATTACKED YOH-DONO.
シュウウ
TSHHH?

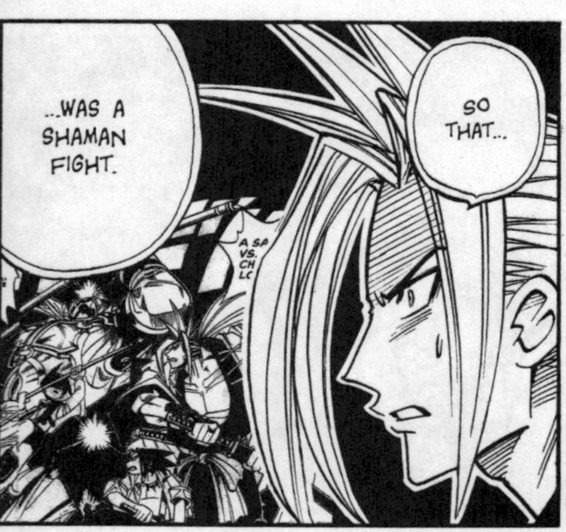
SO THAT...
...WAS A SHAMAN FIGHT.

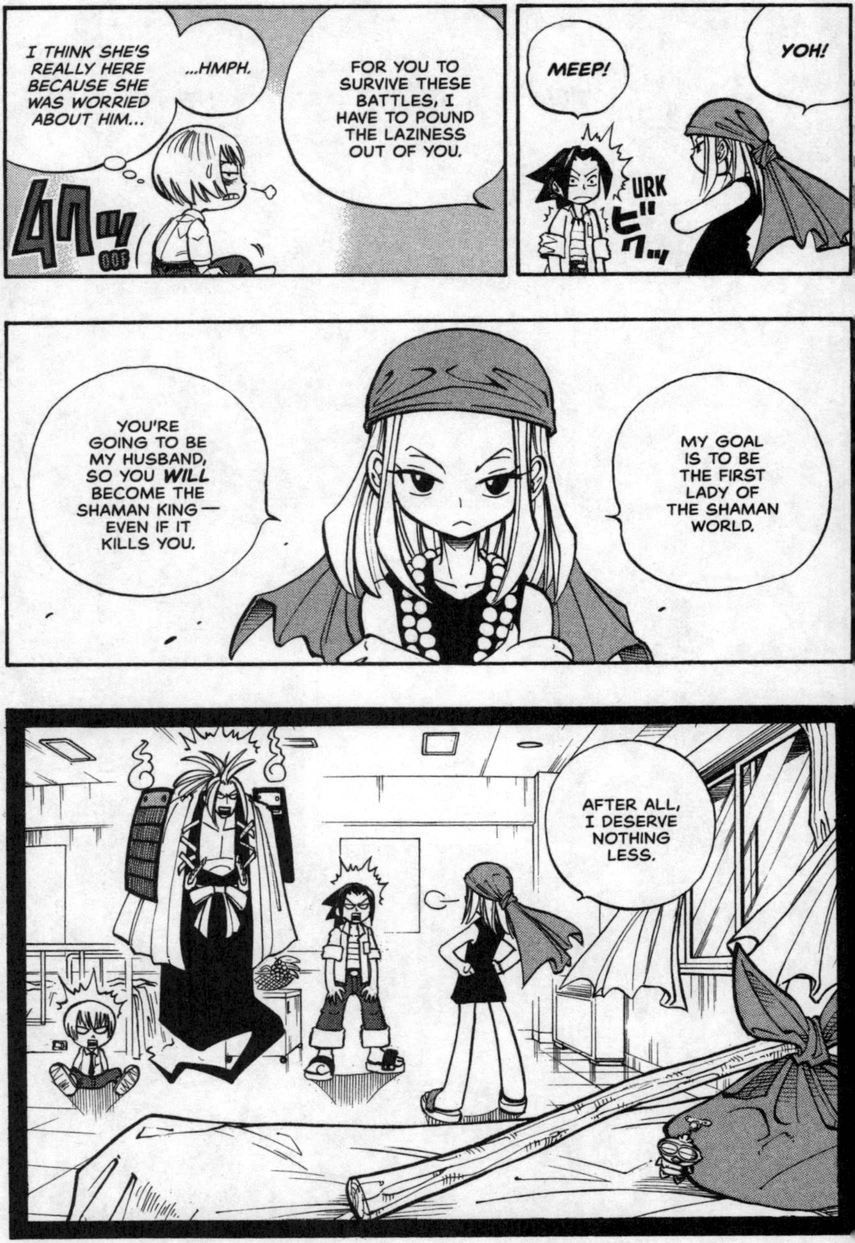
YOH!
MEEP!
URK
FOR YOU TO SURVIVE THESE BATTLES, I HAVE TO POUND THE LAZINESS OUT OF YOU.
...HMPH.
I THINK SHE'S REALLY HERE BECAUSE SHE WAS WORRIED ABOUT HIM...
OOF
MY GOAL IS TO BE THE FIRST LADY OF THE SHAMAN WORLD.
YOU'RE GOING TO BE MY HUSBAND, SO YOU *WILL* BECOME THE SHAMAN KING—EVEN IF IT KILLS YOU.
AFTER ALL, I DESERVE NOTHING LESS.

SHAMAN
KING
2

Shako-chan Mascot

(A reproduction of a famous
Jomon-era Japanese figurine,
sometimes sold at tourist
shops in Japan.)

Chapter 11: The Shaman Life

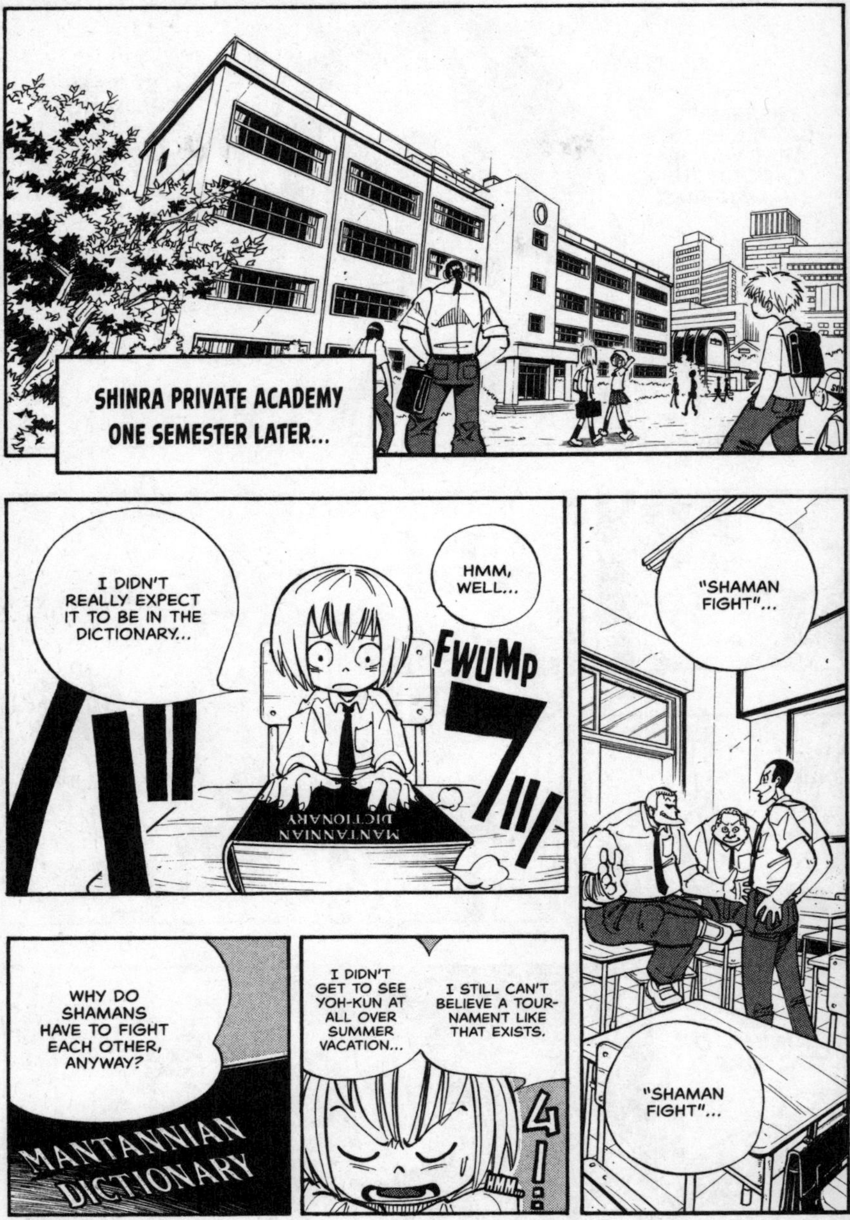
SHINRA PRIVATE ACADEMY
ONE SEMESTER LATER...
"SHAMAN FIGHT"...
"SHAMAN FIGHT"...
HMM, WELL...
I DIDN'T REALLY EXPECT IT TO BE IN THE DICTIONARY...
FWUMP
MANTANNIAN DICTIONARY
I STILL CAN'T BELIEVE A TOURNAMENT LIKE THAT EXISTS.
I DIDN'T GET TO SEE YOH-KUN AT ALL OVER SUMMER VACATION...
HMM...
WHY DO SHAMANS HAVE TO FIGHT EACH OTHER, ANYWAY?
MANTANNIAN DICTIONARY

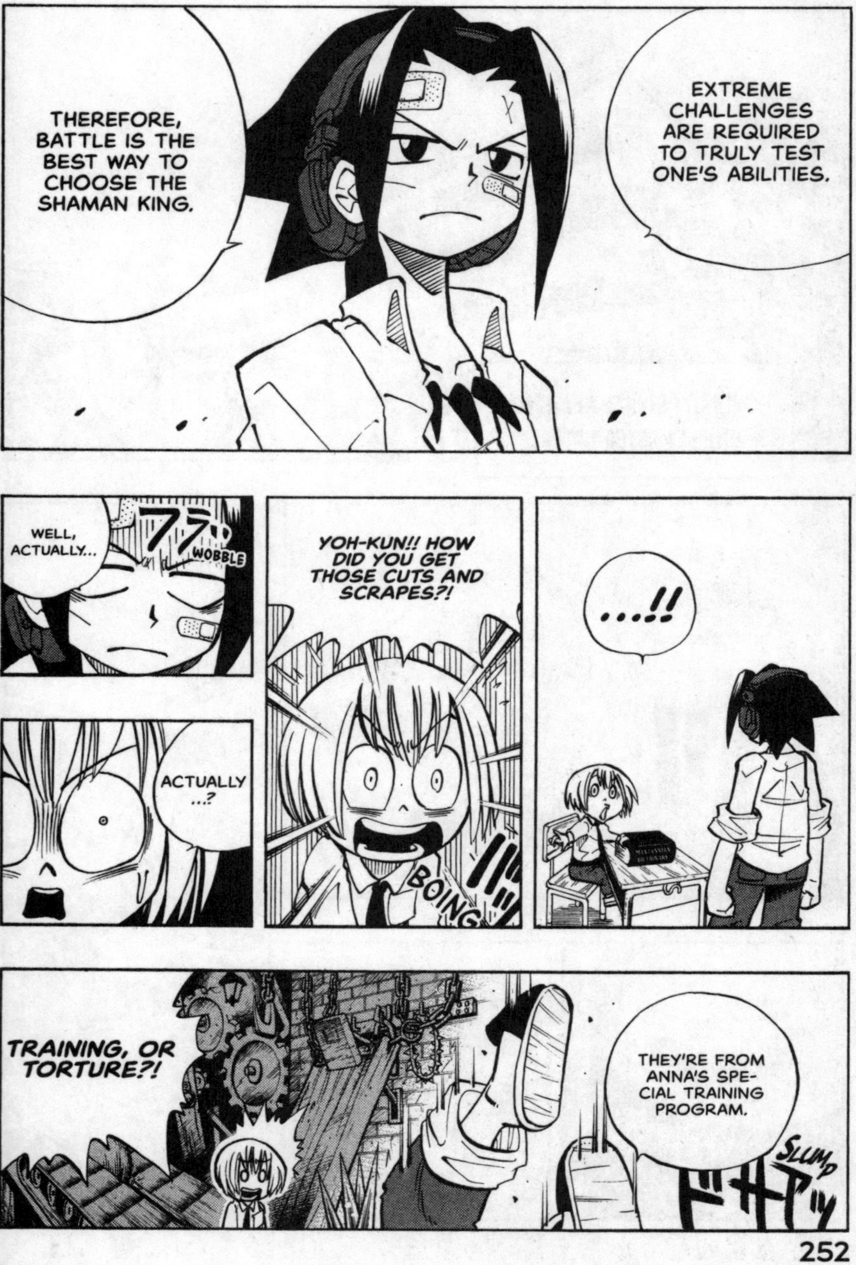
EXTREME CHALLENGES ARE REQUIRED TO TRULY TEST ONE'S ABILITIES.
THEREFORE, BATTLE IS THE BEST WAY TO CHOOSE THE SHAMAN KING.
...!!
YOH-KUN!! HOW DID YOU GET THOSE CUTS AND SCRAPES?!
BOING
WELL, ACTUALLY...
フラ
WOBBLE
ACTUALLY ...?
THEY'RE FROM ANNA'S SPE- CIAL TRAINING PROGRAM.
SLUMP
ドサアッ
TRAINING, OR TORTURE?!

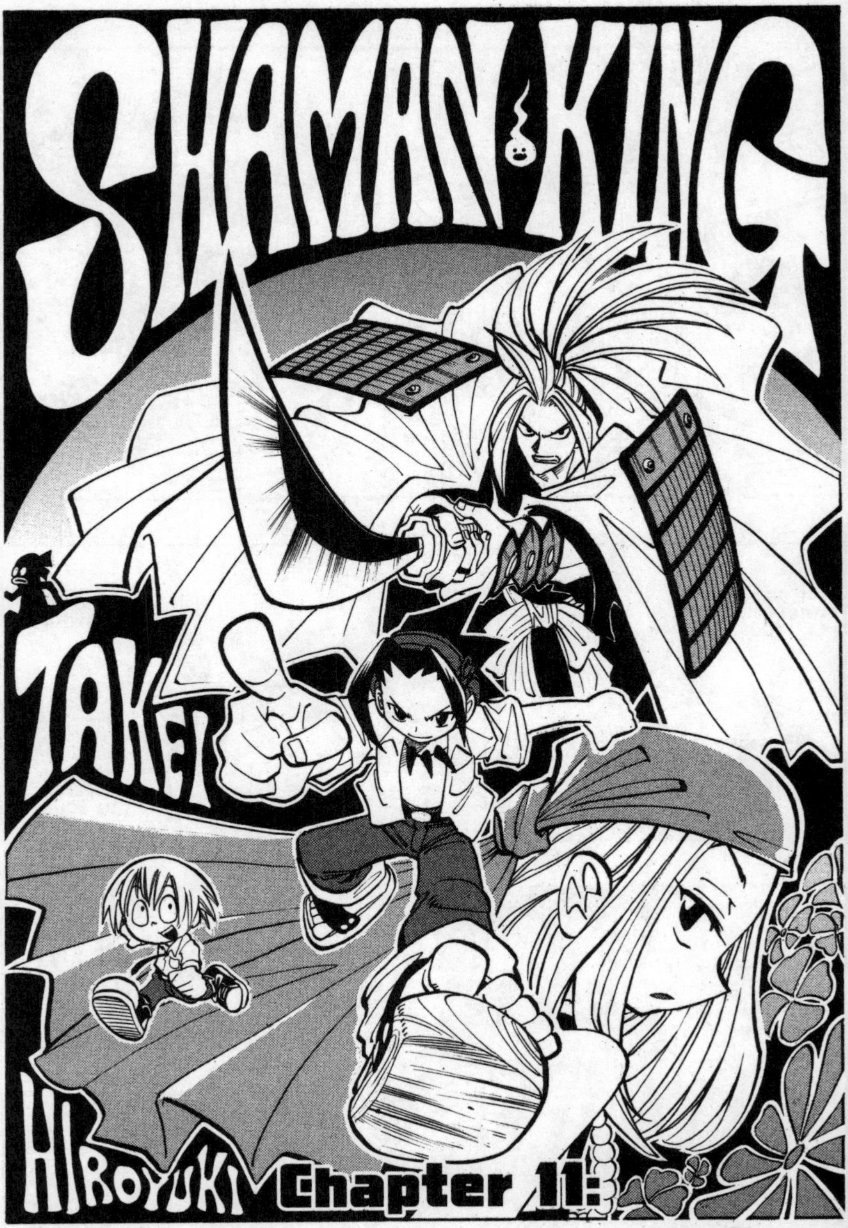
SHAMAN KING
TAKEI
HIROYUKI
Chapter 11:

The Shaman Life

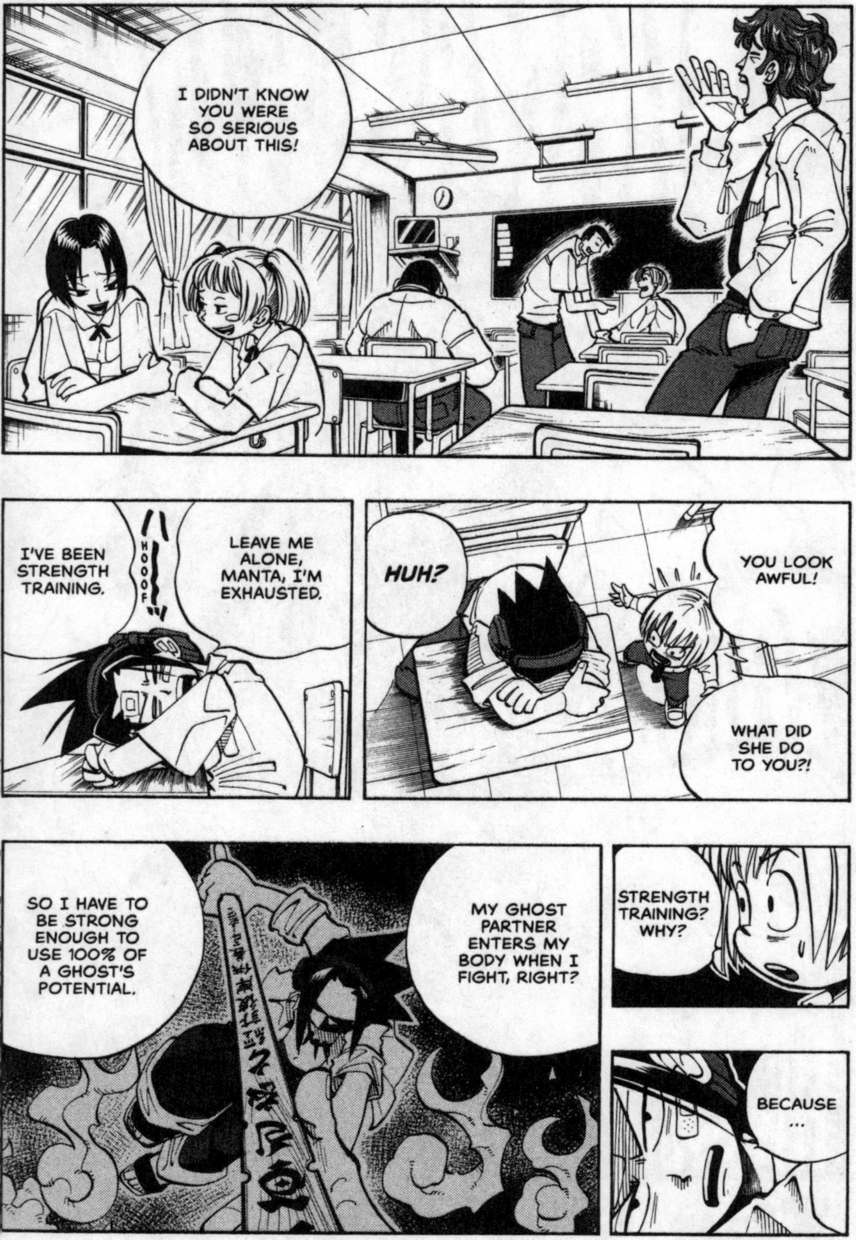
I DIDN'T KNOW YOU WERE SO SERIOUS ABOUT THIS!
YOU LOOK AWFUL!
HUH?
WHAT DID SHE DO TO YOU?!
LEAVE ME ALONE, MANTA, I'M EXHAUSTED.
HOOOF
I'VE BEEN STRENGTH TRAINING.
STRENGTH TRAINING? WHY?
BECAUSE ...
MY GHOST PARTNER ENTERS MY BODY WHEN I FIGHT, RIGHT?
SO I HAVE TO BE STRONG ENOUGH TO USE 100% OF A GHOST'S POTENTIAL.

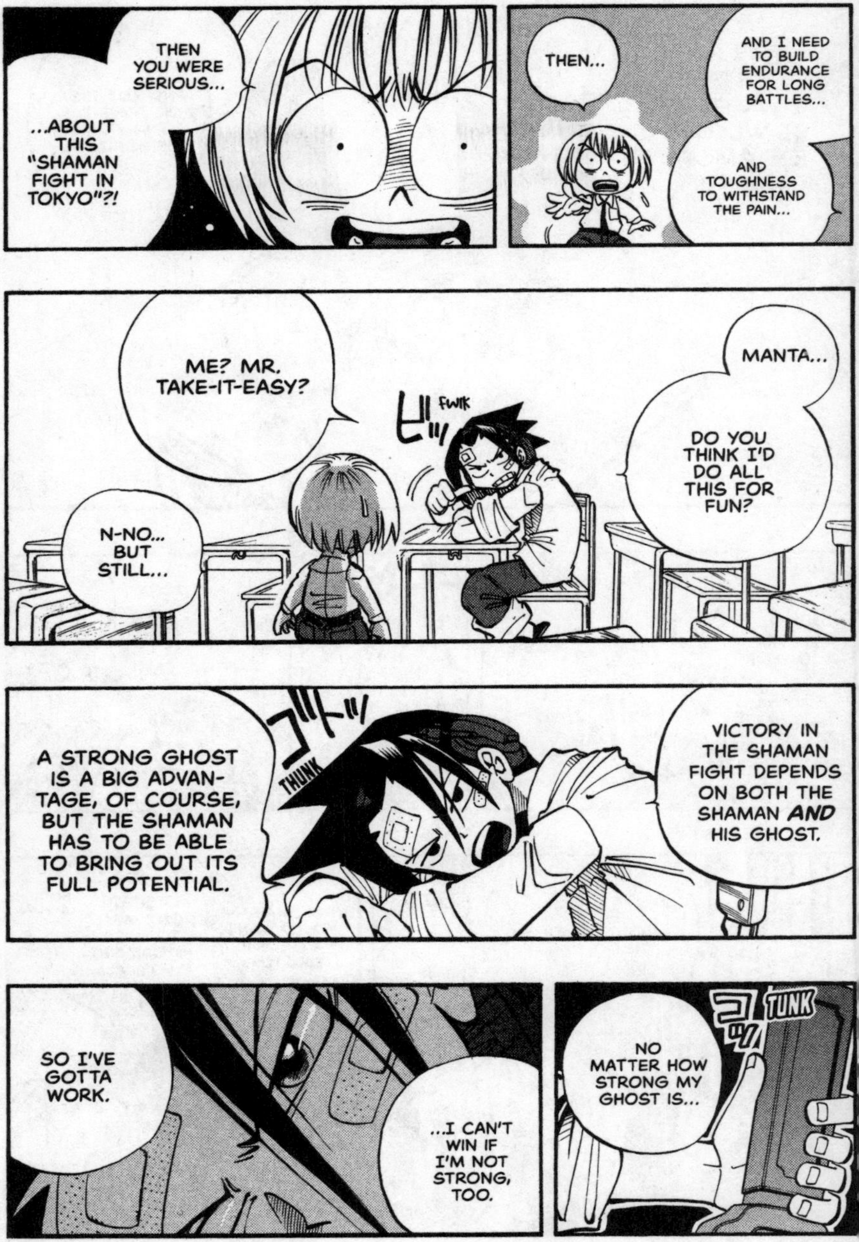
AND I NEED TO BUILD ENDURANCE FOR LONG BATTLES...
AND TOUGHNESS TO WITHSTAND THE PAIN...
THEN...
THEN YOU WERE SERIOUS...
...ABOUT THIS "SHAMAN FIGHT IN TOKYO"?!
MANTA...
DO YOU THINK I'D DO ALL THIS FOR FUN?
FWIK
ME? MR. TAKE-IT-EASY?
N-NO... BUT STILL...
VICTORY IN THE SHAMAN FIGHT DEPENDS ON BOTH THE SHAMAN *AND* HIS GHOST.
THUNK
A STRONG GHOST IS A BIG ADVANTAGE, OF COURSE, BUT THE SHAMAN HAS TO BE ABLE TO BRING OUT ITS FULL POTENTIAL.
TUNK
NO MATTER HOW STRONG MY GHOST IS...
...I CAN'T WIN IF I'M NOT STRONG, TOO.
SO I'VE GOTTA WORK.

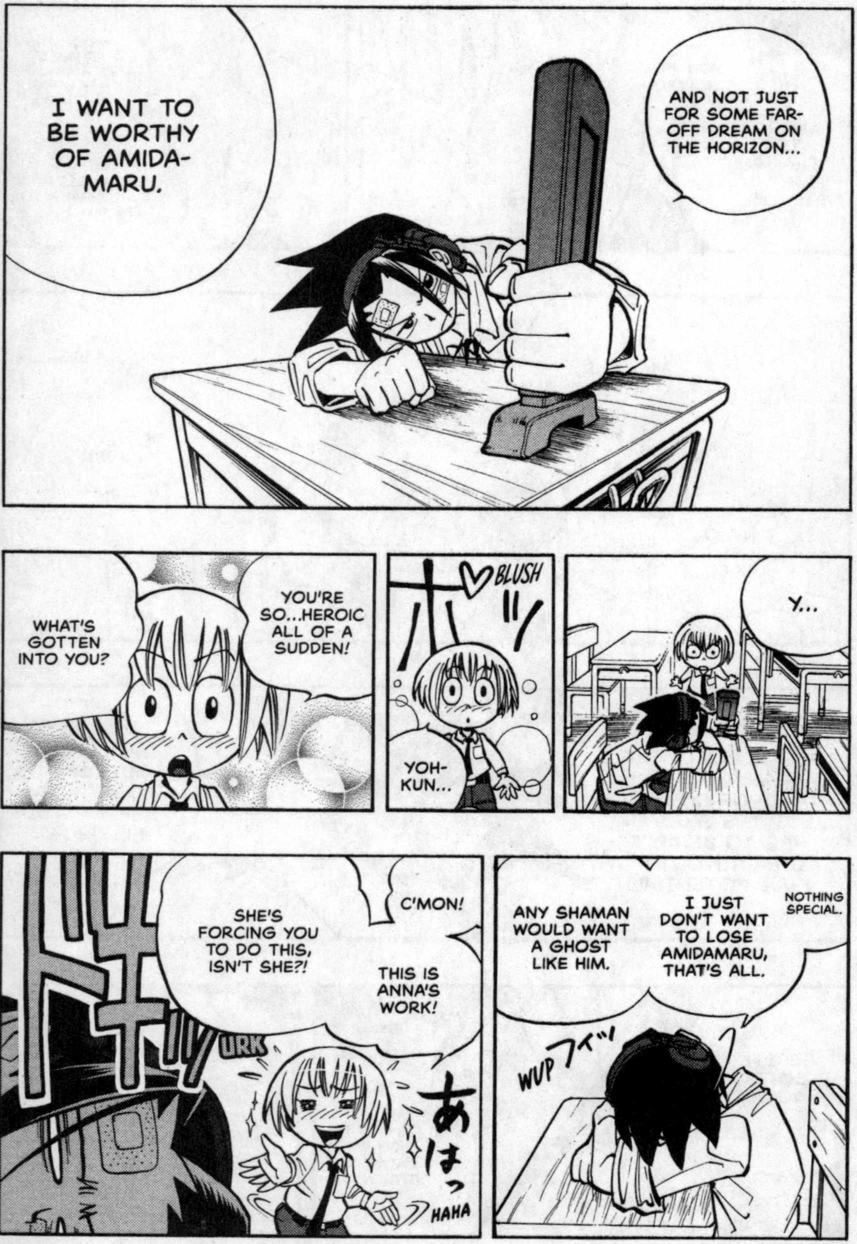
AND NOT JUST FOR SOME FAR-OFF DREAM ON THE HORIZON...
I WANT TO BE WORTHY OF AMIDA-MARU.
Y...
BLUSH
YOH-KUN...
YOU'RE SO...HEROIC ALL OF A SUDDEN!
WHAT'S GOTTEN INTO YOU?
NOTHING SPECIAL.
I JUST DON'T WANT TO LOSE AMIDAMARU, THAT'S ALL.
ANY SHAMAN WOULD WANT A GHOST LIKE HIM.
WUP
C'MON!
THIS IS ANNA'S WORK!
SHE'S FORCING YOU TO DO THIS, ISN'T SHE?!
URK
HAHA

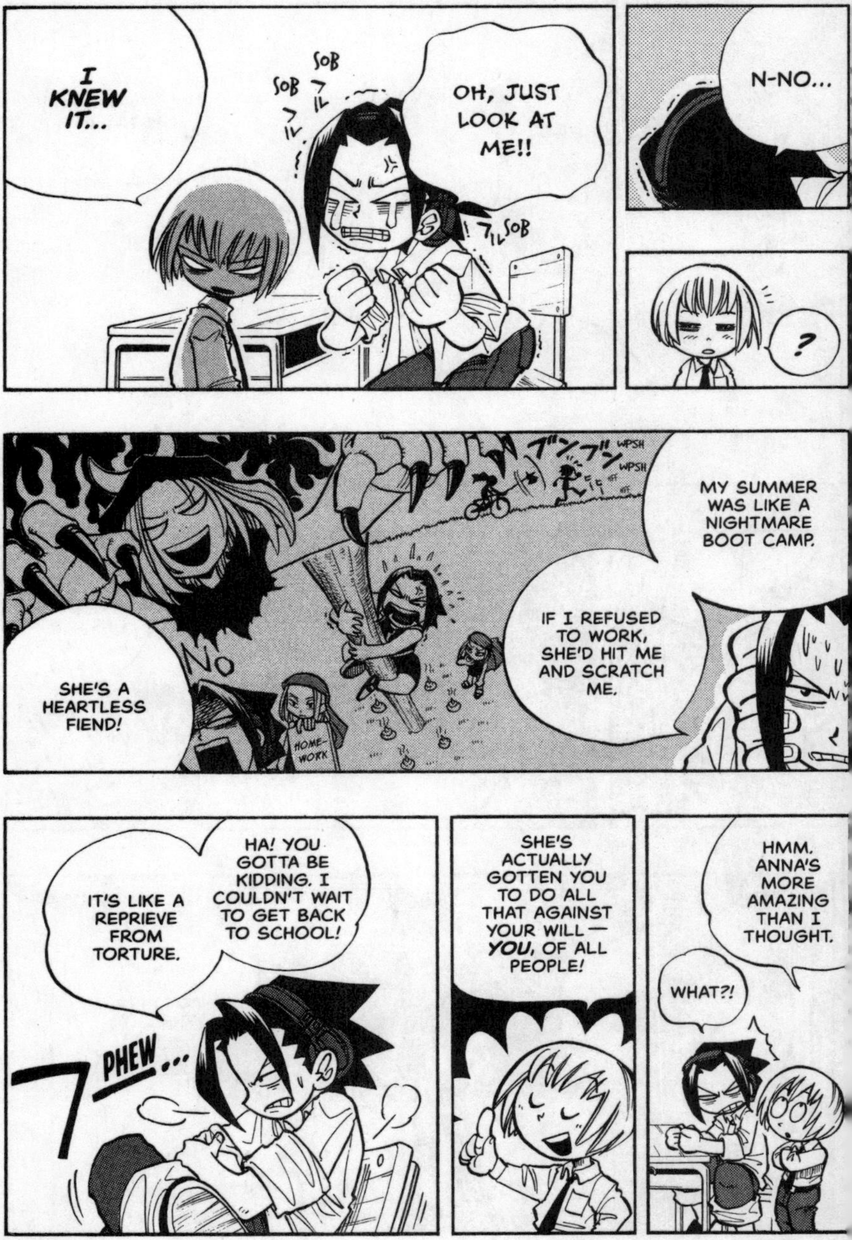
N-NO...
?
OH, JUST LOOK AT ME!!
SOB
SOB
SOB
I KNEW IT...
MY SUMMER WAS LIKE A NIGHTMARE BOOT CAMP.
WPSH
WPSH
IF I REFUSED TO WORK, SHE'D HIT ME AND SCRATCH ME.
No
HOME-WORK
SHE'S A HEARTLESS FIEND!
HMM. ANNA'S MORE AMAZING THAN I THOUGHT.
WHAT?!
SHE'S ACTUALLY GOTTEN YOU TO DO ALL THAT AGAINST YOUR WILL—*YOU*, OF ALL PEOPLE!
HA! YOU GOTTA BE KIDDING. I COULDN'T WAIT TO GET BACK TO SCHOOL!
IT'S LIKE A REPRIEVE FROM TORTURE.
PHEW...

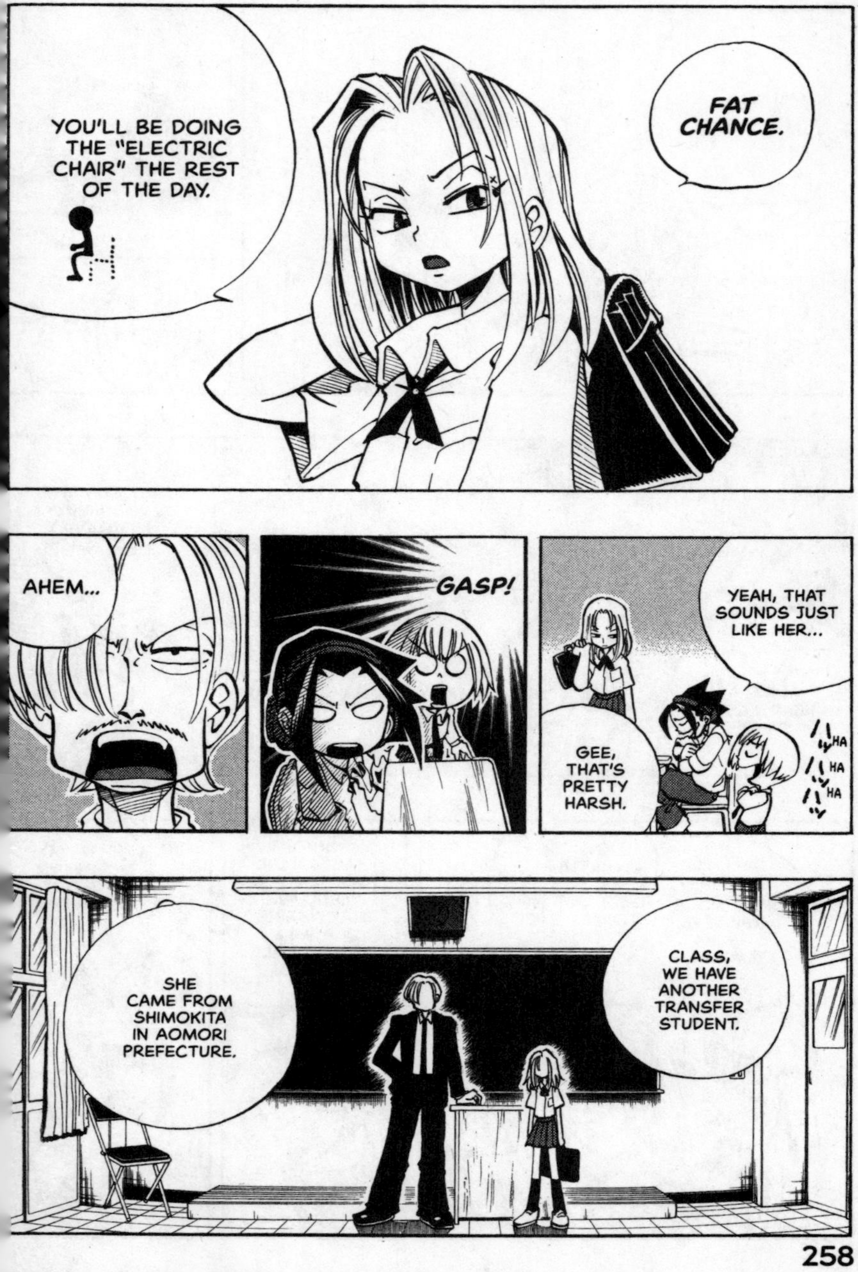
FAT CHANCE.
YOU'LL BE DOING THE "ELECTRIC CHAIR" THE REST OF THE DAY.
YEAH, THAT SOUNDS JUST LIKE HER...
HA HA HA
GEE, THAT'S PRETTY HARSH.
GASP!
AHEM...
CLASS, WE HAVE ANOTHER TRANSFER STUDENT.
SHE CAME FROM SHIMOKITA IN AOMORI PREFECTURE.

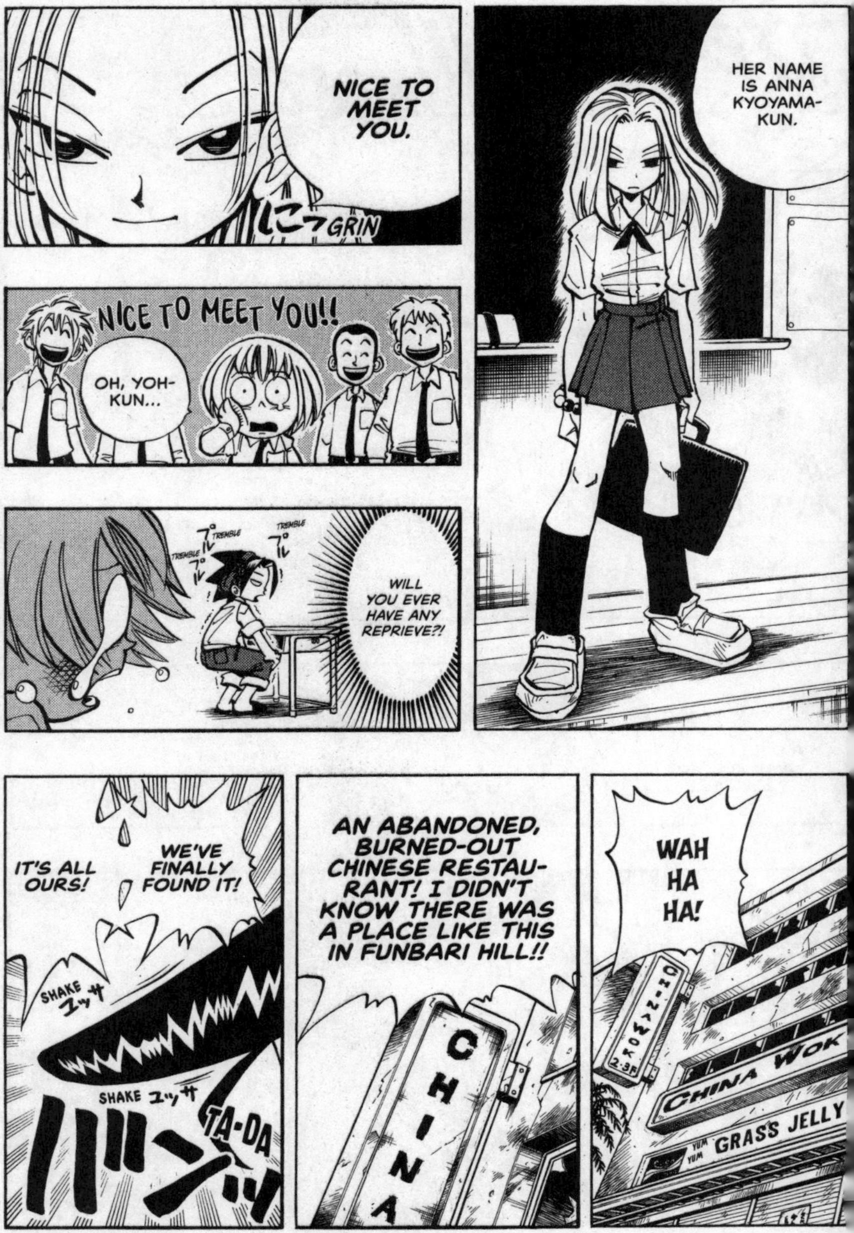
HER NAME IS ANNA KYOYAMA-KUN.
NICE TO MEET YOU.
GRIN
NICE TO MEET YOU!!
OH, YOH-KUN...
TREMBLE
TREMBLE
TREMBLE
WILL YOU EVER HAVE ANY REPRIEVE?!
WAH HA HA!
CHINA WOK
CHINA WOK
YUM YUM GRASS JELLY
AN ABANDONED, BURNED-OUT CHINESE RESTAURANT! I DIDN'T KNOW THERE WAS A PLACE LIKE THIS IN FUNBARI HILL!!
CHINA
WE'VE FINALLY FOUND IT!
IT'S ALL OURS!
SHAKE
SHAKE
TA-DA

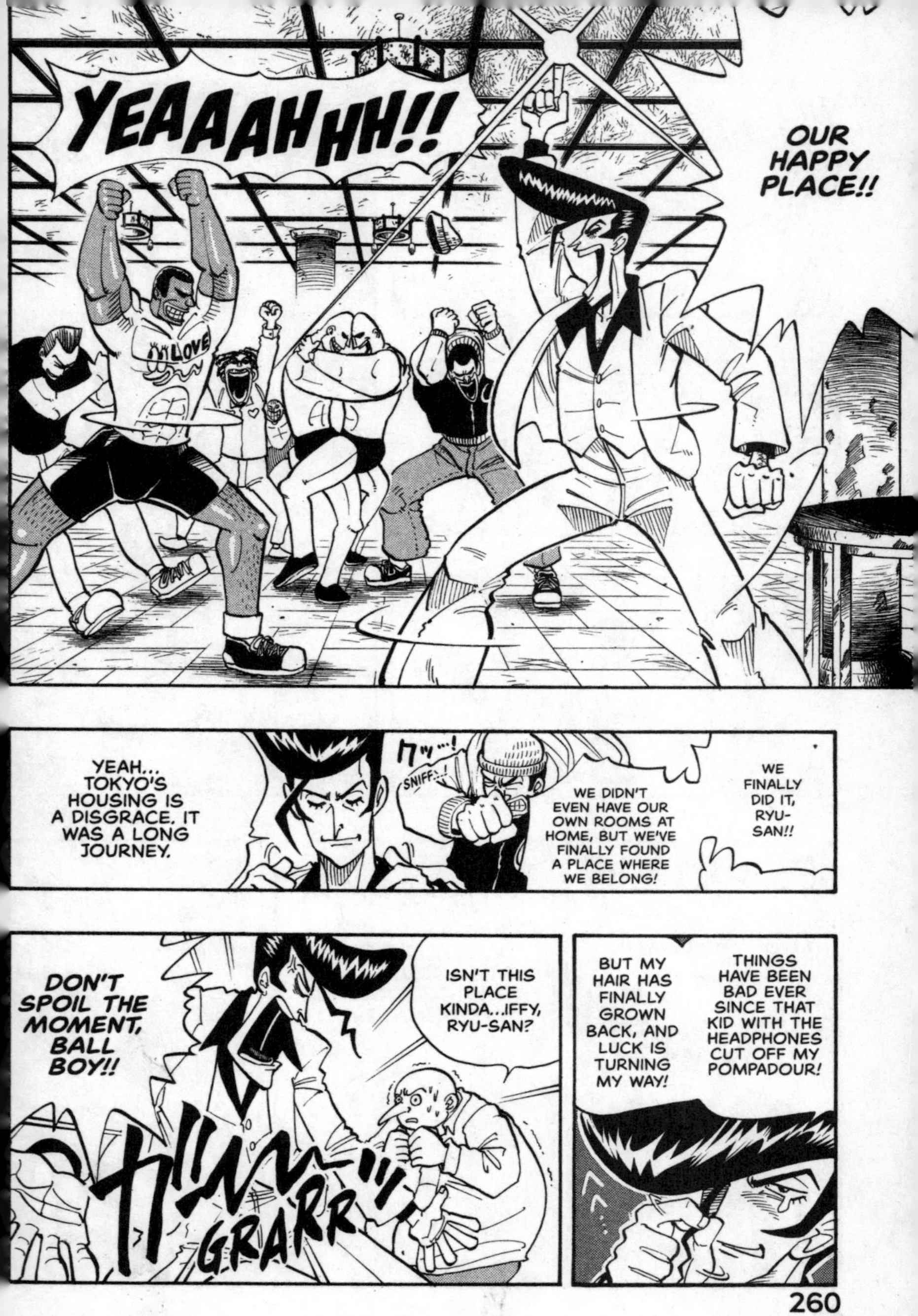

OUR HAPPY PLACE!!
YEAAAHHH!!
WE FINALLY DID IT, RYU-SAN!!
WE DIDN'T EVEN HAVE OUR OWN ROOMS AT HOME, BUT WE'VE FINALLY FOUND A PLACE WHERE WE BELONG!
SNIFF...!
YEAH... TOKYO'S HOUSING IS A DISGRACE. IT WAS A LONG JOURNEY.
THINGS HAVE BEEN BAD EVER SINCE THAT KID WITH THE HEADPHONES CUT OFF MY POMPADOUR!
BUT MY HAIR HAS FINALLY GROWN BACK, AND LUCK IS TURNING MY WAY!
ISN'T THIS PLACE KINDA...IFFY, RYU-SAN?
DON'T SPOIL THE MOMENT, BALL BOY!!
GRARR

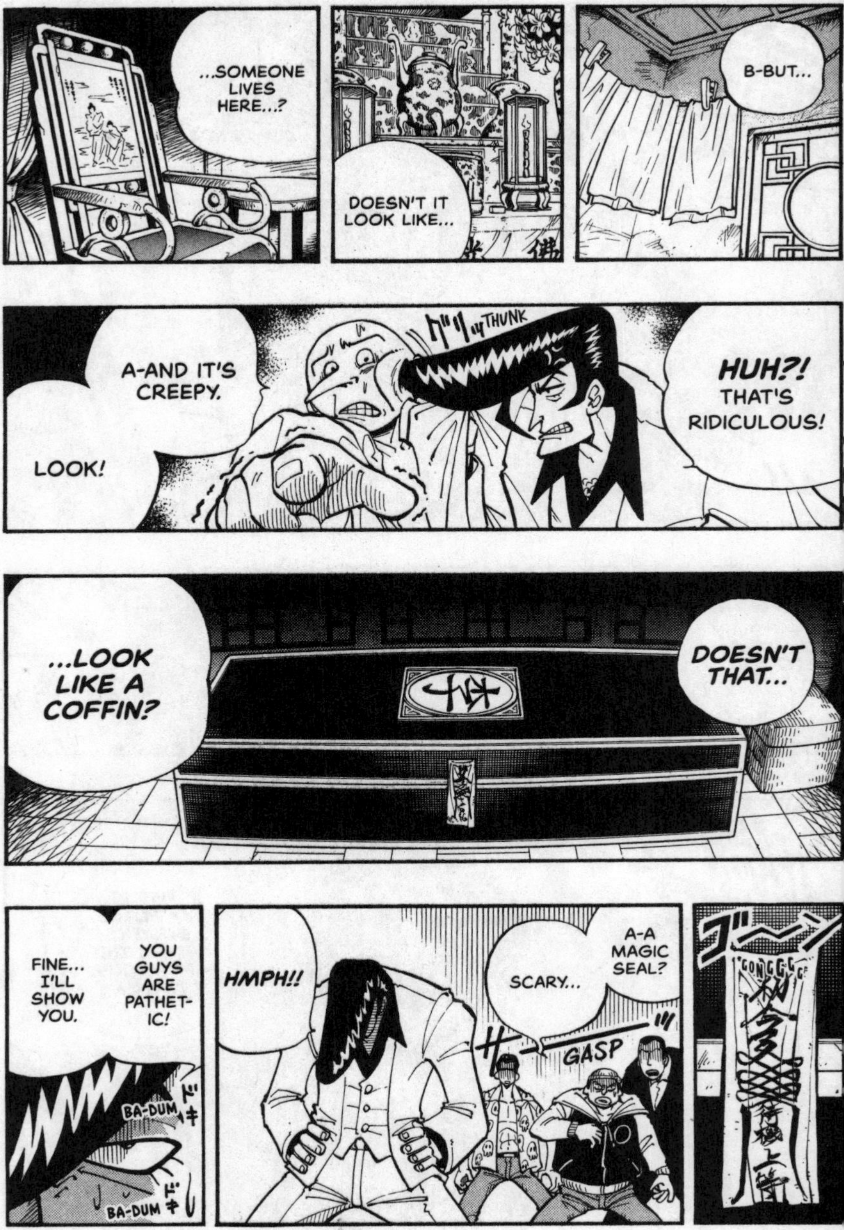
B-BUT...
DOESN'T IT LOOK LIKE...
...SOMEONE LIVES HERE...?
HUH?! THAT'S RIDICULOUS!
グリッ THUNK
A-AND IT'S CREEPY.
LOOK!
DOESN'T THAT...
...LOOK LIKE A COFFIN?
ゴ〜ン GONGGG
A-A MAGIC SEAL?
SCARY...
GASP
HMPH!!
YOU GUYS ARE PATHETIC!
FINE... I'LL SHOW YOU.
ドキ BA-DUM
ドキ BA-DUM

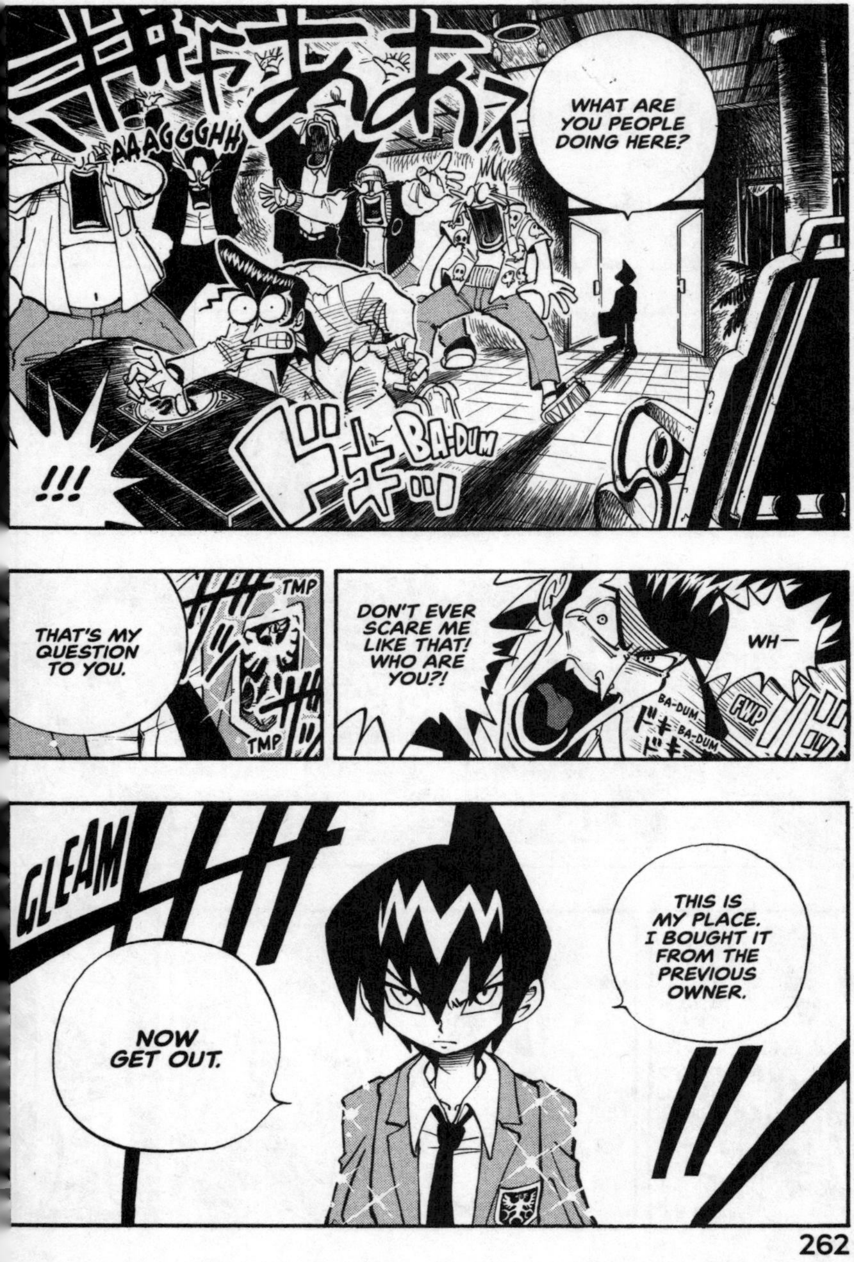
WHAT ARE YOU PEOPLE DOING HERE?
AAAGGGHH
BA-DUM
!!!
WH—
FWP
BA-DUM
BA-DUM
DON'T EVER SCARE ME LIKE THAT! WHO ARE YOU?!
TMP
THAT'S MY QUESTION TO YOU.
TMP
THIS IS MY PLACE. I BOUGHT IT FROM THE PREVIOUS OWNER.
GLEAM
NOW GET OUT.

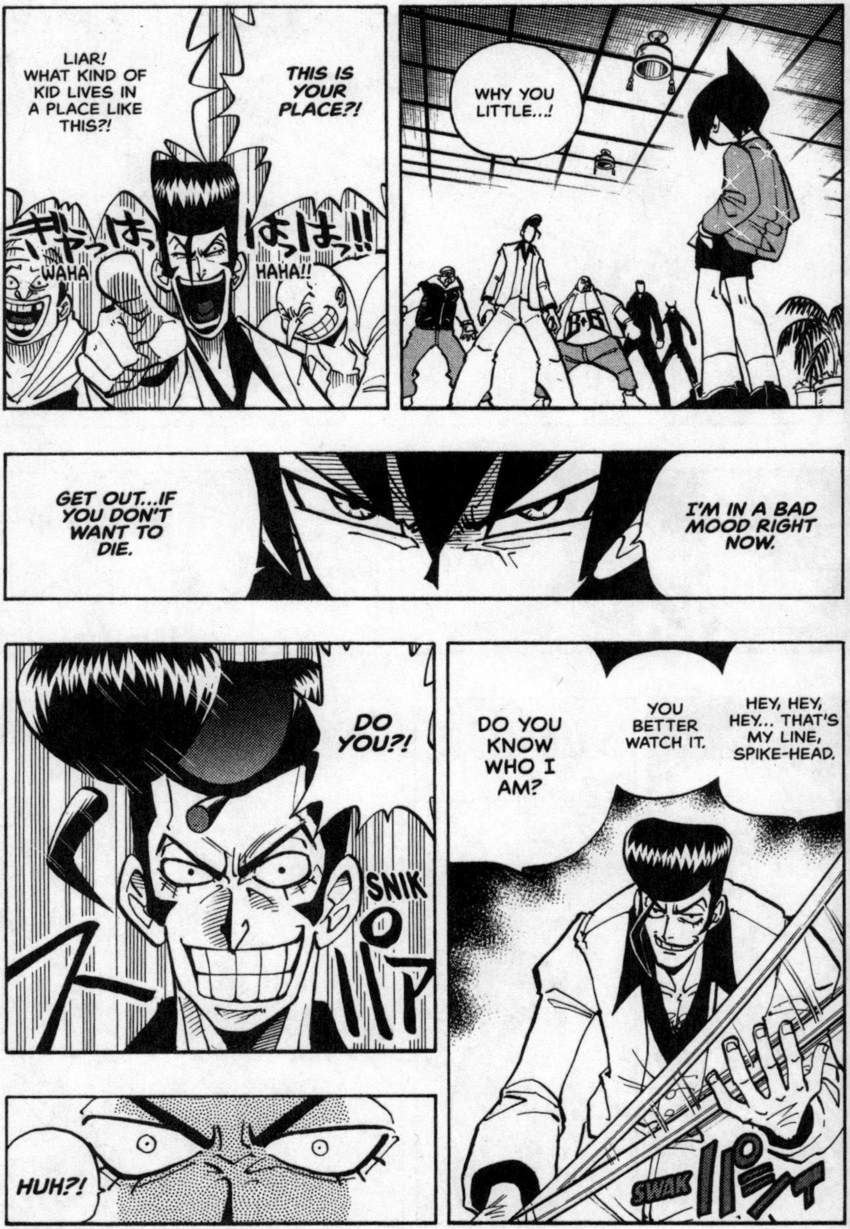
WHY YOU LITTLE...!
THIS IS YOUR PLACE?!
LIAR! WHAT KIND OF KID LIVES IN A PLACE LIKE THIS?!
ぎゃっはっはっはっ!!
HAHA!!
WAHA
I'M IN A BAD MOOD RIGHT NOW.
GET OUT...IF YOU DON'T WANT TO DIE.
HEY, HEY, HEY... THAT'S MY LINE, SPIKE-HEAD.
YOU BETTER WATCH IT.
DO YOU KNOW WHO I AM?
SWAK
DO YOU?!
SNIK
HUH?!

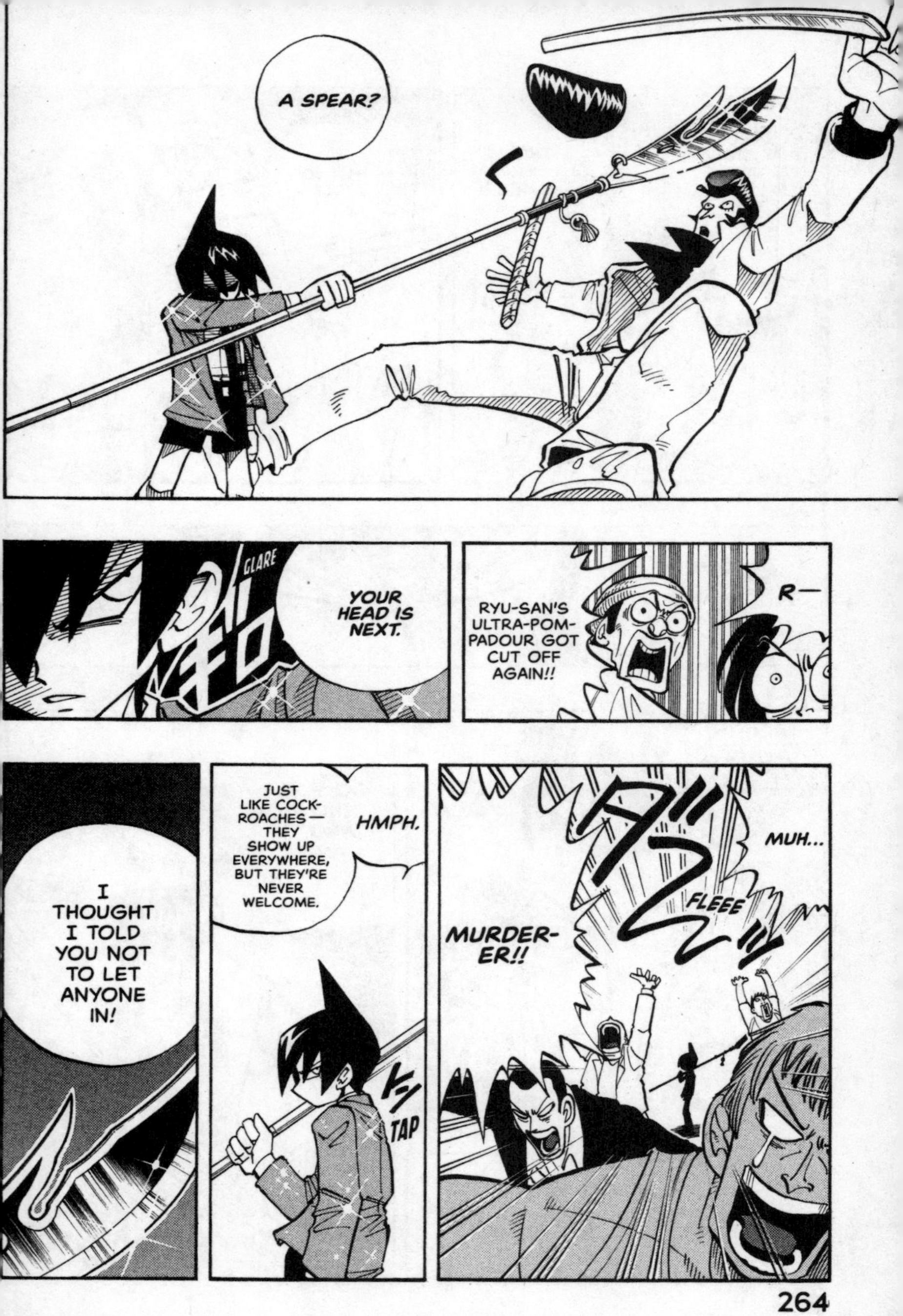
A SPEAR?
R—
RYU-SAN'S ULTRA-POMPADOUR GOT CUT OFF AGAIN!!
GLARE
YOUR HEAD IS NEXT.
MUH...
FLEEE
MURDER-ER!!
HMPH.
JUST LIKE COCK-ROACHES— THEY SHOW UP EVERYWHERE, BUT THEY'RE NEVER WELCOME.
TAP
I THOUGHT I TOLD YOU NOT TO LET ANYONE IN!

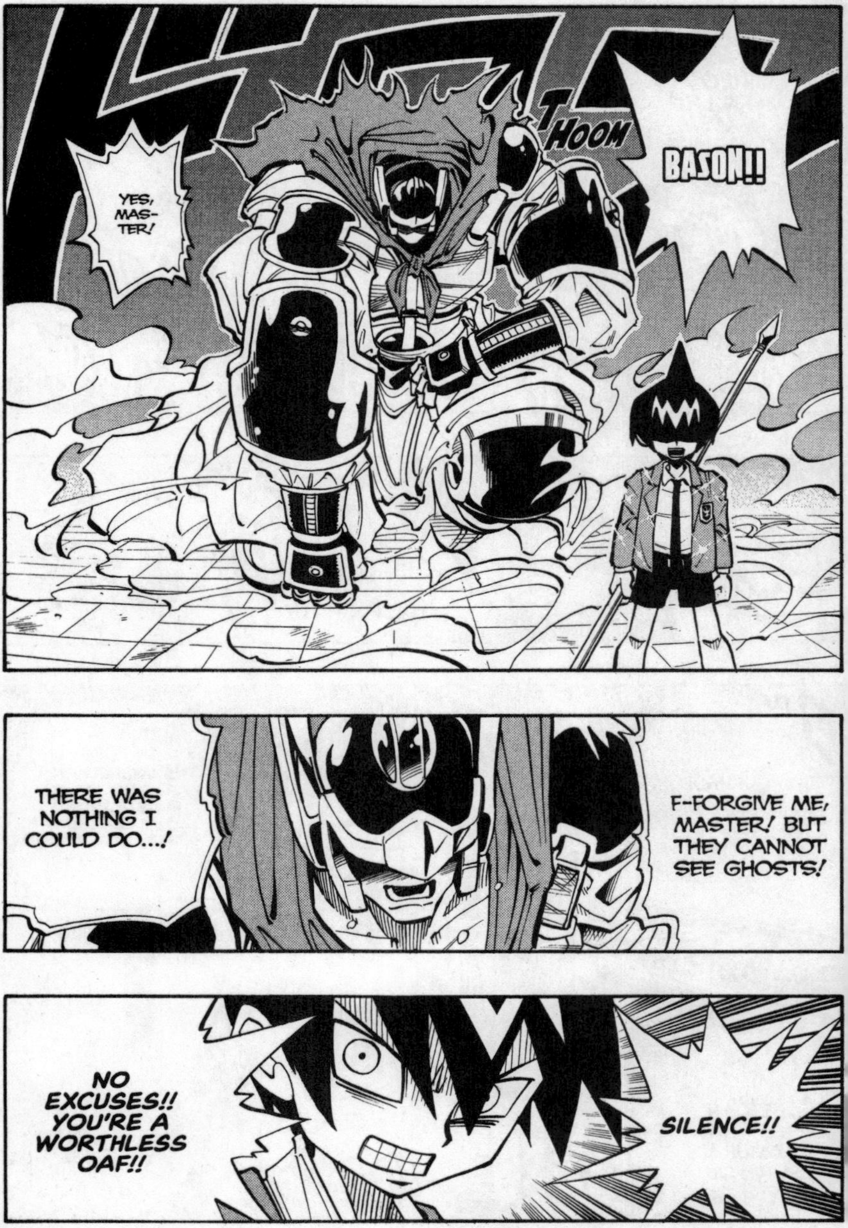
BASON!!
THOOM
YES, MAS-TER!
F-FORGIVE ME, MASTER! BUT THEY CANNOT SEE GHOSTS!
THERE WAS NOTHING I COULD DO...!
SILENCE!!
NO EXCUSES!! YOU'RE A WORTHLESS OAF!!

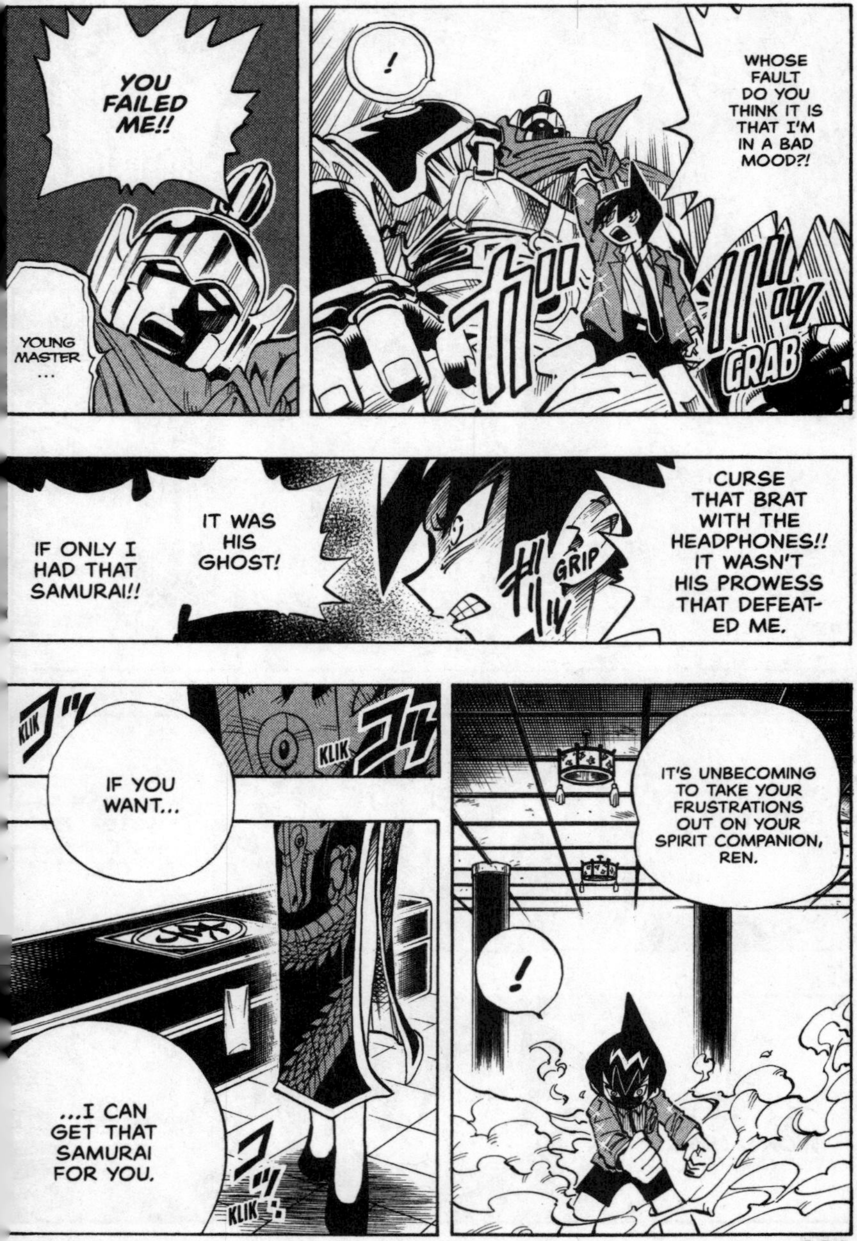
WHOSE FAULT DO YOU THINK IT IS THAT I'M IN A BAD MOOD?!
!
GRAB
YOU FAILED ME!!
YOUNG MASTER ...
CURSE THAT BRAT WITH THE HEADPHONES!! IT WASN'T HIS PROWESS THAT DEFEATED ME.
GRIP
IT WAS HIS GHOST!
IF ONLY I HAD THAT SAMURAI!!
IT'S UNBECOMING TO TAKE YOUR FRUSTRATIONS OUT ON YOUR SPIRIT COMPANION, REN.
!
KLIK
KLIK
IF YOU WANT...
...I CAN GET THAT SAMURAI FOR YOU.
KLIK

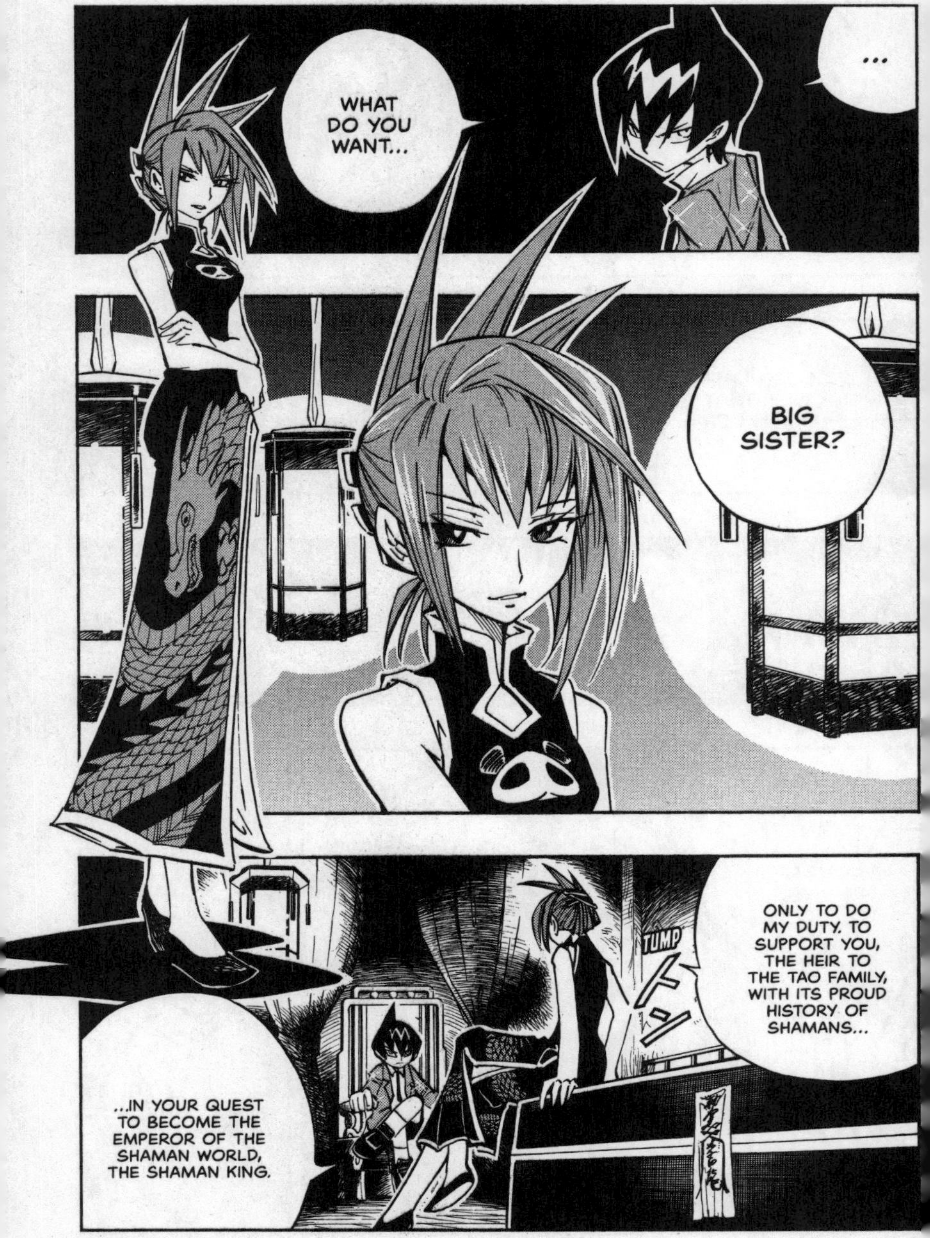

...
WHAT DO YOU WANT...
BIG SISTER?
ONLY TO DO MY DUTY. TO SUPPORT YOU, THE HEIR TO THE TAO FAMILY, WITH ITS PROUD HISTORY OF SHAMANS...
TUMP
...IN YOUR QUEST TO BECOME THE EMPEROR OF THE SHAMAN WORLD, THE SHAMAN KING.

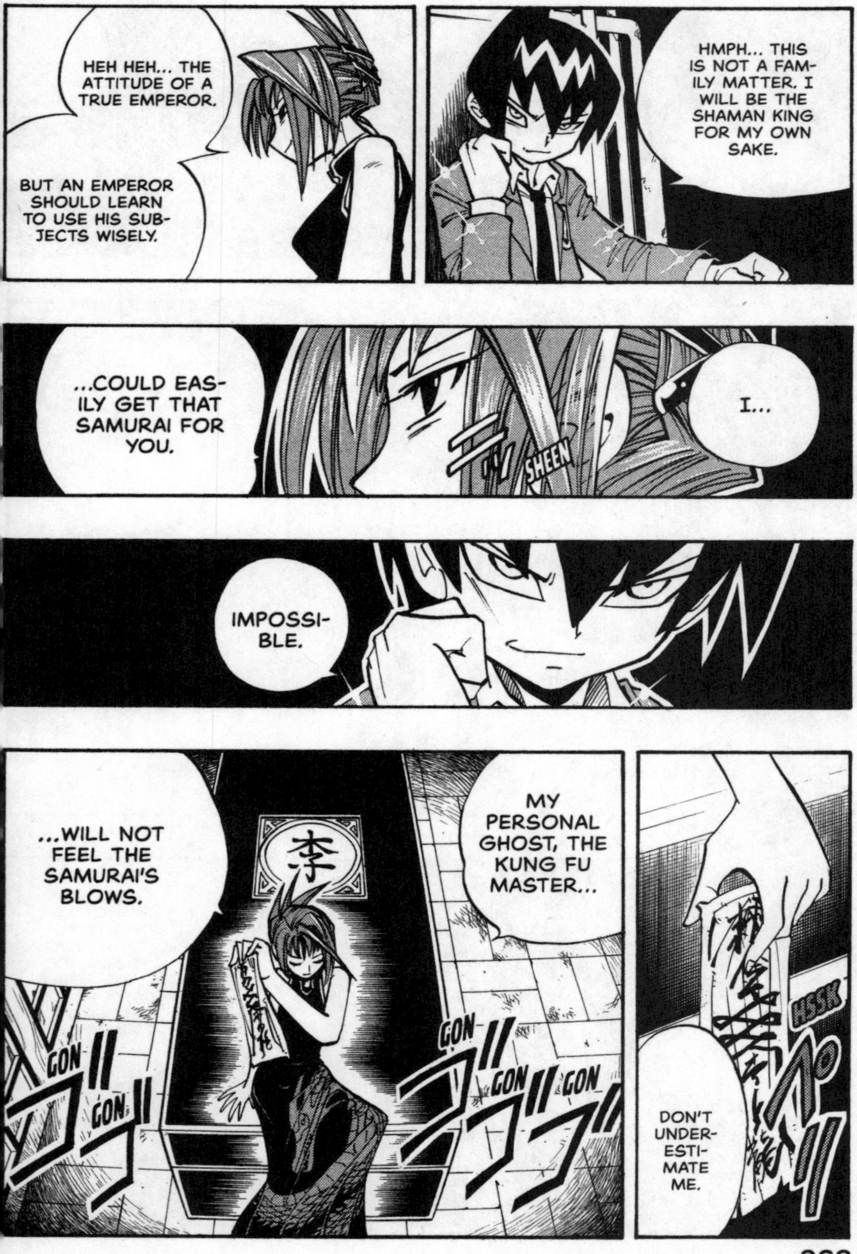
HMPH... THIS IS NOT A FAMILY MATTER. I WILL BE THE SHAMAN KING FOR MY OWN SAKE.
HEH HEH... THE ATTITUDE OF A TRUE EMPEROR.
BUT AN EMPEROR SHOULD LEARN TO USE HIS SUBJECTS WISELY.
I...
SHEEN
...COULD EASILY GET THAT SAMURAI FOR YOU.
IMPOSSIBLE.
HSSK
DON'T UNDERESTIMATE ME.
MY PERSONAL GHOST, THE KUNG FU MASTER...
...WILL NOT FEEL THE SAMURAI'S BLOWS.
GON
GON
GON
GON
GON

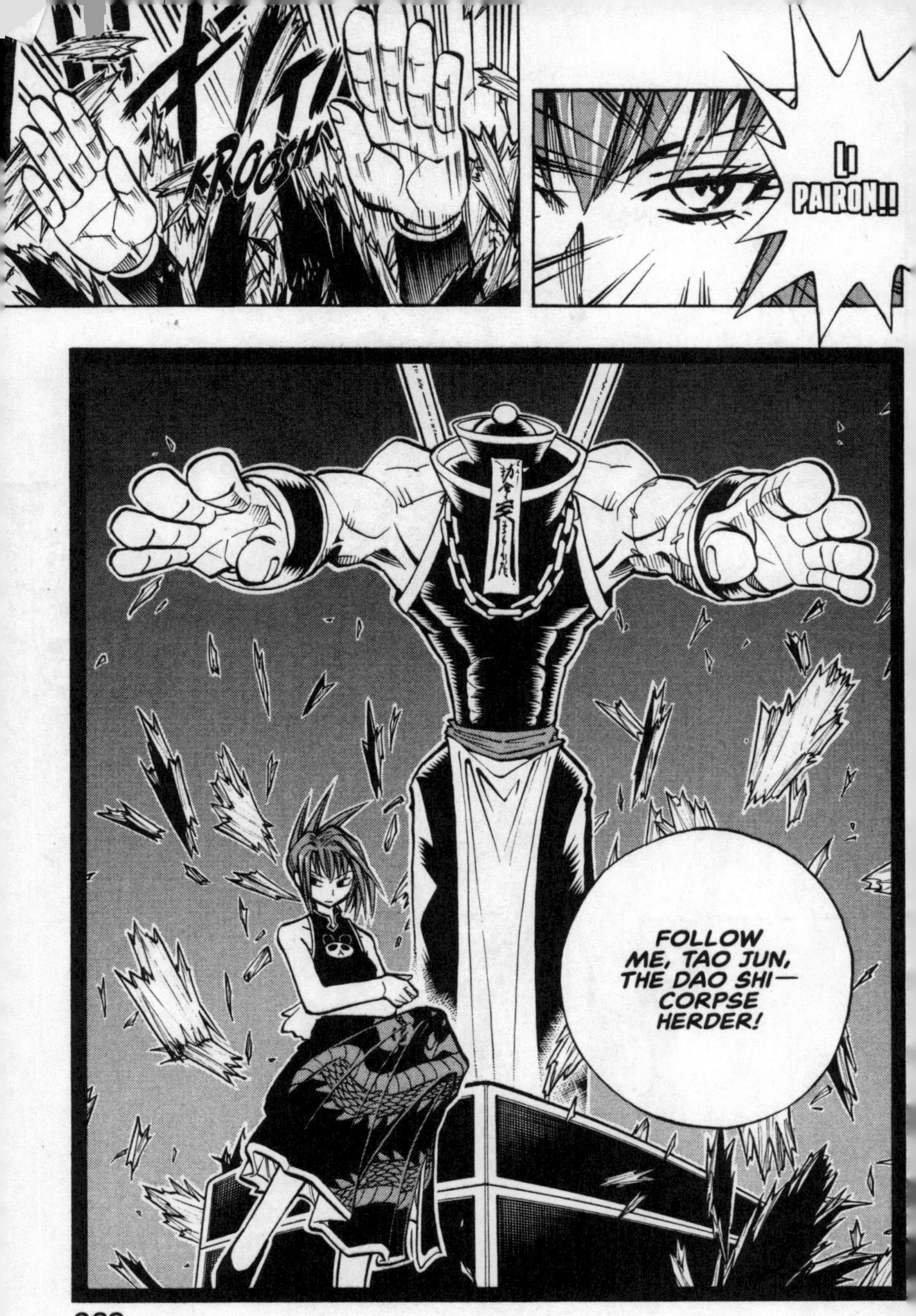
LI
PAIRON!!
KROOSH
FOLLOW ME, TAO JUN, THE DAO SHI—CORPSE HERDER!

SHAMAN KING CHARACTER FILE No.6

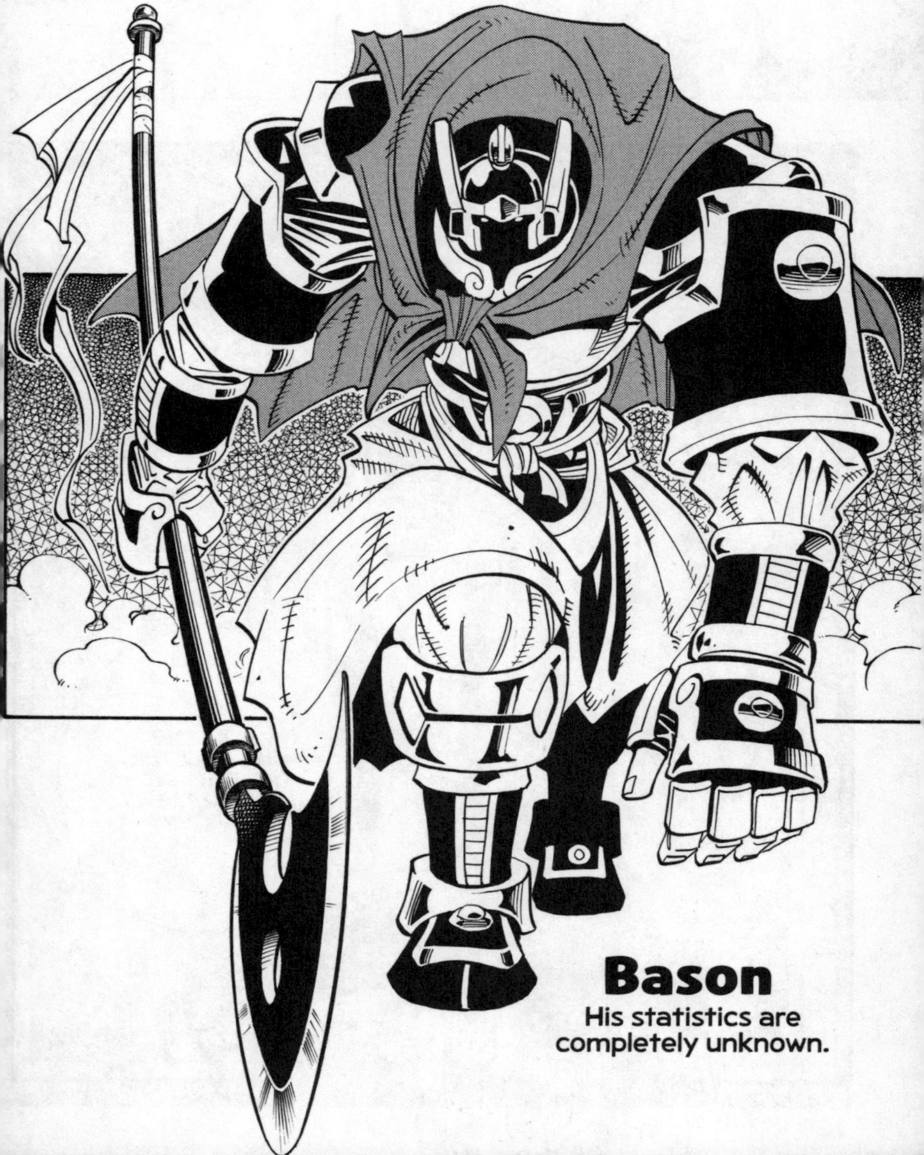

Bason

His statistics are completely unknown.

Chapter 12:

Kung Fu Master

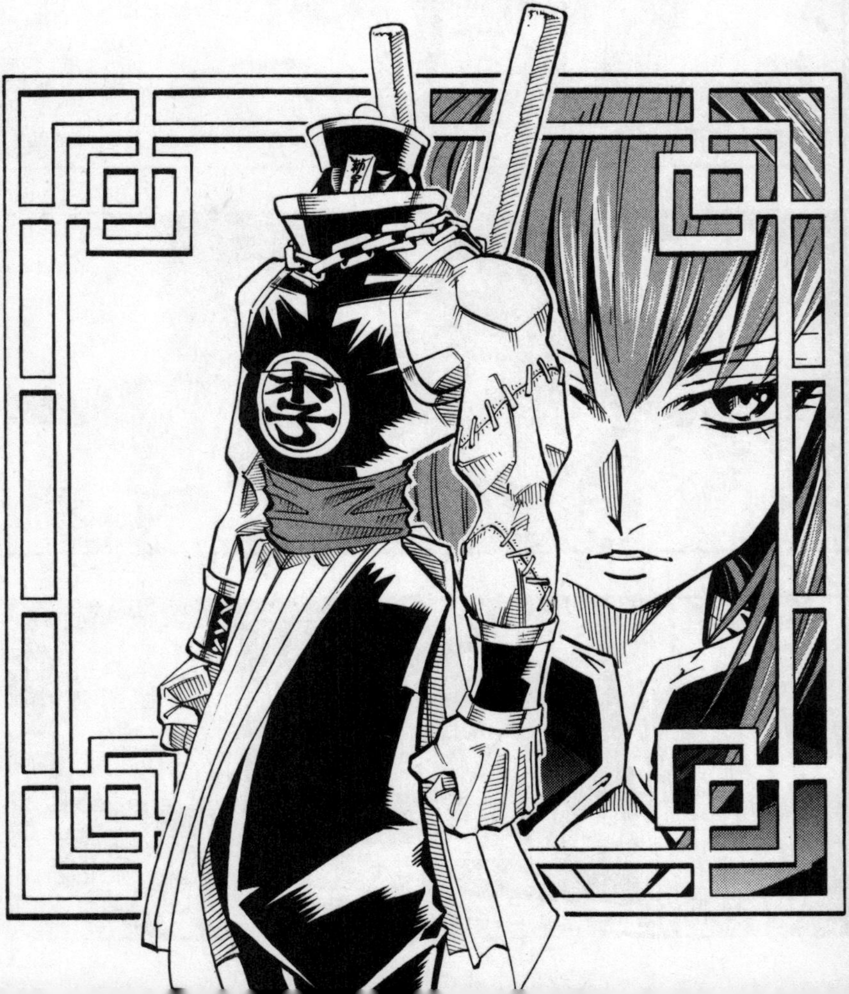

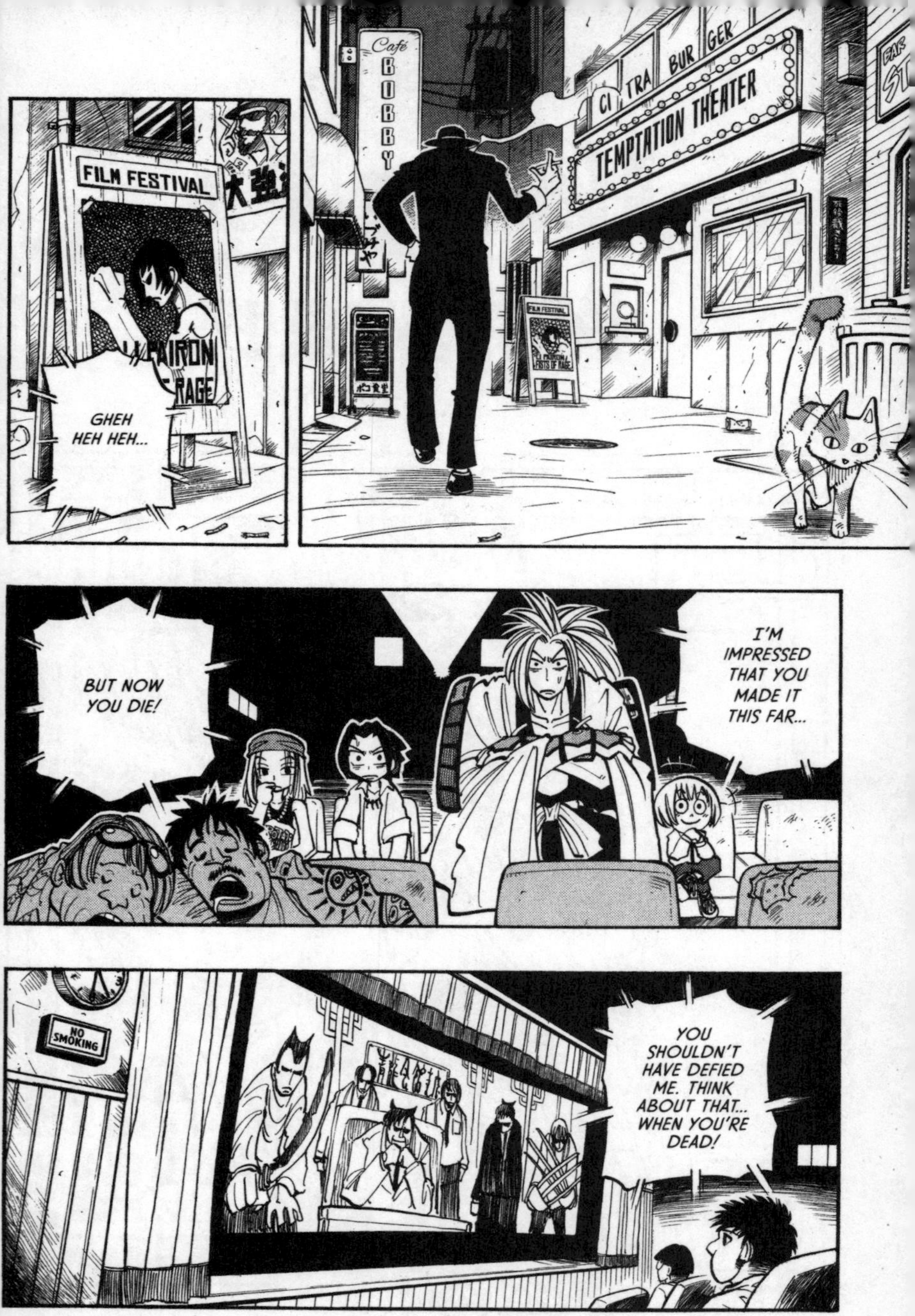
Café
BOBBY
CI TRA BUR GER
TEMPTATION THEATER
FILM FESTIVAL
LI PAIRON
FISTS OF RAGE
FILM FESTIVAL
GHEH HEH HEH...
I'M IMPRESSED THAT YOU MADE IT THIS FAR...
BUT NOW YOU DIE!
YOU SHOULDN'T HAVE DEFIED ME. THINK ABOUT THAT... WHEN YOU'RE DEAD!
NO SMOKING

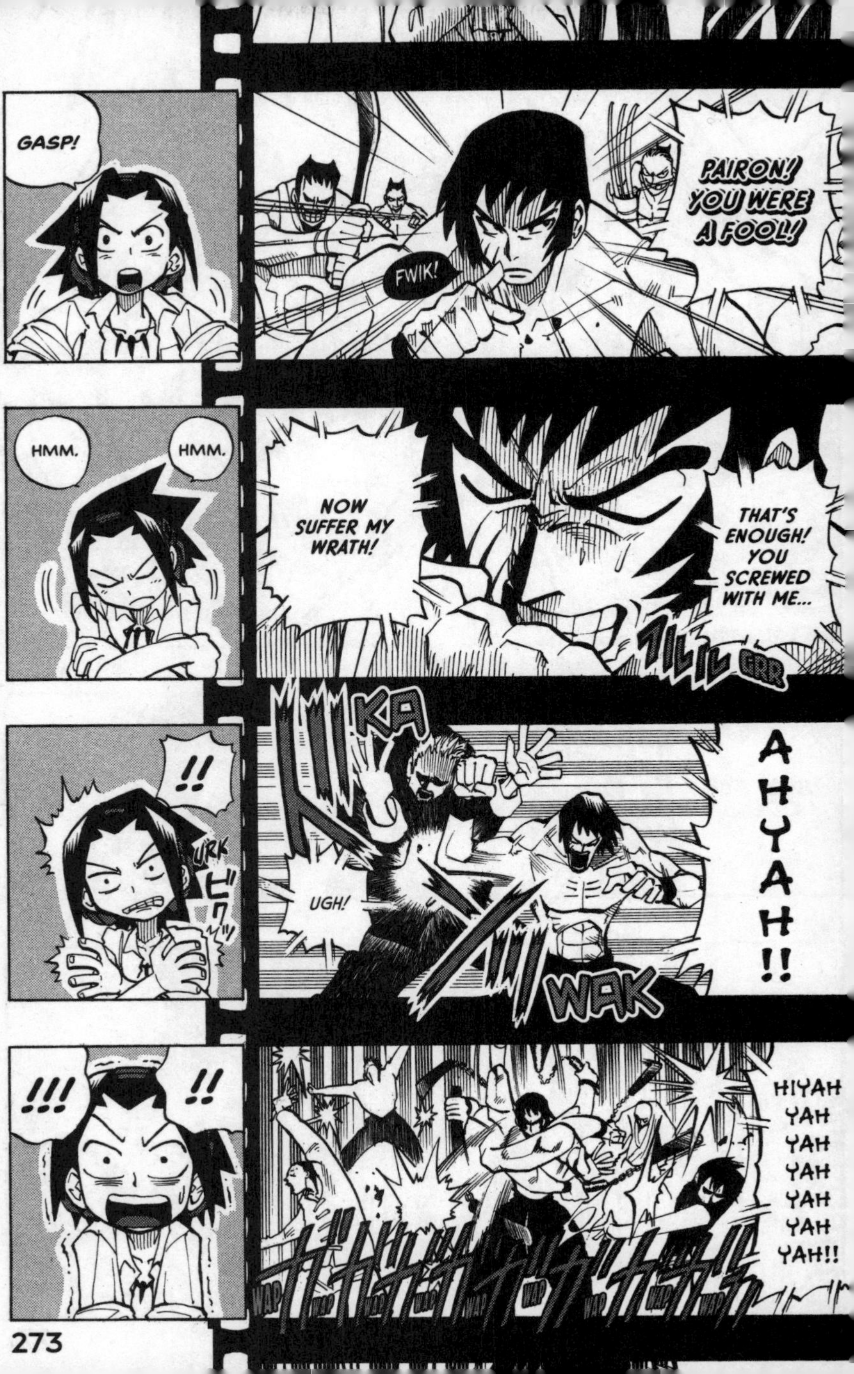
PAIRON! YOU WERE A FOOL!
FWIK!
GASP!
THAT'S ENOUGH! YOU SCREWED WITH ME...
NOW SUFFER MY WRATH!
GRR
HMM.
HMM.
AHYAH!!
KA
UGH!
WAK
!!
URK
HIYAH YAH YAH YAH YAH YAH YAH!!
WAP
!!
!!!

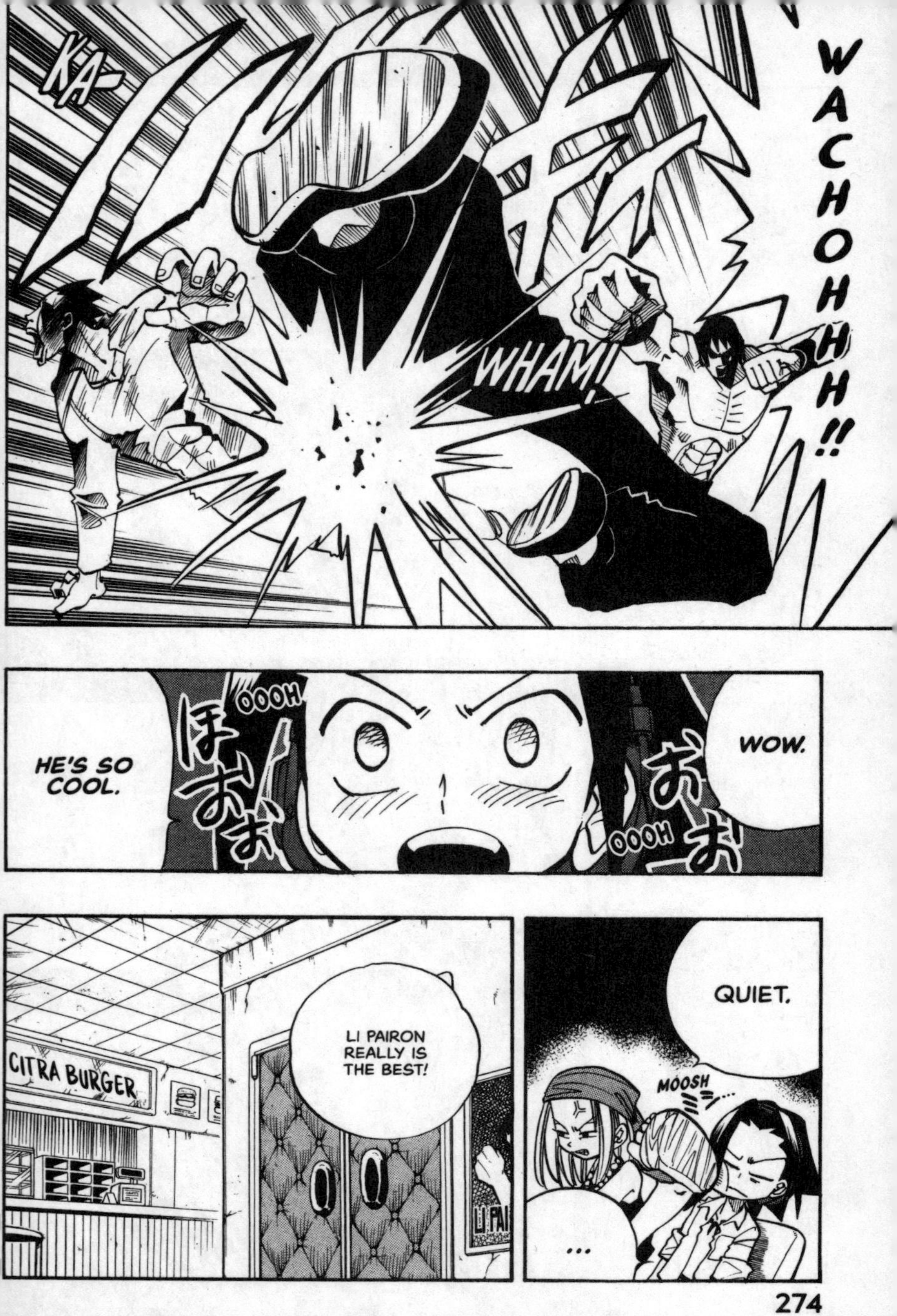
WACHOHHHH!!
KA-
WHAM!
WOW.
おお
OOOH
ほおお
OOOH
HE'S SO COOL.
QUIET.
MOOSH
...
LI PAIRON REALLY IS THE BEST!
CITRA BURGER

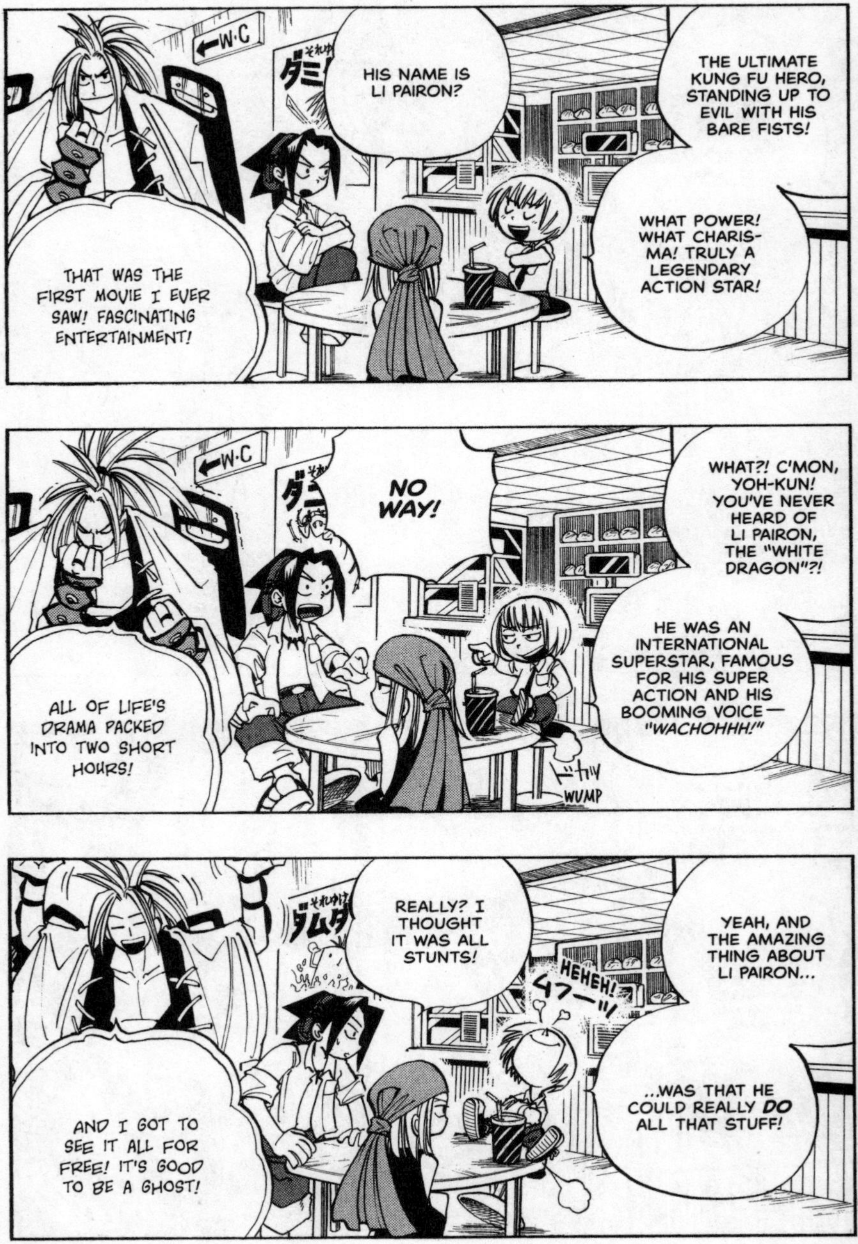
THE ULTIMATE KUNG FU HERO, STANDING UP TO EVIL WITH HIS BARE FISTS!
WHAT POWER! WHAT CHARIS-MA! TRULY A LEGENDARY ACTION STAR!
HIS NAME IS LI PAIRON?
THAT WAS THE FIRST MOVIE I EVER SAW! FASCINATING ENTERTAINMENT!
WHAT?! C'MON, YOH-KUN! YOU'VE NEVER HEARD OF LI PAIRON, THE "WHITE DRAGON"?!
HE WAS AN INTERNATIONAL SUPERSTAR, FAMOUS FOR HIS SUPER ACTION AND HIS BOOMING VOICE— "WACHOHHH!"
NO WAY!
ALL OF LIFE'S DRAMA PACKED INTO TWO SHORT HOURS!
WUMP
YEAH, AND THE AMAZING THING ABOUT LI PAIRON...
HEHEH!
...WAS THAT HE COULD REALLY DO ALL THAT STUFF!
REALLY? I THOUGHT IT WAS ALL STUNTS!
AND I GOT TO SEE IT ALL FOR FREE! IT'S GOOD TO BE A GHOST!

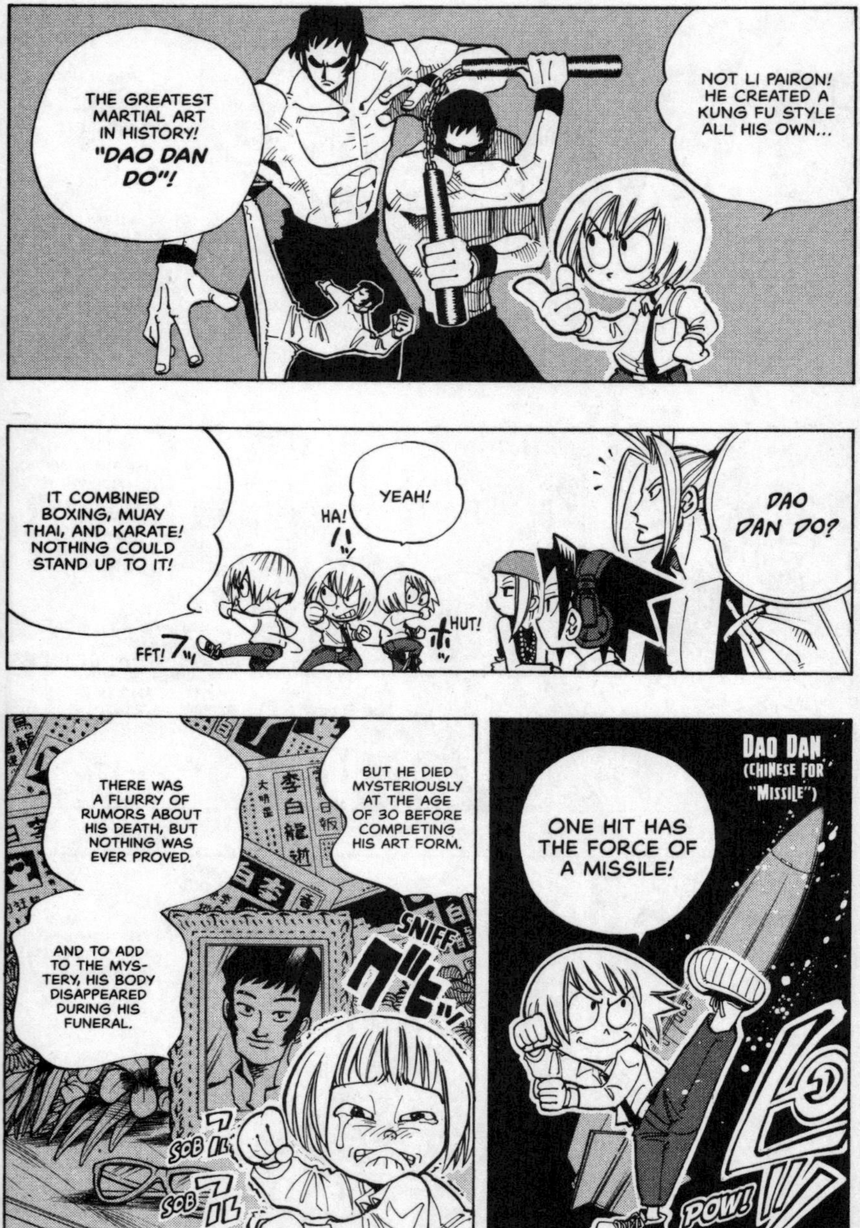
NOT LI PAIRON! HE CREATED A KUNG FU STYLE ALL HIS OWN...
THE GREATEST MARTIAL ART IN HISTORY! "DAO DAN DO"!
DAO DAN DO?
YEAH!
HA!
IT COMBINED BOXING, MUAY THAI, AND KARATE! NOTHING COULD STAND UP TO IT!
HUT!
FFT!
DAO DAN (CHINESE FOR "MISSILE")
ONE HIT HAS THE FORCE OF A MISSILE!
POW!
BUT HE DIED MYSTERIOUSLY AT THE AGE OF 30 BEFORE COMPLETING HIS ART FORM.
THERE WAS A FLURRY OF RUMORS ABOUT HIS DEATH, BUT NOTHING WAS EVER PROVED.
SNIFF
AND TO ADD TO THE MYSTERY, HIS BODY DISAPPEARED DURING HIS FUNERAL.
SOB
SOB

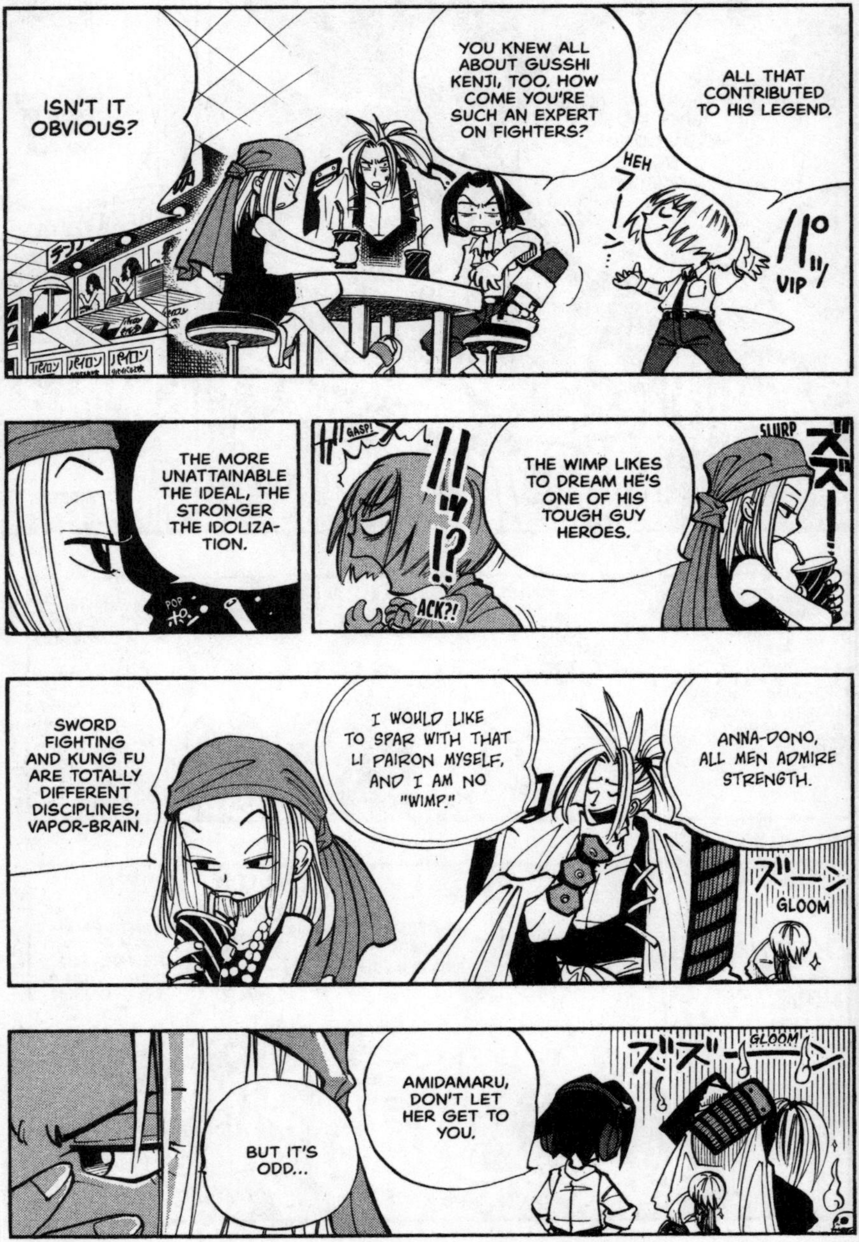
ALL THAT CONTRIBUTED TO HIS LEGEND.
HEH
VIP
YOU KNEW ALL ABOUT GUSSHI KENJI, TOO. HOW COME YOU'RE SUCH AN EXPERT ON FIGHTERS?
ISN'T IT OBVIOUS?
SLURP
THE WIMP LIKES TO DREAM HE'S ONE OF HIS TOUGH GUY HEROES.
GASP!
ACK?!
THE MORE UNATTAINABLE THE IDEAL, THE STRONGER THE IDOLIZATION.
POP
ANNA-DONO, ALL MEN ADMIRE STRENGTH.
GLOOM
I WOULD LIKE TO SPAR WITH THAT LI PAIRON MYSELF, AND I AM NO "WIMP."
SWORD FIGHTING AND KUNG FU ARE TOTALLY DIFFERENT DISCIPLINES, VAPOR-BRAIN.
GLOOM
AMIDAMARU, DON'T LET HER GET TO YOU.
BUT IT'S ODD...

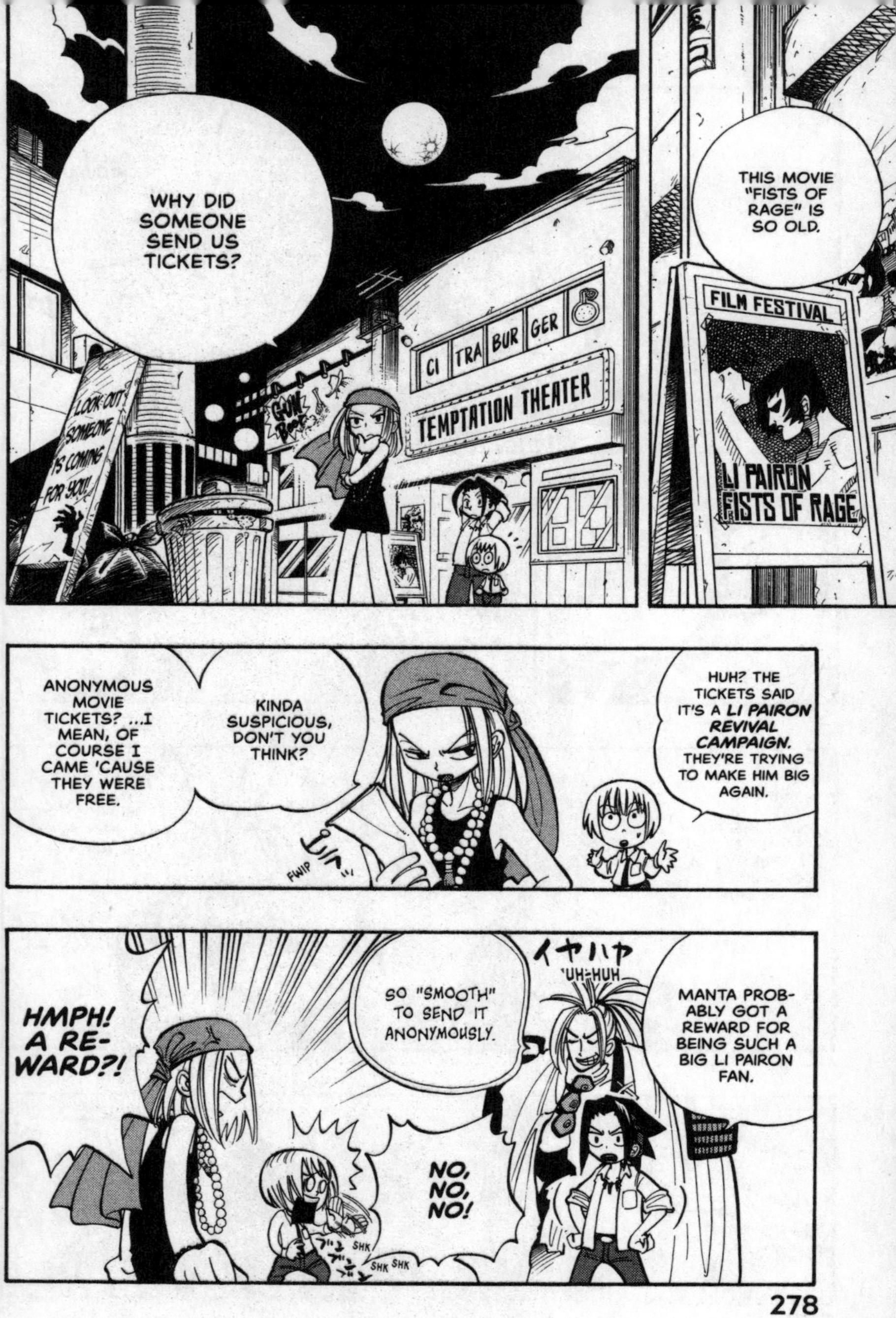
THIS MOVIE "FISTS OF RAGE" IS SO OLD.
FILM FESTIVAL
LI PAIRON FISTS OF RAGE
WHY DID SOMEONE SEND US TICKETS?
CI TRA BUR GER
TEMPTATION THEATER
LOOK OUT SOMEONE IS COMING FOR YOU!!
HUH? THE TICKETS SAID IT'S A LI PAIRON REVIVAL CAMPAIGN. THEY'RE TRYING TO MAKE HIM BIG AGAIN.
KINDA SUSPICIOUS, DON'T YOU THINK?
ANONYMOUS MOVIE TICKETS? ...I MEAN, OF COURSE I CAME 'CAUSE THEY WERE FREE.
FWIP
MANTA PROB-ABLY GOT A REWARD FOR BEING SUCH A BIG LI PAIRON FAN.
イヤハヤ
UH-HUH
SO "SMOOTH" TO SEND IT ANONYMOUSLY.
HMPH! A RE-WARD?!
NO, NO, NO!
SHK SHK SHK

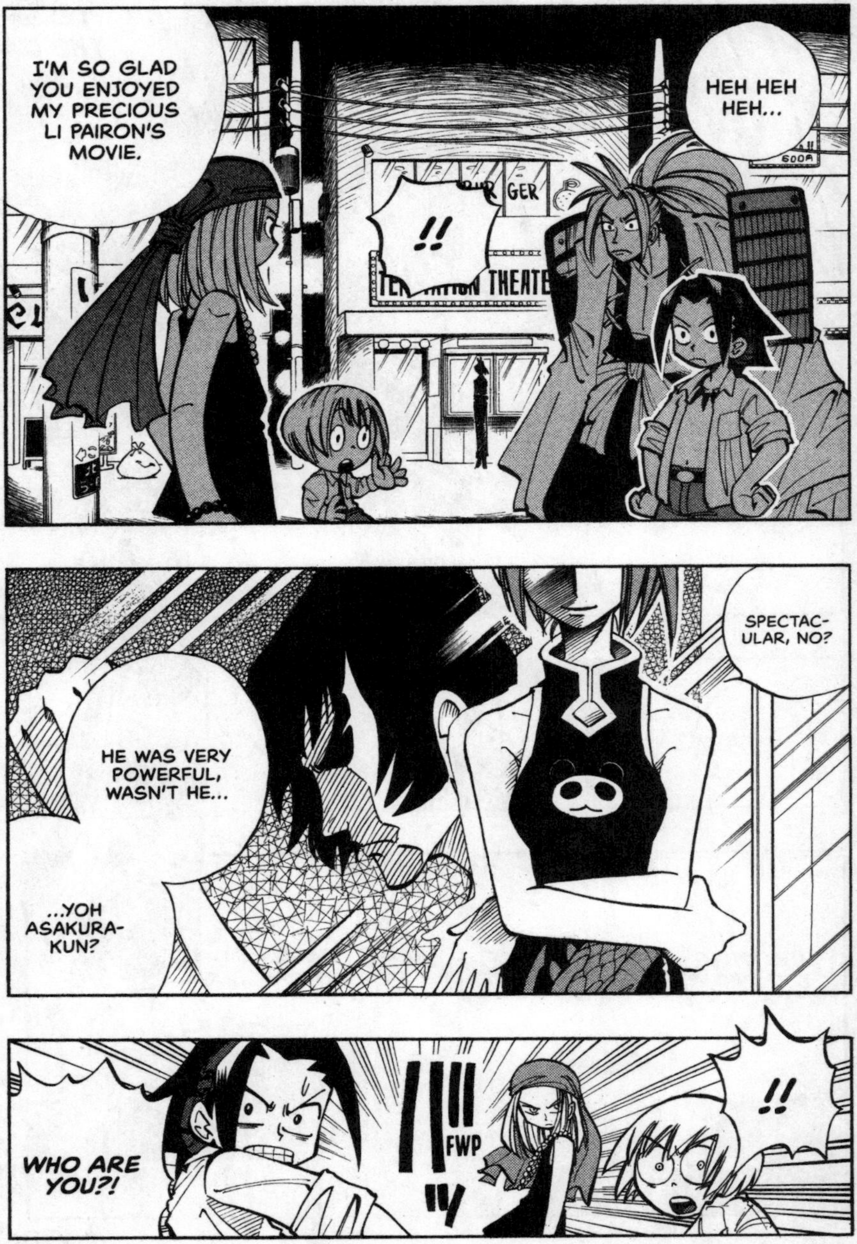

HEH HEH HEH...
I'M SO GLAD YOU ENJOYED MY PRECIOUS LI PAIRON'S MOVIE.
!!
SPECTAC-ULAR, NO?
HE WAS VERY POWERFUL, WASN'T HE...
...YOH ASAKURA-KUN?
!!
FWP
WHO ARE YOU?!

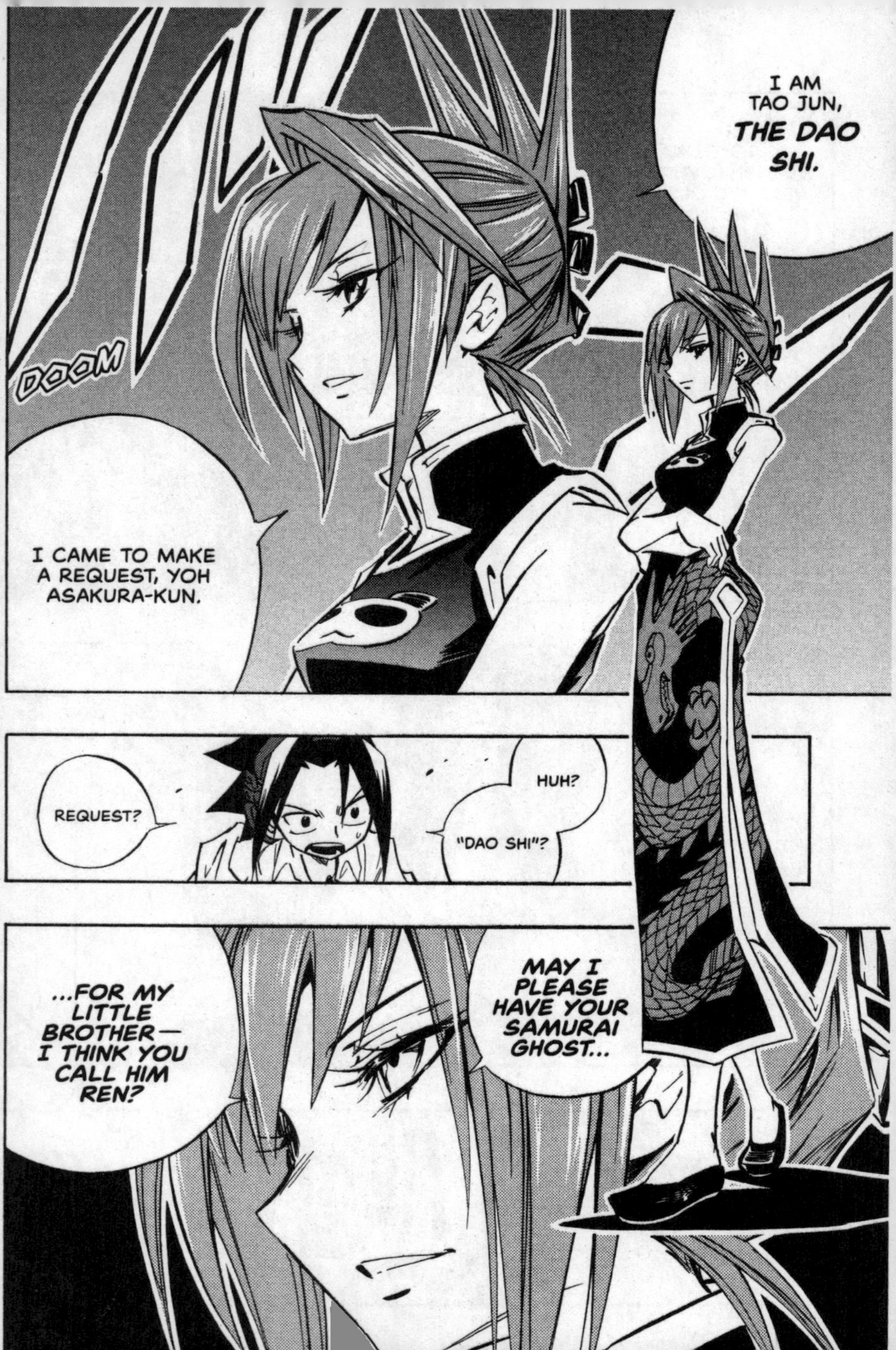
I AM TAO JUN, THE DAO SHI.
DOOM
I CAME TO MAKE A REQUEST, YOH ASAKURA-KUN.
HUH? "DAO SHI"?
REQUEST?
MAY I PLEASE HAVE YOUR SAMURAI GHOST...
...FOR MY LITTLE BROTHER— I THINK YOU CALL HIM REN?

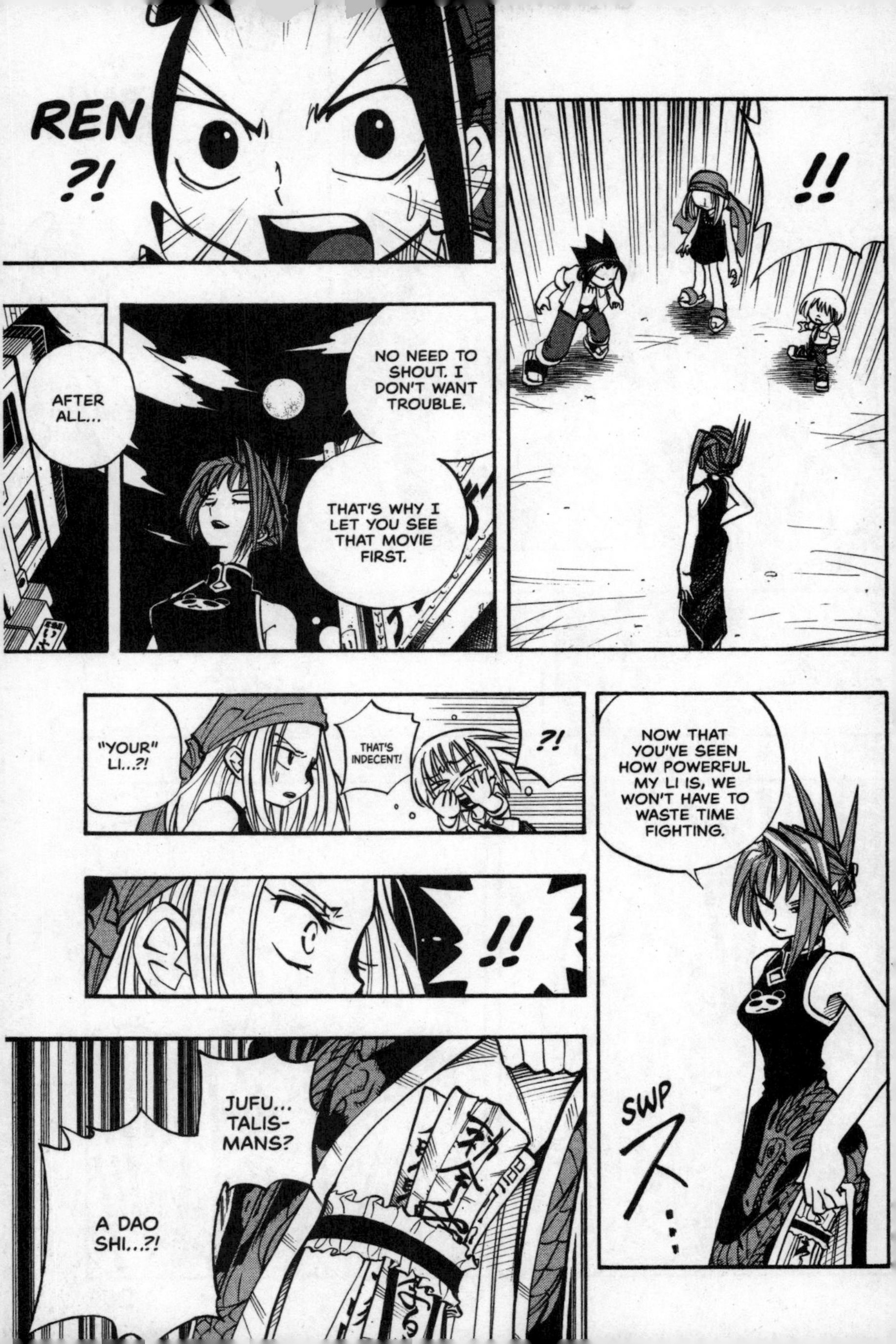
!!
REN ?!
NO NEED TO SHOUT. I DON'T WANT TROUBLE.
AFTER ALL...
THAT'S WHY I LET YOU SEE THAT MOVIE FIRST.
NOW THAT YOU'VE SEEN HOW POWERFUL MY LI IS, WE WON'T HAVE TO WASTE TIME FIGHTING.
SWP
?!
THAT'S INDECENT!
"YOUR" LI...?!
!!
JUFU... TALISMANS?
A DAO SHI...?!

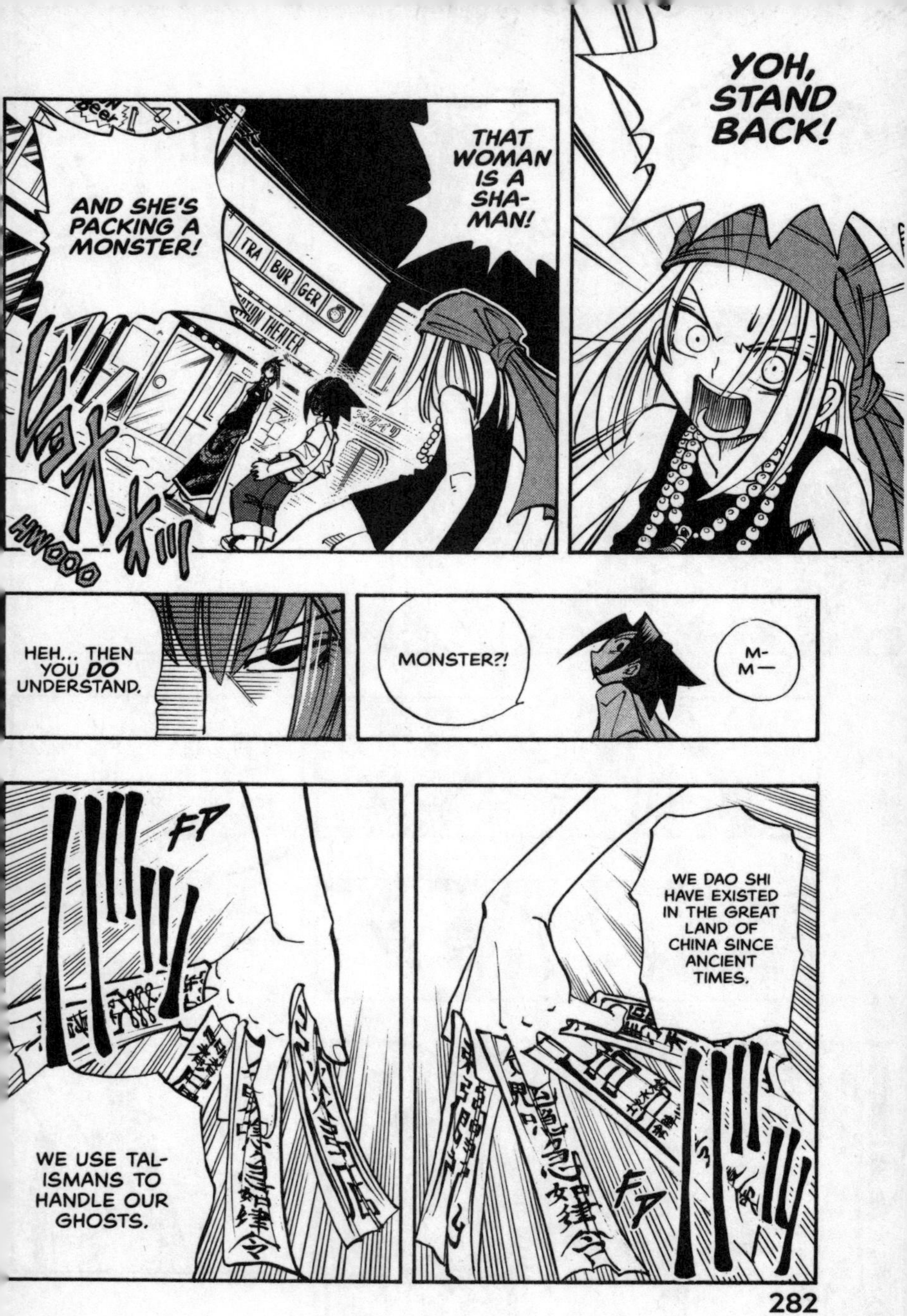
YOH, STAND BACK!
THAT WOMAN IS A SHAMAN!
AND SHE'S PACKING A MONSTER!
HWOOO
TRA BUR GER
M-M—
MONSTER?!
HEH... THEN YOU DO UNDERSTAND.
WE DAO SHI HAVE EXISTED IN THE GREAT LAND OF CHINA SINCE ANCIENT TIMES.
FP
FP
WE USE TALISMANS TO HANDLE OUR GHOSTS.

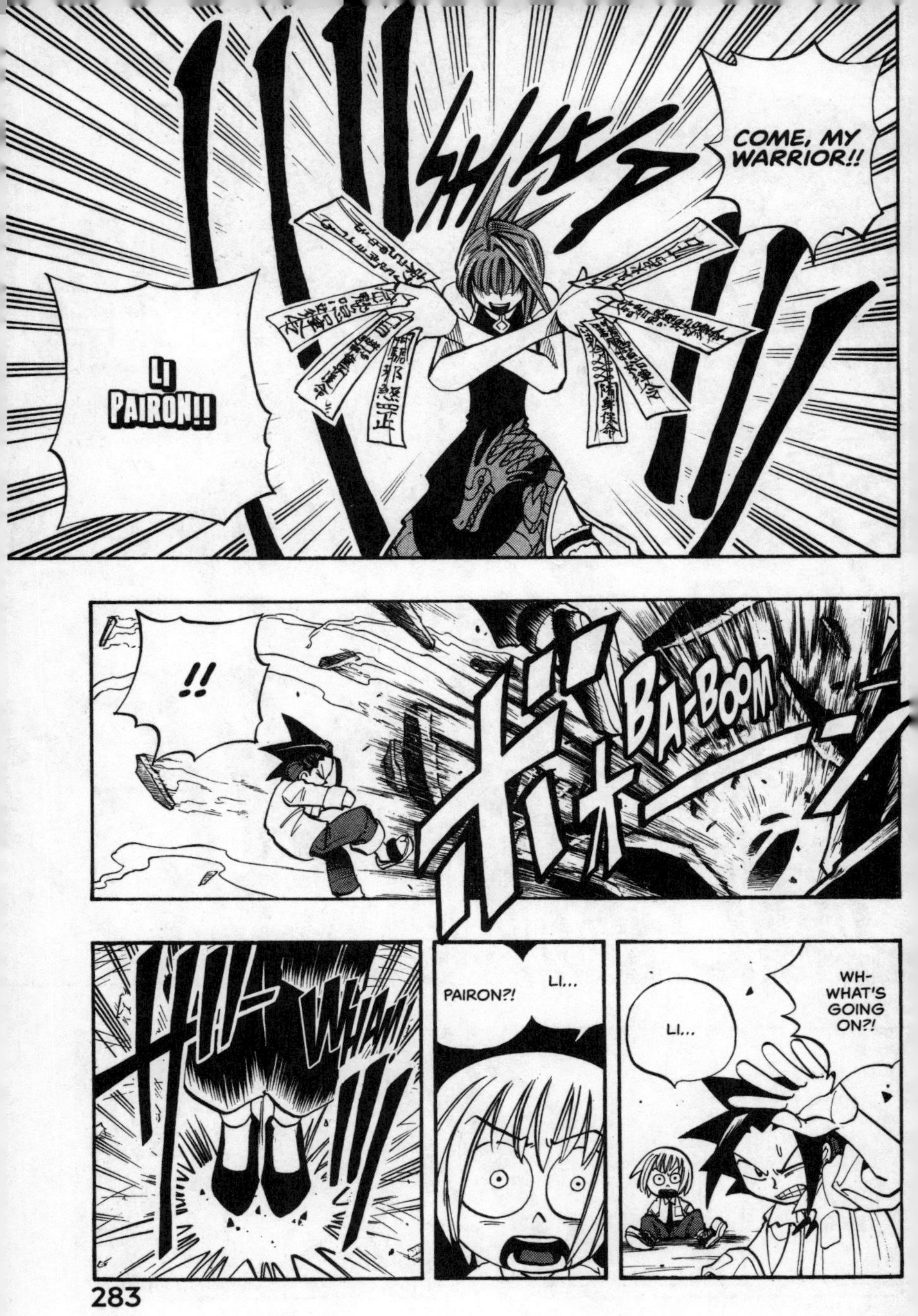
COME, MY WARRIOR!!
LI PAIRON!!
BA-BOOM
!!
WH-WHAT'S GOING ON?!
LI...
LI...
PAIRON?!
WHAM!

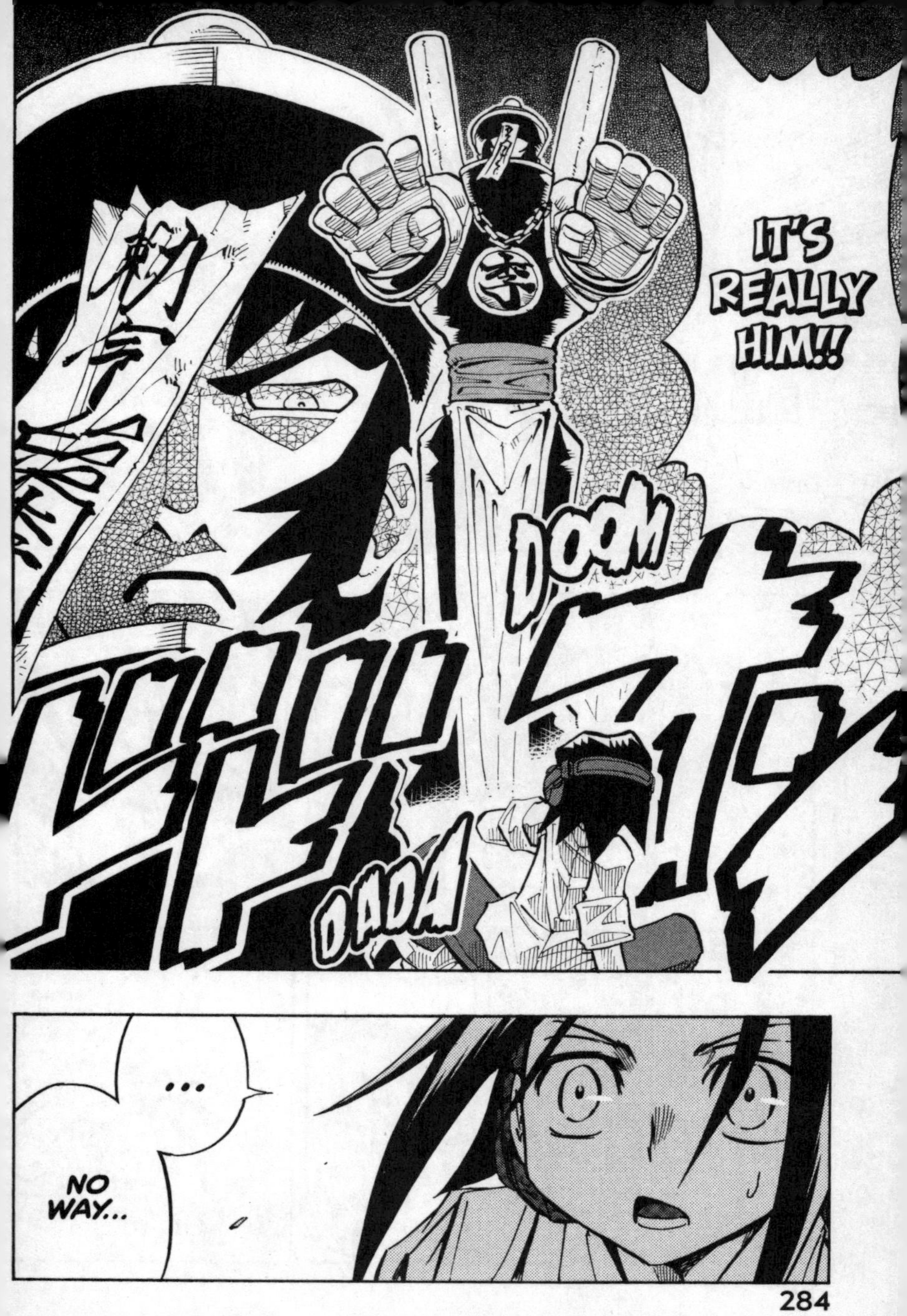
IT'S REALLY HIM!!
DOOM
DADA
...
NO WAY...

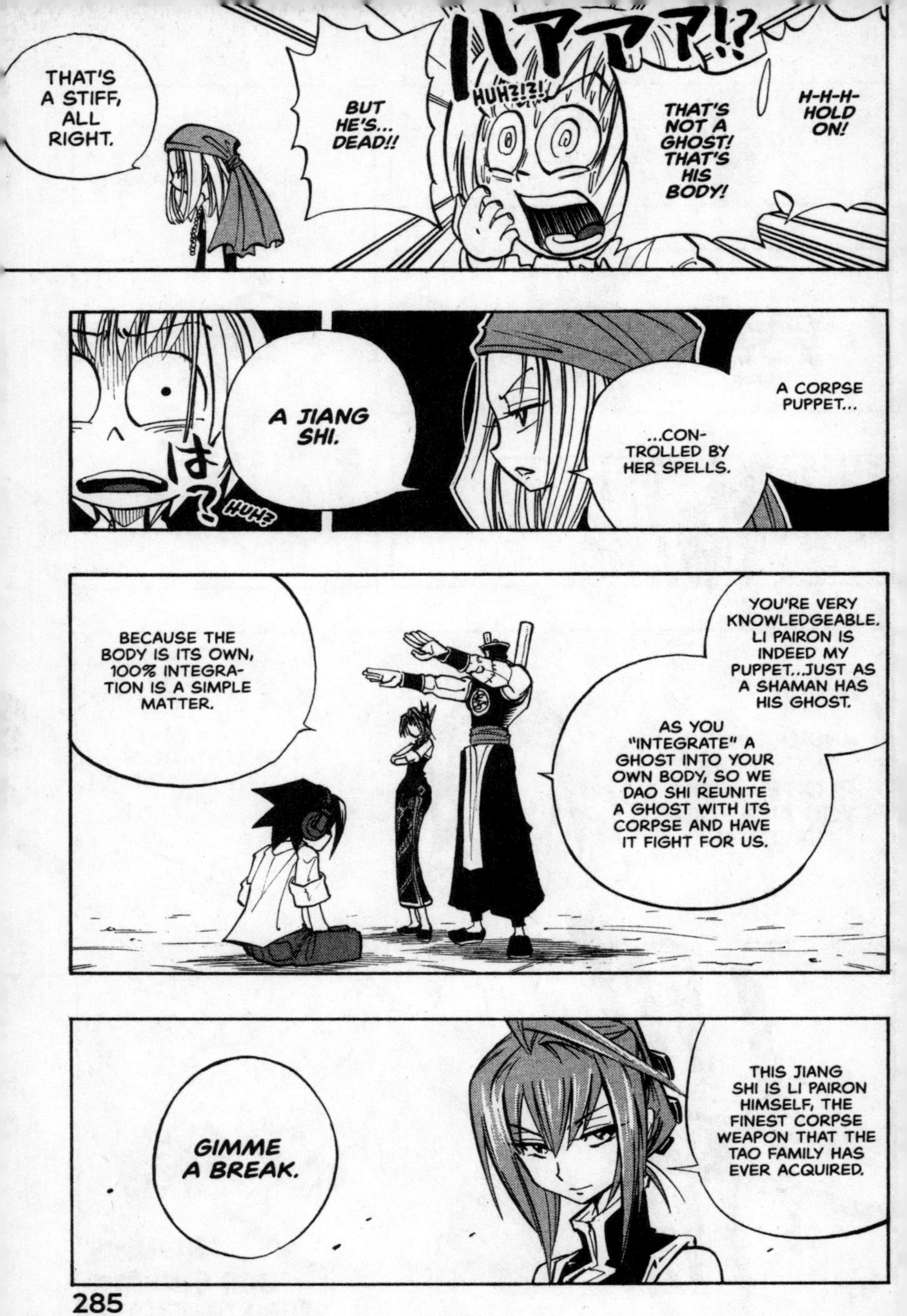
H-H-H-HOLD ON!
THAT'S NOT A GHOST! THAT'S HIS BODY!
ハアアア!!?
HUH?!?!
BUT HE'S... DEAD!!
THAT'S A STIFF, ALL RIGHT.
A CORPSE PUPPET...
...CON-TROLLED BY HER SPELLS.
A JIANG SHI.
は?
HUH?
YOU'RE VERY KNOWLEDGEABLE. LI PAIRON IS INDEED MY PUPPET...JUST AS A SHAMAN HAS HIS GHOST.
AS YOU "INTEGRATE" A GHOST INTO YOUR OWN BODY, SO WE DAO SHI REUNITE A GHOST WITH ITS CORPSE AND HAVE IT FIGHT FOR US.
BECAUSE THE BODY IS ITS OWN, 100% INTEGRA-TION IS A SIMPLE MATTER.
THIS JIANG SHI IS LI PAIRON HIMSELF, THE FINEST CORPSE WEAPON THAT THE TAO FAMILY HAS EVER ACQUIRED.
GIMME A BREAK.

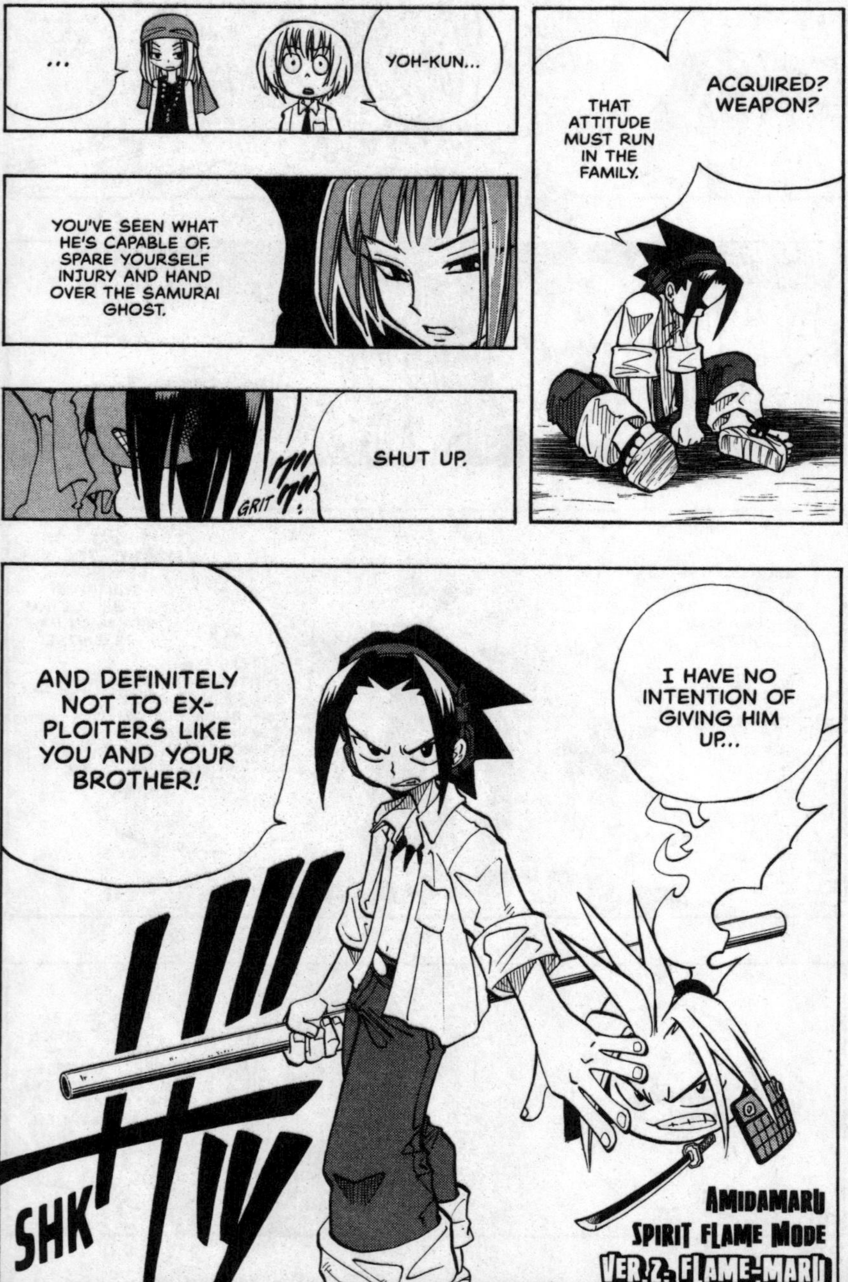
ACQUIRED? WEAPON?
THAT ATTITUDE MUST RUN IN THE FAMILY.
YOH-KUN...
...
YOU'VE SEEN WHAT HE'S CAPABLE OF. SPARE YOURSELF INJURY AND HAND OVER THE SAMURAI GHOST.
SHUT UP.
GRIT
I HAVE NO INTENTION OF GIVING HIM UP...
AND DEFINITELY NOT TO EX-PLOITERS LIKE YOU AND YOUR BROTHER!
SHK
AMIDAMARU
SPIRIT FLAME MODE
VER.2. FLAME-MARU

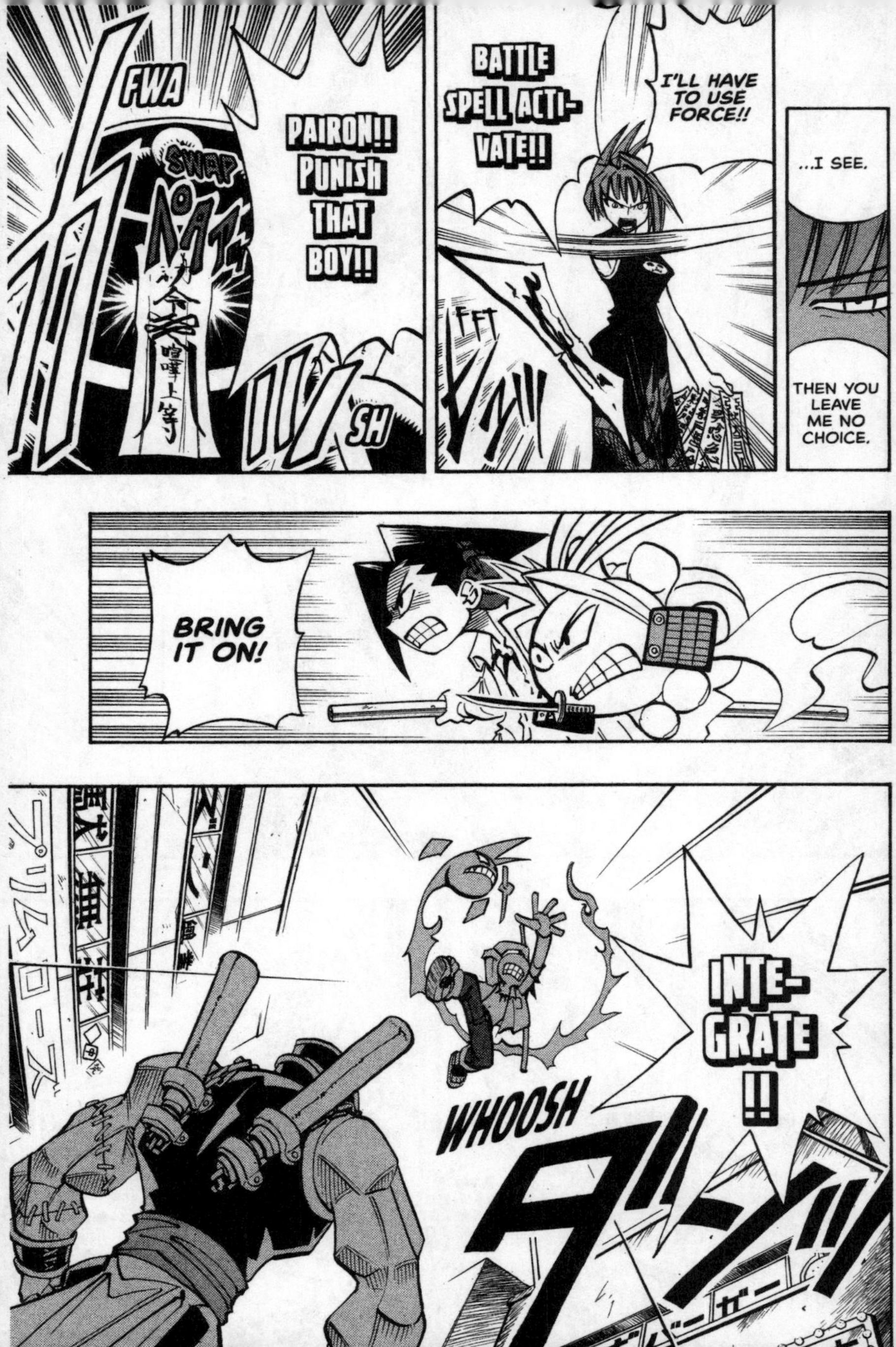
...I SEE.
THEN YOU LEAVE ME NO CHOICE.
I'LL HAVE TO USE FORCE!!
BATTLE SPELL ACTI-VATE!!
FFT
PAIRON!! PUNISH THAT BOY!!
FWA
SWAP
SH
BRING IT ON!
INTE-GRATE!!
WHOOSH

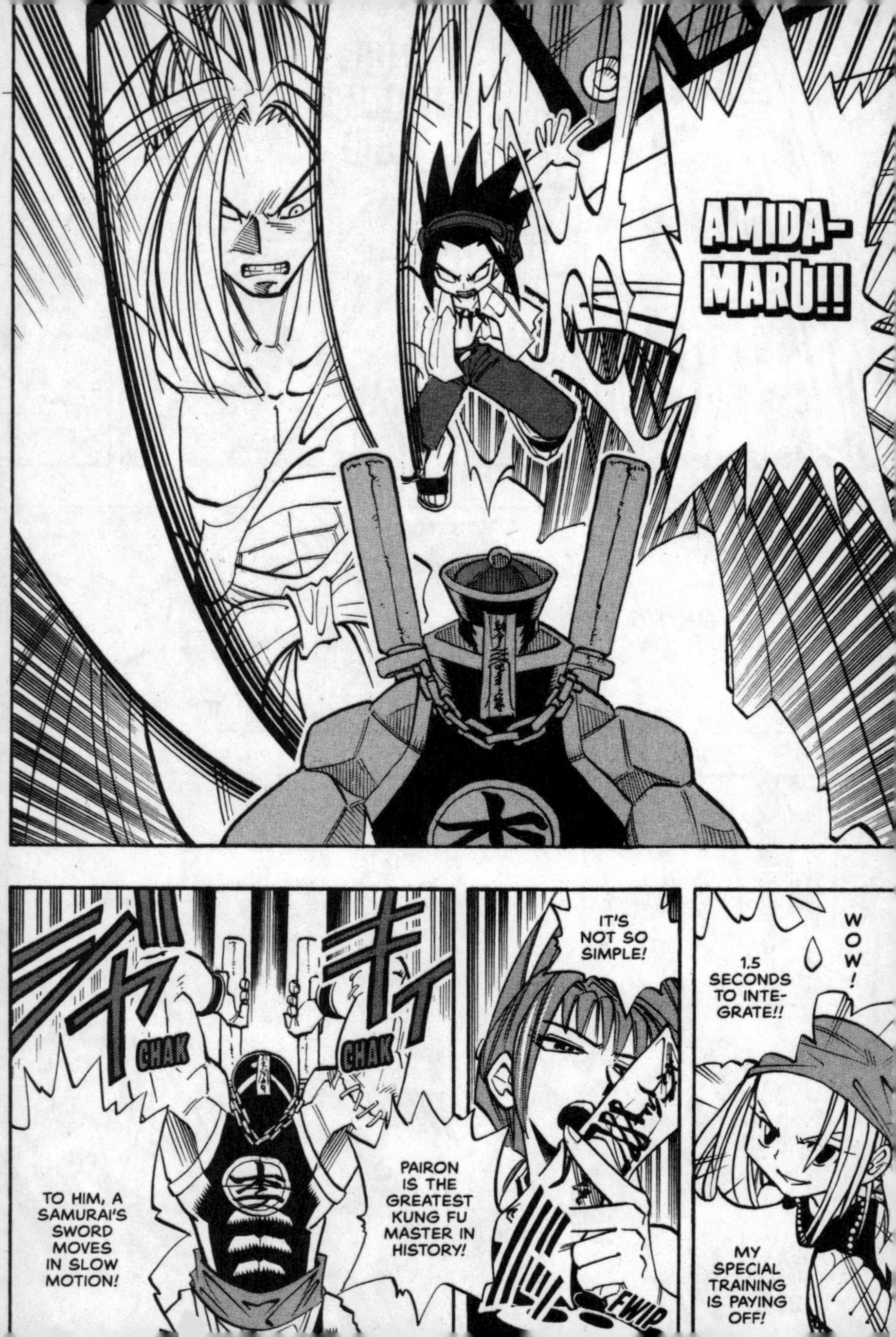

AMIDA-
MARU!!
WOW!
1.5 SECONDS TO INTEGRATE!!
MY SPECIAL TRAINING IS PAYING OFF!
IT'S NOT SO SIMPLE!
PAIRON IS THE GREATEST KUNG FU MASTER IN HISTORY!
FWIP
CHAK
CHAK
TO HIM, A SAMURAI'S SWORD MOVES IN SLOW MOTION!

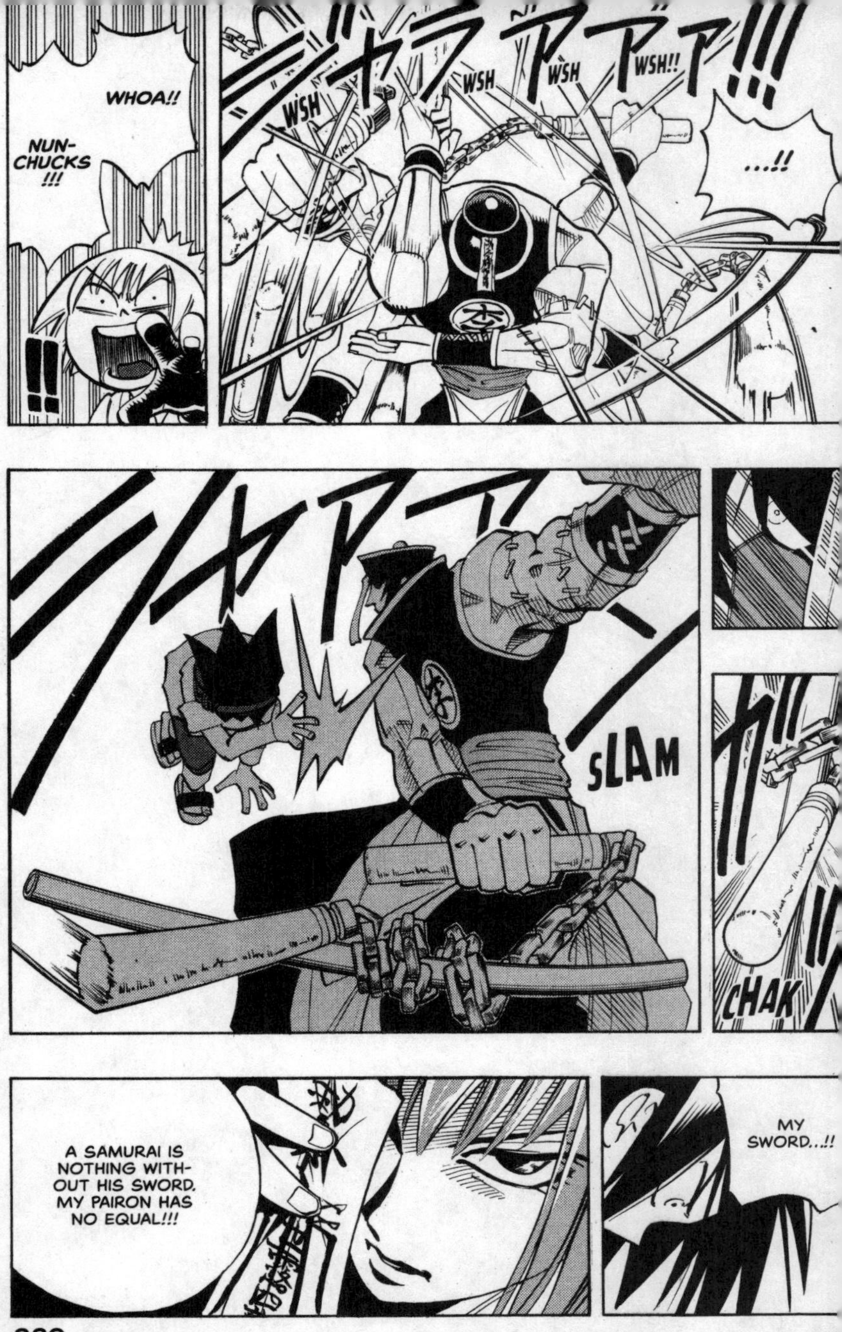
WSH
WSH
WSH
WSH!!
...!!
WHOA!!
NUN-CHUCKS!!!
!!
CHAK
SLAM
MY SWORD...!!
A SAMURAI IS NOTHING WITHOUT HIS SWORD. MY PAIRON HAS NO EQUAL!!!

SHAMAN
KING
2

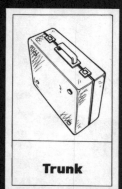

Trunk

Chapter 13: The Corpse Puppet

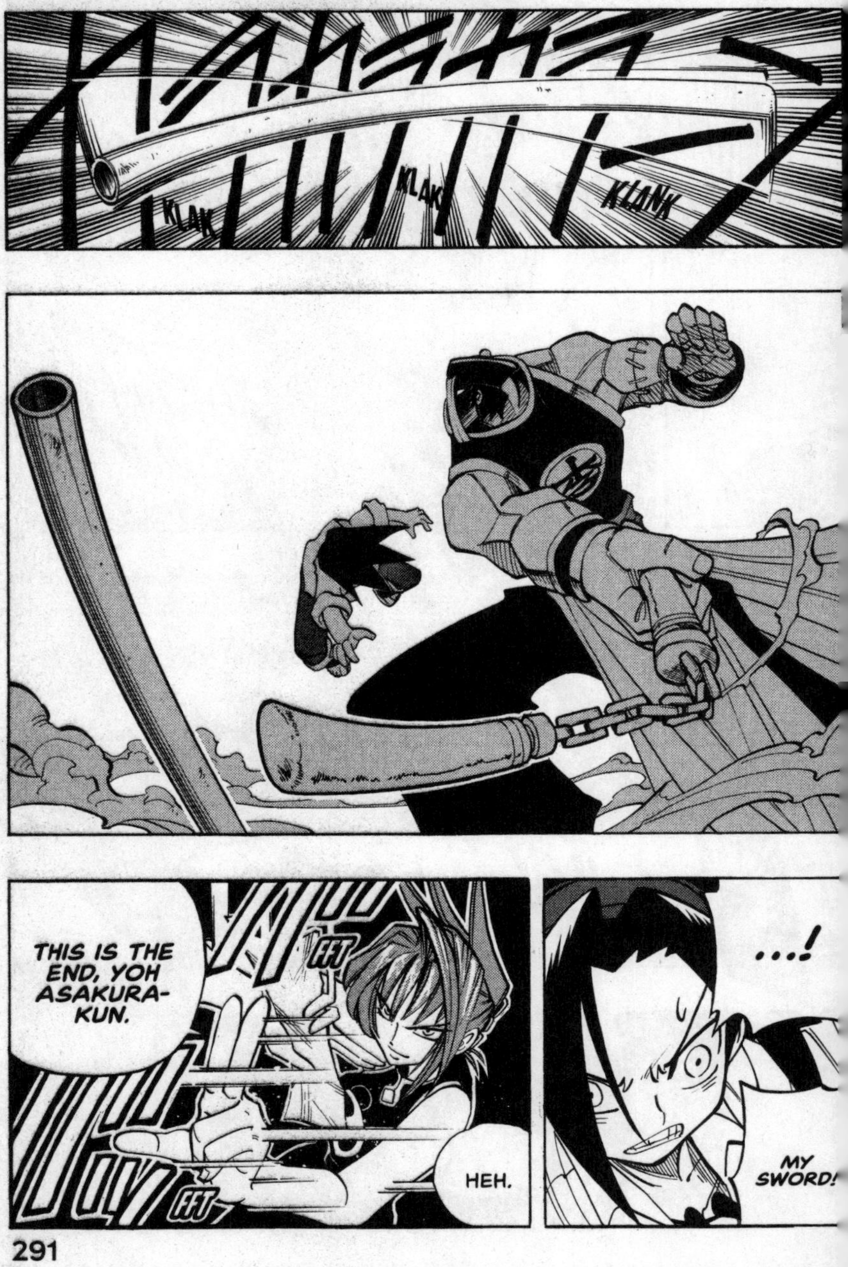
KLANK
KLAK
KLAK
...!
MY SWORD!
THIS IS THE END, YOH ASAKURA-KUN.
FFT
HEH.
FFT

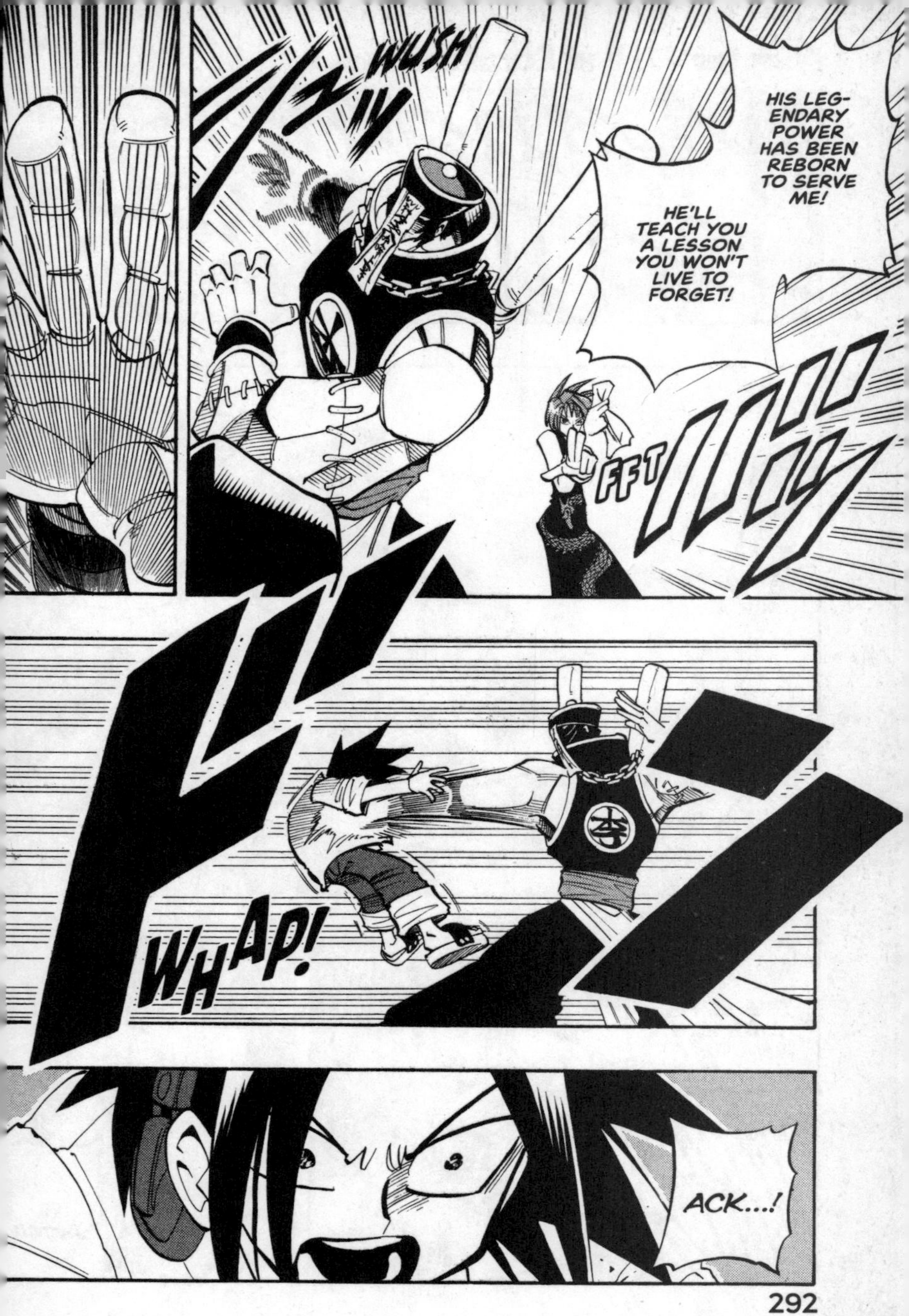
HIS LEG-
ENDARY
POWER
HAS BEEN
REBORN
TO SERVE
ME!
HE'LL
TEACH YOU
A LESSON
YOU WON'T
LIVE TO
FORGET!
WUSH
FFT
WHAP!
ACK...!

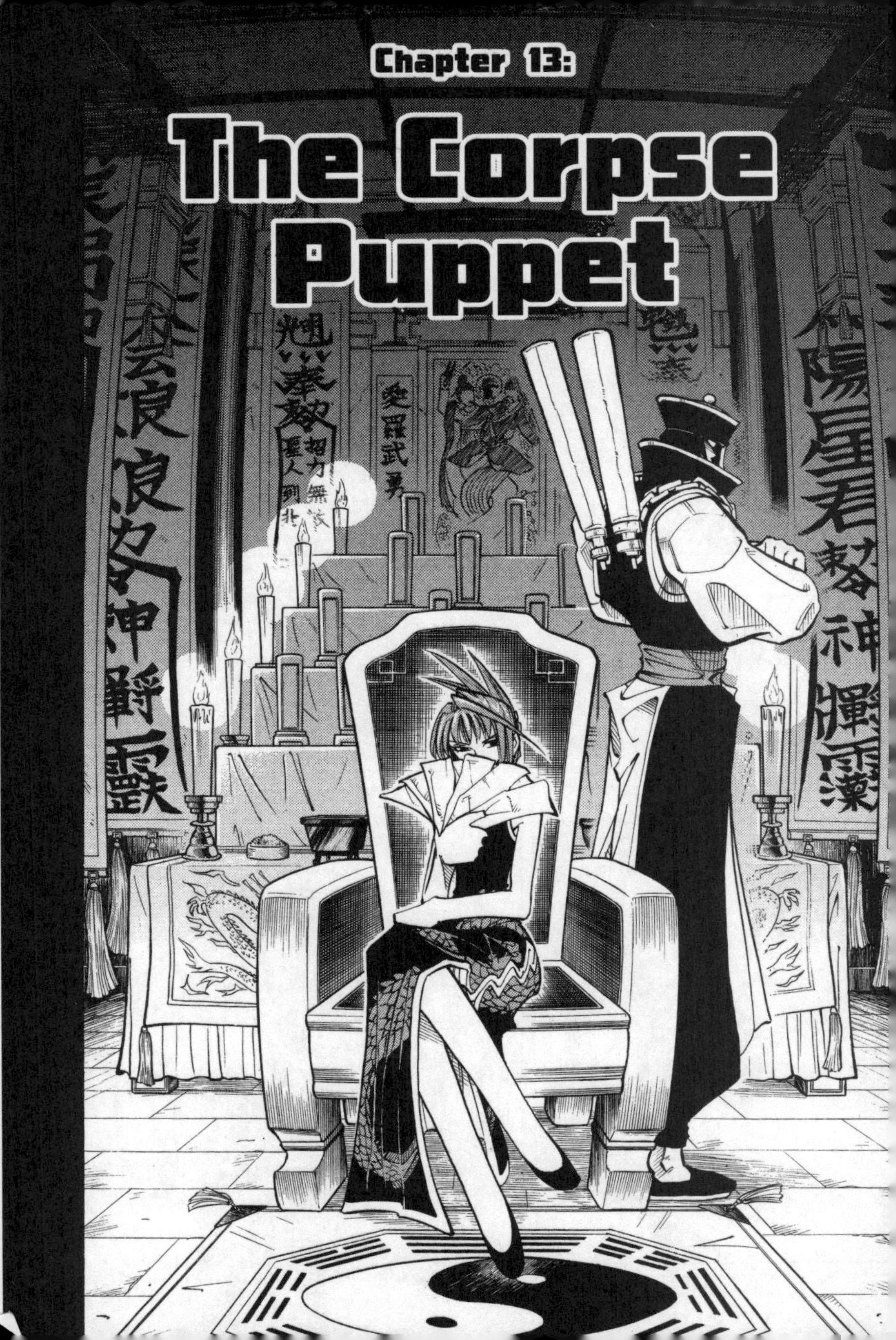
Chapter 13:
The Corpse Puppet

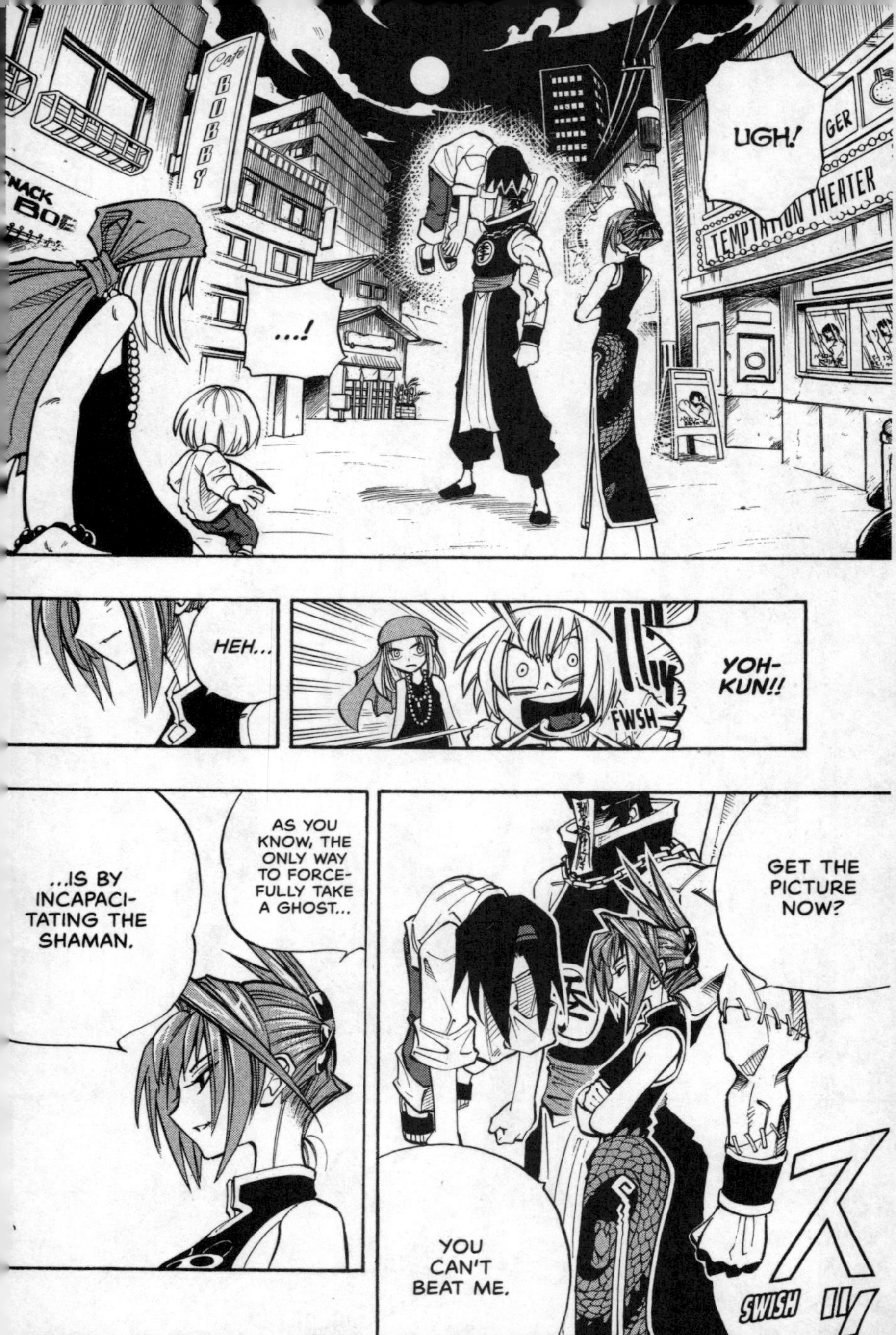
UGH!
GER
TEMPTATION THEATER
...!
Café BOBBY
SNACK BOE
YOH-KUN!!
FWSH
HEH...
GET THE PICTURE NOW?
YOU CAN'T BEAT ME.
SWISH
AS YOU KNOW, THE ONLY WAY TO FORCE-FULLY TAKE A GHOST...
...IS BY INCAPACI-TATING THE SHAMAN.

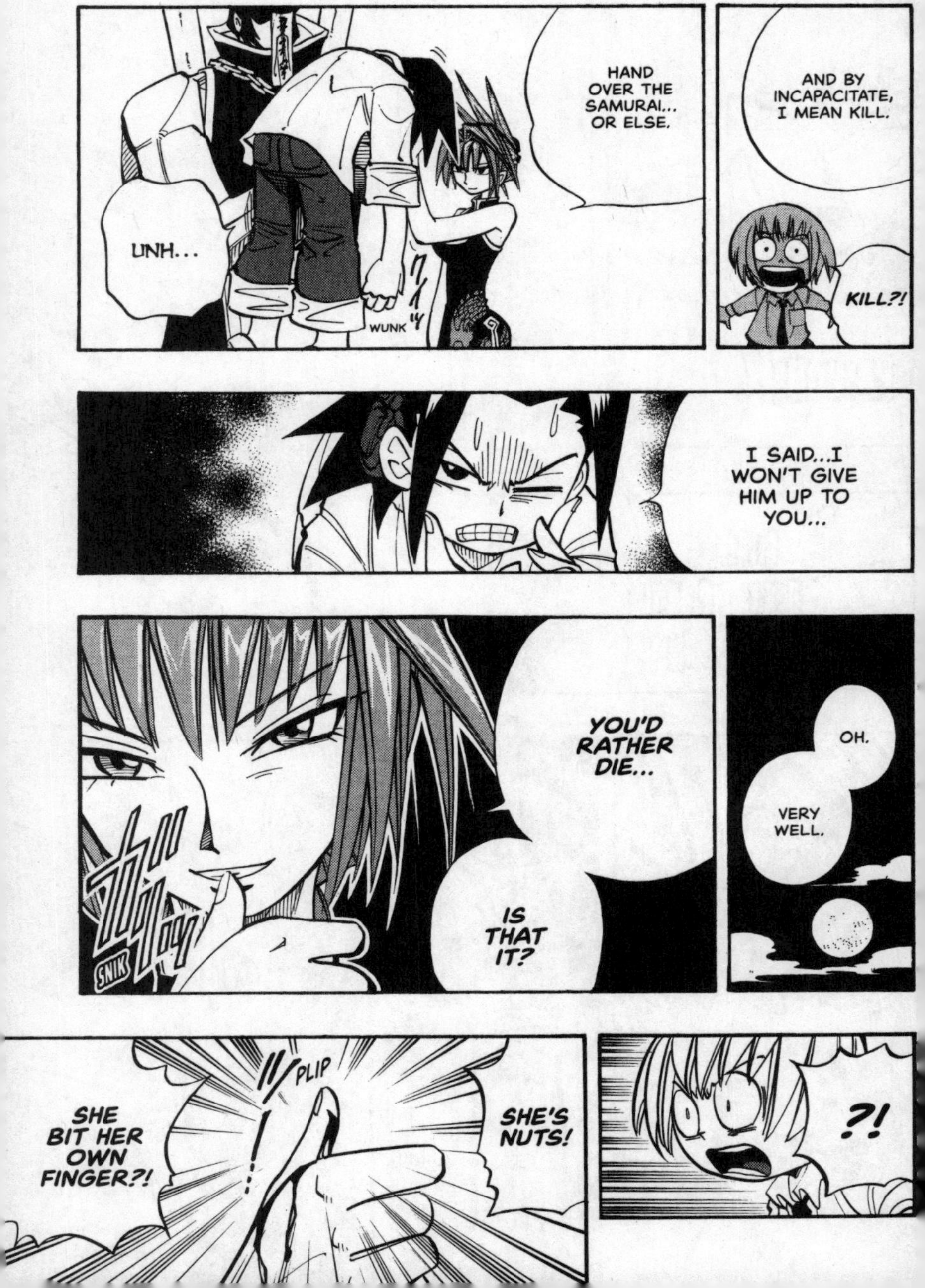
AND BY INCAPACITATE, I MEAN KILL.
KILL?!
HAND OVER THE SAMURAI... OR ELSE.
WUNK
UNH...
I SAID...I WON'T GIVE HIM UP TO YOU...
OH.
VERY WELL.
YOU'D RATHER DIE...
IS THAT IT?
SNIK
?!
PLIP
SHE'S NUTS!
SHE BIT HER OWN FINGER?!

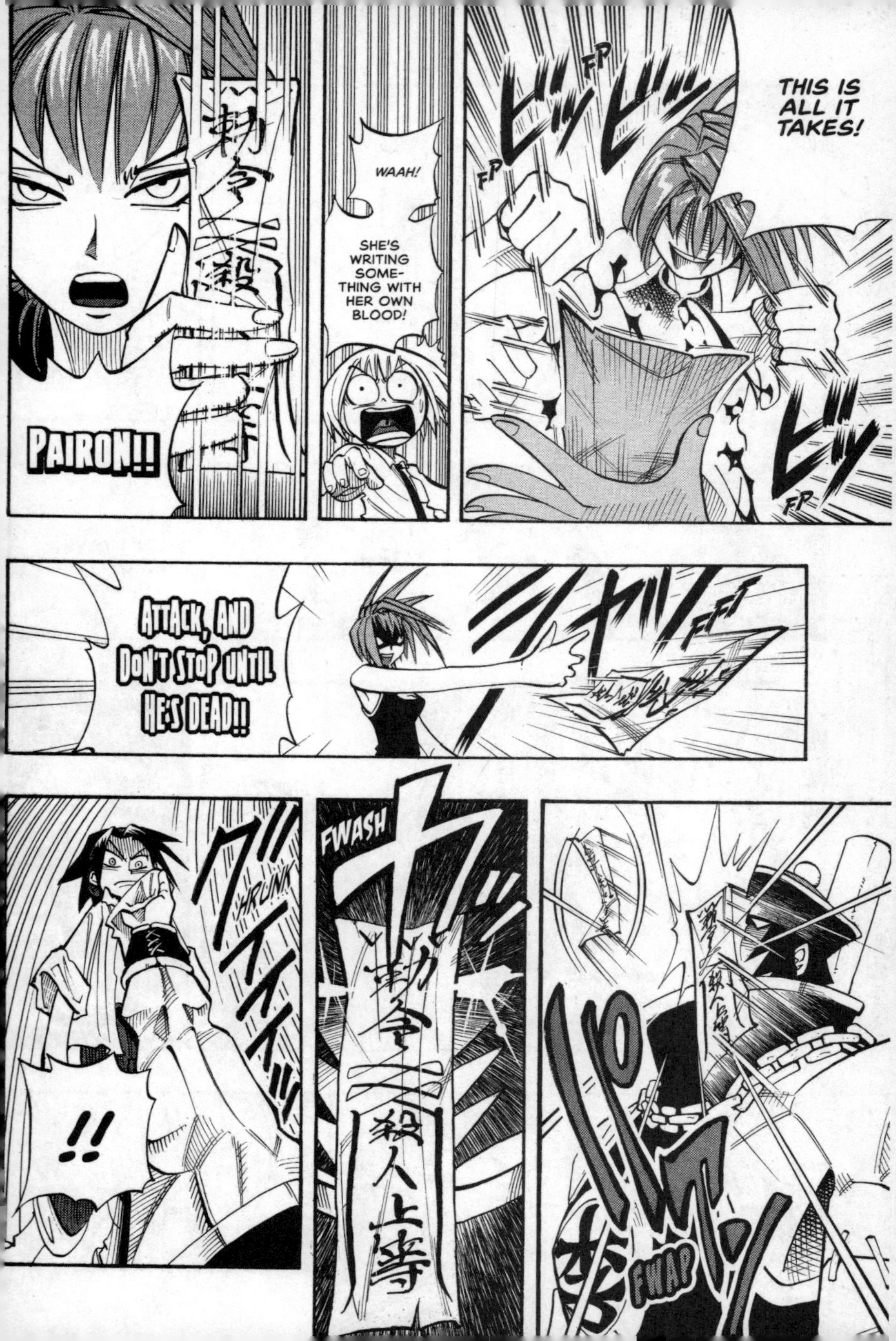
THIS IS ALL IT TAKES!
FP
FP
FP
WAAH!
SHE'S WRITING SOME-THING WITH HER OWN BLOOD!
PAIRON!!
FFT
ATTACK, AND DON'T STOP UNTIL HE'S DEAD!!
FWAP
FWASH
勅令
殺人上等
HRUNK
!!

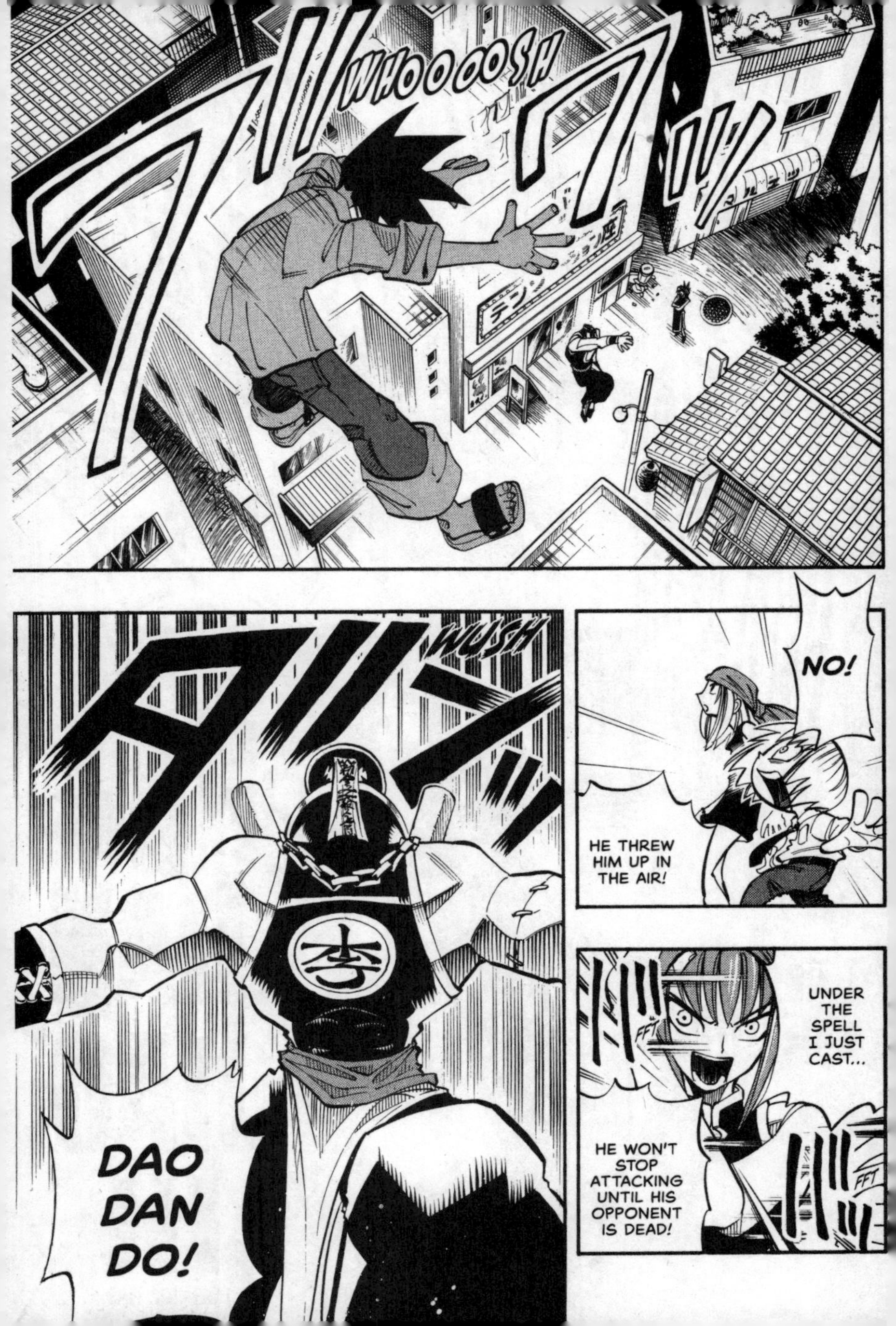
WHOOOOSH
NO!
HE THREW HIM UP IN THE AIR!
UNDER THE SPELL I JUST CAST...
FFT
HE WON'T STOP ATTACKING UNTIL HIS OPPONENT IS DEAD!
FFT
WUSH
DAO DAN DO!

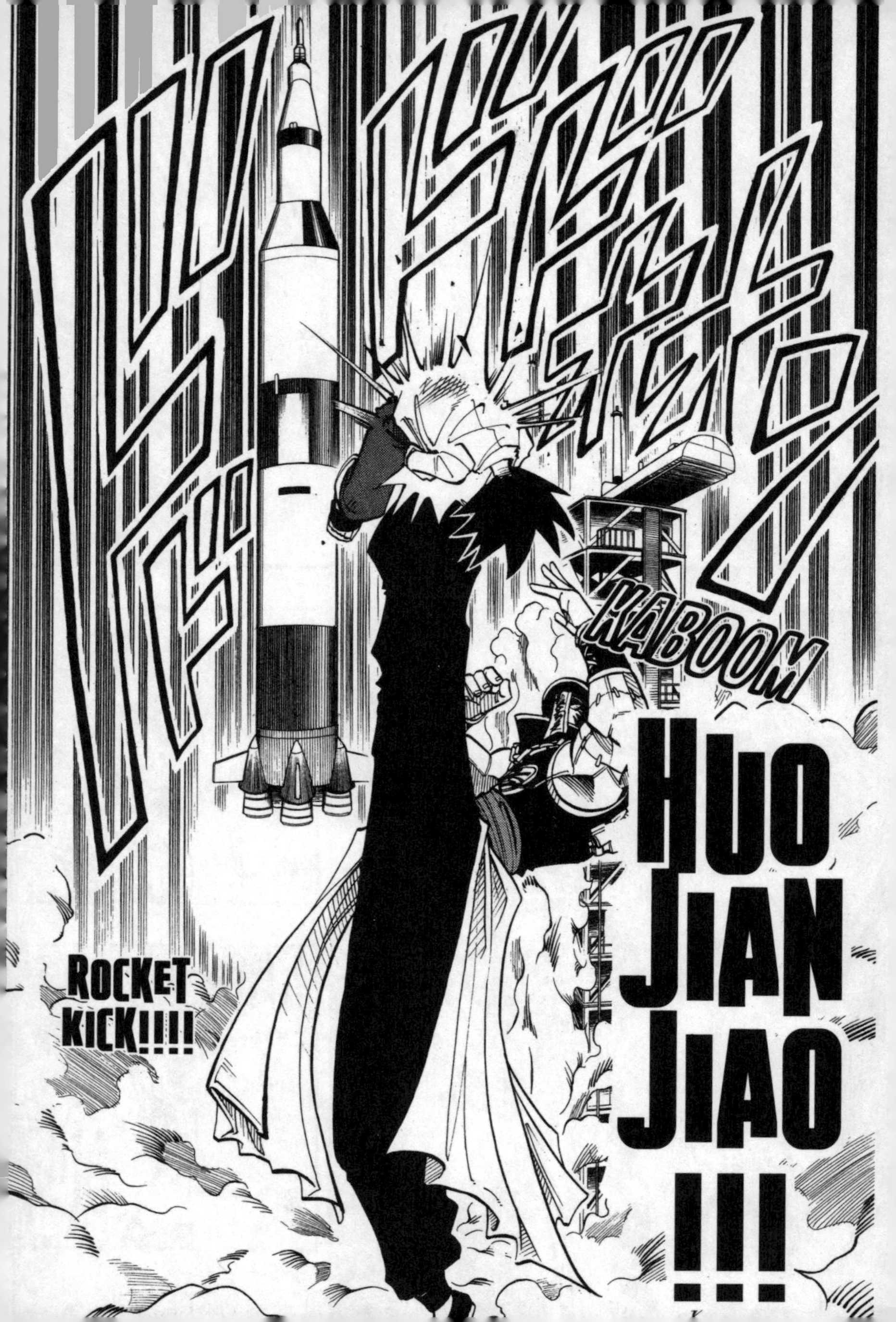
KABOOM
HUO JIAN JIAO !!!
ROCKET KICK!!!!

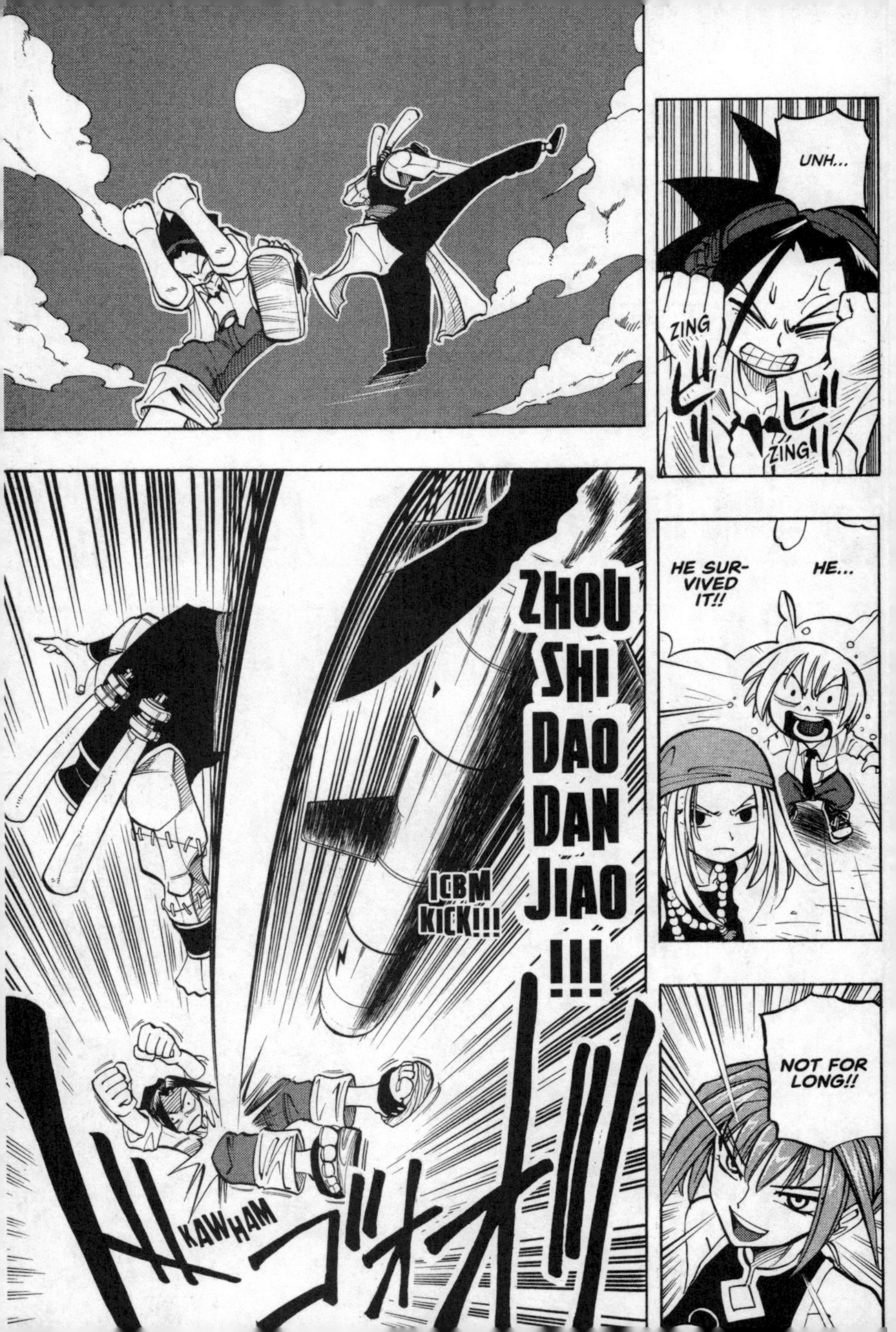
UNH...
ZING
ZING
HE...
HE SUR-VIVED IT!!
NOT FOR LONG!!
ZHOU SHI DAO DAN JIAO !!!
ICBM KICK!!!
KAWHAM

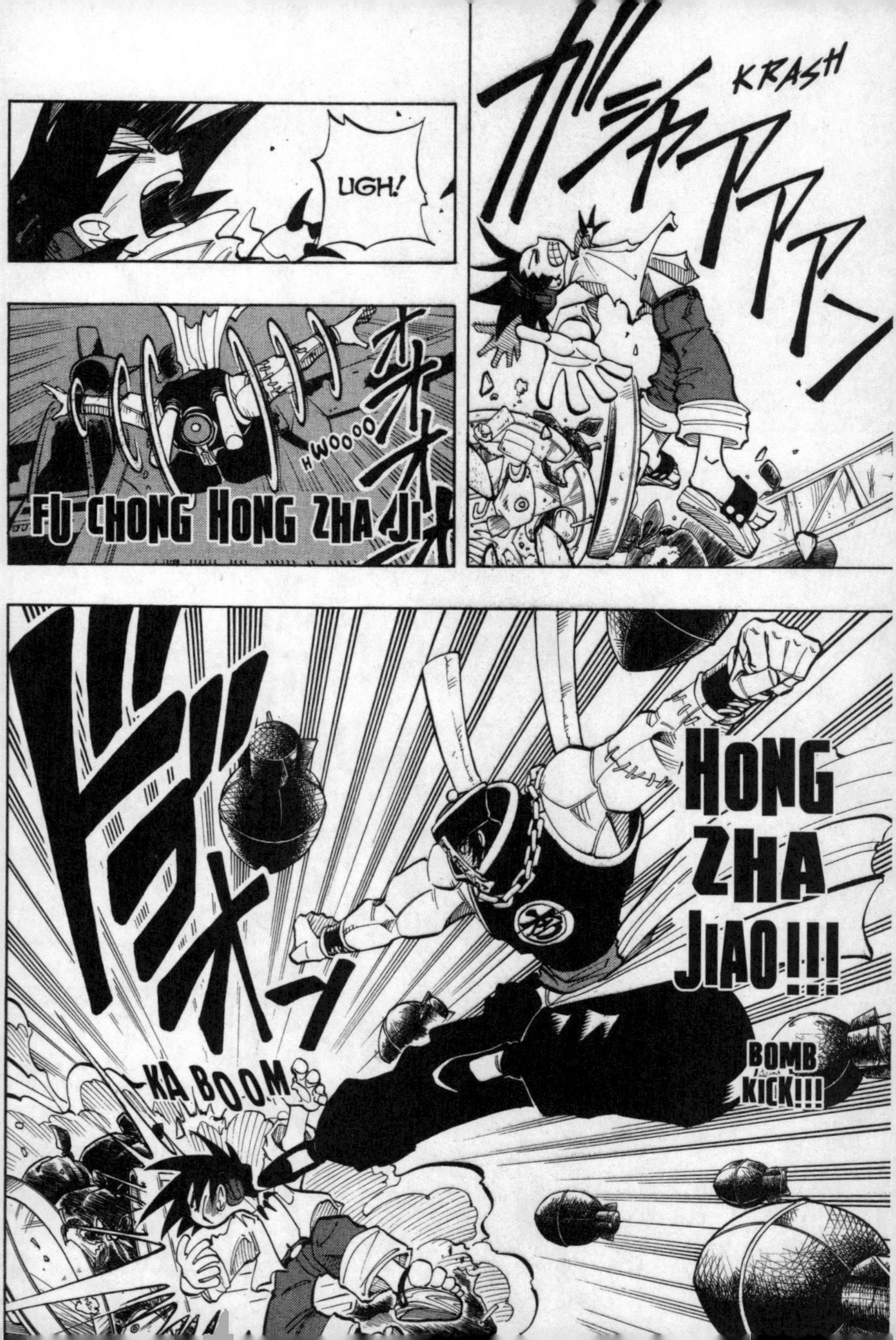
KRASH
UGH!
HWOOOO
FU CHONG HONG ZHA JI
HONG ZHA JIAO!!!
BOMB KICK!!!
KA BOOM

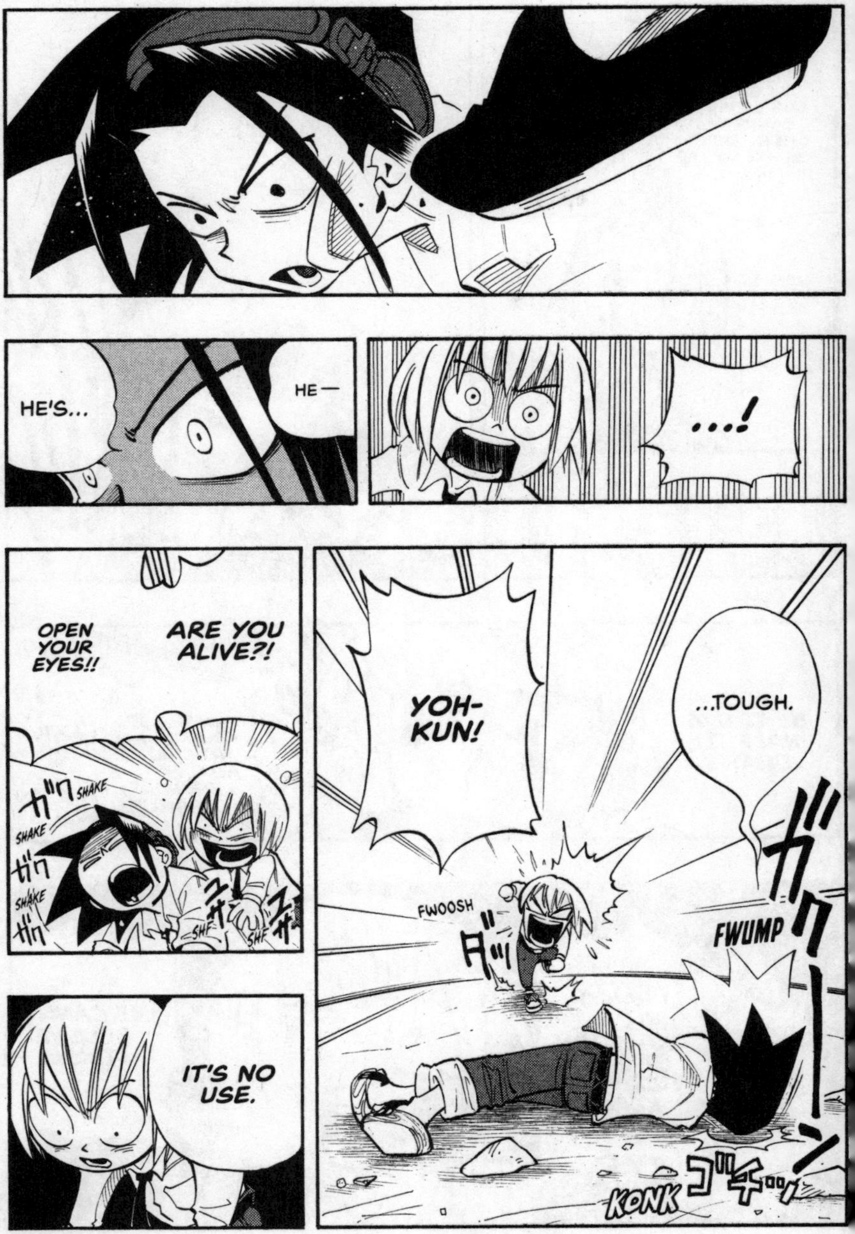
...!
HE—
HE'S...
...TOUGH.
YOH-KUN!
FWUMP
FWOOSH
KONK
ARE YOU ALIVE?!
OPEN YOUR EYES!!
SHAKE
SHAKE
SHAKE
SHF
SHF
IT'S NO USE.

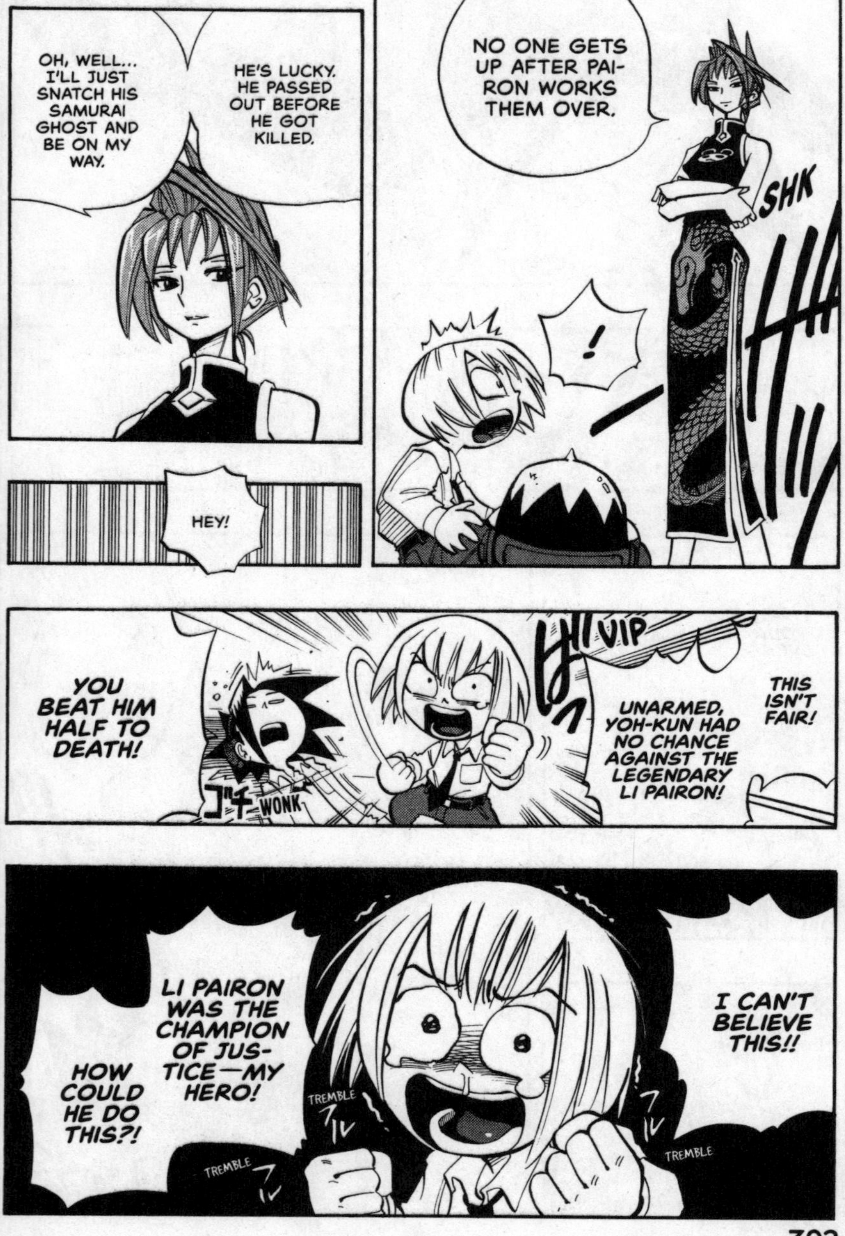
NO ONE GETS UP AFTER PAI-RON WORKS THEM OVER.
SHK
!
HE'S LUCKY. HE PASSED OUT BEFORE HE GOT KILLED.
OH, WELL... I'LL JUST SNATCH HIS SAMURAI GHOST AND BE ON MY WAY.
HEY!
THIS ISN'T FAIR!
UNARMED, YOH-KUN HAD NO CHANCE AGAINST THE LEGENDARY LI PAIRON!
VIP
YOU BEAT HIM HALF TO DEATH!
WONK
I CAN'T BELIEVE THIS!!
TREMBLE
LI PAIRON WAS THE CHAMPION OF JUS-TICE—MY HERO!
HOW COULD HE DO THIS?!
TREMBLE
TREMBLE

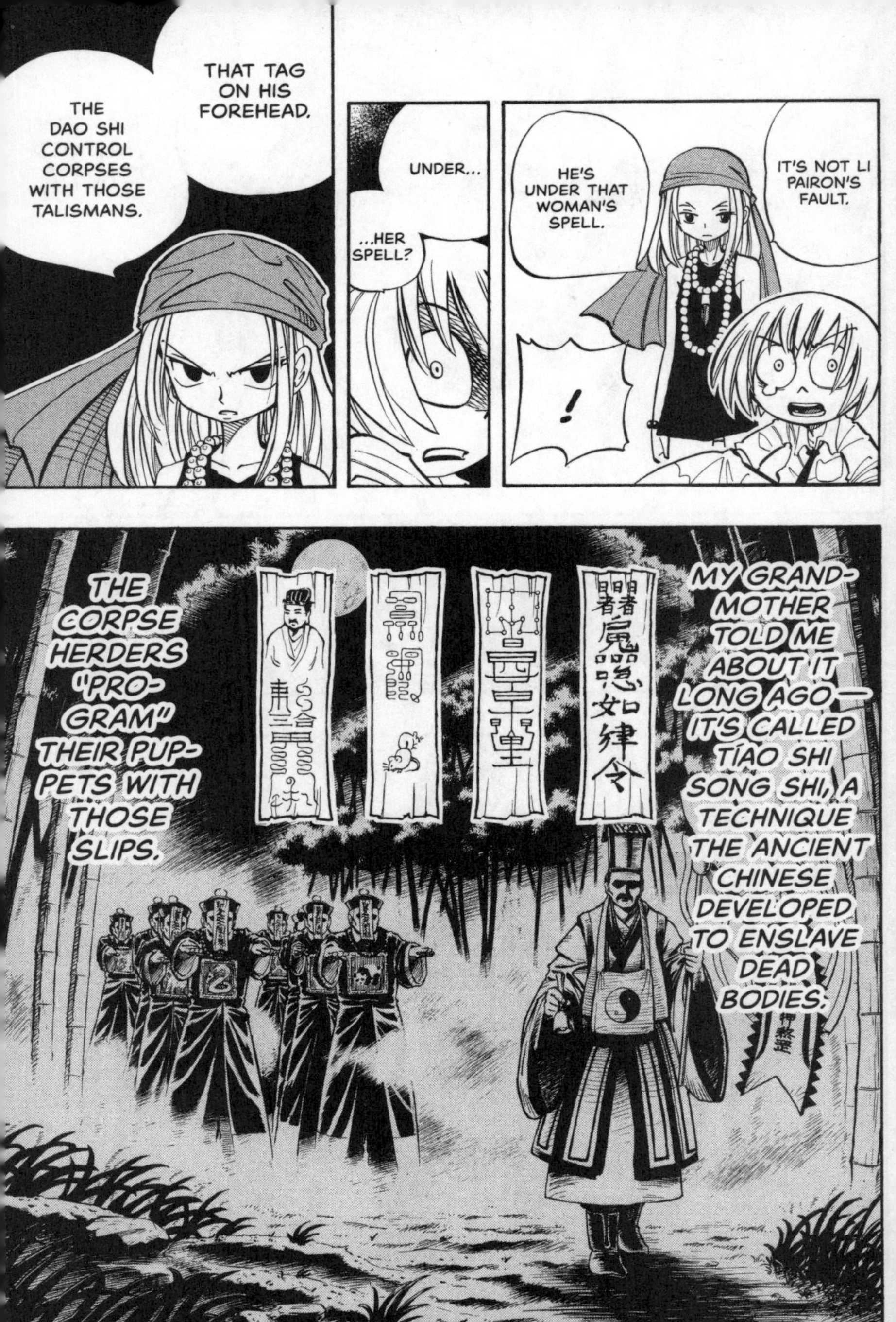
IT'S NOT LI PAIRON'S FAULT.
HE'S UNDER THAT WOMAN'S SPELL.
!
UNDER...
...HER SPELL?
THAT TAG ON HIS FOREHEAD.
THE DAO SHI CONTROL CORPSES WITH THOSE TALISMANS.
MY GRANDMOTHER TOLD ME ABOUT IT LONG AGO—IT'S CALLED TIAO SHI SONG SHI, A TECHNIQUE THE ANCIENT CHINESE DEVELOPED TO ENSLAVE DEAD BODIES.
THE CORPSE HERDERS "PRO-GRAM" THEIR PUP-PETS WITH THOSE SLIPS.

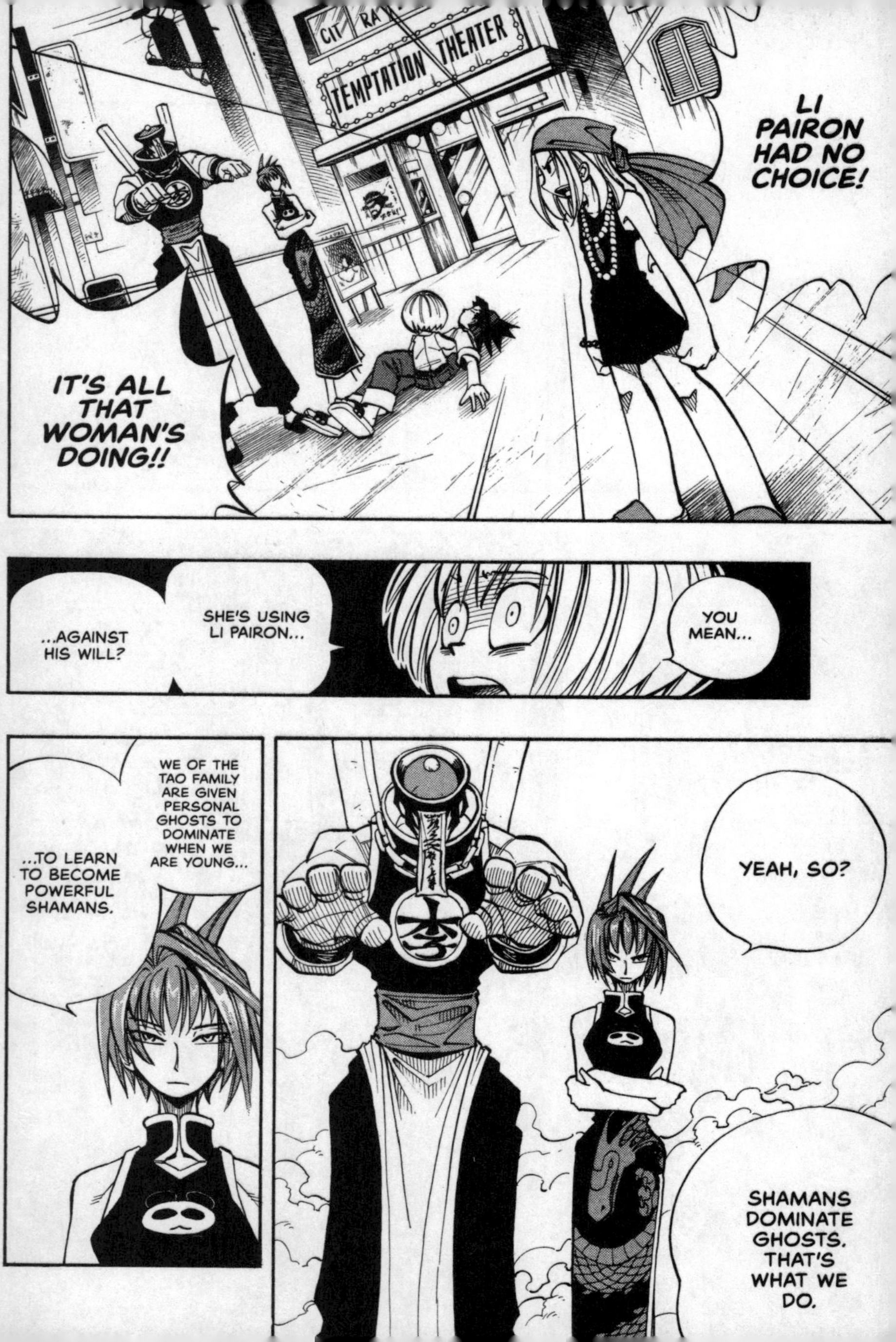
TEMPTATION THEATER
LI PAIRON HAD NO CHOICE!
IT'S ALL THAT WOMAN'S DOING!!
YOU MEAN...
SHE'S USING LI PAIRON...
...AGAINST HIS WILL?
YEAH, SO?
SHAMANS DOMINATE GHOSTS. THAT'S WHAT WE DO.
WE OF THE TAO FAMILY ARE GIVEN PERSONAL GHOSTS TO DOMINATE WHEN WE ARE YOUNG...
...TO LEARN TO BECOME POWERFUL SHAMANS.

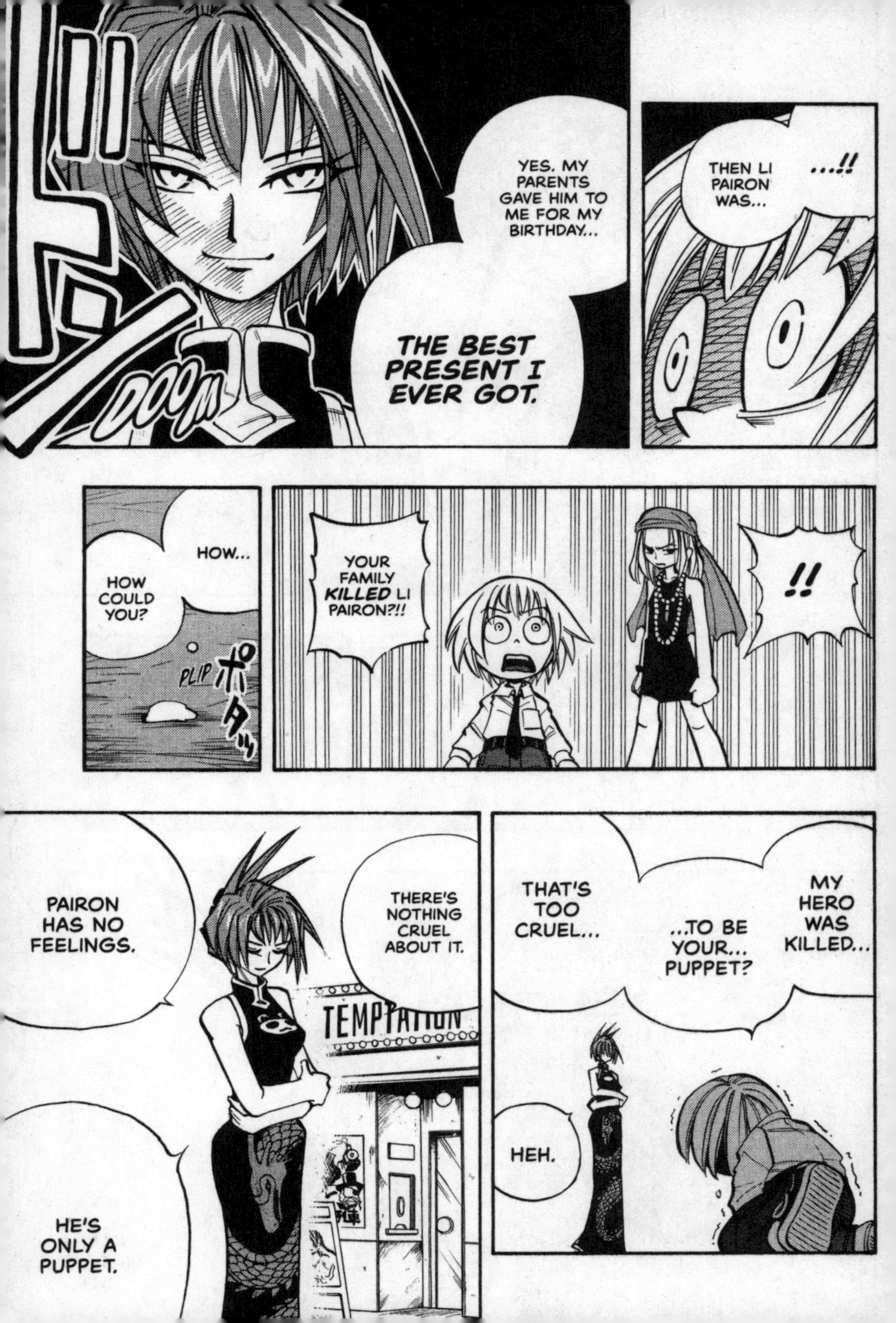
THEN LI PAIRON WAS...
...!!
YES. MY PARENTS GAVE HIM TO ME FOR MY BIRTHDAY...
THE BEST PRESENT I EVER GOT.
DOOM
YOUR FAMILY KILLED LI PAIRON?!!
!!
HOW...
HOW COULD YOU?
PLIP
ポタッ
MY HERO WAS KILLED...
...TO BE YOUR... PUPPET?
THAT'S TOO CRUEL...
HEH.
THERE'S NOTHING CRUEL ABOUT IT.
PAIRON HAS NO FEELINGS.
TEMPTATION
HE'S ONLY A PUPPET.

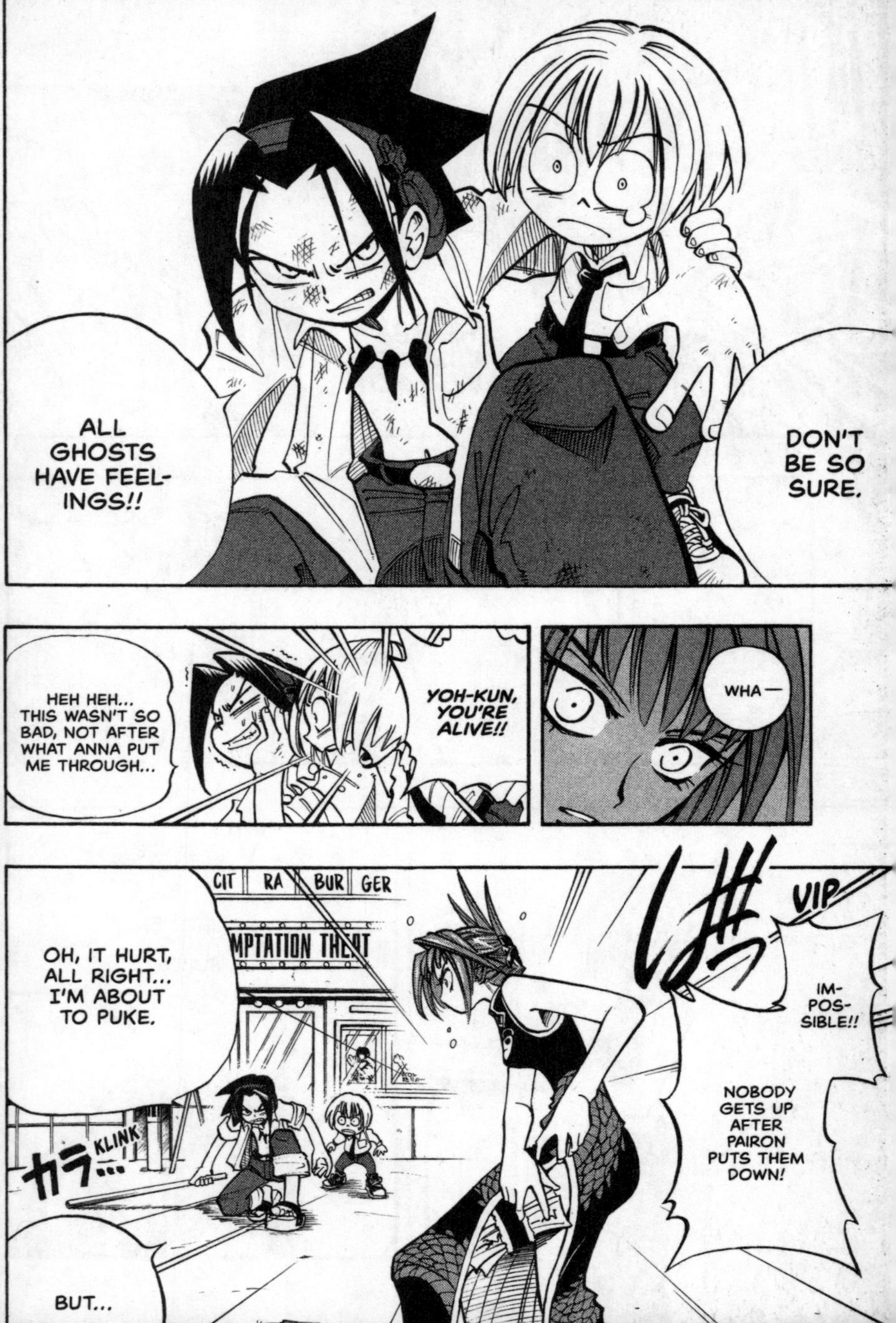
DON'T BE SO SURE.
ALL GHOSTS HAVE FEELINGS!!
WHA—
YOH-KUN, YOU'RE ALIVE!!
HEH HEH... THIS WASN'T SO BAD, NOT AFTER WHAT ANNA PUT ME THROUGH...
VIP
IMPOSSIBLE!!
NOBODY GETS UP AFTER PAIRON PUTS THEM DOWN!
CIT RA BUR GER
MPTATION THEAT
OH, IT HURT, ALL RIGHT... I'M ABOUT TO PUKE.
カラ... KLINK
BUT...

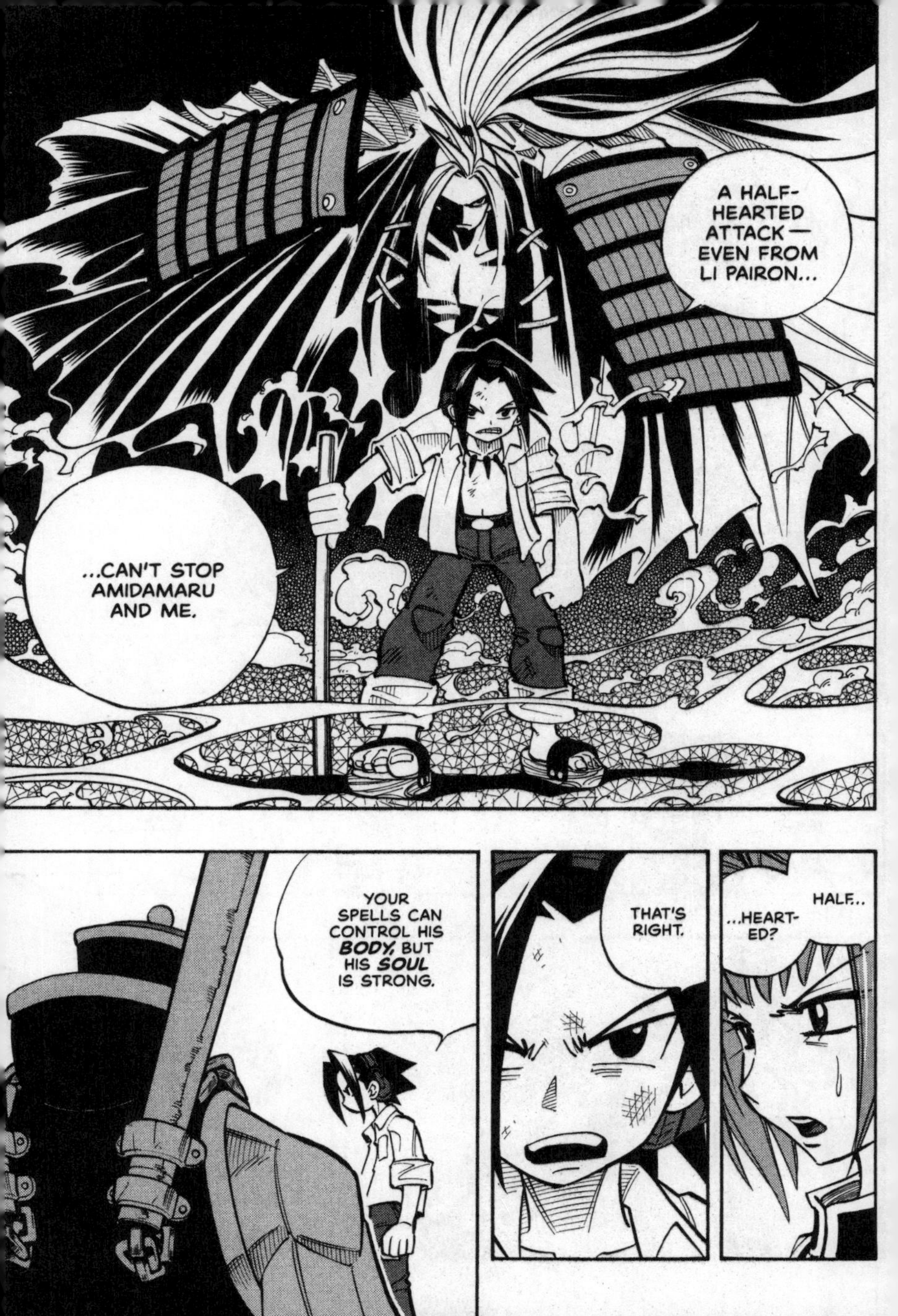
A HALF-HEARTED ATTACK—EVEN FROM LI PAIRON...
...CAN'T STOP AMIDAMARU AND ME.
HALF...
...HEART-ED?
THAT'S RIGHT.
YOUR SPELLS CAN CONTROL HIS BODY, BUT HIS SOUL IS STRONG.

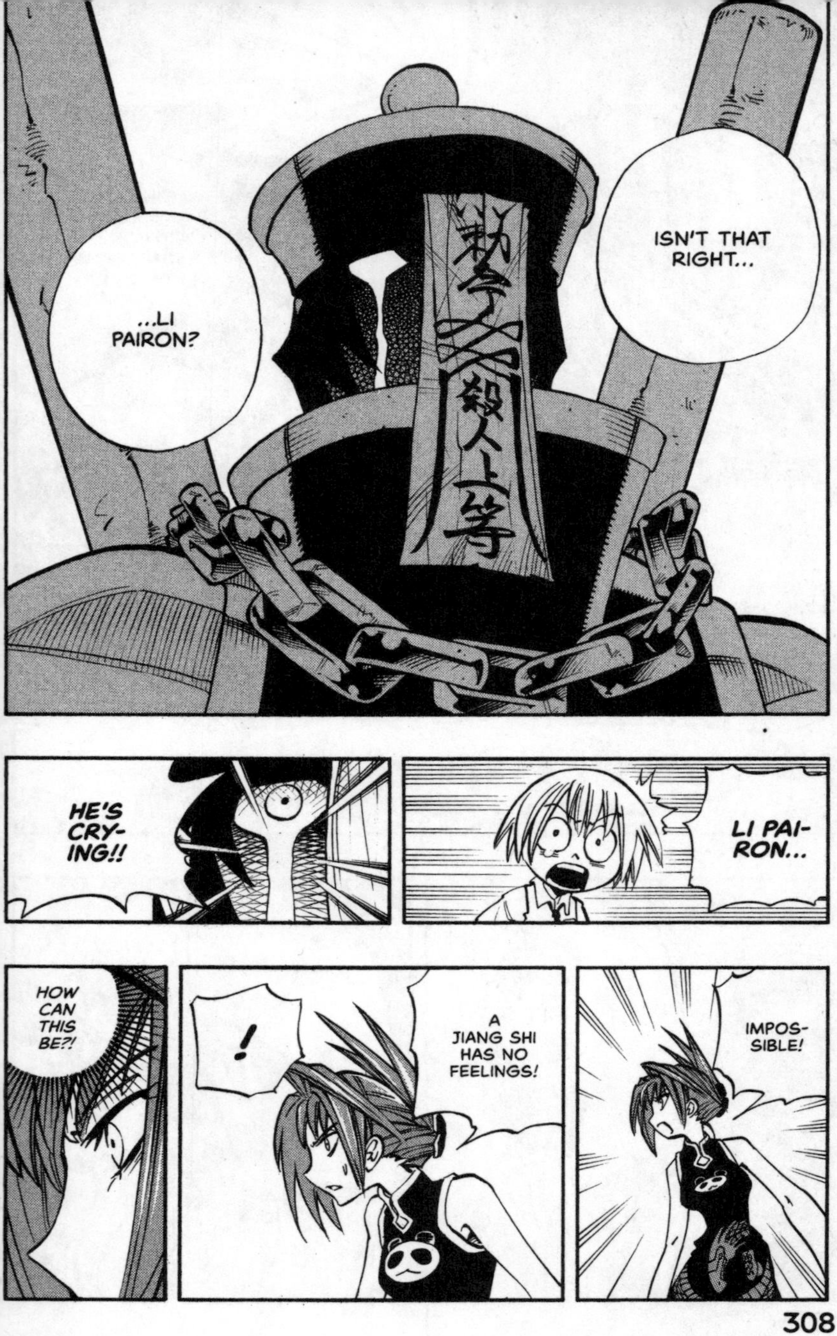
ISN'T THAT RIGHT...
...LI PAIRON?
LI PAI-RON...
HE'S CRY-ING!!
IMPOS-SIBLE!
A JIANG SHI HAS NO FEELINGS!
!
HOW CAN THIS BE?!

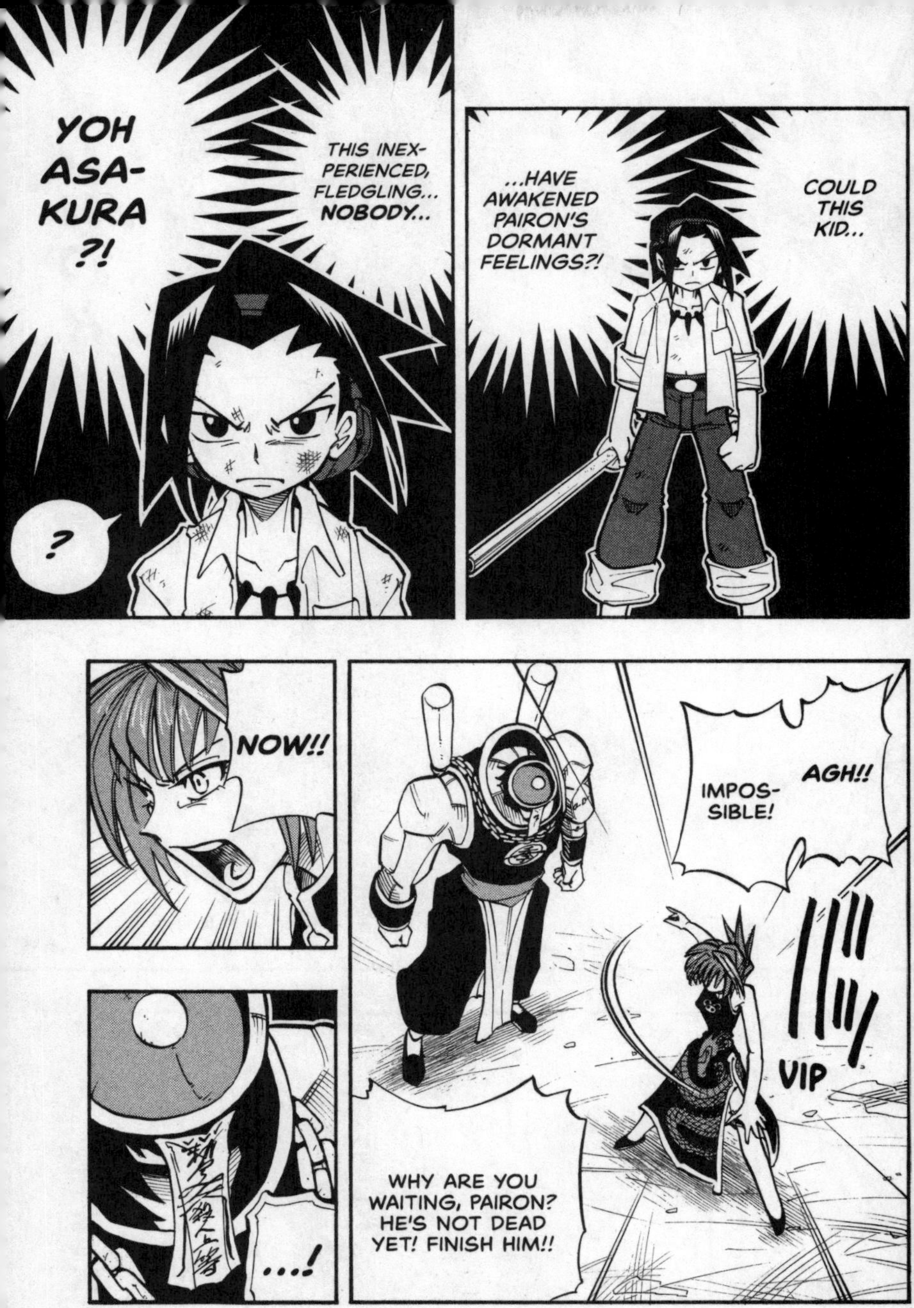
COULD THIS KID...
...HAVE AWAKENED PAIRON'S DORMANT FEELINGS?!
THIS INEX-PERIENCED, FLEDGLING... NOBODY...
YOH ASA-KURA ?!
?
AGH!!
IMPOS-SIBLE!
VIP
WHY ARE YOU WAITING, PAIRON? HE'S NOT DEAD YET! FINISH HIM!!
NOW!!
...!

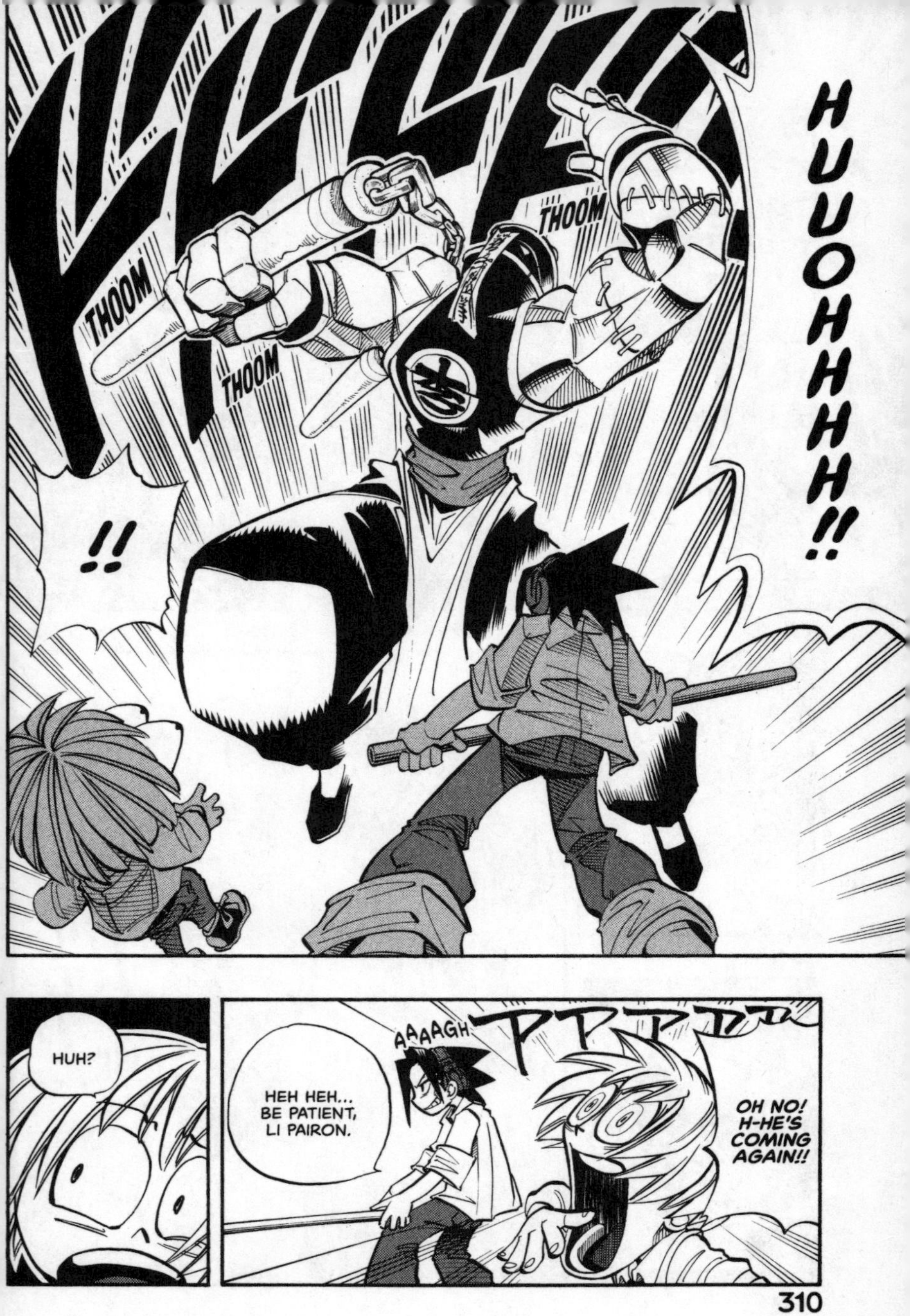
HUUOHHHHH!!
THOOM
THOOM
THOOM
!!
OH NO! H-HE'S COMING AGAIN!!
AAAAGH
HEH HEH... BE PATIENT, LI PAIRON.
HUH?

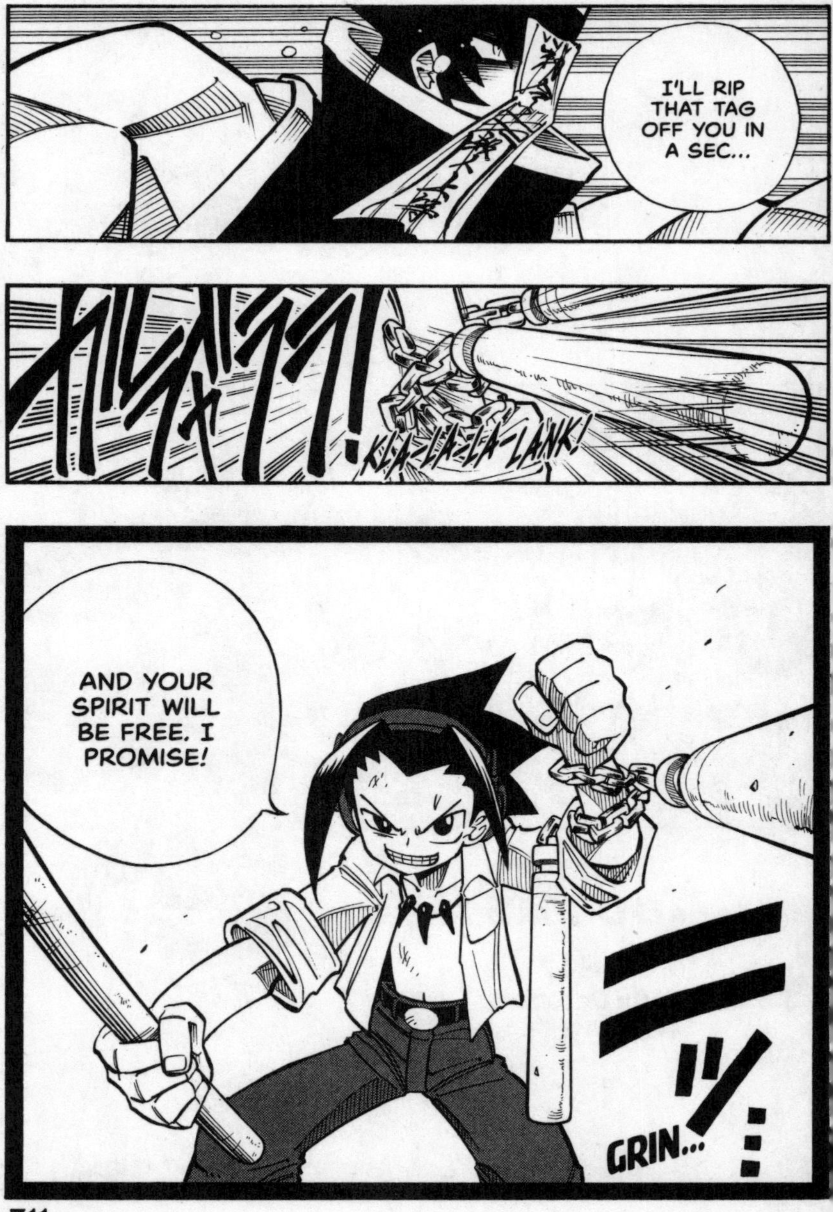
I'LL RIP THAT TAG OFF YOU IN A SEC...
KLA-LA-LA-LANK!
AND YOUR SPIRIT WILL BE FREE. I PROMISE!
GRIN...

SHAMAN KING CHARACTER FILE No.7

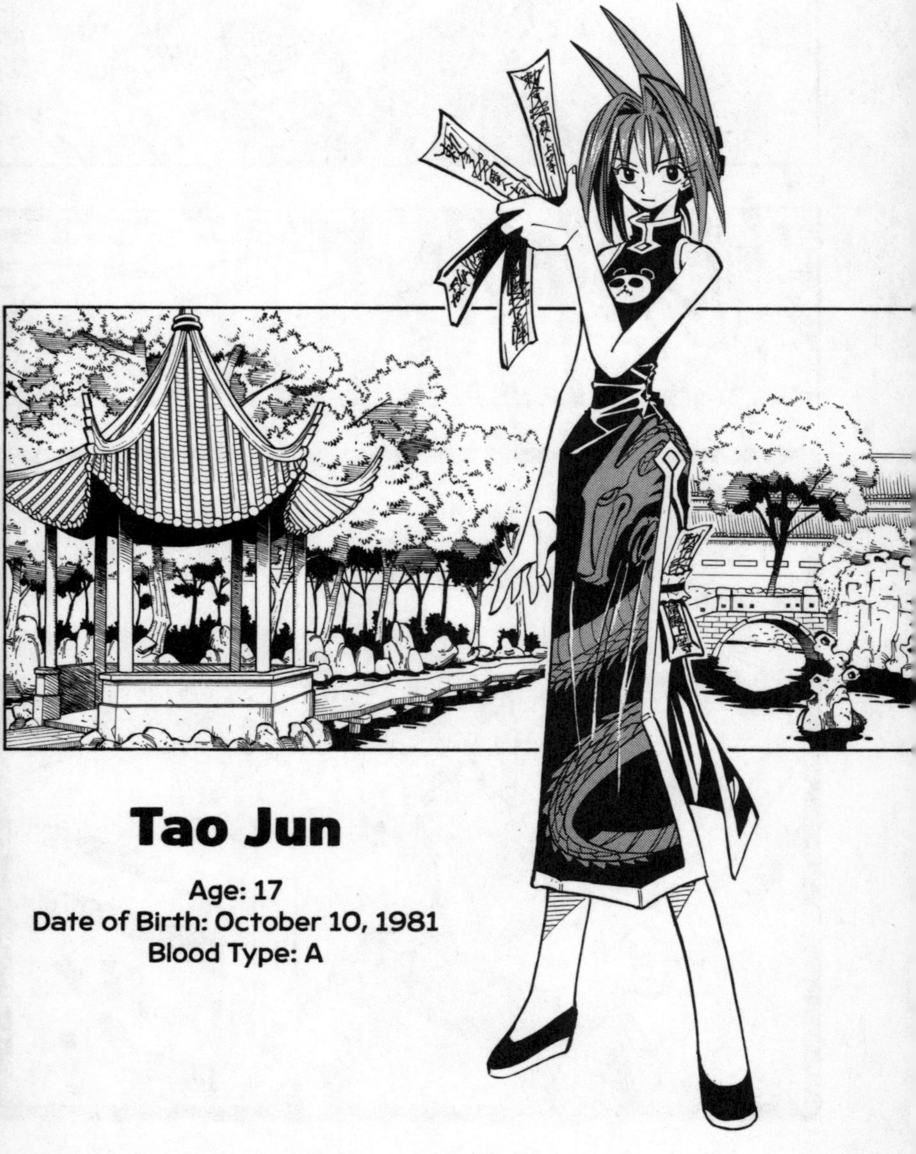

Tao Jun

Age: 17
Date of Birth: October 10, 1981
Blood Type: A

Chapter 14:

Run, Manta, Run

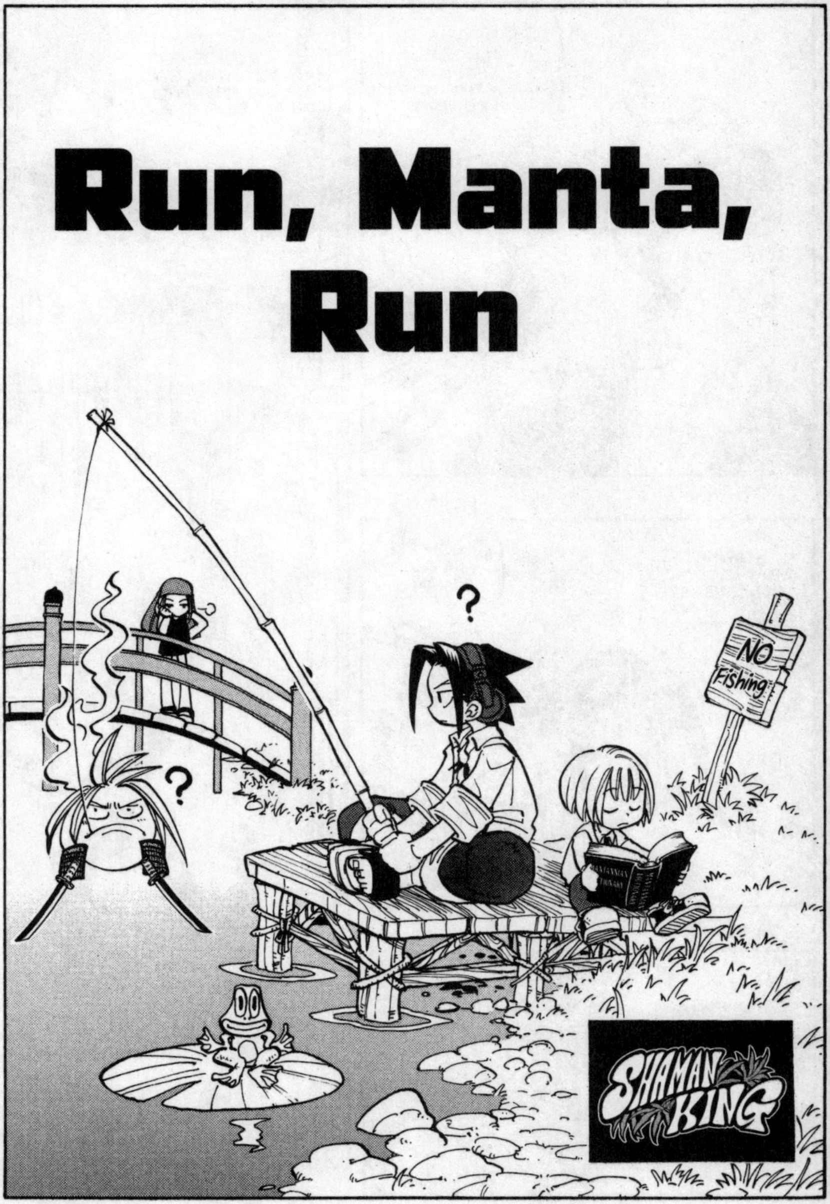
?
?
NO Fishing
SHAMAN KING

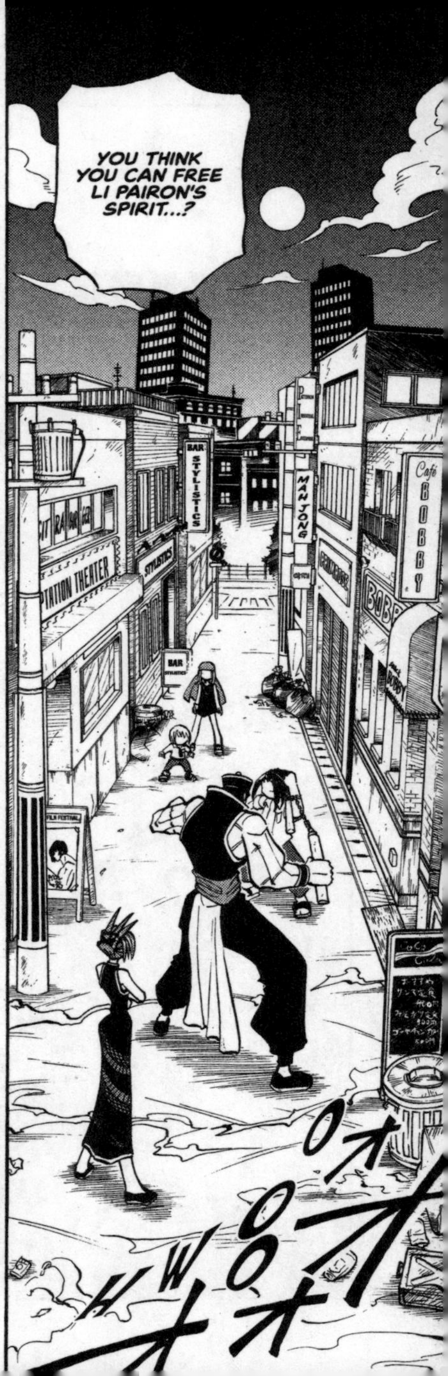
YOU THINK YOU CAN FREE LI PAIRON'S SPIRIT...?
HWOOO
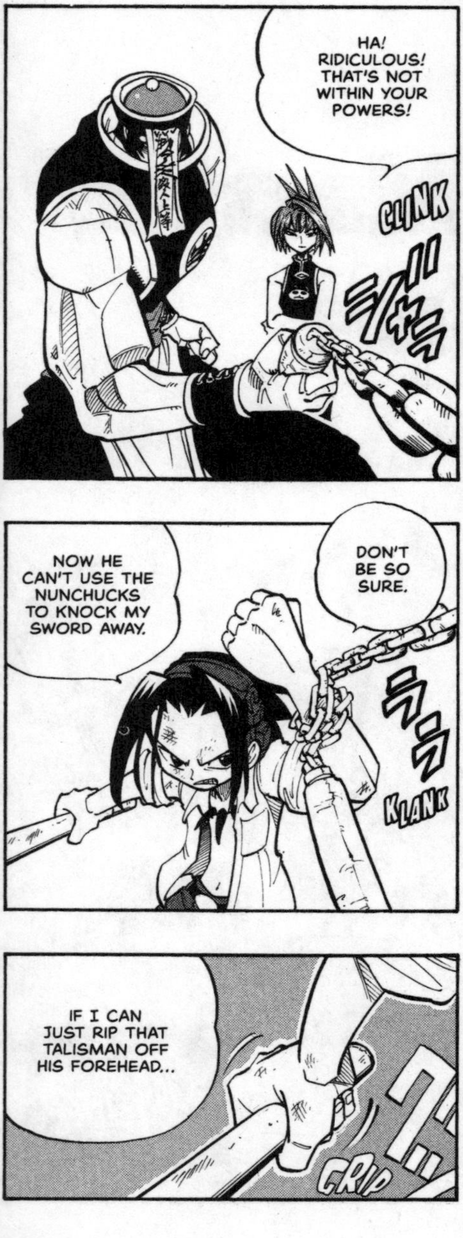
HA! RIDICULOUS! THAT'S NOT WITHIN YOUR POWERS!
CLINK
DON'T BE SO SURE.
NOW HE CAN'T USE THE NUNCHUCKS TO KNOCK MY SWORD AWAY.
KLANK
IF I CAN JUST RIP THAT TALISMAN OFF HIS FOREHEAD...
GRIP

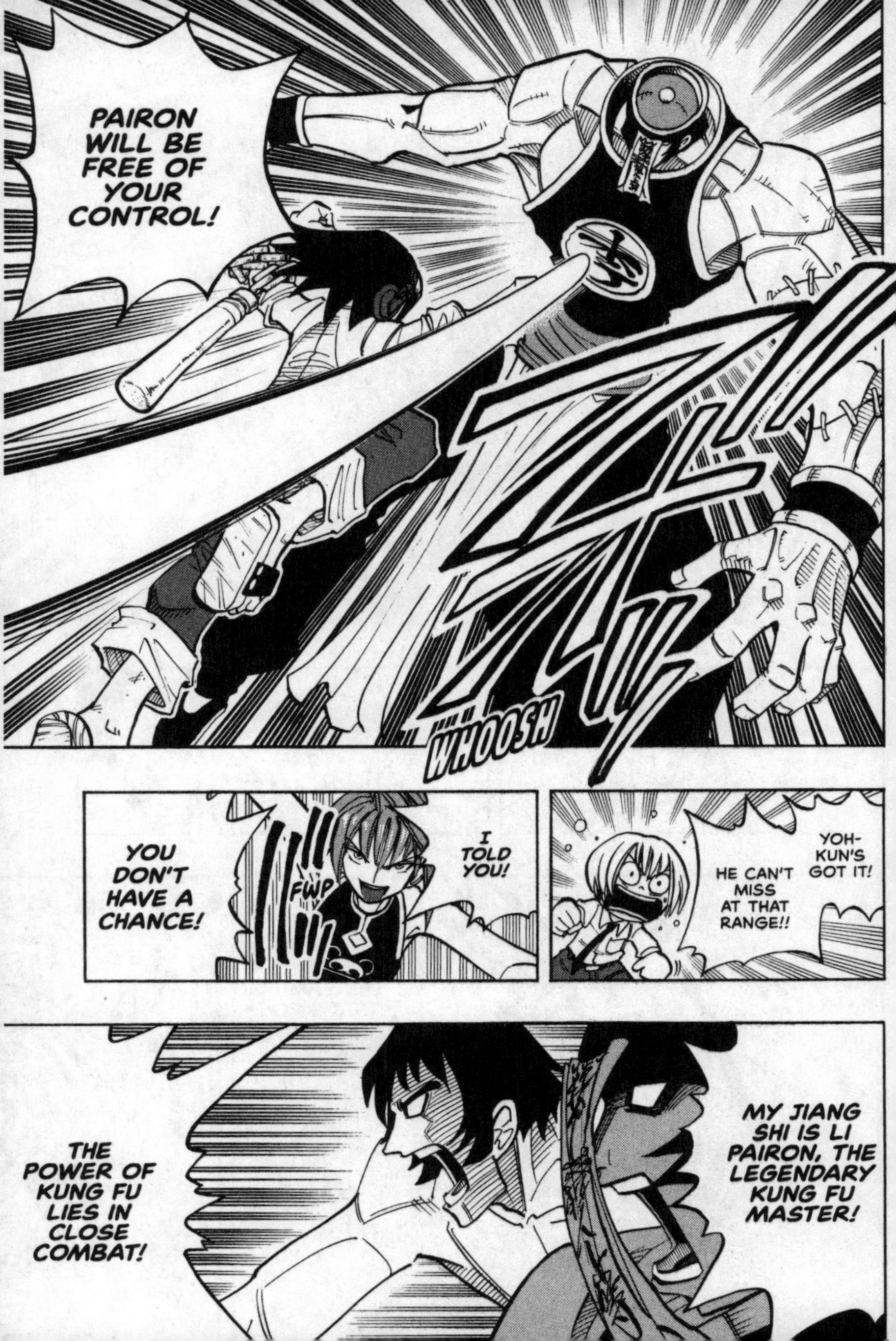
PAIRON WILL BE FREE OF YOUR CONTROL!
WHOOSH
YOH-KUN'S GOT IT!
HE CAN'T MISS AT THAT RANGE!!
I TOLD YOU!
FWP
YOU DON'T HAVE A CHANCE!
MY JIANG SHI IS LI PAIRON, THE LEGENDARY KUNG FU MASTER!
THE POWER OF KUNG FU LIES IN CLOSE COMBAT!

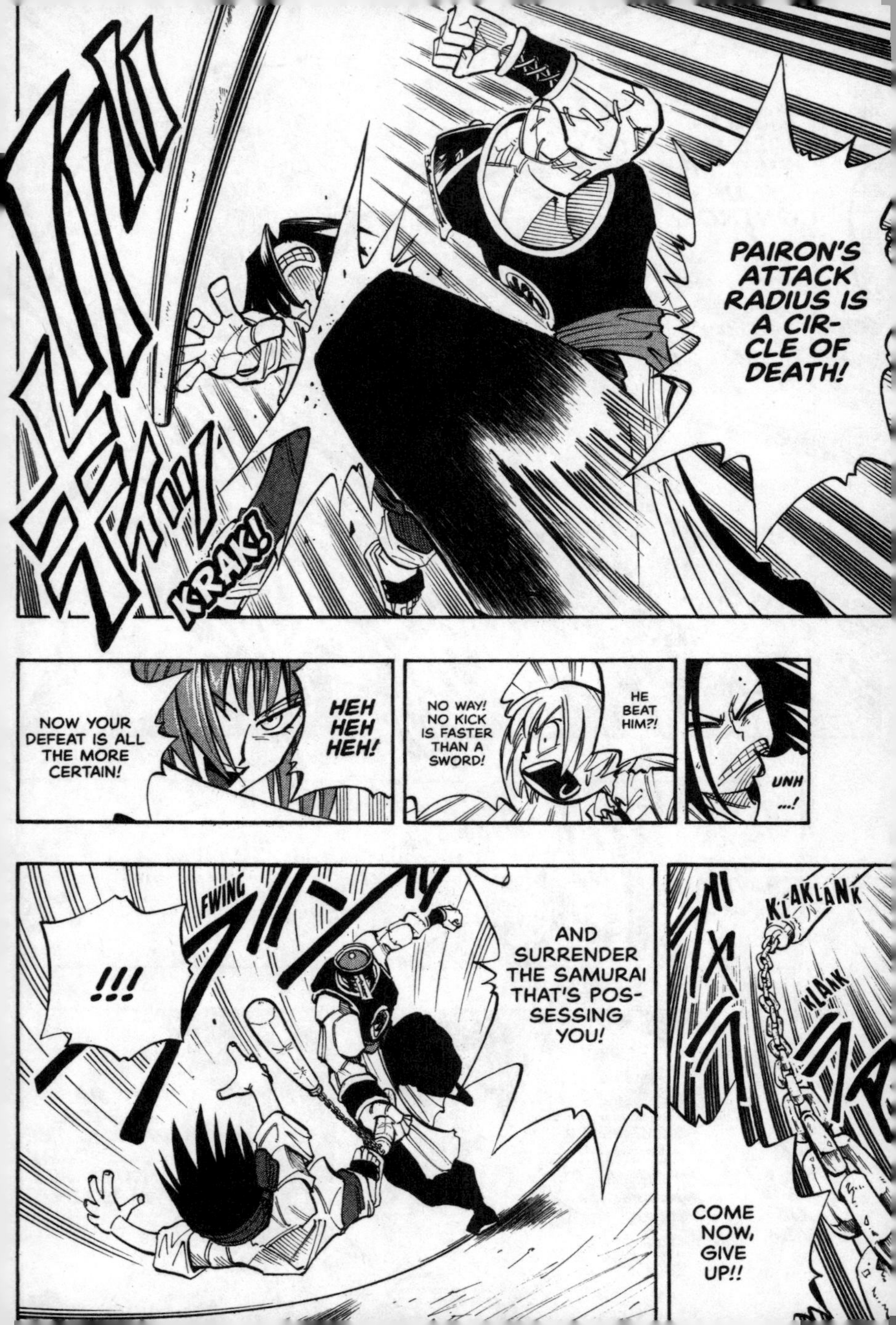
PAIRON'S ATTACK RADIUS IS A CIR-CLE OF DEATH!
KRAK!
UNH ...!
HE BEAT HIM?!
NO WAY! NO KICK IS FASTER THAN A SWORD!
HEH HEH HEH!
NOW YOUR DEFEAT IS ALL THE MORE CERTAIN!
KLAKLANK
KLANK
COME NOW, GIVE UP!!
AND SURRENDER THE SAMURAI THAT'S POS-SESSING YOU!
FWING
!!!

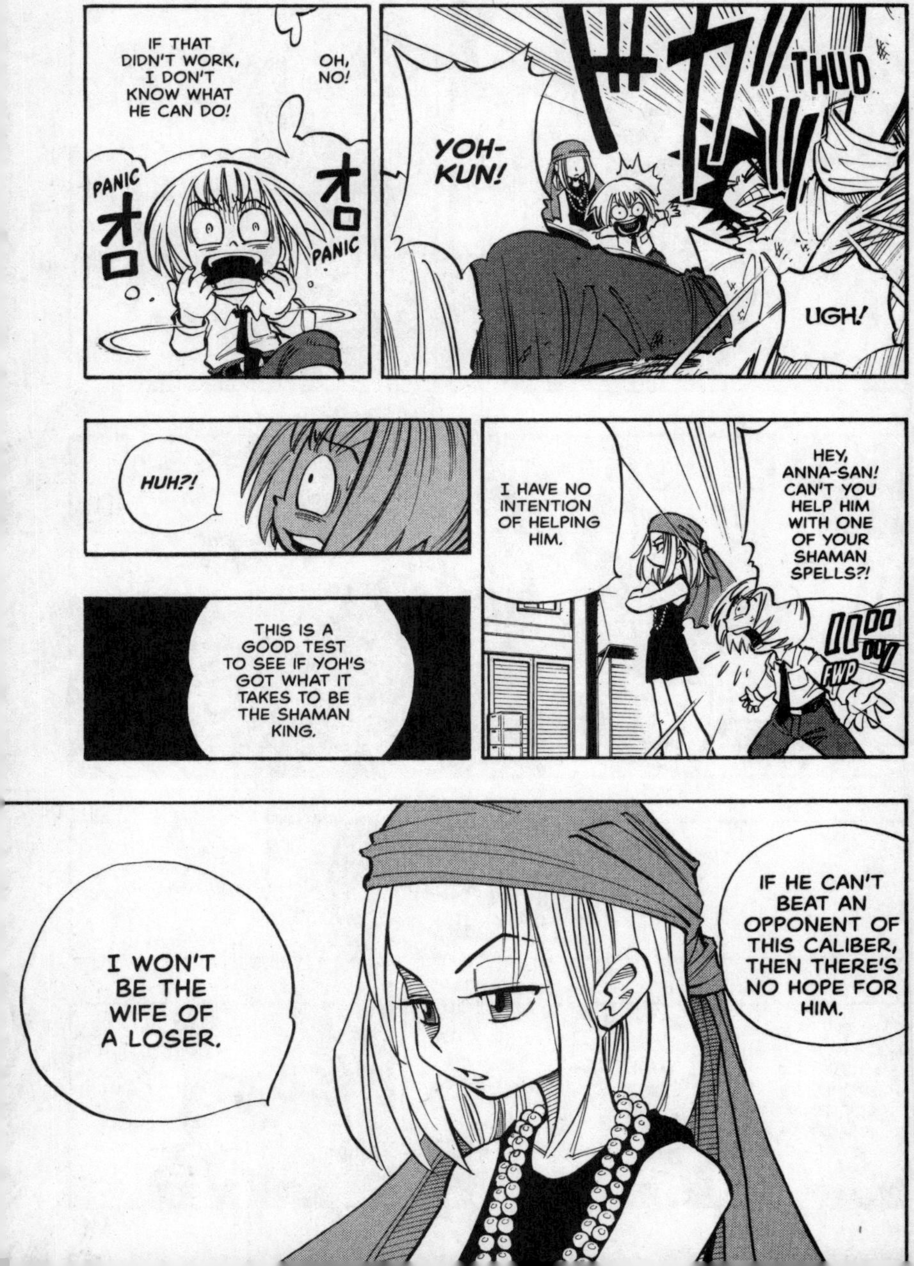
THUD
YOH-KUN!
UGH!
OH, NO!
IF THAT DIDN'T WORK, I DON'T KNOW WHAT HE CAN DO!
オロ PANIC
PANIC オロ
HEY, ANNA-SAN! CAN'T YOU HELP HIM WITH ONE OF YOUR SHAMAN SPELLS?!
FWP
I HAVE NO INTENTION OF HELPING HIM.
HUH?!
THIS IS A GOOD TEST TO SEE IF YOH'S GOT WHAT IT TAKES TO BE THE SHAMAN KING.
IF HE CAN'T BEAT AN OPPONENT OF THIS CALIBER, THEN THERE'S NO HOPE FOR HIM.
I WON'T BE THE WIFE OF A LOSER.

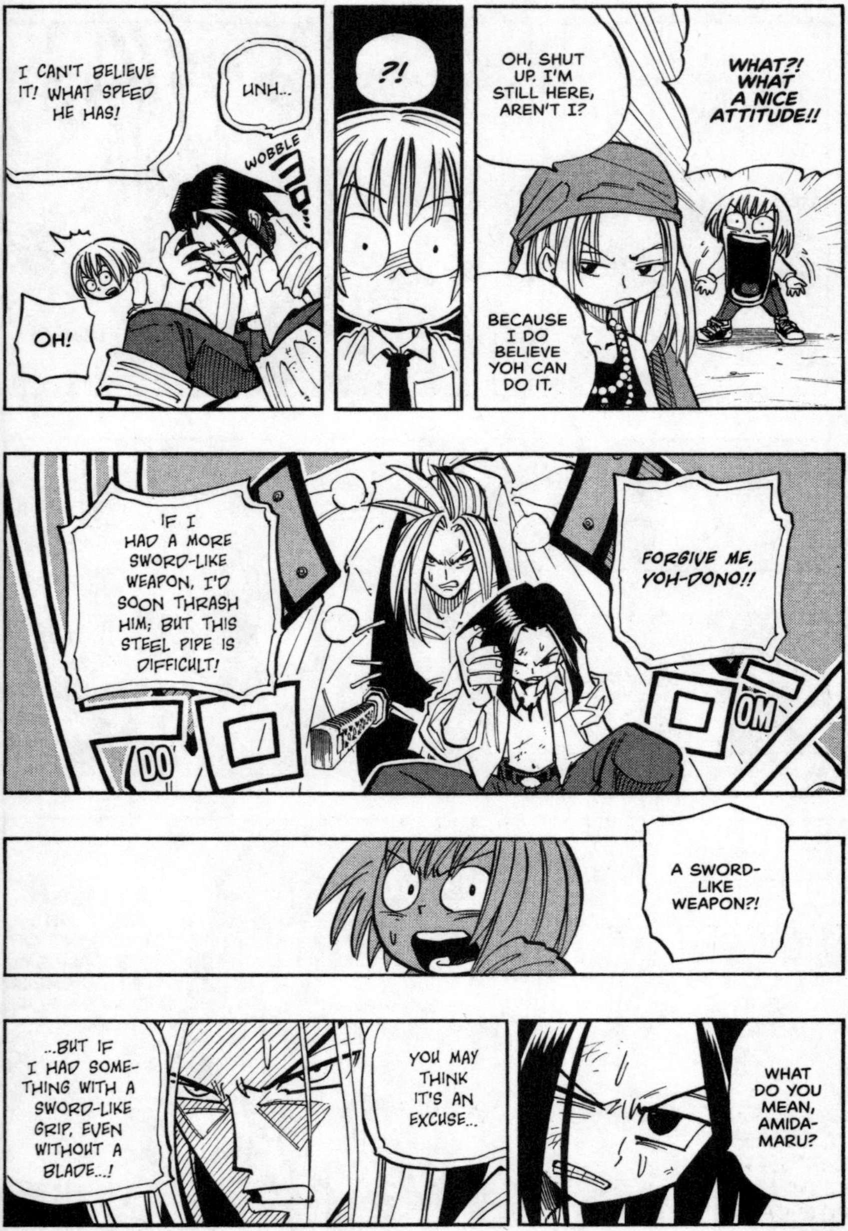
WHAT?! WHAT A NICE ATTITUDE!!
OH, SHUT UP. I'M STILL HERE, AREN'T I?
BECAUSE I DO BELIEVE YOH CAN DO IT.
?!
UNH...
I CAN'T BELIEVE IT! WHAT SPEED HE HAS!
WOBBLE
OH!
FORGIVE ME, YOH-DONO!!
IF I HAD A MORE SWORD-LIKE WEAPON, I'D SOON THRASH HIM; BUT THIS STEEL PIPE IS DIFFICULT!
OM
DO
A SWORD-LIKE WEAPON?!
WHAT DO YOU MEAN, AMIDA-MARU?
YOU MAY THINK IT'S AN EXCUSE...
...BUT IF I HAD SOME-THING WITH A SWORD-LIKE GRIP, EVEN WITHOUT A BLADE...!

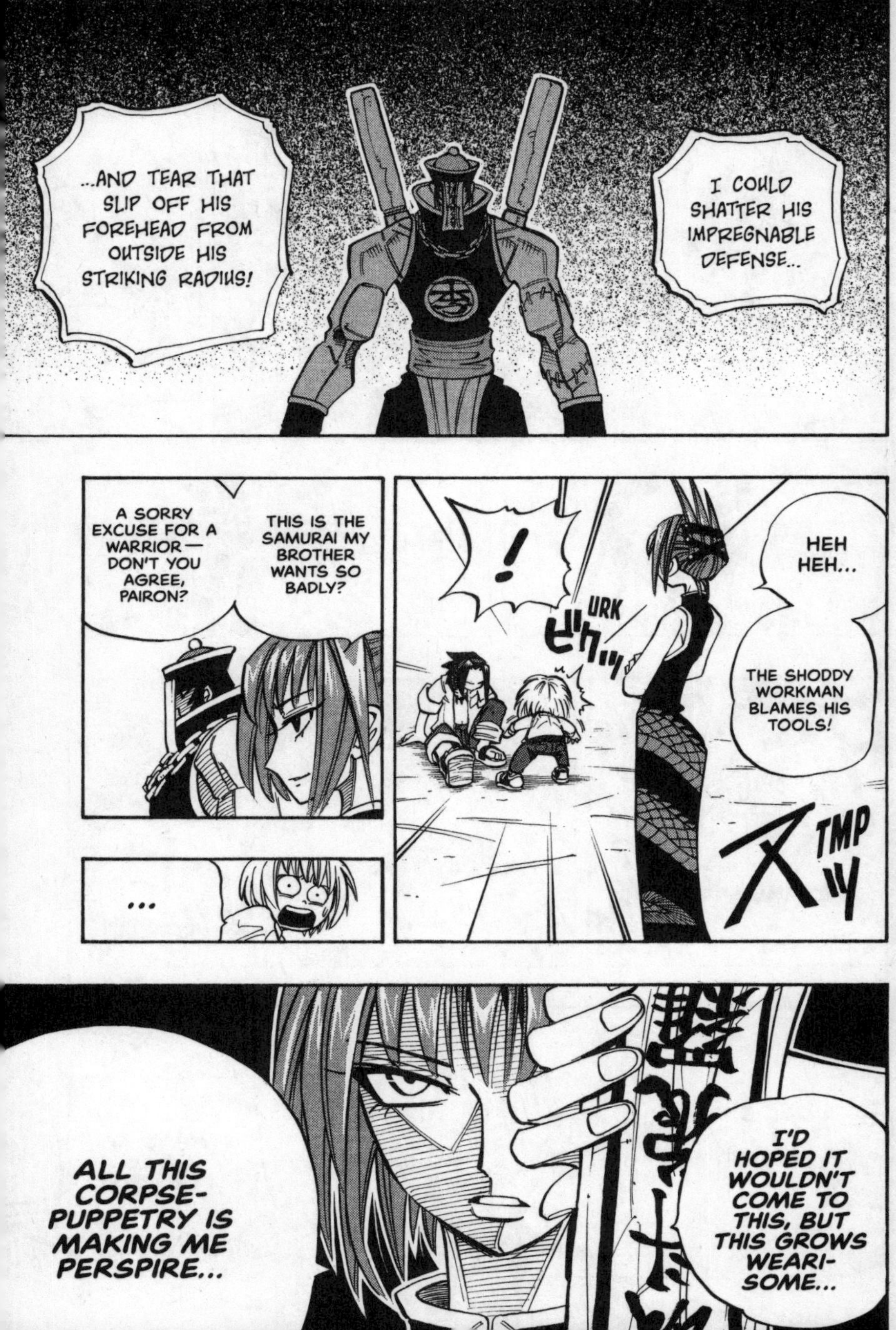
I COULD SHATTER HIS IMPREGNABLE DEFENSE...
...AND TEAR THAT SLIP OFF HIS FOREHEAD FROM OUTSIDE HIS STRIKING RADIUS!
HEH HEH...
THE SHODDY WORKMAN BLAMES HIS TOOLS!
!
URK
ビクッ
TMP
スッ
THIS IS THE SAMURAI MY BROTHER WANTS SO BADLY?
A SORRY EXCUSE FOR A WARRIOR—DON'T YOU AGREE, PAIRON?
...
I'D HOPED IT WOULDN'T COME TO THIS, BUT THIS GROWS WEARI-SOME...
ALL THIS CORPSE-PUPPETRY IS MAKING ME PERSPIRE...

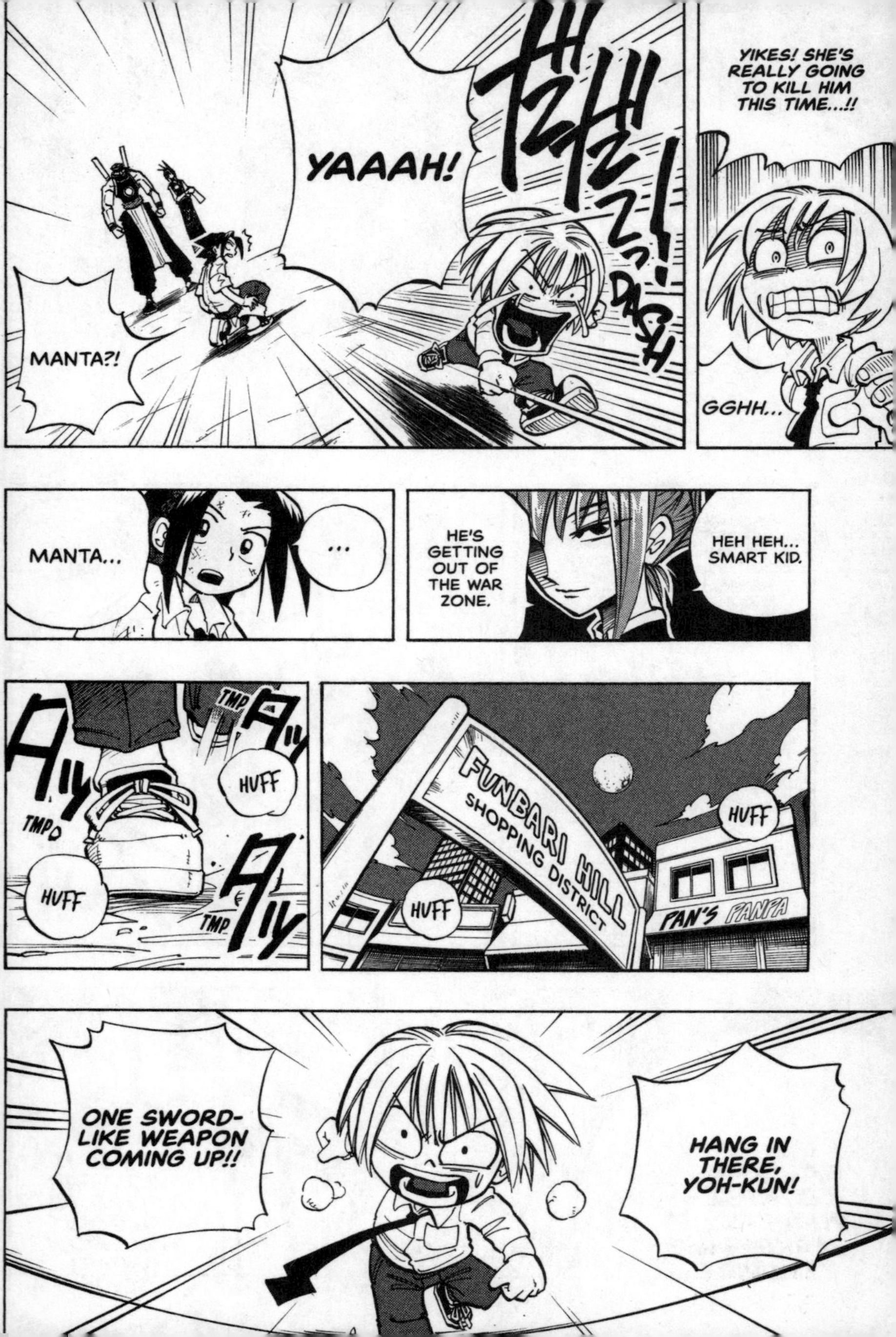
YIKES! SHE'S REALLY GOING TO KILL HIM THIS TIME...!!
GGHH...
YAAAH!
DASH
MANTA?!
HEH HEH... SMART KID.
HE'S GETTING OUT OF THE WAR ZONE.
...
MANTA...
FUNBARI HILL SHOPPING DISTRICT
HUFF
HUFF
PAN'S PANPA
TMP
HUFF
TMP
TMP
HUFF
HANG IN THERE, YOH-KUN!
ONE SWORD-LIKE WEAPON COMING UP!!

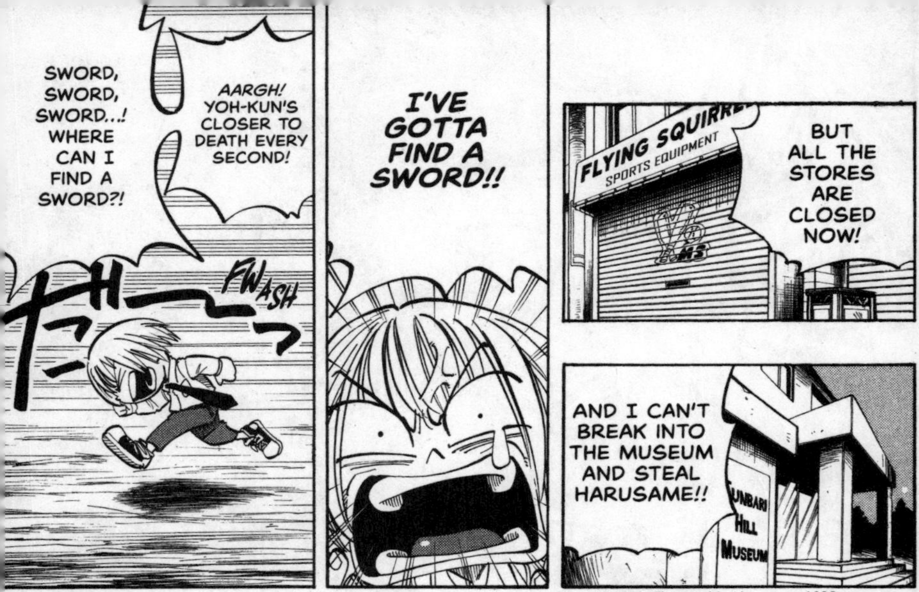
BUT ALL THE STORES ARE CLOSED NOW!
FLYING SQUIRREL
SPORTS EQUIPMENT
AND I CAN'T BREAK INTO THE MUSEUM AND STEAL HARUSAME!!
HILL
MUSEUM
I'VE GOTTA FIND A SWORD!!
AARGH! YOH-KUN'S CLOSER TO DEATH EVERY SECOND!
SWORD, SWORD, SWORD...! WHERE CAN I FIND A SWORD?!
FWASH

Harusame—The sword Amidamaru used 600 years ago.

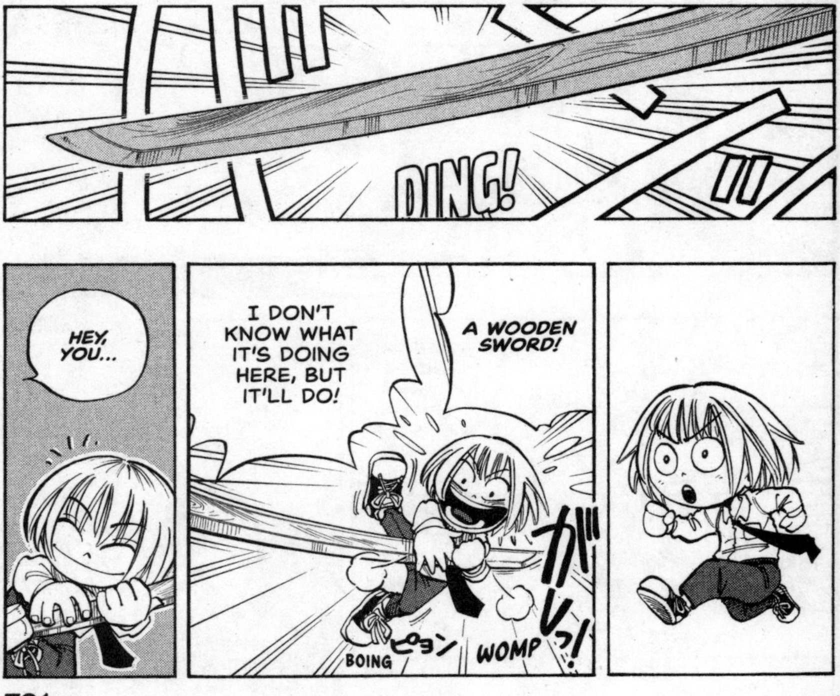
DING!
A WOODEN SWORD!
I DON'T KNOW WHAT IT'S DOING HERE, BUT IT'LL DO!
BOING
WOMP
HEY, YOU...

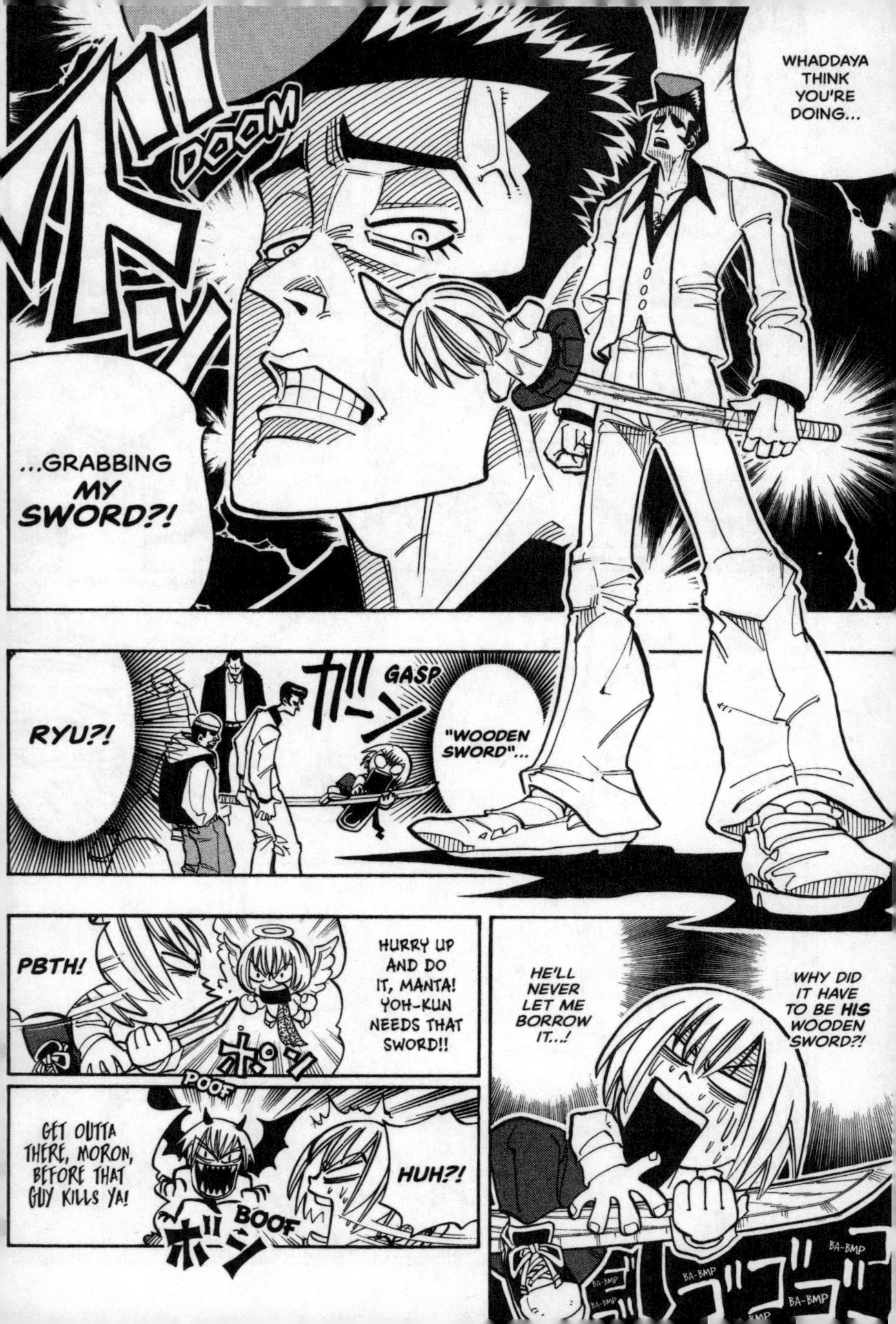
WHADDAYA THINK YOU'RE DOING...
DOOOM
...GRABBING MY SWORD?!
GASP
"WOODEN SWORD"...
RYU?!
WHY DID IT HAVE TO BE HIS WOODEN SWORD?!
HE'LL NEVER LET ME BORROW IT...!
BA-BMP
BA-BMP
BA-BMP
BA-BMP
HURRY UP AND DO IT, MANTA! YOH-KUN NEEDS THAT SWORD!!
PBTH!
POOF
HUH?!
GET OUTTA THERE, MORON, BEFORE THAT GUY KILLS YA!
BOOF

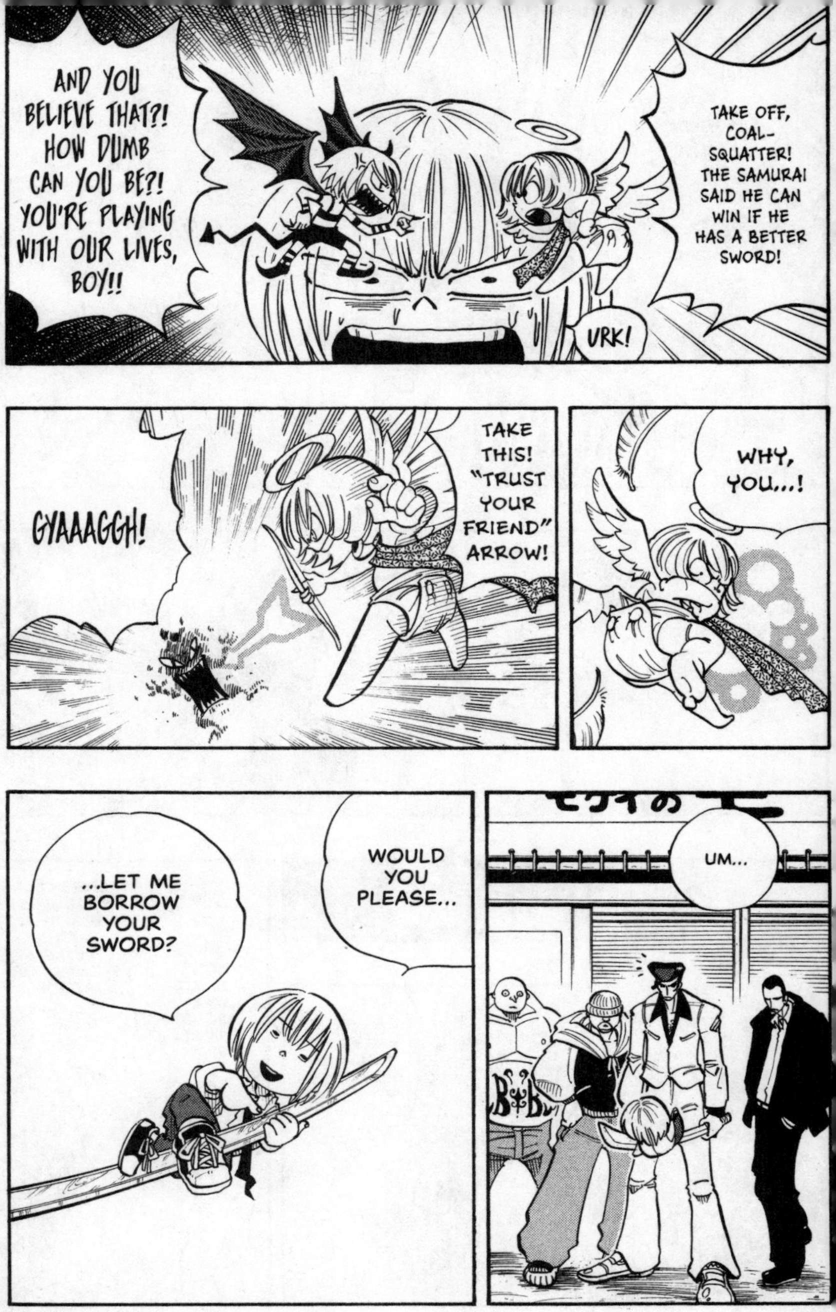
TAKE OFF, COAL-SQUATTER! THE SAMURAI SAID HE CAN WIN IF HE HAS A BETTER SWORD!
AND YOU BELIEVE THAT?! HOW DUMB CAN YOU BE?! YOU'RE PLAYING WITH OUR LIVES, BOY!!
URK!
WHY, YOU...!
TAKE THIS! "TRUST YOUR FRIEND" ARROW!
GYAAAGGH!
UM...
WOULD YOU PLEASE...
...LET ME BORROW YOUR SWORD?

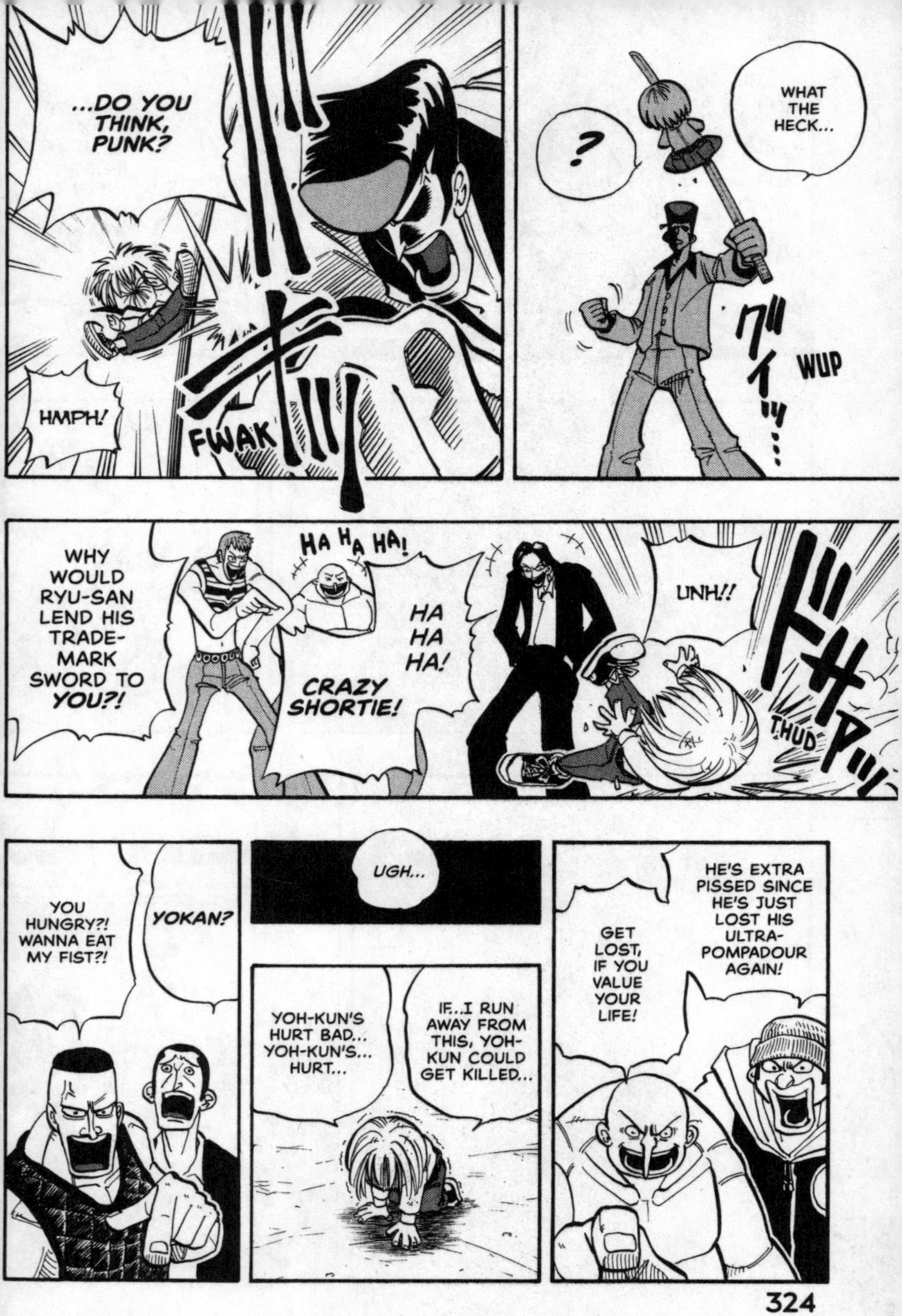
WHAT THE HECK...
?
グイッ
WUP
...DO YOU THINK, PUNK?
HMPH!
FWAK
UNH!!
THUD
HA HA HA!
HA HA HA!
CRAZY SHORTIE!
WHY WOULD RYU-SAN LEND HIS TRADE-MARK SWORD TO YOU?!
HE'S EXTRA PISSED SINCE HE'S JUST LOST HIS ULTRA-POMPADOUR AGAIN!
GET LOST, IF YOU VALUE YOUR LIFE!
UGH...
IF..I RUN AWAY FROM THIS, YOH-KUN COULD GET KILLED...
YOH-KUN'S HURT BAD... YOH-KUN'S... HURT...
YOKAN?
YOU HUNGRY?! WANNA EAT MY FIST?!

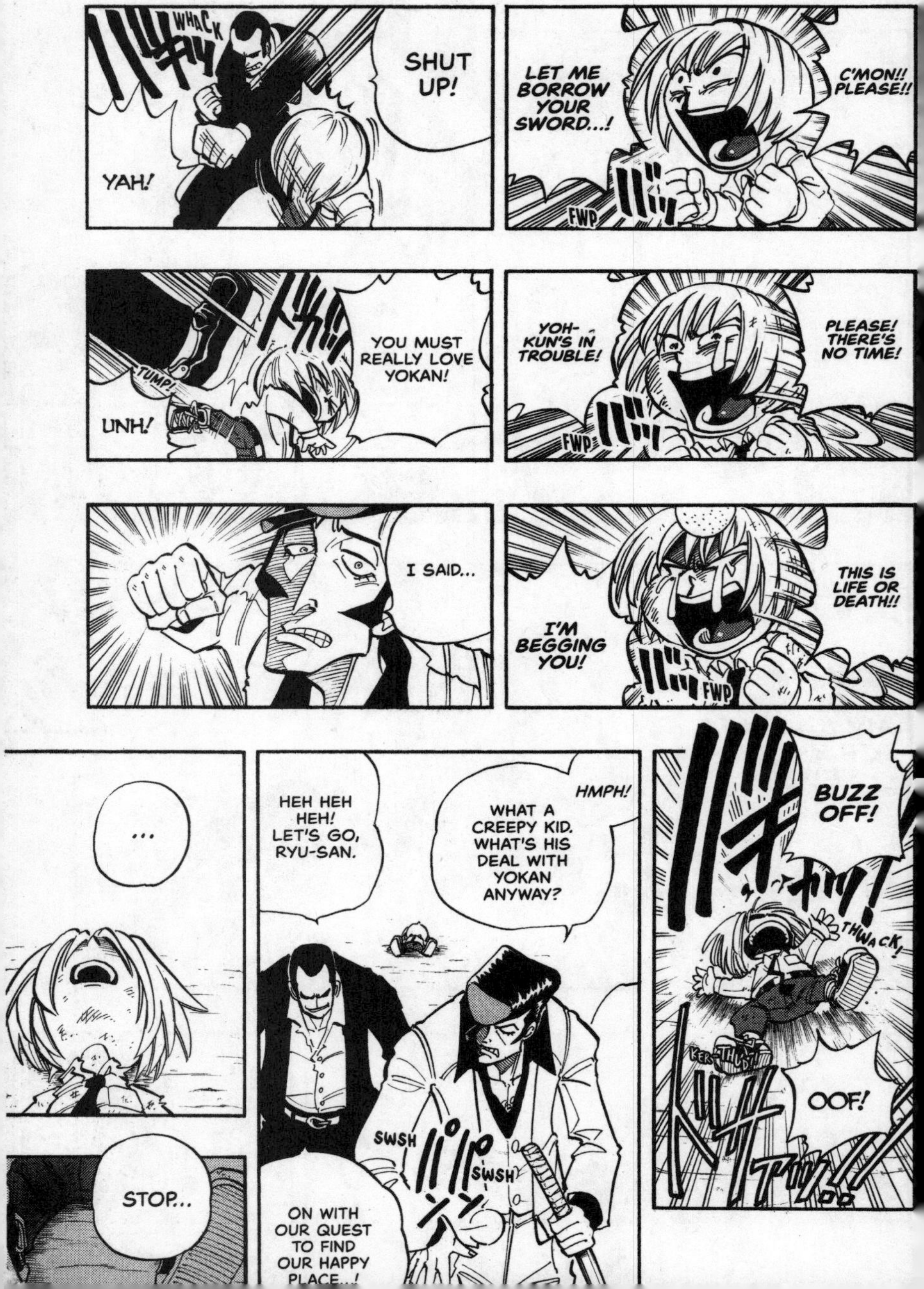
C'MON!! PLEASE!!
LET ME BORROW YOUR SWORD...!
FWP
SHUT UP!
WHACK
YAH!
PLEASE! THERE'S NO TIME!
YOH-KUN'S IN TROUBLE!
FWP
YOU MUST REALLY LOVE YOKAN!
TUMP!
UNH!
THIS IS LIFE OR DEATH!!
I'M BEGGING YOU!
FWP
I SAID...
BUZZ OFF!
THWACK!
KER-THUD!
OOF!
HMPH!
WHAT A CREEPY KID. WHAT'S HIS DEAL WITH YOKAN ANYWAY?
HEH HEH HEH! LET'S GO, RYU-SAN.
SWSH
SWSH
ON WITH OUR QUEST TO FIND OUR HAPPY PLACE...!
...
STOP...

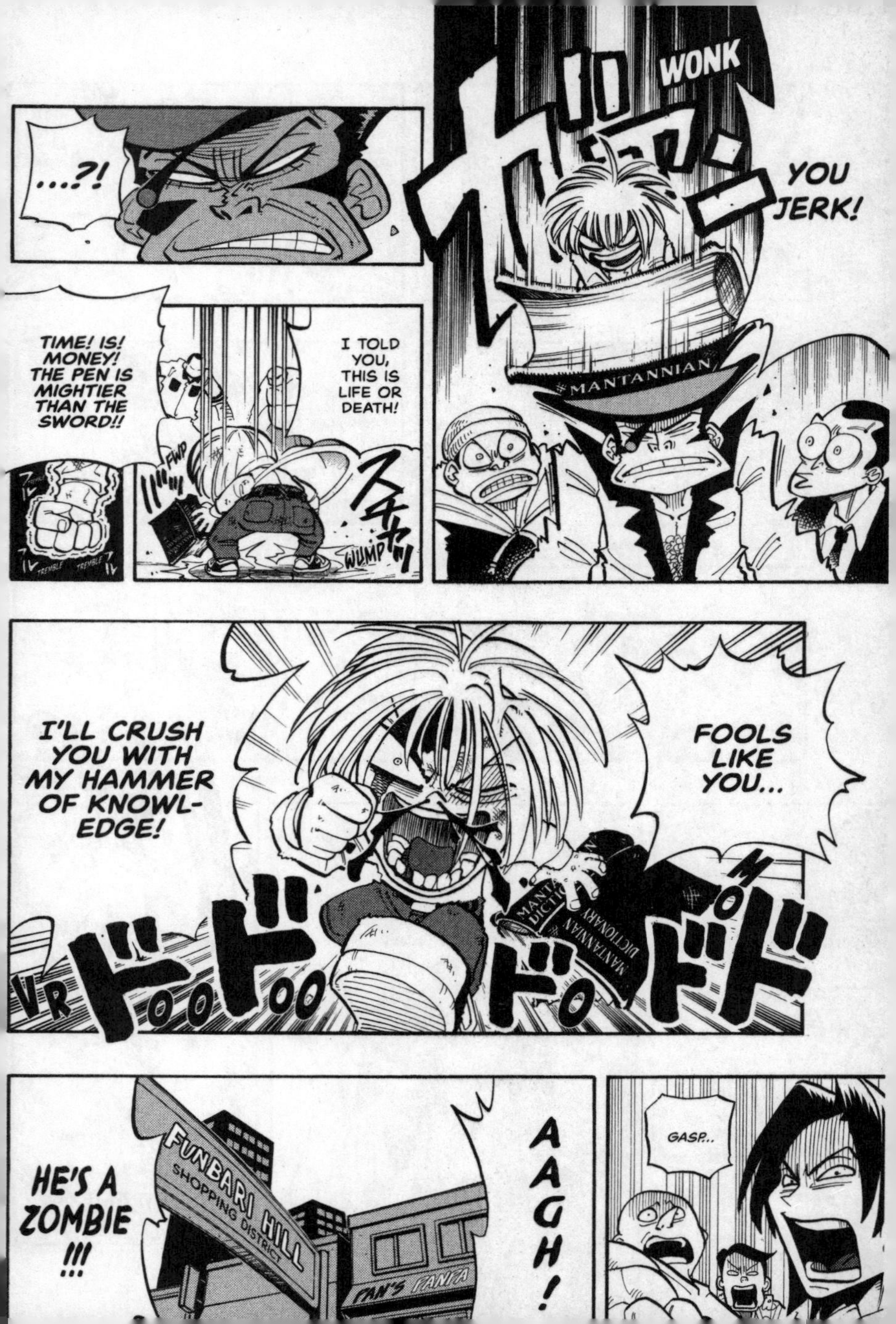
WONK
YOU JERK!
#MANTANNIAN
...?!
I TOLD YOU, THIS IS LIFE OR DEATH!
TIME! IS! MONEY! THE PEN IS MIGHTIER THAN THE SWORD!!
FWP
WUMP
TREMBLE TREMBLE
FOOLS LIKE YOU...
I'LL CRUSH YOU WITH MY HAMMER OF KNOWL- EDGE!
MO
MANTANNIAN DICTIONARY
VR
GASP...
AAGH!
HE'S A ZOMBIE!!!
FUNBARI HILL
SHOPPING DISTRICT

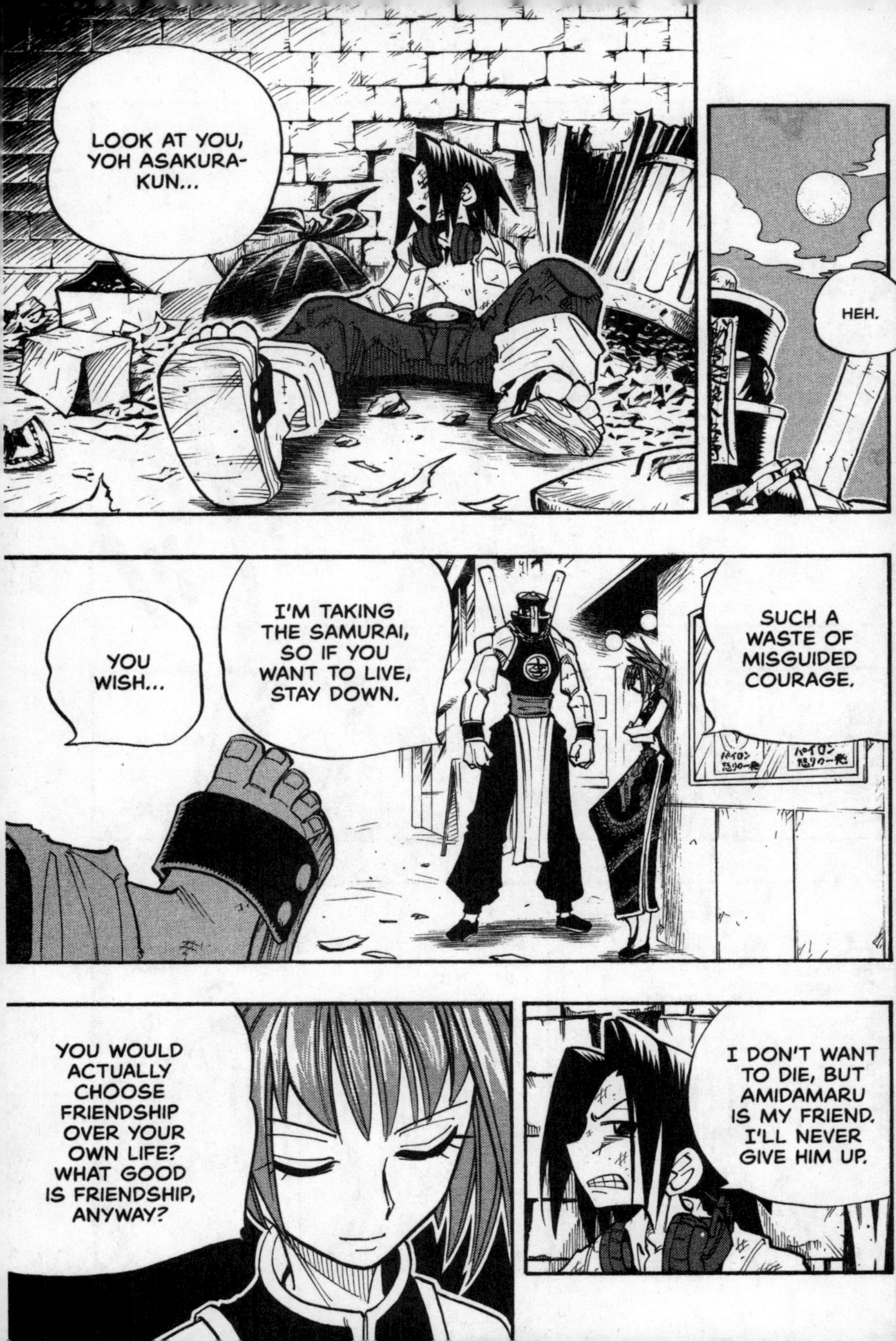
HEH.
LOOK AT YOU, YOH ASAKURA-KUN...
SUCH A WASTE OF MISGUIDED COURAGE.
I'M TAKING THE SAMURAI, SO IF YOU WANT TO LIVE, STAY DOWN.
YOU WISH...
I DON'T WANT TO DIE, BUT AMIDAMARU IS MY FRIEND. I'LL NEVER GIVE HIM UP.
YOU WOULD ACTUALLY CHOOSE FRIENDSHIP OVER YOUR OWN LIFE? WHAT GOOD IS FRIENDSHIP, ANYWAY?

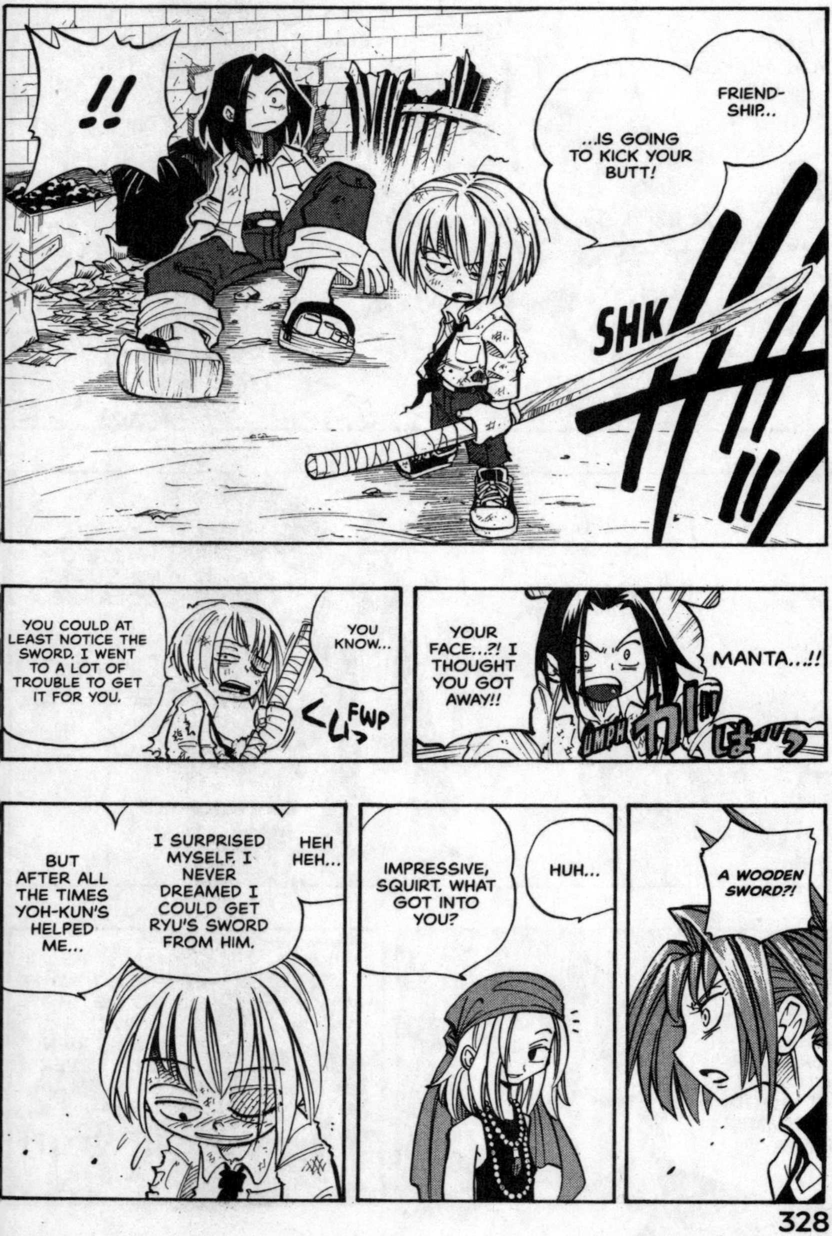
FRIEND-SHIP...
...IS GOING TO KICK YOUR BUTT!
!!
SHK
MANTA...!!
YOUR FACE...?! I THOUGHT YOU GOT AWAY!!
UMPH
YOU KNOW...
YOU COULD AT LEAST NOTICE THE SWORD. I WENT TO A LOT OF TROUBLE TO GET IT FOR YOU.
FWP
A WOODEN SWORD?!
HUH...
IMPRESSIVE, SQUIRT. WHAT GOT INTO YOU?
HEH HEH...
I SURPRISED MYSELF. I NEVER DREAMED I COULD GET RYU'S SWORD FROM HIM.
BUT AFTER ALL THE TIMES YOH-KUN'S HELPED ME...

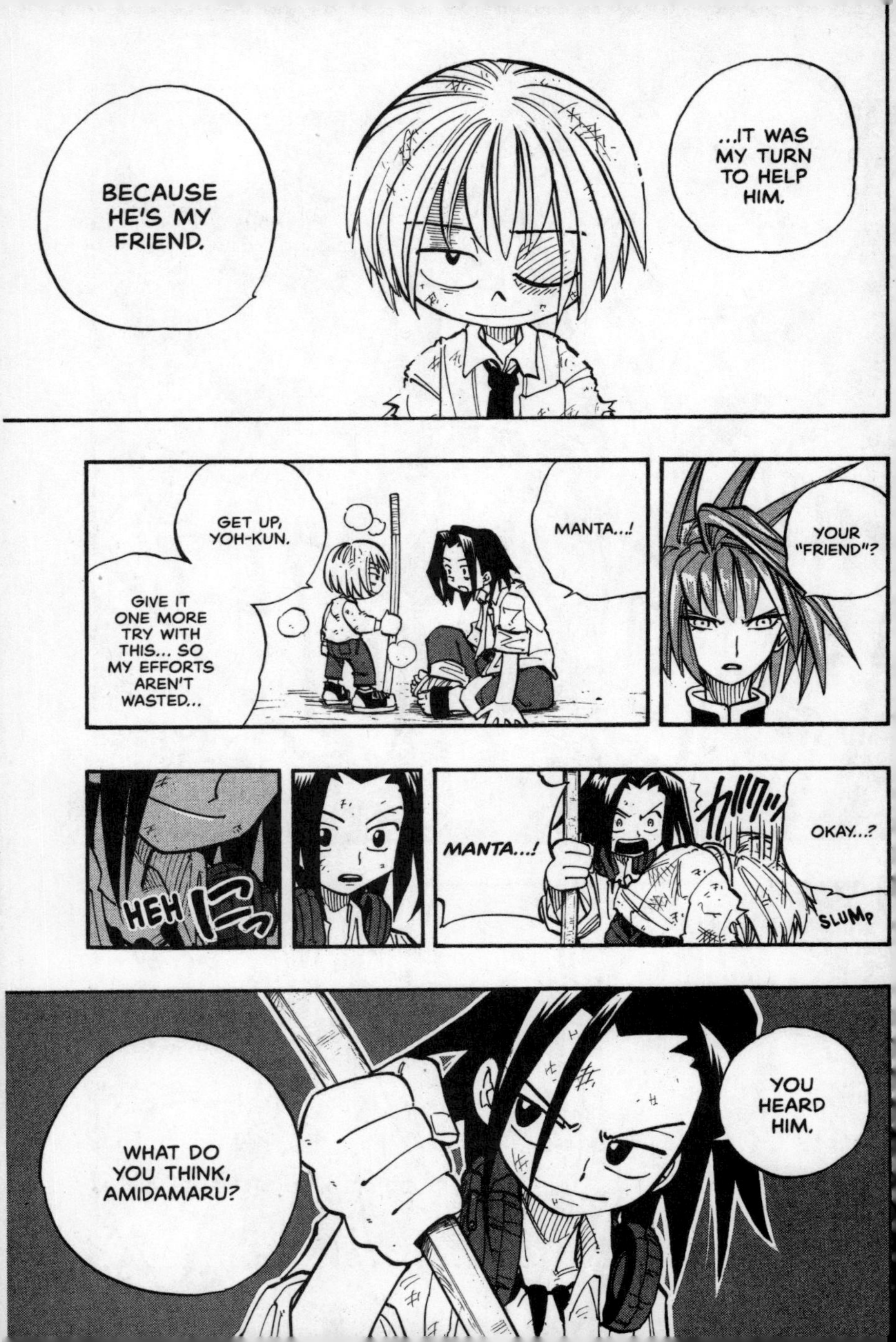
...IT WAS MY TURN TO HELP HIM.
BECAUSE HE'S MY FRIEND.
YOUR "FRIEND"?
MANTA...!
GET UP, YOH-KUN.
GIVE IT ONE MORE TRY WITH THIS... SO MY EFFORTS AREN'T WASTED...
OKAY...?
SLUMP
MANTA...!
HEH
YOU HEARD HIM.
WHAT DO YOU THINK, AMIDAMARU?

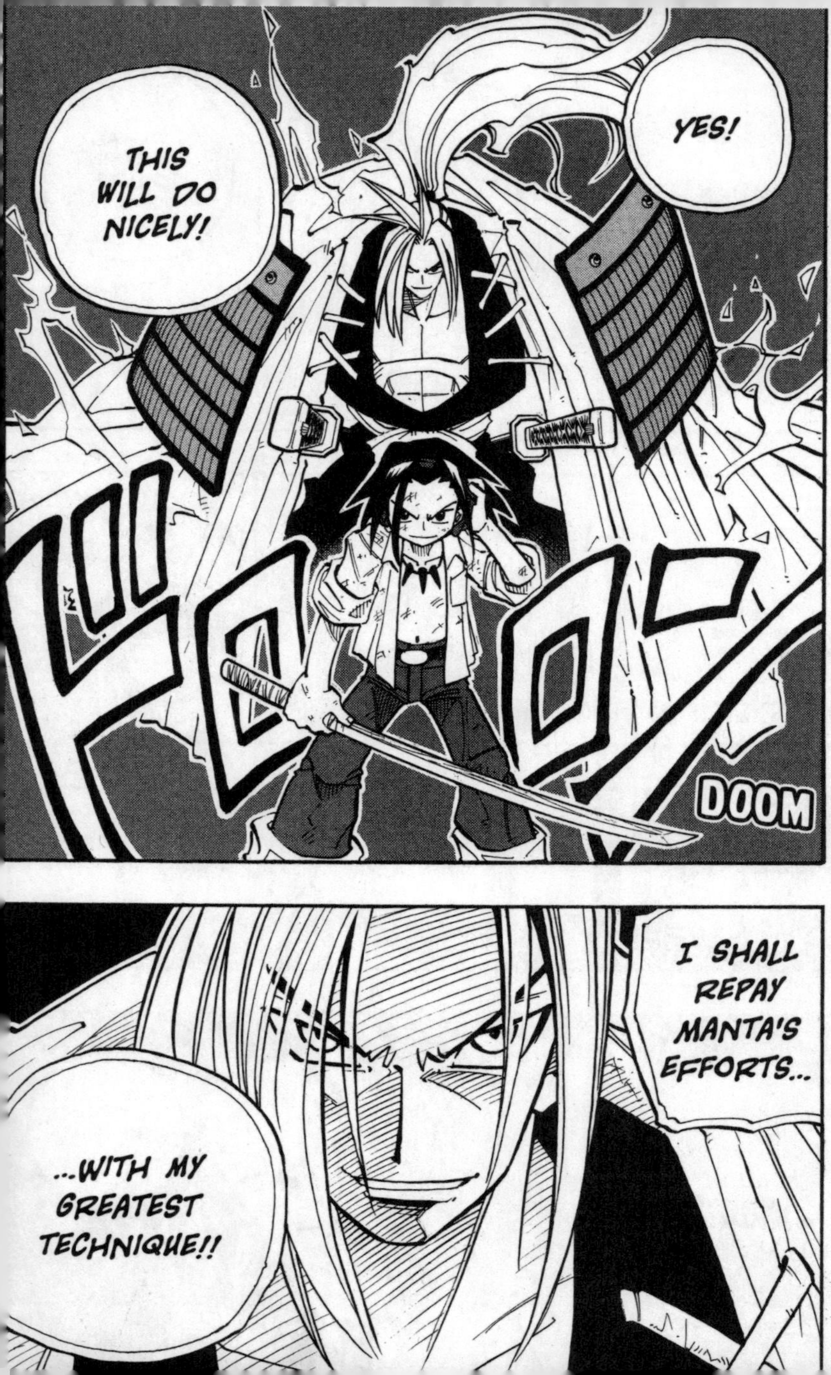
YES!
THIS WILL DO NICELY!
DOOM
I SHALL REPAY MANTA'S EFFORTS...
...WITH MY GREATEST TECHNIQUE!!

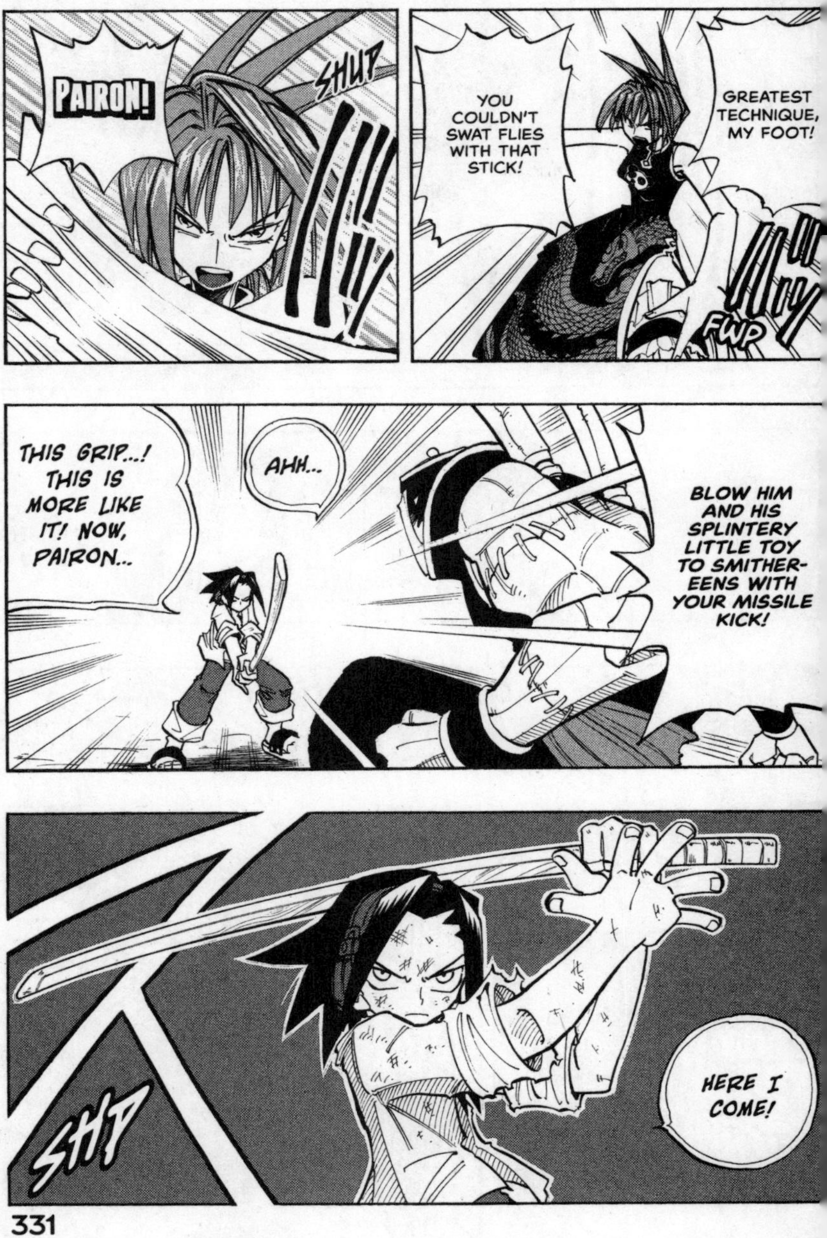
GREATEST TECHNIQUE, MY FOOT!
YOU COULDN'T SWAT FLIES WITH THAT STICK!
FWP
PAIRON!
SHUP
BLOW HIM AND HIS SPLINTERY LITTLE TOY TO SMITHER-EENS WITH YOUR MISSILE KICK!
AHH...
THIS GRIP...! THIS IS MORE LIKE IT! NOW, PAIRON...
HERE I COME!
SHP

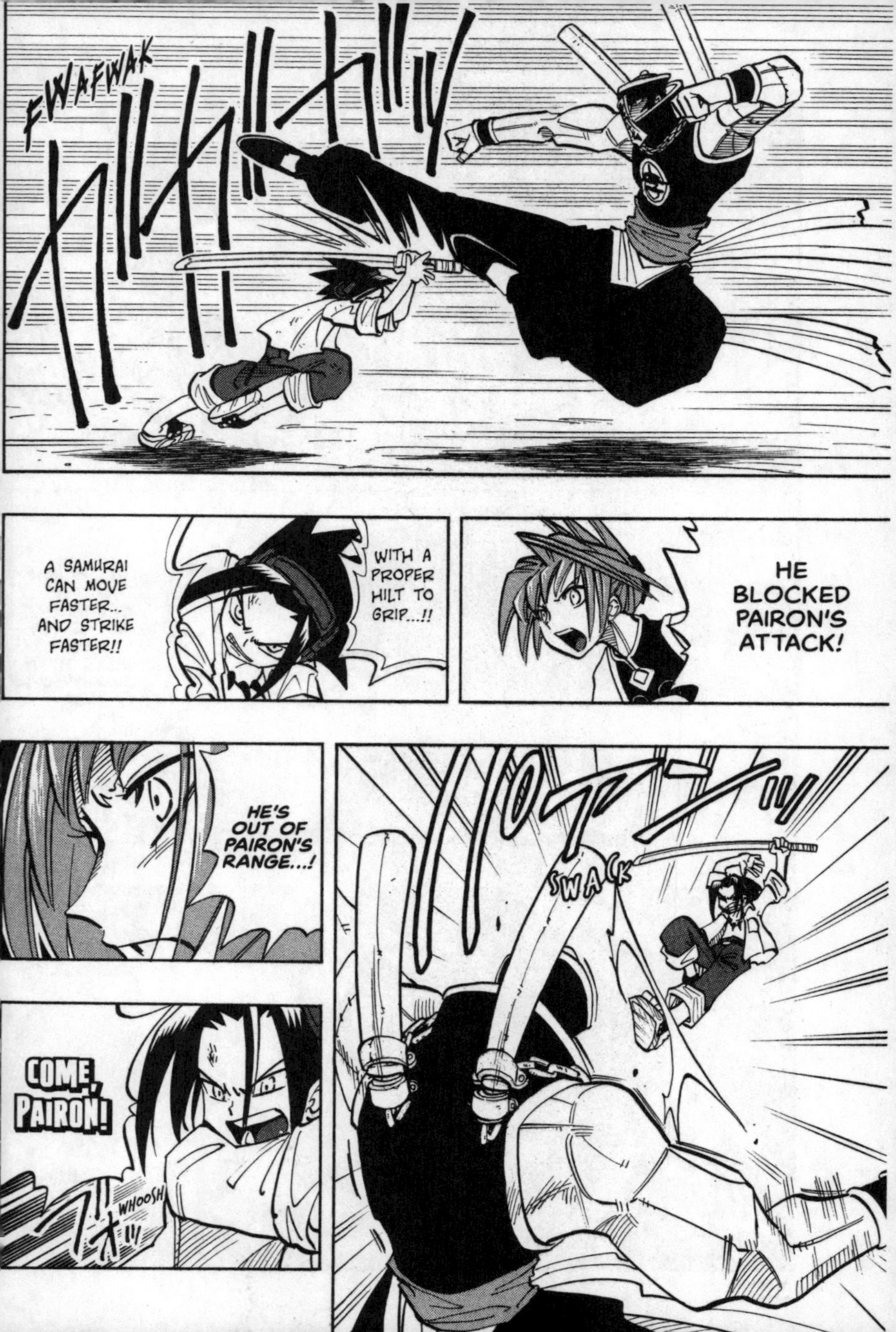
FWAFWAK
HE BLOCKED PAIRON'S ATTACK!
WITH A PROPER HILT TO GRIP...!!
A SAMURAI CAN MOVE FASTER... AND STRIKE FASTER!!
SWACK
HE'S OUT OF PAIRON'S RANGE...!
COME, PAIRON!
WHOOSH

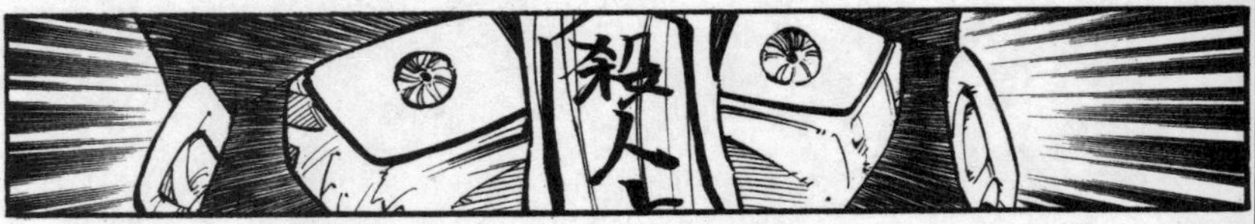
殺人

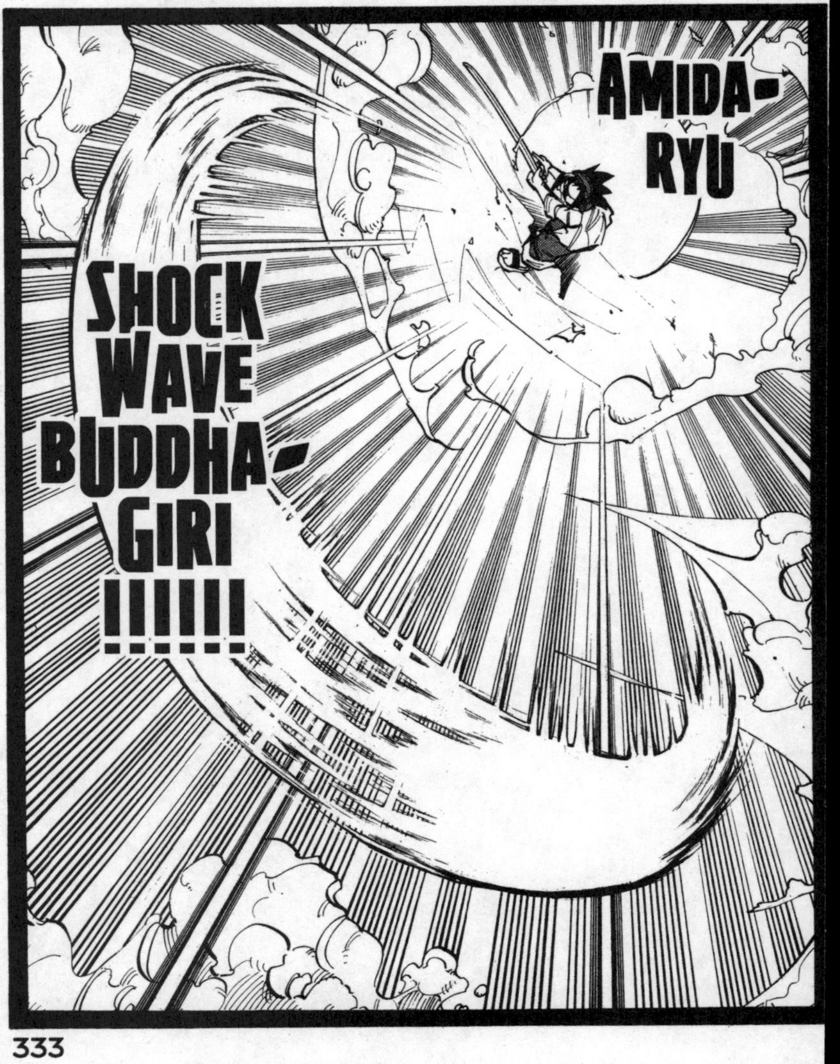
AMIDA-RYU
SHOCK WAVE BUDDHA-GIRI!!!!!!

SHAMAN
KING
2

O-Fuda

Chapter 15: Fists of Rage

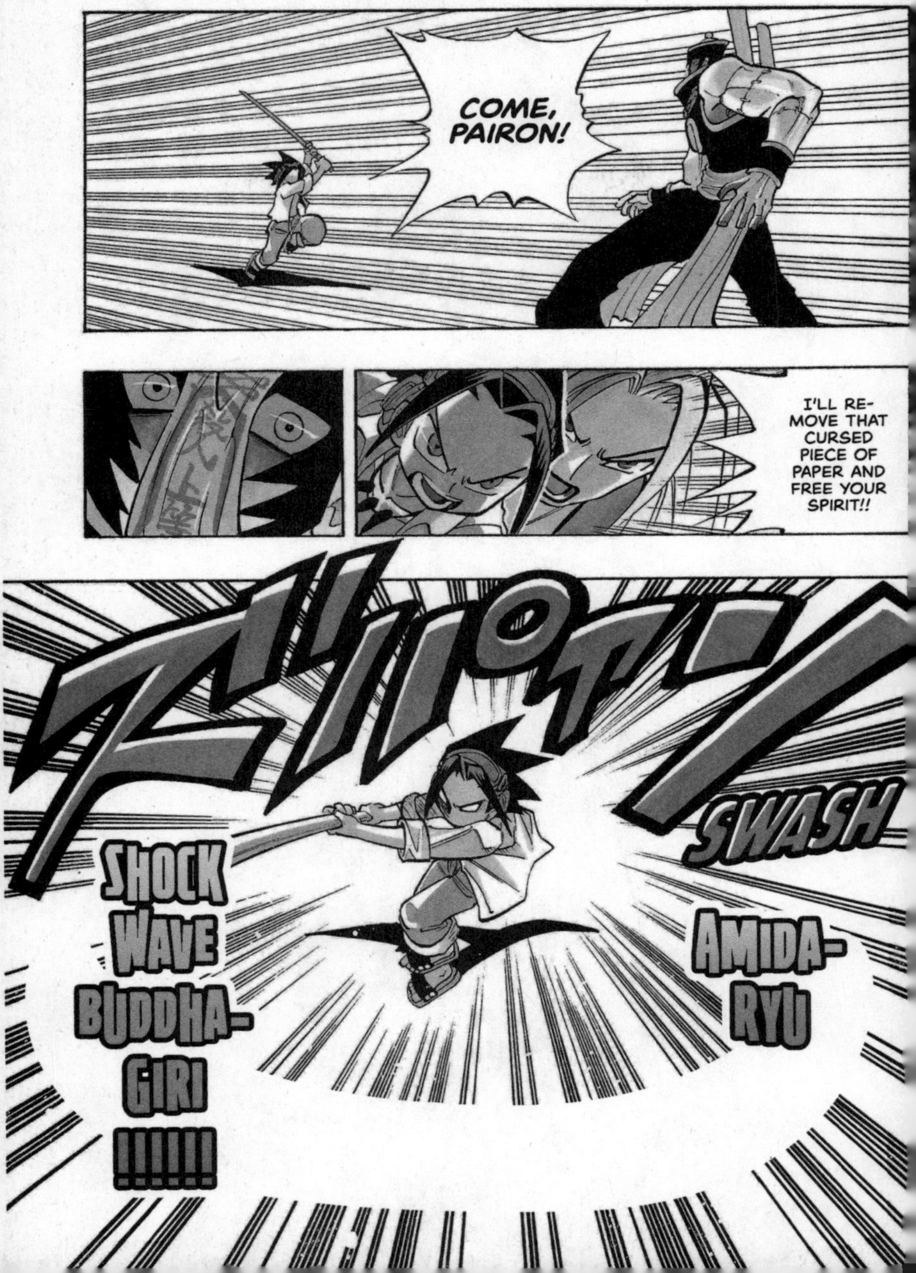
COME, PAIRON!
I'LL REMOVE THAT CURSED PIECE OF PAPER AND FREE YOUR SPIRIT!!
SWASH
AMIDA-RYU
SHOCK WAVE BUDDHA-GIRI!!!!!!!

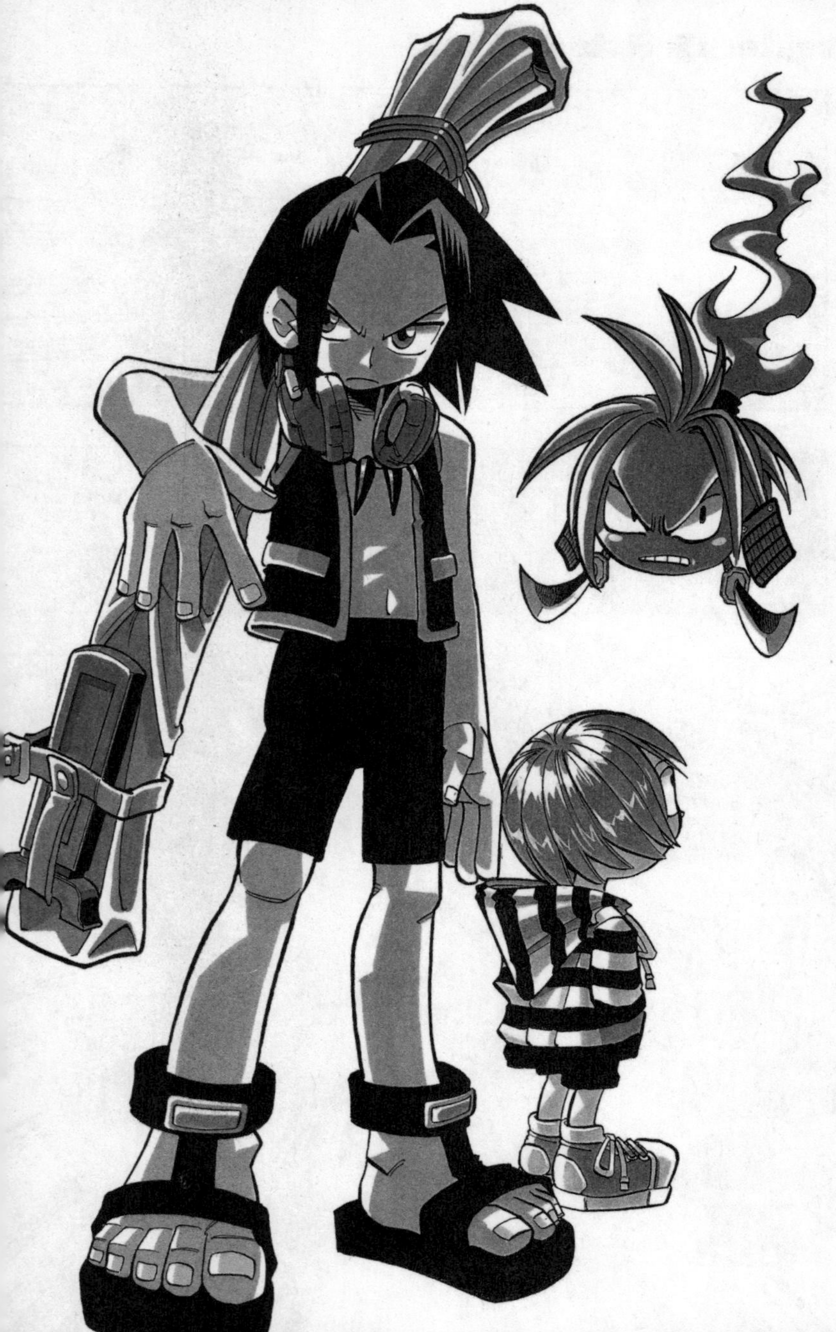

Chapter 15:

Fists of Rage

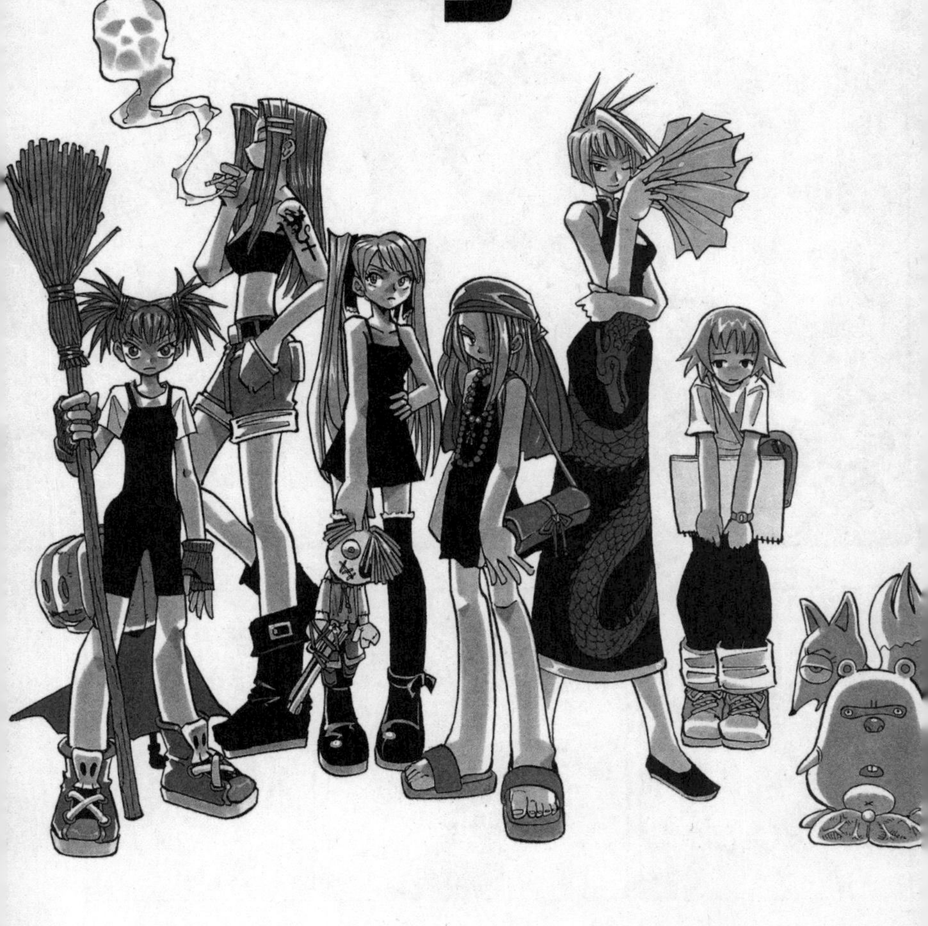

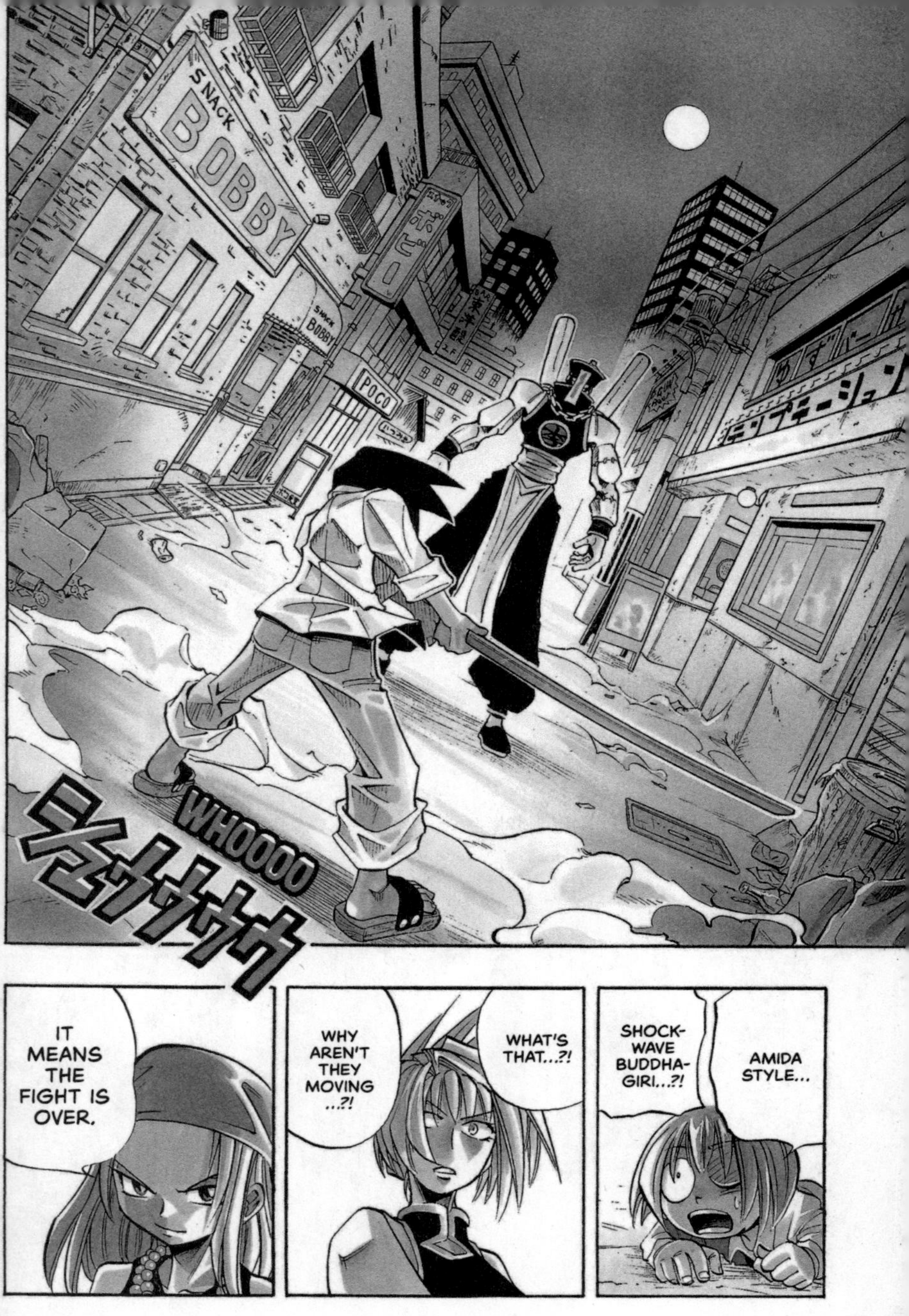
SNACK BOBBY
SNACK BOBBY
POCO
WHOOOOO
SHOCK-WAVE BUDDHA-GIRI...?!
AMIDA STYLE...
WHAT'S THAT...?!
WHY AREN'T THEY MOVING...?!
IT MEANS THE FIGHT IS OVER.

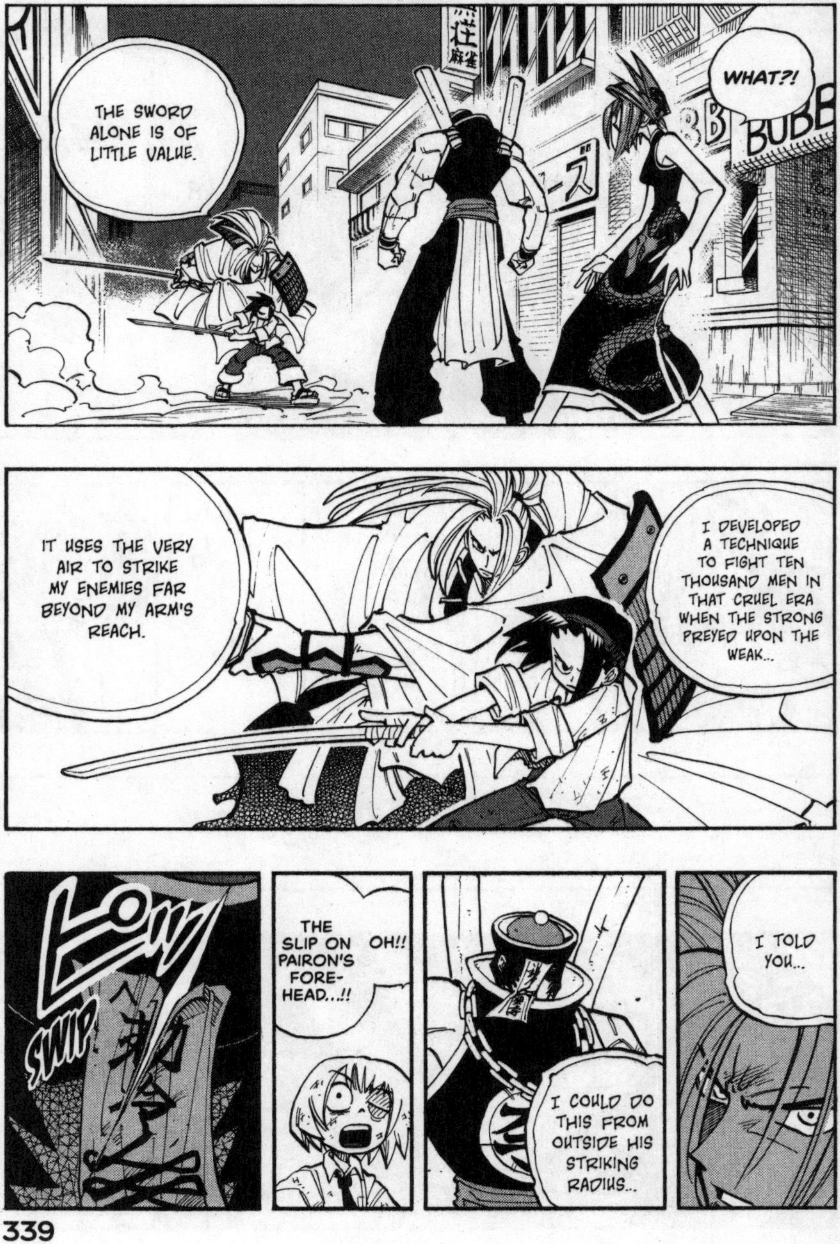
WHAT?!
BUBB
THE SWORD ALONE IS OF LITTLE VALUE.
I DEVELOPED A TECHNIQUE TO FIGHT TEN THOUSAND MEN IN THAT CRUEL ERA WHEN THE STRONG PREYED UPON THE WEAK...
IT USES THE VERY AIR TO STRIKE MY ENEMIES FAR BEYOND MY ARM'S REACH.
I TOLD YOU...
I COULD DO THIS FROM OUTSIDE HIS STRIKING RADIUS...
OH!!
THE SLIP ON PAIRON'S FORE-HEAD...!!
SWIP

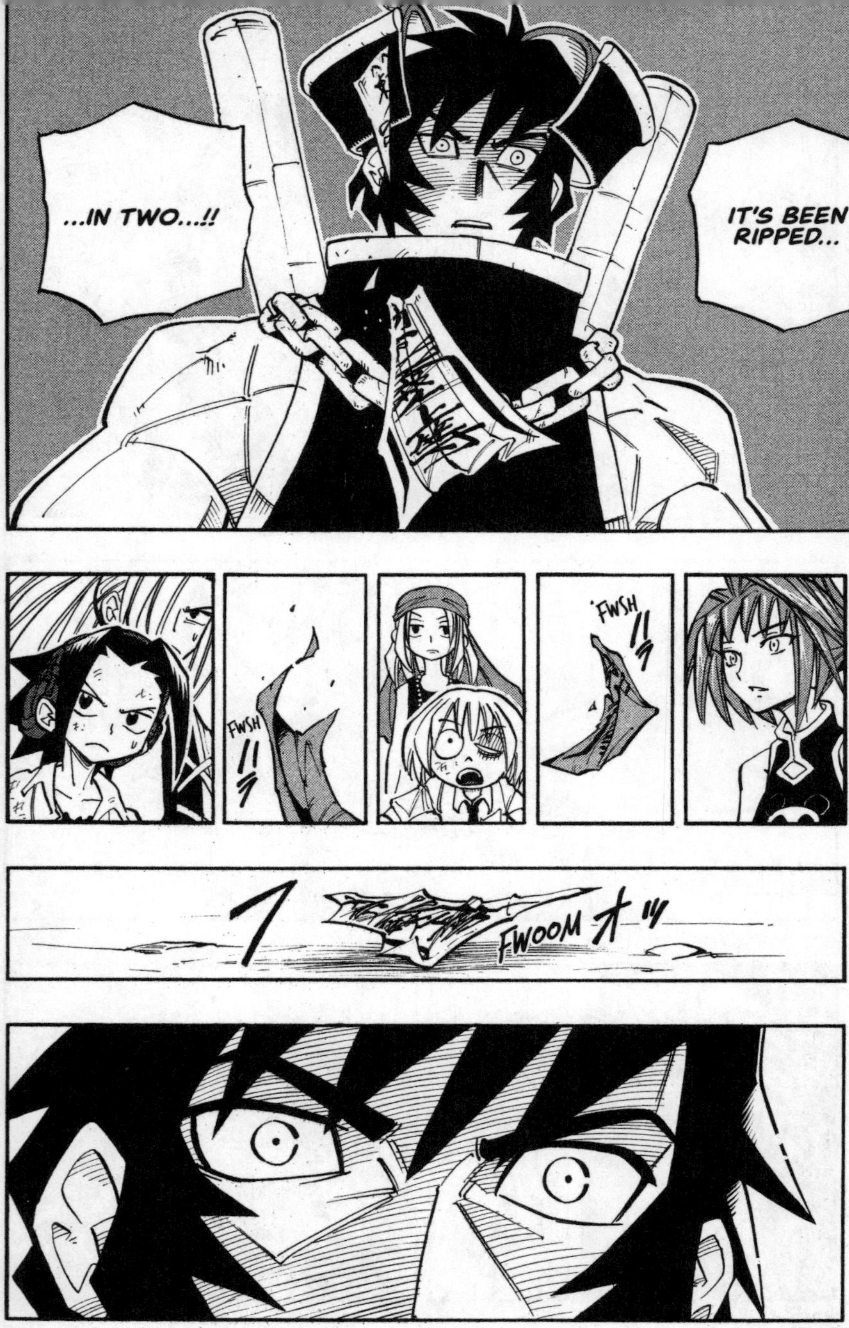
IT'S BEEN RIPPED...
...IN TWO...!!
FWSH
FWSH
FWOOM オッ

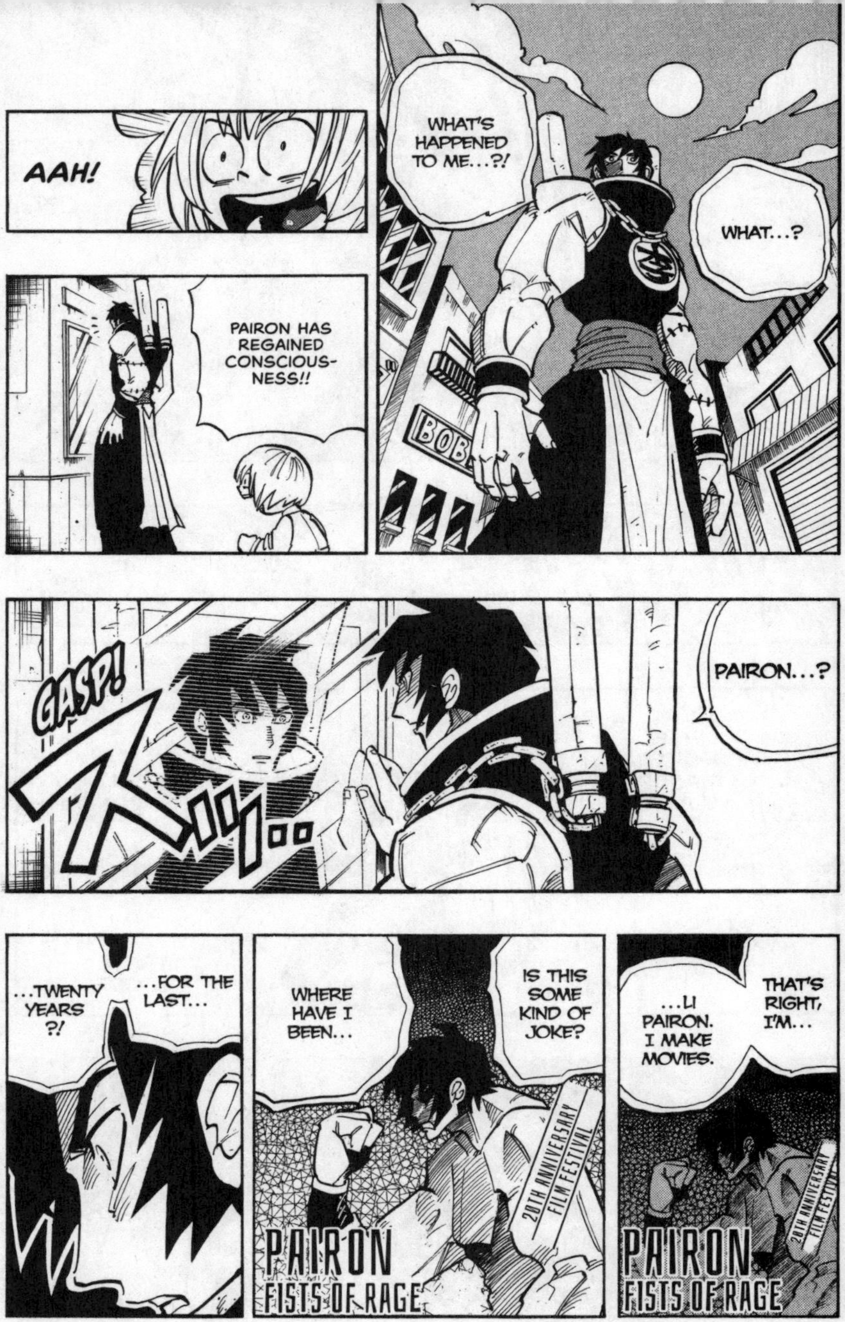
WHAT...?
WHAT'S HAPPENED TO ME...?!
AAH!
PAIRON HAS REGAINED CONSCIOUS-NESS!!
PAIRON...?
GASP!
THAT'S RIGHT, I'M...
...LI PAIRON. I MAKE MOVIES.
20TH ANNIVERSARY FILM FESTIVAL
PAIRON FISTS OF RAGE
IS THIS SOME KIND OF JOKE?
WHERE HAVE I BEEN...
20TH ANNIVERSARY FILM FESTIVAL
PAIRON FISTS OF RAGE
...FOR THE LAST...
...TWENTY YEARS?!

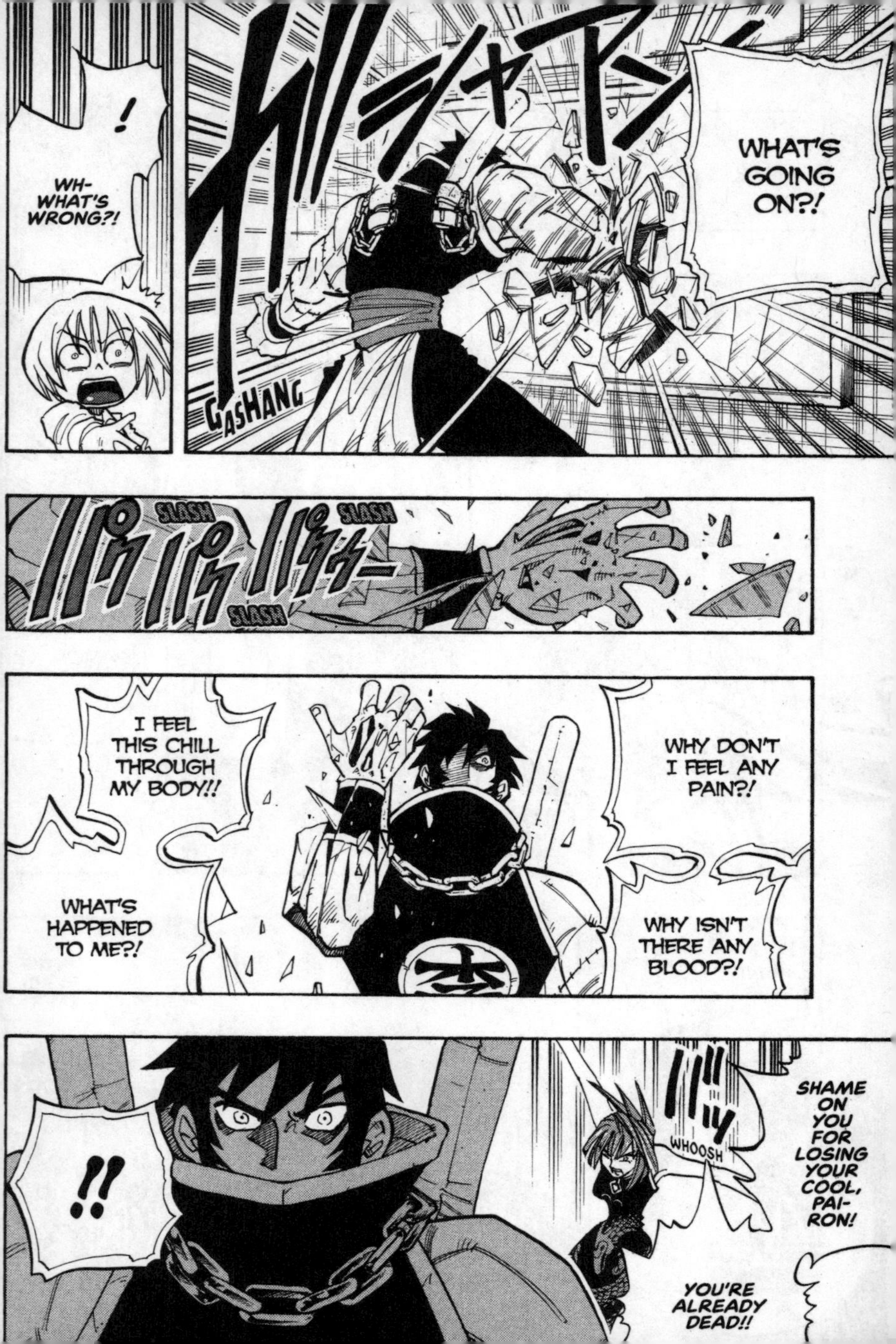
WHAT'S GOING ON?!
GASHANG
!
WH-WHAT'S WRONG?!
SLASH
SLASH
SLASH
WHY DON'T I FEEL ANY PAIN?!
I FEEL THIS CHILL THROUGH MY BODY!!
WHY ISN'T THERE ANY BLOOD?!
WHAT'S HAPPENED TO ME?!
SHAME ON YOU FOR LOSING YOUR COOL, PAI-RON!
WHOOSH
YOU'RE ALREADY DEAD!!
!!

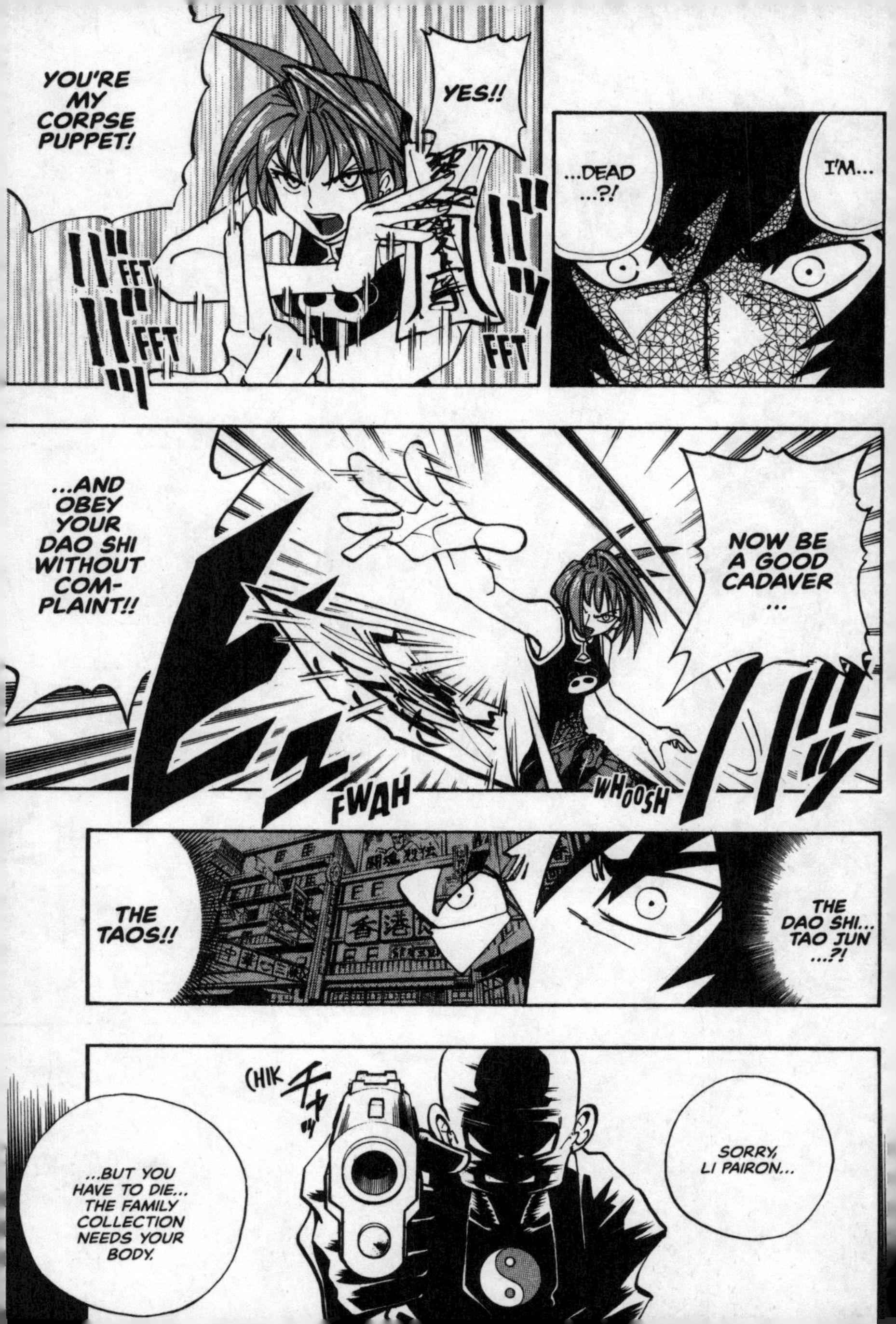
I'M...
...DEAD ...?!
YES!!
YOU'RE MY CORPSE PUPPET!
FFT
FFT
FFT
NOW BE A GOOD CADAVER ...
...AND OBEY YOUR DAO SHI WITHOUT COM-PLAINT!!
WHOOSH
FWAH
THE DAO SHI... TAO JUN ...?!
THE TAOS!!
SORRY, LI PAIRON...
CHIK
...BUT YOU HAVE TO DIE... THE FAMILY COLLECTION NEEDS YOUR BODY.

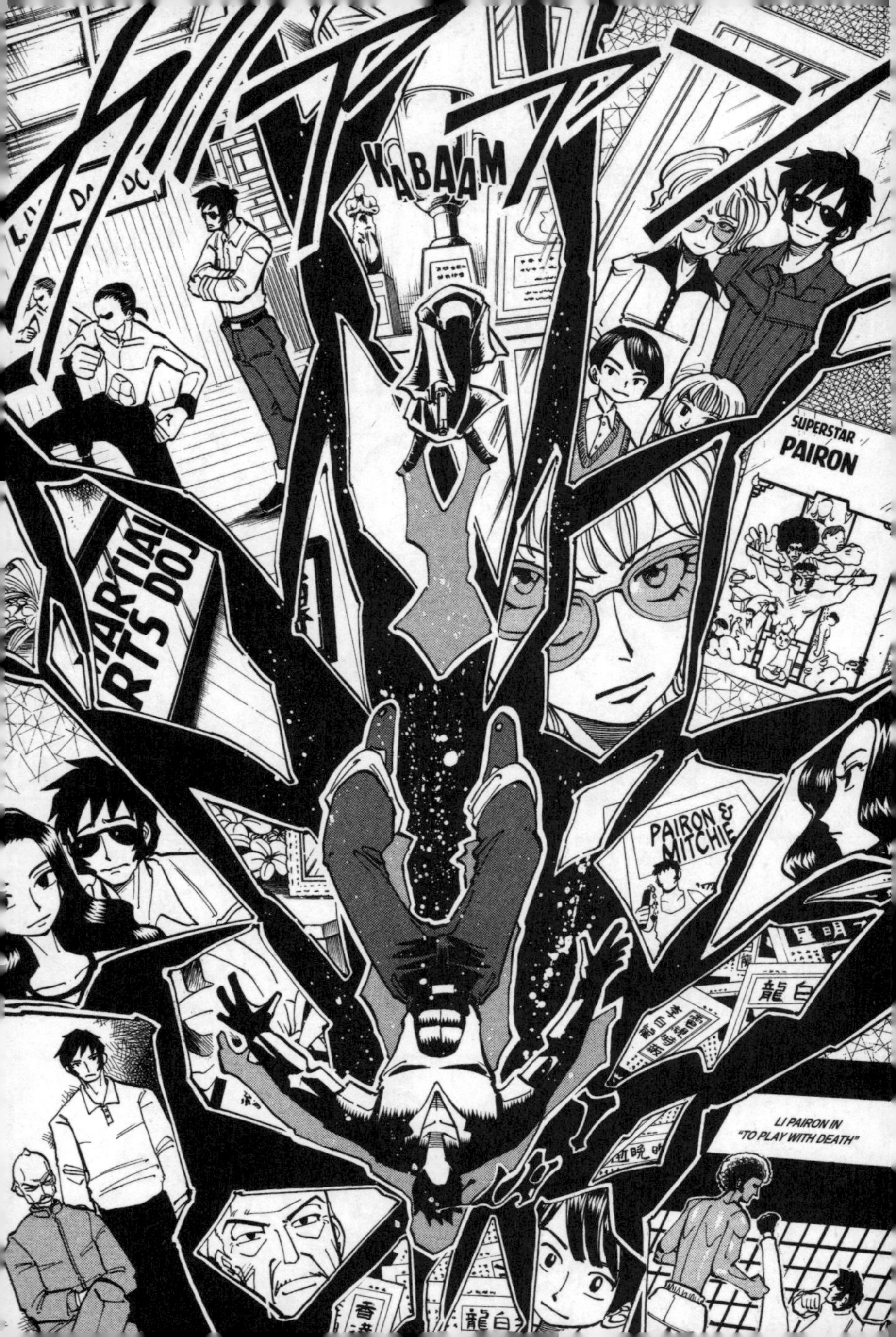
KABAAM
SUPERSTAR
PAIRON
ARTIAL
RTS DOJ
PAIRON &
MITCHIE
LI PAIRON IN
"TO PLAY WITH DEATH"

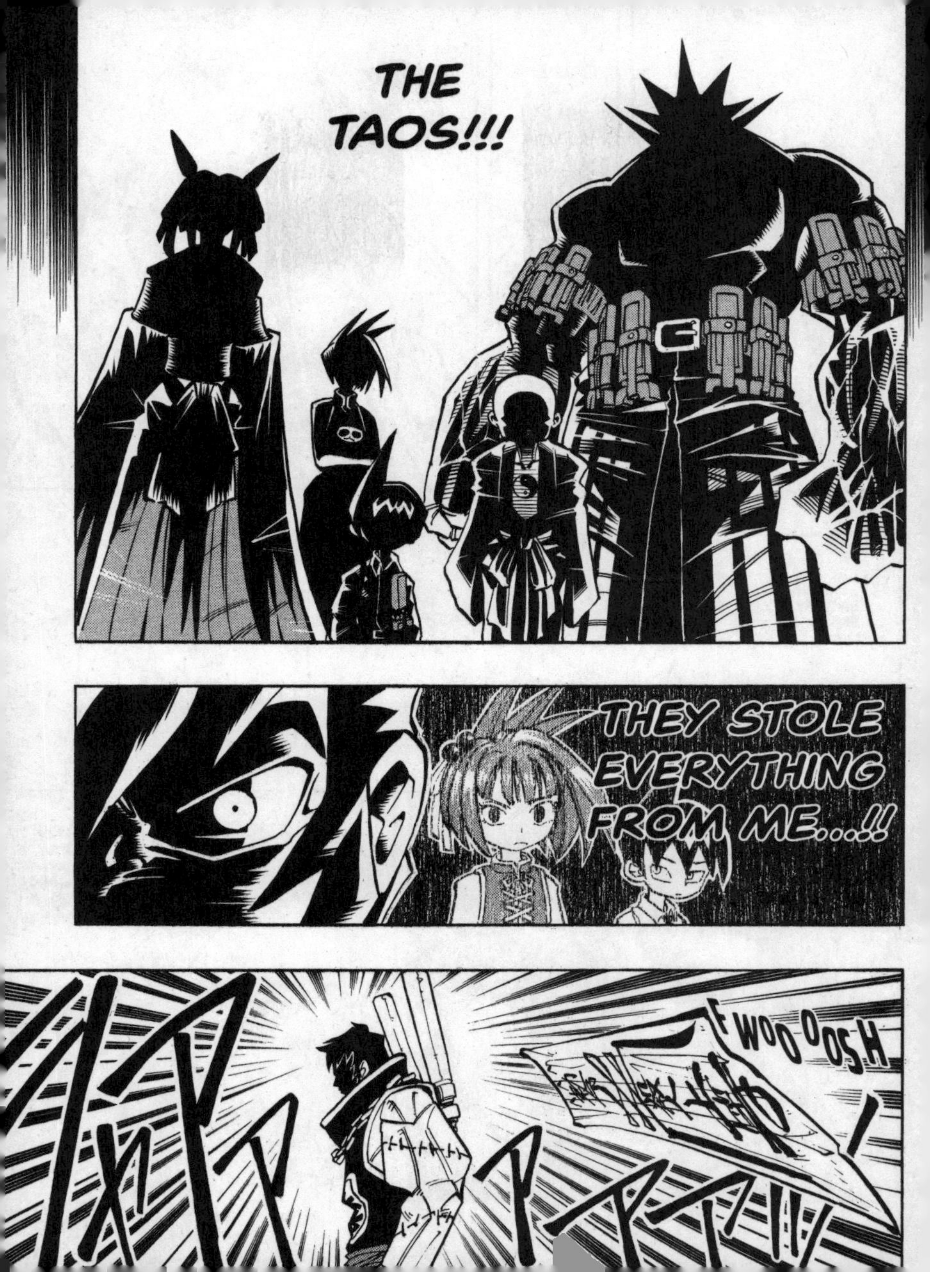
THE TAOS!!!
THEY STOLE EVERYTHING FROM ME...!!
WOO OOSH

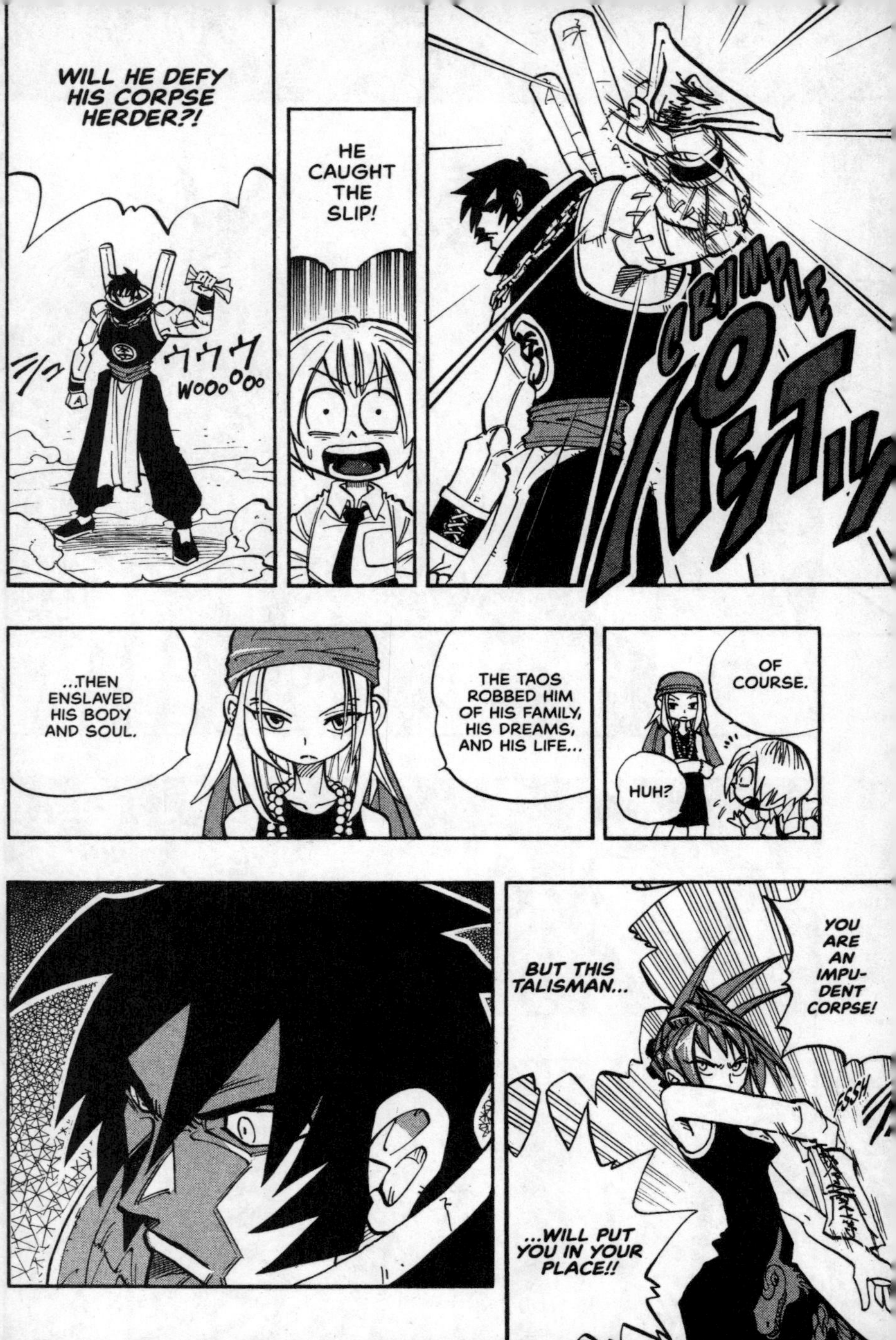
CRUMPLE
HE CAUGHT THE SLIP!
WILL HE DEFY HIS CORPSE HERDER?!
ウウウ
WOOOOOO
OF COURSE.
HUH?
THE TAOS ROBBED HIM OF HIS FAMILY, HIS DREAMS, AND HIS LIFE...
...THEN ENSLAVED HIS BODY AND SOUL.
YOU ARE AN IMPUDENT CORPSE!
BUT THIS TALISMAN...
FSSH
...WILL PUT YOU IN YOUR PLACE!!

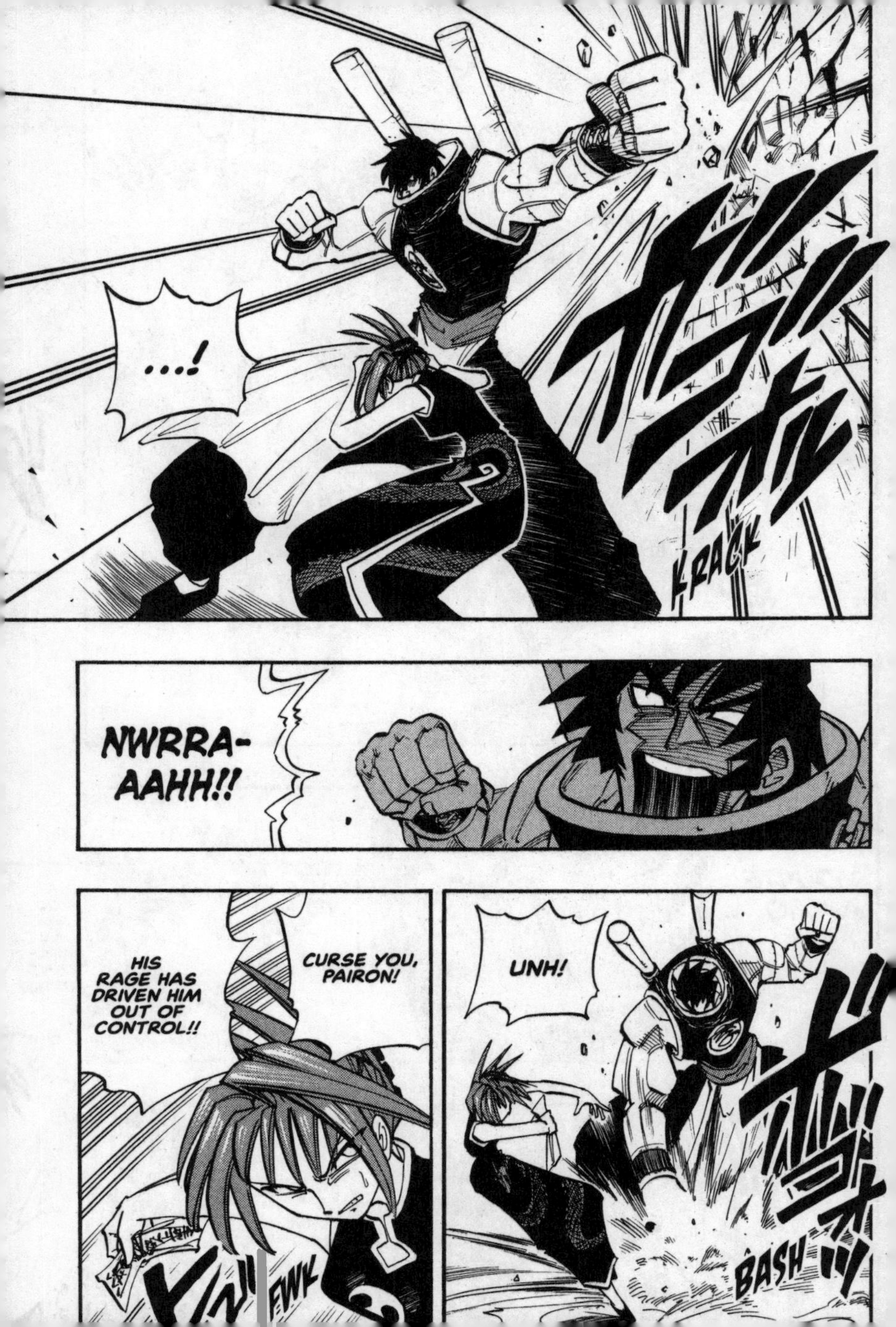
...!
KRACK
NWRRA-AAHH!!
UNH!
BASH
CURSE YOU, PAIRON!
HIS RAGE HAS DRIVEN HIM OUT OF CONTROL!!
FWK

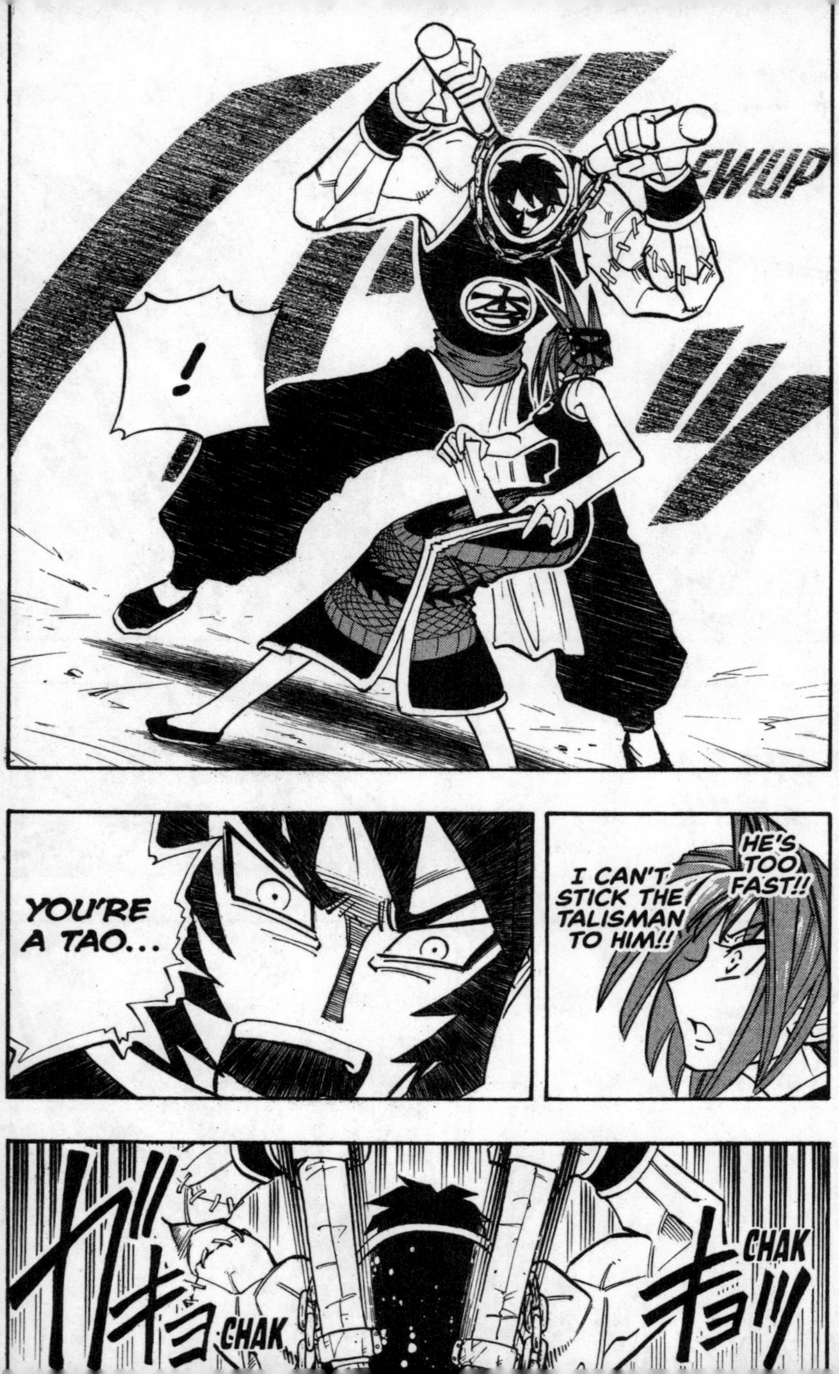
!
FWUP
HE'S TOO FAST!!
I CAN'T STICK THE TALISMAN TO HIM!!
YOU'RE A TAO...
CHAK
CHAK

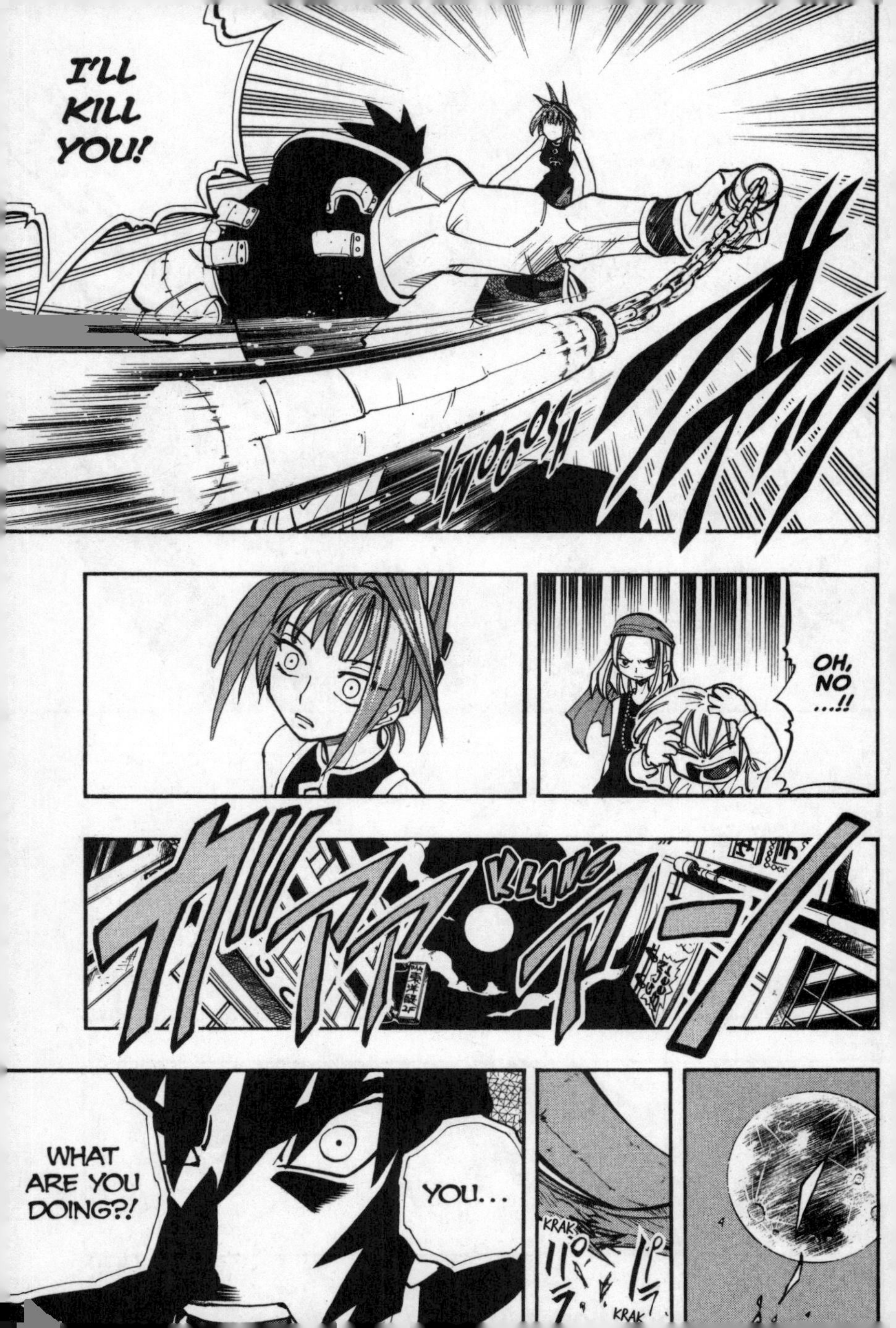
I'LL KILL YOU!
WOOOSH
OH, NO ...!!
KLANG
KRAK
KRAK
YOU...
WHAT ARE YOU DOING?!

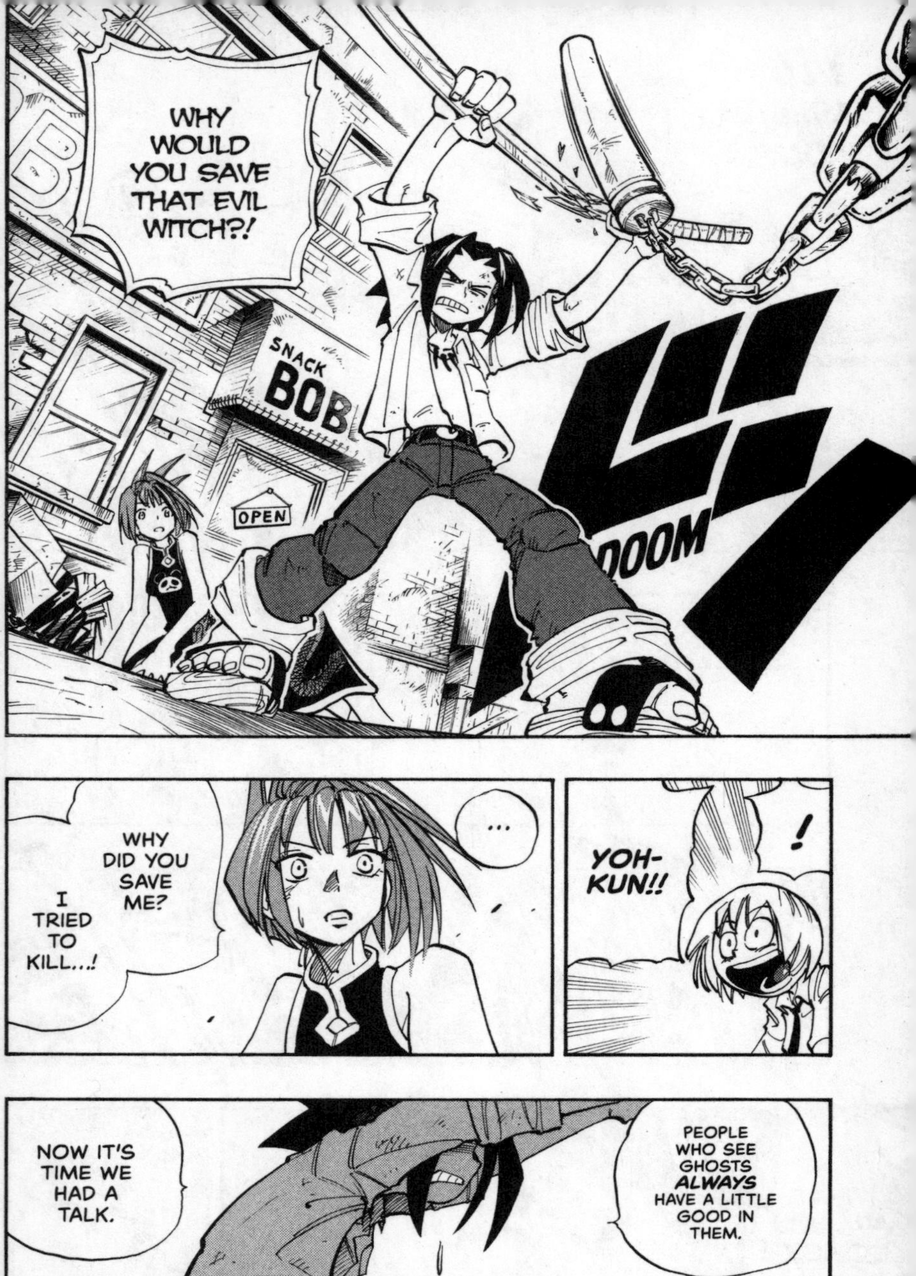
WHY WOULD YOU SAVE THAT EVIL WITCH?!
SNACK BOB
OPEN
DOOM
!
YOH-KUN!!
...
WHY DID YOU SAVE ME?
I TRIED TO KILL...!
PEOPLE WHO SEE GHOSTS **ALWAYS** HAVE A LITTLE GOOD IN THEM.
NOW IT'S TIME WE HAD A TALK.

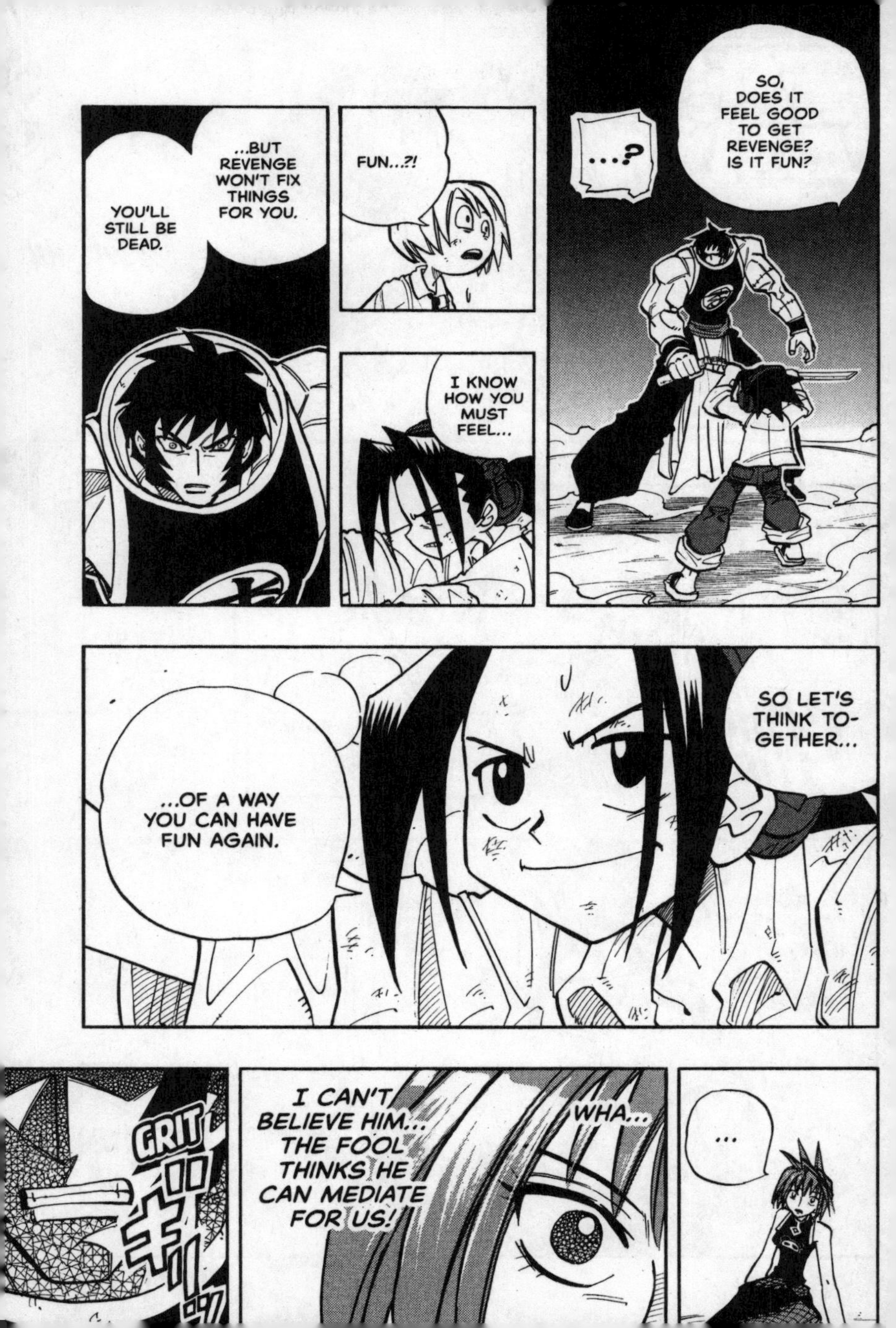
SO, DOES IT FEEL GOOD TO GET REVENGE? IS IT FUN?
...?
FUN...?!
I KNOW HOW YOU MUST FEEL...
...BUT REVENGE WON'T FIX THINGS FOR YOU.
YOU'LL STILL BE DEAD.
SO LET'S THINK TO-GETHER...
...OF A WAY YOU CAN HAVE FUN AGAIN.
...
WHA...
I CAN'T BELIEVE HIM... THE FOOL THINKS HE CAN MEDIATE FOR US!
GRIT

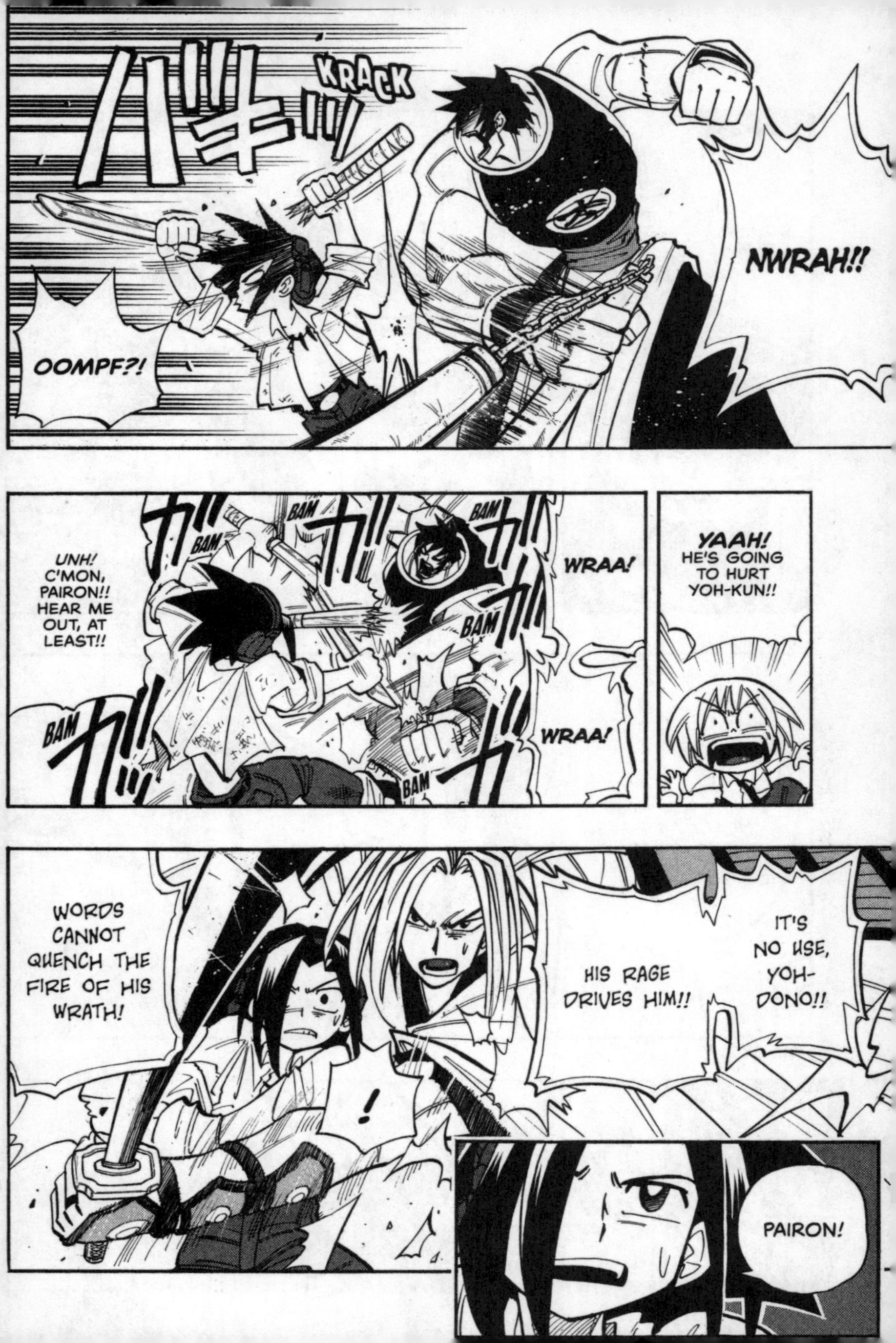
NWRAH!!
KRACK
OOMPF?!
YAAH! HE'S GOING TO HURT YOH-KUN!!
WRAA!
BAM
BAM
BAM
UNH! C'MON, PAIRON!! HEAR ME OUT, AT LEAST!!
BAM
WRAA!
BAM
BAM
IT'S NO USE, YOH-DONO!!
HIS RAGE DRIVES HIM!!
WORDS CANNOT QUENCH THE FIRE OF HIS WRATH!
!
PAIRON!

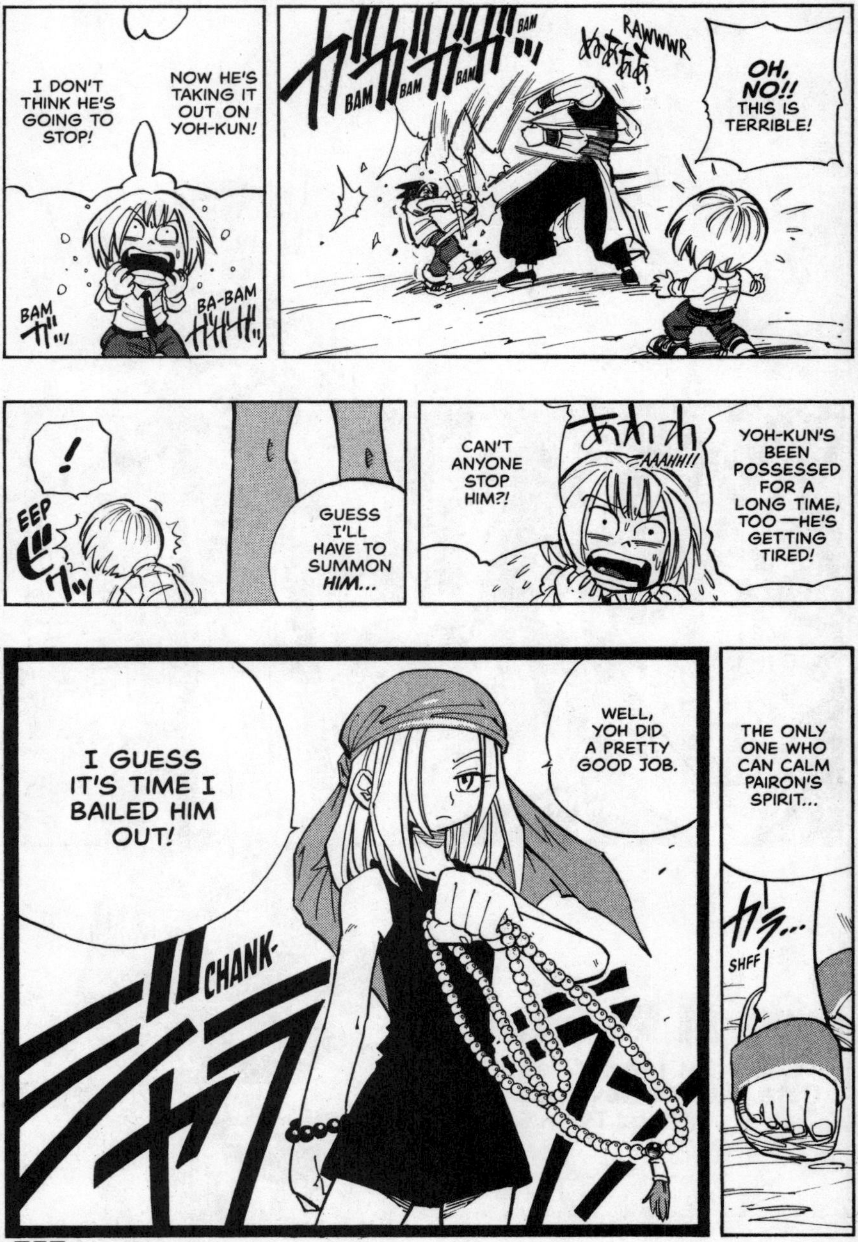
RAWWWR
BAM
BAM
BAM
BAM
OH, NO!! THIS IS TERRIBLE!
NOW HE'S TAKING IT OUT ON YOH-KUN!
I DON'T THINK HE'S GOING TO STOP!
BAM
BA-BAM
YOH-KUN'S BEEN POSSESSED FOR A LONG TIME, TOO—HE'S GETTING TIRED!
AAAHH!!
CAN'T ANYONE STOP HIM?!
GUESS I'LL HAVE TO SUMMON HIM...
!
EEP
THE ONLY ONE WHO CAN CALM PAIRON'S SPIRIT...
SHFF
WELL, YOH DID A PRETTY GOOD JOB.
I GUESS IT'S TIME I BAILED HIM OUT!
CHANK

SHAMAN KING CHARACTER FILE No.8

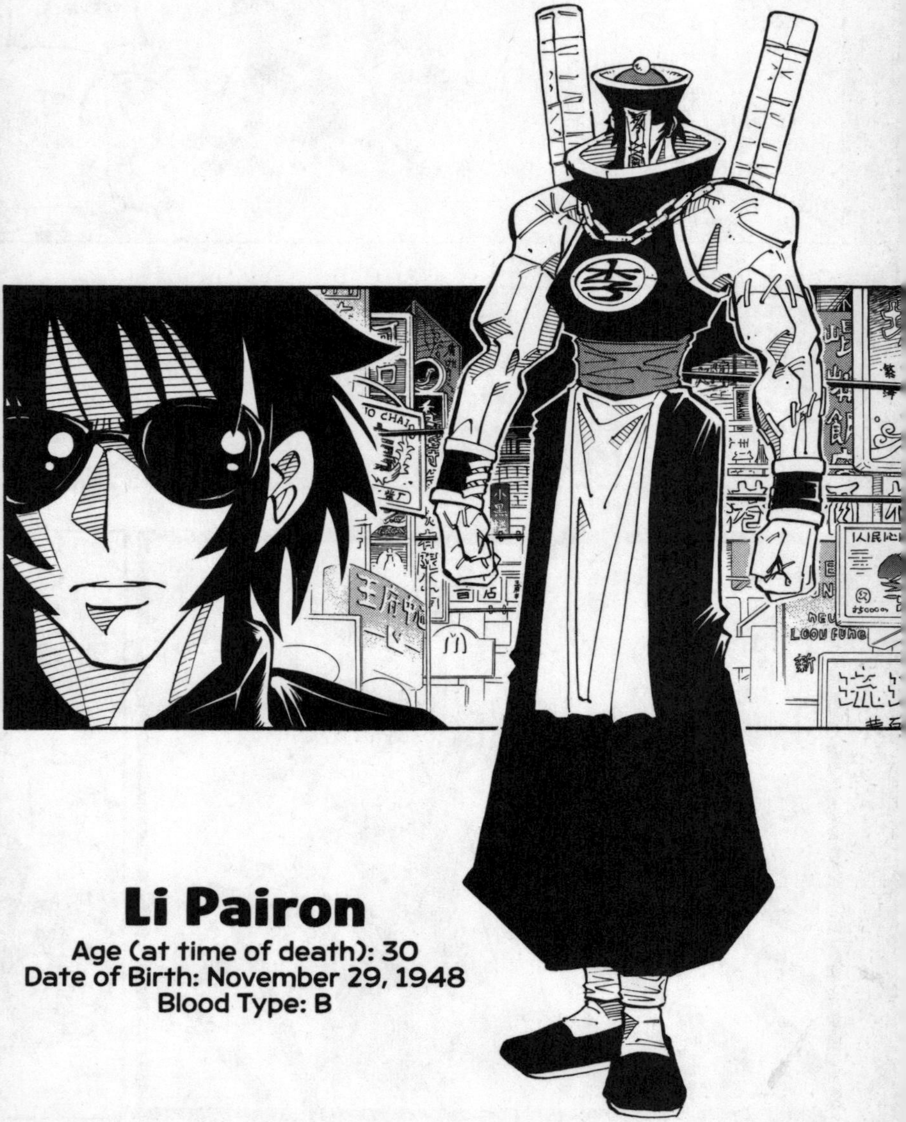

Li Pairon

Age (at time of death): 30
Date of Birth: November 29, 1948
Blood Type: B

Chapter 16:

Raising the Dead

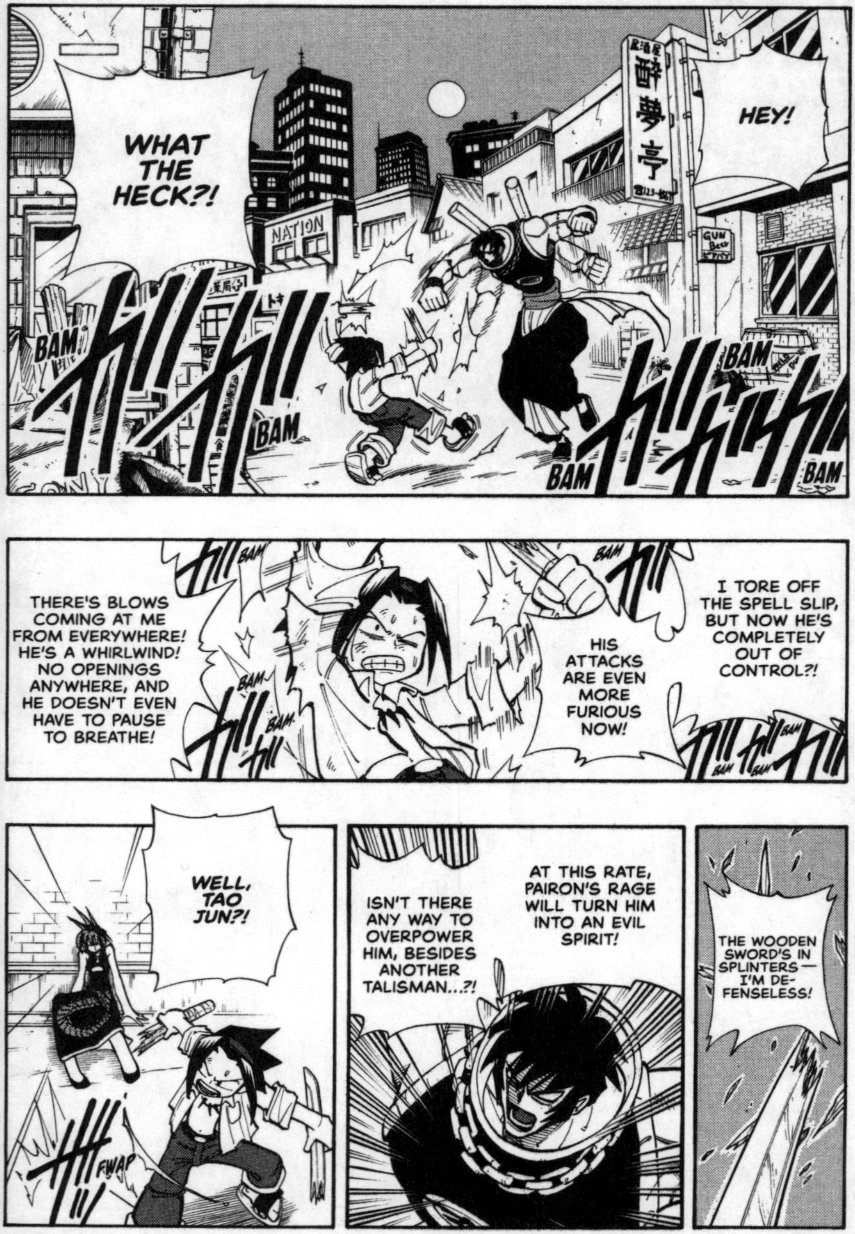
HEY!
WHAT THE HECK?!
BAM
BAM
BAM
BAM
BAM
I TORE OFF THE SPELL SLIP, BUT NOW HE'S COMPLETELY OUT OF CONTROL?!
HIS ATTACKS ARE EVEN MORE FURIOUS NOW!
THERE'S BLOWS COMING AT ME FROM EVERYWHERE! HE'S A WHIRLWIND! NO OPENINGS ANYWHERE, AND HE DOESN'T EVEN HAVE TO PAUSE TO BREATHE!
THE WOODEN SWORD'S IN SPLINTERS— I'M DEFENSELESS!
AT THIS RATE, PAIRON'S RAGE WILL TURN HIM INTO AN EVIL SPIRIT!
ISN'T THERE ANY WAY TO OVERPOWER HIM, BESIDES ANOTHER TALISMAN...?!
WELL, TAO JUN?!
FWAP

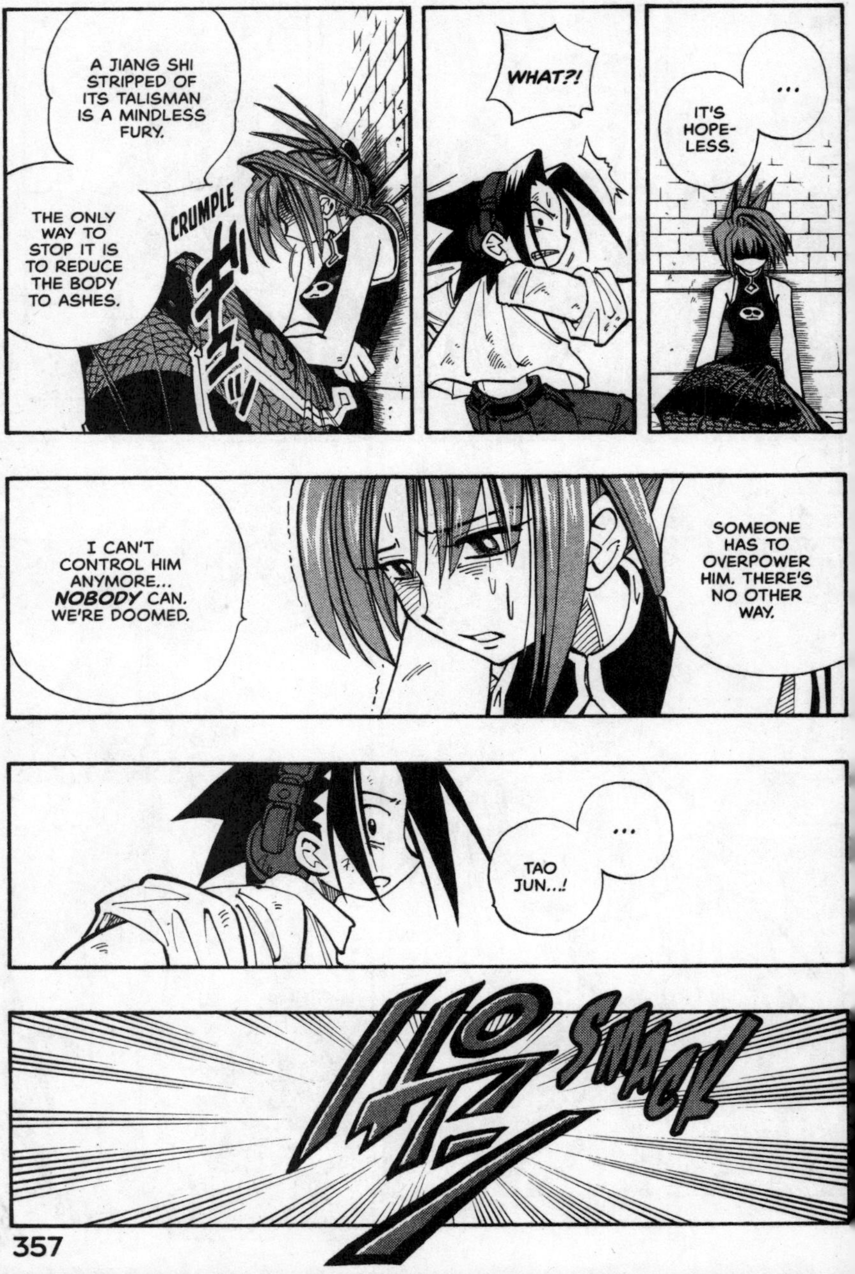
...
IT'S HOPE-LESS.
WHAT?!
A JIANG SHI STRIPPED OF ITS TALISMAN IS A MINDLESS FURY.
THE ONLY WAY TO STOP IT IS TO REDUCE THE BODY TO ASHES.
CRUMPLE
SOMEONE HAS TO OVERPOWER HIM. THERE'S NO OTHER WAY.
I CAN'T CONTROL HIM ANYMORE... ***NOBODY*** CAN. WE'RE DOOMED.
...
TAO JUN...!
SMACK

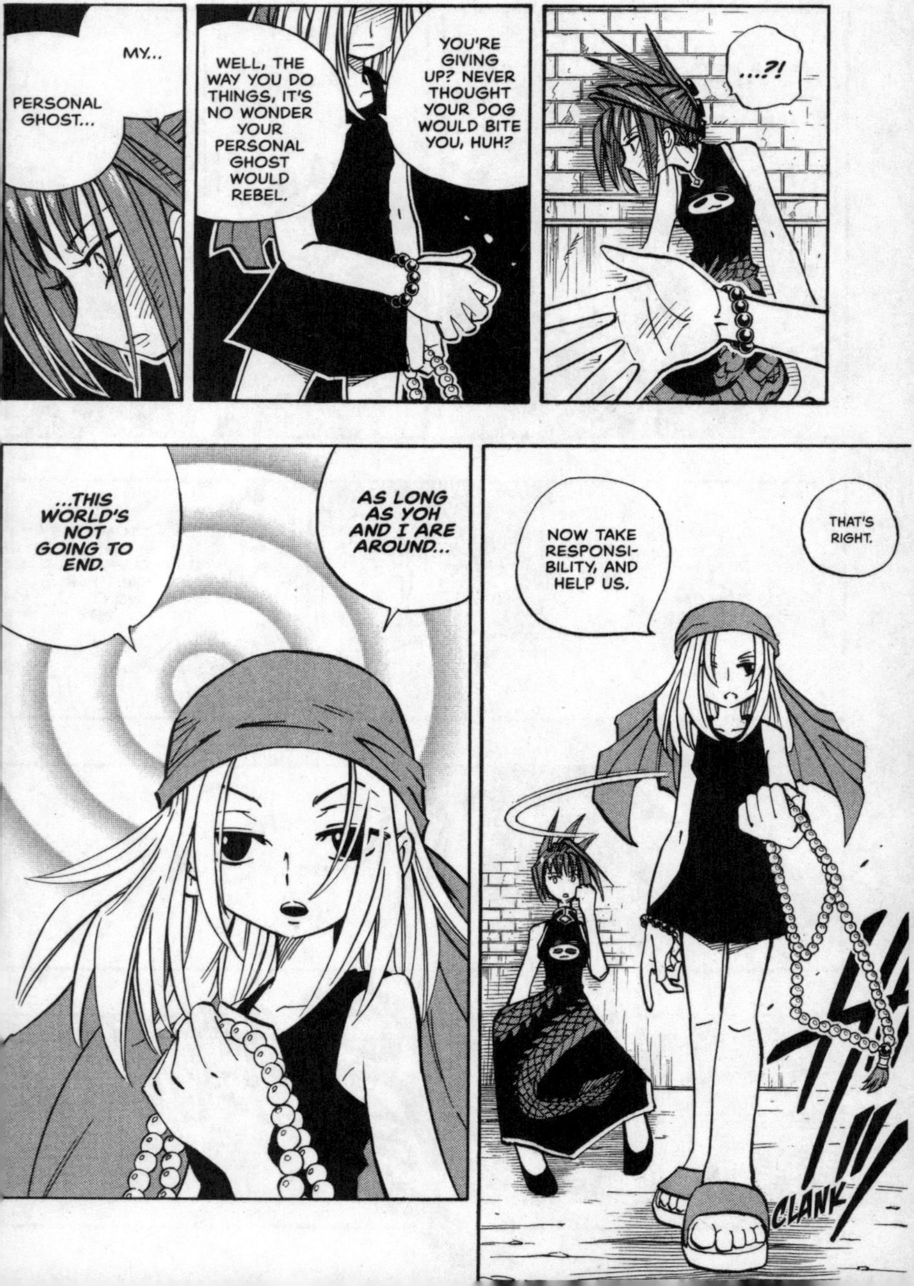
...?!
YOU'RE GIVING UP? NEVER THOUGHT YOUR DOG WOULD BITE YOU, HUH?
WELL, THE WAY YOU DO THINGS, IT'S NO WONDER YOUR PERSONAL GHOST WOULD REBEL.
MY...
PERSONAL GHOST...
THAT'S RIGHT.
NOW TAKE RESPONSIBILITY, AND HELP US.
CLANK
AS LONG AS YOH AND I ARE AROUND...
...THIS WORLD'S NOT GOING TO END.

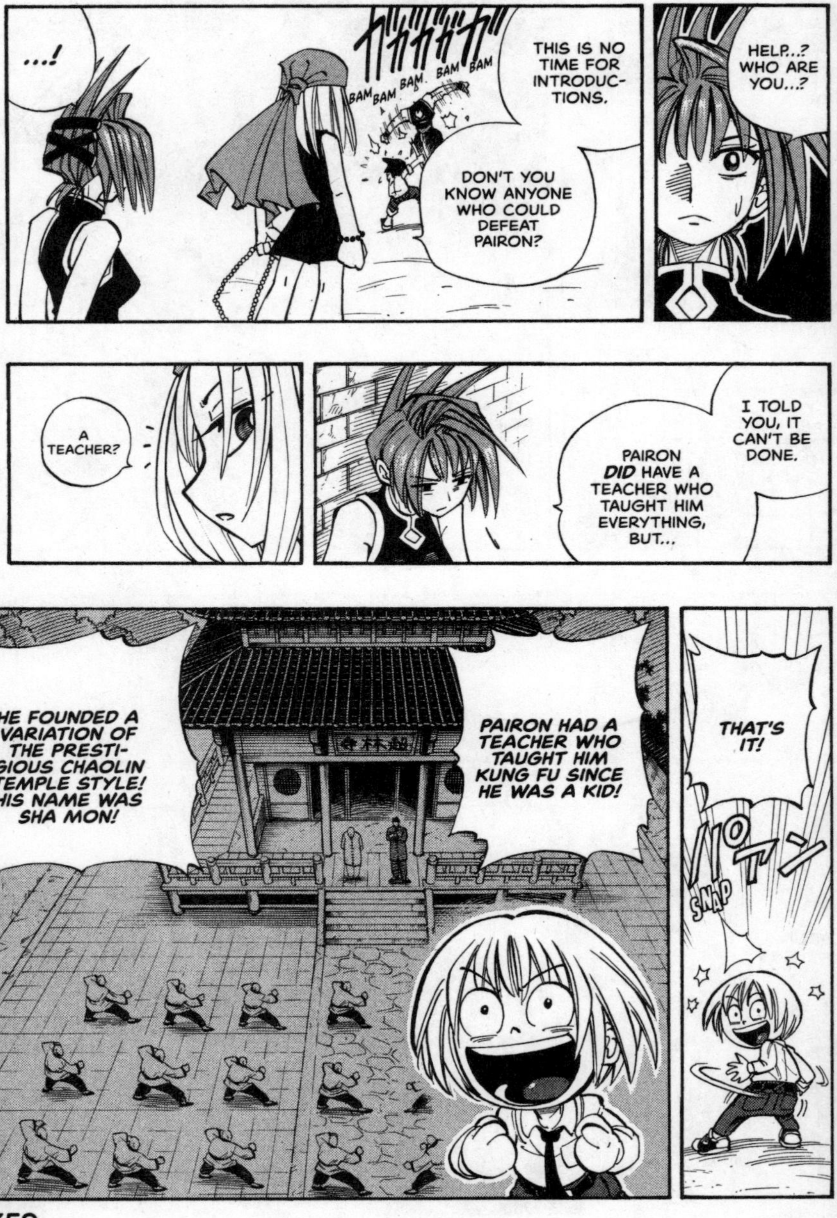
HELP...? WHO ARE YOU...?
THIS IS NO TIME FOR INTRODUCTIONS.
DON'T YOU KNOW ANYONE WHO COULD DEFEAT PAIRON?
BAM BAM BAM BAM BAM
...!
I TOLD YOU, IT CAN'T BE DONE.
PAIRON DID HAVE A TEACHER WHO TAUGHT HIM EVERYTHING, BUT...
A TEACHER?
THAT'S IT!
SNAP
PAIRON HAD A TEACHER WHO TAUGHT HIM KUNG FU SINCE HE WAS A KID!
HE FOUNDED A VARIATION OF THE PRESTIGIOUS CHAOLIN TEMPLE STYLE! HIS NAME WAS SHA MON!

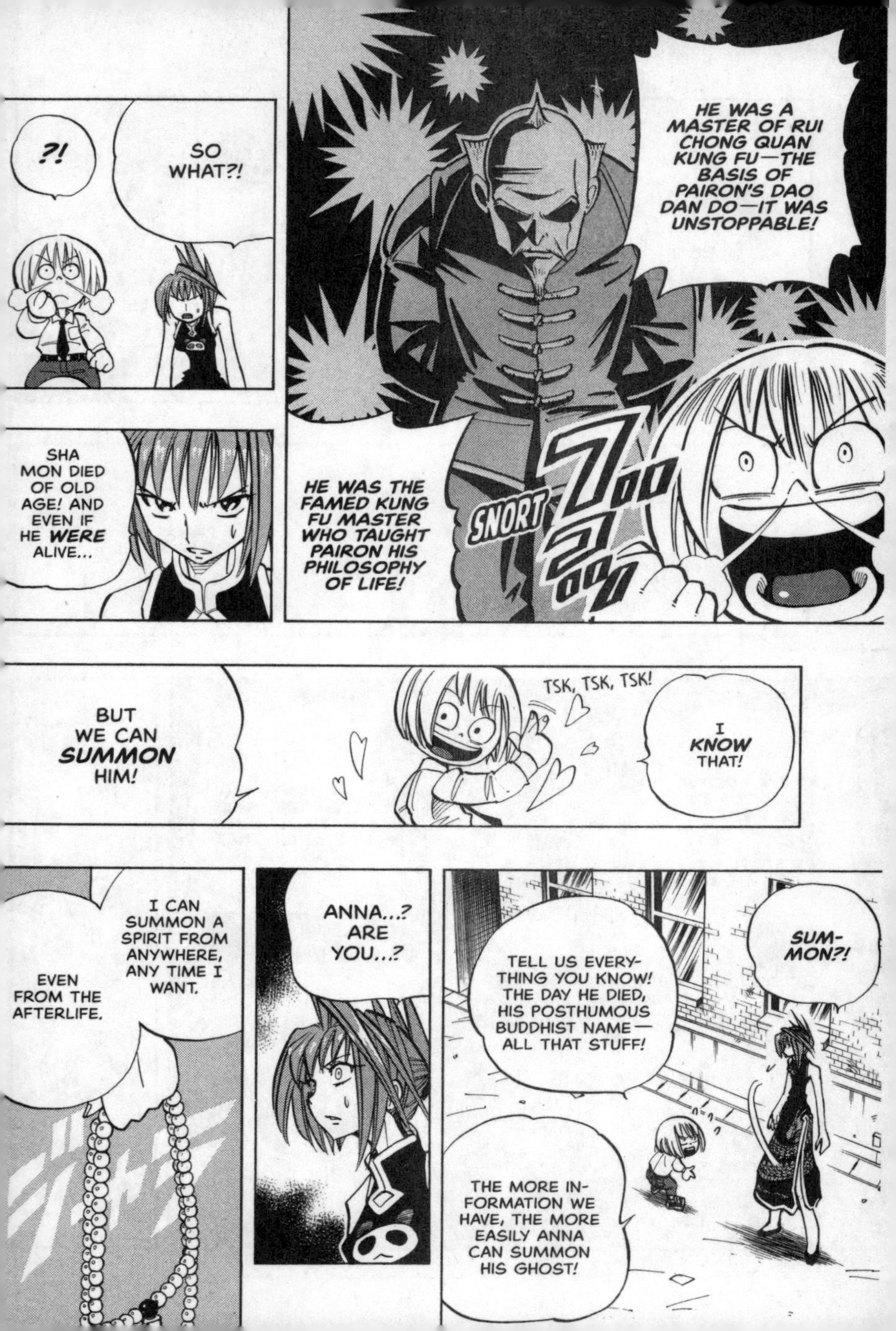
HE WAS A MASTER OF RUI CHONG QUAN KUNG FU—THE BASIS OF PAIRON'S DAO DAN DO—IT WAS UNSTOPPABLE!
SNORT
HE WAS THE FAMED KUNG FU MASTER WHO TAUGHT PAIRON HIS PHILOSOPHY OF LIFE!
SO WHAT?!
?!
SHA MON DIED OF OLD AGE! AND EVEN IF HE **WERE** ALIVE...
I **KNOW** THAT!
TSK, TSK, TSK!
BUT WE CAN **SUMMON** HIM!
SUM-MON?!
TELL US EVERYTHING YOU KNOW! THE DAY HE DIED, HIS POSTHUMOUS BUDDHIST NAME—ALL THAT STUFF!
THE MORE INFORMATION WE HAVE, THE MORE EASILY ANNA CAN SUMMON HIS GHOST!
ANNA...? ARE YOU...?
I CAN SUMMON A SPIRIT FROM ANYWHERE, ANY TIME I WANT.
EVEN FROM THE AFTERLIFE.

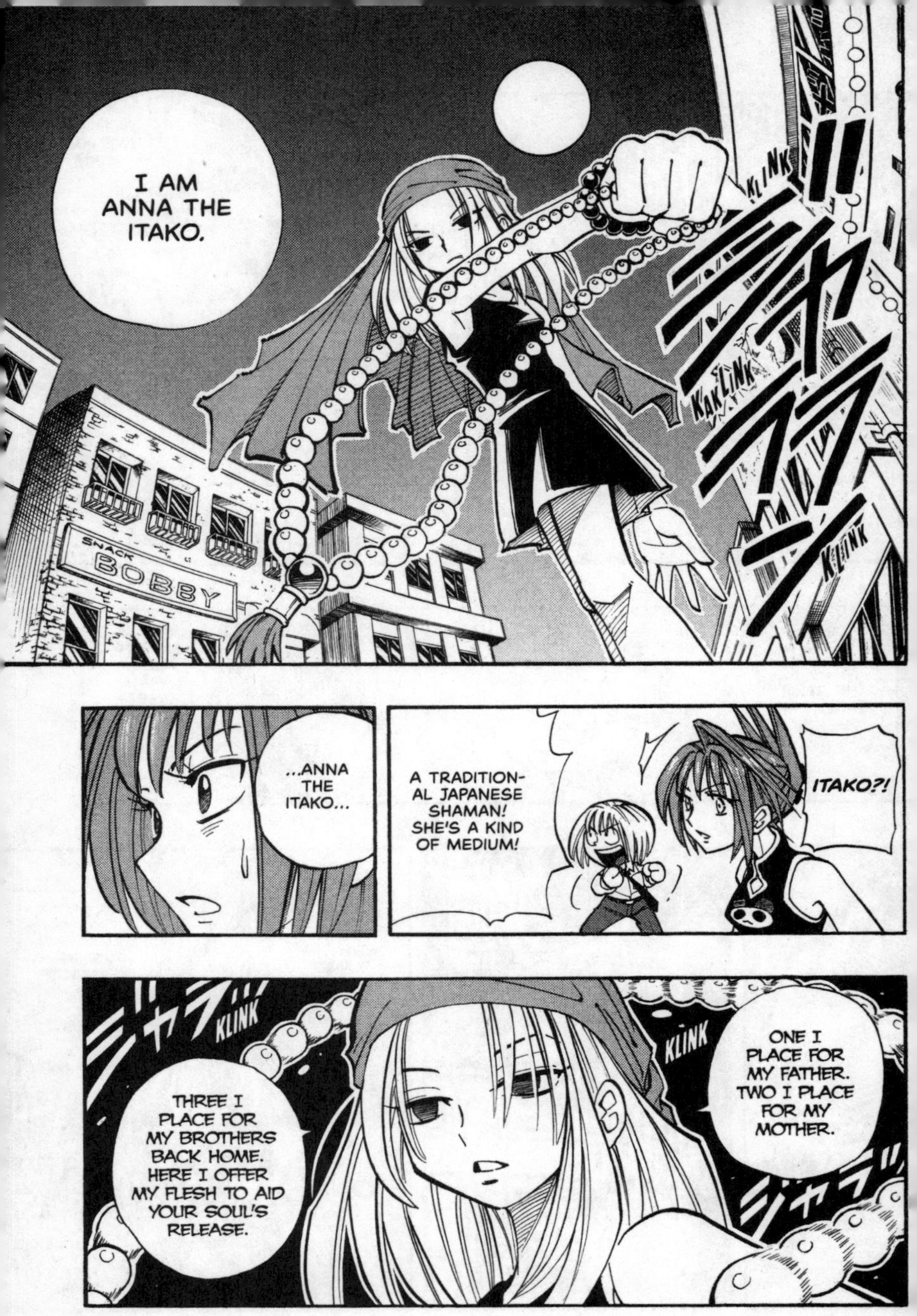
KLINK
KAK KLINK
KLINK
I AM ANNA THE ITAKO.
ITAKO?!
A TRADITION-AL JAPANESE SHAMAN! SHE'S A KIND OF MEDIUM!
...ANNA THE ITAKO...
ONE I PLACE FOR MY FATHER. TWO I PLACE FOR MY MOTHER.
KLINK
KLINK
THREE I PLACE FOR MY BROTHERS BACK HOME. HERE I OFFER MY FLESH TO AID YOUR SOUL'S RELEASE.

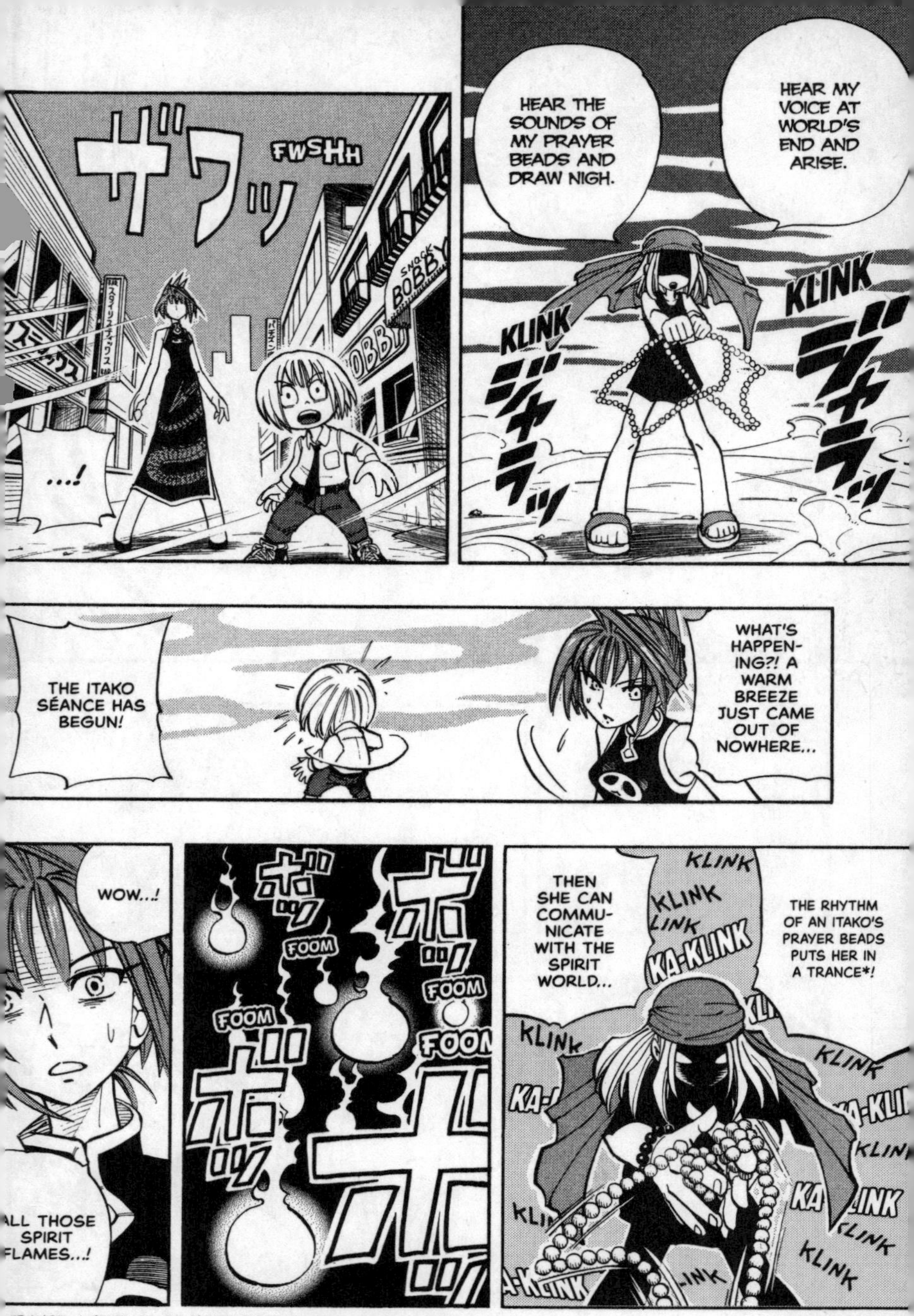
HEAR MY VOICE AT WORLD'S END AND ARISE.
HEAR THE SOUNDS OF MY PRAYER BEADS AND DRAW NIGH.
KLINK
KLINK
FWSHH
...!
WHAT'S HAPPENING?! A WARM BREEZE JUST CAME OUT OF NOWHERE...
THE ITAKO SÉANCE HAS BEGUN!
THE RHYTHM OF AN ITAKO'S PRAYER BEADS PUTS HER IN A TRANCE*!
THEN SHE CAN COMMUNICATE WITH THE SPIRIT WORLD...
KLINK
KLINK
KA-KLINK
FOOM
FOOM
FOOM
FOOM
WOW...!
ALL THOSE SPIRIT FLAMES...!

TRANCE: A STATE OF CONSCIOUSNESS WHICH ALLOWS COMMUNICATION WITH ANOTHER SPIRITUAL PLANE.

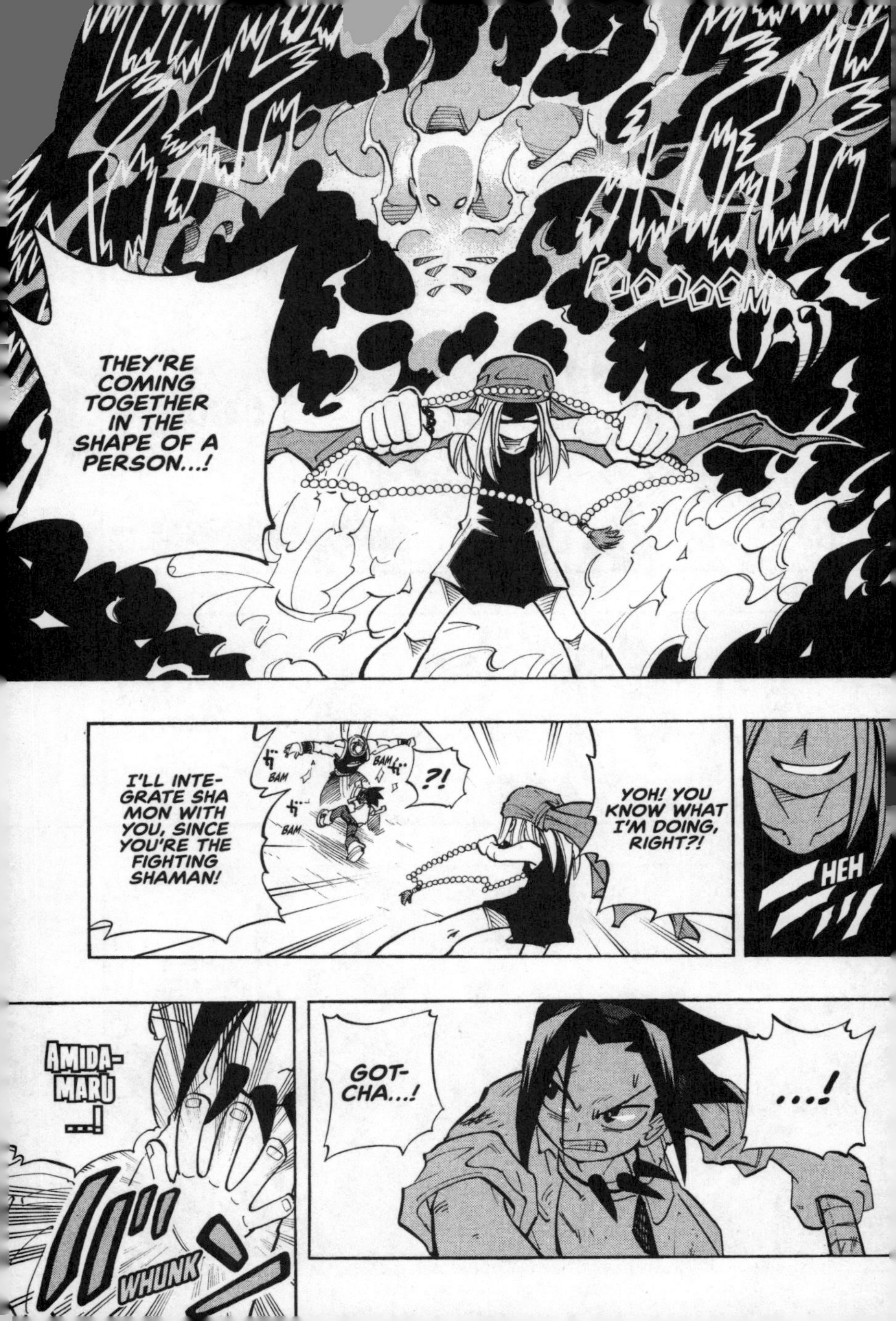
THEY'RE COMING TOGETHER IN THE SHAPE OF A PERSON...!
HEH
YOH! YOU KNOW WHAT I'M DOING, RIGHT?!
?!
I'LL INTE-GRATE SHA MON WITH YOU, SINCE YOU'RE THE FIGHTING SHAMAN!
BAM
BAM
BAM
...!
GOT-CHA...!
AMIDA-MARU ...!
WHUNK

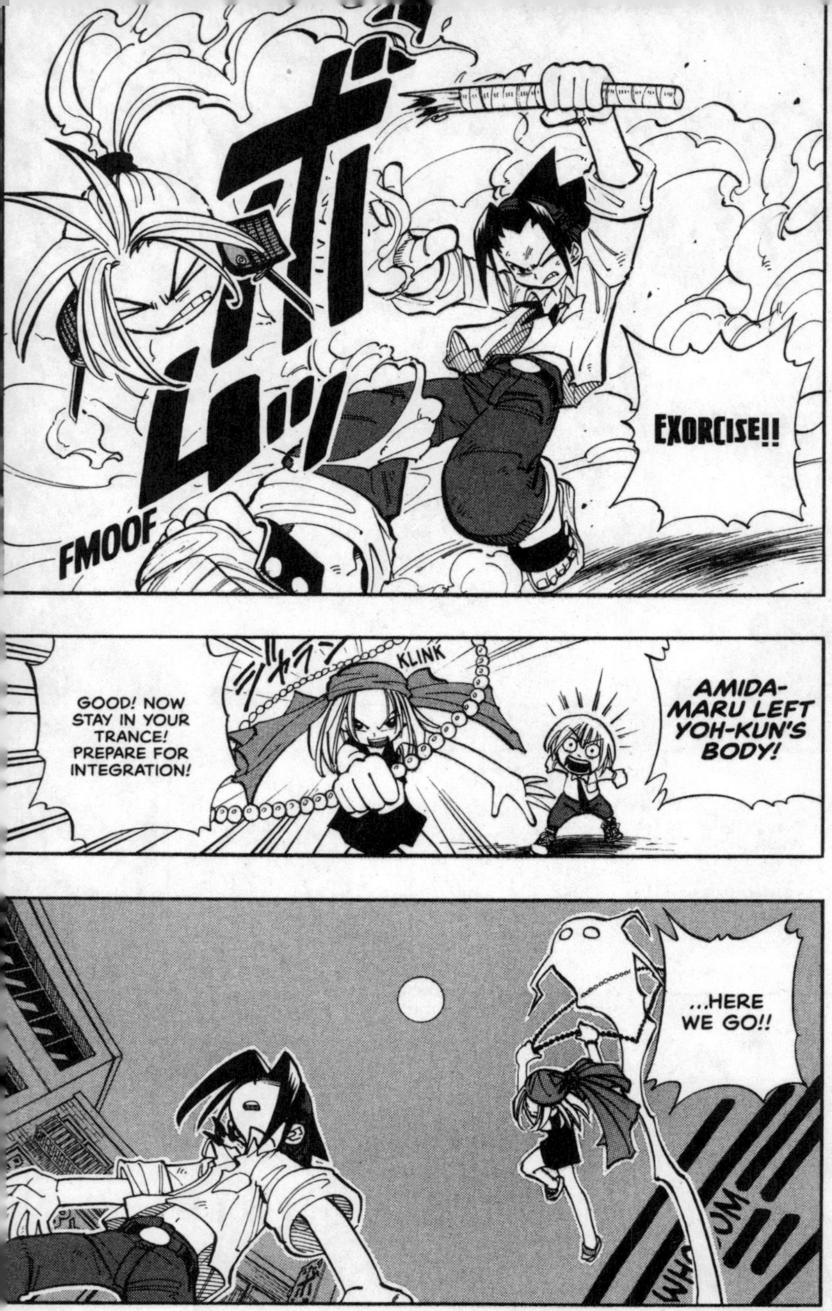
EXORCISE!!
FMOOF
AMIDA-MARU LEFT YOH-KUN'S BODY!
KLINK
GOOD! NOW STAY IN YOUR TRANCE! PREPARE FOR INTEGRATION!
...HERE WE GO!!

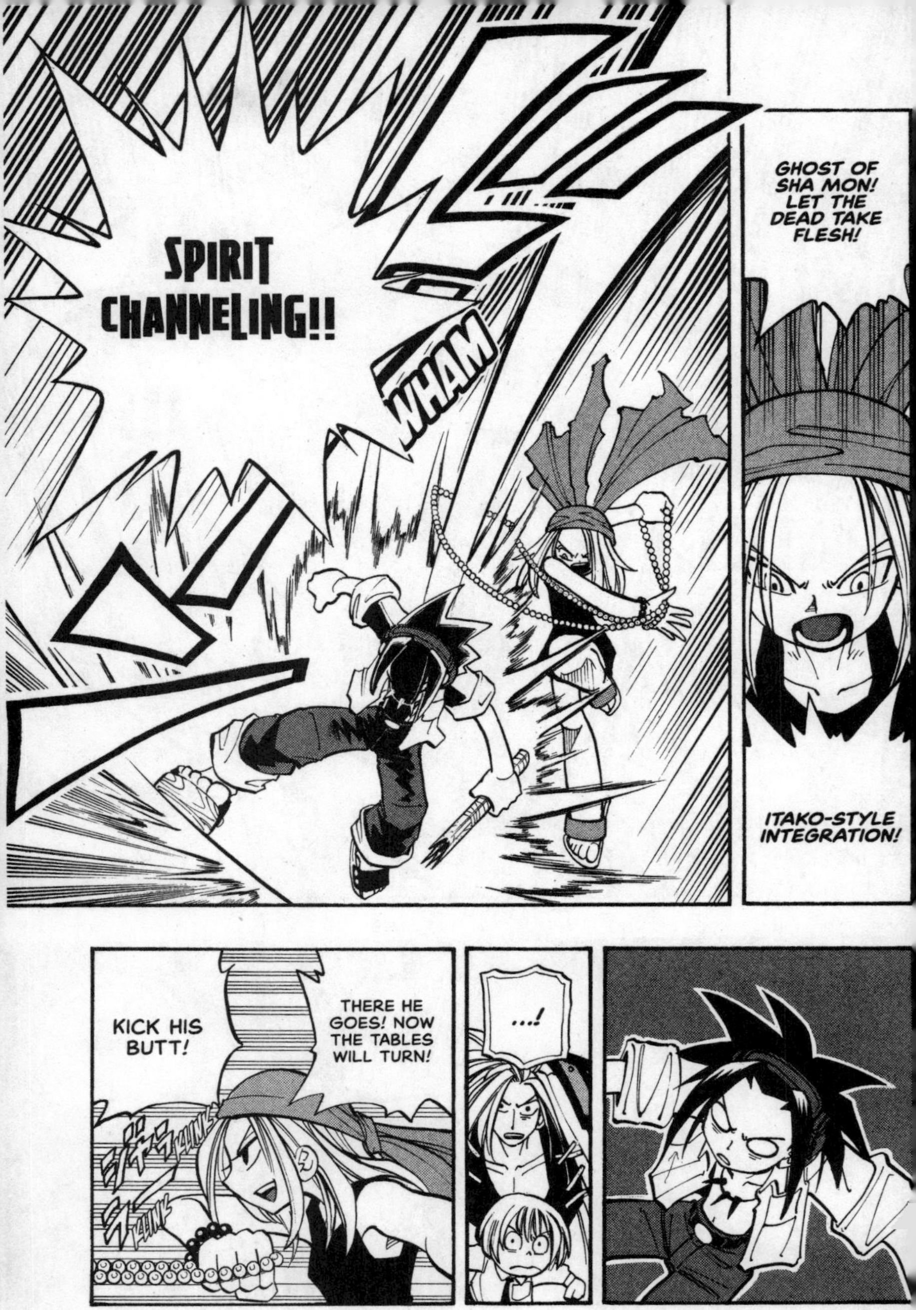
GHOST OF SHA MON! LET THE DEAD TAKE FLESH!
ITAKO-STYLE INTEGRATION!
SPIRIT CHANNELING!!
WHAM
...!
THERE HE GOES! NOW THE TABLES WILL TURN!
KICK HIS BUTT!

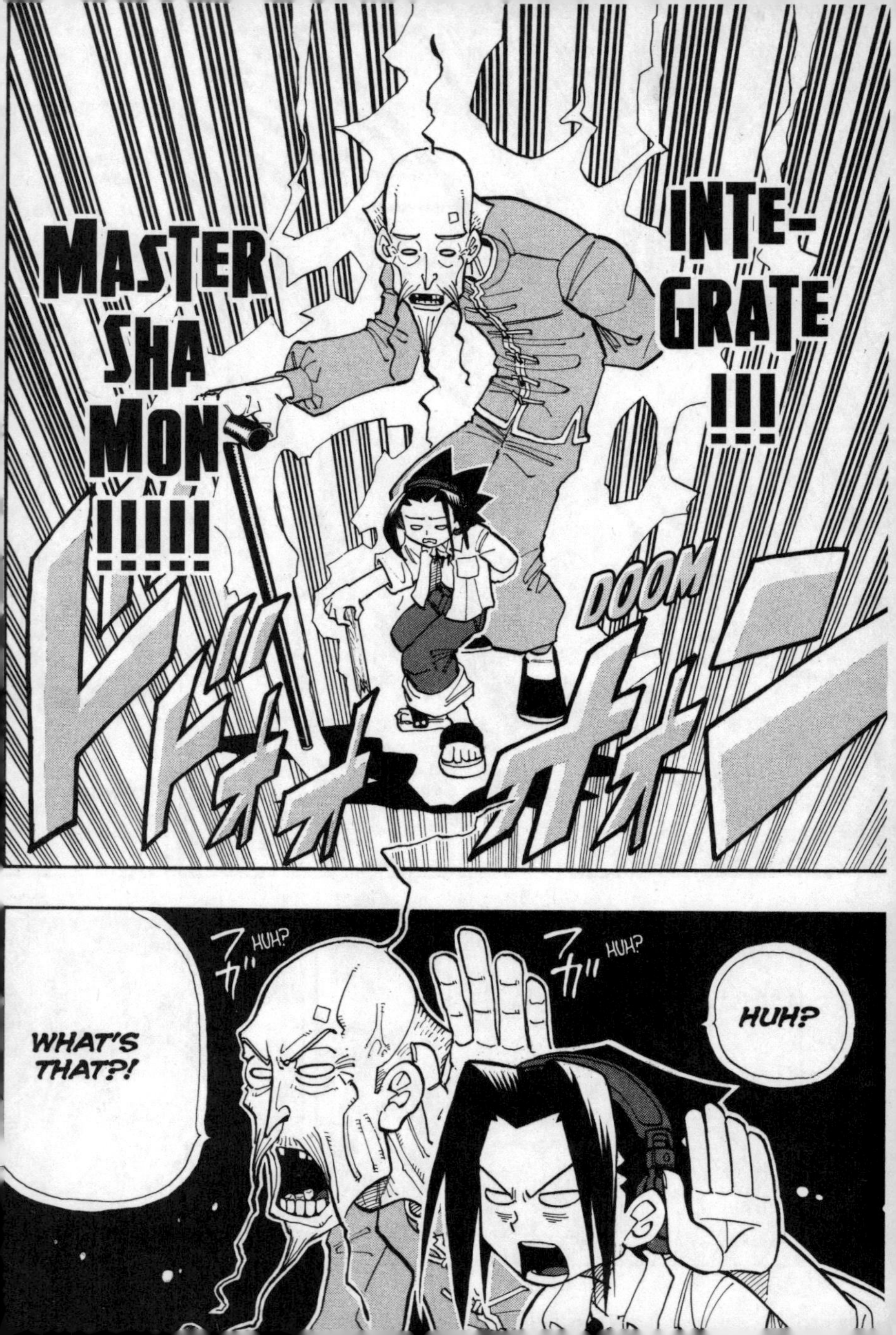
INTE-GRATE!!!
MASTER SHAMON!!!!!
DOOM
HUH?
HUH?
HUH?
WHAT'S THAT?!

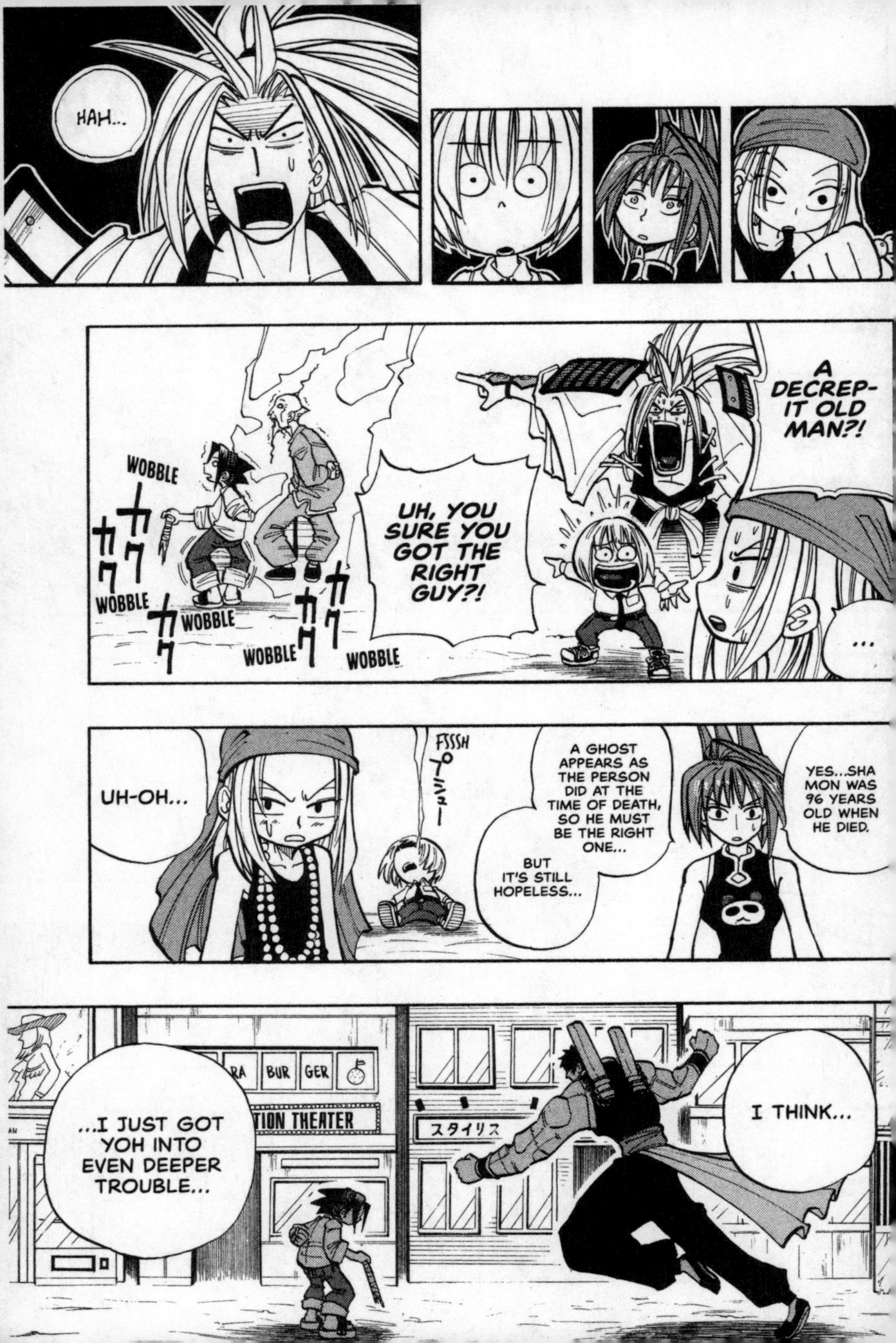
HAH...
A DECREP-IT OLD MAN?!
...
UH, YOU SURE YOU GOT THE RIGHT GUY?!
WOBBLE
カク
WOBBLE
カク
WOBBLE
カク
WOBBLE
カク
WOBBLE
YES...SHA MON WAS 96 YEARS OLD WHEN HE DIED.
A GHOST APPEARS AS THE PERSON DID AT THE TIME OF DEATH, SO HE MUST BE THE RIGHT ONE...
BUT IT'S STILL HOPELESS...
FSSSH
UH-OH...
I THINK...
スタイリス
RA BUR GER
TION THEATER
...I JUST GOT YOH INTO EVEN DEEPER TROUBLE...

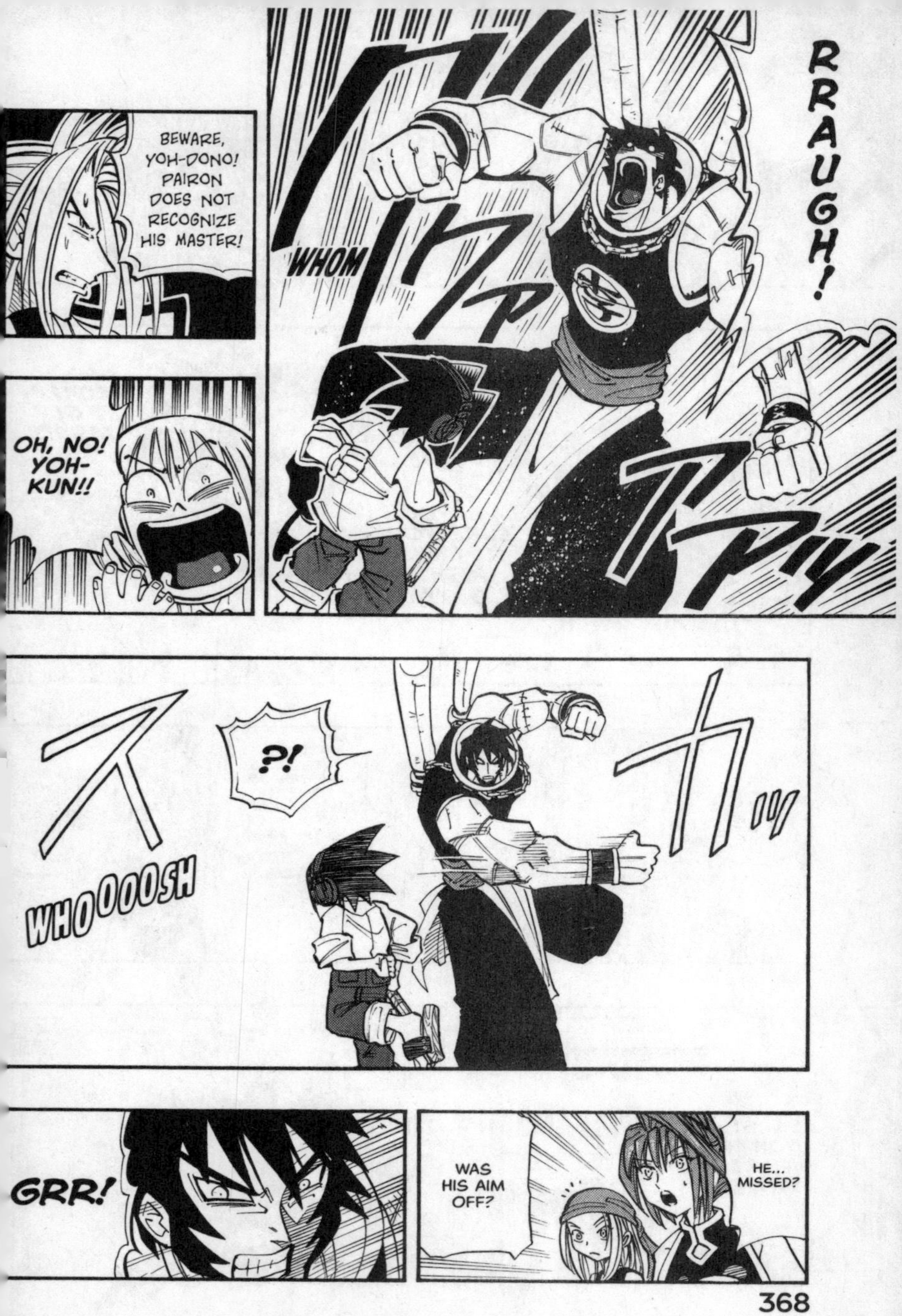
RRAUGH!
WHOM
BEWARE, YOH-DONO! PAIRON DOES NOT RECOGNIZE HIS MASTER!
OH, NO! YOH-KUN!!
?!
WHOOOOSH
HE... MISSED?
WAS HIS AIM OFF?
GRR!

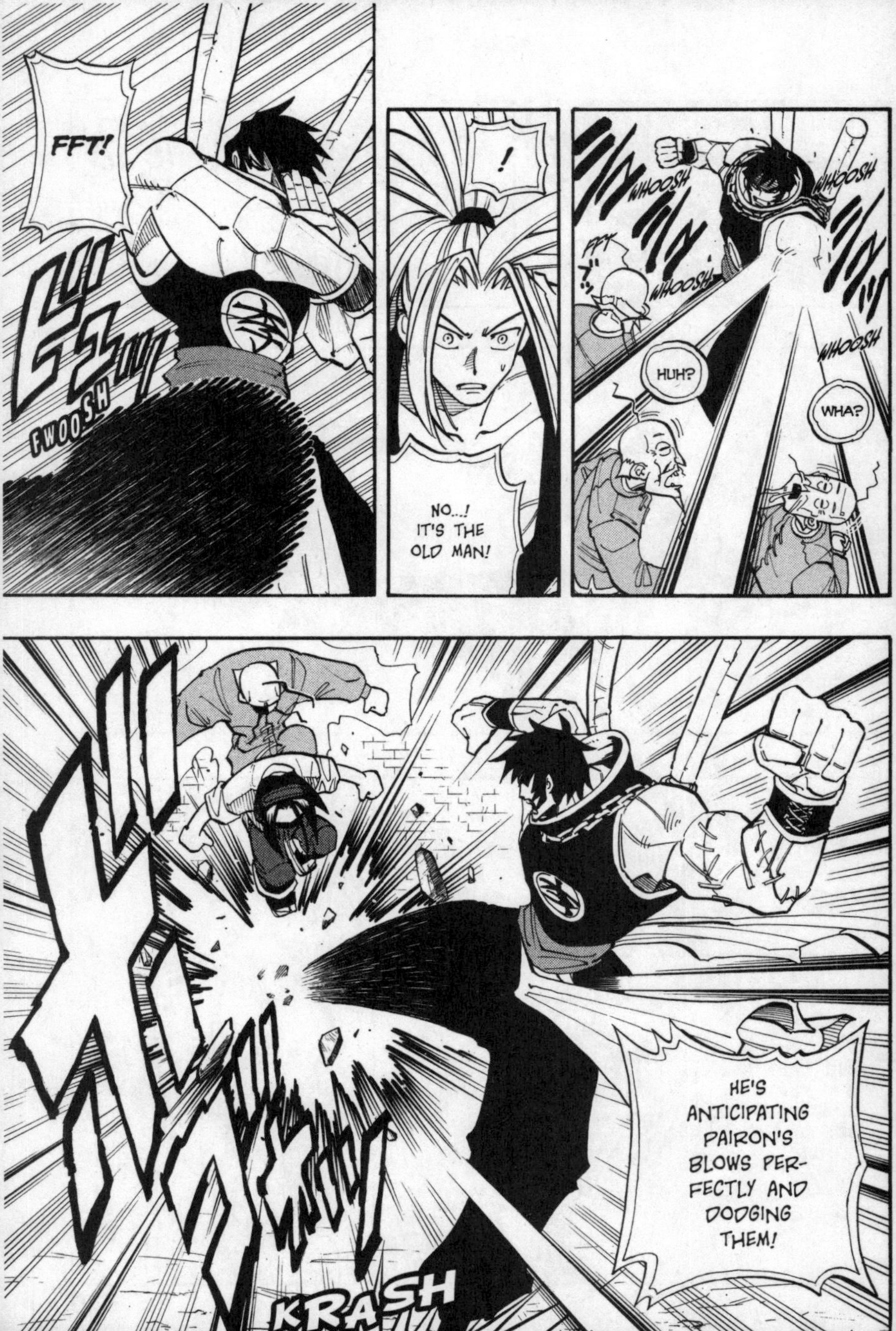
WHOOSH
WHOOSH
WHOOSH
WHOOSH
HUH?
WHA?
!
NO...! IT'S THE OLD MAN!
FFT!
FWOOSH
HE'S ANTICIPATING PAIRON'S BLOWS PER-FECTLY AND DODGING THEM!
KRASH

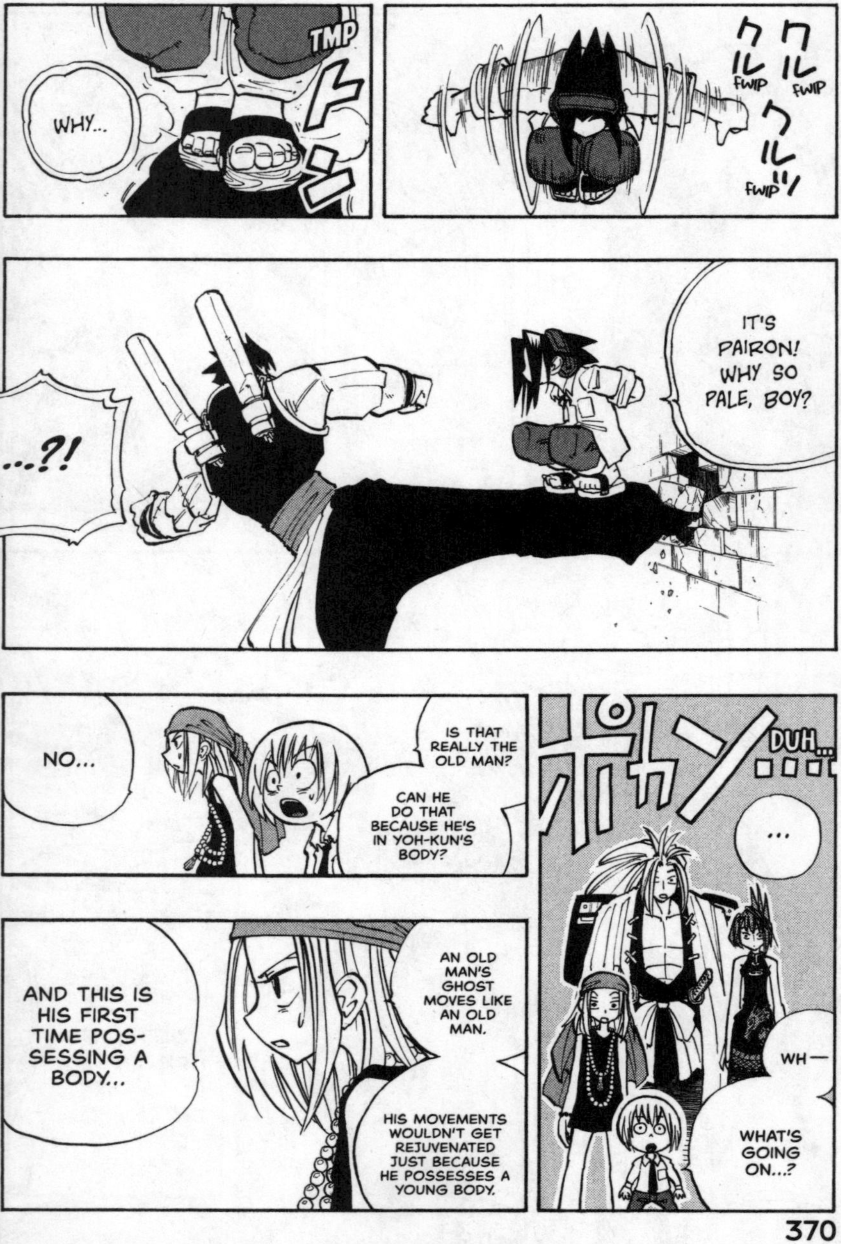
FWIP
FWIP
FWIP
TMP
WHY...
IT'S PAIRON! WHY SO PALE, BOY?
...?!
DUH...
...
WH—
WHAT'S GOING ON...?
IS THAT REALLY THE OLD MAN?
CAN HE DO THAT BECAUSE HE'S IN YOH-KUN'S BODY?
NO...
AN OLD MAN'S GHOST MOVES LIKE AN OLD MAN.
HIS MOVEMENTS WOULDN'T GET REJUVENATED JUST BECAUSE HE POSSESSES A YOUNG BODY.
AND THIS IS HIS FIRST TIME POS-SESSING A BODY...

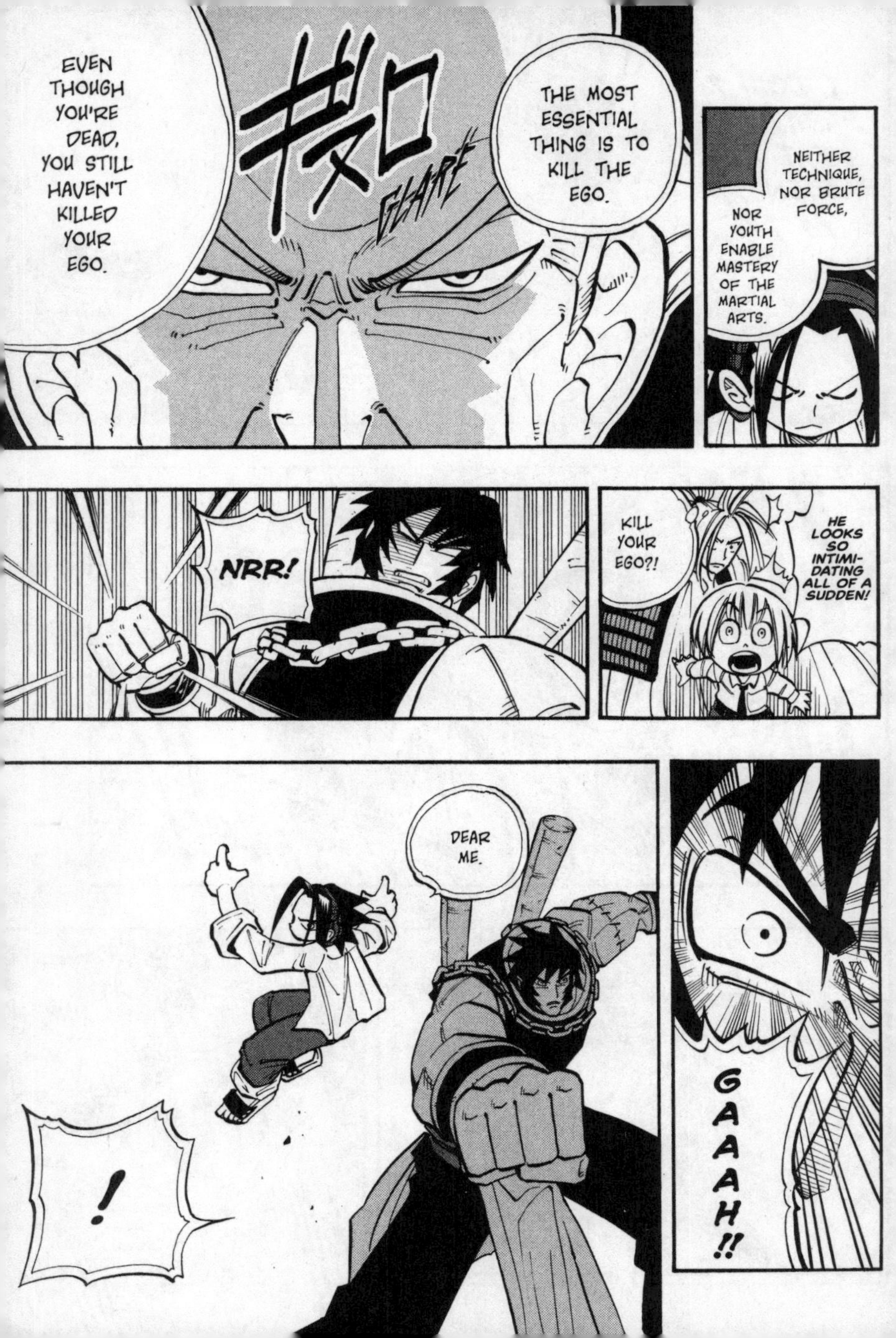
NEITHER TECHNIQUE, NOR BRUTE FORCE,
NOR YOUTH ENABLE MASTERY OF THE MARTIAL ARTS.
THE MOST ESSENTIAL THING IS TO KILL THE EGO.
ギロ
GLARE
EVEN THOUGH YOU'RE DEAD, YOU STILL HAVEN'T KILLED YOUR EGO.
HE LOOKS SO INTIMIDATING ALL OF A SUDDEN!
KILL YOUR EGO?!
NRR!
GAAAH!!
DEAR ME.
!

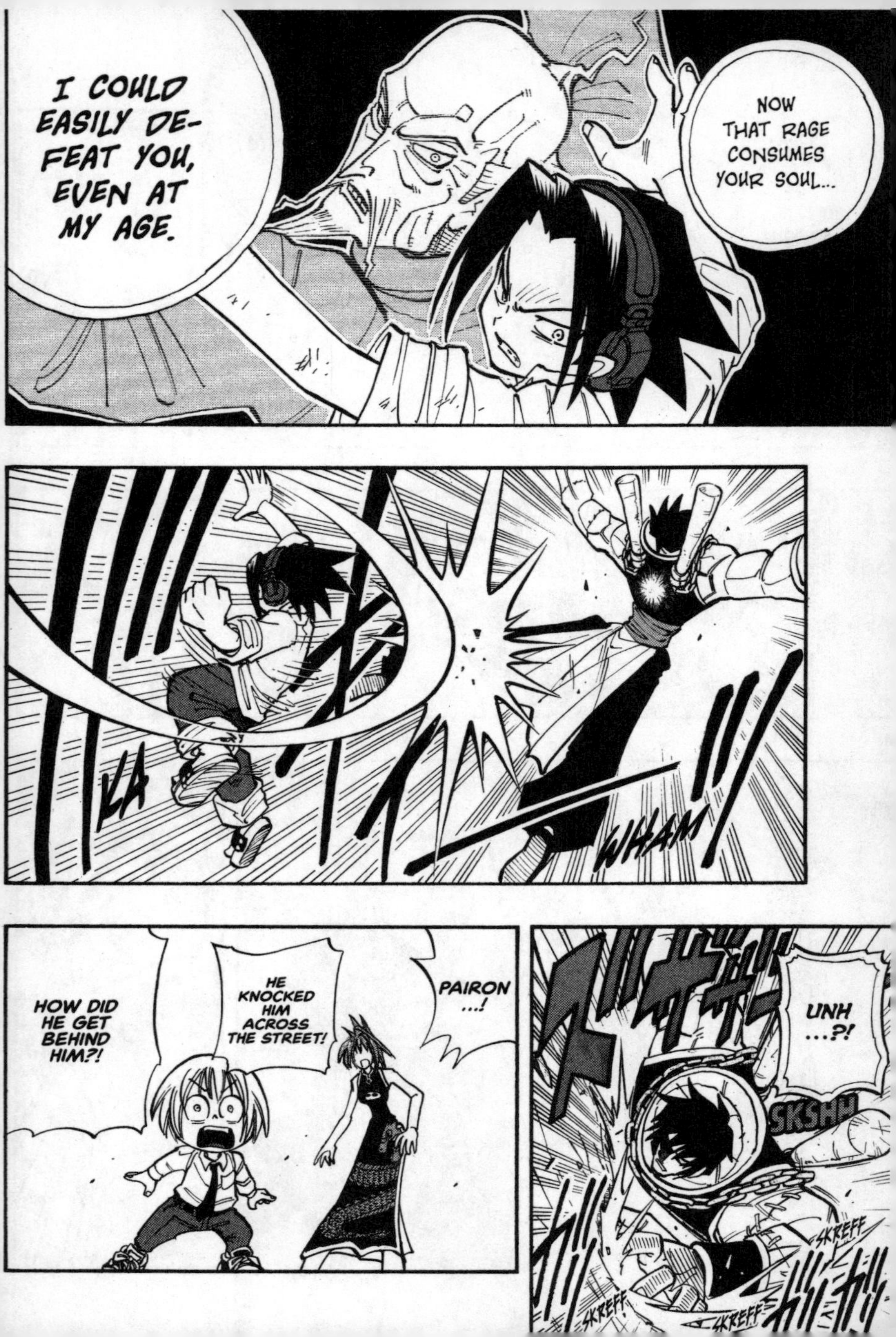
NOW THAT RAGE CONSUMES YOUR SOUL...
I COULD EASILY DE-FEAT YOU, EVEN AT MY AGE.
WHAM
KA
UNH ...?!
SKSHH
SKREFF
SKREFF
SKREFF
PAIRON ...!
HE KNOCKED HIM ACROSS THE STREET!
HOW DID HE GET BEHIND HIM?!

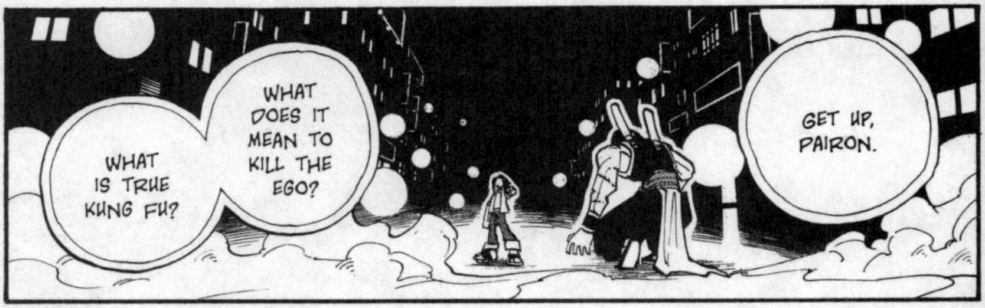
GET UP, PAIRON.
WHAT DOES IT MEAN TO KILL THE EGO?
WHAT IS TRUE KUNG FU?

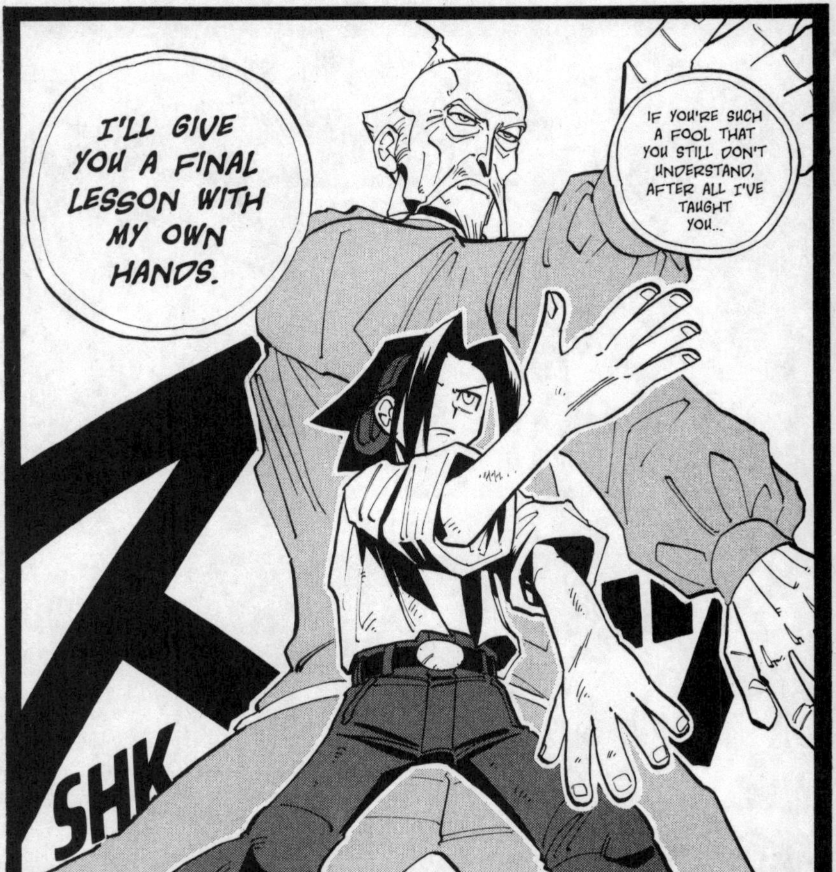
IF YOU'RE SUCH A FOOL THAT YOU STILL DON'T UNDERSTAND, AFTER ALL I'VE TAUGHT YOU...
I'LL GIVE YOU A FINAL LESSON WITH MY OWN HANDS.
SHK

SHAMAN
KING
2

Pointed Hair
(???)

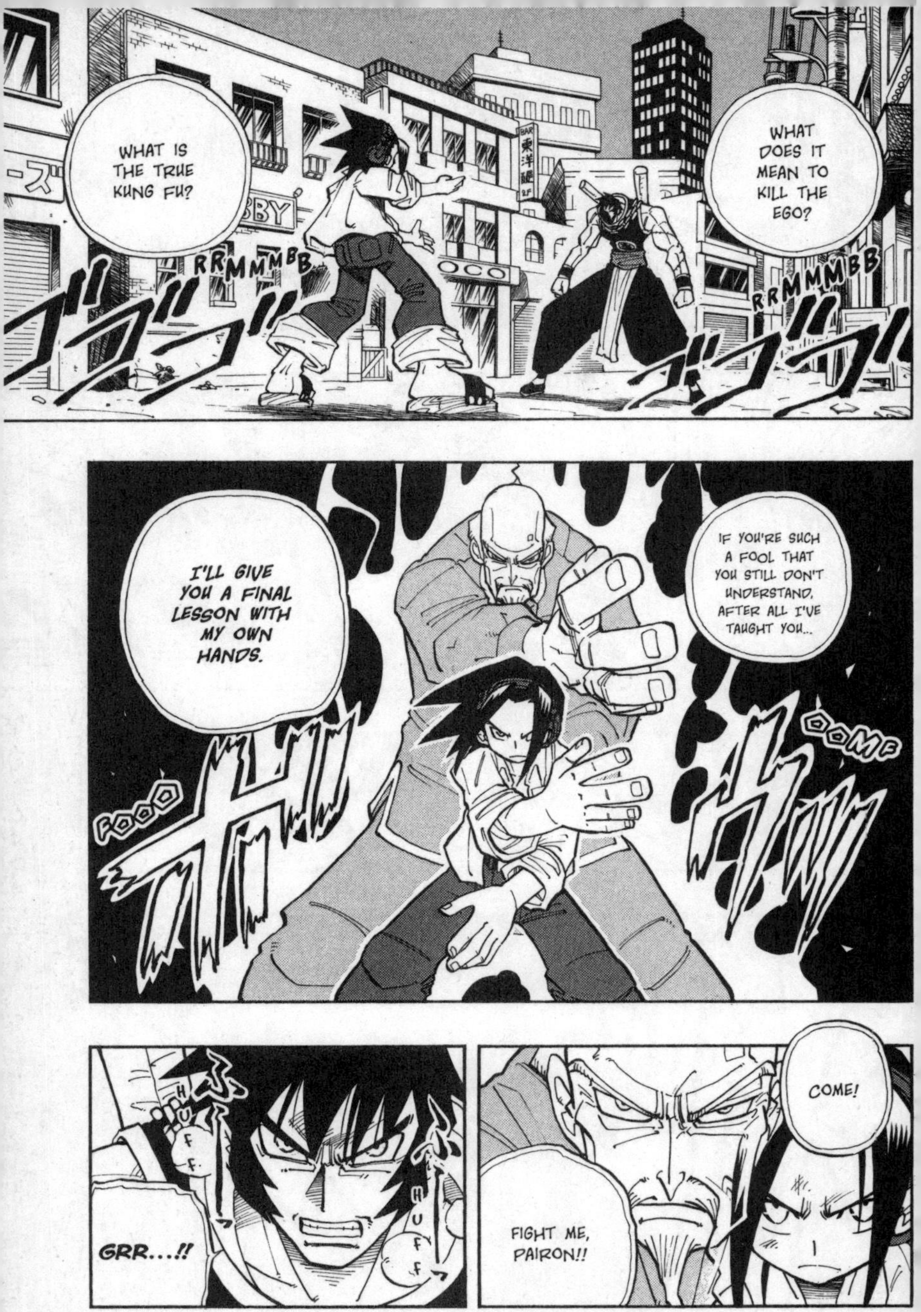
WHAT DOES IT MEAN TO KILL THE EGO?
RRMMMBB
WHAT IS THE TRUE KUNG FU?
RRMMMBB
IF YOU'RE SUCH A FOOL THAT YOU STILL DON'T UNDERSTAND, AFTER ALL I'VE TAUGHT YOU...
I'LL GIVE YOU A FINAL LESSON WITH MY OWN HANDS.
OOMP
FOOO
COME!
FIGHT ME, PAIRON!!
HUFF
HUFF
GRR...!!

Chapter 17: Pairon's Path to Dao Dan Do

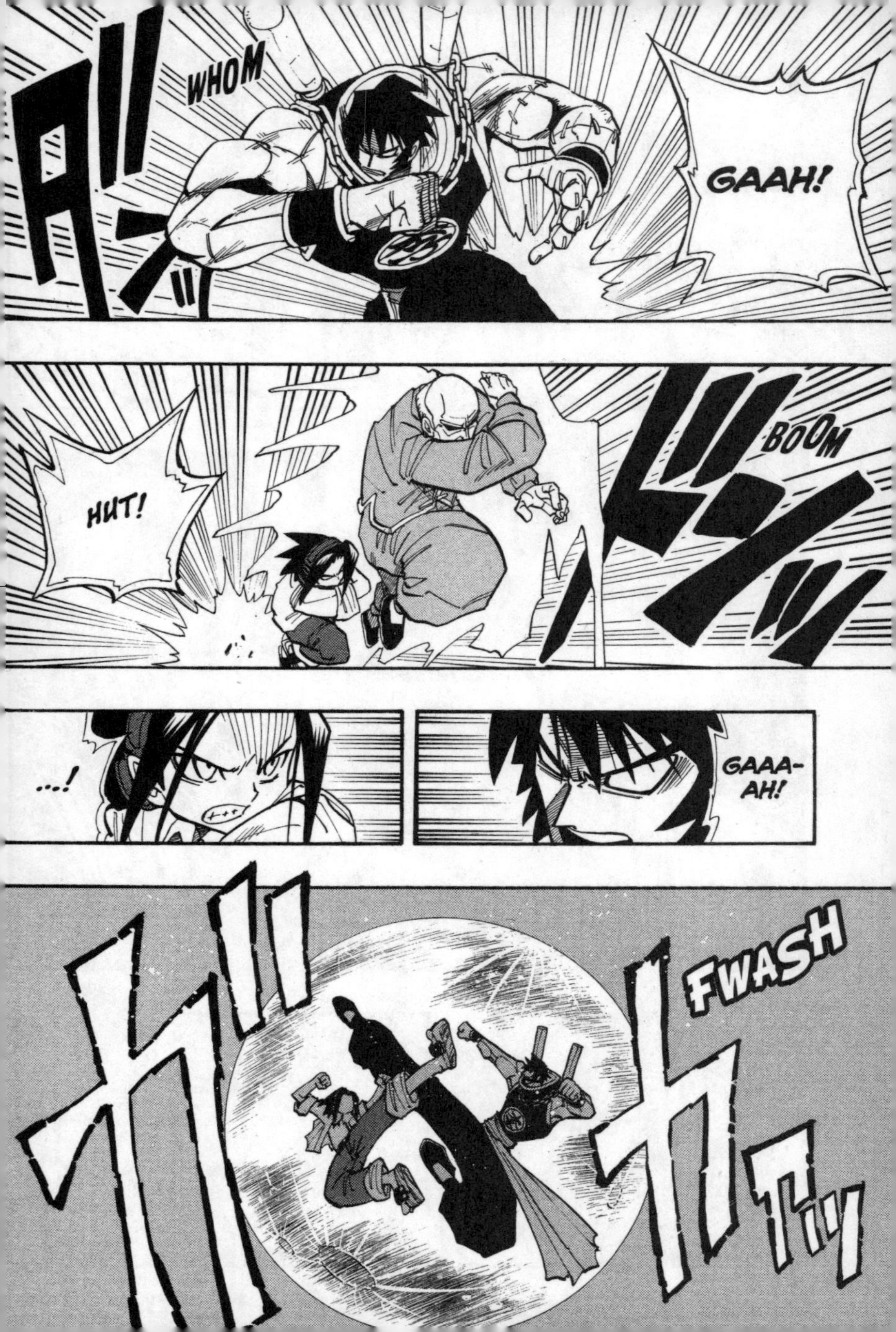
GAAH!
WHOM
BOOM
HUT!
GAAA-AH!
...!
FWASH

Chapter 17:

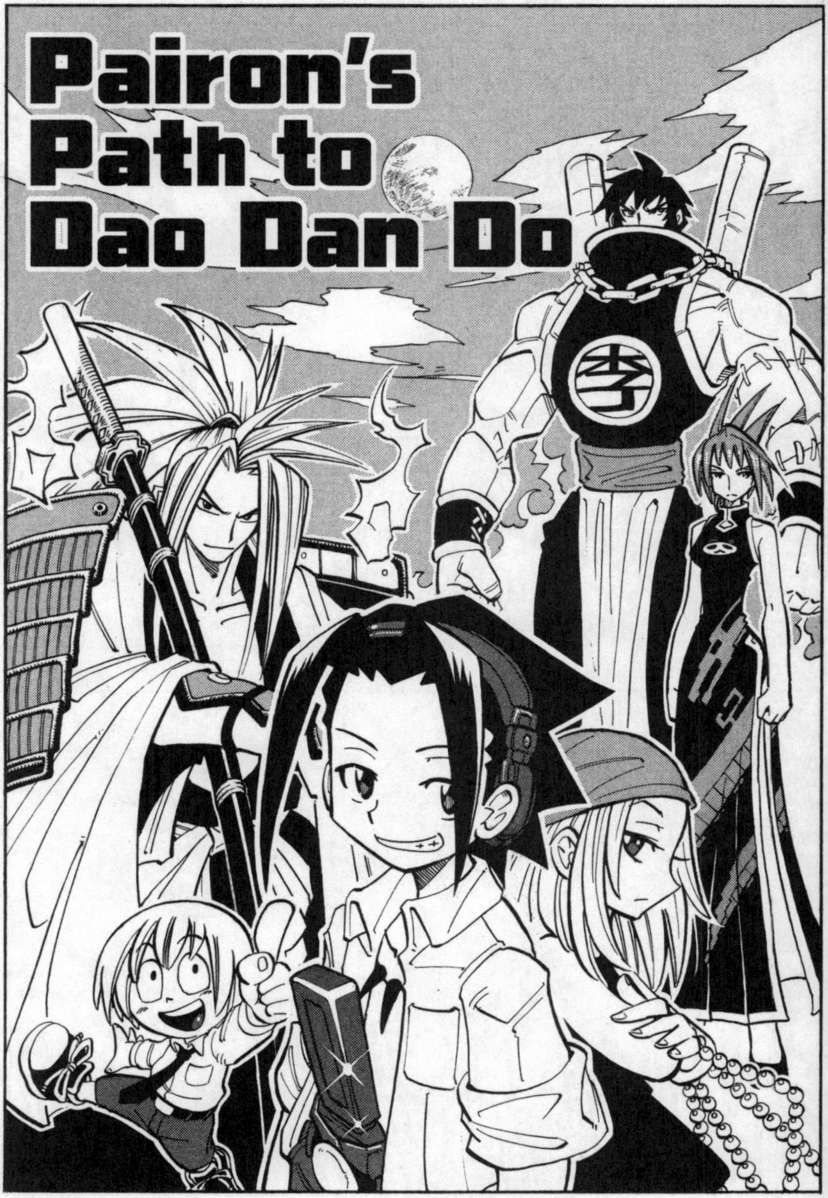
Pairon's Path to Dao Dan Do

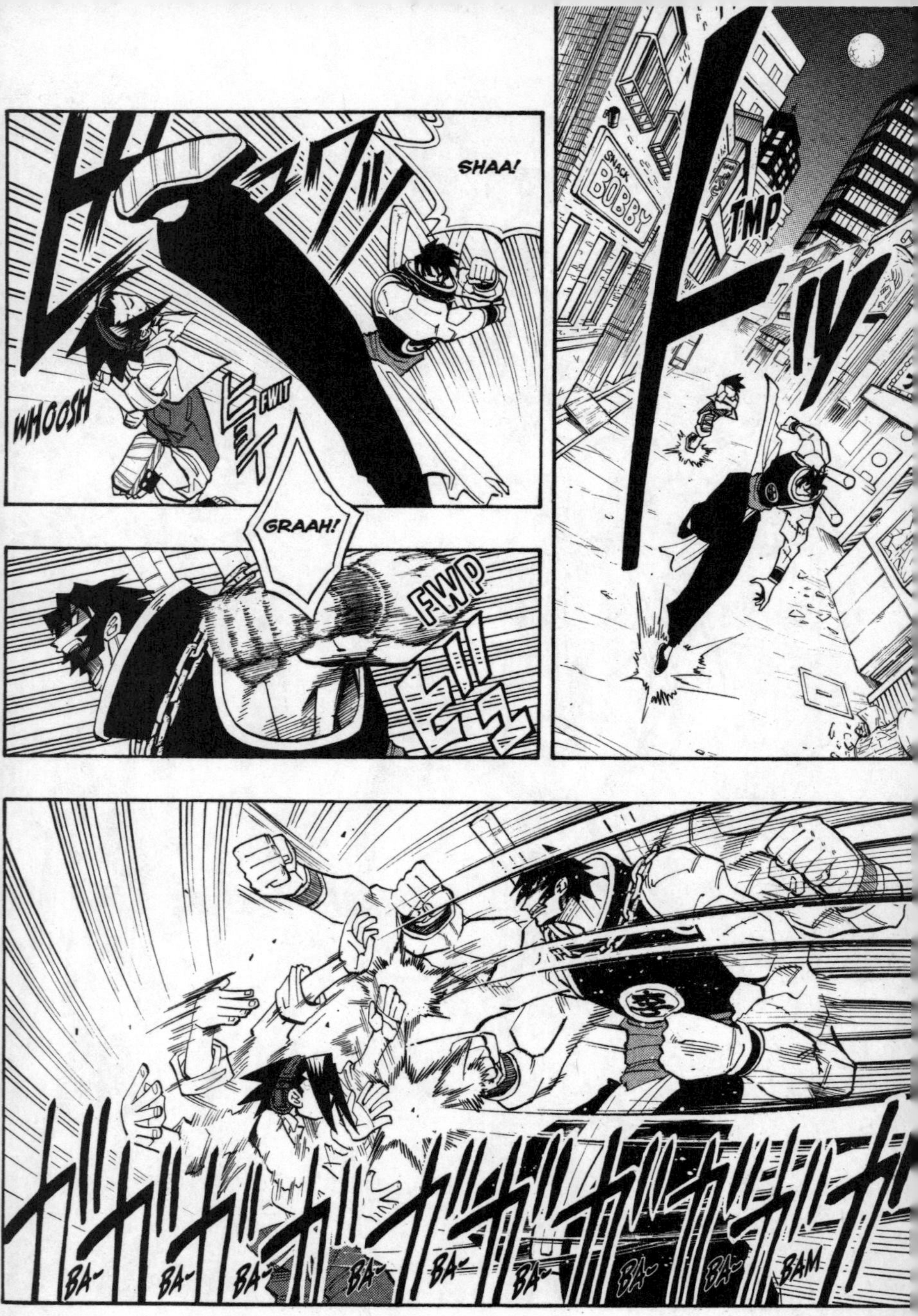
SNACK
BOBBY
TMP
SHAA!
WHOOSH
FWIT
GRAAH!
FWP
BA-
BA-
BA-
BA-
BA-
BA-
BA-
BA-
BAM

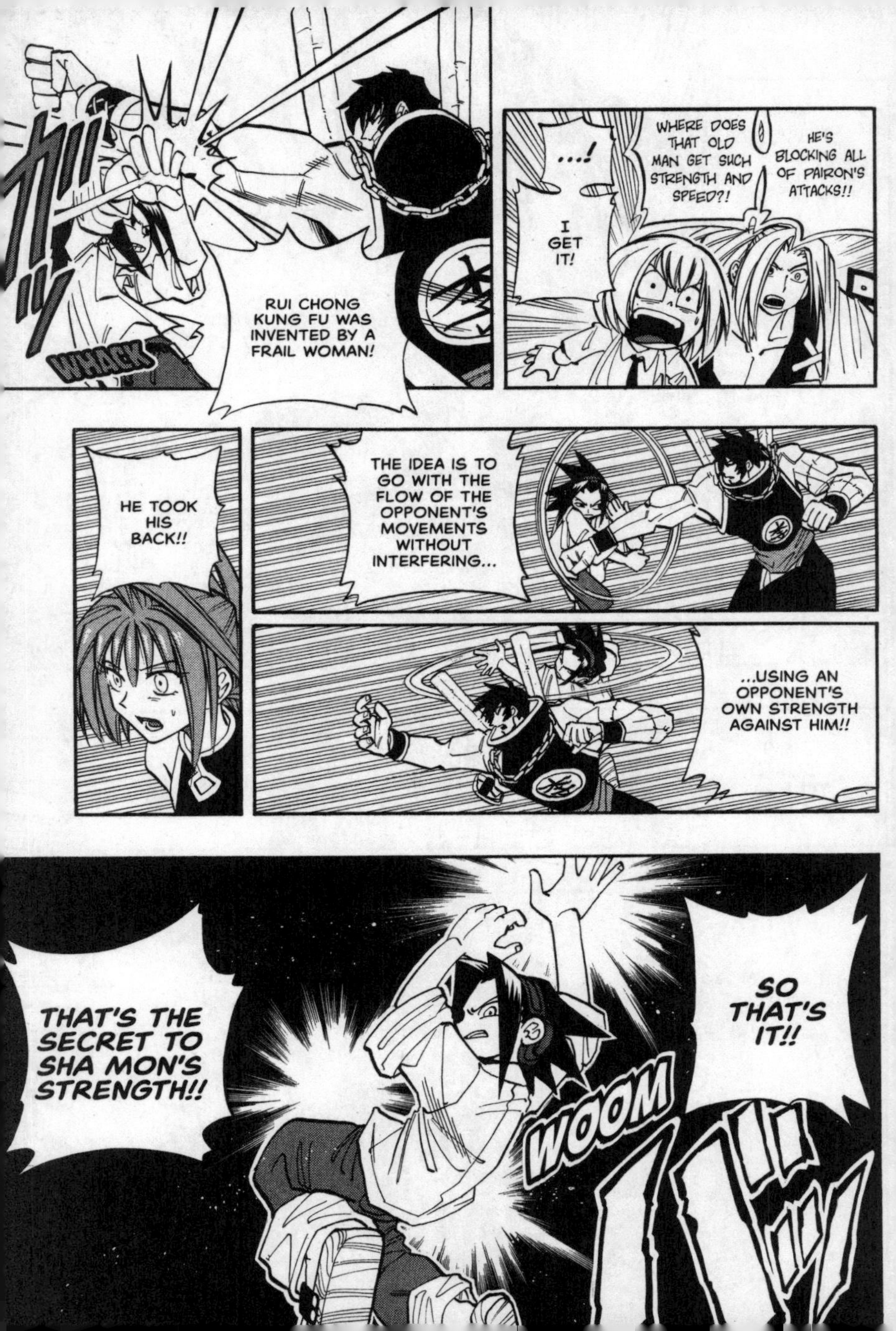
HE'S BLOCKING ALL OF PAIRON'S ATTACKS!!
WHERE DOES THAT OLD MAN GET SUCH STRENGTH AND SPEED?!
...!
I GET IT!
RUI CHONG KUNG FU WAS INVENTED BY A FRAIL WOMAN!
WHACK
THE IDEA IS TO GO WITH THE FLOW OF THE OPPONENT'S MOVEMENTS WITHOUT INTERFERING...
...USING AN OPPONENT'S OWN STRENGTH AGAINST HIM!!
HE TOOK HIS BACK!!
SO THAT'S IT!!
WOOM
THAT'S THE SECRET TO SHA MON'S STRENGTH!!

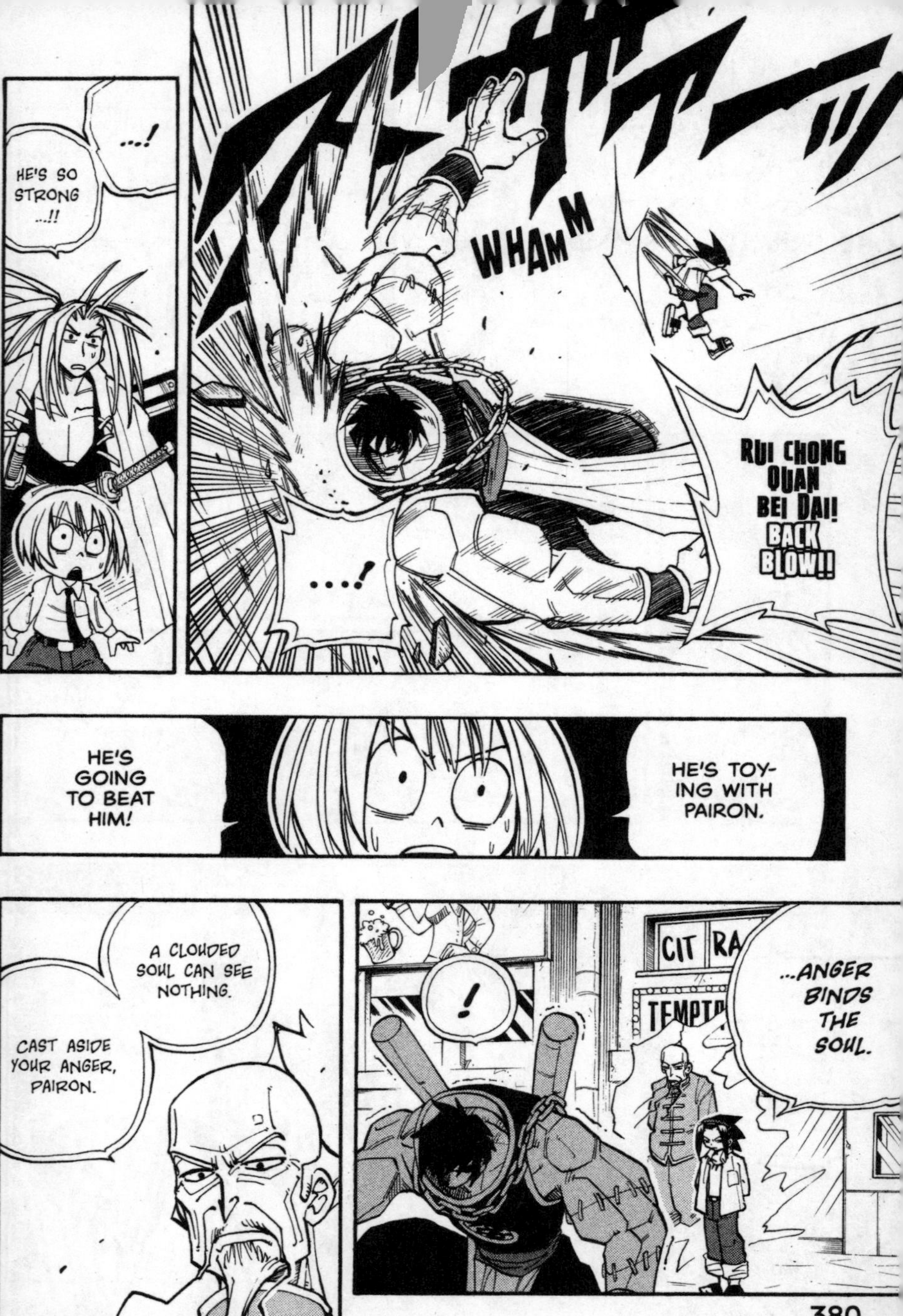
WHAMM
RUI CHONG QUAN BEI DAI! BACK BLOW!!
...!
...!
HE'S SO STRONG ...!!
HE'S TOY-ING WITH PAIRON.
HE'S GOING TO BEAT HIM!
...ANGER BINDS THE SOUL.
!
A CLOUDED SOUL CAN SEE NOTHING.
CAST ASIDE YOUR ANGER, PAIRON.

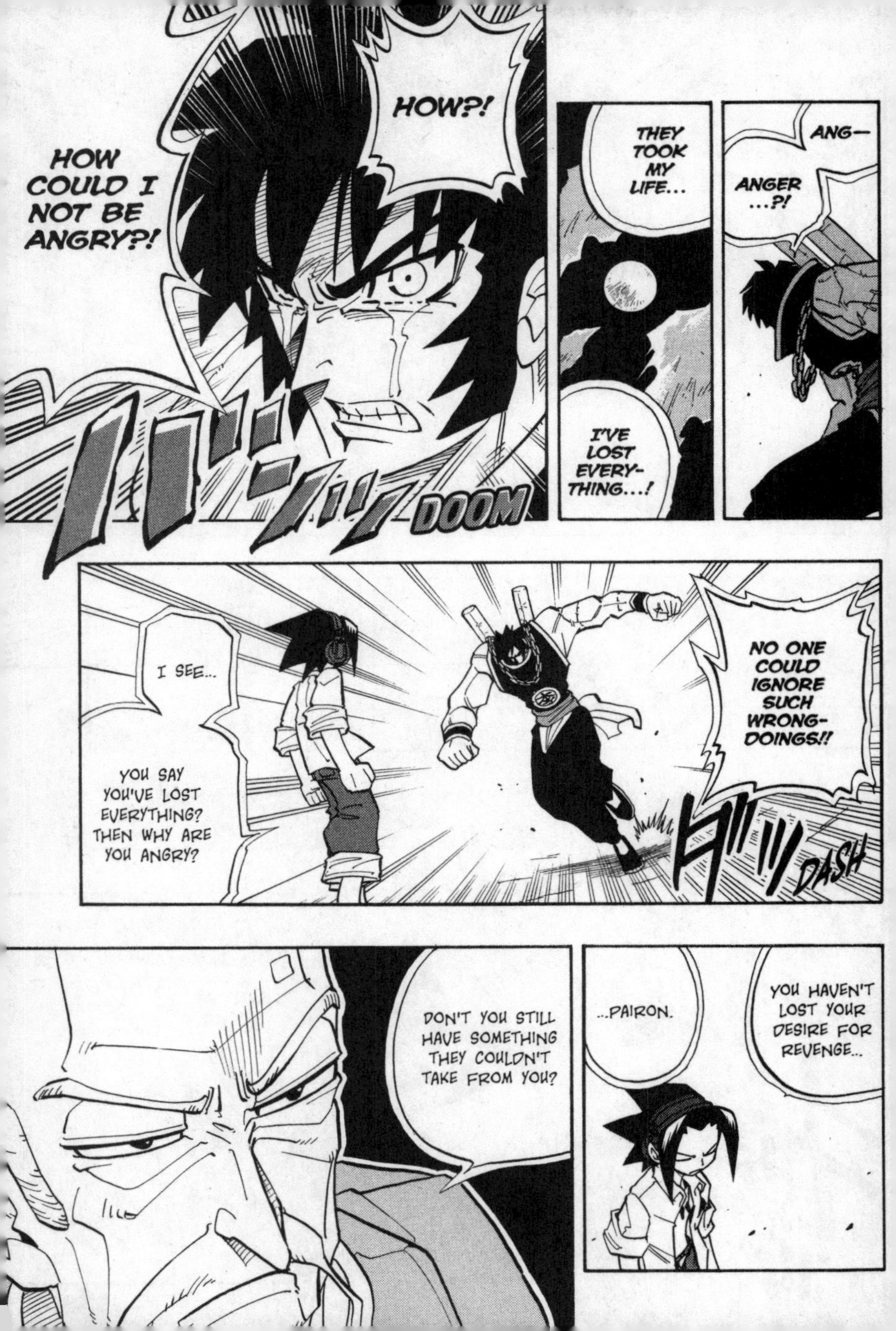
ANG—
ANGER ...?!
THEY TOOK MY LIFE...
I'VE LOST EVERY-THING...!
HOW?!
HOW COULD I NOT BE ANGRY?!
DOOM
NO ONE COULD IGNORE SUCH WRONG-DOINGS!!
DASH
I SEE...
YOU SAY YOU'VE LOST EVERYTHING? THEN WHY ARE YOU ANGRY?
YOU HAVEN'T LOST YOUR DESIRE FOR REVENGE...
...PAIRON.
DON'T YOU STILL HAVE SOMETHING THEY COULDN'T TAKE FROM YOU?

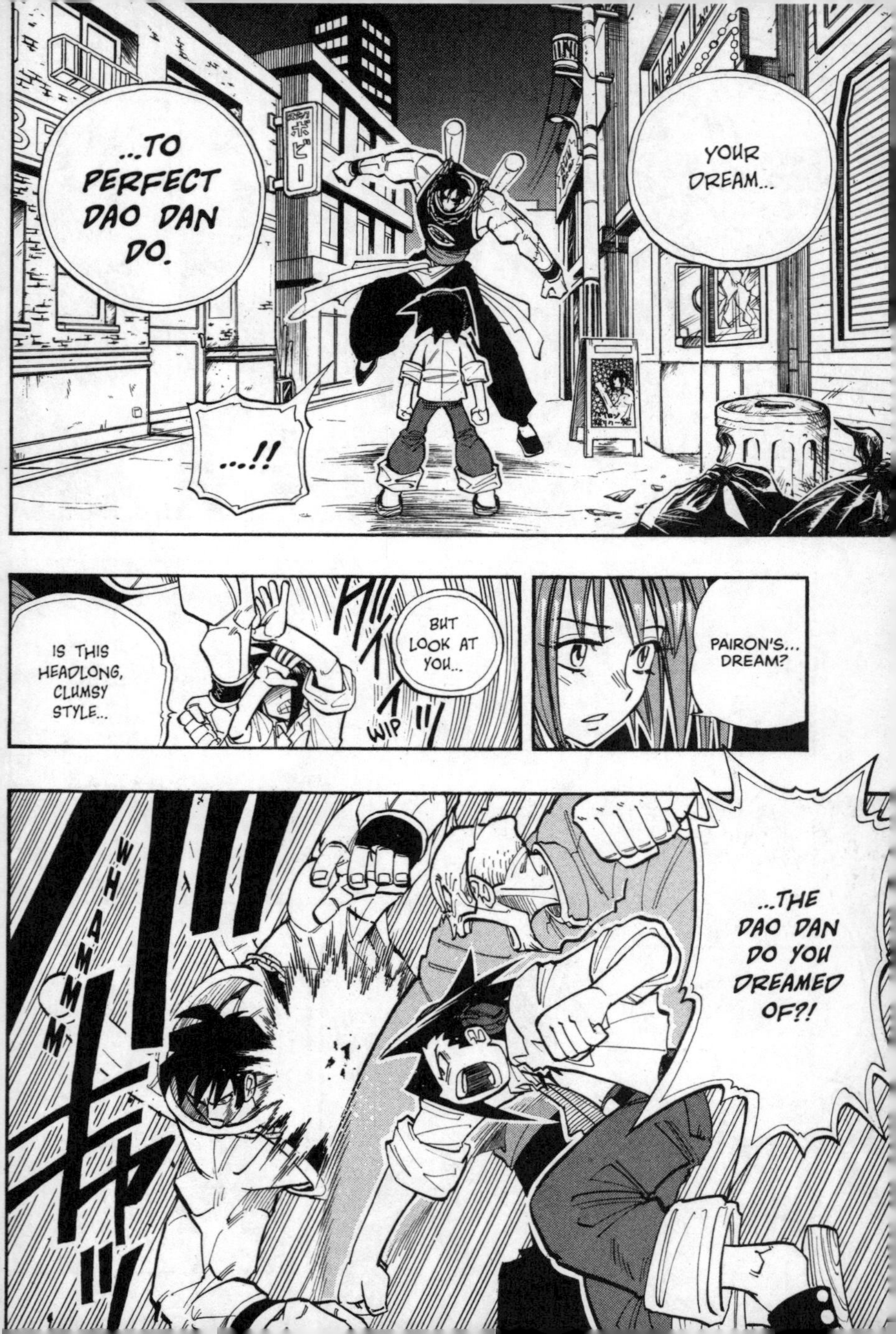
YOUR DREAM...
...TO PERFECT DAO DAN DO.
...!!
PAIRON'S... DREAM?
BUT LOOK AT YOU...
WIP
IS THIS HEADLONG, CLUMSY STYLE...
...THE DAO DAN DO YOU DREAMED OF?!
WHAMMM

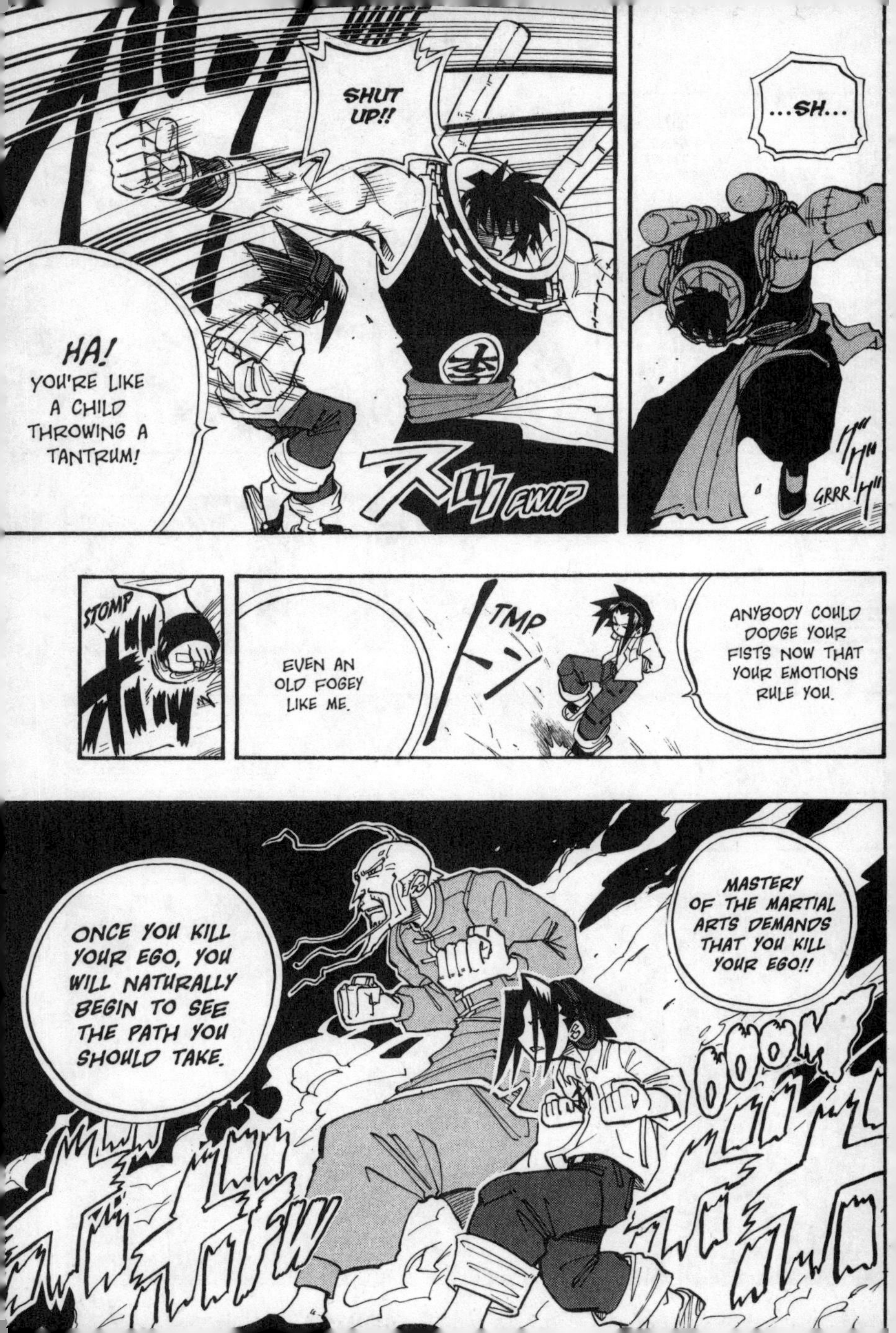
...SH...
GRRR
SHUT UP!!
HA! YOU'RE LIKE A CHILD THROWING A TANTRUM!
FWIP
ANYBODY COULD DODGE YOUR FISTS NOW THAT YOUR EMOTIONS RULE YOU.
TMP
EVEN AN OLD FOGEY LIKE ME.
STOMP
MASTERY OF THE MARTIAL ARTS DEMANDS THAT YOU KILL YOUR EGO!!
ONCE YOU KILL YOUR EGO, YOU WILL NATURALLY BEGIN TO SEE THE PATH YOU SHOULD TAKE.

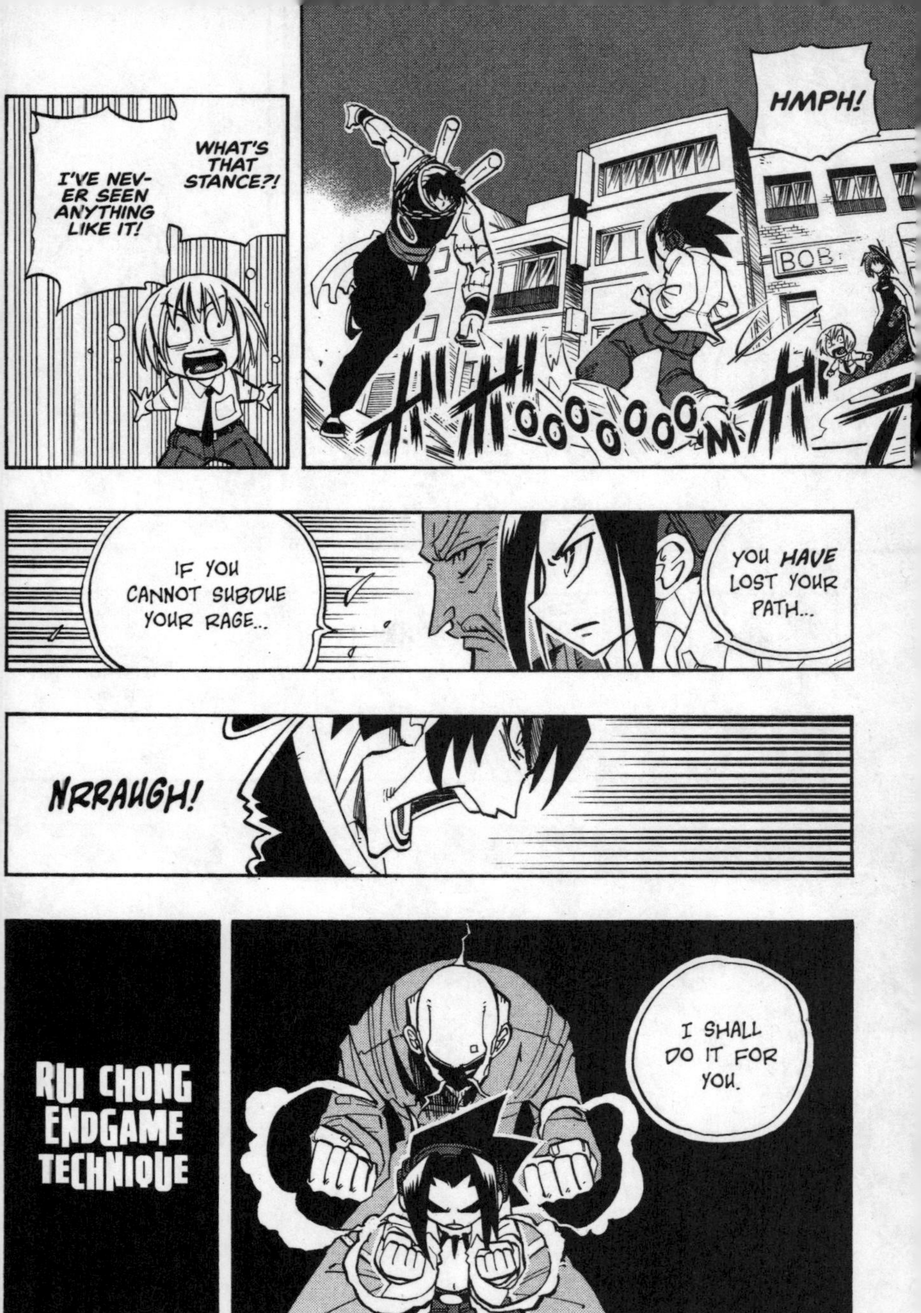

HMPH!
BOB
OOOOOOOM
WHAT'S THAT STANCE?!
I'VE NEV-ER SEEN ANYTHING LIKE IT!
YOU *HAVE* LOST YOUR PATH...
IF YOU CANNOT SUBDUE YOUR RAGE...
NRRAUGH!
I SHALL DO IT FOR YOU.
RUI CHONG ENDGAME TECHNIQUE

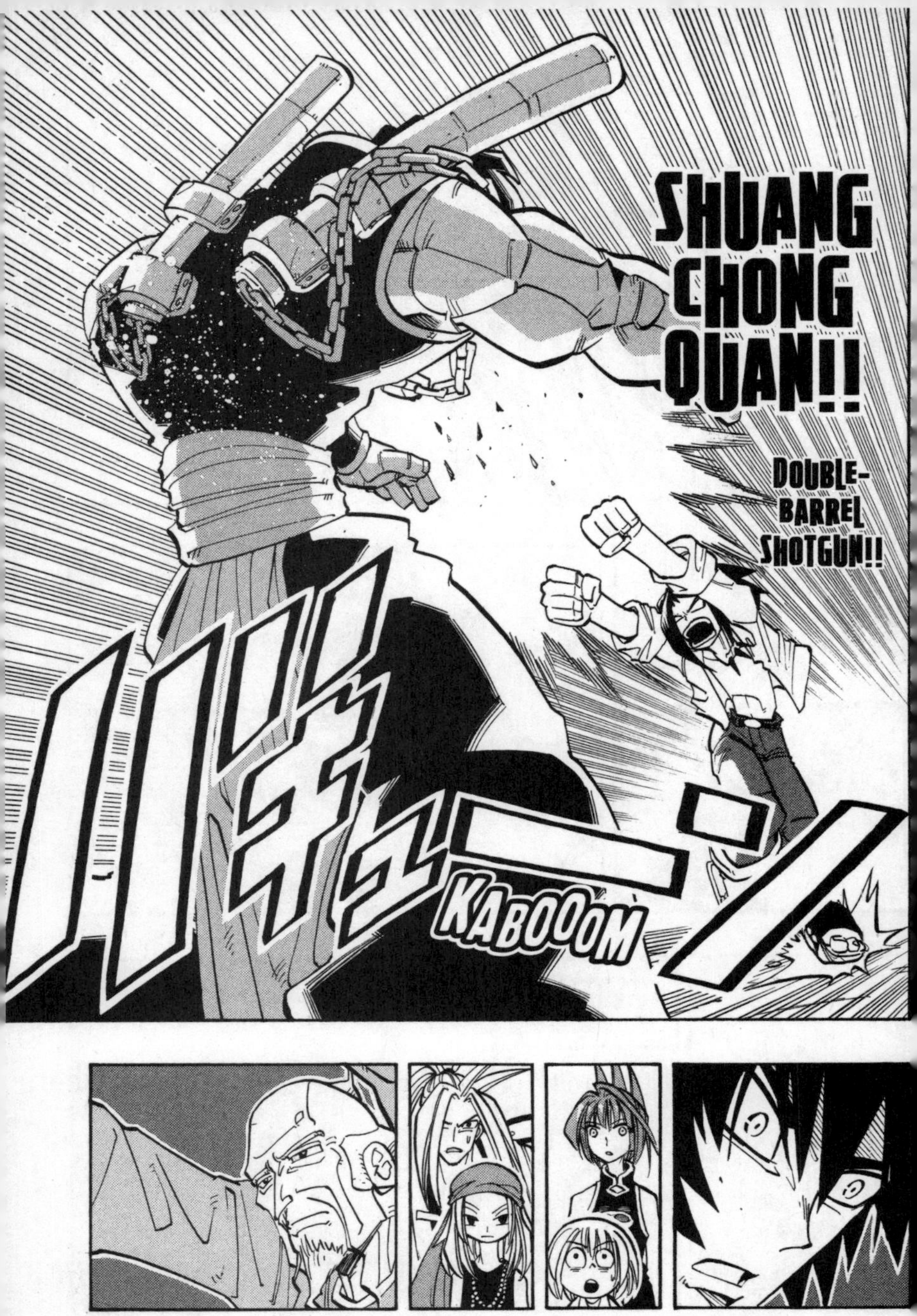
SHUANG CHONG QUAN!!
DOUBLE-BARREL SHOTGUN!!
KABOOOM

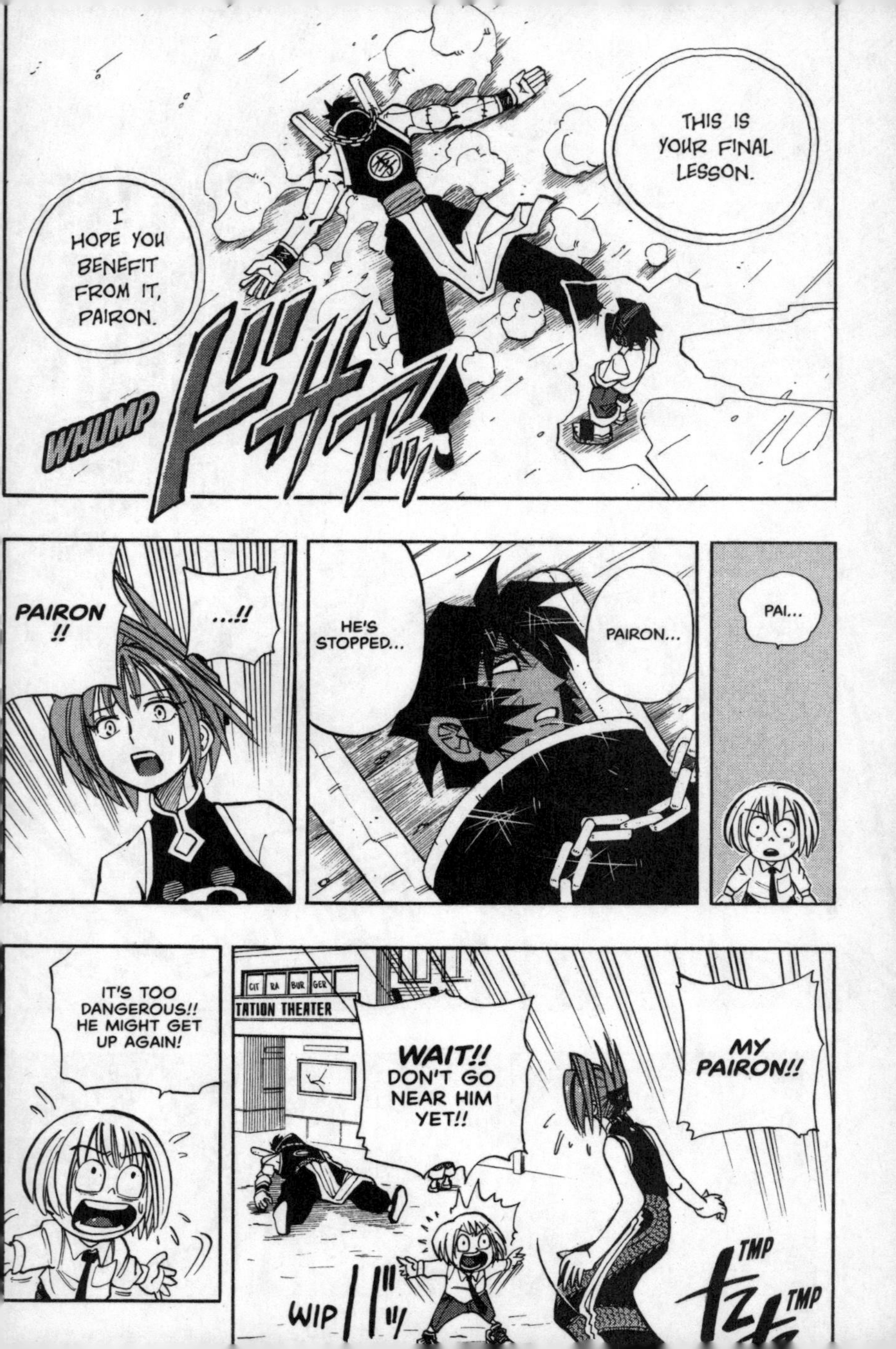
THIS IS YOUR FINAL LESSON.
I HOPE YOU BENEFIT FROM IT, PAIRON.
WHUMP
PAI...
PAIRON...
HE'S STOPPED...
...!!
PAIRON !!
MY PAIRON!!
TMP
TMP
WAIT!! DON'T GO NEAR HIM YET!!
CIT RA BUR GER
TATION THEATER
WIP
IT'S TOO DANGEROUS!! HE MIGHT GET UP AGAIN!

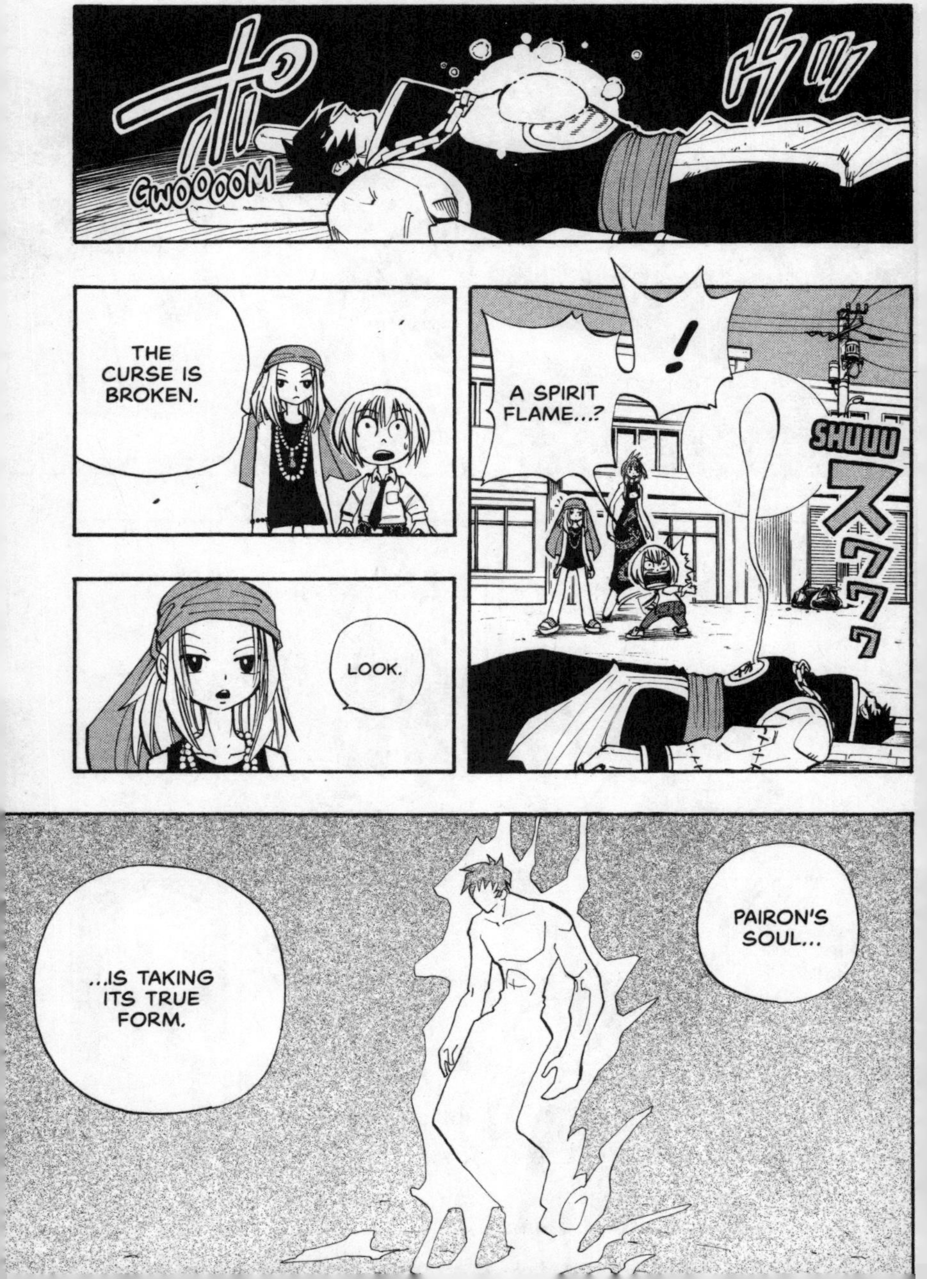
GWOOOOM
!
A SPIRIT FLAME...?
SHUUU
スワワワ
THE CURSE IS BROKEN.
LOOK.
PAIRON'S SOUL...
...IS TAKING ITS TRUE FORM.

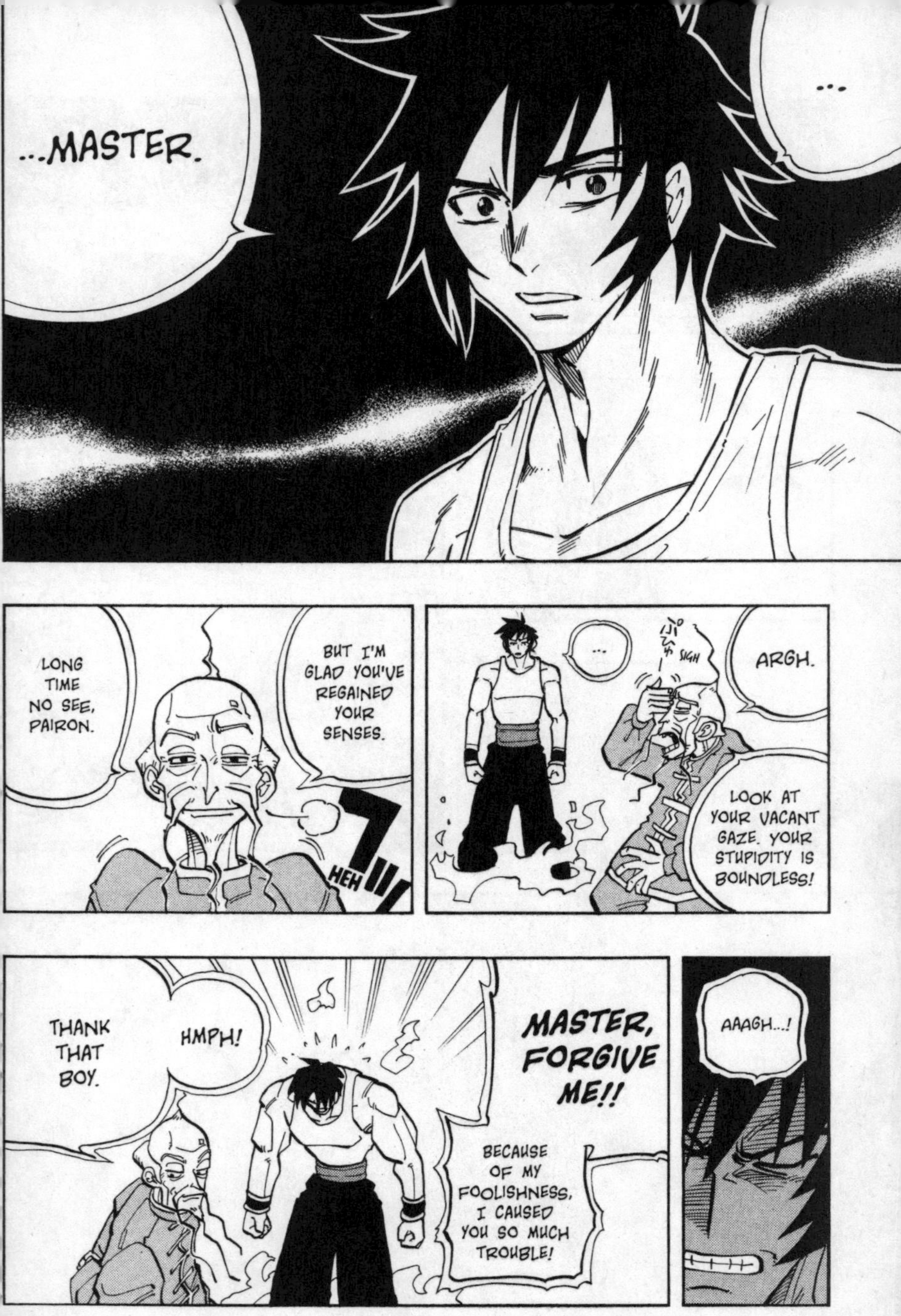
...
...MASTER.
ARGH.
...
SIGH
LOOK AT YOUR VACANT GAZE. YOUR STUPIDITY IS BOUNDLESS!
BUT I'M GLAD YOU'VE REGAINED YOUR SENSES.
LONG TIME NO SEE, PAIRON.
HEH
AAAGH...!
MASTER, FORGIVE ME!!
BECAUSE OF MY FOOLISHNESS, I CAUSED YOU SO MUCH TROUBLE!
HMPH!
THANK THAT BOY.

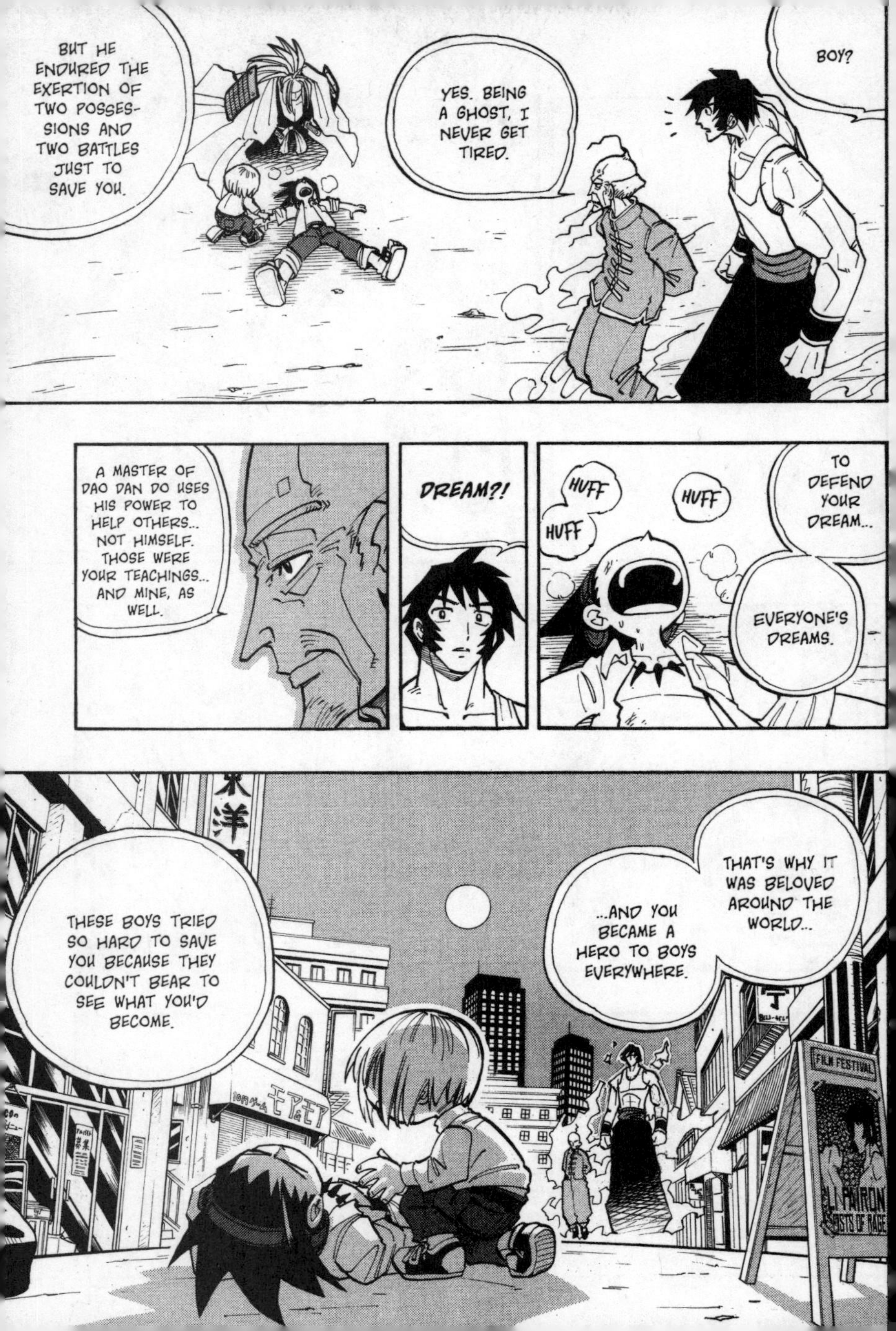
BOY?
YES. BEING A GHOST, I NEVER GET TIRED.
BUT HE ENDURED THE EXERTION OF TWO POSSESSIONS AND TWO BATTLES JUST TO SAVE YOU.
TO DEFEND YOUR DREAM...
EVERYONE'S DREAMS.
HUFF
HUFF
HUFF
DREAM?!
A MASTER OF DAO DAN DO USES HIS POWER TO HELP OTHERS... NOT HIMSELF. THOSE WERE YOUR TEACHINGS... AND MINE, AS WELL.
THAT'S WHY IT WAS BELOVED AROUND THE WORLD...
...AND YOU BECAME A HERO TO BOYS EVERYWHERE.
THESE BOYS TRIED SO HARD TO SAVE YOU BECAUSE THEY COULDN'T BEAR TO SEE WHAT YOU'D BECOME.
FILM FESTIVAL

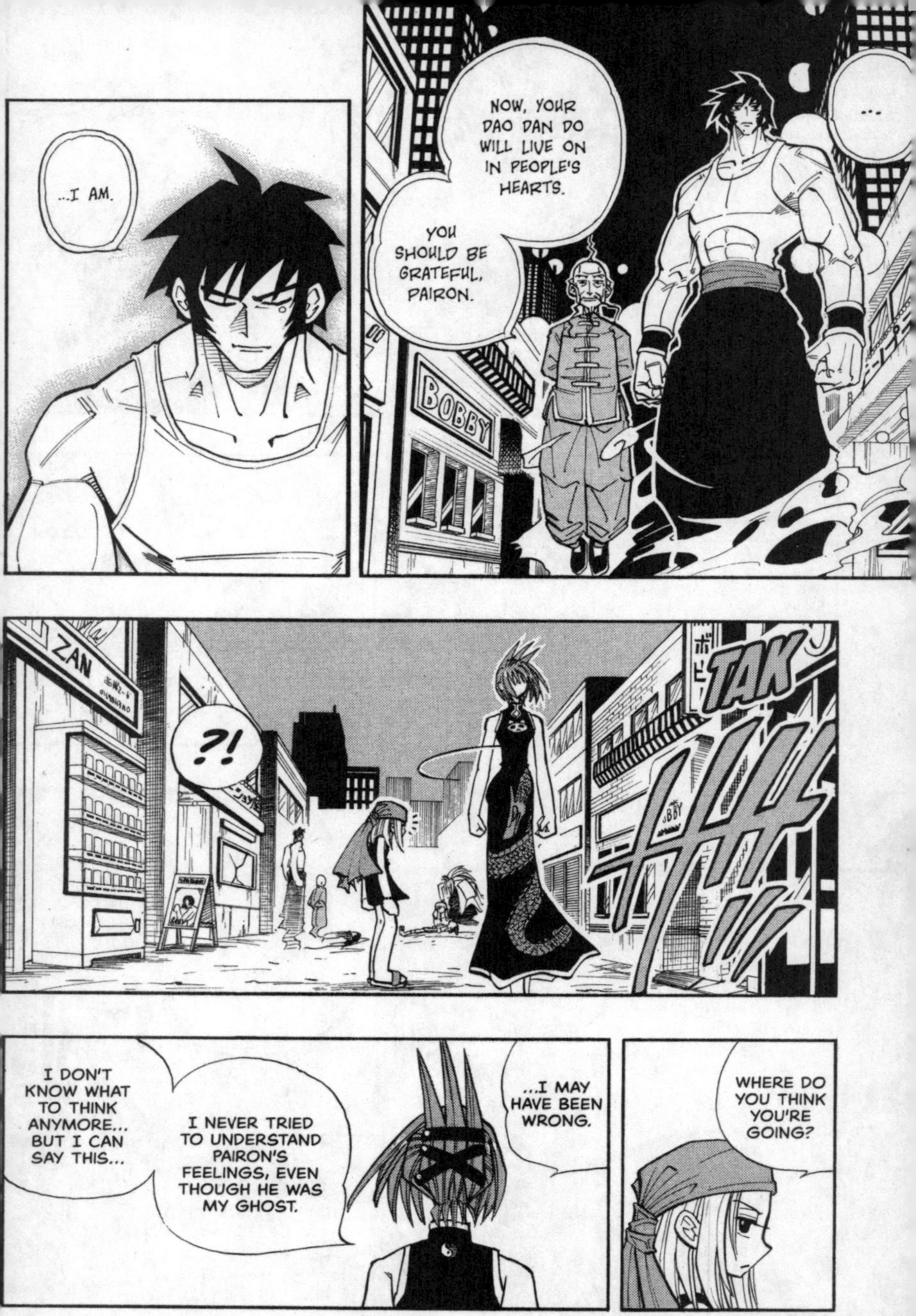
...
NOW, YOUR DAO DAN DO WILL LIVE ON IN PEOPLE'S HEARTS.
YOU SHOULD BE GRATEFUL, PAIRON.
BOBBY
...I AM.
TAK
?!
ZAN
WHERE DO YOU THINK YOU'RE GOING?
...I MAY HAVE BEEN WRONG.
I NEVER TRIED TO UNDERSTAND PAIRON'S FEELINGS, EVEN THOUGH HE WAS MY GHOST.
I DON'T KNOW WHAT TO THINK ANYMORE... BUT I CAN SAY THIS...

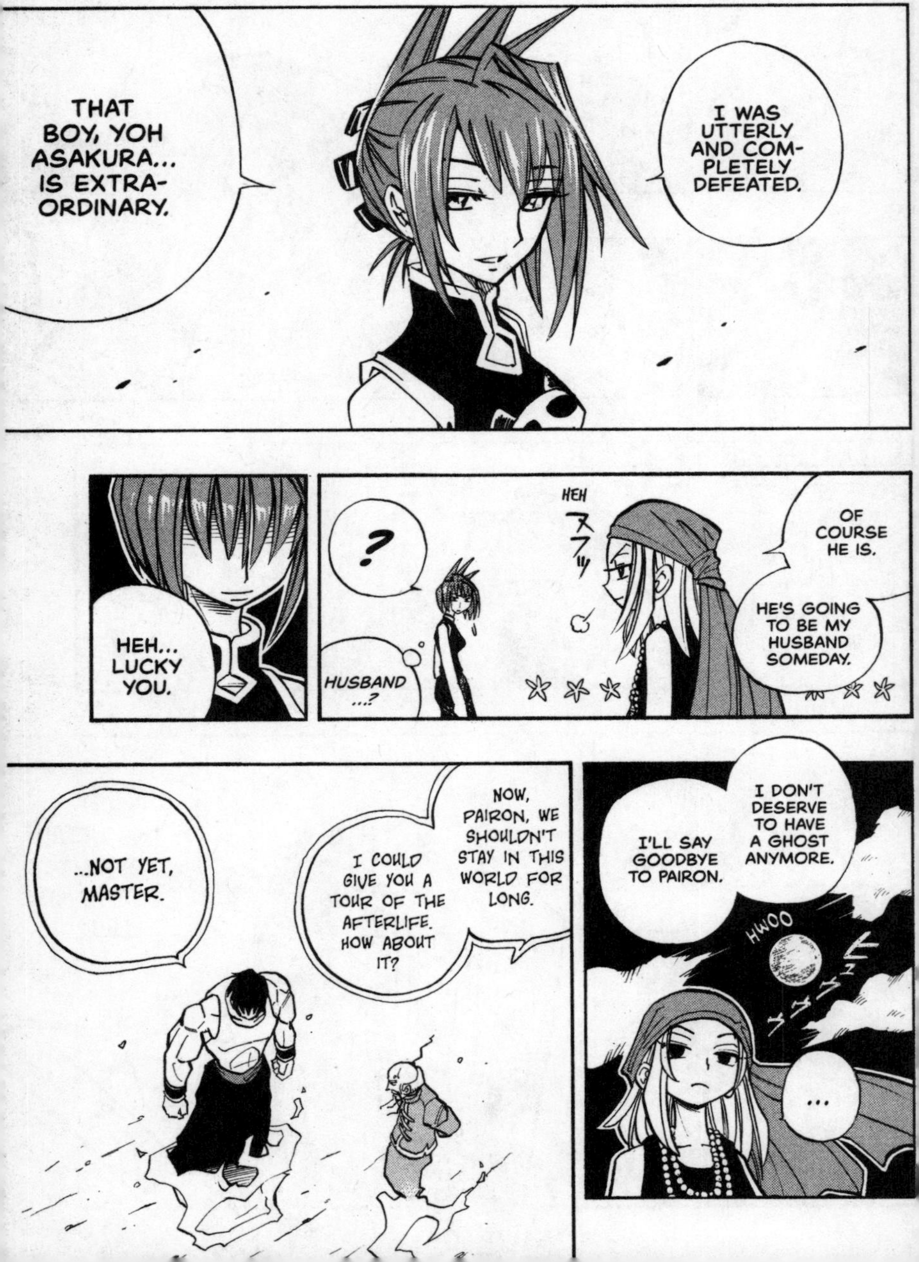
I WAS UTTERLY AND COMPLETELY DEFEATED.
THAT BOY, YOH ASAKURA... IS EXTRAORDINARY.
OF COURSE HE IS.
HE'S GOING TO BE MY HUSBAND SOMEDAY.
HEH
?
HUSBAND ...?
HEH... LUCKY YOU.
I DON'T DESERVE TO HAVE A GHOST ANYMORE.
I'LL SAY GOODBYE TO PAIRON.
HWOO
...
NOW, PAIRON, WE SHOULDN'T STAY IN THIS WORLD FOR LONG.
I COULD GIVE YOU A TOUR OF THE AFTERLIFE. HOW ABOUT IT?
...NOT YET, MASTER.

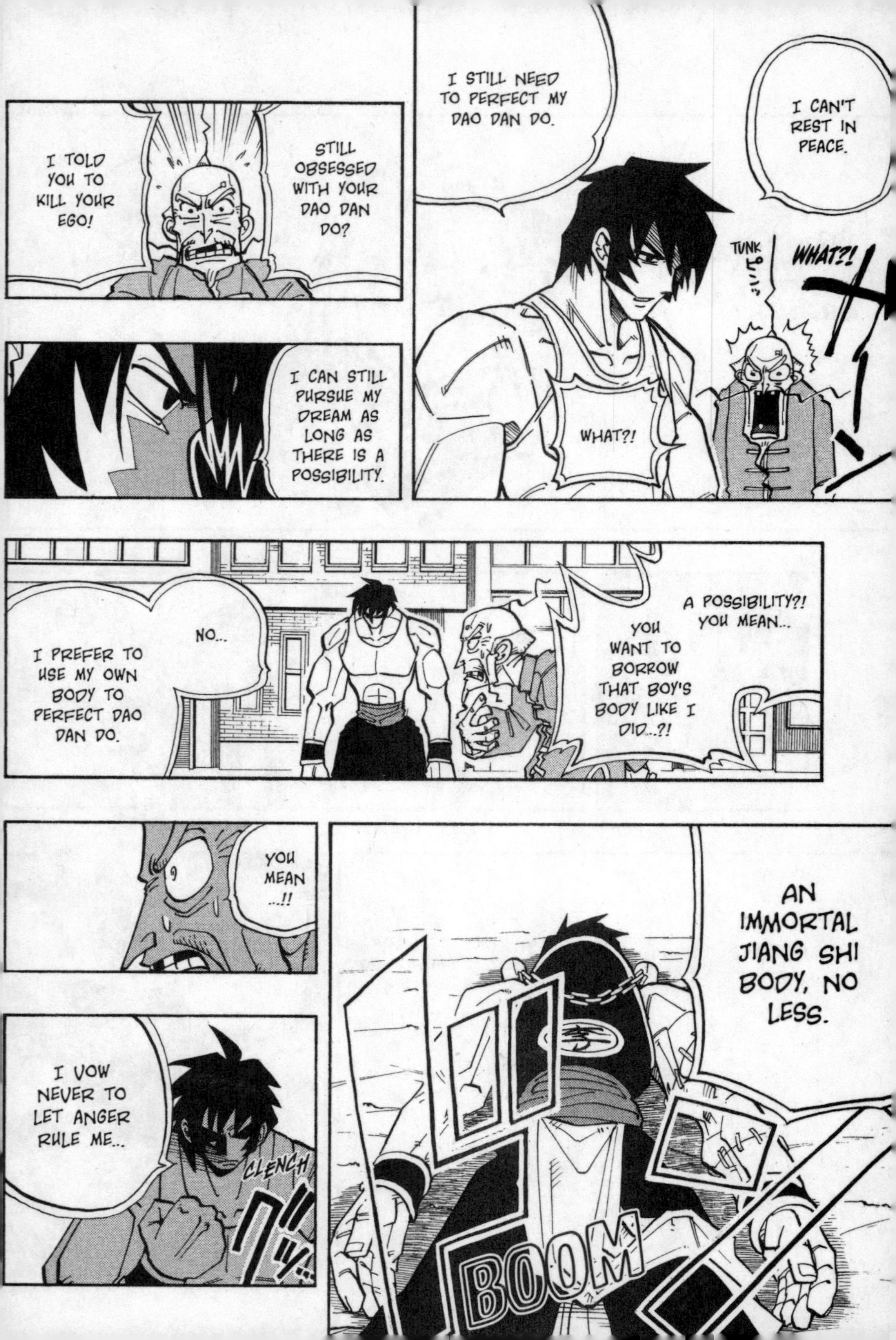
I STILL NEED TO PERFECT MY DAO DAN DO.
I CAN'T REST IN PEACE.
WHAT?!
TUNK
WHAT?!
STILL OBSESSED WITH YOUR DAO DAN DO?
I TOLD YOU TO KILL YOUR EGO!
I CAN STILL PURSUE MY DREAM AS LONG AS THERE IS A POSSIBILITY.
A POSSIBILITY?! YOU MEAN...
YOU WANT TO BORROW THAT BOY'S BODY LIKE I DID...?!
NO...
I PREFER TO USE MY OWN BODY TO PERFECT DAO DAN DO.
AN IMMORTAL JIANG SHI BODY, NO LESS.
BOOM
YOU MEAN ...!!
I VOW NEVER TO LET ANGER RULE ME...
CLENCH

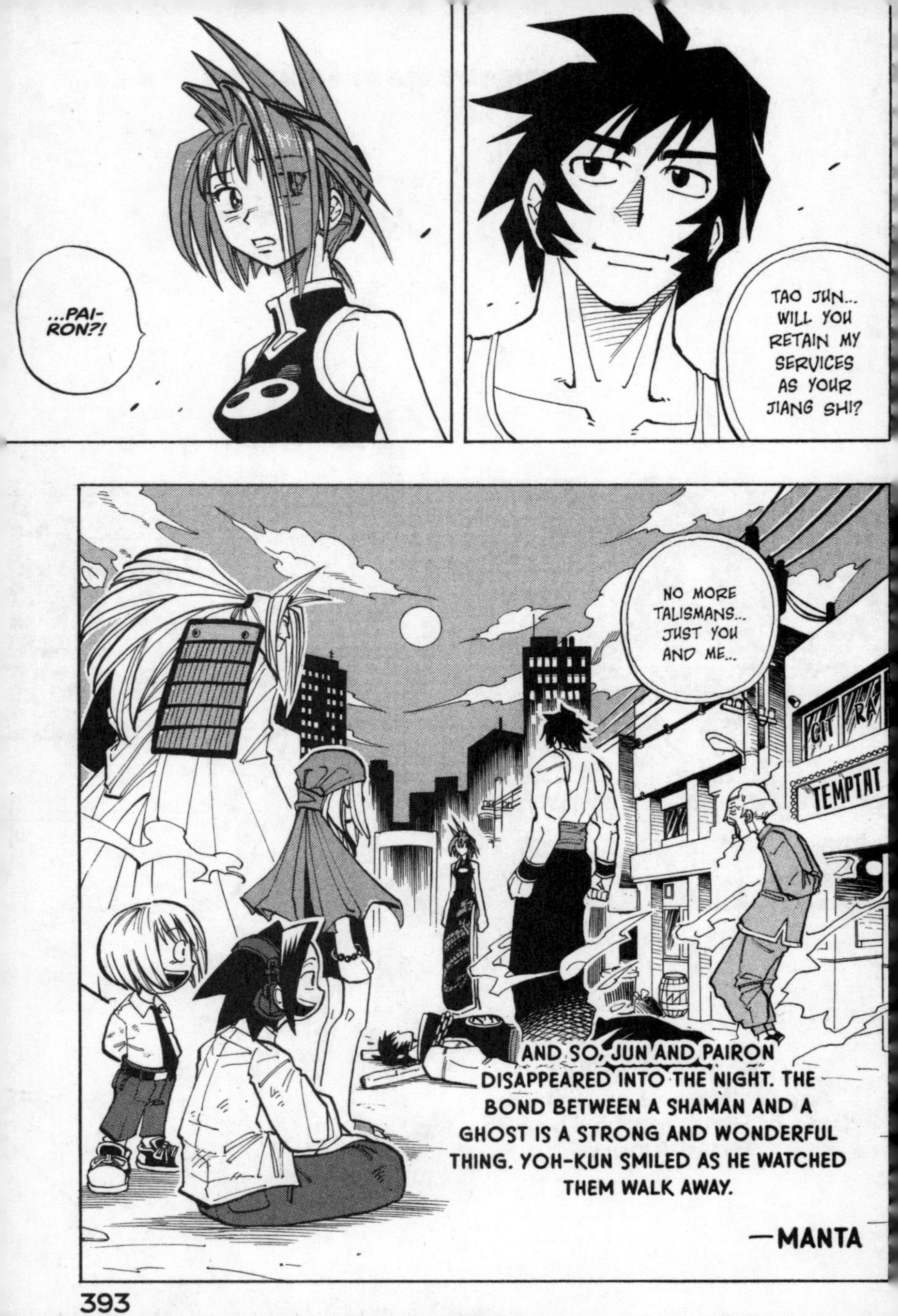
TAO JUN... WILL YOU RETAIN MY SERVICES AS YOUR JIANG SHI?
...PAI-RON?!
NO MORE TALISMANS... JUST YOU AND ME...
CIT RA
TEMPTAT
AND SO, JUN AND PAIRON DISAPPEARED INTO THE NIGHT. THE BOND BETWEEN A SHAMAN AND A GHOST IS A STRONG AND WONDERFUL THING. YOH-KUN SMILED AS HE WATCHED THEM WALK AWAY.
—MANTA

SHAMAN KING CHARACTER FILE No.9

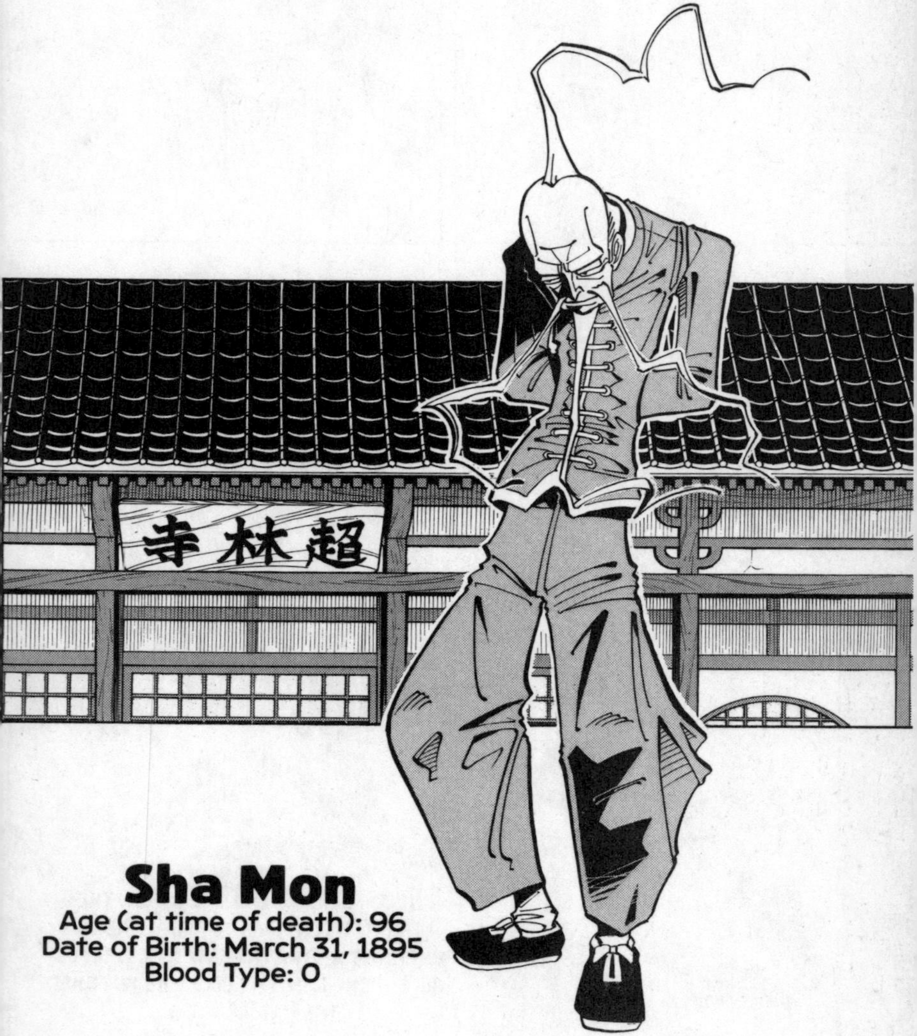
超林寺

Sha Mon

Age (at time of death): 96
Date of Birth: March 31, 1895
Blood Type: O

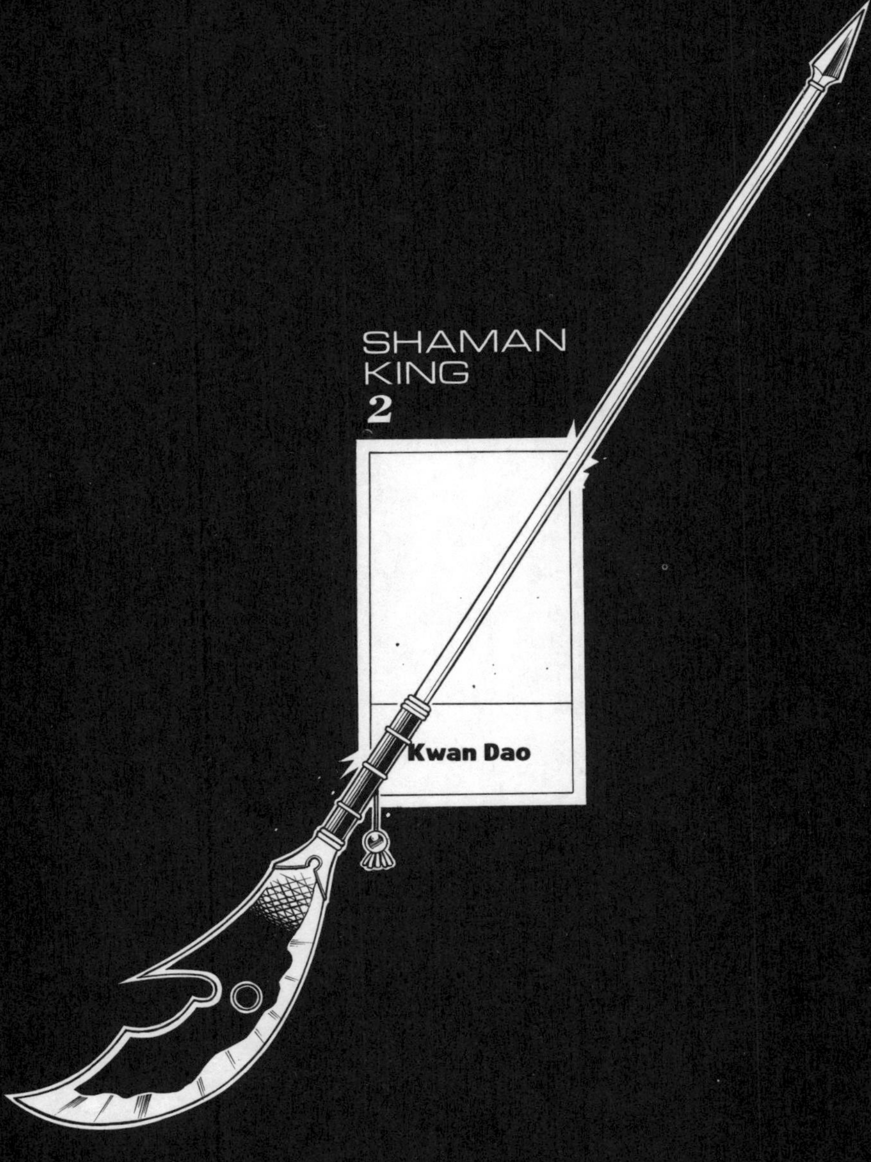
SHAMAN
KING
2
Kwan Dao

SHAMAN KING

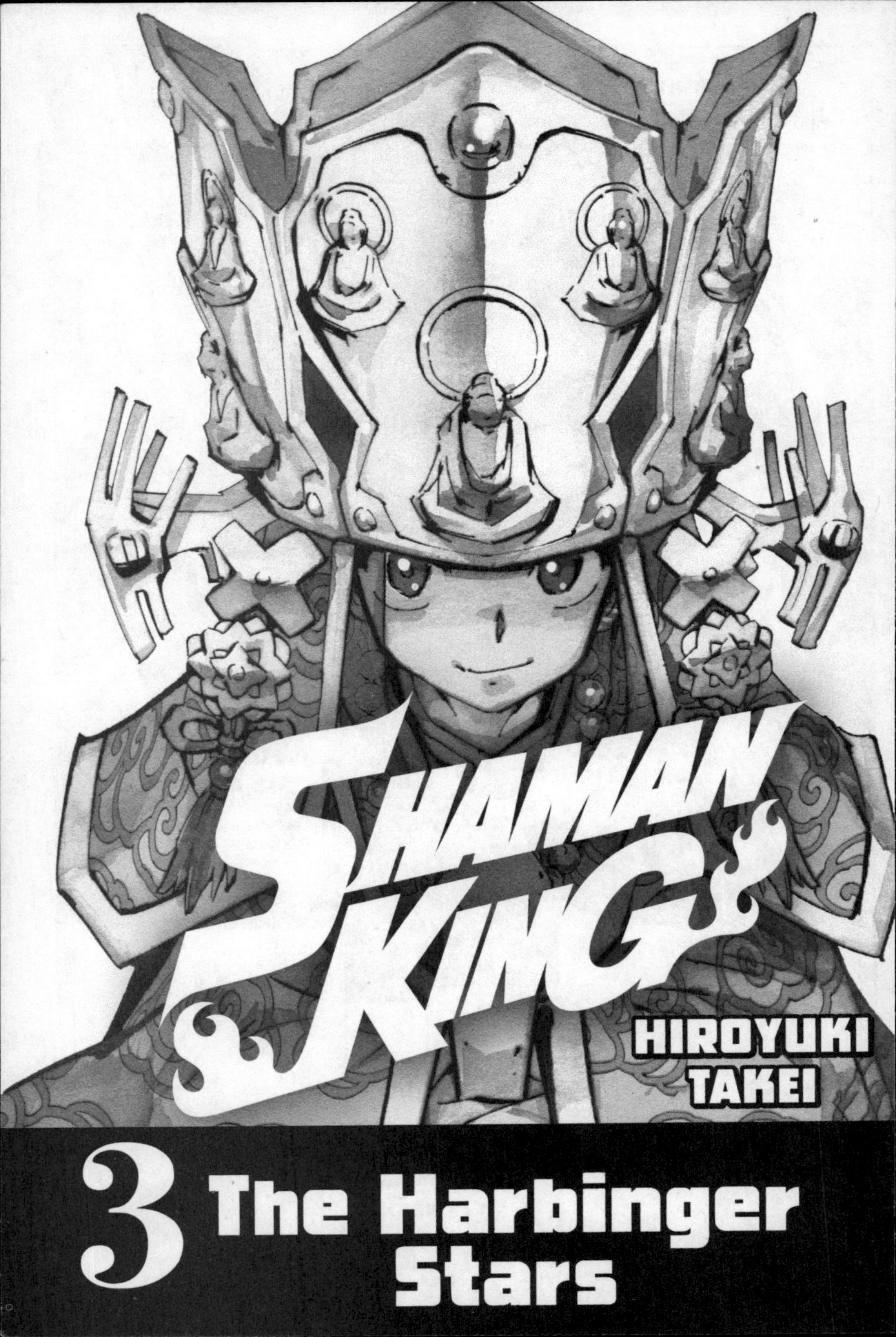
SHAMAN KING
HIROYUKI TAKEI

3 The Harbinger Stars

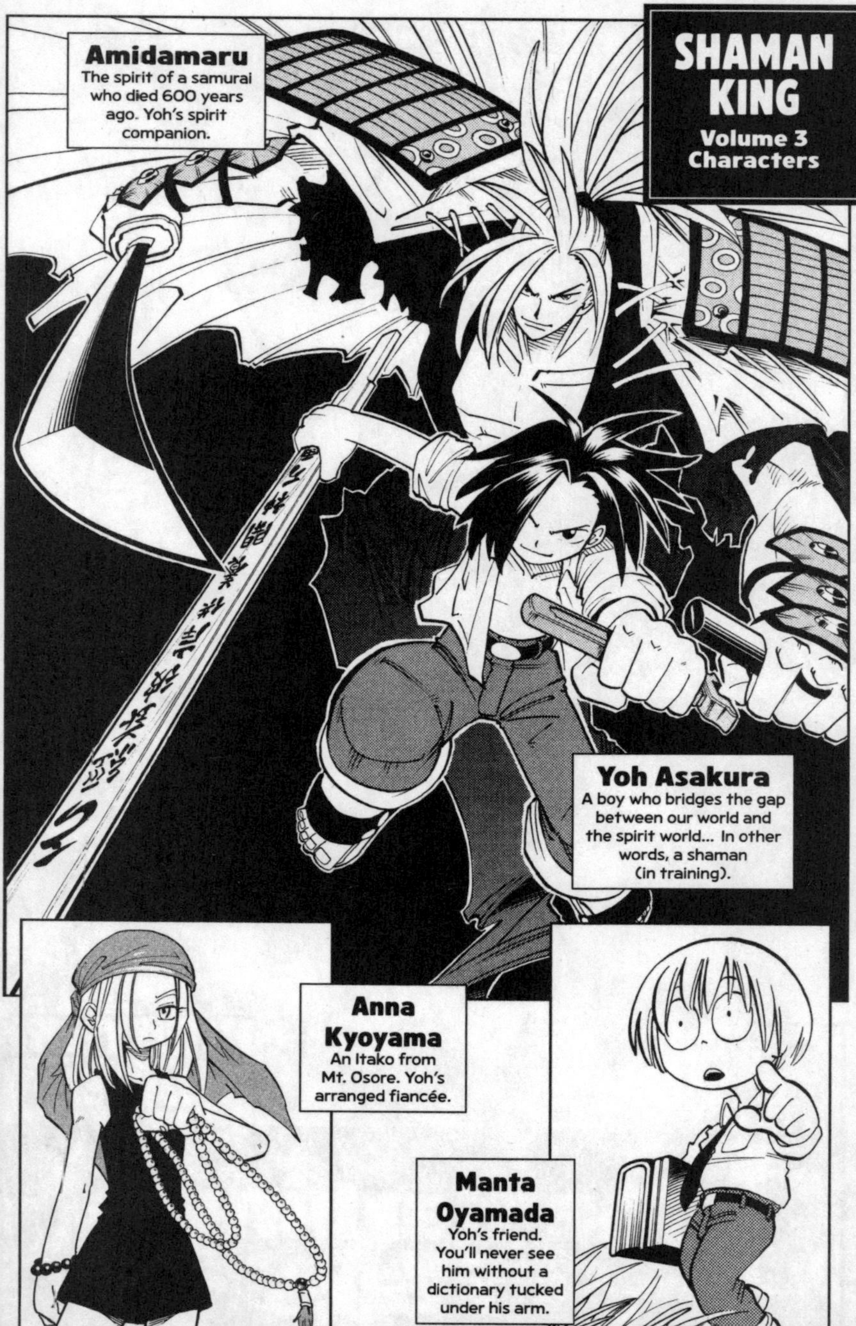
SHAMAN KING
Volume 3 Characters
Amidamaru
The spirit of a samurai who died 600 years ago. Yoh's spirit companion.
Yoh Asakura
A boy who bridges the gap between our world and the spirit world... In other words, a shaman (in training).
Manta Oyamada
Yoh's friend. You'll never see him without a dictionary tucked under his arm.
Anna Kyoyama
An Itako from Mt. Osore. Yoh's arranged fiancée.

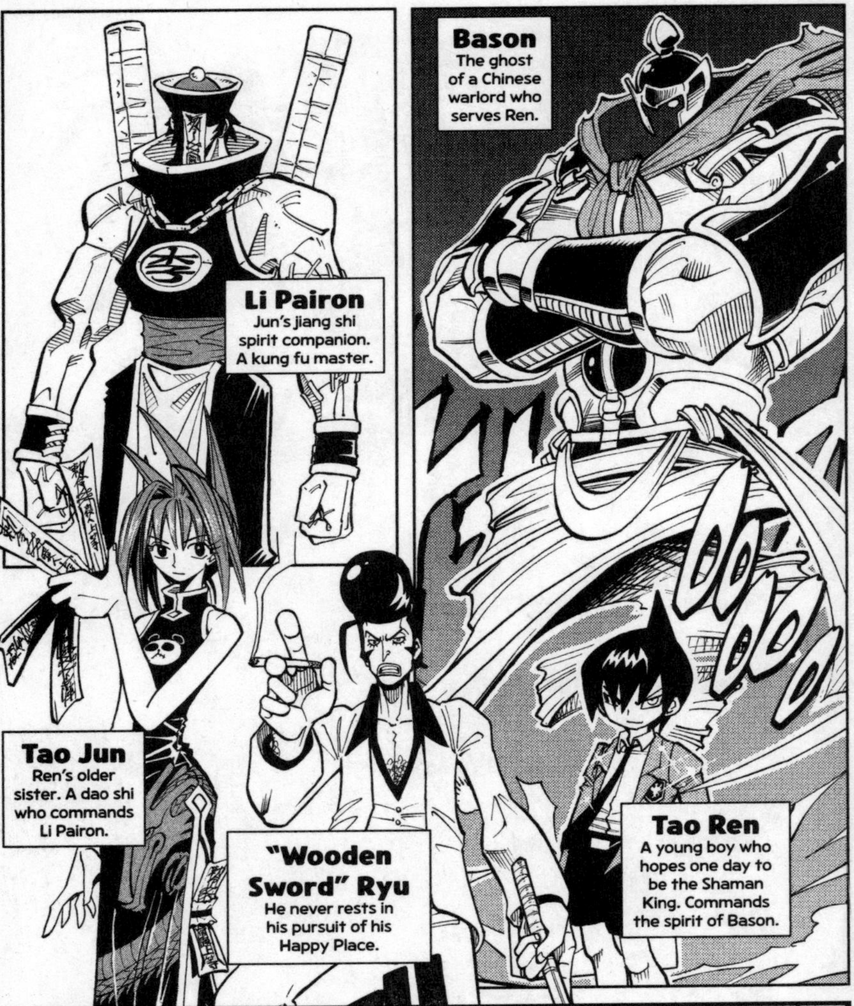
Bason
The ghost of a Chinese warlord who serves Ren.
Tao Ren
A young boy who hopes one day to be the Shaman King. Commands the spirit of Bason.
Li Pairon
Jun's jiang shi spirit companion. A kung fu master.
"Wooden Sword" Ryu
He never rests in his pursuit of his Happy Place.
Tao Jun
Ren's older sister. A dao shi who commands Li Pairon.

THE STORY SO FAR

This kid named Yoh Asakura-kun transferred to my class from Izumo... and it turns out he's a shaman! It seems shamans can bridge the gap between the spirit world and our world, commune with gods and spirits, and even draw on their strength. He came here to hone his abilities and took the ghost of Amidamaru, a samurai who died 600 years ago, as his spirit companion. With the help of his fiancée, Anna, Yoh is in training for the ultimate event: the Shaman Fight in Tokyo, the once every 500 years tournament to see who can channel the "Ruler of Spirits" and become the Shaman King. Yoh has already defeated the brother-sister pair of Ren and Jun... What dangers await him next?

SHAMAN KING 3

The Harbinger Stars

3

Chapter 18: Happy Place Trekkers

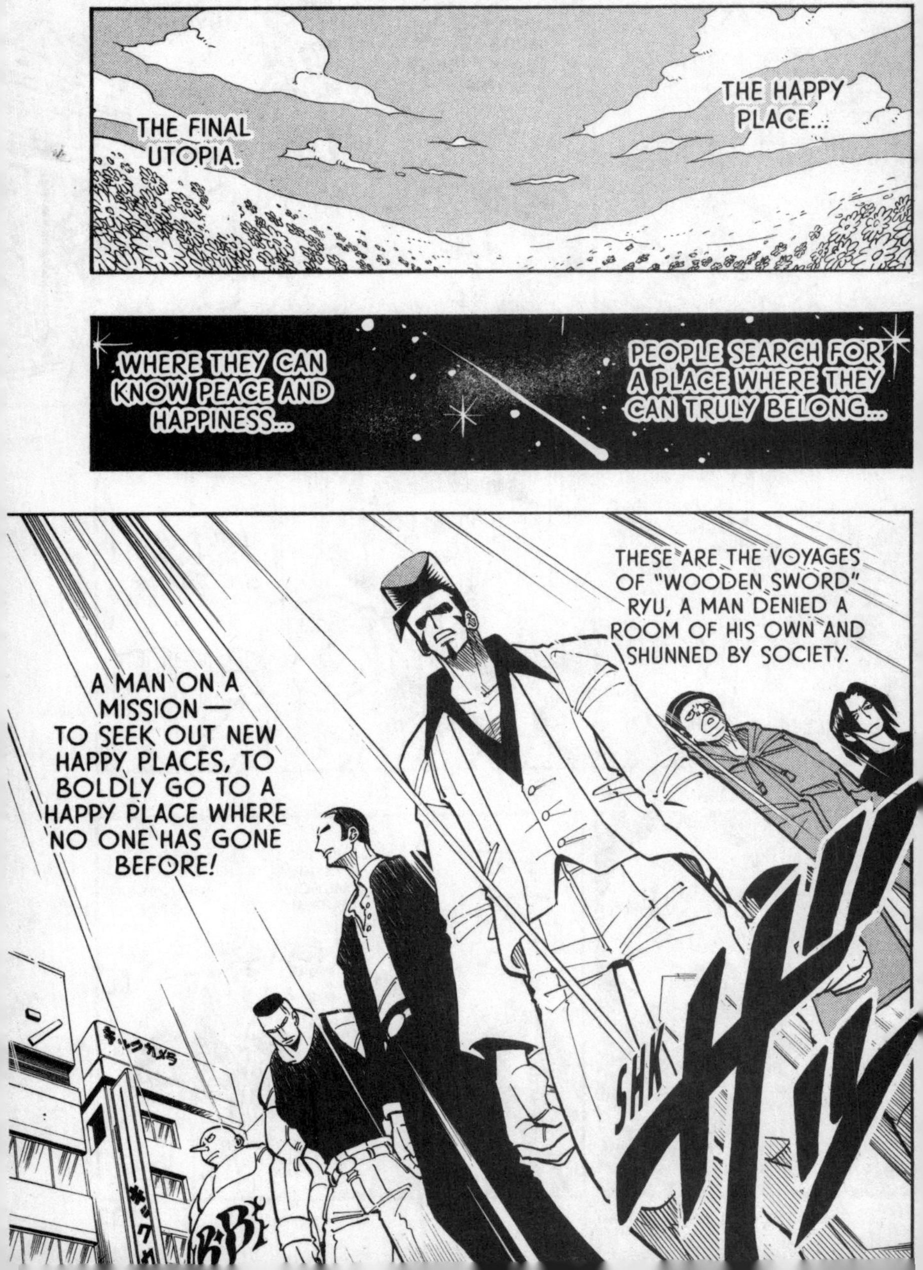

THE HAPPY PLACE...
THE FINAL UTOPIA.
PEOPLE SEARCH FOR A PLACE WHERE THEY CAN TRULY BELONG...
WHERE THEY CAN KNOW PEACE AND HAPPINESS...
THESE ARE THE VOYAGES OF "WOODEN SWORD" RYU, A MAN DENIED A ROOM OF HIS OWN AND SHUNNED BY SOCIETY.
A MAN ON A MISSION— TO SEEK OUT NEW HAPPY PLACES, TO BOLDLY GO TO A HAPPY PLACE WHERE NO ONE HAS GONE BEFORE!
SHK

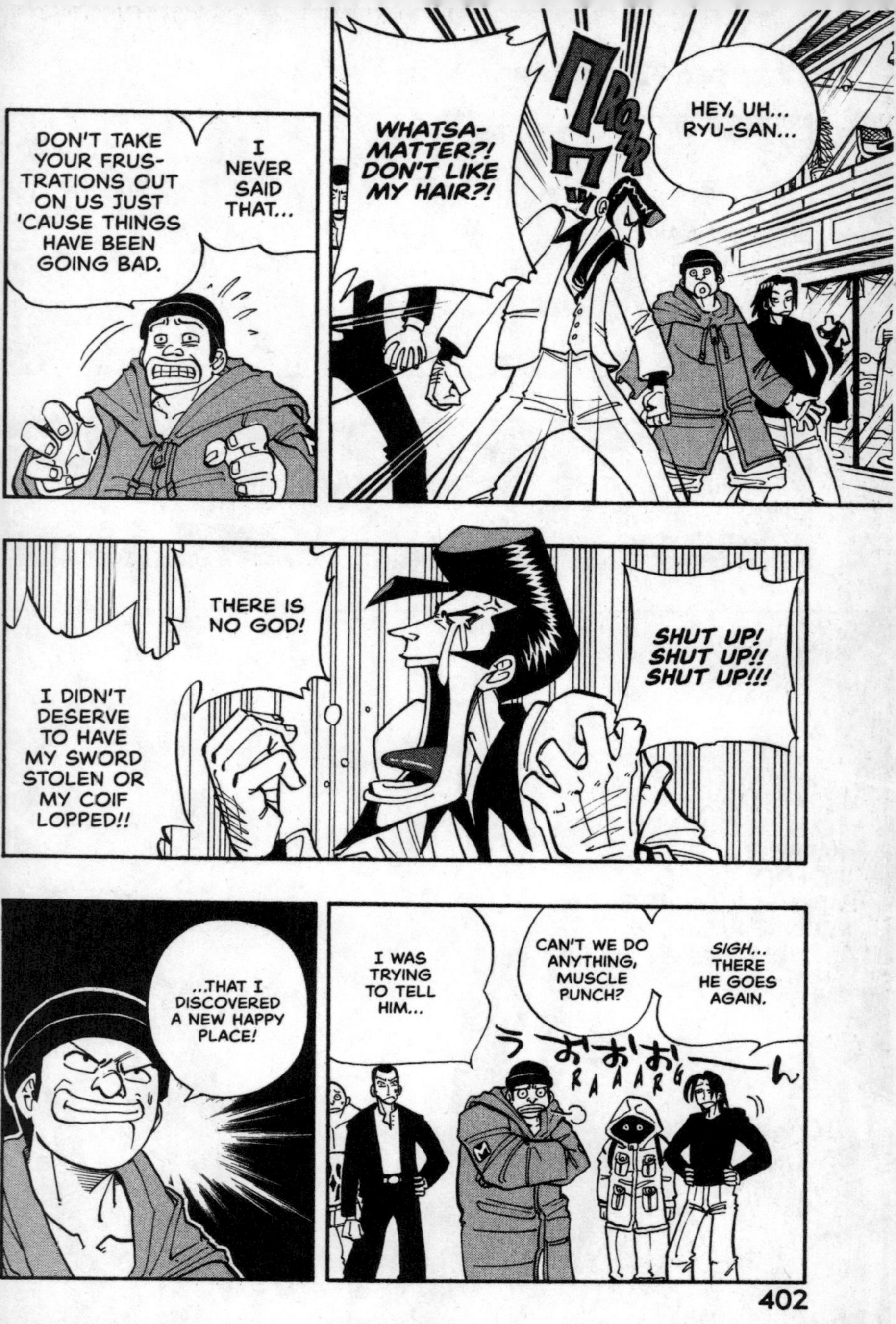
HEY, UH... RYU-SAN...
WHATSA-MATTER?! DON'T LIKE MY HAIR?!
ROAR
I NEVER SAID THAT...
DON'T TAKE YOUR FRUS-TRATIONS OUT ON US JUST 'CAUSE THINGS HAVE BEEN GOING BAD.
SHUT UP! SHUT UP!! SHUT UP!!!
THERE IS NO GOD!
I DIDN'T DESERVE TO HAVE MY SWORD STOLEN OR MY COIF LOPPED!!
SIGH... THERE HE GOES AGAIN.
CAN'T WE DO ANYTHING, MUSCLE PUNCH?
I WAS TRYING TO TELL HIM...
うおおおーーん
RAAARG
...THAT I DISCOVERED A NEW HAPPY PLACE!

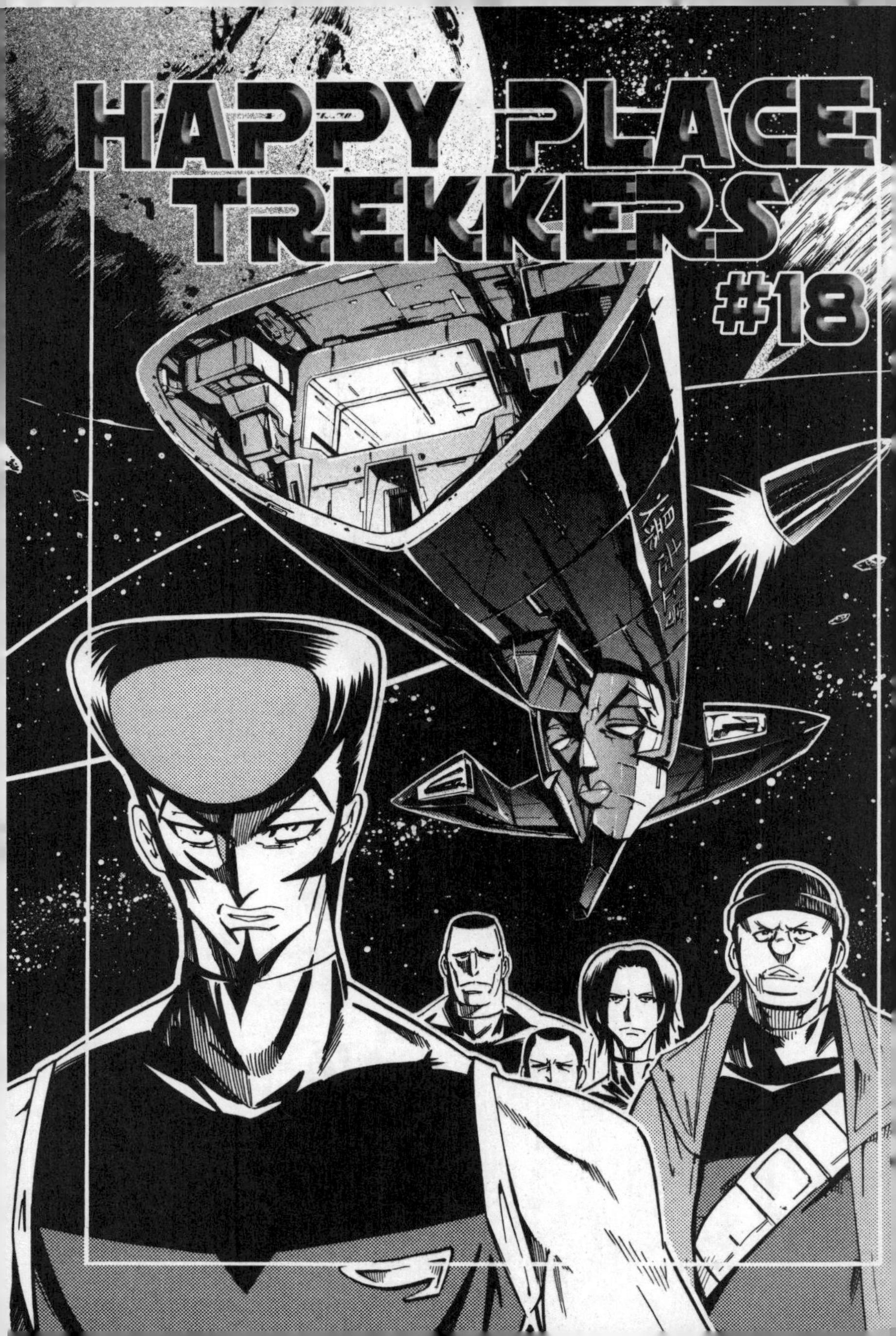
HAPPY PLACE TREKKERS
#18

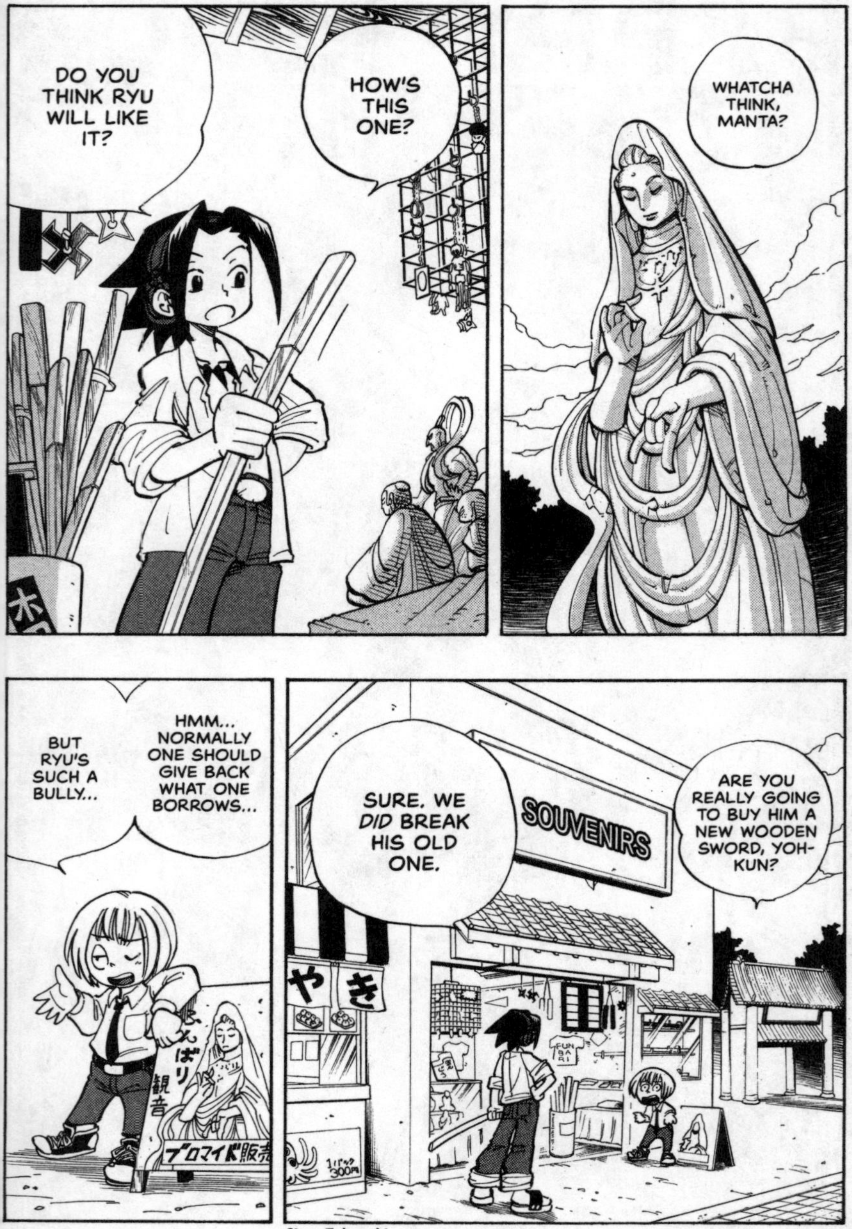
WHATCHA THINK, MANTA?
HOW'S THIS ONE?
DO YOU THINK RYU WILL LIKE IT?
ARE YOU REALLY GOING TO BUY HIM A NEW WOODEN SWORD, YOH-KUN?
SURE. WE *DID* BREAK HIS OLD ONE.
SOUVENIRS
HMM... NORMALLY ONE SHOULD GIVE BACK WHAT ONE BORROWS...
BUT RYU'S SUCH A BULLY...

Sign: Takoyaki

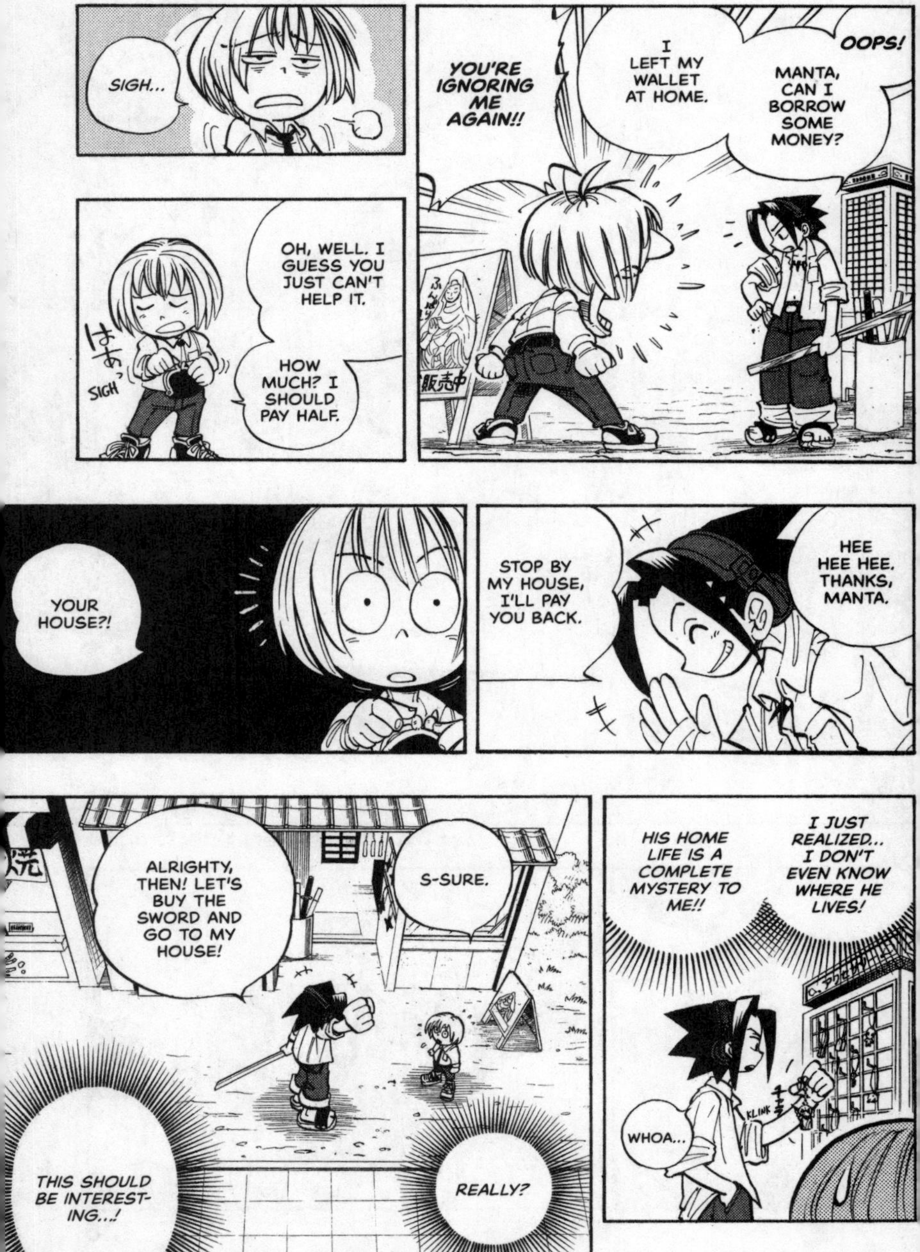
OOPS!
MANTA, CAN I BORROW SOME MONEY?
I LEFT MY WALLET AT HOME.
YOU'RE IGNORING ME AGAIN!!
販売中
SIGH...
OH, WELL. I GUESS YOU JUST CAN'T HELP IT.
HOW MUCH? I SHOULD PAY HALF.
はあっ
SIGH
HEE HEE HEE. THANKS, MANTA.
STOP BY MY HOUSE, I'LL PAY YOU BACK.
YOUR HOUSE?!
I JUST REALIZED... I DON'T EVEN KNOW WHERE HE LIVES!
HIS HOME LIFE IS A COMPLETE MYSTERY TO ME!!
KLINK
WHOA...
S-SURE.
ALRIGHTY, THEN! LET'S BUY THE SWORD AND GO TO MY HOUSE!
REALLY?
THIS SHOULD BE INTERESTING...!

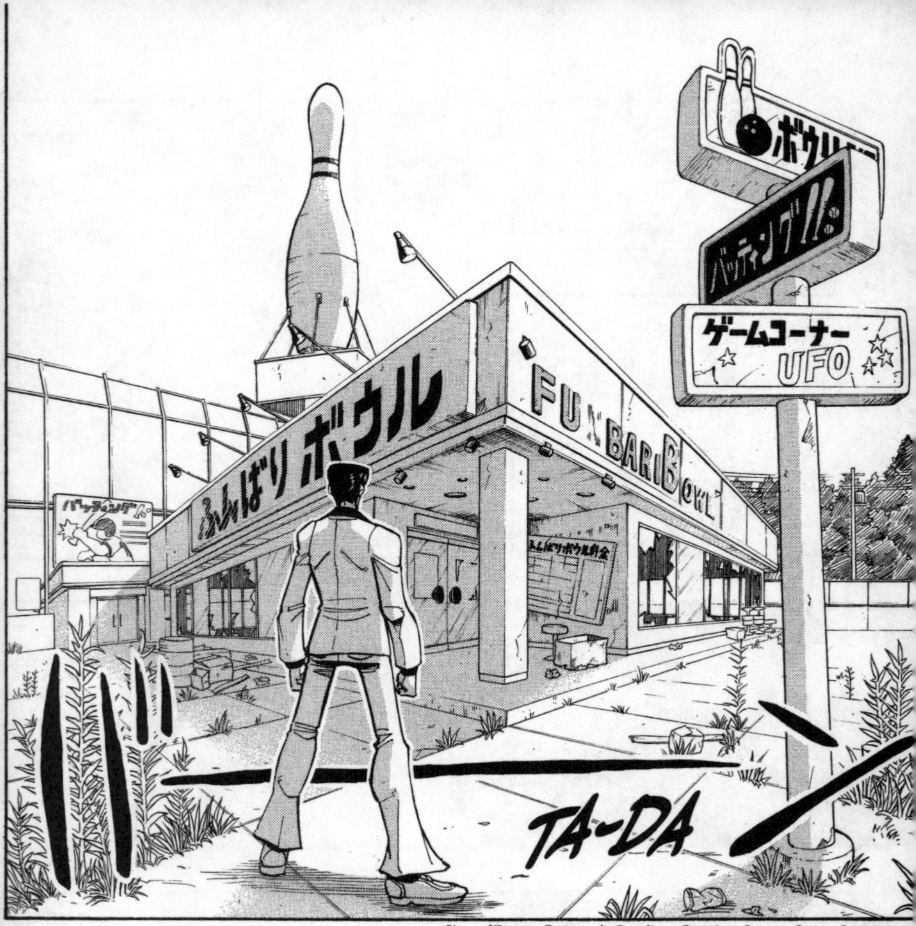
ゲームコーナー
UFO
ふんばり ボウル
TA-DA

Signs (Top to Bottom): Bowling, Batting Cages, Game Corner

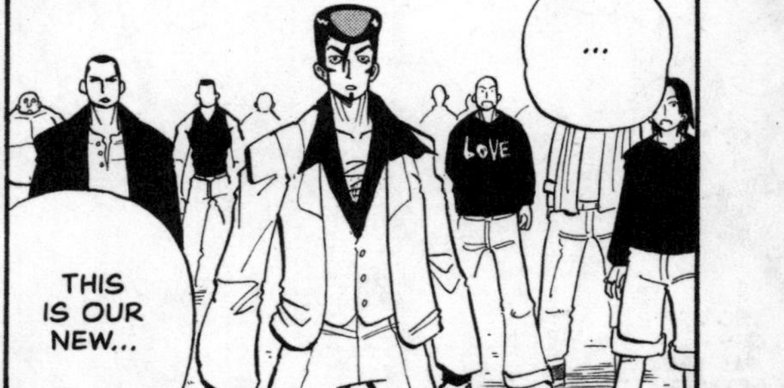
...
THIS IS OUR NEW...

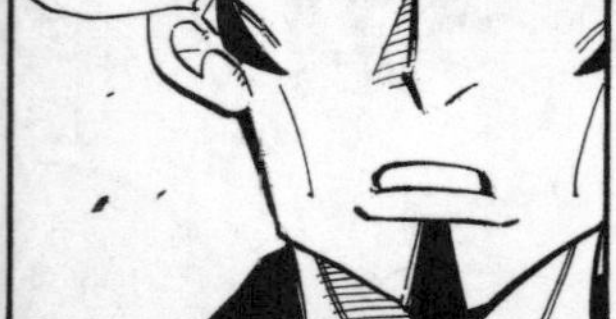
...HAPPY PLACE...?!

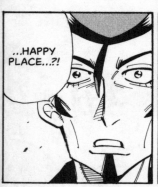

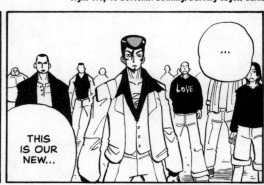

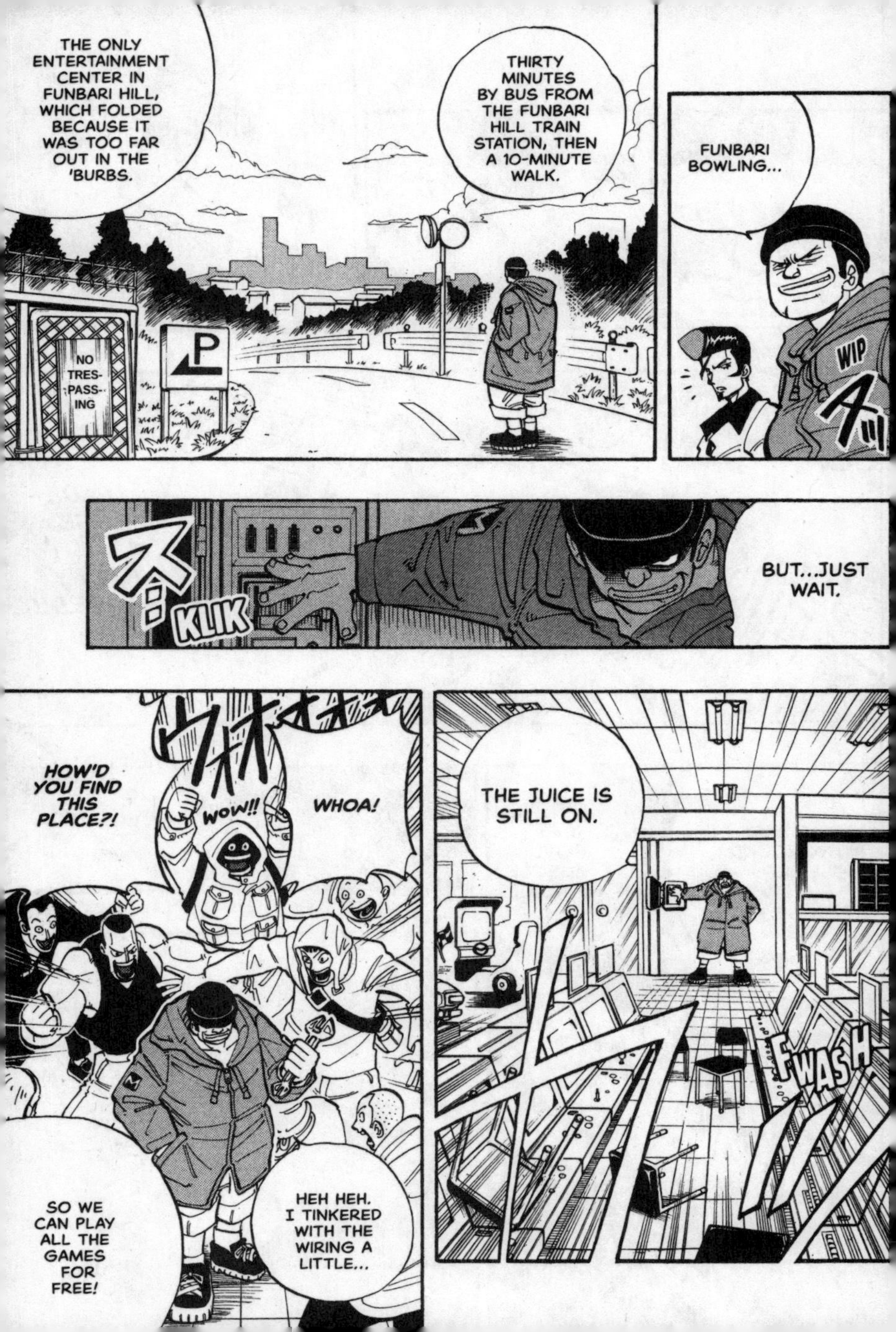
FUNBARI BOWLING...
WIP
THIRTY MINUTES BY BUS FROM THE FUNBARI HILL TRAIN STATION, THEN A 10-MINUTE WALK.
THE ONLY ENTERTAINMENT CENTER IN FUNBARI HILL, WHICH FOLDED BECAUSE IT WAS TOO FAR OUT IN THE 'BURBS.
P
NO TRES-PASS-ING
BUT...JUST WAIT.
KLIK
THE JUICE IS STILL ON.
FWASH
WHOA!
WOW!!
HOW'D YOU FIND THIS PLACE?!
HEH HEH. I TINKERED WITH THE WIRING A LITTLE...
SO WE CAN PLAY ALL THE GAMES FOR FREE!

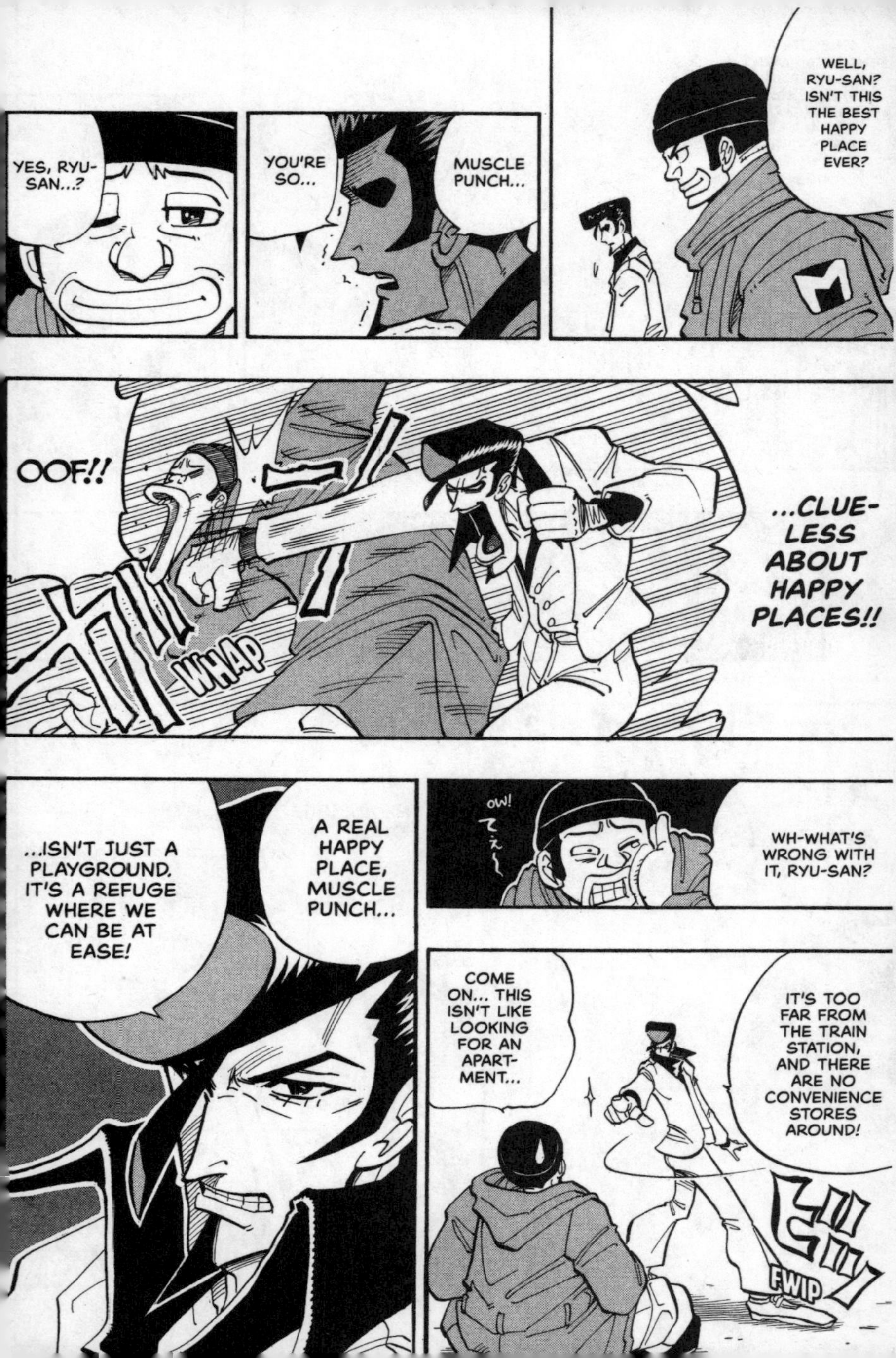
WELL, RYU-SAN? ISN'T THIS THE BEST HAPPY PLACE EVER?
MUSCLE PUNCH...
YOU'RE SO...
YES, RYU-SAN...?
...CLUELESS ABOUT HAPPY PLACES!!
OOF!!
WHAP
WH-WHAT'S WRONG WITH IT, RYU-SAN?
OW!
てぇ〜
IT'S TOO FAR FROM THE TRAIN STATION, AND THERE ARE NO CONVENIENCE STORES AROUND!
COME ON... THIS ISN'T LIKE LOOKING FOR AN APARTMENT...
FWIP
A REAL HAPPY PLACE, MUSCLE PUNCH...
...ISN'T JUST A PLAYGROUND. IT'S A REFUGE WHERE WE CAN BE AT EASE!

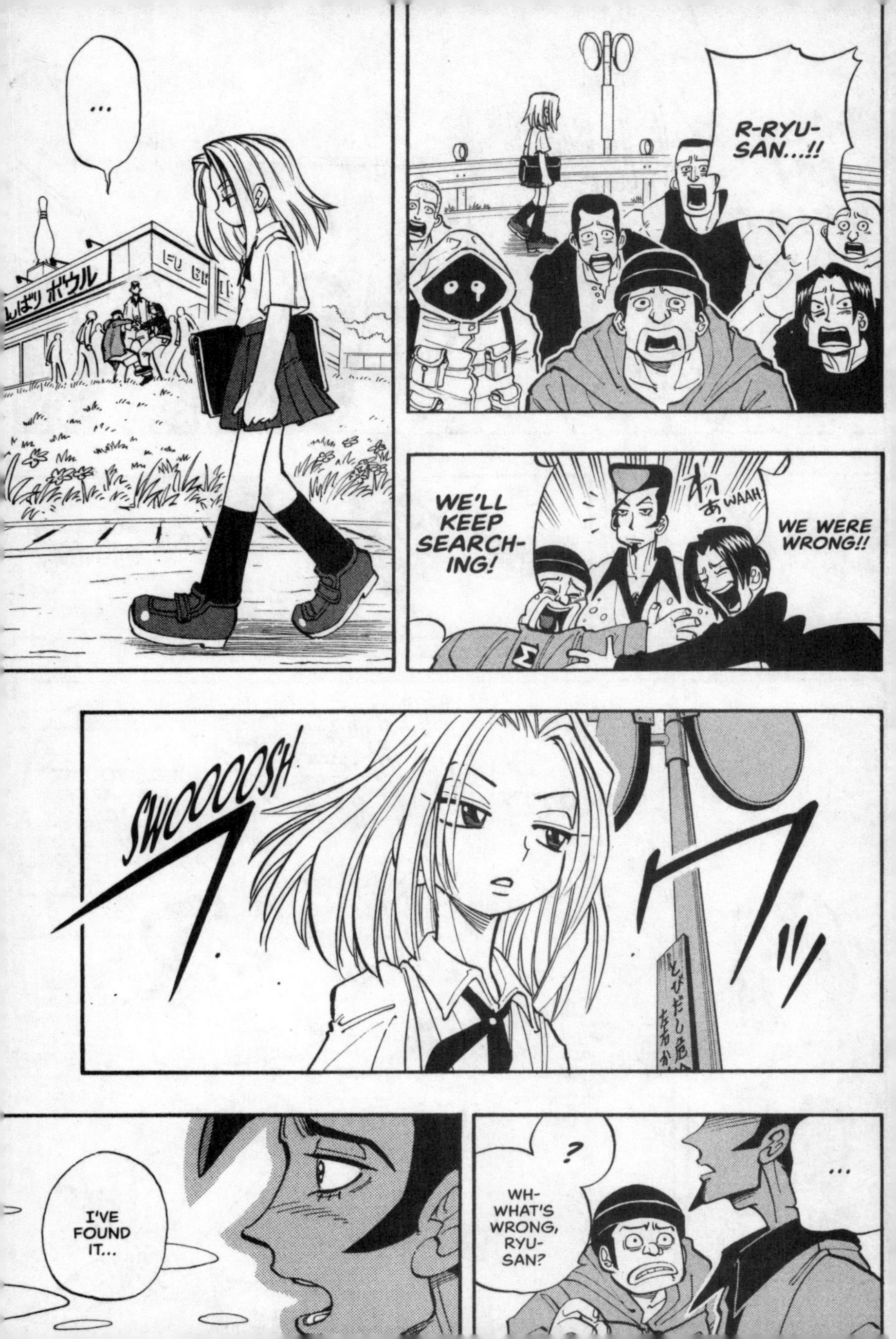
R-RYU-SAN...!!
WAAH
WE WERE WRONG!!
WE'LL KEEP SEARCHING!
...
SWOOOOSH
...
?
WH-WHAT'S WRONG, RYU-SAN?
I'VE FOUND IT...

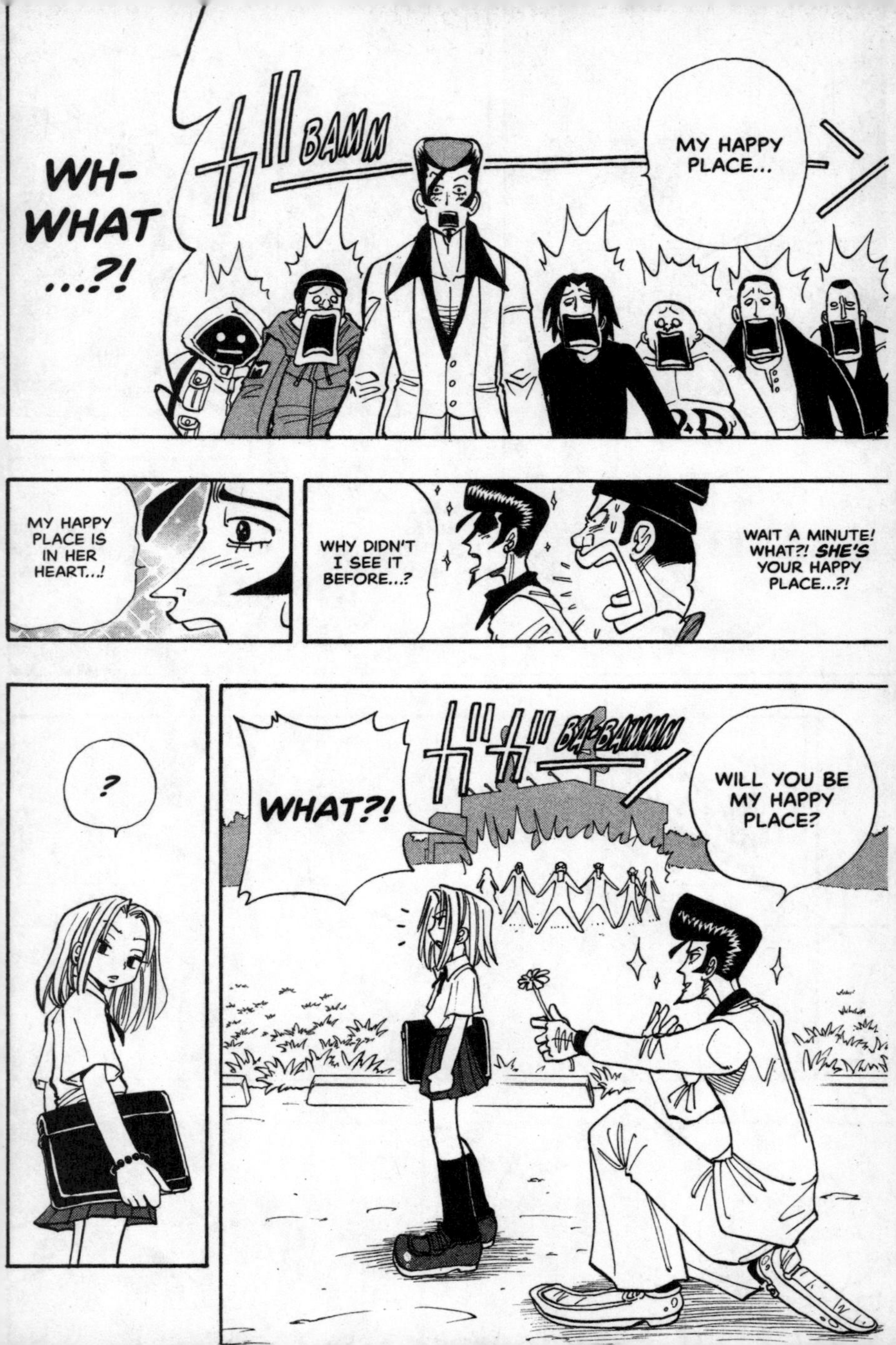
MY HAPPY PLACE...
BAMM
WH- WHAT ...?!
WAIT A MINUTE! WHAT?! *SHE'S* YOUR HAPPY PLACE...?!
WHY DIDN'T I SEE IT BEFORE...?
MY HAPPY PLACE IS IN HER HEART...!
WILL YOU BE MY HAPPY PLACE?
BA-BAMMM
WHAT?!
?

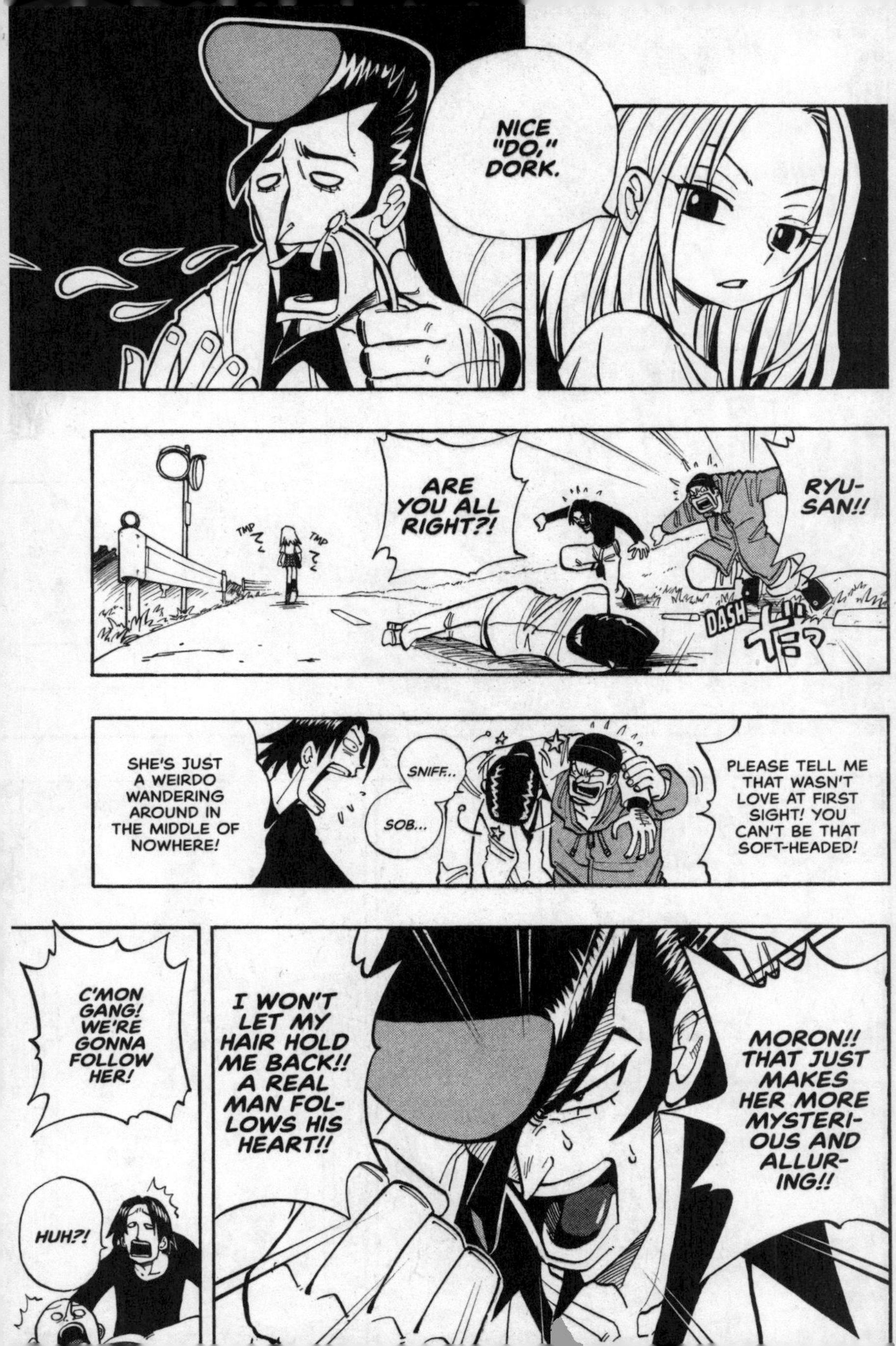
NICE "DO," DORK.
RYU-SAN!!
ARE YOU ALL RIGHT?!
DASH
TMP
TMP
PLEASE TELL ME THAT WASN'T LOVE AT FIRST SIGHT! YOU CAN'T BE THAT SOFT-HEADED!
SNIFF...
SOB...
SHE'S JUST A WEIRDO WANDERING AROUND IN THE MIDDLE OF NOWHERE!
MORON!! THAT JUST MAKES HER MORE MYSTERI-OUS AND ALLUR-ING!!
I WON'T LET MY HAIR HOLD ME BACK!! A REAL MAN FOL-LOWS HIS HEART!!
C'MON GANG! WE'RE GONNA FOLLOW HER!
HUH?!

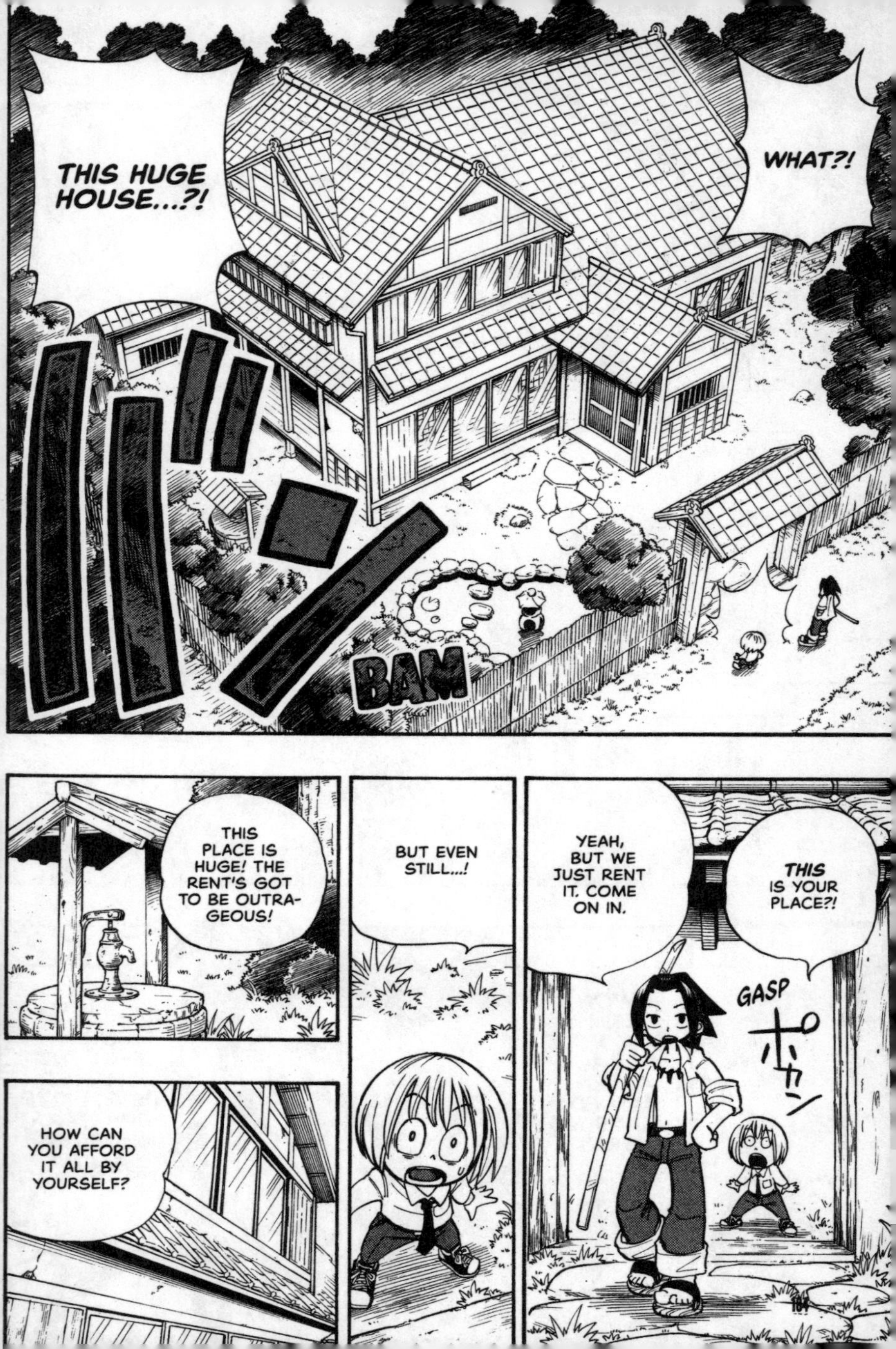
WHAT?!
THIS HUGE HOUSE...?!
BAM
THIS IS YOUR PLACE?!
GASP
ポカン
YEAH, BUT WE JUST RENT IT. COME ON IN.
BUT EVEN STILL...!
THIS PLACE IS HUGE! THE RENT'S GOT TO BE OUTRA-GEOUS!
HOW CAN YOU AFFORD IT ALL BY YOURSELF?

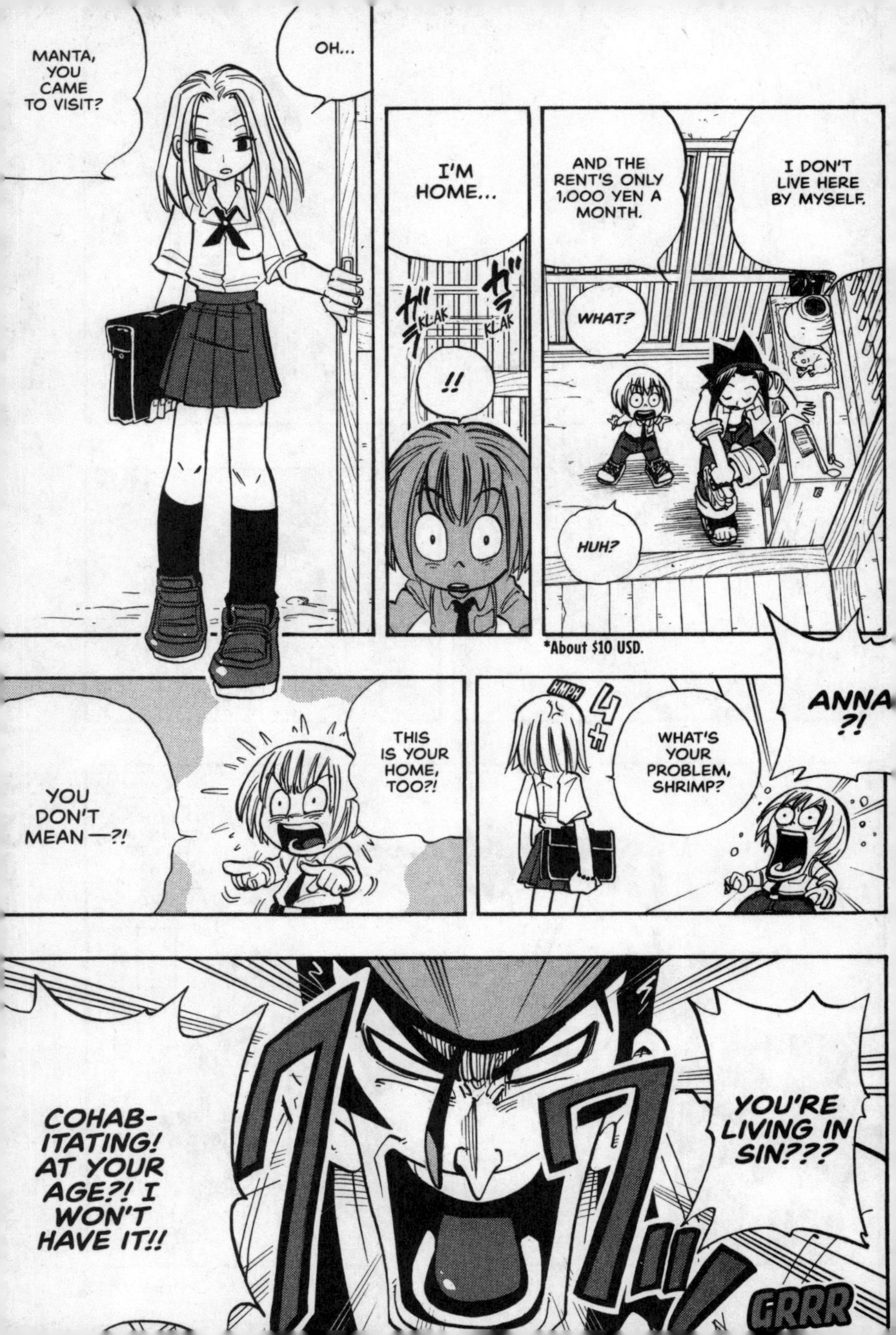
I DON'T LIVE HERE BY MYSELF.
AND THE RENT'S ONLY 1,000 YEN A MONTH.
WHAT?
HUH?
I'M HOME...
KLAK
KLAK
!!
OH...
MANTA, YOU CAME TO VISIT?
*About $10 USD.
ANNA?!
HMPH
WHAT'S YOUR PROBLEM, SHRIMP?
THIS IS YOUR HOME, TOO?!
YOU DON'T MEAN—?!
YOU'RE LIVING IN SIN???
COHAB-ITATING! AT YOUR AGE?! I WON'T HAVE IT!!
GRRR

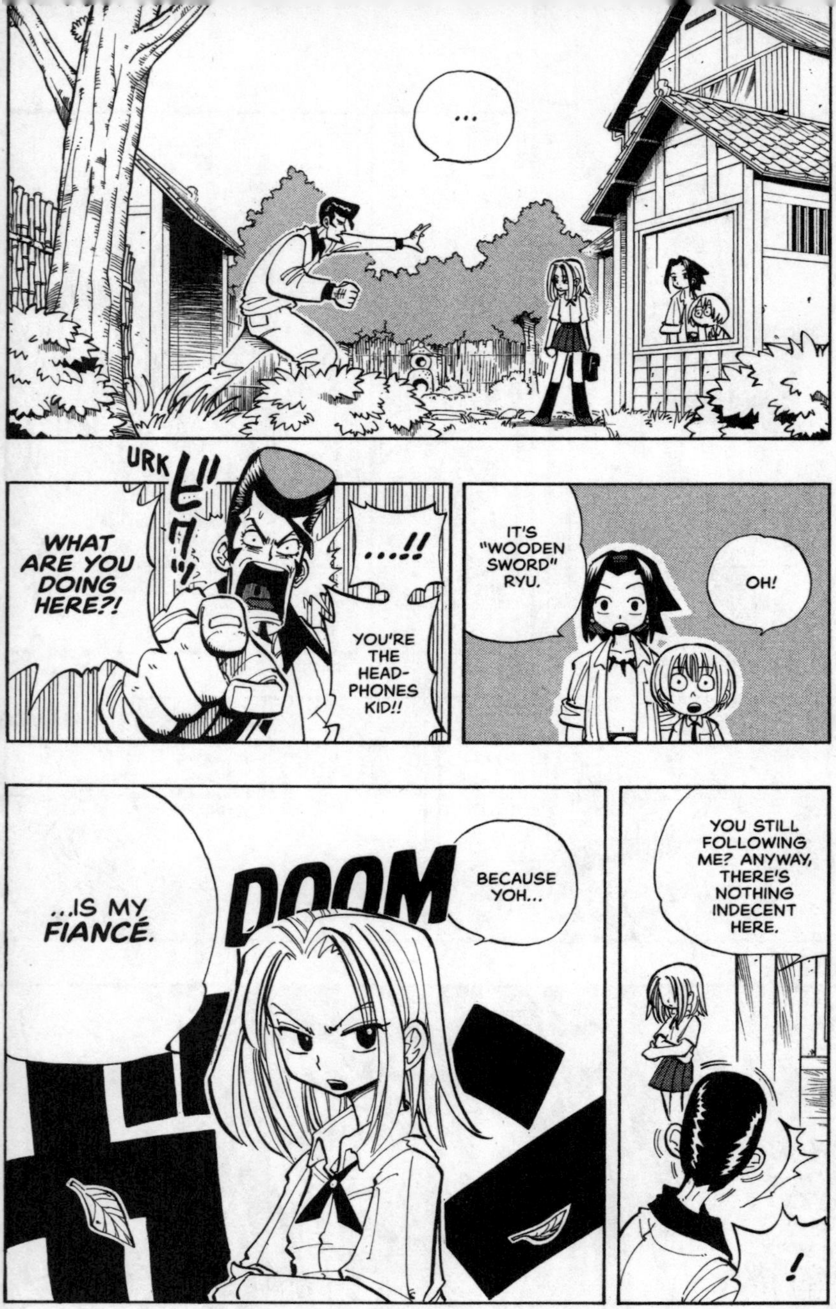
...
IT'S "WOODEN SWORD" RYU.
OH!
...!!
YOU'RE THE HEAD-PHONES KID!!
URK ビクッ
WHAT ARE YOU DOING HERE?!
YOU STILL FOLLOWING ME? ANYWAY, THERE'S NOTHING INDECENT HERE.
!
BECAUSE YOH...
DOOM
...IS MY FIANCÉ.

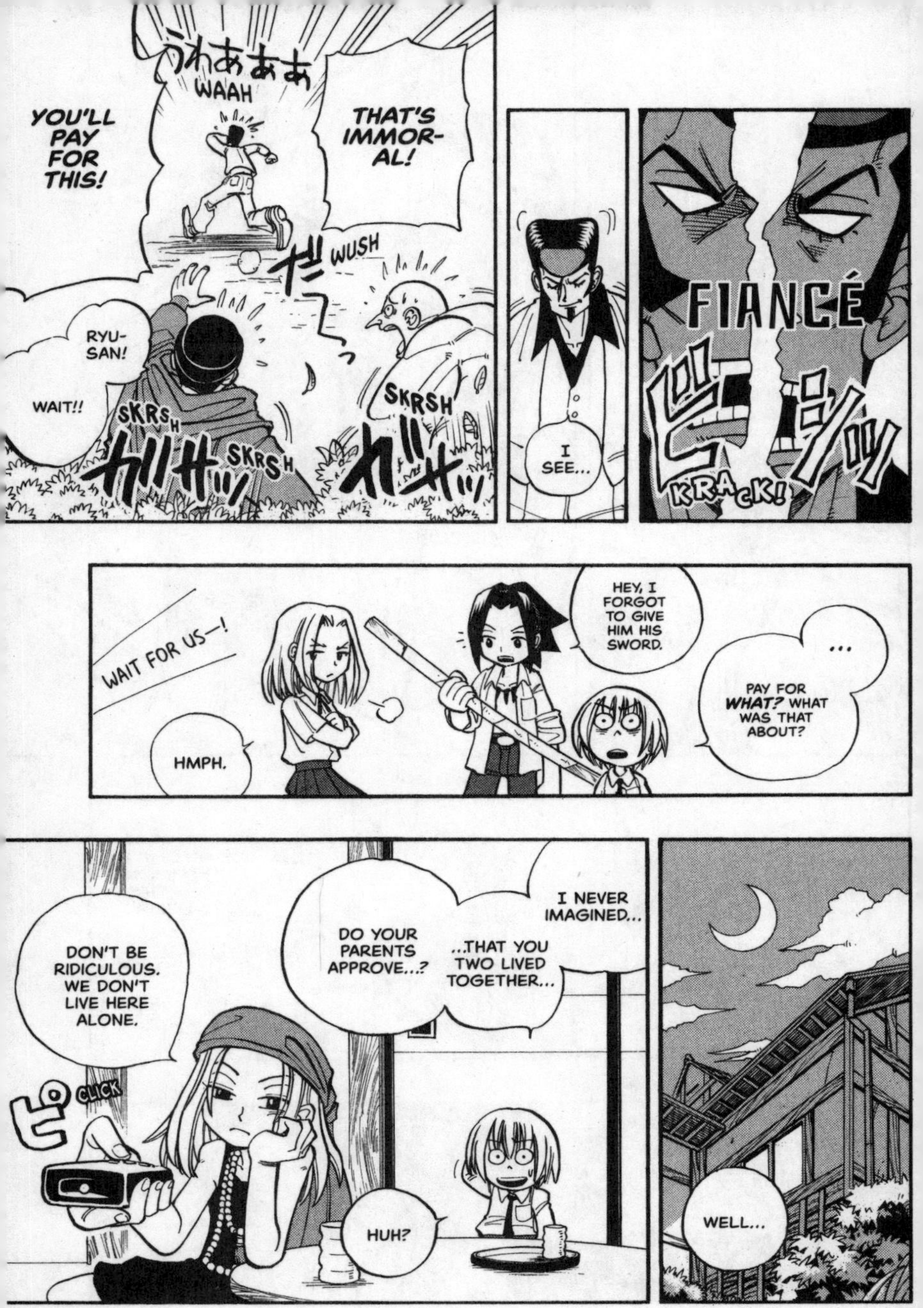
FIANCÉ
KRACK!
I SEE...
うわあああ
WAAH
THAT'S IMMORAL!
YOU'LL PAY FOR THIS!
WUSH
SKRSH
RYU-SAN!
WAIT!!
SKRSH
SKRSH
HEY, I FORGOT TO GIVE HIM HIS SWORD.
...
PAY FOR *WHAT?* WHAT WAS THAT ABOUT?
WAIT FOR US—!
HMPH.
WELL...
I NEVER IMAGINED...
...THAT YOU TWO LIVED TOGETHER...
DO YOUR PARENTS APPROVE...?
DON'T BE RIDICULOUS. WE DON'T LIVE HERE ALONE.
CLICK
HUH?

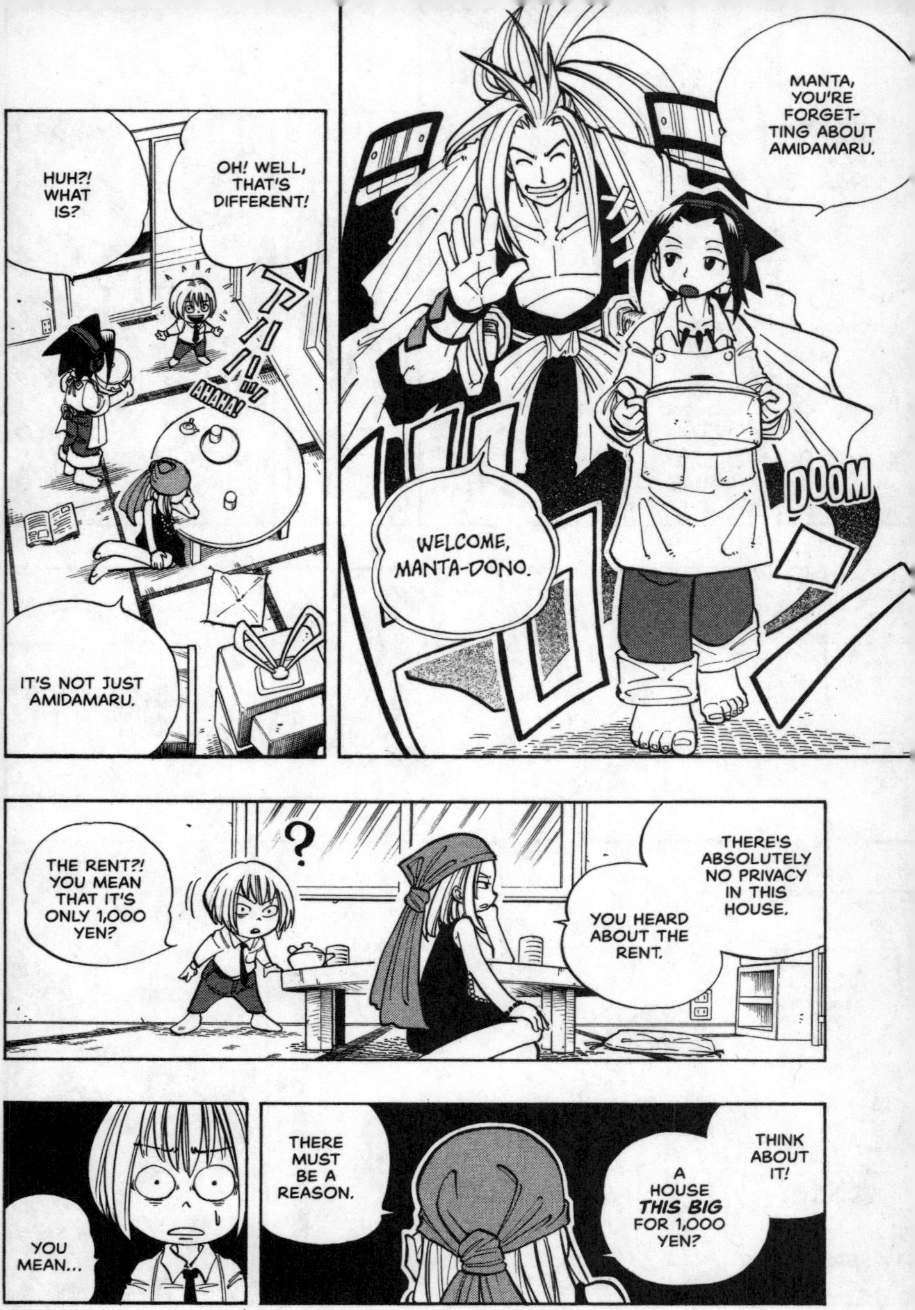
MANTA, YOU'RE FORGET-TING ABOUT AMIDAMARU.
DOOM
WELCOME, MANTA-DONO.
OH! WELL, THAT'S DIFFERENT!
HUH?! WHAT IS?
AHAHA!
IT'S NOT JUST AMIDAMARU.
THERE'S ABSOLUTELY NO PRIVACY IN THIS HOUSE.
YOU HEARD ABOUT THE RENT.
?
THE RENT?! YOU MEAN THAT IT'S ONLY 1,000 YEN?
THINK ABOUT IT!
A HOUSE THIS BIG FOR 1,000 YEN?
THERE MUST BE A REASON.
YOU MEAN...

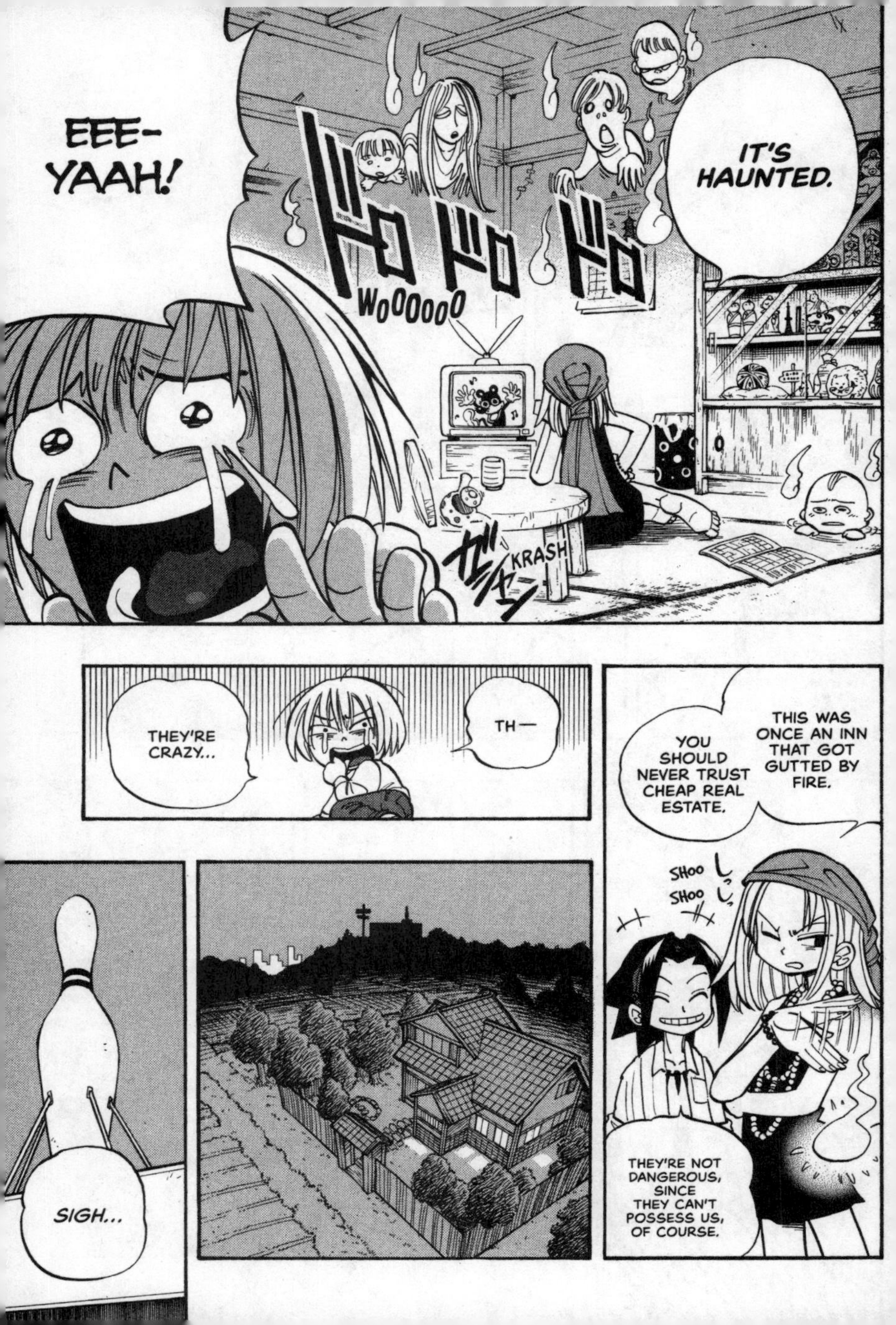
IT'S HAUNTED.
EEE-YAAH!
ドロドロドロ
WOOOOOO
KRASH
THIS WAS ONCE AN INN THAT GOT GUTTED BY FIRE.
YOU SHOULD NEVER TRUST CHEAP REAL ESTATE.
SHOO SHOO
しっしっ
THEY'RE NOT DANGEROUS, SINCE THEY CAN'T POSSESS US, OF COURSE.
TH—
THEY'RE CRAZY...
SIGH...

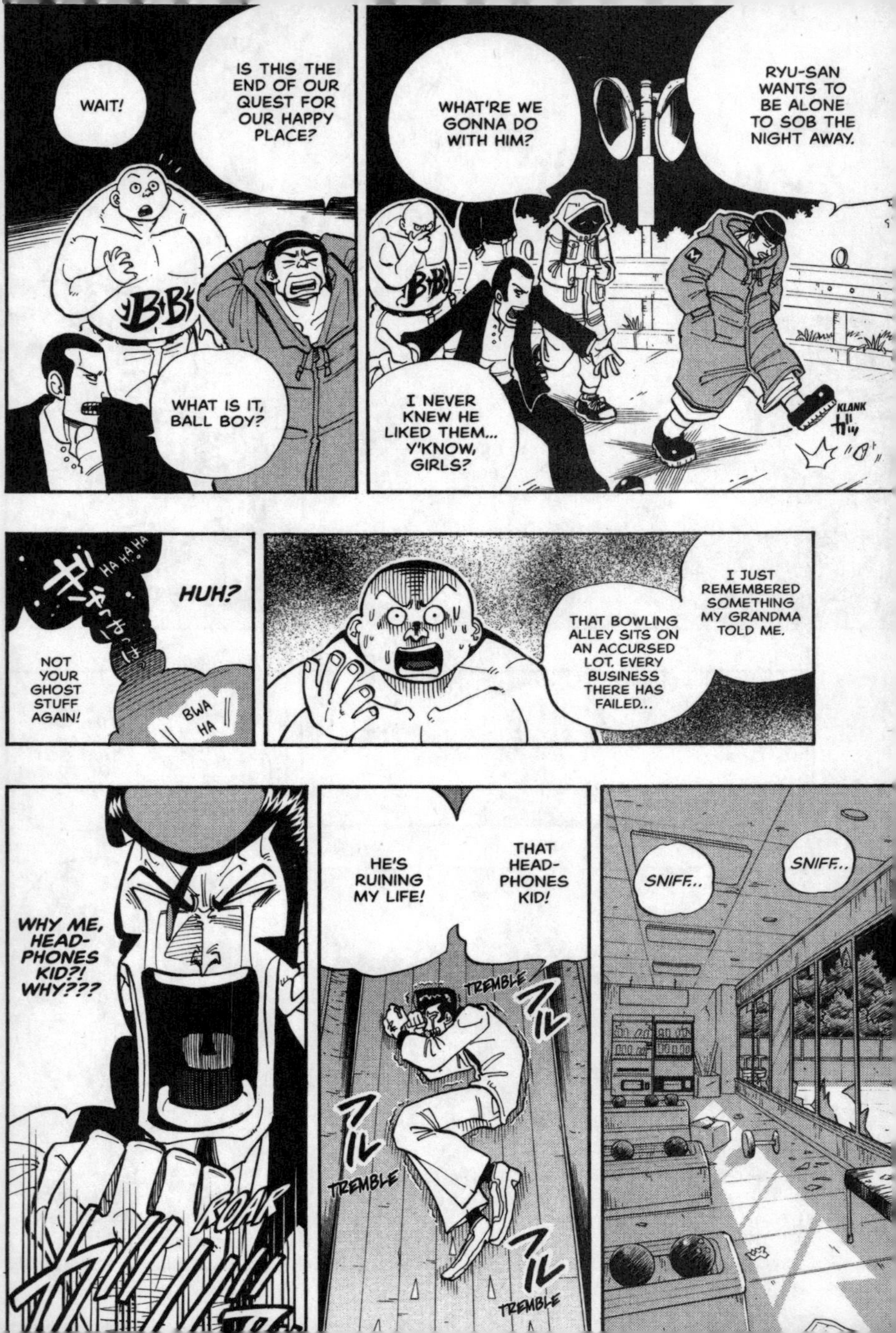
RYU-SAN WANTS TO BE ALONE TO SOB THE NIGHT AWAY.
WHAT'RE WE GONNA DO WITH HIM?
KLANK
I NEVER KNEW HE LIKED THEM... Y'KNOW, GIRLS?
IS THIS THE END OF OUR QUEST FOR OUR HAPPY PLACE?
WAIT!
WHAT IS IT, BALL BOY?
I JUST REMEMBERED SOMETHING MY GRANDMA TOLD ME.
THAT BOWLING ALLEY SITS ON AN ACCURSED LOT. EVERY BUSINESS THERE HAS FAILED...
HUH?
HA HA HA
NOT YOUR GHOST STUFF AGAIN!
BWA HA
SNIFF...
SNIFF...
THAT HEADPHONES KID!
HE'S RUINING MY LIFE!
TREMBLE
TREMBLE
TREMBLE
WHY ME, HEADPHONES KID?! WHY???
ROAR

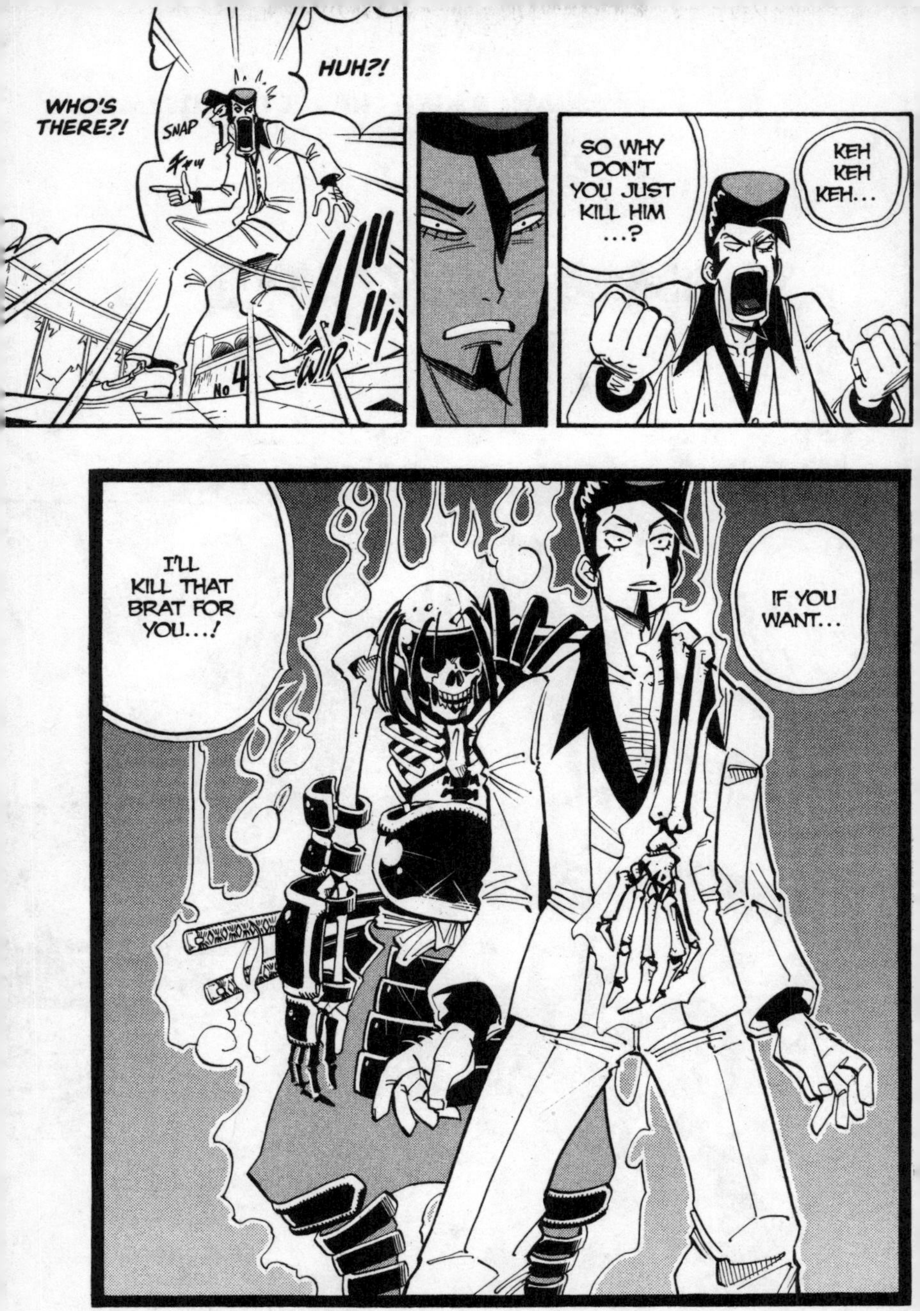
KEH KEH KEH...
SO WHY DON'T YOU JUST KILL HIM ...?
HUH?!
WHO'S THERE?!
SNAP
WIP
No 4
IF YOU WANT...
I'LL KILL THAT BRAT FOR YOU...!

SHAMAN KING CHARACTER FILE No.10

YOH ASAKURA
1989

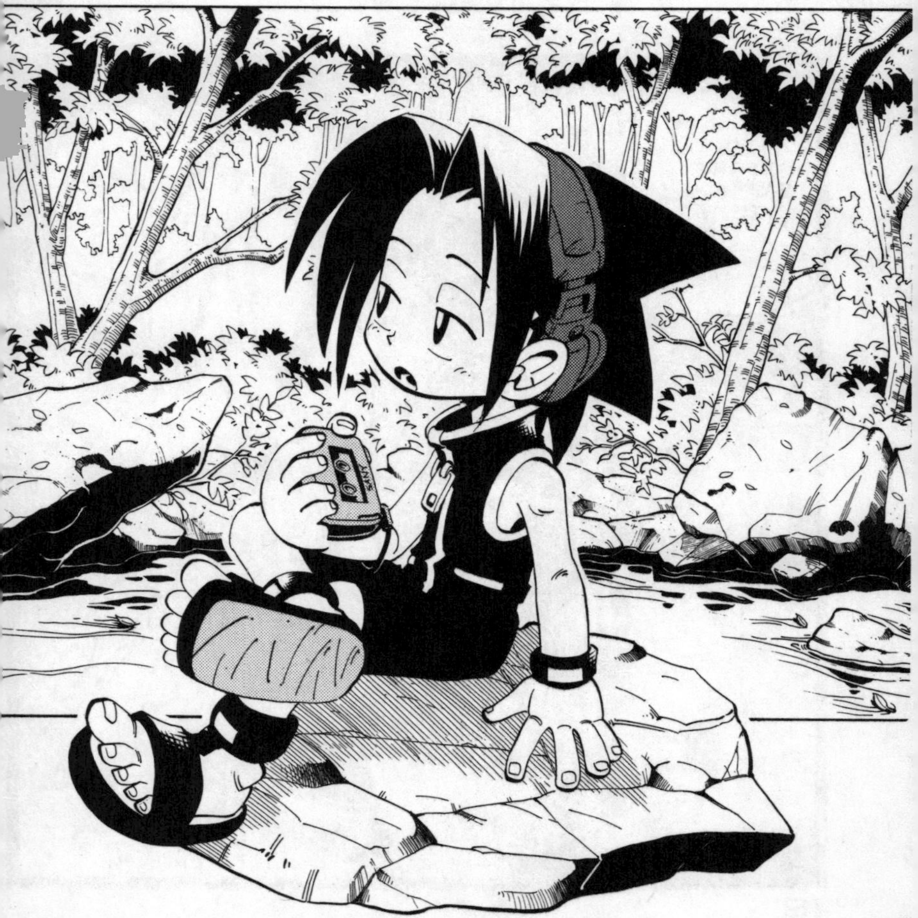

Chapter 19: The 600-Year Curse

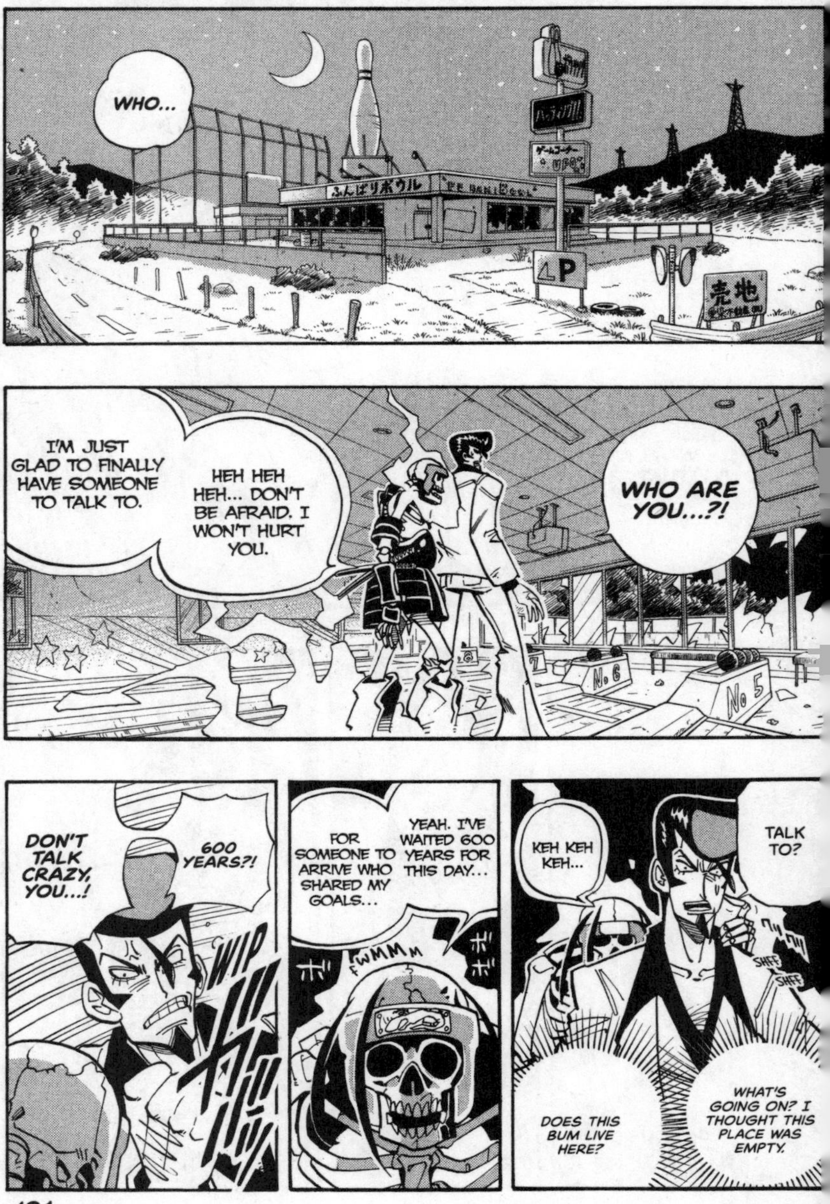
WHO...
ふんばりボウル
P
売地
WHO ARE YOU...?!
HEH HEH HEH... DON'T BE AFRAID. I WON'T HURT YOU.
I'M JUST GLAD TO FINALLY HAVE SOMEONE TO TALK TO.
No 5
No. 6
TALK TO?
KEH KEH KEH...
SHFF
SHFF
WHAT'S GOING ON? I THOUGHT THIS PLACE WAS EMPTY.
DOES THIS BUM LIVE HERE?
YEAH. I'VE WAITED 600 YEARS FOR THIS DAY...
FOR SOMEONE TO ARRIVE WHO SHARED MY GOALS...
FWMMM
600 YEARS?!
DON'T TALK CRAZY, YOU...!
WIP

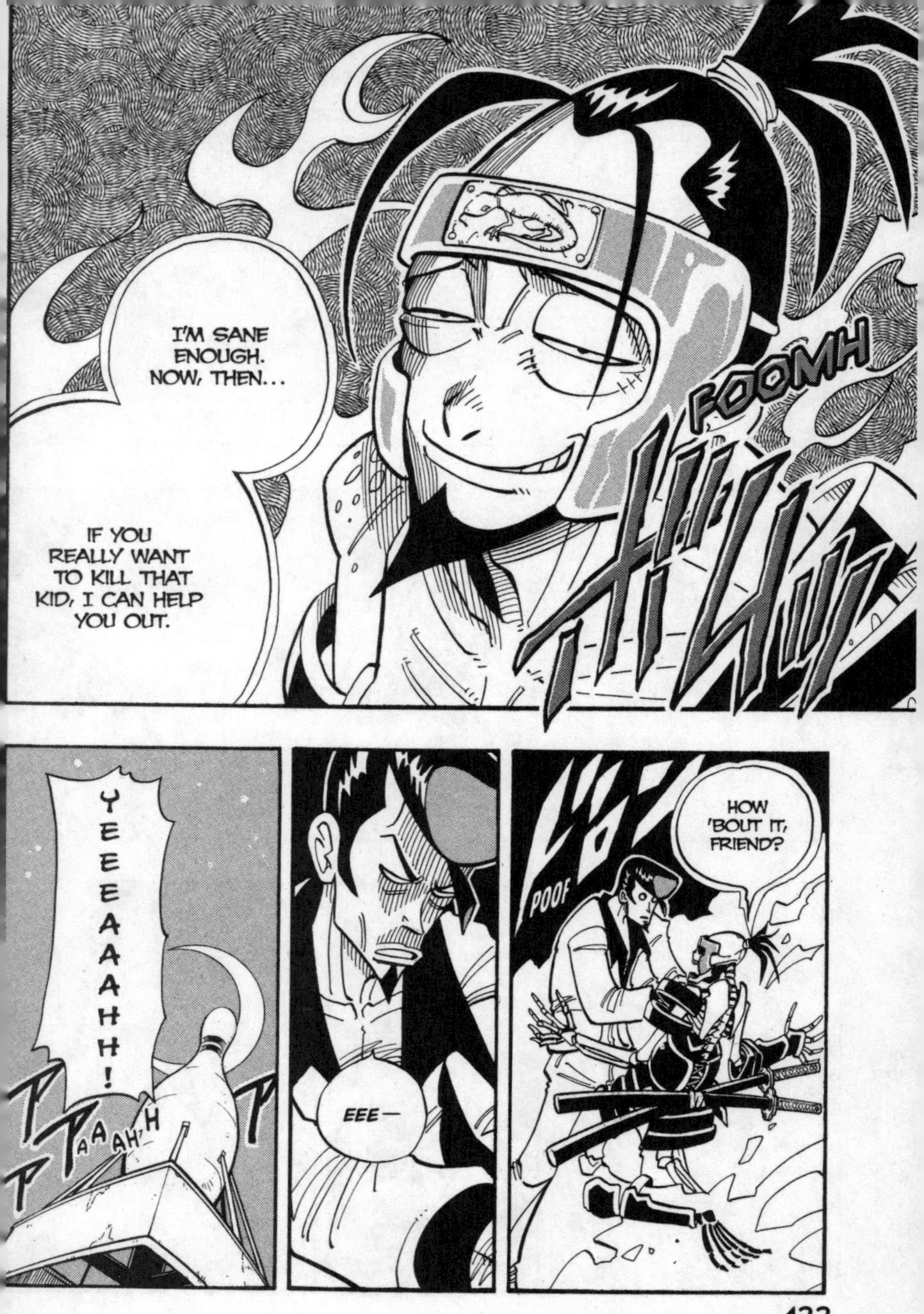
I'M SANE ENOUGH. NOW, THEN...
IF YOU REALLY WANT TO KILL THAT KID, I CAN HELP YOU OUT.
FOOMH
POOF
HOW 'BOUT IT, FRIEND?
EEE—
YEEEEAAAAAHH!

Chapter 19:

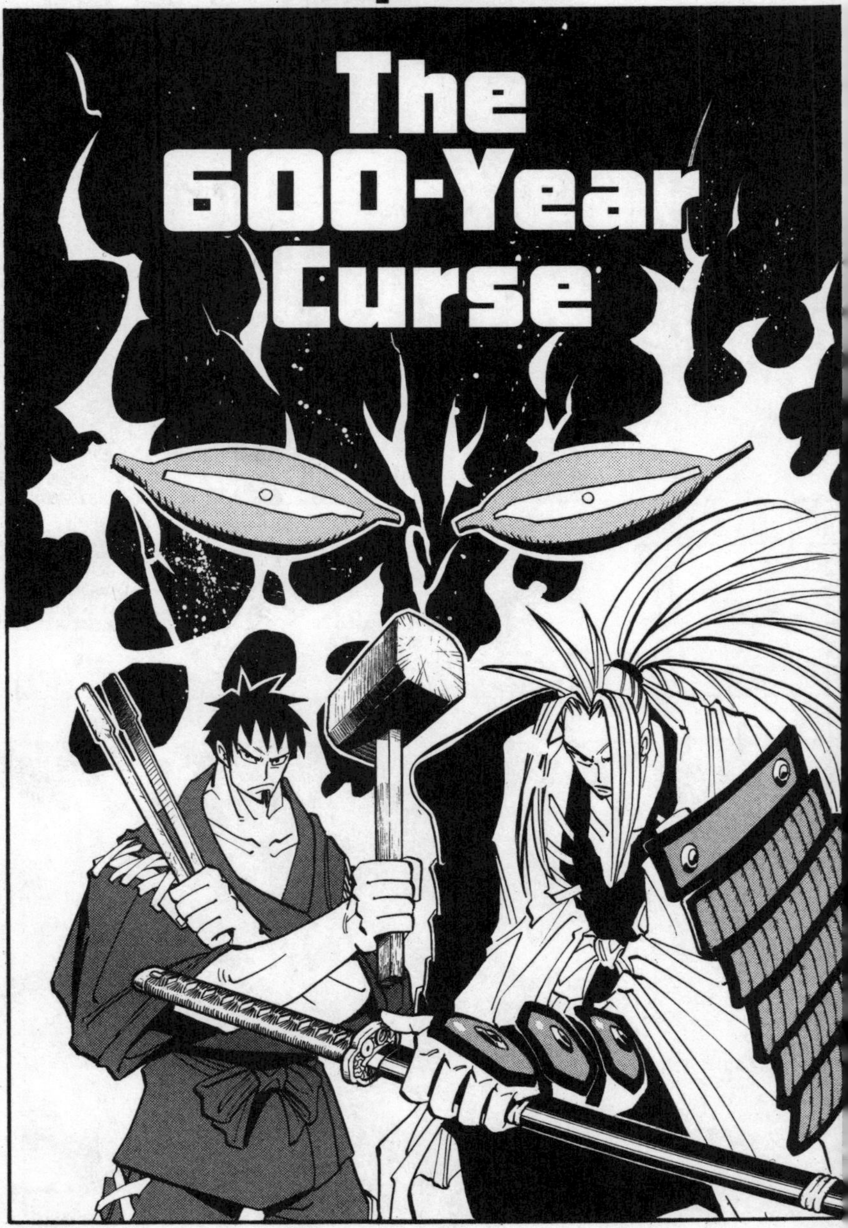
The 600-Year Curse

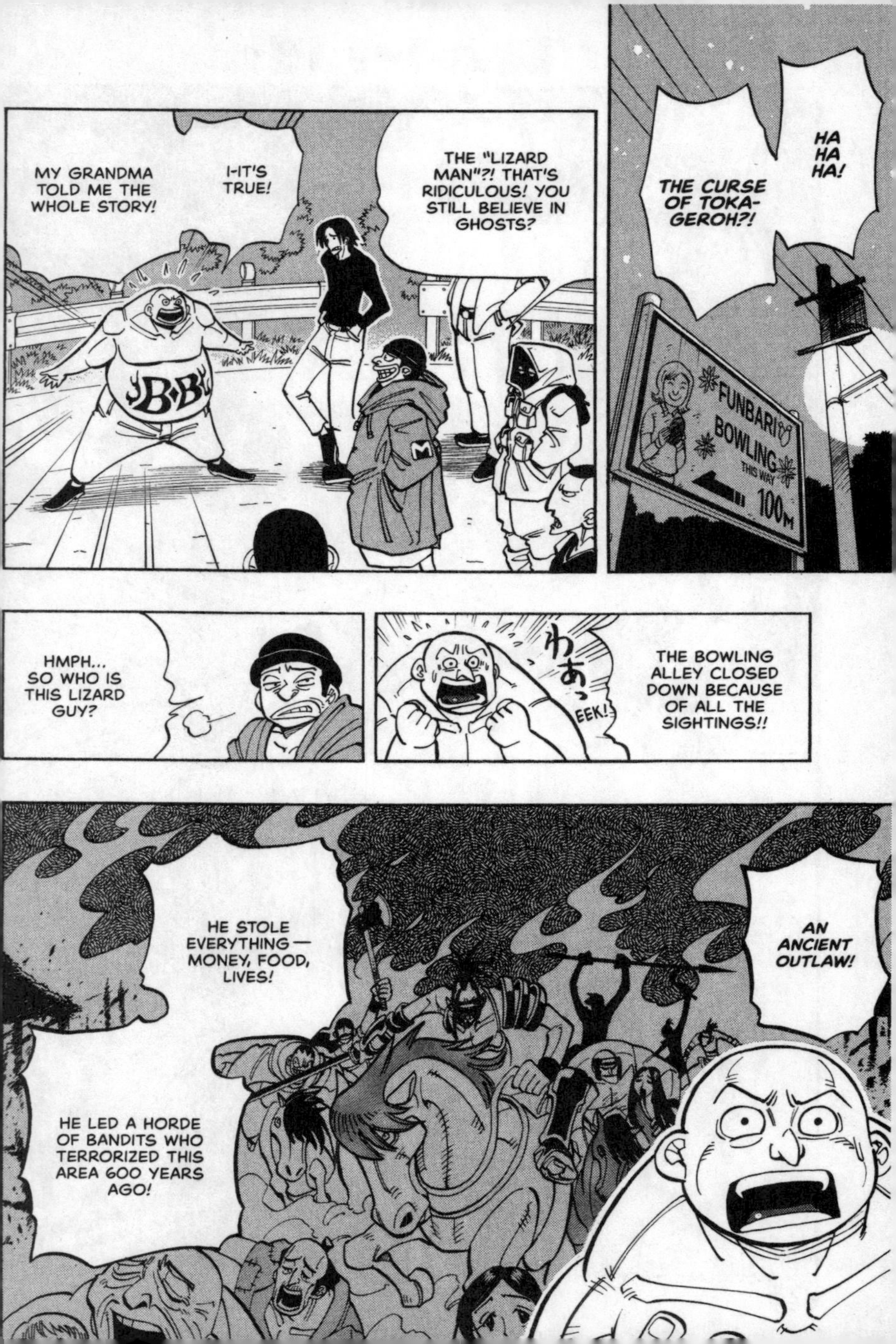
HA HA HA!
THE CURSE OF TOKA-GEROH?!
FUNBARI BOWLING THIS WAY 100M
THE "LIZARD MAN"?! THAT'S RIDICULOUS! YOU STILL BELIEVE IN GHOSTS?
I-IT'S TRUE!
MY GRANDMA TOLD ME THE WHOLE STORY!
わあっ
EEK!
THE BOWLING ALLEY CLOSED DOWN BECAUSE OF ALL THE SIGHTINGS!!
HMPH... SO WHO IS THIS LIZARD GUY?
AN ANCIENT OUTLAW!
HE STOLE EVERYTHING— MONEY, FOOD, LIVES!
HE LED A HORDE OF BANDITS WHO TERRORIZED THIS AREA 600 YEARS AGO!

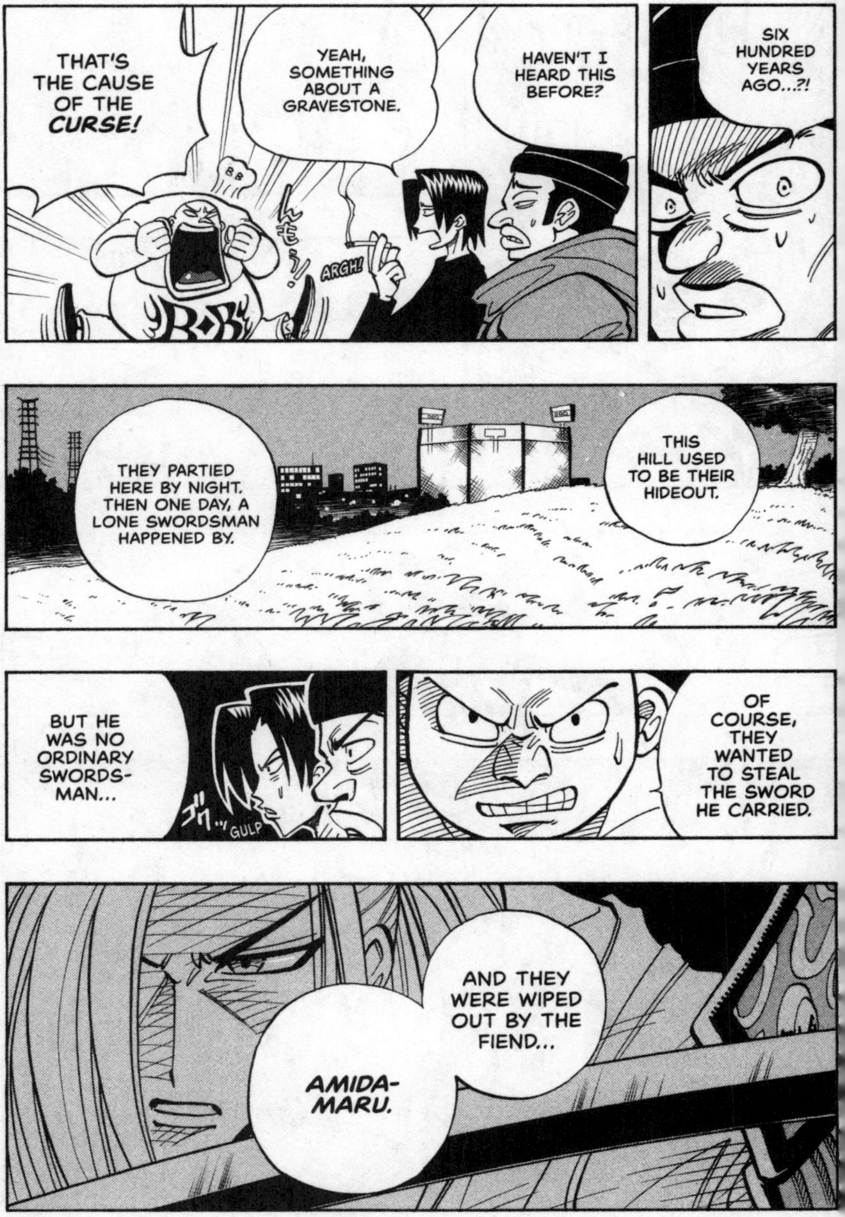
SIX HUNDRED YEARS AGO...?!
HAVEN'T I HEARD THIS BEFORE?
YEAH, SOMETHING ABOUT A GRAVESTONE.
THAT'S THE CAUSE OF THE *CURSE!*
BB
んもう!
ARGH!
THIS HILL USED TO BE THEIR HIDEOUT.
THEY PARTIED HERE BY NIGHT. THEN ONE DAY, A LONE SWORDSMAN HAPPENED BY.
OF COURSE, THEY WANTED TO STEAL THE SWORD HE CARRIED.
BUT HE WAS NO ORDINARY SWORDS-MAN...
ゴク…
GULP
AND THEY WERE WIPED OUT BY THE FIEND...
AMIDA-MARU.

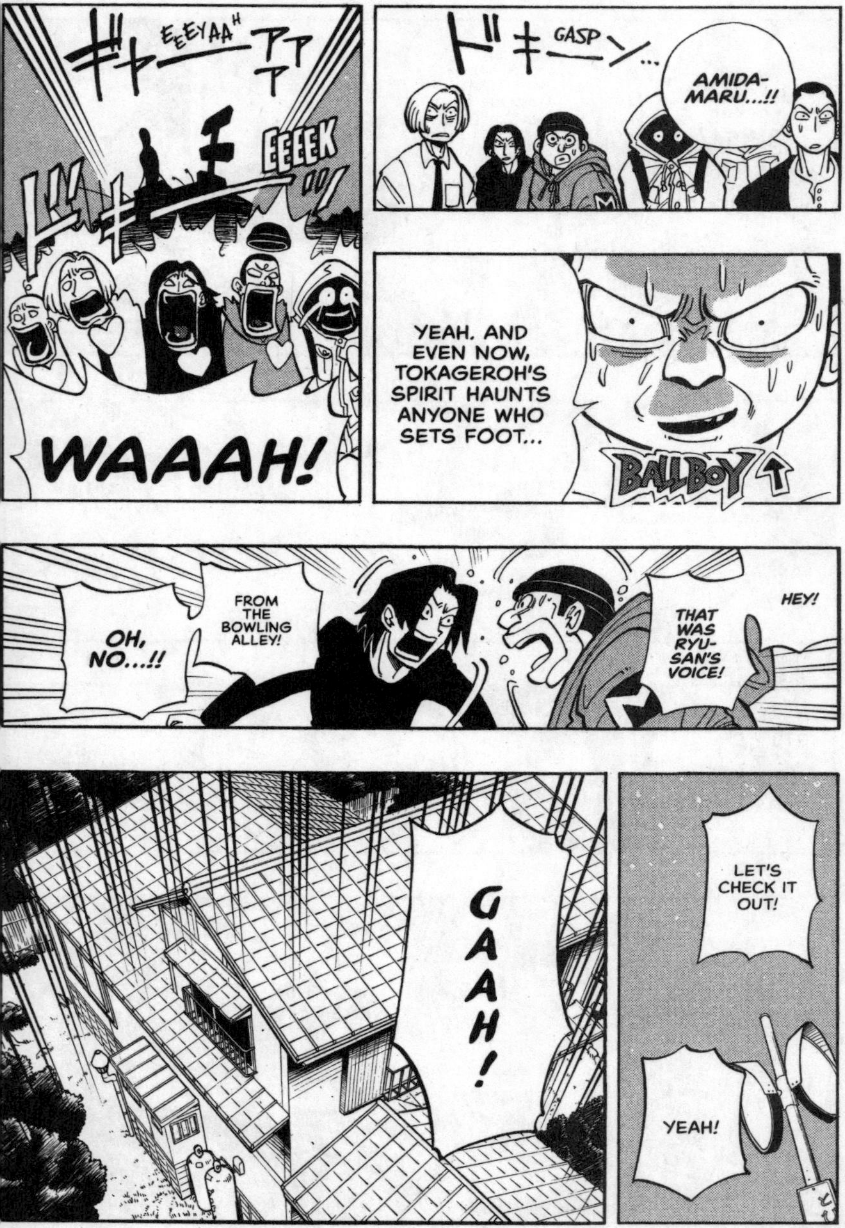
GASP
AMIDA-MARU...!!
YEAH. AND EVEN NOW, TOKAGEROH'S SPIRIT HAUNTS ANYONE WHO SETS FOOT...
BALLBOY
EEEYAAH
EEEEK
WAAAH!
HEY!
THAT WAS RYU-SAN'S VOICE!
FROM THE BOWLING ALLEY!
OH, NO...!!
LET'S CHECK IT OUT!
YEAH!
GAAAH!

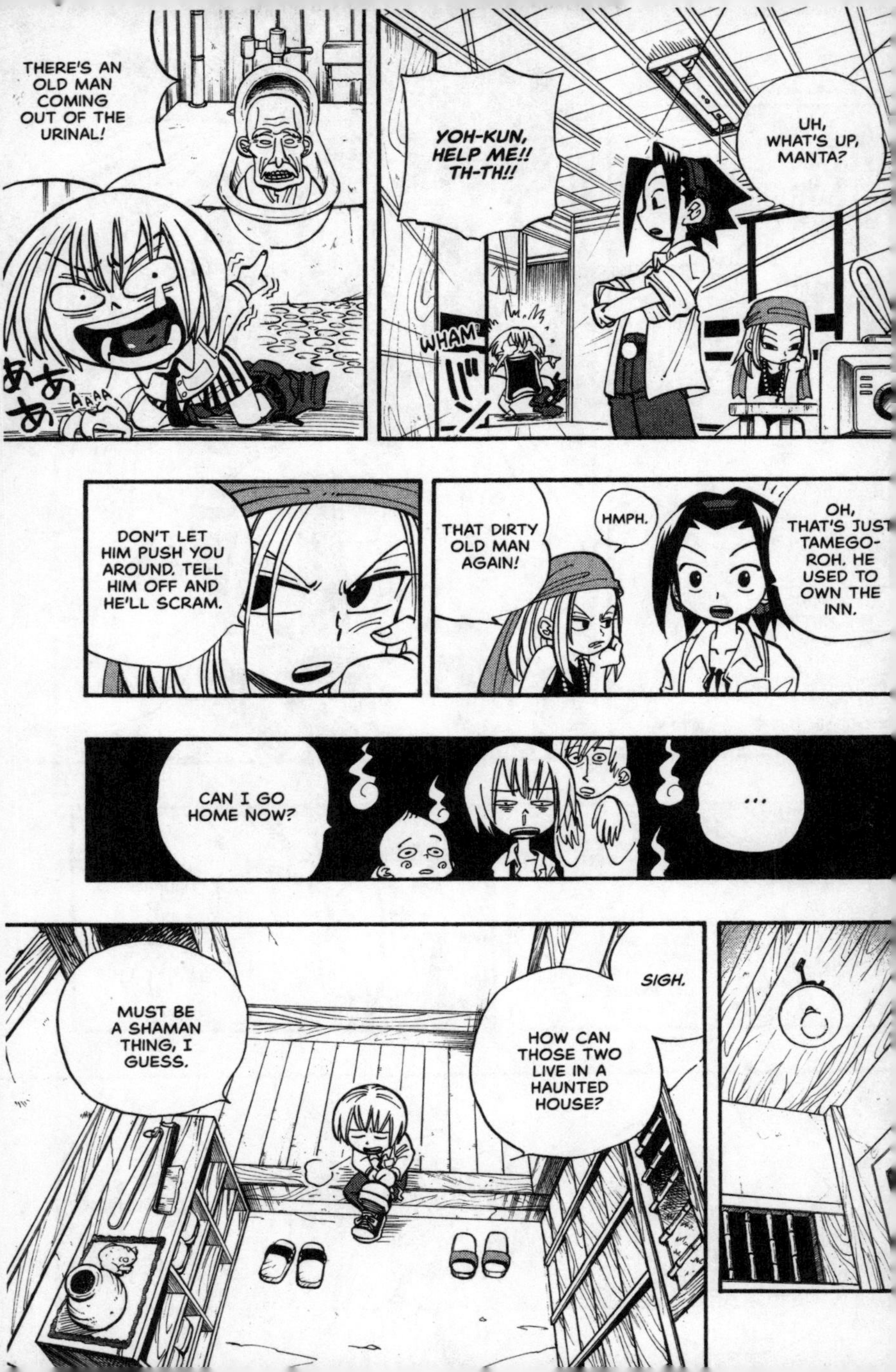
UH, WHAT'S UP, MANTA?
YOH-KUN, HELP ME!! TH-TH!!
WHAM
THERE'S AN OLD MAN COMING OUT OF THE URINAL!
あああ
AAAA
OH, THAT'S JUST TAMEGO-ROH. HE USED TO OWN THE INN.
HMPH.
THAT DIRTY OLD MAN AGAIN!
DON'T LET HIM PUSH YOU AROUND. TELL HIM OFF AND HE'LL SCRAM.
...
CAN I GO HOME NOW?
SIGH.
HOW CAN THOSE TWO LIVE IN A HAUNTED HOUSE?
MUST BE A SHAMAN THING, I GUESS.

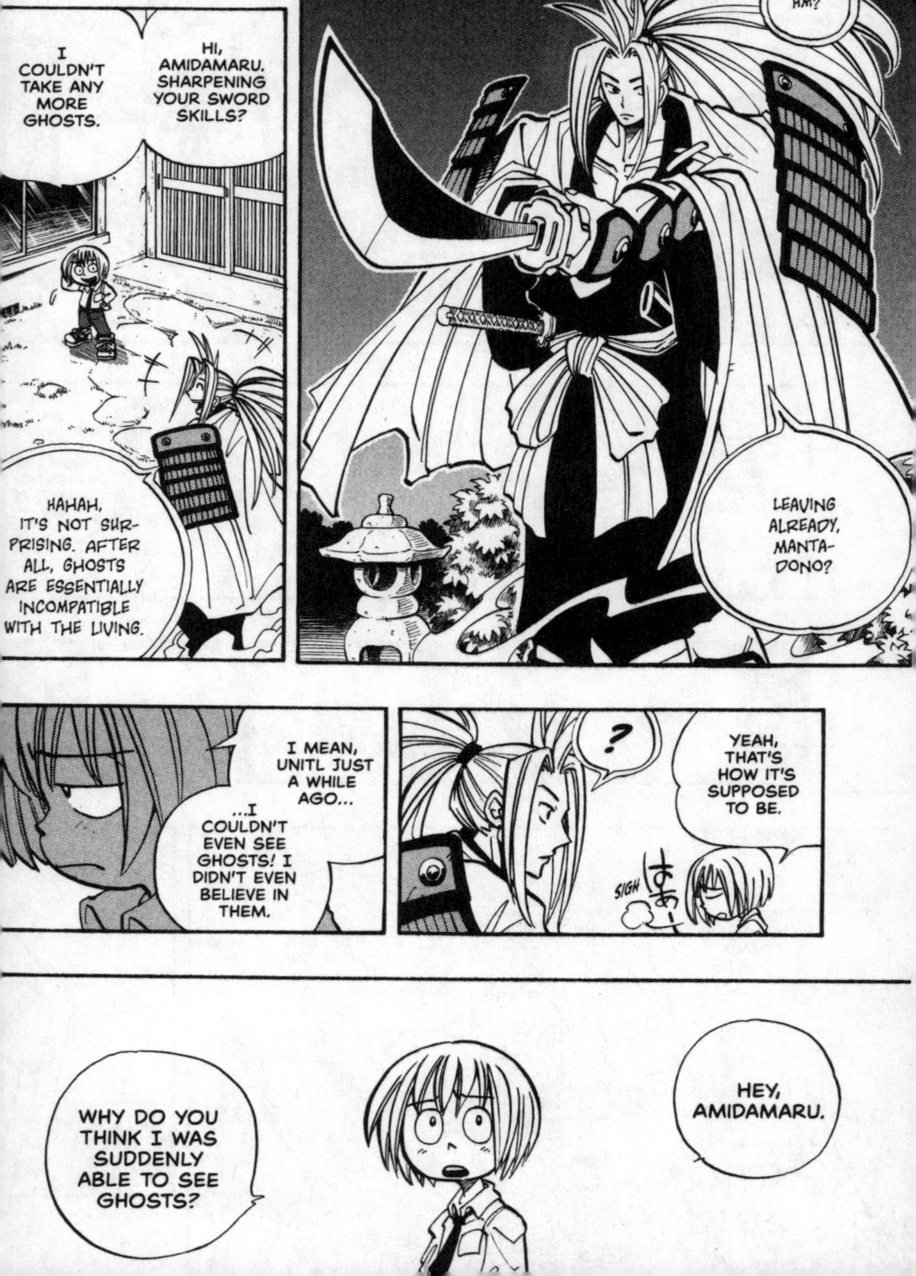
HM?
LEAVING ALREADY, MANTA-DONO?
HI, AMIDAMARU. SHARPENING YOUR SWORD SKILLS?
I COULDN'T TAKE ANY MORE GHOSTS.
HAHAH, IT'S NOT SURPRISING. AFTER ALL, GHOSTS ARE ESSENTIALLY INCOMPATIBLE WITH THE LIVING.
YEAH, THAT'S HOW IT'S SUPPOSED TO BE.
?
SIGH
I MEAN, UNITL JUST A WHILE AGO...
...I COULDN'T EVEN SEE GHOSTS! I DIDN'T EVEN BELIEVE IN THEM.
HEY, AMIDAMARU.
WHY DO YOU THINK I WAS SUDDENLY ABLE TO SEE GHOSTS?

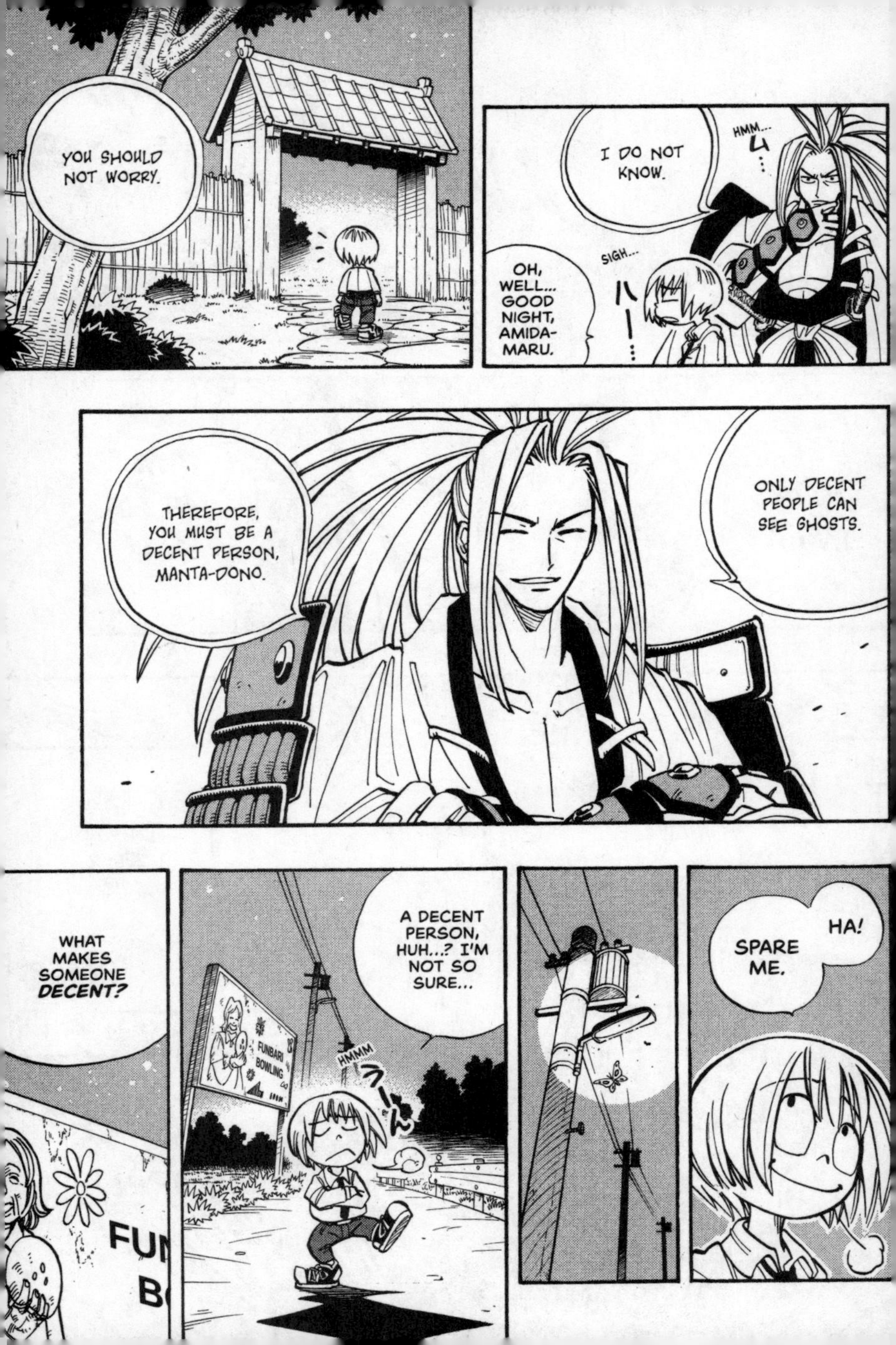
HMM...
I DO NOT KNOW.
SIGH...
OH, WELL... GOOD NIGHT, AMIDA-MARU.
YOU SHOULD NOT WORRY.
ONLY DECENT PEOPLE CAN SEE GHOSTS.
THEREFORE, YOU MUST BE A DECENT PERSON, MANTA-DONO.
HA!
SPARE ME.
A DECENT PERSON, HUH...? I'M NOT SO SURE...
HMMM
FUNBARI BOWLING
WHAT MAKES SOMEONE *DECENT?*

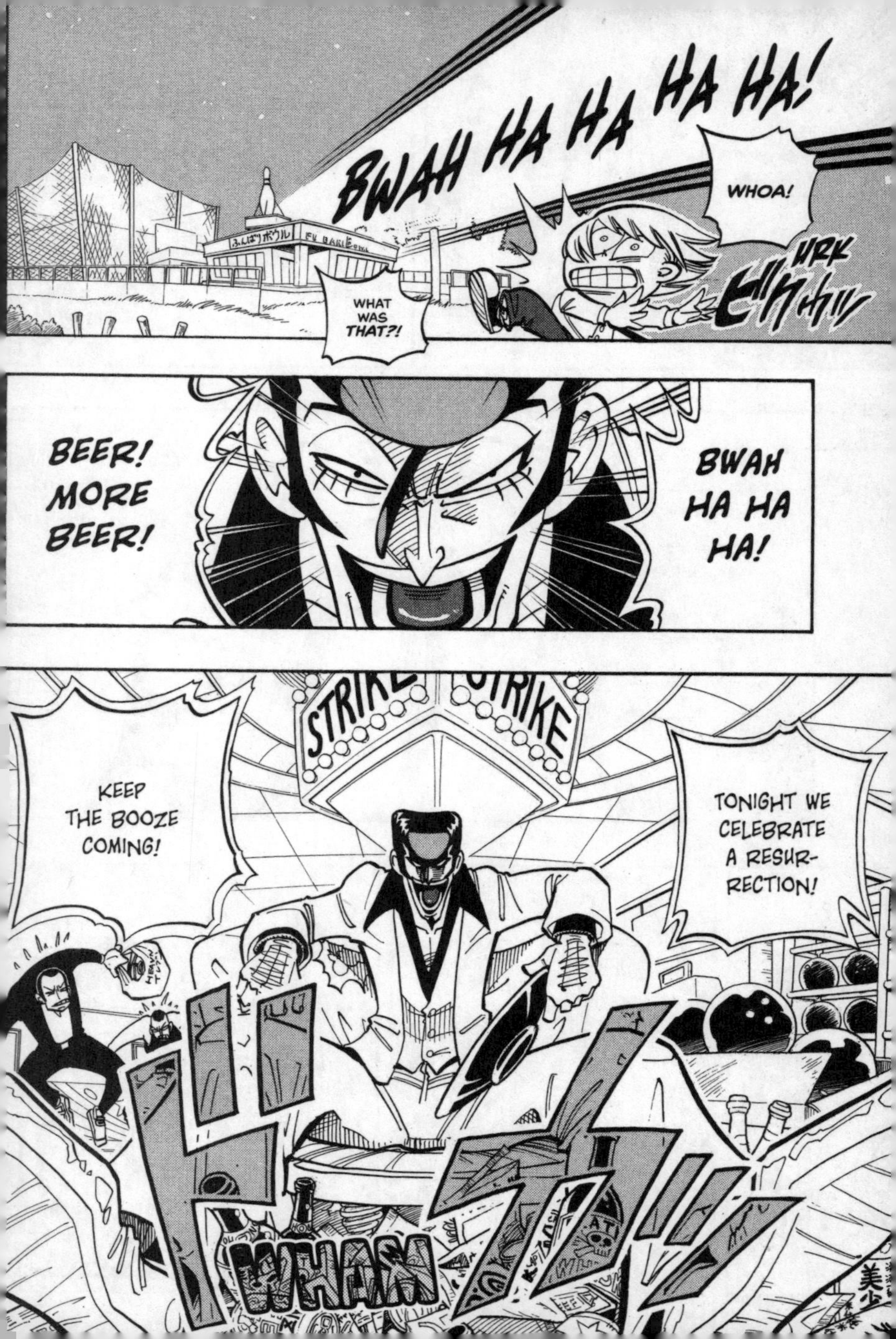
BWAH HA HA HA HA!
WHOA!
HURK
WHAT WAS THAT?!
BWAH HA HA HA!
BEER! MORE BEER!
STRIKE
STRIKE
TONIGHT WE CELEBRATE A RESURRECTION!
KEEP THE BOOZE COMING!
WHAM

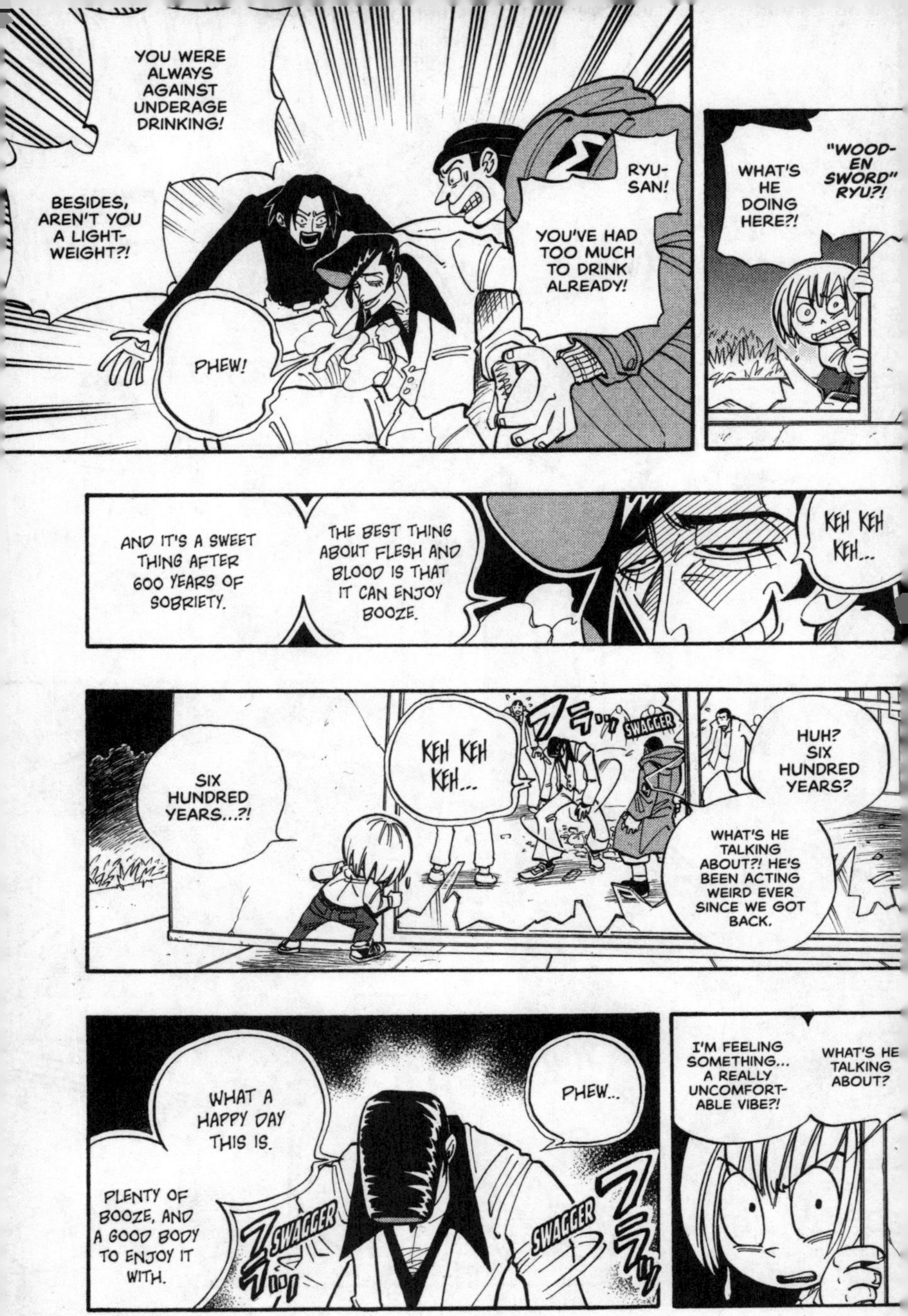
"WOODEN SWORD" RYU?!
WHAT'S HE DOING HERE?!
RYU-SAN!
YOU'VE HAD TOO MUCH TO DRINK ALREADY!
YOU WERE ALWAYS AGAINST UNDERAGE DRINKING!
BESIDES, AREN'T YOU A LIGHT-WEIGHT?!
PHEW!
KEH KEH KEH...
THE BEST THING ABOUT FLESH AND BLOOD IS THAT IT CAN ENJOY BOOZE.
AND IT'S A SWEET THING AFTER 600 YEARS OF SOBRIETY.
HUH? SIX HUNDRED YEARS?
WHAT'S HE TALKING ABOUT?! HE'S BEEN ACTING WEIRD EVER SINCE WE GOT BACK.
SWAGGER
KEH KEH KEH...
SIX HUNDRED YEARS...?!
WHAT'S HE TALKING ABOUT?
I'M FEELING SOMETHING... A REALLY UNCOMFORT-ABLE VIBE?!
PHEW...
WHAT A HAPPY DAY THIS IS.
SWAGGER
SWAGGER
PLENTY OF BOOZE, AND A GOOD BODY TO ENJOY IT WITH.

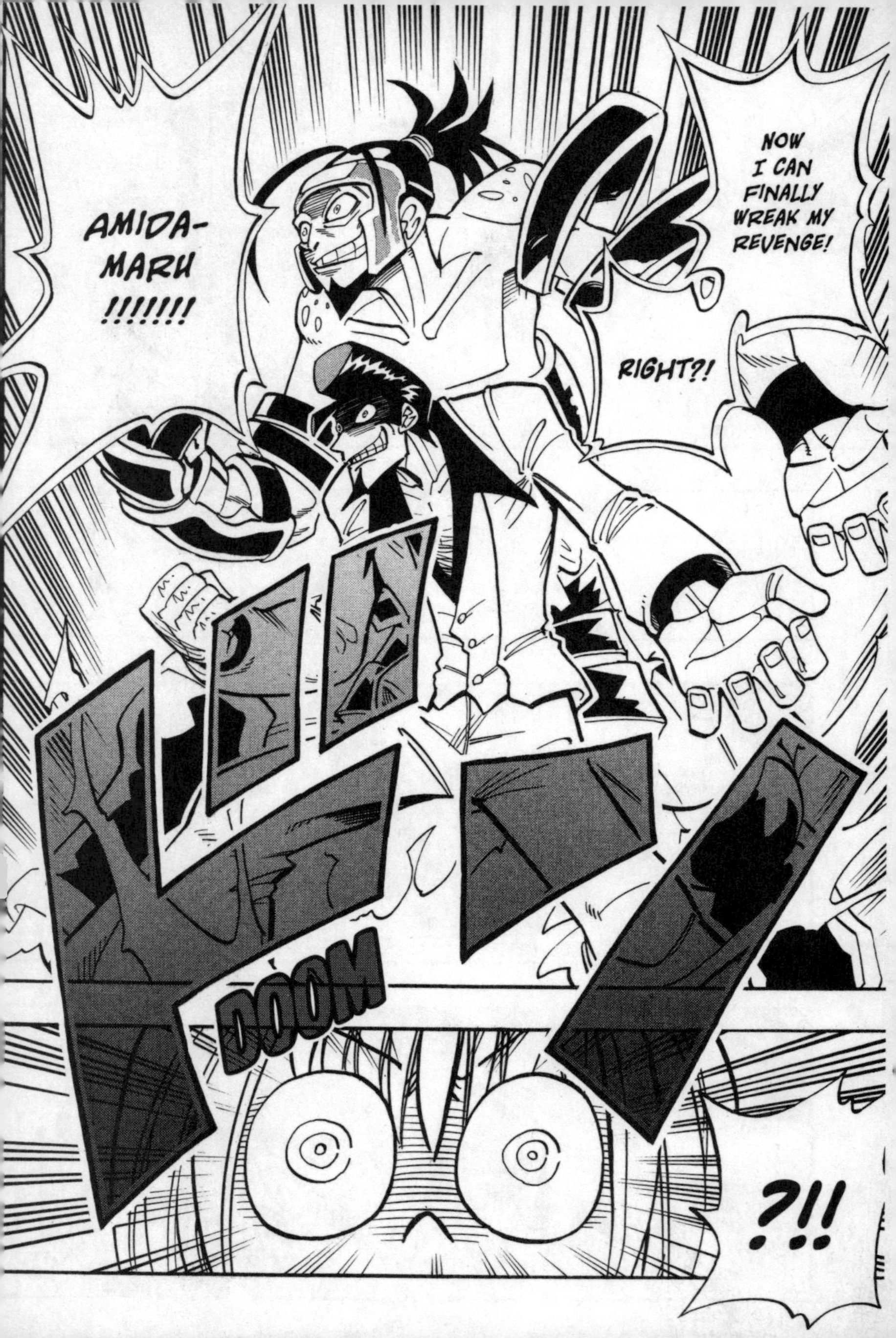
NOW I CAN FINALLY WREAK MY REVENGE!
RIGHT?!
AMIDA-MARU !!!!!!!
DOOM
?!!

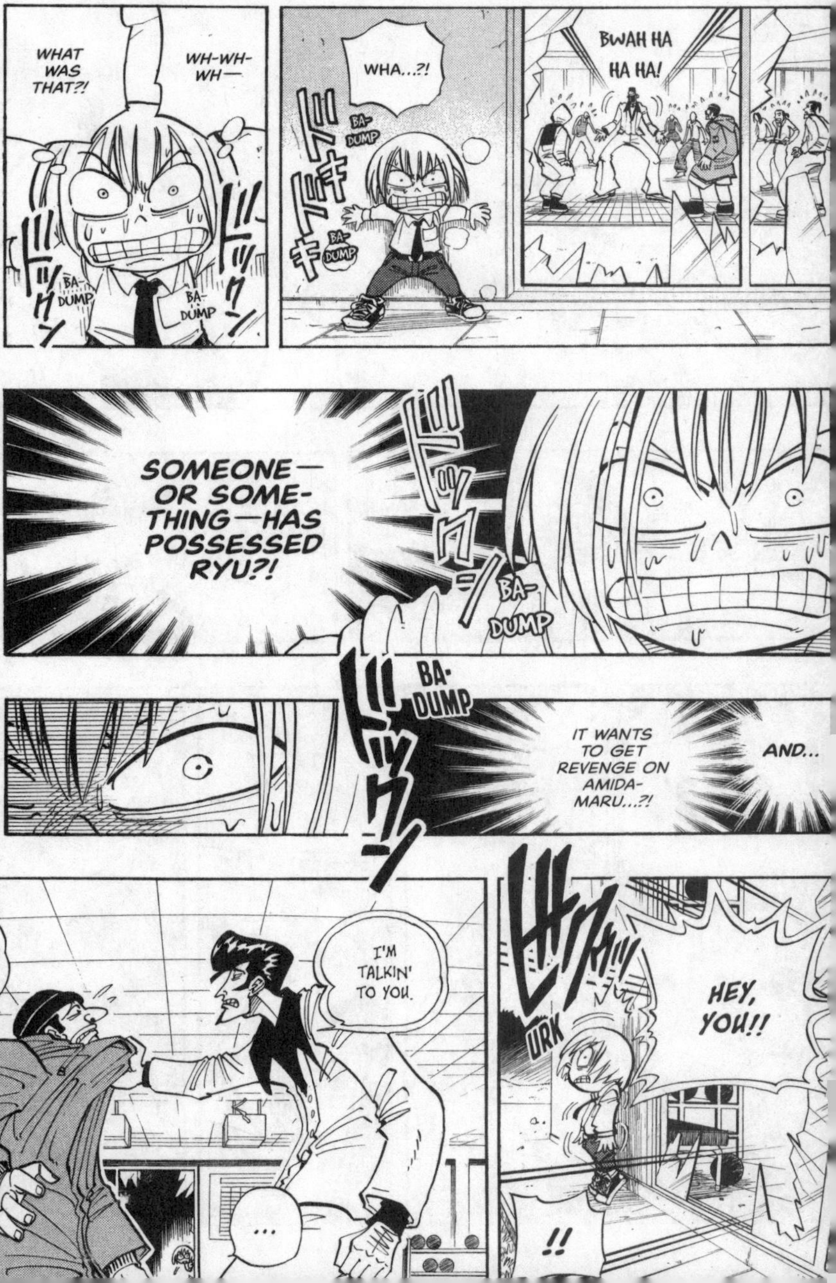
BWAH HA HA HA!
WHA...?!
BA-DUMP
BA-DUMP
WH-WH-WH—
WHAT WAS THAT?!
BA-DUMP
BA-DUMP
BA-DUMP
SOMEONE—OR SOME-THING—HAS POSSESSED RYU?!
BA-DUMP
AND...
IT WANTS TO GET REVENGE ON AMIDA-MARU...?!
HEY, YOU!!
URK
!!
I'M TALKIN' TO YOU.
HUH...?
...

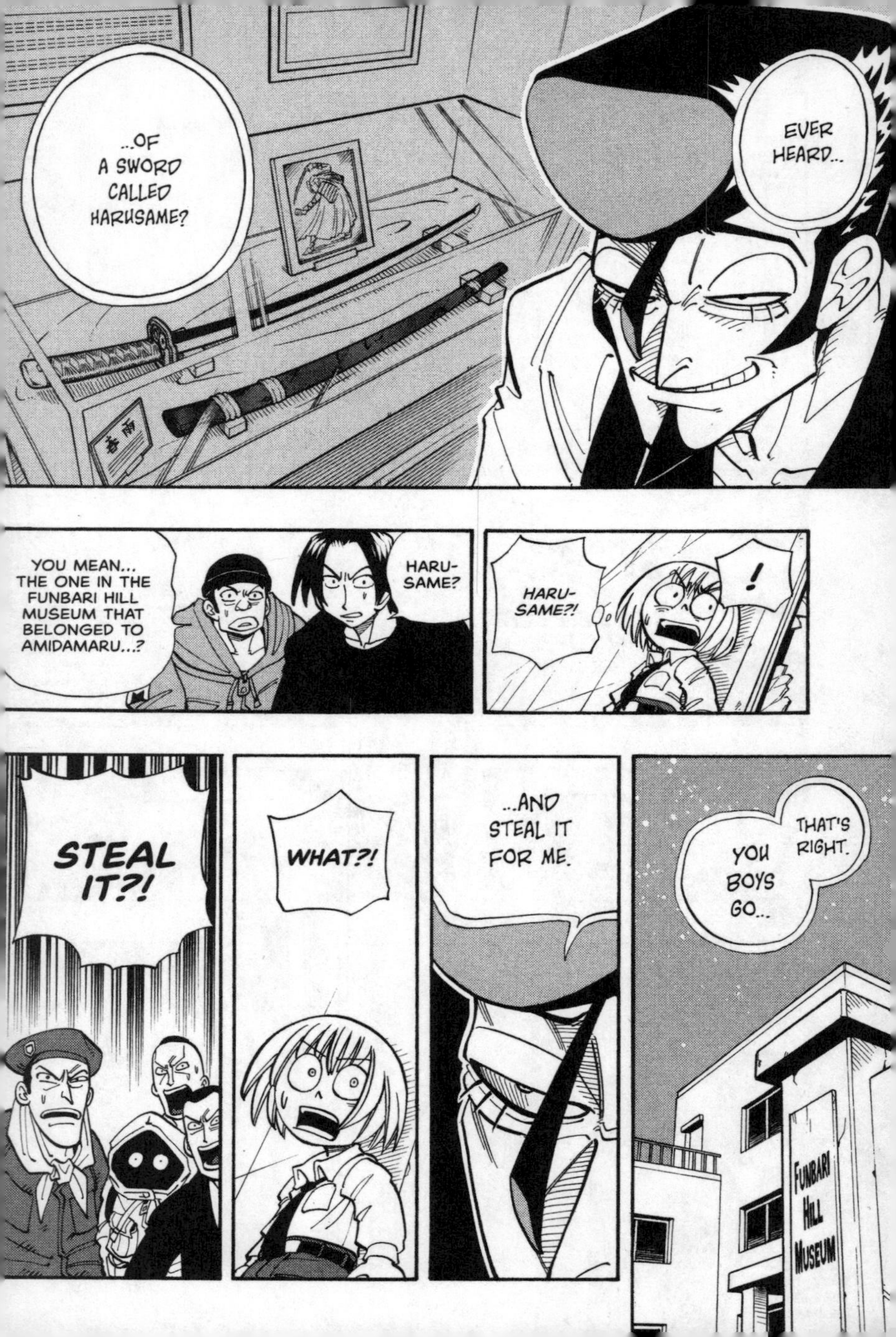
EVER HEARD...
...OF A SWORD CALLED HARUSAME?
!
HARU-SAME?!
HARU-SAME?
YOU MEAN... THE ONE IN THE FUNBARI HILL MUSEUM THAT BELONGED TO AMIDAMARU...?
THAT'S RIGHT.
YOU BOYS GO...
FUNBARI HILL MUSEUM
...AND STEAL IT FOR ME.
WHAT?!
STEAL IT?!

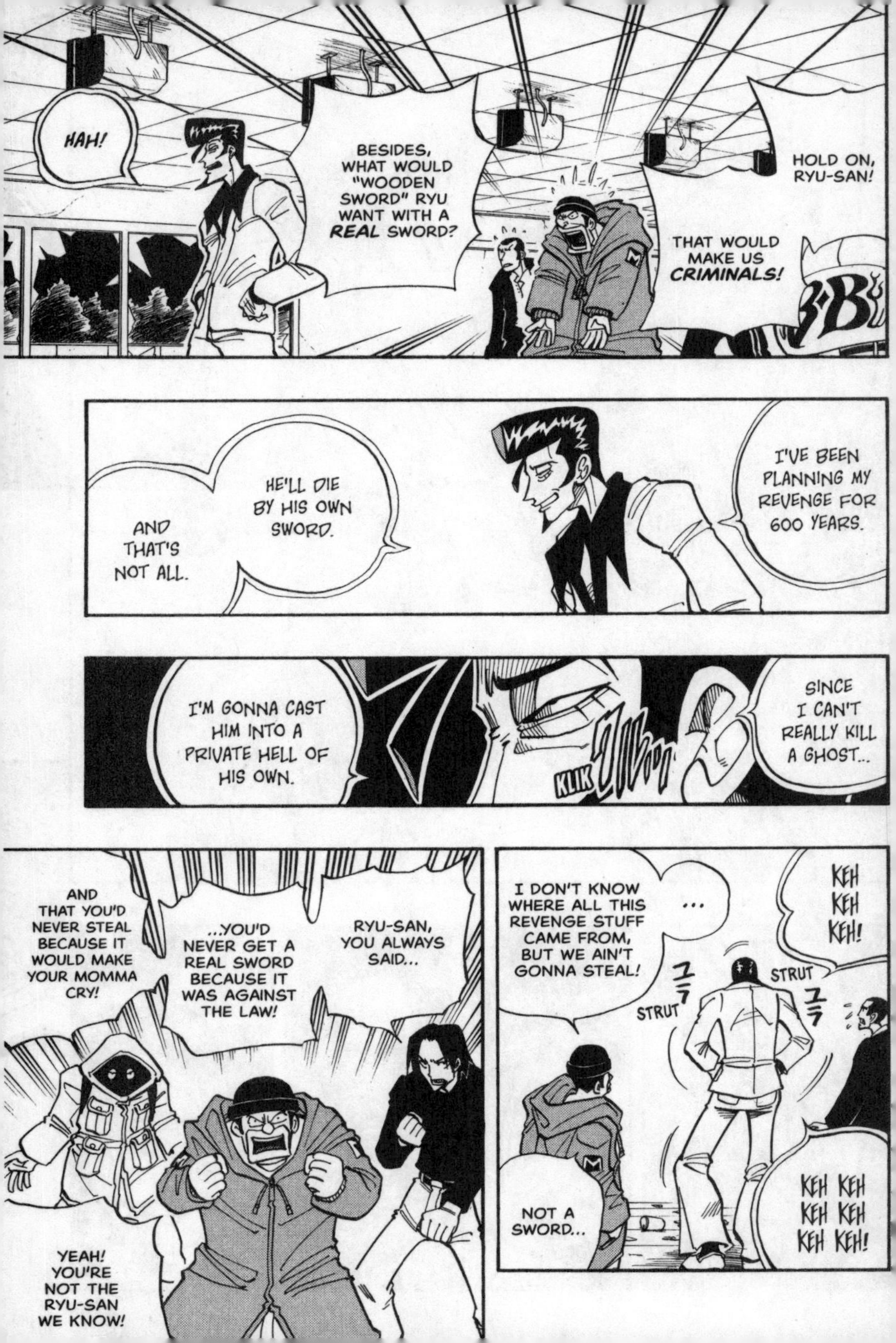
HOLD ON, RYU-SAN!
THAT WOULD MAKE US CRIMINALS!
BESIDES, WHAT WOULD "WOODEN SWORD" RYU WANT WITH A REAL SWORD?
HAH!
I'VE BEEN PLANNING MY REVENGE FOR 600 YEARS.
HE'LL DIE BY HIS OWN SWORD.
AND THAT'S NOT ALL.
SINCE I CAN'T REALLY KILL A GHOST...
KLIK
I'M GONNA CAST HIM INTO A PRIVATE HELL OF HIS OWN.
KEH KEH KEH!
STRUT
STRUT
...
I DON'T KNOW WHERE ALL THIS REVENGE STUFF CAME FROM, BUT WE AIN'T GONNA STEAL!
KEH KEH KEH KEH KEH KEH!
NOT A SWORD...
RYU-SAN, YOU ALWAYS SAID...
...YOU'D NEVER GET A REAL SWORD BECAUSE IT WAS AGAINST THE LAW!
AND THAT YOU'D NEVER STEAL BECAUSE IT WOULD MAKE YOUR MOMMA CRY!
YEAH! YOU'RE NOT THE RYU-SAN WE KNOW!

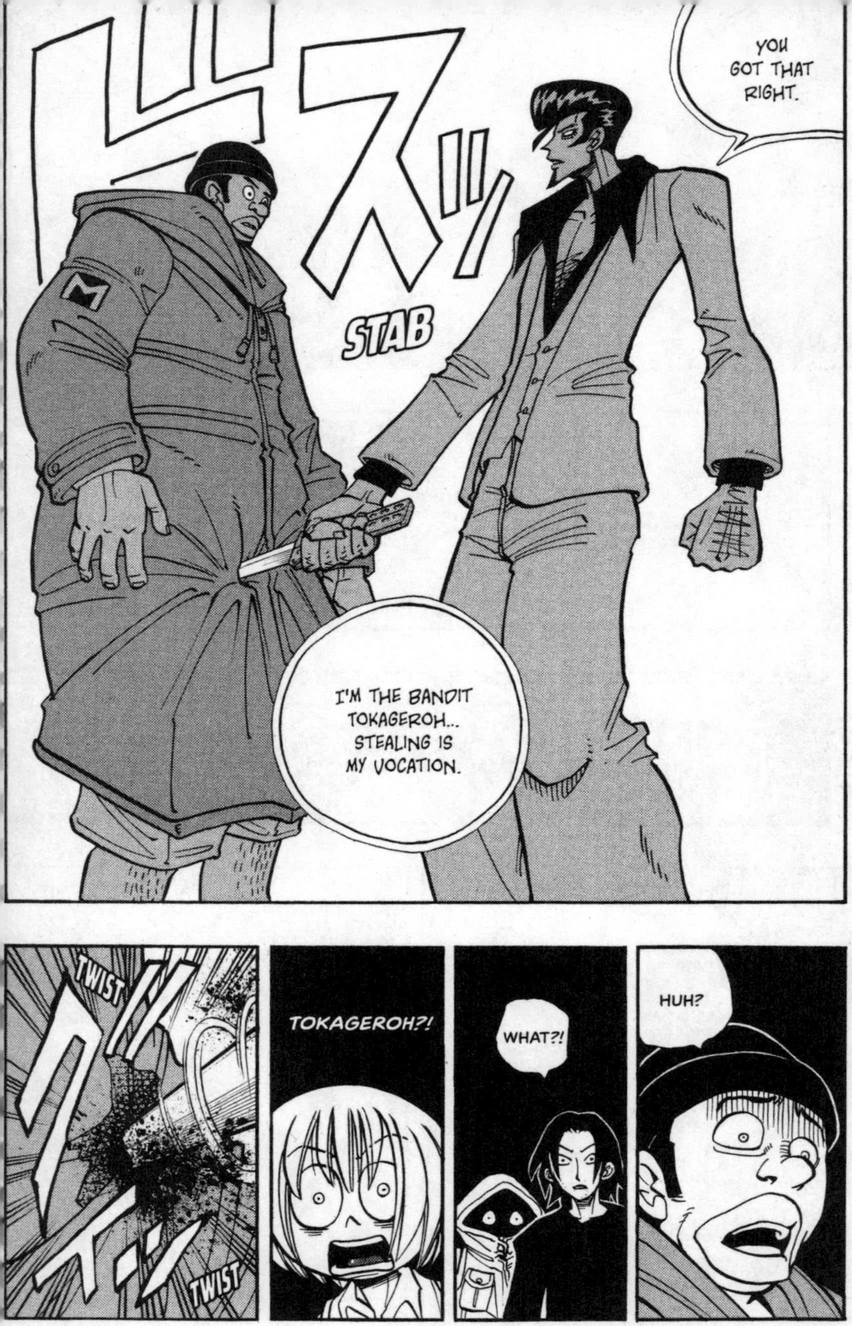
YOU GOT THAT RIGHT.
STAB
I'M THE BANDIT TOKAGEROH... STEALING IS MY VOCATION.
HUH?
WHAT?!
TOKAGEROH?!
TWIST
TWIST

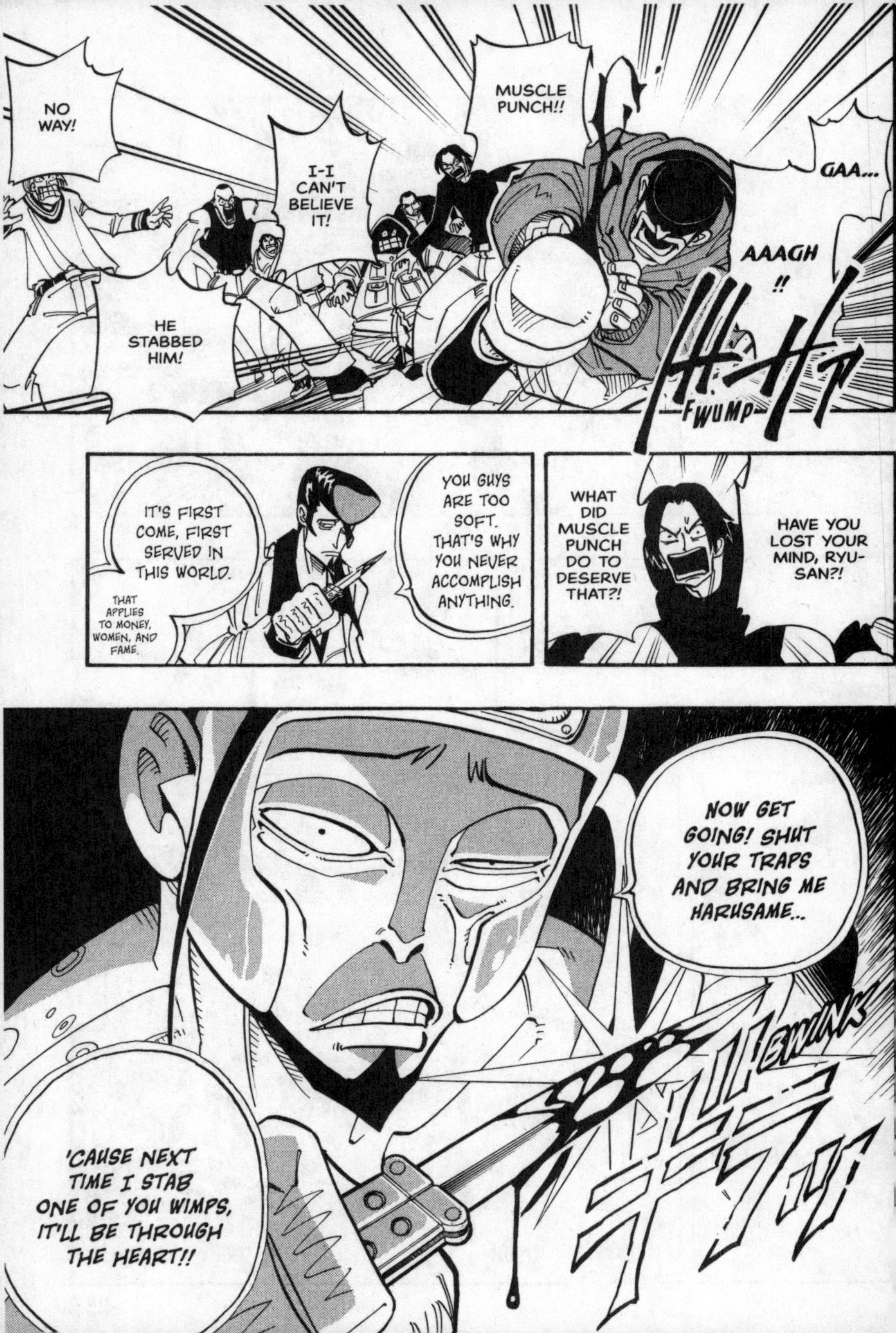
GAA...
AAAGH!!
FWUMP
MUSCLE PUNCH!!
I-I CAN'T BELIEVE IT!
NO WAY!
HE STABBED HIM!
HAVE YOU LOST YOUR MIND, RYU-SAN?!
WHAT DID MUSCLE PUNCH DO TO DESERVE THAT?!
YOU GUYS ARE TOO SOFT. THAT'S WHY YOU NEVER ACCOMPLISH ANYTHING.
IT'S FIRST COME, FIRST SERVED IN THIS WORLD.
THAT APPLIES TO MONEY, WOMEN, AND FAME.
NOW GET GOING! SHUT YOUR TRAPS AND BRING ME HARUSAME...
'CAUSE NEXT TIME I STAB ONE OF YOU WIMPS, IT'LL BE THROUGH THE HEART!!

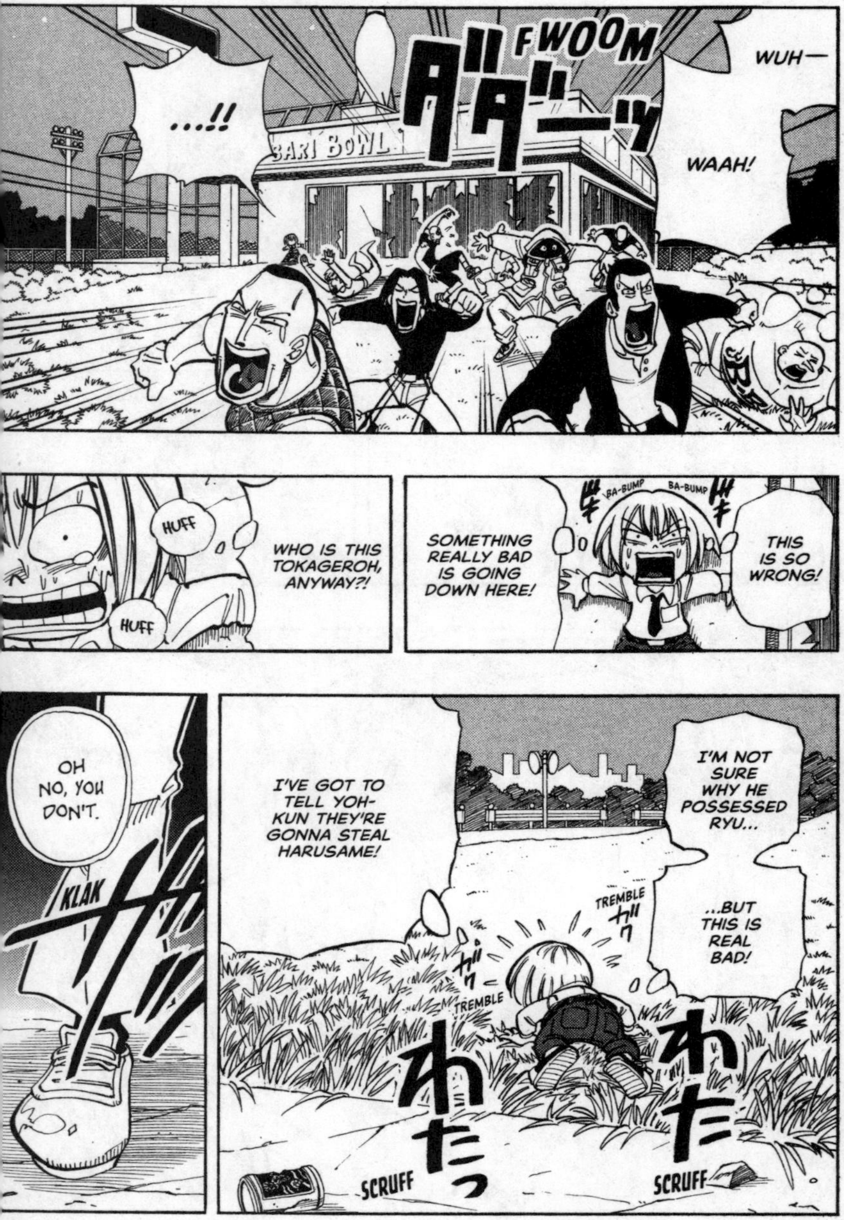
WUH—
WAAH!
FWOOM
BARI BOWL
...!!
BA-BUMP BA-BUMP
THIS IS SO WRONG!
SOMETHING REALLY BAD IS GOING DOWN HERE!
WHO IS THIS TOKAGEROH, ANYWAY?!
HUFF
HUFF
I'M NOT SURE WHY HE POSSESSED RYU...
...BUT THIS IS REAL BAD!
I'VE GOT TO TELL YOH-KUN THEY'RE GONNA STEAL HARUSAME!
TREMBLE
TREMBLE
わた
SCRUFF
わたっ
SCRUFF
OH NO, YOU DON'T.
KLAK

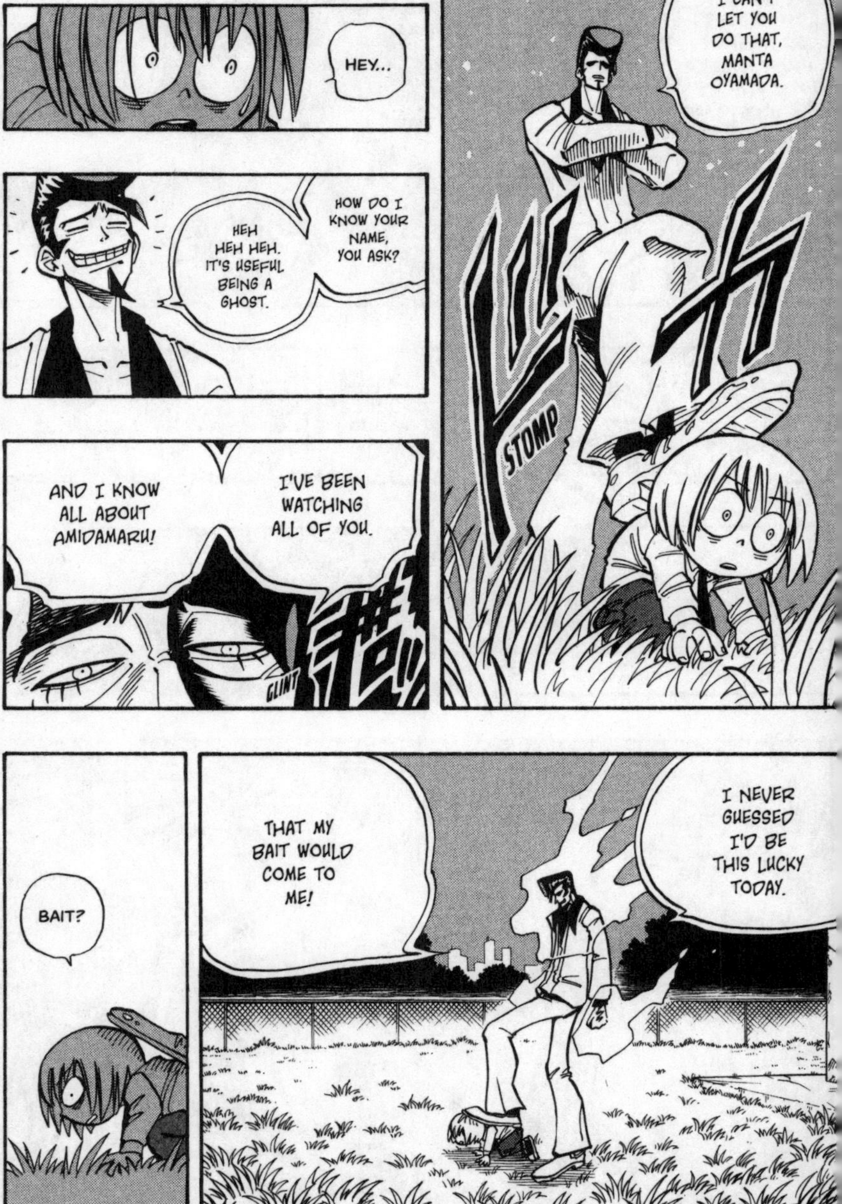
I CAN'T LET YOU DO THAT, MANTA OYAMADA.
STOMP
HEY...
HOW DO I KNOW YOUR NAME, YOU ASK?
HEH HEH HEH. IT'S USEFUL BEING A GHOST.
I'VE BEEN WATCHING ALL OF YOU.
AND I KNOW ALL ABOUT AMIDAMARU!
GLINT
I NEVER GUESSED I'D BE THIS LUCKY TODAY.
THAT MY BAIT WOULD COME TO ME!
BAIT?

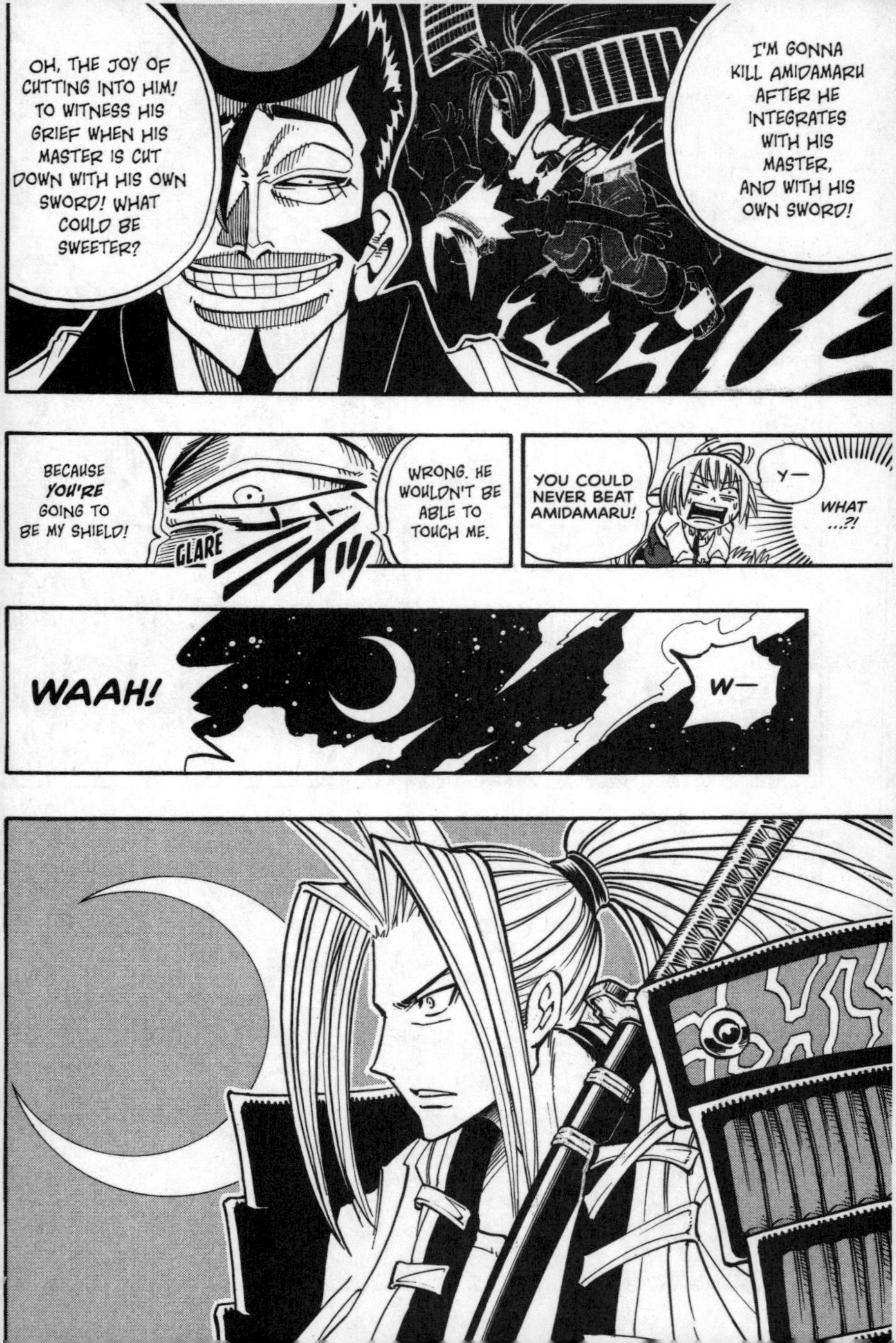

I'M GONNA KILL AMIDAMARU AFTER HE INTEGRATES WITH HIS MASTER, AND WITH HIS OWN SWORD!
OH, THE JOY OF CUTTING INTO HIM! TO WITNESS HIS GRIEF WHEN HIS MASTER IS CUT DOWN WITH HIS OWN SWORD! WHAT COULD BE SWEETER?
Y—
WHAT ...?!
YOU COULD NEVER BEAT AMIDAMARU!
WRONG. HE WOULDN'T BE ABLE TO TOUCH ME.
BECAUSE YOU'RE GOING TO BE MY SHIELD!
GLARE
W—
WAAH!

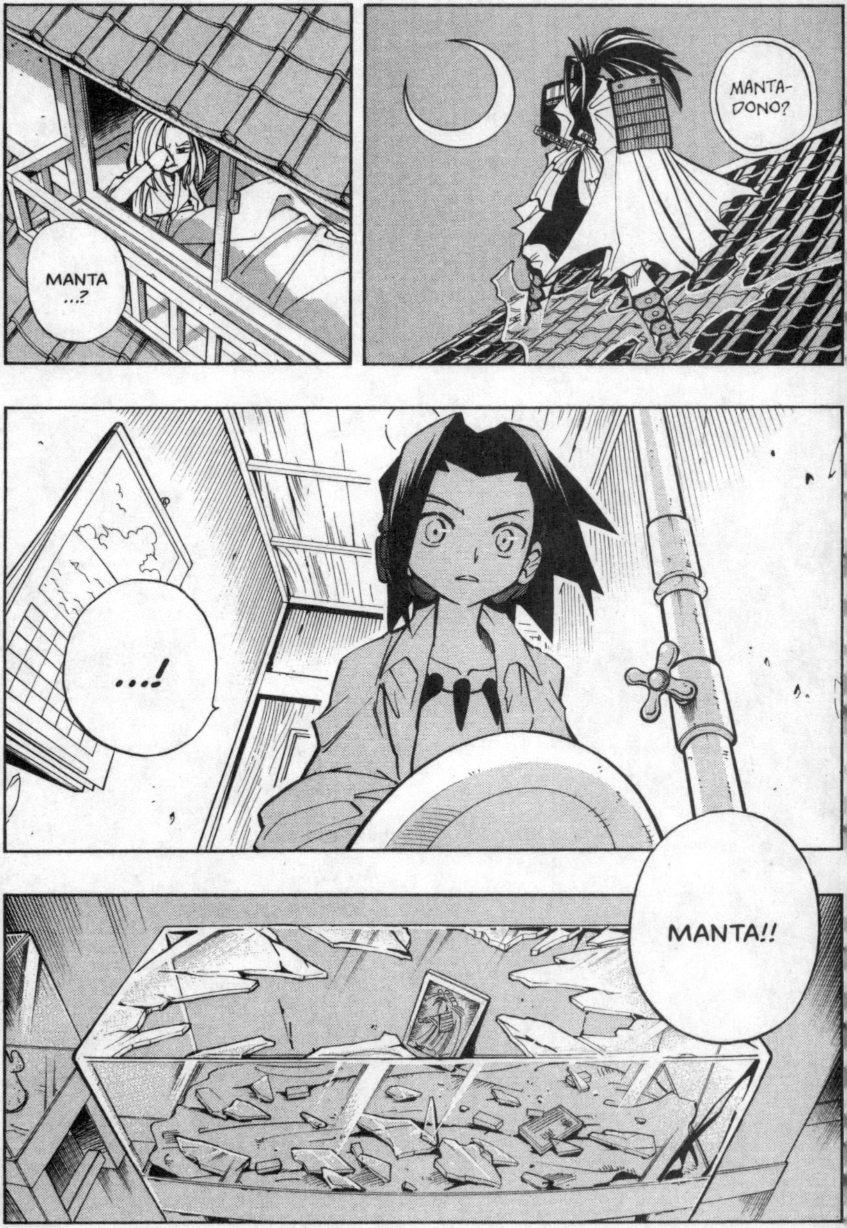
MANTA-DONO?
MANTA ...?
...!
MANTA!!

SHAMAN
KING
3

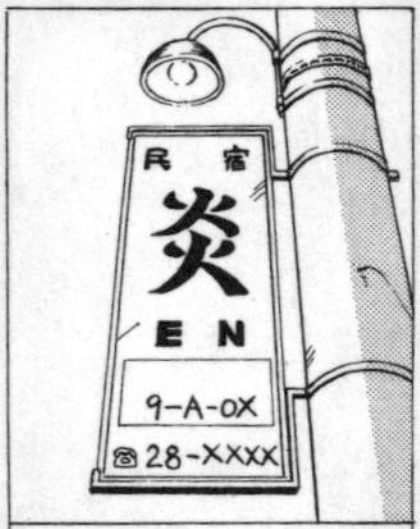
民 宿
炎
EN
9-A-OX
☎ 28-XXXX

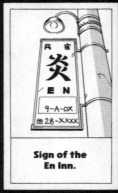

Sign of the En Inn.

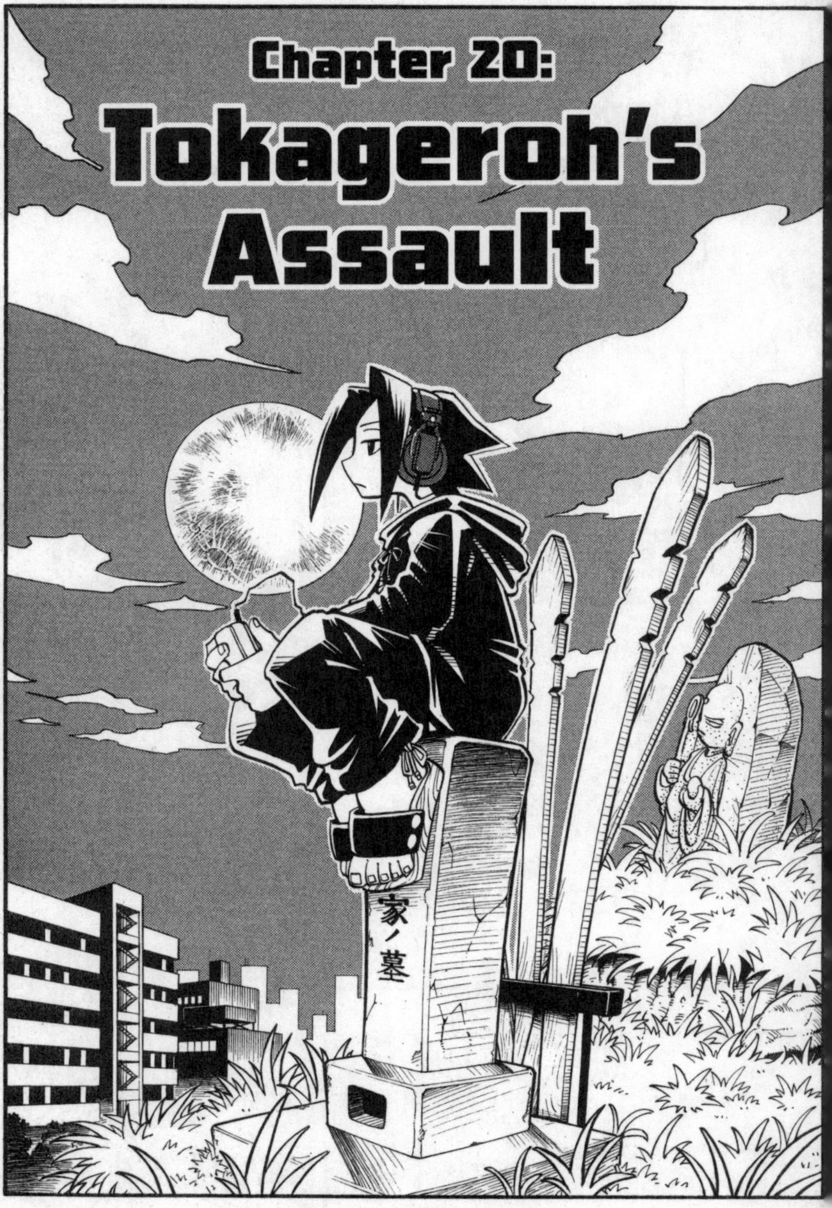
Chapter 20:
Tokageroh's Assault
家ノ墓

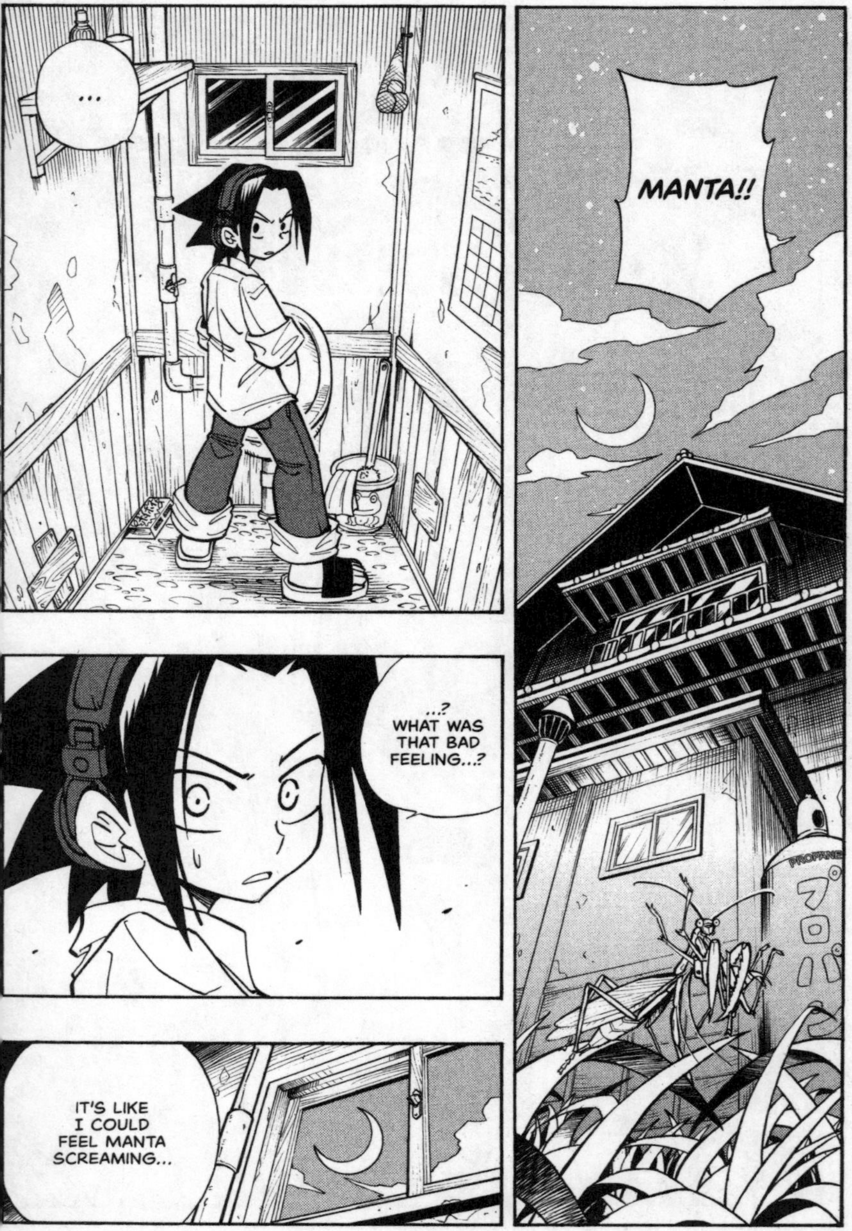
MANTA!!
PROPANE
...
...?
WHAT WAS
THAT BAD
FEELING...?
IT'S LIKE
I COULD
FEEL MANTA
SCREAMING...

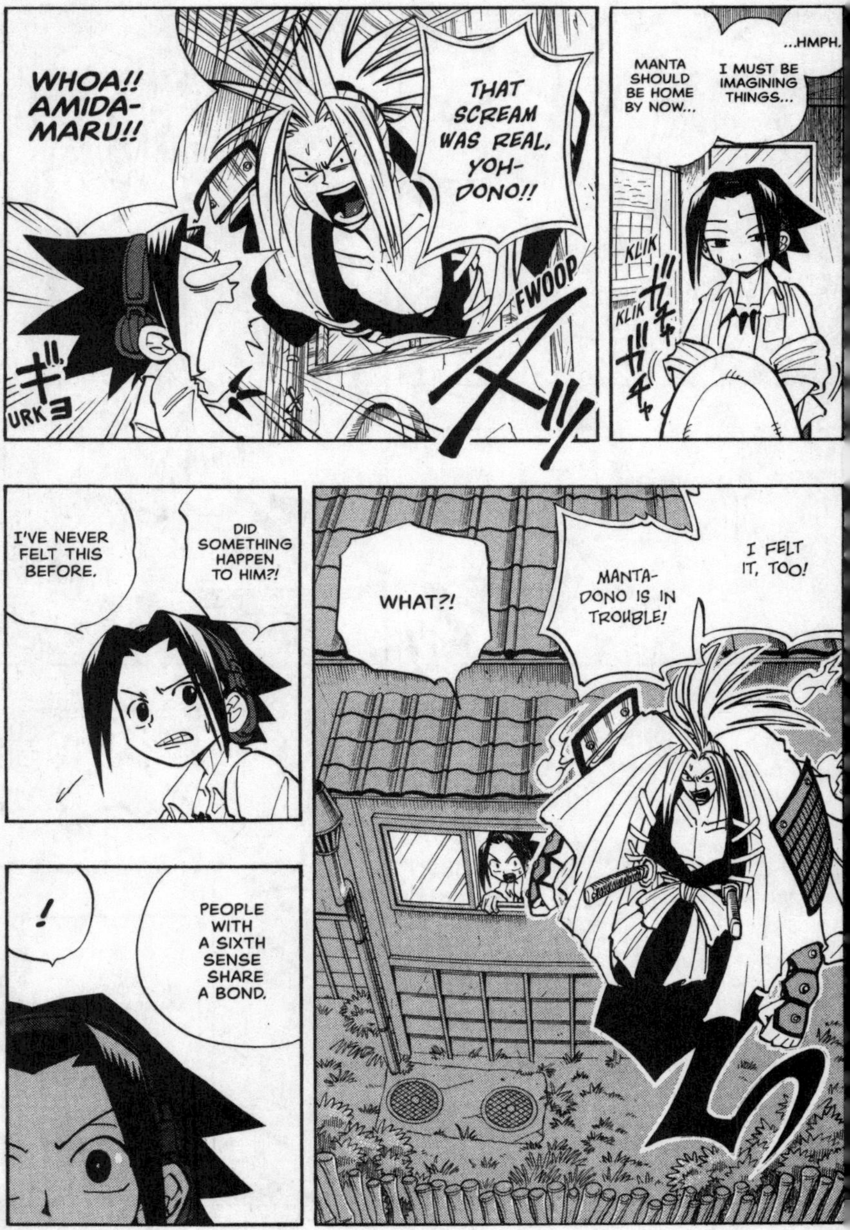
...HMPH.
I MUST BE IMAGINING THINGS...
MANTA SHOULD BE HOME BY NOW...
KLIK
KLIK
THAT SCREAM WAS REAL, YOH-DONO!!
FWOOP
WHOA!! AMIDA-MARU!!
URK
I FELT IT, TOO!
MANTA-DONO IS IN TROUBLE!
WHAT?!
DID SOMETHING HAPPEN TO HIM?!
I'VE NEVER FELT THIS BEFORE.
PEOPLE WITH A SIXTH SENSE SHARE A BOND.
!

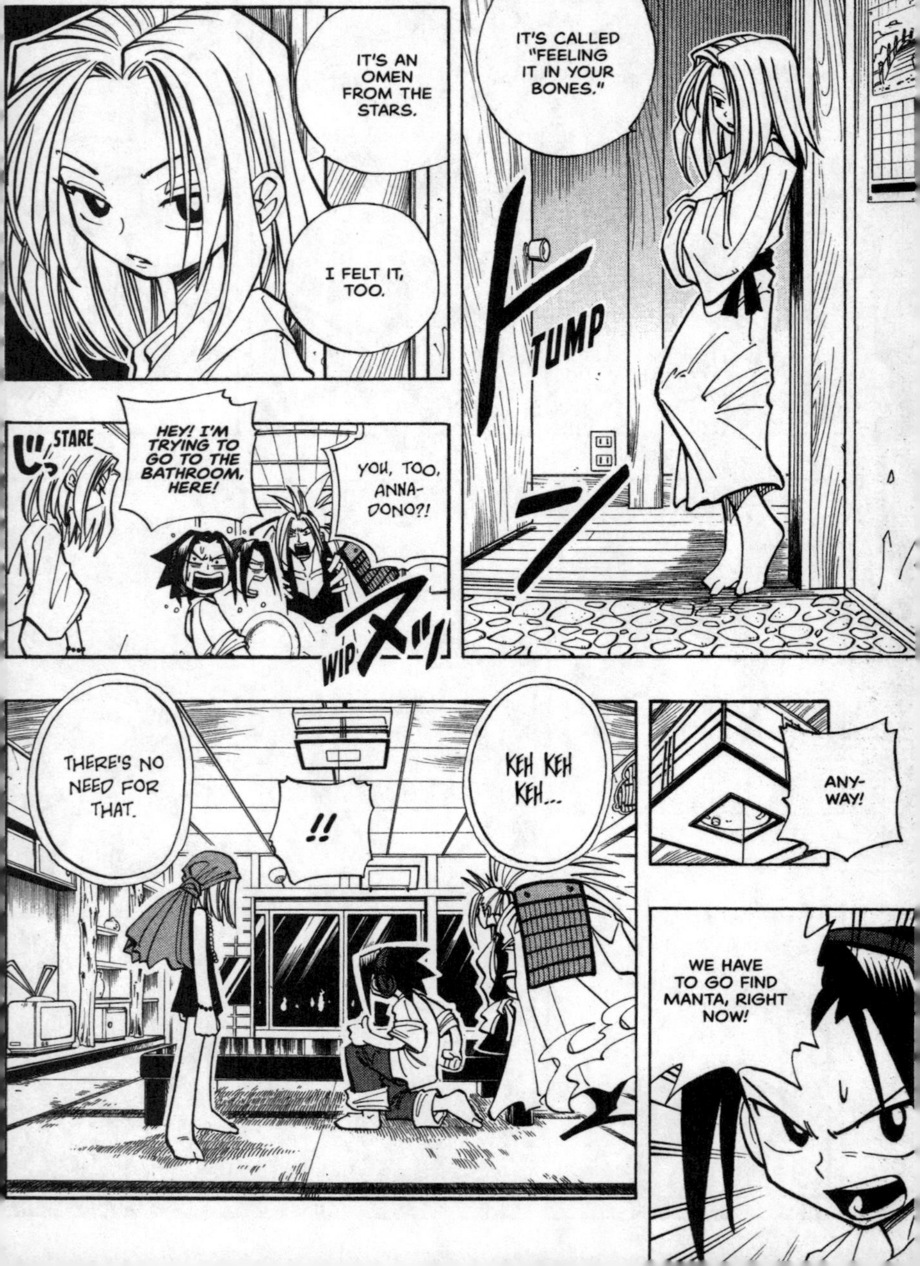
IT'S CALLED "FEELING IT IN YOUR BONES."
TUMP
IT'S AN OMEN FROM THE STARS.
I FELT IT, TOO.
YOU, TOO, ANNA-DONO?!
HEY! I'M TRYING TO GO TO THE BATHROOM, HERE!
STARE
WIP
ANY-WAY!
WE HAVE TO GO FIND MANTA, RIGHT NOW!
KEH KEH KEH...
!!
THERE'S NO NEED FOR THAT.

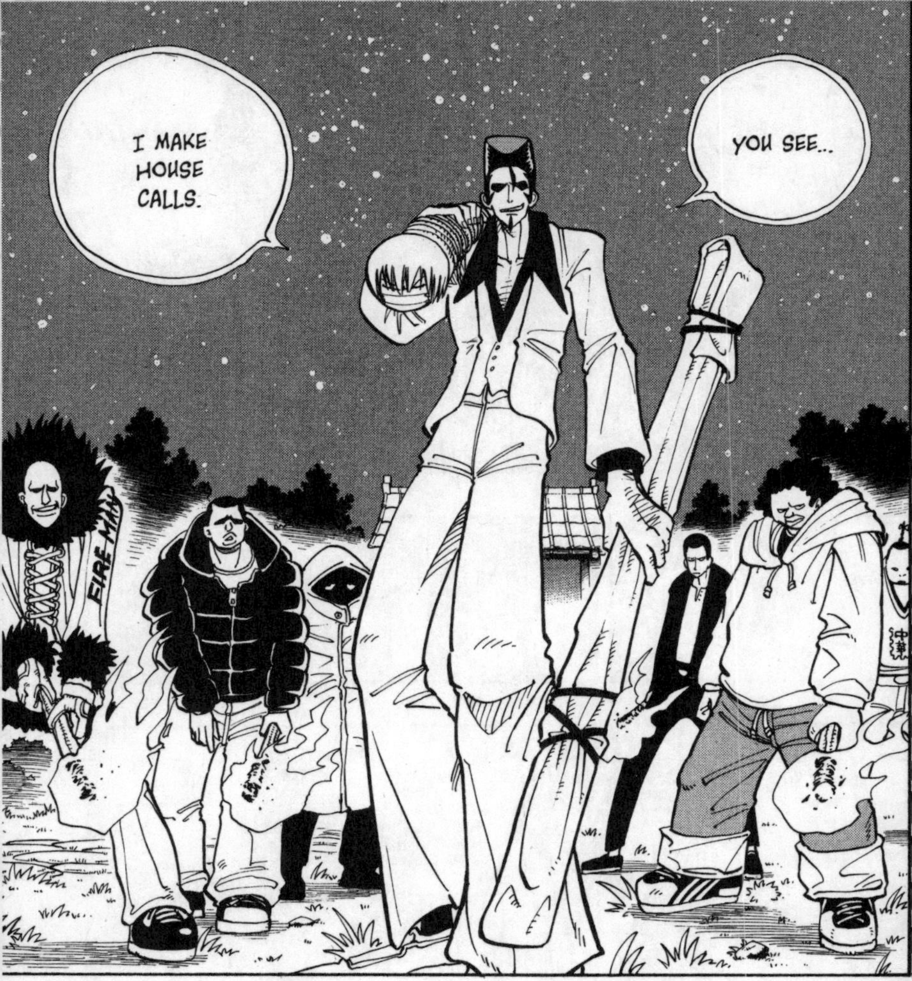
YOU SEE...
I MAKE HOUSE CALLS.
FIRE MAN

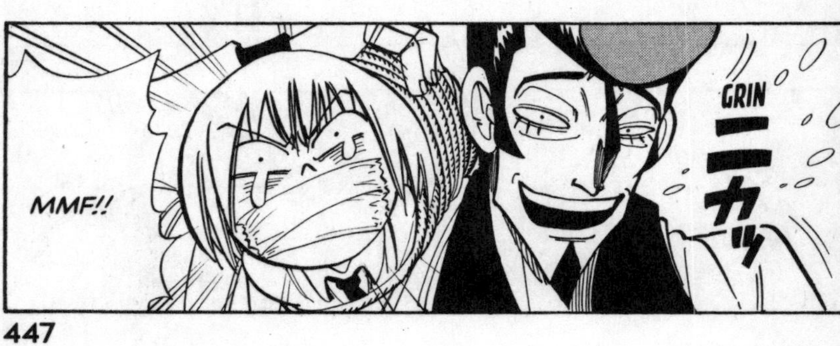
GRIN
ニカッ
MMF!!

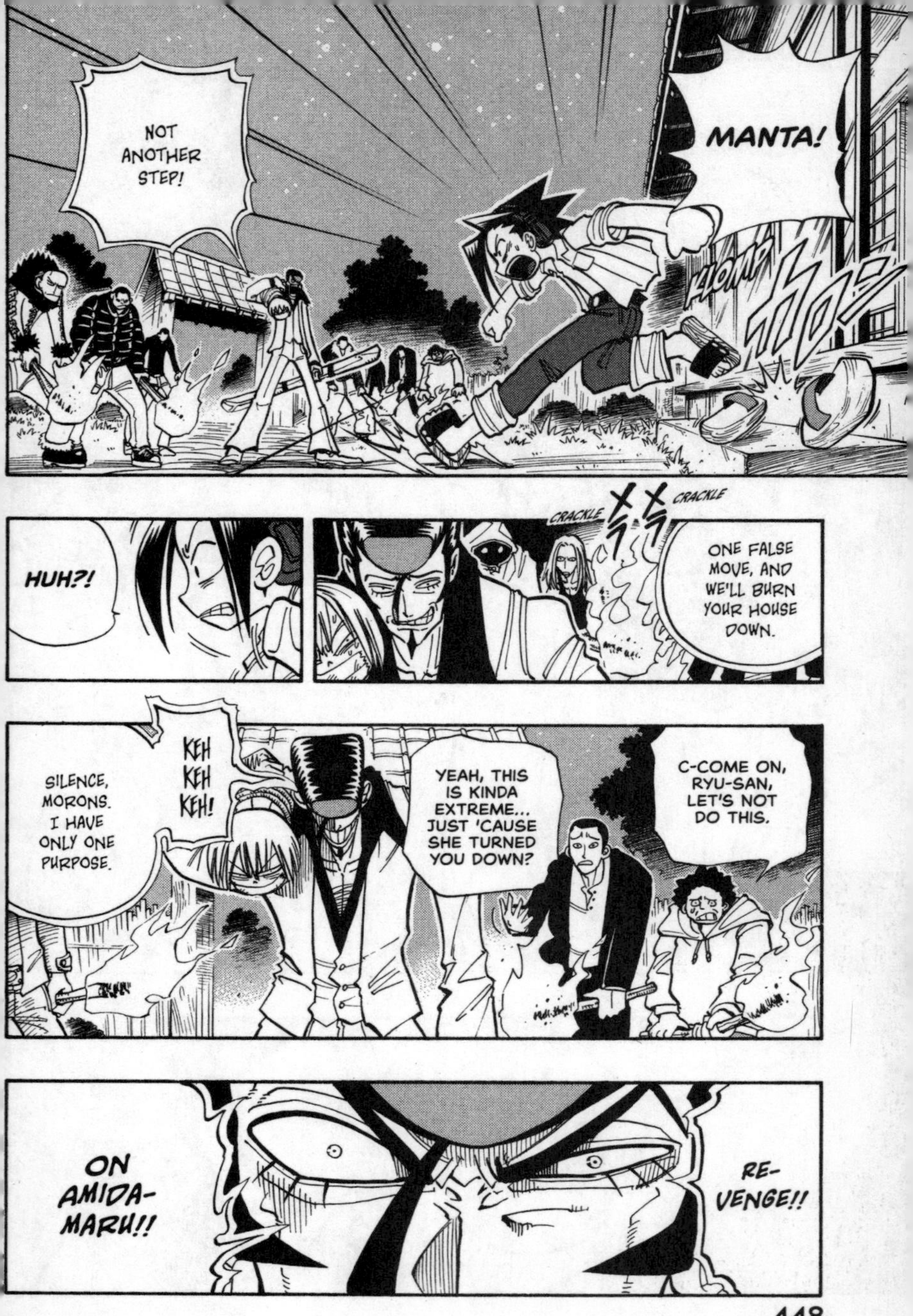
MANTA!
KLOMP
NOT ANOTHER STEP!
CRACKLE
CRACKLE
ONE FALSE MOVE, AND WE'LL BURN YOUR HOUSE DOWN.
HUH?!
C-COME ON, RYU-SAN, LET'S NOT DO THIS.
YEAH, THIS IS KINDA EXTREME... JUST 'CAUSE SHE TURNED YOU DOWN?
KEH KEH KEH!
SILENCE, MORONS. I HAVE ONLY ONE PURPOSE.
RE-VENGE!!
ON AMIDA-MARU!!

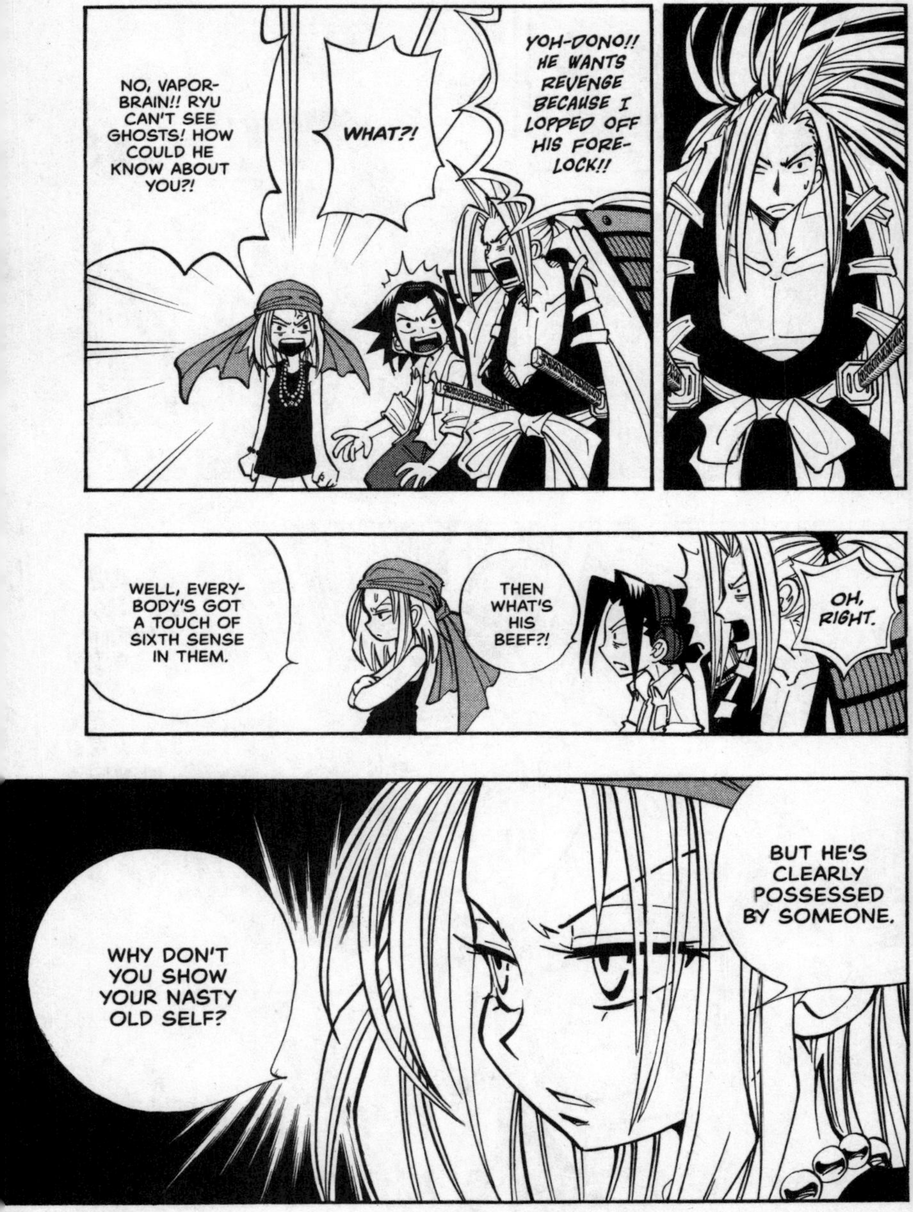
YOH-DONO!! HE WANTS REVENGE BECAUSE I LOPPED OFF HIS FORE-LOCK!!
WHAT?!
NO, VAPOR-BRAIN!! RYU CAN'T SEE GHOSTS! HOW COULD HE KNOW ABOUT YOU?!
OH, RIGHT.
THEN WHAT'S HIS BEEF?!
WELL, EVERY-BODY'S GOT A TOUCH OF SIXTH SENSE IN THEM.
BUT HE'S CLEARLY POSSESSED BY SOMEONE.
WHY DON'T YOU SHOW YOUR NASTY OLD SELF?

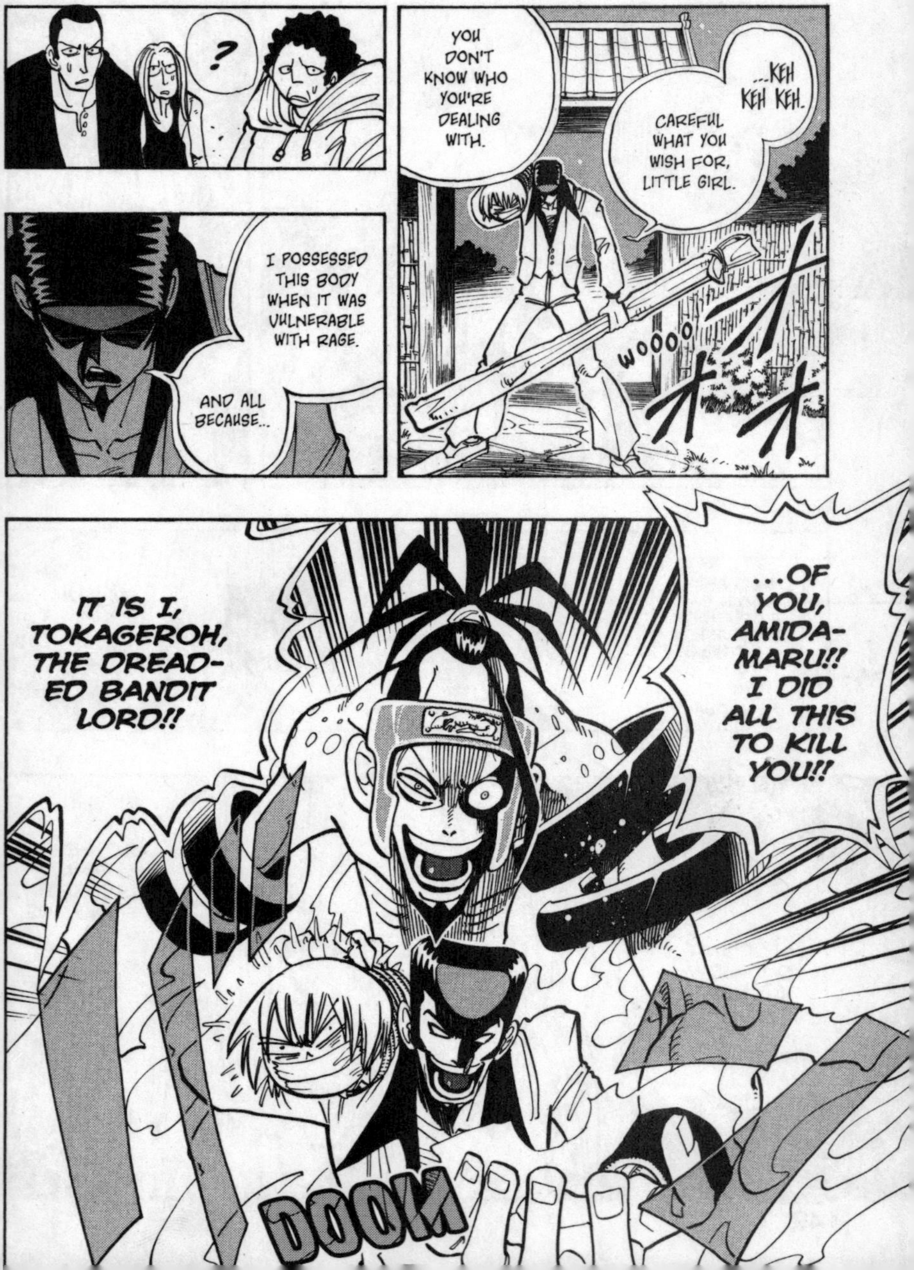
...KEH KEH KEH.
YOU DON'T KNOW WHO YOU'RE DEALING WITH.
CAREFUL WHAT YOU WISH FOR, LITTLE GIRL.
WOOOO
?
I POSSESSED THIS BODY WHEN IT WAS VULNERABLE WITH RAGE.
AND ALL BECAUSE...
...OF YOU, AMIDA-MARU!! I DID ALL THIS TO KILL YOU!!
IT IS I, TOKAGEROH, THE DREAD-ED BANDIT LORD!!
DOOM

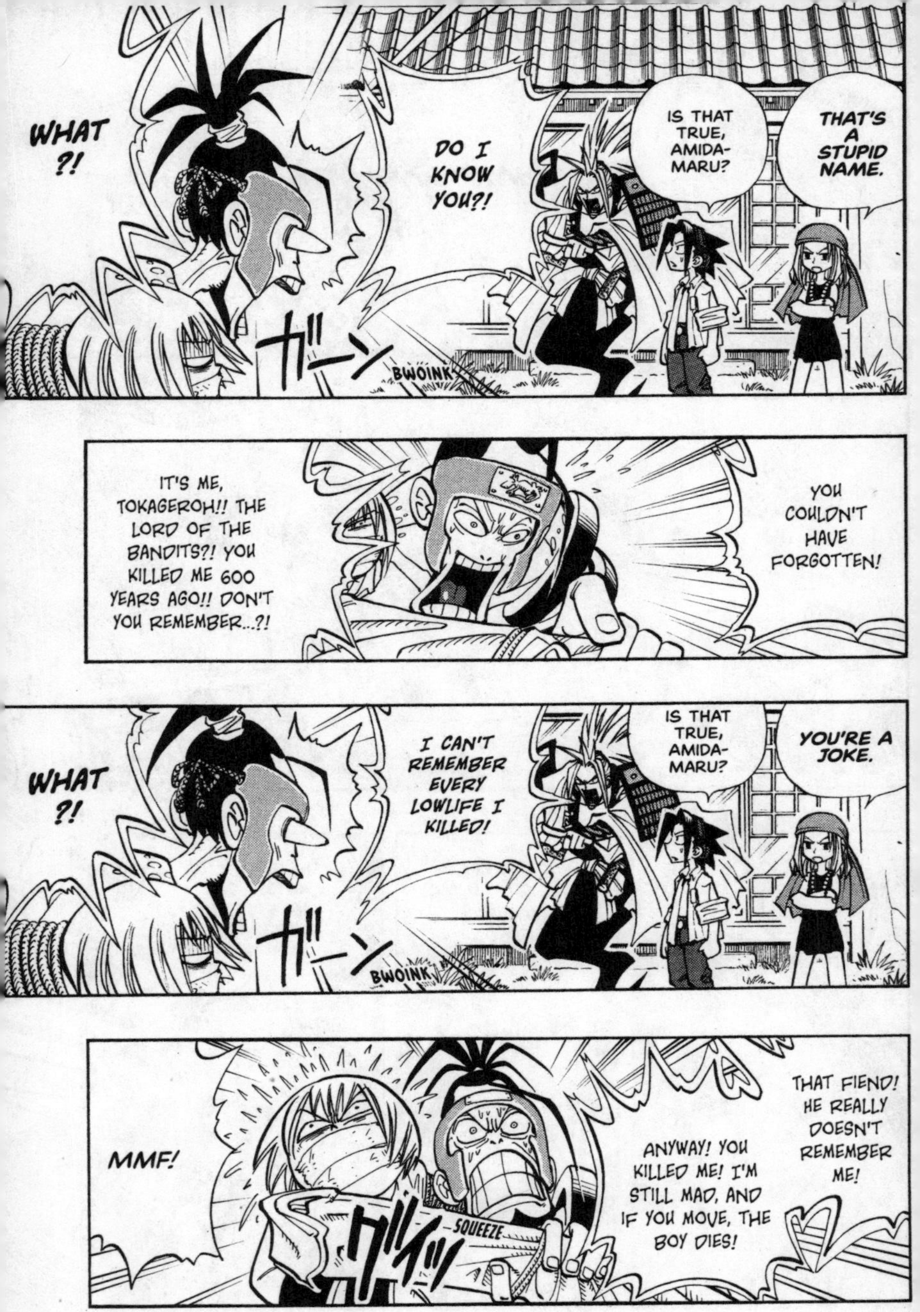
THAT'S A STUPID NAME.
IS THAT TRUE, AMIDA-MARU?
DO I KNOW YOU?!
WHAT ?!
ガーン
BWOINK
YOU COULDN'T HAVE FORGOTTEN!
IT'S ME, TOKAGEROH!! THE LORD OF THE BANDITS?! YOU KILLED ME 600 YEARS AGO!! DON'T YOU REMEMBER...?!
YOU'RE A JOKE.
IS THAT TRUE, AMIDA-MARU?
I CAN'T REMEMBER EVERY LOWLIFE I KILLED!
WHAT ?!
ガーン
BWOINK
THAT FIEND! HE REALLY DOESN'T REMEMBER ME!
ANYWAY! YOU KILLED ME! I'M STILL MAD, AND IF YOU MOVE, THE BOY DIES!
MMF!
グイッ
SQUEEZE

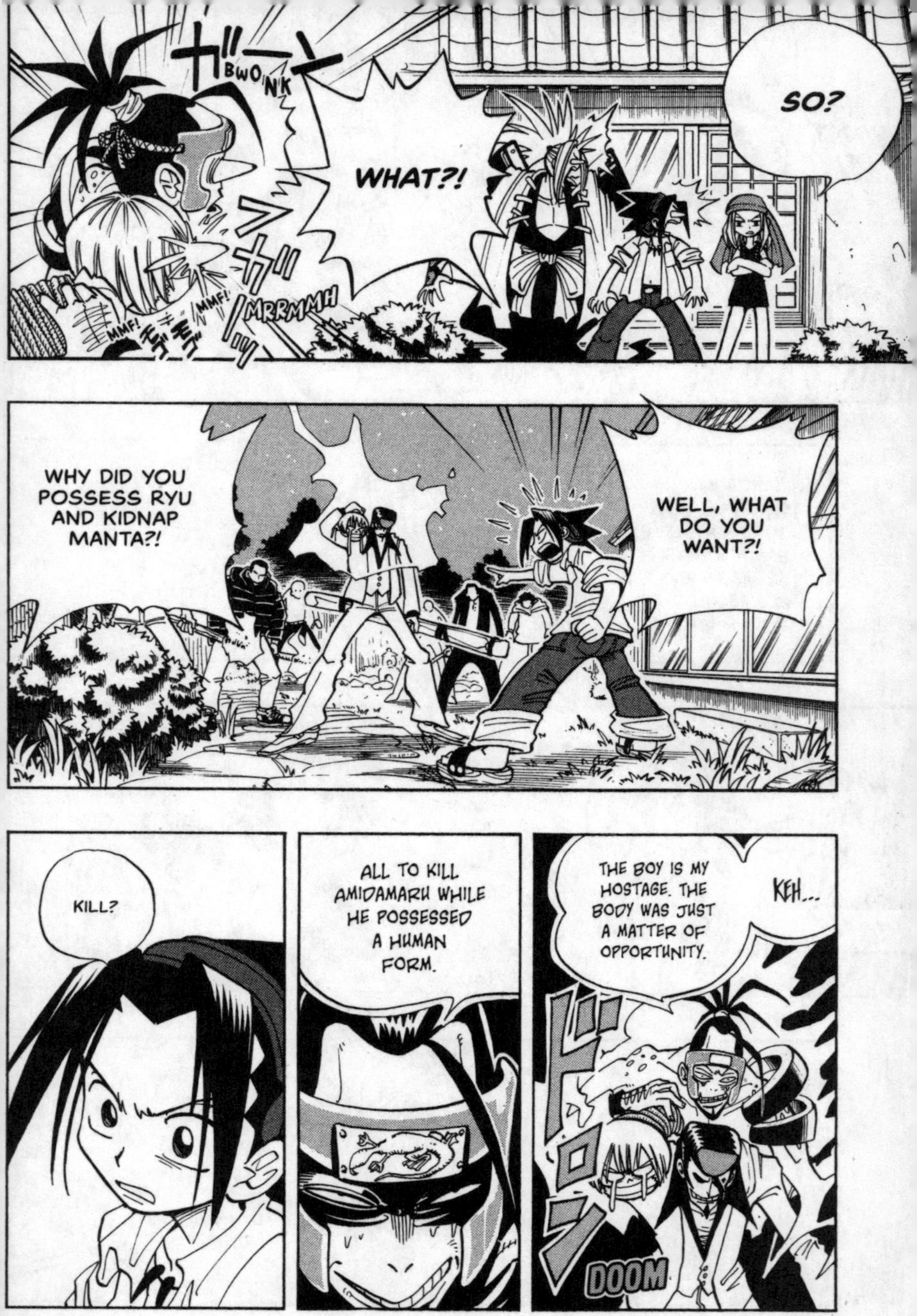
SO?
WHAT?!
BWONK
MRRMMH
MMF!
MMF!
WELL, WHAT DO YOU WANT?!
WHY DID YOU POSSESS RYU AND KIDNAP MANTA?!
THE BOY IS MY HOSTAGE. THE BODY WAS JUST A MATTER OF OPPORTUNITY.
KEH...
DOOM
ALL TO KILL AMIDAMARU WHILE HE POSSESSED A HUMAN FORM.
KILL?

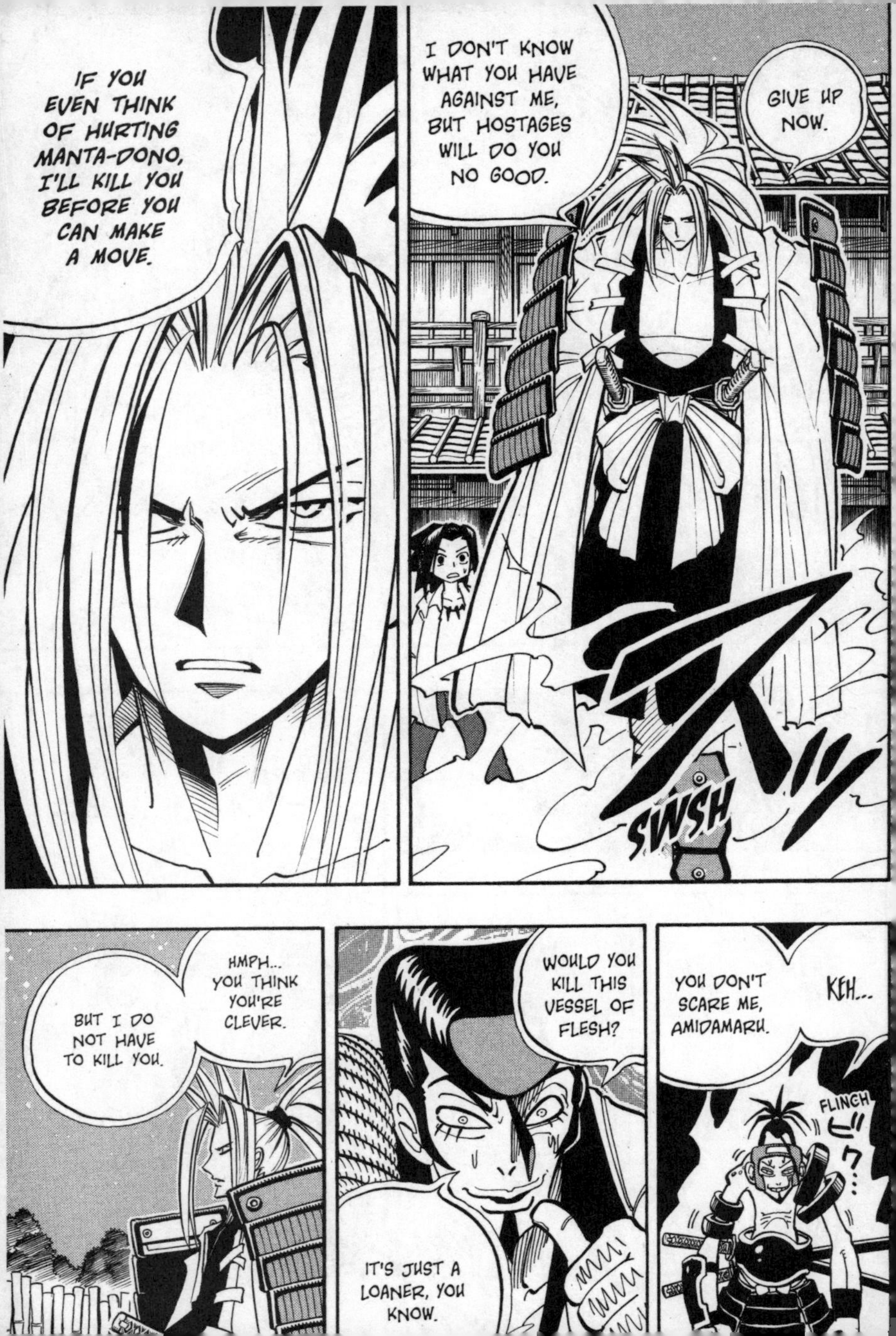
I DON'T KNOW WHAT YOU HAVE AGAINST ME, BUT HOSTAGES WILL DO YOU NO GOOD.
GIVE UP NOW.
SWSH
IF YOU EVEN THINK OF HURTING MANTA-DONO, I'LL KILL YOU BEFORE YOU CAN MAKE A MOVE.
KEH...
YOU DON'T SCARE ME, AMIDAMARU.
FLINCH
WOULD YOU KILL THIS VESSEL OF FLESH?
IT'S JUST A LOANER, YOU KNOW.
HMPH... YOU THINK YOU'RE CLEVER.
BUT I DO NOT HAVE TO KILL YOU.

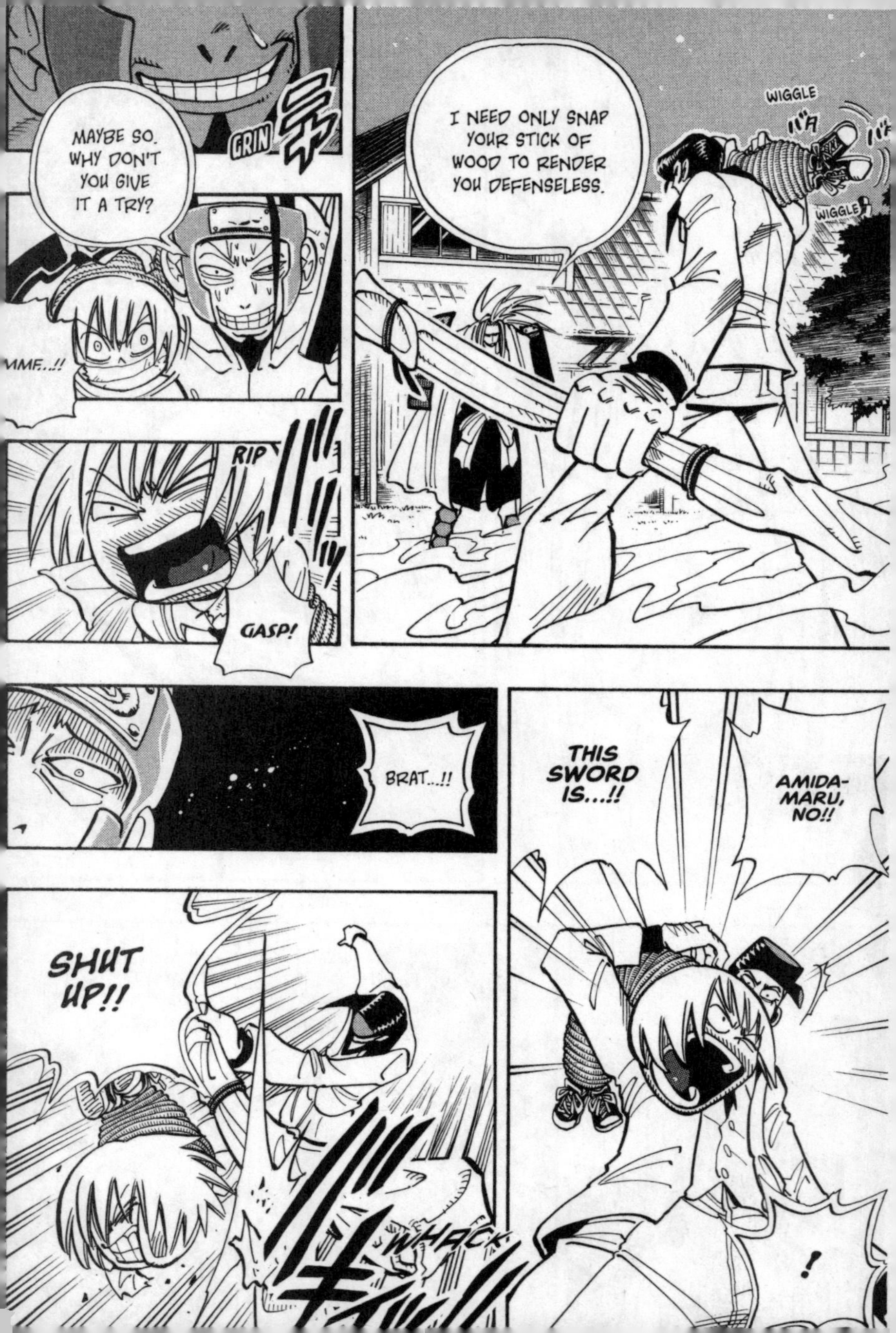

I NEED ONLY SNAP YOUR STICK OF WOOD TO RENDER YOU DEFENSELESS.
WIGGLE
WIGGLE
GRIN
MAYBE SO. WHY DON'T YOU GIVE IT A TRY?
MMF...!!
RIP
GASP!
AMIDA-MARU, NO!!
THIS SWORD IS...!!
!
BRAT...!!
SHUT UP!!
WHACK

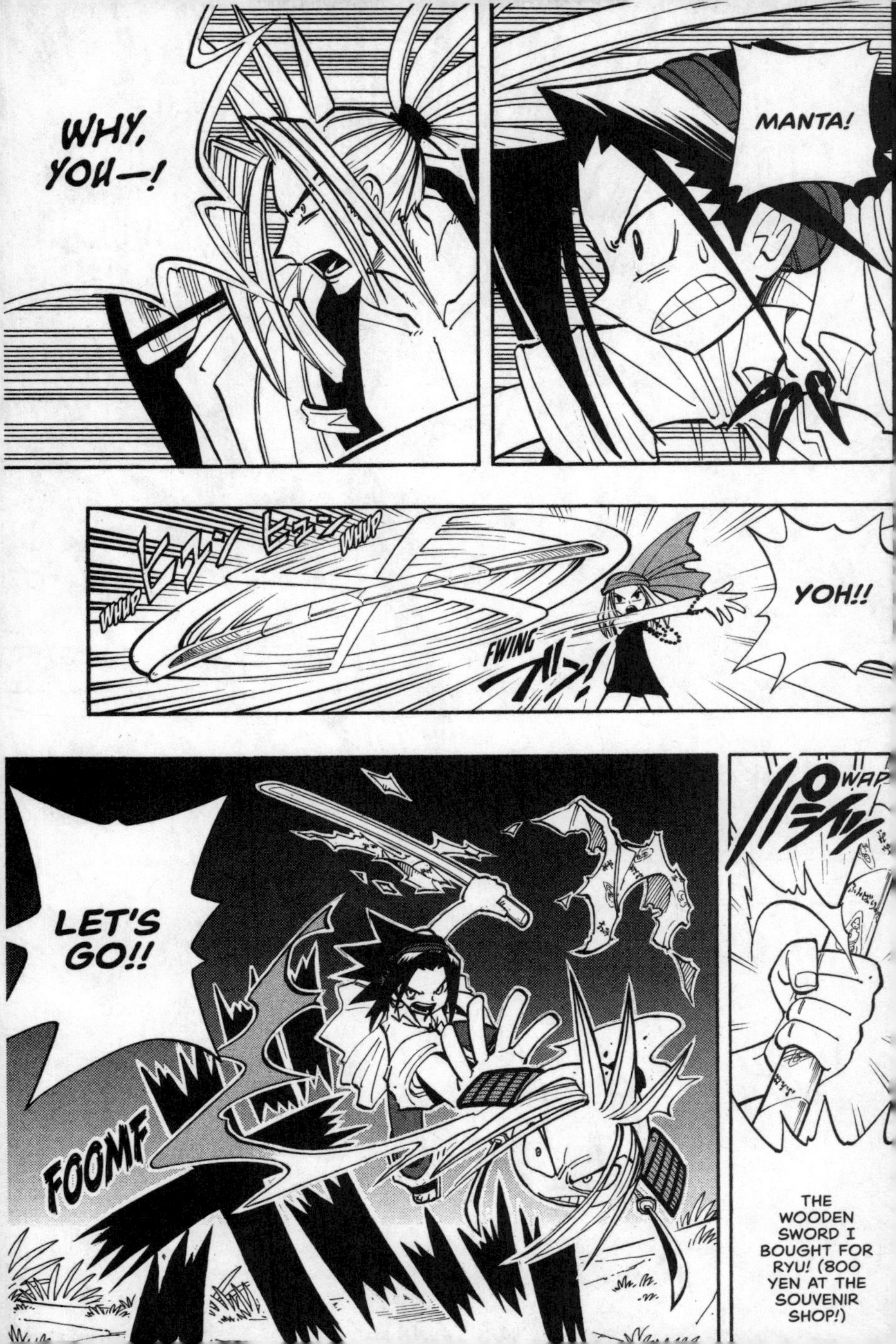
MANTA!
WHY, YOU—!
YOH!!
WHUP
WHUP
FWING
WAP
THE WOODEN SWORD I BOUGHT FOR RYU! (800 YEN AT THE SOUVENIR SHOP!)
LET'S GO!!
FOOMF

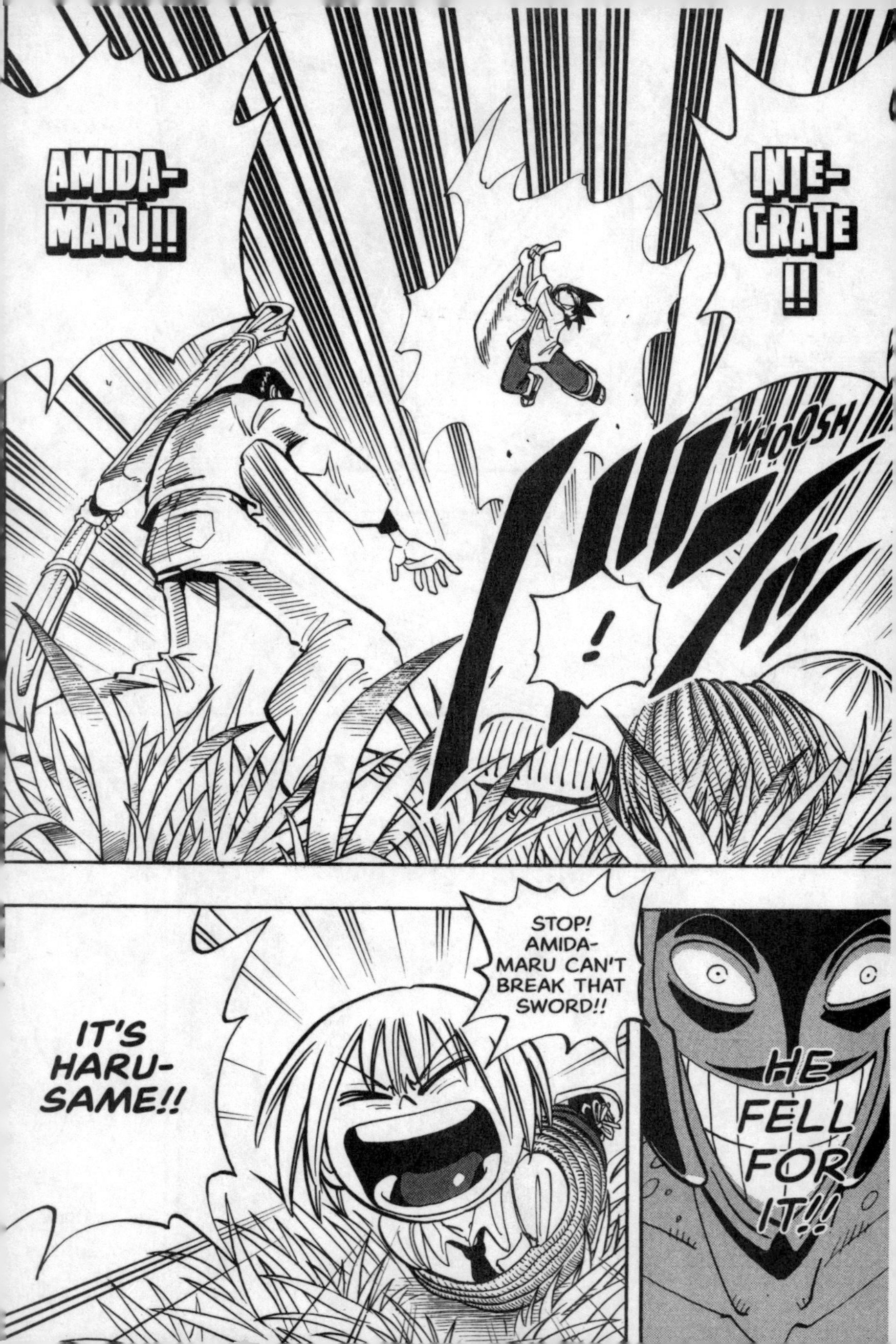
INTE-GRATE!!
AMIDA-MARU!!
WHOOSH
!
HE FELL FOR IT!!
STOP! AMIDA-MARU CAN'T BREAK THAT SWORD!!
IT'S HARU-SAME!!

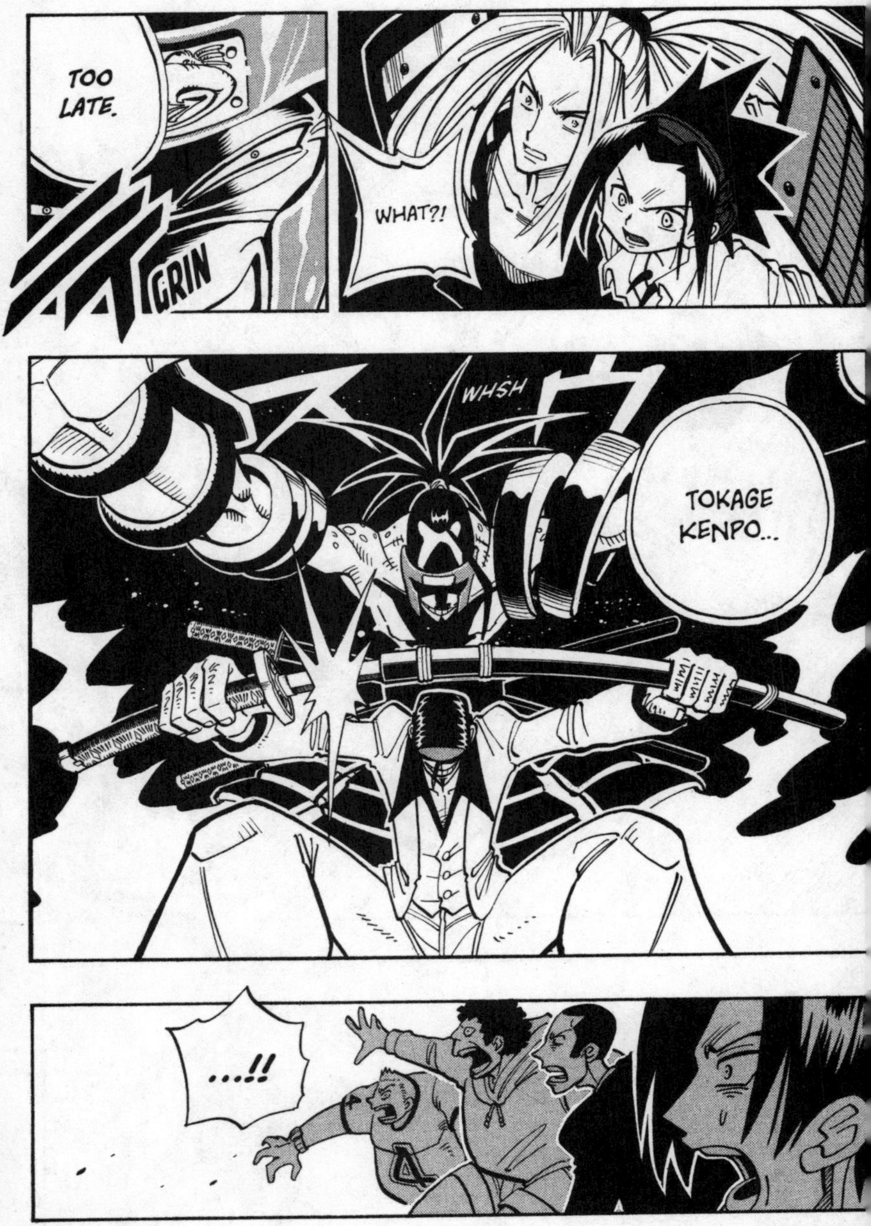
WHAT?!
TOO LATE.
GRIN
TOKAGE KENPO...
WHSH
...!!

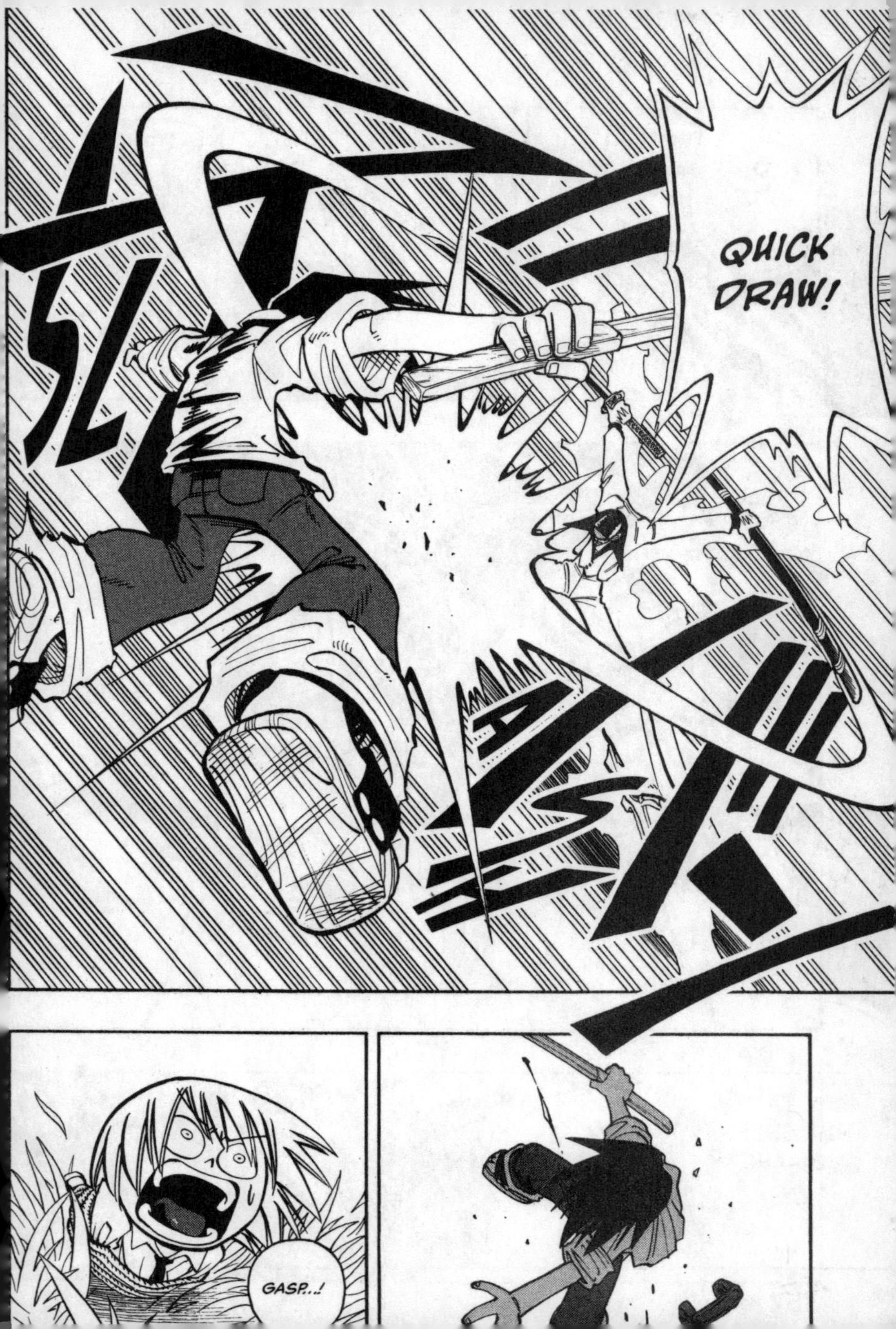
QUICK DRAW!
SLASH
GASP..!

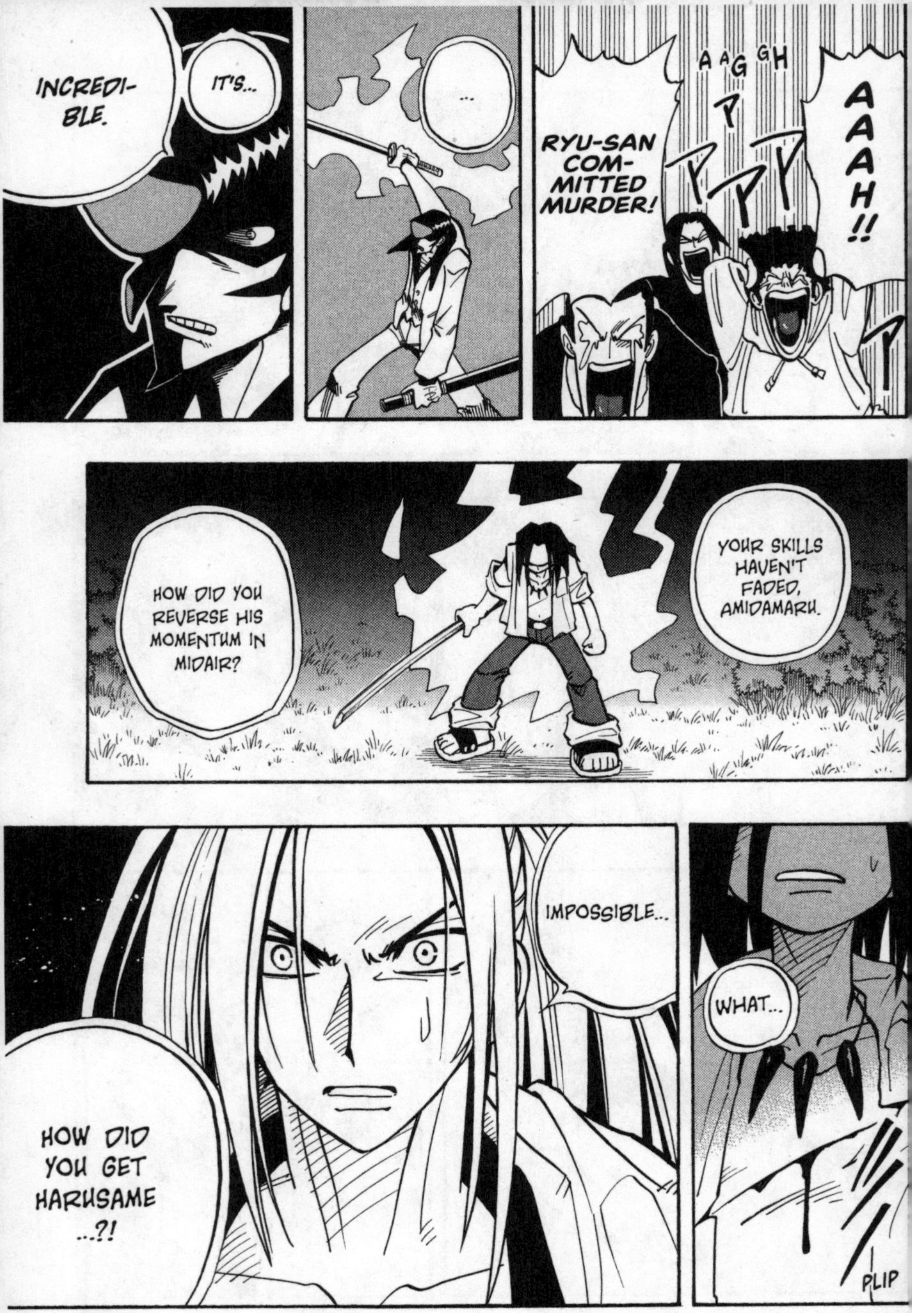
AAAAH!!
AAGGH
PPPP
RYU-SAN COMMITTED MURDER!
...
IT'S...
INCREDIBLE.
YOUR SKILLS HAVEN'T FADED, AMIDAMARU.
HOW DID YOU REVERSE HIS MOMENTUM IN MIDAIR?
WHAT...
PLIP
IMPOSSIBLE...
HOW DID YOU GET HARUSAME ...?!

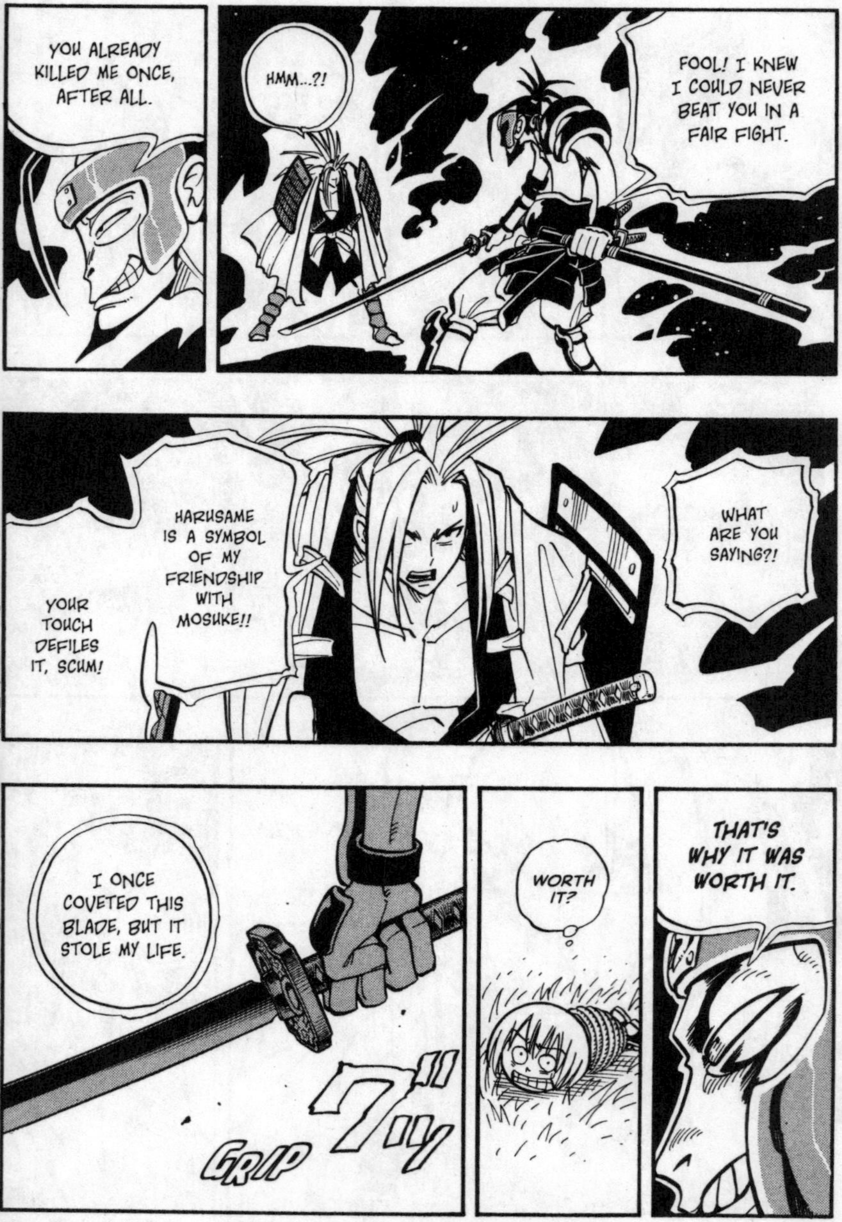
FOOL! I KNEW I COULD NEVER BEAT YOU IN A FAIR FIGHT.
HMM...?!
YOU ALREADY KILLED ME ONCE, AFTER ALL.
WHAT ARE YOU SAYING?!
HARUSAME IS A SYMBOL OF MY FRIENDSHIP WITH MOSUKE!!
YOUR TOUCH DEFILES IT, SCUM!
THAT'S WHY IT WAS WORTH IT.
WORTH IT?
I ONCE COVETED THIS BLADE, BUT IT STOLE MY LIFE.
GRIP

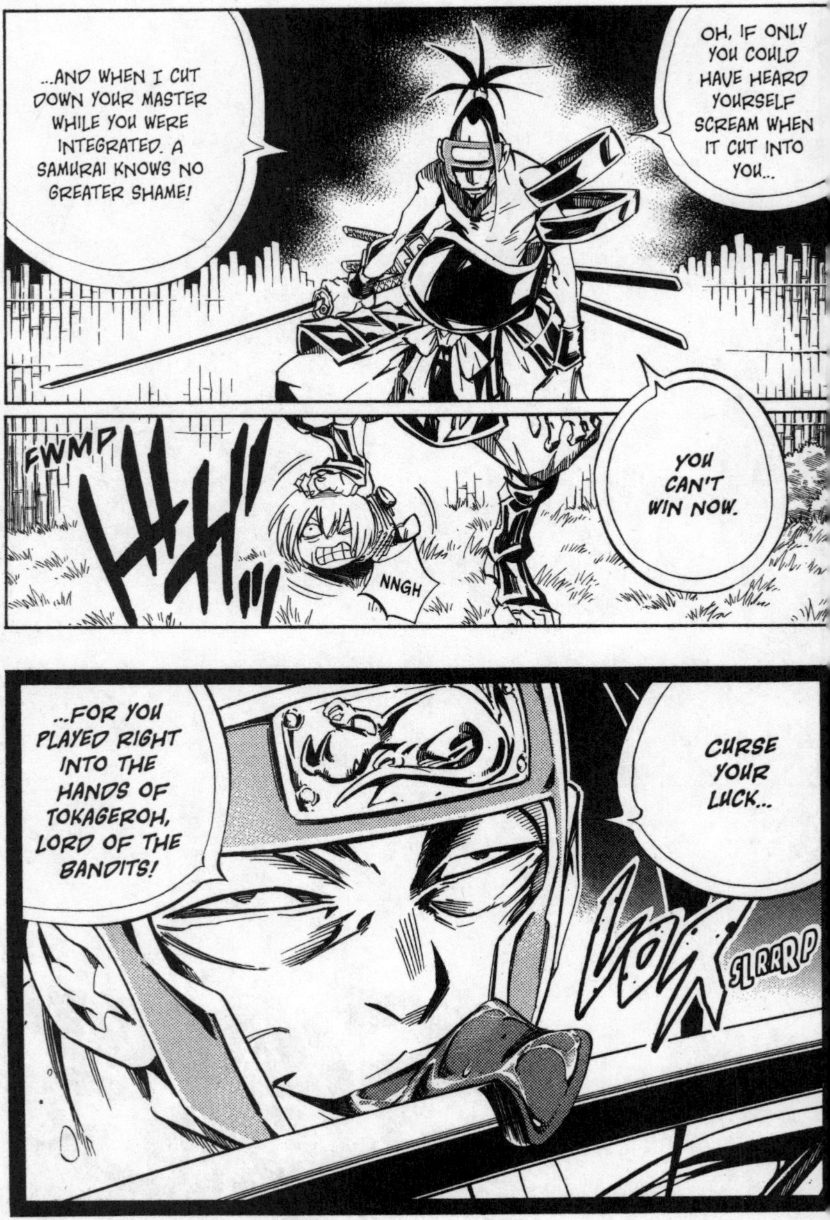
OH, IF ONLY YOU COULD HAVE HEARD YOURSELF SCREAM WHEN IT CUT INTO YOU...
...AND WHEN I CUT DOWN YOUR MASTER WHILE YOU WERE INTEGRATED. A SAMURAI KNOWS NO GREATER SHAME!
YOU CAN'T WIN NOW.
NNGH
FWMP
CURSE YOUR LUCK...
SLRRRP
...FOR YOU PLAYED RIGHT INTO THE HANDS OF TOKAGEROH, LORD OF THE BANDITS!

SHAMAN KING

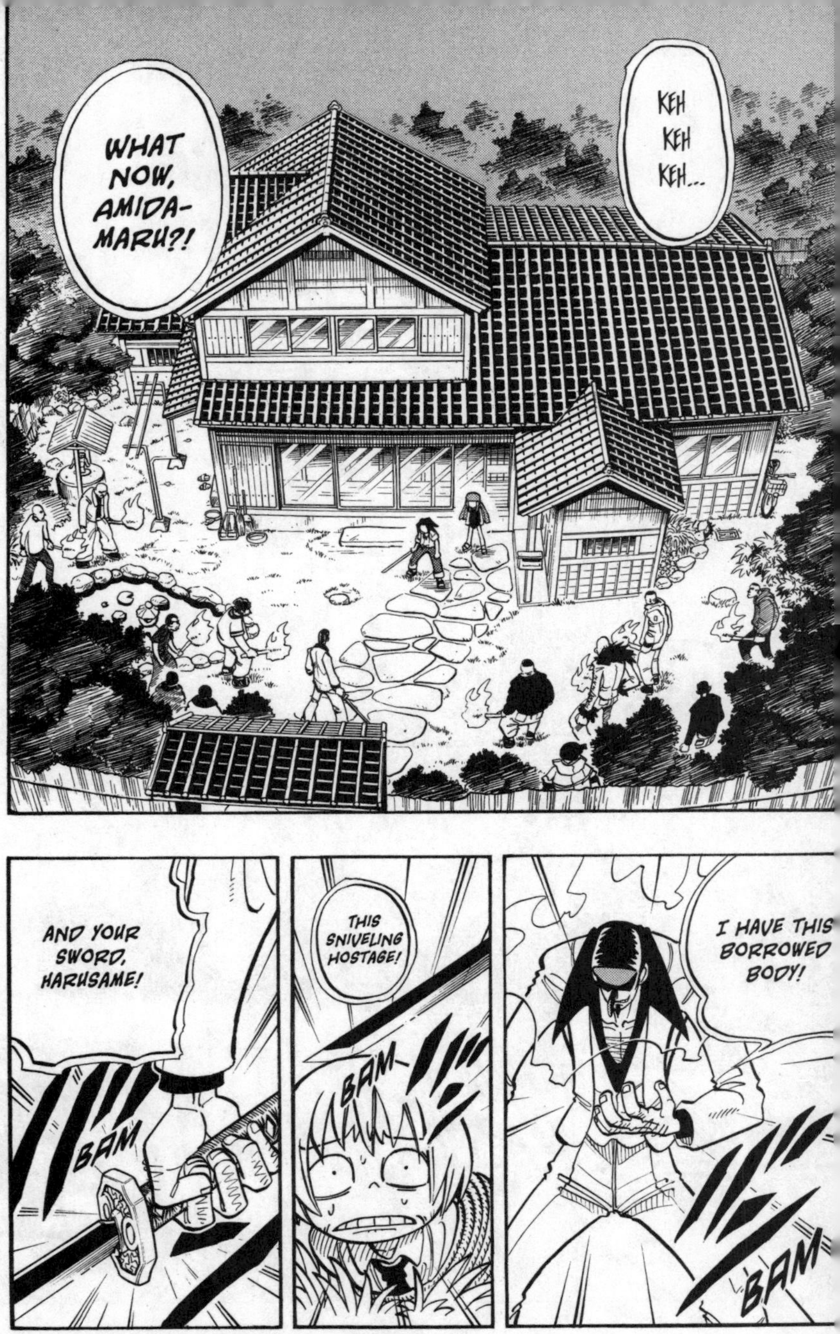
KEH KEH KEH...
WHAT NOW, AMIDA-MARU?!
I HAVE THIS BORROWED BODY!
BAM
THIS SNIVELING HOSTAGE!
BAM
AND YOUR SWORD, HARUSAME!
BAM

Chapter 21: Spring Rain

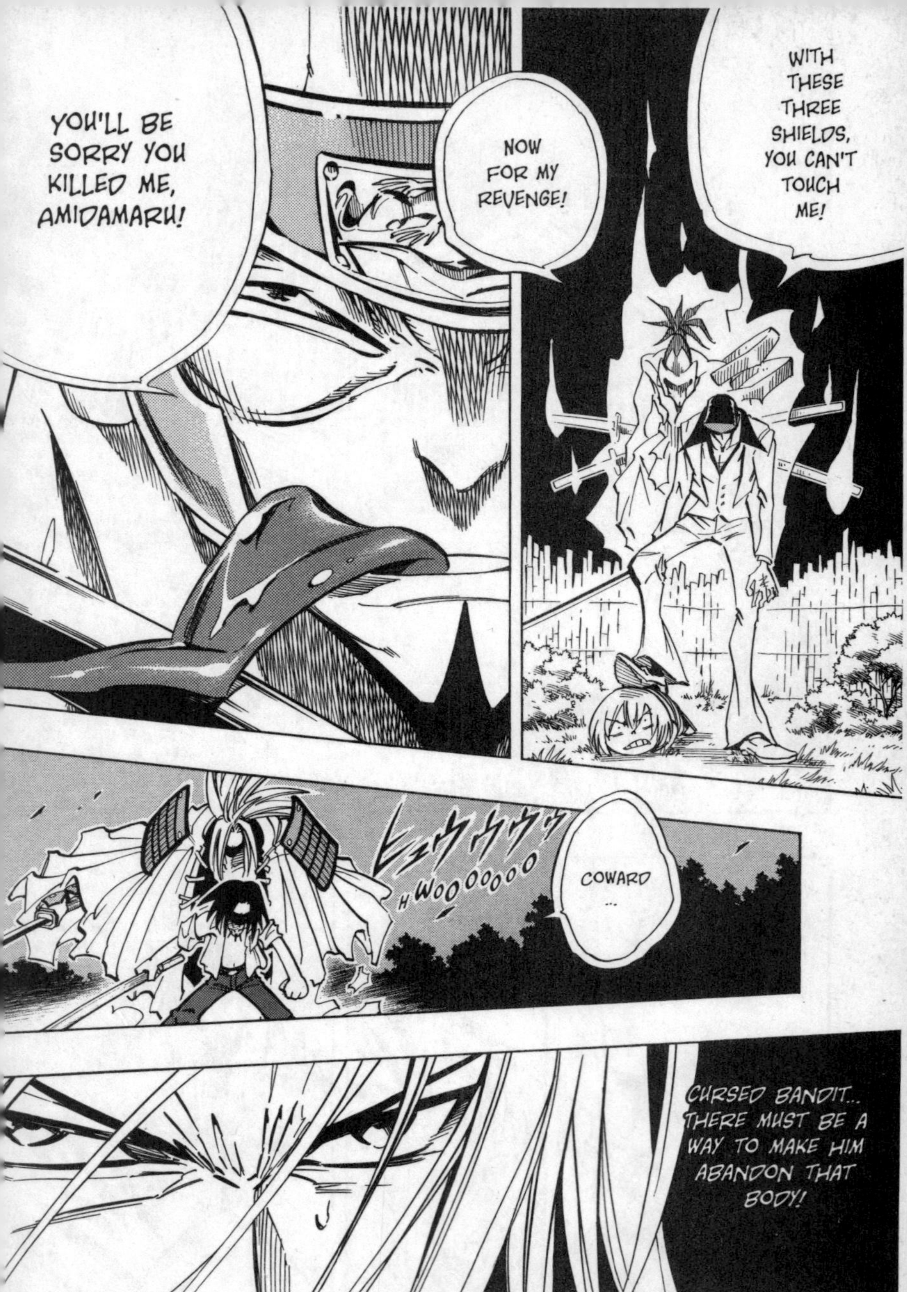
WITH THESE THREE SHIELDS, YOU CAN'T TOUCH ME!
NOW FOR MY REVENGE!
YOU'LL BE SORRY YOU KILLED ME, AMIDAMARU!
COWARD ...
ヒュウウウウ
HWOOOOOOO
CURSED BANDIT... THERE MUST BE A WAY TO MAKE HIM ABANDON THAT BODY!

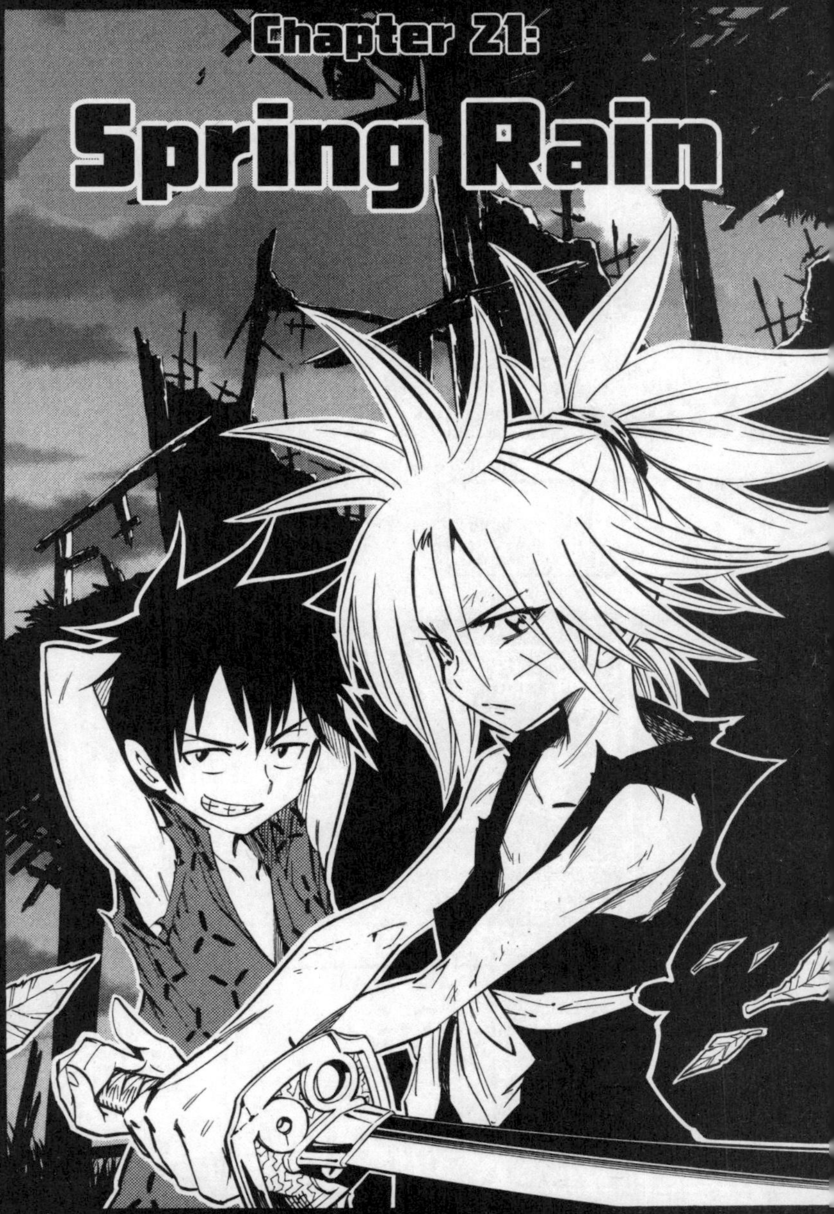
Chapter 21:
Spring Rain

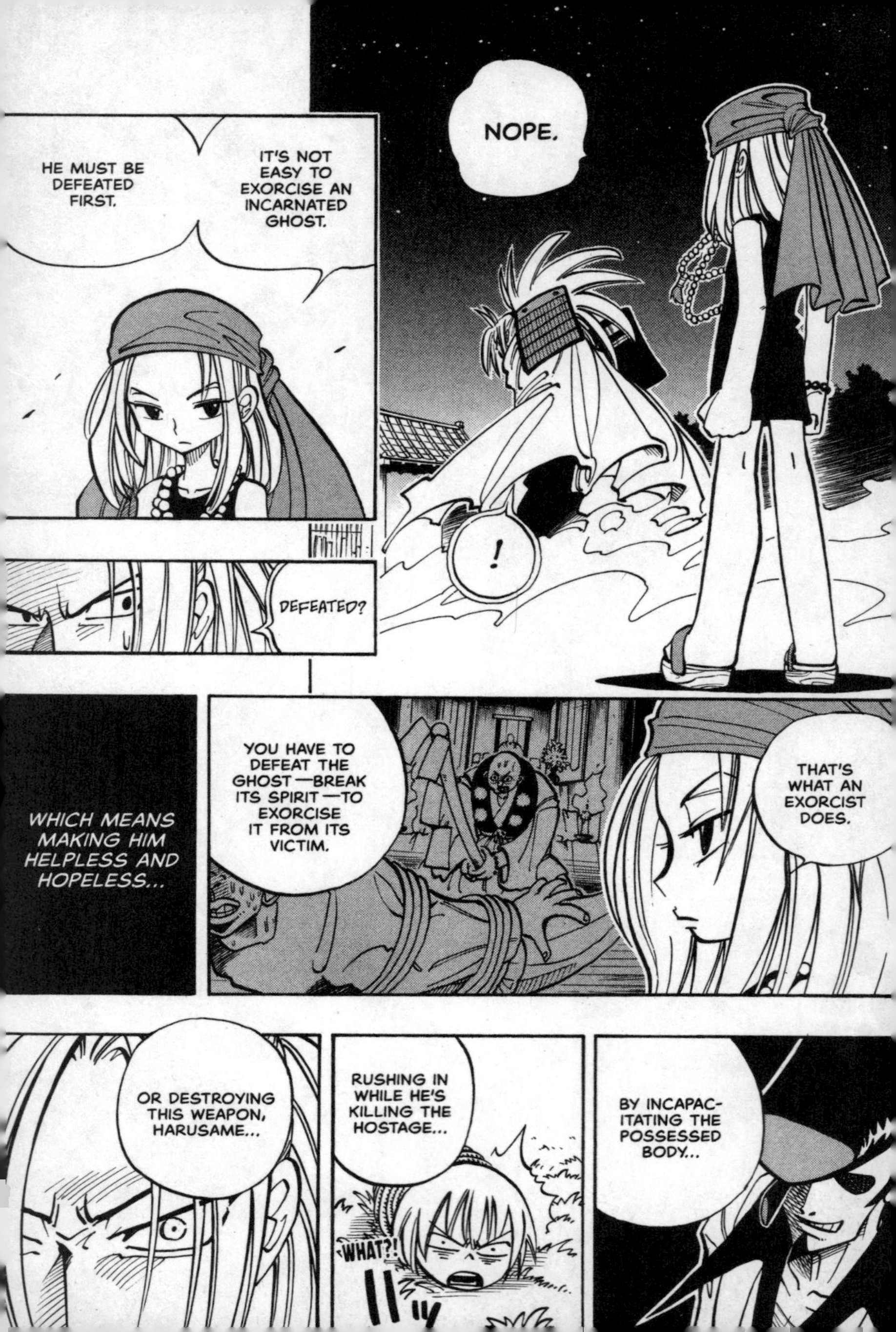
NOPE.
!
IT'S NOT EASY TO EXORCISE AN INCARNATED GHOST.
HE MUST BE DEFEATED FIRST.
DEFEATED?
THAT'S WHAT AN EXORCIST DOES.
YOU HAVE TO DEFEAT THE GHOST—BREAK ITS SPIRIT—TO EXORCISE IT FROM ITS VICTIM.
WHICH MEANS MAKING HIM HELPLESS AND HOPELESS...
BY INCAPAC-ITATING THE POSSESSED BODY...
RUSHING IN WHILE HE'S KILLING THE HOSTAGE...
WHAT?!
OR DESTROYING THIS WEAPON, HARUSAME...

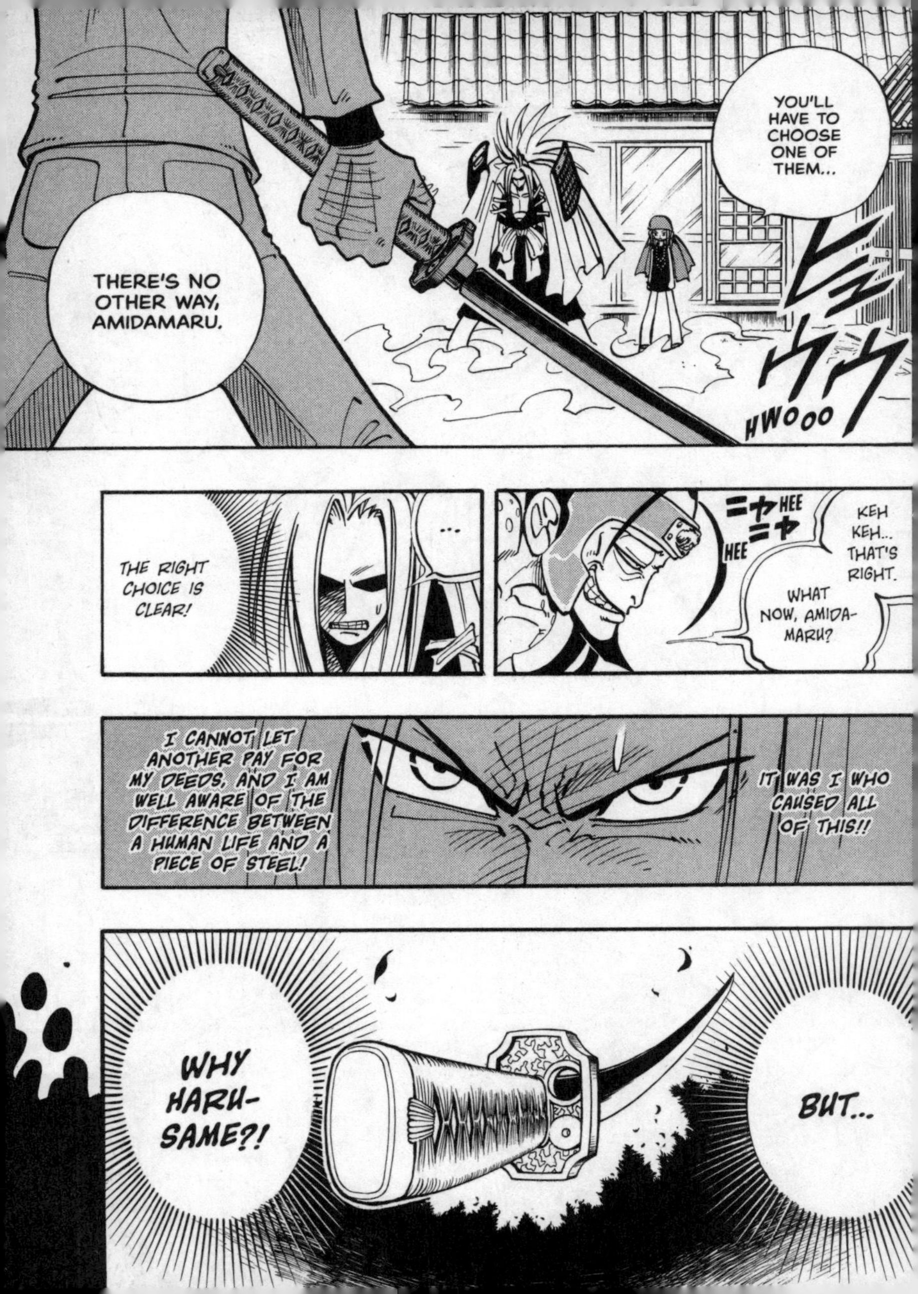

YOU'LL HAVE TO CHOOSE ONE OF THEM...
HWOOO
THERE'S NO OTHER WAY, AMIDAMARU.
HEE HEE
KEH KEH... THAT'S RIGHT.
WHAT NOW, AMIDA-MARU?
...
THE RIGHT CHOICE IS CLEAR!
IT WAS I WHO CAUSED ALL OF THIS!!
I CANNOT LET ANOTHER PAY FOR MY DEEDS, AND I AM WELL AWARE OF THE DIFFERENCE BETWEEN A HUMAN LIFE AND A PIECE OF STEEL!
BUT...
WHY HARU-SAME?!

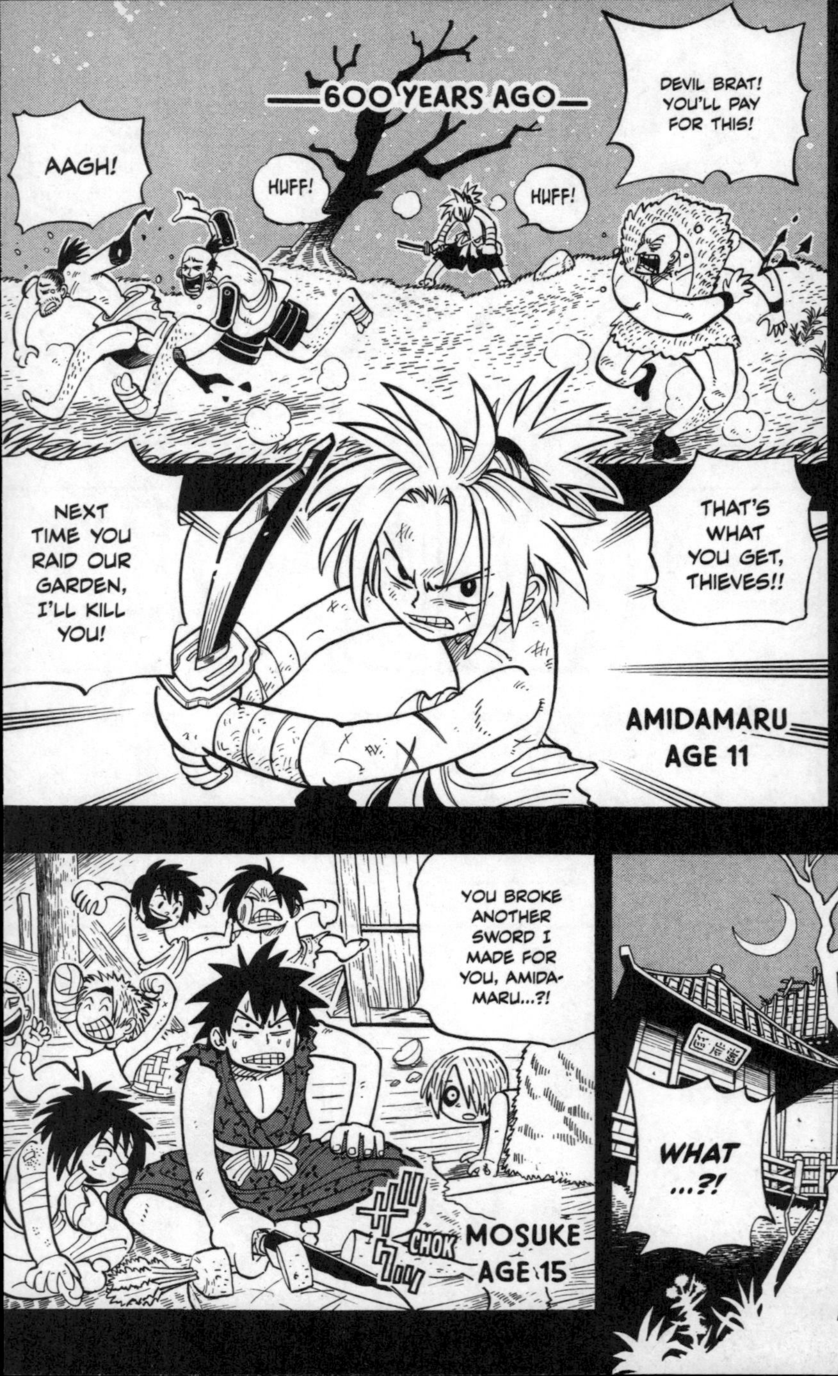
—600 YEARS AGO—
DEVIL BRAT! YOU'LL PAY FOR THIS!
HUFF!
HUFF!
AAGH!
THAT'S WHAT YOU GET, THIEVES!!
NEXT TIME YOU RAID OUR GARDEN, I'LL KILL YOU!
AMIDAMARU AGE 11
WHAT ...?!
YOU BROKE ANOTHER SWORD I MADE FOR YOU, AMIDA-MARU...?!
CHOK
MOSUKE AGE 15

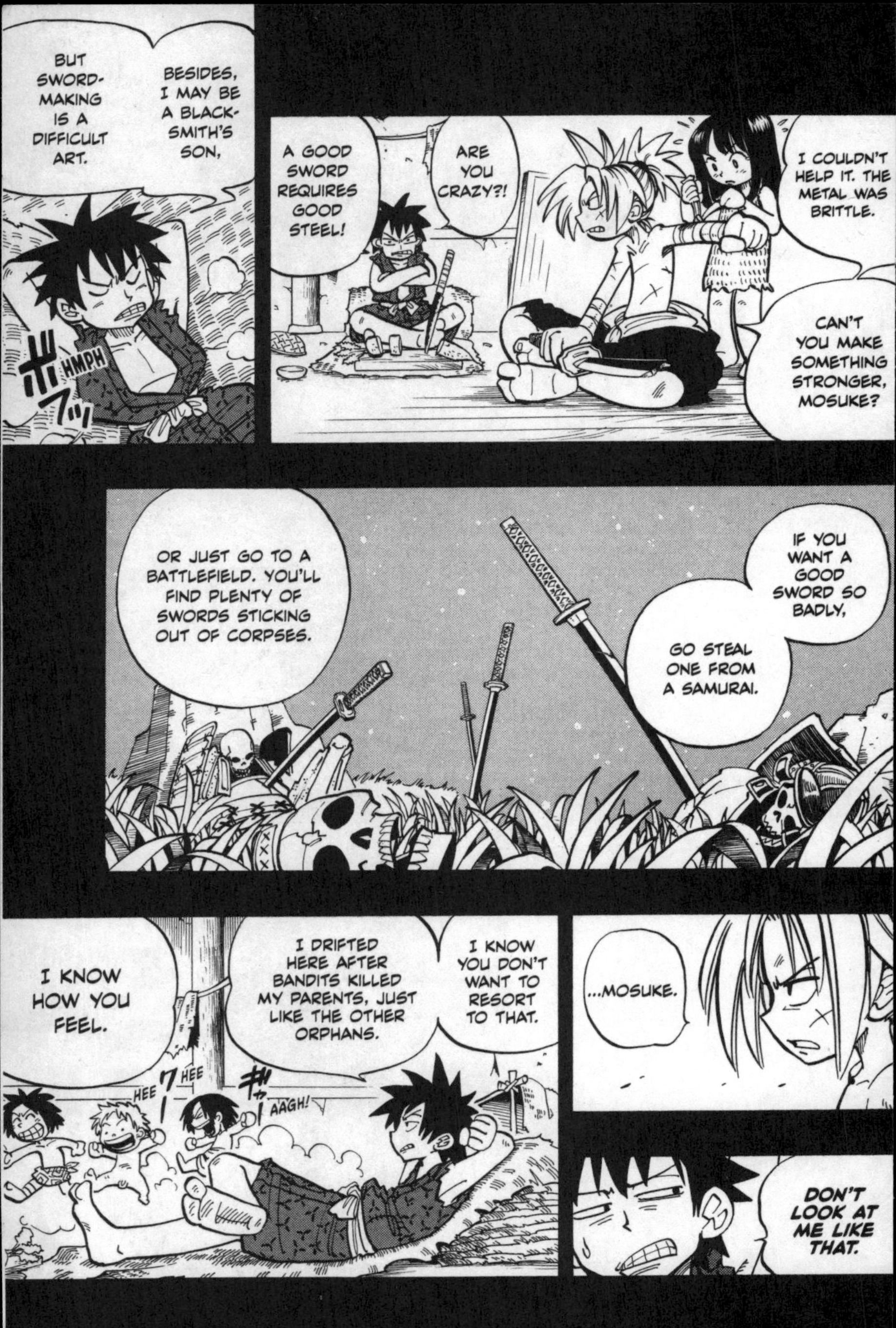
I COULDN'T HELP IT. THE METAL WAS BRITTLE.
CAN'T YOU MAKE SOMETHING STRONGER, MOSUKE?
ARE YOU CRAZY?!
A GOOD SWORD REQUIRES GOOD STEEL!
BESIDES, I MAY BE A BLACKSMITH'S SON,
BUT SWORD-MAKING IS A DIFFICULT ART.
HMPH
IF YOU WANT A GOOD SWORD SO BADLY,
GO STEAL ONE FROM A SAMURAI.
OR JUST GO TO A BATTLEFIELD. YOU'LL FIND PLENTY OF SWORDS STICKING OUT OF CORPSES.
...MOSUKE.
DON'T LOOK AT ME LIKE THAT.
I KNOW YOU DON'T WANT TO RESORT TO THAT.
I DRIFTED HERE AFTER BANDITS KILLED MY PARENTS, JUST LIKE THE OTHER ORPHANS.
I KNOW HOW YOU FEEL.
HEE
HEE
AAGH!

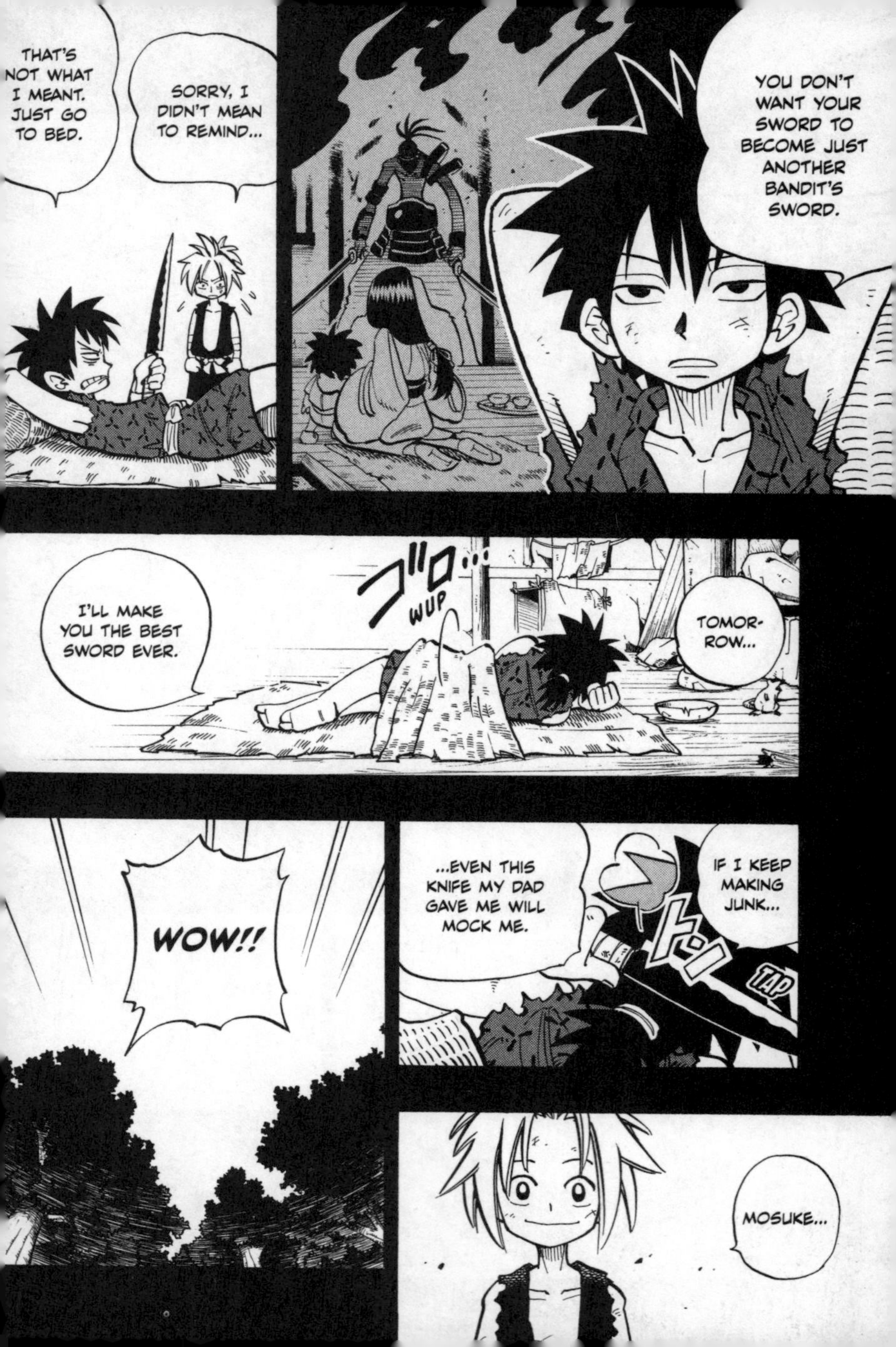
YOU DON'T WANT YOUR SWORD TO BECOME JUST ANOTHER BANDIT'S SWORD.
SORRY, I DIDN'T MEAN TO REMIND...
THAT'S NOT WHAT I MEANT. JUST GO TO BED.
TOMOR-ROW...
ゴロ...
WUP
I'LL MAKE YOU THE BEST SWORD EVER.
IF I KEEP MAKING JUNK...
...EVEN THIS KNIFE MY DAD GAVE ME WILL MOCK ME.
TAP
MOSUKE...
WOW!!

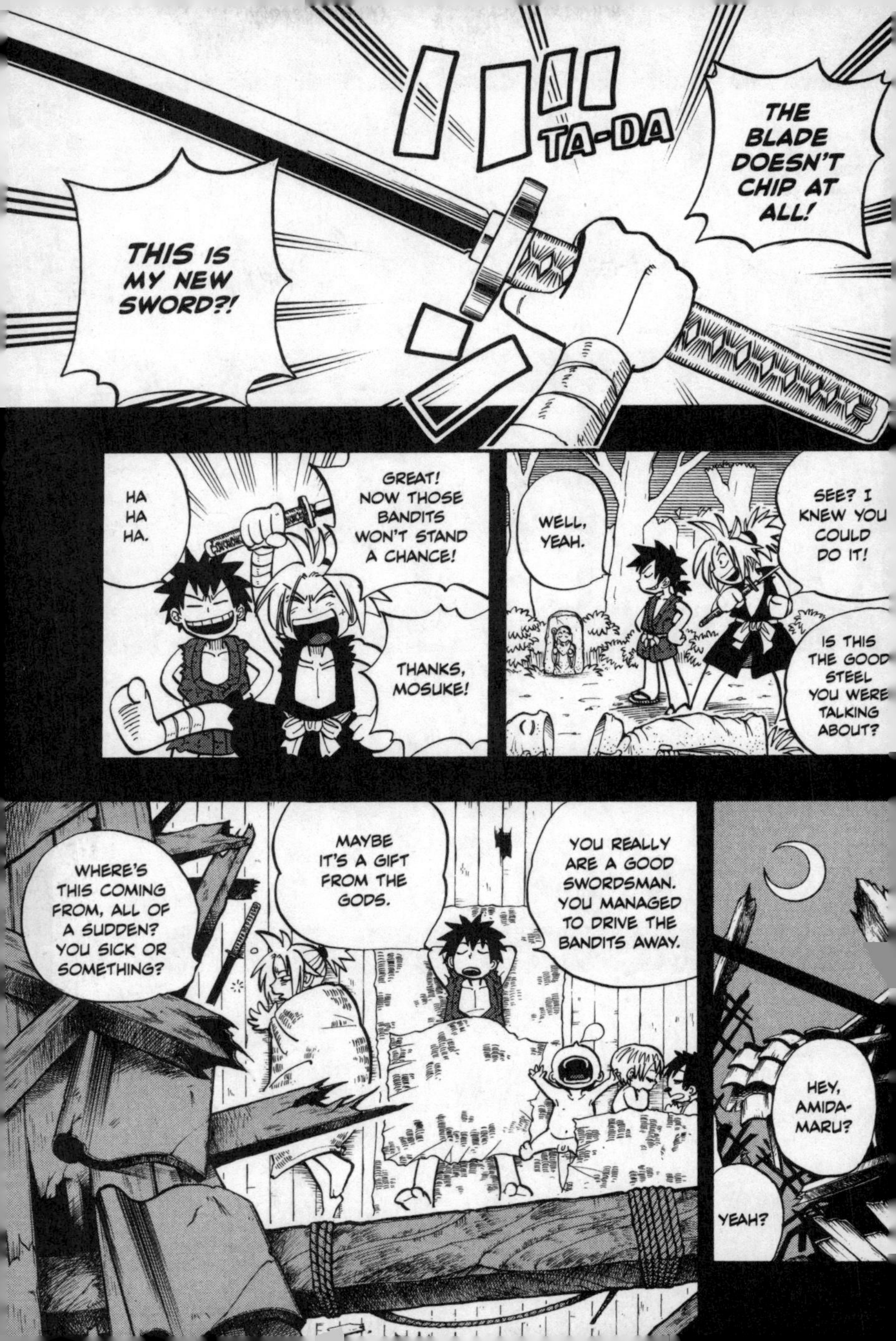
THE BLADE DOESN'T CHIP AT ALL!
TA-DA
THIS IS MY NEW SWORD?!
SEE? I KNEW YOU COULD DO IT!
WELL, YEAH.
IS THIS THE GOOD STEEL YOU WERE TALKING ABOUT?
GREAT! NOW THOSE BANDITS WON'T STAND A CHANCE!
HA HA HA.
THANKS, MOSUKE!
HEY, AMIDA-MARU?
YEAH?
YOU REALLY ARE A GOOD SWORDSMAN. YOU MANAGED TO DRIVE THE BANDITS AWAY.
MAYBE IT'S A GIFT FROM THE GODS.
WHERE'S THIS COMING FROM, ALL OF A SUDDEN? YOU SICK OR SOMETHING?

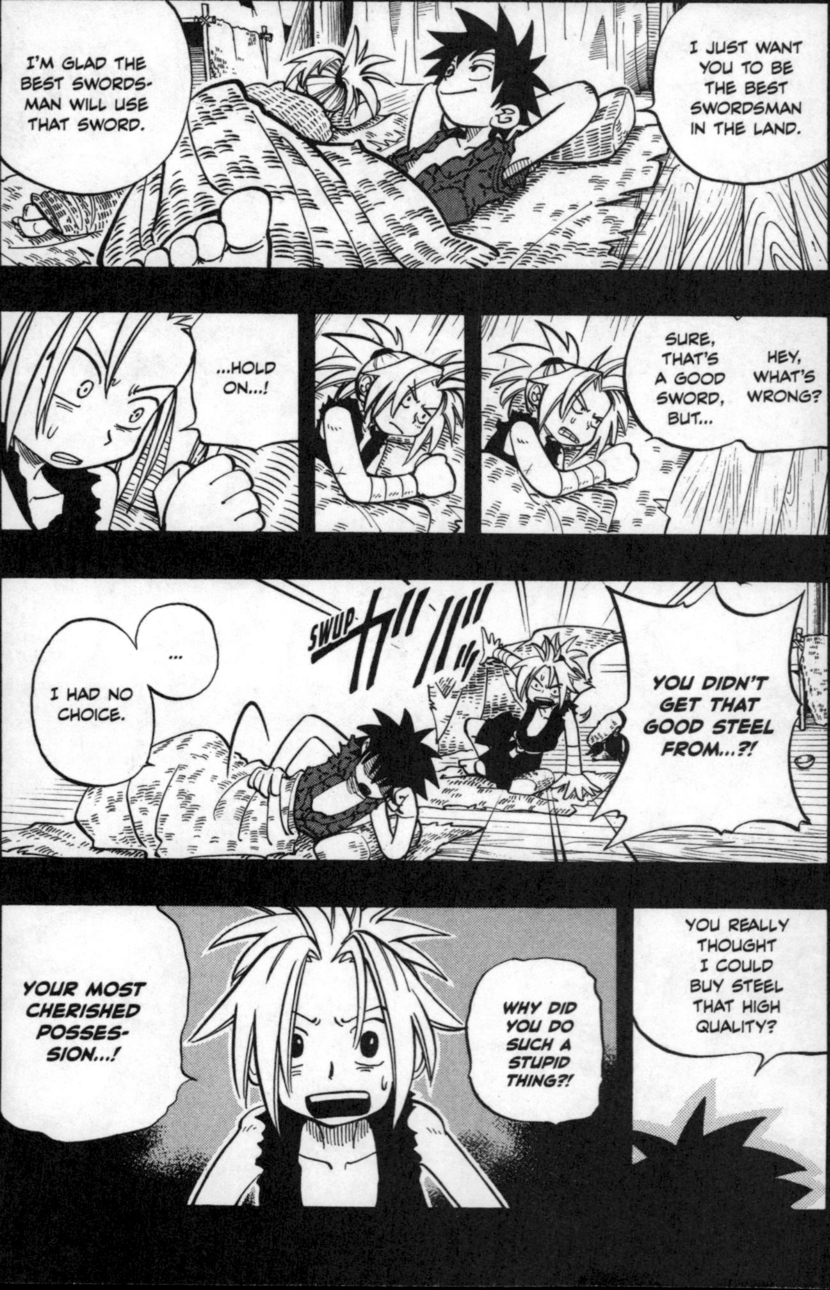
I JUST WANT YOU TO BE THE BEST SWORDSMAN IN THE LAND.
I'M GLAD THE BEST SWORDS-MAN WILL USE THAT SWORD.
HEY, WHAT'S WRONG?
SURE, THAT'S A GOOD SWORD, BUT...
...HOLD ON...!
YOU DIDN'T GET THAT GOOD STEEL FROM...?!
SWUP
...
I HAD NO CHOICE.
YOU REALLY THOUGHT I COULD BUY STEEL THAT HIGH QUALITY?
WHY DID YOU DO SUCH A STUPID THING?!
YOUR MOST CHERISHED POSSES-SION...!

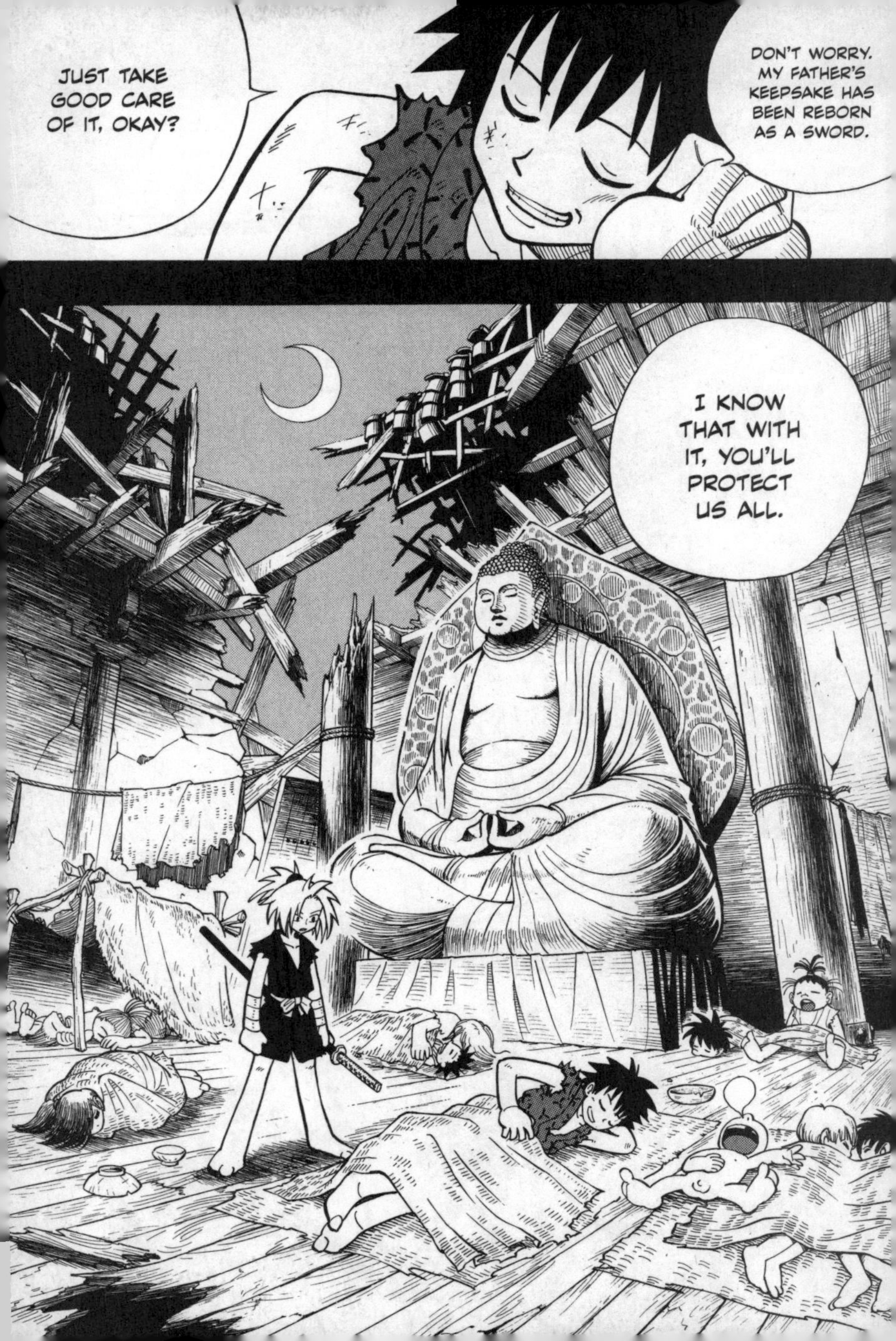
DON'T WORRY. MY FATHER'S KEEPSAKE HAS BEEN REBORN AS A SWORD.
JUST TAKE GOOD CARE OF IT, OKAY?
I KNOW THAT WITH IT, YOU'LL PROTECT US ALL.

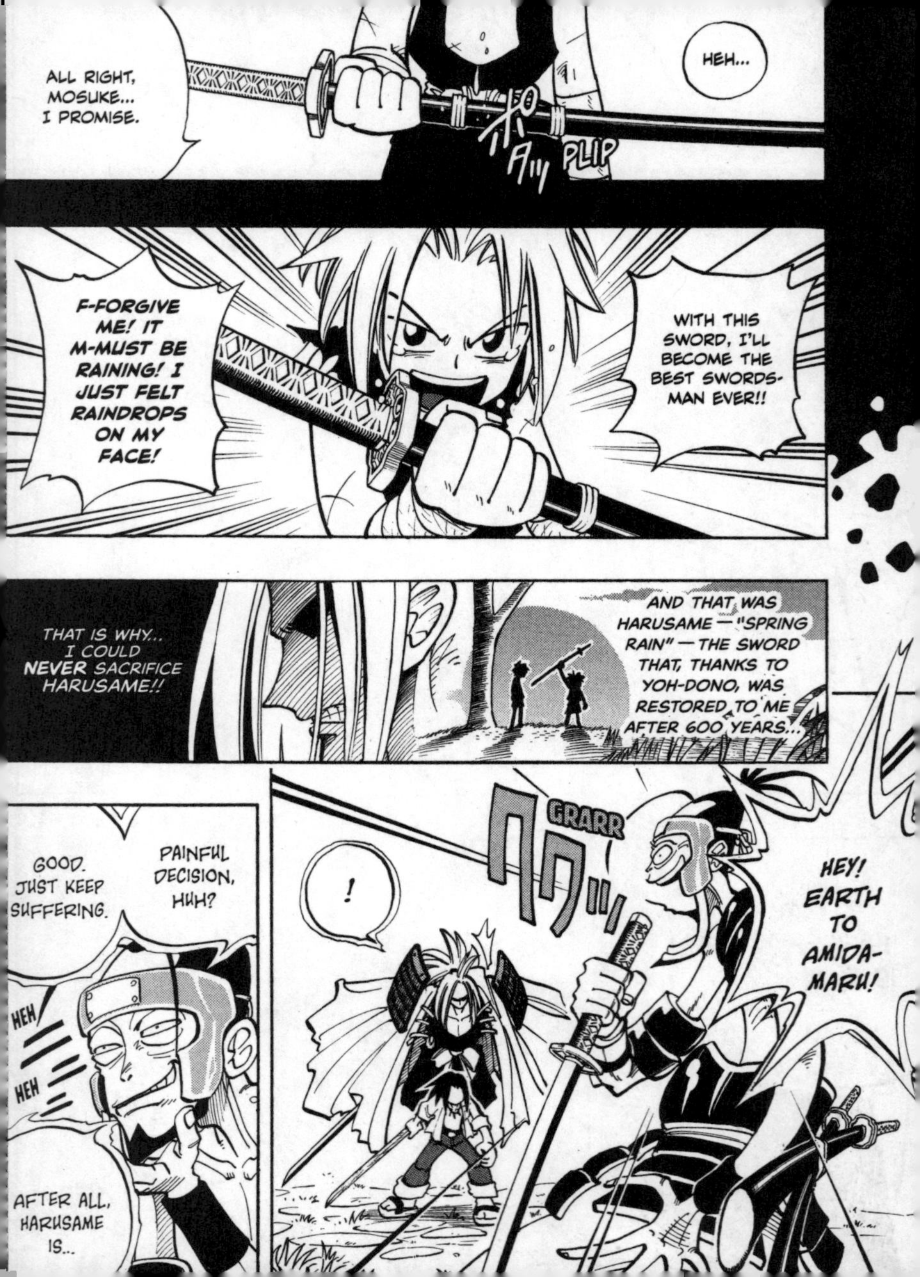
HEH...
ALL RIGHT, MOSUKE... I PROMISE.
PLIP
WITH THIS SWORD, I'LL BECOME THE BEST SWORDS-MAN EVER!!
F-FORGIVE ME! IT M-MUST BE RAINING! I JUST FELT RAINDROPS ON MY FACE!
AND THAT WAS HARUSAME—"SPRING RAIN"—THE SWORD THAT, THANKS TO YOH-DONO, WAS RESTORED TO ME AFTER 600 YEARS...
THAT IS WHY... I COULD NEVER SACRIFICE HARUSAME!!
HEY! EARTH TO AMIDA-MARU!
GRARR
!
PAINFUL DECISION, HUH?
GOOD. JUST KEEP SUFFERING.
HEH
HEH
AFTER ALL, HARUSAME IS...

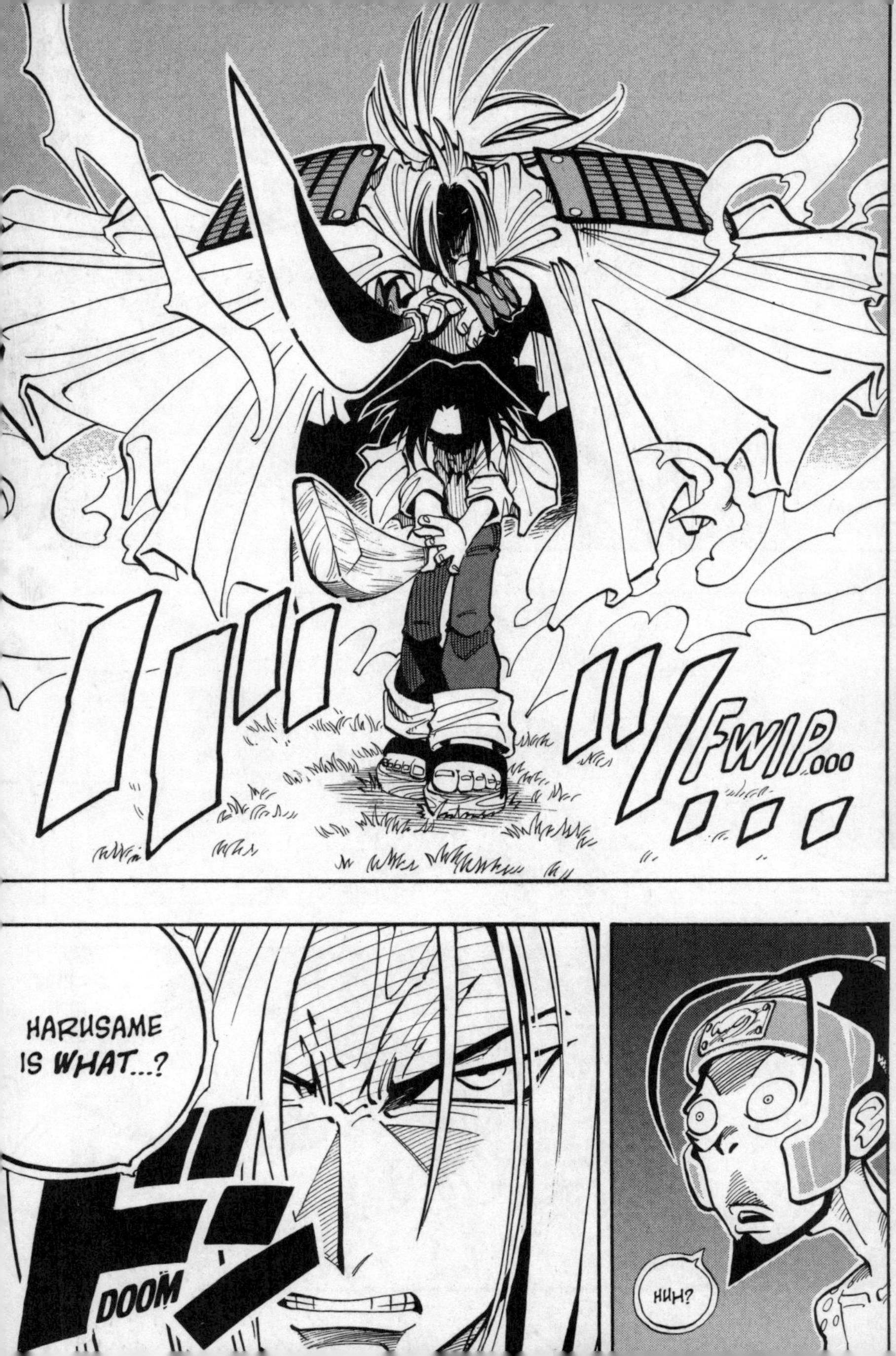
FWIP...
HUH?
HARUSAME IS WHAT...?
DOOM

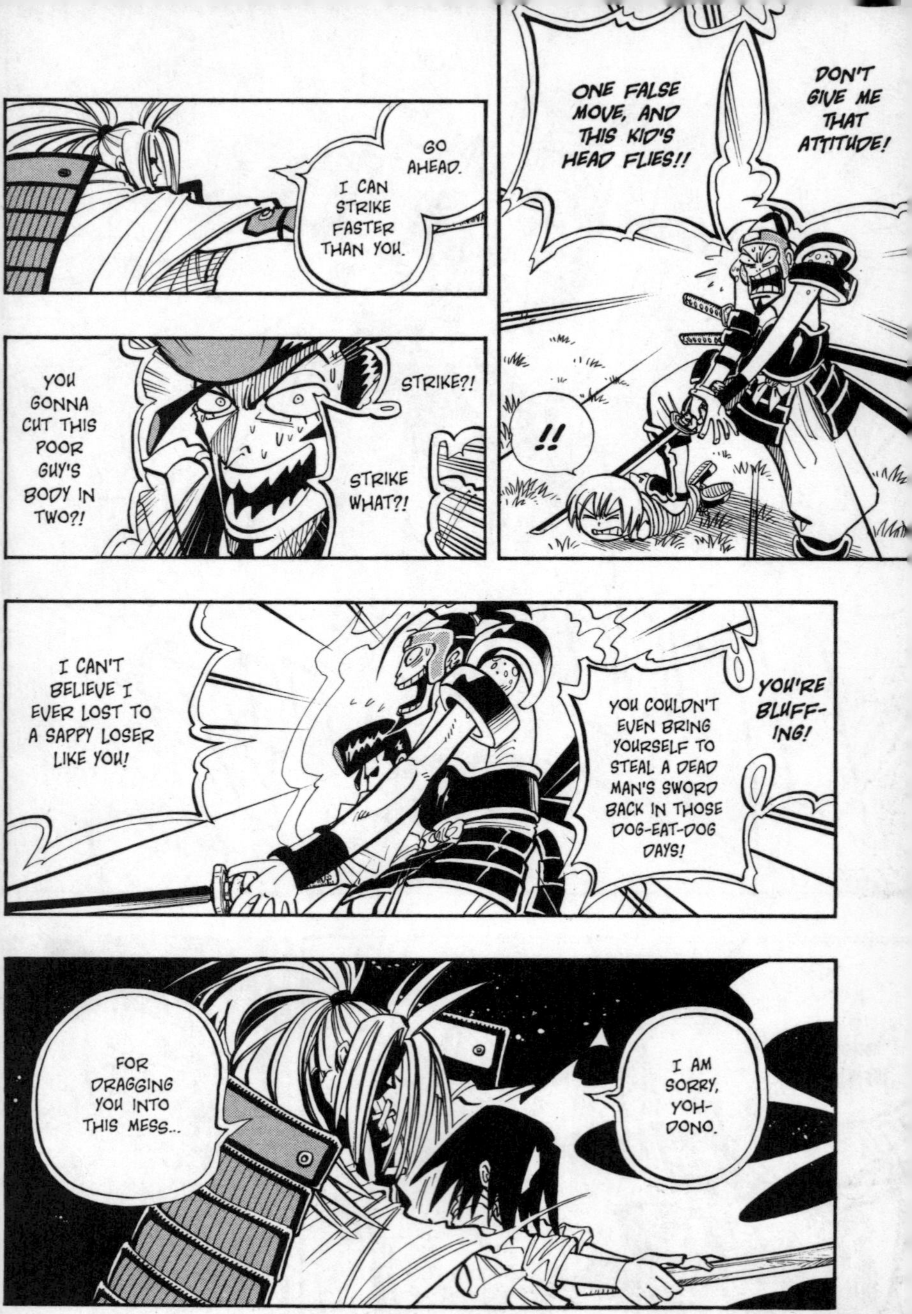
DON'T GIVE ME THAT ATTITUDE!
ONE FALSE MOVE, AND THIS KID'S HEAD FLIES!!
!!
GO AHEAD.
I CAN STRIKE FASTER THAN YOU.
STRIKE?!
STRIKE WHAT?!
YOU GONNA CUT THIS POOR GUY'S BODY IN TWO?!
YOU'RE BLUFF-ING!
YOU COULDN'T EVEN BRING YOURSELF TO STEAL A DEAD MAN'S SWORD BACK IN THOSE DOG-EAT-DOG DAYS!
I CAN'T BELIEVE I EVER LOST TO A SAPPY LOSER LIKE YOU!
I AM SORRY, YOH-DONO.
FOR DRAGGING YOU INTO THIS MESS...

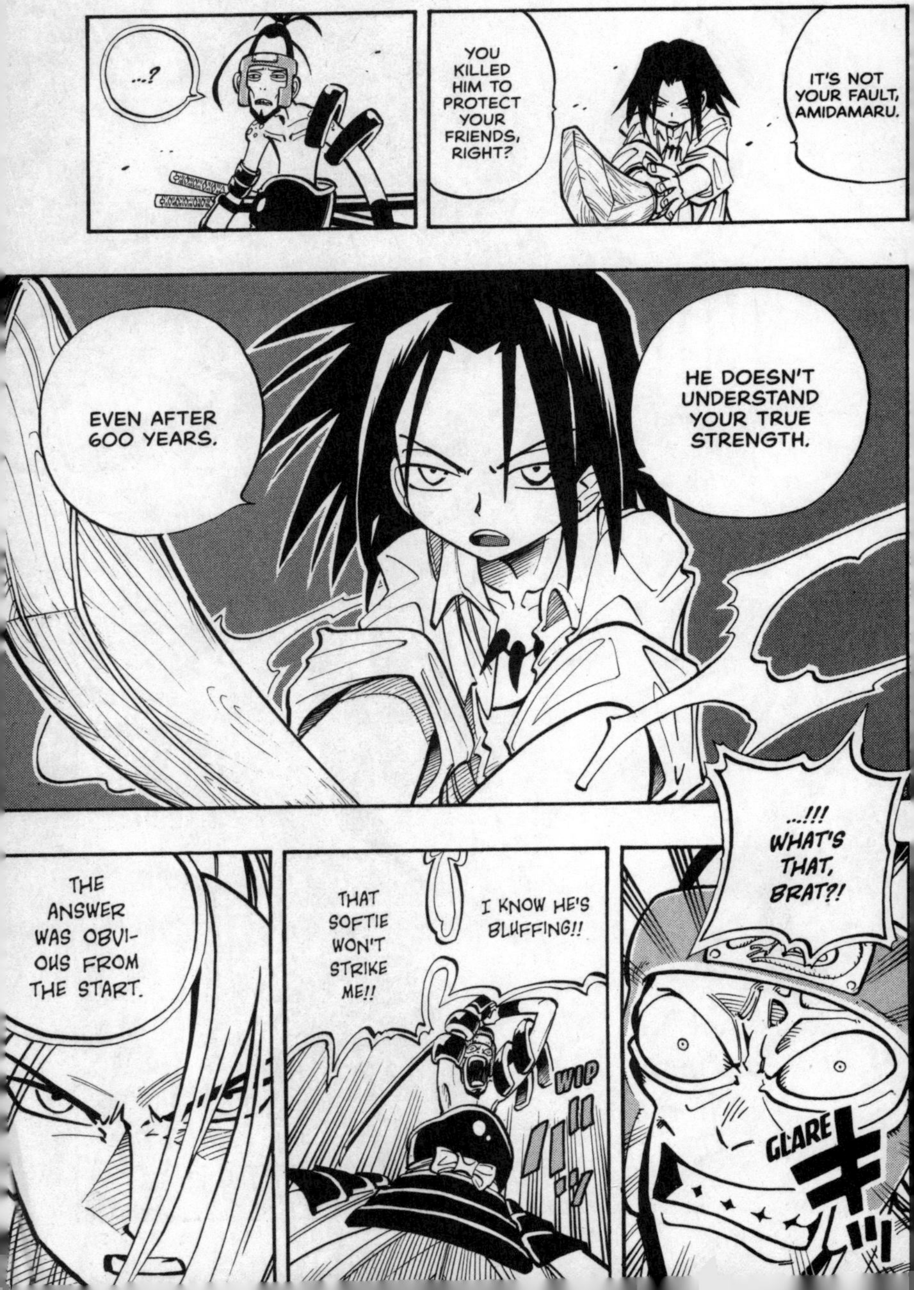
IT'S NOT YOUR FAULT, AMIDAMARU.
YOU KILLED HIM TO PROTECT YOUR FRIENDS, RIGHT?
...?
HE DOESN'T UNDERSTAND YOUR TRUE STRENGTH.
EVEN AFTER 600 YEARS.
...!!! WHAT'S THAT, BRAT?!
GLARE
キッ
I KNOW HE'S BLUFFING!!
THAT SOFTIE WON'T STRIKE ME!!
WIP
THE ANSWER WAS OBVIOUS FROM THE START.

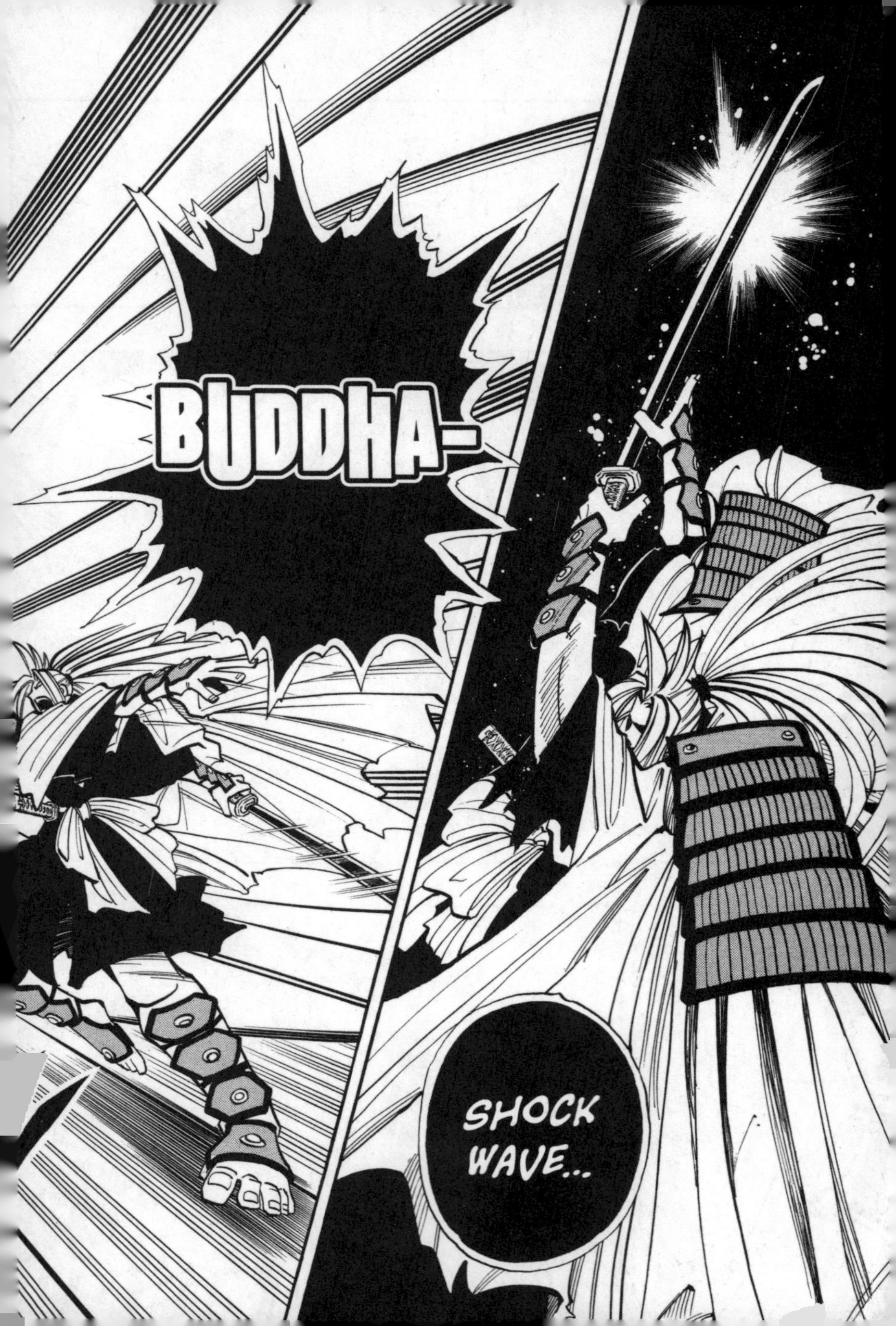
BUDDHA-
SHOCK WAVE...

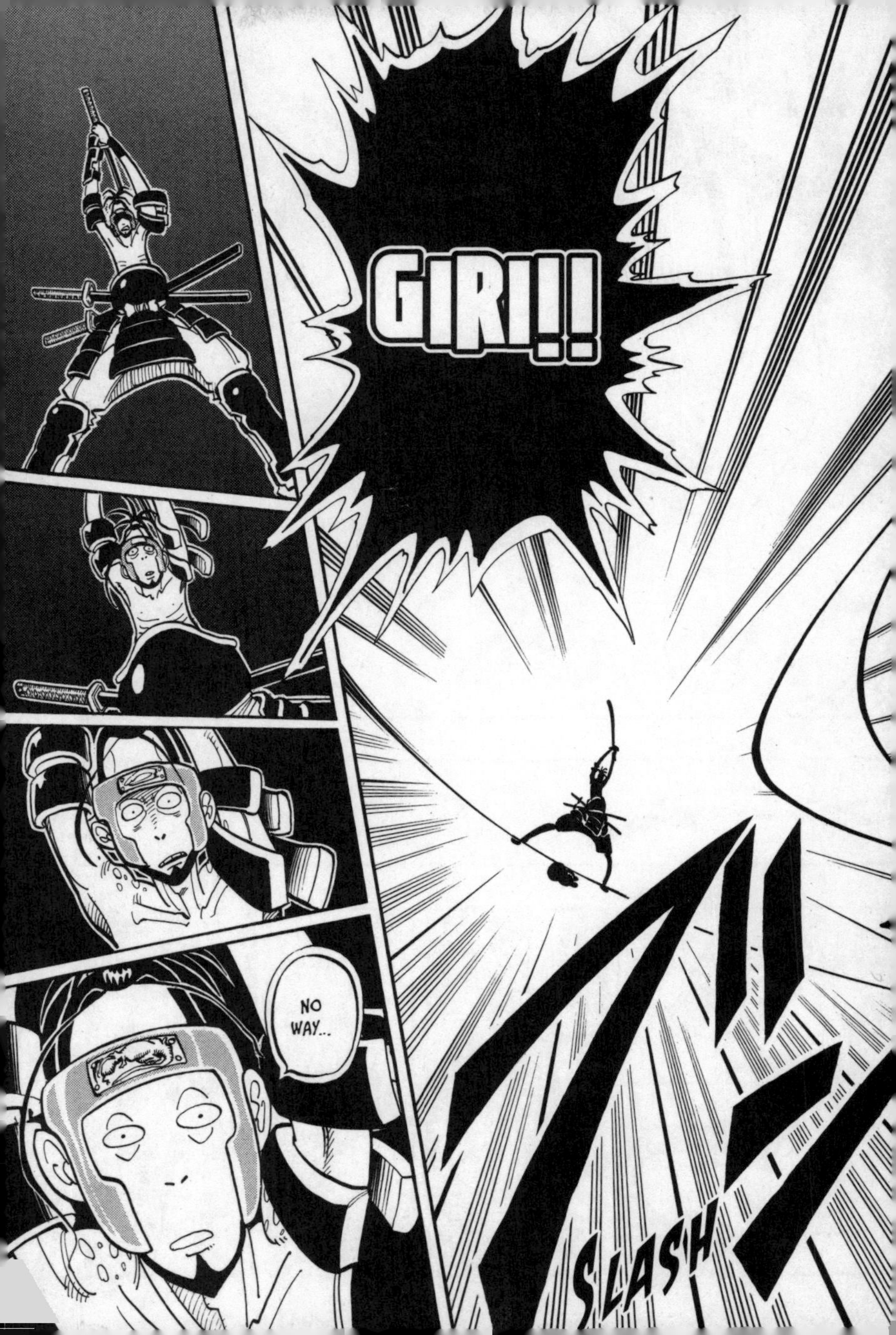
GIRI!!
SLASH
NO WAY...

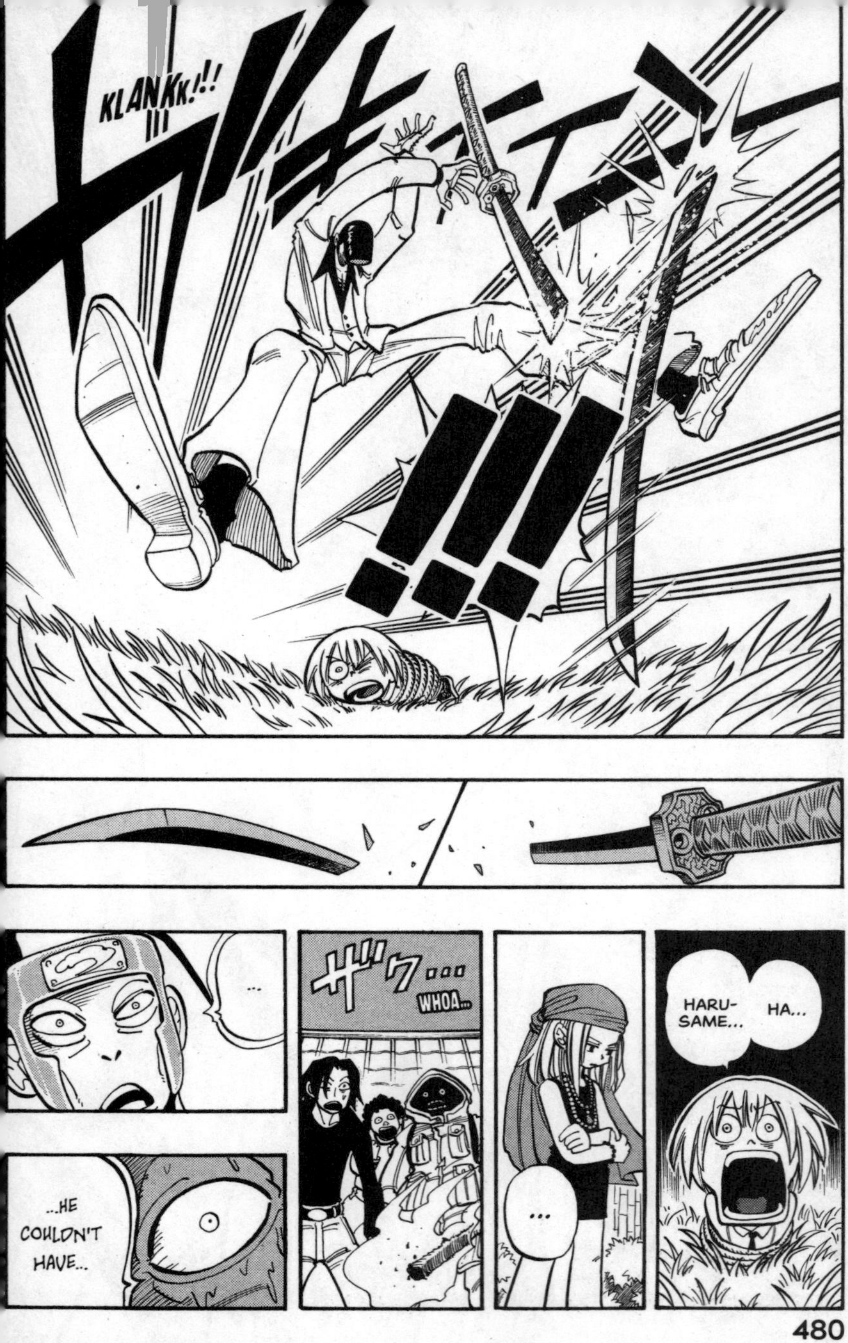
KLANKK!!!
HA...
HARU-SAME...
...
WHOA...
...
...HE COULDN'T HAVE...

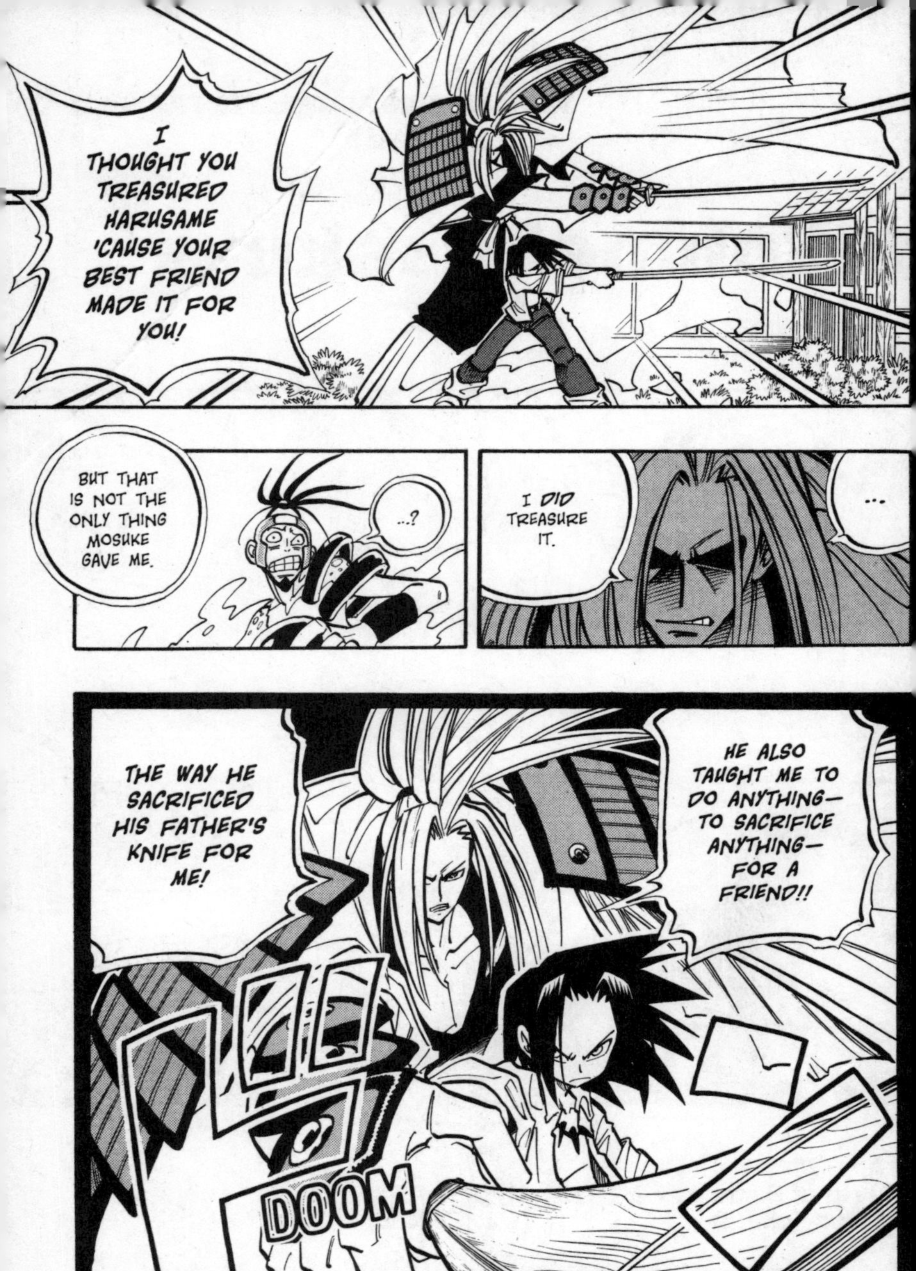
I THOUGHT YOU TREASURED HARUSAME 'CAUSE YOUR BEST FRIEND MADE IT FOR YOU!
...
I DID TREASURE IT.
BUT THAT IS NOT THE ONLY THING MOSUKE GAVE ME.
...?
THE WAY HE SACRIFICED HIS FATHER'S KNIFE FOR ME!
HE ALSO TAUGHT ME TO DO ANYTHING— TO SACRIFICE ANYTHING— FOR A FRIEND!!
DOOM

SHAMAN KING CHARACTER FILE No.11

Yohmei Asakura
1989

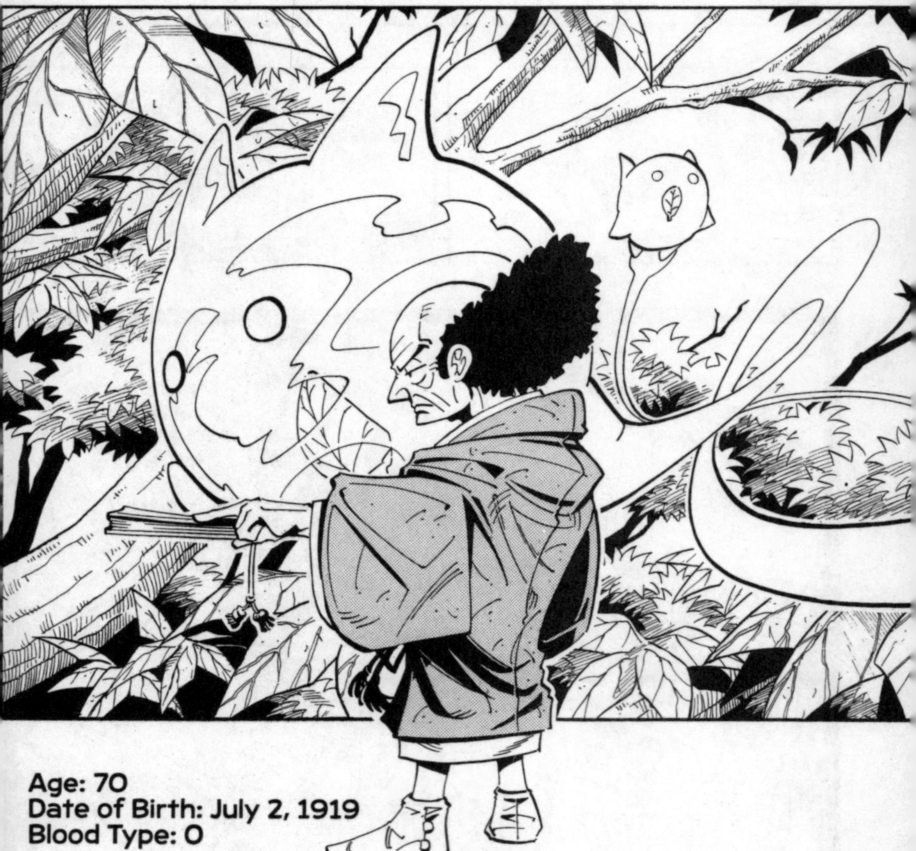

Age: 70
Date of Birth: July 2, 1919
Blood Type: O

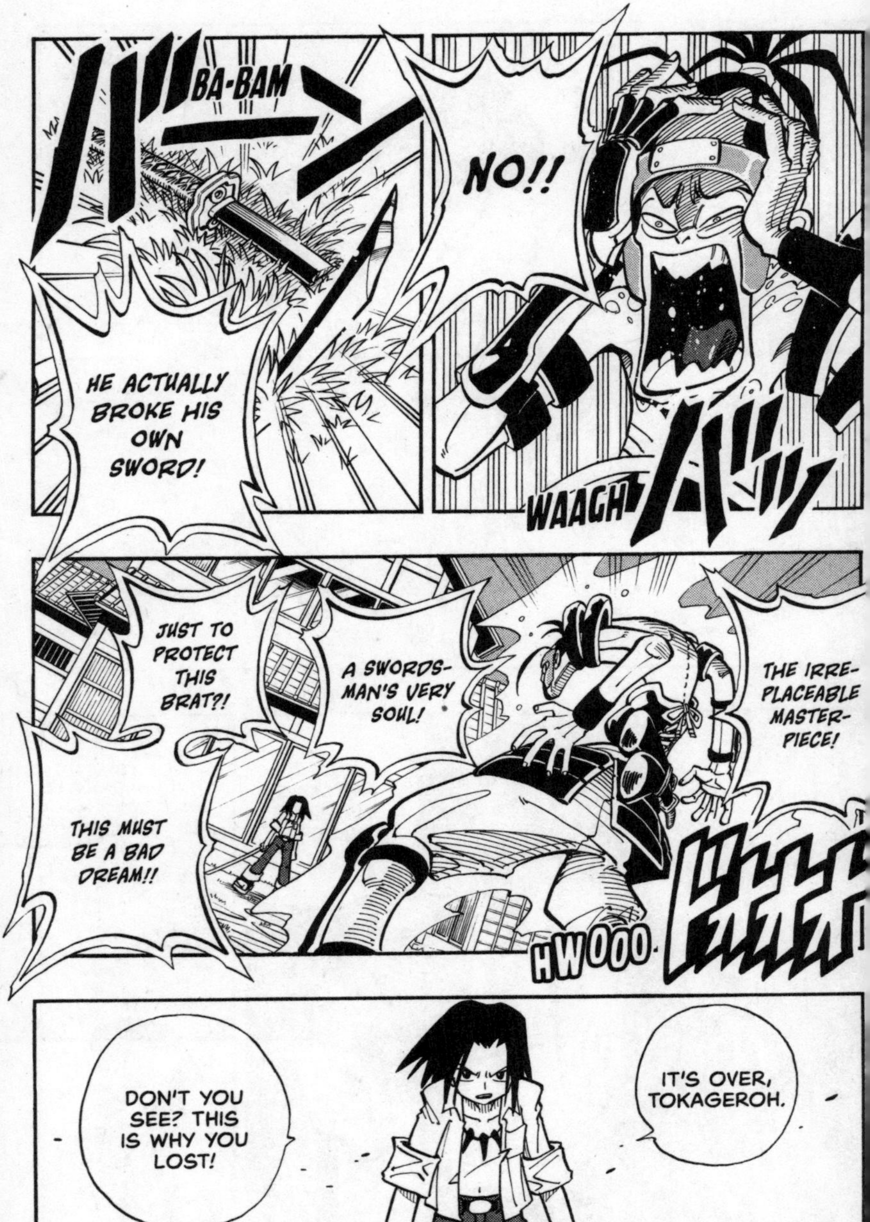
NO!!
WAAGH
BA-BAM
HE ACTUALLY BROKE HIS OWN SWORD!
THE IRRE-PLACEABLE MASTER-PIECE!
A SWORDS-MAN'S VERY SOUL!
JUST TO PROTECT THIS BRAT?!
HWOOO
THIS MUST BE A BAD DREAM!!
IT'S OVER, TOKAGEROH.
DON'T YOU SEE? THIS IS WHY YOU LOST!

Chapter 22: Our Ryu

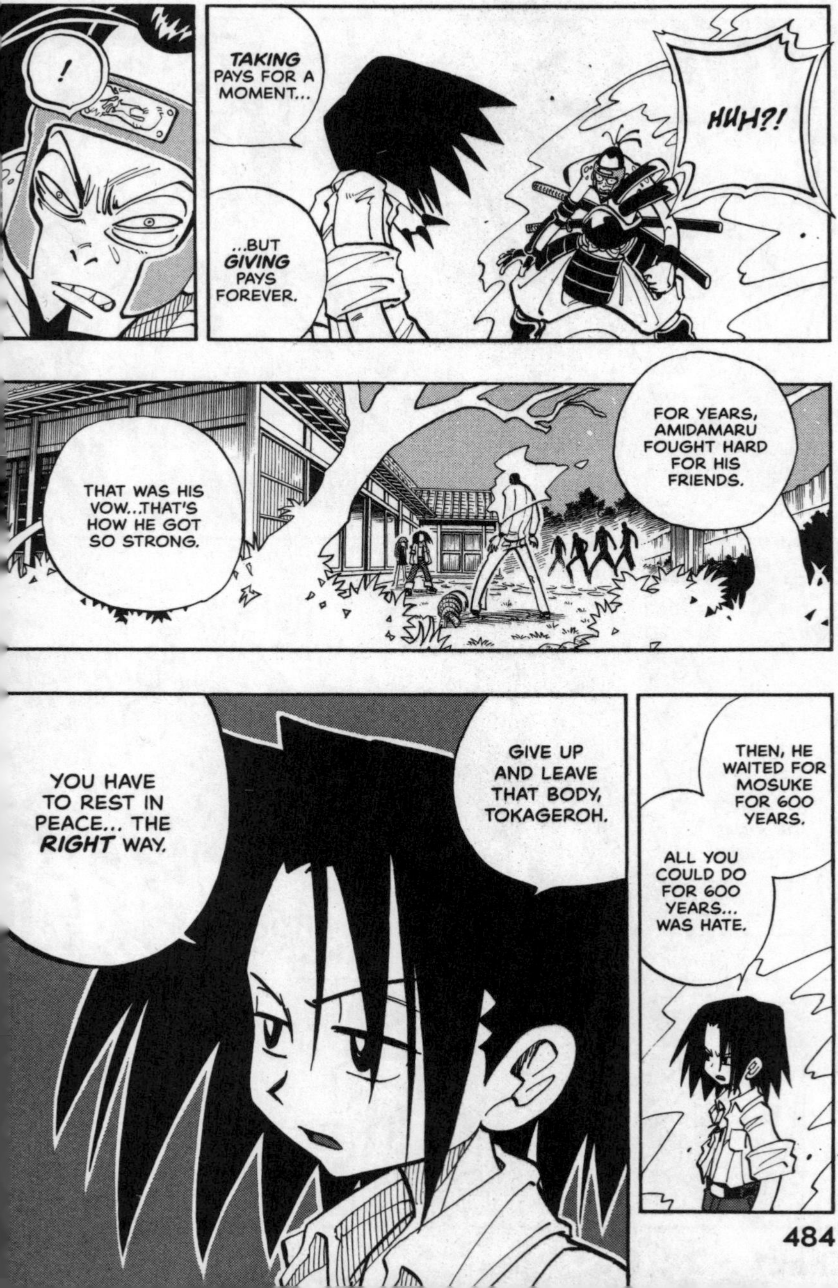
HUH?!
TAKING PAYS FOR A MOMENT...
...BUT GIVING PAYS FOREVER.
!
FOR YEARS, AMIDAMARU FOUGHT HARD FOR HIS FRIENDS.
THAT WAS HIS VOW...THAT'S HOW HE GOT SO STRONG.
THEN, HE WAITED FOR MOSUKE FOR 600 YEARS.
ALL YOU COULD DO FOR 600 YEARS... WAS HATE.
GIVE UP AND LEAVE THAT BODY, TOKAGEROH.
YOU HAVE TO REST IN PEACE... THE RIGHT WAY.

Chapter 22: Our Ryu

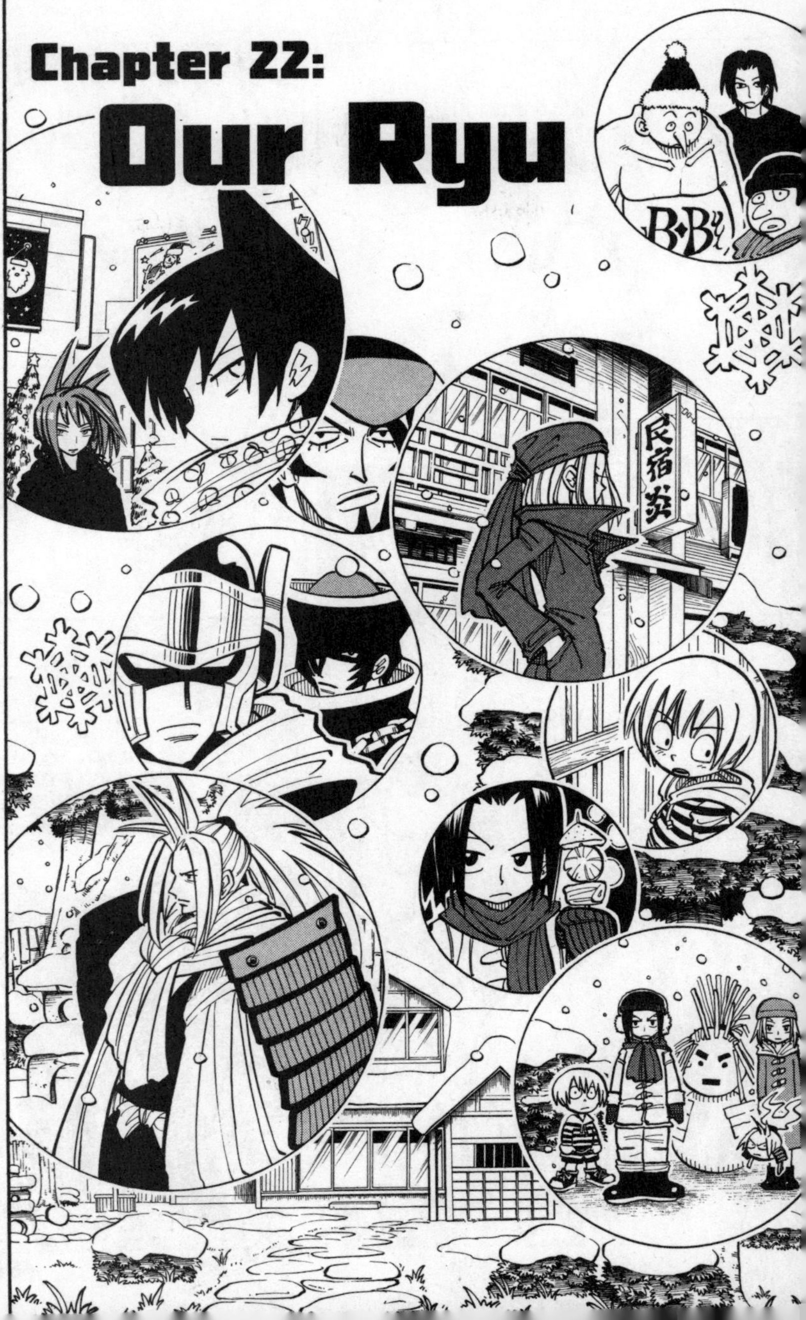
B·B
民宿炎

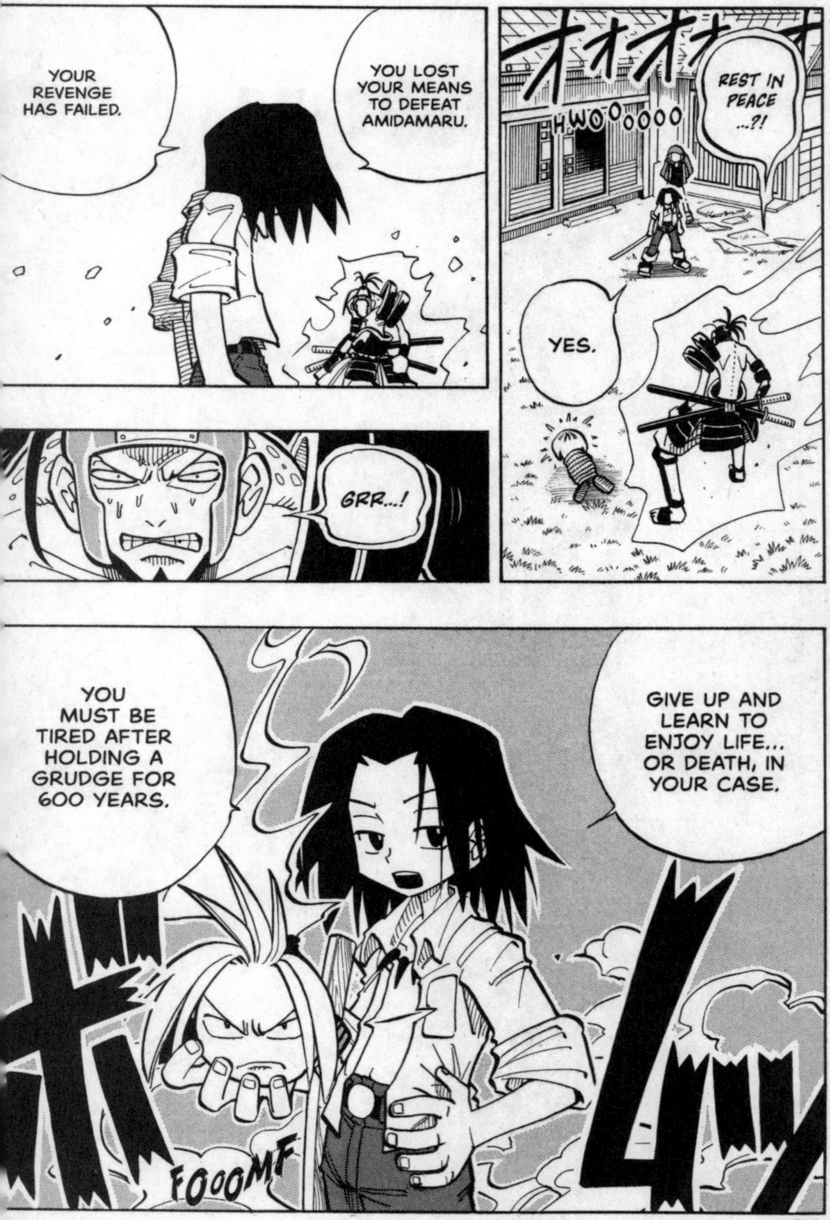
HWOOOOOO
REST IN PEACE ...?!
YES.
YOU LOST YOUR MEANS TO DEFEAT AMIDAMARU.
YOUR REVENGE HAS FAILED.
GRR...!
GIVE UP AND LEARN TO ENJOY LIFE... OR DEATH, IN YOUR CASE.
YOU MUST BE TIRED AFTER HOLDING A GRUDGE FOR 600 YEARS.
FOOOMF

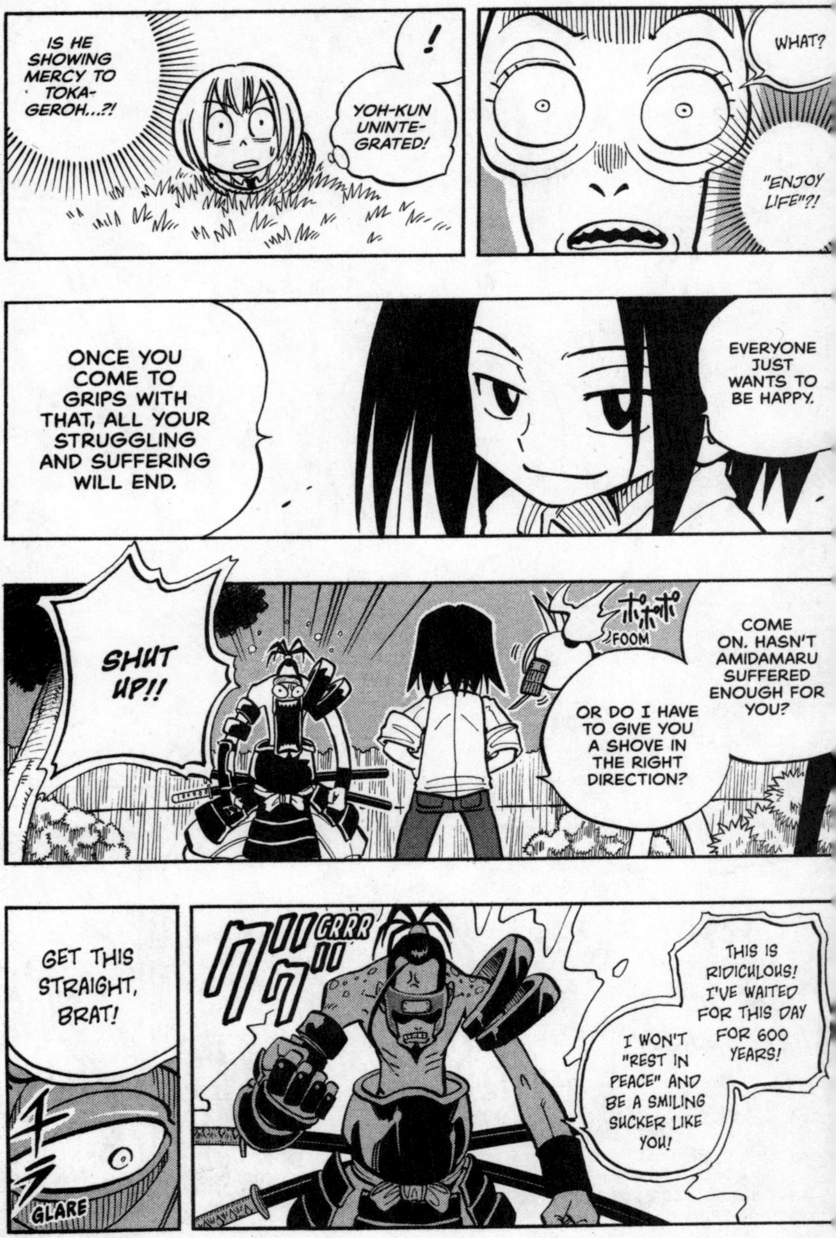
WHAT?
"ENJOY LIFE"?!
!
YOH-KUN UNINTE-GRATED!
IS HE SHOWING MERCY TO TOKA-GEROH...?!
EVERYONE JUST WANTS TO BE HAPPY.
ONCE YOU COME TO GRIPS WITH THAT, ALL YOUR STRUGGLING AND SUFFERING WILL END.
COME ON. HASN'T AMIDAMARU SUFFERED ENOUGH FOR YOU?
ポポポ
FOOM
OR DO I HAVE TO GIVE YOU A SHOVE IN THE RIGHT DIRECTION?
SHUT UP!!
THIS IS RIDICULOUS! I'VE WAITED FOR THIS DAY FOR 600 YEARS!
GRRR
I WON'T "REST IN PEACE" AND BE A SMILING SUCKER LIKE YOU!
GET THIS STRAIGHT, BRAT!
GLARE

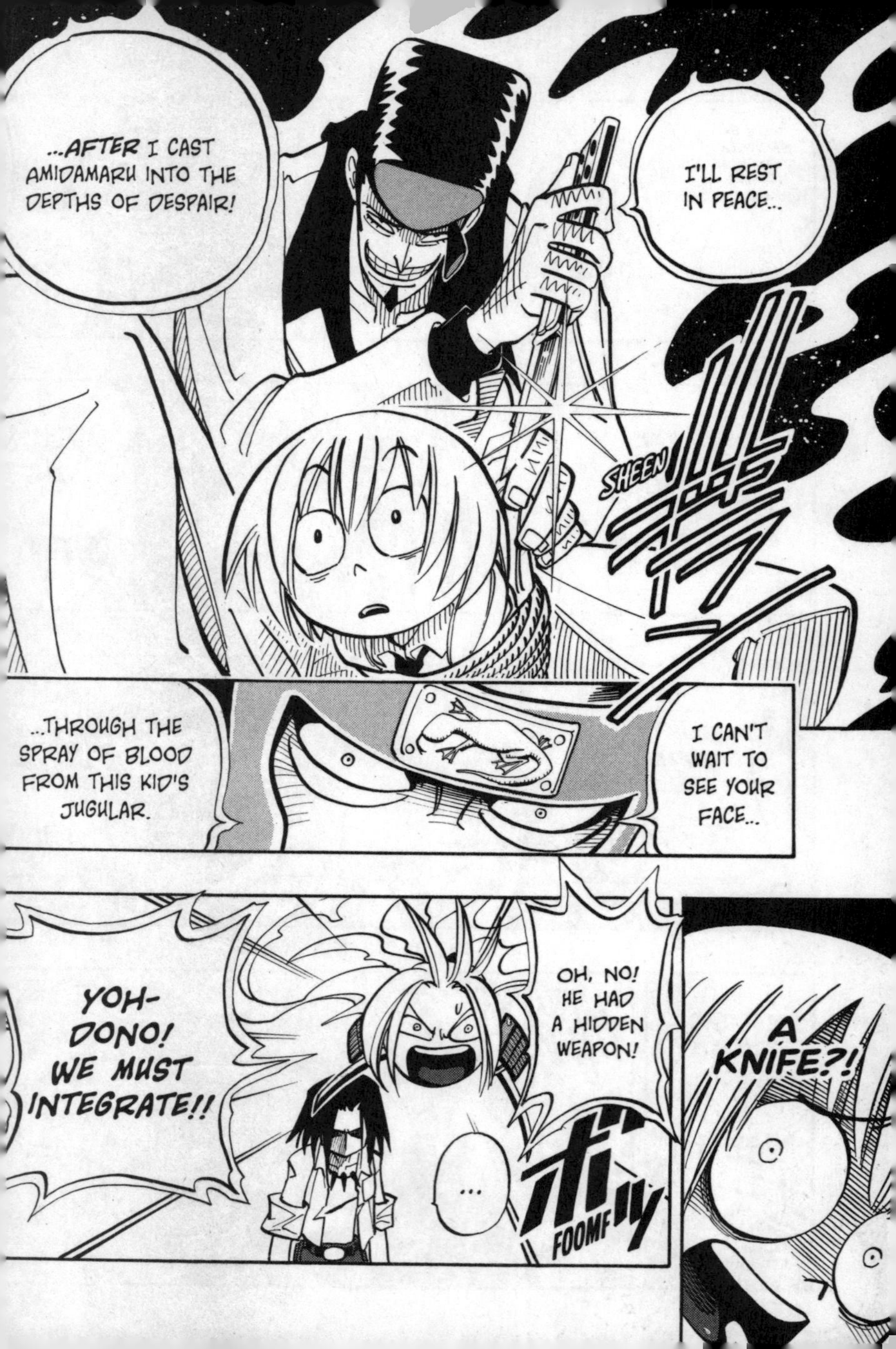
I'LL REST IN PEACE...
...AFTER I CAST AMIDAMARU INTO THE DEPTHS OF DESPAIR!
SHEEN
I CAN'T WAIT TO SEE YOUR FACE...
...THROUGH THE SPRAY OF BLOOD FROM THIS KID'S JUGULAR.
A KNIFE?!
OH, NO! HE HAD A HIDDEN WEAPON!
YOH-DONO! WE MUST INTEGRATE!!
...
FOOMF

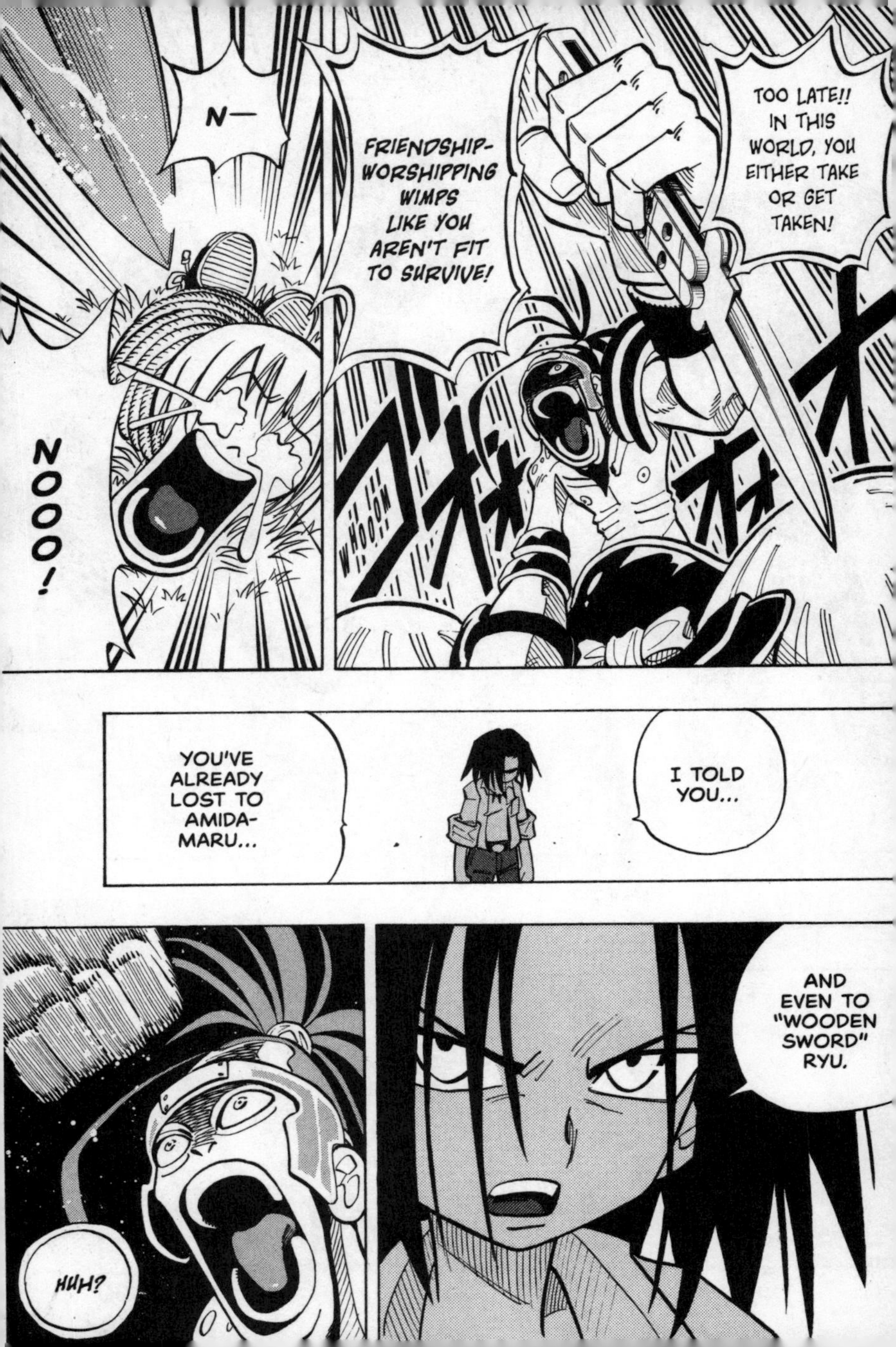
TOO LATE!! IN THIS WORLD, YOU EITHER TAKE OR GET TAKEN!
FRIENDSHIP-WORSHIPPING WIMPS LIKE YOU AREN'T FIT TO SURVIVE!
WHOOOM
N—
NOOOO!
I TOLD YOU...
YOU'VE ALREADY LOST TO AMIDA-MARU...
AND EVEN TO "WOODEN SWORD" RYU.
HUH?

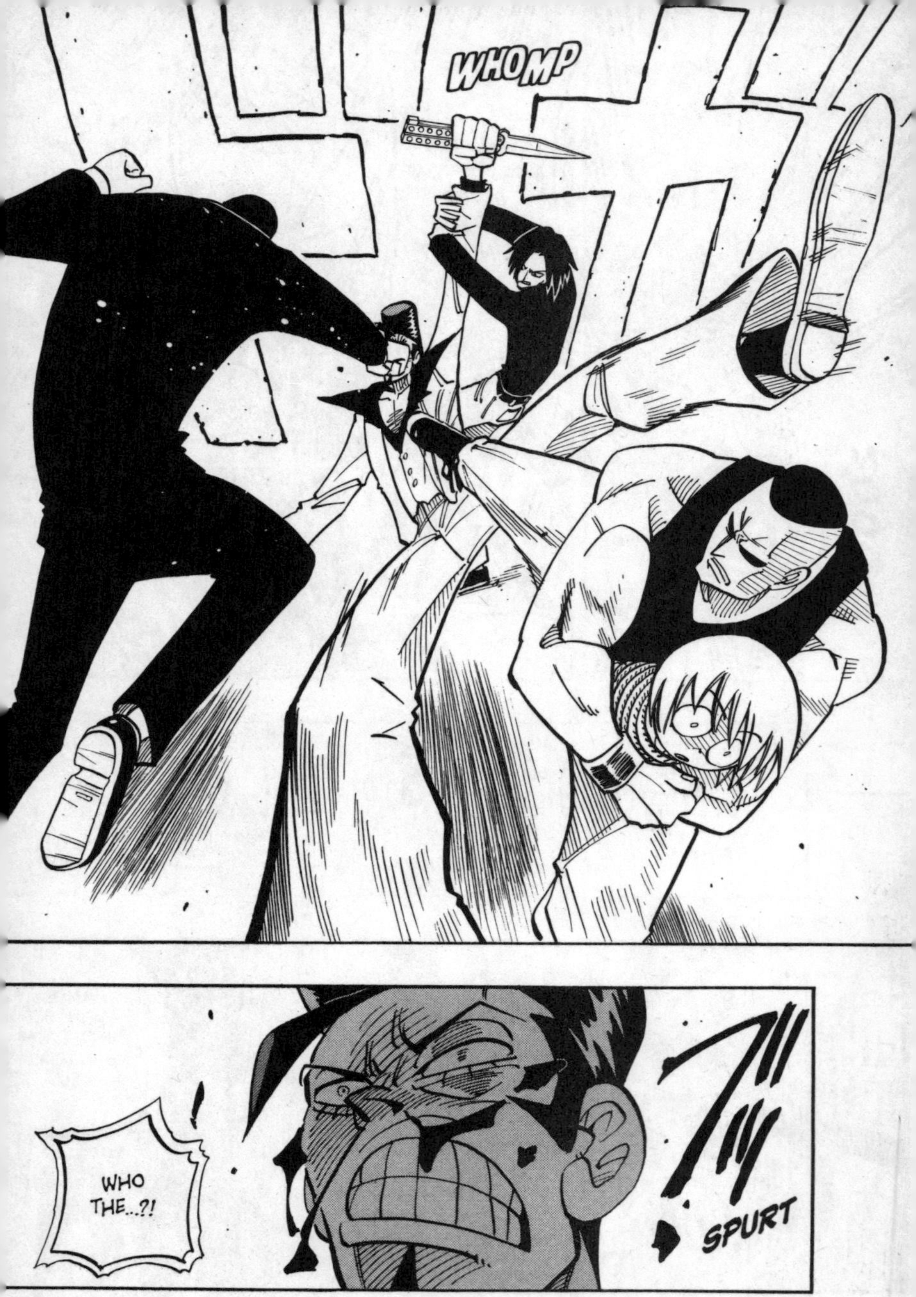
WHOMP
SPURT
WHO THE...?!

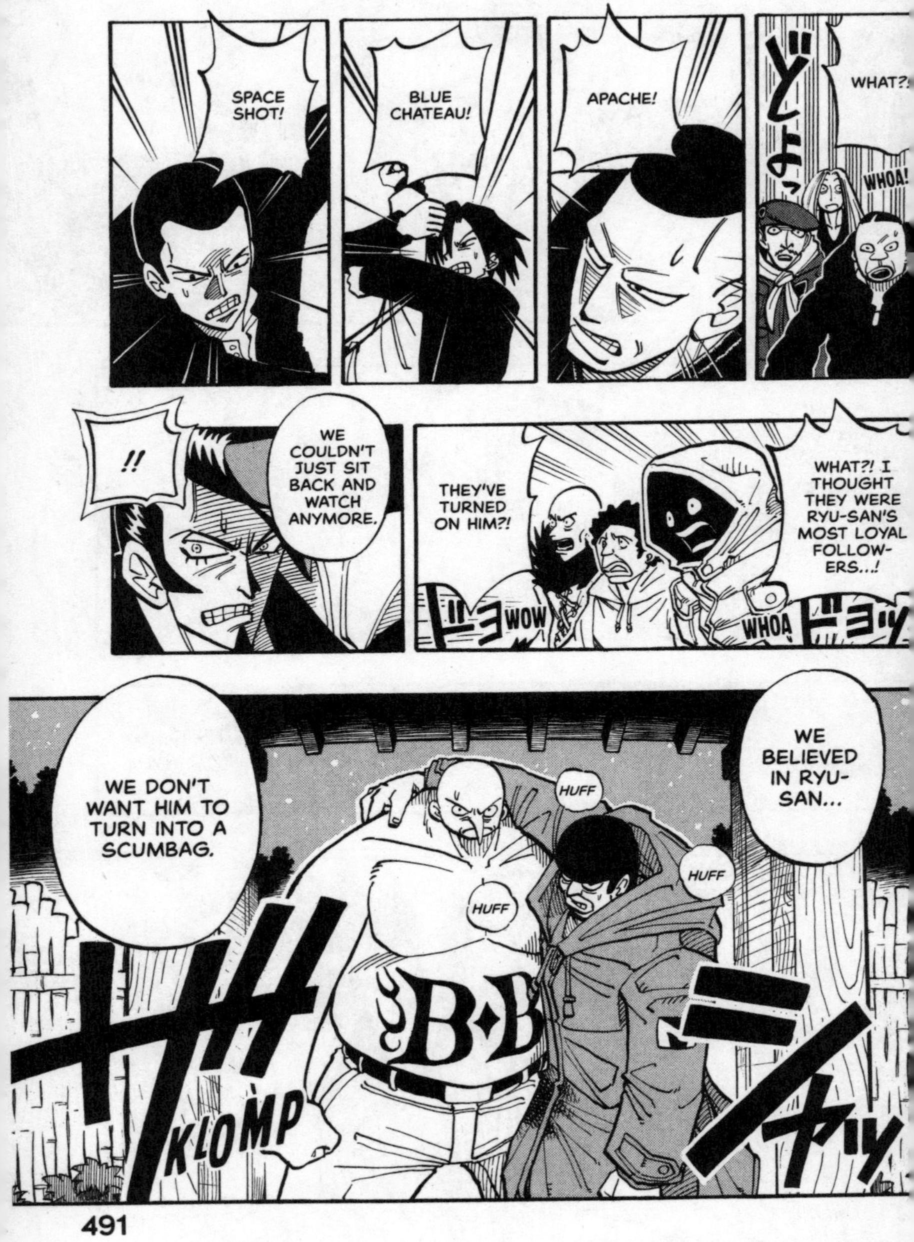
WHAT?!
どよっ
WHOA!
APACHE!
BLUE CHATEAU!
SPACE SHOT!
WHAT?! I THOUGHT THEY WERE RYU-SAN'S MOST LOYAL FOLLOWERS...!
THEY'VE TURNED ON HIM?!
WHOA
ドヨッ
WOW
WE COULDN'T JUST SIT BACK AND WATCH ANYMORE.
!!
WE BELIEVED IN RYU-SAN...
HUFF
HUFF
HUFF
WE DON'T WANT HIM TO TURN INTO A SCUMBAG.
KLOMP

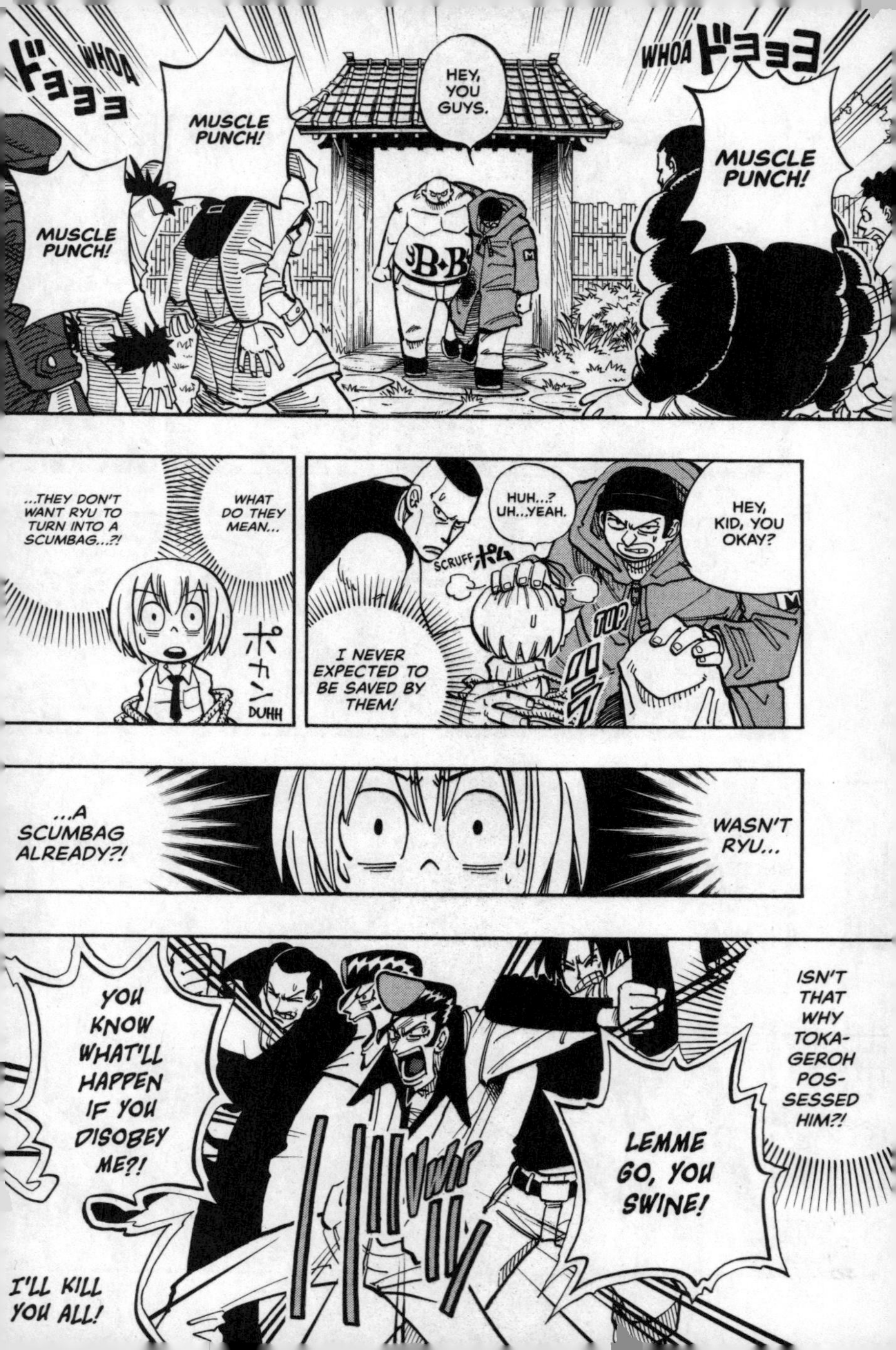
WHOA ドヨヨヨ
MUSCLE PUNCH!
HEY, YOU GUYS.
WHOA ドヨヨヨ
MUSCLE PUNCH!
MUSCLE PUNCH!
HEY, KID, YOU OKAY?
HUH...? UH...YEAH.
SCRUFF ポム
TUP
I NEVER EXPECTED TO BE SAVED BY THEM!
WHAT DO THEY MEAN...
...THEY DON'T WANT RYU TO TURN INTO A SCUMBAG...?!
ポカン DUHH
WASN'T RYU...
...A SCUMBAG ALREADY?!
ISN'T THAT WHY TOKA-GEROH POS-SESSED HIM?!
LEMME GO, YOU SWINE!
YOU KNOW WHAT'LL HAPPEN IF YOU DISOBEY ME?!
I'LL KILL YOU ALL!

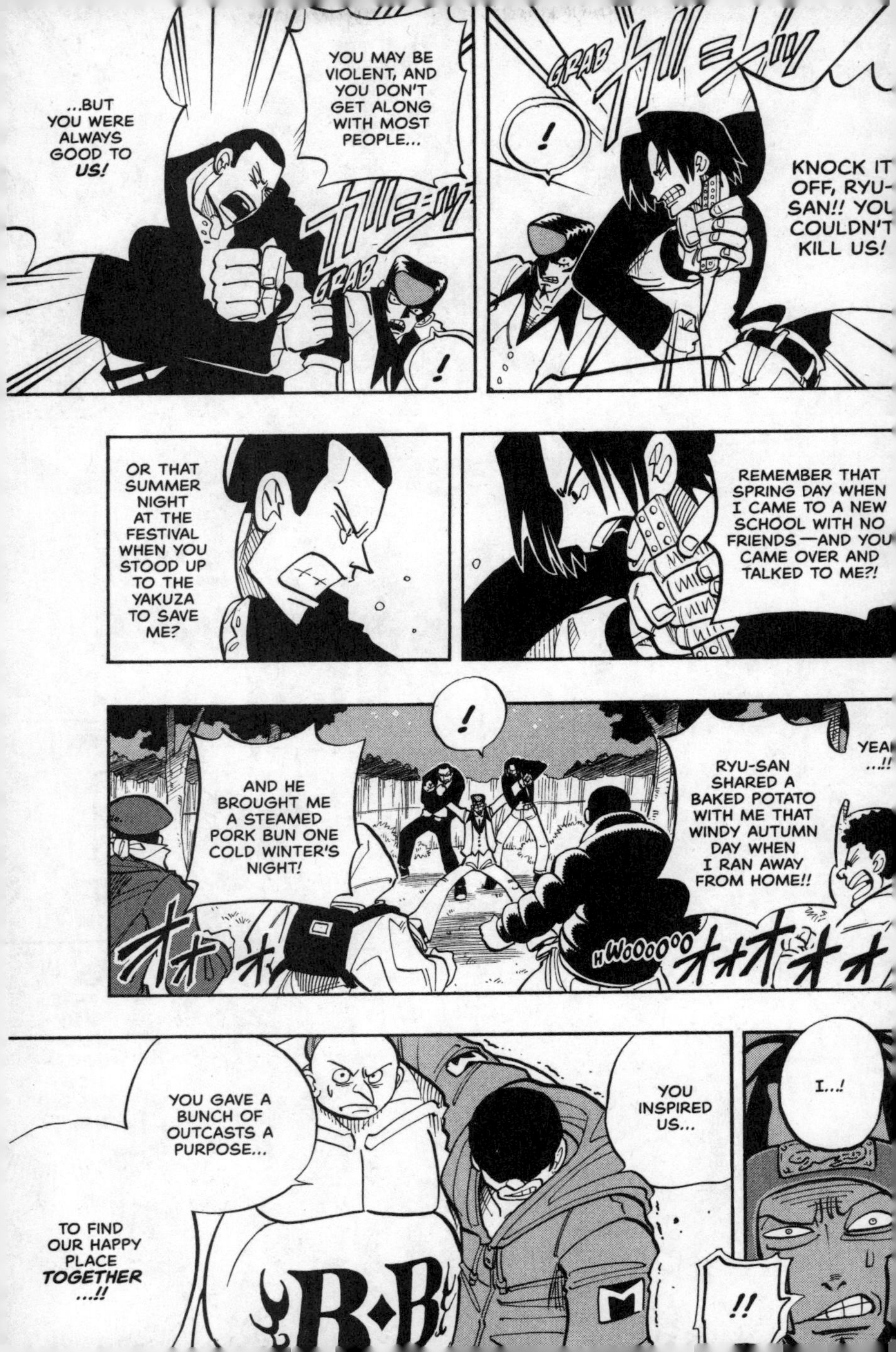
GRAB
!
KNOCK IT OFF, RYU-SAN!! YOU COULDN'T KILL US!
YOU MAY BE VIOLENT, AND YOU DON'T GET ALONG WITH MOST PEOPLE...
...BUT YOU WERE ALWAYS GOOD TO *US!*
GRAB
!
REMEMBER THAT SPRING DAY WHEN I CAME TO A NEW SCHOOL WITH NO FRIENDS—AND YOU CAME OVER AND TALKED TO ME?!
OR THAT SUMMER NIGHT AT THE FESTIVAL WHEN YOU STOOD UP TO THE YAKUZA TO SAVE ME?
YEA ...!!
RYU-SAN SHARED A BAKED POTATO WITH ME THAT WINDY AUTUMN DAY WHEN I RAN AWAY FROM HOME!!
!
AND HE BROUGHT ME A STEAMED PORK BUN ONE COLD WINTER'S NIGHT!
HWOOOOOO
I...!
!!
YOU INSPIRED US...
YOU GAVE A BUNCH OF OUTCASTS A PURPOSE...
TO FIND OUR HAPPY PLACE *TOGETHER* ...!!

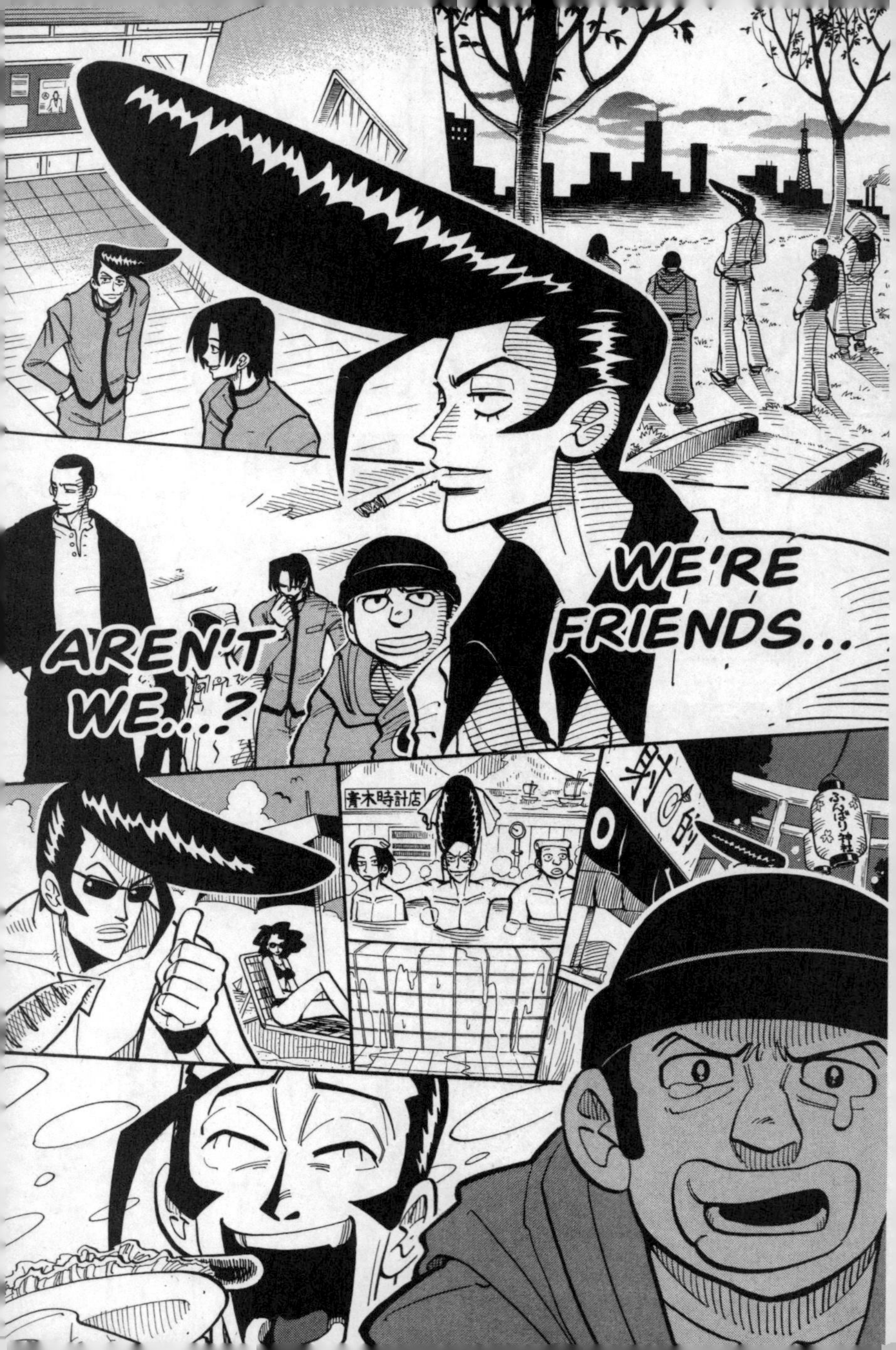
WE'RE FRIENDS...
AREN'T WE...?
ふんばり神社
青木時計店

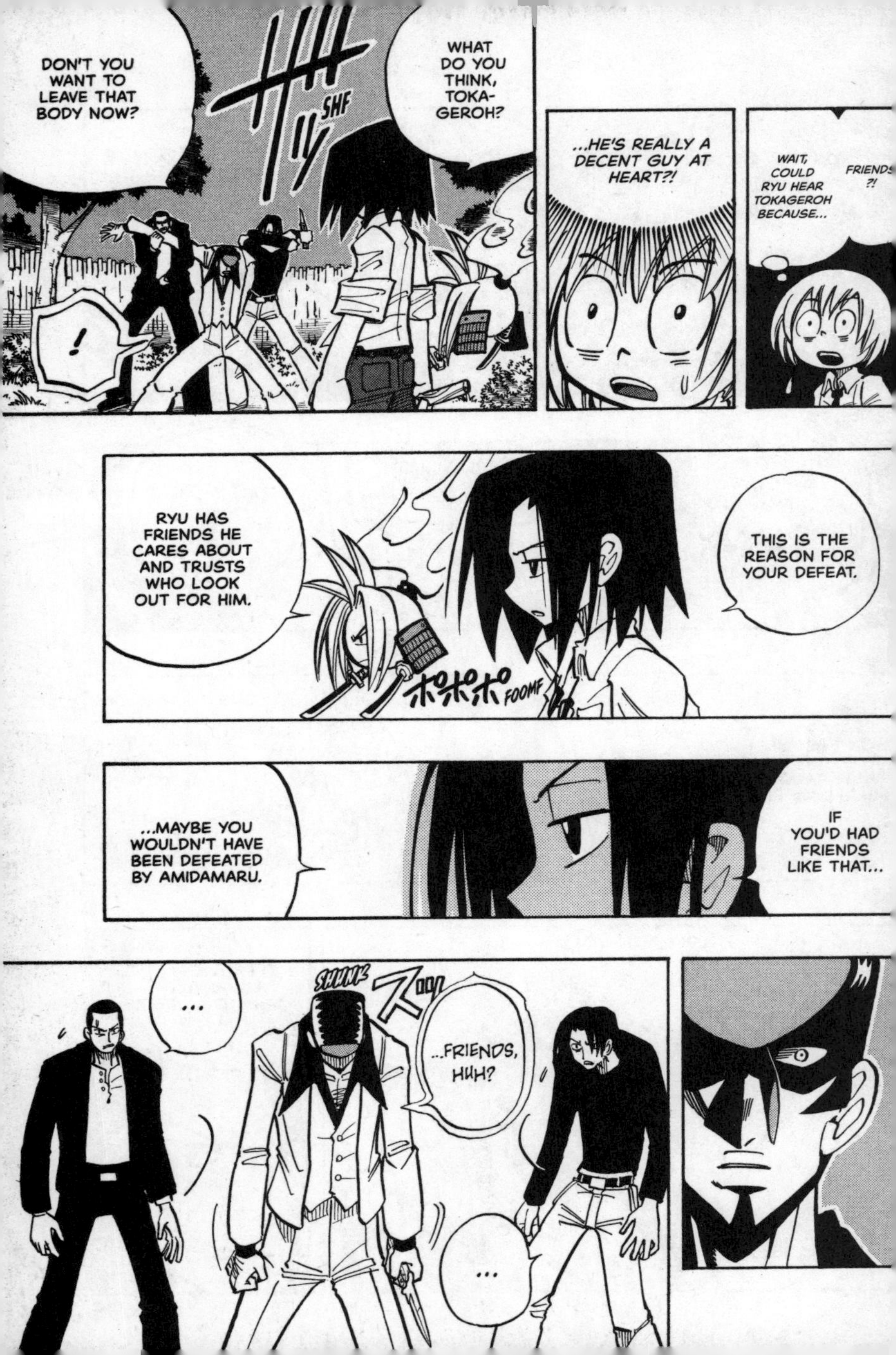
FRIENDS?!
WAIT, COULD RYU HEAR TOKAGEROH BECAUSE...
...HE'S REALLY A DECENT GUY AT HEART?!
WHAT DO YOU THINK, TOKAGEROH?
SHF
DON'T YOU WANT TO LEAVE THAT BODY NOW?
!
THIS IS THE REASON FOR YOUR DEFEAT.
RYU HAS FRIENDS HE CARES ABOUT AND TRUSTS WHO LOOK OUT FOR HIM.
ポポポ FOOMF
IF YOU'D HAD FRIENDS LIKE THAT...
...MAYBE YOU WOULDN'T HAVE BEEN DEFEATED BY AMIDAMARU.
...FRIENDS, HUH?
SHUNK
...
...

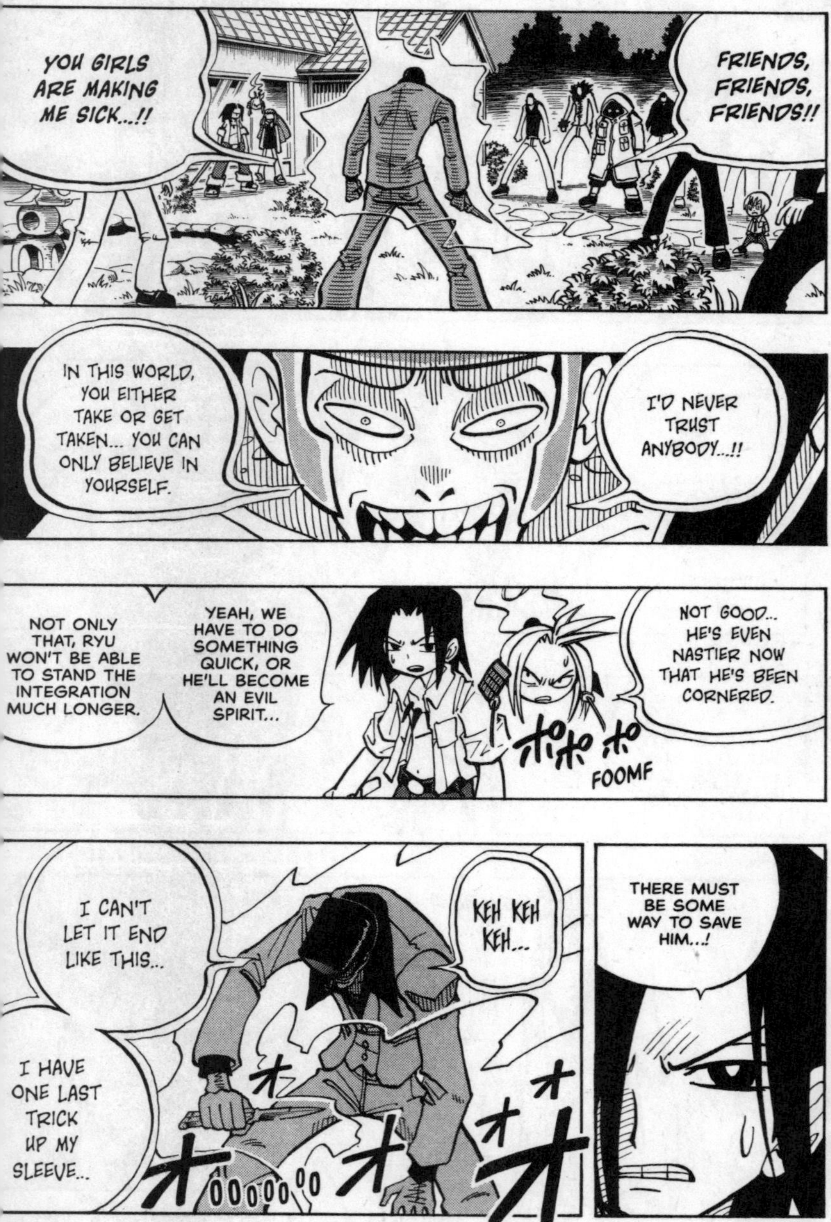

FRIENDS, FRIENDS, FRIENDS!!
YOU GIRLS ARE MAKING ME SICK...!!
I'D NEVER TRUST ANYBODY...!!
IN THIS WORLD, YOU EITHER TAKE OR GET TAKEN... YOU CAN ONLY BELIEVE IN YOURSELF.
NOT GOOD... HE'S EVEN NASTIER NOW THAT HE'S BEEN CORNERED.
ポポポ
FOOMF
YEAH, WE HAVE TO DO SOMETHING QUICK, OR HE'LL BECOME AN EVIL SPIRIT...
NOT ONLY THAT, RYU WON'T BE ABLE TO STAND THE INTEGRATION MUCH LONGER.
THERE MUST BE SOME WAY TO SAVE HIM...!
KEH KEH KEH...
I CAN'T LET IT END LIKE THIS...
I HAVE ONE LAST TRICK UP MY SLEEVE...
オオオオオ
OOOOOOO

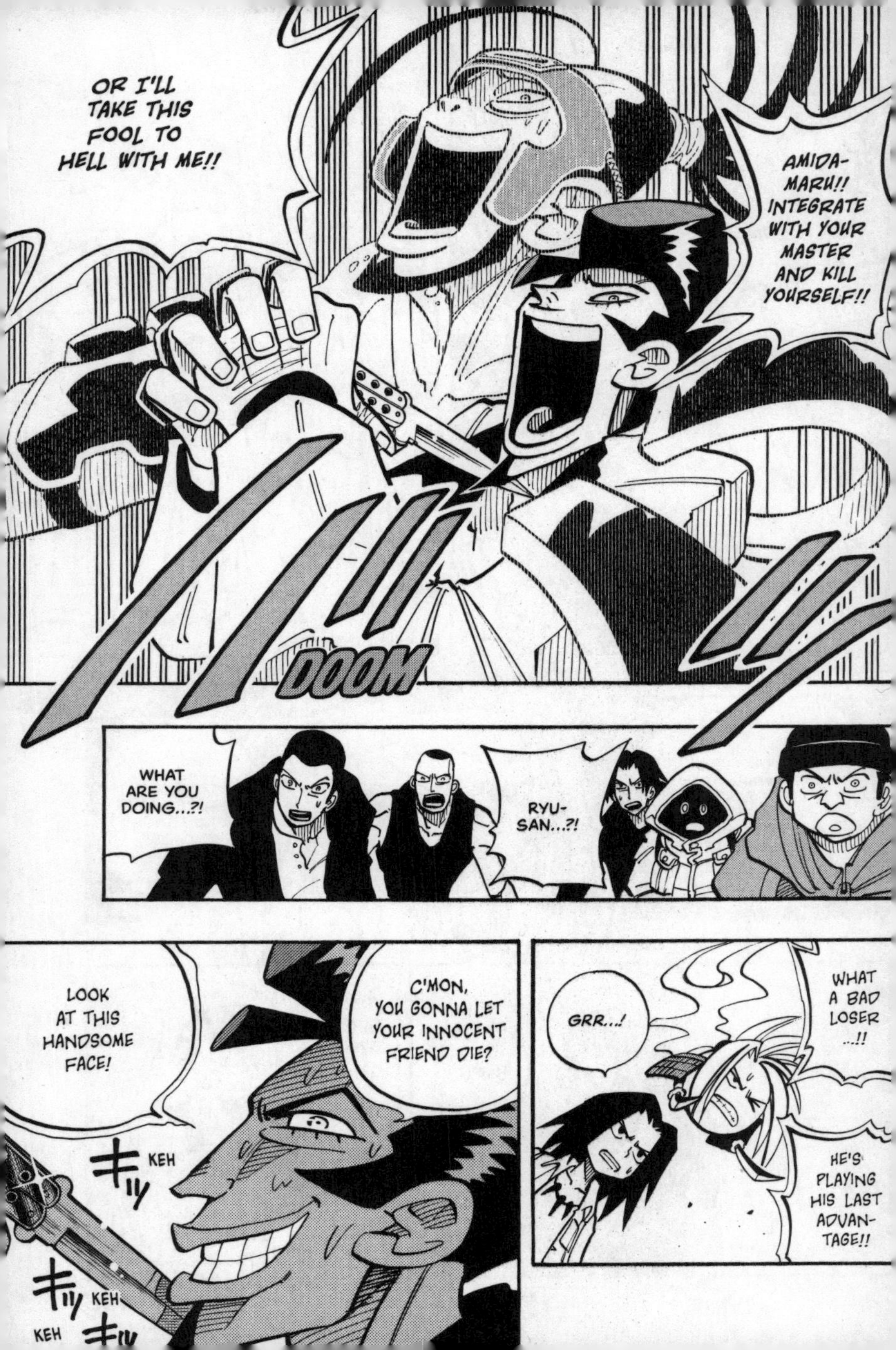
AMIDA-MARU!! INTEGRATE WITH YOUR MASTER AND KILL YOURSELF!!
OR I'LL TAKE THIS FOOL TO HELL WITH ME!!
DOOM
RYU-SAN...?!
WHAT ARE YOU DOING...?!
WHAT A BAD LOSER ...!!
HE'S PLAYING HIS LAST ADVAN-TAGE!!
GRR...!
C'MON, YOU GONNA LET YOUR INNOCENT FRIEND DIE?
LOOK AT THIS HANDSOME FACE!
キッ KEH
キッ KEH
キッ KEH

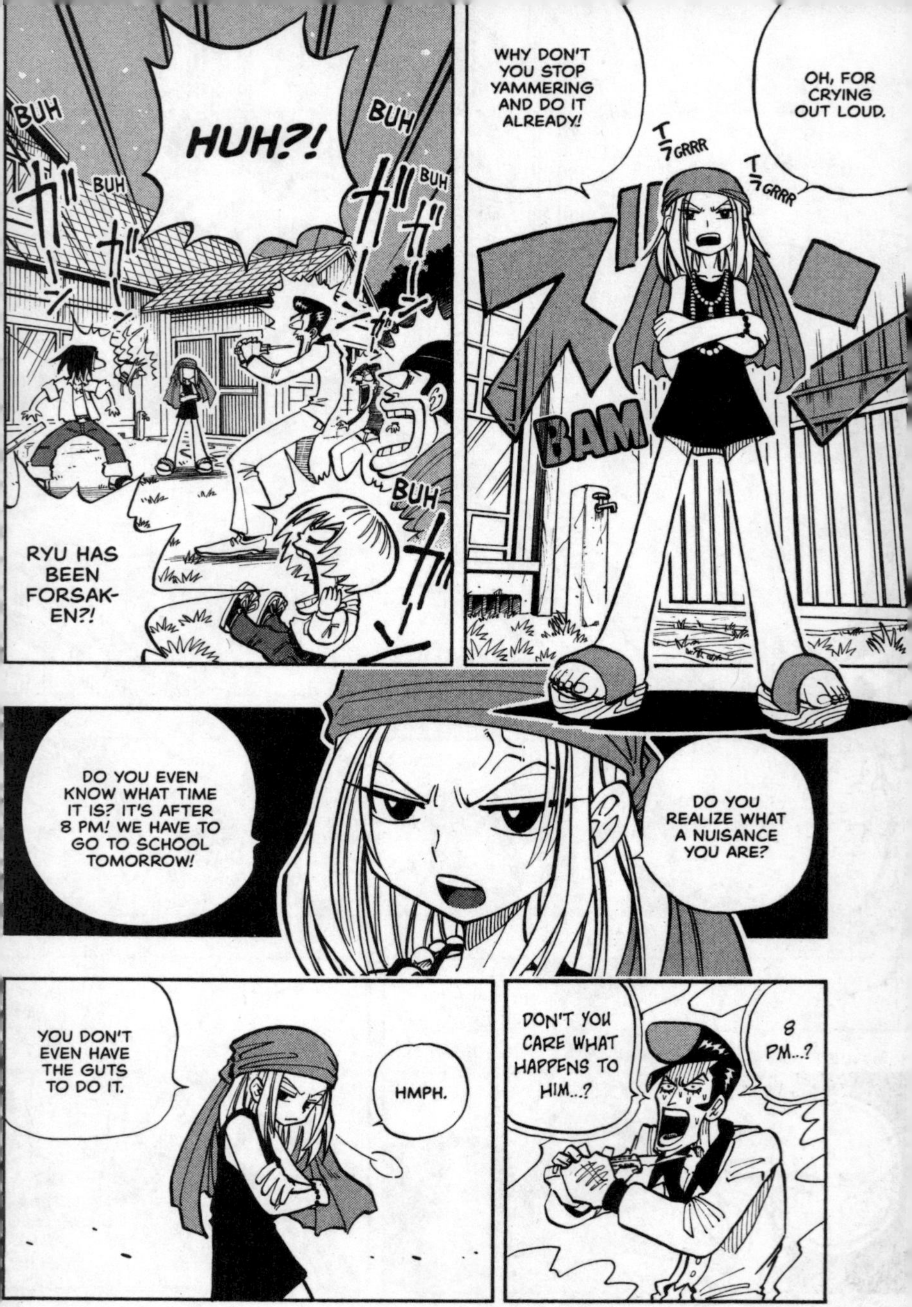
OH, FOR CRYING OUT LOUD.
WHY DON'T YOU STOP YAMMERING AND DO IT ALREADY!
GRRR
GRRR
BAM
HUH?!
BUH
BUH
BUH
BUH
BUH
RYU HAS BEEN FORSAK-EN?!
DO YOU REALIZE WHAT A NUISANCE YOU ARE?
DO YOU EVEN KNOW WHAT TIME IT IS? IT'S AFTER 8 PM! WE HAVE TO GO TO SCHOOL TOMORROW!
8 PM...?
DON'T YOU CARE WHAT HAPPENS TO HIM...?
HMPH.
YOU DON'T EVEN HAVE THE GUTS TO DO IT.

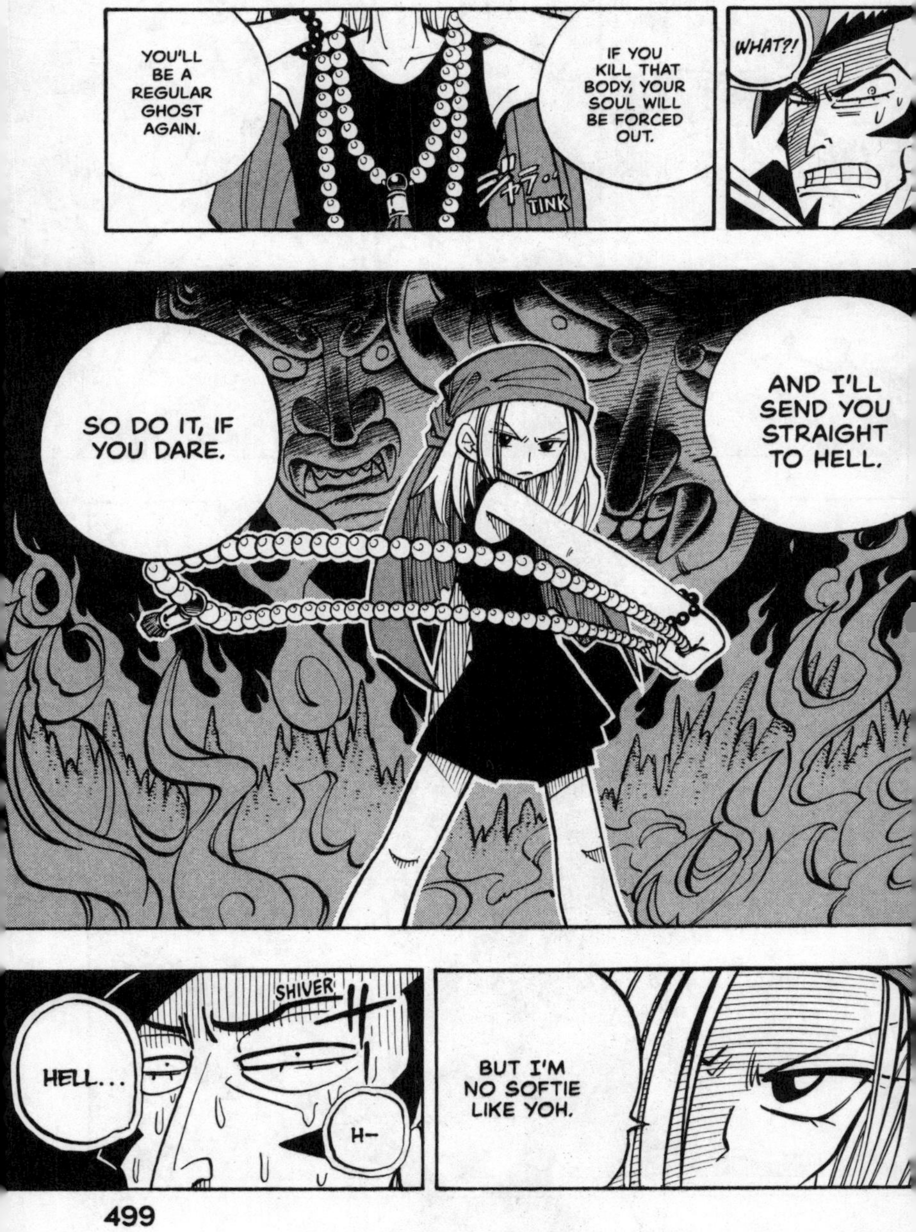
WHAT?!
IF YOU KILL THAT BODY, YOUR SOUL WILL BE FORCED OUT.
YOU'LL BE A REGULAR GHOST AGAIN.
ジャラ…
TINK
SO DO IT, IF YOU DARE.
AND I'LL SEND YOU STRAIGHT TO HELL.
BUT I'M NO SOFTIE LIKE YOH.
SHIVER
HELL...
H--

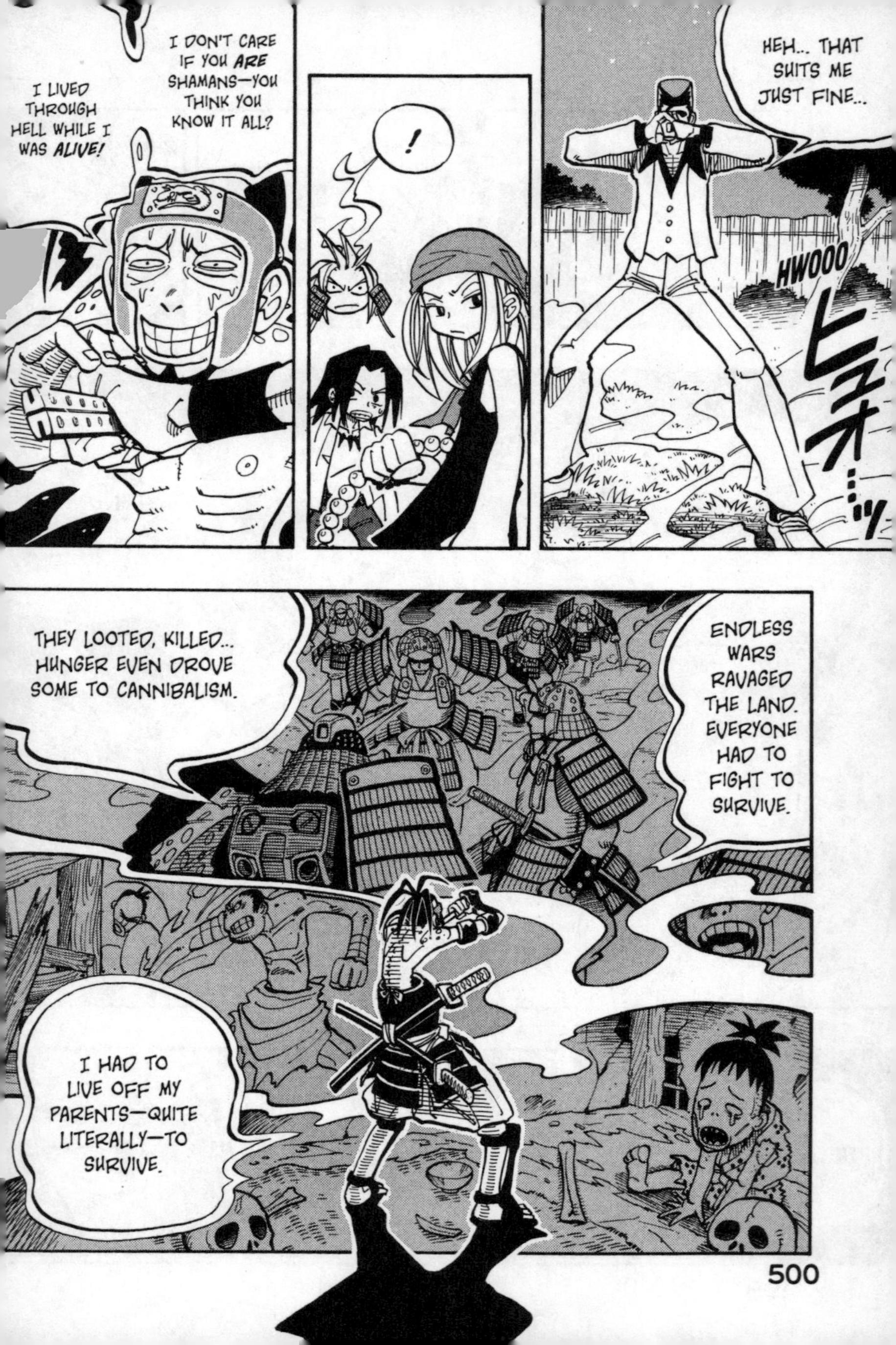
HEH... THAT SUITS ME JUST FINE...
HWOOO
ヒュオ…ッ
!
I DON'T CARE IF YOU ARE SHAMANS—YOU THINK YOU KNOW IT ALL?
I LIVED THROUGH HELL WHILE I WAS ALIVE!
ENDLESS WARS RAVAGED THE LAND. EVERYONE HAD TO FIGHT TO SURVIVE.
THEY LOOTED, KILLED... HUNGER EVEN DROVE SOME TO CANNIBALISM.
I HAD TO LIVE OFF MY PARENTS—QUITE LITERALLY—TO SURVIVE.

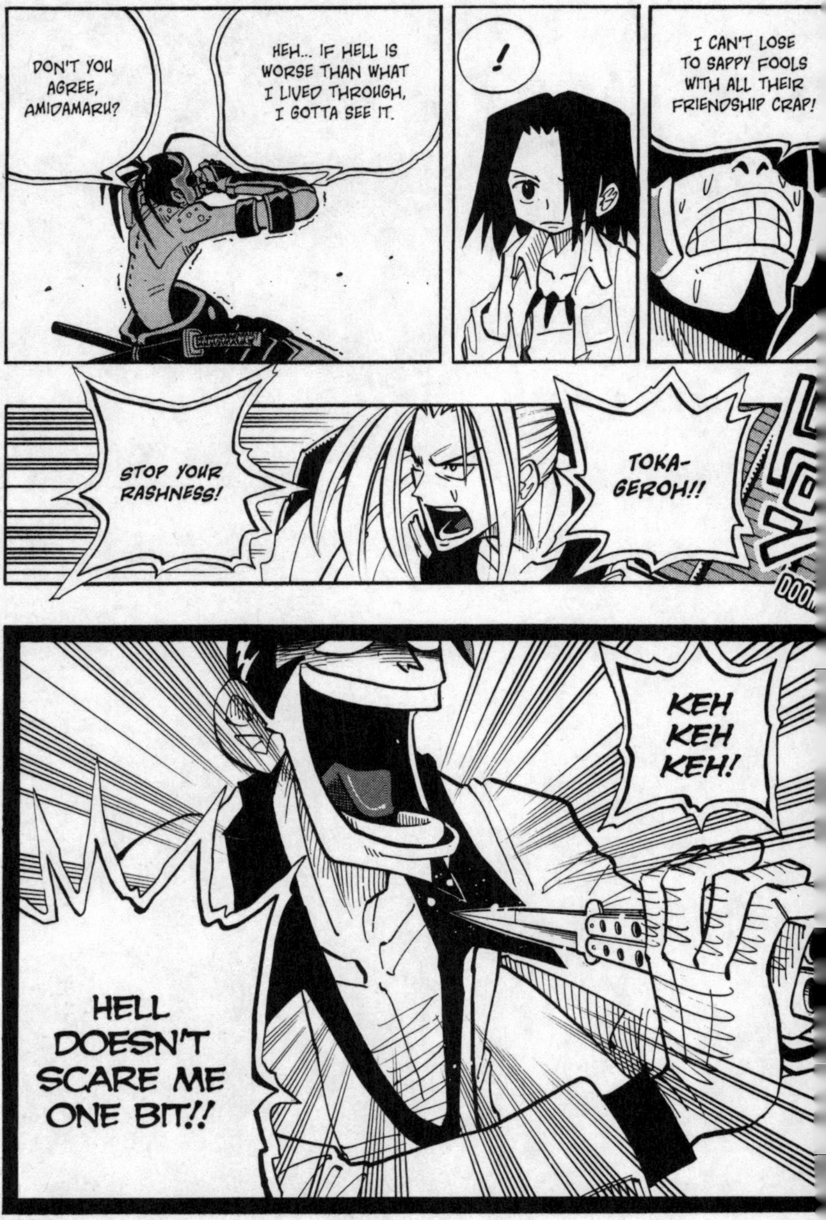
I CAN'T LOSE TO SAPPY FOOLS WITH ALL THEIR FRIENDSHIP CRAP!
!
HEH... IF HELL IS WORSE THAN WHAT I LIVED THROUGH, I GOTTA SEE IT.
DON'T YOU AGREE, AMIDAMARU?
DOOM
TOKA-GEROH!!
STOP YOUR RASHNESS!
KEH KEH KEH!
HELL DOESN'T SCARE ME ONE BIT!!

SHAMAN
KING
3

Tamegoroh
Toilet-haunting spirit

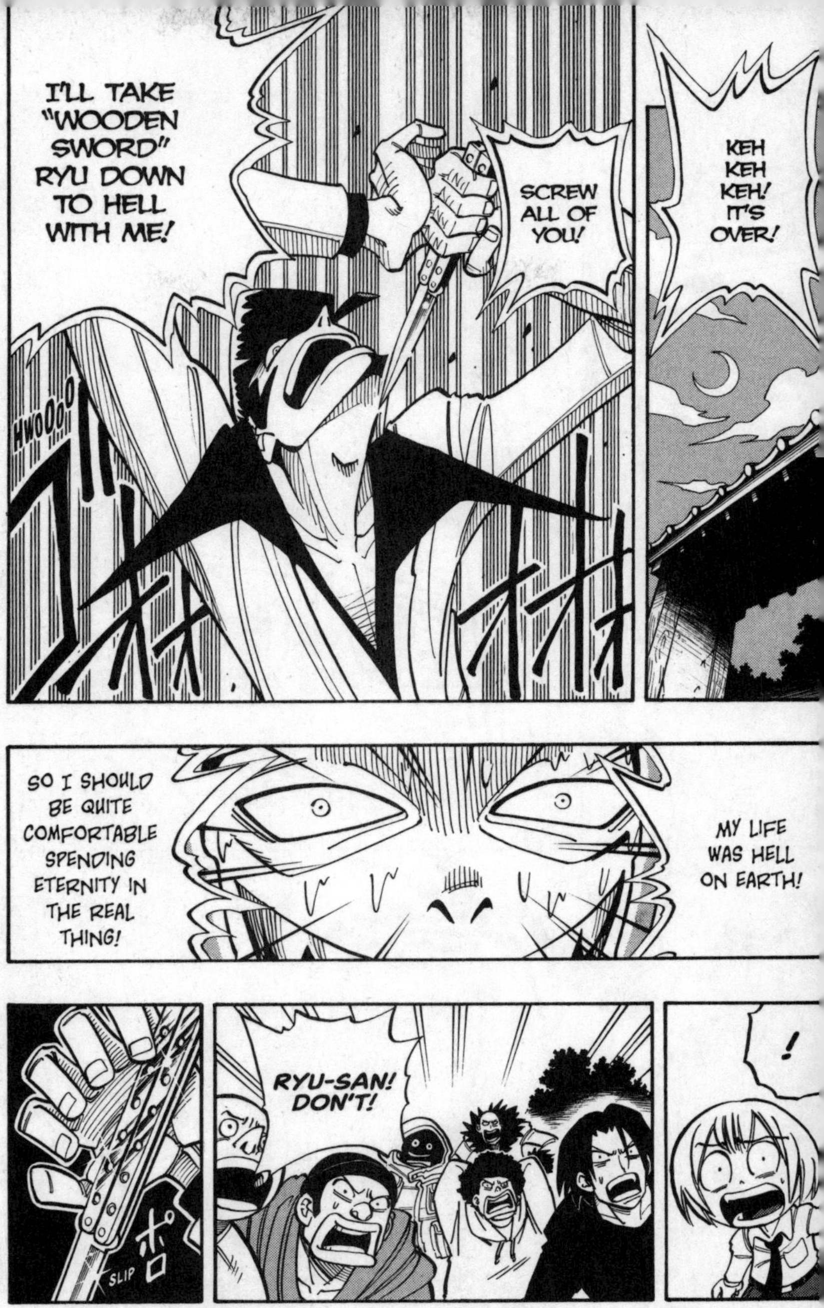
KEH KEH KEH! IT'S OVER!
SCREW ALL OF YOU!
I'LL TAKE "WOODEN SWORD" RYU DOWN TO HELL WITH ME!
HWOOOO
MY LIFE WAS HELL ON EARTH!
SO I SHOULD BE QUITE COMFORTABLE SPENDING ETERNITY IN THE REAL THING!
!
RYU-SAN! DON'T!
SLIP

Chapter 23: Tokageroh's Blues

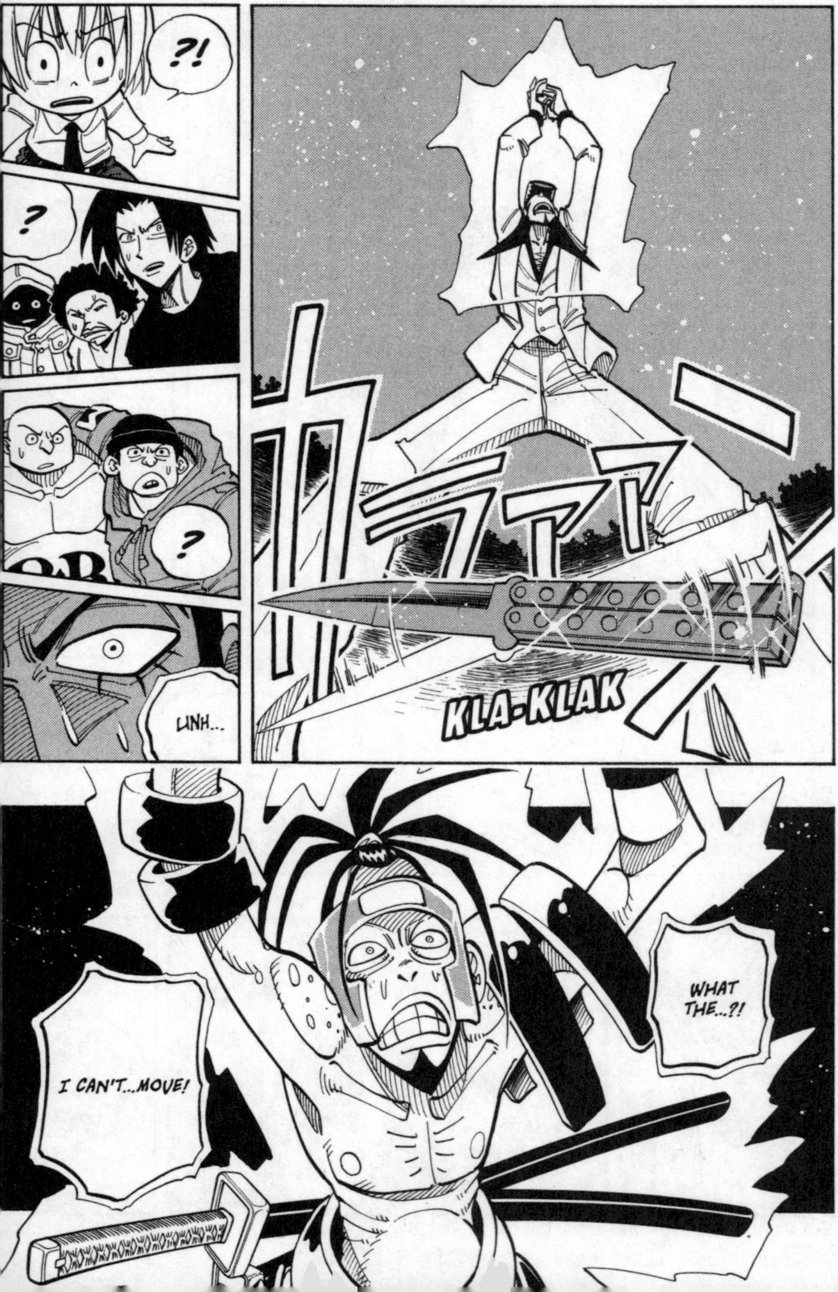
カラアー
KLA-KLAK
?!
?
?
UNH...
WHAT THE...?!
I CAN'T...MOVE!

Chapter 23: Tokageroh's Blues

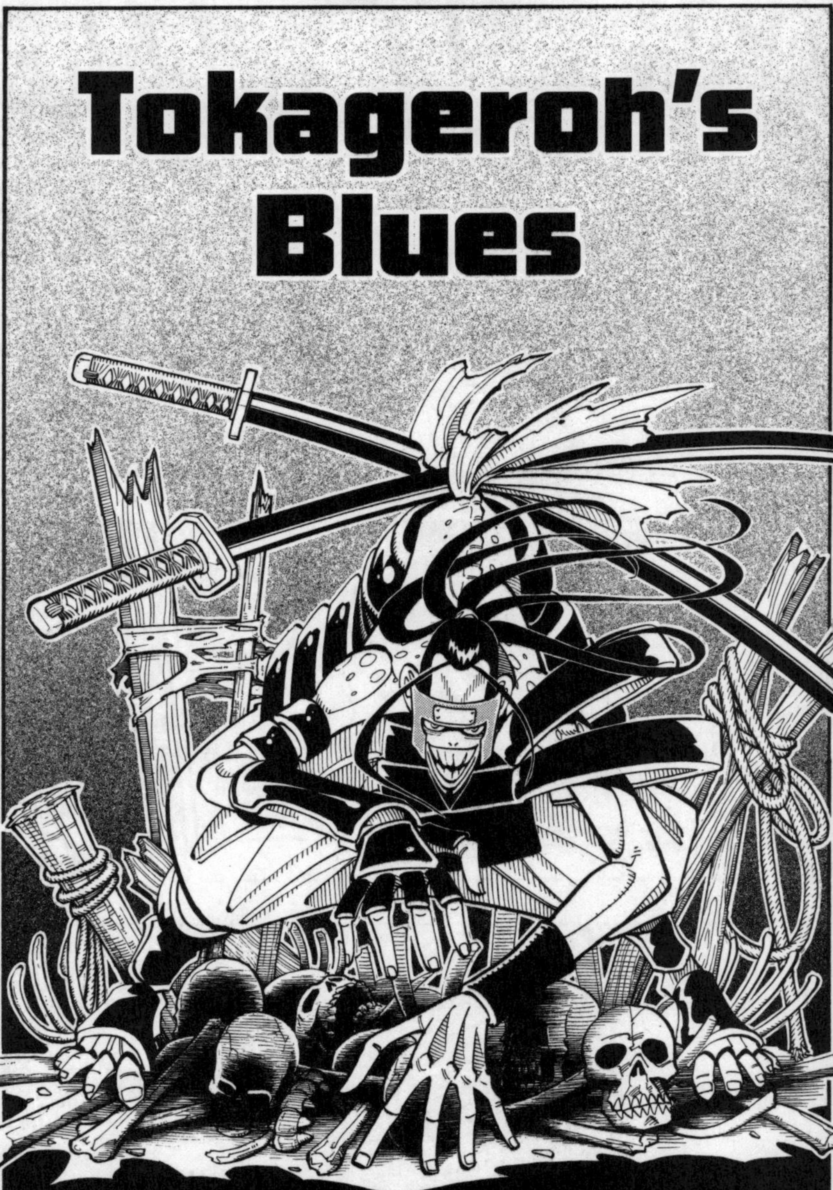

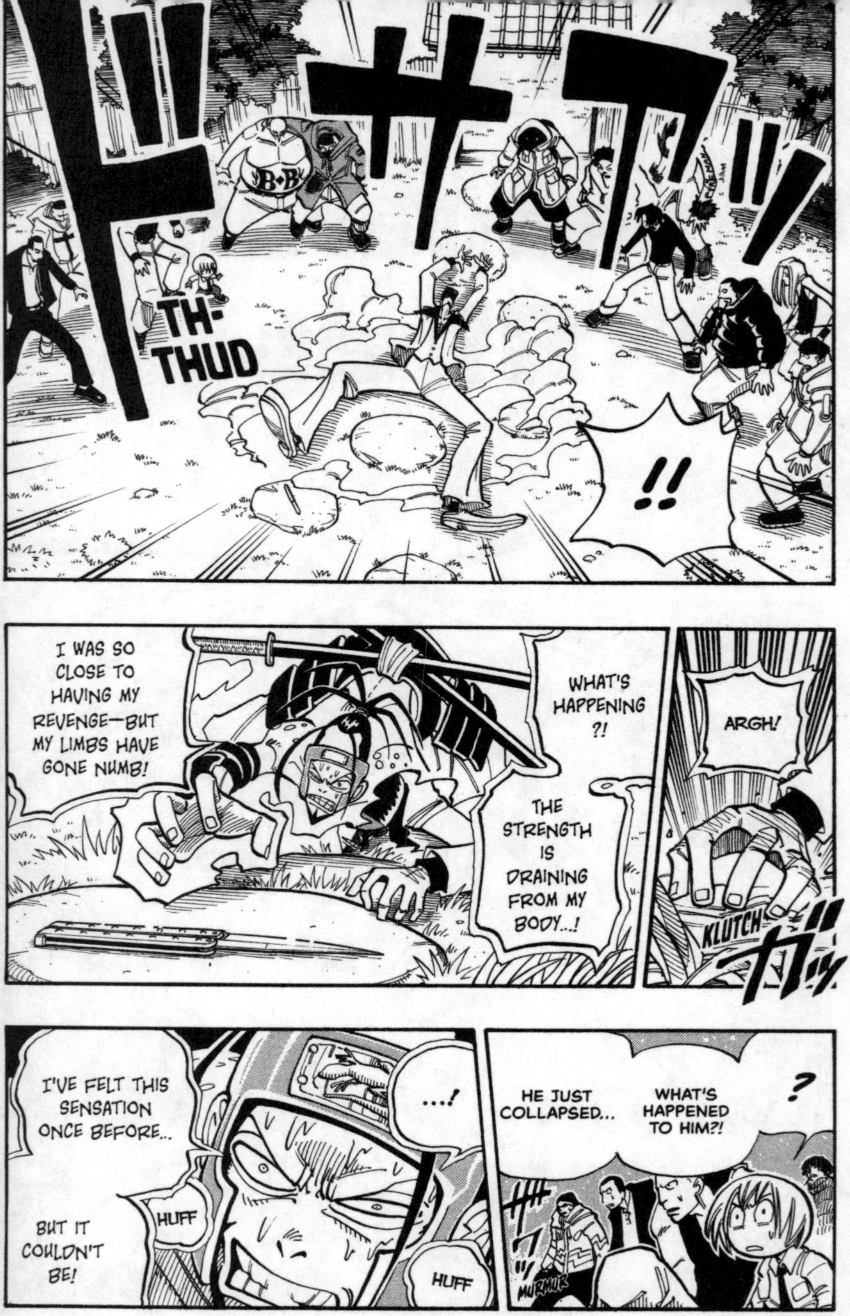
TH-THUD
!!
ARGH!
KLUTCH
WHAT'S HAPPENING?!
THE STRENGTH IS DRAINING FROM MY BODY...!
I WAS SO CLOSE TO HAVING MY REVENGE—BUT MY LIMBS HAVE GONE NUMB!
?
WHAT'S HAPPENED TO HIM?!
HE JUST COLLAPSED...
MURMUR
...!
I'VE FELT THIS SENSATION ONCE BEFORE...
HUFF
HUFF
BUT IT COULDN'T BE!

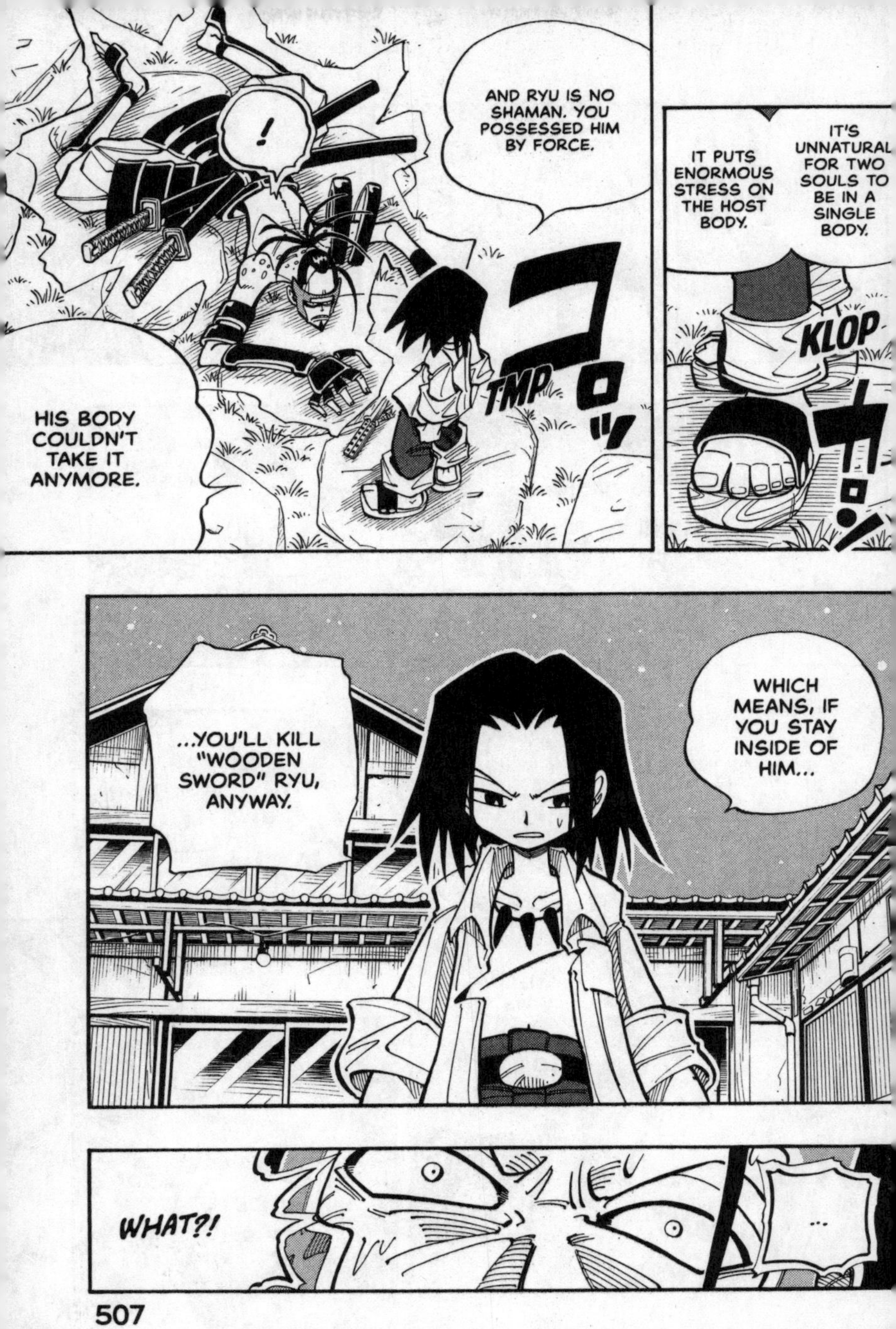
IT'S UNNATURAL FOR TWO SOULS TO BE IN A SINGLE BODY.
IT PUTS ENORMOUS STRESS ON THE HOST BODY.
KLOP
AND RYU IS NO SHAMAN. YOU POSSESSED HIM BY FORCE.
!
TMP
HIS BODY COULDN'T TAKE IT ANYMORE.
WHICH MEANS, IF YOU STAY INSIDE OF HIM...
...YOU'LL KILL "WOODEN SWORD" RYU, ANYWAY.
...
WHAT?!

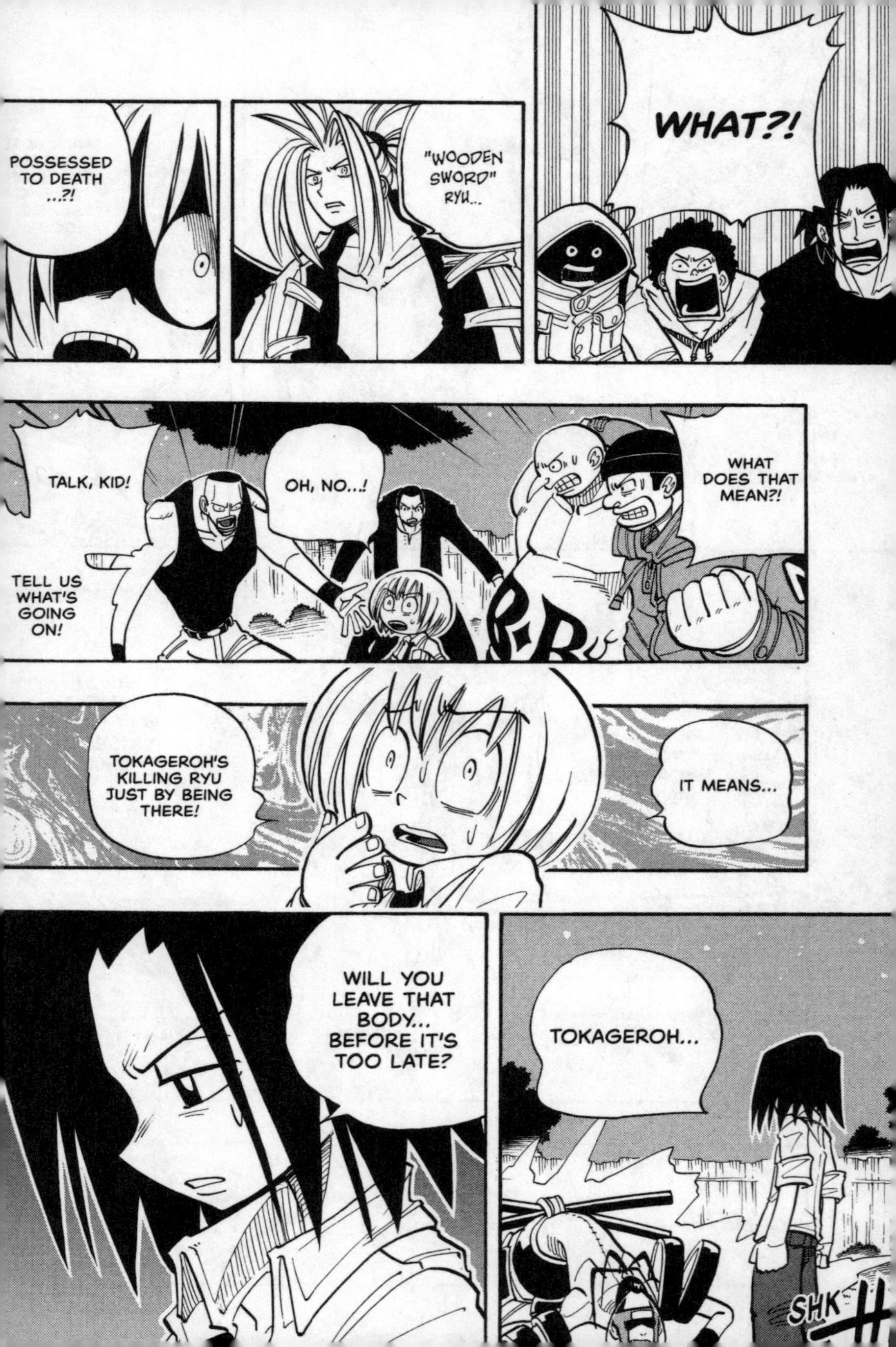
WHAT?!
"WOODEN SWORD" RYU...
POSSESSED TO DEATH ...?!
WHAT DOES THAT MEAN?!
OH, NO...!
TALK, KID!
TELL US WHAT'S GOING ON!
IT MEANS...
TOKAGEROH'S KILLING RYU JUST BY BEING THERE!
TOKAGEROH...
SHK
WILL YOU LEAVE THAT BODY... BEFORE IT'S TOO LATE?

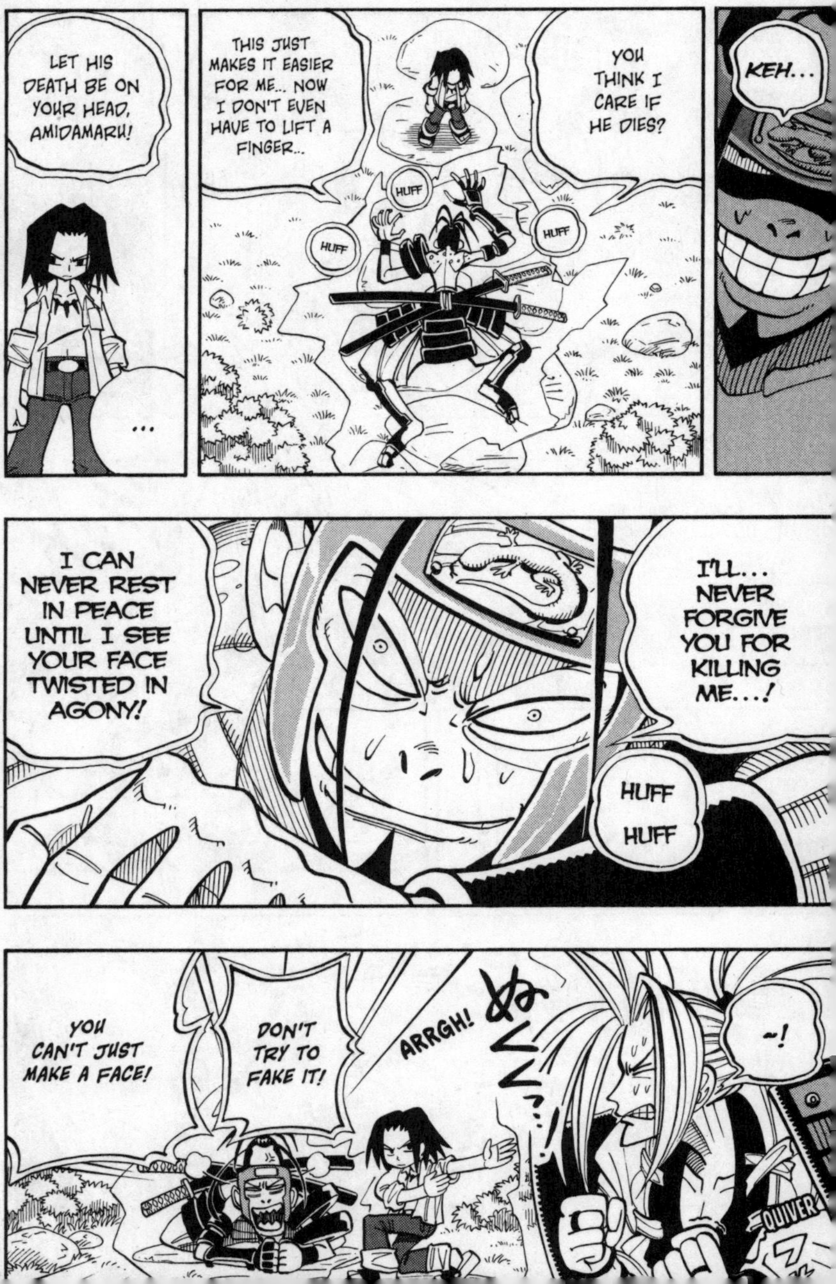
KEH...
YOU THINK I CARE IF HE DIES?
THIS JUST MAKES IT EASIER FOR ME... NOW I DON'T EVEN HAVE TO LIFT A FINGER...
HUFF
HUFF
HUFF
LET HIS DEATH BE ON YOUR HEAD, AMIDAMARU!
...
I'LL... NEVER FORGIVE YOU FOR KILLING ME...!
HUFF HUFF
I CAN NEVER REST IN PEACE UNTIL I SEE YOUR FACE TWISTED IN AGONY!
~!
QUIVER
ぬくく
ARRGH!
DON'T TRY TO FAKE IT!
YOU CAN'T JUST MAKE A FACE!

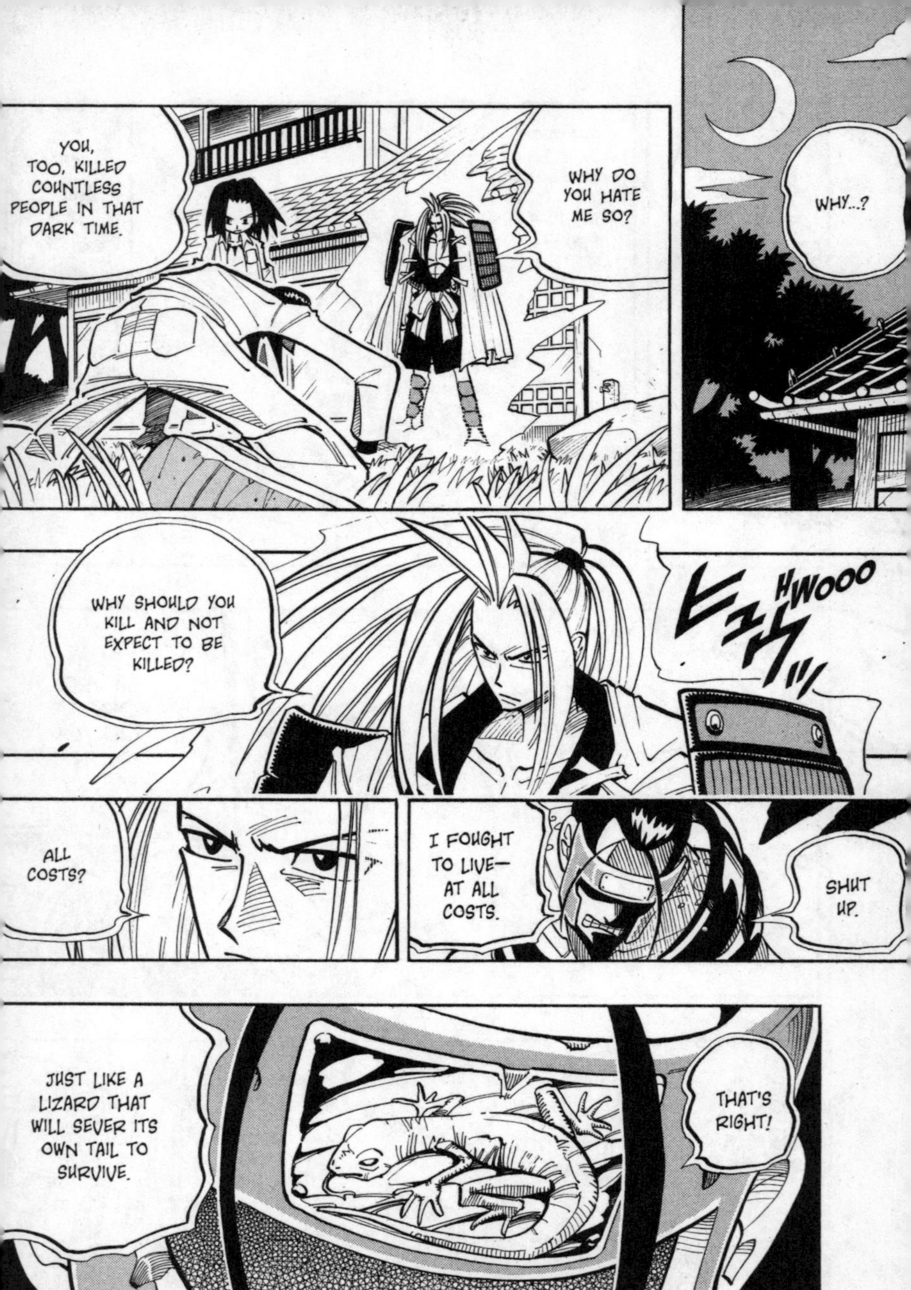
WHY...?
WHY DO YOU HATE ME SO?
YOU, TOO, KILLED COUNTLESS PEOPLE IN THAT DARK TIME.
HWOOO
WHY SHOULD YOU KILL AND NOT EXPECT TO BE KILLED?
SHUT UP.
I FOUGHT TO LIVE— AT ALL COSTS.
ALL COSTS?
THAT'S RIGHT!
JUST LIKE A LIZARD THAT WILL SEVER ITS OWN TAIL TO SURVIVE.

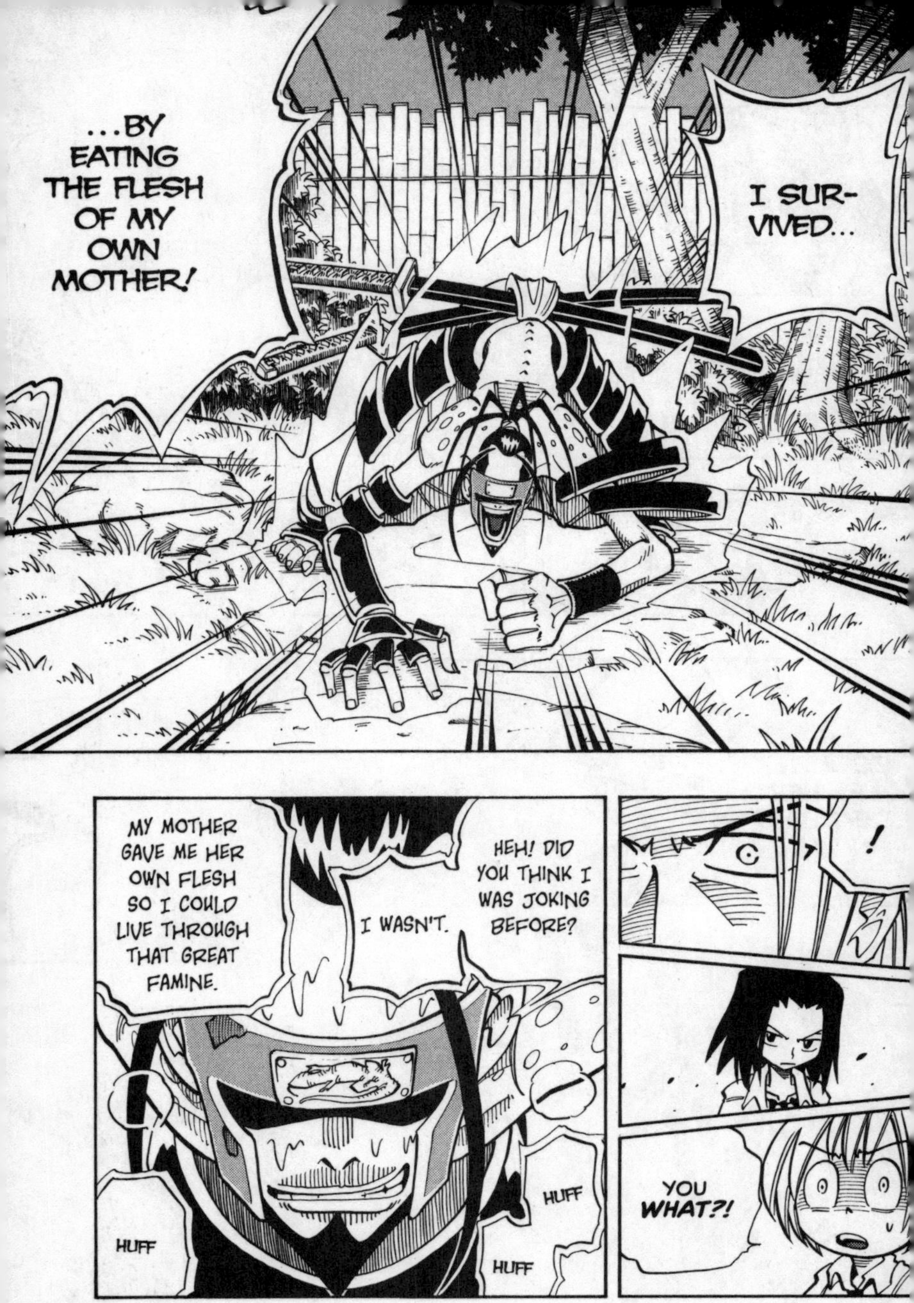
I SURVIVED...
...BY EATING THE FLESH OF MY OWN MOTHER!
!
YOU WHAT?!
HEH! DID YOU THINK I WAS JOKING BEFORE?
I WASN'T.
MY MOTHER GAVE ME HER OWN FLESH SO I COULD LIVE THROUGH THAT GREAT FAMINE.
HUFF
HUFF
HUFF

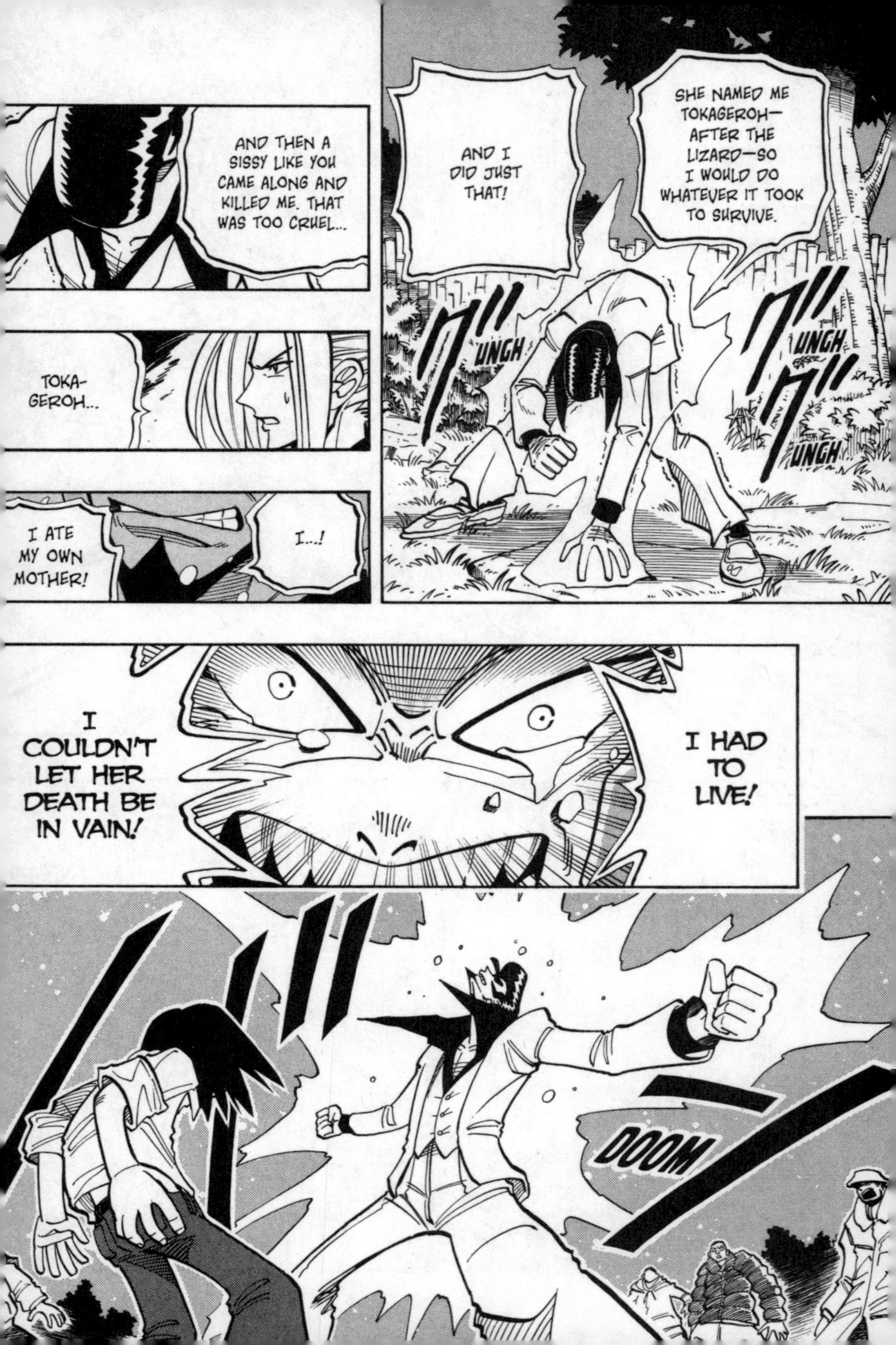
SHE NAMED ME TOKAGEROH— AFTER THE LIZARD—SO I WOULD DO WHATEVER IT TOOK TO SURVIVE.
AND I DID JUST THAT!
UNGH
UNGH
UNGH
AND THEN A SISSY LIKE YOU CAME ALONG AND KILLED ME. THAT WAS TOO CRUEL...
TOKA-GEROH...
I...!
I ATE MY OWN MOTHER!
I HAD TO LIVE!
I COULDN'T LET HER DEATH BE IN VAIN!
DOOM

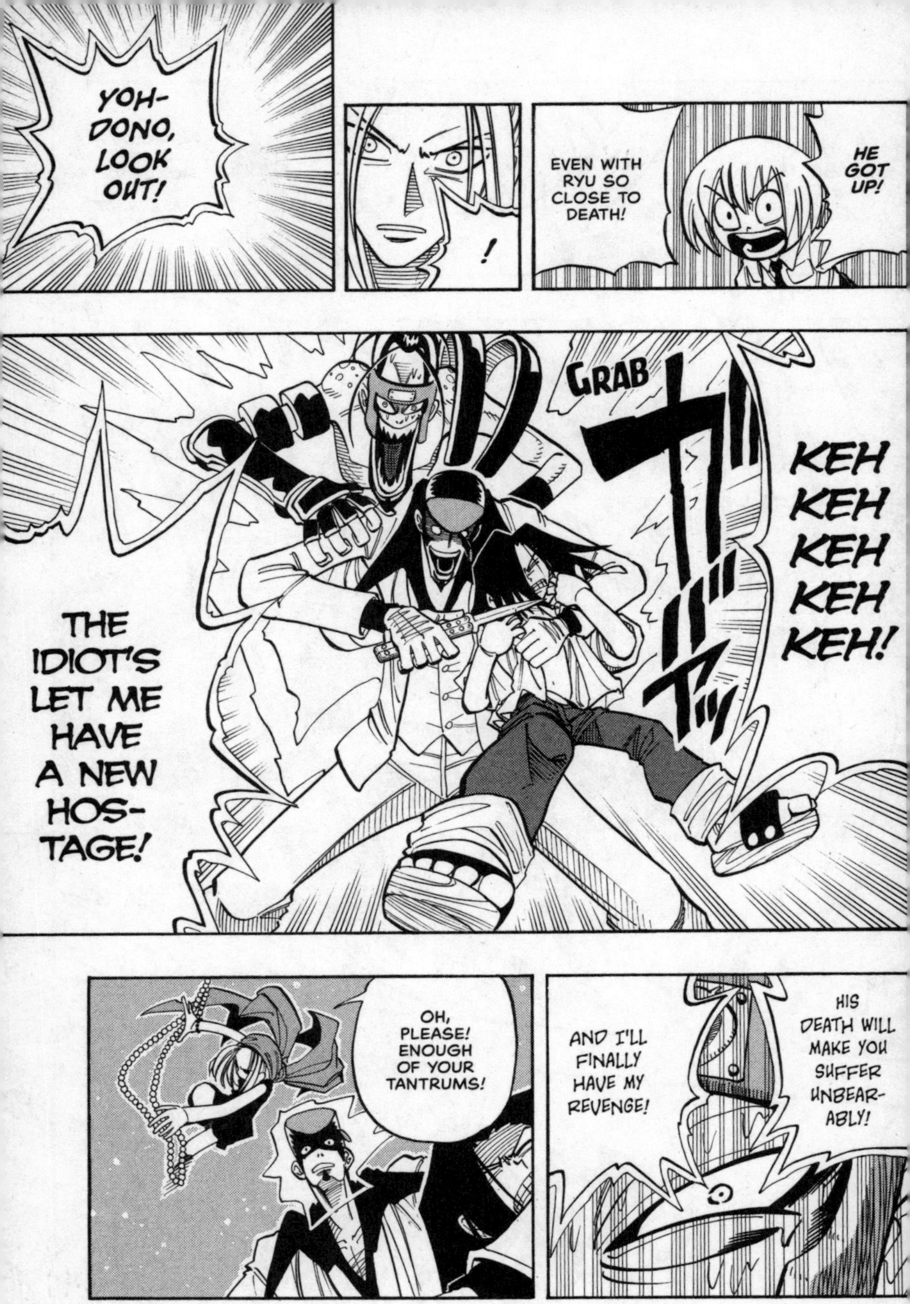
HE GOT UP!
EVEN WITH RYU SO CLOSE TO DEATH!
!
YOH-DONO, LOOK OUT!
GRAB
KEH KEH KEH KEH KEH!
THE IDIOT'S LET ME HAVE A NEW HOSTAGE!
HIS DEATH WILL MAKE YOU SUFFER UNBEARABLY!
AND I'LL FINALLY HAVE MY REVENGE!
OH, PLEASE! ENOUGH OF YOUR TANTRUMS!

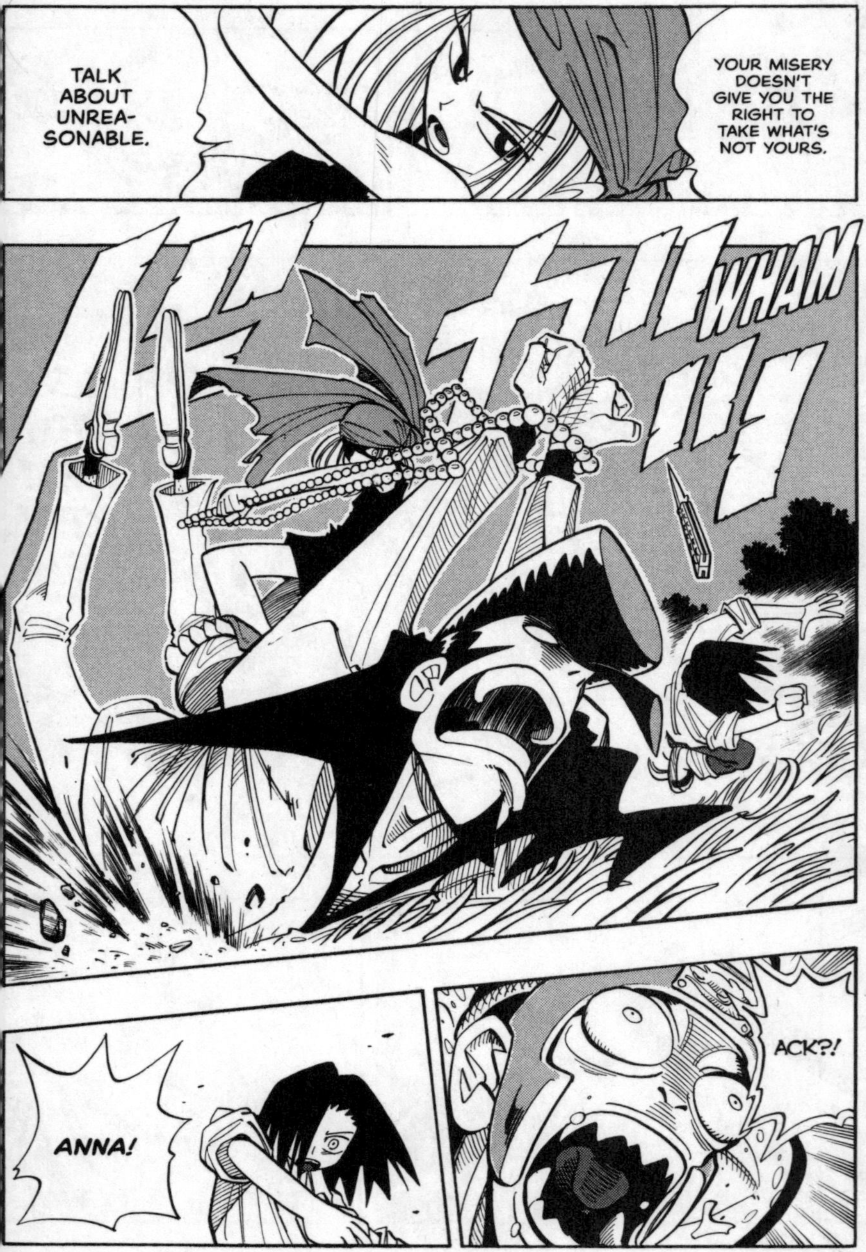
YOUR MISERY DOESN'T GIVE YOU THE RIGHT TO TAKE WHAT'S NOT YOURS.
TALK ABOUT UNREA-SONABLE.
WHAM
ACK?!
ANNA!

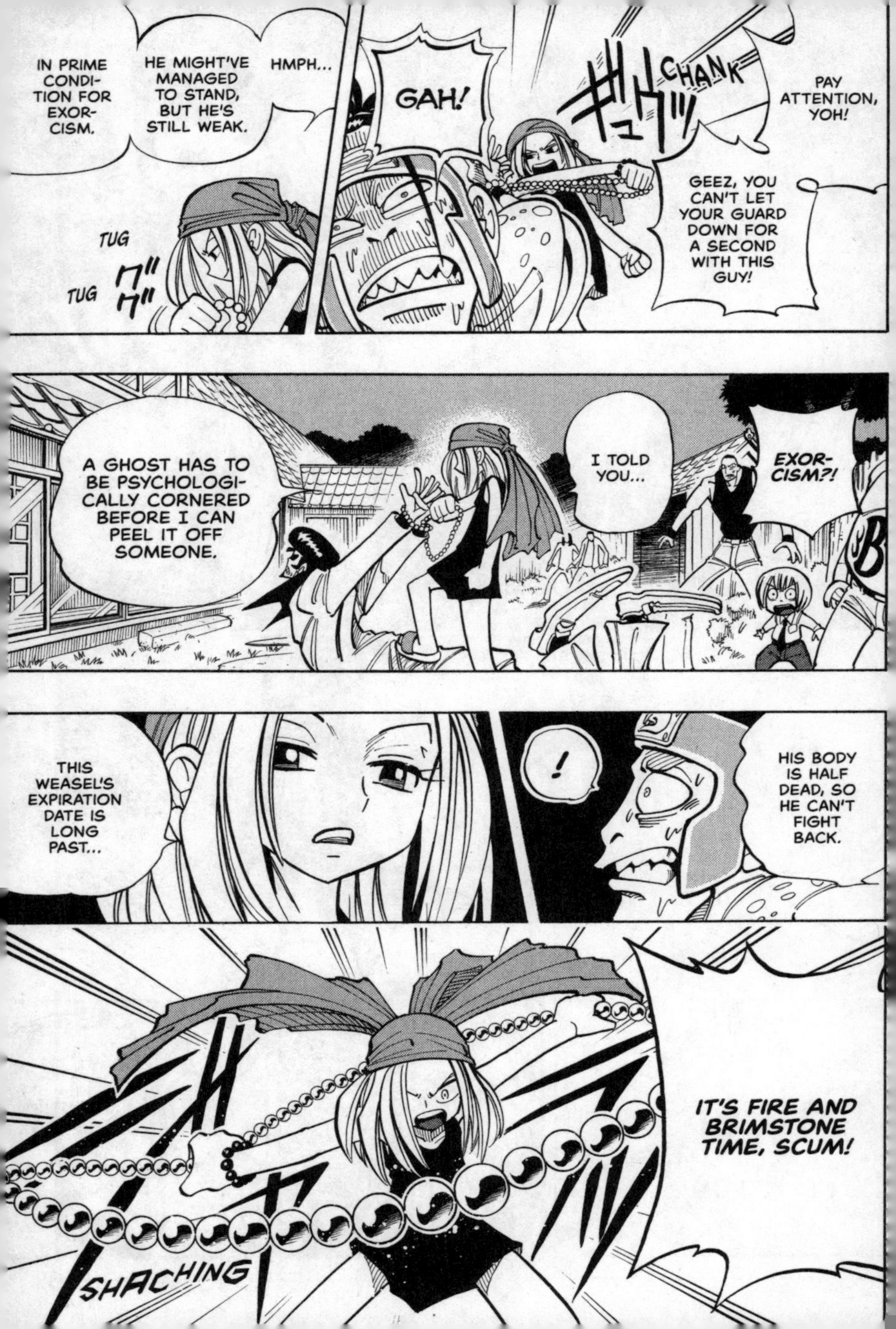
CHANK
PAY ATTENTION, YOH!
GEEZ, YOU CAN'T LET YOUR GUARD DOWN FOR A SECOND WITH THIS GUY!
GAH!
HMPH...
HE MIGHT'VE MANAGED TO STAND, BUT HE'S STILL WEAK.
IN PRIME CONDITION FOR EXORCISM.
TUG
TUG
EXORCISM?!
I TOLD YOU...
A GHOST HAS TO BE PSYCHOLOGICALLY CORNERED BEFORE I CAN PEEL IT OFF SOMEONE.
HIS BODY IS HALF DEAD, SO HE CAN'T FIGHT BACK.
!
THIS WEASEL'S EXPIRATION DATE IS LONG PAST...
IT'S FIRE AND BRIMSTONE TIME, SCUM!
SHACHING

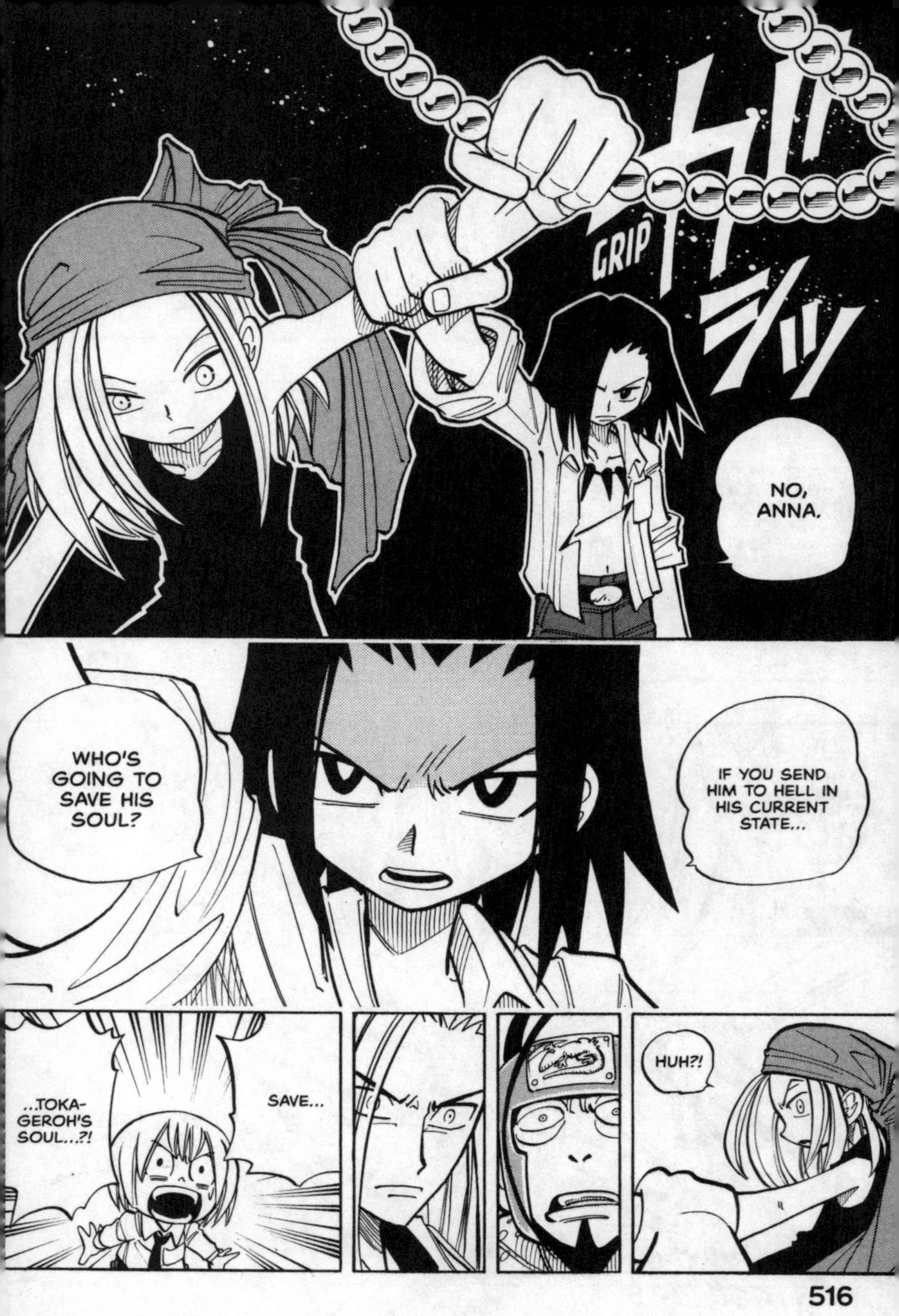
GRIP
NO, ANNA.
IF YOU SEND HIM TO HELL IN HIS CURRENT STATE...
WHO'S GOING TO SAVE HIS SOUL?
HUH?!
SAVE...
...TOKA-GEROH'S SOUL...?!

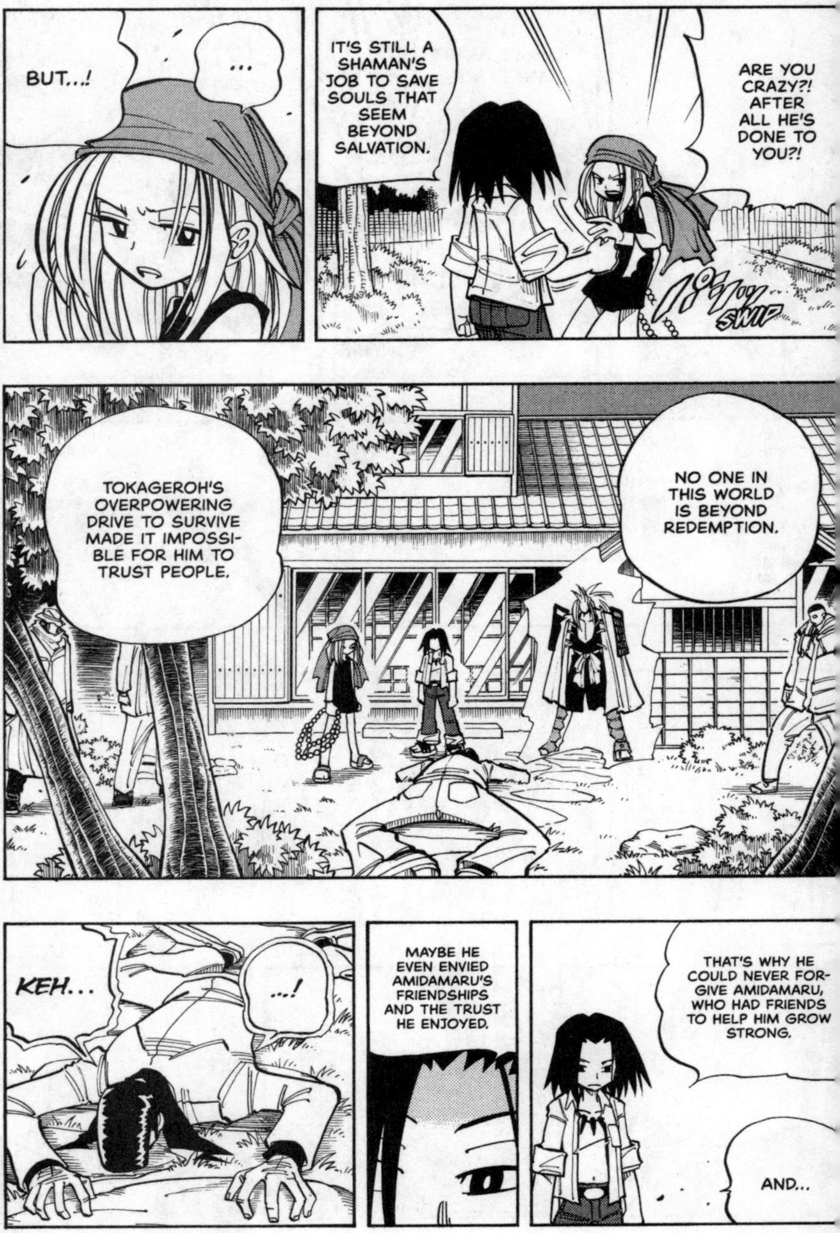
ARE YOU CRAZY?! AFTER ALL HE'S DONE TO YOU?!
IT'S STILL A SHAMAN'S JOB TO SAVE SOULS THAT SEEM BEYOND SALVATION.
SWIP
...
BUT...!
NO ONE IN THIS WORLD IS BEYOND REDEMPTION.
TOKAGEROH'S OVERPOWERING DRIVE TO SURVIVE MADE IT IMPOSSIBLE FOR HIM TO TRUST PEOPLE.
THAT'S WHY HE COULD NEVER FORGIVE AMIDAMARU, WHO HAD FRIENDS TO HELP HIM GROW STRONG.
AND...
MAYBE HE EVEN ENVIED AMIDAMARU'S FRIENDSHIPS AND THE TRUST HE ENJOYED.
...!
KEH...

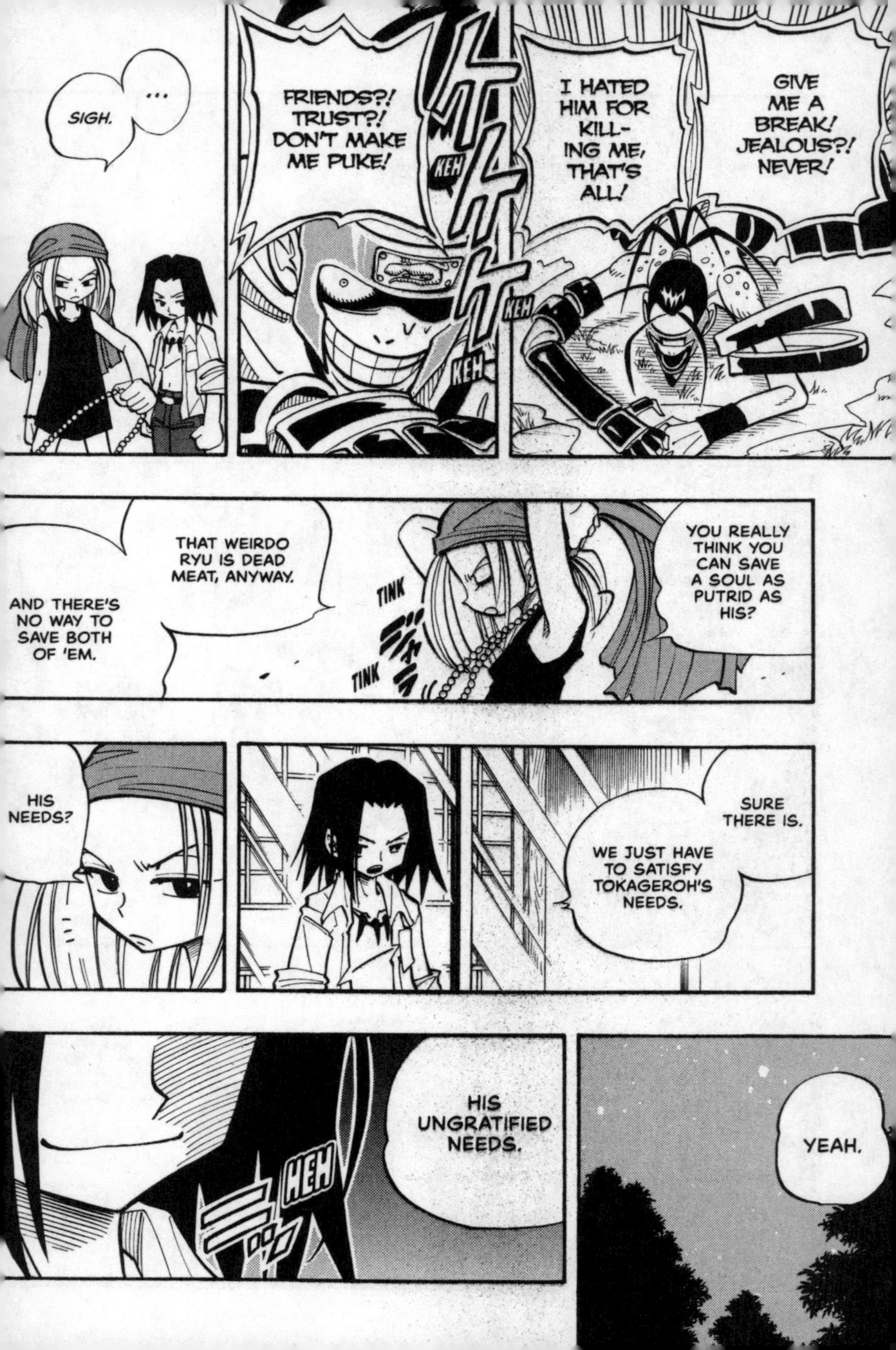
GIVE ME A BREAK! JEALOUS?! NEVER!
I HATED HIM FOR KILL-ING ME, THAT'S ALL!
FRIENDS?! TRUST?! DON'T MAKE ME PUKE!
KEH
KEH
KEH
...
SIGH.
YOU REALLY THINK YOU CAN SAVE A SOUL AS PUTRID AS HIS?
TINK
TINK
THAT WEIRDO RYU IS DEAD MEAT, ANYWAY.
AND THERE'S NO WAY TO SAVE BOTH OF 'EM.
SURE THERE IS.
WE JUST HAVE TO SATISFY TOKAGEROH'S NEEDS.
HIS NEEDS?
YEAH.
HIS UNGRATIFIED NEEDS.
HEH

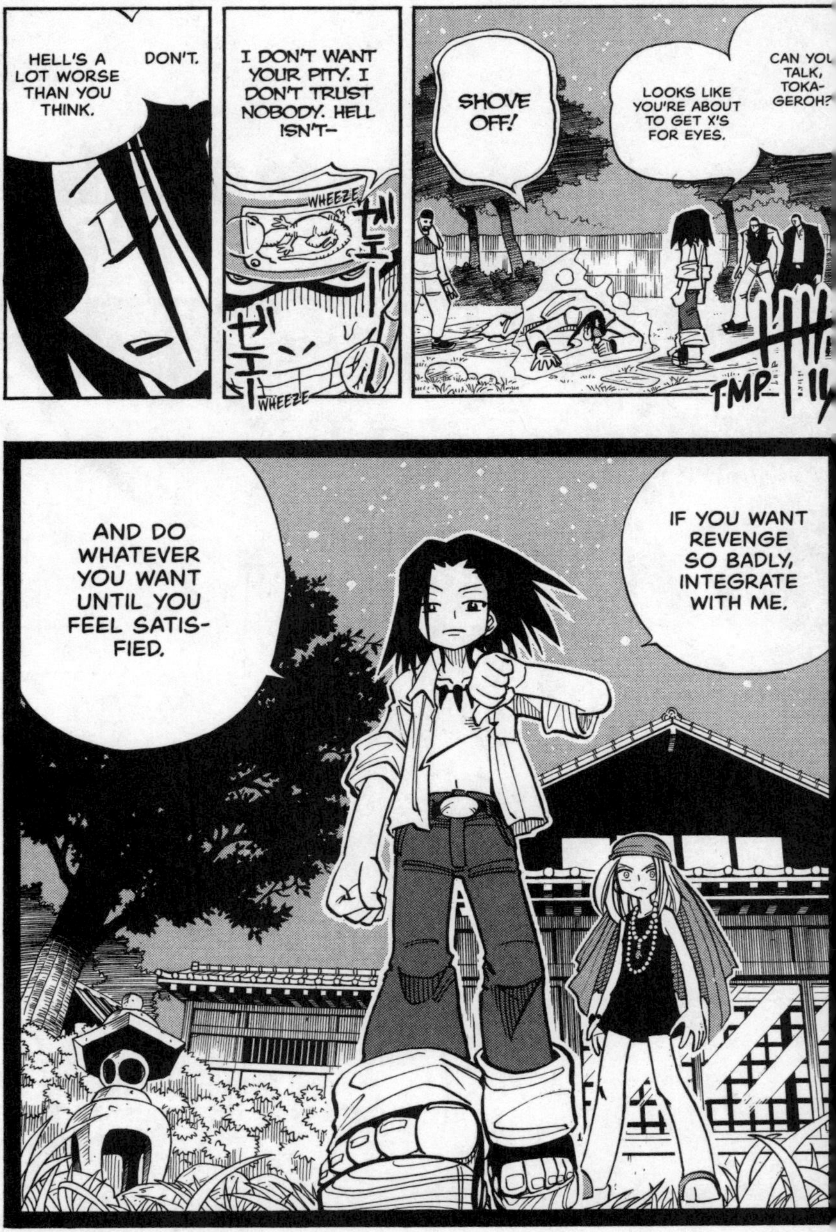
CAN YOU TALK, TOKA-GEROH?
LOOKS LIKE YOU'RE ABOUT TO GET X'S FOR EYES.
SHOVE OFF!
TMP
I DON'T WANT YOUR PITY. I DON'T TRUST NOBODY. HELL ISN'T–
WHEEZE
WHEEZE
DON'T.
HELL'S A LOT WORSE THAN YOU THINK.
IF YOU WANT REVENGE SO BADLY, INTEGRATE WITH ME.
AND DO WHATEVER YOU WANT UNTIL YOU FEEL SATIS-FIED.

SHAMAN KING CHARACTER FILE No.12

Mosuke
1999

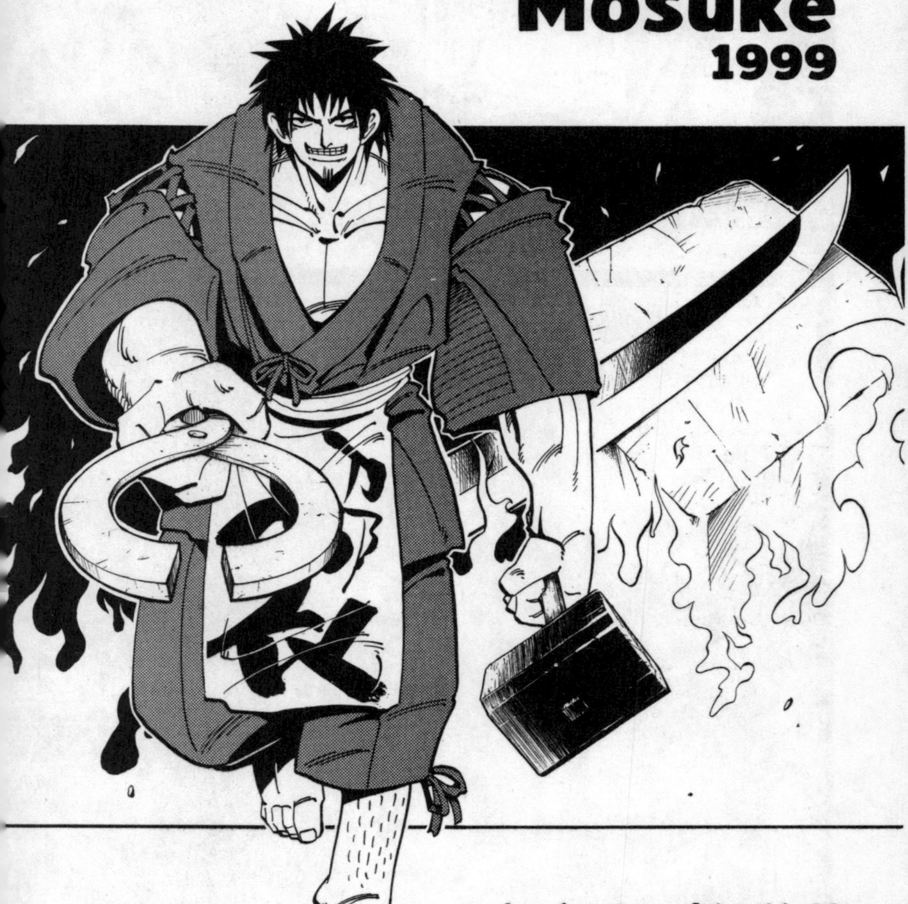

Age (at time of death): 28
Date of Birth: August 13, 1383
Blood Type: B

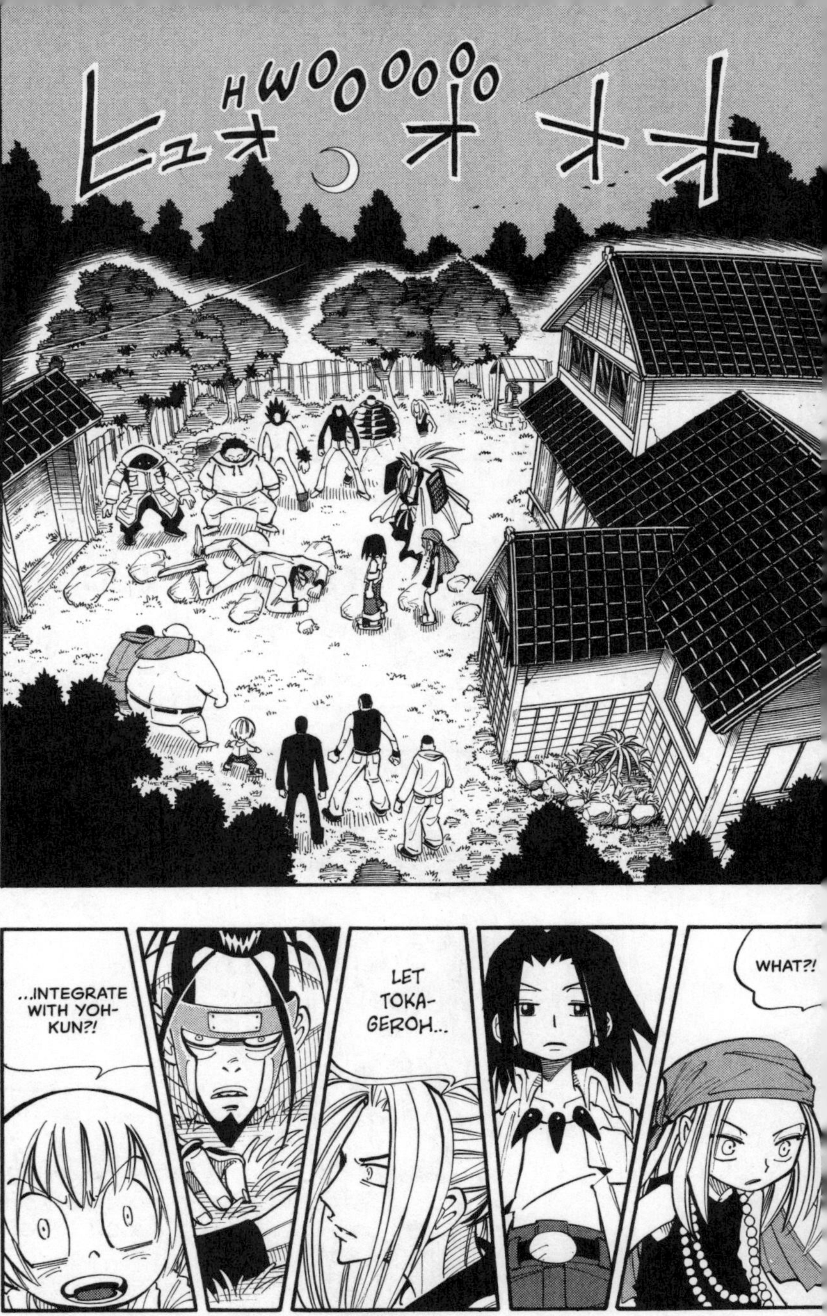
ヒュオオオオ
HWOOOOOO
WHAT?!
LET TOKA-GEROH...
...INTEGRATE WITH YOH-KUN?!

Chapter 24: The Integral Tokageroh

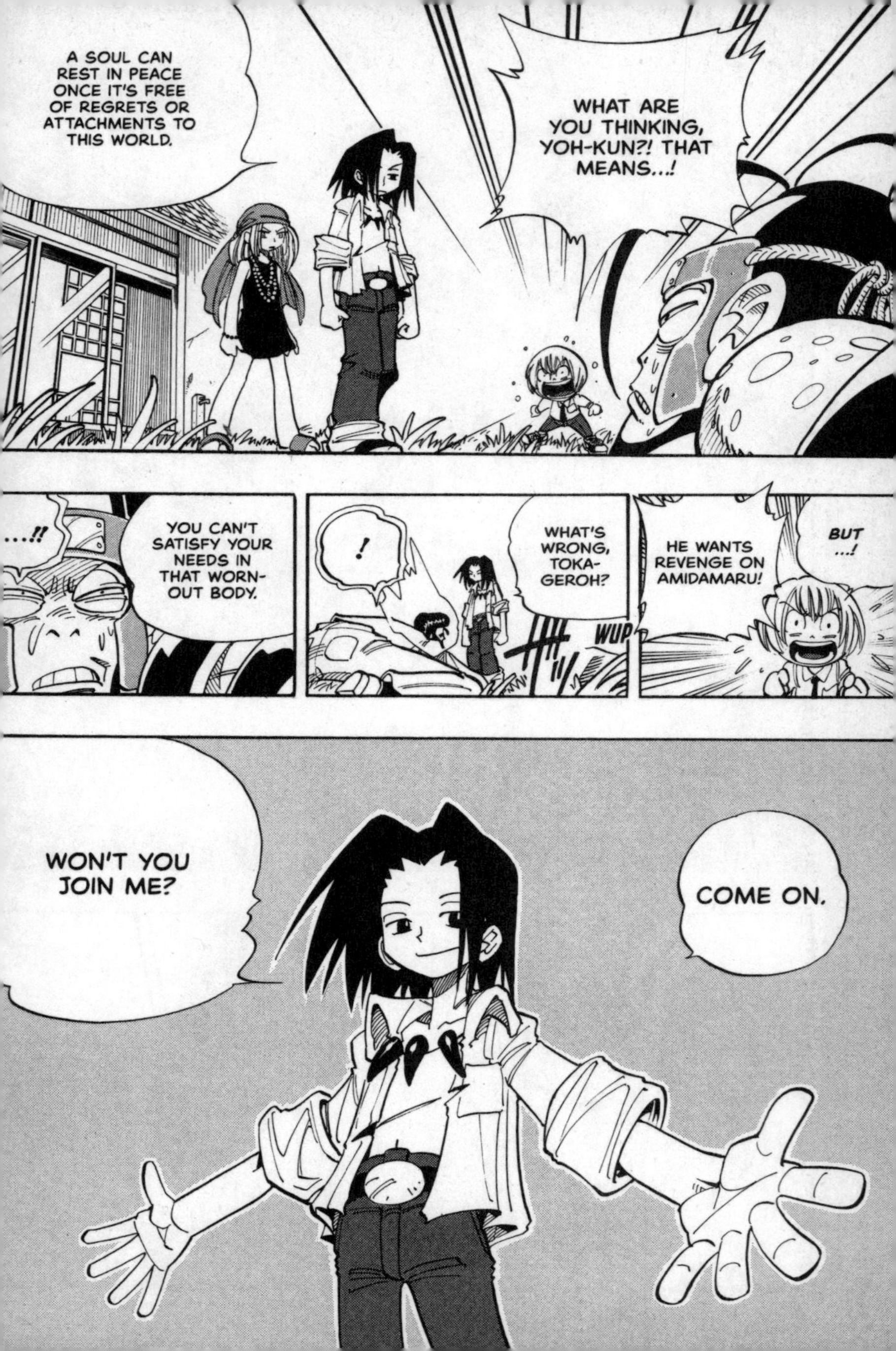
WHAT ARE YOU THINKING, YOH-KUN?! THAT MEANS...!
A SOUL CAN REST IN PEACE ONCE IT'S FREE OF REGRETS OR ATTACHMENTS TO THIS WORLD.
BUT ...!
HE WANTS REVENGE ON AMIDAMARU!
WHAT'S WRONG, TOKA-GEROH?
WUP
!
YOU CAN'T SATISFY YOUR NEEDS IN THAT WORN-OUT BODY.
...!!
COME ON.
WON'T YOU JOIN ME?

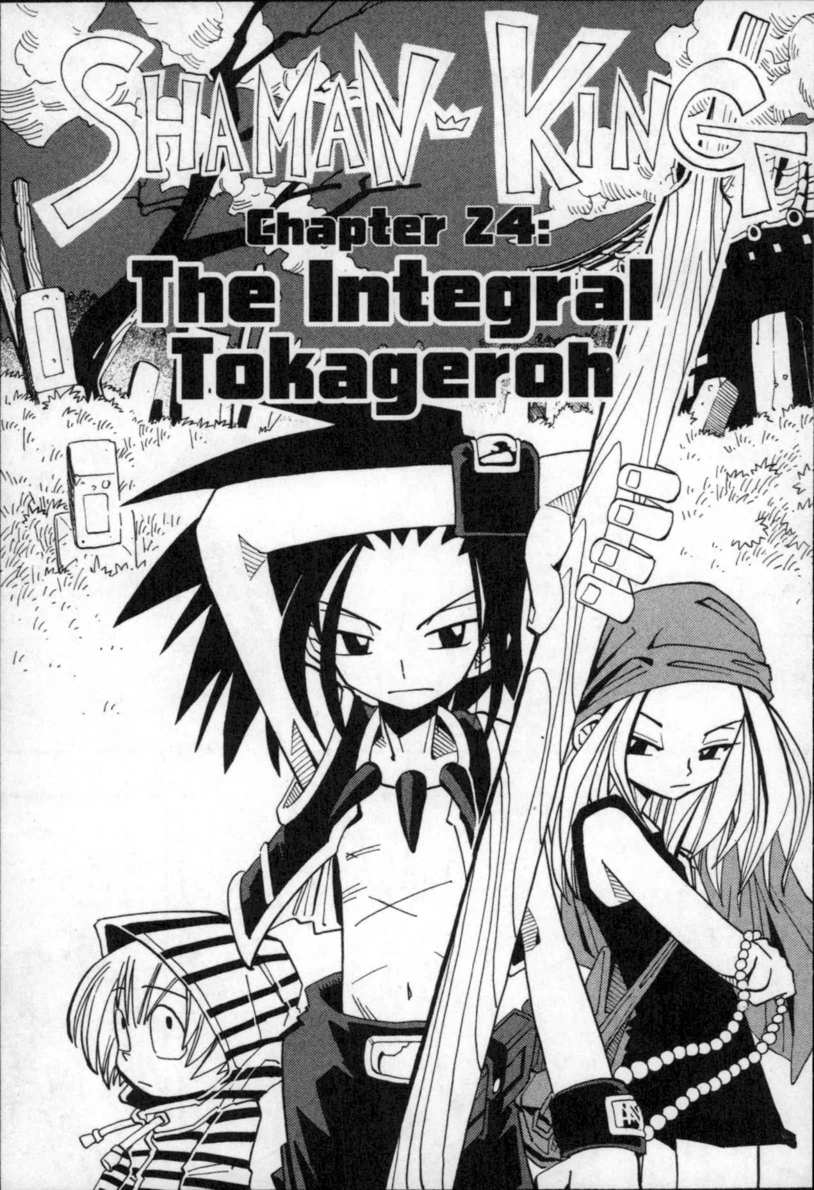
SHAMAN KING
Chapter 24:
The Integral Tokageroh

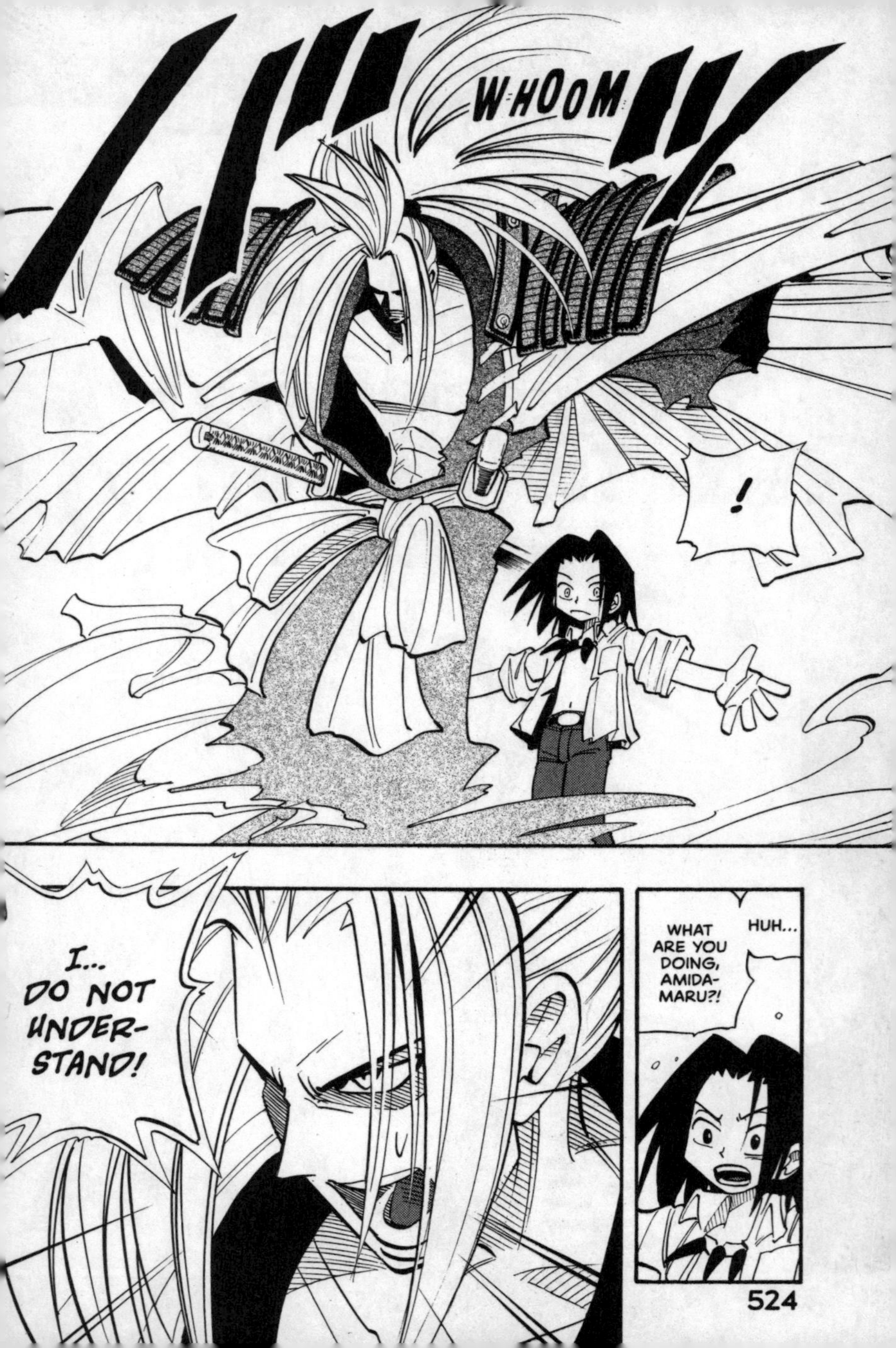
WHOOM
!
HUH...
WHAT ARE YOU DOING, AMIDA-MARU?!
I... DO NOT UNDER-STAND!

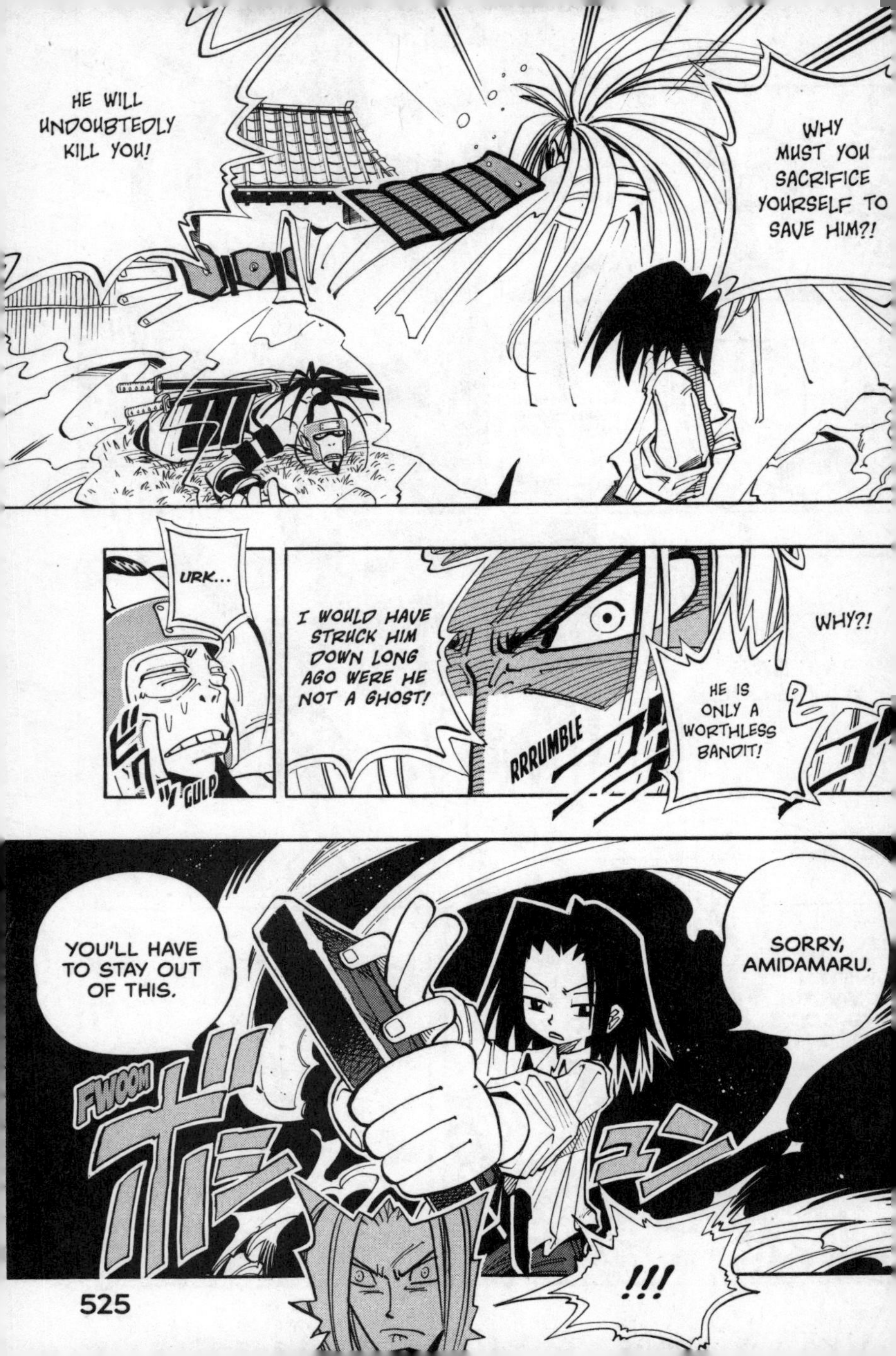
WHY MUST YOU SACRIFICE YOURSELF TO SAVE HIM?!
HE WILL UNDOUBTEDLY KILL YOU!
WHY?!
HE IS ONLY A WORTHLESS BANDIT!
RRRUMBLE
I WOULD HAVE STRUCK HIM DOWN LONG AGO WERE HE NOT A GHOST!
URK...
GULP
SORRY, AMIDAMARU.
YOU'LL HAVE TO STAY OUT OF THIS.
FWOOM
!!!

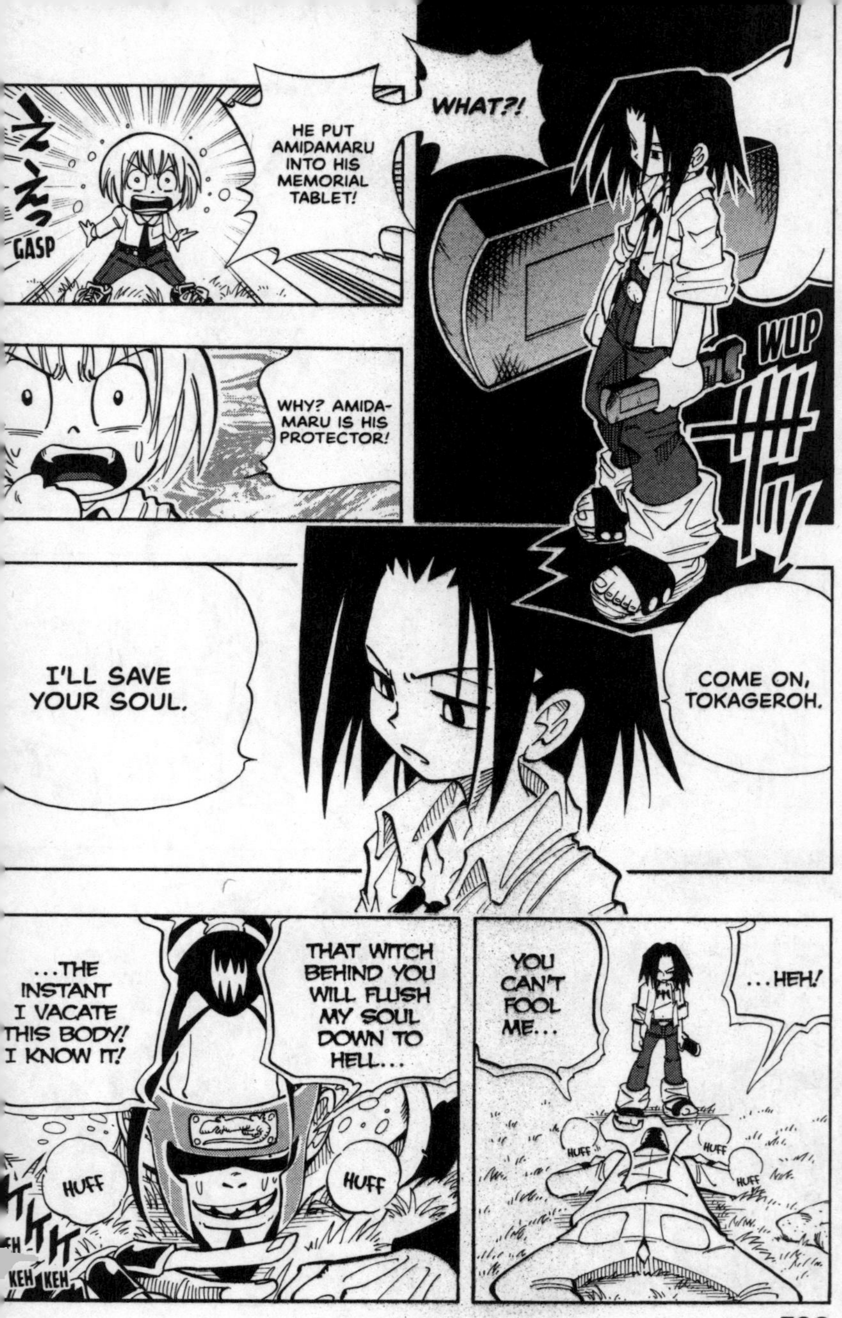
WHAT?!
WUP
HE PUT AMIDAMARU INTO HIS MEMORIAL TABLET!
ええっ
GASP
WHY? AMIDAMARU IS HIS PROTECTOR!
COME ON, TOKAGEROH.
I'LL SAVE YOUR SOUL.
...HEH!
YOU CAN'T FOOL ME...
HUFF
HUFF
HUFF
THAT WITCH BEHIND YOU WILL FLUSH MY SOUL DOWN TO HELL...
...THE INSTANT I VACATE THIS BODY! I KNOW IT!
HUFF
HUFF
KEH KEH

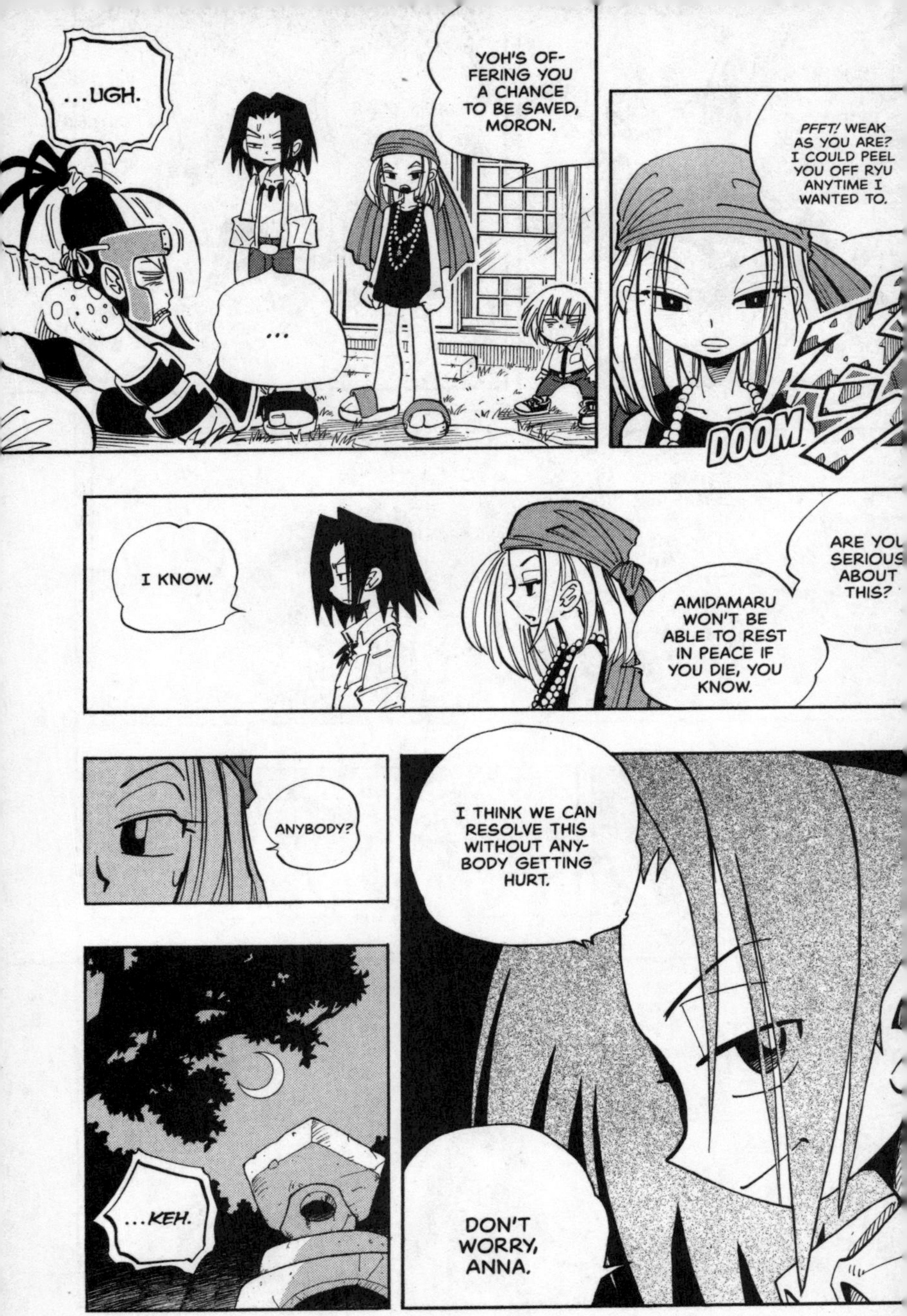
PFFT! WEAK AS YOU ARE? I COULD PEEL YOU OFF RYU ANYTIME I WANTED TO.
DOOM
YOH'S OF-FERING YOU A CHANCE TO BE SAVED, MORON.
...UGH.
...
ARE YOU SERIOUS ABOUT THIS?
AMIDAMARU WON'T BE ABLE TO REST IN PEACE IF YOU DIE, YOU KNOW.
I KNOW.
I THINK WE CAN RESOLVE THIS WITHOUT ANY-BODY GETTING HURT.
DON'T WORRY, ANNA.
ANYBODY?
...KEH.

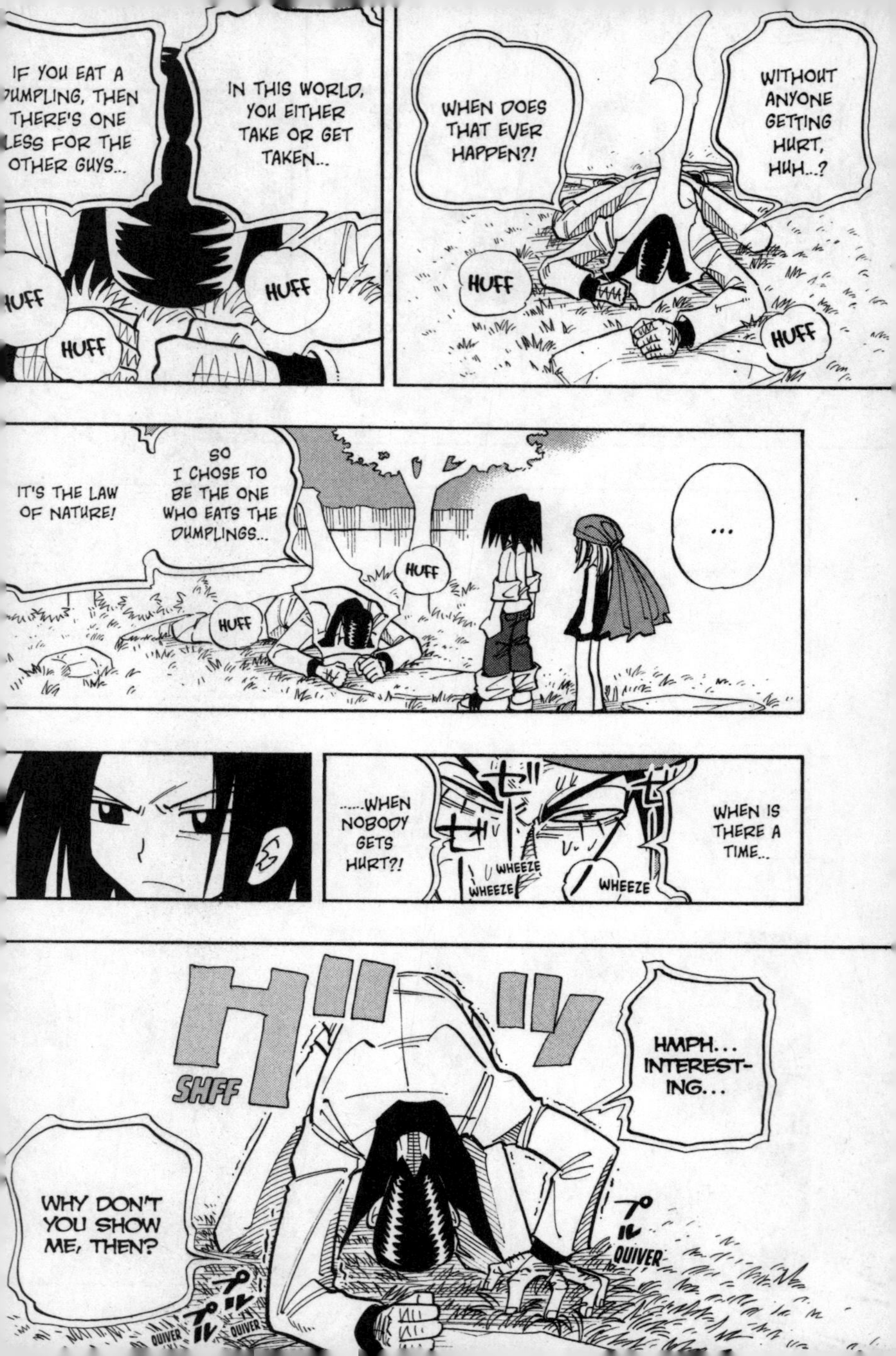

WITHOUT ANYONE GETTING HURT, HUH...?
WHEN DOES THAT EVER HAPPEN?!
HUFF
HUFF
IN THIS WORLD, YOU EITHER TAKE OR GET TAKEN...
IF YOU EAT A UMPLING, THEN THERE'S ONE LESS FOR THE OTHER GUYS...
HUFF
HUFF
...
SO I CHOSE TO BE THE ONE WHO EATS THE DUMPLINGS...
IT'S THE LAW OF NATURE!
HUFF
HUFF
WHEN IS THERE A TIME...
......WHEN NOBODY GETS HURT?!
WHEEZE
WHEEZE
WHEEZE
HMPH... INTERESTING...
SHFF
WHY DON'T YOU SHOW ME, THEN?
QUIVER
QUIVER
QUIVER

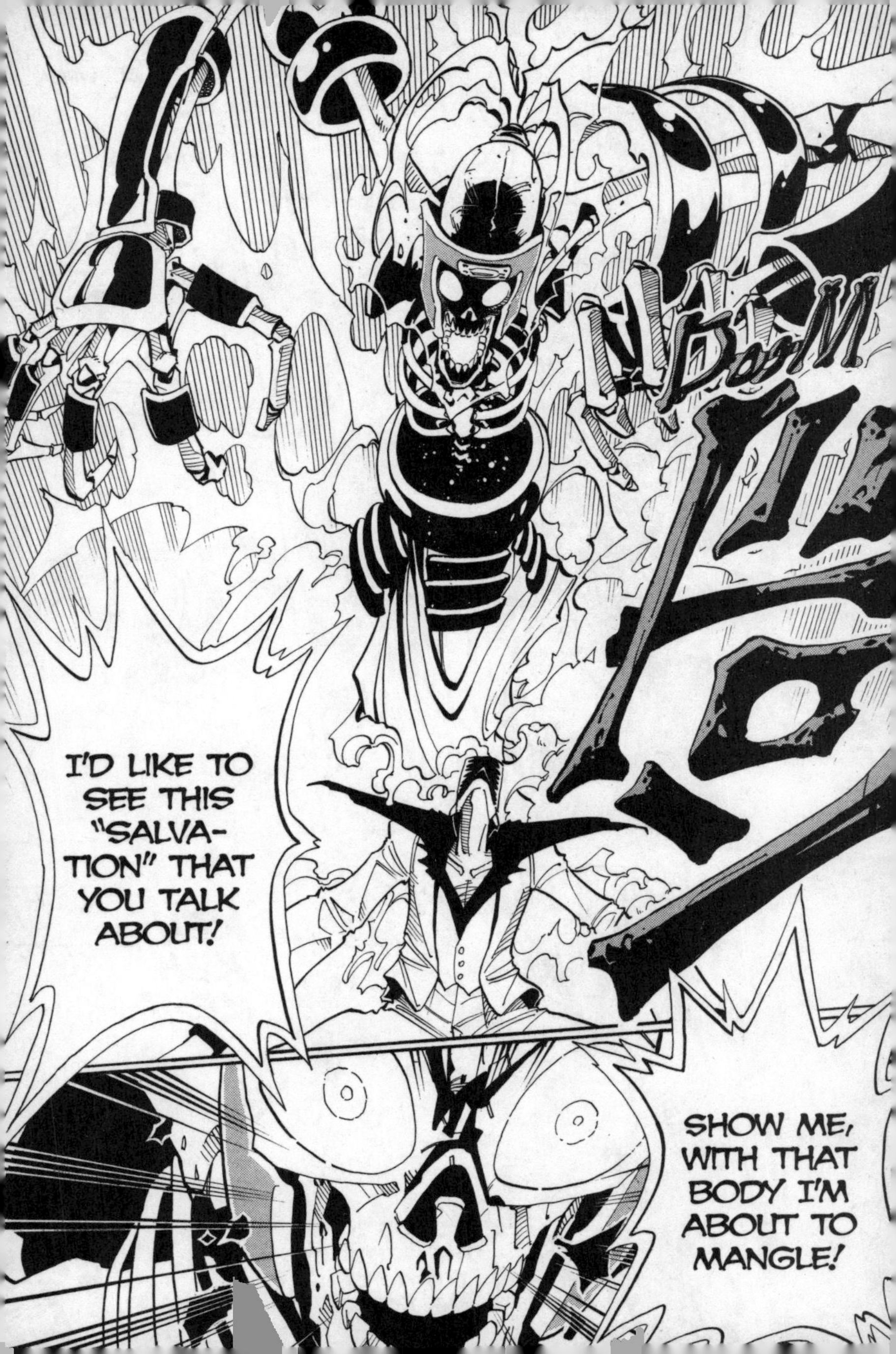
I'D LIKE TO SEE THIS "SALVATION" THAT YOU TALK ABOUT!
SHOW ME, WITH THAT BODY I'M ABOUT TO MANGLE!

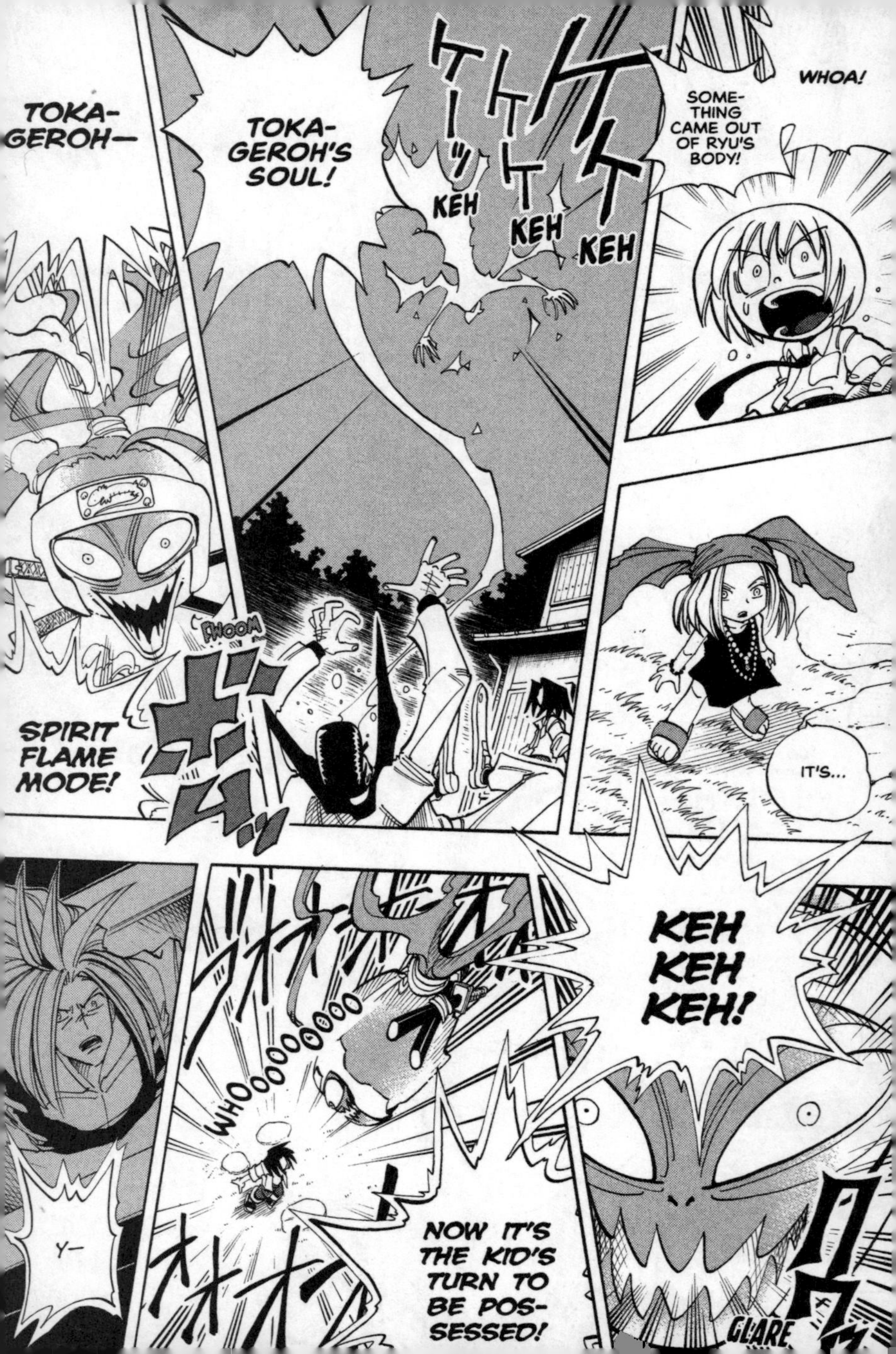
WHOA!
SOMETHING CAME OUT OF RYU'S BODY!
IT'S...
TOKA-GEROH'S SOUL!
KEH
KEH
KEH
TOKA-GEROH—
FWOOM
SPIRIT FLAME MODE!
KEH KEH KEH!
NOW IT'S THE KID'S TURN TO BE POSSESSED!
GLARE
WHOOOOOOOOO
Y—

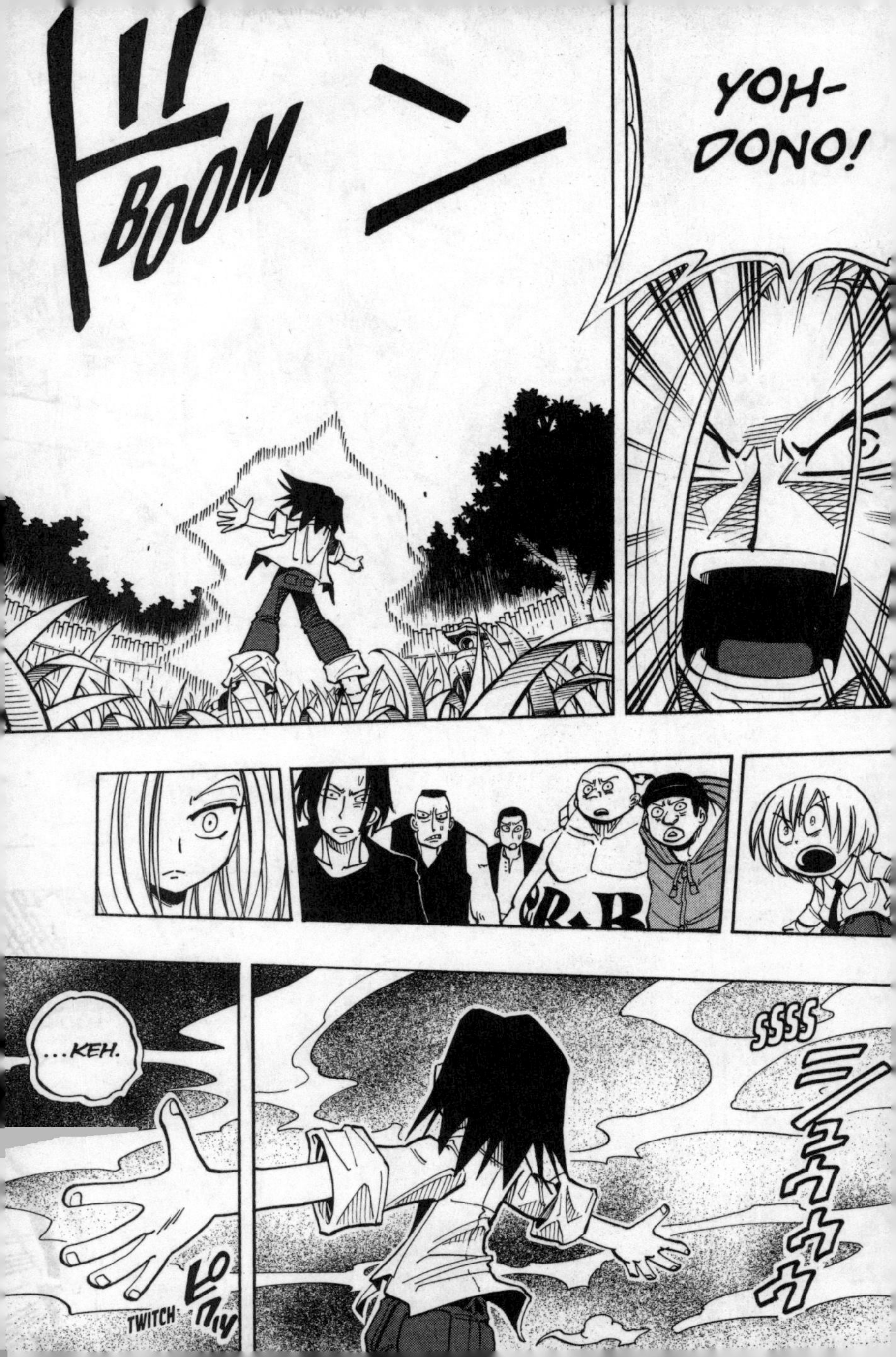
YOH-DONO!
BOOM
SSSS
...KEH.
TWITCH

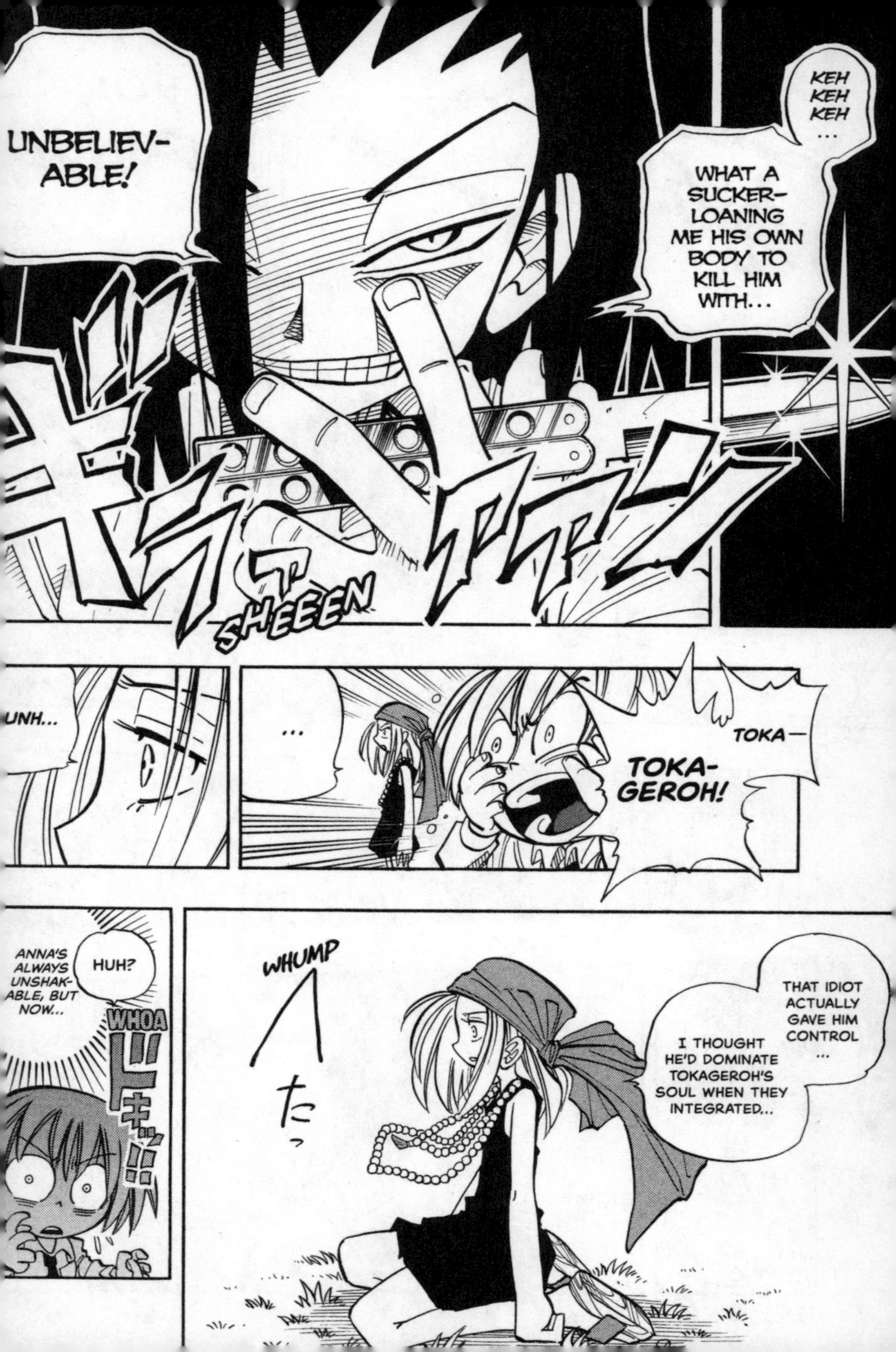
KEH KEH KEH ...
WHAT A SUCKER— LOANING ME HIS OWN BODY TO KILL HIM WITH...
UNBELIEV-ABLE!
SHEEEN
TOKA—
TOKA-GEROH!
...
UNH...
THAT IDIOT ACTUALLY GAVE HIM CONTROL ...
I THOUGHT HE'D DOMINATE TOKAGEROH'S SOUL WHEN THEY INTEGRATED...
WHUMP
HUH?
ANNA'S ALWAYS UNSHAK-ABLE, BUT NOW...
WHOA

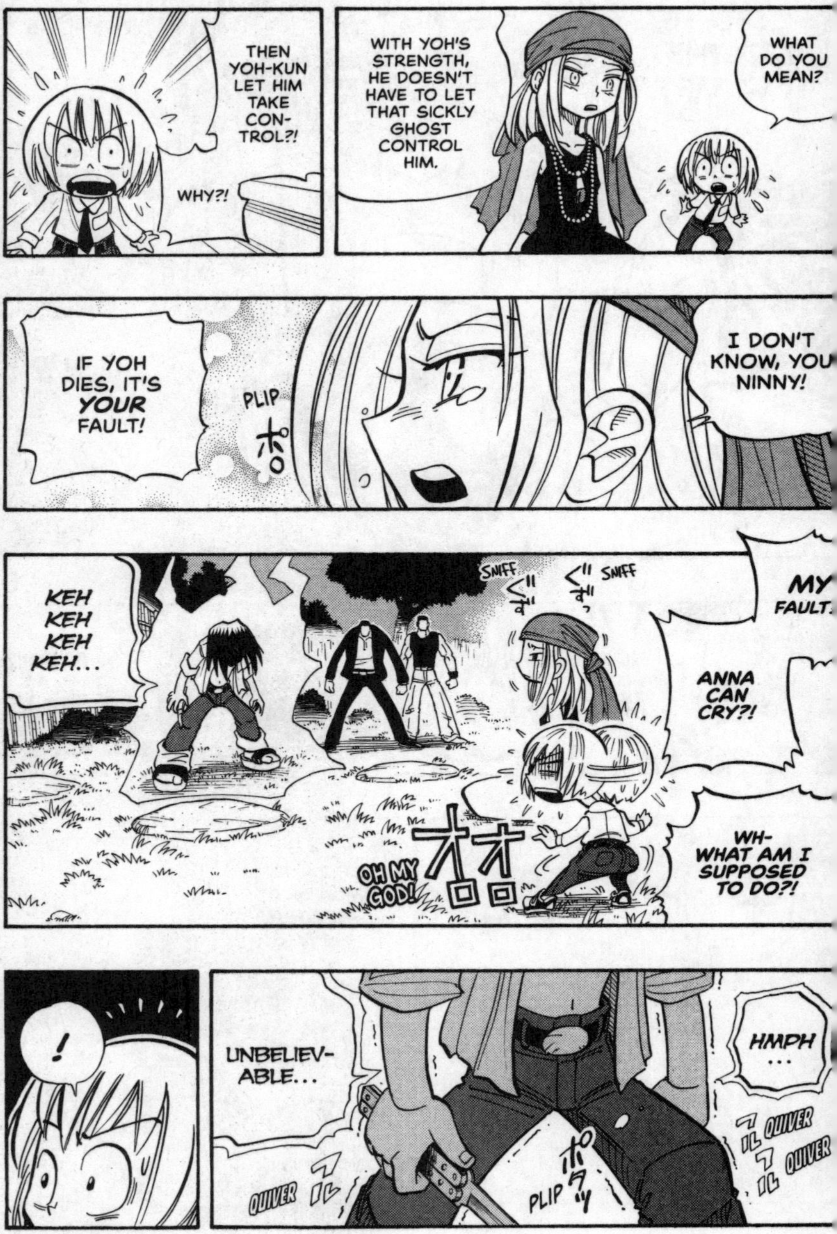
WHAT DO YOU MEAN?
WITH YOH'S STRENGTH, HE DOESN'T HAVE TO LET THAT SICKLY GHOST CONTROL HIM.
THEN YOH-KUN LET HIM TAKE CON-TROL?!
WHY?!
I DON'T KNOW, YOU NINNY!
ポ
PLIP
IF YOH DIES, IT'S *YOUR* FAULT!
MY FAULT...
ぐず SNIFF
ぐず SNIFF
ANNA CAN CRY?!
WH- WHAT AM I SUPPOSED TO DO?!
OH MY GOD!
KEH KEH KEH KEH...
HMPH...
フル QUIVER
フル QUIVER
ポタッ
PLIP
UNBELIEV-ABLE...
フル
QUIVER
!

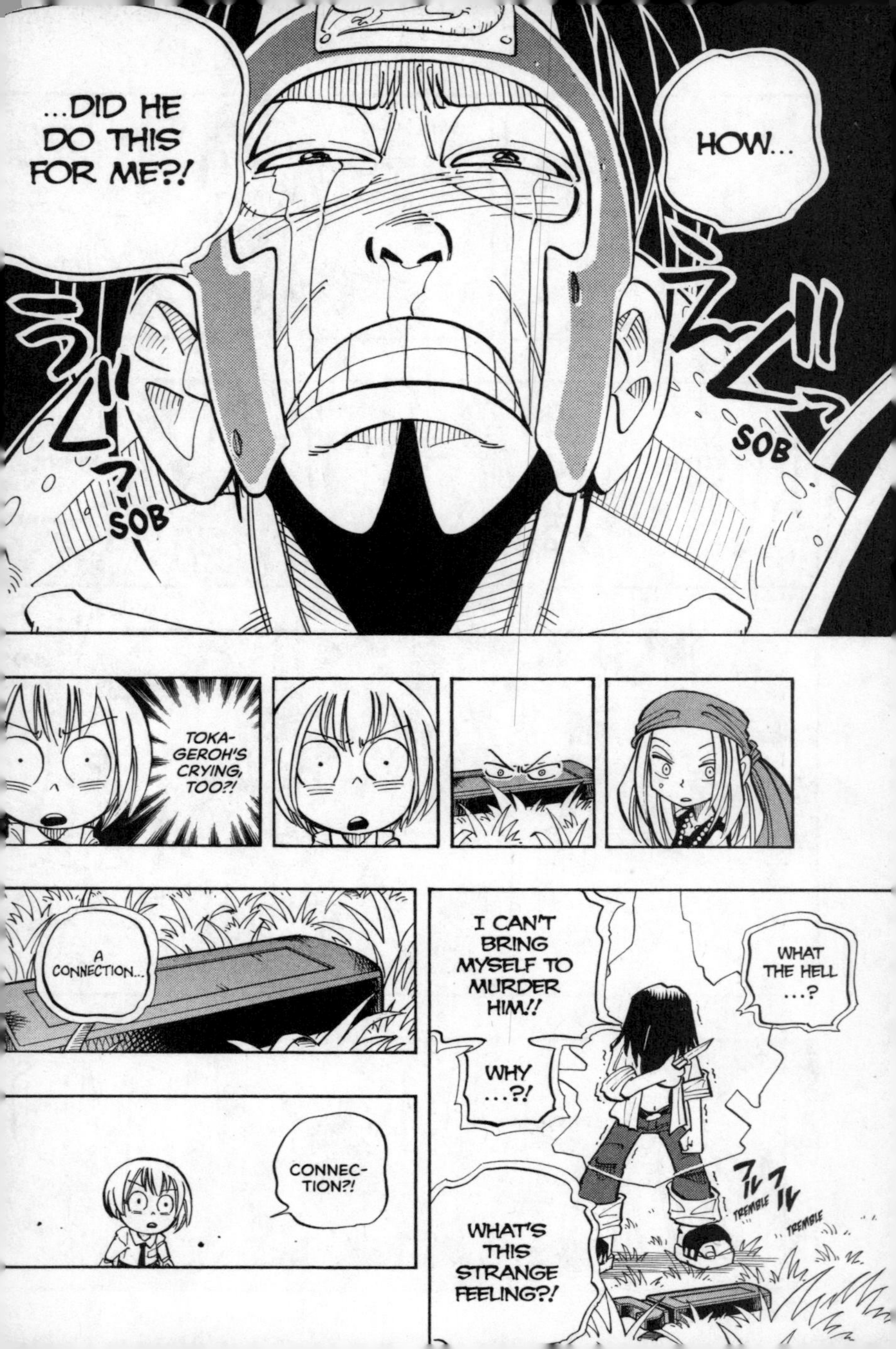
HOW...
...DID HE DO THIS FOR ME?!
SOB
SOB
TOKA-GEROH'S CRYING, TOO?!
WHAT THE HELL ...?
I CAN'T BRING MYSELF TO MURDER HIM!!
WHY ...?!
WHAT'S THIS STRANGE FEELING?!
TREMBLE
TREMBLE
A CONNECTION...
CONNECTION?!

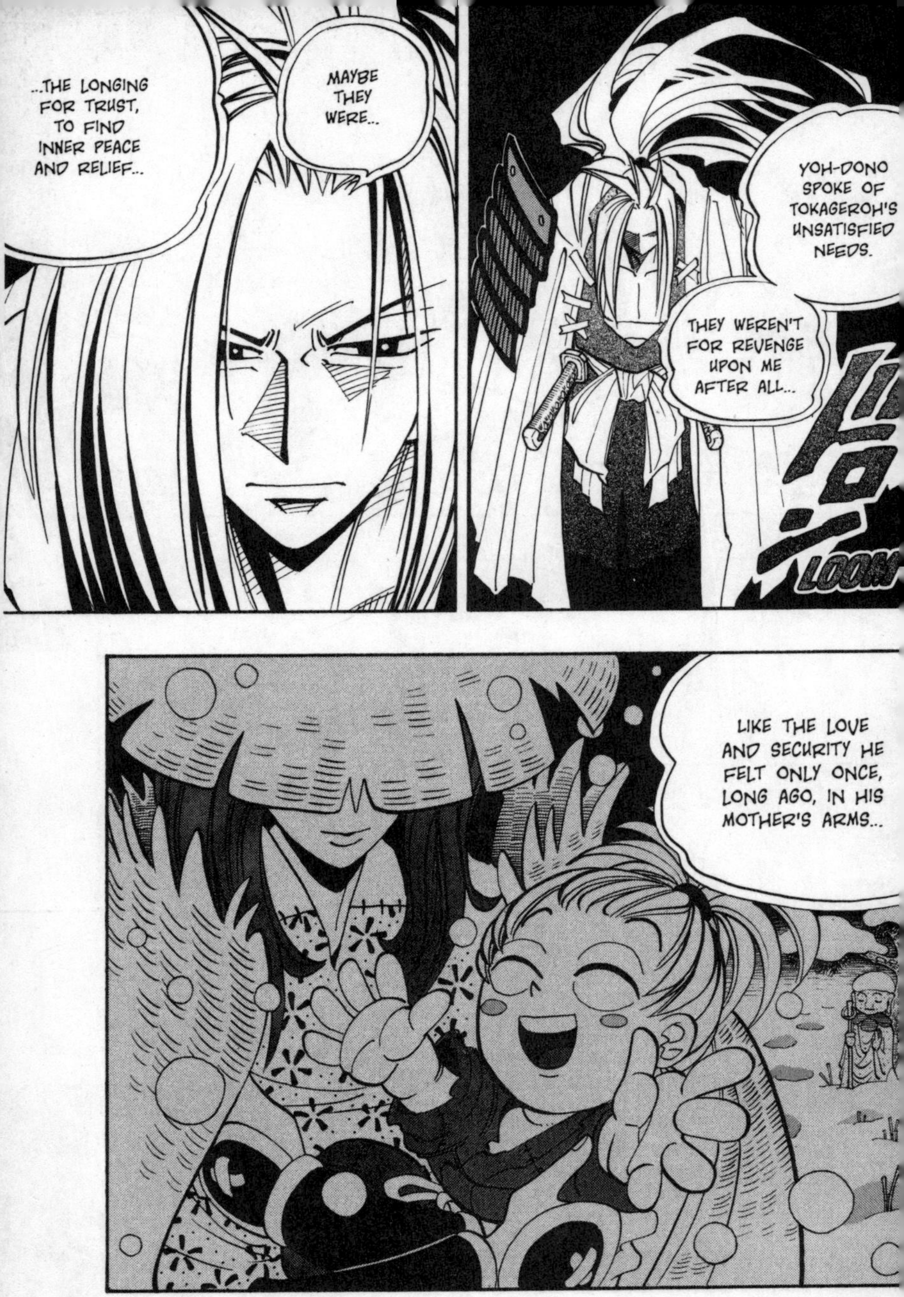
YOH-DONO SPOKE OF TOKAGEROH'S UNSATISFIED NEEDS.
THEY WEREN'T FOR REVENGE UPON ME AFTER ALL...
LOOM
MAYBE THEY WERE...
...THE LONGING FOR TRUST, TO FIND INNER PEACE AND RELIEF...
LIKE THE LOVE AND SECURITY HE FELT ONLY ONCE, LONG AGO, IN HIS MOTHER'S ARMS...

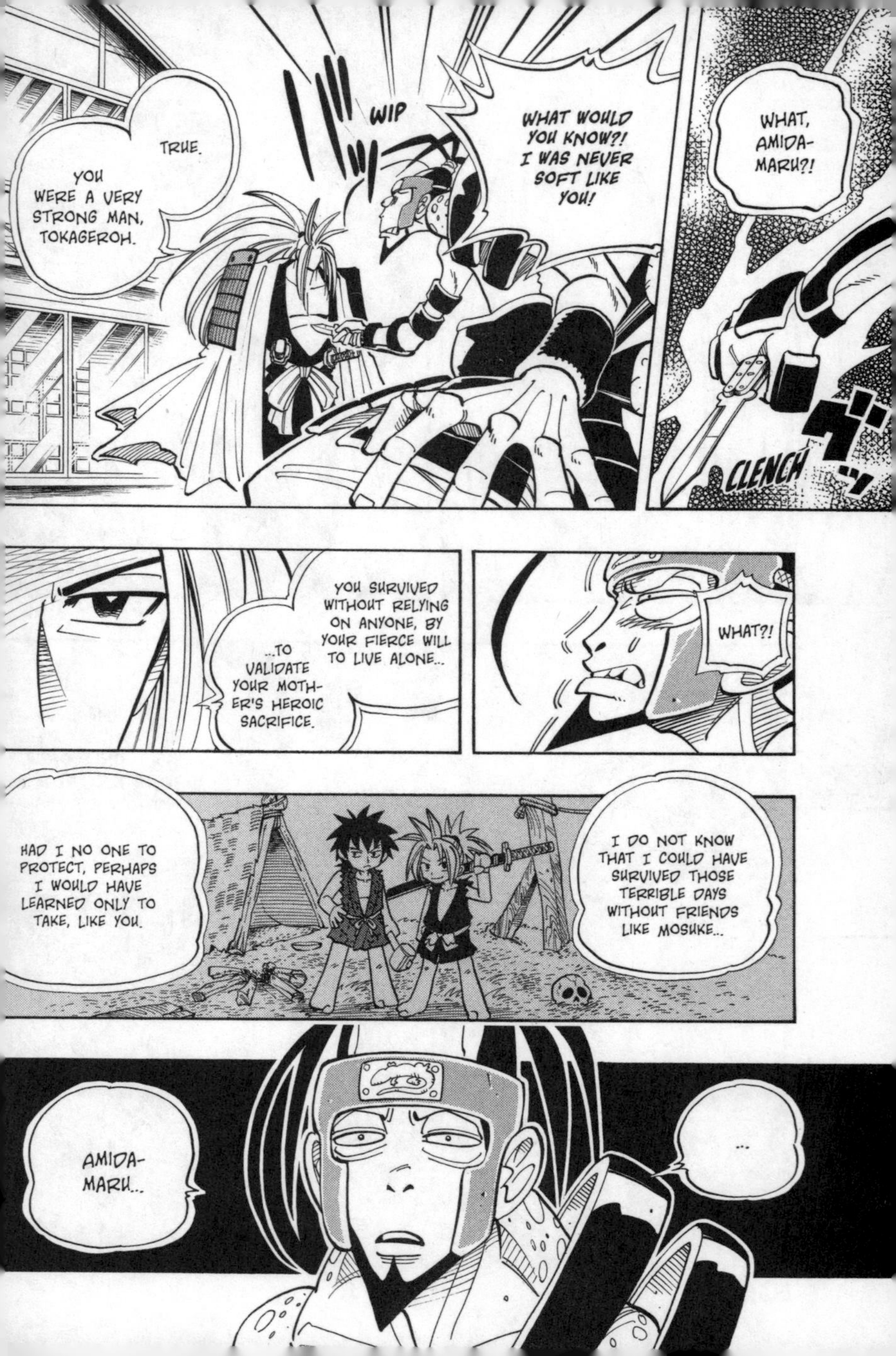

WHAT, AMIDA-MARU?!
CLENCH
WHAT WOULD YOU KNOW?! I WAS NEVER SOFT LIKE YOU!
WIP
TRUE.
YOU WERE A VERY STRONG MAN, TOKAGEROH.
WHAT?!
YOU SURVIVED WITHOUT RELYING ON ANYONE, BY YOUR FIERCE WILL TO LIVE ALONE...
...TO VALIDATE YOUR MOTHER'S HEROIC SACRIFICE.
I DO NOT KNOW THAT I COULD HAVE SURVIVED THOSE TERRIBLE DAYS WITHOUT FRIENDS LIKE MOSUKE...
HAD I NO ONE TO PROTECT, PERHAPS I WOULD HAVE LEARNED ONLY TO TAKE, LIKE YOU.
...
AMIDA-MARU...

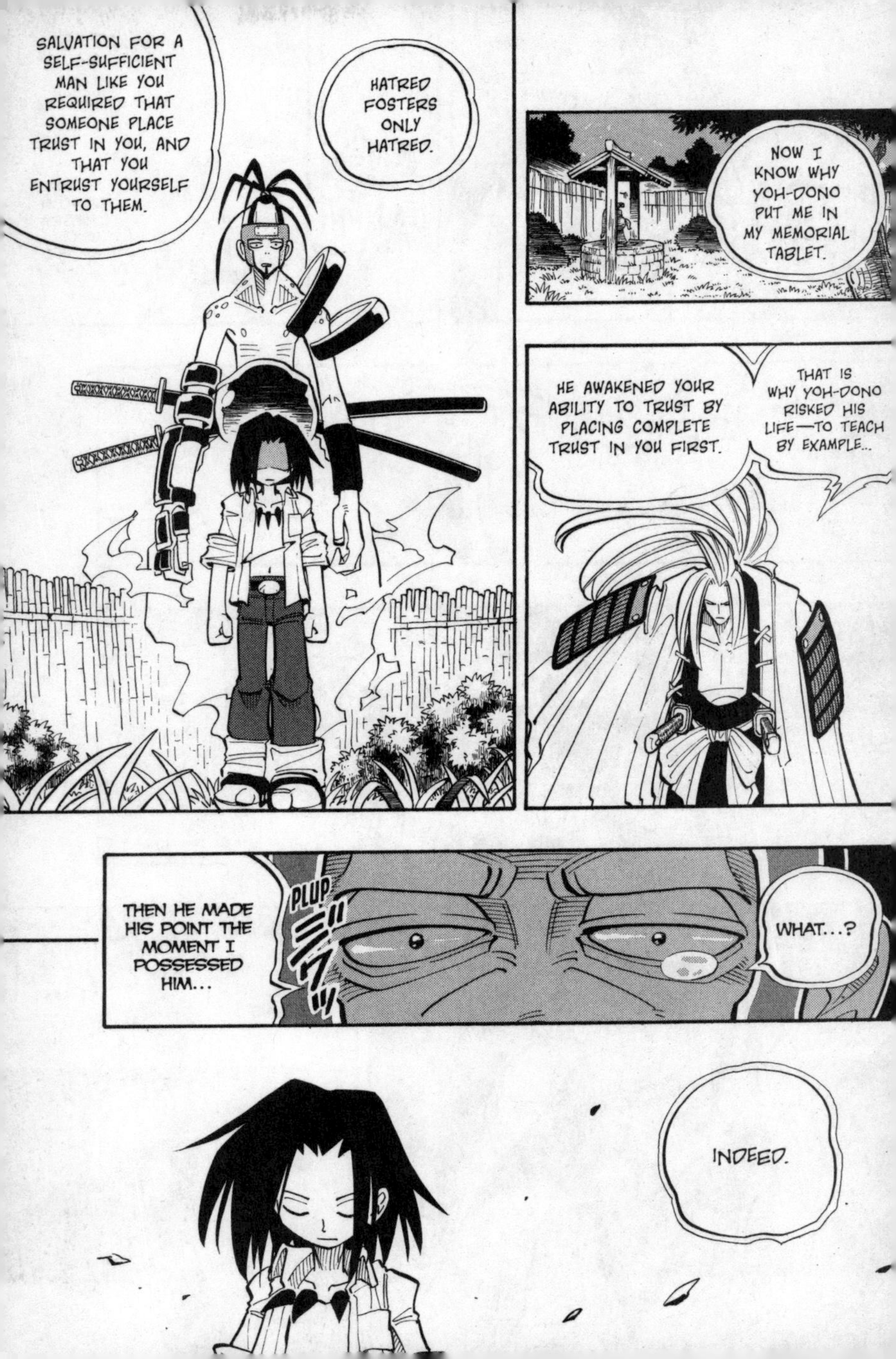
NOW I KNOW WHY YOH-DONO PUT ME IN MY MEMORIAL TABLET.
THAT IS WHY YOH-DONO RISKED HIS LIFE—TO TEACH BY EXAMPLE...
HE AWAKENED YOUR ABILITY TO TRUST BY PLACING COMPLETE TRUST IN YOU FIRST.
HATRED FOSTERS ONLY HATRED.
SALVATION FOR A SELF-SUFFICIENT MAN LIKE YOU REQUIRED THAT SOMEONE PLACE TRUST IN YOU, AND THAT YOU ENTRUST YOURSELF TO THEM.
WHAT...?
PLUP
THEN HE MADE HIS POINT THE MOMENT I POSSESSED HIM...
INDEED.

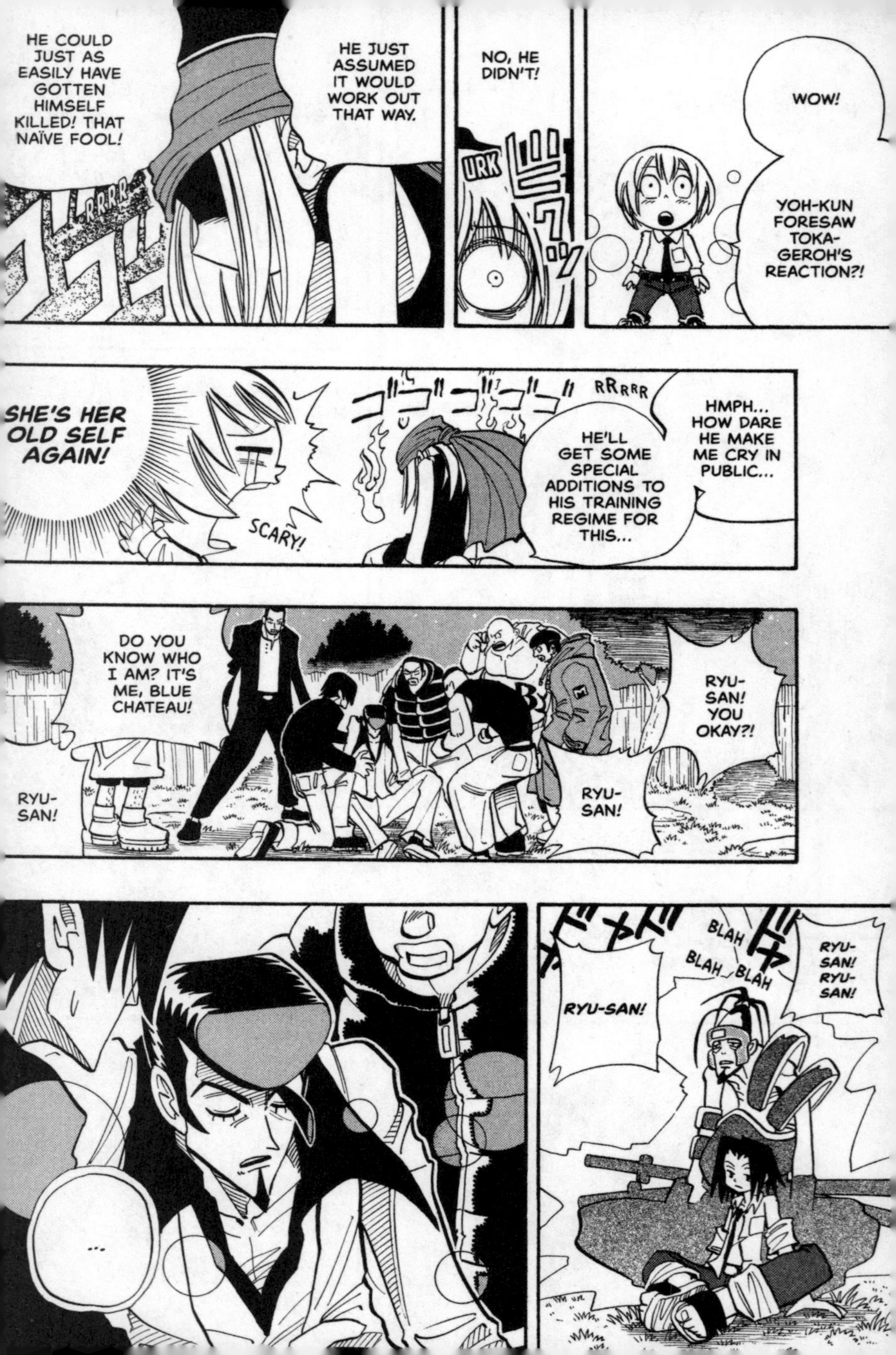
WOW!
YOH-KUN FORESAW TOKA-GEROH'S REACTION?!
NO, HE DIDN'T!
URK
HE JUST ASSUMED IT WOULD WORK OUT THAT WAY.
HE COULD JUST AS EASILY HAVE GOTTEN HIMSELF KILLED! THAT NAÏVE FOOL!
RRRR
HMPH... HOW DARE HE MAKE ME CRY IN PUBLIC...
RRRRR
HE'LL GET SOME SPECIAL ADDITIONS TO HIS TRAINING REGIME FOR THIS...
SCARY!
SHE'S HER OLD SELF AGAIN!
RYU-SAN! YOU OKAY?!
RYU-SAN!
DO YOU KNOW WHO I AM? IT'S ME, BLUE CHATEAU!
RYU-SAN!
RYU-SAN! RYU-SAN!
BLAH BLAH BLAH
RYU-SAN!
...

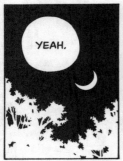

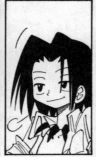

HAVING FRIENDS...
...AIN'T SO BAD, I GUESS.
YEAH.
DUMP-LINGS TASTE BETTER...
...WHEN YOU SHARE THEM WITH FRIENDS.
SLUMP

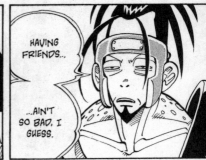

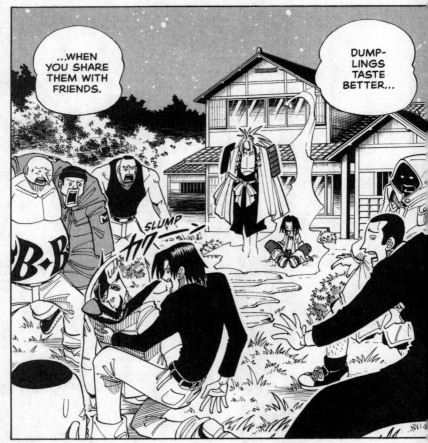

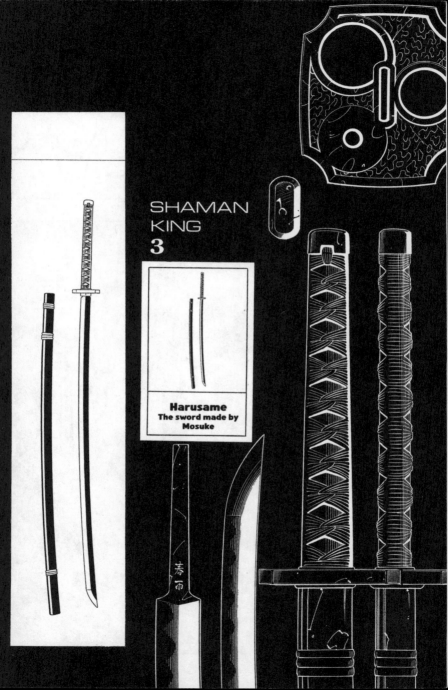

SHAMAN
KING
3

Harusame
The sword made by
Mosuke

Chapter 25: Ryu's Gratitude

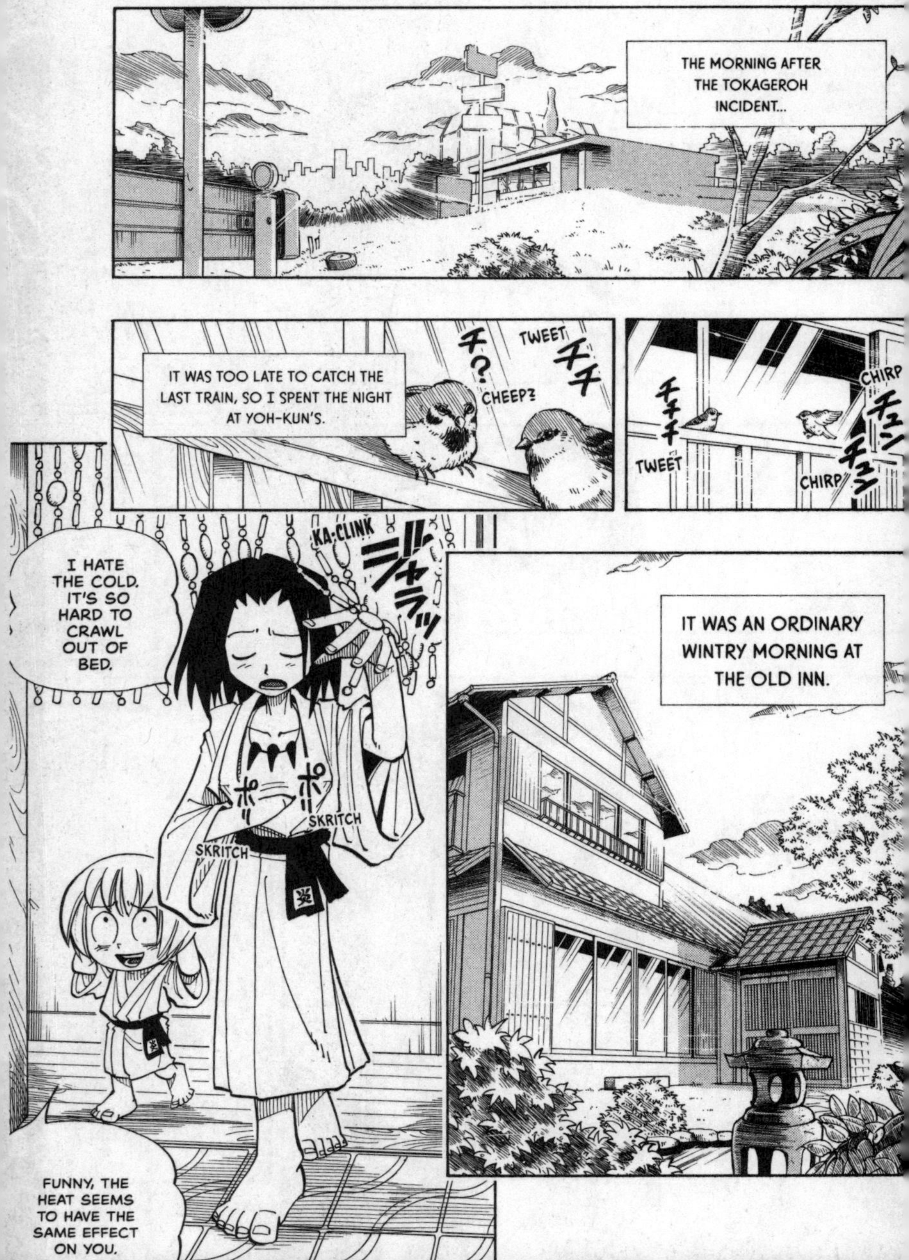

THE MORNING AFTER THE TOKAGEROH INCIDENT...
CHIRP
CHIRP
TWEET
TWEET
CHEEP?
IT WAS TOO LATE TO CATCH THE LAST TRAIN, SO I SPENT THE NIGHT AT YOH-KUN'S.
IT WAS AN ORDINARY WINTRY MORNING AT THE OLD INN.
KA-CLINK
I HATE THE COLD. IT'S SO HARD TO CRAWL OUT OF BED.
SKRITCH
SKRITCH
FUNNY, THE HEAT SEEMS TO HAVE THE SAME EFFECT ON YOU.

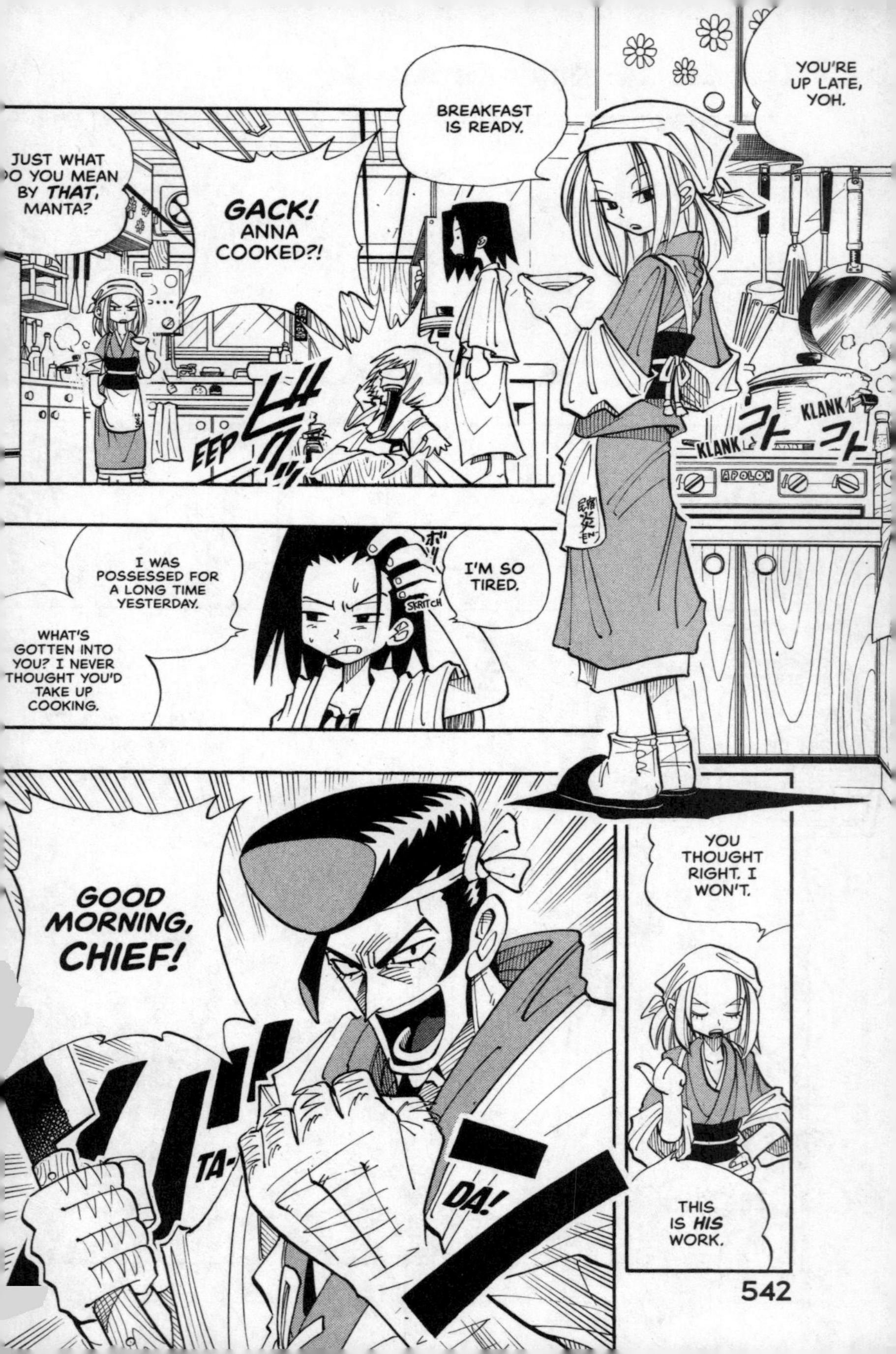

YOU'RE UP LATE, YOH.
BREAKFAST IS READY.
KLANK
KLANK
APOLON
GACK! ANNA COOKED?!
EEP
JUST WHAT O YOU MEAN BY THAT, MANTA?
I'M SO TIRED.
SKRITCH
I WAS POSSESSED FOR A LONG TIME YESTERDAY.
WHAT'S GOTTEN INTO YOU? I NEVER THOUGHT YOU'D TAKE UP COOKING.
YOU THOUGHT RIGHT. I WON'T.
THIS IS HIS WORK.
GOOD MORNING, CHIEF!
TA-
DA!

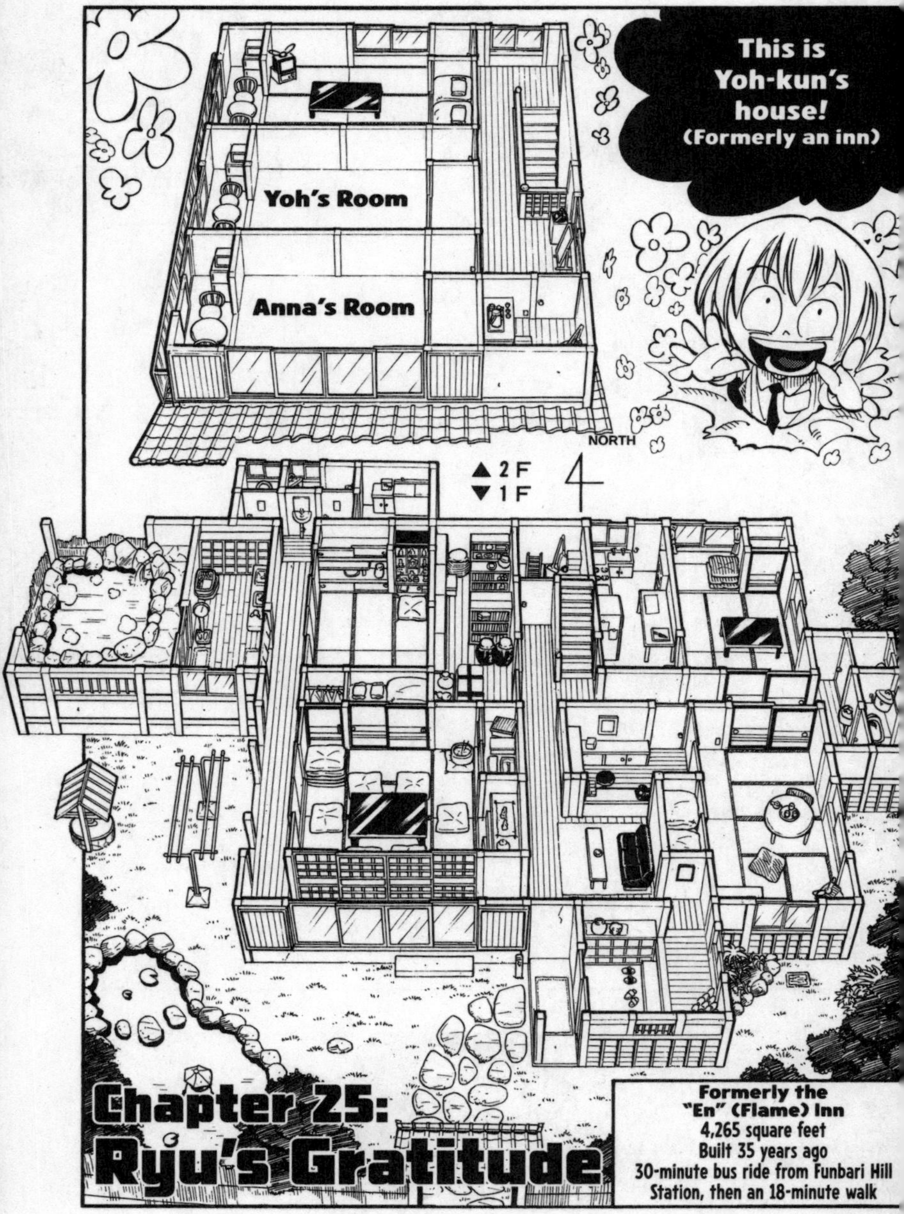
This is Yoh-kun's house! (Formerly an inn)
Yoh's Room
Anna's Room
NORTH
▲2F
▼1F
Chapter 25: Ryu's Gratitude
Formerly the "En" (Flame) Inn
4,265 square feet
Built 35 years ago
30-minute bus ride from Funbari Hill Station, then an 18-minute walk

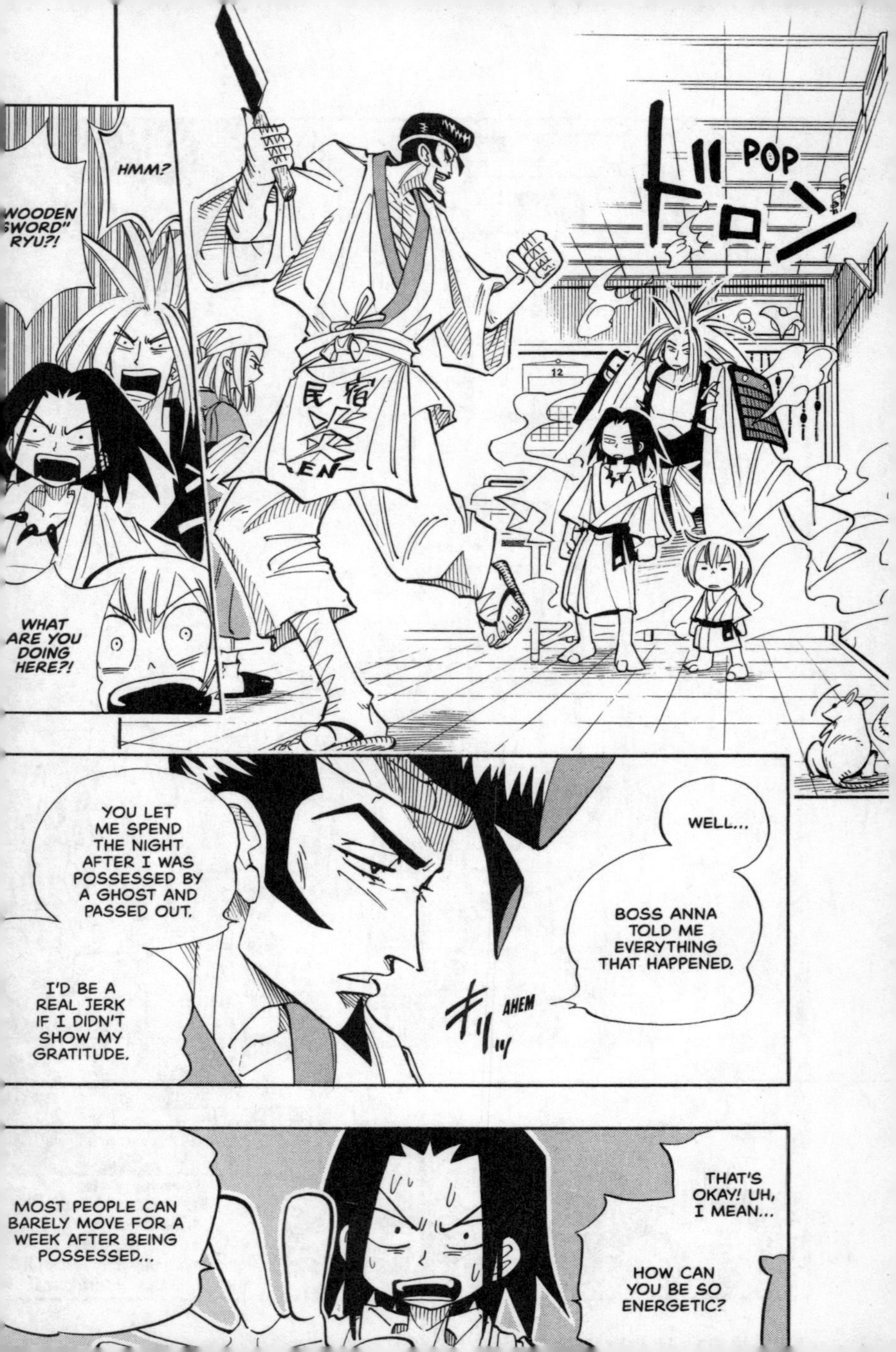
ドロン
POP
HMM?
WOODEN SWORD" RYU?!
WHAT ARE YOU DOING HERE?!
民宿 炎
EN
WELL...
BOSS ANNA TOLD ME EVERYTHING THAT HAPPENED.
キリッ
AHEM
YOU LET ME SPEND THE NIGHT AFTER I WAS POSSESSED BY A GHOST AND PASSED OUT.
I'D BE A REAL JERK IF I DIDN'T SHOW MY GRATITUDE.
THAT'S OKAY! UH, I MEAN...
HOW CAN YOU BE SO ENERGETIC?
MOST PEOPLE CAN BARELY MOVE FOR A WEEK AFTER BEING POSSESSED...

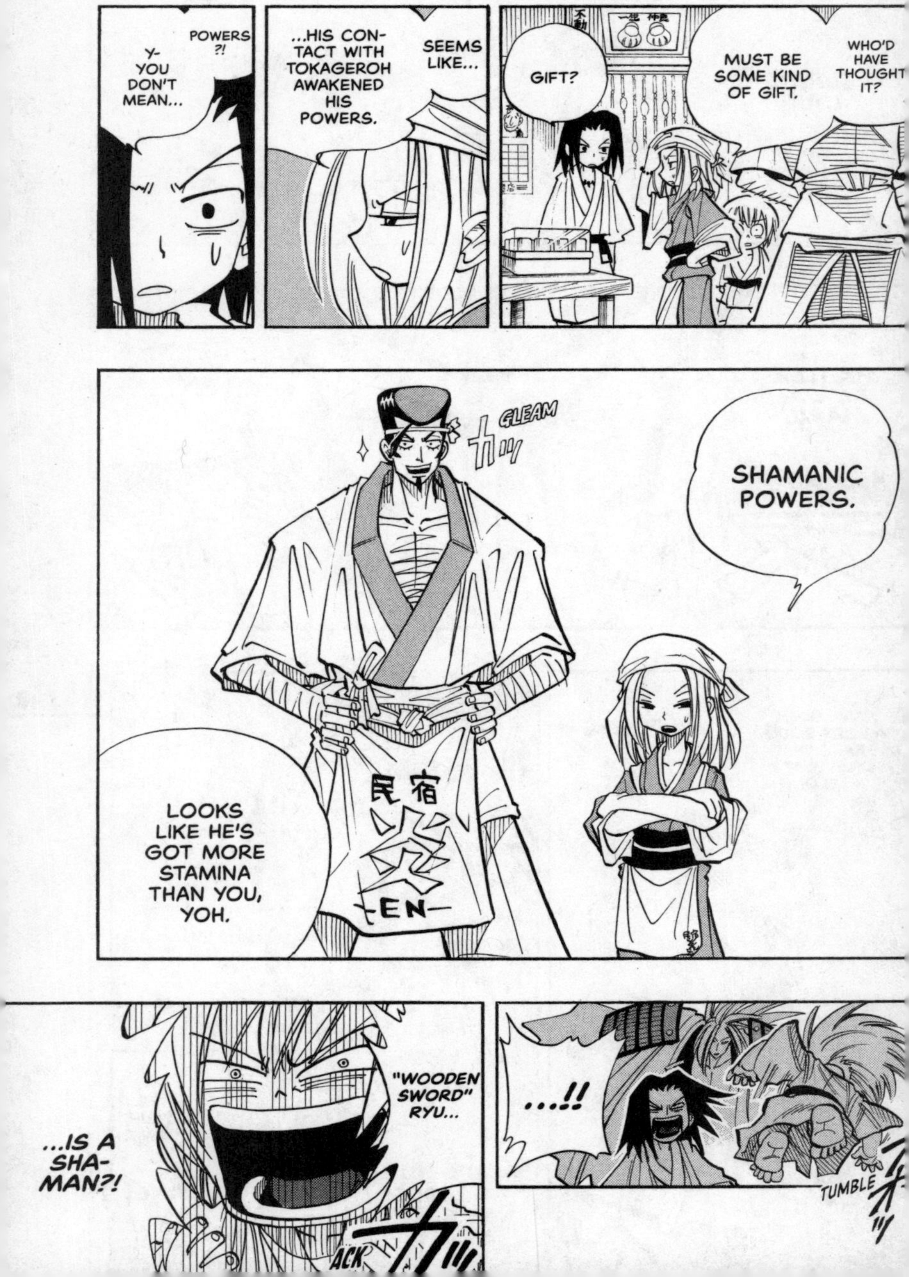
WHO'D HAVE THOUGHT IT?
MUST BE SOME KIND OF GIFT.
GIFT?
SEEMS LIKE...
...HIS CON-TACT WITH TOKAGEROH AWAKENED HIS POWERS.
POWERS ?!
Y-YOU DON'T MEAN...
SHAMANIC POWERS.
GLEAM
民宿
炎
EN
LOOKS LIKE HE'S GOT MORE STAMINA THAN YOU, YOH.
...!!
TUMBLE
"WOODEN SWORD" RYU...
...IS A SHA-MAN?!
ACK

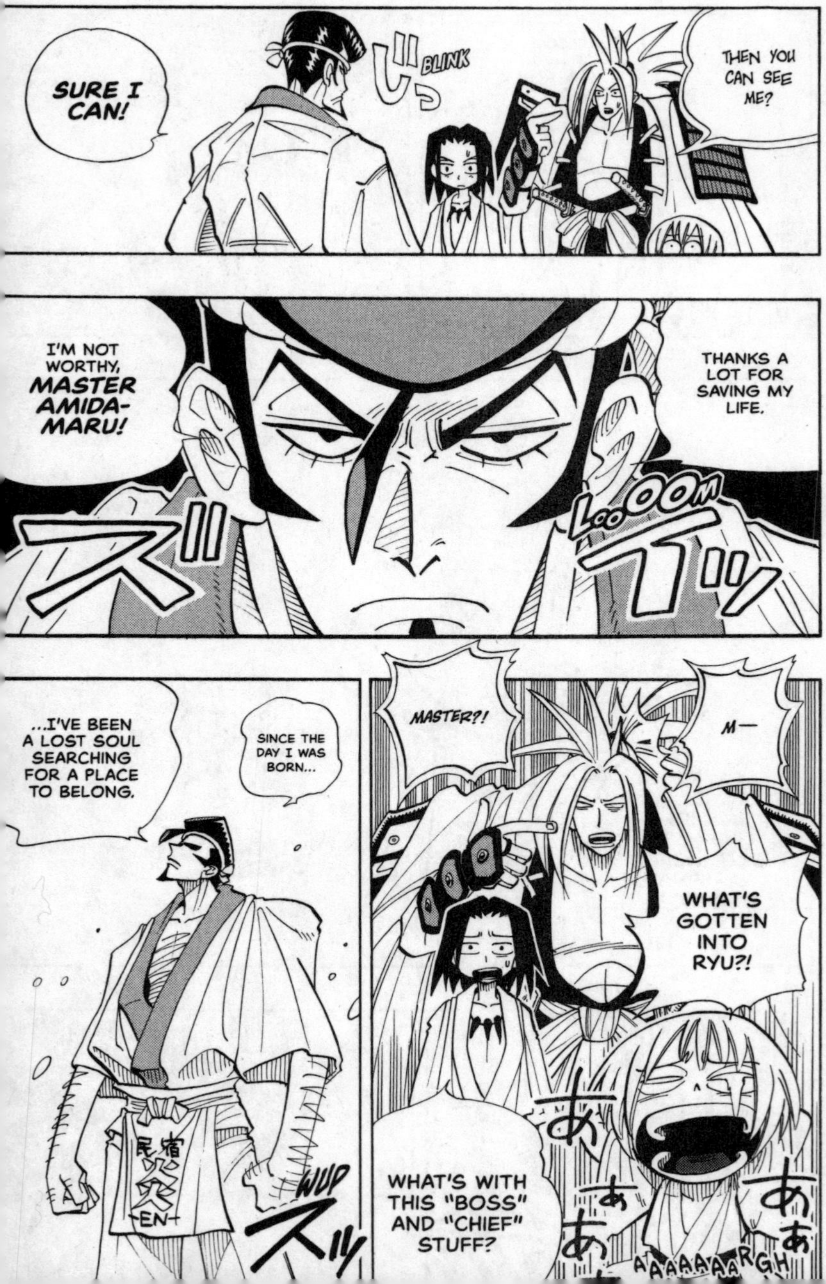
THEN YOU CAN SEE ME?
BLINK
SURE I CAN!
THANKS A LOT FOR SAVING MY LIFE.
LOOOM
I'M NOT WORTHY, MASTER AMIDA-MARU!
M—
MASTER?!
WHAT'S GOTTEN INTO RYU?!
WHAT'S WITH THIS "BOSS" AND "CHIEF" STUFF?
AAAAAAARGH
SINCE THE DAY I WAS BORN...
...I'VE BEEN A LOST SOUL SEARCHING FOR A PLACE TO BELONG.
民宿 炎
-EN-
WUP

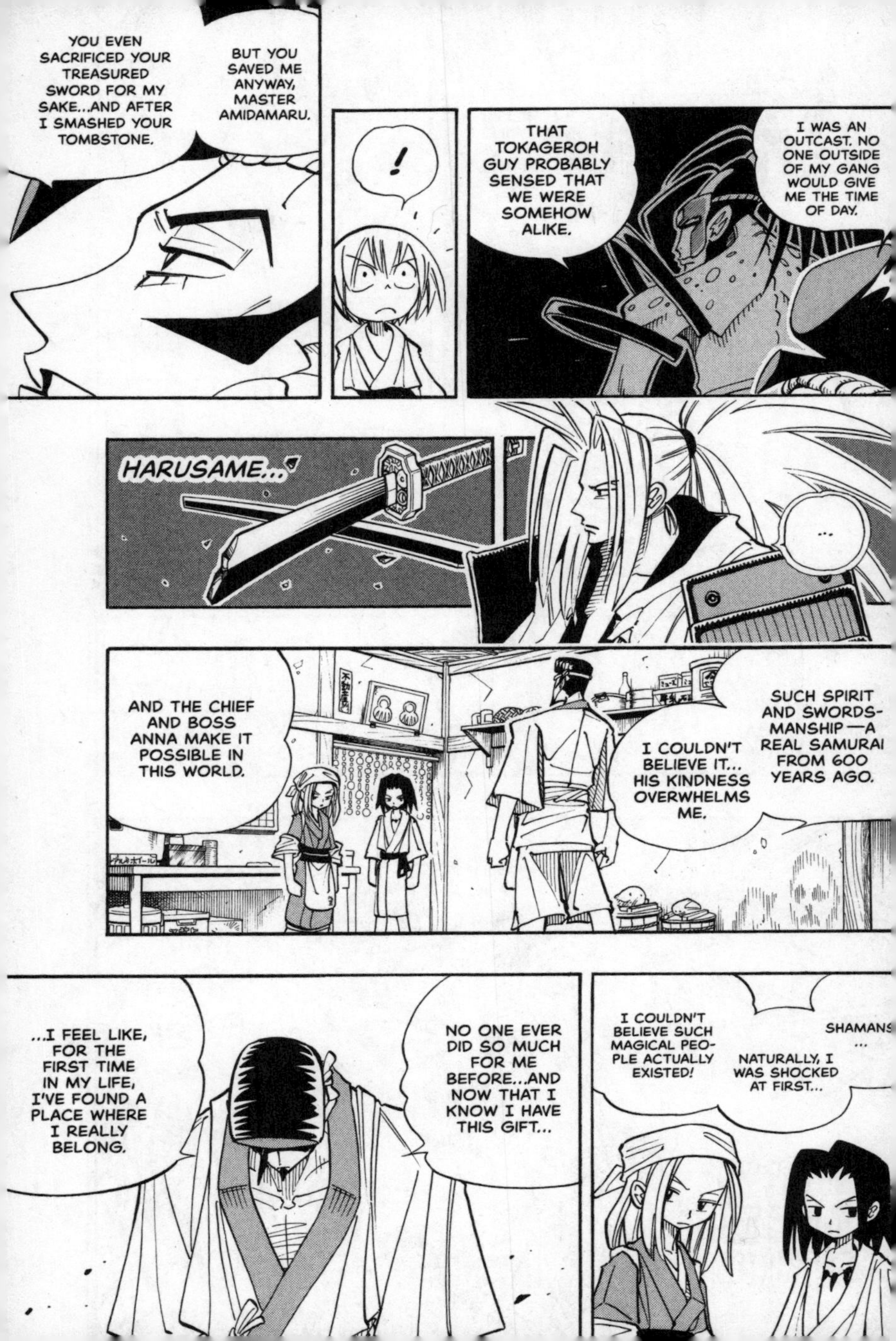
I WAS AN OUTCAST. NO ONE OUTSIDE OF MY GANG WOULD GIVE ME THE TIME OF DAY.
THAT TOKAGEROH GUY PROBABLY SENSED THAT WE WERE SOMEHOW ALIKE.
!
BUT YOU SAVED ME ANYWAY, MASTER AMIDAMARU.
YOU EVEN SACRIFICED YOUR TREASURED SWORD FOR MY SAKE...AND AFTER I SMASHED YOUR TOMBSTONE.
...
HARUSAME...
SUCH SPIRIT AND SWORDSMANSHIP—A REAL SAMURAI FROM 600 YEARS AGO.
I COULDN'T BELIEVE IT... HIS KINDNESS OVERWHELMS ME.
AND THE CHIEF AND BOSS ANNA MAKE IT POSSIBLE IN THIS WORLD.
SHAMANS...
NATURALLY, I WAS SHOCKED AT FIRST...
I COULDN'T BELIEVE SUCH MAGICAL PEOPLE ACTUALLY EXISTED!
NO ONE EVER DID SO MUCH FOR ME BEFORE...AND NOW THAT I KNOW I HAVE THIS GIFT...
...I FEEL LIKE, FOR THE FIRST TIME IN MY LIFE, I'VE FOUND A PLACE WHERE I REALLY BELONG.

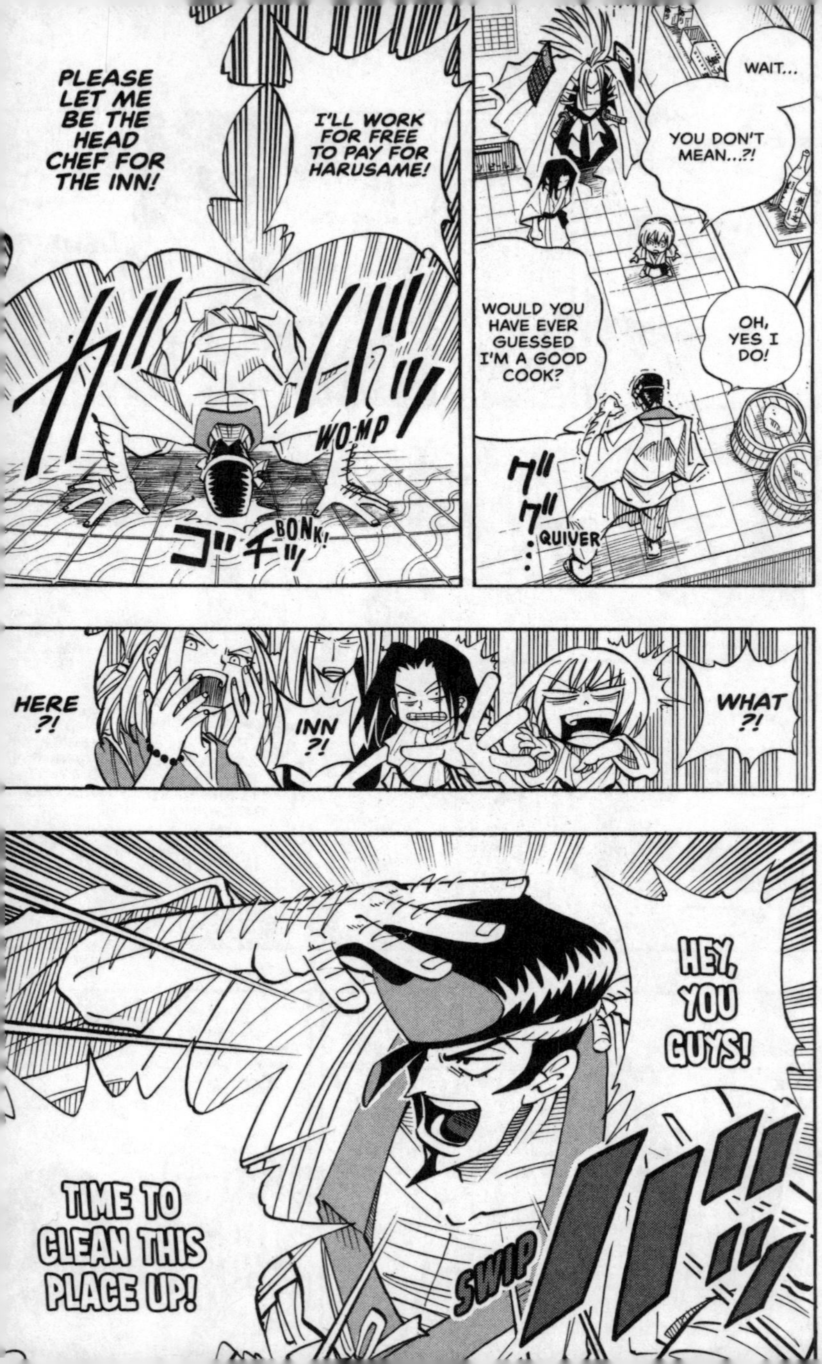
WAIT...
YOU DON'T MEAN...?!
OH, YES I DO!
WOULD YOU HAVE EVER GUESSED I'M A GOOD COOK?
QUIVER
I'LL WORK FOR FREE TO PAY FOR HARUSAME!
PLEASE LET ME BE THE HEAD CHEF FOR THE INN!
WOMP
BONK!
WHAT?!
INN?!
HERE?!
HEY, YOU GUYS!
TIME TO CLEAN THIS PLACE UP!
SWIP

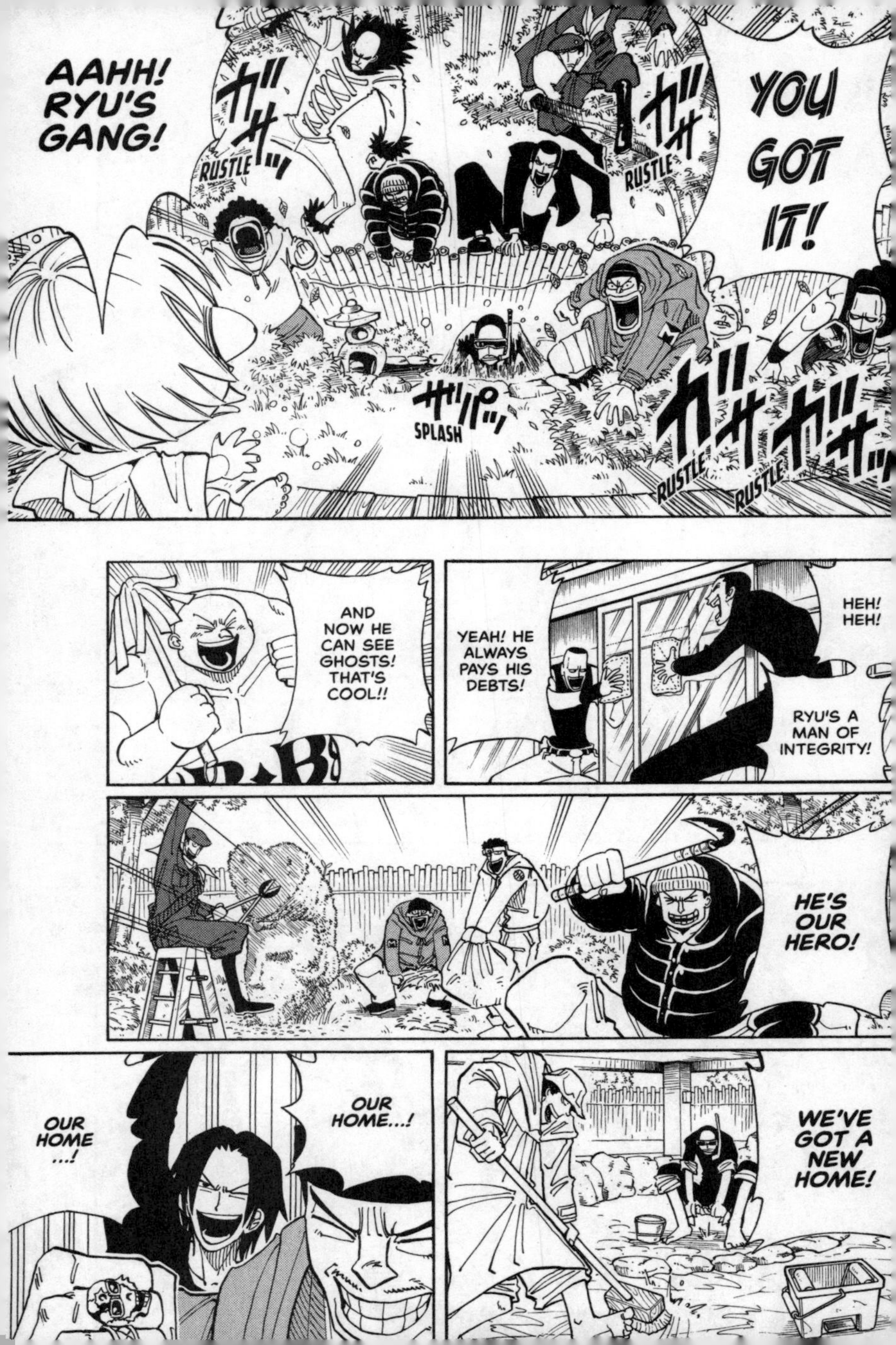
YOU GOT IT!
ガサガサッ
RUSTLE RUSTLE
ガサッ
RUSTLE
ザパッ
SPLASH
ガサッ
RUSTLE
AAHH! RYU'S GANG!
HEH! HEH!
RYU'S A MAN OF INTEGRITY!
YEAH! HE ALWAYS PAYS HIS DEBTS!
AND NOW HE CAN SEE GHOSTS! THAT'S COOL!!
HE'S OUR HERO!
WE'VE GOT A NEW HOME!
OUR HOME...!
OUR HOME ...!

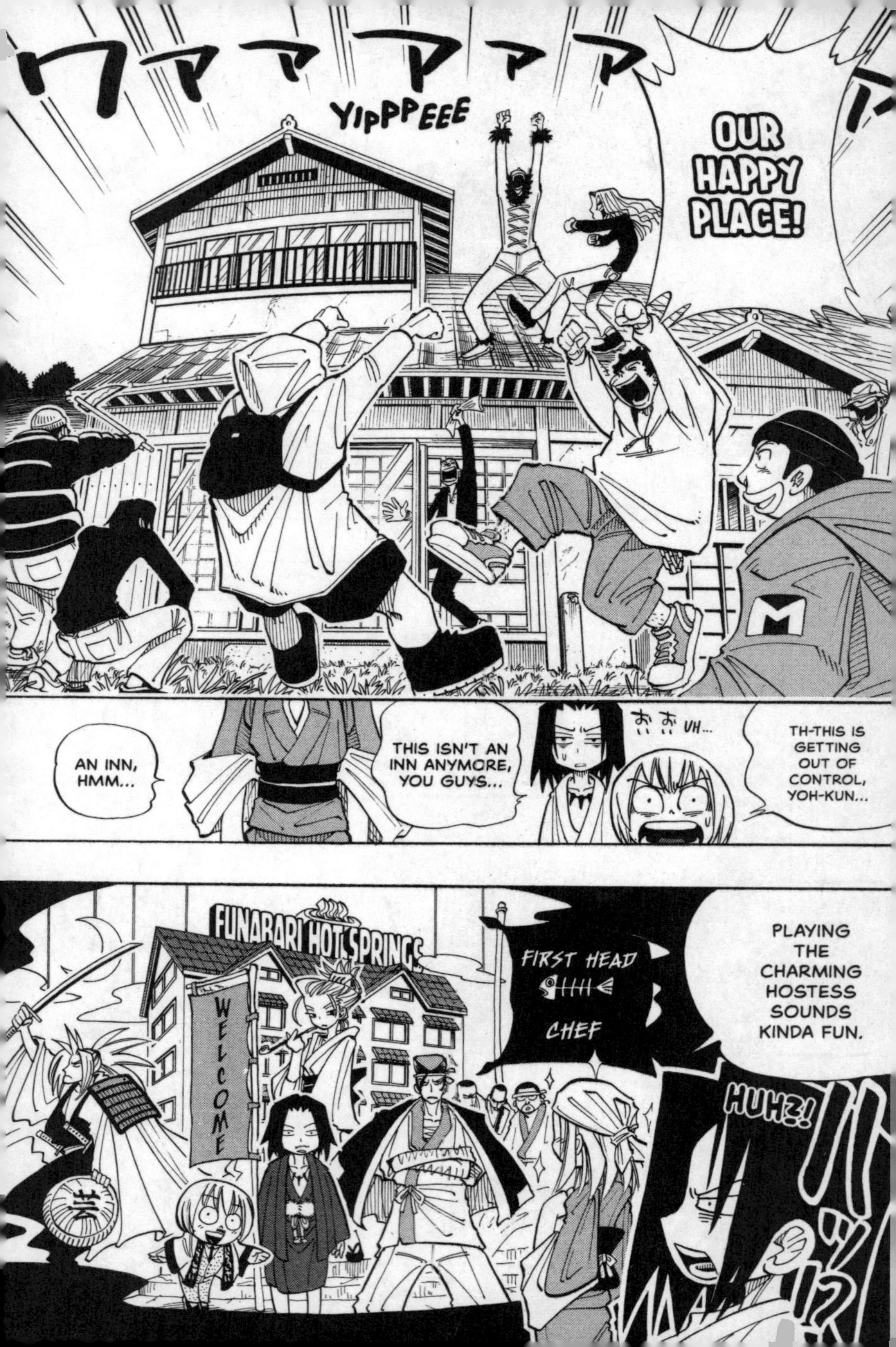
YIPPPEEE
OUR HAPPY PLACE!
TH-THIS IS GETTING OUT OF CONTROL, YOH-KUN...
おお UH...
THIS ISN'T AN INN ANYMORE, YOU GUYS...
AN INN, HMM...
PLAYING THE CHARMING HOSTESS SOUNDS KINDA FUN.
HUH?!
FIRST HEAD CHEF
FUNABARI HOT SPRINGS
WELCOME

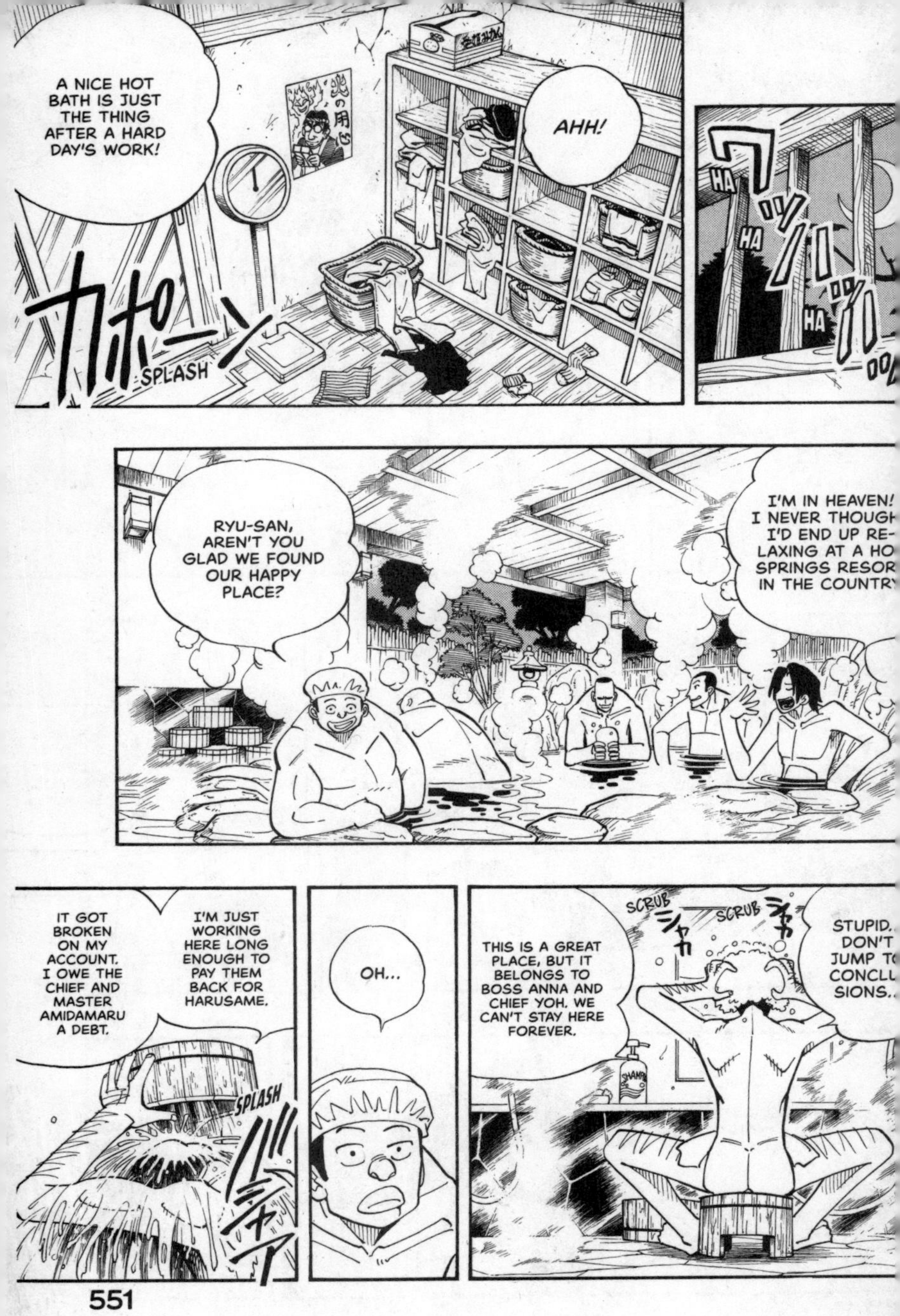
HA HA HA
AHH!
A NICE HOT BATH IS JUST THE THING AFTER A HARD DAY'S WORK!
カポーン
SPLASH
I'M IN HEAVEN! I NEVER THOUGH I'D END UP RE- LAXING AT A HO SPRINGS RESOR IN THE COUNTRY
RYU-SAN, AREN'T YOU GLAD WE FOUND OUR HAPPY PLACE?
STUPID. DON'T JUMP T CONCLU SIONS...
SCRUB
SCRUB
THIS IS A GREAT PLACE, BUT IT BELONGS TO BOSS ANNA AND CHIEF YOH. WE CAN'T STAY HERE FOREVER.
OH...
I'M JUST WORKING HERE LONG ENOUGH TO PAY THEM BACK FOR HARUSAME.
IT GOT BROKEN ON MY ACCOUNT. I OWE THE CHIEF AND MASTER AMIDAMARU A DEBT.
SPLASH

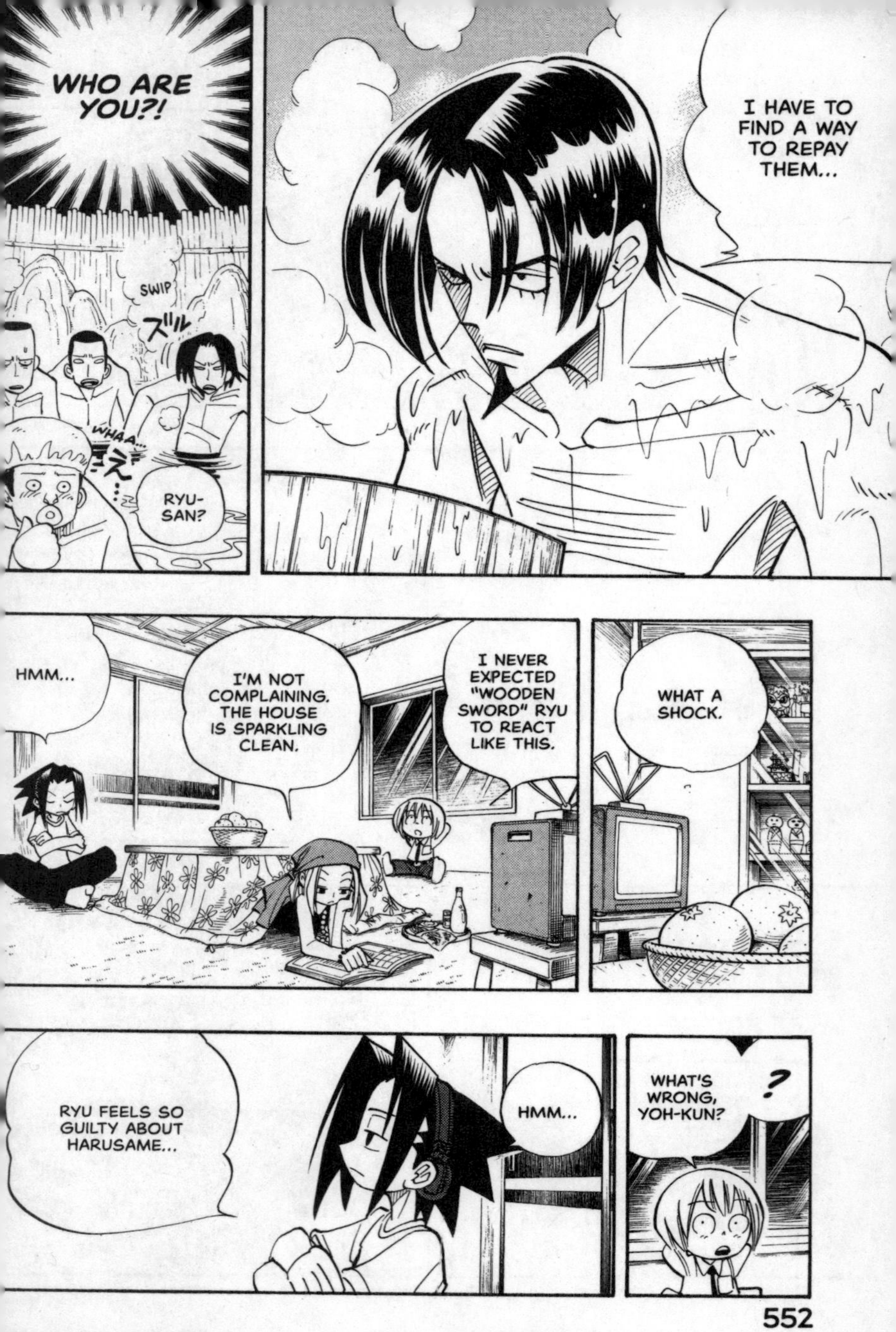
I HAVE TO FIND A WAY TO REPAY THEM...
WHO ARE YOU?!
SWIP
ズル
WHAA...
えぇ
RYU-SAN?
WHAT A SHOCK.
I NEVER EXPECTED "WOODEN SWORD" RYU TO REACT LIKE THIS.
I'M NOT COMPLAINING. THE HOUSE IS SPARKLING CLEAN.
HMM...
WHAT'S WRONG, YOH-KUN?
?
HMM...
RYU FEELS SO GUILTY ABOUT HARUSAME...

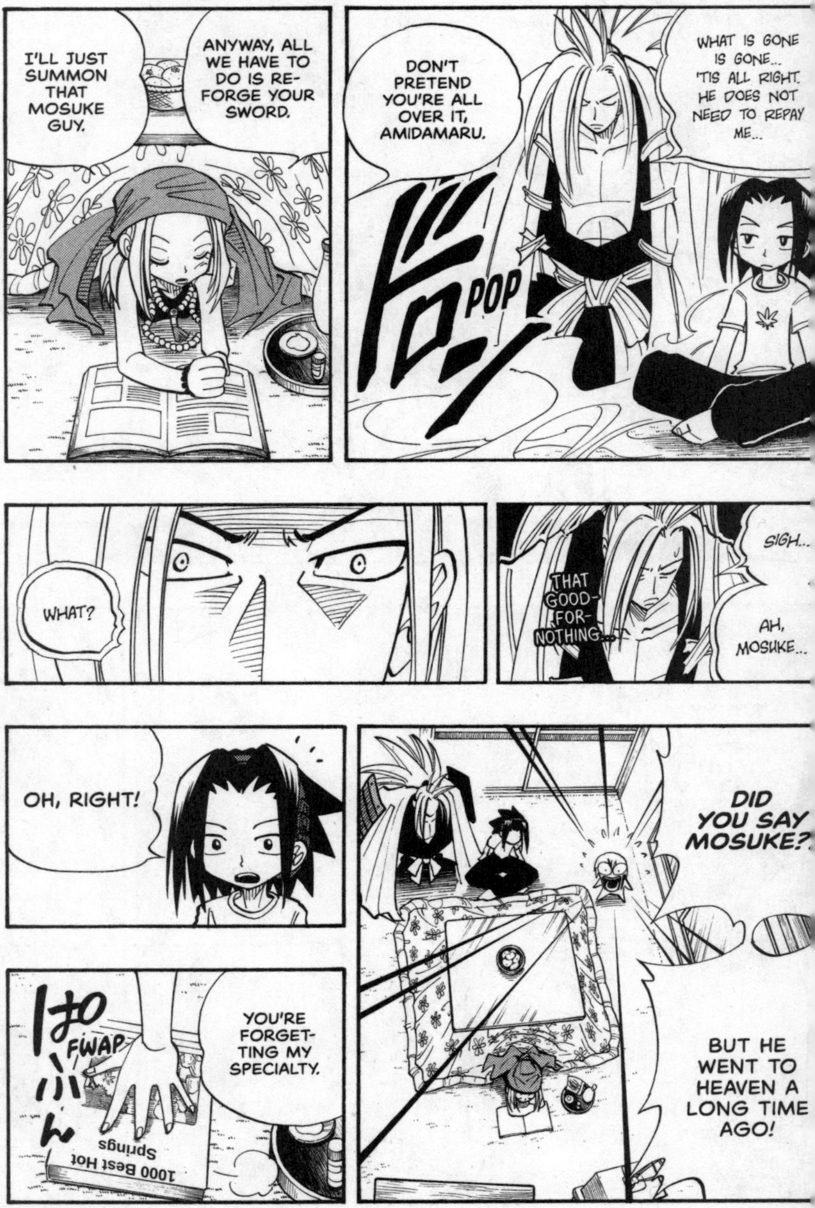
WHAT IS GONE IS GONE... 'TIS ALL RIGHT. HE DOES NOT NEED TO REPAY ME...
DON'T PRETEND YOU'RE ALL OVER IT, AMIDAMARU.
POP
ANYWAY, ALL WE HAVE TO DO IS RE-FORGE YOUR SWORD.
I'LL JUST SUMMON THAT MOSUKE GUY.
SIGH...
AH, MOSUKE...
THAT GOOD-FOR-NOTHING...
WHAT?
DID YOU SAY MOSUKE?!
BUT HE WENT TO HEAVEN A LONG TIME AGO!
OH, RIGHT!
YOU'RE FORGETTING MY SPECIALTY.
FWAP
1000 Best Hot Springs

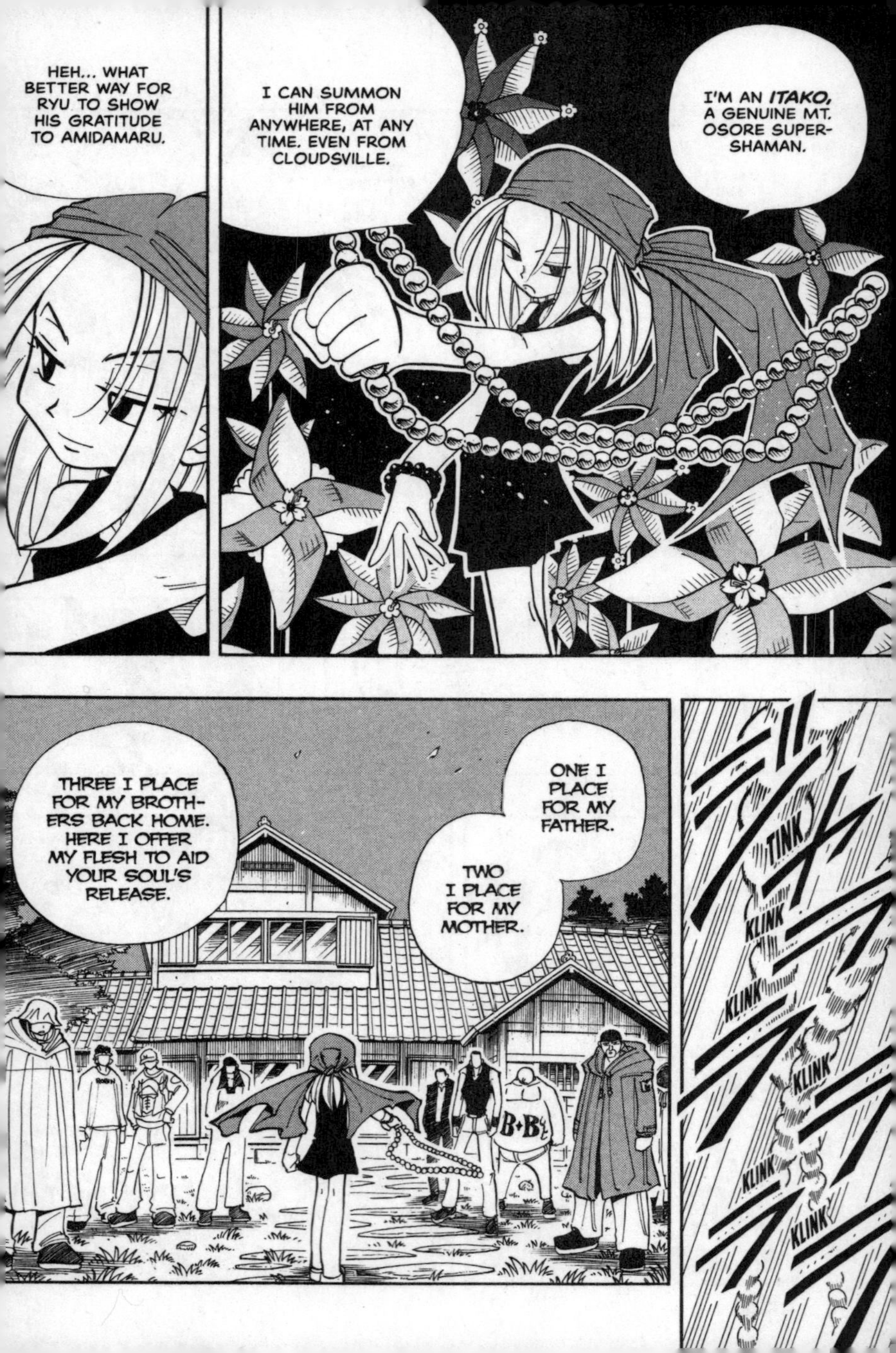
I'M AN *ITAKO,* A GENUINE MT. OSORE SUPER-SHAMAN.
I CAN SUMMON HIM FROM ANYWHERE, AT ANY TIME. EVEN FROM CLOUDSVILLE.
HEH... WHAT BETTER WAY FOR RYU TO SHOW HIS GRATITUDE TO AMIDAMARU.
TINK
KLINK
KLINK
KLINK
KLINK
KLINK
ONE I PLACE FOR MY FATHER.
TWO I PLACE FOR MY MOTHER.
THREE I PLACE FOR MY BROTHERS BACK HOME. HERE I OFFER MY FLESH TO AID YOUR SOUL'S RELEASE.

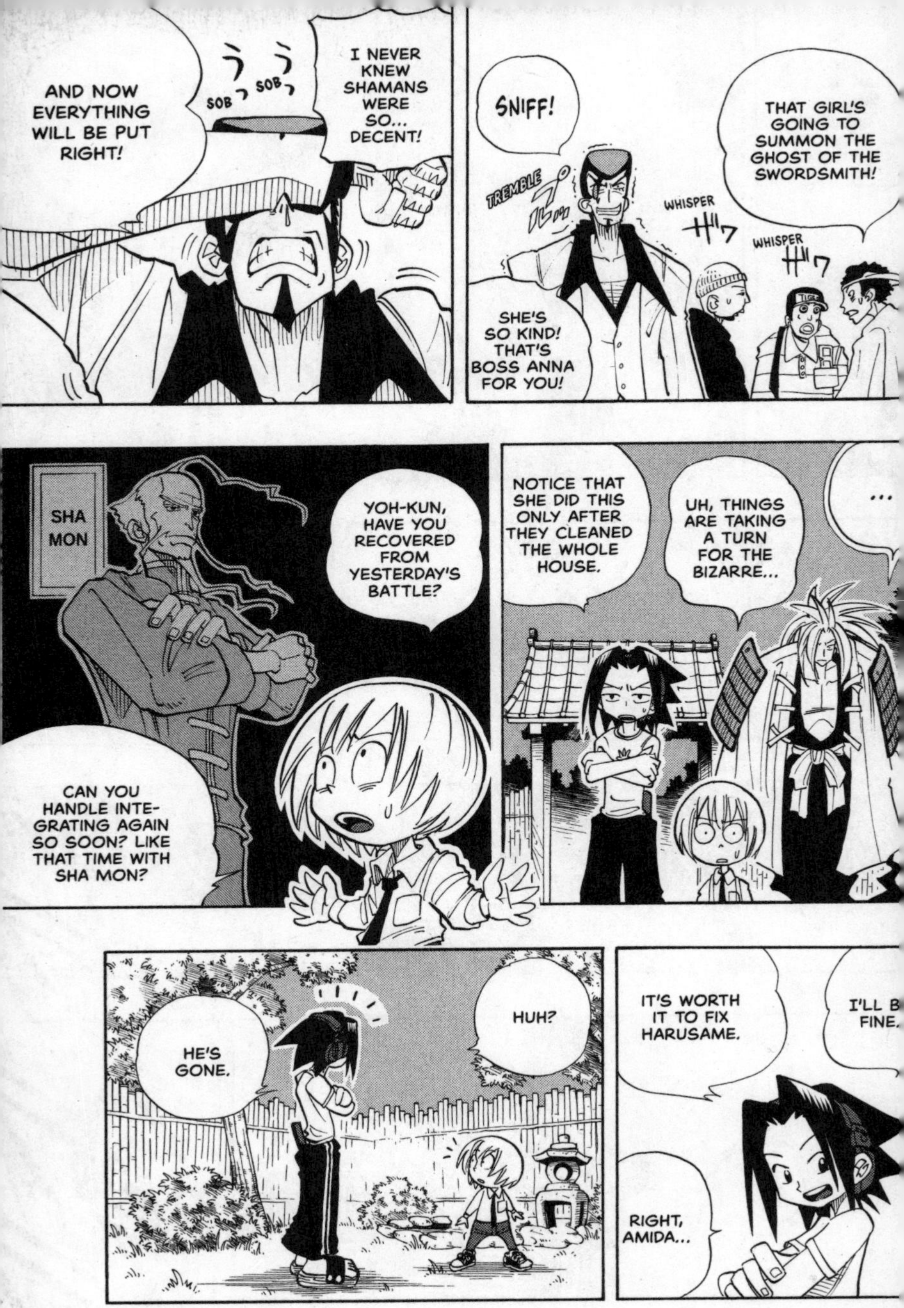
THAT GIRL'S GOING TO SUMMON THE GHOST OF THE SWORDSMITH!
WHISPER
WHISPER
SNIFF!
TREMBLE
SHE'S SO KIND! THAT'S BOSS ANNA FOR YOU!
I NEVER KNEW SHAMANS WERE SO... DECENT!
SOB SOB
AND NOW EVERYTHING WILL BE PUT RIGHT!
...
UH, THINGS ARE TAKING A TURN FOR THE BIZARRE...
NOTICE THAT SHE DID THIS ONLY AFTER THEY CLEANED THE WHOLE HOUSE.
YOH-KUN, HAVE YOU RECOVERED FROM YESTERDAY'S BATTLE?
SHA MON
CAN YOU HANDLE INTE-GRATING AGAIN SO SOON? LIKE THAT TIME WITH SHA MON?
I'LL B FINE.
IT'S WORTH IT TO FIX HARUSAME.
RIGHT, AMIDA...
HUH?
HE'S GONE.

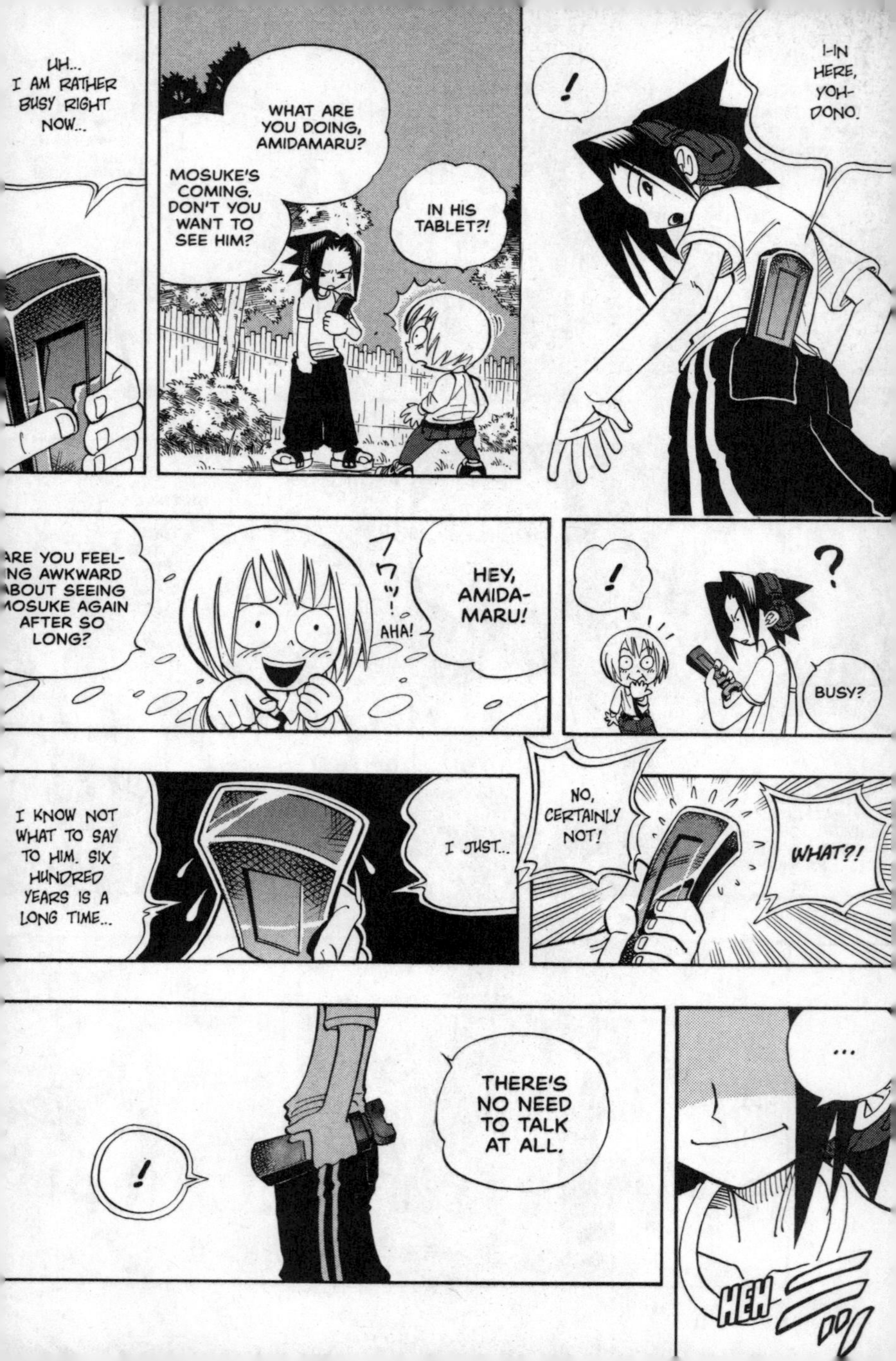
!
I-IN HERE, YOH-DONO.
WHAT ARE YOU DOING, AMIDAMARU?
IN HIS TABLET?!
MOSUKE'S COMING. DON'T YOU WANT TO SEE HIM?
UH... I AM RATHER BUSY RIGHT NOW...
?
!
BUSY?
HEY, AMIDA-MARU!
フワッ!
AHA!
ARE YOU FEELING AWKWARD ABOUT SEEING MOSUKE AGAIN AFTER SO LONG?
WHAT?!
NO, CERTAINLY NOT!
I JUST...
I KNOW NOT WHAT TO SAY TO HIM. SIX HUNDRED YEARS IS A LONG TIME...
...
HEH
THERE'S NO NEED TO TALK AT ALL.
!

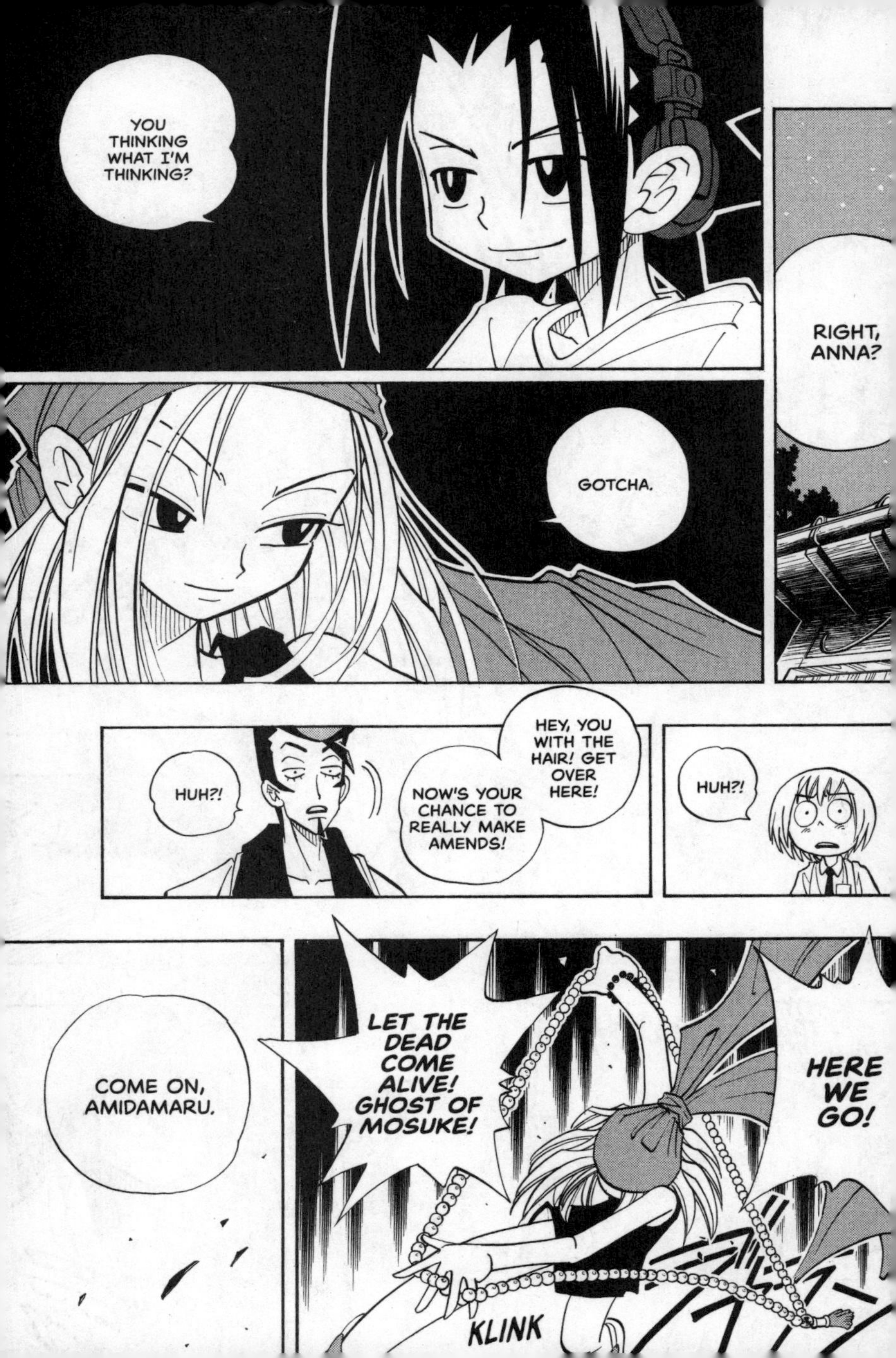
RIGHT, ANNA?
YOU THINKING WHAT I'M THINKING?
GOTCHA.
HUH?!
HEY, YOU WITH THE HAIR! GET OVER HERE!
NOW'S YOUR CHANCE TO REALLY MAKE AMENDS!
HUH?!
HERE WE GO!
LET THE DEAD COME ALIVE! GHOST OF MOSUKE!
KLINK
COME ON, AMIDAMARU.

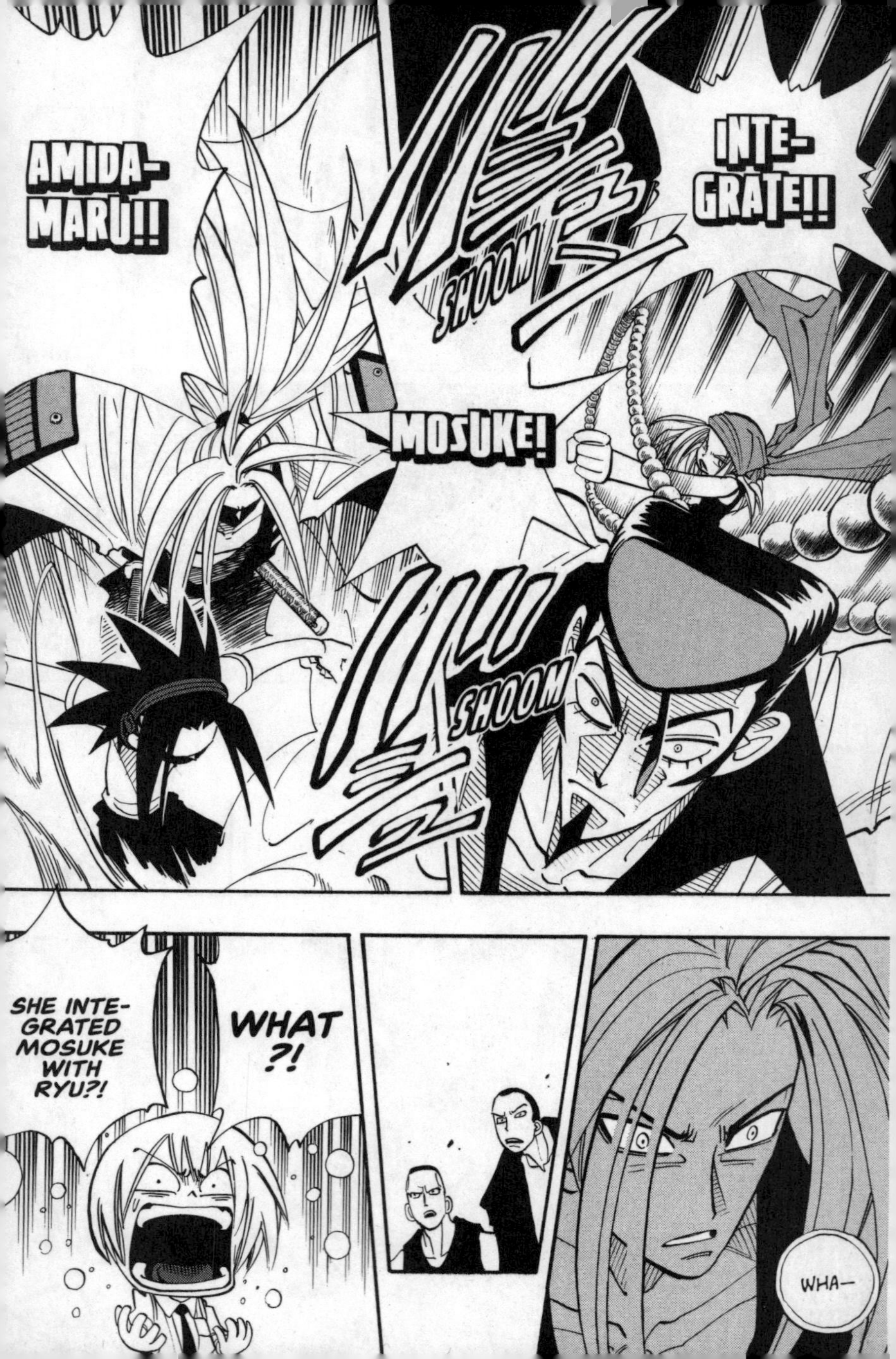
INTE-
GRATE!!
SHOOM
MOSUKE!
AMIDA-
MARU!!
SHOOM
WHA—
WHAT
?!
SHE INTE-
GRATED
MOSUKE
WITH
RYU?!

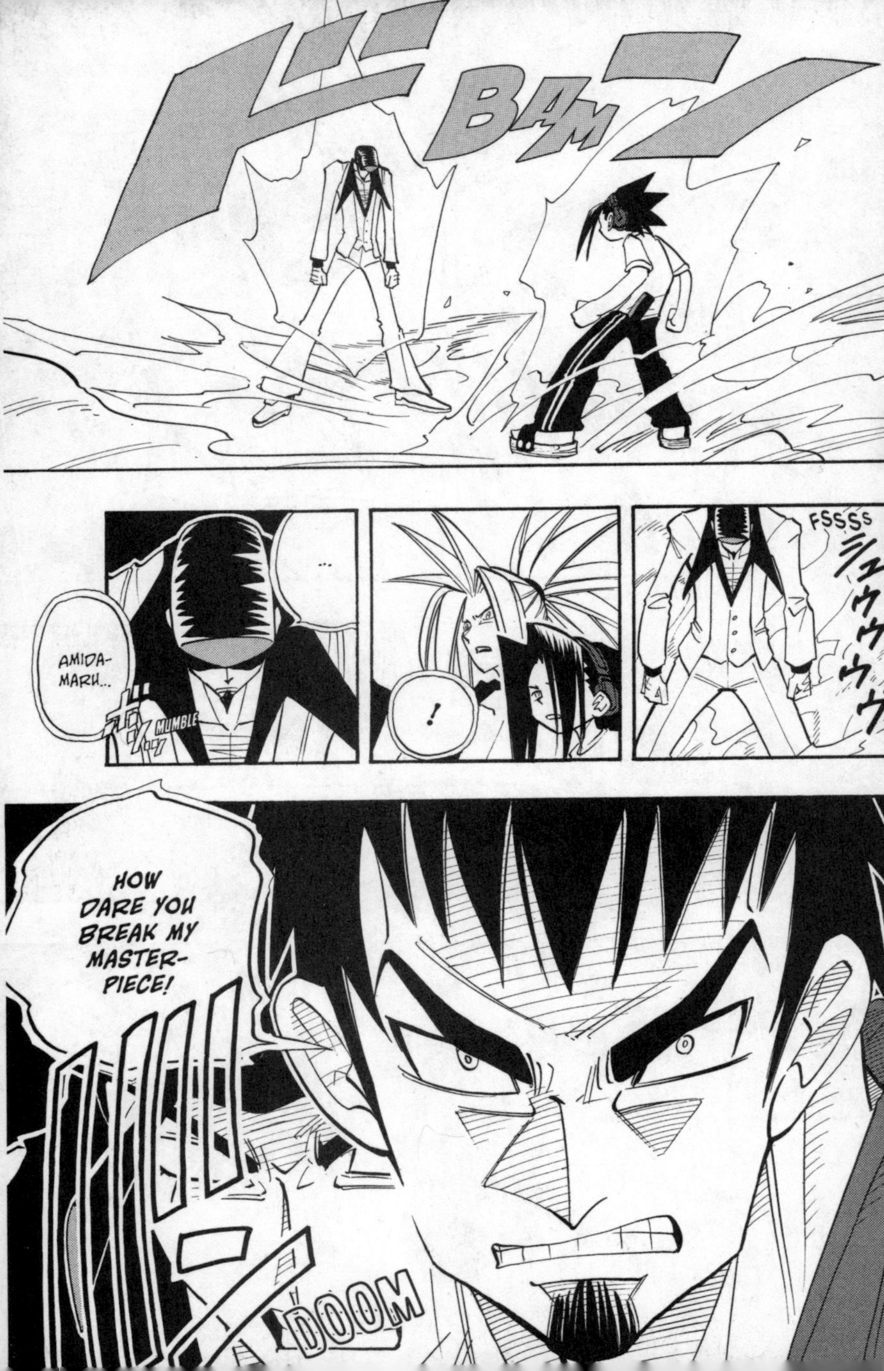
BAM
FSSSS
!
...
AMIDA-MARU...
MUMBLE
HOW DARE YOU BREAK MY MASTER-PIECE!
DOOM

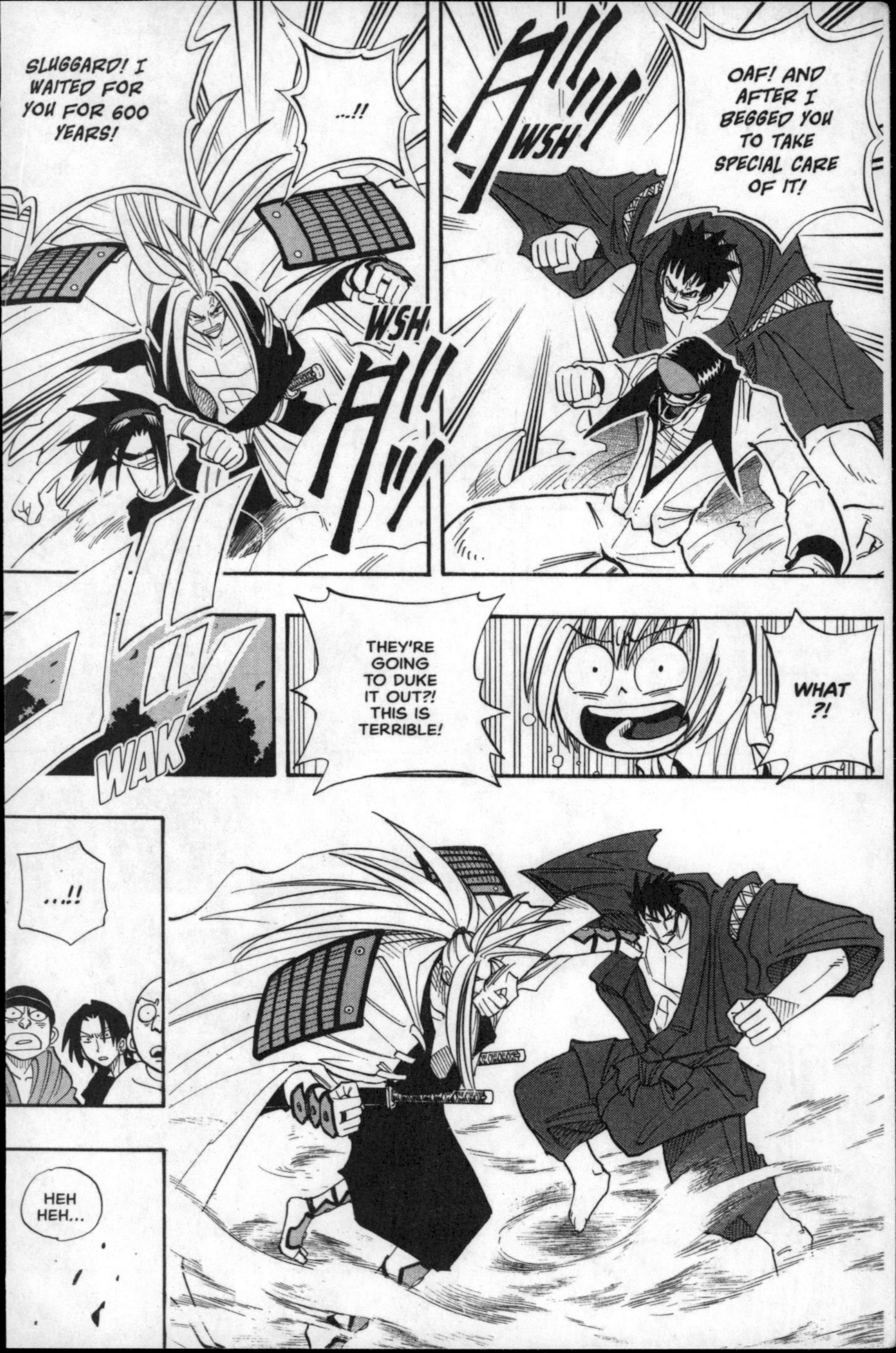
WSH
OAF! AND AFTER I BEGGED YOU TO TAKE SPECIAL CARE OF IT!
...!!
SLUGGARD! I WAITED FOR YOU FOR 600 YEARS!
WSH
WHAT?!
THEY'RE GOING TO DUKE IT OUT?! THIS IS TERRIBLE!
WAK
...!!
HEH HEH...

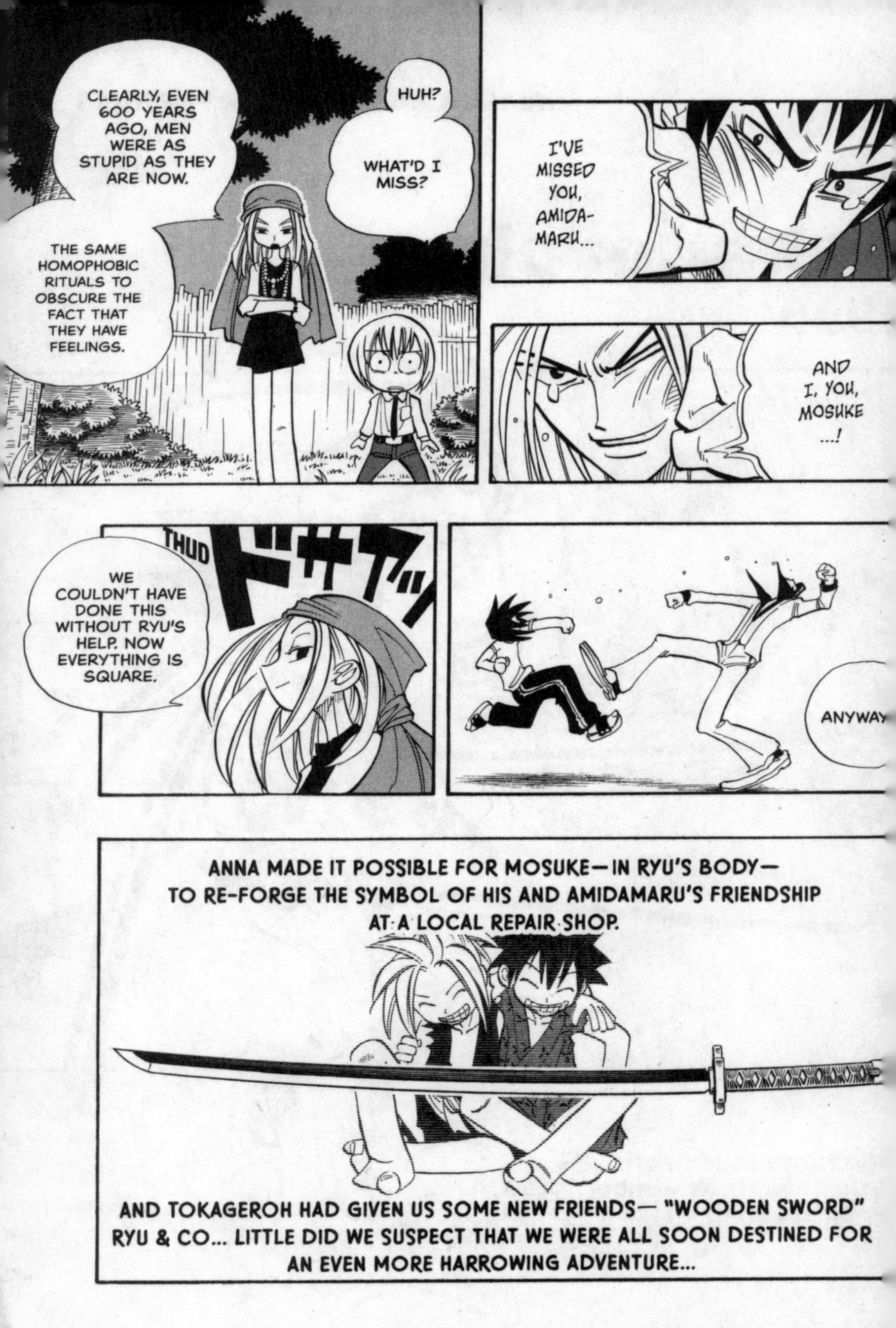
I'VE MISSED YOU, AMIDA-MARU...
AND I, YOU, MOSUKE ...!
HUH?
WHAT'D I MISS?
CLEARLY, EVEN 600 YEARS AGO, MEN WERE AS STUPID AS THEY ARE NOW.
THE SAME HOMOPHOBIC RITUALS TO OBSCURE THE FACT THAT THEY HAVE FEELINGS.
ANYWAY
THUD
WE COULDN'T HAVE DONE THIS WITHOUT RYU'S HELP. NOW EVERYTHING IS SQUARE.
ANNA MADE IT POSSIBLE FOR MOSUKE—IN RYU'S BODY—
TO RE-FORGE THE SYMBOL OF HIS AND AMIDAMARU'S FRIENDSHIP
AT A LOCAL REPAIR SHOP.
AND TOKAGEROH HAD GIVEN US SOME NEW FRIENDS— "WOODEN SWORD" RYU & CO... LITTLE DID WE SUSPECT THAT WE WERE ALL SOON DESTINED FOR AN EVEN MORE HARROWING ADVENTURE...

Tokageroh

999

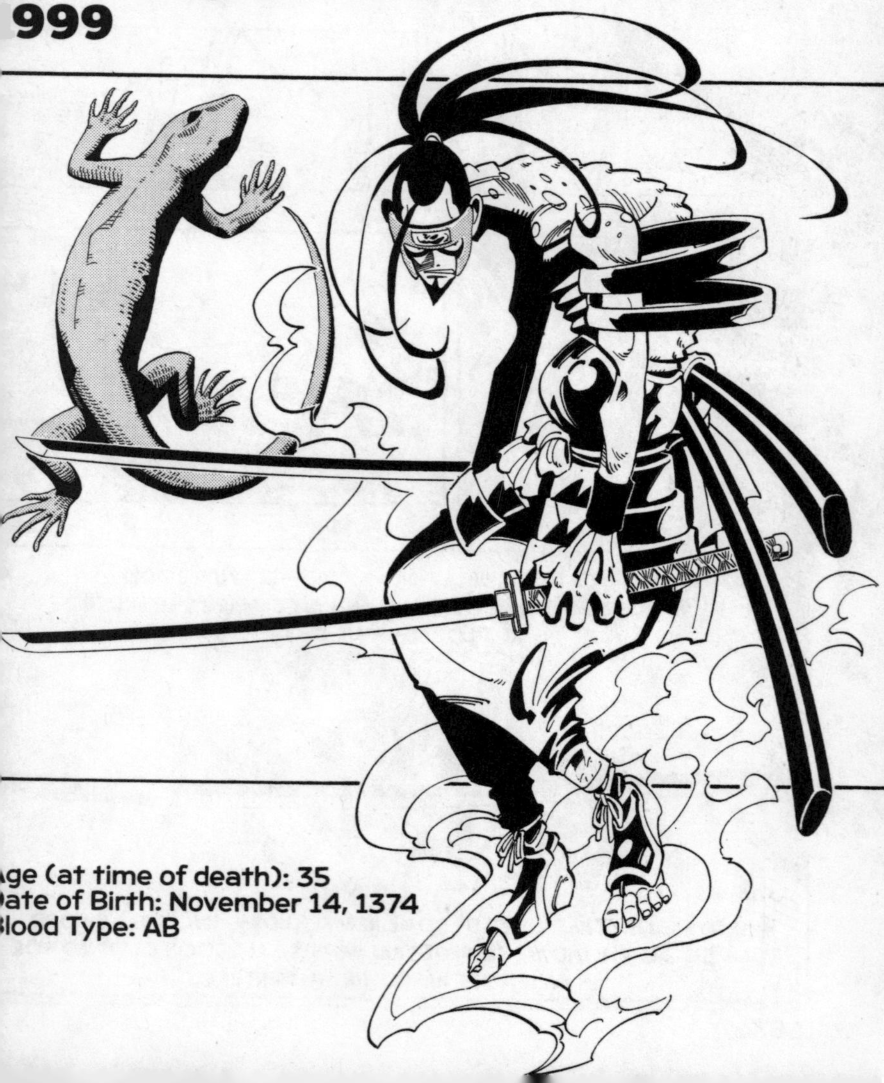

Age (at time of death): 35
Date of Birth: November 14, 1374
Blood Type: AB

Chapter 26:

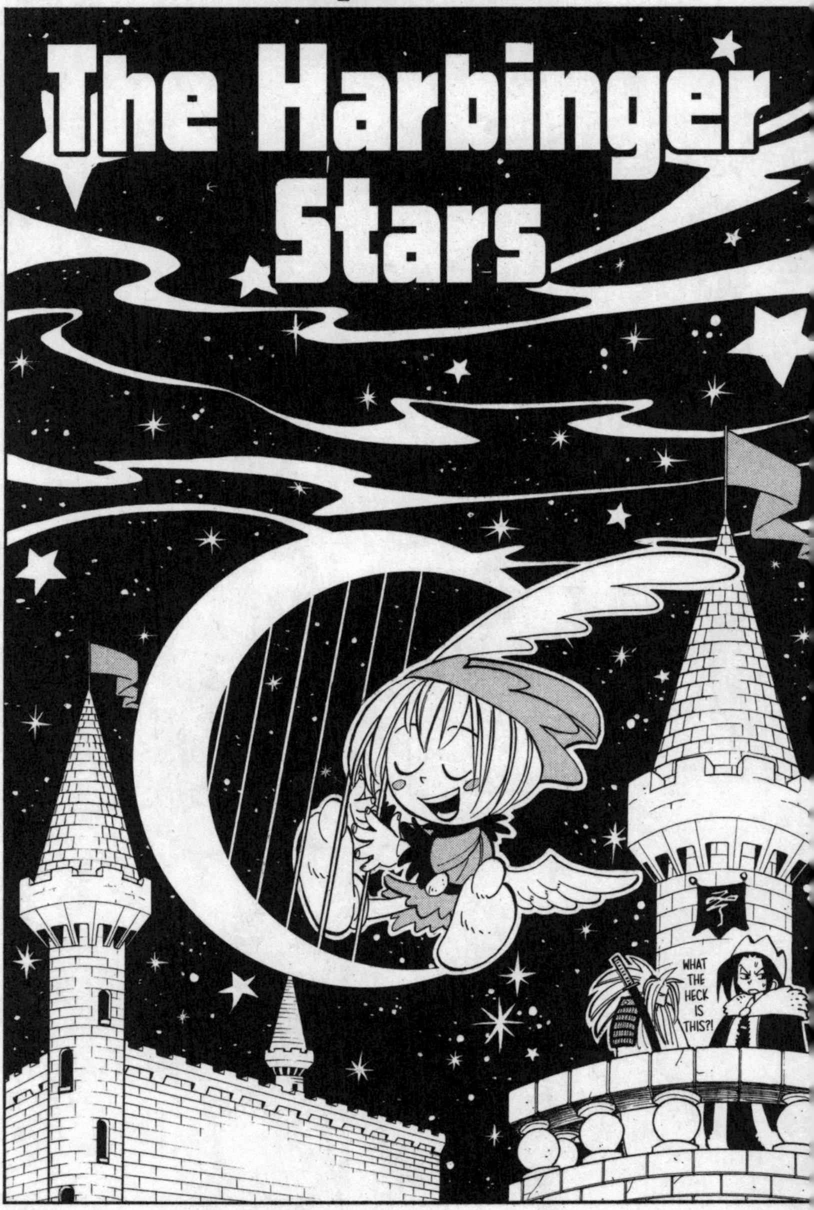
The Harbinger Stars
WHAT THE HECK IS THIS?!

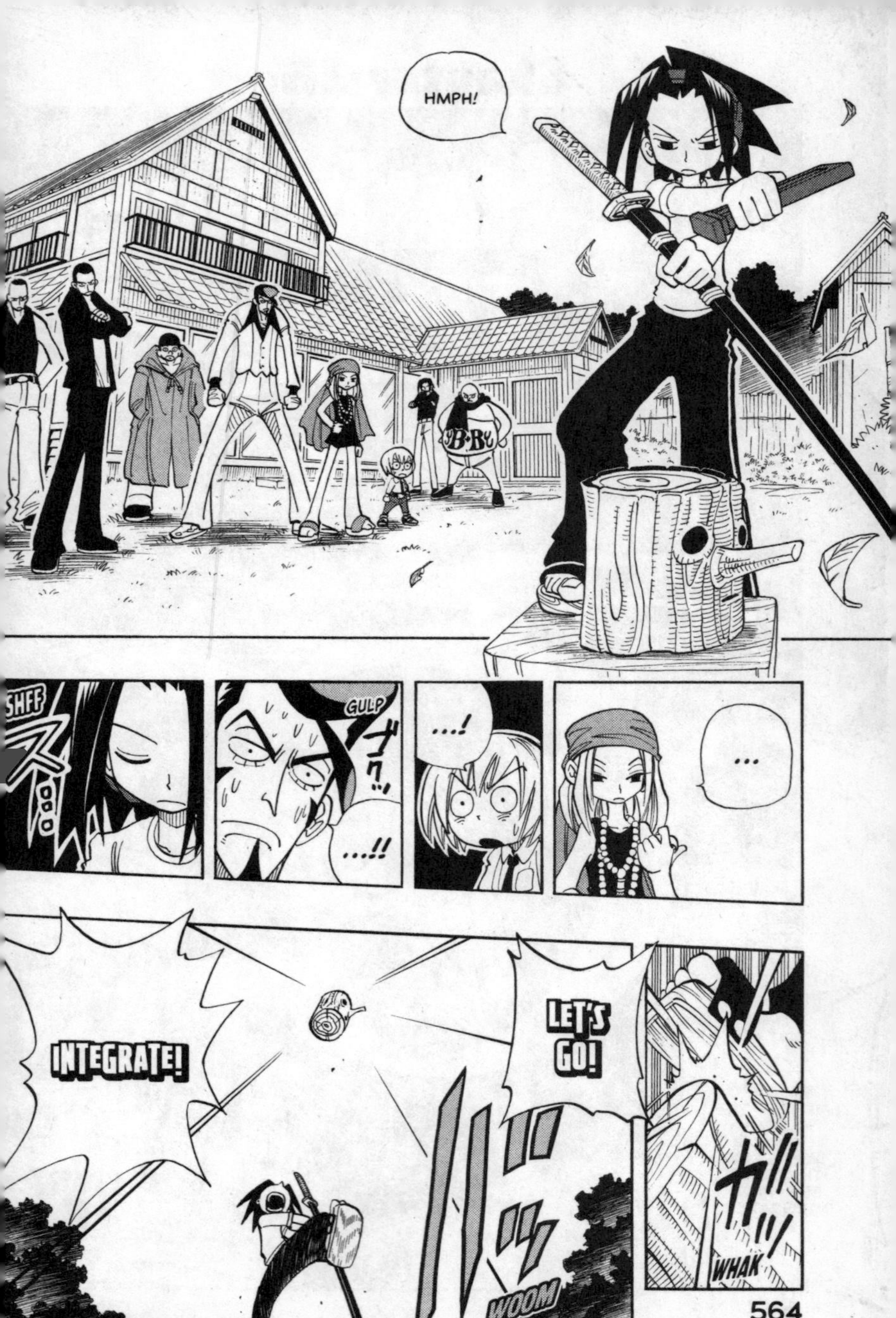
HMPH!
...
...!
GULP
...!!
SHFF
WHAK
LET'S GO!
INTEGRATE!
WOOM

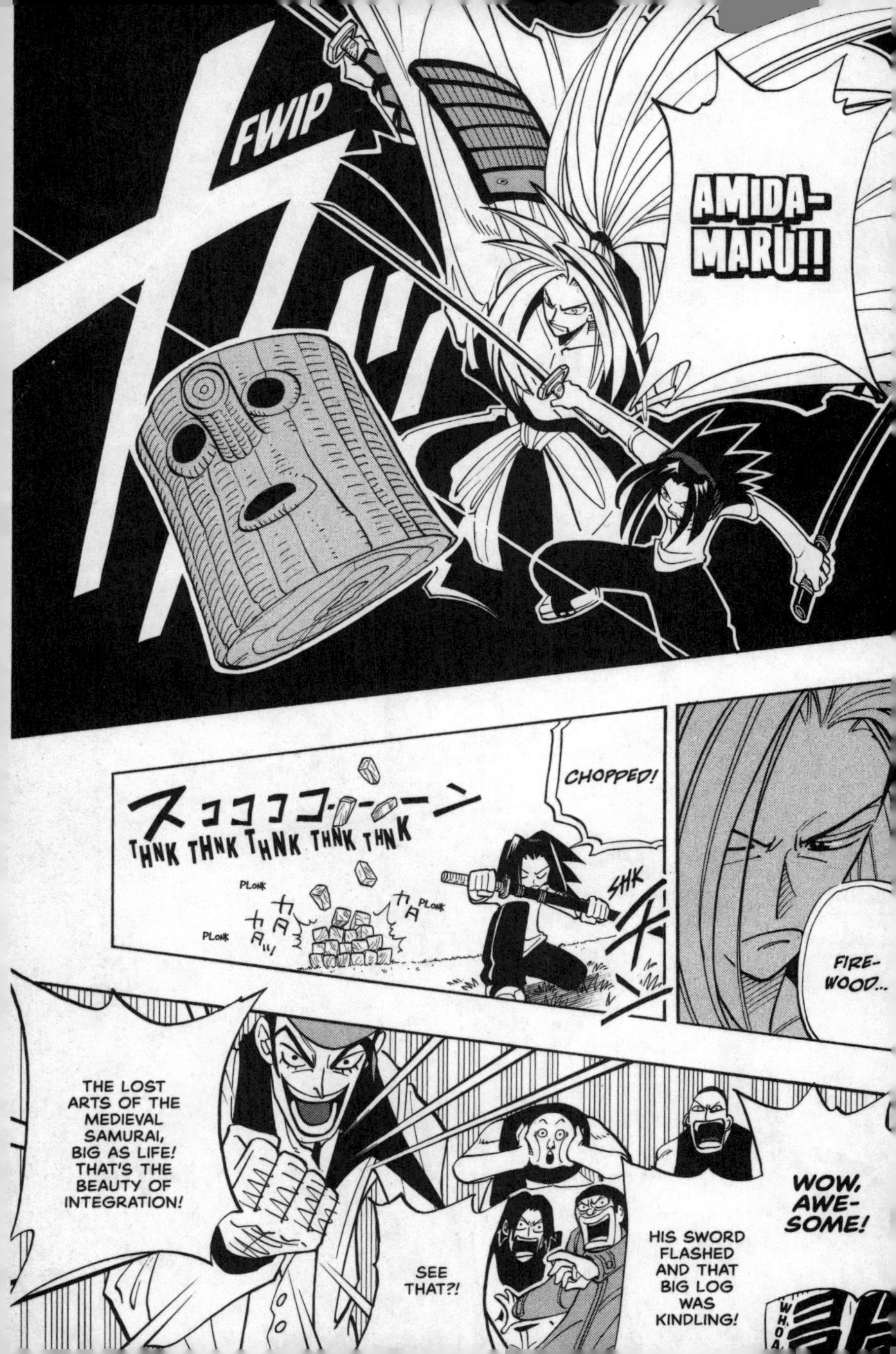

AMIDA-MARU!!
FWIP
FIRE-WOOD...
CHOPPED!
スココココーーーン
THNK THNK THNK THNK THNK
SHK
PLONK
PLONK
PLONK
WOW, AWE-SOME!
WHOA
HIS SWORD FLASHED AND THAT BIG LOG WAS KINDLING!
SEE THAT?!
THE LOST ARTS OF THE MEDIEVAL SAMURAI, BIG AS LIFE! THAT'S THE BEAUTY OF INTEGRATION!

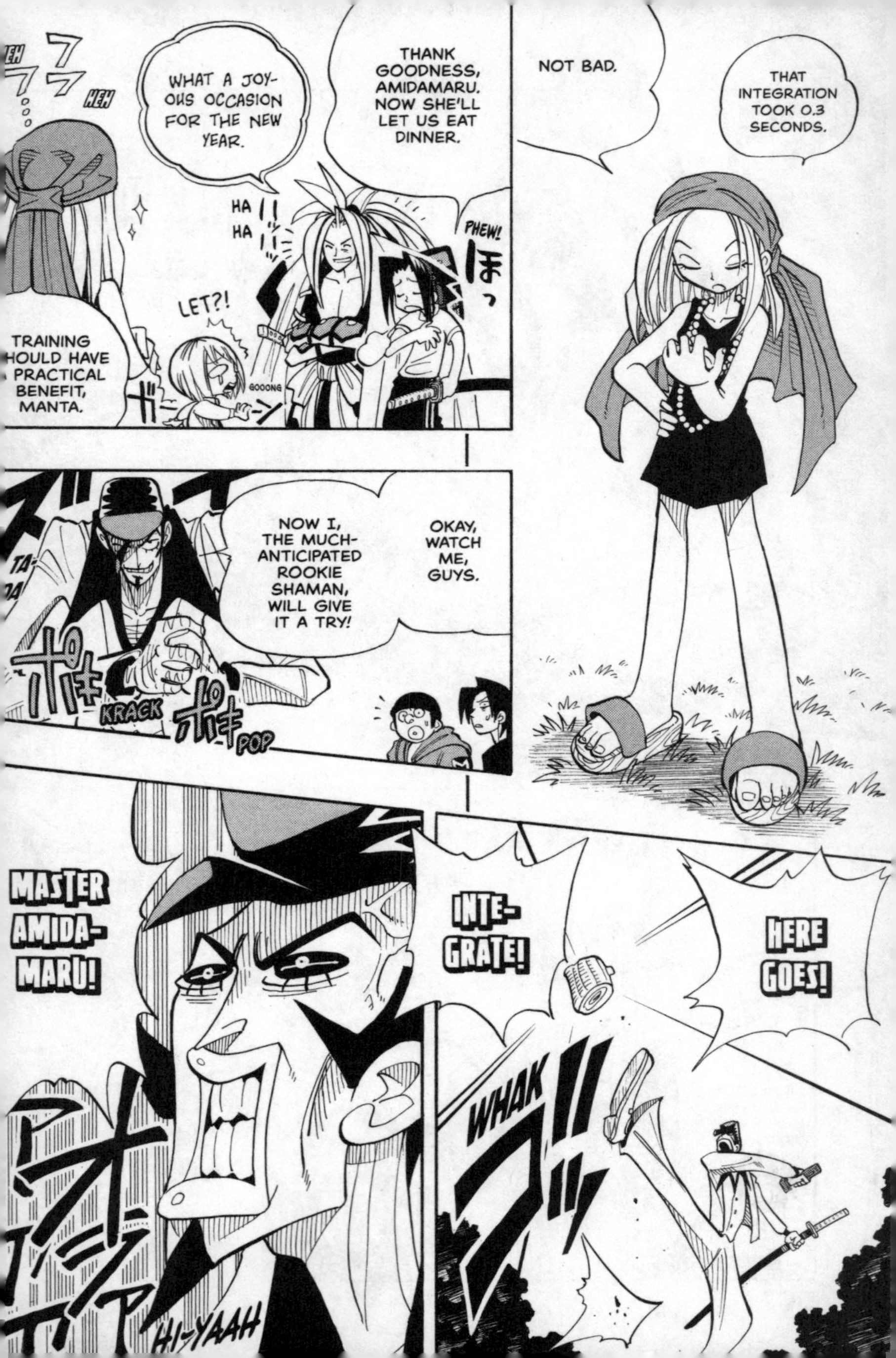
THAT INTEGRATION TOOK 0.3 SECONDS.
NOT BAD.
PHEW!
ほっ
THANK GOODNESS, AMIDAMARU. NOW SHE'LL LET US EAT DINNER.
HA HA
WHAT A JOY-OUS OCCASION FOR THE NEW YEAR.
HEH
フフ
LET?!
GOOONG
ガーン
TRAINING HOULD HAVE PRACTICAL BENEFIT, MANTA.
OKAY, WATCH ME, GUYS.
NOW I, THE MUCH-ANTICIPATED ROOKIE SHAMAN, WILL GIVE IT A TRY!
TA-DA
ポキ
KRACK
ポキ
POP
HERE GOES!
INTE-GRATE!
WHAK
MASTER AMIDA-MARU!
HI-YAAH

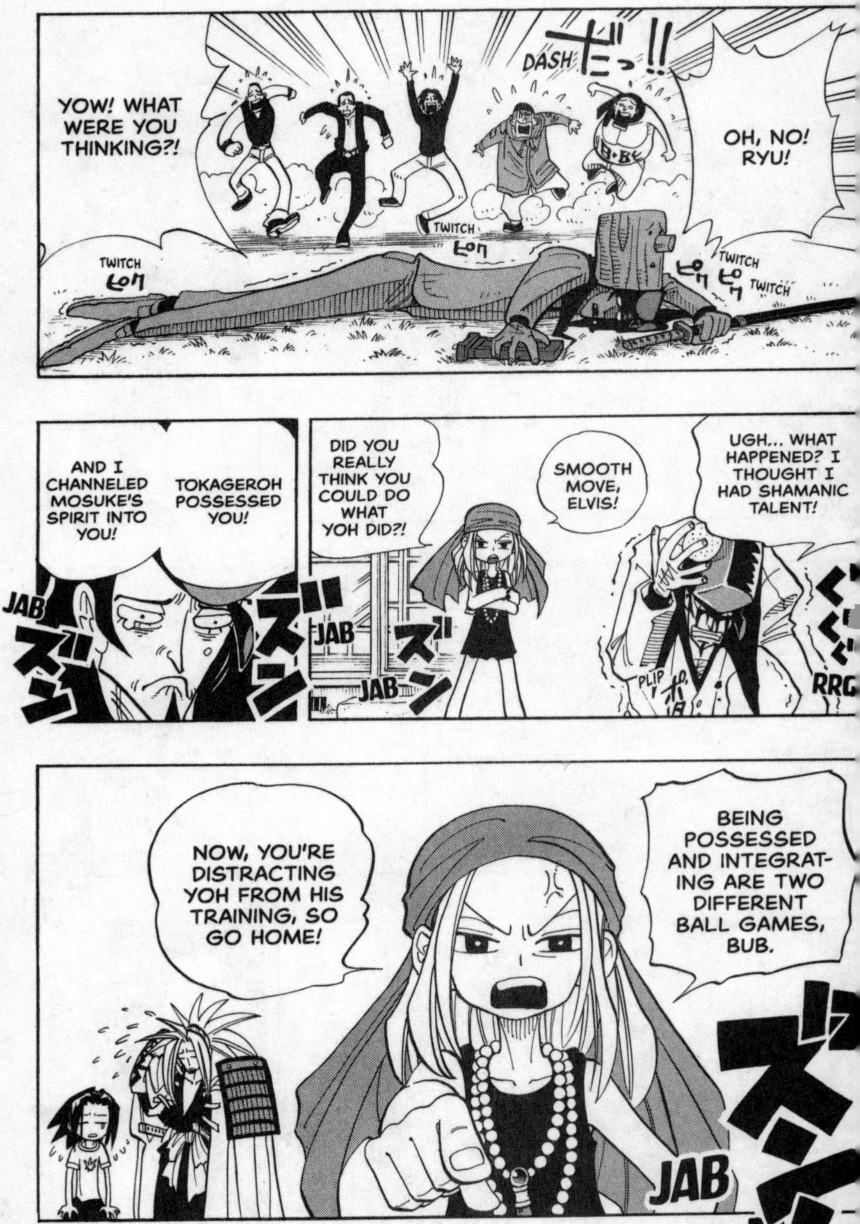
OH, NO! RYU!
DASH
YOW! WHAT WERE YOU THINKING?!
TWITCH
TWITCH
TWITCH
TWITCH
UGH... WHAT HAPPENED? I THOUGHT I HAD SHAMANIC TALENT!
RRG
PLIP
SMOOTH MOVE, ELVIS!
DID YOU REALLY THINK YOU COULD DO WHAT YOH DID?!
JAB
JAB
TOKAGEROH POSSESSED YOU!
AND I CHANNELED MOSUKE'S SPIRIT INTO YOU!
JAB
BEING POSSESSED AND INTEGRATING ARE TWO DIFFERENT BALL GAMES, BUB.
JAB
NOW, YOU'RE DISTRACTING YOH FROM HIS TRAINING, SO GO HOME!

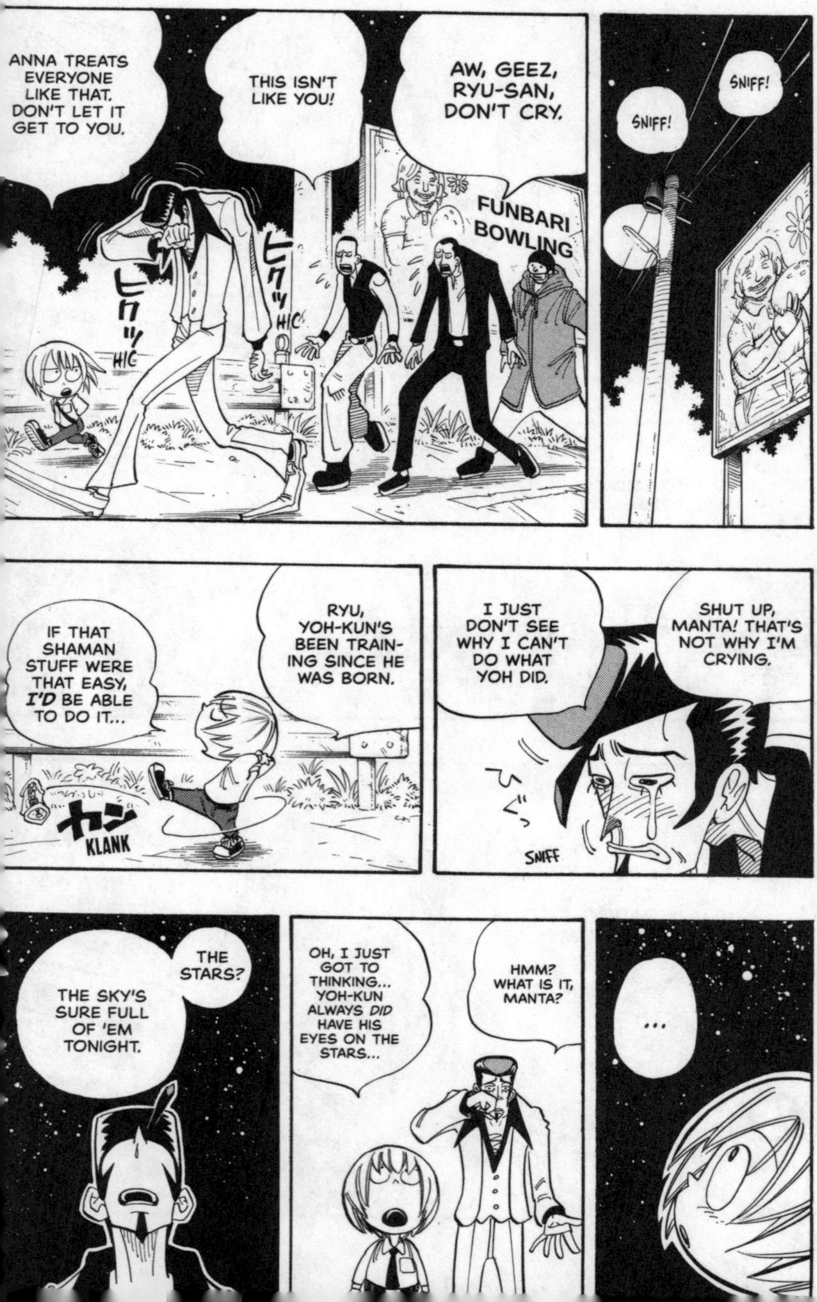
SNIFF!
SNIFF!
AW, GEEZ, RYU-SAN, DON'T CRY.
THIS ISN'T LIKE YOU!
ANNA TREATS EVERYONE LIKE THAT. DON'T LET IT GET TO YOU.
FUNBARI BOWLING
ヒクッ HIC
ヒクッ HIC
SHUT UP, MANTA! THAT'S NOT WHY I'M CRYING.
I JUST DON'T SEE WHY I CAN'T DO WHAT YOH DID.
ひぐっ SNIFF
RYU, YOH-KUN'S BEEN TRAIN-ING SINCE HE WAS BORN.
IF THAT SHAMAN STUFF WERE THAT EASY, *I'D* BE ABLE TO DO IT...
カン KLANK
...
HMM? WHAT IS IT, MANTA?
OH, I JUST GOT TO THINKING... YOH-KUN ALWAYS *DID* HAVE HIS EYES ON THE STARS...
THE STARS?
THE SKY'S SURE FULL OF 'EM TONIGHT.

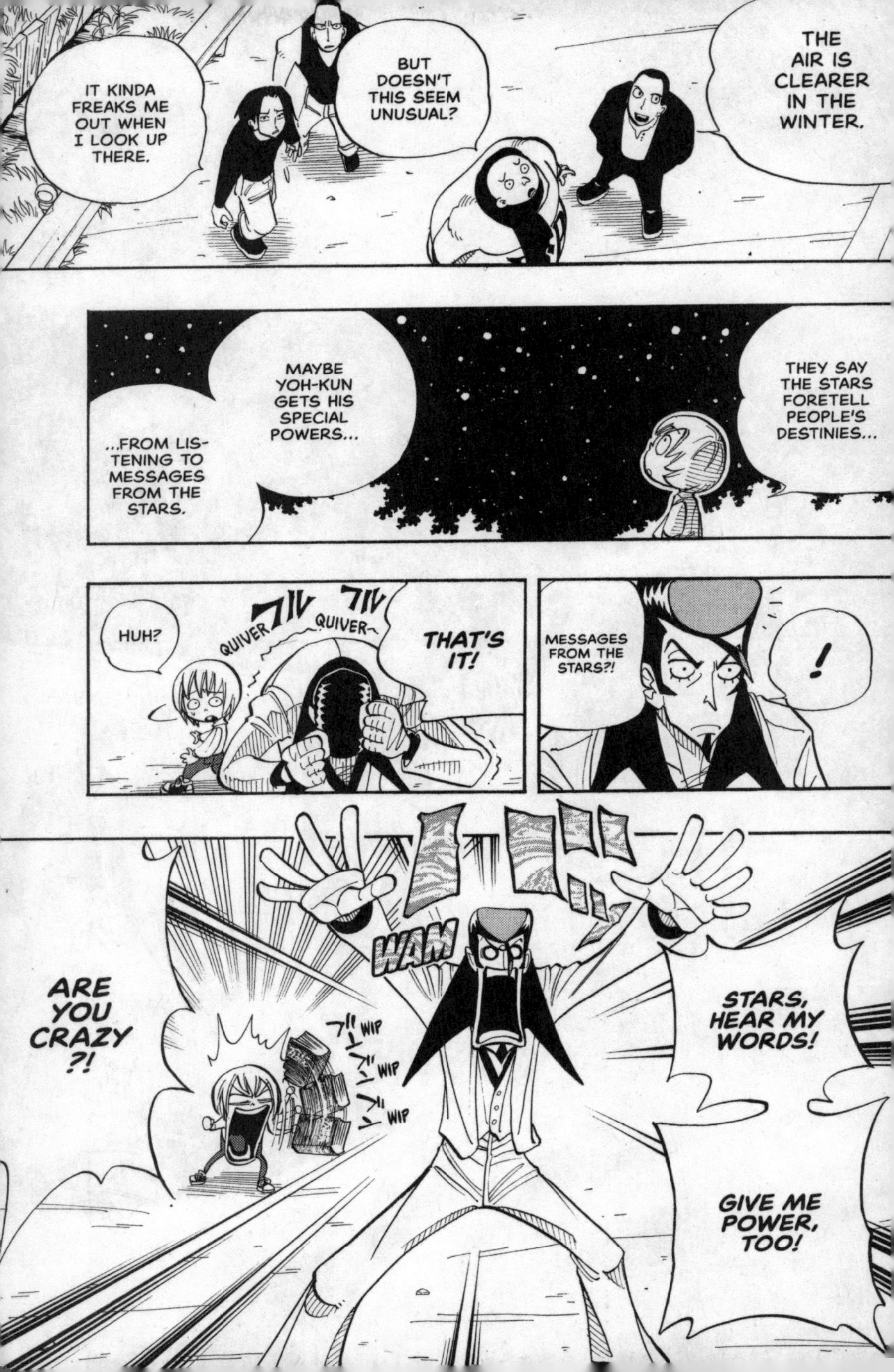
THE AIR IS CLEARER IN THE WINTER.
BUT DOESN'T THIS SEEM UNUSUAL?
IT KINDA FREAKS ME OUT WHEN I LOOK UP THERE.
THEY SAY THE STARS FORETELL PEOPLE'S DESTINIES...
MAYBE YOH-KUN GETS HIS SPECIAL POWERS...
...FROM LIS-TENING TO MESSAGES FROM THE STARS.
!
MESSAGES FROM THE STARS?!
THAT'S IT!
フル QUIVER
フル QUIVER
HUH?
STARS, HEAR MY WORDS!
GIVE ME POWER, TOO!
WAM
WIP
WIP
WIP
ARE YOU CRAZY?!

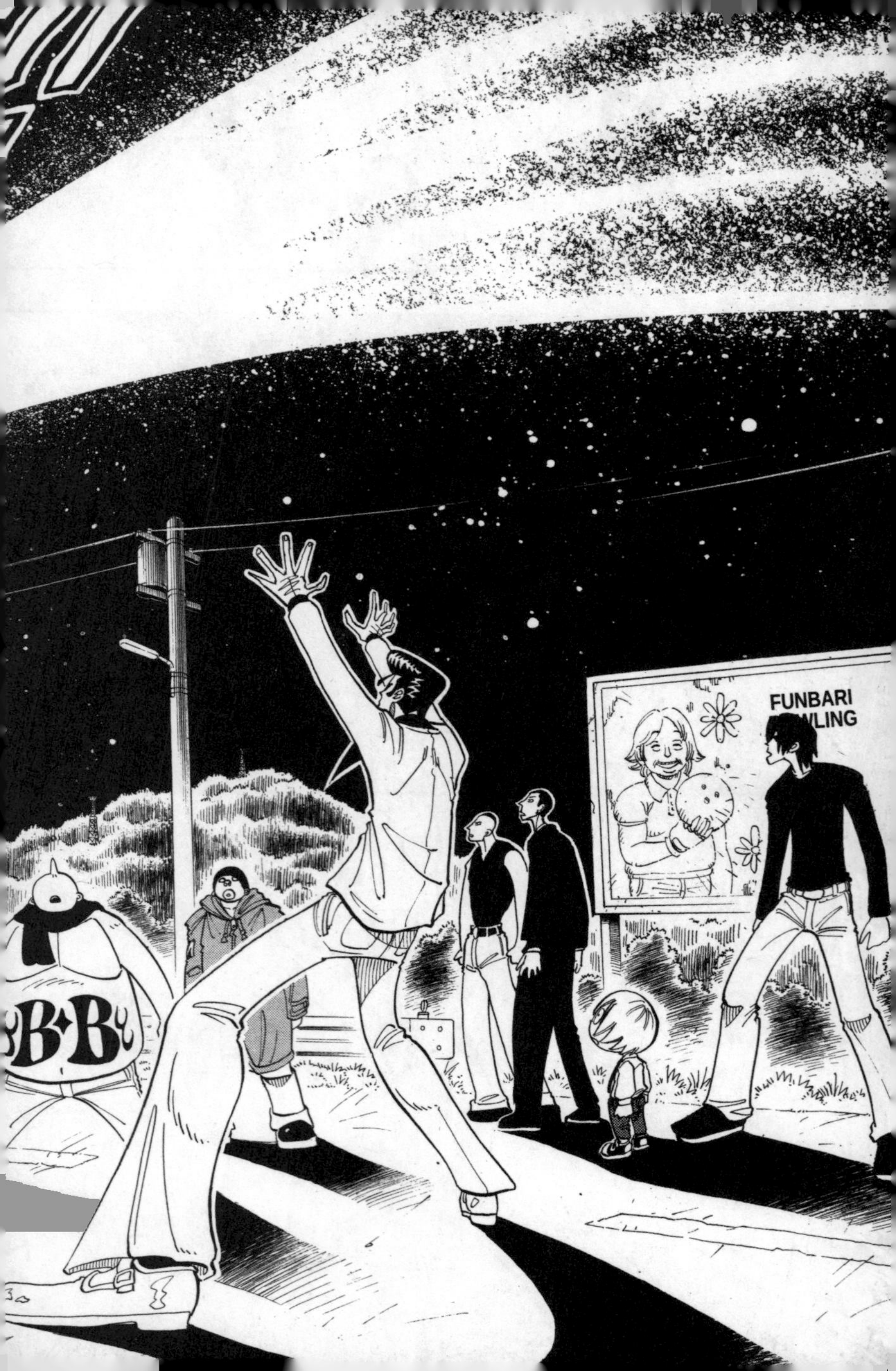
FUNBARI
WLING

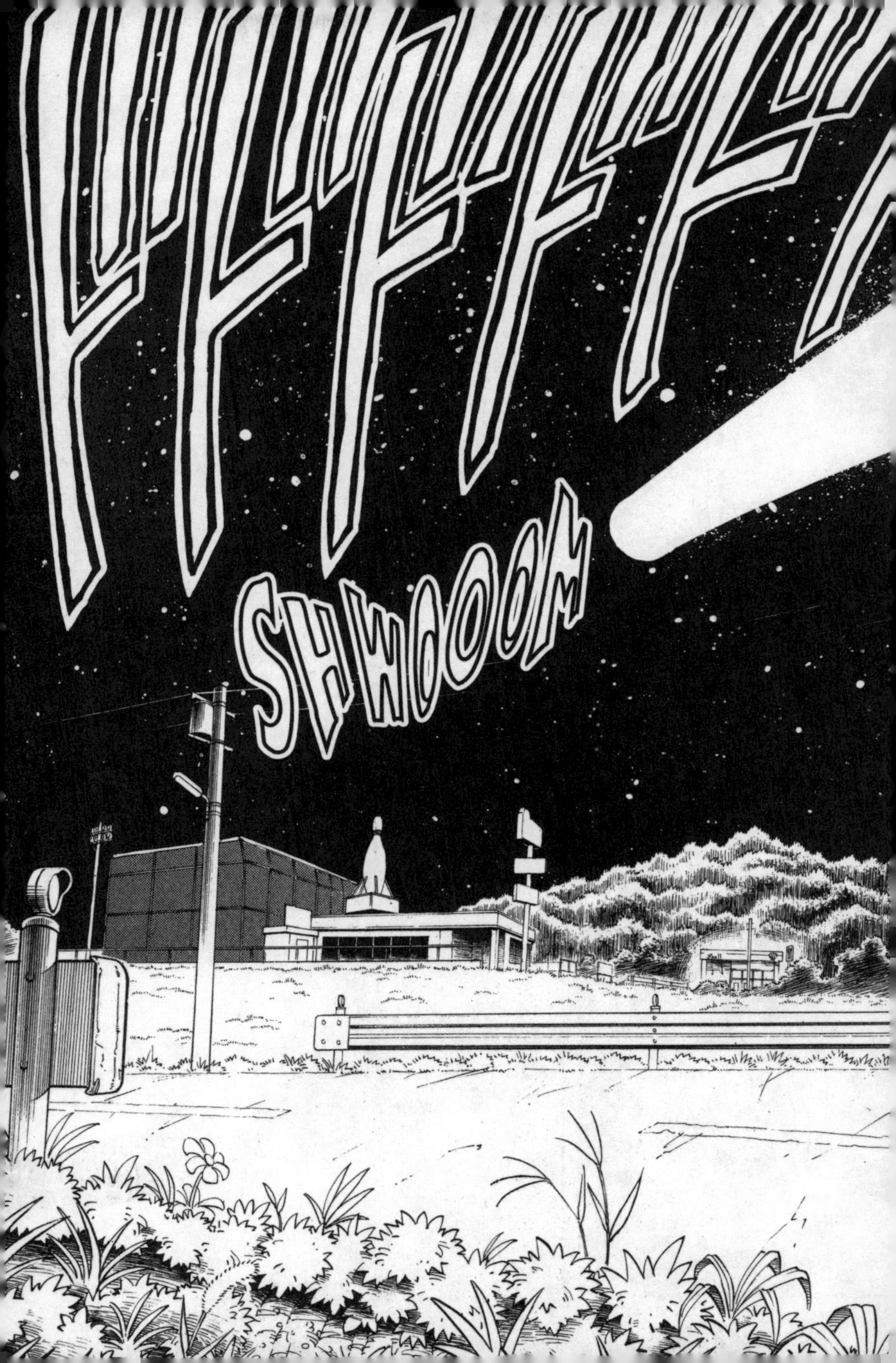
SHWOOOM

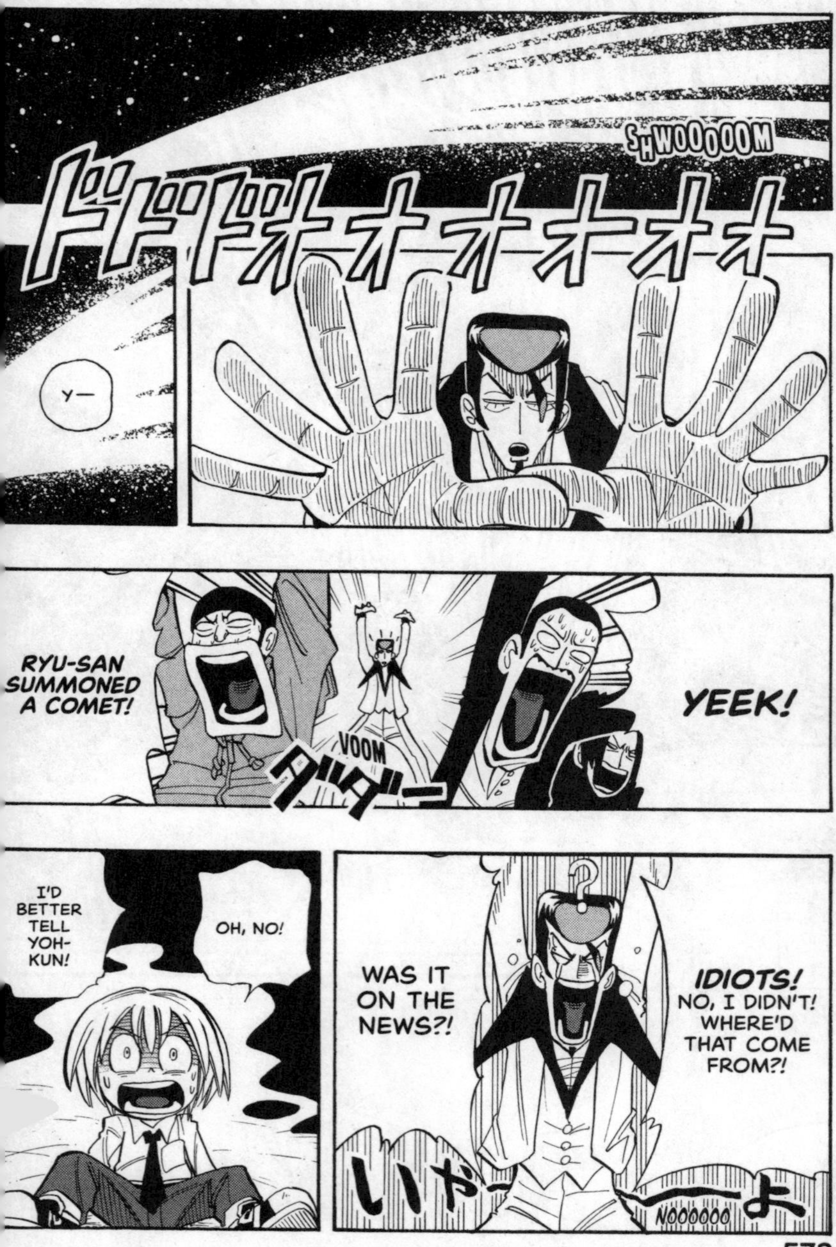
SHWOOOOOM
Y—
YEEK!
VOOM
RYU-SAN SUMMONED A COMET!
IDIOTS! NO, I DIDN'T! WHERE'D THAT COME FROM?!
WAS IT ON THE NEWS?!
NOOOOOO
OH, NO!
I'D BETTER TELL YOH-KUN!

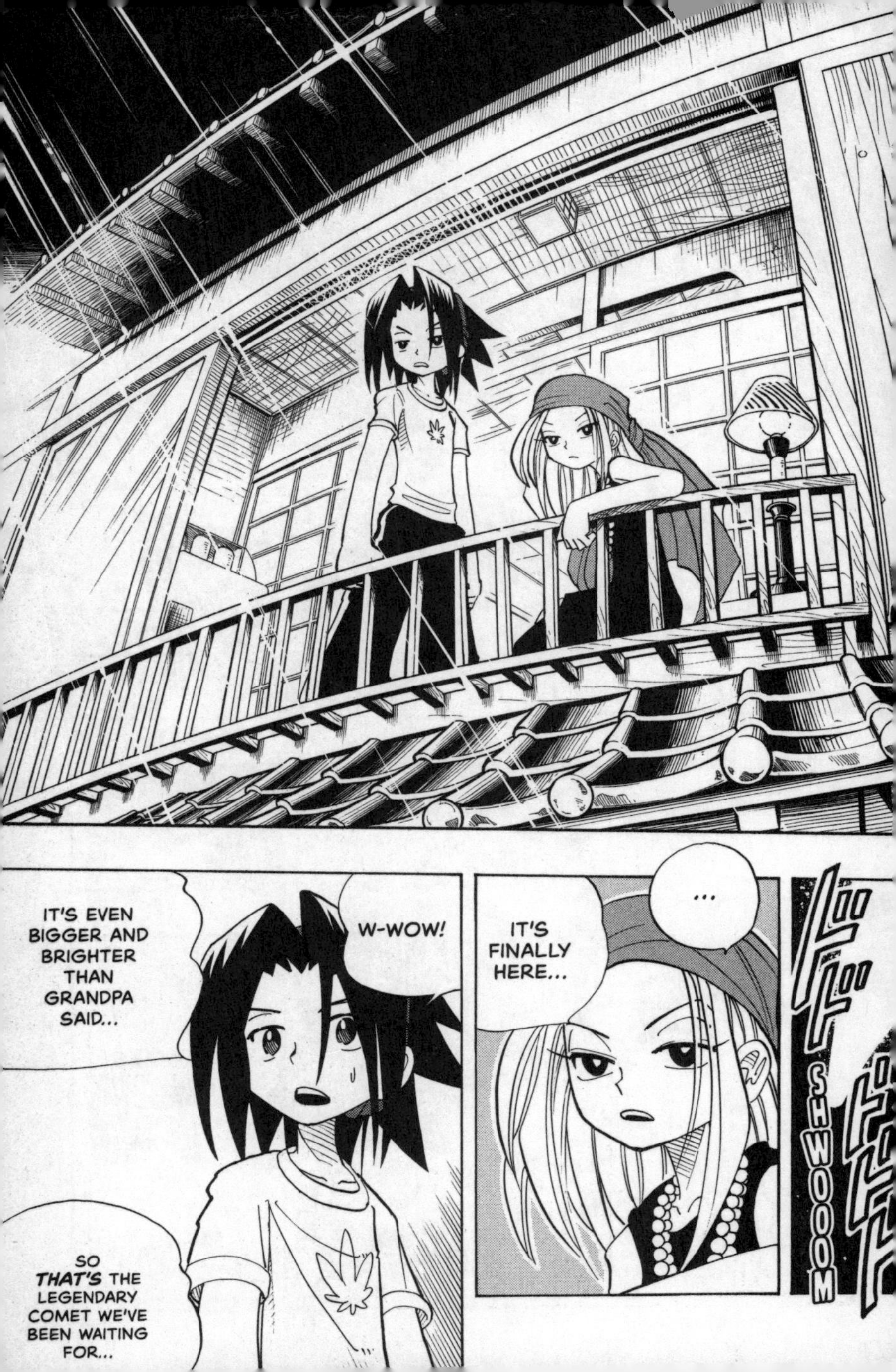
SHWOOOM
...
IT'S FINALLY HERE...
W-WOW!
IT'S EVEN BIGGER AND BRIGHTER THAN GRANDPA SAID...
SO *THAT'S* THE LEGENDARY COMET WE'VE BEEN WAITING FOR...

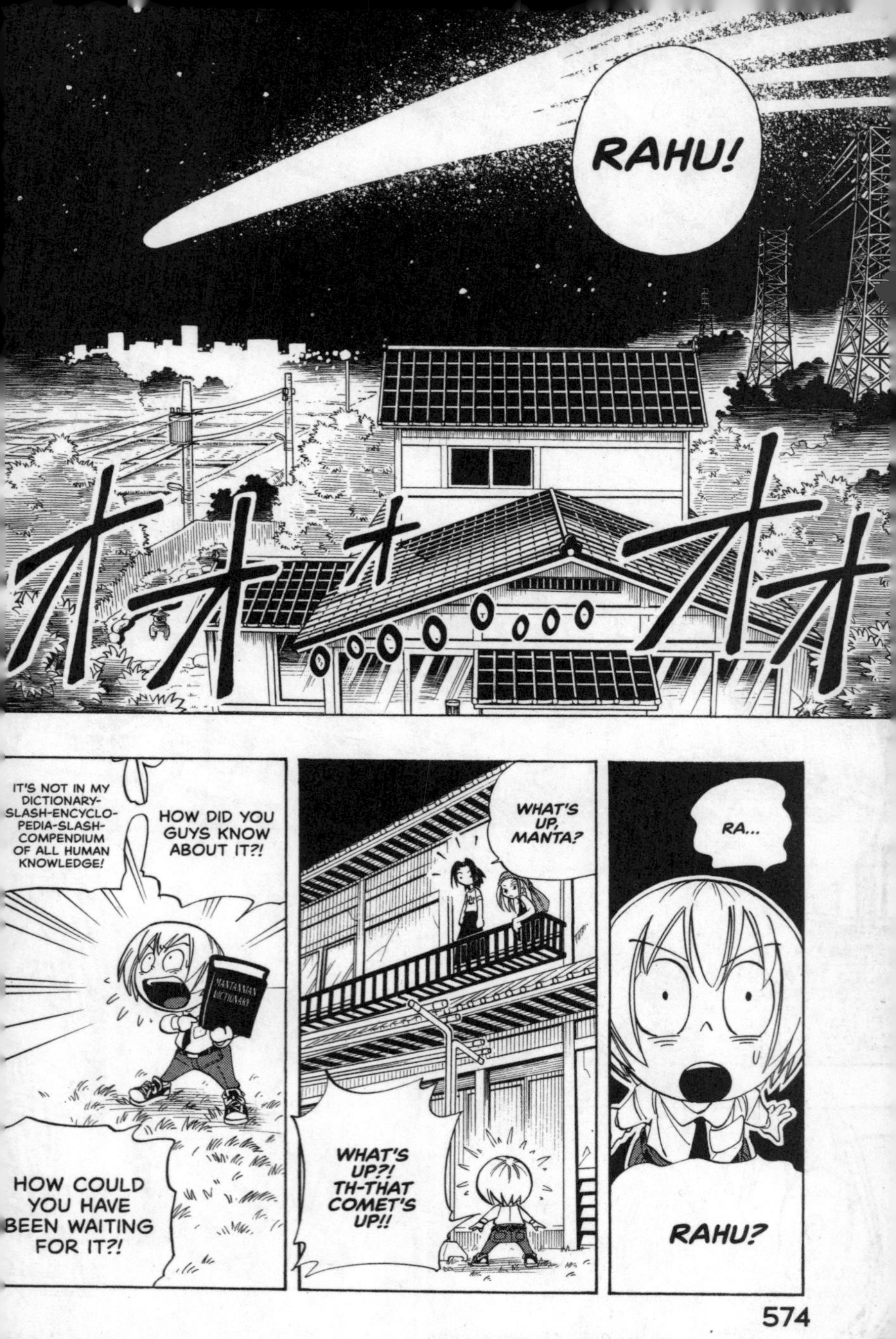
RAHU!
オオォ……オオ
RA...
RAHU?
WHAT'S UP, MANTA?
WHAT'S UP?! TH-THAT COMET'S UP!!
HOW DID YOU GUYS KNOW ABOUT IT?!
IT'S NOT IN MY DICTIONARY-SLASH-ENCYCLOPEDIA-SLASH-COMPENDIUM OF ALL HUMAN KNOWLEDGE!
MANTANIAN DICTIONARY
HOW COULD YOU HAVE BEEN WAITING FOR IT?!

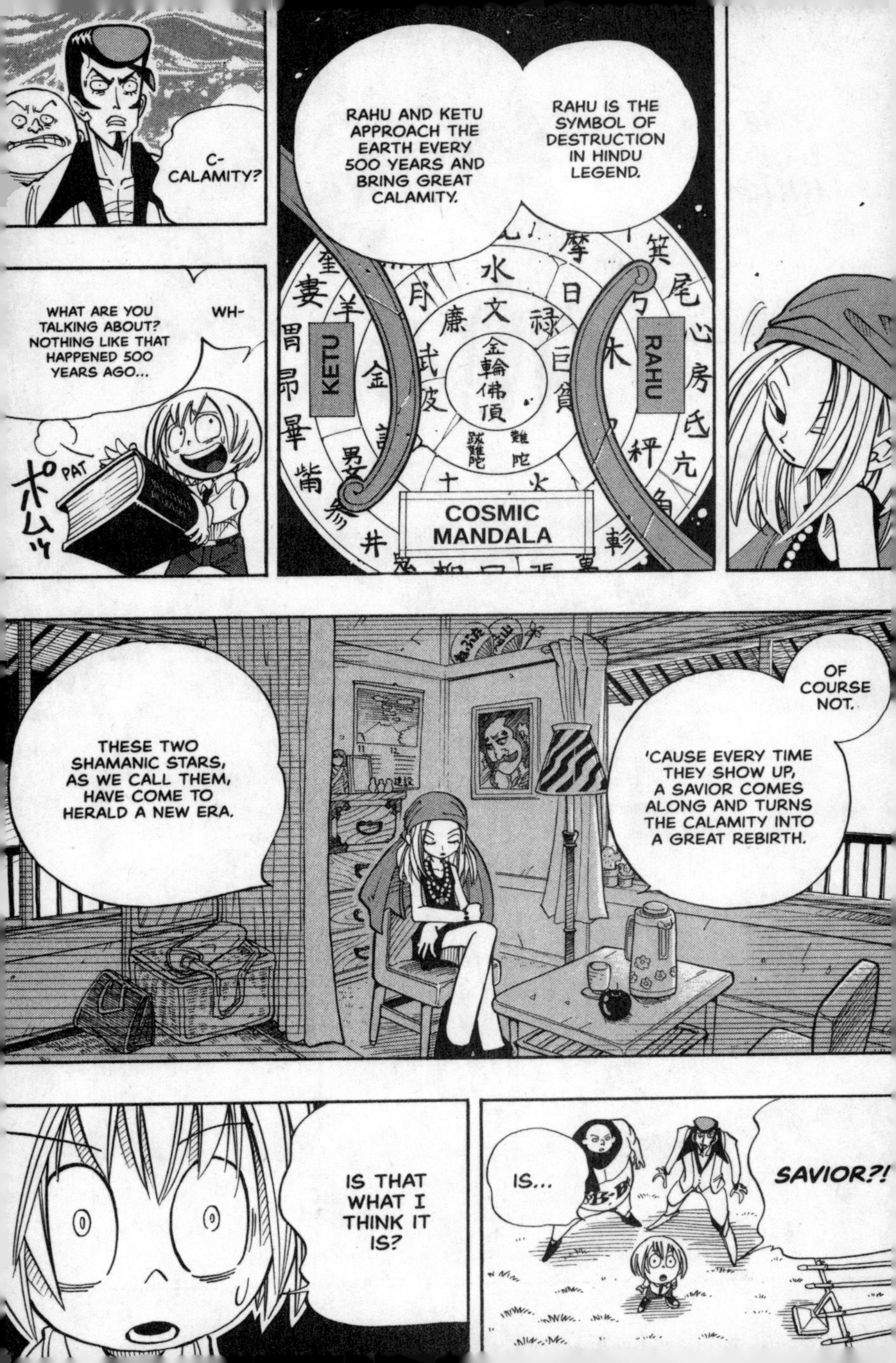
RAHU IS THE SYMBOL OF DESTRUCTION IN HINDU LEGEND.
RAHU AND KETU APPROACH THE EARTH EVERY 500 YEARS AND BRING GREAT CALAMITY.
RAHU
KETU
COSMIC MANDALA
C- CALAMITY?
WH-
WHAT ARE YOU TALKING ABOUT? NOTHING LIKE THAT HAPPENED 500 YEARS AGO...
PAT
OF COURSE NOT.
'CAUSE EVERY TIME THEY SHOW UP, A SAVIOR COMES ALONG AND TURNS THE CALAMITY INTO A GREAT REBIRTH.
THESE TWO SHAMANIC STARS, AS WE CALL THEM, HAVE COME TO HERALD A NEW ERA.
SAVIOR?!
IS...
IS THAT WHAT I THINK IT IS?

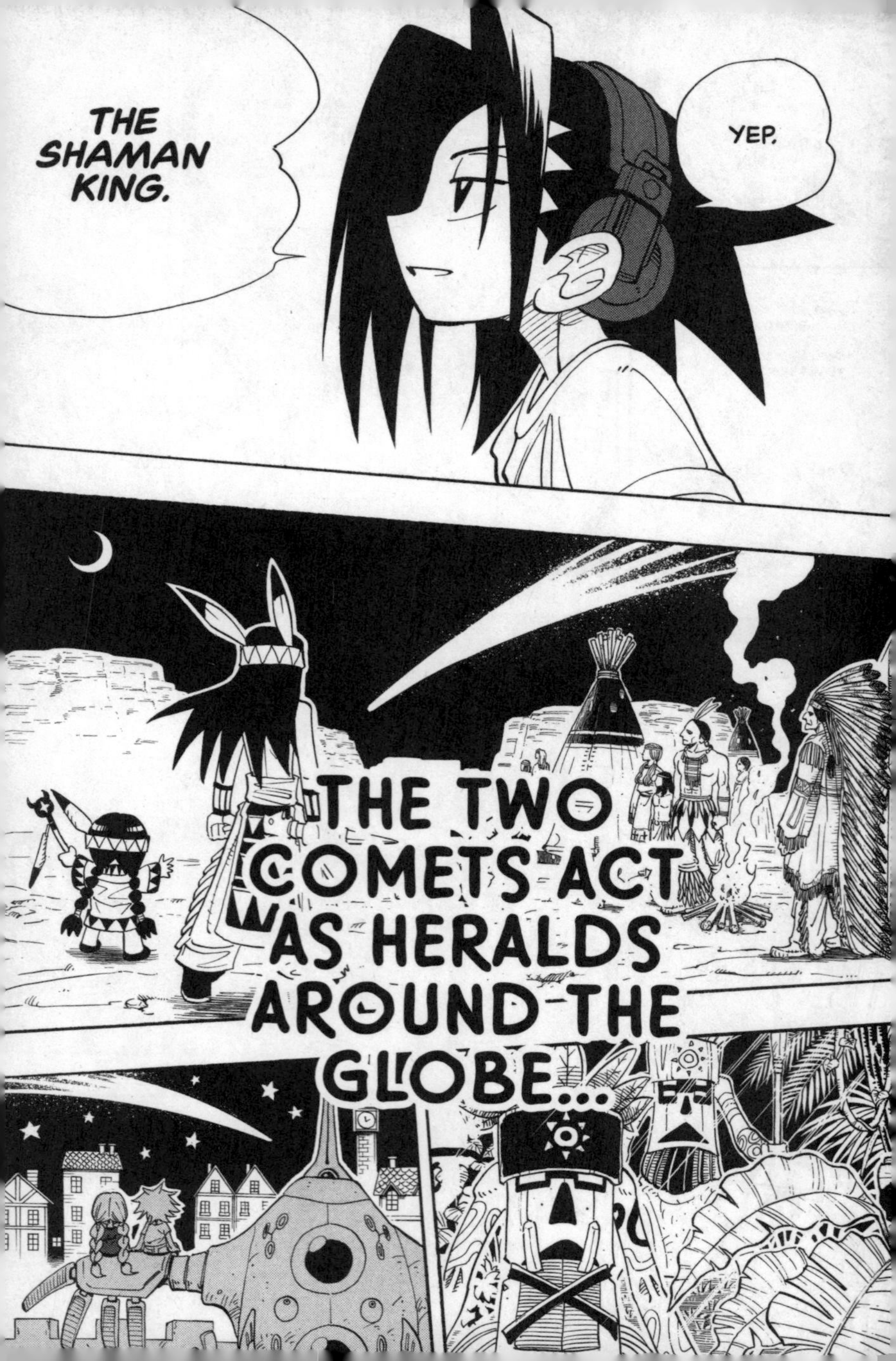
THE SHAMAN KING.
YEP.
THE TWO COMETS ACT AS HERALDS AROUND THE GLOBE...

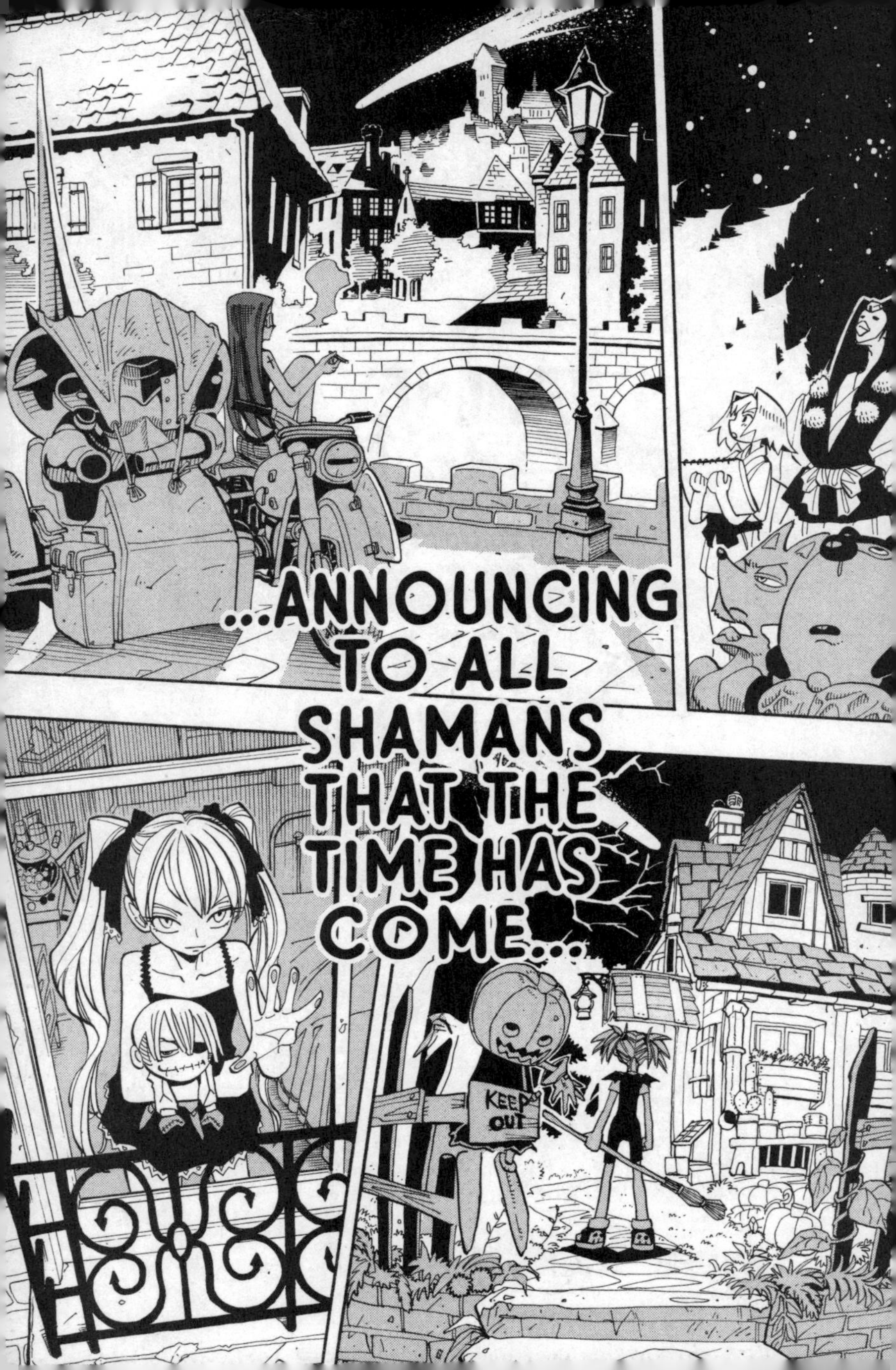
...ANNOUNCING TO ALL SHAMANS THAT THE TIME HAS COME...
KEEP OUT

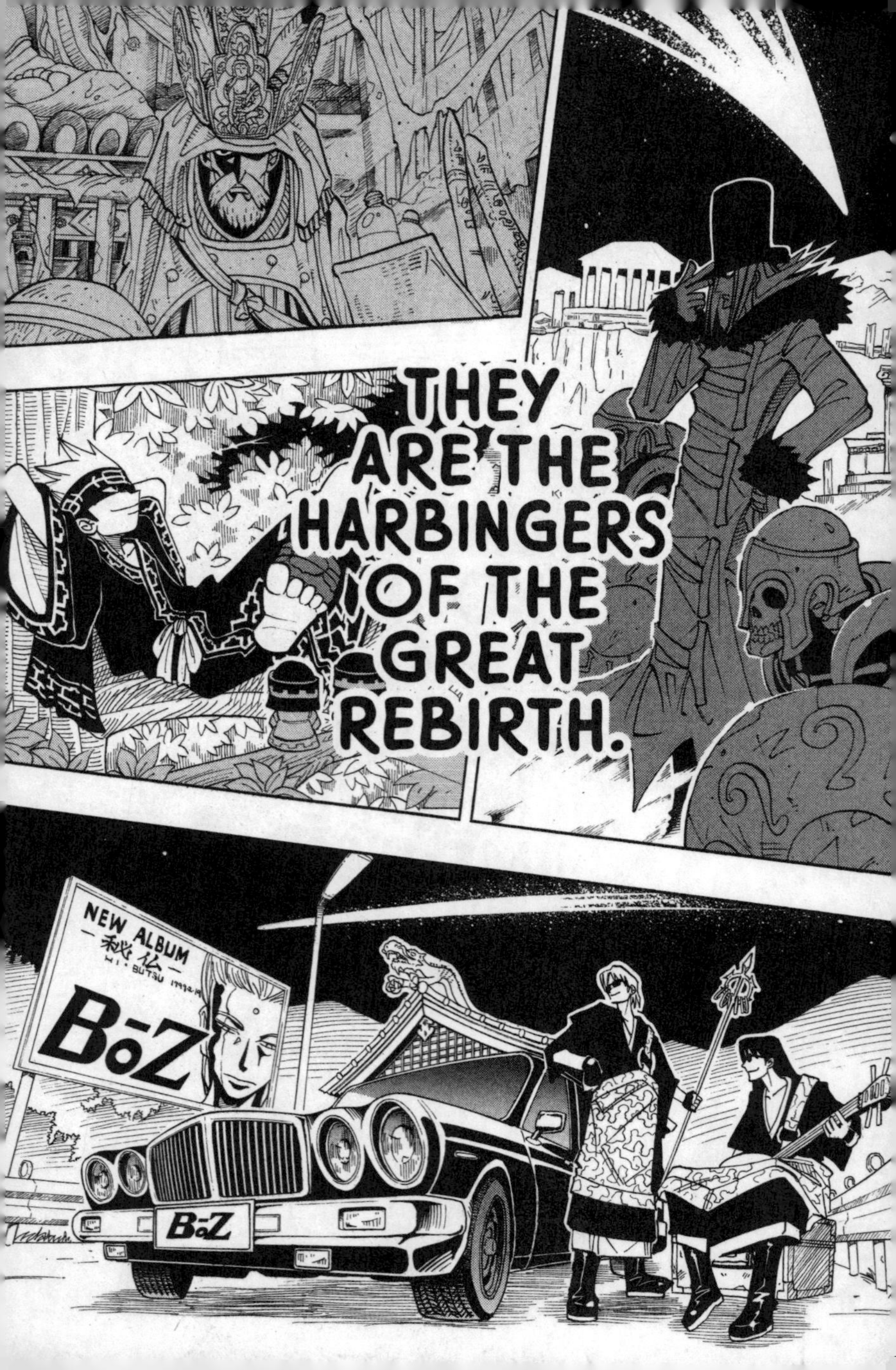
THEY ARE THE HARBINGERS OF THE GREAT REBIRTH.
NEW ALBUM
— 秘仏 —
B-Z
B-Z

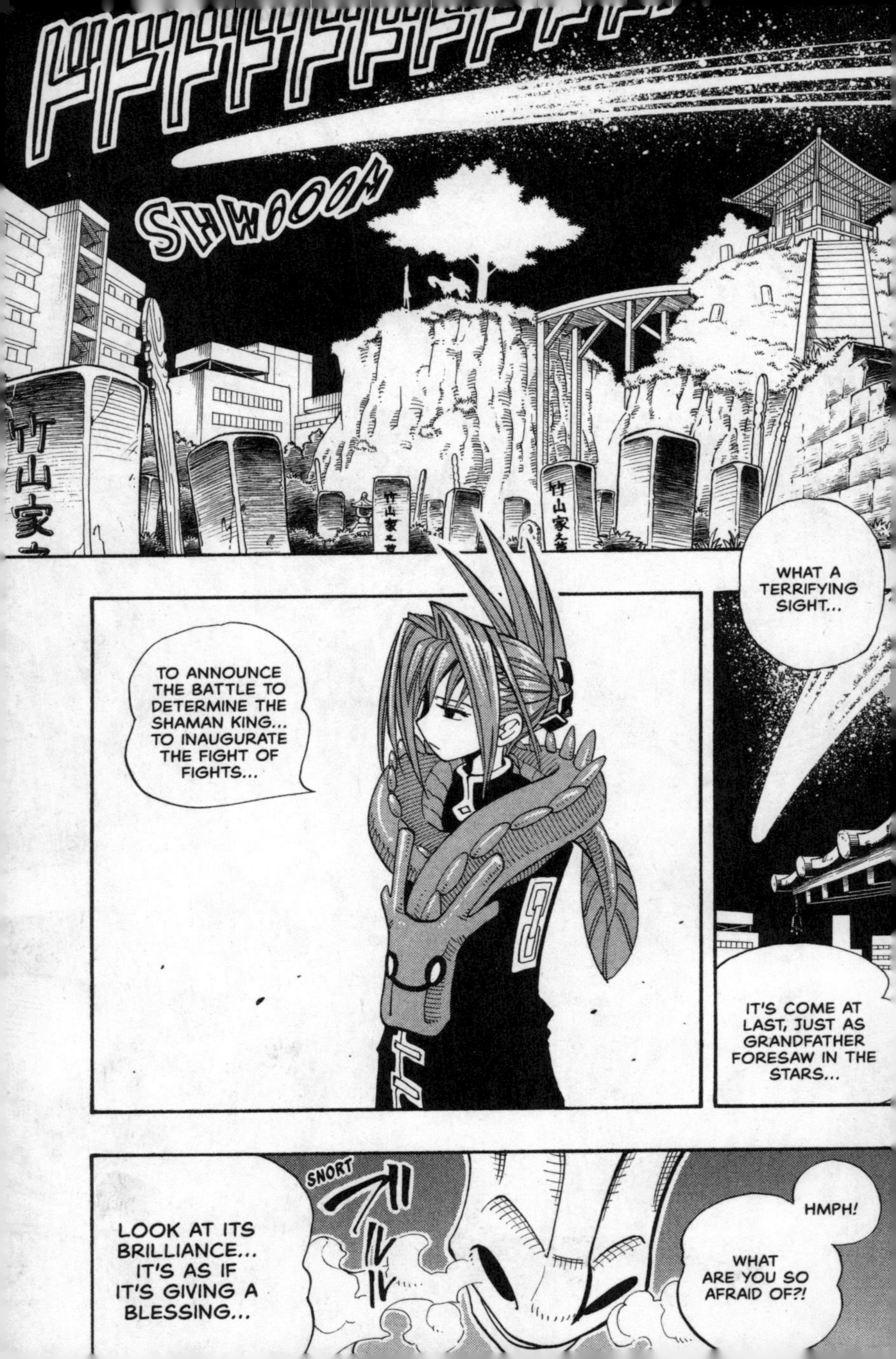
SHWOOOM
WHAT A TERRIFYING SIGHT...
IT'S COME AT LAST, JUST AS GRANDFATHER FORESAW IN THE STARS...
TO ANNOUNCE THE BATTLE TO DETERMINE THE SHAMAN KING... TO INAUGURATE THE FIGHT OF FIGHTS...
HMPH!
WHAT ARE YOU SO AFRAID OF?!
SNORT
LOOK AT ITS BRILLIANCE... IT'S AS IF IT'S GIVING A BLESSING...

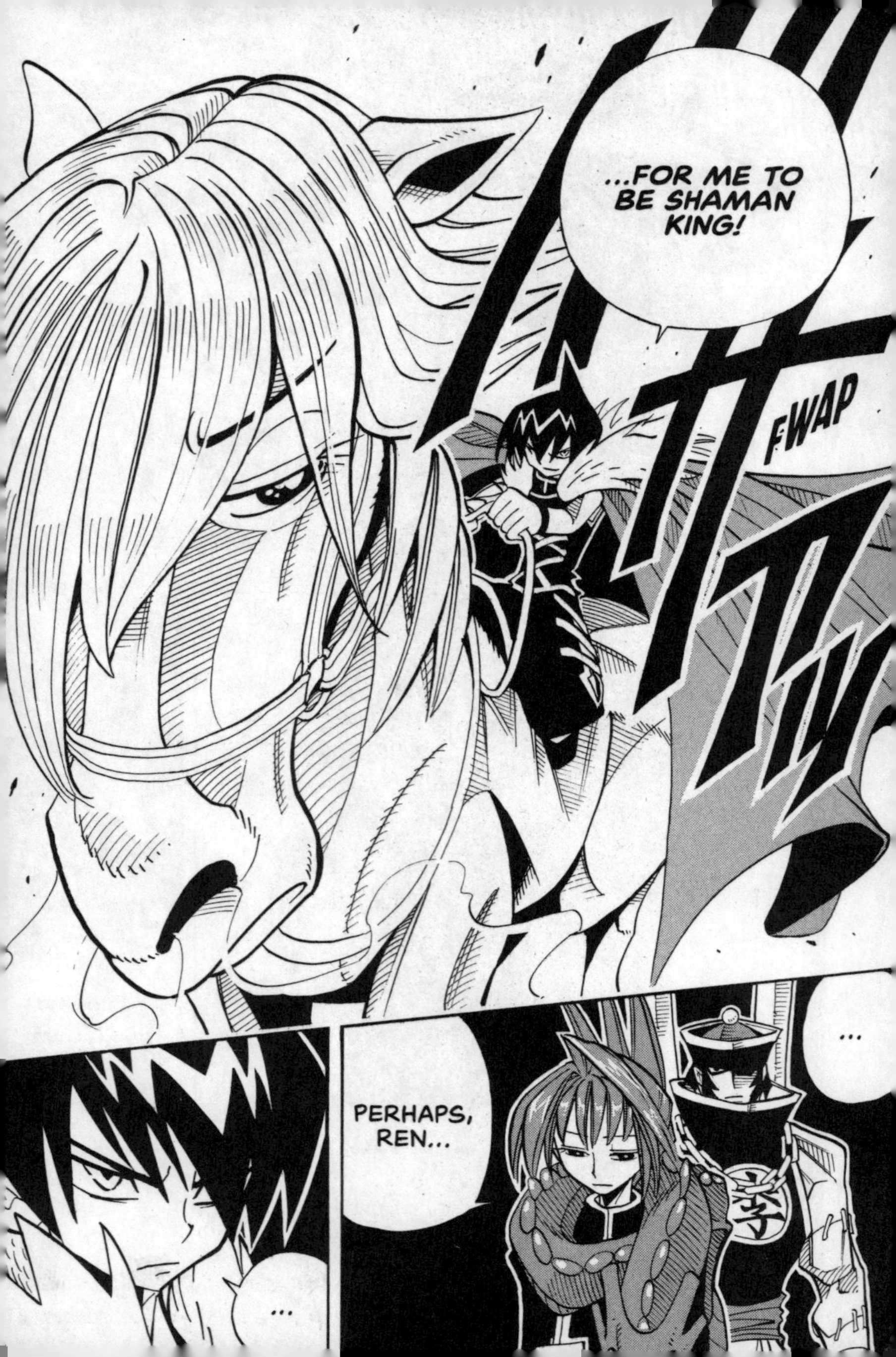
...FOR ME TO BE SHAMAN KING!
FWAP
...
PERHAPS, REN...
...

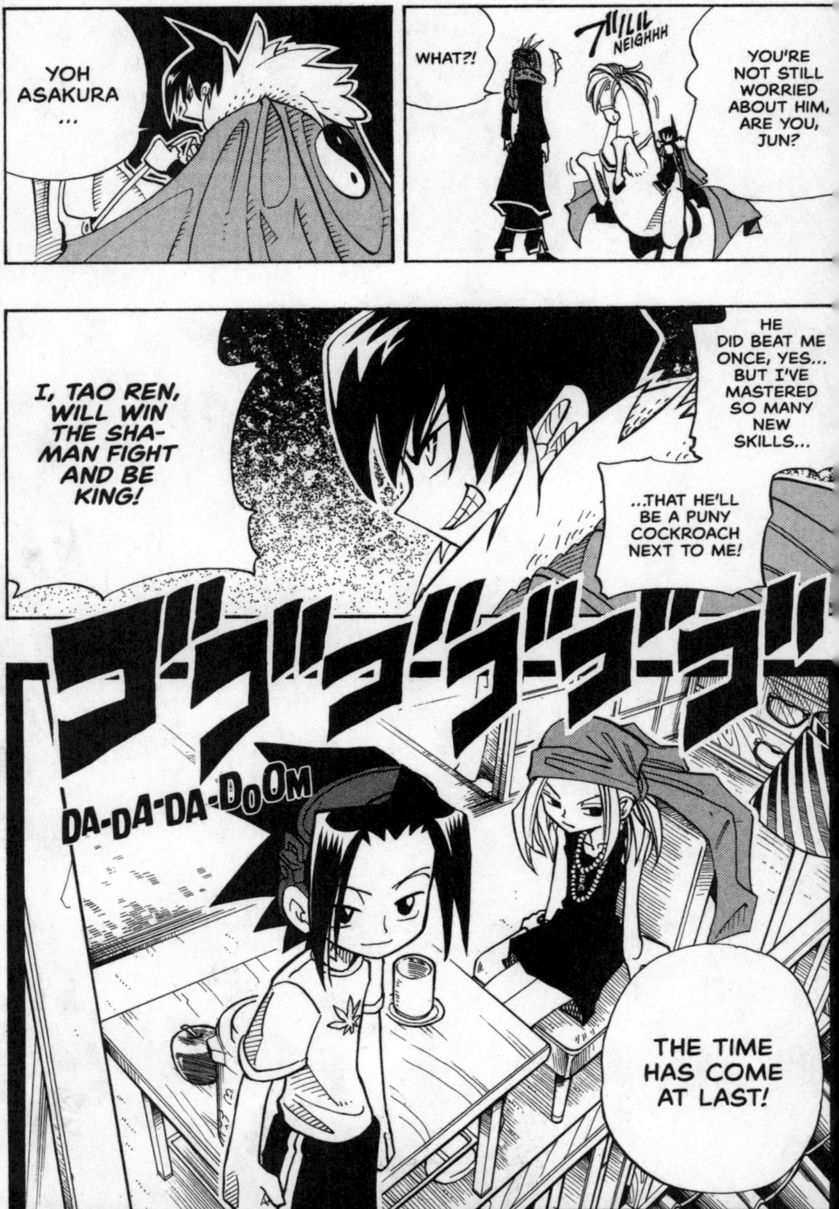
YOU'RE NOT STILL WORRIED ABOUT HIM, ARE YOU, JUN?
NEIGHHH
WHAT?!
YOH ASAKURA ...
HE DID BEAT ME ONCE, YES... BUT I'VE MASTERED SO MANY NEW SKILLS...
...THAT HE'LL BE A PUNY COCKROACH NEXT TO ME!
I, TAO REN, WILL WIN THE SHA-MAN FIGHT AND BE KING!
DA-DA-DA-DOOM
THE TIME HAS COME AT LAST!

To be continued in Shaman King Omnibus 2!

SHAMAN KING

Translation Notes

Cram school, page 8

Manta is going to *juku*, an additional form of schooling many Japanese students attend. They might review the lessons from the day's school classes, or they might tackle additional material. *Juku* are especially aimed at helping students pass Japan's notoriously challenging entrance exams. As Manta's in middle school, he's probably studying to get into high school (which isn't part of compulsory education in Japan, thus individual schools often require exams), but high school students also often attend *juku* to help them prepare for college entrance examinations.

Namu Amida Butsu, page 9

Meaning "In the name of the Buddha Amida," this is the standard funerary invocation in Japan. It's also sometimes repeated as a mantra by followers of Amida, either to focus themselves on their devotions, or hopes that they'll be reborn into Amida's promised land when they die.

Leaves, page 10

It's worth noting that Japanese kanji characters can be pronounced one of two ways: by their *kunyomi*, or Japanese reading, or their *onyomi*, or Chinese-derived reading. When kanji appear by themselves as a single word, they're typically read with their *kunyomi* pronunciation, whereas when multiple kanji appear in the same word, they typically use their *onyomi* pronunciation. However, there are a lot of exceptions: for example, the *kunyomi* reading of the Japanese character for leaf is read as *ha*, and the *onyomi* reading is read as *yoh*, and is the sole character in Yoh's first name.

First Year, Class C, page 14

In Japanese schools, students are assigned to a homeroom where they spend most of the school day, and it's the teachers, not the students, who move from room to room between periods. These homerooms are designated with a combination of a number, representing the class year, and a letter. So 3-B, for example, would be third year, class B. (The individual classes are sometimes known in Japanese as *kumi*, or groups.)

-kun, page 16

An honorific often attached to the names of boys or younger men. As with most honorifics, though, there's some nuance to the exact use of *-kun*, and it can in principle be used in many cases of superiors addressing or referring to juniors or subordinates, such as a boss mentioning an employee.

Izumo, page 16

Located on the western half of the main Japanese island of Honshu, the ancient province of Izumo (literally "the land of clouds emerging" and now part of Shimane Prefecture) was one of the points of origin of the political powers that would eventually become the modern Japanese state. Moreover, the great shrine of Izumo (Izumo Taisha, or more formally Izumo Ōyashiro) was and remains one of the most important shrines of Japan's native Shinto religion. In ancient poetry, the area was conventionally known as *yakumo tatsu Izumo* or "Izumo of the eight clouds rising." Yoh himself uses the first-person pronoun *oira* (as opposed to, say, *ore*), which might be a sign that he speaks in an Izumo, or at least a rural, dialect.

dono, page 42

n honorific used for people who are viewed as substantially more important than the speaker, such as amurai, lords, important priests, and so on. -*Dono* is no longer used much in everyday life (a Japanese speaker shing to express this level of respect would probably just use -*sama*), but it's still seen frequently in manga nd other popular media because it can easily and quickly lend a sense of antiquity to a scene or character.

arusame, page 65

he individual characters that make up the name of Amidamaru's sword come from the words *haru*, meaning ring, and *ame*, meaning rain. Together, the two characters can be read as *harusame*, meaning spring rain, or unu, a type of thin noodles made from bean or potato starch.

ord, page 68

first, Amidamaru addresses this character as *ryoushu-sama*, literally "honored territorial ruler." He later fers to them as his *tono-sama*, or "honored *tono*." A *tono* (which is the same character as the honorific ono mentioned above) is often a local lord or ruler. Although "lord" is sometimes used to translate the word aimyō, referring to a provincial ruler or warlord, that term isn't used here. While the exact history of the ord is somewhat complex, *daimyō* in its modern form and usage probably hadn't emerged yet at the time of is flashback, around 1399, so it's appropriate that Amidamaru uses other expressions.

endo, page 81

terally meaning "way of the sword," kendo is the modern descendent of Japan's traditional sword arts. rictly speaking, the old arts are called *kenjutsu* ("art of the sword"), while kendo is a form of sport or mpetition, typically utilizing bamboo weapons (*shinai*) rather than live steel. While kendo matches are ss fatal than old-fashioned sword duels, though, they're fought with the same intensity, and the practice kendo is intended to cultivate the same dedication and virtue in the practitioner as the old warriors are ought to have possessed. Because getting hit with a bamboo sword is less deadly, but still not necessarily easant, kendo practitioners in competitions wear distinctive outfits including large, solid armor that covers e head and chest to protect themselves.

leep paralysis, page 124

Japan, it is believed that sleep paralysis (*kanashibari*, literally "bound or fastened in metal," from the kanji ne, or metal, and *shibaru*, to bind, tie, or fasten) is caused by ghosts.

athroom sandals, page 182

s considered inappropriate to wear outdoor footwear into many buildings in Japan, but it's also inappro-iate to wear your indoor sandals into parts of a building where the floor might not be clean, especially e bathroom. Instead, there will be a pair (or, in a school, several pairs) of sandals at the bathroom door ecifically to be used there. You leave your indoor slippers at the door and put on a pair of bathroom slippers, en trade back when you come out. Leaving the bathroom with the toilet slippers still on is just as much a ux pas as entering the bathroom wearing your regular indoor footwear.

Tathagata, page 200

Tathagata (referred to in Japanese as *nyorai*, or "perfected one") is a suffix of high-ranking Buddhist deitie
In Pali and Sanskrit, Tathāgata is also the name that Buddha uses to refer to himself. The term means bo
one who has thus gone (*tathā-gata*) and one who has thus come (*tathā-āgata*).

Mt. Sanbe, page 214

A volcano located in Shimane. Although it's somewhere in the middle of the modern prefecture, it was on t
border of the old province of Izumo, discussed earlier. A local myth holds that when the pieces of the Japane
islands were pulled together, Mt. Sanbe was one of the anchors to which a rope was attached.

Onmyōji, page 216

Sometimes called yin-yang diviners, onmyōji were wonder-workers—somewhere between priests and shama
—who used the forces of yin (the dark, feminine energy) and yang (the bright, masculine energy) to perfo
spells, divine the future, and exorcise spirits, among other things. Their art was known as *onmyōdō* or *in'yō
both of which mean "the way of yin and yang."

Shikigami, page 216

Shikigami—the kanji literally mean "ritual-deity"—are, in essence, the familiars of onmyōji. They are gho
or spirits summoned by the practitioner to perform some task, though shikigami can be volatile and requ
careful handling on the part of the conjurer. Anime fans might recognize them as the tiny paper dolls th
follow Chihiro in a scene in Hayao Miyazaki's movie *Spirited Away*.

Itako, page 217

Itako are a kind of shrine maiden (*miko*; see below), particularly in the northern Tōhoku (northeaster
region. They specialize in channeling spirits and performing as mediums for the dead. (In Japanese, a medi
is said to perform *kuchiyose* or "drawing near to the mouth"-that is, speaking for or as the deceased.) Wom
who become itako are typically blind, either from birth or because of circumstances later in life. This mea
that in traditional society, becoming an itako was one of very few ways for a blind woman to survive a
make a living for herself.

Mt. Osore, page 217

Located in Aomori Prefecture (see below) at the northern extremity of the island of Honshu, Mt. Osore
home to a major Buddhist temple, Bodai-ji. The temple is situated in the caldera of a volcano, though t
mountain has been dormant so long that no eruption is recorded in any written source. (It's perhaps n
unrelated, though, that Mt. Osore literally means "the terrible mountain" or, if you will, "Mt. Fear.") Once
year, itako (see above) gather at this mountain to channel the dead together in a group ritual.

Aomori Prefecture, page 217

Aomori is the northernmost prefecture on the island of Honshu, home to the spiritually important Mt. Oso
(see above).

Miko, page 218

A miko is a shrine maiden or attendant at a Shinto shrine. They often dress in white overgarments and r
trousers, an outfit that will be familiar to many anime fans.

ao shi, page 280

dao shi is a Daoist (or Taoist) spellcaster. Note that the term dao shi is Mandarin Chinese, and the syllable "shi" is pronounced differently than it is in Japanese. It's close to the English word "shirt" without the t. The Japanese equivalent of this term, which uses the same kanji, would be dōshi.

okan, page 324

Yōkan is a Japanese sweet treat (wagashi) made mainly from red bean paste and agar gelatin, giving it a thick, chewy texture. As used in this scene, it's a play on words: Manta refers to "Yoh-kun," to which the bully replies, "Yōkan? You hungry?! Wanna eat my fist?!"

Buddha-giri, page 333

Yohmidamaru's attack name, Buddha-giri, roughly translates to Buddha Slash (with giri coming from the Japanese term "to cleave" or "to chop").

o-fuda, page 334

Also called jufu, these sacred slips of paper are often inscribed with charms or curses.

"The sword alone is of little value," page 339

This is a Japanese proverb meaning the sword can only strike one enemy at a time, but tactics can defeat ten thousand men at once.

Kwan Dao, page 395

The ancient Chinese halberd (long-hafted cutting weapon) used by Bason. Also known as a Guan Dao.

The "Lizard Man", page 424

In addition to the lizard-encrusted headband that Tokageroh is seen wearing on page 422, the tokage in Tokageroh's name is Japanese for "lizard," earning him the following moniker.

Tokage Kenpo, page 457

The name of the stance Tokageroh takes here literally translates to "lizard style."

Yakuza, page 493

The yakuza represent organized crime in Japan. They're often represented in popular culture as having their own kind of nobility, adhering to a criminal's code of honor and striving not to harm common people. Despite this popular image, the yakuza are, and remain, a criminal organization that can do financial and physical harm to people and companies.

Rahu and Ketu, page 575

Rahu (pronounced Ragoh in Japanese) and Ketu (pronounced Keito in Japanese) are two of Hindu mythology's nine Navagraha, or celestial bodies. In addition to Rahu and Ketu, which represent the north, or ascending, and the south, or descending, lunar nodes respectively, the Navagraha also include Surya (the Sun), Chandra (the Moon), Budha (Mercury), Shukra (Venus), Mangala (Mars), Brihaspati (Jupiter), and Shani (Saturn).

EDENS ZERO
エデンズゼロ

HIRO MASHIMA IS BACK! JOIN THE CREATOR OF *FAIRY TAIL* AS HE TAKES TO THE STARS FOR ANOTHER THRILLING SAGA!

EDENS ZERO © Hiro Mashima/Kodansha, Ltd.

A high-flying space adventure! All the steadfast friendship and wild fighting you've been waiting for...IN SPACE!

At Granbell Kingdom, an abandoned amusement park, Shiki has lived his entire life among machines. But one day, Rebecca and her cat companion Happy appear at the park's front gates. Little do these newcomers know that this is the first human contact Granbell has had in a hundred years! As Shiki stumbles his way into making new friends, his former neighbors stir at an opportunity for a robo-rebellion... And when his old homeland becomes too dangerous, Shiki must join Rebecca and Happy on their spaceship and escape into the boundless cosmos.

THE MAGICAL GIRL CLASSIC THAT BROUGHT A GENERATION OF READERS TO MANGA, NOW BACK IN A DEFINITIVE, HARDCOVER COLLECTOR'S EDITION!

CARDCAPTOR SAKURA
COLLECTOR'S EDITION
CLAMP

I
DELUXE EDITION
Cardcaptor Sakura
CLAMP

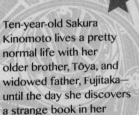

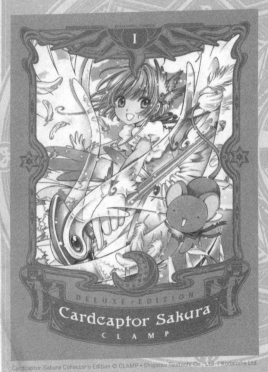

Ten-year-old Sakura Kinomoto lives a pretty normal life with her older brother, Tōya, and widowed father, Fujitaka—until the day she discovers a strange book in her father's library, and her life takes a magical turn...

- A deluxe large-format hardcover edition of CLAMP's shojo manga classic
- All-new foil-stamped cover art on each volume
- Comes with exclusive collectible art card

KC KODANSHA COMICS

The boys are back, in 400-page hardcovers that are as pretty and badass as they are!

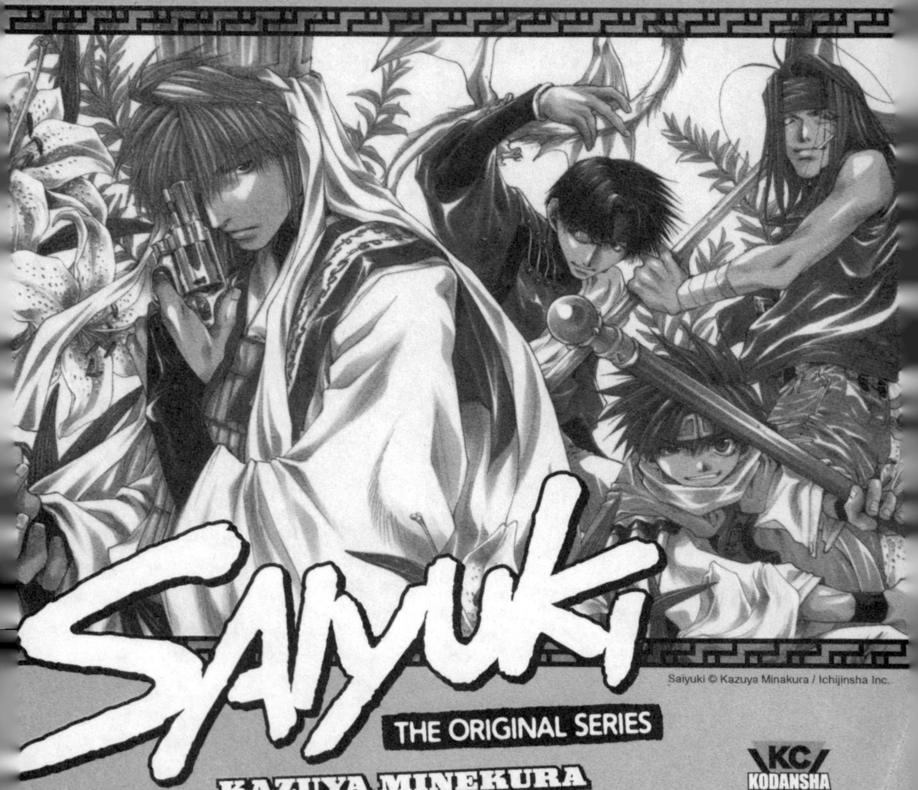
Saiyuki
Saiyuki © Kazuya Minakura / Ichijinsha Inc.
THE ORIGINAL SERIES
KAZUYA MINEKURA
KC
KODANSHA COMICS

"AN EDGY COMIC LOOK AT AN ANCIENT CHINESE TALE." —YALSA

Genjo Sanzo is a Buddhist priest in the city of Togenkyo, which is being ravaged by yokai spirits that have fallen out of balance with the natural order. His superiors send him on a journey far to the west to discover why this is happening and how to stop it. His companions are three yokai with human souls. But this is no day trip — the four will encounter many discoveries and horrors on the way.

FEATURES NEW TRANSLATION, COLOR PAGES, AND BEAUTIFUL WRAPAROUND COVER ART!

A Kodansha Comics Trade Paperback Original
Shaman King Omnibus 1 copyright © 2020 Hiroyuki Takei
English translation copyright © 2021 Hiroyuki Takei

Published in the United States by Kodansha Comics, an imprint of
Kodansha USA Publishing, LLC, New York.

Publication rights for this English edition arranged through
Kodansha Ltd., Tokyo.

First published in Japan in 2020 by Kodansha Ltd., Tokyo.

ISBN 978-1-64651-200-3

Original cover design by Toru Fukushima (Smile Studio)

Printed in the United States of America.

www.kodanshacomics.com

9 8 7 6 5 4 3 2
Translation: Lillian Olsen, Erin Procter
Lettering: Jan Lan Ivan Concepcion
Retouching: Jan Lan Ivan Concepcion, Kai Kyou
Additional Lettering: Nicole Roderick
English Adaptation: Lance Caselman
Editing: Tiff Joshua TJ Ferentini, Jason Thompson
YKS Services LLC/SKY Japan, INC.
Kodansha Comics edition cover design by Phil Balsman

Publisher: Kiichiro Sugawara

Director of publishing services: Ben Applegate
Associate director of operations: Stephen Pakula
Publishing services managing editor: Noelle Webster
Assistant production manager: Emi Lotto, Angela Zurlo
Logo and character art ©Kodansha USA Publishing, LLC

HOW TO READ MANGA

FOLLOW
AND KEE
BACKWA
YOU GET

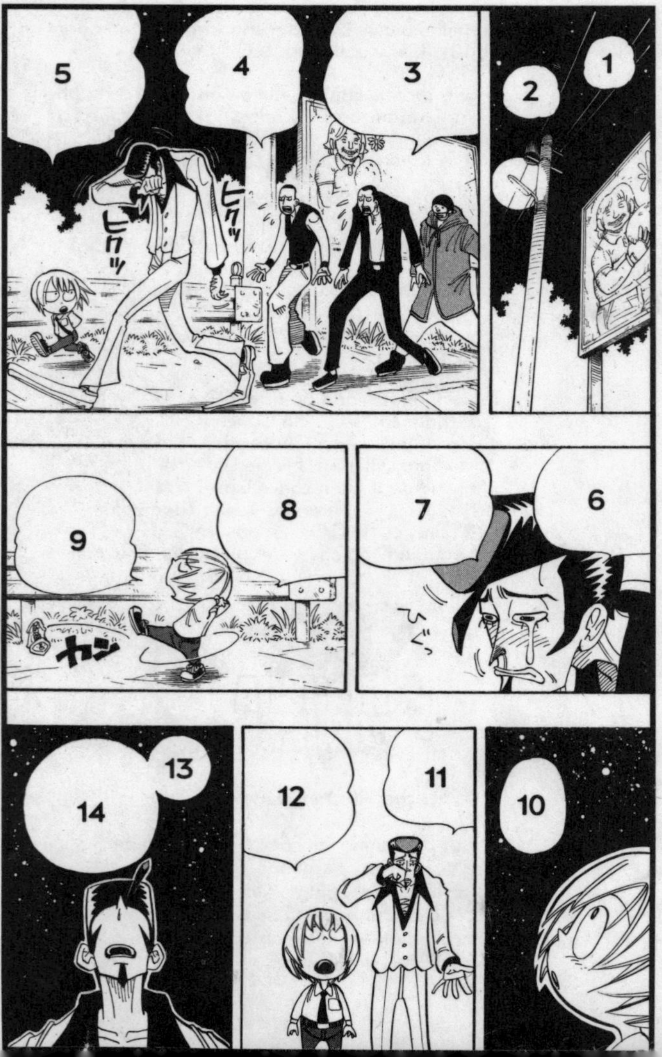
1
2
3
ヒクッ
ヒクッ
4
5
6
7
ひぐっ
8
9
カン
10
11
12
13
14